A New and Complete History of the Holy Bible As Contained in the Old and New Testaments: From the Creation of the World to the Full Establishment of Christianity ; Containing a Clear and Comprehensive Account of Every Remarkable Transaction Recorded in Th

Robert Sears

JUDGMENT OF SOLOMON.

"AND THE KING SAID, DIVIDE THE LIVING CHILD IN TWO." 1st KINGS III., 25

A

NEW AND COMPLETE HISTORY

OF THE

HOLY BIBLE,

AS CONTAINED IN THE

OLD AND NEW TESTAMENTS,

FROM THE

CREATION OF THE WORLD TO THE FULL ESTABLISHMENT OF CHRISTIANITY:

CONTAINING

A CLEAR AND COMPREHENSIVE ACCOUNT OF EVERY REMARKABLE TRANSACTION
RECORDED IN THE SACRED SCRIPTURES DURING A PERIOD OF
UPWARD OF FOUR THOUSAND YEARS.

WITH COPIOUS NOTES, CRITICAL AND EXPLANATORY,

FORMING AN

ILLUSTRATED COMMENTARY OF THE SACRED TEXT.

WITH NUMEROUS ENGRAVINGS.

PART I.—THE OLD TESTAMENT HISTORY.

BY ROBERT SEARS.

AIDED BY THE WRITINGS OF OUR MOST CELEBRATED BIBLICAL SCHOLARS, AND OTHER LEARNED
PERSONS, WHO HAVE MADE THE SCRIPTURES THEIR STUDY.

TWO VOLUMES IN ONE.

SECOND EDITION.

NEW YORK:
PUBLISHED BY SEARS & WALKER,
114 FULTON STREET, AND 122 NASSAU STREET.

BOSTON : SAXTON AND PEIRCE, 133½ WASHINGTON STREET.—PHILADELPHIA : R. S. H. GEORGE ;
THOMAS, COWPERTHWAIT, AND CO. ; AND B. R. LOXLEY.—PITTSBURGH, PA. : R. G. BERFORD.
ALBANY, N. Y. : W. C. LITTLE.—UTICA, N. Y. : BENNETT, BACKUS, AND HAWLEY.—HAMIL-
TON, N. Y. : GRIGGS AND GRANT.—BALTIMORE : J. H. BESORE.—CHARLESTON, S. C. : SILAS
HOWE.—PENFIELD, GA. : W. RICHARDS.—NATCHEZ, MISS. : H. M. GROSVENOR.—ST. JOHN,
N. B. : G. AND E. SEARS.—HALIFAX, N. S. : JOSEPH GRAHAM.

AND SOLD BY BOOKSELLERS GENERALLY, AND THE PUBLISHERS' AUTHORIZED AGENTS
THROUGHOUT THE UNITED STATES AND BRITISH PROVINCES.

MDCCCXLIV.

STEREOTYPED BY REDFIELD & SAVAGE,
13 Chambers Street, New York.
R. CRAIGHEAD, PRINTER, 112 FULTON ST.

PREFACE.

It is impossible duly to estimate the change produced in the world since the rapid multiplication of books by the modern facilities of printing has brought at least some measure of Knowledge to every man's door. Indisputably, much advantage has resulted from the wide promulgation of Truth; but it may be doubted whether a habit of superficial reading has not also been fostered, and whether the mind, instead of being concentrated on a little which is most important, has not, in traversing a larger field, gathered much that is of no value. Perhaps its fine gold has been alloyed, and its wine diluted with water. Perhaps, when heretofore The Bible was the principal subject of study, its attention has been since diverted from that to merely human expositions.

> " Hast thou ever heard
> Of such a book ? The author, God himself ;
> The subject, God and man, salvation, life,
> And death—eternal life, eternal death—
> Dread words ! whose meaning has no end, no bounds ;
> Most wondrous book ! bright candle of the Lord !
> Star of eternity ! the only star
> By which the bark of man could navigate
> The sea of life, and gain the coast of bliss
> Securely ! only star which rose on Time,
> And, on its dark and troubled billows, still,
> As generation, drifting swiftly by,
> Succeeded generation, threw a ray
> Of heaven's own light, and to the hills of God,
> The eternal hills, pointed the sinner's eye.
> By prophets, seers, priests, and sacred bards,
> Evangelists, apostles, men inspired,
> And by the Holy Ghost, anointed set
> Apart, and consecrated to declare
> To earth the counsels of the Eternal One,
> This book, this holiest, this sublimest book
> Was sent."

The Bible, therefore, ought to be the beginning and the end of all religious reading; it is the standard by which everything else must be measured—the touchstone by which every other book must be tried. Other authors are valuable as they direct our attention to this; they are profitable only as they derive their knowledge from this source. They must make their continual appeal " to the law, and to the testimony; if they speak not according to this word, it is because there is no light in them." The errors which have been introduced into the world have sprung either from the perversion or from the neglect of The Bible. Men have put away the divine teacher, and have leaned to their own understandings, or they have not chosen to receive its declarations in simplicity of heart, and have put interpretations upon them which they never were intended to bear. And as even in the best and wisest book that ever proceeded altogether from a human pen, there is much that is uncertain, and much that is imperfect, no man can be assured of his security in the way of truth, unless he is perpetually examining the guides which men have set up, by that light which was given from on high to be a lantern to his path.

We consider the present volume as Scripture itself, teaching the knowledge of its own divine precepts, and urging the practice of them by interesting examples. Young Persons of superior education, whose natural inquisitiveness has been quickened by intelligence, are especially intended to be benefited by it, aiding them in their studies, while eagerly inquiring for sacred knowledge, and seeking, with deeply-felt interest, for a more comprehensive acquaintance with the Oracles of God.

There is not among the many interesting traits of Christian character with which the history of the early Christians abounds, one that stands out more frequently in beautiful and prominent relief, than the tender solicitude and the winning arts which they employed to imbue the susceptible minds of the young with the knowledge and the faith of the Scripture. While they were fondled on the knee, and still watched by the careful eyes of their nurse, the first words they were taught to lisp and articulate were the sacred names of God and the Saviour. And the whole range of nursery knowledge and amusement was comprised in narratives and pictures, illustrating episodes in the life of the holy child, or parables the most simple and interesting in the ministry of Christ. As their minds expanded, they were taught, along with the grand doctrines of Scripture, which, according to the approved fashion of those days, were rendered familiar by apposite similitudes from nature, the Proverbs of Solomon, and those passages of the sacred volume which relate particularly to the economy of life.

Religion, in short, was the grand basis of education, the only subject which, during the first years of life, they allowed their children to be taught; and in order to present it to their minds with the greater attractions, and entwine it with their earliest and purest associations, they adopted the happy expedient of wedding it to the graces of poetry, and rendering it more memorable by the melody of numbers. From the earliest period of Christian antiquity there were authors who, like Watts in modern times, " condescended to lay aside the scholar, the philosopher, and the wit, to write little poems of devotion, adapted to the wants and capacities of children," and these, set to well-known and favorite airs, borrowed from the profaner songs of the heathen, were sung by the Christians at their family concerts, which enlivened their meals, and by which alone the still and peaceful tranquillity of their homes was ever broken. Ere long, their children were taught common, and frequently short-hand writing, in lines taken from the Psalms, or in words of sententious brevity, in which the leading doctrines of the gospel were stated; and at a later period, when the progress of toleration allowed Christian seminaries to be erected, the school-books in use consisted chiefly of passages of the Bible versified, and of the poetical pieces which illustrated or enforced the great subjects of faith and duty. The most celebrated of these were compositions of the two Apollinaries, grammarians of high reputation in Syria—the elder of whom, in imitation of Homer, wrote the Antiquities of the Jews in heroic verse, down to the reign of Saul, while the first of the sacred story he described in such metrical forms as corresponded to the verses of the Greek tragedians, and the lyrical ballads of Pindar. The department undertaken by his son was that of reducing the history of the evangelists and the epistles of Paul into the form and style of Plato's dialogues; and with so much taste and elegance were both of these works compiled, that on their first appearance they took their place among the most esteemed productions of the Fathers. Besides these, there was a collection of miscellaneous poems on sacred subjects, and in all sorts of verse, by the famous Gregory Nazianzen, in very extensive circulation. By means of these, and of many other evangelical books which have long ago become the prey of time, the Christian youth were intro-

duced to the elements of pure and undefiled religion, and their taste for knowledge and the beauties of learning created and formed by works in which salvation was held up as the one thing needful, and no achievements described, no
characters lauded, but such as were adorned with the fruits of righteousness.
Thus did the pious care of the primitive Christians intermingle religion with all
the pursuits and recreations of the young, and never allow them to engage in the
study of science, or to plunge into the business of the world, until they had been
first taught to view everything in the spirit and by the principles of the Word of
GOD.

"A NEW AND COMPLETE UNIVERSAL HISTORY OF THE HOLY BIBLE" has
long been needed. We have, with great care, study, and expense, been enabled
to present one to the public. Commentators, lexicographers, oriental travellers,
and biblical critics of the greatest name, have been extensively consulted in preparing this work. The attention of the reader is respectfully requested to the
copious supply of notes, critical and explanatory, at the foot of the pages, designed to render the publication intelligible and instructive to all classes of readers. Literature, profane and sacred, is here united with the arts of printing and
engraving, to produce a work, which shall be a valuable addition to the biblical
literature of our country. Something more, however, than a mere compiler is
required to do it justice. Patient labor will effect much; but without searching
discrimination, without great power of original conception, a dull and ponderous
work will be the result, the perusal of which will take up as much time as did
the composition of it, and leave as little clear and pleasing impression on the
reader, as the author had distinct conception of his subject, or real love for it.
The Scripture History ought, least of all, to be overlaid with tediousness. Too
little is understood of the character of the revealed dispensations, and the mode
in which they were communicated; and that writer does a great benefit to his
race who familiarizes the Sacred History, by giving a plain and easy narration of
the events which it records, and elucidating the circumstances and peculiarities
of the people who were originally concerned in them.

In preparing the present Work we have endeavored to blend instruction and
entertainment in such a manner that, while the reader is sensibly pleased, he
will find himself imperceptibly improved, and be amazed at his extensive knowledge of the Scriptures, acquired in so rapid a manner. A complete HISTORY
OF THE BIBLE is indeed absolutely necessary to accompany that sacred book, in
order to elucidate many important matters, which, in this age, might not be understood by many pious and well-disposed people. The sacred writers, for instance, often named places which they did not describe, because those to whom
their writings were addressed well knew them. It is our business, therefore, to
point out the situation, together with the ancient and modern state of those
places. They mentioned customs peculiar to the early ages, and oriental countries in which they lived, and which we have here illustrated with great care
and expense.

The Editor refers here with pleasure to the gratifying reception his former publications have met with—more than FIFTY THOUSAND COPIES of his different
volumes having been circulated throughout the United States and British North
America, within the short period of two years—his own expectations of their
success having been more than fully realized. It would be unnatural, if not irre-
ligious, for him not to feel honored and delighted with the numerous favorable
testimonials, relative to their character and design, he has received from the public press, both political and religious; together with the unsolicited recommendations of numerous leading Clergymen of all denominations, Instructers of
Youth, Sunday School Teachers, &c., beside knowing the fact, that there is, at

the present time, a continual and growing demand for them throughout the country.

We respectfully offer the present volume to the patronage of Christian Pastors, Instructers, and Parents. In preparing it for the press, we have found much more labor than we expected, to render the whole instructive and agreeable to modern and intelligent readers. In every part of it we have studied brevity, and labored at condensation. Without this, it would have been an easy matter to double its size with more extended matter, or additional notes; but these, however, in various respects desirable, have been omitted, for the purpose of preserving the size of the volume within moderate limits, that it might be more generally possessed by every class of Christians. "THE BIBLE," says an amiable and universally-admired writer, " is a light to our feet, and a lamp to our path. It points us to the Way, the Truth, and the Life. It is our guide while we live, and our trust when we die. It is the charter of our salvation, and the pledge of our immortality. If there were but one Bible in the world, all the wealth of that world would not be adequate to the value of that Bible." Another old writer observes : " HAPPY IS THE MAN THAT FINDETH WISDOM, AND THE MAN THAT GETTETH UNDERSTANDING ; FOR THE MERCHANDISE OF IT IS BETTER THAN THE MERCHANDISE OF SILVER, AND THE GAIN THEREOF THAN FINE GOLD. SHE IS MORE PRECIOUS THAN RUBIES ; AND ALL THE THINGS THOU CANST DESIRE ARE NOT TO BE COMPARED UNTO HER. LENGTH OF DAYS IS IN HER RIGHT HAND ; AND IN HER LEFT HAND RICHES AND HONOR. HER WAYS ARE WAYS OF PLEASANTNESS, AND ALL HER PATHS ARE PEACE." Proverbs, iii. 13–17.

DESCRIPTION OF THE FRONTISPIECE.

THE JUDGMENT OF SOLOMON;

AFTER THE ORIGINAL, BY PETER PAUL RUBENS.

THEN came there two women unto the king, and stood before him. And the one woman said, O my Lord, I and this woman dwell in one house : and I was delivered of a child with her in the house. And it came to pass the third day after that I was delivered, that this woman was delivered also : and we were together ; there was no stranger with us in the house, save we two in the house, and this woman's child died in the night ; because she overlaid it. And she arose at midnight, and took my son from beside me, while thine handmaid slept, and laid it in her bosom, and laid her dead child in my bosom. And when I rose in the morning to give my child suck, behold it was dead : but when I had considered it in the morning, behold it was not my son which I did bear. And the other woman said, Nay ; but the living is my son, and the dead is thy son. And this said, No ; but the dead is thy son, and the living is my son. Thus they spake before the king.

Then said the king, The one saith, This is my son that liveth, and thy son is dead : and the other saith, Nay ; but thy son is dead, and my son is the living. And the king said, Bring me a sword. And they brought a sword before the king. And the king said, Divide the living child in two, and give half to the one, and half to the other. Then spake the woman whose the living child was, unto the king, for her bowels yearned upon her son, and she said, O my Lord, give her the living child, and in no wise slay it. But the other said, Let it be neither mine nor thine, but divide it. Then the king answered and said, Give *her* the living child, and in no wise slay it : she is the mother thereof.

And all Israel heard of the judgment which the king had judged : and they feared the king, for they saw that the wisdom of God was in him, to do judgment. (1 Kings, iii. 16–28.)

Such a mode of decision as this which Solomon adopted, was not unknown, under absolute monarchies, in the east.

Ariopharnes, king of Thrace, being appointed to arbitrate between three young men, each claiming to be the son of the king of the Cimmerians, discovered the real son by desiring each to shoot an arrow into the dead body of him they called their father. Two of the claimants obeyed without hesitation, but the third refused, upon which the arbitrator judged him to be the genuine prince.

LIST OF THE PRINCIPAL ILLUSTRATIONS

IN THE

HISTORY OF THE BIBLE.

PART I.—OLD TESTAMENT.

PART II.—NEW TESTAMENT HISTORY.

DESCRIPTION OF THE NEW TESTAMENT FRONTISPIECE.

CHRIST BEARING HIS CROSS.

FROM THE ORIGINAL BY AUDRAN.

WHEN Pilate therefore heard that saying, he brought Jesus forth, and sat down in the judgment-seat, in a place that is called the Pavement, but in the Hebrew, Gabbatha. And it was the preparation of the passover, and about the sixth hour: and he saith unto the Jews, Behold your King! But they cried out, Away with him, away with him, crucify him. Pilate saith unto them, Shall I crucify your king? The chief priests answered, We have no king but Cæsar. Then delivered he him therefore unto them to be crucified. And they took Jesus, and led him away. And he bearing his cross went forth into a place called the place of a scull, which is called in the Hebrew, Golgotha: Where they crucified him, and two others with him, on either side one, and Jesus in the midst.—JOHN xix. 13–18.

The path "Via dolorosa," by which our Saviour was conducted from the palace of Pilate to Mount Calvary, is still pointed out by old traditions, with a pardonable minuteness of detail. The house in which Christ was condemned is a ruined Roman edifice, containing several spacious apartments, to each of which is assigned some particular destination in the narrative of Christ's last sufferings on earth. In one he was mocked, in another buffeted, and scourged in a third. An arch that is thrown across the street, is called the arch of "Ecce Homo," from its proximity to the window at which the Redeemer was shown to the people, wearing a crown of thorns, and clothed in a purple robe. At two places, within the length of the Via dolorosa, which is about an English mile, the Saviour is said to have sunk beneath his burden, and at a third, he placed his hand against the wall to support him from falling; credulity professes to discover the impression of his sacred hand in the stone. At a station less than one hundred yards still further, the soldiers, compassionating his weakness, compelled Simon the Cyrenian to succeed to the burden of the cross, and carry it to that spot where the great oblation for the sins of the world was offered.

CONTENTS OF THE WHOLE WORK.

The whole calculated to enlighten the understanding, purify the heart, and promote that KNOWLEDGE by which we may obtain happiness in this world, and eternal salvation in that which is to come.

BOOKS OF THE OLD AND NEW TESTAMENTS.

OLD TESTAMENT BOOKS,—HISTORICAL, MORAL, AND DEVOTIONAL.

NAMES.	AUTHORS.	DATES IN YEARS B. C.
Genesis	Moses	From 4004 to 1635
Job	Moses	2180 or 2130
Exodus	Moses	From 1635 to 1490
Leviticus	Moses	1490
Numbers	Moses	From 1490 to 1451
Deuteronomy	Moses	1451
Joshua	Joshua	From 1451 to 1425
Judges	Samuel	From 1425 to 1120
Ruth	Samuel	From 1241 to 1231
1 Samuel } 2 Samuel }	{ Samuel, Nathan, Gad and others	From 1171 to 1055 From 1055 to 1015
Psalms	David and others	{ At various times—Those by David from 1060 to 1015
Solomon's Song	Solomon	About 1010
Proverbs	Solomon	About 1000
Ecclesiastes	Solomon	About 977
1 Kings { 2 Kings {	{ Nathan, Gad, Ahijah, Iddo, Isaiah, and others	1 Kings from 1015 to 896 2 Kings from 896 to 562
1 Chronicles } 2 Chronicles }	Ezra and others	From 4001 to 562
Ezra	Ezra	From 536 to 450
Esther	Ezra	From 521 to 495
Nehemiah	Nehemiah	From 455 to 420

PROPHETICAL BOOKS IN CHRONOLOGICAL ORDER.

NAMES.	BETWEEN THE YEARS B. C	KINGS OF JUDAH.	KINGS OF ISRAEL.
Jonah	856 and 784	{ Joash, Amaziah, or Azariah,	Jehu and Jehoahaz, or Joash and Jeroboam II.
Amos	810 and 725	Uzziah, ch. i. 1	Jeroboam II.
Hosea	810 and 725	Uzziah, Jotham, Ahaz, Hezekiah	Jeroboam II.
Isaiah	810 and 698	{ Uzziah, Jotham, Ahaz, Heze- kiah and Manasseh	Zechariah, Shallum, Mena- hem, Pekaiah, Pekah & Hosea
Joel	810 and 660 or later	Uzziah or Manasseh	Do.
Micah	758 and 699	{ Jotham, Ahaz, and Hezekiah, ch. i. 1	Pekah and Hosea.
Nahum	720 and 698	Hezekiah, close of his reign.	
Zephaniah	640 and 609	Josiah, ch. i. 1.	
Jeremiah	628 and 586	Josiah and Captivity.	
Lamentations	About 588	Captivity.	
Habakkuk	612 and 598	Jehoiakim.	
Daniel	606 and 534	Captivity.	
Obadiah	588 and 583	After Nebuchadnezzar's siege.	
Ezekiel	595 and 536	Captivity.	
Haggai	520 and 518	After the return from Babylon.	
Zechariah	520 and 510	After the return from Babylon.	
Malachi	436 and 397	After the return from Babylon.	

NEW TESTAMENT BOOKS.

BOOKS.	AUTHORS.	WHERE WRITTEN.	FOR WHOSE USE.	A. D.
1. Matthew, in Hebrew.	Matthew	Judea	Hebrew Christians	38
— in Greek	Matthew	Judea	Gentile Do.	60
2. Thessalonians I.	Paul	Corinth	Do. Do.	54
3. Thessalonians II.	Paul	Corinth	Do. Do.	54
4. Galatians	Paul	Corinth	Do. Do.	54
5. Corinthians I.	Paul	Ephesus	Do. Do.	59
6. Romans	Paul	Ephesus	Do. Do.	60
7. Corinthians II.	Paul	Macedonia	Do. Do.	60
8. James	James	Judea	Jewish nation	61
9. Mark	Mark	Rome	Gentile Christians	62
10. Ephesians	Paul	Rome	Do. Do.	62
11. Philippians	Paul	Rome	Do. Do.	63
12. Colossians	Paul	Rome	Do. Do.	63
13. Philemon	Paul	Rome	Philemon	62
14. Hebrews	Paul	Italy	Hebrew Christians	63
15. Luke	Luke	Greece	{ Theophilus and Gentile } Christians	63
16. Acts	Luke	Greece	Do. Do	64
17. Timothy I.	Paul	Macedonia	Timothy	65
18. Titus	Paul	Macedonia	Titus	65
19. Peter I.	Peter	Babylon or Rome	General	64
20. Jude	Jude	Unknown	Do.	65
21. Peter II.	Peter	Babylon or Rome	Do.	65
22. Timothy II.	Paul	Rome	Timothy	66
23. John I.	John	Ephesus	General	65
24. John II.	John	Ephesus	Lady Electa	69
25. John III.	John	Ephesus	Gaius	69
26. Revelation	John	Patmos	General	97
27. John	John	Ephesus	Do.	96

TO THE READER.

THE providence of GOD is particularly manifested in the preservation of the Holy Scriptures. To the Jews were committed the Oracles of God; and so faithful have they been to this sacred trust, that when copies of the law or the prophets were transcribed, they not only diligently compared the one with the other, but even counted the number of letters in each book, and compared the numbers.

No sooner did the gospel spread through the nations, than it was found necessary to translate the Bible for each into its proper language. Some affirm that the five books of Moses and that of Joshua were translated into Greek before the days of Alexander the Great. But the most remarkable translation of the Old Testament is called the Septuagint, which, if the opinion of some eminent writers is to be credited, was made in the reign of Ptolemy Philadelphus, about 280 years before the Christian era. At any rate, it is undoubtedly the most ancient that is now extant, and on many accounts deserving notice, though not to be put on a level with the Hebrew text, as has been sometimes done.

Other translations of the Old Testament into Greek were made, from A. D. 128 to 200. It is generally believed that the church of Antioch was favored with a Syrian version of the Bible in the year 100. The Ethiopians of Abyssinia have a version of the Bible, which they ascribe to Frumentius, of the fourth century. Chrysostrom, who lived in the end of the fourth, and Theodoret, who lived in the middle of the fifth century, both inform us that they had the Syrian, Indian, Persian, Armenian, Ethiopic, Scythian, and Samaritan versions. The ancient Egyptians had the Scriptures translated into their language. The Georgians have a version in their ancient language. The Old Testament of all these versions, except the Syrian, is taken from the Septuagint.

The famous Latin translation of the Bible called the Vulgate, which is now, and has been for many ages, of authority in the church of Rome, is of great antiquity. It is by some said to have been written, or at least copied and improved, by St. Jerome in the fourth century; probably the last was the case, for there existed before his time a Latin version, which Augustine calls the Italian, Jerome the Vulgate, and Gregory Nazeazen the ancient version. In the year 1200, Peter de Vaux translated the Bible into French; and about the same time the Spanish translation was made. There have been many translations both into French and Spanish since that time. The Polish version was published A. D. 1390; and the first Italian version, A. D. 1471. Luther composed his version of the Bible, in the German language, between the years 1521 and 1532; and what is remarkable, not only the Popish translations, but those of the Protestants, for a considerable time after the reformation, were made, not from the Hebrew of the Old, and Greek of the New Testament, but from the Latin of the Vulgate. We are told that early in the sixteenth century the Bohemians took their first version from the Vulgate; but that toward the close of that century eight divines were employed to compose another from the original text.

We will now give some account of the translations of the Bible into the English language. There have been some who have affirmed that Adelme, Bishop of Sherborn, who lived in the beginning of the eighth century, translated the Psalms into the Saxon tongue. That, however, is uncertain, as some of the best historians make no mention of it; yet it is possible, as he was a man of great parts, and of great learning for those times, and said to be the first Englishman who wrote in the Latin language. About the same time, or a little after, Bede, commonly called the Venerable Bede, translated some parts of the New Testament—some say the whole Bible, but that is not probable. Near two hundred years later, King Alfred translated the Psalms into the same language. In 1382, Wickliff finished his translation of the Bible, which is yet extant; that is to say, there are copies of it in some public and private libraries. All these translations were made from the Vulgate. In the reign of Henry the Eighth, several editions of the Old and New Testaments were published in English: one of the most remarkable is that of William Tyndal in 1530. The translation of the New Testament was made from the original Greek, but probably the Old Testament either from the Latin of the Vulgate, or the Greek of the Septuagint. This was soon followed by the improvements of Coverdale and Mathews. By order of the king, Tonstal, Bishop of Durham, and Heath, Bishop of Rochester, made a new translation, which was published in 1541; but, not pleasing Henry, it was suppressed by authority. In the reign of King Edward the Sixth, another translation was made, two editions of which were published, one in 1549, and the other in 1551. In the reign of Queen Elizabeth, another translation was made, which, being revised by some of the most learned of the bishops, went by the name of the Bishops' Bible. This professed to be translated from the Hebrew of the Old Testament, and the Greek of the New, though in some instances, when there was a difference, it preferred the Septuagint to the Hebrew.

This last circumstance, with some others, induced King James the First to select fifty-four persons, eminent in learning, and particularly well acquainted with the original languages in which the Old and New Testaments were written, to make a new translation of the whole Bible. In the year 1607, forty-seven of those persons, the other seven probably having died, assembled together, and arranged themselves into committees, to each of which a portion was given to translate. They were favored not only with the best translations, but with the most accurate copies, and the various readings of the original text. After about three years' assiduous labor, they severally completed the parts assigned them. They then met together; and while one read the translation newly formed, the rest had each a copy of the original text in his hand, or some one of the ancient versions, and when any difficulty occurred they stopped, till by common consultation it was determined what was most agreeable to the inspired original. This translation was first published A. D. 1610, and is the one which has been, ever since that time, generally approved by men of learning and piety of all denominations.

A

NEW AND COMPLETE

HISTORY OF THE BIBLE.

PART I.

CONTAINING THE HISTORY OF THE OLD TESTAMENT.

INTRODUCTORY OBSERVATIONS.

THE word BIBLE signifies *The Book;* and is applied by way of eminence to that sacred volume which was written by Divine authority and which contains the will of GOD revealed to man. It comprises the Old Testament and the New, or the Jewish and Christian Scriptures,* and consists of history, prophecy, doctrines, precepts, and devotional exercises. In some of the larger editions of the Bible there is a set of pieces called the *Apocrypha,* inserted between the two Testaments; but as they are not attended with evidences of Divine authority, they make no part of the Bible. These apocryphal books appear to contain a portion of authentic history, and many moral lessons, with much fiction and some gross absurdities.

The first five books of the Old Testament (which are called the Pentateuch), have all along been considered as written by Moses;† the others, chiefly by those whose names they bear; or where they do not appear under the name of any person, by some one qualified and authorized for that purpose. The books of the New Testament show the names of the writers to whom they are ascribed, except the "Acts of the Apostles," which bears no name, but evidently appears to have been written by the Evangelist Luke.‡

The Holy Scriptures are the gracious gift of GOD, an invaluable blessing vouchsafed to mankind. They carry with them indubitable marks of their Divine original; and that they are "written by inspiration of GOD," has been demonstrated "by many infallible proofs." The attempts of infidelity, to overturn or weaken the evidence in their favor, have tended only to illustrate and confirm them. But while the outworks of revelation are ably defended, it becomes every sincere inquirer to search out with great diligence the sacred treasures deposited therein. Here, alas! what negligence do we discover! As if it were enough to know that the Bible is the word of GOD, we are willingly ignorant of all it contains; or else we take up with some crude, undigested notion of divine things, which we have received merely upon trust. The truth, excellence, and importance of the Scriptures, are by most persons assented to; but, it is feared, few only, in comparison, are giving a serious and diligent attention to them. Every attempt, therefore, to illustrate the Bible, one of the oldest and most important books in the world—a book that has GOD for its author, and the eternal happiness of the human race for its end, deserves the most serious attention of all

---

* The word Scriptures signifies *the Writings.*
† Except the latter part of Deuteronomy, containing an account of the death of Moses.
‡ Compare the first chapter of Luke with the first of Acts.

those, especially, who profess the Christian religion. To answer this valuable purpose, is the design of the present volume. Not merely for entertainment, but for "instruction in righteousness," and to excite men to search the Scriptures for themselves, it is intended. One would think that curiosity, alone, would prompt persons to their study. For we shall hereby become acquainted with knowledge the most sublime, and events the most wonderful. But a far nobler motive than curiosity should recommend this duty to us. We are called to it by the highest authority; nor can we neglect it, without a manifest contempt of GOD, who, in that sacred book, makes known his will, and requires our unfeigned obedience. The external evidences in favor of the Bible, and the internal marks of Divine authority which it carries, together with its power on the hearts and consciences of men, have been sufficient in all ages, to convince the humble and candid inquirer after TRUTH, that the religion therein contained is from GOD—"the word of the living GOD," and is "able to make us wise unto salvation."

The importance and value of the Old Testament, in the study of either ancient or sacred history, all must admit.* With its general advantages as a text-book, comprising every species of knowledge that is useful and entertaining, every reader should be acquainted. But there are some more peculiar to it; the first of which is, that the New Testament can not be understood without the Old. The apostles often cite it, and more frequently allude to it; and our blessed LORD taking his leave of his disciples, says: "These are the words which I spake unto you, while I was still with you; that all must be fulfilled, which was written of me in the law of Moses, and in the prophets, and in the Psalms." Luke xxiv. 44.

CHRIST being the end of the law, many things which are spoken of in the Old Testament, relate to CHRIST and his servants, as well in a literal as an allegorical sense: "Our Fathers," saith St. Paul, "were all under the cloud, and all passed through the sea, and were all baptized unto Moses, and in that cloud, and that sea; and did all eat the same spiritual food, and did all drink the same spiritual drink; for they drank of the spiritual rock that followed them, and that rock was CHRIST. Now all these things were types unto them, and were written to admonish us, upon whom the ends of the world are come."

Another great advantage is, that the Old Testament is a magazine furnished, with a variety of figures, examples, doctrines, and sententious oracles, not only relating to faith, but to a good life, that thence we may furnish ourselves with directions on all occasions. Thus our blessed LORD, by the example of Noah, and Lot's wife, stirs up the slothful to watchfulness, Luke xvii. 27, 32. He threatens the obstinate

---

* The formation of man, with all his full-grown powers of body and mind—primeval rectitude, federal character and fall—the promised Saviour and his predicted victories—the patriarchal age—the deluge—the foundation of the new world—the settlement of the mother country—the division of the earth—the confusion of tongues, and the dispersion—the early settlement of Egypt—the rise and fall of the Assyrian empire, *even to the names of all its successive princes* from the first to the last—the origin, peculiarities, and overthrow of the Hebrew state—the progress and decline of Canaan, Persia, and Media,—are all familiar topics of Biblical history. Ancient cities, too,—Thebes—the No-Ammi of Nahum—Nineveh, Jerusalem, Babylon, with all that rendered them the wonders of the world, would be traced to the remote darkness of the fabulous age, but for the Old Testament. The only authentic history of these remote events and kingdoms is in the Pentateuch and in the prophets. Before the days of Moses, there were no historical records either in Assyria, Egypt, Phœnicia, Chaldea, or Greece. No other historian has lived at so remote a period as the exodus from Egypt. Dr. Winder shows, at considerable length, that Moses is the only man who had any considerable *materials* for Egyptian history; as the ancient learning of Egypt must have been chiefly lost by the excision of the first-born and the disasters of the Red sea. Since the priests the more common depositories of learning, usually attended in their wars, the people who were left behind must have been chiefly the common people; so that for a long time after this disaster, Egypt was involved in ignorance and darkness; nor is this nation subsequently mentioned in the Hebrew Scriptures until the reign of Solomon. "Moses was the father of history." Infidels have affirmed, there were *astronomical calculations* in Babylon that reached back to a period much farther than the Mosaic history; which therefore, if true, invalidate the entire account given by Moses. This assertion has received a very conclusive refutation from the astronomical calculations of Bedford. But there is a fact stated by Gillies, in his history of Greece, that confirms the calculations of Bedford. This historian states, that, after the conquest of Babylon by Alexander, he "eagerly demanded the astronomical calculations that had been carefully preserved in that ancient capitol about nineteen centuries. By the order of Alexander they were faithfully transcribed and transmitted to Aristotle," who was the preceptor of this prince. And "they re-mounted to twenty-two hundred and thirty-four years beyond the Christian era," a period not even so remote as the deluge. There is no history that can be so safely relied on, or that is so ancient, as the Mosaic history. Every other attempt at history, until the reigns of David and Solomon, is but a mass of shapeless, rearranged tradition, as corrupt as it is fabulous. Long after this time, indeed, the pages of writers, esteemed the most authentic, are disfigured by absurd and disgusting fictions. This defect in the annals of earlier times must be everywhere and deeply felt, if we exclude the information obtained from the Bible. There only is the deficiency supplied. Sanconiathan, Berosus, Ctesias, and Manetho are the oldest human historians; but "Moses was five hundred years before the first and more than a thousand before the last."

Jews, by the remembrance of Sodom and Nineveh, and the queen of the South; and terrifies the uncharitable rich with the words of Abraham to Dives in hell: " They have Moses and the prophets, let them hear them," Luke xvi. 29. St. Paul, as hath been before observed, says: " All these things were done to them for examples to us, that we should avoid those judgments God had afflicted them with for their fornication, idolatry, murmuring," &c.

The last advantage we shall mention is, that, as the Old Testament had the honor to precede the New, so it gave witness to it as John the Baptist did to Christ; both he, Moses, and the prophets, going before him to prepare the way, " to give knowledge of salvation to his people, to give light to them that sat in darkness and in the shadow of death, and to guide our feet into the way of peace." In confirmation of which, Moses and Elias appeared at the transfiguration of Christ on the Mount, bearing witness of him, and speaking of his departure, Luke ix. 31. Indeed, so great is the force of the gospel-truths, that comparing the transactions of our Saviour's life, with what was foretold of them, none can doubt of the completion of those predictions in him only. But none go so far in the eulogies of Moses and the law, as our blessed Lord himself. " There is one that accuseth you, even Moses; had ye believed on him, ye would have believed on me; for he wrote of me: but if ye believe not his writings, how shall ye believe my words, John v. 45, 46.

Having said thus much of those incomparable histories and other excellent things contained in the Old Testament, it may not be improper to say something of the writers or compilers of them. And first of Moses.

And here, considering the dignity of that great and excellent legislator, to whom God did the honor of speaking face to face, it may seem almost a presumption to attempt his character. We shall only say, that, for some thousands of years, the sun did not behold his equal. He was from his infancy brought up in a court, where he received all the advantages of a royal education. He was skilled in Egyptian learning, conversing at court till he was forty years old: at which time, being divinely inspired, he withdrew from the court of Pharaoh, and, disdaining to be thought the son of Pharaoh's daughter, chose rather to suffer affliction with the people of God, than enjoy the pleasures of a sinful life. Being obliged to flee to Midian, he undertook the humble employment of feeding sheep. In which time God appeared to him in the bush, and gave him a commission to be ruler and leader of his people.

But if we inquire more particularly into the character of this excellent person, we shall find him the most honored mortal that ever was born, till the Son of God appeared to bless the form in human shape. He was prophet, prince, and poet. For the first we have his own acknowledgment: " The Lord thy God shall raise up unto thee a prophet like unto me, from among thy brethren," Deut. xviii. 15. For the second, God himself invested him with royal power, when he gave him a commission to deliver and govern his people, Exod. iii. 10. That he was a poet appears from those eleven Psalms ascribed to him, from Psalm lxxxix. to Psalm c. Besides the many personal favors God bestowed upon this great man, he was pleased to honor him with his commendation, that he was the most faithful of his servants, to whom he would communicate his will by express words, Numb. xii. 7, 8. And indeed, if we consider the frequent interviews between God and Moses, the conveyance of the law by him, and his daily pleading for the people in the tabernacle, where God more immediately revealed himself, we may justly call him the secretary of the Divine wisdom. We shall not need to advance his character by enumerating his wondrous works in Egypt: his miraculous conduct of the Israelites through the Red sea; his furnishing them with food from heaven: his producing water by a miracle; and his vindicating God's honor and his own reputation from the calumnies of their enemies by a just execution on Korah and his associates. Whoever examines his administration, will find in it the most refined polity and most exact economy that ever adorned the character of the most illustrious legislator; for he had to do with a most obstinate rebellious people, and whom he governed with such dexterity, that he always brought them to a sense of their duty. Nor was his humility the least embellishment of his character; for though the Israelites had often provoked him by their reproaches, and apostacy, and sometimes threatened to stone him, unmoved he beheld their ingratitude, and, instead of revenging himself by threats and punishments, he humbly addressed himself to God in their behalf, to deprecate the judgments they deserved. And for this virtue God himself expressly distinguishes him with this eulogy, that " he was the meekest man upon earth."

As to the other writers of the Old Testament, little need be said. The first catalogue of sacred books was made by the Jews, but by whom is not certainly known. It is highly probable, it was by Ezra, who collected all the sacred books of the Old Testament, and showing the collection to the Jews, it was received and approved by the whole nation.

The five books written by Moses, contain the history of nearly three thousand years, from the creation till his death. The prophets who succeeded him, wrote in thirteen books, all that happened from his death to the reign of Artaxerxes.

It is not certain whether Joshua wrote the book that goes by his name; but it is very probable it was written by his command, and soon after his death; for Moses had often, during his administration, ordered him to write the most remarkable occurrences in a book. It contained a history of about seventeen years.

Some are of opinion, that every judge wrote what was transacted in his days; and that all these transactions were collected either by Samuel or Ezra. The book of Judges contains the history of three hundred years and upward, from the death of Joshua to the death of Samson. As for the story of Ruth, it is certain she lived in the time of the judges, probably under Shamgar.

The four books that follow, contain the history of near six hundred years. The first book of Samuel to the twenty-fifth chapter, was written by Samuel himself; the prophets Gad and Nathan finished it, and wrote the second book of Samuel. The two books of Kings were written by Jeremiah or Ezra.

The two books of Chronicles were written after the four former. It is generally believed they were composed by Ezra, who collected them partly out of the other books of the Bible, and partly out of the papers which were yet extant in his days, but since lost.

Ezra wrote that book which is called by his name: and contains the history of eighty-two years, from the first year of Cyrus to the twentieth of Artaxerxes Longimanus.

The book of Nehemiah was certainly written by himself, and contains the history of about thirty-one years, from the reign of Artaxerxes to the beginning of the reign of Darius.

The time and author of the book of Esther are very uncertain. Some think it was written by Ezra, or Joachim the priest, the grandson of Jozedec.

As to the story of Job, some have questioned the truth of it; but Job being mentioned in Holy Writ with so much applause, it would be criminal to doubt it.[*] The time in which he lived is difficult to be ascertained, as well as the author. Some say, it was written by himself, others by Moses. These are but conjectures. It is generally believed that Job lived before Moses, and that his afflictions befell him when the children of Israel were in the wilderness. Some are of opinion, that he was descended of Nahor, Abraham's brother; others from Esau, which last is most probable.

CHAPTER I.

HAVING made these introductory observations, we begin with the first transaction that is recorded in history. It is the most awful and glorious that imagination can conceive, namely, THE CREATION OF THE WORLD. " To whom are the heavens above us, the world which we inhabit, and the various objects with which it is filled, indebted for their existence?" A mild but majestic voice replies from the sacred oracle, " In the beginning, God created the heavens, and the earth, and all that is therein." Stupendous work! and worthy the amazing power of that Supreme Being by whom it was executed. The idea of creation is very sublime; but our familiarity with the term may have rendered us insensible of its magnificent character. It is, indeed, so vast, that many of the ancient philosophers denied the possibility of creation, and hence assigned the attribute of eternity to matter[†] making it, in this re-

[*] See Ezekiel xiv. 14; James v. 11.
[†] We know, from the infallible testimony of God, that men and other animals which inhabit the earth, the seas, and the air; all the immense varieties of herbs and plants of which the vegetable kingdom con-

spect, " equal to GOD." But we have not so studied the history of the universe; and our readers, we trust, have learned a better lesson from the oracles of GOD.

In the book of Genesis, the " beginning" of everything is ascribed to the creative power of GOD; and we are informed that over the formless and chaotic earth, darkness reigned, and " that the Spirit of GOD moved" or brooded " upon the face of the waters," bringing order out of confusion, light out of darkness, and this beauteous earth into a fit condition for the residence of man, and the subsistence of animal and vegetable life. The Almighty architect said, " LET THERE BE LIGHT, AND THERE WAS LIGHT." With respect to this expression, Longinus, that great judge of the beautiful and sublime, says, " It is the most noble and lofty example of sublimity that imagination can conceive; it commands things into existence, speaks with the voice of supernatural authority, and is the language of GOD." " And GOD saw the light that it was good, and he divided the light from the darkness, calling the light day, and the darkness night; and the evening and the morning were the first day." Surprising display of OMNIPOTENCE to illuminate a whole system in so short a time, and appoint the proper portions of light and darkness to every part of the universe!*

Who, with an intelligent mind and a sensitive heart, can look upon the glorious

sists; the globe of the earth, the expanse of the ocean, and the wonders of the skies, were all produced by the power of the ETERNAL. Matter, however, under all the varieties of its form, the relative disposition of its parts, and the motions communicated to it, is but an inferior part of the works of creation. From the faculty of thought, and the powers of perception and reflection of which we are conscious, we feel assured that we are animated by a much higher and nobler principle than brute matter.

* THE CREATION OF LIGHT.—We were considerably affected in our younger days by the long-standing objection that Moses made light to exist before the creation of the sun; as books then usually taught, what some still fancy, that there could not have been light without this luminary. But not choosing, on such an important point, to attach our faith to any general assertion, we sought to find out if any investigator of the nature of light had perceived any distinction in its qualities or operation which made it a fluid, or matter independent of the sun. It was not easy, before the year 1790, to meet with the works of any student of nature on such a subject, as it had been little attended to; but we at length saw the fact asserted by Henckel, a German of the old school, of some value in his day; and soon afterward some experiments were announced in England, which confirmed the supposition. It has been a favorite point of attention with us ever since; and no truth in philosophy seems to be now more fully ascertained than that light has a distinct existence, separate and independent of the sun. This is a striking confirmation of the Mosaic record; for that expressly distinguishes the existence and operation of light from the solar action upon it, and from that radiation of it which is connected with his beams and presence. By Moses, an interval of three days is placed between the luminous creation and the appearance and position of the sun and moon. Light was therefore operating, by its own laws and agencies, without the sun, and independently of his peculiar agency, from the first day to the fourth of our terrestrial fabrication. But from the time that the sun was placed in his central position, and his rays were appointed to act on our earth, they have been always performing most beneficial operations, essential to the general course of things. They have also been ascertained by Dr. Herschel to have a power of heating distinct from their production of light and color—an interesting discovery, connected with more consequences and inferences than have yet been noticed. The glory of Sir Isaac Newton began by his discovering that light was not simple and homogeneous, but that it consisted of seven rays of different colors, and of different and invariable degrees of refrangibility. The same degree of this belonged always to the same color, and the same color to the same degree of refrangibility. Red, yellow, and blue, are the primary colors; white light their compound. An opposing theory to this has been gradually growing up from the time of Des Cartes, and is now maintained by several men of no small name and powers in science, which considers light to be an undulating vibration of an ethereal medium universally diffused, and not, as Newton thought, an emanation of particles direct from the sun. La Place preferred the opinion that " light is an emanation from a luminous body." But the newer system comes nearest to the Mosaic fact that light was a distinct production anterior to the sun; and appears to be gaining ground in philosophical minds. Perhaps some harmonizing combination of both theories may reconcile all the phenomena, and best explain the true nature and operation of light. It seems most probable that light is an ethereal fluid now universally diffused, and pervading all things, and not an emanation from the sun; but that this luminary has a direct and additional agency upon it, whose effects we daily see. It may not be impertinent to suggest that light seems, like heat, to have two states, active and latent. The active state causes its visible phenomena, and our sensation of daylight. When this subsides, by the sun's departure, into its latent state, our sense of darkness, or night, is produced. The solar rays again emerging on it, have the power of changing its latent state into its active visibility. Light has also the property of being absorbed by, and, we would add, of combining with, all substances; with some wholly, which are then black; with others, the most numerous cases, only in part; and then that portion of them which is not so absorbed emanates from the substance in the color which comes from them to the eye. After having for many years attended to the phenomena of light, we can not but consider it to be a universally-diffused fluid. Thus far the idea would accord with the undulatory theory; but many facts lead us also to conclude that it actually enters into the composition of all or most substances, and, like heat, becomes a latent part of them. From these it is extricable, with more or less rapidity, without the interference of the solar ray, as in the burning of all inflammable bodies, when it passes into its active and visible state. When the two liquids of nitrous gas and oil of turpentine burst into a flame on being mixed, without the approach of any fire, we think we see a striking instance of latent and combined light passing suddenly into the free and active state. So when that brilliant blaze occurs on dipping the iron wire into oxygen gas, it seems to be the latent light combined in the gas, evolving from it instantaneously into its visible form. The sun has nothing to do with these phenomena, nor with any of our artificial illuminations. All these may be deemed latent light, emerging from its combinations into free and active visibility. Yet most of the Newtonian principles and laws concerning it are confirmed by the phenomena which suggested them; and so is much of the new system by those facts which have been adduced in its support. Hence it is most probable that both theories have a foundation in truth, but require some further additions and modifications on each side to make them consistent with each other, and to remove the apparent contradictions which now keep them in the state of controversial hostility.

scenes and objects around him, without emotion; and, if piety be an inmate of his bosom, without adoring reverence and filial love to Him who made them all? And yet it is most true that the beauties and sublimities of the natural world are exhibited in vain to the generality of mankind. Engaged in other pursuits, or degraded by evil passions, or besotted by self-indulgence, the most magnificent, and the most soothing scenes which mark the power or the goodness of GOD, are equally unnoticed and despised by many who ought to feel most interested in them.

> Wandering oft, with brute unconscious gaze
> Man marks not" HIM,—" marks not the mighty hand,
> That, ever busy, wheels the silent spheres,—
> And as, on earth, this grateful change revolves,
> With transport touches all the springs of life."

The waters being still dispersed over the face of chaos, the Almighty was pleased to separate them from each other, and restrain their current within proper bounds. He divided those above the firmament from those beneath, and parted the waters of the earth from the watery atmospheres. The firmament* formed on this occasion was called heaven, and, with the separation of the waters, completed the second day of the creation. Light being formed, and the waters separated from each other, the Almighty, on the third day, commanded that the waters beneath the firmament should be gathered together, and dry land appear. The waters, accordingly, fled into deep valleys, and recesses of the earth, the lofty mountains raised their towering heads, and the lesser hills displayed their pleasing summits. As the great Creator designed the earth for the future habitation of man and beast, it was no sooner separated from the waters, than he gave it a prolific virtue, and endowed it with the power of vegetation. The surface was immediately covered with grass for cattle, which was succeeded by herbs, plants, and fruit-trees, proper for the nourishment of man. All those were instantly in a state of perfection, that they might be ready for the use of those inhabitants for whom they were designed.†

The Almighty Creator, having prepared such necessaries as he thought proper on earth, for the use of its intended inhabitants, on the fourth day formed those two great luminaries of heaven called the Sun and Moon! the former of which he appointed to rule the day, and the latter the night. He likewise formed the planets, fixed their gravitation and vicissitudes, and appointed their regular courses, that they might divide time and distinguish the seasons. By means of these luminaries the atmosphere was rarified, and by their influence on the planets, was promoted the office of vegetation.

The creation of the first four days consisting of things inanimate, on the fifth GOD pronounced his omnipotent fiat, for the production of living creatures, saying, "Let the waters bring forth abundantly the moving creature that hath life, and fowls‡ that they may fly above the earth in the open firmament of heaven." He was pleased to form these creatures of different shapes and sizes; some very large,‖ to show the wonders of his creating power, and others exceeding small, to display the goodness of his indulgent providence. After he had created them, he gave them his blessing, by bidding them, *be fruitful and multiply;* enduing them, at the same time, with a power to propagate, in a prolific manner, their respective species. And thus were completed the works of the fifth day.

In the beginning of the sixth day GOD created the terrestrial animals, which the sacred historian has divided into three classes, namely,

* The Hebrew word which we translate *firmament,* signifies a curtain, or anything stretched out and extended. The term is not only applied to the sky, but to the atmosphere, and in this place seems particularly to refer to that extent of airy matter which encompasses the earth, and separates the clouds from the waters on the earth.

† Though the first fruits of the earth were all produced without any seeds, by the bare command of God, yet, to perpetuate the same, each kind contained its own seed, which being sown in the earth, or falling, when ripe, from the plants themselves, should continue in succession to the end of the world.

‡ From this expression, some are of opinion that fowls derive their origin from the water as well as the fishes; while others, with equal reason, suppose them to have been made out of the earth, agreeably to the following passage in Gen. ii. 19: "Out of the ground God formed every beast of the field, and every fowl of the air." But these two texts are easily reconciled, when we consider that neither denies what the other asserts. It is to be observed, that some fowls live mostly in the water, others partly on land and partly on water, while a third sort live altogether on land. This diversity countenances the opinion of many of the ancients, that they were made partly out of the water, or of both mixed together.

‖ The words in the text are, *And God created great whales.* But this expression must not be confined to the whale alone; it undoubtedly implies fish of an enormous size, of which there are various species, that differ both in their form and magnitude.

1. Beasts, or wild creatures, such as lions, tigers, bears, wolves, &c.

2. Cattle, or domestic animals, for the use of men, such as bulls and cows, sheep, hogs, horses, asses, &c.

3. Creeping things, such as serpents, worms, and various kinds of insects.

The omnipotent Creator having made these abundant preparations, crowned his work with the formation of the grand object, MAN, for whose use they were designed. He said, *Let us make man in our own image, after our likeness.** And, to show that the creature he was now about to form should be the master-piece of the creation, and (under his auspices) have supremacy over the whole, he further says, *and let him have dominion over the fish of the sea, and over the fowl of the air, and over the cattle, and over all the earth, and over every creeping thing that creepeth upon the earth.* In the formation of man's body, GOD made choice of the dust of the earth, after which, having infused into him an immortal spirit, or, as the text says, *breathed into his nostrils the breath of life, he became a living soul.*†

As soon as Adam began to feel a sense of his existence (having been by his great Creator invested with knowledge as well as power), he was greatly alarmed at the animals that he saw surround him; but the Almighty to ease his mind, assured him, that all the creatures on the earth should be subject to his authority, and to convince him of the great power with which he had invested him, appointed them to appear before him. This was accordingly done, upon which, as they passed, Adam readily gave them such appellations as distinguish their species, and were suitable to their natures.‡

Adam greatly admired the animals to whom he had given names; but, when he saw them all in couples, he was concerned that he alone was without a companion, whose society might contribute to his happiness. The Almighty, knowing his anxiety, threw him into a sound sleep, during which he took away one of his ribs, and, after closing up the orifice, formed it into the body of a woman,|| gave her breath, and, like Adam, she became *a living soul.*

This was certainly the last act§ of the whole creation, which, by the almighty power of GOD, was made perfect in the space of six days; at the close of which the great Creator took a survey of the whole, and pronounced it *good*, or properly adapted to the uses for which it was intended. The next day (which was the seventh from the beginning of the creation¶) GOD set apart as a time of solemn rest from his labors. He blessed and sanctified it; and to impress mankind with a just sense of his infinite wisdom, power, and goodness, ordered it ever after to be kept sacred.**

---

* What a noble and majestic expression was this, and how consistent with the nature of that Almighty Being by whom it was spoken! In the formation of other creatures, God says, Let the earth or the waters bring them forth; but here (as if man was to be made only a little lower than the angels) he says, *Let us make him in our image* - that is, let us make him like ourself; let us endue him with all those noble faculties that will raise him above the animal creation, and make him not only to bear our image in the lower world, but also qualify him for the enjoyment of those blessings that are to be found at our right hand, to the full extent of eternity.

† Josephus says, that after God had created man, he called him Adam, which in the Hebrew signifies *red*, from the earth with which he was made being of that color.

‡ The great poet, Milton, on this occasion, expresses himself as follows:

"As thus he spake, each bird and beast, behold
Approaching, two and two ; these cowering low
With blandishment ; each bird stooped on his wing.
I named them as they passed, and understood
Their nature, with such knowledge God endued
My sudden apprehension !"

|| The general name for woman, in the Hebrew tongue, is *Issa;* but this woman, being the *first*, was (after the fall) called *Eve*, which signifies *the mother of human kind.*

§ Though the sacred historian does not, *in a particular manner*, mention the formation of Eve till some time after that of Adam, yet it is not in the least to be doubted but they were both created on the same day. This, indeed, evidently appears from the relation of the works of the sixth day, Gen. ii. 27, where, after the words, *God created man in his own image*, are added, *male and female created he them.*

¶ It is not directly ascertained at what time or season of the year the world was made ; but, from the trees being laden with fruit (of which history informs us our first parents did eat), it is most reasonable to suppose that it was at or near the autumnal equinox.

** Thus was the seventh day appointed by God, from the very beginning of the world, to be observed as a day of rest by mankind, in memory of the great benefits received in the formation of the universe. It has been a question, among the learned, whether any sabbath was observed before the promulgation of the law by Moses ; but the most judicious commentators agree that Adam and Eve constantly observed the seventh day, and dedicated it in a peculiar manner to the service of the Almighty ; and that the first Sabbath, which Philo (one of the most ancient writers) calls *the birth-day of the world*, was celebrated in Paradise itself ; which pious custom, being transmitted from our first parents to their posterity, became in time so general, that the same Philo calls it the universal festival of mankind.

When Adam first beheld the fair partner of his life, who was presented to him by ner Almighty Creator, he was struck with a secret sympathy, and, finding her of his own likeness and complexion, he exclaimed with rapture,* *This is now bone of my bone, and flesh of my flesh.* He easily foresaw that the love and union which were now, to take place between them were to be lasting. The Divine Hand which conducted the woman to Adam did it in the light of a matrimonial father; and having joined them together, he pronounced this benediction, *Be fruitful and multiply, and replenish the earth;* intimating, that, as he had given them dominion over every part of the creation, they, by being themselves fruitful in the procreation of children, might live to see the earth replenished with a numerous progeny.

To facilitate the intended happiness of our first parents, the Almighty Creator had provided for their residence a most delightful spot called Eden,† which was watered by an extensive river divided into four streams. It was furnished with all kinds of vegetables, among which were two remarkable trees, one called the *Tree of Life,*‡

* The joy and transport of Adam, on his first sight of Eve, is thus beautifully expressed by Milton:

"————————————On she came,
Led by her heavenly Maker (though unseen)
And guided by his voice; not uninformed
Of nuptial sanctity and marriage rites.
Grace was in all her steps, heaven in her eye,
In every gesture dignity and love.
I, overjoyed, could not forbear aloud:
'This turn hath made amends; thou hast fulfilled
Thy words, Creator bounteous and benign!
Giver of all things fair, but fairest this
Of all thy gifts!'"

† There is probably no subject on which such a diversity of opinions has been entertained as concerning the site of the Paradise in which the progenitors of mankind were placed. Mohammedans even believe that it was in one of the seven heavens from which Adam was cast down upon the earth after the fall. "Some," says Dr. Clarke, "place it in the third heaven, others in the fourth; some within the orbit of the moon, others in the moon itself; some in the middle regions of the air, or beyond the earth's attraction; some on the earth, others under the earth, and others within the earth." Every section of the earth's surface has also, in its turn, had its claim to this distinction advocated. From this mass of conflicting opinions we shall select the two which have been supported by the most eminent authorities, and which seem to have the strongest probabilities in their favor.

It has been assumed that in whatever situation, otherwise probable, the marks by which Moses characterizes the spot are to be found, there we may suppose that we have discovered the site of Paradise. In fixing the first probability, the all but unquestionable fact that the known rivers Euphrates and Tigris are mentioned as two of the four rivers of Eden, is of the greatest importance; and therefore the most exact inquirers have not sought for the spot at any point distant from those rivers. The Euphrates and Tigris being thus identified with two of the rivers of Eden, there has remained a great latitude in the choice of a site for the garden, some looking for it near the source of those rivers, and others seeking it in the low and flat plains through which they flow in the lower part of their course.

The first position places Eden in Armenia, near the sources of the four great rivers Euphrates, Tigris (Hiddekel), Phasis (Pison), and the Araxes (Gihon). The similarity of sound between Phasis and Pison is considered to strengthen this opinion, as does also the similarity of meaning between the Hebrew name Gihon and the Greek Araxes, both words denoting swiftness.

One consideration that induced a preference for this site is, that the advocates of this opinion considered "heads," as applied to the rivers which went forth from the garden, to mean "sources," which would therefore render it natural to look for the terrestrial paradise in a mountainous or hilly country, which only could supply the water necessary to form four heads of rivers. But others, those who would fix the site toward the other extremity of the two known rivers, reckon it sufficient, and indeed more accordant with the text, to consider the "four heads" not as sources, but as channels—that is, that the Euphrates and Tigris united before they entered the garden, and after leaving it divided again, and entered the Persian gulf by two mouths; thus forming four channels, two above and two below the garden, each called by a different name. "The river or channel," says Dr. Wells, "must be looked upon as a highway crossing over a forest, and which may be said to divide itself into four ways, whether the division be made above or below the forest." With this view, some writers are content to take the present Shat-ul-Arab (the single stream which is formed by the confluence of the Tigris and Euphrates, and which afterward divides to enter the gulf) as the river that went through the garden; but as Major Rennell has shown that the two great rivers kept distinct courses to the sea until the time of Alexander, although at no great distance of time afterward they became united, other writers are contented to believe that such a junction and subsequent divergence did, either in the time of Moses or before the deluge, exist in or near the place indicated. The deluge must have made great changes in the beds of these and many other rivers, and inferior agencies have alone been sufficient greatly to alter the ancient channels of the Tigris and Euphrates. This is not only rendered obvious by an inspection of the face of the country, but the memory of such events is preserved by local traditions, and they are even specified in the writings of the Arabian geographers and historians. Thus, then, of the two most probable conjectures, one fixes the terrestrial Paradise in Armenia, between the sources of the Euphrates, Tigris, Phasis, and Araxes; and the other identifies the *land* of Eden with the country between Bagdad and Bussorah; and, in that land, some fix the *garden* near the latter city, while others, more prudently, only contend that it stood in some part of this territory where an ancient junction and subsequent separation of the Euphrates and Tigris took place.

‡ This tree is supposed to have been so called from its having in it a virtue not only to repair the animal spirits, as other nourishment does, but likewise to preserve and maintain them in the same equal temper and state wherein they were created; that is to say, without affecting the party who used it with pain, disease, and decay.

and the other the *Tree of Knowledge*,* by the latter of which *Good* and *Evil* were to be distinguished. Into this earthly paradise did the Almighty conduct Adam and Eve, giving them orders to take care of the garden, and superintend the plants. He granted them permission to eat of the fruit of every tree, except that of the *Tree of Knowledge of Good and Evil*. This he strictly charged them not even to touch, on the penalty of incurring his displeasure, and thereby entailing upon themselves and their descendants, mortality, diseases, and death. With this small restraint GOD left them in the garden of Eden, where everything was pleasing to the sight, and accommodated to their mutual enjoyment.

Thus fixed in the most beautiful situation, possessed of innocence, devoid of guilt, and free from care, the happiness of our first parents appeared complete:

> " Perfection crowned with wondrous frame,
> And peace and plenty smiled around ;
> They felt no grief, they knew no shame,
> But tasted heaven on earthly ground."

But, alas! their bliss was transient, their innocence fleeting, and their exemption from care very short.

All animals at this time were social in their tempers, except the serpent,† who was equally subtle and envious. This malignant creature, viewing the felicity of the first pair with those painful sensations which are natural to depravity of heart, determined to allure them from their innocence, and stimulate them to the crime of disobedience. In consequence of this infernal design, he began by persuading Eve to taste the prohibited Tree of Knowledge, telling her,‡ that, by so doing, both herself and her husband would immediately be sensible of the difference between Good and Evil,' acquire much additional happiness, and even not be inferior, in point of wisdom, to GOD himself.

Unhappily the artifices of the serpent prevailed. Eve gazed on the tempting fruit till her appetite was inflamed; its beautiful hue made her fancy it a most delicious food; and she at length sacrificed her duty to gratify her curiosity. She stretched forth her presumptuous hand, took of the baneful fruit, and ate her own destruction.

> " ———————— She plucked, she ate ;
> Earth felt the wound, and nature from her seat,
> Sighing through all her works, gave sign of wo
> That all was lost."

Pleased with the taste of the fruit, and fancying herself already in possession of that additional happiness the serpent had promised her, she flew to Adam, and enticed him to participate in her crime.

> " ———————— He scrupled not to eat
> Against his better knowledge—
> Earth trembled from her entrails, as again
> In pangs, and Nature gave a second groan :
> Sky lowered, and muttering thunder, some sad drops
> Wept, at completing of the mortal sin."

Remorse, the natural consequence of guilt, now opened their eyes to each other's nakedness. No longer shielded by innocence from shame, they were mutually shocked at the reciprocal indecency of their appearance : art was now substituted to conceal what their criminality rendered too obvious; they contrived aprons made of fig-leaves, and highly applauded themselves for acquiring, at the expense of their integrity, the faculty of invention, to remove difficulties which their former simplicity prevented their perceiving.

While they were in a state of innocence, they no sooner heard the voice of GOD ap-

---

* There are various opinions concerning the nature and properties of the *Tree of Knowledge*, which was forbidden to our first parents. Some think it had a baneful quality, directly opposite to that of the Tree of Life ; while others imagine it is thus called by the sacred historian, because, directly after Adam and Eve had eaten of it, they became sensible of the good they had lost, and the evil they had incurred, by their disobedience.

† It is generally thought that this was the work of Satan, who, to effect his purposes, assumed the figure of a serpent.

‡ It may appear strange to some that the serpent should be here represented as having the power of speech, and that Eve, on that account, should not have been greatly alarmed. Josephus and some others allege that all animals were endued with speech and reason before the fall. But other interpreters more plausibly observe, that the meaning here must be that the serpent, by his actions, conveyed the same ideas to the mind of Eve as words of the same import would have done. For example, she seeing the serpent eat of the forbidden fruit without receiving any damage, concluded it was innocent, and was therefore induced by his example to make the trial herself.

proach them, than they ran with ecstasy to meet him, and with humble joy welcomed his gracious visits; but now their Maker was become a terror to them, and they a terror to each other. Their consciences painted their transgression in the blackest colors, all hope was banished, and nothing remained but horror and despair.

When, therefore, after their transgression, they heard the voice of the LORD in the garden, instead of running to meet him as before with cheerfulness and joy, they flew to the most retired part of it, in order to conceal themselves from his sight.* But the Almighty soon called them from their dark retreat; and, after a short examination, they both acknowledged their guilt. The man attempted to excuse himself by laying the blame on the woman, and pleaded her persuasions as the cause of his criminality. The woman endeavored to remove the crime from herself to the serpent; but the Almighty thought proper to make all three the objects of his distributive justice. As the serpent had been the original cause of this evil, GOD first passes sentence on him, which was, that (instead of going erect as he did before the fact) he should ever after creep on his belly, and thereupon become incapable of eating any food, except what was mingled with dust. The woman was given to understand that she had entailed upon herself sorrow from conception, pain in childbirth, and subjection to her husband. The punishment of Adam consisted in a life of perpetual toil and slavery,† in order to keep in due subjection those passions and appetites, to gratify which he had transgressed the divine command.

The awful decree being thus solemnly pronounced, as well on the author of the offence, as the offenders themselves, the Almighty, to enhance their sense of the crime, and the tokens of his resentment, expelled the guilty pair from the blissful regions of paradise, after which he placed at the east end of the garden a guard of angels, in order not only to prevent their re-entrance, but to secure the forbidden fruit from the unhallowed hands of polluted mankind.

Thus, by this original pollution, fell our first parents, who, from the happiest condition that can be conceived, plunged themselves into a state of wretchedness, and thereby entailed misery on their descendants.

> "They ate the apple, it is true;
> We taste the wormwood and the gall,
> And to these distant ages rue
> The dire effects of Adam's fall."

CHAPTER II.

In the space of two years after the expulsion of our first parents from Paradise, the human race was increased by Eve's being delivered of two sons, the first of whom she called Cain,‡ and the latter Abel.‖ As these two brothers were of different dispositions, so, when they grew up to years of maturity, they followed different employments. Abel, the younger was just in his dealings, and amiable in his temper. Firmly believing that GOD saw all his actions, and knew their motives, he carefully avoided offending his beneficent Maker, and, in the simplicity of a shepherd's life, took a pleasure in practising all the social virtues. On the contrary, Cain was perversely wicked, and avariciously craving. His attention was principally directed to

---

* Milton makes Adam, on this occasion, express himself as follows:
> "—————— How shall I behold the face
> Henceforth of God or angel, erst with joy
> And raptures oft beheld?— O! might I here
> In solitude live savage, in some glade
> Obscured, where highest woods impenetrable
> To star or sunlight) spread their umbrage broad,
> And brown as evening; cover me, ye pines!
> Ye cedars, with innumerable boughs,
> Hide me, where I never may see them more!"

† The words in the text are, *in the sweat of thy face shalt thou eat bread*; which implies that labor alone should produce what, if he had not transgressed, nature would have spontaneously bestowed.

‡ As soon as Eve was delivered of her first child, she cried out, in a transport of joy, *I have gotten a man from the Lord*: being persuaded that this son was the *promised seed* mentioned by the Almighty in the sentence he passed on the serpent: *I will put enmity between thee and the woman, and between thy seed and her seed: it shall bruise thy head, and thou shalt bruise his heel.* In consequence of this persuasion, Eve called her first son Cain, which signifies *possession* or *acquisition*.

‖ The word *Abel*, in the Hebrew language, signifies *vanity*, and, according to some, was given him as an intimation of the little esteem his mother had for him in comparison of her first-born.

husbandry; but with all the benefits arising from cultivation, he was perpetually dissatisfied at what the earth produced, and, from his natural vile disposition, was guilty of the first murder ever committed.

It was customary, even in the infancy of the world, to make acknowledgments to God by way of oblation. This being agreed on by these two brothers, Cain offered the produce of his husbandry, and such fruits as nature bestowed by the assistance of art. Abel's oblation consisted of the milk of his herds, and the firstlings of his flocks. The Almighty was pleased to prefer the latter, being the simple productions of nature, to the former, which, no doubt, he considered as the interested offerings of laborious avarice. This preference raised the resentment of Cain, whose soul was so impressed with hatred toward his brother, that he even showed it in his countenance.

The Almighty, knowing the secrets of Cain's heart, condescended, in his great goodness, to expostulate with him to the following effect: "That his respect to true goodness was impartial, wherever he found it; and that, therefore, it was purely his own fault that his offering was not equally accepted: that piety was the proper disposition for a sacrificer, and that if herein he would emulate his brother, the same tokens of divine approbation should attend his oblations: that it was madness in him to harbor any revengeful thought against his brother, because, if he proceeded to put them into execution, a dreadful punishment would immediately follow."

This kind admonition from the Almighty had so little effect upon Cain, that, instead of being sensible of his fault, and endeavoring to amend, he grew more and more incensed against his brother, and at length formed the resolution of gratifying his revenge by depriving him of his existence. Accordingly, going one day to Abel, and pretending the greatest kindness and affection, he asked if he would walk with him in the fields, as the weather was remarkably fine and pleasant. Abel, little suspecting the horrid design of his brother, readily complied with his request, when the latter had no sooner got him to a convenient spot, than he fell upon him and killed him;* after which, to prevent discovery, he dug a hole, and interred the body.

But it was not long before Cain was called to an account for this horrid deed. The all-seeing God, from whom no secrets can be hid, appeared before him, and demanded the reason of his brother's absence. Sensible of the enormity of his crime, Cain attempted to reply; but guilt, for a time, tied his tongue. At length, in faltering accents, he tried to evade what he did not dare positively to answer. He pretended to be surprised at not having seen his brother for some time; and likewise observed, that he was neither the guardian of Abel, nor empowered to watch his motions.

On this the Almighty charged Cain, in direct terms, with the murder of his brother; and, after expressing to him the atrociousness of the crime, and how much it cried to heaven for vengeance, proceeded to pass sentence on him. "Now," says he, "art thou cursed from the earth, which hath opened her mouth to receive thy brother's blood from thy hand. When thou tillest the ground it shall not henceforth yield unto thee her strength; a fugitive and a vagabond shalt thou be in the earth."

The wretched criminal, struck with the severity of this denunciation, convinced of the atrocious nature of his offence, and deploring the misery of his situation, exclaimed, "My punishment is greater than I can bear." He was apprehensive of meeting with worse evils than his sentence really imported; and that he should not only feel the miseries of banishment, but likewise be subjected to the loss of his life by the hands of his fellow-creatures. But, to ease his mind in this last respect, the Almighty was pleased to declare to him, that whoever should slay him, vengeance should be taken on them seven fold. He likewise set a particular mark on him, whereby he might escape his supposed danger; for it was the divine intent to punish him by the prolongation of his life, during the remainder of which he should be loaded with infamy, and under all the horrors of a guilty conscience.

In consequence of the divine sentence, Cain left his parents and relations, and went into a strange country. He was banished from that sacred spot where the Almighty had given frequent manifestations of his glorious presence; and though by the divine decree no person was permitted to hurt him, yet the consciousness of his own guilt made him fearful of everything he saw or heard. After wandering about

* As warlike instruments were not at this time in use, it is generally supposed that Cain murdered Abel by knocking out his brains either with a stone or a piece of wood; but in whatever manner it was done, this we know, from the words of divine revelation, that Cain was the first murderer, and Abel the person first murdered.

a considerable time through different countries, he at length settled with his family in the land of Nod. Here he lived for a course of years, in which time his descendants being greatly increased, in order to keep them together, he built a city, and called it after the name of his son Enoch, which, in the Hebrew tongue, signifies a dedication.

From the loins of Cain, in regular succession, came Lamech, the son of Methuselah, who introduced polygamy by marrying two wives, the one named Adah, and the other Zillah. Among the children by the former of these wives he had two sons, namely, Jabal and Jubal, the first of whom made great improvements in the management of cattle, and the other invented the psaltery, and first gave melody to music. By Zillah he had Tubal-Cain, who was celebrated for his great strength, excelled in martial exercises, and first discovered the art of forging and polishing metals. Lamech had likewise a daughter called Naamah (which denotes *fair* and *beautiful*), who is supposed to have been the first person that found out the art of spinning and weaving.

Having said thus much of Cain and his posterity, we must now return to our primitive parents, Adam and Eve. The death of the righteous Abel and the banishment of Cain afflicted them to the heart; and they continued some time in the deepest lamentation. At length the Almighty was pleased to alleviate their affliction by a promise that they should have another son, who should be a comfort and consolation to them in their old age. Accordingly, in the proper course of time, Eve was delivered of another boy, whom they called Seth, which signifies *substitute*, or *appointed*, because God was pleased to send him instead of " Abel, whom Cain slew." At this time Adam was one hundred and thirty years old, after which he lived eight hundred years, and begat several other children, both sons and daughters.

The male posterity of Adam, in the line of Seth, was as follows:—

When Seth was one hundred and five years old, he had a son named Enos, in whose days the sacred historian informs us that men began to institute stated forms and ceremonies in the worship of Almighty God. After the birth of Enos, Seth lived eight hundred and seven years, so that the whole of his life was nine hundred and twelve years.

Enos, at the age of ninety, had a son, whom he named Cainan; after which he lived eight hundred and fifteen years; in the whole nine hundred and five.

Cainan, when seventy, had a son named Mahalaleel; after which he lived eight hundred and forty years; in all nine hundred and ten.

Mahalaleel, when sixty-five, had a son named Jared; after which he lived eight hundred years; in all eight hundred and sixty-five.

Jared, when one hundred and sixty-two, had a son named Enoch;[*] after which he lived eight hundred years; in all nine hundred and sixty-two.

Enoch, when sixty-five, had a son named Methuselah; after which he lived three hundred years; in all three hundred and sixty-five.

Methuselah, when one hundred and eighty-seven, had a son named Lamech; after which he lived seven hundred and eighty-two years; in all nine hundred and sixty-nine.

Lamech, when one hundred and eighty-two, had a son named Noah; after which he lived five hundred and ninety-five years; in all seven hundred and seventy-seven.

And Noah, when five hundred years old, had three sons, Shem, Ham, and Japhet; from whom the world was replenished after the general deluge.

This is the genealogy which Moses gives us of the posterity of Adam, in the line of Seth; and if we consider the prodigious length of men's lives in this age, the strength of their constitutions from a temperate life, and the advanced years in which they begat children, the number of inhabitants previous to the flood must have been very immense.

The descendants of Seth, and those of Cain, lived separate for a considerable time, the former despising the latter on account of their natural cruelty. The Sethites, who adhered to the service of God, and diligently attended to their religious duties, were styled the "Sons of God;" in distinction to which the descendants of Cain, who led profligate and impious lives, were termed the "sons and daughters of men."

---

* Of all the posterity of Adam, the most remarkable is Enoch, who, for his distinguished piety and virtue, was exempted from mortality, being immediately, that is, without passing through the valley of the shadow of death, translated to the heavenly mansions.

After the death of Adam,* the Sethites retired from the plain where they had hitherto resided, to the mountains opposite paradise; and, for some time, continued to live in the fear of God, and to preserve the strictest rules of piety and virtue. In the course of time, the descendants of Cain, who were now become very numerous, spread themselves over all that part of the country which had been left by the Sethites, even to the confines of the mountains where Seth had fixed his abode; and here they continued that abandoned course of life they had followed before their removal.

By this close connexion, the Sethites had frequent opportunities of seeing the daughters of Cain, who being exceeding beautiful, they were so captivated with their charms, that they entered into nuptial alliances with them; and from this intercourse were born men of a very gigantic size, who were no less remarkable for their daring wickedness, than for their bold and adventurous undertakings. Thus did the example of the wicked family of Cain prevail, and, by degrees, destroy all the remains of religious duties in the posterity of Seth. The righteous Noah used his utmost efforts to convince them of the enormity of their conduct; but all his admonitions were in vain: the bent of their thoughts had taken another turn, and their whole study and contrivance was, how to gratify their inordinate passions.

This universal depravity of mankind so offended the Almighty, that, as the sacred historian informs us, he " repented that he had made man on the earth "† and, as a proper punishment for their offences, thought of destroying not only the whole of the human race (Noah and his family excepted), but also the brute creation, which he had formed for the use of ungrateful man. But before the Almighty fixed the resolution of executing his design, he thought proper to give one chance to the principal objects of his resentment, which was, that if, in the space of one hundred and twenty years, they should forsake their evil ways, repent, and reform, his mercy should be at liberty to interpose and reverse their doom. This he communicated to his servant Noah, who, for his great justice and piety, had found favor in his sight; and for which his family (consisting only of eight persons) were to be exempted from the general destruction.

Notwithstanding the merciful and beneficent promises of the Almighty, yet such was the corrupt state of mankind at this time, and so lost were they to every sense of virtue, that they still prosecuted their vicious courses, and subjected themselves to the consequences of the divine displeasure. Finding, therefore, that all lenity and forbearance tended to no purpose, except to make them more bold and licentious, God at length made known to his servant Noah his awful determination of involving them, and the earth they inhabited, in one general destruction, by a flood of water. He likewise assured him that as he had, in a particular manner, testified his fidelity to his Maker, he would take care to preserve him and his family, together with such other creatures as were necessary for the restoration of their species from the general calamity. To effect this, he gave him orders to make an ark, or large vessel of gopher-wood,‡ and, that it might be secured from the violence of the waves, to pitch it both within and without. The form and dimensions of this building are thus described by the sacred historian: " And this is the form which thou shalt make it of: the length of the work shall be three hundred cubits, the breadth of it fifty cubits, and the height of it thirty cubits. A window shalt thou make to the ark,

---

* The sacred historian does not inform us at what exact period Adam paid the debt of nature, nor in what place his remains were deposited. The ancient Arabians tell us that he was buried at Hebron, in the cave of Machpelah, which Abraham, many ages after, bought for a burying-place for himself and family. They likewise say that when Adam found his end approaching, he called his son Seth, and the other branches of his numerous family, to whom he gave a strict charge that they should always live separate, and have no manner of intercourse with the impious family of the murderer Cain.

† This expression must not be taken in the literal sense of the words, *for God is not the son of man that he should repent*; but it is a figurative expression, and adapted to our apprehensions. The meaning, therefore, is, that as all men were corrupt, and turning a deaf ear to his preacher Noah, the Almighty was determined to destroy man whom he had created.

‡ When we consider that כפר and κυπαρισσος have the same radical consonants, we are at once led to select a species of cypress as the " gopher-wood," or rather the gopher-tree in question. The wood of the cypress possesses an unrivalled fame for its durability, and its resistance to those injuries which are incident to other kinds of wood. The divine appointment had doubtless a reason founded in the nature of things, and no better reason can be found than the matchless excellence of the wood recommended. The compact and durable nature of the cypress rendered it peculiarly eligible for sacred purposes: hence we find it was employed in the construction of coffins among the Athenians, and mummy-cases among the Egyptians. The *cupressus sempervirens*, a straight and elegant tree of the cone-bearing family, seems therefore to have the best title to the credit of having furnished the material for the most important vessel that was ever constructed.

and in a cubit shalt thou finish it above; and the door of the ark shalt thou set in the side thereof; with lower, second, and third stories shalt thou make it."*

Having received these instructions from God, Noah, in obedience to the divine command, immediately set about the arduous work, which he finished, according to God's direction, seven days before the rain began to fall, having been encouraged so to do by an assurance from his Maker, that though he meant to destroy the world in general, yet he would establish his covenant with him.

The ark being finished, the Almighty commanded Noah to take into it "every living thing of all flesh," both cattle and beasts of the field, birds and fowls of the air, and reptiles of all kinds; of the unclean only one pair each, but of the clean, seven pair. That he should likewise make a proper provision of food for the different animals; and, having placed them in their respective apartments, should then enter the ark himself, taking with him his wife, together with his sons and their wives.

All things being adjusted agreeably to the divine direction, Noah entered the ark, with his family, in the six hundredth year of his age; and on the seventeenth day of the second month (which was seven days after his entrance) the whole face of nature began to wear a gloomy aspect, and to appear as if the earth was to be finally dissolved, and all things return to their primitive chaos. The windows or cataracts of heaven were opened, and the earth was overspread with a dreadful inundation. In vain did sinful mortals seek for protection, or endeavor to shelter themselves from the common destruction; for mountains and valleys were soon alike, and every refuge was banished their sight. For forty days and nights did the rain continue to fall, without the least intermission; when at length the ark began to float, and, in process of time, was elevated above the highest mountains. A dismal scene now presented itself! the earth, with all its beautiful variety of nature and art, was no more! nothing appeared to the sight but a watery desert, abounding with wrecks of the once lovely creation.†

The Almighty having thus avenged himself of a sinful world, and reflecting upon Noah, and the poor remains of his creatures in the ark, caused a drying north wind to arise, the flood-gates of heaven to be stopped, and the falling of the waters to cease; by which means the deluge began to abate, and the waters gradually subsiding, in process of time the earth again appeared.

The first discovery Noah made of the cessation of the flood was, from the ark

* There is much difference of opinion about the form of the ark. The common figures are given under the impression that it was intended to be adapted to progressive motion; whereas no other object was sought than to construct a vessel which should *float* for a given time upon the water. For this purpose it was not necessary to place the ark in a sort of boat, as in the common figures; and we may be content with the simple idea which the text gives, which is that of an enormous oblong box, or wooden house, divided into three stories, and apparently with a sloping roof. The most moderate statement of its dimensions makes the ark by far the largest of vessels ever made to float upon the water. As the measurements are given, the only doubt is as to which of the cubit measures used by the Hebrews is here intended. It seems that the standard of the original cubit was the length of a man's arm from the elbow to the end of the middle finger, or about eighteen inches. This was the *common* cubit; but there was also a *sacred* cubit, which some call a hand's breadth (three inches) larger than the common one; while others make the sacred cubit twice the length of the common. The probability is that there were two cubit measures beside the common; one being of twenty-one inches, and the other of three feet. Some writers add the geometrical cubit of nine feet. Shuckford says we must take the common or shortest cubit as that for the ark; and Dr. Hales, taking this advice, obtained the following result: "It must have been of the burden of 42,413 tons. A first-rate man-of-war is between 2,200 and 2,300 tons; and, consequently, the capacity or stowage of eighteen such ships, the largest in present use, and might carry 20,000 men, with provisions for six months, besides the weight of 1,800 cannon and all military stores. It was then by much the largest ship ever built."

† THE DELUGE.—*From the original by Nicholas Poussin.*—Several great masters have treated this subject, but none of their productions have acquired the celebrity of our engraving, by Poussin. All others have chosen but partial scenes or episodes—either the beginning or the end—of this terrible infliction. Poussin alone has ventured to imbody the whole of this all-engulfing cataclysm, and show its frightful catastrophe: he alone has dared to render that tremendous sentence: "All flesh died that moved upon the earth, both of fowl and of cattle, and of beast, and of every creeping thing that creepeth upon the earth, and every man." The air is laboring with the full-swollen clouds; the rain descends in torrents; the sun, obscured, throws but a dull and feeble light; the overwhelming floods have long confounded the hills with the plains, and already reached the summits of the highest mountains. The foaming waves in the centre of the awful scene, rolling in irresistible volumes, dash against the rock the frail bark of one who had vainly leaped thereon to find a refuge, and now raises his imploring hands to inexorable Heaven. In front a family are still struggling to escape their fate; while the ark floats away in the distance. Never was execution more adapted to its subject—abounding in gloomy and terrific images, presented with appalling truth. This chef d'œuvre was the last labor of Poussin: he finished it in 1664, at the age of 70, and died in the following year.

The Deluge.]—Genesis vii., 11-24.

resting on the mountains of Ararat.* This was about the beginning of May, and about the middle of the following month the tops of the mountains appeared. But Noah (who, no doubt, was glad to see the appearance of anything substantial after so long a confinement), wisely considering, that though the mountains were visible, the valleys might be yet overflowed, waited forty days longer before he attempted any further discovery. At the expiration of that time, opening the window of the ark, he let go a raven, supposing that the scent of dead bodies would allure him to fly a considerable distance. Encouraged by the absence of the raven for seven days, he let fly a dove, which, finding no resting-place, returned to its old habitation. Seven days after he sent out the same bird, which then returned with an olive-branch in its mouth, a happy certainty that the waters were removed from the place where the olive-tree stood. Still, however, determined not to be too hasty, he remained in the ark seven days more, when sending out the dove a third time, and she not returning, he concluded that the waters were entirely withdrawn. In consequence of this he made the necessary preparations for leaving the ark; but, mindful of God's directions, ventured not forth till fifty-five days after, in order that the earth might be properly dry for his reception. Having, at the expiration of that period, received God's positive command to leave the ark, he accordingly came out of it on the twenty-seventh day of the second month, bringing with him every creature that had been retained for replenishing the earth. Thus ended Noah's long and melancholy confinement, which, from the time of his entering the ark to that of his leaving it, amounted exactly to one solar year.

The first thing Noah did, after quitting the ark, was to erect an altar, on which he offered sacrifices to God, for his great goodness in preserving him and his family from the general destruction. The Almighty, knowing the purity of Noah's intentions, was so well pleased with his conduct, that he gave him his divine assurance that he would never more "curse the ground for man's sake," nor should the earth ever be again destroyed by a general deluge. In confirmation of this, he appointed a bow† to appear in the heavens as a token, and which was now to be the ratification of the truth of his promise.

Having, by this divine promise, eased the mind of Noah, who was fearful of a second deluge, the Almighty, after blessing him and his sons, granted them many singular privileges, such as far exceeded those he had bestowed on our primitive parents. Before the flood, mankind had no other food than vegetables; but now the Almighty, after giving Noah and his sons the same dominion over the creation as he had done Adam, permitted them to kill any creatures they thought proper for food, only with this restriction, that they should not eat "the blood thereof." This restraint was certainly laid by God to prevent the shedding of human blood, against which he denounces the following sentence: "Whoso sheddeth man's blood, by

---

* It is generally admitted that the mountain on which the ark rested lies in Armenia; although there are some who contend that it must be sought in Cashgar, on the extension eastward of the great Caucasian chain. The investigations of recent Biblical critics have, however, tended to strengthen the original conviction in favor of the Armenian mountain. The particular mountain to which people of different nations and religions concur in awarding this distinction is situated in N. lat. 39° 30', and E. long. 44° 30', in the vast chain of Taurus, and nearly in the centre between the southern extremities of the Black and the Caspian seas. Its summit is elevated 17,260 feet above the level of the sea, and is always covered with snow, as indeed is the whole mountain, for three or four months in the year. It is a very grand object, being not merely a high summit in a chain of elevated mountains, but standing as it were apart and alone; the minor mountains, which seem to branch out from it and decline away in the distance, being so perfectly insignificant in comparison, that the sublime effect of this most magnificent mountain is not at all impaired, or its proportions hidden by them. This great mountain is separated into two heads, distinguished as the Great and Little Ararat, which perhaps accounts for the plural expression, "mountains," of the text. The heads form distinct cones, separated by a wide chasm or glen, which renders the distance between the two peaks 12,000 yards. One of them is much smaller than the other, and forms a more regular and pointed cone: it is also much lower, and its summit is clear of snow in summer. The Armenians, who have many religious establishments in its vicinity, regard the mountain with intense veneration, and are firmly persuaded that the ark is still preserved on its summit.

† "*I do set my bow in the cloud.*"—The rather equivocal sense of the word "set" in English has occasioned a very mistaken impression, which has led to some cavils, which the use of the more proper word "appoint" would have prevented. As it stands, it has been understood to say that the rainbow was at this time first produced: whereas, as its appearance is occasioned by the immutable laws of refraction and reflection, as applied to the rays of the sun striking on drops of falling rain, we know that the phenomenon must have been occasionally exhibited from the beginning of the world, as at present constituted. Accordingly, the text says no more than that the rainbow was then appointed to be a token of the covenant between God and man. Our engraving is a view of MOUNT ARARAT, from the hills above Erivan, drawn by A. W. Calcatt, from a sketch made on the spot by J. Morier, Esq.

Mount Ararat, from the hills above Erivan. "And the ark rested upon the mountains of Ararat."—Gen. vii., 4.

man shall his blood be shed." With these grants and promises, God gave the same encouragement to Noah and his family that he did to our first progenitors, by telling them to "be fruitful and multiply, and replenish the earth."

Though the deluge had destroyed all the inhabitants of the earth (except what were retained in the ark for forming the *new* world), yet the vegetable part of the creation still existed, and, in a short time, by the genial warmth of the sun, again appeared in all its glory.

Previous to the flood, Noah had directed his attention to husbandry,* and the earth having now resumed its former appearance, he betook himself to the same employment. Among other improvements, he planted a vineyard, and, prompted by natural curiosity to taste the fruit of his own labor, invented a machine for extracting the juice from the grape. Pleased with the taste of the liquor, and being unacquainted with the strength of it, he unwisely gave a loose to indulgence, and, by drinking too freely, became quite intoxicated. In consequence of this, he laid himself down to sleep in his tent, where, either from the rustling of the wind, or the discomposure of his body, he was uncovered on that part which natural modesty teaches us to conceal.

This circumstance produced the first instance of human degeneracy after the flood. The *old* world was destroyed for the wickedness of its inhabitants, and therefore it might have been expected that the *new* world would have been filled with people of a better disposition: but, as in the ark there were unclean as well as clean beasts, so in the family of Noah there were two good sons and one naturally wicked, the two former being Shem and Japhet, and the latter Ham.

The unseemly situation of Noah, from his intoxication, was first discovered by this wicked son, who, instead of covering his father's nakedness and concealing his shame, exposed his weakness, and made him the subject of his scorn and derision. But his brothers were far from being pleased with his conduct: possessed of filial piety, and moved at the indecent posture of their aged parent, they no sooner saw him than they ran and fetched a garment, and immediately covered that nakedness which their pious modesty would not permit them to behold.

When Noah recovered from the stupefaction into which the wine had thrown him, and was informed of the unworthy manner in which his son Ham had treated him, he cursed his race, in the person of Canaan, his grandson: "Cursed," said he, "be Canaan: a servant of servants shall he be to his brethren." On the contrary, reflecting how respectfully his other two sons behaved, he rewarded their pious care with giving each his blessing; all which, in process of time, was fulfilled in their posterity.

These are all the particulars given us by the sacred historian relative to Noah, except that he lived three hundred and fifty years after the deluge, and paid the debt of nature at the age of nine hundred and fifty. At what exact period he died we are not informed, neither the place of his interment; but, according to oriental tradition, his remains were deposited in some part of Mesopotamia.

CHAPTER III.

It is not in the least to be doubted but that Noah and his family, for some years after the flood, continued to reside in the neighborhood of the mountains of Armenia, where the ark had rested. But his descendants, in the course of time, having a numerous progeny, the greater part of them quitted their primitive spot, and directing their course eastward, came at length to the plain of Shinar, on the banks of the river Euphrates. Attracted by the beauty of the place, the convenience of its situation, and the natural fertility of the soil, they resolved not to proceed any further, but to make this their fixed place of residence.

Having formed this resolution, in order to render themselves conspicuous to future

* It is conceived that Noah considerably advanced agriculture by inventing more suitable implements than had previously been in use. We find no grounds for this conjecture in the text; but it is by no means unlikely that the demand upon his mechanic ingenuity in the construction of the ark had qualified him for improving the agricultural implements previously in use.

Babylon—inundated.

generations, they determined to erect a city,* and in it a building of such stupendous height as should be the wonder of the world. Their principal motives in doing this were, to keep themselves together in one body, that by their united strength and counsels, as the world increased, they might bring others under their subjection, and thereby become masters of the universe.

The idea of the intended tower gave them the most singular satisfaction, and the novelty of the design induced them to enter upon its construction with the greatest alacrity. One inconvenience, however, arose, of which they were not apprized, namely, there being no stone in the country wherewith to build it. But this defect was soon supplied by the nature of the soil, which being clayey, they soon converted into bricks, and cemented them together with a pitchy substance, called bitumen, the country producing that article in great abundance.

As the artificers were numerous, the work was carried on with great expedition, and in a short time the walls were raised to a great height. But the Almighty, being dissatisfied with their proceedings, thought proper to interpose, and totally put an end to their ambitious project; so that this first attempt of their vanity became only a monument of their folly and weakness.

Though the descendants of Noah were at this time exceedingly numerous, yet they all spoke one language.† In order, therefore, to render their undertaking ineffectual, and to lessen the towering hopes of these aspiring mortals, the Almighty formed the resolution of confounding their language. In consequence of this, a universal jargon suddenly took place, and the different dialects caused such a distraction

---

* BABYLON.—This city arose from the building of Babel, and became the famous capital of Chaldea. This most celebrated metropolis of the East, enlarged by Belus, and further extended by Queen Semiramis, about the year 1200 B. C., reached its summit of magnificence under Nebuchadnezzar, about the year 570 B. C., or when further embellished by his daughter-in-law Nitocris. Its magnitude was 480 furlongs, or 60 miles in compass, being an exact square of 15 miles on each side. Its walls were built of brick laid in bitumen, 87 feet thick, and 350 feet high, on which were 250 towers, or, according to some, 316. The materials for building the wall were dug from a vast ditch or moat, which was lined with brick-work, and, being filled with water from the river Euphrates, surrounded the city as a defence. The city had 100 gates of solid brass, one at each end of its 50 streets, 150 feet wide: these crossed the city; so that the whole was divided into 676 squares, four and a half furlongs on each side, around which were houses, the inner parts being reserved for gardens, pleasure-grounds, and fields. Facing the wall, on every side, was a row of houses, with a street between, of 200 feet wide; and the city was divided into equal parts by the river Euphrates, over which was a bridge, and at each end of it a palace, communicating with each other under the river by a subterraneous passage. Near to the old palace stood the tower of Babel: this prodigious pile, being completed, consisted of eight towers, each 75 feet high, rising one upon another, with an out side winding staircase, to its summit, which, with its chapel on the top, reached an elevation of 660 feet In this chapel was a golden image 40 feet high, valued at $17,500,000, and the whole of the sacred utensils were reckoned worth $200,000,000! Besides these wonders, were the hanging gardens, on a series of elevated terraces, the uppermost equalling the height of the city walls, and having a reservoir, supplied by a machine with water from the river. This great work was designed by Nebuchadnezzar to represent a hilly country, for the gratification of his wife Amytis, a native of Media. Babylon flourished for nearly 200 years in this scale of grandeur; during which idolatry, pride, cruelty, and every abomination, prevailed among all ranks of the people; when GOD, by his prophets, denounced its utter ruin, and which was accordingly accomplished, commencing with Cyrus taking the city, after a siege of two years, in the year 538 B. C., to emancipate the Jews, as foretold by the prophets. By successive overthrows, this once "glory of the Chaldees' excellency," this "lady of kingdoms," has become a "desolation," "without an inhabitant," and its temple a vast heap of rubbish! Daniel ii. vi., Isaiah xiii. xlv., Jeremiah l. li. "Birs Nemroud," as the ancient tower of Babel is called, Mr. Rich says, "is a mound of an oblong form, the total circumference of which is 762 yards. At the eastern side it is cloven by a deep furrow, and is not more than 50 or 60 feet high; but on the western side it rises in a conical figure to the elevation of 198 feet, and on its summit is a solid pile of brick, 37 feet high by 28 in breadth, diminishing in thickness to the top, which is broken and irregular, and rent by a large fissure extending through a third of its height. It is perforated by small holes, disposed in rhomboids. The fire-burnt bricks of which it is built have inscriptions on them: and so excellent is the cement, which appears to be lime-mortar, that it is nearly impossible to extract one whole. The other parts of the summit of this hill are occupied by immense fragments of brick-work, of no determinate figure, tumbled together, and converted into solid vitrified masses, as if they had undergone the action of the fiercest fire, or had been blown up with gunpowder, the layers of brick being perfectly discernible." These ruins proclaim the divinity of the Holy Scriptures!

† LANGUAGE, or human speech, Genesis xi. 1: this most certainly was originally given to our first parents by the inspiration of God, who, therefore, exercised Adam in giving names to the creatures, Gen. ii. 19, 20. Learned men call the most ancient language the "Shemitish," as spoken by the descendants of Shem, the son of Noah. This, however, was soon divided into three dialects: many other languages are now found to exist, Daniel iii. 4; of which the origin is declared in the Bible to have been effected by the Divine interposition at Babel, Genesis xi. 7. The Shemitish dialects were: 1. Aramæan, spoken in Syria, Mesopotamia, and Chaldea, subdivided into the Syriac and Chaldee dialects. 2. Hebrew or Canaanitish dialect, spoken in Phenicia and its colonies. 3. Arabic, spoken with variations in Arabia and Ethiopia. Hebrew bears marks of being the most ancient of the oriental languages; and in it the Old Testament, which contains the most ancient records in existence, was written, except Daniel, ii. 4, vii. 28, Ezra iv. 8, vi. 18, vii. 12-26. The New Testament was written in the Greek language. Seventy-two distinguished languages are spoken of; but five which are the chief, viz. Hebrew, Greek, Latin, Germanic, and Sclavonic. The English is a compound of all these, and, with the French, is most esteemed. Ours, it seems probable, is destined by Divine Providence to become the universal language of mankind, through the intelligence, influence, and Christian missions of Great Britian and America.

of thought, that, incapable of understanding or making known to each other their respective ideas, they were thrown into the utmost disorder. By this awful stroke of divine justice they were not only deprived of prosecuting their intended plan, but of the greatest pleasure a social being can enjoy, namely, mutual converse and agreeable intercourse. We are not, however, to suppose that each individual had a peculiar dialect or language to himself, but only the several tribes or families, which are supposed to have been about seventy in number. These, detaching themselves according to their respective dialects, left the spot, which, before the consequences of their presumption, they had considered as the most delightful on earth, and took up their temporary residences in such places as they either pitched on by choice, or were directed to by chance.

Thus did the Almighty not only defeat the designs of those ambitious people, but likewise accomplished his own, by having the world more generally inhabited than it otherwise would have been. The spot on which they had begun to erect their tower was, from the judgment that attended so rash an undertaking, called Babel.*

The confusion of tongues, and dispersion of the family of Noah, happened one hundred and one years after the flood, as is evident from the birth of Peleg, the son of Eber, who was the great-grandson of Shem, and born in the one hundred and first year after that memorable period. He received his name from this singular circumstance, the word *Peleg*, in the Hebrew language, signifying *partition* or *dispersion*.

The descendants of Noah being now dispersed, in process of time, from their great increase, they scattered themselves to distant parts of the earth, and, according to their respective families, settled in different parts of the world. Some took up their residence in Asia, some in Africa, and others in Europe. But by what means they obtained possession of the several countries they inhabited, the sacred historian has not informed us. It is, however, natural to suppose, that their respective situations did not take place from chance, but mature deliberation; and that a proper assignment was made of such and such places, according to the divisions and subdivisions of the different families.

In order to ascertain a proper idea of the manner in which the world was populated after the flood, and confusion of tongues, we shall give the genealogy of Noah's three sons, and describe the respective parts of the earth possessed by their descendants; in doing which, we shall, agreeably to the manner of Moses, begin with those of Japheth, who, though usually mentioned last, was the eldest son of Noah.

It is to be observed that the grand-children of Noah made it an invariable rule to give their own names to the countries of which they became possessed, and where they settled, in order to perpetuate their memories to future posterity.

The sons of Japheth were seven in number, who spread themselves over Asia, from the mountains Taurus and Auranus to the river Tanais, and then entering Europe, penetrated as far as Spain, distinguishing the countries, as they proceeded, by their own proper appellations, viz.:† Gomer gave title to the Gomorites, now called Galatians, or Gauls, by the Greeks. Magog founded the Magogites, since styled Scythians, or Tartars. From Media originated the Medeans or Medes. Javan was the founder of the Ionians and Greeks in general. Tubal, of the Iberians, or Spaniards: and Mashech, of the Meschinians or Cappadocians: and Tiras, of the Thiræans or Thracians.

Gomer had three sons, the eldest of whom, Ashkanaz, took possession of Ascania (which is part of the Lesser Phrygia). The second son, named Riphah, possessed

* BABEL (*confusion* or *mixture*), a tower commenced, as is generally supposed, during the life of Noah, under the direction of Nimrod, a grandson of Ham, and about A. M. 1770, or 113 years after the deluge, though some place this work two or three hundred years later, Genesis x. 10, xi. 1-9. Nimrod is believed to have formed a system of idolatry for his adherents, designing, by this means, to establish a national union under his government, thereby frustrating the Divine designs, which required their dispersion, to repeople the earth. This impious attempt occasioned their miraculous confusion of speech, on which account the building ceased, and the purpose of God was accomplished in the replenishing of the world by the scattered people. How far the work had proceeded we are not informed; but it is believed that, besides three years in preparing materials, twenty-two had been expended in the undertaking, and that the tower had been carried up several stories, laying the foundation for the city of Babylon.

† Several of these nations still retain the names given them by their founder; others have lost their original appellations; and some are distinguished by terms corrupted from the primitive denominations. The Greeks principally occasioned these innovations; for, when power gave them importance, they arrogated to themselves the glory of antiquity; corrupted the names of other nations to give them a more modern appearance; and pretended that, from the emigrations of their predecessors, the surrounding realms were peopled, for which reason they took the liberty to prescribe laws for their observance, as they had invented appellations for their distinction.

5

himself of the Riphaan mountains; and Togarmah, the third son, took Galatia and part of Cappadocia.

Javan had four sons, namely, Elishah, who seated himself in Peloponnesus; Tarshish, in part of Spain; Kittim, in Italy; and Dodanim, in France.

By these, and the colonies which, in process of time, proceeded from them, not only a considerable part of Asia, but all Europe, with the adjacent islands, were well stocked with inhabitants descended from Japheth, who, though thus dispersed spoke the same language, and, for a time at least, preserved a correspondence with the respective tribes or families to which they originally belonged.

The descendants of SHEM, the second son of Noah (from whom originated the Hebrew nation), were five sons, who possessed themselves of those parts of Asia which extend from the Euphrates to the Indian ocean. Elam, the eldest, took possession of a country in Persia, at first called after himself, but, in the time of Daniel, it obtained the name of Susiana. Ashur founded the Assyrian empire, in which he built several cities, particularly one called Nineveh;* Arphaxad founded Chaldea;

* NINEVEH (MOUSOUL).—*Drawn by J. M. W. Turner, from a sketch made on the spot by the late Claudius James Rich, Esq.*— Nineveh, the splendid metropolis of the Assyrian empire, was anciently a city of great importance. It was founded by Asshur, the son of Shem (Genesis x. 11), and by the Greeks was called Ninus, to whom they referred its foundation. It was erected on the banks of the Tigris, and was of great extent: according to Diodorus Siculus, it was fifteen miles long, nine broad, and forty-eight in circumference. It was surrounded by walls 100 feet high, on the top of which three chariots could pass together abreast, and was defended by 1,500 towers, each of which was 200 feet high. In the time of the prophet Jonah (who lived between 810 and 785 B.C.) it was "an exceeding great city of three days' journey"—wherein were more than sixscore thousand persons that could not discern between their right hand and their left hand." Jonah iii. 3; iv. 11. Its destruction, which that prophet had announced within forty days, was averted by the general repentance and humiliation of the inhabitants. (iii. 4-10.) That repentance, however, was of no long continuance; for the prophet Nahum, soon after, predicted, not only the utter destruction of Nineveh, which was accomplished one hundred and fifteen years afterward, but also the manner in which it was to be effected. "While they were folden together as thorns, they were devoured as the stubble fully dry." (Nahum i. 10.) "Nineveh is laid waste: who will bemoan her?" (iii. 7.) The Medians, under the command of Arbaces, being informed, by some deserters, of the negligence and drunkenness which prevailed in the camp of the Ninevites, assaulted them unexpectedly by night, discomfited them, and became masters of their camp, and drove such of the soldiers as survived the defeat into the city. "The gates of the river shall be opened, and the palace shall be dissolved" (Nahum ii. 6); and Diodorus Siculus relates that "there was an old prophecy that Nineveh should not be taken till the river became an enemy to the city; and in the third year of the siege, the river, being swollen with continual rains, overflowed part of the city, and broke down the wall for twenty furlongs. Then the king" (Sardanapalus) "thinking that the oracle was fulfilled, and the river become an enemy to the city, built a large funeral pile in the palace, and collecting together all his wealth, and his concubines, and his eunuchs, burnt himself and the palace with them all; and the enemy entered the breach which the waters had made, and took the city." What was predicted, therefore, in Nahum i. 8, was literally fulfilled: "With an overflowing flood will he make an utter end of the place thereof." Nahum (ii. 9) promises the enemy much spoil of gold and silver; and we read in Diodorus that Arbaces carried away many talents of silver and gold to Ecbatana, the royal city of the Medes. According to Nahum (i. 8, iii. 15) the city was to be destroyed by fire and water; and from Diodorus we learn that it was actually destroyed by fire and water. Nineveh was taken a second time, by Cyaxares and Nabopolassar, from Chinaladin, king of Assyria, A. M. 3378, after which it no more recovered its former splendor. It was entirely ruined in the time of Lucian of Samosata, who lived in the reign of the emperor Hadrian: it was rebuilt under the Persians, but was destroyed by the Saracens about the seventh century. Its utter destruction, as foretold by Nahum (i. ii. iii.) and by Zephaniah (ii. 13-15) has been so entirely accomplished, that no certain vestiges of it have remained. Several modern writers are of opinion that the ruins on the eastern bank of the river Tigris, opposite to the modern town of Mousoul, point out the site of ancient Nineveh. The late learned and intelligent political resident at Bagdad, Claudius James Rich, Esq. (from one of whose drawings, never before engraved, our view is taken), states, that on this spot there is an enclosure of a rectangular form, corresponding with the cardinal points of the compass, the area of which offered no vestiges of building, and is too small to contain a town larger than Mousoul: but it may be supposed to answer to the palace of Nineveh. Four mounds are observable, the longest of which runs north and south, and consists of several ridges of unequal height, the whole appearing to extend four or five miles in length. These mounds, as they show neither bricks, stones, nor any other materials of building, but are in many places overgrown with grass, resemble the mounds left by intrenchments and fortifications of Roman camps. On the first of these, which forms the southwest angle, is erected the village of Nebbi Yunus, where is shown the *supposed* tomb of the prophet Jonah or Jonas. The next, which is the largest of all, Mr. Rich conjectured to be the monument of Ninus. It is situated near the western face of the enclosure, and is called Koyunjuk Tepé. Its form is that of a truncated pyramid, with regular steep sides and a flat top; and it is composed of stones and earth, the latter predominating sufficiently to admit of the summit being cultivated by the inhabitants of the village of Koyunjuk, which is built on the northeastern extremity of this artificial mound. Its greatest height, as measured by Mr. Rich, was 178 feet; the length of the summit east and west, 1,850 feet; and its breadth, north and south, 1,147 feet. A short time before Mr. Rich visited these remains, out of a mound on the north face of the boundary, "there was dug an immense block of stone, on which were sculptured the figures of men and animals. So remarkable was this fragment of antiquity, that even Turkish apathy was roused, and the pacha and most of the principal people of Mousoul went to see it. One of the spectators particularly recollected, among the sculptures of this stone, the figure of a man on horseback, with a long lance in his hand, followed by a great many others on foot. The stone was soon afterward cut into small pieces for repairing the buildings of Mousoul, and this inestimable specimen of the arts and manners of the earliest ages was irrecoverably lost." These ruins evidently indicate the former existence of some very extensive edifices, which most probably belonged to ancient Nineveh, and which attest the literal accomplishment of the prophecy that that "rejoicing city

Nineveh.

Lud, Lydia; and Aram that part of Syria which extends itself to the Mediterranean seas.

Aram had four sons, namely, Uz, who seated himself in the country called Damascus; Hul took possession of Armenia; Mash, of the mountain Masius; Gether, of a part of Mesopotamia.

Arphaxad was the father of Salah, whose son Eber gave name to the Hebrew nation. Joctan, the first-born of Eber, had thirteen children, all of whom settled themselves in that part of the world which is situated between Syria and the river Cophene in Judea. The youngest son of Eber was Peleg, who, as we have before observed, was so called because, at the time of his birth, the dispersion of the people took place.

The descendants of HAM (the youngest son of Noah) were four sons, namely, Cush, who took up his residence in that part of Armenia lying towards Egypt; Mizraim,* in both Upper and Lower Egypt; Phutt, in part of Lybia; and Canaan, in that part of the country which was afterward called by his name.

Cush, the eldest son of Ham, had several children, namely, Seba, who settled on the southwest of Arabia; Havilah fixed himself in that part of the country situated on the river Pison, where it leaves the Euphrates, and runs into the Arabian Gulf; Saptah took up his residence on the same shore, a little to the north of his brother Havilah; Raamah and Sabtecha, together with the two sons of the former (namely, Sheba and Dedan), settled themselves on the same coast, farther to the east; and Nimrod, the last son of Cush, was founder of the Babylonish empire.

Besides the three sons of Mizraim (who, after the death of their father, divided his territory into three parts), he had three others, namely, Ludim and Lehabim, who peopled Lybia; and Caslubim, who seated himself at Castisots, near the entrance of Egypt from Palestine. Caslubim had two sons, namely, Philistim and Caphthorim, the former of whom established the country of the Philistines, between the borders of Canaan and the Mediterranean sea; and the latter, after his father's death, took possession of his territories.

The sons of Canaan were, Sidon, the founder of the Sidonians, who lived in Phœnicia; Heth, the founder of the Hittites, who lived near Hehron; Emor, the founder of the Amorites, who lived in the mountains of Judea; and Arva, the founder of the Arvadites,† who resided near Sidon. But whether the other sons of Canaan settled in this country or not, can not be ascertained with any certainty; only this we know, that they must have taken up their residence somewhere between Sidon and Gerar, and Admah and Zoboim; those places being the boundaries of the land they possessed.

Thus we find that, in the first dispersion of the people over the world, the descendants of Japheth not only possessed all Europe, but also a considerable portion of Asia. The posterity of Shem had in their possession the Greater and Lesser Asia, and probably all the countries to the east, as far as China. The descendants of Ham possessed all Africa, with a great part of Asia.

which dwelt carelessly" should "become a desolation, dry like a wilderness, a place for beasts to lie down in." Zephaniah ii. 13, 15.
There are appearances of mounds and ruins extending for several miles to the southward, the space between which is a level plain, over every part of the face of which broken pottery and the other usual remains of ruined cities are seen scattered about.

* After the death of Mizraim (who was king of Egypt), the country he possessed was, by three of his sons, divided into as many kingdoms, viz: *Anamim* was king of Tanis, or lower Egypt, called afterward Delta; *Napthukim*, of Naph, or Memphis, in Upper Egypt; and *Pathrusim* founded the kingdom of Pathros, or Thebes in Thebais.

† The Arvadites are said by Josephus to have occupied and given their name to the small island of Aradus, called Arvad and Arphad in the Scriptures (2 Kings xix. 13; Ezekiel xxvii. 8); and the inhabitants of which are by Ezekiel mentioned along with the Sidonians, as taking an active part in the maritime commerce of Tyre. This island, which is about one league from the shore, and not above a mile in circumference, ultimately became the port and chief town of this enterprising and prosperous section of the Phœnician people; and there was a time when even Romans regarded with admiration its lofty houses, built with more stories than those of Rome, and its cisterns hewn in the rock. All this, except the cisterns and some fragments of wall, has passed away; but Arvad is still the seat of a town, and, being a mart of transit, its inhabitants are still engaged in commerce. Though the island was the favorite seat of the people, as their wealth and peace were there safe from the wars and troubles of the continent, and their shipping needed not to hazard the dangers of the coast, they were by no means without possessions on the main land; for their dominion along the shore extended from Tortosa (also Tartous, anciently Antaradus) which lay opposite their island, northward to Jebilee. They were, therefore, the most northerly of the Phœnician people. See Joseph. Antiq. i. 6, 2; Strabo, Geog. v. 15; Pococke, ii. 27; Volney, ii. 148. Buckingham's Arab Tribes, 522.

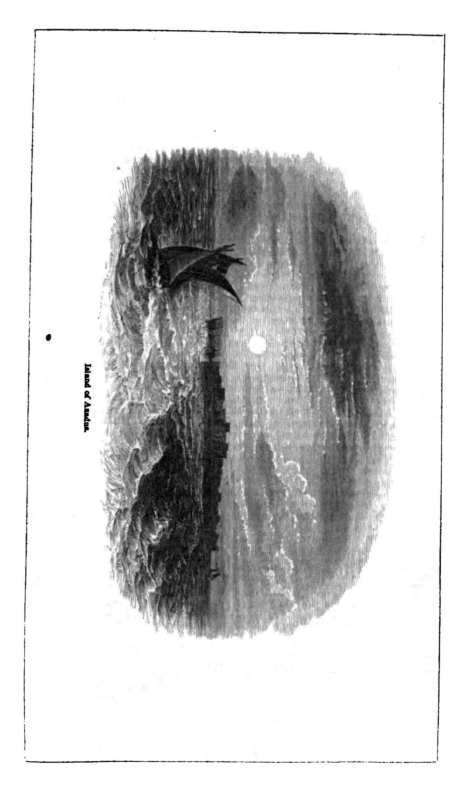

Island of Azalea.

But before we quit the genealogy of Noah's descendants, it will be necessary to mention some further particulars relative to the posterity of his second son Shem, from whom the Hebrews took their rise, and who will be found the principal objects of the succeeding history.

About two years after the flood, at which time Shem was one hundred years old, he had a son named Arphaxad; after which time he lived five hundred years; so that the whole of his life was exactly six hundred years.

Arphaxad, when thirty-five, had a son named Salah; after which he lived four hundred and three years; in all four hundred and thirty-eight.

Salah, when thirty, had a son named Eber (from whom his descendants were called Hebrews), after which he lived four hundred and three years; in all four hundred and thirty-three.

Eber, when thirty-four, had a son named Peleg, in whose time the earth came to be divided; after which he lived four hundred and thirty years; in all four hundred and sixty-four.

Peleg, when thirty, had a son named Reu, after which he lived two hundred and nine years; in all two hundred and thirty-nine.

Reu, when thirty-two, had a son named Serug; after which he lived two hundred and seven years; in all two hundred and thirty-nine.

Serug, when thirty, had a son named Nahor; after which he lived two hundred years; in all two hundred and thirty.

Nahor, when twenty-nine, had a son named Terah; after which he lived one hundred and nineteen years; in all one hundred and forty-eight.

Terah was the father of the first great patriarch after Noah, namely, Abraham. He had likewise two other sons, the one called Nahor, and the other Haran. The last of these, who was the eldest of the three, died before his father, at Ur,* in Chaldea, the place of his nativity. He left behind him a son named Lot, and two daughters, the elder of whom, called Milchah, was espoused to her uncle Nahor, and the younger, named Sarai, was married to her uncle Abram.

A universal depravity of human nature now displayed itself in all parts of the world, but more particularly in the city of Ur, where the practice of idolatry was carried to its utmost height. In consequence of this, Terah resolved to leave his abode, that he might no longer be an eye-witness of the iniquity of the people. Having formed this resolution, he quitted Ur, and taking with him his son Abram and his wife, together with his grandson Lot, set out with an intent of visiting the land of Canaan. In his journey he stopped at a place called Haran (or Charran), a city of Mesopotamia, where, being seized with a violent illness, he was compelled to make it the place of his residence. The violence of the disorder prevailing over the power of medicine, nature at length gave way, and Terah died at Haran, in the two hundred and fifth year of his age.

CHAPTER IV.

At the close of the preceding chapter, we observed that Terah, the father of Abram, left his native place, in order to go into the land of Canaan. It is here to be observed, that his conduct in this respect certainly arose from divine direction,

---

* Ur of the Chaldees.—The birthplace of Abraham has been generally regarded as a town; but such orientalists as have of late years had occasion to express an opinion on the subject, have been rather disposed to regard it as the name of a district. As such, there is little reason to question that it is that which the sacred text indicates, as it comprehends both the towns in which the names mentioned in this part of the history have been sought. Of these, one is the town called by the Syrians Urhoi, and by the Arabians Orfah, or Urfah, which the Moslems firmly believe to be the Ur of the text; and the Jews and Christians of the country acquiesce in this conclusion. This town is situated at the foot of the mountains of Osroene, at the head of the great plain which was formerly so called, and is still a place of some consideration. Cartwright says: "The air of this city is very healthful, and the country fruitful. It is built nearly four-square, the west side standing on the side of a rocky mountain, and the east part trendeth into a spacious valley, replenished with vineyards, orchards, and gardens. The walls are very strong, furnished with great store of artillery, and contain in circuit three English miles; and for the gallantness of its sight it was once reckoned the metropolitical seat of Mesopotamia." This traveller, as well as one who preceded him, Rauwolf heedless of the analogy of name, regards Urfah rather as representing Haran than Ur.

the Almighty having thought proper to select this family out of the rest of mankind, by making Abram "Father of the faithful," or worshippers of the true God.

It is evident that God had revealed himself to Abram, previous to his removal from Ur, as appears from the account of the inspired penman: "The Lord had said unto Abram,"* &c., Gen. xii. 1. He had commanded him to leave the country in which he resided, and to travel into another he should point out to him. He likewise promised to make him father of a mighty people, and in him to bless all the families on the earth.

Abram, fully persuaded, in his own mind, of the truth of the divine promise (though he knew not the difficulties that might attend his removal, nor even the country in which he was to settle), immediately after the decease of his father, prepared himself to go to the land which God should appoint, and, by a strict attention to the divine commands, prove at once his faith and obedience.

Accordingly, taking with him his nephew Lot, his wife Sarai, and the rest of his family, together with all his effects, he set out on his journey, which he prosecuted with all convenient expedition, till he came (by the divine guidance) into the land of Canaan.† Desirous of making some survey of the country, he stopped in the plain‡ of Moreh, not far from the city of Sichem,‖ then inhabited by the Canaanites. Here he erected an altar, in order to pay his devotions to God, who was so well pleased with his conduct, that he gave him fresh assurances of his favor and protection, and that, in process of time, the whole land in which he then dwelt should be possessed by his descendants.

After staying some time in the plains of Moreh, Abram removed with his family into the more mountainous part of the country, situated between Bethel and Hai. Here he likewise erected an altar, that he might not be deficient in the discharge of that duty which he was conscious of owing to his great and omnipotent benefactor.

From Bethel he proceeded farther to the south; but was interrupted in his progress by a dreadful famine, which raged with great violence throughout the whole country. In consequence of this, he formed the resolution of going to Egypt, that being the only place where relief could be obtained under such calamities.§

Being apprized of the natural libertinism of the Egyptians, Abram was exceeding anxious concerning his wife Sarai, fearing lest her extraordinary beauty might provoke their lascivious attention. Though she was at this time in the sixty-sixth year of her age,¶ yet she still retained those personal charms which, in that country,

---

* In what manner God revealed himself to Abram, the sacred historian has not told us. It was probably by a voice from the Shechinah, or symbol of the Divine presence; for St. Stephen expressly says: "The God of Glory appeared unto him before he dwelt in Charran." Acts vii. 2.

† This country fell to the lot of Canaan, the son of Ham, to which he gave his own name. Canaan was about 200 miles long, and nearly 60 broad, lying along the eastern border of the Mediterranean sea. David and Solomon governed several provinces beyond the limits of Canaan, which enlarged their kingdom, 1 Kings, iv. 21-24. Canaan was bounded on the north by the mountains of Lebanon in Syria, on the east by Arabia Deserta, on the south by the wilderness of Arabia Petrea and Idumea, and on the west by the land of the Philistines and the Mediterranean sea. Besides the name of its first possessor, Canaan has been variously denominated as the Land of the Hebrews, Genesis xl. 15; Palestine, Exodus xv. 14; the Land of Promise, Hebrews xi. 9; the Land of Israel, Judah, Judea, the Holy Land, Zechariah ii. 12. Canaan has been the theatre of the most extraordinary transactions which have ever taken place under the Divine government upon earth. This is the country where the chief patriarchs walked with God— where the theocracy of Israel was established—where the prophets received most of their divine inspirations—where the temple of Jehovah was erected under his special direction—where the incarnate Son of God accomplished the work of human redemption—and where the apostles were miraculously endowed with the gifts of the Holy Spirit, to fulfil their commission as ambassadors for Christ to invite sinners of all nations into the kingdom of Messiah for the blessings of pardon, purity, and immortality, in the eternal glory of God. Canaan, in the times of David and Solomon, contained a population of about 5,000,000; but now it has only about 1,500,000 inhabitants. Since the destruction of Jerusalem by the Romans, it has been the scene of strange revolutions, especially during the crusades, profanely called holy wars: it now forms two wretched provinces, Acre and Damascus, under the miserable government of pachas, subject or tributary to the sultan of Turkey. The population consists of Turks, Syrians, Bedouin Arabs, Copts, Druses of Lebanon, Roman, Armenian, and Greek Christians, and Jews.

‡ The Septuagint and most other versions call it the Oak of Moreh, from a large oak that grew on it; but our translation renders it plain.

‖ This city, after the ruin of Samaria by Salmanesar, was the capital of the Samaritans; and Josephus says it was still so in the time of Alexander the Great. It was situated ten miles from Shiloh, forty from Jerusalem, and fifty-two from Jericho.

§ It appears from this circumstance, that Egypt had been soon formed into a kingdom after mankind were dispersed by the confusion of languages. Its first name was Mizraim, which signifies straightness; it being closed on the north by the Mediterranean sea, on the west and south by mountains, and on the east by the Red sea, or Indian gulf. Nicolaus Damascus, a heathen author, says, that Abram went out of Chaldea into Canaan, now called Judea, but, in consequence of a great famine raging there, he removed to Egypt, in which were abundance of all kinds of provisions.

¶ It may appear somewhat strange that Sarai should have such personal charms at so advanced an age: but it must be remembered that as in those days they were longer lived than at present, so their charms were proportionally durable.

might endanger the life of him who should pass for her husband. After some deliberation, Abram concluded that the safest way would be for her to conceal her marriage; upon which, communicating his fears to Sarai, and she approving of his plan, it was mutually agreed between them, that wherever they took up their residence, instead of his wife, she should pass for his sister.

The apprehensions that Abram had formed were soon verified, after his arrival in Egypt. The distinguished charms of his wife attracted the notice of several principal Egyptians, and she soon became the subject of popular conversation. The king, being informed of her beauty, was excited to gratify his curiosity by the sight of so amiable a stranger. Accordingly, Sarai was, by his order, conducted to court, and placed in the apartments allotted for his concubines. Here she remained several days, during which Abram (her supposed brother) was treated with great civility, and on her account (though the king had not yet seen her) complimented with many valuable presents.

A feeling mind may, in some degree, conceive the distress each party must naturally be susceptible of on this trying occasion. Sarai was a beautiful woman, in the power of a loose and vicious monarch, and destitute of all protection but from the hands of the Almighty. While her husband, who should be the only guardian of her person, dare not own her as his wife, lest the rage of lust and strength of power should deprive him of his existence.

To relieve them from this distressed situation, the Almighty was pleased to interpose in their behalf: and, in order to deter Pharaoh* and his nobles from any dishonorable attempts on Sarai, he suddenly afflicted them with various diseases and bodily infirmities. Not being able to account for this singular circumstance, they at length suspected that it was occasioned by the confinement of Sarai, who, instead of being the sister of Abram, must certainly be his wife. In consequence of these suspicions, the king sent for Abram, and expostulated with him on his misconduct, in having spread a false report, which might have been attended with a breach on his wife's chastity. After saying this he ordered him immediately to quit his kingdom, permitting him to take not only his own effects, but the presents that had been made him in consequence of his supposed sister.

The famine in Canaan, which had occasioned Abram to go into Egypt, was happily ceased; so that his leaving the place was not only in conformity to the king's command, but agreeable to his own inclinations. Abram directed his course the same way he had come, and on his arrival at Bethel, where he had erected an altar, he offered on it a sacrifice of thanks to God for his happy escape from Egypt, and safe return into the land of Canaan.

Abram and his nephew Lot had hitherto lived with great unanimity on the same spot; but their families and possessions being now greatly increased, inconveniences took place. They found themselves particularly distressed for want of provision for their cattle, which, probably, arose partly from the late famine, and partly from the great number of Canaanites, who possessed the most fertile parts of the land. This want of pasture-ground occasioned frequent disputes between the herdsmen of Abram and those of Lot; so that the former, fearing lest the contention which prevailed among the servants might end in a rupture between themselves, resolved, in a friendly manner, to propose a separation from Lot. In doing this, such was his great prudence and condescension, that, though superior in every respect to his nephew, he gave him his choice of settlement in that part of the country he should best approve. "If," says he, "thou wilt take the left hand, then I will go to the right; or, if thou depart to the right hand, then I will go to the left."

This generous and friendly proposition was readily agreed to by Lot, who, after taking a view of the country, chose the plains near Sodom and Gomorrah, which, being watered by the streams of Jordan,† was not only pleasant, but exceedingly fertile.

* What this king's name was, or indeed any of the Egyptian monarchs, can not be ascertained. The name *Pharaoh* was a title of dignity common to all, in the same manner as that of Cæsar assumed by the Roman Emperors.
† This river, being the principal stream of Palestine, has acquired a distinction much greater than its geographical importance could have given. It is sometimes called "the river," by way of eminence, being in fact almost the only stream of the country which continues to flow in summer. The river rises about an hour and a quarter's journey (say three or three miles and a quarter) northeast from Banias, the ancient Cæsarea Philippi, in a plain near a hill called Tel-el-kadi. Here there are two springs near each other, one smaller than the other, whose waters very soon unite, forming a rapid river, from twelve to fifteen yards

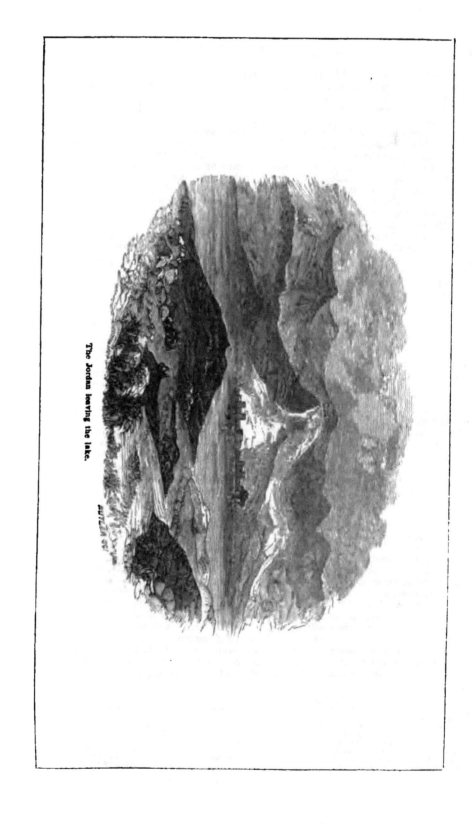

The Jordan leaving the lake.

These matters being adjusted, Abram and Lot parted, the former continuing at Bethel, and the latter retiring to the spot he had chosen for his future residence.

Some time after Lot's departure, the Almighty, ever mindful of his faithful servant Abram, again appeared to him in a vision, and not only renewed the promise he had before made, of enlarging his posterity, but, bidding him cast his eyes round the kingdom, confirmed the gift of all the land which he beheld, to him and his descendants.

These divine assurances were acceptably received by Abram, who, desirous of seeing the different parts of the country promised to his posterity, removed from Bethel, and took up his residence in the plain of Mamre, at a small distance from Hebron. Here (as was his usual custom, wherever he pitched his tent) he erected an altar, in order to discharge his religious duties, by offering sacrifices to the Lord

In a short time after Abram had settled himself at Mamre, by the natural affability of his temper, and the respect shown him on that account, he acquired the intimacy and friendship of some of the most considerable Canaanites, particularly three, named Mamre, Aner, and Eschol; the former of whom was of such importance as to give name to the country in which he lived.

This alliance was not only agreeable to Abram, but, in the course of time, proved infinitely serviceable, as will appear from the following circumstances. Chederlaomer, king of Elam, had for some years held five petty princes (of which number the king of Sodom was one) in a tributary subjection to him. Weary with this subjection, they at length determined to shake off the yoke they had so long borne; to effect which they confederated together, and, joining their respective forces, prepared themselves to march against their oppressor.

The king of Elam, being informed of their intentions, resolved, if possible, to frustrate their designs. He accordingly raised a powerful army, and, in conjunction with three other kings, his allies, immediately advanced to meet the enemy. The revolted kings, seeing him at a distance, took the field, with a firm resolution of trying the fate of a pitched battle. The place allotted for determining the dispute was the valley of Siddim, which was full of pits of bitumen, or soil of a clayey nature. For some time the victory appeared doubtful; but at length the five tributary kings were put to the route: one part of their army was entirely cut to pieces, and the other fled to the neighboring mountains, leaving their cities a prey to the conquerors. Lot, who happened at this time to reside in Sodom, was involved in the calamity of the city, being not only plundered of all his possessions, but carried away among the rest of the captives. One of the soldiers belonging to the vanquished, happening to make his escape, immediately hastened to Abram, to whom he related the particulars of the battle, and the hapless fate of his nephew. The faithful patriarch, anxious for Lot, determined to pursue the victors, and, if possible, not only rescue him, but the whole of the captives. He accordingly armed all his own servants, the number of whom amounted to three hundred and eighteen, and, accompanied by his three friends and associates, Mamre, Eschol, and Aner, set out in pursuit of the victors, whom, after a march of about seventy leagues, he overtook near Dan. Availing himself of the covert of the night, he put his forces into proper disposition, and immediately charged the enemy on all quarters. So sudden and vigorous an attack on an army fatigued with a late engagement, and revelling in the spoils of conquest, had the desired effect, for Abram, in a short time, obtained a complete victory. Chederlaomer, the king of Elam, was, among many others, slain, and his whole army being routed, Abram's victorious party pursued them as far as Hobah, a small place situated near Damascus. The enemy, from the great consternation into which they had been thrown, by the suddenness of the attack, fled so precipitately, that they left behind them not only the captives, but likewise the booty of which they had

across, which rushes over a stony bed into the lower plain, where it is joined by a river which rises to the northeast of Banias. A few miles below their junction the now considerable river enters the small lake of Houle, or Semechonitis (called "the waters of Merom" in the Old Testament). This lake receives several other mountain-streams, some of which seem to have as good claim to be regarded as forming the Jordan with that to which it is given in the previous statement; and it would perhaps be safest to consider the lake formed by their union as the real source of the Jordan. After leaving the lake, the river proceeds about twelve miles to the larger lake, called by various names, but best known as the Sea of Galilee: after leaving which, it flows about seventy miles farther, until it is finally lost in the Dead or Salt sea. It discharges into that sea a turbid, deep, and rapid stream, the breadth of which is from two to three hundred feet. The whole course of the river is about one hundred miles in a straight line, from north to south; but, with its windings, it probably does not describe a course of less than one hundred and fifty miles.

possessed themselves. The whole of these fell into the hands of Abram, and among them his nephew Lot, who, being thus happily recovered, returned, with all his substance, to his former habitation.

Abram having, by this conquest, signalized both his valor and fidelity, was highly caressed by those whose cause he had so gallantly espoused. The first person who came to congratulate him on the occasion was the king of Sodom, who, in thankful acknowledgment of the benefits received from his important services, offered him all his booty which he had retaken belonging to him, desiring only the restoration of those prisoners who were his subjects. But Abram's righteous soul disdained to take advantage of the unfortunate; and therefore, after reserving to his associates·that part of the plunder to which their services entitled them, he restored to the king both his subjects and property, evincing, through the whole of his conduct, the most distinguished fidelity, intrepid courage, and inflexible justice.

The next person who congratulated Abram on his success was Melchisedek,* king of Salem, who, on his return from the battle, accommodated both him and his men with a refreshment of bread and wine which he had provided on the occasion. Being a priest as well as king, he first blessed Abram for being the instrument of so public a deliverance, and then the Almighty, for having given him such uncommon success; in return for which, the victorious patriarch presented him with the tenth part of the spoils he had taken from the enemy.

As Abram had now acted in the public capacity of a warrior, and might reasonably expect that the kings whom he had routed would recruit their scattered forces, and prepare for a second attack, he was fearful of the consequences. But the Almighty, in order to fortify his mind against all disagreeable apprehensions, even from the most potent princes of the earth, appeared to him in a vision, and informed him that he had undertaken his defence, and would ever reward his faithfulness. "Fear not," says he, "Abram, I am thy shield, and thy exceeding great reward."

Hitherto the pious patriarch had listened to God's promises without the least shadow of distrust; but on this fresh assurance he ventured, for the first time, to expostulate with his great protector, not knowing how these things could possibly be accomplished, while himself continued without an heir to his body, and that, to all appearance, he must be obliged to leave his substance to Eliezer his steward.

The troubles of Abram on this head were soon removed by the beneficence of the Almighty, who told him that not his servant, but a son of his own, begotten of his body, should be his heir, and that from him should descend a race as "innumerable as the stars in heaven."

Abram was so encouraged by this joyful intelligence, that he ventured to beg of God that he would be pleased to give him some sensible token whereby he might be assured of so distinguished a blessing. The Almighty thought proper to comply with his request, and that they might enter into a formal covenant on the occasion, ordered him to take a heifer, a goat, and a ram, each of three years old, together with a pigeon and a turtle-dove, and offer them up as a sacrifice.

The pious patriarch readily obeyed the divine command, and, having killed the beasts, cut them in halves, laying each opposite to the other; but the fowls he left whole. After doing this, he walked between the dissected bodies, making his solemn vows to God of perpetual obedience to his will; and then sat himself down to prevent birds of prey from injuring the sacrifice.

About the time of sunset Abram fell into a deep sleep, during which it was revealed to him that he was not to expect an immediate accomplishment of the divine promise; for though himself was to die in peace, and at a good old age, yet his posterity were, after that, to sojourn and be afflicted in a strange country, for the space of four hundred years; after which the Almighty would not only punish their oppressors, but would likewise safely establish them in the land he had promised.

After this revelation Abram soon awoke, and while he was reflecting on what he had heard, the Almighty, in confirmation of the assurances he had given him, and as a ratification of his part of the covenant, caused the symbol of his divine presence to appear before him. It consisted of a *smoking furnace* and a *burning lamp*, which passed between the divided pieces of the victims, and totally consumed them.

---

* Who this extraordinary person was, has been a subject of great dispute; but the most rational opinion is, that he was one of the princes of Canaan, who on account of his great piety and goodness, was called Melchizedek, which, in the Hebrew language, signifies *King of Righteousness*

Sarai, the wife of Abram, desired a son no less fervently than her husband. But she had been considered barren before she left Mesopotamia; she was now seventy-five years of age; and she had waited ten years since their hearts were first gladdened by the promise of an heir. She therefore thought the case was hopeless as regarded herself; and began to reflect that, although a son had been promised to Abram, it had not been said, and did not necessarily follow, that this son should be the fruit of her own womb. Explaining these views to the patriarch, she prevailed upon him to resort to a custom of the time, of which there are still some traces in the East, under which the man takes a secondary wife, whose children become his undoubted heirs, equally with any other children he may have; and if the woman is the slave or attendant of the chief wife, or is provided by the chief wife, the children are, in a legal point of view, considered hers: and, in the same point of view, the condition of the actual mother remains unchanged, though in practice it necessarily sustains some modification from the operation of the feelings arising from the connexions which are formed, especially when her children are grown up. The female whom Sarai proposed to Abram as her substitute was her own handmaid, a woman of Egypt, named Hagar, who may be supposed to have been one of the female slaves whom the king of Egypt gave to the patriarch.*

In due time it was known that Hagar had conceived, and the prospect of becoming the mother of Abram's long-promised heir had a mischievous effect upon her mind, leading her to treat her mistress with disrespect. Sarai, through whose preference and management all this had been brought about, was stung to the quick by this treatment, and complained of it to Abram with some sharpness, insinuating that, without some encouragement from him, Hagar durst not be so impertinent to her. The patriarch himself, respecting the rights of his wife, and displeased at Hagar's presumption (which those who know anything of Oriental women of her class, will believe to have been very coarsely and offensively manifested), reminded Sarai that the Egyptian was still her bond-servant, and that her authority was sufficient to prevent or punish the treatment of which she complained. Being thus assured that he would not interfere, Sarai proceeded to a more unsparing exercise of the powers with which she was invested, than the raised spirits of the Egyptian bondmaid could brook; and she therefore fled, directing her course towards her own country. It is a terrible and perilous thing for a woman, alone and on foot, to pass the desert which lies between the land of Canaan and Egypt; and we know not how one might do it and live. Nor did Hagar accomplish this enterprise; for she was as yet but upon the borders of the desert, and was tarrying for refreshment and rest by a well of water, when an angel of God appeared to her, and persuaded her to return and submit herself to her mistress; encouraging her to obedience by the assurance that the child she then bore in her womb would prove a son, whom she was directed to name Ishmael (God attendeth), because the Lord had attended to her affliction. She was also assured that this son should be the parent of a numerous race; and that while in his character, as typifying that also of his descendants, he should be wild and fierce as the desert ass—his hand against every man, and every man's hand against him—he should never be expelled or rooted out from the domain which God would give to him.† Thus instructed and encouraged, Hagar returned to her master's camp in the valley of Mamre; and in due season brought forth a son, to whom, in obedience to the angel's direction, Abram gave the name of Ishmael.

At this time Abram was eighty-six years of age; and lest, in the excess of his joy, he should mistake this child for the heir of the promises which had been made him, about thirteen years after, the Almighty again appeared to him in a vision, and renewed his former covenant; to ratify which he was pleased to institute the rite of circumcision, by commanding that every male child, of eight days old, whether born in the house or bought with money, should be circumcised, on the penalty of being cut off from the benefits of the covenant. As a further mark of his divine respect, he changed our patriarch's name from Abram to Abraham, and his wife's from Sarai to Sarah;‡ and to complete his happiness, again promised that he should yet have a son by her.

* It is not unlikely that Hagar had been given to Sarai as her personal attendant while she was in Pharaoh's harem, and that she was allowed to retain her as such when she departed.
† This is the best interpretation we can give to the expression, " and in the face of all his brethren shall he dwell."
‡ The difference in the sound of these words is very trifling, but in the sense, it is considerable. The

Women of Egypt—lower class.

Though this promise gave great satisfaction to Abraham, yet his mind was agitated on account of Ishmael, his first-born, for whom he had a most paternal affection. He was suspicious that, on the birth of a child by the free woman, he might be deprived of that descended from the bond-woman; and therefore, falling prostrate on the ground, he began to intercede with God in behalf of Ishmael: " O," says he, " that Ishmael might live before thee!" But the Almighty thought proper to remove his fears, by assuring him that the great blessings in the covenant were not designed for Ishmael, but for a son to be born of Sarah, which should happen within the course of the year, and that his name should be called Isaac. That he might not, however, seem wholly to neglect his request for Ishmael, he promised to "make him a great nation," and the father of twelve princes; but at the same time told him, that the covenant made should only be established in the son begotten of Sarah.

This was the whole substance of the vision; and as soon as it was ended, Abraham delayed not (according to the divine command) to circumcise himself, his son Ishmael, and all the males in his family. And this ordinance the Hebrews have ever since very religiously observed.*

CHAPTER V.

THE great wealth of the inhabitants of Sodom and Gomorrah had introduced luxury, which, as usual, soon produced licentiousness. The fatal consequences of this were, irreverence to God, inhospitality to strangers, and the indulgence of the most abominable vices. These enormities highly offended the Almighty, who, in order to punish the people, denounced his vengeance both against them and their country. But, previous to the execution of the fatal sentence, he thought proper to intimate his intentions to his faithful servant Abraham.

At this time the pious patriarch resided at Mamre; and as he was sitting one day at the door of his tent, he saw at a distance three persons, whom he took for travellers. Being naturally of a hospitable disposition, when they came up to him he arose from his seat, and, in a polite manner, asked them to partake of such refreshment as his habitation afforded. His civility being accepted, an entertainment was immediately prepared for the unknown guests, which being set before them, they, to all appearance, seemed to eat. While they were at table, one of them inquired after Sarah, and being told she was in the tent, he then addressed himself to Abraham, and assured him that he had still in remembrance the case of his wife Sarah, who, before the end of the year, should certainly be delivered of a son. From this circumstance Abraham was convinced that these three visiters were messengers from heaven, and that one of them was the peculiar representative of the Almighty.

Sarah had listened attentively to the discourse that had passed between her husband and his guests; but, considering the advanced age both of herself and him, she regarded not their prediction, and even laughed within herself at the improbability of such an event. This disrespectful behavior being observed by the stranger, he, in an angry tone, asked her the reason of it. Struck with terror, she attempted to deny it; upon which he dismissed her with this gentle reproof: that it was exceedingly wrong in her to mistrust what he had said, since "nothing was impossible with God."

This finished the conversation, immediately after which the three guests prepared themselves to depart, and Abraham, understanding they were going towards Sodom,

---

word *Abram*, signifies *high father*; but *Abraham* implies the *father of a great multitude*, as he certainly was, according to the Divine promise, "a father of many nations have I made thee," Gen. xvii. 5.

The word *Sarai* signifies, *my princess*, or chief of my family only; but *Sarah* implies, *Princess or chief of multitudes*, according to the words in the text, " She shall be a mother of nations, kings of people shall be of her," Gen. xvii. 16.

* CIRCUMCISION—the cutting off the small skin of the prepuce, as the rite was enjoined upon Abraham with the male part of his family, to be the sign of the covenant of God with the patriarch, when he renewed to him the promise of the Messiah (Gen. xvii. 10-26). Physicians have regarded circumcision as medically beneficial; and it was practised by the Arabians, Israelites, and Saracens, the descendants of Abraham; but especially by the Israelites, to whom it was ordained as the initiatory ordinance of the Hebrew church. This, however, with all the Levitical ceremonies, was abolished by the perfect mediation of CHRIST (Acts xv. 1-24; Col. iii. 11). The Israelites are called the circumcision, and the Gentiles the uncircumcision, Rom. iv. 9.

CIRCUMCISION OF THE HEART: this is the thing signified by the original ceremony, the cutting off of every evil affection by the renewal of the soul in holiness to secure devotedness of heart in the true service of GOD as promised by Moses, Phil. iii. 3; Col. ii. 11; Deut. x. 16.

courteously offered to attend them some part of the way. As they journeyed together, God was pleased to manifest his peculiar regard to Abraham, in foretelling the dreadful judgment he intended to inflict on Sodom and the neighboring cities, which instance of his kindness was founded upon an assurance that he would command not only his children, but his household also, to persevere in the true fear and worship of their divine Creator.

This intelligence was communicated to Abraham by one of the angels (the immediate representative of God), the other two having gone before with great haste, to reach, as soon as possible, the place of their destiny. So melancholy a piece of news greatly afflicted Abraham, who, from an assurance of the divine favor, ventured to intercede in behalf of those wicked people. Not doubting but the supreme and equitable Judge of the earth would listen to mercy, he begged of him not to punish the innocent with the guilty. He made five petitionary propositions, lessening the supposed number of pious inhabitants in Sodom from fifty to ten, earnestly beseeching of God that, could even so small a number be found, he would, on their account, withdraw his avenging rod, and avert the impending danger. This request being granted, the angel departed, and Abraham returned home, happy in the thought of having received such peculiar manifestations of the divine love.

In the mean time, the two other guests, who went before (and were, indeed, the ministering angels whom God had appointed to execute his judgment on the Sodomites), pursued their journey towards the city, whither they arrived in the evening. Lot happened at this time to be sitting at the gate of the city; as soon, therefore, as he saw the angels, he arose, and, after proper salutations, invited them to his house, in order to refresh themselves. For some time the divine messengers declined the offer; but at length, from the strength of Lot's importunities, they were prevailed on to accept the invitation.

It being soon rumored about the city that Lot had strangers with him, great numbers of the vile inhabitants assembled together, and, surrounding the house, commanded him, in a peremptory manner, to deliver them up. Lot thought at first to appease them by mild and soft words; and, therefore, stepping out of the house, and shutting the door after him, he begged of them not to offer any insult to his guests, who had committed themselves to his care and protection. This not having the desired effect, in order to appease their rage, and, if possible, to preserve the laws of hospitality inviolate, he offered to give up his two virgin daughters to their discretion. But so abandoned were these wretches to wickedness, and so deaf to every remonstrance, that they even refused this offer, and threatened Lot with very severe treatment, if he did not immediately comply with their request.

Finding Lot was resolute, and totally disregarded their threats, they determined to effect that by force which they could not obtain by any other means. Accordingly, pressing forward, they attempted to break open the door; but the divine messengers prevented their design. By an exertion of supernatural power, they forced their way out of the house, took in their host, and then, shutting the door, struck the rioters with a temporary blindness; so that, not being able to find the house, they were obliged to desist from their diabolical intentions.

All things being now quiet, the two angels acquainted Lot with the purport of their embassy. They told him they were come to execute the divine vengeance on that execrable place and its neighborhood; and therefore, if he had any friends for whose safety he was concerned, to acquaint them of their danger, that thereby they might escape the general destruction.

In the city were two young men, who had been betrothed to Lot's daughters, to whom he immediately repaired, and informed them of the approaching event, at the same time advising them, for their safety, to leave the place and go with him; but, instead of listening to his advice, they totally despised it, and profanely ridiculed the idea of the threatened destruction.

In the morning, soon after daylight, one of the angels, observing Lot not to prepare for his departure with that expedition he knew to be necessary, rather chastised him for his conduct. The cause of this delay certainly arose from hopes that the dreadful sentence against those wretched people might be reversed; but his hopes were in vain, for, instead of ten righteous persons, that Abraham had capitulated for, no more than four, and all those of Lot's family (himself included), were appointed to escape the dreadful judgment. Knowing, therefore, the necessity of immediate departure, the angel took Lot, his wife, and his two daughters by the hands, and conducted them out of the city. The divine messenger told him to make all the expedition possible, and, to avoid the common ruin, pursue his course to the neighboring mountains.

Lot, observing the mountains to which he was directed were at a considerable distance, began to despair of reaching them in a proper time, and therefore entreated the angel that he might be permitted to escape to a small city, not far from Sodom, then called Bela, but afterward Zoar. This request was granted, and that city, on their account, escaped the general destruction. Before the angel left them, he urged them to make all possible haste, as the divine commission could not be put in execution till they were safely arrived at the place of their destination. He likewise enjoined them not, upon any account whatever, to look behind them, but to keep their eyes fixed on the place allotted for their refuge.

Having said this the angel departed, and Lot, with his family, pursued their journey toward Zoar. After travelling some way, Lot's wife, either from forgetfulness of the prohibition, or out of respect to the place of her habitation, indiscreetly looked back. This misconduct was attended with the most fatal consequences: she was immediately turned into a pillar of salt,* and became a standing monument of the vengeance of the Almighty on disobedient and obstinate offenders.

Lot and his daughters, strictly observing the divine injunction, hastened toward Zoar, whither they had no sooner arrived, than the vengeance of the Almighty began to appear in all its horrors. The angry heavens poured down showers of liquid fire†

---

* She was overwhelmed and smothered in the spray of the igneous and saline matters which filled the air; and which, gathering and hardening around her, left her incrusted body with some resemblance to a mass of rock salt.

† The examination of the agencies which it pleased GOD to employ in effecting this great overthrow is a subject which need not interrupt the present narrative. It suffices now to mention, that the destruction was sudden and overwhelming, and not only did it overthrow and devour the cities of the plain, and all the inhabitants, and all the growth of the ground, and every living thing, but it cut off the Jordan in its course, and absorbed the very plain itself: the surface of which, once blooming like another Eden, no man has beheld since that day; but, instead thereof, a bitter, sulphureous and fetid lake, the Lake of Death, which has, from that hour to this, remained one of the wonders of the earth. The following brief description of the Dead sea (see engraving), will, we hope, be read with interest:—

The celebrated lake, which occupies the site of Sodom and Gomorrah, is variously called in Scripture the Sea of the Plain (Deut. iii. 17, iv. 49), being situated in a valley with a plain lying to the south of it, where those cities once flourished, with the other cities of the plain; the Salt sea (Deut. iii. 17, Josh. xv. 5), from the extremely saline and bitter taste of its waters; the Salt sea eastward (Num. xxxiv. 3), and the East sea (Ezek. xlvii. 18; Joel ii. 20), from its situation relatively to Judæa. At present it is called Bahret-Lout, or the sea of Lot. By Josephus and other writers, it was called the Lake Asphaltites, from the abundance of bitumen found in it. The most familiar name, the Dead sea, is in allusion to the ancient tradition, erroneously but generally received, that no animal can exist in its stagnant and hydro-sulphuretted waters, which, though they look remarkably clear and pure, are nauseous in the extreme. A chymical analysis of one hundred grains of the water gave the following results as to the substances, and proportions of them, which it holds in solution:—

| Muriate of lime | - | - | - | 3.920 | Soda | - | - | - | - | 10.360 |
| Magnesia | - | - | - | 10.246 | Sulphate of lime | - | - | .054 |

From this analysis it will readily be concluded that such a liquid must be equally salt and bitter. The acrid saltness of its waters, indeed, is much greater than that of the sea: and the land which surrounds this lake, being equally impregnated with that saltness, refuses to produce any plants, except a few stunted thorns, which wear the brown garb of the desert. Bodies sink or float upon it in proportion to their specific gravity: and although the water is so dense as to be favorable to swimmers, no security is found against the common accident of drowning. This sea, when viewed from the spot where the rapid Jordan daily discharges into it 6,090,000 tons of muddy water, takes a southeasterly direction visible for ten or fifteen miles, when it disappears in a curve toward the east. The expanse of the Dead sea, at the embouchure of the Jordan, has been supposed not to exceed five or six miles: though the mountains, which skirt each side of the valley of the Dead sea, are apparently separated by a distance of eight miles. The mountains on the Judæan side are lower than the mountains of Moab, on the Arabian side. The latter chain at its southern extremity is said to consist of dark granite, and of various colors. The shores at the northern extremity are remarkably flat, and strewed with vast quantities of driftwood, white and bleached by the sun, which is brought down by the swelling of Jordan. It is not certainly known whether there has been any visible increase or decrease in the waters of the Dead sea. Some have imagined that it finds a subterraneous passage to the Mediterranean, or that there is a considerable suction in the plain, which forms its western boundary; but Dr. Shaw has long since accounted for it, by the quantity which is daily evaporated.

As the Dead sea advances toward the south, it evidently increases in breadth. Its dimensions have been variously estimated by different travellers. Pliny states its total length to be one hundred miles, and its greatest breadth twenty-five: the Jewish historian Josephus, who measured this lake, found that in length it extended about five hundred and eighty stadia, and in breadth one hundred and fifty; according to our standard, somewhat more than seventy miles by nineteen. With this measurement nearly coincides the estimate of Dr. Shaw, who appears to have ascertained its dimensions with accuracy, and who computes its length to be about seventy-two English miles, and its greatest breadth about nineteen. Whoever has once seen the Dead sea, will ever after have its aspect impressed upon his memory: it is in truth a gloomy and fearful spectacle. The precipices, in general, descend abruptly into the lake, the surface of which is generally unruffled, from the hollow of the basin (in which it lies) scarcely admitting the free passage necessary for a strong breeze. It is, however, for the same reason, subject to whirlwinds or squalls of short duration. A profound silence, awful as death, hangs over the lake: its shores are rarely visited by any

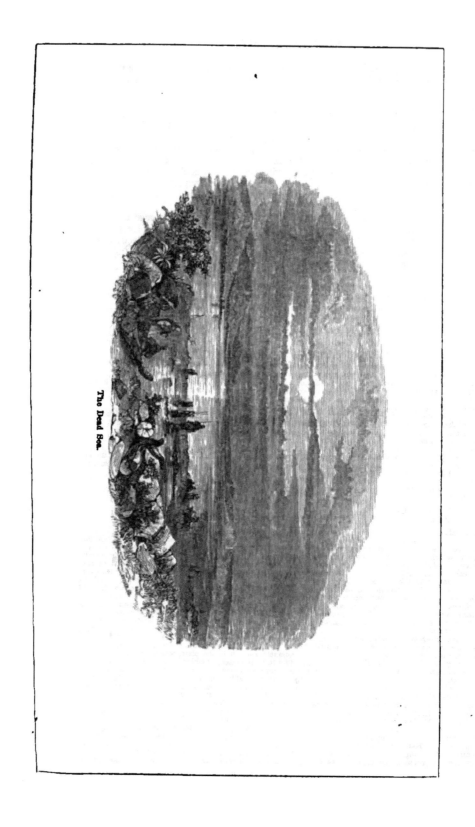

The Dead Sea.

on Sodom and Gomorrah, and the other wicked cities of the plain; and in a short time the whole was reduced to a state of irreparable destruction.

When Lot beheld the dreadful calamity that had befallen the cities of Sodom and Gomorrah, he began to think himself not safe in Zoar; he therefore withdrew to the mountains to which he was first directed, and, for want of a proper habitation, lived for some time with his daughters in a cave. In his caverned retreat a new and unexpected evil befell Lot. His daughters, like all eastern women, and especially all women of Bedouin parentage, looked upon the possession of children as the best and brightest hope of their existence; but they saw none on earth whom they might expect to marry. They knew not that any of their father's family and connexions existed, to become their husbands; and the example of their sisters, who had perished in Sodom with their husbands, made them afraid, if willing, to entertain the notion of a marriage with Canaanitish husbands. They therefore most wickedly managed, on two successive nights, to intoxicate their father with wine, and in that condition, and without his clear knowledge of what was done, to procure issue by him. A son to each daughter was the result of this transaction. The eldest daughter gave to her son the name of Moab ("from a father"), and the younger called hers Ben-Ammi ("son of my people"), which latter name, intimating the mother's satisfaction in the fact that the child was a son of her own race, corroborates the view we have taken of the motives by which the women were influenced, and which seems to us far preferable to the notion that they supposed that all the inhabitants of the earth, except their father and themselves, were destroyed in the overthrow of Sodom. We do not see how it is possible that they could have entertained any such impression. Be this as it may, the sons which were born to them were the progenitors of the Moabites and Ammonites,—nations well known in a later age for their enmity to the house of Israel. Thus much of Lot, of whom the sacred history takes no further notice. We now proceed to consider the peculiar dispensation of Providence with respect to his faithful servant Abraham.

At the time of the destruction of Sodom and Gomorrah, the pious patriarch resided at Mamre; but as soon as he beheld that fatal catastrophe, struck with a proper sense of the Divine vengeance, and the great power he had over his creatures, he removed thence to the southward, and took up his residence in Gerar, one of the principal cities in Palestine.

On his first entering this place, he had recourse to the same policy he had before practised when in Egypt, and an agreement was made between him and his wife that they should pass for brother and sister. Abimelech,* the king of Gerar, supposing this to be their real affinity, and being captivated with the person of Sarah, who, though far advanced in years, possessed some distinguished charms, ordered her to be brought to his palace, with an intent of making her his concubine. But the Almighty warned him in a dream from committing the iniquitous act, by assuring him, that if he took to his bed a woman, whose husband was a prophet, his conduct should be punished with immediate death.

In consequence of this, Abimelech sent for Abraham, whom he severely reprimanded for having endeavored to impose on him, by calling her his sister whom he

footstep, save that of the wild Arab; and its desolate but majestic features are well suited to the tales related concerning it by the inhabitants of the country, who hold it in superstitious dread, and speak of it with terror.

We can not forbear subjoining the lively account which Mr. Stephens gives of the " water of the Dead sea:"

" From my own experience I can almost corroborate the most extravagant accounts of the ancients. I know, in reference to my own specific gravity, that in the Atlantic and Mediterranean I can not float without some little movement of the hands, and even then my body is almost totally submerged; but here, when I threw myself upon my back, my body was half out of the water. It was an exertion even for my lank Arabs to keep themselves under. When I struck out in swimming it was extremely awkward, for my legs were continually rising to the surface, and even above the water. I could have lain and read there with perfect ease. In fact I could have slept; and it would have been a much easier bed than the bushes at Jericho. It was ludicrous to see one of the horses: as soon as his body touched the water, he was afloat, and turned over on his side: he struggled with all his force to preserve his equilibrium; but the moment he ceased moving, he turned over on his side again, and almost on his back, kicking his feet out of water and snorting with terror. The worst of my bath was, after it was over, my skin was covered with a thick glutinous substance, which it required another ablution to get rid of; and after I had wiped myself dry, my body burnt and smarted as if it had been turned round before a roasting fire. My face and ears were incrusted with salt; my hairs stood out, 'each particular hair on end,' and my eyes were irritated and inflamed, so that I felt the effects of it for several days. In spite of all this, however, revived and refreshed by my bath, I mounted my horse a new man."

* The kings of Gerar were generally called by the title of Abimelech, in the same manner as those of Egypt were called by that of Pharaoh.

knew to be his wife.* In excuse for the fiction Abraham alleged he did it for his own safety, being apprehensive that, had it been known she was his wife, he might, in order to possess her, have robbed him of his existence. He farther said, that the report he had given of her being his sister was not, in fact, a falsity, for though she was not born of the same woman, yet she was begot by the same man.

This apology pacified the king, who not only restored Abraham his wife, but also gave him many valuable presents, with full permission to settle himself in any part of his dominions.

The Almighty had not only threatened the king with death should he violate the chastity of Sarah, but also afflicted him and all the women belonging to him with a kind of impotence. Abraham, therefore, in return for Abimelech's civility, prayed to God to remove these imperfections, which he being pleased to grant, the king's disability left him, and the queen, with the rest of the women belonging to him, were restored to their natural fertility.

Soon after this the Divine promise (made by the Almighty to Abraham) was fulfilled. The time appointed was now elapsed, and Sarah brought forth a son, whom Abraham, agreeably to the sacred injunction, called Isaac ;† and on the eighth day he was circumcised.

Sarah having long considered Ishmael as the presumptive heir of her family, had reared and continued to treat him with the most affectionate tenderness. But on the birth of Isaac she became apprehensive with respect to his inheritance, imagining, that in case of Abraham's death, Ishmael's superiority of years would give him every advantage over her own son. Stimulated by such fears, she resolved to get rid of Ishmael, and it was not long before an opportunity offered for accomplishing her design.

Though Sarah was far advanced in life (being now upward of ninety years old) yet, by the Divine power, nature was completely perfect.‡ She was bountifully sup-

---

* ABRAHAM'S EQUIVOCATION.—This was not a subject which the fertile fancies of Abraham's rabbinical descendants were likely to leave unimproved. Accordingly, we have a Talmudical story, which tells us that, on approaching Egypt, the patriarch put Sarah in a chest, which he locked up, that none might behold her dangerous beauty. "But when he was come to the place of paying custom, the collectors said, 'Pay us the custom.' And he said, 'I will pay the custom.' They said to him, 'Thou carriest clothes.' And he said, 'I will pay for the clothes.' Then they said to him, 'Thou carriest gold ;' and he answered them, 'I will pay for my gold.' On this they said to him further, 'Surely thou bearest the finest silk ;' and then he replied, 'I will pay custom for the finest silk.' Then said they, 'Certainly it must be pearls that thou takest with thee ;' and he only answered, 'I will pay for pearls.' Seeing that they could name nothing of value for which the patriarch was not willing to pay custom, they said. 'It can not be but that thou open the box, and let us see what is within.' So they opened the box, and the whole land of Egypt was brightly illumined by the lustre of Sarah's beauty."

† The word Isaac implies laughter, and alludes to the smile of disbelief which appeared in Sarah's countenance when the angel informed her that she should become pregnant.

‡ PRIMITIVE LONGEVITY.—We need not remind the reader that the age of man before the deluge made a near approach to a thousand years, but, after that event, rapidly declined to the present standard (which it had certainly reached before the time of David), at which it has remained, unaffected but by local influences. Many reasons have been given for the antediluvian longevity, and for the subsequent abridgment of human life ; but they all fail in some point or other, excepting that which, proceeding on the observation that air is the agent by which, under all circumstances, the duration of life is most affected, infers that the superior purity of the air before the deluge—or, more properly, its superior fitness for the conservation of the living principle in man—was the operating cause of the long duration of antediluvian life ; and that the gradual but quick contraction of man's life, which afterward took place, was probably owing to some signal deterioration, caused by the deluge, in the wholesome properties of the primitive air. How the deluge may have produced such a change is another question, into which we need not enter.

At the time this history opens, the duration of life was about threefold that to which it ultimately fell ; and, notwithstanding the gradual abridgment which took place, it remained twofold till about the time of the departure of the Israelites from Egypt. Terah himself died at the age of 205, which must have seemed but a reasonable old age, as it is considerably within the age attained by any of his ancestors, except his own father Nahor, who died prematurely at 148 years of age.

But the operation of the abridging influence is best shown by figures, thus : Noah lived 950 years ; Shem, 600 ; Arphaxad, 438 ; Salah, 433 ; Eber, 464 ; Peleg, 230 ; Reu, 239 ; Serug, 230 ; Nahor, 148 ; Terah, 205. Here we see that Noah, nearly two thirds of whose life had passed before the deluge, lived as long as an antediluvian ; whereas his son Shem, most of whose life passed after the deluge, has one third of the average duration of antediluvian life struck off from his. His son Arphaxad was born two years after the flood, and therefore may be taken to represent the first generation of entire postdiluvians, whose term of life is made one third shorter than that of the semi-antediluvians, and (in two generations) is reduced to one half that of the pure antediluvians. A rest at this point of reduction was allowed for three generations, after which the existing term of life was again halved, reducing it to a quarter of the antediluvian term. After three more generations, another reducing process commenced, not, as before, by abrupt halving of the previous term of life, but by a gradual reduction, which in about 500 years reduced the previous term of 230-'40 years to about one half, or 120 years ; and in about 500 years more, we find that this term also had been nearly halved and brought down to the present standard ; for at that time it is that David said : "The days of our years are threescore years and ten : and if by reason of strength they be fourscore years, yet is their strength labor and sorrow." Psalm xc. 10. The progress of the abridgment may be illustrated by a few more figures. Abraham died at the age of 175, being 40 years less than his father's age ; and yet he is said to have died "in a good old age ; an old man and full of years :" in like

plied with food for her infant son, whom she suckled herself, and at the usual time weaned him. On this joyful occasion Abraham made a great feast, in the height of which Sarah observed that Ishmael treated her son with derision and contempt. Enraged at this circumstance, as soon as the guests were gone, she communicated the particulars to her husband, and importuned him to turn both Ishmael and his mother from their habitation, intimating, that the son of a bond-woman had no title to that heirship which solely belonged to her son Isaac.

The good old patriarch now found himself in a very intricate situation. He loved Ishmael, and was loth to part with him. Not knowing, therefore, in what manner to proceed on so trying an occasion, he applied himself to God, who was pleased to confirm what Sarah had requested. At the same time the Almighty promised Abraham that he would make Ishmael (because he was his son) a populous nation, though his portion and inheritance was not to be in that land which was all along designed for the descendants of Isaac.

Thus was it determined, by the Divine appointment, that Hagar should once more become a wanderer; nor could the fondness of Abraham for his son Ishmael prevent her fate: it was the Lord's command, nor durst the patriarch refuse to obey.

Early in the morning, therefore, Abraham, calling Hagar to him, told her she must leave his house, and that her son must be the partner of her banishment. Hagar was of course greatly surprised at this sudden command, but finding her master absolute, she was obliged to submit. That she might not be distressed for want of proper refreshment, he supplied her with a quantity of provisions, together with a large bottle of water, having done which he gave her a final dismission.

After travelling some days in the dreary wilderness of Beersheba, her provisions grew short, and her bottle of water was quite exhausted. It unfortunately happened that Ishmael was at this time in a high fever, and Hagar not being able to get water to quench his thirst, there was little hope of his existing much longer. Thus distressed, she knew not what to do, but at length, to shelter her son in some degree from the violent heat of the weather, she placed him under a tree, and retired at some distance, that she might not be a spectator of the dying pangs of her beloved Ishmael.

A melancholy scene now took place: the feeble tongue of the child begged relief from its tender parent, whose woes were doubled by her inability to give it the least assistance; his pressing demands could only be answered by a flow of tears, and the only prospect before them was despair and death. But the ears of boundless mercy are ever open to the cries of distress, and the Lord of Omnipotence is ever ready to relieve the indigent.

While Hagar was lamenting her direful situation, a Divine agent appeared before her, and, for her present relief, directed her to a well of water which she had not

manner, Isaac, who lived to 180, is said to have been "old and full of days." And if these expressions do not imbody the ideas of a writer who, from living in a later day, when the term of man's life was much shortened, naturally considered these as extreme old ages, we should be entitled from them to conclude—as was probably true after all—that a man was in those days called old with reference to the age at which his contemporaries, rather than his predecessors, died. The patriarchs were very sensible that the term of life was undergoing abridgment. Thus, when Jacob stood before the Egyptian king, and was asked his age, he replied : "The days of the years of my pilgrimage are a hundred and thirty years : few and full of evil have the days of the years of my life been, and have not attained unto the days of the years of the life of my fathers in the days of their pilgrimage." He lived to 147 years. His son Levi lived to 137 years ; and another of his sons, Joseph, only to 110 years. Amram, the son of Levi, lived to exactly the same age as his father ; and Moses and Aaron, the two sons of Amram, both lived to 120. Our information of the steps by which life declined to "threescore years and ten" before the time of David, is less distinct.

But we principally wish to remind the reader of the probability—or rather the moral certainty—that the seasons of life, its childhood, youth, maturity, and age, were distributed over the whole period of life, however long, in much the same proportions as at present ; so that the prime and old age commenced later and ended later than under a more abridged term of life. Thus, we should not suppose, that when the term of life was 140 years, a man of seventy was constitutionally older than one of thirty-five is now. This seems so obvious as to require little argument ; and we are not disposed to discuss the question even were argument needed. But we may just observe that there is not wanting much positive proof in favor of this view. Thus we see those whose ages when their eldest son was born is recorded, are only in one instance under thirty—and that one instance is in the case of a man (Terah's father) whose whole age little exceeded half the average of his time. We see, also, that none of the Hebrew patriarchs had a son before he was forty. And when we take into account the general disposition to early marriages in the East, this may show that the age of manhood was reached much later than it has been since ; and the activity and vigor, mental and bodily, which these same persons evince at an age far passing the present extreme term of life, shows that constitutional old age began late in proportion. The admiration which the beauty of Sarah excited when she was nearly seventy years of age, also affords a strong corroborative illustration. The subject is one of considerable interest, and deserves a more attentive consideration than it can here obtain.

before perceived. Having filled the bottle, she gave some of the water to Ishmael, who was greatly refreshed with it, and, in a few days, so far recovered from his illness as to be able, with his mother, to pursue their journey. Hagar's intentions were, at first, to have gone into Egypt, but she now altered her mind, and fixed her abode in the wilderness of Paran, where Ishmael (whose health and strength were now greatly increased) in a short time became so expert an archer, that he was able to obtain a sufficiency of provisions both for himself and mother.

When Ishmael grew up to the years of maturity, his mother, who was an Egyptian, married him to a woman of her own country. By this woman he had twelve sons,* whose descendants dispersed themselves in that part of the country situated between Havilah and Shur, that is, in several parts of Arabia Petræa, the western part whereof, toward Egypt, is, in scripture, called Shur, and the eastern part, toward the Persian gulf, Havilah.

In the meantime, Abraham continued to reside in the land of Palestine; and as his riches and power every day increased, Abimelech grew jealous of him, being fearful that he might, some time or other, endeavor to supplant him in the government. To prevent this, by the advice of his general Phicol, he formed a solemn league of friendship with Abraham, and thereby removed those fears which, for some time, had given him great uneasiness. A dispute had arisen between the servants of Abimelech and those of Abraham, relative to a well, which the latter had dug; but after a proper explanation, the matter was adjusted to the satisfaction of all parties, the well being declared the property of Abraham.†

The place where Abimelech and Abraham entered into this solemn covenant was, thenceforth, called Beersheba.‡ Here Abraham intending to end his days, should it be the will of Providence for him so to do, planted a grove‖ for a place of worship,

---

* The names of these sons were as follow: Nebajoth, Kedar, Adbeel, Mibsam, Mishma, Dumah, Massa, Hadar, Tema, Jetur, Naphish, and Kedemah: "twelve princes according to their nations." Gen. xxv. 13, &c.

† It may perhaps, at first view, appear strange that a dispute of any consequence should have arisen on account of a well of water· but it must be remembered, that, in those hot and dry countries, a well of water was an inestimable treasure, and the digging it a work of prodigious labor, which arose from the rockiness of the soil, and the great depth it was necessary to dig before they could find a spring.

‡ The word *Beer*, in the Hebrew language, signifies a *well*, and *Shebo* an *oath*, so that the Jews called it the *Well of the Oath*; because of the oath that Abraham and Abimelech had made at that place.

‖ WORSHIP IN GROVES (*See Engraving*).—The use of groves as places of primitive worship is natural and easily understood, though it could only have arisen in an early state of society, or be preserved where society remained in a primitive condition. It was the thought of a people who had not made any advances in architecture—who dwelt in tents or in huts—and who, while they did not feel that these dwellings were unsuitable or inadequate for themselves, could not but be sensible that they were so unimpressive, that it seemed revolting to associate with them, in any more formal service of worship, the idea of that God who fills all nature, and of whose grandeur they had no unworthy notions. They therefore preferred to seek intercourse with him, and to render him their service amid the vastness of his own creation, and under the shadow of those ancient woods, which insensibly inspire us with awe, and fill us with reverential feelings, which turn and vent themselves upon whatever has been customarily before the mind as the proper object of its reverence. Happy when that object is God!—as it was to the patriarchs. There is no doubt that men had this use for groves, almost universally, before any temples existed; but it is not so clear to us that, as some suppose, groves were used for religious purposes, before even altars were known. But Noah constructed an altar as soon as he left the ark; and this use of groves must, therefore, have been antediluvian, if it existed before altars: and this is certainly more than we know. It is certain, however, that, under the operation of the ideas we are tracing, altars were placed in the groves; and the next step was probably to build a hut near at hand to contain the implements of sacrifice; and when men had begun to build in their groves, the idea of a chapel or oratory for use in inclement weather, and when the trees were, in winter, bare of foliage, would naturally have been suggested. When, at last, the increased resources of constructive art, coupled with a weaker and more humanized idea of God, led men to entertain the bold idea of rearing fabrics—"temples made with hands"—which might make impressions on the mind worthy of his worship and service, the influence of old habits and old associations still operated. Most nations took care, when in their power, to plant groves around these buildings, for the most part with an enclosing ditch, hedge, or wall; and these groves were not only consecrated to the gods in whose honor the temples in the midst of them had been built, but were themselves places of sanctuary for criminals who fled to them for refuge.

As to the corruptions which became, in the end, associated with groves, and which led Moses to prohibit them very strictly, and to command that the groves which were found, in the land of Canaan, consecrated to idols, should be cut down, another opportunity will be afforded us of considering this part of the subject. Meanwhile, we only wish to call attention to the point alluded to in the text, respecting some points of analogy in this matter between the practices and the ideas of the patriarchs and those of the Celtic Druids. Among them we seem to find preserved, down to a late date, many of the ideas and practices which equally belong to the patriarchal ages, and which are doubtless to be regarded as relics of the religion which was common to all men in the first ages, and which they carried with them to the several places of their dispersion. In process of time these primitive institutions were in almost every country wofully corrupted, or, indeed lost, in various modifications of ceremony, idolatry, and unbelief. The Hebrew patriarchs doubtless exhibit in purity the religion of anterior ages, and what had been the sole religion of mankind; and thus he who studies the history of religious notions and practices is supplied with a test which enables him to ascertain the traces of this primitive religion, which may have been preserved in different and distant nations. Now, we know not of any people who preserved, mixed with many and awful corruptions, so many traces of this ancient religion as existed in the Druidical institutions

and in it erected an altar, that he might not be anywise deficient in the discharge of his religious duties.

The Almighty, in his wise Providence, had, in divers instances, and on many occasions, put Abraham's faith and obedience to the test; but now he resolved to try him in the tenderest point, in which every tie of parental affection bound him, and to give up which required a degree of resignation uncommon to the best of men. He is required, by his God, to sacrifice his son—to embrue his hands in the blood of his darling offspring.

Ishmael was now no more to him; he had parted with him at the divine command, and had transferred his affections solely on Isaac; and this son, this *only* son, who had been given him by Divine promise, and in whom all his future expectations of happiness centred, must fall a victim by the unalterable decree of Heaven. Hard task to flesh and blood! Severe trial to human nature! But if the flesh shuddered, the spirit was absolute: God commands—the patriarch obeys.

Early, therefore, the next morning, Abraham arose, and, without giving any notice to his family, prepared himself for the appointed business. He sat out, accompanied only by his son Isaac, and attended by two servants, who led an ass laden with provisions, together with the wood, instruments, and other things necessary for the sacrifice. After travelling three days he came within sight of the spot God had appointed for the dreadful scene, which was a particular mountain in the land of Moriah. Here he ordered his servants to stop with the ass, while he and his son went to a spot at some distance to perform their religious duties.

Abraham having laden his son with the wood and other materials for a burnt-offering, they proceeded on their journey. The harmless Isaac, ignorant of the design of his pious and affectionate parent, went cheerfully on with him, and the good old patriarch, relying on the faithfulness of the Divine promise, overcame the strugglings of a natural affection, which might have retarded his compliance with the will of God, and proceeded with a resolution worthy the *father of the faithful.*

As they approached near the appointed place for executing the awful injunction, Isaac, recollecting that a proper victim (the most essential requisite for the sacrifice) was wanting, innocently asked his father, where was the lamb for the burnt-offering? Such a question, at such a time, was enough to have startled any heart less firm than Abraham's; but, fixed in the resolution to obey the divine command, he coolly replied, " My son, God will provide one himself."

Being now arrived at the spot which the Almighty had directed, the first thing Abraham did was to erect an altar; after which, having prepared the instruments, and laid the wood in order, he embraced his son, and then bound him. Here the sacred historian, like a great painter, hath drawn a veil over the sorrow of Abraham, and the resignation of Isaac, that the imagination of the reader might paint to him more forcibly the struggles of the parent, and the agonies of the son, than words can possibly express.

Every preparation being now made, Abraham, taking up the knife, stretched forth his hand to give the finishing stroke to the life of his son; when, behold! God is satisfied with the faith and obedience of the father, and the piety and resignation of the son. The voice of a heavenly messenger is suddenly heard, saying unto Abraham, "Lay not thy hand upon the lad, neither do thou anything unto him." The uplifted arm was now withheld, and the fatal blow happily averted. The divine sound intimated, that the Almighty neither delighted in human sacrifices, nor wished to make a father the murderer of a son whom he had bestowed on him as a peculiar favor; but that the command had been given to try if his obedience to God exceeded his feelings as a man, and if his natural affections could submit to his religious duties.

and religion of the Celtes. It is true they had idols, and that many wild notions were entertained, and many horrid rites practised by them; but, amid all, they believed in one Supreme Being, to whom all other gods were far inferior. His symbol was the oak, and him, exclusively, they worshipped amid the groves. They never had images of him, or erected temples to him; and Tacitus, speaking of the Senones, who were a branch of the Celtes, and had the same religion, tells us that its principle consisted in the acknowledgment that the Deity whom they worshipped in the groves, the God without name, was he who governed all things, on whom all things depended, and whom all beings were bound to obey.

There are other resemblances which would render our position more clear if we could bring them into one view. But the purpose of the present note does not require this; and we need only now observe, that these remarkable analogies between the patriarchal (or say the Hebrew) and Druidical religions are late discoveries of our own day; but the antiquity and wisdom of the Druidical religion, and its conformities with that of the Jews, were adduced so long ago as the time of Celsus, in opposition to what that writer was pleased to consider the novelties of the gospel.

Cromlech at Plas Newydd.

Druidical Circle.—Jersey.

When the divine voice ceased, the pious patriarch, turning his eyes from the dear, though intended victim, beheld a ram fastened by his horns in a thicket. Convinced in his mind that this was the gracious substitute of Providence, he immediately flew to it with raptures, and having slain it with that knife which was intended for the destruction of his son, brought it to the altar and presented it (instead of the before-destined Isaac) as a burnt-offering, to his great and benevolent benefactor.

This infallible token of Abraham's obedience was so satisfactory to the Almighty, that he was pleased to renew his gracious promise to him with enlarged abundance; and even to confirm the same by a solemn oath. "By myself have I sworn, for because thou hast done this thing, and hast not withheld thy son, thine only son, from me."

Having thus complied with the will of God, and received a most convincing testimony of the divine approbation, Abraham and Isaac returned to the servants, and they all went joyfully together to Beersheba, at that time the place of Abraham's residence. In memory of this singular transaction, the pious patriarch called the place where it happened, "Jehovah-jirah," in allusion to the answer he gave to his son's question, "God will provide himself a lamb."

When Abraham returned home, he received the agreeable intelligence of the increase of his family, namely, that Milcah, his brother Nahor's wife, had brought him a numerous issue.* But the joy he received on this account was soon damped by a circumstance which happened in his own family, namely, the loss of his wife Sarah, who died at Kirjath-arba (afterward called Hebron), in the one hundred and twenty-seventh year of her age.

At the time of Sarah's death, Abraham was at Beersheba; but he no sooner heard of the melancholy event than he immediately repaired to Hebron, in order to perform the last offices due to his departed wife. As he was a stranger in the country, and had no land there of his own, he could not give her honorable interment without first obtaining the consent of the people. He therefore addressed himself to a general assembly of the principal inhabitants, entreating them to allow him the liberty of burying his wife in their country. This request being readily granted, Abraham bowed to the assembly in acknowledgment for the favor; after which he told them he should be glad to purchase a piece of ground as a sepulchre for himself and family, and begged of them to entreat Ephron, the prince of the country, to sell him the cave of Machpelah.

This request being likewise granted, and application made to Ephron, he generously offered the patriarch not only the cave, but also the whole field in which it stood, as a burying-place. Abraham acknowledged the bounty of the offer; but as he had ever acted on a principle of strict justice, he desired the prince to fix a price on the field; and that, on such condition, he would take possession of it for the purposes intended.

The prince, finding the patriarch resolute, asked four hundred shekels (a sum greatly beneath its real value). The purchase was made before all the people of Hebron, and the field, together with the cave, was formally assigned over to Abraham and his heirs for ever.

This matter being adjusted, Abraham, after the usual ceremonies of mourning were over, buried his wife in the cave he had then purchased, and in which his own remains were afterward deposited.

Abraham, being now far advanced in years, and apprehending he had not much longer to live, was desirous of seeing his own son Isaac married, and settled in the world, before his departure out of this transitory life. He therefore called to him his household steward, an old and trusty servant, to whom he related his intention of marrying his son; and obtained from him an oath,† that (in case he died first) he

* The names of the children of Nahor, by Milcah, were as follows: Huz, Buz, Kemuel, Cheshed, Hazo, Pildash, Jidlaph, and Bethuel. The last of these begat Rebecca, who was afterward the wife of Isaac.

† The great anxiety of the patriarchs to secure the marriage of their sons to women of their own clan or family appears everywhere, and is even indicated in the precise mention which is made of marriages which took place against this regulation—as in the cases of Ishmael and Esau. Such a desire has always prevailed wherever the distinction of clans or tribes has been strongly marked, for the sake of keeping up its property, blood, and peculiar feelings, and of compacting its union and influence; and these ordinary motives acquired increased intensity in the instance of the Hebrew patriarchs in consequence of the general idolatry or superstition into which all the surrounding nations had fallen, and which alone would have sufficed to preclude intermarriages with them. This consideration, separately from any other, has always prevented the Jews from forming matrimonial connexions with any but the daughters of Israel. Their law forbade such marriages in the strictest manner; and we shall find instances of their being severely punish-

should procure a wife for him among his own kindred, and not from the daughters of the Canaanites. Having obtained this solemn oath, Abraham told his servant to go into Mesopotamia, which was the place of his nativity, and there choose a wife, out of his own kindred, for his son Isaac. On receiving these orders, the servant asked him this question: "If," says he, "the woman refuse to follow me into the land of Canaan, must I return and fetch thy son to her?" The patriarch immediately answered in the negative, as no consideration could prevail on him to suffer his son to return to a land which he himself had left on account of the inhumanity and idolatry of its inhabitants. To encourage the servant in the prosecution of his intended expedition, Abraham assured him that a heavenly messenger would conduct him to the place whence he should bring a wife unto his son; and that if the woman pitched on should refuse to follow him, he should be free from the oath he had taken, and be considered as having properly discharged the business with which he was intrusted.

These matters being settled, Eliezer (for that was the name of this trusty servant) set out on his embassy, attended by a number of servants and camels, agreeably to the importance of his business, and the dignity of the person by whom he was employed.

After undergoing great fatigue, both from the badness of the roads and the want of water, this trusty servant, with his attendants, reached Mesopotamia, and repaired to Haran,* a city belonging to his master's brother Nahor. When he had arrived near the entrance of the city, he stopped at the public well (whither it was customary for the young women of the place to come every morning and evening for water), in order to refresh the camels.†

ed, and of the deep disgust which they inspired. They were neither to take the females of other nations, nor give their own females to them (Deut. vii. 3, 4); and the reason was, "For they will turn away thy sons from following me." While this principle inhibited marriages with other nations, there was another law which preserved the integrity of property in the respective tribes, by directing that daughters having any inheritance should not marry out of the tribe of their father, (Num. xxxvi). "So shall not the inheritance of the children of Israel remove from tribe to tribe." These principles, taken from the subsequent laws of the Hebrews, afford the best explanation of the conduct of the patriarchs with regard to the marriages of their sons. Among the Bedouin Arabs there is no regulation precluding the intermarriages of different tribes; but in practice a man seldom takes a wife from any other tribe than his own; and still more rarely, although there is no national or religious difference, will a Bedouin give his daughter in marriage to the inhabitant of a town, or to a cultivator or artisan. Some tribes never do so; but others are rather less strict. So, as Ward informs us, among the Hindoos, the parents who find employment at a distance from their original homes, always marry their children in their own country and among their old acquaintance.

* "CHARRAN," as given by St. Stephen, is the proper reading of this name, and is, therefore, different from the name of Abram's brother, which is truly spelt Haran. The site of this place is very questionable. Most writers on scriptural geography identify it with the place called Charræ by the Greeks and Romans, and renowned in history for the defeat of Crassus. But we are inclined to think that this identification is scarcely compatible with that which finds Ur in Urfah; for not only is this Charran in the same plain with Urfah, but is actually, at almost all times, visible from it, being distant not above eight hours' ride to the south; so that a removal to this distance hardly corresponds with the historical intimations which refer to it. There are three other sites to which different writers refer the Charran of our history. One is Oruros, on the Euphrates, about fifty miles below the embouchure of the Chaboras: the second is Haræ, about twenty miles to the east-northeast of Palmyra; and the third, Carræ, about thirty-eight miles northeast from Damascus. All these places would, however, be out of the way in proceeding from Urfah to the land of Canaan, excepting the one near Damascus, which, on many grounds, we should hold to offer the preferable claim, were it not that the account of Jacob's journey to the same place expressly informs us that Haran was in Mesopotamia, on which ground the site, with the mention of which we commenced this note, must still be held to have a little the preference, notwithstanding the objections which apply to it, as none of the others answer to this condition. We think it very likely that the site of Ur, and more than likely that the site of Haran, are yet to be found.

† Water is usually drawn in the evening, and frequently in the cool of the morning also. Fetching water is one of the heaviest of the many heavy duties which devolve upon the females in the East, and one which the most sensibly impresses us with a sense of their degraded condition. The usage varies in different countries. Among the Arabs and other nomades, and also in many parts of India, it is the exclusive employment of the women, without distinction of rank. But in Turkey and Persia the poorer women only are subject to this servile employment, respectable families being supplied daily by men who make the supplying of water a distinct business. The tents of the Bedouins are seldom pitched quite near to the well from which they obtain their water; and if the distance is not more than a mile, the men do not think is necessary that the water should be brought upon the camels; and, unless there are asses to be employed on this service, the women must go every evening, sometimes twice, and bring home at their backs long and heavy leathern bags full of water. The wells are the property of tribes or individuals, who are not always willing that caravans should take water from them; and in that case, a girl is sometimes posted at the well to exact presents from those who wish to have water. It is not likely that Abraham's servant travelled without a leathern bucket to draw water, and it is therefore probable that he abstained from watering his ten camels until he should have obtained permission. The women, when they are at the wells in the evening, are generally obliging to travellers, and ready to supply such water as they may require for themselves or their beasts. The women of towns in Turkey and Persia have seldom far to go, except under peculiar circumstances in the situation or soil of the place, or quality of its water. Their water-vessel depends much upon the distance; if rather far, a skin will probably be preferred as most convenient for carrying a good quantity; but if near, an earthern jar will often be chosen. The present well seems to have been quite near the town, and we concur in the translation which renders Rebecca's vessel "a pitcher." The

Having been properly instructed by his master in the fear of God, and being sensible of the importance of the business, as well as fearful of not executing it to his master's satisfaction, he made a mental prayer to God, beseeching him to direct him, by a certain sign, to a proper object of choice for his young master. He had no sooner solicited this divine assistance than his request was immediately complied with, and the sign given was, that she who, at his desire, permitted him to drink of her water, would be the person appointed by God for the wife of his servant Isaac.

Soon after this, Rebecca, the daughter of Bethuel, came to the well, with her pitcher, for water; after she had filled it, the servant (having taken notice that she was exceedingly beautiful) accosted her in a very humble manner, begging that she would give him a draught of the water, he being exceedingly thirsty. Rebecca readily consented, and not only gave him to drink, but also went several times to the well to fetch water for the refreshment of his camels.*

This propitious occurrence highly delighted Abraham's servant, who, after paying some general compliments to her beauty and benevolence, made inquiry concerning her family and relations. To which the lovely virgin replied, that she was the daughter of Bethuel, the son of Nahor, and kinswoman to Abraham.

This intelligence gave fresh spirits to the faithful messenger, who was now convinced that God approved of the alliance between Rebecca and Isaac. He therefore presented to her a pair of gold ear-rings, and some other female ornaments, requesting her to accept them as a token of his esteem for her virtues, and a grateful return

---

word (kad) is different from that (chemits) rendered "bottle" in the narrative of Hagar's expulsion: and is the same word used to describe the vessels in which Gideon's soldiers concealed their torches, and which they broke to produce a crashing and alarming noise. The women contrive to draw an enjoyment even out of this irksome duty, as it affords the best opportunity they have of meeting and talking together, and of displaying their finery to each other. They by no means appear to the worst advantage, as to dress, at the wells; and this circumstance shows that Abraham's servant might there, without any incongruity, invest Rebecca with the ornaments he had brought. To a traveller in the East, the best opportunities of making his observations on the females will occur in the evening at the wells. Eliezer was aware of this, and regarded the opportunity as favorable for his purpose. It appears that the unmarried females even of towns went unveiled, or only partially veiled, on ordinary occasions, in these early times. Now all go veiled; and the more extended use of the veil in modern times has probably, in one respect, operated favorably for the women, by exonerating those in families decently circumstanced from the very heavy duty of fetching water, the proper management of the veil being scarcely compatible with the performance of this laborious office. Accordingly we find that this duty devolves more exclusively on the females, without distinction of rank, in those Asiatic countries or tribes where the women are not obliged to veil their faces, as in India, and among the Arabian and other-nomade tribes. We have already noticed the Arabian usage In consequence of the modifications which we venture to think that the extended use of the veil has produced among the inhabitants of towns west of the Indus, it is perhaps in India we are to look for the most precise parallels to the patriarchal customs. Accordingly we find, that in many parts of India, women of the first distinction draw water daily from the public wells. They always fetch it in earthern jars carried upon their heads. Sometimes two or three jars are carried at once, one upon the other, forming a pillar upon the bearer's head. As this necessarily requires the most perfect steadiness, the habit gives to the females a remarkably erect and stately air. It seems that it is a distinction to carry the jar on the shoulder; and Forbes, in his "Oriental Memoirs," relates an anecdote of an intelligent native who, when this highly interesting passage was read to him, inferred that Rebecca was of "high caste," from her carrying the pitcher on her shoulder. The text, however, does not necessarily imply that she carried the jar erect upon her shoulder, but quite as probably means that it was carried at the back, the handle being held over the shoulder by the hand or leathern strap.

* The pastoral poetry of classical antiquity, which has been imitated more or less in all nations, has rendered us familiar with the idea of females of birth and attractions acting as sheperdesses long after the practice itself has been discontinued, and the employment has sunk into contempt. When nations originally pastoral settled in towns, and adopted the refinements of life, the care of the sheep ceased to be a principal consideration, and gradually devolved upon servants or slaves, coming to be considered a mean employment, to which the proprietor or his household only gave a general and superintending attention. The respectability of the employment in these patriarchal times is not evinced by our finding the daughter of so considerable a person as Laban engaged in tending the flocks, for in the East all drudgery devolves upon the females; but by our finding the sons of such persons similarly engaged in pastoral duties, which in Homer also appears to have been considered a fitting employment for the sons of kings and powerful chiefs. We are not aware that at present, in the East, the actual care of a flock or herd is considered a dignified employment. Forbes, in his "Oriental Memoirs," mentions, that in the Bramin villages of the Concan, women of the first distinction draw the water from wells, and tend the cattle to pasture, "like Rebecca and Rachel." But in this instance it can not be because such employments have any dignity in them, but because the women are obliged to perform every servile office. So, among the Bedouin Arabs, and other nomade nations, the immediate care of the flocks devolves either upon the women or the servants; but most generally the latter, as the women have enough to occupy them in their multifarious domestic duties. However, among some tribes, it is the exclusive business of the young unmarried women to drive the cattle to pasture. "Among the Sinai Arabs," says Burckhardt, "a boy would feel himself insulted were any one to say, 'Go and drive your father's sheep to pasture;' these words, in his opinion, would signify, 'You are no better than a girl.'" These young women set out before sunrise, three or four together, carrying some water and victuals with them, and they do not return until late in the evening. Throughout the day they continue exposed to the sun, watching the sheep with great care, for they are sure of being severely beaten by their father should any be lost. These young women are in general civil to persons who pass by, and ready enough to share with them their victuals and milk. They are fully able to protect their flocks against any ordinary depredation or danger, for their way of life makes them as hardy and vigorous as the men.

Camels.

for her distinguished condescension. As it grew late, and he had valuable property about him, he entreated permission, for that night, to reside at the house of her relations. Rebecca, in a most engaging manner, permitted him this convenience, but begged that she might previously apprize the family of so unexpected a visiter. Accordingly, having accepted the presents, she immediately hastened home, leaving Eliezer full of contemplation and acknowledgments to the divine favor for the happy incident.

As soon as Rebecca entered the house, her brother Laban, observing the bracelets on her arms, asked her by what means she had obtained such costly ornaments. Rebecca acquainted him with every particular that had happened, from her going out till her return; upon which Laban immediately went to the well, where finding Eliezer and his attendants, he brought them home with him, and ordered proper provision to be made both for him and his retinue.

As soon as Eliezer had paid the necessary compliments to Rebecca's family, he informed them of the nature of his embassy, the great success that had attended him in his journey, and the fortunate incident of his meeting Rebecca without the city. He likewise gave them an ample account of the state of his master's family; of the wealth and prosperity wherewith God had blessed him; of the son and heir which he had given him in his old age; and of the large expectances which this heir had, not only from the prerogative of his birth, but from the donation and entail of all his father's possessions. Having thus minutely related every particular relative to his embassy, he demanded an immediate answer, saying, till that was obtained, he could not, with any satisfaction, take the least refreshment.

From the very singular circumstances that had occurred in the course of Eliezer's journey, Laban and Bethuel* were of opinion that Divine Providence was materially concerned in the whole affair. Concluding, therefore, that it would be exceedingly wrong to refuse Eliezer's request, they readily consented, and told him he might take Rebecca to her intended husband as soon as he thought proper.

This business being settled, the trusty servant presented Rebecca with jewels of silver and gold, and fine raiment, which he had brought with him for the purpose.

He likewise gave some considerable presents† to her mother and the rest of the family; and the remainder of the evening was dedicated to mirth and festivity.

Early in the morning, Eliezer, being impatient to acquaint his master with the success of his embassy, desired to be dismissed. This request greatly surprised the family, who, influenced by natural affection, desired that Rebecca might be permitted to tarry with them a few days, to take, perhaps, a last farewell. But the diligent and faithful steward would not admit of no delay; upon which, the matter being referred to Rebecca herself, she agreed to go with him whenever he thought proper. Accordingly, the necessary preparations being made, and the bridal blessing bestowed, she took her leave, attended by her nurse (whose name was Deborah) and other servants appointed on the occasion.

When Eliezer came within some distance of his master's house, it happened that Isaac was then walking in the fields, meditating on the beauties of nature, and the beneficence of that Being who formed the creation. Seeing at a distance his servants and camels on the road, he hastened to meet them, anxious to know the result of Eliezer's embassy. As he approached near, Rebecca asked who he was; and being informed, she immediately alighted from her camel, threw a veil‡ over her face, and waited to receive the first compliments of her intended husband.

* This Bethuel could not be the father of Rebecca, because, had that been the case, it would have been improper to have had Laban either named before him, or to have given answer to Abraham's messenger when his father was by; and, therefore, since Josephus makes the damsel tells Eliezer that her father had been dead long ago, and that she was left to the care of her brother Laban, this Bethuel (who is here named after Laban, and never more taken any notice of during the whole transaction) must have been some younger brother of the family.
† Dr. Shaw, who resided many years in the East, tells us, that among the Arabians, the person who settles a marriage contract, first adorns the espoused person with jewels, and then makes presents to her relations, according to their rank. He adds, that, on such occasions, it is expressly stipulated what sum of money the husband shall settle on the wife; what jewels she shall wear; how many suits of raiment she shall have; and, lastly, how many slaves shall be allowed to attend her.
‡ Whether veiled before or not, she now " covered herself"—her whole person—with the ample enveloping veil with which brides are still conducted to the bridegroom. Rosenmuller, in illustration of this passage, quotes an ancient father (Tertullian), who, with an express reference to the same text, observes, as a custom still existing in his time, that the heathen brides were also conducted to their husbands covered with a veil. It is still all but universal in the East, and it will be observed that it is used, not only by the females whose faces are always concealed both before and after marriage, but by those who display

When Isaac came up to Rebecca, he addressed her with great respect, and immediately conducted her to his mother's tent, which had been previously fitted up for her reception, and designed for her future habitation. A few days after they were joined in wedlock, and Isaac grew so fond of her, that his mind was greatly relieved from that perturbation with which, for three years, it had been loaded, for the loss of his affectionate mother. Such was the pious regard children had for their parents in those days; and such was the amiable example set by Isaac for all who should follow!

Some time after Isaac's marriage, his father, though far advanced in life, yet still possessing great strength of constitution, made an addition to his family, by taking another wife, whose name was Keturah, and by whom he had six sons. But, lest they should interfere with Isaac in his inheritance of Canaan, as they grew up he portioned them off, and sent them towards the east, where, settling in Arabia and Syria, they became, in time, the rulers of different nations.

These are the last circumstances mentioned by the sacred historian, relative to the great patriarch Abraham, who at length, worn out with bodily infirmities, quietly gave up the ghost, in the one hundred and seventy-fifth year of his age, leaving behind him a name famous to all posterity. He was buried by his two sons, Ishmael and Isaac, in the cave of Machpelah, where, about forty years before, he had deposited the remains of his beloved Sarah.

Ishmael, the eldest son of Abraham, though not his heir, lived many years after his father. He died at the age of one hundred and seven, leaving behind him twelve sons.*

part or the whole of their faces on all ordinary occasions. It is, in fact, the indispensable costume for the occasion. Whether the bridal veil was distinguished from other veils does not appear; but we observe that one of red silk or muslin is affected by the Persians on such an occasion, although the ordinary veils are white or blue; and Dr. Russel, in his account of a Maronite marriage, observes that the bride's veil was of the same color. Thus we see that Rebecca, by enveloping her person in a veil, put herself into the costume usual for a bride when conducted to the tent or house of her husband.

* THE ISHMAELITES.—We know not whence the strange opinion arose that the whole Arabian nation is descended from Ishmael, and that, consequently, the names of the Ishmaelites and Arabs are co-extensive, unless from the Chaldee and Arabic paraphrasts, and from other Jewish writers, whose historical authority, at all times of the least possible value, becomes a perfect nullity when open to any obvious influence, such as the wish to represent Abraham as the father of so great and wide-spread a nation as the Arabians. The whole testimony of the oriental writers, and all the inferences deducible from the sacred narrative, are opposed to this conclusion. The Arabians have a history anterior to Ishmael; and it would be preposterous to suppose that Arabia, even to its deserts, was not occupied before his time.

According to the Arabian writers, Arabia was occupied a few generations after the flood by the successive settlement within it of variously-descended tribes, all of whom ultimately gave way to the races from which the present Arabs claim to be descended, either from being destroyed by them or lost in them. These latter proceed from two stocks, of which the most ancient is that of Kahtan, the same who is in the Bible called Joktan, a son of Eber; and the other that of Adnan, who descended in a direct line from Ishmael. To the posterity of the former is given the distinguishing title of eminence, al Arab al Araba (equivalent to "a Hebrew of the Hebrews" among the Jews), that is, the genuine or pure Arabs: while those of Ishmael receive that of al Arab al Mostáreba, meaning naturalized or mixed Arabs. But some writers, who wish to be more precise, apply the first and most honorable title to the most ancient and lost tribes to which we have alluded, while the descendants of Kahtan obtained the name of Motáreba, which likewise signifies mixed Arabs, though in a nearer degree than Mostáreba; those who acknowledged Ishmael for their ancestor (through Adnan) being the more distant graft. Considering the origin of Ishmael, it is no wonder that those supposed to be descended from him should have no claim to be admitted as pure Arabs; but as he is alleged to have contracted an alliance with the Jorhamites (descended from Jorham, a son of Kahtan) who possessed Hejaz, by marrying the daughter of their emir Modad, whence, and by subsequent intermarriages his descendants became blended with them into one nation, their claim to be regarded as Mostáreba is beyond dispute.

There is considerable uncertainty in the descents from Ishmael to Adnan, which is the reason why the Arabs have seldom attempted to trace their genealogies higher than the latter, whom they therefore look upon as the founder of their tribes. The account of this Adnan does not commence, however, till 122 B.C.; so that the uncertainties extend over a period of about 1800 years. This is a very awful circumstance at the first view, but the line of descent is not compromised by it, notwithstanding. The uncertainties refer merely to the numbers and names of the generations which fill the interval, and arise from the contracted manner in which genealogies, extending over a long series of ages, were necessarily kept. Thus they do not specify all the generations from A to Z, in this way:—" Z, the son of Y; Y, the son of X; X, the son of W," and so on up to A: but knowing it to be a matter of perfect notoriety and unquestionable truth that Z is descended from some eminent ancestor, say S, and that it is equally notorious and unquestionable that the remote ancestor of this S was M, and that M was descended from G, and G from A,—they may omit the intermediate ancestors, through whom Z descended from S, and S from M, and M from G, and G from A, and state the matter thus: " Z, the son of S, the son of M, the son of G, the son of A:" and it may occur that not only the names but even the numbers of the generations between A and Z may, in the course of time, become involved in great uncertainty through their not being given in detail in the genealogies, while the truth yet remains certain and unquestionable that Z is descended from A through G, M, and S. Hence, it is not questioned that Adnan is descended from Ishmael, and a certain number, eight or ten, of illustrious names are mentioned to mark out the line of descent, while the names of the mass of intermediate ancestors is lost, and even the numbers of their generations may be a subject of fair dispute without the main question being touched. It is, therefore, surprising to see some able writers so much in the dark as to imagine, that, because the Arabian writers give us only some eight or

CHAPTER VI:

WHEN Isaac married Rebecca, he was forty years old, and lived with her nearly twenty years before she had issue. He had been so long uneasy on this account, that he at length prayed to God to grant him an heir, who being pleased to listen to his request, bestowed that blessing he had so earnestly wished for, and the long barren Rebecca now conceived, to the great satisfaction both of herself and husband.

After Rebecca had been pregnant some months, the struggles of the children (for she had twins within her) gave her such pain and uneasiness, that she began, in a manner, to wish herself not with child. Unable to account for the cause of her extreme pains, she went to consult the divine oracle, and received for answer, that the two children, which she then bore, should be the heads of two different nations, and that they would long contest for superiority; but that, in process of time, the glories acquired by the *elder* would be eclipsed by the more resplendent transactions of the *younger*.

When the time of Rebecca's delivery arrived, the child that first entered the world was covered all over with red hair,* for which reason his parents called him Esau; and the other came so close after him, that he took hold of his heel with his hand, and was therefore called Jacob, to denote (what he afterward proved) the supplanter of his brother.

As these two children grew up, they became very different in their tempers, and when they arrived at the age of maturity, followed different employments. Esau, the elder, being strong and active, delighted in the chase, and thereby frequently supplying his father with venison, obtained his particular affection; while Jacob, who was of a more courteous disposition, by staying at home in the tent, and employing himself in family offices, became the favorite of his mother.

Esau having one day greatly fatigued himself with hunting, returned home just at the time his brother Jacob had prepared a mess of pottage† for his own refreshment

ten names to mark the line of descent, they were absurd enough to suppose that that eight or ten generations sufficed to cover the long interval between Ishmael and Adnan. We have dwelt on this subject the rather because this Arabian manner of proceeding suffices to clear up some difficulties which the Hebrew genealogies offer.

It must not be inferred that the Arabs undervalue the descent from Ishmael in comparison with that from Kahtan, on account of their applying to it a less honorable designation. This is by no means the case; for, on the contrary, they set a high value, like the Jews, on the privilege of being descended from Abraham; and this distinction is, in the eyes of the modern Arabs, greatly enhanced by the circumstance that Mohammed belonged to this race, and gloried in being descended from Ishmael and Abraham.

Of the personal history of Ishmael the Arabians give a highly *embellished* account, which it is not necessary in this place to repeat. In those circumstances which seem most entitled to consideration, as not incompatible with his scriptural history, we are somewhat inclined to suspect that they apply to him actions and events which really belong, if they are at all real, to some of his descendants. For instance, that Ishmael ever was in Hejaz, or formed any important connexions there, seems to us very doubtful; but there is nothing in this that might not be very probably true of one of his descendants, after the tribe had increased, and had formed alliances among the Arabs of the Kahtan races. We therefore attach little weight to the statement of his marriage to the daughter of the king of the Jorhamites, though we should not be prepared to doubt it merely on the ground that the scripture tells us that he married an Egyptian woman, since his Arabian wife might have been the second. In fact, much that the Arabians tell us about Ishmael proceeds on the grievous misconception that Abraham himself lived in Hejaz, and that there all the events of his later history took place.

The account of the descent of numerous Arabian tribes from Ishmael is not open to the same doubts or difficulty, and is, indeed, so clear in itself, and so universally acknowledged, that the object of the present note has not been to prove this, but to indicate the historical certainty that *all* the Arabians could not, and did not, claim to be descended from him.

* This expression, according to some commentators, is taken two ways, namely, either that Esau was, at his birth, covered with red hair, or that the color of his skin was red, like a coat of red hair. He was called Esau, from the word *Eschau*, which in the Hebrew language, signifies a *hair-cloth*; as Jacob was named from *Hekel*, the *heel*, and signifies a supplanter, or one that taketh hold of, or trippeth up another's heels.

† The *edom*, or red pottage, was prepared, we learn from this chapter, by seething lentils (*adashim*) in water; and subsequently, as we may guess from a practice which prevails in many countries, adding a little *manteca*, or suet, to give them a flavor. The writer of these observations has often partaken of this self-same " red pottage," served up in the manner just described, and found it better food than a stranger would be apt to imagine. The mess had the redness which gained for it the name of *edom*; and which, through the singular circumstance of a son selling his birthright to satisfy the cravings of a pressing appetite, it imparted to the posterity of Esau in the people of Edom. The lentil (or *Lens seculenta* of some writers, and the *Ervum lens* of Linnæus) belongs to the leguminous or podded family. The stem is branched, and the leaves consist of about eight pairs of smaller leaflets. The flowers are small, and with the upper division of the flower prettily veined. The pods contain about two seeds, which vary from a tawny red to a black. It delights in a dry, warm sandy soil. Three varieties are cultivated in France—" small brown," " yellowish," and the " lentil of Provence." In the former country they are dressed and eaten during Lent as a haricot; in Syria they are used as food after they have undergone the simple process of being parched in a pan over the fire.

Esau, being almost spent with hunger, was so struck with the looks of the pottage, that he anxiously begged of his brother to let him participate of the repast. But Jacob (who was probably so instructed by his mother) refused to comply with his request, unless on the following conditions; namely, that he would immediately make over to him his birth-right. Esau reflecting on the danger to which he was daily subject, from the nature of his employment, set no great value on what Jacob required; and the latter, perceiving his disposition to comply (that he might have the right more firmly conveyed to him), proposed his doing it by way of oath. Notwithstanding the singularity of the request, Esau complied with it, and the bargain being made, he ate very greedily of the food prepared by his brother. Thus did the unthinking Esau dispose of his birth-right, with all the privileges* belonging to it, for so simple a thing as a mess of pottage.

Isaac, at this time, lived at Beersheba, but a dreadful famine happening in the land of Canaan, he resolved (as his father Abraham had done on a similar occasion) to avoid its consequences by retiring to Egypt. He accordingly proceeded as far as Gerar, a city belonging to the Philistines. But here he was interrupted in his intended journey by the interposition of the Almighty, who, in a dream, charged him not to go into Egypt, but to tarry in the country where he then was; and at the same time assured him, that he would not only secure him from the danger of the famine, but, in performance of the oath which he had sworn to his father Abraham, would cause his descendants (to whom he would give the whole land of Canaan in possession) to multiply exceedingly.

In conformity to the divine command, Isaac determined to fix his residence at Gerar, where he made use of the same stratagem his father had formerly done in the same place, and from the same motive. Fearful lest the charms of his wife Rebecca might attract the particular notice of some of the city, and thereby endanger his own safety, it was agreed between them, that, instead of his wife, she should pass for his sister. This deception succeeded for a time, but at length was discovered by Abimelech† the king, who, from a window, observed such familiarities pass between them, as convinced him they were man and wife.

In consequence of this discovery, Abimelech sent for Isaac, whom he accused of dissimulation, telling him, that from the freedom he had observed between him and Rebecca, he was sure she was his wife; and that the imposition he had endeavored to lay on the people might have been attended with consequences disgraceful to himself.

Isaac, conscious of the justness of the accusation, did not attempt to disprove the charge, but urged, in vindication of his conduct, that he did it to preserve that life, which, otherwise, he thought in the most imminent danger. This apology was admitted by Abimelech, who not only forgave him the offence, but immediately issued an edict, that whoever should presume to offer any injury either to him or his wife, should be punished with death.

Having received these tokens of friendship from Abimelech, Isaac thought himself happy under his protection, and, intending to make Gerar his fixed place of residence, employed himself in husbandry, and the rearing of flocks, for the future support of himself and family. The great success that attended his endeavors, by means of his beneficent Creator, soon raised the envy and indignation of the Philistines. In the space of one year only, during his residence at Gerar, so prolific was the land he sowed that, to the great astonishment of his neighbors, it yielded him a hundred fold.

* It should be understood, that previously to the establishment of a priesthood under the Law of Moses, the first-born had not only a preference in the secular inheritance, but succeeded exclusively to the priestly functions which had belonged to his father, in leading the religious observances of the family, and performing the simple religious rites of these patriarchal times. The secular part of the birthright entitled the first-born to a "double portion" of the inheritance; but writers are divided in opinion as to the proportion of this double share. Some think that he had one half, and that the rest was equally divided among the other sons; but a careful consideration of Gen. xlvii. 5–22, in which we see that Jacob transfers the privilege of the first-born to Joseph, and that this privilege consisted in his having one share more than any of his brethren, inclines us to the opinion of the Rabbins, that the first-born had merely twice as much as any other of his brethren. It is certainly possible, but not very likely, that in the emergency, Esau bartered all his birthright for a mess of pottage; but it seems more probable that Esau did not properly appreciate the value of the sacerdotal part of his birthright, and therefore readily transferred it to Jacob for a trifling present advantage. This view of the matter seems to be confirmed by St. Paul, who calls Esau a "profane person," for his conduct on this occasion; and it is rather for despising his spiritual than his temporal privileges, that he seems to be liable to such an imputation.

† This Abimelech was probably the son of him with whom Abraham had formerly made a covenant. It is reasonable to suppose that Abimelech was only a title commonly used for the kings of the Philistines, in the same manner as Cæsar was by the Roman emperors, and Pharaoh for the kings of Egypt.

This so irritated the Philistines, that, in order to oblige him to leave the country, they filled up the wells which had been formerly dug by his father's servants; and Abimelech himself, to satisfy the resentment of the people, ordered him to quit Gerar, telling him, that as he had sufficiently improved his fortune under his protection, he might now give the like opportunity to others, by leaving the place, and retiring to a more distant part of the country.

Finding to what a degree the people were incensed against him, Isaac, to preserve his property, as well as secure his person, left the place, and retired to the valley of Gerar, which was at some distance from the city, and where Abraham had formerly fed his cattle. Having settled himself here, he opened the wells (which had been dug by his father and filled up by the Philistines) and called them by their ancient names. In the course of their labors, Isaac's servants discovered a new well of fine springing water; but a dispute arising between them and some neighboring herdsmen, the latter claiming the well as found upon their ground, Isaac resolved to leave the place; and by way of perpetuating the circumstance called it *Esek*, which, in the Hebrew language, signifies *contention*. Removing some way farther, Isaac's servants dug another well, which being likewise claimed by the Philistines, he was obliged to relinquish it, and therefore, called the place *Sitnah*, which signifies *enmity.**

Being quite tired out with repeated insults from the Philistines, in order to prevent the like in future, he removed to the most distant part of their country. Here he dug another well; and not meeting with any opposition, he called it *Rehoboth*, which signifies *enlargement*, because his flocks had now room to feed and range the country in search of fresh pasturage: " for now," said he, " the Lord hath made room for us, and we shall be fruitful in the land."

After residing a short time on this spot Isaac returned to Beersheba,† where, on the very night of his arrival, the Almighty was pleased to appear to him in a vision, promising him his favor and protection, and that he would bless him, and multiply

---

* The cause of these differences seems to have been, that a question arose whether wells dug by Abraham's and Isaac's people within the territories of Gerar belonged to the people who digged them, or to those who enjoyed the territorial right. The real motive of the opposition of the people of Gerar, and their stopping up the wells made by Abraham, seems to have been to discourage the visits of such powerful persons to their territory; for otherwise the wells would have been suffered to remain on account of their utility to the nation. Stopping up the wells is still an act of hostility in the East. Mr. Roberts says that it is so in India, where one person who hates another will sometimes send his slaves in the night to fill up the well of the latter, or else to pollute it by throwing in the carcases of unclean animals. The Bedouin tribes in the country traversed by the great pilgrim-caravan which goes annually from Damascus to Mecca, receive presents of money and vestments to prevent them from injuring the wells upon the line of march, and which are essential to the very existence of the multitudes who then traverse this desert region. However, of all people in the world, none know so well as the Arabs the value of water, and the importance of wells, and hence they never wantonly do them harm. They think it an act of great merit in the sight of God to dig a well; and culpable in an equal degree to destroy one. The wells in the deserts are in general the exclusive property either of a whole tribe, or of individuals whose ancestors dug them. The possession of a well is never alienated; perhaps because the Arabs are firmly persuaded that the owner of a well is sure to prosper in all his undertakings, since the blessings of all who drink his water fall upon him. The stopping of Abraham's wells by the Philistines, the re-opening of them by Isaac, and the restoration of their former names—the commemorative names given to the new wells, and the strifes about them between those who had sunk them and the people of the land—are all circumstances highly characteristic of those countries in which the want of rivers and brooks during summer renders the tribes dependant upon the wells for the very existence of the flocks and herds which form their wealth. It would seem that the Philistines did not again stop the wells while Isaac was in their country. It is probable that the wells successfully sunk by Isaac did not furnish water sufficient for both his own herds and those of Gerar, and thus the question became one of exclusive right. Such questions often lead to bitter and bloody quarrels in the East; and it was probably to avoid the last result of an appeal to arms that Isaac withdrew out of the more settled country toward the desert, where he might enjoy the use of his wells in peace.

† BEERSHEBA.—In the Biblical Repository for April, 1839, we have a very valuable and interesting "Report of Travels in Palestine and the Adjacent Regions, in 1838; *undertaken for the illustration of Biblical Geography* by the Rev. Prof. E. Robinson and Rev. E. Smith;" in which we find a notice of the discovery of the site of Beersheba, about thirty miles to the south of Hebron. Our readers will not fail to be gratified at being enabled to obtain the view, conveyed in the following description, of a place of such great interest in the history of the patriarchs :—

‡ "After crossing another elevated plateau, the character of the surface was again changed. We came upon an open rolling country; all around were swelling hills, covered in ordinary seasons with grass and rich pasturage, though now arid and parched with drought. We now came to Wady Lebu; and on the north side of its water-course we had the satisfaction of discovering the site of ancient Beersheba, the celebrated border city of Palestine, still bearing in Arabic the name of Bir Seba. Near the water-course are two circular wells of excellent water, nearly forty feet deep. They are both surrounded with drinking troughs of stone, for the use of camels and flocks; such as doubtless were used of old for the flocks that then fed on the adjacent hills. Ascending the low hills north of the wells, we found them strewed with the ruins of former habitations—the foundations of which are distinctly to be traced. These ruins extend over a space of half a mile long by a quarter of a mile broad. Here, then, is the place where Abraham and Isaac and Jacob often lived! Here Samuel made his three sons judges; and from here Elijah wandered out into the southern desert, and sat down under the *rethem*, or shrub of broom, just as our Arabs sat down under it every day and every night. Over these swelling hills the flocks of the patriarchs roved by thousands. we now only found a few camels, asses, and goats."

Great Officer on a Journey.

his seed, for the sake of his faithful servant Abraham. In grateful acknowledgment of this repeated instance of the divine goodness, Isaac, intending to continue here, first built an altar for religious worship, and then ordered his servants to clear out the well which had been formerly dug by his father.

Isaac had not long returned to Beersheba, when Abimelech, touched with a sense of the unworthy treatment he had received, both from him and his subjects, as well as fearing his just resentment, should he become powerful hereafter, thought it most prudent to avoid future trouble, by endeavoring either to renew the old league which had been formerly made with his father Abraham, or to enter into a new one. Accordingly, taking with him the chief of his nobility, together with the captain-general of his forces, he went, in great pomp, to Beersheba, in order to pay honor and respect to Isaac. At the first interview Isaac, to show that he still retained a sense of the injuries he had formerly done him, received his visit very coolly, and, with apparent surprise, asked, how he came to offer respect to a person, for whom, by his conduct and behavior, he had long discovered an utter aversion? Abimelech, conscious of his error, made the best excuse the nature of the case would admit. He told him he had long been convinced that the divine favor attended him in all his undertakings, and that he might not be thought to oppose God, he was come to renew the covenant between his people and Abraham's posterity, and was ready to engage in the same conditions and obligations.

Isaac, being naturally of a quiet and easy disposition, readily admitted this apology from Abimelech, whom, with his attendants, he entertained with great liberality. The articles for a treaty of friendship were agreed on that same evening, and the next morning confirmed by a solemn and mutual oath; after which Abimelech took his leave, and returned home.

Soon after the departure of Abimelech, the servants of Isaac informed him, that, in the well they had been clearing out, and which formerly belonged to Abraham, they had found a spring of most excellent water. This event happening on the same day that the league of friendship had been confirmed between Isaac and Abimelech, he called it (as his father had done before on a similar occasion) *Beersheba, the well of the oath,* " i. e. the well wherein water was delivered, on the day that Abimelech and I entered into a treaty of peace, and ratified the same with the solemnity of an oath."

A circumstance now occurred, which gave great uneasiness both to Isaac and his wife. Their two sons were arrived at the age of forty, and Esau had taken two wives from among the Hittites, one of whom was Judith, the daughter of Beeri, and the other Bashemath, the daughter of Elon, both women of respectable families in Canaan. These marriages he had contracted without his parents' privity, knowing that his father had determined not to form any alliance with the idolatrous Canaanites. Rebecca was so incensed at Esau's conduct, that the little affection she before had for him, was now entirely alienated; but such was the power of natural affection in Isaac, and such his over-fondness for an obdurate and perverse son, that knowing the error past repair, he made a virtue of necessity, and forgave what he could not remedy.

Isaac, becoming very old,* imperfect in his eyesight, and apprehensive that his dissolution was near at hand, resolved to bestow that parental benediction on his son Esau, which he had long intended. Accordingly, calling him one day to his private apartment, he first related the occasion of his sending for him, and then desired him to take his hunting instruments, to go into the fields, kill some venison,† and dress it to his palate, that his spirits might be refreshed, and his mind properly disposed, for giving him that solemn blessing which should crown his future prosperity.

While Isaac was relating his intentions to Esau, Rebecca had so planted herself as to hear all that passed. She, therefore, determined, if possible, to deprive him of the intended blessing, and, by stratagem, get it conferred on her favorite son Jacob. As soon, therefore, as Esau was well gone, Rebecca, calling her son Jacob, told him what she had heard, namely, that his father was going to bestow a benediction, which was final and irrevocable, on his brother; but that, if he would listen to, and follow her directions, she doubted not of getting the honor bestowed on him.

* Isaac was at this time 137 years old, so that there is no wonder he should be imperfect in his sight. It appears that he was still ignorant of Esau having sold his birth-right; for he loved him as his first-born son, and designed to bestow on him the blessing.

† Venison was the principal article of food, in these early ages, next to vegetables, and it is very likely the aged patriarch longed for some. According to all the accounts we have of the people in the Eastern countries, they had always a feast prepared before they bestowed their blessing on their first-born son.

Jacob promising to pay a strict obedience to whatever his mother should command, she ordered him to go immediately to the flocks, and bring two kids, with which, she said, she would make savory meat, such as should resemble venison, and be agreeable to the palate of his father. Jacob made some hesitation at complying with this injunction, intimating, that if his father should discover the deception, instead of a blessing, he would pronounce on him a curse. As a farther ground of objection, he observed, that, as Esau was remarkably hairy, and he naturally smooth, his father, to supply the defect of sight, might handle him, in which case a discovery must unavoidably follow. But these objections bore no weight with Rebecca, who, determined to put her design into execution, told him, whatever bad consequences ensued, she would take all upon herself: "Upon me," said she, "be thy curse, my son; only obey my voice."*

Jacob, being thus encouraged by his mother, threw off his diffidence, and going to the fold, brought with him, as he was directed, two fat kids. Rebecca immediately killed them, and taking the choicest parts, dressed them in such manner, by the assistance of savory sauce, as to make the whole strongly resemble venison. Having thus prepared the food, she dressed Jacob in his brother's best attire, and covering his hands and neck with the skins of the kids, gave him the dish, ordering him immediately to take it to his father.

Jacob, agreeably to his mother's directions, went with the food to Isaac's apartment, which he had no sooner entered, than the good old man (not being able to distinguish objects from the imperfection of his sight) with surprise asked, who he was. To which Jacob replied, "I am Esau, thy first-born: I have punctually obeyed thy command; arise, therefore, and eat of my venison, that thy soul may bless me." Isaac, astonished at the haste with which his desire was executed, inquired of him how it happened that he had so quickly got the venison? To this he answered, "Because the Lord thy God brought it to me." Being, however, still diffident as to his person, Isaac ordered him to approach near, that, by feeling him, he might be convinced whether or not it was really and verily his son Esau. Jacob accordingly went close to his aged father, who, feeling the hairy skin on his hands and neck, exclaimed, with great surprise, "The hands are the hands of Esau, but the voice is the voice of Jacob." He then put the question to him forcibly, saying, "Art thou my very son Esau?" To which Jacob, without the least hesitation, answered, "I am."

The good old man, being now satisfied, arose from his couch, ate of his son's pretended venison, and drank a cup or two of wine; after which he bid him come near that he might bestow on him the promised blessing. The scent arising from Jacob's garments gave great satisfaction to Isaac. He smelt, and praised them: "The smell of my son," said he, "is as the smell of a field, which the Lord hath blessed."† He then, in a kind of ecstacy of pleasure, embraced and kissed his pretended first-born; and, after wishing him all heavenly and earthly blessings,‡ at length dismissed him.

* From a circumspect view of Rebecca's conduct throughout the whole of this affair, it appears evident that she had been made acquainted with the Divine will concerning the channel in which the grand promise was to pass. She therefore resolved to do her part toward preventing the ill effects of Isaac's partial fondness for his eldest son Esau, who had already indicated so unworthy a disposition. To this end she incites her son Jacob (as it appears) to an act of deceit, and, being confident of the propriety of her conduct, absolves him from all guilt or blame. The expression, "Upon me be thy curse, my son," is as much as to say, I will warrant thee success; I am so fully persuaded of the rectitude of the proceeding, that I fear no evil from it, but will readily bear it all if any happens. A stronger proof than this can not be given of Rebecca's full confidence in the propriety of her proceeding. Indeed, it does not appear that the least blame is laid upon Rebecca for her conduct: on the contrary, Isaac himself confirms the blessing which Jacob had by her means acquired; whence we must necessarily conclude that she acted upon right motives, and with a full persuasion of the Divine pre-appointment and approbation. Many particular circumstances, if we were fully informed of the state of the family, might possibly be urged in her behalf; but this alone is sufficient to vindicate her from all blame. She had certainly been pre-informed that Jacob should have the pre-eminence, and therefore she acted religiously in preventing her husband from any endeavor to counteract the Divine will. Let it, however, be observed, that her case is so peculiar that it can not be drawn into example; and, detached from that important and discriminating circumstance of God's will revealed to her, her conduct would, unquestionably, be deemed blameable.

† It is evident, from mention being here made of the smell of Jacob's garments, that the people in the most early times perfumed their clothes, especially when they approached a person of superior rank; and this custom is still preserved in most parts of Asia. The comparison between the smell of the garments and that of the field is very just; for in the Eastern countries, where they have a long continuance of drought, nothing can be more sweet and delightful than the scent arising from a field after a refreshing shower.

‡ The prayer which Josephus makes Isaac offer up to God on this occasion is to the following effect:— "Eternal and Supreme Being! Creator of all things! thou hast already showered down innumerable favors on my family, and promised still greater blessings in future. Ratify, O Lord, those gracious assurances, and despise not the prayers of infirm age. Protect this child from all calamities; grant him

A short time after Jacob had left his father's tent, Esau entered it, and, bringing with him the venison he had been directed to prepare, invited his aged parent, in the same dutiful manner his brother had previously done, to arise, and eat of it. Isaac, surprised at this address, hastily asked, "Who art thou?" On being answered that it was his elder son Esau, he appeared, for some time, thunderstruck; but at length recovering himself, he asked, who, and where, that person was, who had been with him before, and taken away the blessing, which he neither could nor would revoke.

When the disappointed Esau heard these words from his father, he exclaimed, in the bitterness of his soul, "Bless me, even me also, O my father." Isaac then told him that his brother Jacob had, by stratagem, obtained that blessing he had designed for him; upon which Esau complained of his double perfidy, first, in artfully obtaining his birth-right, and then in robbing him of his father's benediction. He wept bitterly for some time, and then pathetically asked his father if he had not in reserve a blessing for him, repeating the importunate request, "Bless me, even me also, O my father."

Isaac, no doubt, was greatly grieved to hear the lamentations of Esau for so great a loss; but what could he do? he had already bestowed the choicest of his blessings on Jacob, and as they were gone he could not recall them. At length, however, in order to pacify the afflicted Esau, he told him that his posterity should become a great people, and live by dint of the sword; and that though they might become subject to the descendants of Jacob, yet in process of time they would shake off their yoke, and erect a dominion of their own.*

When Esau came coolly to reflect on the loss he had sustained by the artifices of his brother, he resolved, as soon as a proper opportunity should offer, to be revenged on him. The respect he had for his father laid a restraint on the execution of his design. As Isaac was far advanced in years, and exceedingly infirm, Esau imagined his existence was of short duration, and therefore determined to wait till his father's death, immediately after which he resolved to put a period to the life of his brother.

Esau having accidentally dropped some hints of his design, they soon came to the ears of his mother, who, anxious for the future welfare of her favorite Jacob, acquainted him with the horrid intentions of his brother. She told him that the most prudent method he could take would be to absent himself till his brother's anger was in some degree abated, and that the most proper place for him to fly to was the house of his uncle Laban in Mesopotamia : that thither he might retire for a time, and as soon as she found his brother's resentment was assuaged, she would not fail to recall him. She said the thoughts of separating gave her great affliction, though nothing in comparison with the misery she must feel, should she in one day be robbed of them both—of him, by the hands of his brother ; and of his brother, by the hand of justice.

Jacob, who ever listened to and obeyed the counsel of his mother, was very ready to comply with her proposal; but at the same time was unwilling to depart without the consent of his father, which, in this case, he was fearful of obtaining. Rebecca soon hit upon a stratagem to remove this seeming difficulty. She immediately repaired to Isaac, to whom she complained of the great concern under which she labored on account of Esau having taken wives from among the daughters of the Hittites. She then intimated her fears lest Jacob should follow his example; to prevent which she earnestly recommended that he might be sent to Mesopotamia, and there choose a wife from among her own kindred.

Though Isaac was unacquainted with the drift of his wife's complaint, yet, being a pious man, and knowing that the promise made to Abraham, and renewed in him, was to be completed in the issue of Jacob, he readily assented to Rebecca's proposal.

---

length of days, peace of mind, and as much wealth as may appear consistent with his happiness here. In fine, render him, O Lord, the dread of his enemies, and the glory of his family and friends."

* The Edomites, or Idumæans (the descendants of Esau), were, for a considerable time, much more powerful than the Israelites, who were descended from Jacob, till, in the days of David, they were entirely conquered. See 2 Samuel viii. 14. After this they were governed by deputies, or viceroys, appointed by the kings of Judah, and for a long time were kept in total subjection to the Jews. In the days of Jehoram, the son of Jehoshaphat, they expelled their viceroy, and set up a king of their own (see 2 Kings viii. 20), which fulfilled the latter part of Isaac's prophecy. For some generations after this they lived independent of the Jews ; and, when the Babylonians invaded Judea, they not only took part with them, but greatly oppressed the inhabitants after their departure. Their animosity against the descendants of Jacob evidently appears, indeed, to have been hereditary ; nor did they ever cease, for any considerable time, from broils and contentions, till, at length, they were conquered by Hyrcanus, and reduced to the necessity either of embracing the Jewish religion or quitting their country. Preferring the former, they were intermixed with the Jews, and became one nation, so that in the first century after the birth of Christ the name of Idumæan was totally annihilated.

Calling, therefore, his son Jacob, he first bestowed on him his blessing, and then strictly enjoined him never to marry a Canaanitish woman. To prevent so improper an alliance, he ordered him to go to his uncle Laban, in Mesopotamia, and provide himself with a wife from his family. Jacob promised to obey his father's orders, upon which the good old man, after repeating his blessing, dismissed him.

When Esau understood that his father had again blessed Jacob, and sent him into Mesopotamia to avoid marrying any of the daughters of Canaan, he began seriously to reflect on his own misconduct, and to lament having, by the indiscreet alliances he had formed, incurred the displeasure of his aged parents. To reinstate himself, therefore, if possible, in his father's esteem, he took a third wife, whose name was Mahalath, the daughter of his uncle Ishmael. This marriage certainly took place both from duty and affection; but, unfortunately for Esau, it was not attended with the wished-for consequences.

Early the next morning, after Jacob received his father's charge and blessing, he left Beersheba, and proceeded on his journey toward Haran. Determined strictly to obey his father's commands, he travelled the most private ways he could find, shunned the houses of the Canaanites, and, when night came on, took up his lodging in the open air, near a place called Luz, having only the spangled sky for his canopy, and a hard stone for his pillow. Notwithstanding the uneasiness of his situation, he slept soundly, during which he dreamed that he saw a ladder set upon the earth, the top of which reached to heaven, and on the rounds of it were a number of angels, some ascending and others descending. On the summit of the ladder appeared the Almighty, who promised him all those privileges he had before done to Abraham and his father Isaac; and that, wherever he went, he might be assured of the divine protection. " Behold I am with thee, and will keep thee in all places whither thou goest, and will bring thee again into this land: for I will not leave thee until I have done that which I have spoken to thee of."*

This dream made such an impression on Jacob's mind, that, as soon as he awoke, he paid an awful reverence to the place, and after a short contemplation of what had passed, thus exclaimed: " This is none other than the house of God, and this is the gate of heaven!" Having said this, he arose, and taking the stone which had been substituted for a pillow, he set it upright, poured oil on it, and, in pious commemoration of the vision, called the place " Bethel," which, in the Hebrew language, signifies " the house of God."†

* There is something very noble and sublime in the representation of this vision. The ladder which reached from earth to heaven is a proper image of the providence of God, whose care extends to all things in heaven and on earth. The angels are represented ascending and descending on this mysterious ladder, because these ministering spirits are always active in the execution of the wise designs of Providence, and appointed the special guardians of the just: they ascend to receive, and descend to execute, the commands of God. And, lastly, by the representation of the Divine Majesty appearing above the ladder, is meant, that though the conduct of Providence is often above the reach of human comprehension, yet the whole is directed by infinite wisdom and goodness; and though in this vale of misery we can see only a few lower steps of the ladder, nearest to the earth, yet it hath a top that reacheth unto heaven: and were it possible for us to trace the chain of causes and effects to their source, we should see them gradually ascend higher and higher, till they terminate at length in the Supreme Being, the first and proper cause of all, who presides over and directs the complicated scheme of Providence, from the creation of the world to the consummation of all things. Certainly nothing could have been a more seasonable relief to Jacob, or filled his heart with greater joy, than the pleasing assurance, that though he was an exile from his native country, and wandering alone over the solitary wastes, yet he was still in the presence of his Maker whose powerful arm would constantly protect him from all dangers, and under whose wings he should be absolutely safe.

† Nothing can be more natural than this act of Jacob, for the purpose of marking the site and making a memorial of an occurrence of such great interest and importance to him. The true design of this humble monument seems to have been, however, to set this anointed pillar as an evidence of the solemn vow which he made on that occasion. This use of a stone, or stones, is definitely expressed in Gen. xxxi. 48 and 52. Mr. Morier, in his " Second Journey through Persia," notices a custom which seems to illustrate this act of Jacob. In travelling through Persia, he observed that the guide occasionally placed a stone on a conspicuous piece of rock, or two stones one upon another, at the same time uttering some words which were understood to be a prayer for the safe return of the party. This explained to Mr. Morier what he had frequently observed before in the East, and particularly on high roads leading to great towns, at a point where the towns are first seen, and where the oriental traveller sets up his stone, accompanied by a devout exclamation in token of his safe arrival. Mr. Morier adds : " Nothing is so natural, in a journey over a dreary country, as for a solitary traveller to set himself down fatigued, and to make the vow that Jacob did : ' If God will be with me, and keep me in the way that I go, and will give me bread to eat, and raiment to put on, so that I may reach my father's house in peace,' &c., then will I give so much in charity ; or, again, that, on first seeing the place which he has so long toiled to reach, the traveller should sit down and make a thanksgiving, in both cases setting up a stone as a memorial." The writer of this note has himself often observed such stones without being aware of their object, until happening one day to overturn one that had been set upon another, a man hastened to replace it, at the same time informing him that to displace such stones was an act unfortunate for the person so displacing it, and unpleasant to others. The writer afterward observed, that the natives studiously avoided displacing any of these stones, " set up for

Previous to his departure from this memorable spot, in order to bind himself more strongly to the service of God, he made a most solemn vow to the following effect: "That if he would protect and prosper him in his journey, provide him with common necessaries in his absence, and grant him a happy return to his father's house, to him alone would he direct his religious worship; in that very place where the pillar stood, on his return, would he make his devout acknowledgments, and offer unto him the tenth* of whatever he should gain in the land of Mesopotamia."

After making this solemn vow, the pious traveller proceeded on his journey, and at length arrived at Haran. As he came near the town he saw some shepherds with their flocks not far from a well, which was covered with a large stone. Of these shepherds he made inquiry concerning Laban and his family, and was informed that they were all well, and that it would not be long before Rachel, his daughter, would be there with her flock. Scarce had he received this intelligence when the damsel arrived with her fleecy care, immediately on which Jacob, as a token of respect, rolled away the stone from the mouth of the well,† and watered the sheep in her stead; which done, he saluted her, wept for joy, and told her to whom he belonged.

Elated at this incident, Rachel, leaving Jacob at the well, immediately hastened home, and acquainted her father with what had happened. Laban was so transported at the arrival of his sister's son, that he fled with all expedition to the spot, and, after cordially embracing him, conducted him to his house.

Jacob, after receiving some refreshment, told his uncle the occasion of his leaving home, and related the most material incidents that had happened in the course of his journey. Laban was sufficiently satisfied of the truth of his nephew's relation, and, from the singular circumstances that attended his excursion, was convinced that he was under the immediate care and protection of Divine Providence.

After being a few days with his uncle, Jacob, detesting an inactive life, applied himself to business, by assisting Laban in the care of his flocks, and such other matters as pertained to his interest. Having thus employed him, with great diligence, for the space of a month, his uncle one day entered into private conversation with him, and, among other things, told him he neither expected nor thought it reasonable that he should have his labor for nothing, and therefore, as he intended staying with him for some time, desired him to name such wages as would satisfy him for his services.

Jacob hesitated for some time what answer to give to this request, but at length, thinking on the charms and graces of the beautiful Rachel, who had already captivated his heart, he proposed serving him seven years, on condition of having, at the expiration of that time, Rachel for his wife.

Laban readily consented to this proposal, and Jacob as readily entered on his service. The flattering prospect of possessing so amiable a partner, after the seven years, and the endearments of her pleasing company during the time, rendered that interval of waiting apparently short and light.

When the time of Jacob's servitude had expired, he required Laban to fulfil his contract, by giving him his daughter Rachel in marriage. Laban seemingly assent-

a pillar," by the way-side. The place now pointed out as Bethel contains no indication of Jacob's pillar. The Jews believe that it was placed in the sanctuary of the second temple, and that the ark of the covenant rested upon it; and they add, that after the destruction of that temple, and the desolation of Judæa, their fathers were accustomed to lament the calamities that had befallen them over the stone on which Jacob's head rested at Bethel. The Mohammedans are persuaded that their famous temple at Mecca is built over the same stone.

* This is the second place in which we find mention of the tenth, or tythes, solemnly consecrated to God. Jacob promises to give them in return for his prosperous journey, as his grandfather Abraham had given them in return for his victory over the confederate princes.

† Wells are still sometimes covered with a stone or otherwise, to protect them from being choked up by the drifted sand; and it was probably to prevent the exposure of the well by too frequently removing the stone, that the shepherds did not water their flocks until the whole were assembled together; for it is not to be supposed that they waited because the united strength of all the shepherds was requisite to roll away the stone, when Jacob was able singly to do so. When the well is private property, in a neighborhood where water is scarce, the well is sometimes kept locked, to prevent the neighboring shepherds from watering their flocks fraudulently from it; and even when left unlocked, some person is frequently so far the proprietor that the well may not be opened unless in the presence of himself or of some one belonging to his household. Chardin, whose manuscripts furnished Harmer with an illustration of this text, conjectures, with great reason, that the present well belonged to Laban's family, and that the shepherds dared not open the well until Laban's daughter came with her father's flocks. Jacob, therefore, is not to be supposed to have broken the standing rule, or to have done anything out of the ordinary course; for the oriental shepherds are not at all persons likely to submit to the interference or dictation of a stranger. He however rendered a kind service to Rachel, as the business of watering cattle at a well is very tiresome and laborious.

ed, and, on the occasion, invited all his friends and neighbors to the solemnization of the nuptials. But Laban, desirous of retaining Jacob longer in his service, had projected a scheme for that purpose, the execution of which gave great uneasiness to his nephew. After the entertainment was over, and the company retired, Laban caused Leah, his eldest daughter, to be conducted to Jacob's bed, instead of the beautiful Rachel, to whom he was contracted. When daylight appeared in the morning, and Jacob discovered the deception,* he immediately arose, and going to Laban, expostulated with him on the impropriety of his conduct. Laban, who had prepared an answer for the occasion, told him, in a magisterial tone, that it was an unprecedented thing in that country (and would have been deemed an injury to her sister) to marry the younger before the elder; "but" (continued he, in a milder tone), "if you will fulfil the nuptial week with your wife, and consent to serve another seven years for her sister, I am content to take your word for it, and to give Rachel to you as soon as the seven days" (or nuptial week for Leah) "have expired."

This unfair treatment greatly perplexed Jacob, but his distinguished affection for Rachel made him resolve to obtain her, however dear the purchase. He therefore readily consented to his uncle's secondary terms, and when the nuptial ceremonies for Leah were over, he likewise took Rachel in marriage.

The distinguished charms of Rachel, in preference to those of Leah, made Jacob pay the greatest respect to the former; but his happiness was greatly curtailed by Leah's having four sons† even before Rachel had conceived. This circumstance particularly affected Rachel, who, in a fit of melancholy, one day told her husband that unless *he gave* her children she should certainly die with grief. "Give me," said she, "children, or else I die."‡

Jacob was greatly vexed at this speech of his beloved wife, who seemed to lay the whole fault of her sterility to him. He therefore sharply rebuked her in words to the following effect: "That it was not in his power to work miracles; that the want of children was agreeable to the divine will; and that such uneasy and discontented behavior was the way to prevent, rather than obtain, such a favor."‖

This answer greatly mortifying Rachel, she resolved to supply the defect of herself by the same means that had been practised by her grandmother Sarah. She accordingly made a proposition to Jacob that he should take her handmaiden Bilhah as a concubinary wife, and that if she should bear children they should be accounted hers. Jacob assented to this proposal, and, in the proper course of time, Bilhah was delivered of a son, whom Rachel named Dan, which, in the Hebrew language, signifies "judging." Within a twelvemonth after this Bilhah bore another son, whom Rachel called Naphtali.

By this time Leah imagined she had done bearing children, and, therefore, to imitate her sister's policy, she gave her maid (named Zilpah) to Jacob, by whom she had likewise two sons, the one named Gad, and the other Ashur.

Reuben, the eldest son of Jacob, was now arrived at years sufficient to be trusted by himself, and wandering one day in the fields, about the time of wheat harvest, he happened to meet with some mandrakes,§ which he brought home and presented to

---

* As all marriages in the East were solemnized in the evening, or rather at midnight, and as the bride was veiled, so it was no difficult matter to impose on Jacob, who did not expect any such deceit. Dr. Shaw tells us, that in the Levant the bride is brought home in the dark to her husband, and being introduced to the harem, or apartment for the woman, her mother goes and conducts the bridegroom to her; but he does not see her till the next morning.

† The names of these sons were Reuben, Simeon, Levi, and Judah. *Reuben* signifies *a son given by Divine regard; Simeon* implies, *God hath heard or considered me; Levi* signifies *joined:* and *Judah, praise or thanksgiving.*

‡ This expression furnishes us with a lively picture of human folly in general. If children are to parents like a flowery chaplet, whose beauties blossom with ornament, and whose odors breathe delight, death or some unforeseen misfortune may find means to entwine themselves with the lovely wreath. Whenever our souls eagerly long after some inferior acquisition, it may be truly said, in the words of our Divine Master, "Ye know not what ye ask." Does Providence withhold the thing we long for? It denies in mercy, and only withholds the occasion of our misery, if not the instrument of our ruin. With a sickly appetite we often loathe what is wholesome, and hanker after our bane. Where the imagination dreams of unmingled sweets, there experience frequently finds the bitterness of wo.

‖ It is not to be wondered at that such a man as Jacob should be offended at an expression made use of by his beloved wife, which, in its own nature, was little better than blasphemy. To say, "Give me children," was certainly a high indignity offered to the majesty of Heaven, as none but God can give being to any creature whatever.

§ The Hebrew word *dudaim,* here rendered "mandrakes," has occasioned so much discussion as to evince clearly enough that we know nothing about it. Calmet has an exceedingly long note on this word in his "Commentaire Littéral sur la Genèse," in which he states the different opinions which had in his time been entertained as to the plant really intended by the *dudaim.* Some think that "flowers," or "fine flowers,"

his mother Leah. Pleased with the sight of what the boy had brought, Rachel desired Leah to give her a part; but instead of complying with her request, she gave her this forbidding answer: "That having robbed her of her husband's affections, she could not expect to have any part of her son's present." Notwithstanding this contemptuous answer, Rachel was determined, if possible, to obtain some of the mandrakes, to do which she thought of inducing Leah to comply with her request by a method, which above all others, was most likely to prove effectual. It happened to be her turn that night to enjoy the company of her husband; and, therefore, in order to obtain her ends, she told Leah, if she would oblige her with some of her son's mandrakes, she would waive her pretensions for that night, and resign the right of her husband's bed to her. This proposition being approved of by Leah, the agreement was accordingly made; and as soon as Jacob came home she related what had passed, and asked him to confirm the bargain. Jacob readily assented, and Leah enjoyed his company that night, the consequence of which was that she conceived again, and had a fifth son, whom she called Issachar, which signifies *hire* or *reward*. After this she had another son, whom she named Zebulon; and the last of all, a daughter, called Dinah.

Rachel had long lamented not having issue of her own body; but at length it pleased God to remove her troubles on that head by giving her a son. As soon as she found she had conceived, she exclaimed, with the most expressive joy, "God hath taken away my reproach;"[*] and when the child was born she called his name Joseph, which, in the Hebrew language, signifies *increase*.

Soon after the birth of Joseph the appointed time of Jacob's last servitude being expired, he began to entertain thoughts of returning to his own country, and accordingly begged his uncle to dismiss him and his family. But Laban, who had found by experience no small advantage from his services, entreated him to stay a little longer, promising, at the same time, that if he would comply with his request, he would give him whatever wages he should think proper to ask. In answer to this, Jacob reminded him of the great increase of his substance since it had been under his care, and that he now thought it high time to make some provision for himself and family; so that therefore he was resolved to return to Canaan, unless he could point out to him some method whereby he might improve his fortune, and not longer waste his time in humble servitude.

Laban could not bear the thoughts of parting with Jacob, and therefore again pressed him hard to stay, at the same time offering him his own terms. After some farther controversy, Jacob at length consented to stay with his uncle, on the following conditions: that they should pass through the whole flock both of sheep and goats, and having separated all the speckled cattle from the white, the former should be committed to the care of Laban's sons, and the latter to the care of Jacob; and that whatsoever spotted or brown sheep or goats should, from that time forward, be produced out of the white flock (which he was to keep) should be accounted his hire.

Laban readily consenting to this proposal, the flocks were accordingly separated. The spotted cattle were delivered into the custody of Laban, while the rest were committed to the care of Jacob; and to prevent any intercourse between them, they were placed three days journey apart.

Whether it was from his own observation on the power of fancy in the time of conception, or (what seems much more likely) from the interposition of divine wisdom in furnishing him with the idea; but so it was that he pursued a very extraordinary method to improve his own stock, and at the same time lessen that of Laban. He

in general, are intended; while others fix the sense more definitely to "lilies," "violets," or "jessamines." Others reject flowers, and find that figs, mushrooms, citrons, the fruit of the plantain or banana, or a small and peculiarly delicious kind of melon, are intended. A great number adhere to the "mandrake," which has the sanction of the Septuagint, the Chaldee, the Vulgate, and of many learned commentators. Hasselquist, the naturalist, who travelled in the Holy Land to make discoveries in natural history, seems to concur in this opinion. Calmet, however, is disposed to contend, that the citron is intended; and his arguments deserve the attention of those who are interested in the question. The claims of the plantain, and of the delicate species of melon to which we have alluded, have been strongly advocated since Calmet's time.

[*] Many reasons concur to render the possession of sons an object of great anxiety to women in the East. The text expresses one of these reasons. Sons being no less earnestly desired by the husband than by the wife, a woman who has given birth to sons acquires an influence and respectability, which strengthen with the number to which she is mother. To be without sons is not only a misfortune, but a disgrace to a woman; and her hold on the affections of her husband, and on her standing as his wife, is of a very feeble description. Divorces are easily effected in the East. An Arab has only to enunciate the simple words, *ent taleks*—"thou art divorced"—which, in whatever heat or anger spoken, constitute a legal divorce.

took rods or twigs of the green poplar, hazel and chestnut trees, and stripping off part of the rinds in streaks, caused some of the white to appear on the twigs. These twigs he placed in the watering troughs when the cattle came to drink, at the time in which they usually engender; so that by seeing the speckled twigs they might conceive and bring forth speckled cattle. He also took particular care to place the twigs before the fattest and most healthy, and to avoid putting any before those that were weak and sickly; by which means he might not only obtain for himself the greater number, but also the choicest and most valuable.

This scheme succeeded to his utmost wishes, and in a short time he became exceeding rich and powerful. But the extraordinary increase of his property exposed him to the envy, not only of Laban, but also his sons, the former of whom treated him with great coolness, and the latter frequently accused him of having procured to himself a good estate out of their fortunes.

Jacob, finding himself envied by his uncle and kinsmen, had some thoughts of leaving them, and retiring, with his family and effects, into his own country. This design was, in a short time, ultimately resolved on, in consequence of the Almighty appearing to him in a vision, and ordering him to return to the land of Canaan.

Though Jacob was fully resolved to obey the divine command, yet he thought it most prudent, previous to his departure, to hold a consultation with his two principal wives, namely, Leah and Rachel, in order to obtain their consent. Accordingly, sending for them into the field (which, from its privacy he thought the most proper place for the business) he told them, that for some time past he had observed their father had treated him with great coolness and indifference, and even sometimes with marks of displeasure, though he was not sensible of any just cause for such behavior. He appealed to them concerning his industry and fidelity, and the injustice of their father toward him, first, in having deceived him, and afterward in having so often changed his wages.* He observed, that God had turned all their father's devices to his advantage, had taken away his cattle, and given them to him. He then told them, that the Lord appeared to him in a dream, reminding him of the solemn vow he had made at Bethel, in his journey to Mesopotamia, and that he had commanded him to return to the land of Canaan.

Leah and Rachel, having listened with great attention to what Jacob had said, readily agreed to go with him; and by all means recommended his paying a strict obedience to the divine command.

In consequence of this, Jacob, having made the necessary preparations for his departure, set his wives and children upon camels, taking the advantage of his father-in-law's absence (who was gone to shear his sheep, and which likewise gave Rachel the opportunity of stealing away his images†) he set out upon his journey, taking with him all his cattle, and other property, he had acquired during his stay at Haran.

Jacob had proceeded on his journey three days before Laban received intelligence of his flight, in which time he passed the Euphrates, and having gained the mountains of Gilead, he there stopped, in order to refresh himself and attendants, who by this time were become greatly fatigued with travelling.

Laban no sooner heard that his nephew had absconded, than he immediately pursued him with a mind fully bent on revenge. But in this he was checked by the interposition of the Almighty, who, appearing to him the same night in a vision,

---

* It is to be observed, that when Laban found Jacob so successful in the produce of his flocks, he repented of his bargain, and several times altered the agreement, which God, as many times, turned to Jacob's advantage.

† The Hebrew word which we render *images* is teraphim, a kind of penates, or household-gods which they worshipped as *symbols* of the Deity and consulted as oracles—hence Laban calls them his *gods*. These *teraphims* were afterward known by the name of *talismen*, as they are to this day in most parts of India. Some think those of Laban represented angels, who were supposed to declare the mind of God. Rachel might steal them either for their curiosity or worth; but it is most probable she still retained a tincture of her father's superstition, and designed to make them the objects of her worship in Canaan; for it appears (Gen. xxxv. 4) that Jacob, when he made a thorough reformation in his house, caused them to be taken from her, and buried them under the oak which was by Shechem.

The following is a list of the idols mentioned in scripture: Adram-melech, Isaiah xxxvii. 38; Anamelech, 2 Kings xvii. 31; Ashtaroth, Judges ii. 13; Baal, Numbers xxii. 4; Baalim, 1 Samuel vii. 4 (plural of Baal); Baal-berith, Judges viii. 33; Baal-peor, Numbers xxv. 3; Beelzebub, 2 Kings. i. 2; Bel, Isaiah xlvi. 1; Calf, Exodus xxxii. 4; Castor, Acts xxviii. 11; Chemosh, 1 Kings xi. 7; Dagon, Judges xvi. 23; Diana, Acts xix. 24, 25; Jupiter, Acts xiv. 12; Milcom or Molech, 1 Kings xi. 5–7; Moloch, Leviticus xviii. 21; Nebo, Isaiah xv. 2; Nergal, 2 Kings xvii. 30; Nibhaz, 2 Kings xvii. 31; Nisroch, 2 Kings xix. 37; Pollux, Acts xxviii. 11; Remphan, Acts vii. 43; Rimmon, 2 Kings v. 18, Sheshach, Jeremiah li. 41; Succoth-benoth, 2 Kings xvii. 30; Tammuz, Ezekiel viii. 14; Tartak, 2 Kings xvii. 31; Teraphim, Judges xvii. 5.

threatened him severely if he committed any hostility or violence against his servant Jacob.

In consequence of this when Laban came up with his nephew at Mount Gilead, he only expostulated with him on his want of respect in stealing away his daughters, and thereby preventing them from taking their leave as became his children, or departing in a manner consistent with their rank and dignity. He added that such conduct might have exposed him to his most severe resentment, and that he might have sustained much injury from him who was by far the most powerful. That, indeed, he would have pursued measures of revenge, had he not been diverted therefrom by the immediate prohibition of God himself.

In answer to this Jacob reminded his uncle of the cheat he had put upon him, in making him serve so long for a woman he did not love; the altering of the agreement so many times made between them relative to the sheep; and, lastly, his late strange behavior to him and his family. All these, and many more, he said, were but ill requitals for his care and diligence, as well as the blessings which God had heaped on him for his sake.

Laban had still another thing to lay to Jacob's charge, namely, the stealing of his gods. Fired with resentment at this accusation, Jacob (who knew nothing of Rachel's having taken them) desired him to make the most diligent search for them throughout his family, assuring him, at the same time, that on whomsoever they should be found, that person should immediately be put to death.

In consequence of this Laban proceeded to search the different tents, and having examined those of Jacob, Leah, and her handmaids, without effect, he went to the tent of Rachel, who, conscious of her crime, and fearful of the consequences should she be detected, had just concealed the images in the camel's furniture, on which she sat herself down to rest.

Having taken this precaution, she pleaded as an excuse for not arising to salute him, that she was exceedingly ill, and that to move then might greatly increase her complaint. This excuse was readily admitted by her father, who, after searching every other part of the tent without effect, departed.

When Laban acquainted Jacob with his bad success, the latter upbraided him, in very severe terms, for his unjust suspicions. He then recounted the great services he had done him during a number of years, and concluded with these words, "Except the God of my father had been with me, surely thou hadst sent me away empty."

Laban, conscious that Jacob's charge was most justly founded, made not the least attempt to vindicate his conduct; but, waiving the argument, assumed an air of respect for Jacob, and a fondness for his wives and children; and, in order to remove all further animosity, proposed a treaty of alliance between them, and to erect a monument which should be a standing witness of the same to future ages.

This proposition being agreed to, and the covenant signed, they accordingly raised a pillar or heap of stones,* as a memento of the circumstance; and then took mutual oaths that neither should invade the property of the other. A particular injunction was likewise laid on Jacob, that he should use his wives and children with all becoming tenderness and affection.

The covenant being thus ratified, and sacrifices offered up on the occasion, Jacob entertained his brethren that night in as magnificent manner as the nature of his situation would admit. The next morning Laban took leave of Jacob and his family, and each departed for their respective habitations.

Jacob had been favored with a heavenly vision in his way from Canaan to Mesopotamia; and the Almighty was pleased to favor him again with the like token of his protection on his return. As he was proceeding on his journey, there appeared before him a body of heavenly messengers, which he no sooner saw than he broke out into the following exclamation: "This is God's host;" from which additional mark of divine protection, he called the place Mahanaim.†

* The heap of stones raised by Laban and Jacob in memory of this covenant was called *Gilead*, which, in the Hebrew language, signifies *a heap of witnesses*. This circumstance, in after ages, gave name to the whole country thereabout, which lies on the east of the Sea of Galilee, being part of that ridge of mountains which ran from Mount Lebanon southward on the east of the Holy Land, and included the mountainous region called, in the New Testament, *Trachonitis*.

† The Hebrew word Mahanaim signifies two *hosts* or *camps*, because the angels appeared like two armies drawn up on either side for his protection, according to that beautiful expression of the Psalmist, "The angel of the Lord encampeth round about them that fear him, and delivereth them." Psalm xxxiv. 7.
The place called Mahanaim was situated between Mount Gilead and the brook Jabbok. It was afterward one of the residences of the Levites, and one of the strong places belonging to David.

Mountains of Seir.

Though Jacob had the greatest reason to rely on the protection of the Almighty, yet, as he drew near the confines of Edom, and within the reach of his incensed brother Esau (whom he had highly provoked, and concerning the abatement of whose resentment he had received no account from his mother, though so long absent), he thought it most prudent to send a message to him, in order to allay his anger, and, if possible, regain his fraternal affection.

He accordingly sent messengers to Esau, whose residence was at Mount Seir,* otherwise called the country of Edom, whither he had settled himself soon after his marriage with the daughter of Ishmael.

The message Jacob sent to his brother was to the following effect: that during his residence in Mesopotamia he had acquired prodigious wealth, and that as he was now on his return to his native country, he thought proper to notify his arrival to him, and at the same time to implore his favor and friendship.

The messengers, having discharged their embassy, returned, and gave Jacob such an account as greatly alarmed him. They brought no direct answer from Esau, and only told their master that his brother was coming to meet him at the head of four hundred men.

Jacob, concluding that the design of this mighty retinue was to act against him in a hostile manner, was greatly perplexed, and at a loss in what manner to proceed. He knew, on the one hand, that the number of his people was too small to engage with that of his brother; and, on the other hand, that his baggage was too heavy for flight. At length he came to this conclusion: to divide his company into two bands, so that, if Esau should fall upon one, he might have the chance of escaping with the other.

Such was the plan laid down by Jacob; but as he well knew, from former experience, that his safety depended upon the divine protection, independent of all human creatures, he, in this critical juncture, addressed himself to God in a very humble and submissive prayer, the substance of which was to the following effect: "O thou eternal Majesty of heaven, whom my father worshipped, and who alone art the object of my prayer, permit an unworthy creature to repeat thy own promise to thee. When my family began to increase, thou wast graciously pleased to order me to return to my native country; and, to encourage me, thou promisedst that thou wouldst protect me. What an infinite condescension, O my God, to a poor unworthy creature! The least of all thy mercies is too good for me; and yet thou hast been pleased to show me the greatest. When I crossed Jordan, I had nothing besides my staff; but in thy goodness thou hast caused my family and substance to increase so fast, that I am now possessed of great riches. O God, thou promisedst to make my seed a great nation; and although I know thou couldst suffer them to be killed, and raise them up from the dead, yet, O most merciful Father, be pleased still to preserve them, and

* The term "Mount Seir," or rather the mountains of Seir, must be understood with considerable latitude. It was applied indefinitely to that range of mountains which, under the modern names of Djebal, *Shera*, and Hasma, extends from the southern extremity of the Dead sea to the gulf of Akaba. The reader will recollect the "Ghor," or valley, extending in the same direction, which we have had frequent occasion to mention, and which is supposed to have formed the continued channel of the Jordan before its waters were lost in the Dead sea. Now the mountains of Seir rise abruptly from this valley, and form a natural division of the country, which appears to have been well known to the ancients. The plain to the east of the hilly region which these mountains form, is much more elevated than the level of the Ghor, on the west of the same mountains; in consequence of which, the hills appear with diminished importance as viewed from the eastern or upper plain. This plain terminates to the south by a steep rocky descent, at the base of which begins the desert of Nedjed. It is to a part of this upper plain, and to the mountains which constitute its western limit, that, as Burckhardt thinks, the name of Arabia Petræa, or the Stony, was given by the ancients; the denomination being, however, extended northward, so as to include the eastern plain with the mountains which form the eastern boundary of Palestine so far north as the river Jabbok. Speaking of this region, Burckhardt says: "It might well be called Petræa, not only on account of its rocky mountains, but also of the elevated plain, which is so covered with stones, especially flints, that it may with great propriety be called a stony desert, although susceptible of culture. In many places it is overgrown with herbs, and must once have been thickly inhabited, for the traces of many ruined towns and villages are met with on both sides of the Hadj route between Maan and Akaba, as well as between Maan and the plains of the Haouran, in which direction there are many springs. At present, all this country is desert, and Maan is the only inhabited place in it."—("Travels in Syria;" different parts of which have been analysed to furnish this geographical statement.) The mountains themselves are described by the same traveller as chiefly calcareous, with an occasional mixture of basalt. The mountainous region which they form, of course, differs from the plain which skirts it on the east. The climate is very pleasant. The air is pure; and although the heat is very great in summer, the refreshing breezes which then prevail prevent the temperature from becoming suffocating. The winter, on the other hand, is very cold; deep snow falls, and the frosts sometimes continue to the end of March. This mountainous country is adequately fertile, producing figs, pomegranates, apples, peaches, olives, apricots, and most European fruits. The region has been in all times noted for the salubrity of its air; and Burckhardt observes, there was no part of Syria in which he saw so few invalids.

suffer not my enraged brother to destroy them; I know that thy promise is truth itself, and I will cheerfully trust in thee."

After having thus humbly and earnestly implored the guidance and protection of the Almighty, Jacob determined to pursue another measure in order to appease the anger of his brother, which he imagined to be no less severe than when he left Canaan. Imagining that Esau might consider his first message as an empty piece of formality, he resolved, as he had already informed him of the great wealth of which he was possessed, to send him a very liberal present. He accordingly selected from his stock the following articles, namely; two hundred she-goats and twenty he-goats; two hundred ewes and twenty rams; thirty milch camels with their colts; forty swine and ten bulls; twenty she-asses and ten foals. These being divided into separate droves, he ordered the servants to keep a proper space between them, and strictly charged them, whenever they should meet his brother, to present each to him separately, and to tell him that they were presents sent by Jacob to his lord Esau.

Jacob, having dismissed his servants with this present to his brother, arose early next morning, and, before daylight, sent his wives and children, together with all his substance, forward on their journey, staying himself for some time behind. A short time after the departure of his family and children, being alone, he was accosted by an angel, who, appearing in the shape of a man, began to wrestle with him, which exercise they continued till break of day. The contest was certainly unequal, notwithstanding which, the angel permitted Jacob to prevail; but, to convince him that he did not obtain the victory by means of his own strength, and how easily himself could have made a conquest, he touched the sinews* or hollow of his thigh, which was immediately put out of joint.

The angel then asked Jacob his name, and on being answered, he told him he should hereafter be called Israel,† which signifies "a man that has prevailed with God." After saying this, the angel blessed Jacob, and then departed. In consequence of so singular a circumstance, Jacob called the place where it happened Peniel, which signifies the "face of God," being confident that it must have been a divine agent with whom he had been contending.

Soon after the angel disappeared, Jacob, though lame, made what haste he could to join the company. Having come up with them, they proceeded with great expedition on their journey; but they had not travelled far before Jacob discovered his brother Esau, attended by a considerable body of men, coming toward him. Alarmed at the sight of so powerful a retinue, Jacob immediately divided his family into three companies, placing them at equal distances from each other. The two maid-servants and their sons went first; Leah and her children next; and Rachel and Joseph (the latter of whom was now about six years old) in the rear, while himself led the van.

As soon as Jacob approached his brother, he showed his respect to him by bowing seven times to the ground. Esau, filled with the tenderest sense of fraternal affection, at once removed his brother's fears and compliments by running to him with eager joy, falling on his neck, and most cordially embracing him. He wept over him for some time; after which, seeing his wives and children prostrate themselves before him in the order Jacob had placed them, he returned their civilities with the like tenderness he had done his brother's. Thus was revenge turned into love and pity; and Esau, who once thirsted for his brother's blood, dissolves into tears of joy, and melts with the softest endearments of love and friendship.

Thus transported with this happy interview, Esau surveyed his brother's possessions with pleasure, and expressed his satisfaction at the great success he had met with during his residence in Mesopotamia. He kindly acknowledged the presents Jacob had sent him, but begged he would excuse his accepting them, because they would be superfluous to him, who had already great abundance. Jacob, however, pressed him so earnestly, that he at length agreed to accept them; to make some

* This was the sinew or tendon that keeps the thigh-bone in the socket, not only in the human species, but also in the brute creation; and from this circumstance, even to the present time, the Jews will not eat that part. In the Misnah, one of their books of directions concerning religious ceremonies, they have a whole chapter prescribing the manner in which it is to be cut out of the beast when killed; and it is further enjoined that they shall not eat the sinews of the hips of any animal whatever.

† The words in the text are—"Thy name shall be called no more Jacob, but Israel." This expression clearly evinces the mis-translation of some passages in the scriptures, it being certain that the patriarch was frequently after called Jacob. But this seeming contradiction will be easily adjusted, by substituting the words *not only* for "*no more*:" in which case the sense will read thus: Thou shalt *not only* be called Jacob, but *also* Israel—the latter of which names was at length established in Jacob's descendants.

recompense for which, Esau invited him to Seir, and offered to accompany him the remaining part of the journey. Though Jacob had no design of accepting this offer, yet he did not choose to make a direct refusal. He therefore represented to Esau the tenderness of his children and flocks, and that they could not travel with such expedition as would be agreeable to him. He begged they might not confine him to their slow movements, but that he would return home his own pace, and he would follow with as much expedition as possible. Esau then offered to leave him a number of men to guard and conduct him into his territories; but this compliment Jacob likewise thought proper to decline, upon which, after saluting each other, they parted.

Esau returned immediately to Seir, and expected that his brother would follow him; but Jacob turned another way, and coming to a spot which struck his fancy, he resolved (at least for a time) to settle in it; in consequence of which he built a house for his family, as also proper conveniences for the reception of his cattle.

After staying here some time, Jacob removed to Shechem, and having purchased a piece of ground of Hamor, the prince of the country, he there pitched his tents,* intending to make it his fixed place of residence. He also erected an altar, and called it El-alohe-Israel, which signifies "the great or mighty God of Israel."

Jacob might probably have lived at this place a considerable time, had it not been for an occurrence of a very singular nature. His daughter Dinah, who was at this time about sixteen years of age, and very beautiful in person, being desirous of seeing the dresses and ornaments of the women of that country, rambled abroad from her mother's tent, in order to gratify her curiosity. Young Shechem, the son of Hamor (the king of the country), happening to see her, was so captivated with her charms, that, unable to restrain the force of his passion, he determined, if possible, to possess her. He diligently watched her for some time, till at length, taking the

---

* The use of tents probably arose at first out of the exigencies of pastoral life, which rendered it necessary that men removing from one place to another in search of pasture should have a portable habitation. Accordingly, we find that the first mention of tents is connected with the keeping of cattle (Gen. iv. 20), and to this day tents remain the exclusive residence of only pastoral people. Portability is not the only recommendation of tents to the nomade tribes of the East: the shelter which they offer in the warm but delicious climates of Western Asia is positive enjoyment. Shelter from the sun is all that is needful; and this a tent sufficiently affords, without excluding the balmy and delicate external air, the comparative exclusion of which renders the finest house detestable to one accustomed to a residence in tents. The advantage of tents in this respect is so well understood, even by the inhabitants of towns, that, in many places, those whose circumstances admit it endeavor, so far as possible, to occupy tents during the summer months. This was the constant practice of the late king of Persia, who every year left his capital with all the nobles, and more than half the inhabitants, to encamp in the plain of Sultanieh. Many of the princes, his sons, did the same in their several provinces, and the practice is an old one in Persia. It is true that tents would seem to be rather cheerless abodes in the winter: but it is to be recollected that the nomades have generally the power of changing the climate with the season. In winter the Bedouins plunge into the heart of the desert, and others descend, in the same season, from the mountainous and high lands, where they had enjoyed comparative coolness in summer, to the genial winter climate of the low valleys and plains, which in the summer had been too warm.

It is impossible to ascertain with precision the construction and appearance of the patriarchal tents; but we shall not probably be far from the truth, if we consider the present Arab tent as affording the nearest existing approximations to the ancient model. The common Arab tent is generally of an oblong figure, varying in size according to the wants or rank of the owner, and in its general shape not unaptly compared by Sallust, and after him Dr. Shaw, to the hull of a ship turned upside down. A length of from twenty-five to thirty feet, by a depth or breadth not exceeding ten feet, form the dimensions of a rather large family tent; but there are many larger. The extreme height—that is, the height of the poles which are made higher than the others in order to give a slope to throw off the rain from the roof—varies from seven to ten feet; but the height of the side parts seldom exceeds five or six feet. The most usual-sized tent has nine poles, three in the middle, and three on each side. The covering of the tent among the Arabs is usually black goat's-hair, so compactly woven as to be impervious to the heaviest rain; but the side coverings are often of coarse wool. These tent-coverings are spun and woven at home by the women, unless the tribe has not goats enough to supply its own demand for goat's-hair, when the stuff is bought from those better furnished. The front of the tent is usually kept open, except in winter, and the back and side hangings or coverings are so managed that the air can be admitted in any direction, or excluded at pleasure. The tents are kept stretched in the usual way by cords, fastened at one end to the poles, and at the other to pins driven into the ground at the distance of three or four paces from the tent. The interior is divided into two apartments, by a curtain hung up against the middle poles of the tent. This partition is usually of white woollen stuff, sometimes interwoven with patterns of flowers. One of these is for the men, and the other for the women. In the former, the ground is usually covered with carpets or mats, and the wheat-sacks and camel-bags are heaped up in it, around the middle post, like a pyramid, at the base of which, or toward the bank of the tent, are arranged the camels' pack-saddles, against which the men recline as they sit on the ground. The women's apartment is less neat, being encumbered with all the lumber of the tent, the water and butter, skins, the culinary utensils, &c. Some tents of great people are square, perhaps thirty feet square, with a proportionate increase in the number of poles; while others are so small as to require but one pole to support the centre. The principal differences are in the slope of the roof, and in the part for entrance. When the tent is oblong, the front is sometimes one of the broad, and at other times one of the narrow, sides of the tent. We suspect this difference depends on the season of the year or the character of the locality; but we can not speak with certainty on this point. It will be observed that the tent covering among the Arabs is usually black; but it seems that they are sometimes brown, and occasionally striped white and black. Black tents seem to have prevailed among the Arabs from the earliest times.

Tents.

opportunity of her being alone, he suddenly seized on her, and, by mere dint of violence, obtained his wishes.

But notwithstanding this dishonorable act, Shechem was still so enamored with Dinah's charms, that he most earnestly wished to marry her; and strongly solicited his father to intercede with her friends in his behalf, and to form a treaty with them for that purpose.

Jacob was soon informed of the depredation made on his daughter's chastity, and though greatly incensed at so unjustifiable a proceeding, he resolved not to take any notice of it till his sons (who were then abroad) came home. Accordingly, on their arrival, he told them the injury their sister had sustained, and by whom; upon which their resentment was raised to the greatest height, and they vowed severely to revenge the dishonor thus thrown upon their family.

In the mean time, Shechem having prevailed with his father to use his interest in obtaining for him the beautiful Dinah, they both went together to make the proposal to Jacob, whose sons were with him at the time of their arrival. After the first salutations were over, Hamor, addressing himself to Jacob, told him the great affection his son had for his daughter Dinah, and earnestly entreated him that he would give her to him in marriage. He at the same time proposed that Jacob's family should intermarry with his people, and offered them the privilege of settling and trading in any part of his dominions they thought proper. To strengthen this proposal, young Shechem promised to give Dinah as large a dowry, and her relations as costly presents, as they should desire. In short, he offered them whatever advantages they should please to nominate, bidding them only name their terms, and they should be granted to the uttermost, provided they would but give him Dinah in marriage.

These were certainly very fair offers, and such as evinced that Shechem was desirous of making some recompense for the injury he had done his beloved Dinah. But, instead of accepting these proposals, the treacherous sons of Jacob, who only meditated the most bloody revenge, made the following reply: "That it was not lawful for them to contract an affinity with an uncircumcised nation, but that, if they and their people would consent to be circumcised (as they were), they would then agree to the terms proposed."

Shechem was so enamored with Dinah, and Hamor so fond of his son, that, notwithstanding the singularity of this proposal, they readily agreed to it. Accordingly, leaving Jacob and his son, they immediately repaired to the city, and having convened a general assembly of the inhabitants, they told them "that the Israelites were a wealthy, peaceable, and good-natured people; that they might reap many great advantages from them, and, in process of time, by intermarrying with them, might make all their substance (which was very considerable) their own; but that this could not be done without a general consent to be circumcised."

Captivated with the prospect of great wealth, and influenced by the powerful interest both Hamor and his son had among them, they unanimously assented to the proposal; and on that very day every male of them was circumcised.

This circumstance furnished Simeon and Levi (the sons of Jacob, and brother to Dinah, by the same mother) with an opportunity of wreaking that revenge on the Shechemites which they had privately resolved on for the violation of their sister's chastity. Sensible of the great pain the Shechemites felt in consequence of circumcision, they determined to take advantage of it, by attacking them at a time when they knew they must be totally incapable of making the least resistance. Accordingly, on the third day* after the operation (having properly armed themselves for the purpose), they went (unknown to their father) into the city, and suddenly falling on the inhabitants, put every male to the sword, Hamor and his son not excepted. They then searched the king's palace, where, finding their sister Dinah, they immediately brought her away; after which they plundered the houses of the city, took both women and children captive, and possessed themselves of what property they could, as well in cattle as in other articles; and such things as they could not take with them, they totally destroyed.†

* This was the time, according to most physicians, when fevers generally attended circumcision, occasioned by the violent inflammation of the wound. The Jews themselves observe, that the pain was much more severe on the third day than at any other time after the operation.

† Though the sacred historian only mentions Simeon and Levi to have been the perpetrators of this horrid act of cruelty, yet there is not the least doubt but they had considerable assistance. They, indeed, are

When Jacob (who was totally unacquainted with these unjustifiable proceedings till after they had taken place) first heard of them, he was greatly incensed against his sons, and very severely reprimanded them for committing so treacherous and barbarous an action. But Simeon and Levi paid little attention to their father's rebuke; on the contrary, such were their ideas of the crime committed in the violation of their sister's chastity, that they intimated to him the resentment they had shown was but just for so base an injury.

It is not to be wondered at that this violent outrage, committed in the capital of the Shechemites, should exasperate the whole people of the country against the Israelites. This seems to have been the reason why the Almighty, soon after the transaction happened, commanded the patriarch to remove to Bethel, the place which he had dedicated to his immediate service. Though the sons of Jacob had wholly destroyed one colony of the Canaanites, yet there were great numbers bordering on the spot, who, either in their own defence, or in revenge for the cruel and unjust treatment of their countrymen, might give the good patriarch much disquiet, if not totally destroy him and his family. His omnipotent Creator, therefore, in order to secure him from danger, ordered him to go to Bethel,* there to fix his residence, and erect an altar to the same God who appeared to him when he fled from the presence of his brother Esau.

The obedient and pious Jacob hesitated not to comply with the divine command; but, previous to his setting about the business, he thought it necessary to make a reformation in his family, and cleanse it from the pollutions that might be offensive in so sacred a place. To effect this, he strictly charged not only his own family, but all that belonged to him, to bring out their idols, or strange gods, then clean themselves,† and change their garments, telling them they must go with all expedition to Bethel, the house of their God.

They readily obeyed the patriarch's orders, and delivered up to him not only their idols,‡ but also their ear-rings,‖ all of which Jacob buried in a deep hole under an oak◊ near Shechem.

Jacob, having thus cleansed his family from impurities, set out with them on his

only mentioned because, being own brothers to Dinah both by father and mother, and consequently more concerned to resent the injury done to her honor, they are made the chief contrivers and conductors of it. It is, however, reasonable to imagine, that the rest of Jacob's sons, who were old enough to bear arms, as well as the greatest part of his domestics, were engaged in the execution of this wicked exploit; because it is scarcely conceivable how two men alone should be able to master a whole city, to slay all the men in it, and take all the women captives, who, on this occasion, may be supposed more than sufficient to have overpowered them.

* BETHEL.—The following brief but interesting notice of the site of Bethel has lately been afforded by Professor Robinson. After telling us that the site now bears the name of Beit-in, he proceeds to state that,— "It lies just east of the Nablous road, forty-five minutes northeast of Bireh. Here are ruins of very considerable extent, and among them the foundations of several churches, lying on the point of a low hill between two shallow wadys, which unite below, and run off southeast into a deep and rugged valley. This was evidently a place of note in the early Christian ages, and apparently also in the days of the Crusades. It is now entirely uninhabited; except that a few Arabs, probably from some neighboring village, had pitched their tents here for a time. In the western valley we spread our carpets, and breakfasted on the grass within the limits of what was once an immense reservoir. We obtained here from the Arabs butter of excellent quality, which might have done honor to the days when the flocks of Abraham and Jacob were pastured on these hills."—*Biblical Repository,* April, 1839, p. 420.

† The Hebrew word, which we translate *clean,* properly signifies, *the washing of the body with water.* As there is some analogy between external cleanliness and purity of mind, it may denote the cleansing of the soul by repentance from all those impurities whereby a man becomes morally polluted in the sight of God. In which view, this rite of washing the body with water was used as a sign of inward purification, not only among the idolatrous heathens, but also by the worshippers of the true God, both before and under the law. "Wash ye, make ye clean, put away the evil of your doings from before mine eyes, Isaiah i. 16. And as men should at all times have their souls adorned with this inward purity, so especially when they approach their Maker in the duties of his immediate worship. It was, therefore, highly commendable in Jacob, on this solemn occasion, to enjoin all under his care to cleanse and purify themselves particularly from idolatry, and from those guilty stains lately contracted by shedding innocent blood, as they would otherwise be unfit to hold an intercourse with their God; as if he had said, "Put off your sordid apparel, especially those garments in which you were so lately defiled with blood, and put on your cleanest raiment, as an emblem of your being divested of all impure affections, and clothed with those internal graces and pious dispositions, which are the ornament of the soul, and render it comely in the sight of God.

‡ The greater part of those idols belonged to the Shechemites; but among them were those which Rachel had stole from her father Laban, and which she had probably worshipped (unknown to her father) during her stay at Shechem.

‖ The ear-rings and other jewels worn by these people were consecrated to the honor of that idol whom they worshipped; and on them were engraven some figures. The reason of their wearing them was, to preserve them (as they thought) from any danger or misfortune; and from this act of idolatry we may suppose arose the custom among the papists of wearing the relics and images of their saints.

◊ The oak here mentioned seems to have been the place where these servants of Jacob, who had strange gods, used to meet; and certainly no place could be more proper for burying their idols than the spot on which they had worshipped them.

6

journey to Bethel. In order to ensure their safety, the Almighty, ever mindful of his promise to his chosen people, struck such a terror into the people belonging to the country through which they passed, that, notwithstanding the provocation given by the massacre at Shechem, not a single person presumed to interrupt them, and they travelled to their destined place without the least molestation.

No sooner did Jacob arrive at Bethel,* than, agreeably to the divine command, he erected an altar, which he called El-beth-el; and on which he performed the very vow he had before made when on his journey from Canaan to Mesopotamia.

A short time after Jacob had performed this act of worship, the Almighty was pleased to appear to him again, and to give him fresh assurances of his design to multiply his posterity, and to bestow on him the inheritance of the land of Canaan. As a lasting monument of this additional mark of the divine favor, Jacob erected a pillar of stone, which he consecrated with the usual form, by pouring on it wine and oil.

After being some time at Bethel, Jacob, urged, by filial affection, resolved to leave it, in order to pay a visit to his ancient father at Mamre. Accordingly, taking with him his family, they set out on their journey, intending to stop that night at Ephrath (afterward called Bethlehem), a small place not far distant from Bethel. But before they could reach the intended spot Rachel fell suddenly in labor, and having very severe pangs, the midwife, in order to encourage her, bid her not fear, for she would have another son. She was indeed delivered of a boy, but expired immediately after, having but just a moment's space of time to give him the name of Benoni, which signifies "the son of my sorrow." But Jacob, unwilling to increase the remembrance of so melancholy a circumstance, called him Benjamin, that is, "the son of my right hand," or "my strength;" intimating thereby his peculiar affection for this last pledge of his beloved wife.

The remains of Rachel were deposited at the place where she died, and in order to perpetuate her memory, Jacob erected a monument of stone† over her grave, which the sacred historian tells us was extant in his days.

But this was not the only misfortune that attended Jacob on his journey to Mamre. After travelling some way farther, in order to refresh himself and family, he stopped and pitched his tents on a pleasant spot, at some distance from the tower of Edar.‡ During his stay here his eldest son Reuben, having taken a liking to Bilhah (the concubinary wife which Rachel had given to Jacob), made no scruple of defiling her. Though Jacob took no notice of this disagreeable circumstance at the time it occurred, yet he was greatly afflicted in his mind, and retained a painful sense of it even to his dying day, as is evident from a reproachful hint he gave him a short time before his death.‖

Though these aggravated griefs sat heavy on Jacob's mind, yet he continued his resolution of visiting his aged parent. He accordingly pursued his journey, and at length came to Mamre, the place of his father's abode. It is not to be doubted but, at their first meeting, a reciprocal affection displayed itself, as each must be happy in the sight of the other after so long an absence.

With this circumstance the sacred historian concludes the life of Isaac, who, as

---

* According to the sacred historian (though he does not mention any time) it appears that soon after Jacob's arrival at Bethel, Deborah (Rebecca's nurse) died there. What age she was we are not informed; but it is certain she must have been very old, as she came with Rebecca from Mesopotamia, when she was married to Isaac. Her remains were deposited beneath an oak (as was the custom in those days) called Allon-bachuth, from which the Jews have a tradition that Rebecca died on the same day with her nurse; that word, in the Hebrew language, signifying *mourning*.

† We have no doubt that the original erection by Jacob was merely the most tall and shapely stone which could be found in the neighborhood. The site seems always since to have been marked by some sepulchral erection or other. That which now exists is such as those with which sheikhs and other persons of note are honored. Its date we can not find, but it is certainly modern. The structure which the travellers of the sixteenth and seventeenth centuries figure and describe, had the same general shape, but it was open, in arches, on all sides. The best figure of it is in "Amico's Trattato delle Piante e Immagini di Sacri Edifizi di Terra Santa," 1620. And this was not very ancient; for the travellers of the thirteenth century (as Brocard) describe Rachel's sepulchre as a *pyramidal* monument.

‡ Some commentators are of opinion, that by the tower of Edar is meant the field near Bethlehem where those shepherds were keeping their flock to whom the angels appeared, and gave information of the birth of our Saviour. Among others, one reason which induces them to think so is because the word Edar, in the Hebrew tongue, signifies *a flock*: so that what is here called the *tower of Edar* should be rendered *the tower of the flocks*. Others are of opinion that by *the tower of Edar* is to be understood some place near Jerusalem; it being spoken of by the prophet Micah as the place or stronghold of the daughters of Sion. Se Micah iv. 8.

‖ See Genesis xlix. 4.

he informs us, paid the debt of nature in the one hundred and eightieth year of his age, being five years older than his father Abraham. He had been very infirm, and almost blind, for a considerable time; but was always respectable for his piety, tranquillity, and submission to the will of Heaven. He was buried by his two sons, Esau and Jacob, in the cave of Machpelah, which Abraham purchased of Ephron as a burying-place for his family. It is to be observed that the death of Isaac is here mentioned by way of anticipation, it being certain that he lived some years after Jacob's return from Mesopotamia.

CHAPTER VII.

THE pious Jacob had not long enjoyed the company of his aged father, after his return from Mesopotamia, before a circumstance occurred which gave him great unhappiness. Joseph was his beloved child, as being the son of his dear departed Rachel, besides which, he particularly attracted the attention of his father from his very extraordinary genius. In consequence of these circumstances, Jacob, as a token of his peculiar love to his favorite Joseph, gave him clothes much richer than he did the rest; and, among others, one coat which was made of a changeable or party-colored stuff.* This naturally raised the envy of his brothers; besides which, they had for some time considered him as a spy, because he had told his father of some indiscretions committed by the sons of Bilhah and Zilpah, with whom he was most conversant, by frequently assisting them in the care of their flocks. From these circumstances they treated Joseph with contempt, withheld from him the common offices of civility, and made it their constant study to perplex and torment him.

But what completed the envy and resentment of Joseph's brethren, or, rather, produced an irreconcileable hatred, was his innocently relating to them two dreams, the explanations of which seemed to portend his own future greatness. The substance of the first of these dreams was, that "as he was binding sheaves with his brethren in the field, his sheaf arose and stood upright, while their sheaves round about fell down, and, as it were, made obeisance to his." This dream being considered by his brethren as an indication of his pride and ambition, their malice was greatly increased, but still more so when they heard the substance of the second dream. "Behold," says he, "the sun and the moon and the eleven stars made obeisance to me." When Joseph related this last dream his father was present, on which the good old man, either to appease the anger of his other sons, or check that presumption which in young minds so naturally arises from good omens, reprimanded him in these words: "Shall I and thy brethren come to bow down ourselves to thee to the earth?" But though Jacob thought proper to reprimand his son Joseph, for the reason here assigned, yet, in his own mind, he thought there was something very ominous in the dreams, and that they were predictions of events that would some time or other come to pass.

After Joseph had related these dreams to his brethren (notwithstanding the reprimand given him by his father), instead of their hatred being abated, they grew every

* This party-colored tunic of Joseph has occasioned some speculation; but it would seem that the real point of interest has not been noticed. It would be desirable to know whether the art of interweaving a piece in various colors was at this time discovered or not. Judging from the information which this text gives, it would seem not; for the word which is constantly rendered "colors" may, as in the marginal reading, with more than equal propriety be rendered "pieces;" which makes it probable that the agreeable effect resulting from a combination of colors was obtained by patchwork in the first instance, and in after times by being wrought with a needle. The value and distinction attached to such variegated dresses show that they were not common, and were worked by some elaborate process. This continued long after. In the time of David, such a dress was a distinction for a king's daughter (2 Samuel xiii. 18); and in Judges v. 30, we see ladies anticipating the return of a victorious general with "a prey of divers colors, of divers colors of needlework on both sides." We may, therefore, infer that in these times people generally did not wear variegated dresses, the common use of which must have been consequent on the discovery of the art of interweaving a variegated pattern in the original texture, or of printing it subsequently. Except in Persia, where a robe is usually of one color, most Asiatic people are partial to dresses in which various patterns are interwoven in stripes or flowers; and party-colored dresses have necessarily ceased to form a distinction. The most remarkable illustration of this text which we have seen is given by Mr. Roberts, who states that in India it is customary to invest a beautiful or favorite child with "a coat of many colors," consisting of crimson, purple, and other colors, which are often tastefully sewed together. He adds: "A child being clothed in a garment of many colors, it is believed that neither tongues nor evil spirits will injure him, because the attention is taken from the beauty of the person to that of the garment."

day more and more exasperated; so that they resolved at length to cut him off, and only waited for a convenient opportunity for effecting their purposes.

Some time after this, Jacob, having purchased some land near Shechem, sent all his sons (Joseph excepted) to keep their flocks there. After being absent a long time, and no intelligence received of them by Jacob, he was very anxious for their welfare, fearing lest the inhabitants of the land should revenge on them the loss of their countrymen, who had been put to death by Jacob's sons. To remove these disagreeable apprehensions, he ordered Joseph to go to Shechem, and inquire after the health and welfare of his brethren, and return with all convenient expedition.

Joseph, in obedience to his father's commands, set out for Shechem, which was about sixty miles distant from the place where his father now dwelt. When he came within some distance of Shechem, he happened to meet a stranger, of whom he made inquiry after his brethren. The stranger told him they had removed from Shechem some time, and were gone to a place called Dothan.* Joseph accordingly hastened to Dothan; and no sooner did his brethren see him approaching than their old malice revived, and they determined to embrace this opportunity of destroying him. "Behold" (says one of them to the rest), "this dreamer cometh. Come now, therefore, and let us slay him, and cast him into some pit, and we will say some evil beast has devoured him; and we shall see what will become of his dreams."

This horrid design would certainly have been carried into execution had it not been for the interposition of Reuben, who used the most forcible arguments to dissuade them from embruing their hands in the blood of their brother. As they were, however, determined to show some instance of their resentment, Reuben proposed that they should cast Joseph into the next pit, with a design, no doubt, of taking him out privately and conveying him safe to his father. This proposition being approved of by the rest of the brethren, as soon as Joseph came up to them they immediately seized him, and, after taking off his party-colored garment, threw him into a pit, which at that time happened to be dry. As soon as this was done Reuben withdrew, in order to contrive some means for rescuing his brother, while the rest, insensible of remorse for the deed they had committed, sat down and regaled themselves with such provisions as the place afforded. They were satisfied in their minds that their base ends would soon be answered, and that Joseph must inevitably perish in the pit for the want of food. But the eye of Omnipotence beheld his distress, and interposed in his behalf; for as Reuben had already been the means of preventing his immediate death, so Judah now became the means of delivering him out of the pit.

It happened that while they were regaling themselves they espied at a distance a caravan of Ishmaelites, who were travelling from Mount Gilead into Egypt with spices and other merchandise.† The sight of these furnished Judah with a thought

---

* This place is mentioned as a "city" in 2 Kings vi. 13—15. Eusebius says it was twelve miles south of Samaria. That it was somewhere north of Shechem would appear from the present text. What is meant by the "pit" into which Joseph was cast is an exhausted cistern, or reservoir, in which the rain-water is collected, and of which there are many in Palestine. Many of them are found to be empty in summer, the supply of water they contain being often soon exhausted. Dr. Richardson thus mentions the place which is pointed out as the scene of the affair recorded in this chapter: "Having cleared the intricate defiles of this part of the country, we got upon an extensive open field which bore an abundant crop of thistles, and on which several herds of black cattle were feeding. This, by some, is supposed to be the scene of the infamous conspiracy of which the liberty of Joseph was the temporary victim. A little farther on we arrived at Gib Youssouff, or the pit into which Joseph was cast by his brethren, being a ride of three hours and forty minutes from Mensura. Here there is a large Khan for the accommodation of travellers, and a well of very excellent water, and a very comfortable oratory for a Mussulman to pray in." This place is about two and a half or three days' journey from Shechem, which is nearly equal to the distance between Hebron and Shechem; so that the distance from Hebron to Dothan, if this be Dothan, was about five or six days' journey, which, as Dr. Richardson observes, "is a long way for the sons of Jacob to go to feed their herds, and a still farther way for a solitary youth like Joseph to be sent in quest of them." But we do not consider this distance too great, particularly as we know the place was somewhere beyond Shechem. Indeed the doctor himself admits that it is a very likely place, particularly as it lies in what is still one of the principal roads from the Haouran and Mount Gilead to Egypt. Speaking of the same neighborhood (Nablous or Shechem), Dr. Clarke says: "Along the valley we beheld a company of Ishmaelites coming from Gilead, as in the days of Reuben and Judah, 'with their camels, bearing spicery, and balm, and myrrh,' who would gladly have purchased another Joseph of his brethren, and conveyed him as a slave to some Potiphar in Egypt. Upon the hills around, flocks and herds were feeding as of old; nor, in the simple garb of the shepherds of Samaria, was there anything to contradict the notions we may entertain of the appearance formerly exhibited by the sons of Jacob." He adds, that the morning after his arrival at Nablous, he met caravans coming from Grand Cairo, and noticed others reposing in the large olive plantations near the gates.

† Midianites being also mentioned as denominating this company, we may infer that it was a mixed caravan, and principally composed of Ishmaelites and Midianites. We might call them generally "Arabians," as the Chaldee does. "Here," says Dr. Vincent, "upon opening the oldest history in the world, we find

in what manner he might secure his brother Joseph from certain death, and at the same time answer their ends by getting him totally removed. As the caravan approached, he urged the iniquity of being instrumental to the destruction of their own

the Ishmaelites from Gilead conducting a caravan loaded with the spices of India, the balsam and myrrh of Hadramaut ; and in the regular course of their traffic proceeding to Egypt for a market. The date of this transaction is more than seventeen centuries before the Christian era, and notwithstanding its antiquity, it has all the genuine features of a caravan crossing the Desert at the present hour." (Commerce and Navigation of the Ancients, vol. ii., p. 362.) We can not at this moment enter into the question, which Dr. Vincent assumes, that the Arabians had already become the medium of communication between India and Egypt. As the subject divides itself into two parts, the commerce of the Arabians and that of the Egyptians, we postpone the former, and confine ourselves to a few remarks on the latter. Dr. Vincent calls the Egyptians, with great propriety, the Chinese of antiquity ; and the analogy between the two people might form a subject for very interesting discussion. In the present text we see a caravan of foreigners proceeding to Egypt, their camels laden with articles of luxury ; whence it is an obvious inference that Egypt had then become what it is always recorded to have been, the centre of a most extensive land commerce :—the great emporium to which the merchants brought gold, ivory, and slaves from Ethiopia, incense from Arabia, spices from India, and wine from Phœnicia and Greece : for which Egypt gave in exchange its corn, its manufactures of fine linen, its robes, and its carpets. In after-times, the merchants of the west, of Greece and Rome, resorted to Egypt for its own products, and for the goods brought thither by the oriental merchants. But none of this was done by Egyptians themselves. We never, either in ancient or modern times, read of Egyptian caravans. This doubtless arose in a great degree from the aversion which (in common with all people who observe a certain diet and mode of life prescribed by religion) they entertained to any intercourse with strangers, and which reminds us continually of the restrictive policy of the Japanese in some respects, and of the religious prejudices of Hindoos and strict Mohammedans. Thus, it was a maxim among the Egyptians not to leave their own country, and we have ample evidence that they rarely did so, except in attendance upon the wars and expeditions of their sovereigns, even when their restrictive policy and peculiar customs became relaxed under the Greek and Roman rulers of the country. "They waited," says Goguet, after Strabo, " till other nations brought them the things they stood in need of, and they did this with the more tranquillity, as the great fertility of their country in those times left them few things to desire. It is not at all surprising that a people of such principles did not apply themselves to navigation until very late." Besides, the Egyptians had a religious aversion to the sea, and considered all those as impious and degraded who embarked upon it. The sea was, in their view, an emblem of the evil being (Typhon), the implacable enemy of Osiris ; and the aversion of the priests in particular was so strong, that they carefully kept mariners at a distance, even when the rest of the nation began to pay some attention to sea-affairs. But besides their religious hatred to the sea, and political aversion to strangers, other causes concurred in preventing the cultivation of maritime commerce by the Egyptians. The country produces no wood suitable for the construction of vessels. Therefore, when the later Egyptians and the Greek sovereigns began to attend to navigation, they could not fit out a fleet till they had obtained a command over the forests of Phœnicia, which gave occasion to bloody wars between the Ptolemies and the Seleucidæ for the possession of those countries. The unhealthiness of the Egyptian coast, and the paucity of good harbors, may also be numbered among the circumstances which operated, with others, in preventing attention to maritime affairs. Moreover, all the nations who in those times traded in the Mediterranean were also pirates, who made it a particular branch of their business to kidnap men from the coasts ; and it was therefore natural that a people who had no vessels with which to oppose them or retaliate upon them, should allow them no pretence to land upon their shores.

The indifference of the Egyptians to foreign commerce is demonstrated by the fact that they abandoned the navigation of the Red sea to whatever people cared to exercise it. They allowed the Phœnicians, the Edomites, the Jews, the Syrians, successively, to have fleets there and maritime stations un its shores.' It was not until toward the termination of the national independence that the sovereigns of Egypt began to turn their attention to such matters. The ports of Lower Egypt were ultimately opened to the Phœnicians and Greeks, by Psammeticus, about 656 years B. C. His son, Necho, for the purpose of facilitating commerce, attempted to unite the Mediterranean and Red sea, by means of a canal from the Nile ; but desisted after having lost 100,000 workmen. This work was completed by the Persians, but turned out to be of little practical benefit, either from the failure of the eastern channel of the Nile, or from being choked by the sands drifted from the desert. Failing in this project, Necho contrived to pay great attention to navigation. He caused ships to be built both on the Mediterranean and Red sea, and interested himself in maritime discovery, with a view to the extension of the commercial relations of Egypt. He sent on a voyage of discovery those Phœnician mariners who effected the famous circumnavigation of Africa, sailing from the Red sea, and, after doubling the Cape of Good Hope, returning by the Mediterranean. The maritime power of Egypt increased thenceforward, the clearest proof of which may be found in the fact, that in the reign of Necho's grandson, Apries, the Egyptian fleet ventured to give battle, and actually defeated so experienced a naval power as that of the Phœnicians. The race of sailors which arose were, however, considered as the lowest and most impure of the castes into which the Egyptian people were divided. In the next reign, that of Amasis, the sacred Nile was at last opened to the foreign merchants. Naucratis, a city of Lower Egypt, on the Canopean arm of the Nile, near the site afterward occupied by Alexandria, was assigned to such Greek traders as chose to settle in Egypt. The commercial states of Greece were also permitted to found temples or sanctuaries, in certain places, for the accommodation of their travelling merchants, and which might also serve as staples and marts for the merchandise which they should send into Egypt. This concession was found to have a most favorable operation upon the prosperity of Egypt, and in its ultimate consequences combined with other causes in working a great change in the character and habits of the population, which thenceforward became progressively modified by an infusion of Greek manners and ideas. Such concessions were not in the first instance made without limitations. The Greeks were obliged to enter the Canopean branch of the Nile, and were required to land at Naucratis. If by any accident a ship entered at any other mouth of the river it was detained, and the captain was obliged to swear that he had been compelled to enter against his will. He was then compelled to sail back for Naucratis ; and if this was prevented by the winds, he was required to discharge his cargo, and to send it round the Delta (more inland) in the small vessels in which the Egyptians navigated the Nile. This restriction must have ceased soon after, when the country was subdued by the Persians, and all the mouths of the Nile were equally thrown open. Its subjection to the Persians does not seem to have materially interfered with the growing maritime commerce of Egypt. But Herodotus, who was there in this period, remarks on the characteristic singularity which the Egyptians had carried into their marine and trade. Their ships were built and armed after a fashion quite different from that observed by other nations, and their rigging and cordage were arranged in a manner that appeared very singular and fantastic to the Greeks

brother, by which they would contract an eternal stain of guilt. He therefore advised them to sell him to the Ishmaelites, by which means they would not only save his life, but likewise promote their own interest. This proposal being universally approved of, Joseph was taken out of the pit, and sold to the merchants for twenty pieces of silver; and the merchants, on their arrival in Egypt, sold him again to Potiphar, one of the king's chief officers, and captain of his guards.

Reuben, who was absent while this circumstance happened, came soon after to the pit, in order to assist his brother in making his escape; but, astonished at not finding him there, he ran hastily to his brethren, rent his clothes, and upbraided himself as the cause of his being lost: "The child," said he, "is not, and whither shall I go?" In short, he bewailed himself to such a degree, that his brethren, in order to mitigate his grief, told him in what manner they had disposed of him; upon which Reuben, finding it impossible now to recover him, joined with the rest, in forming a tale for their father which might take from them all suspicion of their being instrumental to the loss of his beloved Joseph.

To effect this purpose, they killed a kid, and dipping Joseph's coat into the blood, took it to their father, telling him they had found it in the field, and were fearful it was their brother's. "This," said they, "have we found; know now whether it be thy son's coat, or no."

The good old patriarch no sooner saw the coat, than he was convinced to whom it belonged, and not suspecting that any human hand could be guilty of such an unnatural cruelty as to murder him, concluded that he had been unhappily devoured by some wild beast. This loss was the most severe he had ever sustained. When his beloved Rachel died, it was in a natural way; but Joseph (according to his present apprehension) is, by a savage animal, barbarously torn in pieces before his time. His grief, therefore, knew no bounds; he rent his clothes, put on sackcloth, and mourned for his beloved son many days: nay, so excessive was his affliction, that when his children in general endeavored to comfort him, it availed nothing, and all the answer he made them was, that he could only cease to mourn when he should follow him in the path of mortality.*

In conformity to the sacred historian, we must here make a short digression from the farther transactions of Joseph, in order to admit some occurrences which are materially connected with the history, and, therefore, must not be suffered to pass unnoticed.†

Some time before Joseph was sold into Egypt, Judah (his father's son by Leah), who had been the means of saving his brother's life, married a Canaanitish woman, named Shuah, by whom he had three sons, viz., Er, Onan, and Shelah.

In process of time, when Er, his eldest son, grew up to years of maturity, he took him a wife whose name was Tamar; but Er, being naturally of a very wicked disposition, the Almighty was pleased to cut him off before he had any children by his wife. In consequence of this Judah (agreeably to the custom of the country) advised Onan, his second son, to marry his brother's widow in order to preserve the succession of his family. Onan seemingly obeyed his father's orders, but not brooking the thoughts that any of his children should inherit his brother's name (which must have been the case had Tamar borne him any) he took a very wicked method of avoiding

---

After all, the Egyptians were not themselves a people addicted to maritime commerce. The Greek rulers of Egypt indeed changed the entire system of Egyptian trade, and the new capital, Alexandria, became the first mart of the world, while the ancient inland capitals, which had arisen under the former system, sunk into insignificance. But it was the Greeks of Egypt, not the Egyptians, who did this. "They became," says Dr. Vincent, "the carriers of the Mediterranean, as well as the agents, factors, and importers of oriental produce: and so wise was the new policy, and so deep had it taken root, that the Romans, upon the subjection of Egypt, found it more expedient to leave Alexandria in possession of its privileges, than to alter the course of trade, or occupy it themselves." (The facts combined in this sketch of Egyptian trade, &c., have been drawn from the works of Vincent, Heeren, Reynier, Goguet, Rennel, and Hales.)

* What an affecting idea is here conveyed to the mind of the reader! The hoary patriarch rends his clothes, covers his aged body with sackcloth, and refuses to be comforted. Thus Achilles in Homer ex presses his grief, on receiving the news of Patroclus' death.

"————————With furious hands he spread
The scorching ashes on his graceful head;
His purple garments, and his golden hairs,
Those he deforms with dust, and these with tears."—POPE.

† Though the past and following events seem to be connected by the sacred writer, yet the marriage of Judah certainly took place long before Joseph was sold into Egypt; and, in all probability, a short time after Jacob's return from his uncle Laban.

it, for which offence he was (as his brother had been before him) punished with sudden death.

Shelah, the third son, being as yet too young for marriage, Judah desired his daughter-in-law Tamar to retire to her father's house, and there remain a widow, till his son became a proper age, at which time he would make him her husband.

Tamar obeyed her father-in-law's commands, and waited till Shelah was come to man's estate; but finding no signs of his intending to fulfil his promise, she determined on revenge for her disappointment, which she effected by the following stratagem.

Shuah, Judah's wife, had been some time dead, and as soon as the usual time of mourning was expired, he went, accompanied by a particular friend, to Timnath, in order to participate of the accustomed amusements of sheep-shearing.

Tamar, having received previous intelligence of his intended excursion, and the time of his going, threw off her widow's habit; and dressing herself like a courtesan, she threw a veil* over her face, and then placed herself between two ways through one of which she knew Judah must necessarily pass in his road to Timnath.

As soon as Judah saw her he took her to be what she appeared, and accordingly, in a very familiar manner, paid his addresses to her. Previous, however, to any farther intimacy, she insisted upon having some reward for her compliance, which he readily agreed to, and promised to send her a kid; but she having a farther design upon him, demanded a pledge for the performance of his promise, which was, his signet,† his bracelet, and his staff. Judah readily complying with this request, they retired together, the consequence of which was that Tamar soon after proved with child.

Agreeably to the promise made by Judah to Tamar, previous to their intercourse, the former sent his friend Hirah (for that was his name) with a kid to redeem his pledge; but when he came to the place the woman was gone, nor could he, upon the strictest inquiry, learn that any such person as he described had been ever there. This circumstance greatly perplexed Judah, who, upon cool reflection, thought it most prudent to let her go with the pledges, fearing, if he should make farther search after her, it might injure his reputation.

About three months after this Judah received intelligence that his daughter-in-law had played the harlot, and that she was certainly with child. Enraged at her incontinence, he ordered her to be brought forth, and, according to the laws of the country, publicly burnt.‡

Tamar, instead of being alarmed at this dreadful sentence pronounced against her, only sent the pledges to Judah, and with them this message: "That the man to whom those belonged was the very person by whom she was with child."

Judah, struck with confusion at the sight of the pledge he so well knew, and reflecting on the injury he had done Tamar in not fulfilling the promise of giving her his son in marriage, he acknowledged her to be less culpable in the whole affair than himself. "She hath," said he, "been more righteous than I."|| Tamar's ends were answered in this stratagem, for Judah immediately took her home to his house, but never after had any intercourse with her.

When the time of Tamar's delivery came, she was brought to bed of twins, whose births were attended with these singular circumstances. One of them having put

---

* That veils were not peculiar to harlots, but worn by the most modest women in those times, there is not the least doubt: yet as harlots were not then allowed to enter into cities, they usually sat in the public ways, and covered their faces with a veil, in order to conceal their infamy; and some assert that the veils they wore differed from those used by modest women. Tamar assumed that character, most probably, to engage Shelah, who was her betrothed husband, and who she might expect would come with his father; but, being disappointed of him, she gratified Judah, in order to be again taken into the family.

† The word here translated a *signet* should have been a ring, which ornaments were then worn according to their different ranks. At that time there could be no occasion for signets, it being most probable that writing was not then known. By the word *bracelets* is generally understood a girdle of twisted silk, which either hung from the neck, or was fastened round the waist somewhat in the form of a child's sash.

‡ It may appear strange that Judah should have such authority as to order this punishment to be inflicted on his daughter-in-law Tamar. But it is to be observed that the ancients supposed every man to be judge or chief magistrate in his own family; so that, though Tamar was a Canaanite, yet, as she married into Judah's family, and brought disgrace upon it, she necessarily lay under the cognizance of him, who may be supposed, from what followed, to have suspended the sentence, till he had made farther inquiry into the nature of her offence.

|| He does not say Tamar was more holy or chaste, but more righteous or just; that is, Judah, not keeping his promise in marrying her to Shelah, provoked her to lay this trap for him, resolving since he would not let her have children by Shelah, she would have them by him. Thus, though she may be deemed more wicked in the sight of God, she appeareth more just in the opinion of Judah.

forth his hand, the midwife immediately tied around it a scarlet thread, in order to distinguish him as the first-born; but the child having withdrawn its hand, the other made its way, and came first into the world. This occasioned his name to be called Pharez, which signifies "breaking forth:" the other was called Zarah, which implies " he ariseth," alluding to the sign he gave of his coming, by putting forth his hand.

What farther circumstances occurred, after this, relative to Tamar, we are not informed; but it is reasonable to suppose that she continued the remainder of her life in the house of Judah, and that she lived the whole time in a state of widowhood.

Having, with the sacred historian, mentioned the before-mentioned particulars elative to Judah and his family, we shall, in like manner, now resume the history of Joseph, and relate the various adventures and enterprises that befell him during his residence in Egypt.

From the time that Joseph had first admission into Potiphar's family, he conducted himself with the greatest diligence and fidelity. By his faithful services he so obtained the favor of his master, that, after some time, he not only dismissed him from every laborious employment, but made him superintendent of his whole property, and committed the charge of his house solely to his care and direction.

Joseph being then appointed principal manager of his master's affairs, both within doors and without, the Lord was pleased to bestow a blessing on the house of the Egyptian; who, by means of Joseph, flourished exceedingly, and being sensible of the cause of his very singular success, daily increased in his good offices toward his faithful servant.

Thus circumstanced, Joseph had reason to hope for a comfortable life, though sold to slavery; and to expect, in time, his liberty, as a reward for his truth and fidelity. But it pleased the Almighty farther to exercise his faith and patience, in order to prepare him for a still brighter display of his grace and goodness toward his chosen people.

Joseph was now about twenty-seven years of age, of a comely form, beautiful complexion, and winning deportment. These united charms not only engaged the attention, but also excited the love of his master's wife, who, when all tacit tokens to draw the youth into an indulgence of her unlawful flame failed, was so fired by her eager passion, that she broke through every rule of decency, and, in plain terms, courted him to her bed. But how great was her surprise when, instead of a ready compliance, as she probably expected, she found herself not only denied, but likewise severely reprimanded for her dissolute and illegal passion! "Behold," said he, "my master wotteth not what is with me in the house, and he hath committed all that he hath to my hand. There is none greater in this house than I; neither hath he kept back anything from me, but thee, because thou art his wife: how then can I do this great wickedness, and sin against God?"[*]

But this repulse, sufficient to have filled with shame a mind not entirely lost to honor and virtue, had no effect on this lewd woman, who determined still, if possible, to obtain her ends. After making several other fruitless attempts, at length a favorable opportunity offered for accomplishing her wishes. It happened one day that Potiphar was engaged abroad on some particular business, and all the servants, except Joseph, were employed about their work in the adjoining fields. In the course of the day (having properly prepared herself for the purpose) Joseph's mistress called him to her apartment, which he had no sooner entered than she addressed herself to him in a language calculated to steal the soul from virtue, and melt the coldest continence into the warmest desires. But Joseph's integrity was not to be shaken. Though her arguments were enforced with all the blandishments of art, they made

* This answer was truly noble, and is highly worthy of imitation: it speaks a mind whose passions are in subjection to the ruling principle of reason and conscience; a mind that had the most delicate sentiments of honor, and the most lively impressions of religion. His honest heart startles at the thought of committing so foul a crime as adultery; and the ingratitude and breach of trust with which it would have been accompanied in him, present it to his mind in the blackest colors; so that these virtuous sentiments concurring with his awful reverence of the Supreme Being, who beholds and judges all the actions of the sons of men, enabled him to repel this violent assault with the utmost horror and indignation. This is an example of the greatest probity and inflexible integrity; an example worthy of the highest commendation. Joseph was then a servant in a strange country: he was tempted by an imperious woman: if he complied, he would be sure of concealment and rewards; he would be sure to enjoy his place, and be advanced; if he resisted, he must expect to be accused and treated as a criminal, be deprived of his place, of his liberty, of his fame, and perhaps of his life too. These are weighty considerations; but he prefers chains, ignominy, and even death itself, to the crime of committing so heinous an action, and sinning against God.

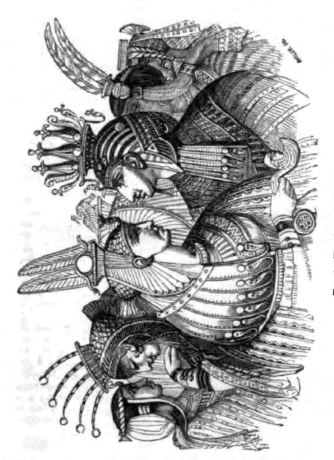

Egyptian Females—official dresses.

not the least impression on him. On the contrary, he again expostulated with her on the heinousness of the crime, begging her not to desire him to commit an act which must be destructive to him and disgraceful to her. But all his reasonings were of none effect: instead of her passion being allayed it was farther inflamed, and at length, breaking through all decency, she caught him by his cloak, and attempted to compel him to compliance. He struggled with his mistress for some time, and finding he had no other way of escaping, he slipped himself from his garment, which he left in her hand, and precipitately fled.

Fired with resentment at the supposed indignity, and fearful of the disgrace that would attend the discovery of her shameful passion, she resolved to shield herself by laying a malicious accusation against Joseph. Accordingly, she began by making a most horrid outcry, which immediately brought in all the servants who were within hearing to her assistance. As soon as they entered the room she showed them Joseph's cloak, and at the same time thus vehemently exclaimed: "See," said she, "he hath brought in a Hebrew unto us to mock us: he came in unto me to lie with me." And farther to engage them in her cause when the affair should come to examination, she craftily added: "And I cried with a loud voice, and when he heard it, he left his garment with me and fled." Having then prepared the servants to confirm her declaration, she laid the cloak by her, in order to produce it as an evidence against Joseph when his master should return.

By the time Potiphar came home she had dressed up the story so well, and expressed the pretended indignity put upon her by the Hebrew* servant (as she called him) with such an air of resentment, that he made no doubt of the truth of her tale. The credulous husband, little suspecting his wife's treachery, was particularly prepossessed with the circumstance of the cloak, and therefore, without making the least inquiry into the merits of the cause, immediately committed Joseph to the king's prison.

Though the innocent Joseph was thus persecuted, in consequence of his base and treacherous mistress, and was thereby bereft both of friends and relations, yet he was not without that divine Friend who had hitherto protected him. He had not been long in prison before his virtuous and obliging deportment gained him the peculiar favor of the keeper, insomuch that he not only intrusted him with the management of the affairs belonging to the prison, but also with the custody of the prisoners themselves.

Some time after Joseph's confinement, it happened that two persons of note (namely, the king's cup-bearer and his chief baker) were, for some offence or other,† committed to the same prison, and being delivered to the care of Joseph, he attended them in person, and by that means an intimacy between them was soon established.

Joseph, going one morning to their apartment, as he was accustomed to do, found them both in a very pensive and melancholy situation. On inquiring the cause of this sudden change, they told him that each had (the preceding night) a very extraordinary dream; and that they were uneasy on account of being in a place where they could not have a person to interpret them. To allay their superstitious humor in trusting to diviners and soothsayers, Joseph told them that the interpretation of dreams did not depend upon rules of art; but, if there was any certainty in them, it must proceed from a divine inspiration. Having said this, he desired that each would relate the particulars of what he had dreamed, and he would give them his opinion with respect to the interpretation.

The cup-bearer told his dream first, the substance of which was as follows: "That in his sleep he fancied he saw a vine with three branches, which, all on a sudden, budded, then blossomed, and at length brought forth ripe grapes: that he held Pharaoh's cup in his hand, pressed the juice into the same, and gave it to the king, who, as usual, took it and drank." This dream Joseph interpreted thus: "The three branches," said he, "denote three days, within which Pharaoh will restore thee to thy place, and thou shalt, as usual, give him to drink, according to the duties of

* She did not call Joseph by his own name, but that of the people to whom he belonged. This she did in order to increase her husband's rage against him, the Egyptians and Hebrews being, at this time, inveterate enemies to each other.

† Some authors are of opinion, that the crime of which these men were accused was that of having embezzled the king's treasure; but the Targum says, they had attempted to poison him. Whatever were their crimes, they must have been very great persons with respect to their birth; for, according to Diodorus Siculus, none but the sons of the chief priests were admitted into those offices.

thy office." He then told the cup-bearer that, if his interpretation proved true, he hoped he would, in his prosperity, remember him, and recommend his case to the king, since the truth was, he had been fraudulently taken from his own country, and thrown into prison, without having been guilty of the least offence.

The baker, hearing so happy an interpretation of the cup-bearer's dream, was the more ready to relate his, which was to this effect: " That while, as he thought, he had on his head three wicker baskets, in the uppermost of which were several kinds of baked meats for the king's table, the birds came, and ate them out of the basket." The interpretation Joseph gave of this dream was, " that the three baskets (even as the three branches had done) signified three days; but that, in the space of that time, the king, having inquired into his conduct, and found him guilty, would order him to be first beheaded, and afterward his body to be hanged on a gibbet, for the fowls of the air to devour his flesh."*

As Joseph had foretold, so it came to pass; for, three days after this, the cup-bearer was restored and the baker hanged. The cup-bearer, however, proved very ungrateful to Joseph, in not using the least endeavors to get his releasement, and he might probably have continued in prison the remainder of his life, had it not been for the following incident.

When Joseph had been more than two years in prison, it happened that Pharaoh the king had in one night two very portentous dreams, which gave him the more uneasiness, because none of the Egyptian Magi† (whom he consulted the next morning) could give him the least explanation of their meaning. While the king was in this state of perplexity on account of his dreams, he received some agreeable intelligence from his cup-bearer, who, recollecting Joseph, told him that while he and the chief baker were under his majesty's displeasure in prison, each of them, in the same night, had a dream, which a young man, a Hebrew, then in prison with them, interpreted exactly, and as the events happened; and that, in his opinion, he had a talent that way much superior to any that had been hitherto consulted.

Pharaoh was so pleased with this intelligence, and so anxious to have his dreams explained, that he immediately despatched a messenger to the prison, with orders to bring Joseph before him. Accordingly, after having shaved himself, and put on his best attire, he left the prison, and being conducted to the palace, was immediately introduced to the king, who, after a short time, related to him his dreams as follows: " That, as he was walking on the banks of the river,‡ he saw seven fat kine come out of it, and feed on the meadow; after which seven others, exceeding lean, and frightful to behold, came also to the river, and devoured the seven fat kine. That after this he dreamed again, and fancied he saw seven full ears of corn, proceeding all from the same stalk, which were, in like manner with the kine, devoured by seven others that were blasted and withered."

When the king had finished relating his dreams, Joseph (after giving him to understand that it was by the assistance|| of God alone he was enabled to be an interpreter of dreams) told him " that the seven kine and seven ears of corn signified the

---

* It may appear strange that the sacred historian should mention the baker's being first beheaded, and afterward hanged. But it is to be observed that this practice was common at that time. Hence Jeremiah says, " princes were hanged up by their hands," intimating that their heads had been previously cut off. See Lamentation v. 12. Also 1 Sam. xxxi. 9, 10.

† The magicians, or interpreters of dreams, were, at that time, a regular body of people in Egypt, and always consulted with respect to their pretended knowledge of future events. Their method of interpretation was from an attentive consideration of the symbols or images that appeared in the dream. Thus, the best they could pretend was no more than conjecture; but they always gave their answers to whatever questions they were asked in such ambiguous words that they could hardly be detected.

‡ The river here mentioned was the Nile, so much celebrated in ancient history. This river has its rise in Numidia, and after running many miles northward through a country scorched with the violent heat of the sun, it enters Upper Egypt with great force, and passes over a cataract or broken rock. Hence it continues its course still north, and receiving the addition of many other rivers, it falls over another cataract, and then continues its course to the Lower Egypt as far as Grand Cairo, after which it divides itself into three branches, in the form of the Greek letter Δ, and then empties itself into the Mediterranean sea. Once every year it overflows the greater part of Lower Egypt, and from that proceeds either scarcity or plenty. If the water rises too high, scarcity ensues, because it lies too long on the ground; and if too low, then there is not a sufficiency to fertilize the soil.

|| The answer Joseph gave the king when he first asked him to interpret his dreams was exceeding modest, and much of the same nature with that given by Daniel to King Nebuchadnezzar. See Daniel ii. 28, 29. He elevates the monarch's mind to the first cause of the dreams which so troubled him, and engages his attention by making him hope he should give him an answer, of which God himself was the author: " It is not," says he, " in me; God shall give Pharaoh an answer of peace." Which was as much as to say, " I have no more skill than those already consulted; from God alone the interpretation must preceed; and he, I trust, will give a favorable one to your dreams."

same thing, and the repetition of the dream only denoted the certainty of the event; that, therefore, as the lean kine seemed to eat up the fat, and the withered ears of corn to consume the full and flourishing; so, after seven years of great plenty, other seven years of extreme famine would succeed, insomuch that the remembrance of plenty would be lost throughout the land of Egypt."

After Joseph had thus interpreted the king's dreams, he advised him to improve the hints given in them, by appointing some wise and prudent person over his whole kingdom, who should take care to build granaries and appoint officers under him in every province, and that these officers should collect and lay up a fifth part of each plentiful year's produce, that a proper supply might be had during the succeeding years of famine.

This careful and prudent advice was highly approved of by the king, who, struck with the extraordinary foresight and sagacity of Joseph, did not long hesitate in fixing on the person thus recommended; for, turning first to his subjects, and then to Joseph, he thus respectively addressed them: "Can we," says he, "find such a one as this is? a man in whom the Spirit of God is. Forasmuch as God has showed thee all this, there is none so discreet and wise as thou art: thou shalt be over my house; and according to thy word shall all my people be ruled: only in the throne will I be greater than thou."

Having said this, Pharaoh appointed Joseph his deputy over the land of Egypt, and immediately invested him with the ensigns of that high station. He took the ring from his own finger, and put it on Joseph's; caused him to be clothed in a robe of fine linen, and put a golden chain about his neck. He ordered him to ride in the chariot next to his; and that wherever he went heralds should go before, to give notice of his coming to the people, who should show their subjection to him by bending the knee as he passed.

Pharaoh having thus bestowed on Joseph the greatest power and highest honors, in order to attach him more strongly to his interest, and make him forget the very thoughts of ever returning to his own country, changed his name from Joseph to Zaphnath-paaneah;* soon after which he procured him an honorable alliance, by marriage, with Asenath, the daughter of Potipherah, priest, or prince of On.†

Joseph's prediction began now to be fulfilled; and the plenteous years having commenced, he entered upon the duties of the high office with which he had been invested. He made a progress throughout the whole kingdom, built granaries in all the principal places, and appointed proper officers to collect and lay up the stipulated quantity of provisions. The same method he invariably pursued every season of the fruitful years, till at length he had amassed such quantities of corn as even to exceed computation.

During the seven years of plenty, Joseph had two sons by his wife Asenath, the first of whom he called Manasseh, intimating that God had made him forget all his toils; and the other he called Ephraim, because he had made him fruitful in the land of his affliction.

The seven years of plenty being expired, those of dearth commenced, according to Joseph's prediction, and the famine was not only spread throughout the land of Egypt, but also the neighboring countries. But, through Joseph's provident care, under the blessing of Divine Providence, Egypt was so well furnished with provisions, as not only to supply its own inhabitants, but also foreigners, with bread and other necessaries of life. The king referred all who applied to him for these articles, to Joseph, who opened the storehouses, and sold to the Egyptians and others, in such quantities, and at such rates, as seemed to him most just and equitable.

The famine having penetrated as far as the land of Canaan, and particularly affected that part of the country where Jacob resided, he, hearing there was corn to be bought in Egypt, sent ten of his sons thither for that purpose. On their arrival they were

---

* The generality of interpreters are of opinion, that this is a Coptic word, and implies *a revealer of secrets,* alluding to Joseph's having interpreted Pharaoh's dreams. It was customary, at this time, for princes to give foreigners a new name, to denote their naturalization, to take away all invidious distinction, and declare them worthy of their most intimate favor and protection.

† On was a famous city in Egypt, situated between the Nile and the Arabian gulf, about twenty miles from Memphis, the metropolis of the kingdom. Here was celebrated an annual festival, in honor of the sun, from which it was afterward called *Heliopolis.* The word we translate *priest* may signify one who ministers at the altar, or one who governs in civil affairs: priests were anciently the chief men of the kingdom; for kings themselves were priests.

directed to apply to Joseph for an order, whom they no sooner approached, than they bowed themselves before him,* as a token of reverence to his dignified office.

Joseph, at first sight, knew his brethren, but did not choose, at present, to make himself known to them, intending to take this opportunity of punishing them for the ill-treatment he had received at their hands. The better to effect his purpose, instead of speaking to them himself, he appointed an interpreter, who, by his directions, with a severe look and angry tone of voice, asked them, whence they came. They answered, "From the land of Canaan to buy provisions;" upon which he charged them with being spies, who came thither for no other purpose but to discover the weakness of the country. They replied, that they came with no other intent than purely to buy corn for their numerous family; and that they were all the sons of one man,† who once, indeed, had twelve, but that the youngest was left at home, and the next to him was dead.

But Joseph still insisted they were spies, and, to put their honesty to the test, made this proposition: "That, since, as they said, they had a younger brother at home, some one of them should be despatched to bring him, while the rest should be kept in confinement till his arrival; and if they did not assent to this he should consider them in no other light than that of spies and enemies." Having said this, he ordered them all to prison, there to remain till they should give a proper answer to the matter proposed.

On the third day of their confinement, Joseph sent for them again, and, showing a more pleasant countenance than he had yet done, told them, by means of his interpreter, that as himself feared God, and was desirous of acting justly by them, he was unwilling that their family should want provision, or that they themselves should suffer, if innocent. He therefore proposed, "That one of them should be confined as a hostage for the rest, while they returned with corn for the family; and that, when they came again, and brought their youngest brother with them, the one confined should be immediately released, and all of them considered as men of honesty and integrity."

Being reduced to a state of extremity, and knowing it was in vain to remonstrate with one, under whose immediate power they were, they unanimously, though no doubt with reluctance, agreed to this proposal. The interpreter was at this time absent, and, supposing no one else understood their language, they, imagining their present distressed situation was a punishment for their cruel treatment of their brother, began, in Joseph's presence, to condemn each other for their barbarous conduct. "Justly," said they, "do we now suffer for our cruelty to our brother, to whom we refused mercy, though he begged it in the anguish of his soul; therefore God is just in sending upon us this distress." Reuben, who was not so culpable as the rest, told them, that all this mischief might have been prevented had they listened to his counsel, and not acted so inhumanly to their innocent brother, for whose sake it was no more than what they might expect, that vengeance, at one time or other, would certainly overtake them.

Though Joseph could counterfeit the stranger in his looks, his mein, and his voice, yet he still retained the brother in his heart. The confusion and distress of his brethren awakened all his fraternal tenderness, and he was obliged to withdraw from their presence to give a vent to his passions. In a short time, however, he returned, and, after commanding Simeon‡ to be bound in their presence, he sent him to prison. Having done this, he set all the rest at liberty, and ordered the officer who distributed the corn, to supply them with what they wanted, and, at the same time, unknown to them, to put each man's money into the mouth of his sack.

* This manner of salutation was common in their own country, but not in use among the Egyptians: a sufficient proof that Jacob's family had little or no acquaintance with the inhabitants of the neighboring kingdoms. But by using the customary form of their family, they fulfilled the dreams of Joseph (as far as they had any relation to themselves) and no doubt brought those dreams to Joseph's remembrance.
† This part of their answer was certainly very pertinent, as it was not probable that a father would have sent his sons, and much less all of them, in one company, upon so dangerous an expedition: nor, that one particular person, or family, would have formed a design against so capital a kingdom as that of Egypt.
‡ The Jewish Rabbies say, that Joseph determined to retain Simeon rather than any other, because it was he who threw him into the pit. This tradition is far from being improbable. It is certain that Reuben was desirous of saving Joseph, and Judah inclined to favor him; so that if Simeon had joined with them, their authority might have prevailed over the rest to save him. We may add to this, that Simeon was a violent man, as is evident from his barbarous treatment of the Shechemites; and that Joseph might think proper to detain him, as it would least afflict his father.

These orders being punctually obeyed, they set out for Canaan, and at the close of their first day's journey, met with a circumstance they little expected. One of them opening his sack to give his ass provender, observed his money in the mouth of it, which, on examination, appeared to be the case with all the rest. This unexpected event gave them great uneasiness, and, looking confusedly at each other, they exclaimed, "What is this God hath done unto us?" They imagined it to be a plot concerted by the viceroy of Egypt, and that he intended, on their return, to make them slaves, by accusing them of theft.

Prosecuting their journey, they at length arrived at the habitation of their venerable parent, to whom they related all the particulars of their journey into the land of Egypt. They informed him of the treatment they had received from the viceroy: that he had accused them of being spies, and that they had no method of clearing themselves, but by leaving Simeon bound in prison, as a pledge, till they should return with Benjamin, on which terms alone their innocence could be justified.

The good old patriarch was sensibly affected at these melancholy tidings, and, in the affliction of his soul, thus complained: "That one way or other, he had been deprived of his children; that Joseph was dead, Simeon was left in Egypt, and now they were going to take Benjamin from him likewise, which were things too heavy for him to bear."

Reuben, finding his father thus unhappily circumstanced, in order to mitigate his affliction, told him he need not be apprehensive of any danger from the absence of Benjamin. He begged that he would put him under his protection, and at the same time assured him, that if he did not bring him safe back, he would readily agree to the loss of his own two sons for such defect.

But this proposal had little weight with Jacob, and, instead of assuaging his grief, only contributed to augment it. Resolved, therefore, not to trust Benjamin with them, he answered Reuben as follows: "My son," said he, "shall not go down with you, for his brother is dead, and he is left alone; if mischief befall him by the way in the which ye go, then shall ye bring down my gray hairs with sorrow to the grave."*

In this state of doubt and perplexity did they spend their time, till the famine every day increasing, and their stock of provisions being nearly consumed, Jacob told his sons to go again into Egypt for a fresh supply; but at the same time took no notice of their obligation to the viceroy to bring with them their youngest brother.

Jacob's sons, knowing their departure without Benjamin would not only argue in them the greatest folly and rashness, but also expose them to the resentment of the viceroy, and, at the same time, thinking it impossible to obtain their father's consent, were reduced to the utmost dilemma. Reuben had already tried his efforts in vain; Judah, therefore, now addressed him in more positive terms, urging at once the absolute and indispensable necessity of taking Benjamin with them, "as the viceroy had most solemnly declared they should not so much as see his face, if, on their return, he was not with them."

Jacob, being now put to his last shifts for the preservation of his favorite son Benjamin, knew not how to act, and, in the fulness of his soul, reproved his sons for having informed the viceroy they had a brother. In answer to this Judah told him, that what was said upon that head proceeded from the simplicity of their hearts; that he inquired so minutely into their circumstances and family, that they could not possibly avoid giving the information he required; and added, that they had little suspicion of his making so singular a demand.

Judah, finding his father waver a little in his resolution, repeated the necessity of their going again into Egypt, and pressed him to consent to give up their brother Benjamin, solemnly promising that, at the hazard of his own life, he would take care, and return him safe into his hands. "Send the lad," said he, "with me, and we will arise and go; that we may live, and not die, both we, and those, and also our little ones: I will be surety for him; of my hand shalt thou require him: if I bring him not unto thee, and set him before thee, then let me bear the blame for ever."

From the strong importunities of Judah, and a proper reflection on the necessity of

* Nothing can be more tender and picturesque than these words of the venerable patriarch. Still affected with the remembrance of his beloved Rachel, he can not think of parting with Benjamin, the only remaining pledge of that love, now Joseph, as he supposes, is no more; for, by her, he had only these two sons. We here seem, as it were, to behold the gray-headed venerable parent pleading with his sons; the beloved Benjamin standing by his side; impatient sorrow in *their* countenances, and, in *his*, all the feeling anxiety of paternal love.

affairs, Jacob was at length induced to comply, and therefore delivered up to them his son Benjamin. But before their departure he advised them, since it must be so, to take a double quantity of money with them, lest there should have been some mistake made in the other that was returned, and the price of what they had already bought demanded. He likewise told them to take some such presents as the country afforded, and what they imagined would be most acceptable to the viceroy. Having said this, he entreated Heaven for their safety, and then dismissed them with an aching heart, though fully resolved to acquiesce in God's good Providence, whatever might be the event.

On their arrival in Egypt, they immediately went to the king's principal granaries, and presented themselves before Joseph, who, seeing their brother Benjamin with them, gave orders to his steward to conduct them to his house, where he designed they should that day dine with him. They now began to have disagreeable apprehensions, fearing this might be a contrivance against them on account of the money which was returned in their sacks. They, therefore, before they entered the house, acquainted the steward with the whole affair; and, to demonstrate their honesty, told him, that besides the money which they found returned, they had brought more with them to buy a fresh quantity of provision. The steward, having been let into the secret, and perceiving the concern they were in, desired them not to make themselves in the least uneasy. He told them, that what they found in their sacks they ought to look upon as a treasure sent from Heaven: he owned that he himself had fairly received their money, and gave them assurance that they would never hear more of it. To convince them that they might rely on what he said, he left them a short time, and then returned with their brother Simeon unbound: after which he acquainted them that they were that day to dine with his master; and, in the meantime, showed them all the tokens of civility due to welcome guests.

As the time was near at hand that Joseph was to come home to dinner, his brethren took care to have their present ready; and, on his entering the apartment, they gave it him in the most humble and submissive manner. He saluted them with the greatest cordiality, and made anxious inquiry concerning the health and welfare of their aged father. To which they submissively replied: "Thy servant, our father, is in good health; he is yet alive."

Though Joseph addressed his brethren in general terms, his attention was principally fixed on his brother Benjamin, who was most near and dear to him. After inquiring of the rest if he was the youngest brother whom they had mentioned, without waiting for an answer, he saluted him in these words, "God be gracious unto thee, my son."[*] His passions were now raised to such a pitch, that, unable to contain the flood of tears that was ready to flow from his eyes, and fearing lest he should discover himself too soon, he retired into an adjoining apartment, and there gave a loose to his fraternal emotions. After a short time, having dried up his tears, and washed his face, that it might not appear he had wept, he returned to the company, and gave immediate orders for the provision to be served up.

In the room where the entertainment was provided were three tables; one for Joseph alone, on account of his dignity; another for his Egyptian guests, who would never eat with the Hebrews,[†] and a third for his brethren.

These last were all placed in exact order according to their seniority, a circumstance which greatly surprised them, for, not knowing their brother Joseph, they could not conceive by what means he had obtained so perfect a knowledge of their respective ages.

During the entertainment Joseph behaved in the most courteous manner, not only to his brethren, but to the whole company. He sent from his own table[‡] messes to each of his brothers; but with this difference, that the one sent to Benjamin was five times larger than any of the rest.[||] This was another mystery they could not account

* Joseph was the only *brother* of Benjamin by his mother Rachel. His calling him *son*, therefore, was only an appellation of courtesy used by superiors in saluting their inferiors, whom they styled sons, with respect to themselves, as fathers of the country.

† The dislike which the Egyptians took to the Hebrews did not arise, as some have imagined, from the latter eating animal food, but from their low degree in life, being shepherds, an employment, which, though esteemed by the Hebrews, was despised by the Egyptians.

‡ It was the custom among the ancients for all the provision to be placed on one table, and the master of the feast to distribute to every one his portion.

|| Joseph certainly did this not only to show his particular regard to Benjamin, but also to observe whether the rest would look upon their younger brother with the same envious eye as they had formerly done upon

for; however, they made themselves easy for the present, and enjoyed the repast which had been so bountifully prepared for them.

The entertainment being over, Joseph's brethren took their leave, and made the necessary preparations for setting off, the next morning, to the land of Canaan, pleased with the thoughts of what had passed, and the satisfaction their aged parent would receive on their safe arrival. But Joseph had one more fright for them still in reserve. He ordered his steward, when he filled their sacks with corn, to return their money (as he had done before) but into Benjamin's sack not only to put his money, but the silver cup likewise, out of which himself was accustomed to drink.*

This being done, early the next morning they proceeded on their journey toward Canaan; but they had not got far when Joseph ordered his steward to pursue them, and upbraid them with ingratitude in having so basely requited his master's civility, as to steal away his cup.

The steward did as he was commanded, and having overtaken them, accused them of theft. Conscious of their innocence, they were not in the least affected at the charge. As a test of their integrity they reminded the steward of their bringing back the money which they found in their sacks in their former journey; and to obviate every suspicion of their being guilty of the accusation laid against them, they offered to stand search under the severest penalties: "With whomsoever of thy servants," said they, "it may be found, let him die, and we also will be my lord's bondmen."

The steward took them at their word, but softened the penalty, by fixing it, that the person on whom the cup should be found should be his servant, and the rest considered as blameless.

Impatient to prove their innocence, every one hastily unloaded his beast, and, as they opened their sacks, the steward searched them; when behold, to their great astonishment and surprise, the cup was found in the sack belonging to Benjamin. It was to no purpose for the poor youth to say anything in his defence: upon such a demonstration none would believe him. As they were all concerned in the disgrace, they rent their clothes, and, without attempting even to palliate the fact, loaded their asses, and, in a mournful manner, returned to the city.

Joseph had remained at home in expectation of their return, and no sooner did they approach his presence than they immediately prostrated themselves before him. Joseph, without giving them time to speak a word in their defence, charged them with the fact, and reprimanded them for their folly in committing a theft, which it was totally out of their power to conceal. "What deed," says he, "is this ye have done? Wot ye not, that such a man as I can certainly divine."†

In the midst of a general horror, Judah, in a very humble tone, addressed himself to Joseph in words to this effect: "We have nothing to offer in our defence; God hath detected our iniquity, and we must remain slaves with him in whose sack the cup was found." But Joseph interrupted him by declaring, that he could by no means do such injustice; for that he only who stole the cup should be his slave, while the rest, whenever they pleased, were at full liberty to return to their father.

Judah, encouraged by finding the viceroy somewhat softened, presumed farther to address him, which he did in the most submissive and pathetic terms. He acquainted him with the whole case between them and their father, in relation to their bringing Benjamin into Egypt, to take away the suspicion of their being spies. He very feelingly described their father's melancholy situation for the loss of his son Joseph; the extreme fondness he had for his son Benjamin; the difficulty they were under to prevail with him to trust him with them, insomuch that himself was forced to become

himself. The custom of allotting the largest portion at the banquets of the ancients to any particular person, by way of preference, was practised in Homer's days, as appears from Agamemnon's speech to Idomeneus:

> "For this in banquets when the generous bowls
> Restore our blood, and raise the warrior's souls,
> Though all the rest with stated rules are bound,
> Unmixed, unmeasured, are thy goblets crowned."

* Joseph ordered this cup to be privately put into Benjamin's sack, in order to make a farther trial of his brethren's temper, and to see whether, moved with envy, they would give up Benjamin, or endeavor to assist him in his danger. It is not likely (as some have thought) that he really designed to have made a pretence for detaining Benjamin; or that he could be ignorant of his father's warm affection to his youngest son.

† This was as much as to say, "You see by my office that I am one of the great ministers of state; while the other diviners are preferred only from the college of priests. As I am, therefore, so superior to them, could you be insensible that it was in my power to divine, or detect your robbery?"

security for his safe return ; and that, if he should go home without him, his father's life was so wrapped up in the child, that he would certainly die with grief. To prevent, therefore, so melancholy a scene, he offered himself as an equivalent for his brother. "I pray thee," said he, "let thy servant abide, instead of the lad, a bondman to my lord, and let the lad go up with his brethren ; for how shall I go up to my father, and the lad be not with me ?"

This moving speech, and generous offer, so operated on the passions of Joseph, that he could no longer contain himself: the force of nature shook his frame, and obliged him to throw off all disguise. Ordering, therefore, the rest of the company to depart, that he might discover himself with more affectionate freedom, they were no sooner gone, than he burst into a flood of tears, and, looking earnestly at his brethren, pathetically exclaimed, "I am Joseph ; doth my father yet live ?"[*]

Conscious guilt, at the very name of that Joseph whom they had so unnaturally treated, struck them dumb, as they now dreaded the power he had of resenting the injuries they had done him. But brotherly love overcame resentment, and banished every desire of revenge. Joseph, observing their confusion, bid them, in the most endearing manner, approach nearer to him, when he assured them, that he was the very brother they had sold into Egypt, and though he had assumed the dignity becoming his office, he still retained the tenderness of a brother. To remove all further apprehensions of danger, he told them, that their selling him into Egypt, was directed by an unforeseen Providence ; and that they had no reason to be angry with themselves for doing it, since they were no more than the instruments in God's hand to bring about what his wise purpose had determined. That himself had no reason to resent it, since, by that means, he had been advanced to the honor and dignity of being governer of all Egypt. And, lastly, that neither his father, nor any of his family, ought to murmur at it, since God appointed this method for the preservation of their lives.[†]

Having said this, he told them that there were yet five years of the famine to come, and therefore he would advise them to hasten home, and, as soon as possible, bring their father, together with all the family, into Egypt. As an inducement for them to leave their own country, he desired them, from him, to address their father to this effect: "that God had made him lord of all Egypt, and that therefore he must not defer coming ; for he would provide Goshen[‡] for the place of his habitation, and there would he carefully nourish not only him but all his family." He acknowledged that this relation must, of course, appear strange to his father; but that he certainly would not doubt the testimony of so many eyewitnesses ; and above all, that he would not fail to believe what was told him by his favorite son Benjamin. He then threw himself upon Benjamin's neck, kissed him, and wept for joy ; and having a little recovered himself, he treated all the rest with like tenderness. His brethren being thus convinced that a perfect reconciliation had taken place between them, took courage, and conversed with him in a manner very different to what they had done previous to this happy discovery.

The rumor had reached the king that Joseph's brethren were come; and it is a pleasing evidence of the esteem in which he was held, and the regard which he had conciliated, that a domestic incident which was calculated to be a satisfaction to him, was highly agreeable to Pharaoh and all his court. The monarch sent for him, and authorized him to express the kindest attentions toward them, and the utmost anxiety for their welfare. He, as well as Joseph, saw that it would be best for them to come

---

[*] There is certainly a distinguished beauty in this interrogation ; and the transition is finely wrought. The soul of Joseph was so full of filial affection for his father, that, before he had finished his sentence, he inquired after him, though but a short time before, they had told him he was alive. And how must such an abrupt declaration affect his brothers ! No wonder they were dumb for some time with astonishment, and unable to answer the question asked.

[†] These passages point out to us the very noble and just ideas which Joseph entertained concerning the providence of God : but, besides this, we may observe a peculiar generosity and tenderness of temper in this apology to his brethren, wherein he endeavors to remove every uneasy apprehension from their minds. Good hearts are always averse to giving pain ; the same benevolence of disposition which makes them zealous to diffuse happiness, makes them tender of inflicting a momentary smart. Joseph was unwilling that his brethren should feel any alloy to their satisfaction which the present event afforded ; and therefore he turned, as it were, from their view the very thought and remembrance of their former unnatural behavior to him, and directed their attention to reflections which were equally comfortable and important.

[‡] This was the most fruitful part of all Lower Egypt, especially for pasturage ; and therefore the most commodious for those who were brought up shepherds and accustomed to a pastoral life. Besides this, it was very conveniently situated, being but a small distance from the city where Pharaoh kept his court.

to Egypt, and he had the consideration to direct that they should be well supplied with provisions on the way, and that they should be furnished with carts,* in which the aged Jacob, with the women and young children, might pass from Canaan to Egypt with more comfort, than by the more ordinary means of conveyance.

It is little to be wondered at that Joseph should very readily obey the king's commands. Accordingly, he furnished them with a proper number of carts for bringing their family and substance, together with a sufficient quantity of provision for their journey as well home as back again. He sent his father a present, consisting of ten asses laden with the choicest dainties Egypt afforded. To his brethren he gave each changes of raiment, but to Benjamin he gave five changes, together with three hundred pieces of silver. Having done this, Joseph dismissed his brethren, giving them, at the same time, a strict charge that they should not *fall out by the way.*†

Thus supplied, and thus circumstanced, the sons of Jacob, with hearts full of joy, prosecuted their journey to Canaan. As soon as their aged father saw them, his drooping spirits revived, more especially when he beheld his sons Benjamin and Simeon, whose return he had little expected. But when they informed him that his son Joseph was likewise alive, and described the great pomp and splendor in which he lived, the good old patriarch was affected indeed; and, unable to bear so much good news at once, fainted in their arms.

When Jacob came again to himself, his sons showed him the presents sent by Joseph, together with the carts that were to carry him and his family into Egypt. The sight of these, with many particulars they related of their brother Joseph, revived his spirits; his doubts and fears vanished, and, in an ecstacy of joy, he exclaimed, " It is enough ! Joseph, my son, is yet alive: I will go and see him before I die."

The necessary preparations being made, Jacob and his family left Hebron, and proceeded on their journey toward Egypt. It might be supposed that the old man's anxiety to see so dear a son, and for whom he had so long mourned, would have made him proceed with the greatest expedition ; but parental affection gave way to religious duties. Being desirous of making proper acknowledgments to God for the benefits already received, as well as to implore his farther protection, he stopped at Beersheba, and there offered up sacrifices to the Lord. The reasons of his choosing this spot on the present occasion were, because it was the place where Abraham and Isaac had lived so long: and at the same time it was in the way to Egypt, being the utmost boundary of Canaan toward the south.

On the evening of the same day that Jacob had performed his religious duties at Beersheba, the Almighty appeared to him in a vision, bidding him not fear to go down into Egypt, since he would be with him and protect him, and in due time, bring his posterity out of it to take possession of the promised land. That as to himself, he should live near his beloved Joseph, die in his arms, and have his eyes closed by his hand.‡

* CARTS.—The Egyptians had no chariots, except perhaps war chariots, suited to bear such a journey as this, and they would have been most unsuitable for the present purpose. Besides, the word for a chariot is different from that which is here employed, although a wheel-carriage of some kind or other is certainly indicated. To indicate that carriage, we have taken the word "cart," as preferable, upon the whole, to that of "wagon"—partly as being less definite. But it does not appear that the Egyptians had any carts, or any wheeled carriages save chariots of war, and light curricles for civil use. The Nile and the numerous canals offered such facilities for carriage and conveyance by water, that the use of carts and wagons does not appear to have been thought of. Carts are indeed represented in the paintings and sculptures of that ancient country; but not as being in use among the Egyptians themselves, but by a people with whom they are at war, apparently a nomade people of Asia, and who are represented as escaping in their carts. Now, we infer, that as the Egyptians had no carts of their own, those which were sent for Jacob were such as they had either taken in war from a people by whom they were used, or had been left behind by the intrusive shepherd-race. As having been used by a pastoral people, they would seem to the king particularly suitable for the removal of a pastoral family. In connexion with preceding statements, and with the conjecture just offered, it deserves to be noticed that the next instance of carts which occurs in the scriptural history is found among the Philistines. 1 Samuel vi. 7. The first of our engravings represents the only kind of wheel-carriage now used in Syria, and that chiefly for agricultural purposes. The second represents the carts of the Tartar nomades of Central Asia, whose usages offer many remarkable resemblances to those of the patriarchs and the early pastoral races with which early Bible history makes us acquainted.

† Joseph was no stranger to the tempers of his brethren, and therefore thought proper to reprove them in this gentle manner. Probably he suspected they might accuse each other with the cruelty they had exercised toward him, or throw envious reflections on Benjamin, because he had been eminently distinguished above the rest.

‡ It must certainly have given great consolation to good old Jacob to find, from the promise of God, that Joseph was to attend him on his death-bed, and to close those eyes that had often assisted him in contemplating the beauties of nature. The custom of *closing the eyes* of persons departed is very ancient, and they were usually the nearest and dearest friends who performed this last office.

BUTLERS.

Modern Syrian Carts of Ancient Form.

Carts of the Tartar Nomades.

Encouraged by this divine promise, Jacob left Beersheba, and cheerfully pursued his journey toward Egypt, his sons taking with them their children and wives in the carts which Joseph had sent for the purpose. They likewise took with them all their cattle and goods; and the whole number of souls descended from Jacob's loins amounted to three score and ten.

As soon as they came to the borders of Egypt (and not far from the land of Goshen) Jacob despatched his son Judah before them, in order to acquaint Joseph with their arrival. This intelligence was very agreeable to Joseph, who immediately ordered his chariot to be got ready, and, with a retinue suitable to his high station, hastened to meet his father, whom he congratulated on his safe arrival at a place where it was in his power to make him happy and comfortable during the remainder of his life. Words can not describe the expressions of filial duty and paternal affection that took place on this occasion. Tears of joy plentifully flowed on both sides. While the son was contemplating the goodness of God in bringing him to the sight of his aged parent, the father, on the other hand, thought all his happiness on earth completed in this interview; and, therefore, in the fulness of his soul, he exclaimed, " Now let me die, since I have seen thy face, because thou art yet alive."

These mutual endearments being over, and Joseph having paid his respects to the whole family, he told his father and brethren that he would go before and acquaint the king with their arrival. As he imagined Pharaoh would be desirous of seeing some of them, he gave them this caution: that in case he should ask of what occupation they were, their answer should be, that they were shepherds, as their ancestors, for many generations, had been before them. By these means, he told them, he might secure the land of Goshen for their residence, which was not only one of the most pleasant parts of Egypt, but the best calculated for feeding their flocks and herds. Besides this, he said, there would be another material advantage, namely, that it would be a happy retreat from the insults of the Egyptians, who were known to have an utter detestation to those who followed a shepherd's life.

Having given this caution, Joseph took with him five of his brothers, and after previously informing Pharaoh that his father and family were arrived at Goshen, presented them before the king. Pharaoh received them with great courtesy, out of respect to Joseph, and, among other questions, asked them of what occupation they were. They answered (agreeably to the directions given them by Joseph) that they were shepherds, as their ancestors, for many generations before, had been: that want of pasturage for their cattle, and sustenance for themselves, had made them leave Canaan, and they humbly beseeched his majesty that they might be permitted to settle in the land of Goshen, that part of the country being best adapted for the purposes of their employment. Pharaoh readily granted their request, and moreover told Joseph, that if any of his brethren were remarkable for their activity and knowledge, he might, if he thought proper, appoint them as superintendents over the royal shepherds.

Joseph's project having so far happily succeeded, he, soon after, introduced his aged parent to Pharaoh, who after receiving him in a very courteous manner, among other questions, asked him his age. Jacob answered, he was a hundred and thirty; upon which the king expressing some surprise from his appearing so strong and healthy, Jacob farther told him, that his life was not, as yet, near so long as some of his ancestors, nor did he look so well as those who were much farther advanced in life, which was owing to the great troubles and perplexities under which he had long labored. Some other questions being asked, and the answers given, Jacob, after wishing the king health and prosperity, took his leave, and returned to Goshen, where Joseph took care to supply him and his family with such an abundance of necessaries as made them insensible of the general calamity.

While Jacob and his family were thus happily circumstanced, by means of the power and affection of Joseph, the Egyptians were in the utmost distress. The dreadful effects of the famine appeared more and more every day, and Joseph keeping up the corn at a very high price, in a short time all the money was brought into the king's coffers. When their money was gone, they were all (except the priests who were furnished from the king's stores) obliged to part with their cattle, their houses, their lands, and, at length, even their liberty, for provision.*

* Whatever those may think who have endeavored to depreciate the conduct of Joseph, it is certain that there was no injustice in Joseph's making the Egyptians pay for the corn which he had bought with Pharaoh's money, and laid up with great care and expense. In demanding their cattle, he had most

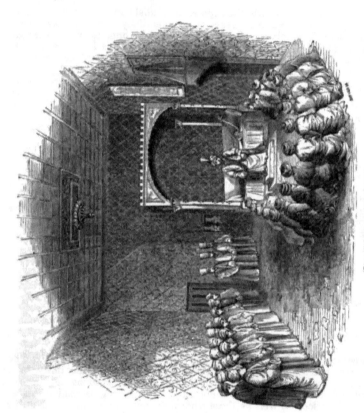

The Sultan on his throne.

All these Joseph purchased of the people in the king's name, and for the king's use; and, to let them see that the purchase was in earnest, and that their liberties and properties were now become the king's, he removed them, from their former places of abode, into different, and very distant parts of the kingdom.

In any other person such conduct might have been considered as arising from an immoderate zeal for absolute power in the king, and an advantage unjustly taken of the necessities of the people; but so Joseph managed the matter as to gain the approbation both of prince and people. When the seventh and last year of the famine was come, he told them they might expect to have a crop the ensuing year; for that the Nile would overflow its banks, and the earth bring forth her fruits as usual. Having made this known, he distributed fresh lands, cattle, and corn to the people, that they might return to their tillage as before; but this he did on the following condition: that thenceforth the fifth part of all the produce of their lands should become the property of the king. "Behold," says he, "I have bought you this day and your land for Pharaoh. Lo, here is seed for you, and ye shall sow the land. And it shall come to pass in the increase, that you shall give the fifth part unto Pharaoh, and four parts shall be your own for seed of the field, and for your food, and for them of your household, and for food for your little ones."

To these conditions the people willingly consented, imputing the preservation of their lives to Joseph's care: "Thou hast saved," said they, "our lives; let us find grace in the sight of my lord, and we will be Pharaoh's servants." From this time it passed into a law, that the fifth part of the produce of the land of Egypt (except what belonged to the priests) should become the property of the crown.

While Joseph was enjoying the fruits of his great success and policy, his family at Goshen (whom he failed not frequently to visit) became not only numerous, but exceeding wealthy. The seven years of famine were succeeded by great plenty, the earth resuming its former fertility, and the whole land abounding in all the usual productions of nature. Seventeen of these years of plenty did Jacob live to see, at the expiration of which nature's lamp grew dim, and life was nearly exhausted; his decayed spirits warn him of his approaching fate, and each drooping faculty beats an alarm to death.

When Jacob found himself thus circumstanced, he sent for his son Joseph, whom he addressed in words to the following effect: "Though the desire of seeing a son so dear to me as you are raised to the height of Egyptian glory, joined to the raging famine which then visited our land, made me willingly come down into this strange country; yet Canaan being the inheritance which God promised to Abraham and his posterity, and where he lies interred with my father Isaac, and some other of our family, in the ground which he purchased of the inhabitants for that purpose; my last and dying request to you is, that you will not suffer me to be buried here, but swear to see me carried to Machpelah, and there deposited with my ancestors. Your great power with the king will easily obtain that favor, which is the last I have to ask."

Joseph not only promised, but likewise swore, strictly to fulfil his father's request; upon which the good old man was so perfectly satisfied, that, after thanking his son for these fresh assurances of his fidelity, he bowed himself in acknowledgment to God, who, besides all his other mercies, had given him this last token of his protection, in assuring him, by Joseph's promise and oath, that he should be removed from Egypt into the promised land.

Joseph, having thus satisfied his father in this particular, took his leave, but not without giving a strict charge to those who attended him, that, upon the very first appearance of danger, they should immediately send for him. He had been but a short time at court, before a messenger arrived with the dismal intelligence that his father was near expiring; upon which, taking with him his two sons, Manasseh and Ephraim, he hastened with all expedition to visit him.

As soon as the feeble patriarch understood that his son Joseph had arrived, it immediately raised his sinking spirits, and he became so far revived as to be able to sit upright in his bed. Desiring his favorite Joseph to approach near him, he began

probably a view to save them; for, as they had not corn for themselves, they could much less have it for their cattle; and, therefore, this was the only way to preserve the lives of both, and to prevent that waste of the corn which must have been made if they had had the keeping and feeding of the cattle themselves; and it is highly probable that he returned them their cattle after the famine, when they were fixed again in their several habitations—otherwise it would have been hardly possible for them to support their families and carry on their business.

with recapitulating all the glorious promises which God had formerly made him concerning his posterity possessing the land of Canaan; and after mentioning the death of Rachel, together with the place where her remains were deposited,* he spoke to the following effect: " How tenderly I loved my dear Rachel, all my family can testify; but this farther proof I now give you of my affection to her. You have two sons born in a foreign country, and who, according to the usual order of inheritance, should have only the portion of grandchildren in the division of the promised land; but, from this day forward, they shall be esteemed my sons, and, as heads of two distinct tribes (for they shall not be called the tribe of Joseph, but the tribes of Ephraim and Manasseh), receive a double portion in that allotment. But it must not be so with the other sons which you may beget after these: they must come in only for the portion of grandchildren. And to you in particular I bequeath that tract of land which, by the force of arms, I took from the Amorites."†

During the time Jacob was thus talking with Joseph concerning himself and children, he had not observed that Joseph's sons were with him, but spoke of them as if they had been absent. At length, turning to Joseph, and observing (as he thought) somebody with him (though he could not discern who it was, ou account of his eyes being dim with age), he asked who he had with him. To which Joseph replied, his sons Ephraim and Manasseh, and at the same time, with great reverence, bowed himself to the ground.

Jacob was greatly rejoiced at this intelligence, and immediately ordered them to be brought near, that he might bestow on them his blessing. Joseph obeyed his father's commands, and placed the children according to the order of their age, that is, Manasseh, as being the first-born, on the right, and Ephraim on the left: but Jacob, crossing his hands, laid his *right* (which carried with it the preference) upon the *younger*, and his *left* upon the *elder* of them. Joseph, observing this, and supposing it to proceed from a mistake, was going to rectify it; but his father told him that what he did was by divine direction, and therefore made Ephraim not only the first in nomination, but gave him a blessing much more extensive than that conferred on his elder brother.

This conversation was hitherto private, being only between Jacob and his favorite son Joseph. But the good old patriarch, finding his dissolution near at hand, ordered all his sons to be brought before him, that, while he had strength to speak, he might take his last farewell, and not only distribute his blessing among them, but likewise foretell what should happen to them and their posterity in future times.

Accordingly, all Jacob's sons being brought before him, he addressed them separately, beginning with Reuben, the eldest.

" Reuben," says he, " thou art my first-born, and, by right of primogeniture, entitled to many privileges and prerogatives in superiority over thy brethren; but, for the crime of incest in polluting thy father's bed, both thou and thy tribe are totally degraded from the privileges of birthright."

Having said this to Reuben, he next addressed himself to Simeon and Levi conjunctively; telling them, that for their impious massacre of Hamor and his people, their tribes should be ever separate, and dispersed among the rest. " I will divide them," says he, " in Jacob, and scatter them in Israel."‡

Jacob, then turning to Judah, prophesied of him to this effect: That to his tribe should the sovereignty belong, and they should be situated in a very fruitful country: that from his name should the whole nation of the Jews derive their appellation; and that the form of government which he then instituted should remain among them until the coming of the Messiah.||

* It is probable that Jacob here mentioned to Joseph the place of Rachel's interment, in hopes that he might, at some convenient opportunity, remove her ashes to the cave of Machpelah.

† There are many particulars in the lives of the patriarchs, and of others, which are not at all mentioned in scripture; and there are some instances of a transient reference to facts of this kind, to things which have been said and done, but are never related. Of this kind, it is reasonable to suppose, is the passage in question; at least, we have no mention in scripture of any portion of land taken from the Amorites by Jacob. All, therefore, which can be said upon the subject must be mere conjecture; of which the most probable is, that the parcel of ground near Shechem, which Jacob purchased of Hamor, is here meant, and which, probably, he took or recovered, by force of arms, from the Amorites, who, it seems, had seized on it after his removal to another part of Canaan.

‡ This prophecy was literally fulfilled; for the Levites were scattered throughout all the other tribes, and Simeon had only a part of the land of Judah for his residence.

|| The words in the text run thus:—Judah, "thou art he whom thy brethren shall praise; thy father's children shall bow down before thee. The sceptre shall not depart from Judah, nor a lawgiver from

Of Zebulun, Jacob prophesied that his tribe should be planted near the seacoasts, and have harbors convenient for shipping;* and of Issachar, that his should prove a pusillanimous people, and be lovers of inglorious ease more than of liberty and renown.†

Jacob, having predicted the fate of, and bestowed his blessings on, the children descended from Leah, proceeds next to those of his two concubinary wives. He began with Dan, the son of Bilhah, whose posterity, he foretold (though descended from a handmaid), should have the same privileges with the other tribes, become a politic people, and greatly versed in the stratagems of war.‡ Of Gad's posterity he

between his feet, until Shiloh come; and unto him shall the gathering of the people be." Many commentators have written largely on this remarkable prophecy related by Jacob to his son Judah.

From the time that our first parents ate of the forbidden fruit, we have seen that the promised seed was, one age after another, more and more circumscribed, although its salutary effects were to be the same. It is first called the seed of the woman; it is next consigned over to Seth; Shem, the younger son of Noah, gets the preference; afterward Abraham is made choice of; from Isaac, the son of Abraham, it goes to his second son Jacob; and here Jacob, by the spirit of prophecy, conveys it to the posterity of Judah.

There are several things to be attended to in this remarkable prophecy, and such as are of the utmost importance for us to know. First, we are told that Judah's brethren should praise him, and that his hand should be in the neck of his enemies. This was remarkably fulfilled in the local situation of the tribe of Judah; for their being so near the Arabians, obliged them to be continually on their guard; and as they were for the most part successful, so it may be justly said that the hand of Judah was in the neck of his enemies, and that his brethren praised him for standing up in their defence. Secondly, it is here said that his father's children should bow down before him, and certainly nothing was ever more literally fulfilled. David, in whose family the royal sovereignty was placed, was of the tribe of Judah, and to him all the other tribes bowed down. But the prophecy conveys a further idea, namely, that from Judah, according to the flesh, the Messiah should come, to whom all nations should bow down; and in the book of Revelations he is called the lion of the tribe of Judah. Thirdly, "the sceptre shall not depart from Judah," &c.; by which we are to understand that there should never be one wanting to sway the regal sceptre, or exercise sovereign authority in the tribe of Judah, till that glorious and Divine Person came, whose kingdom was to have no end, and to whom the people were to be gathered; for the Messiah is, in many places of scripture, called the "desire of all nations." Such is the nature of this remarkable prophecy; and now, in order to prove the concurring authenticity of the Mosaic and Gospel history, let us see in what manner it has been fulfilled.

During the time of Joshua's wars with the Canaanites, the tribe of Judah was more distinguished for its valor than the others; and it appears, from the book of Judges, that they were always the most forward to engage with the common enemy. When it is said that "the sceptre shall not depart from Judah," it implies that it should depart from all those of the other tribes who should enjoy it. Thus it departed from the tribe of Benjamin on the death of Saul; and it is well known that the ten tribes were carried away captive, and incorporated with other nations, while that of Benjamin put itself under the protection of Judah.

From the time of David till the taking of Jerusalem by Nebuchadnezzar, Judah exercised the regal authority; and although ten of the tribes, who followed the idolatry of Jeroboam, had kings, yet they were for the most part subject to those of Judah. It is true, the Jews were also carried captive to Babylon; but during the seventy years they were in that country, they were so far from being treated as slaves, that they were allowed to build houses, and lived in such affluence, that many of them refused to return to their own country when permission was granted them. When Cyrus, the emperor, issued his orders for them to return to the land of Judea, they had rulers among them, for they were expressly mentioned in the royal proclamation. It is certain, that after returning from their captivity they were not so free as before, because they were frequently oppressed by the Persians, Greeks, and Romans; but, for all that, they lived as a distinct people, under their own laws and government. It continued to be the same under the Asmodean princes; and it is well known that Herod the Great married Mariamne, the last female of that line; and in the latter end of his reign the Messiah was born. It is true, the Romans, in some cases, deprived them of the power of judging in cases of treason; but, notwithstanding, we find, in the cases of our Saviour and the apostle Paul, that the Roman prætors or governors never proceeded to judge a criminal till he was condemned by the rulers of the people.

The learned Dr. Shaw says, the blessings given to Judah were very different from all those bestowed on the other tribes. The mountains in Judea abound with so much wine, oil, and milk, that one is surprised at the fertility of a place which, at a distance, has the appearance of barrenness. Grapes and raisins are sent annually in great quantities from Hebron to Egypt, besides several other sorts of fruit.

From these observations, will not the impartial reader declare that this prophecy has been literally fulfilled? and is not the present melancholy state of the Jews a striking proof of its authenticity? Till the Messiah came, they had a regal government; but, because they rejected him, they are now scattered up and down through all nations, without being permitted to enjoy the privileges of any nation whatever. Surely this should convince us that no human testimony can overthrow the evidence brought in support of the Mosaic and Gospel histories.

* It is remarkable that Zebulun is mentioned by Jacob before Issachar, who was the eldest; but this distinction, it is probable, arose from his great superiority and merit. Zebulun's portion of the country was likewise very preferable to Issachar's; for, besides the advantage he had in common with him, and that our Lord chiefly resided in his tribe, and was thence called a Galilean, he is here promised a seacoast, with harbors commodious for ships. If Jacob had been present at the division of the promised land, he could hardly have given a more exact description of Zebulun's lot; for it extended from the Mediterranean sea on the west to the lake of Tiberias, or sea of Galilee, on the east.

† Of all the tribes of Israel, that of Issachar was distinguished for being the most indolent. That part of the country which fell to their share was exceeding fertile; but that fertility only served to enervate the people, so that when they were invaded by foreign enemies, they soon became an easy prey to them, and were often obliged to pay tribute.

‡ The words in the text are, "Dan shall be a serpent by the way, an adder in the path; that biteth the horse's heels so that his rider shall fall backward." It is to be observed, that the part of Canaan which the descendants of Dan inhabited was noted for serpents of a particular species, who were so cunning that they used to lie in wait to bite the feet of passengers. This very justly alluded to the disposition of Dan's descendants, who, when engaged in war, frequently did more execution by craft and stratagem than by force of arms. It is the opinion of the Jews that the prophecy of Dan's destroying his enemies by cunning was more particularly fulfilled, when Sampson, who was of that tribe, pulled down the temple, which crushed himself and the Philistines to death. See Judges xvi. 30.

foretold, that they should be frequently infested with robbers, but should overcome at last.* Of Asher's, that they should be situated in a pleasant and fruitful country ;† and of Naphtali's, that they should spread their branches like an oak, and multiply exceedingly.‡

Jacob, having now done with those children begotten on Leah and his concubinary wives, next directs his attention to the sons of his beloved Rachel. Turning himself to Joseph, he first took some notice of his past troubles, and then set forth the future greatness of his descendants; after which he bestowed his benediction on him in words to the following effect: "The Lord," says he, "even the God of thy fathers, shall bless thee with the dew of heaven and with the fatness of the earth, with the fruit of the womb," that is, with a numerous posterity, "and with plenty of all sorts of cattle. May all the blessings promised to me and my forefathers be doubled upon Joseph's head; may they outtop and outstretch the highest mountains; and prove to him more fruitful and more lasting than they."||

The only one now remaining to receive Jacob's blessing was his youngest son Benjamin, who, no doubt, from having been a great favorite with his father, expected a suitable distinction from the rest of his brethren; but, whether Jacob foresaw that no extraordinary merit or happiness would attend this tribe, or that it should afterward be blended with that of Judah, and consequently share the blessing of that tribe, so it was that he only prophesied of him that his descendants should be of a fierce and warlike disposition; and, "like a ravenous wolf, should shed the blood of their enemies, and in the evening divide the spoil."§

The good old patriarch having thus (by divine direction) foretold the fate of his descendants, he bestowed his blessing on each of his sons separately; after which he reminded them all (but more especially Joseph), that it was his most earnest request they would bury him among his ancestors, in the cave of Machpelah, which had been purchased by Abraham, and where not only the remains of him and his wife Sarah were deposited, but likewise those of Isaac and Rebecca, and where he had also buried his wife Leah.

Having given this last charge, the pious Jacob laid himself gently down in his bed, a short time after which he calmly resigned his soul into the hands of Him who gave it. He died in the one hundred and forty-seventh year of his age, during the last seventeen of which he resided in Egypt.

The loss of so good a father must undoubtedly be very afflicting to the whole family, but none of them expressed their grief with such filial affection as the pious Joseph, who could not behold his aged parent's face, though dead, without kissing and bathing it with his tears. Having thus given vent to his passions, and somewhat recovered himself, he ordered the physicians (according to the custom of the country) to embalm his father's body, and then set about making the necessary preparations for his funeral.

The time that Jacob's family mourned for their father was seventy days, during

* The tribe of *Gad* had their portion of land on the frontiers of the Jewish territories, so that they were continually exposed to the incursions of the bordering Arabs; but, in the course of time, they became so expert in war, that they always repulsed them.

† The tribe or *Asher* possessed that part of the country which reached from Zidon to Mount Carmel: it was so beautiful and fertile a spot, that it not only abounded with all kinds of provisions, but also with the choicest fruits, and most luxuriant productions of the earth.

‡ In the territories allotted to the tribe of *Naphtali* was the country of Genesaret; which (Josephus says) was looked upon as the utmost effort of nature in point of beauty. It was also remarkable for producing some of the best wines in all Palestine. In one part of the prophecy, as related by Moses, it is said, "Naphtali is a hind let loose;" the meaning of which is, that the people should be exceeding swift in the pursuit of their enemies, which, indeed, was the case, in a very peculiar manner, with this tribe.

|| The fruitfulness promised to Joseph in the great increase of his posterity was exemplified in the prodigious number of his two-fold tribe, Ephraim and Manasseh. At the first numbering of the tribes, these produced 72,700 men capable of bearing arms. (See Numb. i. 33–35.) And at the second numbering, 85,200 (Numb. xxvi. 34–37), which by far exceeded the number of either of the other tribes.

§ History sufficiently justifies the truth of this prediction relative to the tribe of Benjamin, for they alone maintained a war with all the other tribes, and overcame them in two battles, though they had sixteen to one. It must, however, be observed, that the comparison does not only respect mere valor and fortitude in defending themselves, but also fierceness in making wars and depredations upon others. But what is chiefly to be regarded in this prophecy is, that the tribe of Benjamin should continue till the final destruction of the Jewish polity. For since the natural morning and evening can not with the least propriety be here understood, and as the Jewish state is the subject of all Jacob's prophecy, we must consider the morning and the night as the beginning and final period of that state; and, consequently, that the tribe of Benjamin would exist till Shiloh came. And this prophecy was fully accomplished; for, upon the division of the kingdom after Solomon's death, the tribe of Benjamin adhered to that of Judah, and formed one people with it; continued to share the same fortune, and by that means existed till the destruction of Jerusalem by the Romans, which happened many years after the other ten tribes were no longer a people.

which Joseph never appeared at court, it being improper for him so to do on such an occasion. In consequence of this, he requested some of the officers about the king to acquaint him that his father, previous to his death, had enjoined him, upon oath, to bury him in a sepulchre belonging to their family, in the land of Canaan; and that therefore he begged permission that he might go and fulfil his last commands; after which he would return to court with all convenient expedition.

Pharaoh not only complied with Joseph's request, but (in compliment to him and his family) gave orders that the chief officers of his household, together with some of the principal nobility of the kingdom, should attend the funeral; who, joined with his own, and his father's whole family, some in chariots and others on horseback, formed one of the most pompous processions ever seen on a similar occasion.

On their arrival in the land of Canaan they halted at a place called "the threshing-floor of Atad,"* where they continued seven days mourning for the deceased. The Canaanites, who inhabited that part of the country, observing the Egyptians mixing themselves in these obsequies, were astonished, and imagining them to be the principals concerned in the funeral lamentation, could not forbear exclaiming, "This is a grievous mourning to the Egyptians!" whence they called the name of - the place Abel-Mizraim, which signifies "the mourning of the Egyptians."

This solemnity being ended, they proceeded on their journey, and at length, arriving at the field of Machpelah, they deposited the remains of Jacob in the cave with his ancestors, after which the whole company returned in solemn procession to Egypt.

During the life of Jacob, Joseph's brethren thought themselves secure; but now their aged father was no more, their former fears returned, and suggested to them the just revenge Joseph might yet take for the great injuries he had received from their hands. In consequence of this, they held a consultation together in what manner to proceed for their own security; the result of which was to form a message (purporting to have been delivered by Jacob), and send it to their brother. This was accordingly done, and the substance of the message was to the following effect: "Thy father commanded, before he died, saying, Thus shall ye say to Joseph: Forgive, I pray thee now, the trespass of thy brethren and their sin; for they did evil unto thee; but pardon them, not only for my sake, but because they are the servants of the God of thy father."

When Joseph read this message, such was his compassionate and forgiving temper, that he could not refrain from weeping. To remove, therefore, the fears and apprehensions of his brethren, he immediately sent for them, and, receiving them with the same kind affection as when their father was alive, excused the actions they had formerly committed to his prejudice in the most obliging manner; and, in order fully to remove their ill-founded fears, dismissed them with the assurance that they should always find in him a constant friend and an affectionate brother.

Though Joseph lived fifty-four years after his father's death, yet the sacred historian does not mention any farther particulars of him except the following; namely, that he lived to see himself the happy parent of a numerous offspring in his two sons, Ephraim and Manasseh, even to the third generation; during which time, it is reasonable to suppose, he continued in high favor with his prince, and in a considerable employment under him.

When Joseph grew old, and found his death approaching, he sent for his brethren, and, with the like prophetic spirit that his father Jacob had done, told them that God, according to his promise, would not fail bringing their posterity out of Egypt into the land of Canaan. At the same time he made them swear, that when it should please God thus to visit them, they should not forget to carry his remains with them, that they might be deposited in the burial-place of his ancestors.

The pious Joseph, having thus bound his brethren by oath to convey his remains to his native land, soon after departed this life, in the one hundred and tenth year of his age. In compliance with the injunction laid, his brethren had the body immediately embalmed, put into a coffin, and carefully secured, till the time should come when the prediction was to be fulfilled of their leaving Egypt, and possessing the land of Canaan.

Thus have we finished the life of the great patriarch Joseph, who is certainly one of the most distinguished characters to be met with either in sacred or profane his-

* This place is supposed to have been situated about two leagues from Jericho, on the other side of the Jordan, and about fifty miles from Hebron.

Peasants in Persia.

tory. To enliven what has already been said of him, we shall conclude this chapter with some general reflections and observations on the whole of his conduct; and likewise point out some of the most distinguished writers, whose accounts of him justly corroborate that given by the sacred historian.

It is observable that Moses is more diffuse on the history of Joseph, than on that of any other of the patriarchs: indeed, the whole is a master-piece of history: there is not only in the manner throughout such a happy, though uncommon mixture of simplicity and grandeur (which is a double character so hard to be united as is seldom met with in compositions merely human), but it is likewise related with the greatest variety of tender and affecting circumstances, which would afford matter for reflections useful for the conduct of almost every part and stage of the life of man.

Consider him in whatever point of view or in whatever light you will, he must appear amiable and excellent, worthy of imitation, and claiming the highest applause. You see him spoken of in the sacred books with the highest honor; as a person greatly in the favor of God, and protected by him wherever he went, even in so extraordinary a manner as to become the observation of others,—as one of the strictest fidelity in every trust committed to him,—of the most exemplary chastity and honor, that no solicitations could overcome,—of the most fixed reverence for God, in the midst of all the corruptions of an idolatrous court and kingdom,—of the noblest resolution and fortitude, that the strongest temptations could never subdue,—of such admirable sagacity, wisdom, and prudence, that made even a prince and his nobles consider him as under divine inspiration,—of that indefatigable industry and diligence which made him successful in the most arduous attempts,—of the most generous compassion and forgiveness of spirit, that the most malicious and cruel injuries could never weaken or destroy,—as the preserver of Egypt and the neighboring nations, and as the stay and support of his own father and family,—as one patient and humble in adversity,—moderate in the use of power and the height of prosperity,—faithful as a servant, dutiful as a son, affectionate as a brother, and just and generous as a ruler over the people;—in a word, as one of the best and most finished characters, and as an instance of the most exemplary piety and strictest virtue.

———

CHAPTER VIII.

THE distinguished happiness which the descendants of Jacob had possessed during the power invested in their great protector Joseph, was, after his death, materially interrupted by the accession of a new king to the throne of Egypt. This monarch beheld, with a jealous eye, not only the prosperity, but also the great increase, of the Israelites, and began to fear that, in case of an invasion, they might possibly take part with the enemy, and thereby divest him of his regal dignity.

In consequence of these conjectures Pharaoh summoned a council of his principal nobility, to whom he stated the absolute necessity of taking some measures to lessen not only the power, but also the great increase of the Israelites, who were to be considered as strangers in the land where they now dwelt, and, in time, might be prejudicial to the public weal.

The council agreed in opinion with the king; upon which it was resolved not only to impose heavy taxes on them, but to confine them likewise to the hard labor of bearing burdens, digging clay, making bricks, and building strong fortresses in different parts of the kingdom; by means of which their spirits would be sunk, their bodies empoverished, and the great increase that had for some time taken place among them in a great measure stopped.*

No sooner was this resolution formed than it was carried into execution. The wretched Israelites were set about the laborious employ to which they were assigned, and that they might not be negligent in the execution of their business, taskmasters were set over them, whose natural dispositions were so cruel, that they did all in their power to make their lives truly miserable.

* In our engraving on the previous page the woman in the foreground is employed in baking bread at the very usual kind of oven—a hole in the ground. The other women are weaving. Both are the principal employments of women among the pastoral tribes, and were such among the Hebrews. It will be remembered that the hangings for the tabernacle were woven by the women, in the wilderness.

But such was the goodness of God in behalf of the poor Israelites, that Pharaoh's project was far from succeeding to his wishes; for the more they were oppressed, the more they multiplied. This so aggravated the king, and increased his jealousy to such a degree, that, in order to obtain his purposes, he hit upon another expedient. He sent for two of the most eminent of the Egyptian midwives (whose names were Shiprah and Puah), to whom he gave a strict charge, that whenever they were called to do their office to any Hebrew woman, if the child were a male they should privately strangle it, but if a female, they might let it live.

The midwives, touched with the cruelty of this injunction, and fully satisfied in their minds that it was better to obey God than man, paid no regard to Pharaoh's orders, but saved both male and female alike. Irritated at their disobedience, the king sent for them, and reprimanded them for their conduct in very severe terms; but they excused themselves by telling him that the Hebrew women were so much stronger in their constitutions than the Egyptians, and so lively, that they were generally delivered before they could reach them.

The judicious as well as humane conduct of the Egyptian midwives was very acceptable to God; but Pharaoh was highly incensed against them, considering the excuse they made as a mere evasion. He therefore determined not to trust them any longer, but to try another expedient, which might more effectively answer the intended purposes, and totally extirpate the whole male race of the Hebrews. To accomplish this end, he issued out an edict,* commanding that every male born among the Israelites should be thrown into the river and drowned, but that all the females should be saved.

It is not to be wondered at that so barbarous an edict should greatly afflict the already distressed Israelites, and that they should concert various methods whereby they might secure their offspring from the consequences of so inhuman a decree. That methods of this nature were used, will appear from the following circumstances.

Some years before this cruel edict was published, one Amram, of the house of Levi, married a woman named Jochebed, of the same tribe. The first child they had was a daughter, whom they called Miriam, and about four years after she was delivered of a son, whom they named Aaron. In the time of this cruel persecution Jochebed was delivered of another son, who being a child of most exquisite beauty, she was particularly anxious for the preservation of its life.

In hopes of accomplishing her wishes, she concealed the child in her house for three months;† but, not being able to secrete him any longer, and fearful that he would fall into the hands of those appointed to drown the male children, she at length resolved to commit him to the Providence of God. Accordingly, having made a little ark or boat of rushes,‡ and well plastered it, both within and without, with pitch or bitumen, she put the child into it, and going privately down the river, left it among the flags by the bank, placing his sister Miriam at a proper distance to observe the event.

But the Providence of God soon interposed in behalf of the helpless infant. A short time after the mother had left it, Pharaoh's daughter,‖ attended by the maids of

* It is the opinion of most commentators, and the learned in general, that this inhuman edict was so abhorred by the Egyptians, that they scarce ever put it in execution; and that it was recalled immediately after the death of the king who enacted it; which time Eusebius and others place in the fourth year after the birth of Moses.

† Josephus, in speaking of this circumstance, relates the following story: "That Amram, finding his wife with child, and fearing the consequences of the king's edict, prayed earnestly to God to put an end to that dreadful persecution; and that God appeared to him and told him, that he would, in due time, free his people from it, and that the son, who shortly would be born unto him, should prove the happy instrument of their glorious deliverance, and thereby eternise his own name." That this made him conceal him as long as he could, but fearing a discovery, he resolved to trust him to the care of Providence, arguing to this effect: that if the child could be concealed (as it was very difficult to do and hazardous to attempt) they must be in danger every moment, but as to the power and veracity of God, he did not doubt of it, but was assured, that whatever he had promised he would certainly make good; and with this trust and persuasion he was resolved to expose him.

‡ Though his ark, or boat, is said to have been made with rushes, it is most probable that it was formed with flags of the tree papyrus, of which the Egyptians made their paper, and which grew particularly on the banks of the Nile. Clemens Alexandrinus expressly says, that the vessel was made of papyrus, the product of the country: and his assertion is confirmed by several other profane writers.

‖ Josephus calls this princess Thurmuthis; and from him Philo, who adds, that she was the king's only daughter and heir: and that being some time married without having issue, she pretended to be big with child, and to be delivered of Moses, whom she owned as her natural son. That he was esteemed so is evident, from what the Apostle to the Hebrews says, namely, "That when Moses was grown up, he scorned to be thought the son of Pharaoh's daughter." See Heb. xi. 24.

honor, came to the river to bathe herself, and seeing the basket at some distance, she ordered one of her attendants to go and bring it out of the flags. Her orders were immediately obeyed, upon which, no sooner did she uncover the child than it made its mourning complaint to her in a flood of tears. This circumstance, joined to the extraordinary beauty of the infant, so moved her heart with compassion, that (notwithstanding she perceived it was one of those children whom her father, in his edict, had ordered to be drowned) she determined to preserve it, and declared her intention of having it brought up under her direction.

By this time Miriam, the child's sister, had mixed herself with the attendants of the princess, and observing with what tenderness she looked upon her brother, and at the same time hearing her intimate her desire of procuring a proper nurse for it, she very officiously offered her service to procure one. The princess accepted this offer, and ordered her to go immediately and bring the person with her, and she would wait her return. Accordingly, the girl hastened with all expedition to the mother, and soon bringing her to the place, the princess delivered the child into her hands, ordering her to take the utmost care of it, and at the same time told her, that whatever expenses attended the rearing of it, she would defray. This, no doubt, was a welcome bargain to the mother, who, taking the child home with her, nursed it openly, her fears being removed by having a royal protection for its security.

When the child was of a proper age, his mother took him to court, in order to show him to the princess. The graces of his person, joined to the beautiful yet noble simplicity of his countenance, so engaged her attention, that she adopted him as her own son, and gave him the name of Moses.[4] That he might be perfectly accomplished, she kept him constantly at court, where he was instructed in all the learning and discipline, both civil and military, used among the Egyptians, and in every other respect treated in a manner becoming the dignity of a prince of the blood.[†]

Moses continued to live in Pharaoh's court till he arrived at the age of maturity, when he resolved to leave it, and associate himself with his persecuted brethren the Israelites. Observing their wretched state of servility, and the cruel manner in which they were treated by their merciless taskmasters, he was greatly affected; and to such a degree was his indignation raised, that, seeing one day an Egyptian treat a Hebrew in a very cruel manner, he immediately stepped up to his assistance, and, not perceiving any person near, slew him, and buried his body in the sand.[‡]

As he was walking out the next day he met with two Hebrews, in strong contest with each other; upon which he admonished them to consider that they were brethren, and endeavored to decide the quarrel between them. But he who was the aggressor, instead of listening to his advice, treated it with contempt, and upbraided him with having been guilty of murder in killing an Egyptian.

Moses (little suspecting that any one had seen the transactions of the preceding day) was greatly alarmed at this circumstance, being apprehensive as it was known by one, it would circulate from him among the multitude, and that it could not be long before it reached the ears of Pharaoh, in which case it might be attended with the most fatal consequences. To remove, therefore, these disagreeable apprehensions, and secure himself from all danger, he resolved to leave Egypt, which he accordingly did, and fled into the land of Midian,[||] a beautiful and fertile country situated to the east of the Red sea.

* The word *Mo*, in the Egyptian language signifies *water*, and *yees*, *saved*; so that the name Moses was very suitable to the circumstance of his being saved from perishing in the water.

† It is uncertain at what age Moses was delivered to the princess. It is, however, reasonable to suppose that his parents had so well instructed him in their religion, and taken such care to let him know both what relation they bore to him, and what hope they had conceived of his being designed by Heaven to be the deliverer of his nation; that he had made no other use of his education, which the princess gave him, than to confirm himself more and more against the superstitions and idolatry of the Egyptians; and to make himself fit to answer those ends, for which, by Providence, he seemed designed.

‡ We may reasonably suppose that the Egyptian whom Moses slew, through indignation at his brethren's wrongs, was one of the task-masters. It has been questioned how far this action of Moses was justifiable. Le Clerc observes, that, as the Egyptian king authorized the oppression of the Israelites, it was fruitless to apply to him for redress of their grievances. The civil magistrate, who ought to have protected injured innocence, was himself become the oppressor; and, consequently, the society, being degenerated into a confederacy, in oppression and injustice, it was as lawful to use private force and resistance, as against a band of robbers and cut-throats. However, we are to remember, that the Divine hand was in all this: and that thus the way was preparing for the grand deliverance of Israel from Egyptian oppression.

|| Midian is supposed to be that part of Arabia Petræa, which bordered on the land of Goshen, and whose metropolis (called Petrea) was situated not far from Mount Horeb. It is generally agreed that the people of this country originated from Midian, the fourth son of Abraham by Keturah, from whom they were called Midianites.

This was the happy spot where majesty, guarded only by rural innocence, submitted to the humble office of a shepherd, and a crook, instead of a sceptre, graced the hand of the peaceful monarch. Here Jethro (the principal man of the country), in quality both of prince and priest, enjoyed the blessings of a quiet reign, and whose daughters (laying aside the distinction of their birth) took more delight in the innocent employment of tending their father's flocks, than in all the gayeties of a luxurious court.

In the plains of Midian was a well to which it was common for all the neighboring people to drive their flocks to water. Moses, having reached this spot, and being greatly fatigued, after quenching his thirst with the water, sat himself down to rest. He had not been long here before the seven daughters of Jethro came to draw water for their flocks; but they had no sooner filled their vessels than some rude shepherds, who came on the like errand, being resolved to have their turn first served, violently seized on the water drawn by the damsels, and thereby greatly frightened them. Moses, disapproving of such ill conduct in the men, interposed in behalf of the women, and, obliging the shepherds to retire, drew more water for them, and gave it to their flocks. The damsels, in the most engaging manner, made their acknowledgments to him for his services, after which they took leave and hastened home.

Jethro expressed great surprise at the quickness of his daughters' return; upon which they informed him that they had met with a stranger at the well, who not only assisted them, but likewise protected them from the insults of several rustics, who had forcibly taken from them the water they had drawn for their cattle. After hearing this story, and not seeing the person who had thus gallantly defended them, Jethro reprehended his daughters for being guilty of ingratitude and incivility, and asked what had become of the generous stranger. They answered they had left him at the well, upon which he ordered them immediately to return, and invite him home.

The daughters obeyed their father's command, and Moses being introduced into the house of Jethro, he treated him with every mark of the most distinguished respect. And so pleased was Moses with the courteous reception he met with, that, after a short time, he expressed his willingness to take up his abode with him and become his shepherd. Jethro very readily accepted this proposal, and, to attach Moses the more strongly to his interest, gave him his daughter Zipporah in marriage. By this wife he had two sons, the eldest of whom he called Gershom, which signifies a "stranger," alluding to his own condition in that country. The younger he called Eliezar, which signifies "God is my help," in grateful acknowledgment of God's having delivered him from the hands of Pharaoh.

After Moses had been some few years in Jethro's family, the king of Egypt, who was upon the throne at the time he left the country, died; but this was not productive of the least benefit to the persecuted Israelites; his successor was no less a tyrant than himself, and their miseries, instead of being mitigated, were daily increased. At length their complaints reached heaven; the Almighty, remembering the covenant which he had made with their forefathers, looked upon them with an eye of compassion; and having resolved, in his secret providence, to make Moses the principal instrument in bringing about their deliverance, he began to prepare him for so distinguished an undertaking.

As Moses was one day attending his father-in-law's sheep, they happened to stray much farther than usual, upon which he followed them as far into the desert as Mount Horeb. He had no sooner arrived here than the angel of the Lord appeared to him in a flame of fire out of the midst of a bush. So uncommon a sight greatly startled Moses, but what increased his astonishment was the continuance of the bush unconsumed, notwithstanding it appeared to be wholly encompassed with flames.

After reflecting some time on this extraordinary circumstance, Moses resolved to approach nearer the bush, in order, if possible, to discover the cause of its seeming to burn, and yet appearing not to be in the least damaged. But the Almighty, to prevent his irreverent approaches, and to strike the greater awe and sense of the divine presence into him, called out of the bush, and forbade him drawing near; and, to make him still more sensible of the sacredness of the place, commanded him to take off his sandals, because the ground on which he stood was holy.

Moses immediately obeyed the divine order, upon which the Almighty discovered himself to him in these words: "I am the God of thy father, the God of Abraham, the God of Isaac, and the God of Jacob." The frightened Moses was struck with such reverence of the divine Majesty, and fear of the effects of his presumption, that he immediately fell on the ground and covered his face, being unable to sustain the refulgency of the divine presence.

When Moses had a little recovered himself, the Almighty, in words to this effect, addressed him: "I have seen," said he, "the affliction of my people which are in Egypt, and have heard their cry by reason of their taskmasters: for I know their sorrows. And I am come down to deliver them out of the hand of their oppressors, and to conduct them to the promised land, a land flowing with milk and honey. Thee have I chosen to be the instrument in this great work: therefore be of good courage, for I will send thee to Pharaoh, to demand liberty of him for my people the children of Israel."

Moses had long laid aside all thoughts of attempting to rescue his brethren, the Israelites, from their thraldom; nor had he any opinion of his own abilities, should he make the attempt, to succeed in so difficult an undertaking. Wherefore, when the Almighty proposed the thing to him, he endeavored to excuse himself, by urging his meanness and insufficiency to take upon him the character of a divine ambassador. "Who am I," said he, "that I should go unto Pharaoh, and that I should bring forth the children of Israel out of Egypt?" But this difficulty the Almighty removed, by assuring him that he would be with him, and assist him in every step he took; that he would enable him, however perplexed and arduous the task, to accomplish it; and for a token of his veracity herein, told him that within a small compass of time he should see those very people, who were now in slavery, set free and worshipping him on that very mountain.

Still unwilling to undertake the task, Moses desired to know what he should say to the people, and by what name he was to call the person who sent him on the message. To which the Almighty replied, that he should tell him it was an eternal, independent, self-existing Being, the God of Abraham, Isaac, and Jacob, by which name he had ever gone, and by which he would continue to go, to all eternity. He then ordered him to go into Egypt, where, on his arrival, he should first assemble together the chief of the Israelites, and acquaint them with his business; after which he should go directly to the king, and demand of him their liberty, at least for three days, that they might retire into the wilderness, in order to sacrifice to their God. This request, he told Moses, the king would not at first grant, but in the end he would be glad to consent, when he should see the divine power displayed in a variety of miracles which would take place on sundry occasions. "I will exert myself," said he, "in many miraculous operations on him and his subjects, and at last he shall permit you to depart; but you shall not go away empty, for ye shall be loaded with the spoils of the Egyptians."

It might be thought that such solemn assurances, even from the mouth of God himself, would have been sufficient to have gained a ready compliance; but Moses, either from the ideas he entertained of the difficulty of the enterprise, or from diffidence of his own abilities, was still desirous of declining the task, and objected, that when he came into Egypt the people would probably doubt his word, and consider him as an impostor.

This objection God immediately removed by showing him a miracle. Asking him what he had in his hand, he replied, a rod; upon which the Almighty ordered him to throw it on the ground, which he had no sooner done than it was immediately turned into a serpent. Moses, frightened at this sudden change of his rod, attempted to run away; but God, to encourage him, bid him take it up by the tail, which he had no sooner done than it resumed its former shape; and to convince him, at the same time, that he should not want credit with the Israelites, he gave him a commission to perform the same miracle before them when he should get into Egypt.

Still farther to remove Moses's scruples, the Almighty was pleased to give him another instance of his great and distinguished power. He ordered him to put his hand into his bosom, which he accordingly did, and on pulling it out, it was covered all over with leprosy. He then told him to put his hand into his bosom again, which he likewise did, and on taking it out the leprosy was gone, and it became as clean as at first. This miracle he likewise commissioned Moses to show the Israelites; and moreover, to arm him sufficiently beyond all doubt, he was pleased to empower him with a third miracle. "If," says he, "they will not believe these two former, thou shalt take of the water of the river, and pour it upon dry land, and the water shall become blood."

Notwithstanding these solemn and repeated assurances of the divine aid, favor, and protection, Moses still endeavored to waive the important office, urging as a farther plea that he wanted eloquence, the great qualification of an ambassador; and that since God had condescended to talk to him, he was much more deficient in his speech than before. But this obstacle the Almighty was likewise pleased to remove, by putting Moses in mind of his omnipotence. "Who," said he, "hath made man's mouth? or who maketh the dumb, or deaf, or the seeing, or the blind? have not I the Lord? Now therefore go, and I will be with thy mouth, and teach thee what thou shalt say."

Hitherto Moses had some shadow of pretence for his unwillingness to go into Egypt; but now, all his objections being answered, he, in very plain terms, desired to be excused from the enterprise, and begged of God that he would be pleased to appoint some other person in his stead.

So long as Moses had anything to plead in excuse for not going, God heard him patiently, and graciously condescended to remove his doubts; but, when all this was done, and he at length gave an absolute refusal, the Almighty was greatly displeased, though at the same time he did not display any instance of his resentment. On the contrary, he resumed Moses's last objection (which he had already answered in general), and showed him, in a more particular manner, how he should supply that defect: "Is not," said he, "Aaron, the Levite, thy brother? He is eloquent,* and I will appoint him to meet thee. Tell him what I have said; and be assured that I will always assist you both, and direct you what to say. He shall be the orator, and thou shalt be to him instead of God. And to strengthen thy commission, and give thee credit among thy people, take this rod in thy hand, for with it shalt thou be enabled to perform many miracles."

Every obstacle being removed, and the most evincing demonstrations of a miraculous power, together with the protection of Divine Providence, given to Moses, he was at length prevailed on to accept the commission. He accordingly went first to his father-in-law Jethro, and, without telling him the occasion, requested permission to go and visit his brethren, who were then in the land of Egypt.

Jethro readily consented to Moses's request; upon which, taking his wife and children with him, he proceeded on his journey. He had not, however, gone far, when an angel appeared to him, and with a stern countenance, and flaming sword in his hand, threatened to kill him, because, either from the persuasions of his wife or from his own neglect, he had not yet circumcised his younger son Eliezar. As soon as Zipporah understood the cause of the Divine displeasure, she immediately took an instrument made of a sharp flint, and with it circumcised the child; which being done, the angry vision, after giving signs that God was appeased, disappeared.†

While Moses was on his journey to Egypt, Aaron, by a Divine revelation, was informed thereof, and ordered to go and meet him in the wilderness. Aaron obeyed the Divine command, and met his brother at a small distance from Mount Horeb. After mutual embraces and endearments, Moses opened to him the purport of his commission, the instructions he had received from God, and the miraculous works he was empowered to perform.

---

* Moses excelled in wisdom and conduct, Aaron, his brother, in eloquence. Such is the wise order of Providence, which has dispensed different gifts to different persons, that they may each be assisting to one another, and knit more firmly the band of society! Thus Polydamus in Homer, Iliad 13, tells Hector, God gives to different men different accomplishments :

> " To some the powers of bloody war belong,
> To some sweet music, and the charm of song ;
> To few, and wondrous few, has Jove assigned
> A wise, extensive, all-considering mind."—POPE.

† The best interpretation that can be given of this extraordinary circumstance is, that Moses having deferred the circumcision of his youngest son (perhaps in compliance to his wife), God was peculiarly offended with him for such neglect ; not only because Moses knew that no child could be admitted a member of the Jewish community, nor be entitled to the blessings of God's covenant with those people, without circumcision ; but also because *his* example was of the greatest consequence : for who would have regarded the law, if the law-giver himself had neglected it? Zipporah, therefore, conscious of her husband's danger, as well as of her own negligence, immediately performed the office herself ; in consequence of which the cause being removed, God's anger also ceased ; and he suffered Moses to pursue his journey. Zipporah is supposed to have performed the office, because Moses was in too great a consternation to do it himself.

The two brothers, being thus joined in the same commission (though Moses was the sovereign), repaired with all expedition to Egypt. Immediately on their arrival they called an assembly of the chief elders of the Israelites, to whom Aaron declared the message which God had sent by Moses; while the latter, to confirm the truth of his divine mission, wrought the several miracles which God had appointed in the presence of the whole assembly. In consequence of this, they all appeared fully convinced that he was a true prophet come from the God of their fathers, who had at length commiserated their afflictions, and sent him now to deliver them from their bondage; and, with this persuasion, they all knelt down and worshipped God.

A few days after this, Moses and Aaron went to Pharaoh's court, and, having obtained admission to the king, requested of him that he would permit the Israelites to go three days' journey into the wilderness, in order to perform a solemn service to the Lord their God. But the haughty tyrant not only refused complying with their request, but most impiously arraigned the divine prerogative, and called in question the existence of the only wise and true God in these presumptuous words: "Who is the Lord, that I should obey his voice to let Israel go? I know not the Lord, neither will I let Israel go."

Pharaoh suspected that the Israelites had a design of revolting from his service, and that they had been laying schemes to get out of his dominions. This to him was an argument that they had too much leisure time from business, and that the most effectual way to check their contrivances would be to curtail their vacant hours; he therefore ordered greater tasks and more work to be laid on them. He reprimanded Moses and Aaron for going among the people and interrupting them in their employments; and strictly charged the task-masters not to allow them any more straw, and yet to exact the same tale of bricks from them without abatement.

The task-masters acquainted their under-officers with this severe injunction, who immediately communicated it to the people, and they were accordingly forced to wander about the country to seek for straw, the task-masters, at the same time, exacting from them their usual number of bricks; and when they were unable to perform their task, the under-officers, who were Israelites, and whom the task-masters had set over them, were called to account and punished.

Not knowing whence this unreasonable severity proceeded, whether from the royal edict or the rigor of the task-masters, the under-officers addressed the king himself; and, in the most humble manner, laid their grievances before him. But so far were they from receiving any redress, that the answer returned them was—that "the king would have his edict fully executed, and insisted on having their full number of bricks, though he was resolved not to allow them any straw."

This answer greatly afflicted the poor Israelites, insomuch that they were almost driven to despair. On their return from the king they happened to meet Moses and Aaron, and supposing them to be the cause of the additional burden laid on them, expressed their grief and resentment in words to this effect: "That they had taken care to infuse an odium into the king against them, and given him a plausible handle to destroy them, which they wished to God might fall on their own heads."

These bitter expressions greatly afflicted Moses, who, retiring to a private place, addressed himself to God in this humble expostulation: "Why," said he, "O Lord, hast thou thus afflicted the people? For since I spoke to Pharaoh in thy name, he hath treated them with more severity than before, and they are more unlikely to be delivered than ever."

The great concern Moses had for the oppression of the Israelites was certainly the cause of his forgetting the promise which God had given him, as also what he had foretold relative to the perverseness of Pharaoh. But, notwithstanding this, the Almighty was pleased to give him fresh assurances of his divine intentions of removing the Israelites from the state of bondage: "I am the Lord," said he, "the Almighty God, that appeared unto Abraham, Isaac, and Jacob. Was I not known to them by my name Jehovah? Be assured that I the Lord, who made a covenant with them to give their posterity the land of Canaan, have heard their complaints and remembered my promise. Therefore, say thus to the children of Israel, I am Jehovah, who exist only of myself, and give existence to all beings. Tell them I will deliver them from the Egyptian slavery, with the power of my Almighty arm, and inflict heavy judgments on them that oppress them. Nor will I only deliver you all from this bondage, but I will take you under my immediate protection: ye shall be my people, and I will be your God. I am Jehovah, the Lord, that promiseth this, and that can and will do it."

Encouraged by this gracious and divine declaration, Moses immediately repaired to the Israelites, to whom he delivered his message as God had commanded. But such was their affliction of mind, in consequence of the increase of their servitude, and which they attributed to have arisen from him, that they paid no attention to what he said. They were prejudiced against him, and rather looked upon him as an enemy than as one who was desirous of procuring their enlargement.

The Almighty, fully resolved to pursue the ends of his Providence, again commanded Moses to go to the king of Egypt and demand the liberty of the Israelites. Having been so roughly dismissed from Pharaoh's presence before, and so unkindly rejected by the Israelites, Moses endeavored to decline the errand by drawing an argument from each circumstance: "Since," says he, "the children of Israel, thine own people, would not hear me, though what I offered was so much to their advantage, how can I expect that so wicked a prince as Pharaoh is should pay any attention to so insignificant a person* as I am, and in a matter so much to his loss?"

To remove this objection, the Almighty was pleased to address himself to Moses in words to this effect: "Consider," said he, "I have made thee as a God† to Pharaoh and Aaron, thy brother, shall be thy interpreter, or orator. Thou shalt tell him all that I have commanded thee, and ye shall demand of Pharaoh the deliverance of my people. And that thou mayest not be discouraged by a repulse, as before, take notice that Pharaoh shall give no credit to what thou sayest, that I may thereby show my power and wonders to him and his people, and deliver the children of Israel by the strength of my hand. For since Pharaoh has begun to harden his heart in contemptuously treating me and abusing my people, I will now permit him to go on in his obstinate humor, that I may exert my power in miraculous operations in the land of Egypt. Therefore, when ye come into Pharaoh's presence, and he shall demand a miracle of you, to convince him of the truth of your mission, thou shalt direct Aaron to cast his rod on the ground before Pharaoh, and it shall be turned into a serpent."

In consequence of these instructions, Moses and Aaron went again to the king, and repeated their demand of his dismissing the Israelites. Pharaoh desired them to show him some miracle, whereby he might be induced to believe, that the God, of whom they had so much spoken, had really sent for them. Upon this Aaron threw down his rod, which had no sooner touched the ground, than it was changed into a living serpent.

Though Pharaoh was somewhat surprised at this incident, yet he was determined, if possible, to make it appear of no great importance. To effect this, he sent for his principal magicians, whom he ordered to try, if, by their magical arts, they could cause the like transmigration. They obeyed the king's commands, and, to his great satisfaction, their attempts succeeded. They threw down their rods, which were immediately changed into serpents, only with this remarkable circumstance, that Aaron's rod swallowed up (while in the figure of a serpent) all those of the magicians, after which it resumed its accustomed form. It might have been supposed, that this would have been sufficient to have convinced the proud monarch of the superior power of the God of Israel; but his heart was so averse to the thoughts of parting with the Hebrews, that it did not in the least affect him.

As this miracle made no impression on the obstinate tyrant, the Almighty resolved to make use of more forcible scourges, and to afflict the Egyptians with such a suc-

* It is remarkable, that in the text Moses here calls himself an uncircumcised person, or rather a man whose lips had not been circumcised. See Exod. vi. 12. By this we are to understand, that he meant no more than that he was not possessed of that fluency of speech which was necessary on so important an occasion. The word *circumcised* is phraseologically used by the Hebrews on several occasions, as when they call any one *uncircumcised in heart, mind,* or *tongue,* they mean no more than that the person spoken of is not so perfect in these particulars as might be wished. Besides, as circumcision was the first and greatest sacrament among them, so uncircumcision was esteemed the greatest scandal and disgrace. The phrase, therefore, naturally and clearly expresses the humble opinion Moses had for himself, his unfitness for such an office, and his inability to persuade or prevail with so haughty a monarch as Pharaoh.

† The word here translated a God, signifies a prince, a counsellor, or governor; and as Moses was to work many wonders in the land of Egypt, so there is no doubt but Pharaoh would look upon him as a person endued with supernatural power. It was then beginning to grow common with the heathen nations, particularly the Egyptians, to rank their great men among the number of their gods; and, therefore, when the Lord here speaks to Moses, he does not say that he made him an object of worship, but only that he would endue him with so much power, that the Egyptians would look upon him as a God.

cession of plagues as should compel them to dismiss the long-enslaved Israelites. Having observed to Moses, that Pharaoh's heart was hardened, he ordered him to take the rod, which had been turned into a serpent, and (in company with his brother Aaron) to throw himself in the way of Pharaoh, at his usual time of coming to the banks of the river Nile. That as soon as he saw the king, he should again demand of him the liberty of the Israelites; and that if he still continued obstinate, as a farther sign that they were messengers from God, he should give the rod to Aaron, who, by striking it on the water, should immediately change it into blood.

In obedience to the divine command, Moses, at the time appointed, went to the bank of the river, soon after which the king arriving, he accosted him in words to this effect: "That he was sent from the Almighty God of the Hebrews, to demand the release of the Israelites, and that if he did not comply with his request, but still remained obstinate, his God should not only afflict him for his perverseness, but bring down the most heavy judgments on his people."

The infidel prince, regardless of the order of God, by these two appointed missionaries, still persisted in his resolution (so little did the first miracle operate on his mind) of detaining the Israelites, and continuing them in their wretched state of bondage. Finding all remonstrances in vain, Moses delivered his rod to Aaron, who, striking the water with it, as God had commanded him, it changed into blood, and so continued for the space of seven days, by means of which the fish were suffocated, and the inhabitants compelled to dig for water to allay their thirst. As it was known that Moses received his education among the Egyptians, Pharaoh concluded, that all this was performed by magic skill. Wherefore, calling for his magicians, he put them upon the like trial; who, taking some water out of the wells they had dug, so artfully changed its color, as to make it appear like blood. Though this was but a delusion, yet Pharaoh was satisfied in his own mind that what Moses and Aaron had done was not the effect of any supernatural power, but a mere trick of art; and therefore still resolved not to permit the departure of the Israelites.

But the Almighty was pleased to display still farther miracles before this impious and obstinate tyrant. When the seven days were expired, and the waters had resumed their natural qualities, Moses, at the command of God, accosted Pharaoh again, and renewed his solicitations for the delivery of the Israelites, threatening, on his refusal, to bring upon the land such prodigious numbers of frogs, as should visit him and his subjects in their most private recesses.

Pharaoh, regardless of these threats, defied him; upon which Moses ordered Aaron to take his rod, and stretch forth his hand with it over the rivers, which in an instant affected all the waters of Egypt, that, not waiting for the slow productions of nature, the animated streams unburdened themselves upon the land in shoals of frogs, which immediately invaded all parts of the country, and infested even the royal palace itself.*

The obstinate and perverse king had again recourse to his magicians, who, by their mimic power, so deluded Pharaoh as to make him believe they had wrought the like miracle. This hardened his heart for a time; but the loathsome plague continuing, and pursuing his people wherever they went, he was at length forced to apply to Moses and Aaron, to whom he promised that the Israelites should have their liberty, provided their God would remove so infestuous a plague. "Entreat the Lord," said he, "that he may take away the frogs from me, and from my people; and I will let the people go that they may do sacrifice unto the Lord."

Moses demanded the time when this should be put to an issue, upon which the next day was conjunctively agreed on. Accordingly, Moses, in order to fulfil his part of the contract, after leaving Pharaoh, retired to a private place, and, addressing himself to God, humbly besought him to remove the plague of the frogs from the land of Egypt. The Almighty was pleased to listen to Moses's solicitations: the frogs soon died, which the people gathered together in heaps; but they were so numerous, that before they could be removed, the scent, which was exceeding obnoxious, spread itself throughout the whole country.

* This plague of the frogs, as well as that of the water being changed into blood, was excellently adapted to subvert the superstitions of Egypt, and to demonstrate the over-ruling power of the Almighty; for as the bank of the river Nile was the grand scene of the magical operations of the Egyptians, in which blood and frogs made a principal part of the apparatus; so, by commanding that river to produce such an infinite multitude of these creatures to annoy them, God, with wonderful propriety, adapted their chastisement to the nature of their crimes: for frogs were not only the instruments of their abominations, but likewise the emblems of those impure demons whom they invoked by their incantations.

River Nile, under its usual appearance.

As Moses had now fulfilled his part of the contract, he naturally expected that Pharaoh would have performed his; but the impious monarch, vainly imagining that the artillery of divine vengeance was now exhausted, unfaithfully broke his word, and still refused to let the Israelites depart.

This breach of promise so offended the Almighty, that he resolved to treat the haughty tyrant in a more severe manner than he had hitherto done. As yet God had given him previous notice of the judgments he intended to denounce, that he might have the opportunity of escaping them; but now, without giving him the least intimation of his design, he commanded Moses to direct Aaron to stretch out his rod, and strike the dust with it, that it might *become lice throughout all the land of Egypt.* Aaron had no sooner obeyed the divine command, than the animated dust was immediately turned into swarms of vermin, which not only infested the human species, but also the beasts of the field. Pharaoh again had recourse to his magicians, who (though they had faintly imitated the former plagues) now attempted this in vain: they owned their art outdone, and acknowledged this to be the inimitable work of a divine hand.

But notwithstanding this, Pharaoh's heart was so hardened, that he would not pay the least attention to the solicitations of Moses; upon which the Almighty was pleased to give him another summons, in words to this effect: " Rise up," says he to Moses, " early in the morning, and meet Pharaoh as he comes to the river: tell him, Thus saith the Lord: let my people go, that they may serve me, or I will send swarms of flies upon thee and thy people, which shall fill their houses, and cover the face of the earth. And that thou mayest know, that this is brought as a judgment upon thee and thy subjects, for oppressing my people, I will, on that day, separate the land of Goshen, in which my servants dwell, from the rest of Egypt, that the flies shall not molest them."

Moses, in conformity to the divine command, delivered this message to Pharaoh, whose obstinacy and perverseness were so great, that he still refused the Israelites to depart. In consequence of this, the next day, clouds of swarming insects filled the air, which in numberless troops descended to the earth, and, with their unusual noise, surprised and affrighted the wretched inhabitants. All attempts to remove this dreadful calamity proved vain and fruitless; their most private recesses could not secure them from the poisonous stings of these obnoxious animals, and a succession of painful misery invaded them on all sides. The magicians beheld, with confusion, this direful plague, and no more attempted to offer any imitation. A general horror was spread throughout the whole country, and every part echoed with the cries of tortured men and cattle.

Not being able longer to endure this dreadful calamity, and finding no likelihood of its being removed, the obstinate Pharaoh sent for Moses and Aaron, and, in a sullen dissatisfied tone, bade them go and sacrifice to their God; but with this injunction, that they should not pass beyond the bounds of Egypt. He was desirous of obtaining relief, but, at the same time, was unwilling to part with a people, from whose slavery he had reaped such great advantage. Being a stranger to the true God, he did not conceive that the Israelites could not acceptably sacrifice to their God while under Egyptian bondage.

Moses, desirous of convincing rather than inflaming, the infidel prince, prudently answered: " We can not sacrifice to our God in this land, for that would be an affront to the Egyptians,* and they will be revenged on us. Permit us, therefore, to avoid their resentment, by going three days' journey into the wilderness, where we can sacrifice to our God in the manner he hath commanded."

In reply to this, the haughty monarch said, " If nothing else will serve you but to go into the desert, I will let you go; but remember, it must not be far. And in return for this concession, I desire you will entreat your God to remove the plague."

Moses promised to intercede for him, but at the same time cautioned him to be sincere in what he said, and not violate his engagements as he had before done. Leaving Pharaoh, Moses retired to a proper place, where he addressed himself to God, be-

---

* The meaning of this expression is, that the animals which they were to sacrifice to the Lord, being those which were worshipped by the Egyptians, it would be such an affront and abomination to them, as would endanger the lives of the Israelites. Herodotus tells us, that the Egyptians esteemed it a profanation to sacrifice any kind of cattle except swine, bulls, calves, and geese; and that heifers, rams, and goats (the usual sacrifices of the Israelites), were, by them, held sacred. It is, therefore, no wonder that the Israelites should wish to offer up their sacrifices in a place detached from the sight of the Egyptians, justly suspecting, that had they not, it might have been attended with fatal consequences.

seeching him to remove the plague of the flies. His prayers were accordingly heard, and the insects soon took their flight. But this obstacle was no sooner removed, than the haughty tyrant reassumed his former obstinacy, and peremptorily forbid the Israelites worshipping their God in the way and manner he had directed.

This additional provocation so incensed the Almighty against Pharaoh, that he again sent Moses to him with this message: "Tell him," said he, "Thus saith the God of the Hebrews, let my people go, that they may serve me, or be assured I will visit all thy cattle that are in the field with a grievous murrain; and to make thee still more sensible of my Omnipotence, I will, by a wonderful distinction, preserve the cattle of my people, while I destroy those of the Egyptians."

Pharaoh paid no more attention to this message than he had done to the former, in consequence of which, the very next day, this awful threat was most severely executed. The generous horse loathed his full manger and loved pastures, and sunk beneath his rider; the ass and camel could no longer support their burdens, or bear their own weight; the laboring ox fell dead before the plough; the harmless sheep died bleating, and the faithful dogs lay gasping by them.

Though this was certainly a most horrid spectacle, yet it made not the least impression on the hardened Pharaoh, who still resolved to brave Heaven with his impious perverseness. Remembering what Moses had said of the preservation of the Israelites' cattle, he sent to Goshen to learn how it had fared with them, and was assured that not one of their cattle had died, or received the least infection. This circumstance was certainly sufficient to have convinced him that it was no casualty, but a direct judgment upon him, seeing that it exactly answered the divine prediction. But notwithstanding this, his heart was so callous, that he still preserved the resolution of not suffering the Israelites to depart.

These means proving ineffectual, the Almighty, in order to make some impression on the mind of this impious monarch, determined to afflict him and his people with a plague, and that without giving him the least notice of his intentions. He accordingly commanded Moses and Aaron to take ashes of the furnace, and throw them into the air in the presence of Pharaoh. This was accordingly done, upon which the ashes soon spread the dire contagion, and the tainted air infected the Egyptian blood with its pernicious influence. The most inveterate biles and ulcers appeared on their flesh, and their whole constitution became a noisome spring of sores. So universal was this plague, that even the magicians (who, it is probable, would willingly have once more tried their skill) were affected, and that in such manner, that they dared not appear in public.

Pharaoh's obstinacy, which before proceeded from an implacable hatred to the chosen people of God, now arose from the mere hardness of his heart, and notwithstanding he must be sensible that the present plague was the immediate effect of a divine and supernatural direction, yet he continued firm in his resolution of detaining the Israelites. But the Almighty, determined to make some impression on him, rendered the very powers of Heaven subservient to his divine purpose, giving this charge to his servant Moses: "Go," says he, "early in the morning, to the king of Egypt, and tell him, that I, the God of the Hebrews, demand the liberty of my people, that they may worship me; which, if he refuse, he may be assured that I will shower my plagues upon him and his people; and I will make him know that I am the only God on earth. Say farther to him: If, when lately I smote the cattle with a murrain, I had smitten thee and thy people with pestilence, thou hadst been cut off from the earth. But I have reserved thee to show my power, and by the judgments I shall inflict will I make known my name to all the world. Oppress not, nor detain my people; for if thou dost, to-morrow, by this time, unless thou submitteth thyself, I will send such a storm of hail from heaven upon Egypt as never was known since it has been a nation. And that thou mayest not lose what cattle the murrain left, which being not in the field escaped that plague, send thy servants, and let them drive them under shelter; for upon every man and beast, which shall be found in the field, the storm shall fall, and they shall surely die."

So careless, as well as impious, was Pharaoh, that even this declaration would not make him submit, though his own life, as well as those of his people, was in imminent danger. But some of them, who had been witnesses of the dreadful wrath of God, made a prudent use of the divine caution, and, housing their cattle in time, they were preserved from the general destruction.

The appointed time being come, Moses, in obedience to the divine command, waved his rod in the air, which soon began to murmur in imperfect sounds, till the full charged clouds, with impetuous force, burst and discharged themselves in such horrid peals of thunder, as to shake the whole frame of nature. This was succeeded by a stormy shower of hail, which covered the ground with the scattered remains of trees and houses, and the dead bodies of men and beasts. Nor did the divine vengeance stop here: the heavens discharged a body of liquid fire, which, darting on the ground, glided over the waters, and filled every place with the most dreadful horror.

The haughty tyrant began now to be impressed with those sensations to which he had hitherto been a stranger. Seeing all nature, as he imagined, ready to dissolve, he melted into penitence, and, sending for Moses and Aaron, confessed himself guilty. " I have sinned this time," said he; " the Lord is righteous, and I and my people are wicked. Entreat the Lord that there be no more mighty thunderings and hail; and I will let you go, and ye shall stay no longer." Moses promised to comply with this request, but at the same time assured him, he knew there was no sincerity in his heart; and that his seeming repentance was only the effect of his fright.

Moses, however, in conformity to his promise, addressed himself to the Almighty, beseeching him to remove the plague; which was no sooner done, than his prediction was verified: for, when Pharaoh found the storm was ceased, and all was calm and serene, his fears totally vanished, his perverseness returned, and he resolved still to keep the Israelites in a state of bondage.

The Almighty was now pleased to make another trial, and to send his servant Moses to apprize the haughty and perfidious tyrant of his intentions. The message he delivered to Moses was prefaced by his reasons (as, indeed, he had done before) why he permitted Pharaoh to continue in his obstinacy; the substance of which, together with the message itself, was to this effect: " I have," says he, " hardened Pharaoh's heart, and the hearts of his servants, that I may show these my wonders before them, and that thou mayest tell, in the hearing of thy sons, and the Israelites to succeeding generations, what prodigies I have wrought in Egypt, that ye may all know that I am the Lord, the Almighty Jehovah. Wherefore, go to Pharaoh, and tell him, Thus saith the Lord God of the Hebrews, Why dost thou persist in thy obstinacy? Let my people go, that they may serve me, or I will bring the locusts into thy land to-morrow, which shall come in such swarms, as to cover the surface of the earth, and devour all the products of it that have escaped the former plagues. And this shall prove such a plague as none of thy predecessors ever saw."

This message Moses carefully delivered to Pharaoh in the presence of his nobles, and, not receiving any answer to it, he retired. As soon as he was gone, Pharaoh's courtiers, still sensibly impressed with the late calamities, and fearful that he was about to call down more plagues upon them, very roughly accosted their king, desiring him to let the Israelites go and serve their God, lest, for his obstinacy, not only himself, but also the whole people of his kingdom, should be totally destroyed.

The importunity of Pharaoh's courtiers prevailed more than God's threats and judgments. He immediately despatched a messenger after Moses and Aaron, who accordingly returning, he told them they might go and serve their God; but under this limitation, that it should only be the men, for that all the women and children should be left behind. This, however, would not do for Moses: he insisted that all the Israelites should go, both old and young, sons and daughters; nay, and their flocks and herds; " for," said he, " we must hold a feast to the Lord, and all must be at it." Pharaoh considered this demand as not only peremptory, but insolent: he therefore bade them look to it, and consider well what they insisted on; after which, in a very threatening manner, he dismissed them.

This repulse occasioned another judgment to be inflicted on the miserable subjects of an infidel king; for Moses, by the divine command, stretched out his hand, with the rod in it, and immediately a scorching wind blew all that day and the succeeding night; the consequence of which was, the next morning there appeared endless legions of locusts, which, in a short time, so devoured the fruits of the earth, that it became, as it were, quite naked: the happy productions arising from the fertile Nile, and all that bountiful nature afforded, were carried off by these airy pillagers, and nothing appeared but horror and desolation throughout the land of Egypt.

The hardened Pharaoh was more sensibly affected at this plague, than he had been at any of the former. He plainly saw that the destruction of the fruits of the earth must be succeeded by the destruction of man and beast. Wherefore, sending for Moses and Aaron, he, in a more suppliant manner, addressed them in words to this effect: "I have, indeed, offended Jehovah your God, in refusing to obey his command, and you, in so often breaking my word with you: forgive me this offence, and entreat your God to avert this judgment, that I and my people perish not by devouring famine."

Moses, once more compassionating the case of the justly afflicted king, addressed himself to the Almighty in his behalf, and the locusts, by the force of a strong westerly wind, were driven into the Red sea. But this plague was no sooner removed than Pharaoh's obstinacy and contempt of God's commands returned, and he again refused the departure of the Israelites.

All these methods to reduce Pharaoh to an obedience of the Divine command proving ineffectual, the Almighty commanded Moses to stretch forth his hand toward heaven, that there might be a universal darkness, such as before had never been known, throughout the land of Egypt.

Moses obeyed the Divine command, immediately on which such solid and thick clouds of darkness invaded the sky, that nature seemed at once to be involved in one dreadful eclipse: the sun no longer enlightened the lower world with his cheerful beams; the moon, with the stars, no more illuminated the air; and so dismal was the aspect of all things, that nature appeared as if about to return to her original chaos.

This dreadful scene of horror lasted three days, and the haughty Pharaoh was so affected at it, that though he had long stood immoveable against the threats and judgments of God, yet he now, fearing a universal dissolution, and frightened at the continual terror of this long night, began seriously to relent, and sending for Moses, thus addressed him:—"Ye may go," said he, "with your little ones, and serve the Lord; but, for my security, I would have you leave your flocks and herds behind."

But this not being absolutely consistent with the Divine command, Moses would not accept it. He told Pharaoh that it was the express command of their God to remove with *all* their substance; and that they knew not in what manner they were to offer sacrifice to their God, nor should they till they came into the wilderness.

The haughty tyrant, incensed at the non-compliance of Moses to what he esteemed a distinguished indulgence, commanded him to be gone, and, with great austerity, told him if he ever appeared before him again, it should cost him his life.

Moses promised Pharaoh he should never again see his face; but, by the Divine command, he once more visited him, and that with a message more severe than any he had yet delivered. "Tell him," says the Almighty to Moses, "in the hearing of his people, Thus saith the Lord, About midnight will I go out into the midst of Egypt. And all the first-born in the land of Egypt shall die, from the first-born of Pharaoh that sitteth upon his throne, even unto the first-born of the female servant that is behind the mill;* and all the first-born of beasts. And there shall be a great cry throughout all the land of Egypt, such as was never before, nor shall be again. But the children of Israel shall not be in the least affected, that ye may know the distinction made by the Lord between you and them. And all thy servants shall come down unto me, saying, Get thee out, and all the people that follow thee; and after that will I go out myself."

Moses delivered this message to Pharaoh in the manner he had been commanded. But the haughty tyrant defied his threats, and still persisted in his obstinacy that the Israelites should not depart from Egypt; upon which Moses, finding him inflexible, turned away and left him.

Previous to the carrying of this last sentence into execution, the Almighty instructed Moses and Aaron in what manner to direct the people to prepare the passover, which

* It was usual for the lowest slaves to be employed in the drudgery of the mill; and therefore the prophet Isaiah uses this idea, to express the abject state of slavery to which Babylon should be reduced: "Come down, and sit in the dust, O virgin daughter of Babylon: sit on the ground, take the mill-stones and grind meal." Isaiah lvii. 1, 2. Dr. Shaw observes, that most families in those countries still grind their wheat and barley at home, having two portable mill-stones for that purpose; the uppermost whereof is turned round by a small handle of wood, or iron, which is placed in the rim. When the stone is large, or expedition is required, then a second person is called in to assist; and, it is usual for the *women* alone to be concerned in this employment, who seat themselves over against each other, with the mill-stones between them. We may see not only the propriety of the expression in this verse, of sitting *behind the mill*, but the force of another, Matt. xxiv. 41, that "Two women shall be grinding at the mill; the one shall be taken, and the other left."

was to be a feast in commemoration of their departure out of Egypt, and was to be held on the day preceding that event.* The directions which, by the Divine command, Moses gave to the people on this occasion, were to the following effect: that every family of Israel (or, if the family was too small, two neighboring families joining together) should, on the tenth† day of the month, take a lamb, or kid, and having shut it up till the fourteenth day, then kill it. That the lamb, or kid, should be a male not above a year old, and without any manner of blemish: that, when they killed it, they should catch the blood in a vessel, and, with a bunch of hyssop dipped in it, sprinkle the side posts of the outer door, after which they should not stir out of the house till the next morning. In the meantime, they were to eat the lamb, or kid (dressed whole and without breaking a bone of it), neither raw nor sodden, but roasted, with unleavened bread and bitter herbs; that if there was more than they could dispense with, they were to bury it; and, lastly, that the posture in which they were to eat it was to be in a hurry, with their clothes‡ on their shoulders and their staves in their hands, as if they were just upon the point of going to depart.

The tremendous night was not long delayed. While the Jews were celebrating this newly instituted feast—at midnight—the destroying angel went forth in a pestilence, and smote all the first-born in the land of Egypt,—"from the first-born of Pharaoh, that sat on his throne, to the first-born of the captive that lay in the dungeon; and all the first-born of cattle." And there was a great cry in Egypt—lamentation and bitter weeping—for there was not a house in which there was not one dead.

The effect of this dreadful blow was exactly such as Moses had foretold. The king, his nobles, and the Egyptian people, rose in sorrow from their beds that night. The shrieks of the living, with the groans of those about to die, breaking in upon the stillness of the night—the darkness of which must greatly have aggravated the horror and confusion of that hour—made the people fancy they were all doomed to destruction, and that the work of death would not cease till they had all perished. The king himself was filled with horror and alarm. Without truly repenting his obduracy, he bitterly lamented its effects. It appeared to him that the only method of arresting the progress of the destruction was to send the Hebrews instantly away—in the fear that every moment they tarried would prove the loss of a thousand lives to Egypt. He therefore sent to Moses and Aaron by that very night—that hour—to tell them, "Get you forth from among my people, both ye and the children of Israel; and go and serve the Lord as ye said; take *also your flocks and herds*, and begone; and bless me also." And the Egyptian people also, says the scriptural narrative, were urgent upon them, to send them away in haste; for they said, "We are all dead men." In their anxiety to get them off, lest every moment of their stay should prove the last to themselves or those dear to them, the Egyptians would have done anything to satisfy and oblige them. This favorable disposition had been foreseen from the beginning, and the Hebrews had been instructed by Moses to take advantage of it, by borrowing ornaments of precious metal—"Jewels of gold and jewels of silver," with rich dresses, from the Egyptians. On the principle that, "all that a man hath he will give for his life," there can be no doubt but that, under circumstances which made them consider their own lives in jeopardy, and when the losses they had sustained were calculated to make their finery seem of small value in their sight, the Egyptians were quite as ready to

* These directions given by the Almighty to Moses are introduced by the following passage: "This month shall be unto you the beginning of months; it shall be the first day of the first month of the year to you." The Jews, like most other nations, began their year, before this event, about the autumnal equinox, in the month Tifri, after their harvest and vintage: but that which was their first month, now became their seventh; as the month of Abib, which answers principally to our March, was, by God's appointment, and in commemoration of this their deliverance, constituted the first month of their sacred year. Abib signifies *the green corn;* and the month was so named, because, about this time, the corn in those countries began to ripen.

† The passover, or feast was to be celebrated on the fourteenth day of the month, so that four days were allowed previous to its being held. In after-times the Jews did not begin their preparations till the thirteenth, or the day preceding the passover: but here, they are ordered to prepare on the tenth day of the month, not only because this being the first time of the celebration of the passover, they might require more time to prepare for a ceremony entirely new, but because, being to depart from Egypt suddenly, and in great haste, they might be perfectly ready, and have no hinderance to make them neglect any part of the duty enjoined.

‡ These clothes were slight thin garments, resembling those which the Arabs now wear, and which they call *hykes.* "These hykes," says Dr. Shaw, "are of various sizes, and of different qualities and fineness. The usual size of them is six yards long and two broad. It serves them for a complete dress in the day; and, as they sleep in their raiments, as the Israelites did of old (Deut. xxiv. 13) it serves likewise for their bed and covering at night."

Ornaments of Egyptian Females.

lend as the Hebrews to borrow. The women also were authorized to borrow from the Egyptian females : and we may easily believe that their exertions added much to the large amount of valuable property which was extracted from the fears of the Egyptians. With whatever understanding these valuable articles were given and received, the ultimate effect is, that in this final settlement, the Hebrews received something like wages—though, as such, inadequate—for the long services they had rendered to the Egyptians.*

So eager were the Egyptians to get them off, that, between persuasions, bribery, and gentle compulsion, the whole body had commenced its march before daybreak, although it was not till midnight that the first-born had been slain. They had no time even to bake the bread for which the dough was ready; and they were, therefore, obliged to leave it in their dough bags, which they carried away, wrapped up in their clothes, with the view of preparing their bread when an opportunity might be offered by their first halt. Hurried as they were, they forgot not the bones of Joseph, which they had kept at hand, and now bore away with them. On they marched, driving before them their cattle and their beasts of burden, laden with their moveables and tents; and themselves, some, doubtless, riding on camels, some on asses; but, from the great number of these required for the women and the children, most of the men doubtless marched on foot. Thus, laden with the spoils of Egypt, they went on their way rejoicing, leaving the Egyptians to the things which belong to mourning and the grave.

We are told that the number of the Israelites who on this eventful night commenced their march was "about six hundred thousand men on foot, besides women and children." The description of "men on foot" denotes, as elsewhere appears, men fit to bear arms, excluding therefore not only those who are too young, but those who are too old for such service. As this prime class of the community is usually in the proportion of one fourth of the whole population, the result would give nearly two millions and a half as the number of the posterity of Jacob. This number is so very high, that it has seemed incredible to many. We must confess, that it is difficult to realize the presence of so vast a host, with their flocks and herds, and to form an idea of the immense area they would cover, were only standing-room given to them, much more where encamped under tents ;—and when we further consider the length and breadth of their moving body on a march, as well as the quantities of water they would require, we may be tempted to conclude that a much smaller number would amply justify the promises of God, and would render many circumstances in the ensuing portion of their history more easy to be understood. Besides this, the ancient manner of notation afforded temptations and facilities for the corruption of numbers, whence it happens that the most disputed texts of Scripture, and those in which, as the copies now stand, there are palpable contradictions, are those which contain numerical statements. We are not insensible to these considerations, and have endeavored to assign them all the weight which they are entitled to bear. But seeing that the present number, high as it is, has some support from collateral evidence, and from

* THE "BORROWED" JEWELS.—Much learning and labor have been bestowed on explanations of this transaction. The most general improvement which has been suggested is, that we should assign the sense of "ask," or "demand," to the word which most versions translate into "borrow :" and the meaning will then be, that the Hebrews availed themselves of the consternation in which they saw the Egyptians, to demand these valuable articles, in compensation for the long service they had rendered. In this explanation one little circumstance is forgotten, which is, the probability that these precious articles were obtained from persons who had never any direct benefit from, or interest in, their services. It seems to us that not so much as is commonly supposed is gained by this alteration. We prefer to adhere to the more received view of the case ; because that seems more in agreement with all the circumstances which surround the transaction. The explanation proceeds on the notion that the Israelites had avowed their intention to escape ; for, had it been presumed that they intended to return, it would have been a piece of the grossest and most fatal madness in them to "demand" this valuable property from the Egyptians in a compulsory manner. But their intention to withdraw altogether was never avowed while they were in Egypt. Moses never avowed it. Even when rather closely pressed on the subject, he persisted, at least by implication, that there was no other object than that of holding a feast to Jehovah at the distance of three days' journey into the wilderness, and the ulterior intention was not distinctly avowed by the move which was made from "Etham on the edge of the wilderness." This, therefore, only being the avowed object of the Israelites, it must have seemed perfectly natural to the Egyptians that they should wish to appear as richly attired as possible at the great feast they were about to celebrate ; and as natural, that they should borrow such articles as they, in their state of bondage and poverty, did not possess. The consternation they were in at the death of their first-born, and their haste to get the Hebrews away, precluded much deliberation. But by the time the Israelites moved from Etham there had been leisure for reflection, and they manifested their sense that the substance with which they parted on that occasion had only been lent, by the haste which they made to recover it, as soon as they became assured that the Hebrews intended to escape.

the considerations to which we have already adverted, and, above all, reflecting that the present number is a positive circumstance, whereas all alteration could only be conjectural,* we deem it the best and safest course to take the number as we find it in the present copies of the Pentateuch. But besides the descendants of Jacob, there was a large "mixed multitude," which went out of Egypt on this occasion. Who they were is not clearly stated; but it would appear that the mass was formed of foreign slaves, belonging to the principal persons among the Hebrews, with a good number, probably, belonging to the Egyptians, who were glad to take the opportunity of escaping with the Israelites. Besides this, there were manifestly a considerable number of Egyptians of the poorer class, who perhaps expected to better their condition in some way, or had other very good reasons for leaving Egypt: indeed, as it did not turn out that the Israelites were anything the better for their presence, we are free to confess that we think it likely they were chiefly such thieves, vagabonds, adventurers, and debtors, as could no longer stay safely in Egypt.

The circumstance that Moses was so well acquainted with the number of the Israelites before they left Egypt, intimates that an account of their numbers had not long before been taken by the Egyptians. That ingeni-

* So conjectural that while some strike off one cipher, reducing 600,000 to 60,000, others are not content without taking off two, thus reaching the certainty to a very convenient and manageable number of 6,000. Another conjecture has been that the 600,000 includes the population, and not merely the men fit to bear arms; but this is precluded by the terms of the text, "besides women and children."

ous people employed very early, if they did not invent, the practice of taking a census of what is called the effective part of the population; and from them, unquestionably, the Israelites, under the direction of Moses, adopted this useful custom. In all such enumerations, in ancient times, the women and children were not included, and their number is never stated. But probably they were able to form an estimate of the proportion which the numbered part of the population bore to the whole; although their conclusions in this matter must have been more uncertain than our own, which have been found on repeated actual enumerations of portions of the entire population which were never included in the ancient enumerations.

The point from which the Hebrew host started on their march was Rameses, one of the " treasure cities" which they had built for Pharaoh in the land of Goshen, and which seems to have become the chief place in the territory they occupied. The difficulties in tracing their march begin at the very first stage.

There are two preliminary questions, satisfactory information on which would much assist us in understanding the early part of their journey. The first is, the situation of Rameses, from which they started; and the second, the point to which their journey was, in the first instance, directed. On the first point no very satisfactory information can be obtained. It is, indeed, not quite clear that any particular locality is intended, or whether the land of Goshen, in the large indefinite sense, may not be denoted by "the land of Rameses." But some information is reflected upon the first by the answer to the second of these questions, which answer is, that the destination which was in the first instance contemplated, was doubtless the wilderness of Sinai. The land of Goshen appears most evidently to have bordered on, if it did not include, part of the tract over which the nearest and most convenient road to the peninsula of Sinai from the banks of the Nile has always passed. This is nearly the line in which, in after ages, a canal was made connecting the Nile with the Gulf of Suez; and that, while it is the nearest route, it is the only one which offers a supply of water, is a consideration which doubtless as much recommended it in ancient times to those going from Egypt to Sinai or Arabia, as it does now recommend it to the great caravan of pilgrimage which yearly journeys from Cairo to Mecca. The route of this caravan is the same, as far as the head of the Gulf of Suez, as one would take which proceeds to the Desert of Sinai. We shall therefore presume that this *was* the route taken.

If the Hebrews were to have gone direct to take possession of the Promised Land, their nearest road would have been " by the way of the Philistines;" that is, by the usual route from Egypt to Gaza. But the Philistines were unquestionably the most powerful and warlike people then in Palestine, and there was already some ill blood between them and the Israelites, and would be likely to offer a most formidable opposition to them at the very first step of their progress. The Hebrews were in fact altogether unfit to face such enemies, or any enemies whatever: they were not yet even fit to be a nation; and therefore, instead of being at once led to their promised heritage, it was the divine will that they should be conducted into the desert, there to be trained, disciplined, and instructed, so as to fit them for their future destinies. Moses knew that their first destination was the wilderness of Sinai; for when the Lord appeared to him in Horeb, it was announced that the bondaged children of Abraham should be brought to worship God in that very mountain.

The Hebrews left Rameses and proceeded on their way. And now it appeared that the Lord provided against their going astray, by placing a miraculous column of cloud to go before them by day and mark out their road; while by night it became a column of fire, and gave light to all the camp. This was important, also, as evincing that Moses was not acting by his own authority, and that, however highly he was entitled to their confidence and respect, they had a more unerring Guide and a more exalted Protector.

Their first day's journey brought them to Succoth. We relinquish the notion which we once entertained that Succoth may have been at or near the place (Birket el Hadj, or Pilgrim's Pool) where the great pilgrim caravan encamps and makes its final arrangements for its journey. We think it, upon the whole, more likely that the point from which the Hebrews departed *in the first instance* may have been in that neighborhood. Succoth, therefore, must be sought somewhere about a day's journey in the direction toward Suez. The name denotes *tents* or *booths,* and it is

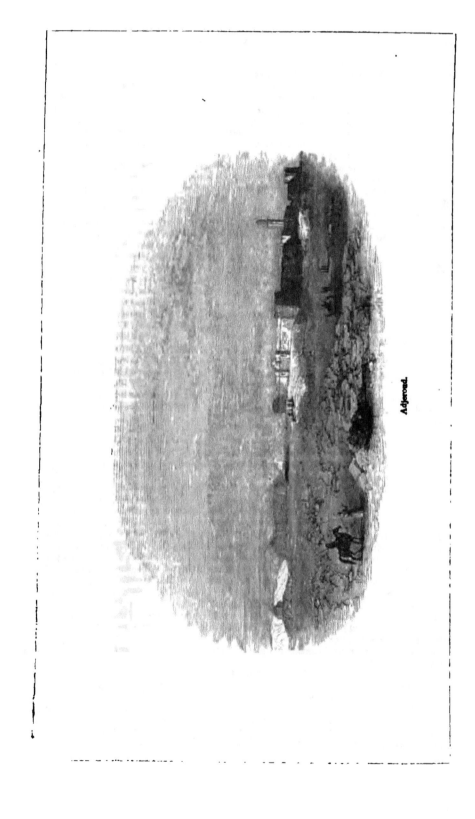

Adjeroed.

useless to seek its site, as the name appears only to denote a place where caravans passing that way usually encamped.

Their next resting-place of which we are told was "Etham, on the edge of the wilderness." But in this, as in other cases, we are not to suppose that the places which are named are the only places at which they rested; and in the present instance the distance may suggest that this Etham was the third rather than the second encampment. The halting-places of caravans are in these desert regions so much determined by the presence of wells, that, in connexion with the circumstance of its being situated "on the edge of the wilderness," there is not much difficulty in concluding that Etham is represented by the modern Adjeroud, which forms the third stage of the pilgrim's caravan, and where there is an old fortress, a small village, and copious well of indifferent water. This place is about eleven miles to the northwest of Suez. The neighborhood seems indeed to be on the edge of the wilderness: for what M. du Bois-Ayme says of Bir-Suez (which *he* identifies with Etham) is true also of Adjeroud, that, in effect, it appears to be toward the extremity of the desert: for hence the sea is seen to make a bend to the west, and by joining the high chain of Mount Attaka to terminate the desert to the south. The journey to this point had been for the most part over a desert, the surface of which is composed of hard gravel, often strewed with pebbles.

They had now arrived near the head of the Red sea, and also, as we suppose, at the limit of the three days' journey into the wilderness for which they had applied. It is therefore evident that their next move must decide their future course, and convey to the Egyptians a clear and decisive intimation of their intentions. If they designed to do as they had all along declared to be their only wish, they would stay at this place, and proceed to celebrate the feast to Jehovah, of which so much had been said: but, if they intended to escape altogether, they would resume their journey, and, passing by the head of the Red sea, strike off into the desert. And here God, who knew that the king of Egypt had so far recovered his consternation that he was determined to pursue and drive them back, if they made any move indicating an intention to escape, directed a move which must have been most unexpected to all parties, and which could not to any indifferent spectator have seemed the result of the most gross and fatal infatuation.

About the head of the Gulf of Suez a desert plain extends for ten or twelve miles to the west and north of the city of that name. On the west this plain is bounded by the chain of Attaka, which comes down toward the sea in a northeasterly direction. Opposite Suez this chain is seen at a considerable distance, but, as we advance southward, the mountains rapidly approach the sea, and proportionately contract the breadth of the valley; and the chain terminates at the sea, and seems, in the distant view, to shut up the valley at Ras-el-Attaka, or Cape Attaka, twelve miles below Suez. But, on approaching this point, ample room is found to pass beyond; and on passing beyond we find ourselves in a broad alluvial plain, forming the mouth of the valley of Bedea. This plain is on the other or southern side nearly shut up by the termination of another chain of these mountains, which extend between the Nile and the western shore of the Red sea. Any further progress in this direction would be impossible to a large army, especially when encumbered with flocks and herds, and with women, children, and baggage; and this from the manner in which the rocks, the promontories, and the cliffs advance on the western shore. And, besides, any advance in this direction would be suicidal to a body desiring to escape from Egypt, as they would have the Red sea between them and Arabia Proper, and could only get involved among the plains and valleys which separate the mountain chains of Egyptian Arabia.

The valley of Bedea, which opens to the Red sea in the broad plain to which we have brought the reader, narrows as it proceeds westward toward the Nile. It forms a fine roadway between the valley of the Nile and the Red sea, and, as such, has in all ages been one of the most frequented routes in all the country, being traversed by all parties and caravans which desire to proceed from the neighborhood of Cairo, or places to the south of Cairo, to Suez, or to places lying beyond the head of the gulf.

Now, the Hebrew host being at Etham, and their next step thence being of the utmost importance, they were directed, not—as might obviously have been expected —to pass round the head of the gulf into the Sinai peninsula, but to proceed southward, between the mountains of Attaka and the *western* shore of the gulf, and, after

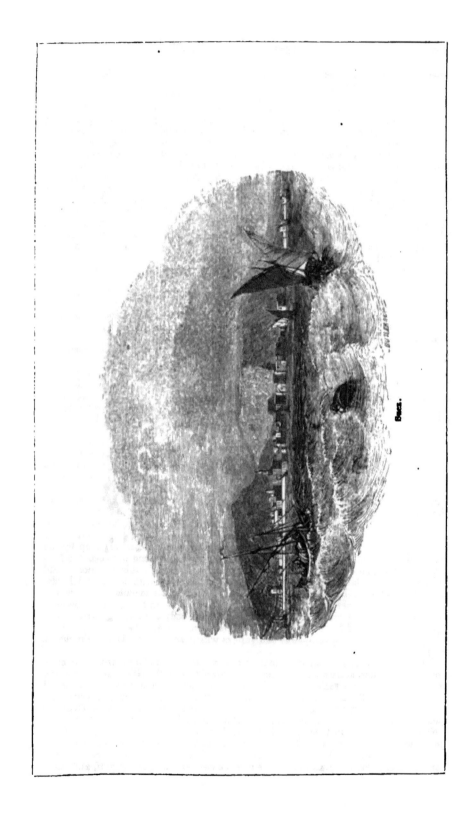

Baez.

passing the Ras-el-Attaka, to encamp in the plain into which the valley of Bedea opens. The more thoroughly any one makes himself acquainted with the topography of this region, the more obvious and reasonable, we are persuaded, will seem to him this explanation of the text—" Turn and encamp before Pi-ha-hiroth [the mouth of the ridge], between Migdol and the sea, over against Baal-zephon: before it ye shall encamp by the sea." As the names Migdol and Baal-zephon are not now recognisable anywhere about the head of the gulf,* no facts or inferences can be deduced from them; but an important confirmation is derived from the circumstance that we are told that, in consequence of the move which was made, the Hebrew host were shut up between the sea and the mountains, without any means of escape, unless through the sea, when the retreat in the rear was cut off.

Many have thought they found cause to wonder at this extraordinary movement, which placed the Hebrews in a position of such inextricable difficulty, forgetting that this was the very purpose of God, that the prospect of an extraordinary advantage might tempt the Egyptians on to their own destruction, and bring them within the reach of those agencies by which God intended to act against them. The wonder which the reader may feel is exactly the wonder which the king of Egypt felt, and by which he was led on to his ruin.

The movement was made; and the thousands of Israel encamped in the plain of Bedea.

The days which had passed had given the Egyptians time to recover from some portion of their panic; and their first feeling of unmixed horror and alarm gave place to considerable resentment and regret, on the king's part, that he had so suddenly conceded all the points which had been contested between him and Moses, and had allowed them all to depart; and as for his subjects, such of them as had a profitable interest in the labors of the Israelites would, to some extent, join in the king's feelings, as soon as their bondsmen took any course to intimate that they intended to escape; and the same intimation would not fail to alarm those who had "lent" to the Hebrews their "jewels of silver and jewels of gold," and who by this time had found leisure to think that they had too easily parted with their wealth. Thus it seems that the course which the Israelites might take after their arrival at Etham was regarded with much anxiety by the Egyptians, who took care to be informed of all their movements.

When, therefore, the king heard not only that they had taken a decisive move from Etham, but, through some astonishing infatuation, had so moved as to become "entangled in the land," and "shut in by the wilderness," he hastened to avail himself of the extraordinary advantage which they had placed in his hands. "He made ready his chariot, and took his people with him." He mustered not less than six hundred chariots, which are said to be "all the [war] chariots of Egypt." This is in correspondence with the sculptures, which show that the Egyptians made great use in war of such chariots as our engraving exhibits. A large body of infantry† was also assembled, and the pursuit commenced. Their light, unencumbered march was no doubt much more quickly performed than that of the Israelites to the same place.

One of the citations in Eusebius from the lost history of Manetho, the Egyptian priest, says: "The Heliopolitans relate that the king with a great army, *accompanied by the sacred animals*, pursued after the Jews, *who had carried off with them the substance of the Egyptians*."‡ This takes notice of two facts not mentioned by Moses, but not at all disagreeing with his statement, namely, that, for their protection against the God of Israel, the Egyptians took with them their sacred animals, by which means the Lord executed judgment upon the [bestial] gods of Egypt, as had been foretold (Exod. xii. 12); and then that to recover the substance which the Hebrews had "borrowed" was one of the objects of the pursuit.

We do not agree with those who think that the king of Egypt came upon the

---

* *Migdol* was probably a *tower*, as the name imports, and may seem to have been on the mountains which hem in the valley. *Baal-zephon*, meaning *the Northern Baal* or *Lord*, would seem to have been a town or temple situated somewhere in the plain of Medea, or over against it on the *eastern* shore of the sea.

† These must be intended by "his army," as distinguished from his "chariots and horsemen." Our engraving, (p. 133) composed from Egyptian sculptures and paintings, shows Egyptian soldiers with the equipments and arms of different corps. The man in the foreground with the round studded shield is, however, not an Egyptian, but belongs to a nation, the soldiers of which are often seen fighting as auxiliaries along with those of Egypt. A native Egyptian soldier, if he has any shield, has it round at the upper end and square at the lower. The charioteer in the background is known to be a king by his head-dress.

‡ " Præp. Evang." lib. x. cap. 27.

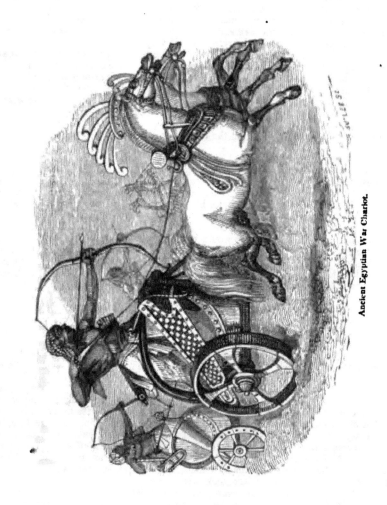

Ancient Egyptian War Chariot.

encamped Hebrews through the valley of Bedea, in the plain at the mouth of which they were encamped. As he was so glad to find how they had "entangled themselves in the land," he was not likely to take a course which would deprive him of all the advantages derivable from their apparent oversight. This he would do by coming upon them through the valley of Bedea; for this would have left open to them the alternative of escaping from their position by the way they entered: whereas, by coming the same way they had come, he shut up that door of escape, and, if they fled before him, left them no other visible resource but to march up the valley of Bedea, back to Egypt, before the Egyptian troops. That this was really the advantage to himself which the king saw in their position, and that it was his object to drive them before him back to Egypt through this valley, or to destroy them if they offered to resist, we have not the least doubt; and it is unlikely that he would take any road but that which would enable him to secure these benefits.

The Egyptians, being satisfied that they had secured their prey, and that it was impossible for their fugitive bondsmen to escape but by returning to Egypt, were in no haste to assail them. They were also, themselves, probably wearied by their rapid march. They therefore encamped for the night—for it was toward evening when they arrived—intending, probably, to give effect to their intentions in the morning.

As for the Israelites, the sight of their old oppressors struck them with terror. There was no faith or spirit in them. They knew not how to value their newly-found liberty. They deplored the rash adventure in which they had engaged; and their servile minds looked back with regret and envy upon the enslaved condition which they had so lately deplored. Moses knew them well enough not to be surprised that they assailed him as the author of all the calamities to which they were now exposed. "Is it because there were no graves in Egypt," said they, "that thou hast taken us away to die in the wilderness? Is not this the word that we did tell thee in Egypt, saying, Let us alone, that we may serve the Egyptians? For it had been better for us to serve the Egyptians than to die in the wilderness." This is one specimen of a mode of feeling and character among this spiritless and perverse people of which Moses had seen something already, and of which he had soon occasion to see much more. One might be disposed to judge of their feelings the more leniently, attributing them to the essential operation of personal slavery in enslaving the mind, by debasing its higher tones of feeling and character, did we not know that the same characteristics of mind and temper constantly broke out among this remarkable people very long after the generation which knew the slavery of Egypt had passed away.

Moses did not deign to remonstrate with them or to vindicate himself. It seems that the Divine intention had been previously intimated to him; for he answered, with that usual emphasis of expression which makes it a pleasure to transcribe his words: "Fear ye not: stand still, and see the salvation of the Lord, which he will show to you this day: for the Egyptians whom ye have seen to-day ye shall see no more again for ever. The Lord shall fight for you, and ye shall hold your peace." They were pacified by this for the present; but there is good reason to suspect, that if measures of relief had long been delayed, they would have given up Moses and Aaron to the Egyptians, and have placed themselves at their disposal. But measures of relief were *not* long delayed. When the night was fully come, the Lord directed Moses to order the people to march forward to the sea; on their arriving at which, the prophet lifted up his rod upon the waters, over which instantly blew a powerful east wind, by which they were divided from shore to shore, so that the firm bottom of hard sand appeared; offering a dry road in the midst of the sea, by which they might pass to the eastern shore. At that instant, also, the pillar of fire which had gone before the Hebrews to guide them on their way was removed to their rear, and, being thus between them and the Egyptians, it gave light to the former in their passage, while it concealed their proceedings and persons from the latter.*

It thus happened that some time passed before the Egyptians discovered that the Israelites were in motion. When they made this discovery, the king determined to

* According to a well-known optical effect, by which we can see by night all that stands between us and the light, but nothing that lies beyond the light. No doubt the pillar gave good light to the Egyptians themselves, but did not enable them to see the Israelites. In like manner the Israelites, doubtless, could not see the Egyptians. A little attention to a matter so perfectly obvious would have spared us some speculations, such as that which gives the pillar a cloudy side and a flaming side, &c.

Ancient Egyptian Soldiers.

follow. It is by no means clear that they knew or thought that they were following them into the bed of the sea. Considering the darkness of the night, except from the light of the pillar, with the confusion of ideas and indistinct perceptions of a people who had not been on the spot long enough to make particular observations, and most of them probably roused from sleep to join in the pursuit, it seems likely that they felt uncertain about the direction, and supposed that they were following some accustomed route by which the Israelites were either endeavoring to escape or to return to Egypt. They may even have thought they were going up the valley of Bedea, although that actually lay in an opposite direction. Anything, however improbable, seems more likely to have occurred to them than that they were passing through the divided sea.

By the time the day broke and the Egyptians became aware of their condition, all the Hebrews had safely reached the other side, and all or nearly all the Egyptians were in the bed of the gulf; the van approaching the eastern shore, and the rear having left the western. The moment of vengeance was come. They found themselves in the midst of the sea, with the waters on their right hand and on their left, and only restrained from overwhelming them by some power they knew not, but which they must have suspected to have been that of the God of the Hebrews. The marine road, ploughed by the multitudes which went before them, became distressing to them; their chariot-wheels dragged heavily along, and very many of them came off from the cars which they supported. The Lord also began to trouble them with a furious warfare of the elements. The Psalmist more than once alludes to this. He exclaims: "The waters saw thee, O God, the waters saw thee, and were afraid:" and then speaks as if every element had spent its fury upon the devoted heads of the Egyptians. The earth shook; the thunders rolled; and most appalling lightnings—the arrows of God—shot along the firmament; while the clouds poured down heavy rains, "hailstones, and coals of fire."* It deserves to be mentioned that this strife is also recorded by the Egyptian chronologer, who reports, "It is said that fire flashed against them in front."

By this time the pursuers were thoroughly alarmed. "Let us flee," said they, from the face of Israel, for JEHOVAH fighteth for them against the Egyptians." But at that instant the Lord gave the word, Moses stretched forth his hand over the sea, and the restrained waters returned and ingulfed them all.

This stupendous event made a profound impression upon the Hebrew mind at large. From that day to the end of the Hebrew polity, it supplied a subject to which the sacred poets and prophets make constant allusions in language the most sublime. Its effect upon the generation more immediately concerned was very strong, and, although they were but too prone to forget it, was more abiding and operative than any which had yet been made upon them. When they witnessed all these things, and soon after saw the carcases of those who had so lately been the objects of such intense dread to them, lying by thousands on the beach, "they feared the Lord, and believed the Lord and his servant Moses."

In the sublime song which Moses composed and sang with the sons of Israel in commemoration of this great event—their marvellous deliverance and the overthrow of their enemies—he, with his usual wisdom, looks forward to important ulterior effects, to secure to the Hebrews the benefit of which may not improbably have formed one of the principal reasons for this remarkable exhibition of the power of Jehovah, and his determination to protect the chosen race. These anticipations, which were abundantly fulfilled, are contained in the following verses:

> "The nations shall hear this and tremble;
> Anguish shall seize the inhabitants of Palestine.
> Then shall the princes of Edom be amazed:
> And dismay shall possess the mighty ones of Moab.
> All the inhabitants of Canaan shall melt away;
> Fear and terror shall fall upon them:
> Through the greatness of thine arm
> They shall become still as a stone,
> Until thy people pass over [Jordan], O JEHOVAH,
> Until thy people pass over whom thou hast redeemed."

On this occasion the first instance is offered of a custom, learned most probably in Egypt, and ever retained by the Hebrew women, of celebrating with dances and

* Psalm xviii. 13–15; lxxvii. 16, 17.

Dance of Females with Timbrels.

timbrels every remarkable event of joy or triumph.   They were now led by Miriam, the sister of Moses and Aaron; and they seem to have taken part as a chorus in the song of the men, by answering:—

> "Let us sing unto the LORD, for he hath triumphed gloriously,
> The horse and his rider hath he thrown into the sea."

As the timbrels of the women were doubtless Egyptian, and the dresses of those of superior rank were probably Egyptian also, we have considered that a similar dance of females, from Egyptian sources, would form a satisfactory illustration.

It will appear, from the opinion we have been induced to entertain respecting the place in which the Israelites encamped, and from which they departed, on the western shore of the gulf, that we concur with those who regard Ain Mousa* as the place, on the eastern shore, where they came up from the bed of the sea, and where they witnessed the overthrow of their oppressors.   That the site is thus distinguished in the local traditions of the inhabitants of Sinai, the name alone suffices to indicate; and, although undue weight should not be attached to such traditions, it would be wrong entirely to disregard them when they support or illustrate conclusions otherwise probable.   We shall, however, content ourselves with adding, descriptively, that a number of green shrubs, springing from numerous hillocks, mark the landward approach to this place.   Here are also a number of neglected palm-trees grown thick and bushy for want of pruning.   The springs which here rise out of the ground in various places, and give name to the spot, are soon lost in the sands.   The water is of a brackish quality, in consequence, probably, of the springs being so near the sea; but it is, nevertheless, cool and refreshing, and in these waterless deserts affords a desirable resting-place.   The view from this place, looking westward, is very beautiful, and most interesting from its association with the wonderful events which it has been our duty to relate.   The mountain chains of Attaka, each running into a long promontory, stretch along the shore of Africa; and nearly opposite our station we view the opening—the Pi-ha-biroth—the "mouth of the ridge," formed by the valley in the mouth of which the Hebrews were encamped before they crossed the sea.   On the side where we stand, the access to the shore from the bed of the gulf would have been easy.   And it deserves to be mentioned, that not only do the springs bear the name of Moses, but the projecting head-land below them, toward the sea, bears the name of Ras Mousa.   Thus do the Cape of Moses and the Cape of Deliverance look toward each other from the opposite shores of the Arabian gulf, and unite their abiding and unshaken testimony to the judgments and wonders of that day in which the right hand of Jehovah was so abundantly "glorified in might."†

---

* The Fountains of Moses.

† As Egypt has been the grand scene of the very important transactions related in this chapter, it may not be improper to close it with a few observations on its learning, language, religion, idolatry, &c.   Egypt (that binds or troubles), an ancient country of Africa, peopled by Mizraim, a son of Ham, the son of Noah, from whom it received its name; and the Arabs still call it Mesr.   Egypt is about six hundred miles long, and from one hundred to three hundred broad: it lies at the northeast corner of Africa, bounded on the north by the Mediterranean sea, on the east by the isthmus of Suez and the Red sea, which divide it from Asia, on the south by Abyssinia, and on the west by Libya.   Egypt was divided into two districts, Upper Egypt, or Thebias, and Lower Egypt, or the Delta.   The river Nile, running through the whole length of the land, from north to south, abounds with fish, crocodiles, and hippopotami; and, by its annual overflowing, the country became one of the most fruitful in the world, so that its majestic waters formed the glory of the king of Egypt, Ezek. xxix. 3–5.   Egypt was, at an early period, famous above every other country, for its progress in the arts and sciences, Acts vii. 22; 1 Kings iv. 29, 30, attracting thither the most celebrated philosophers and historians of Greece, to complete their studies.   Pythagoras, Herodotus, Plato, and many others, sought instruction in Egypt, among its celebrated sages; yet idolatry was carried to such a height, by the wisest instructers of that country, that the Egyptians made gods for their religious worship, not only of the sun and moon, but of their various beasts, oxen, sheep, goats, and cats, and even of leeks, onions, and diseases, and of monsters having no existence, except in their own disordered imaginations.   Divine prophecy has been strikingly illustrated in the history of Egypt, Ezek. xxix. 8–15, xxx. 10–13.   Nebuchadnezzar conquered it, as foretold by the prophet; then it became subject to Persia; and in succession to the Greeks, Romans, Saracens, Mamaluke-slaves, and Turks.   Napoleon Bonaparte conquered it in 1798, in the hope of acquiring India; but the French were expelled by the British, who delivered it up to the Turks, against whom it is now in a state of rebellion.   It has, therefore, had no prince of its own; and it has been "the basest of kingdoms:" the decrees of Heaven have been accomplished, and they will yet be fulfilled, in the triumphs of Christianity, Isa. xi. 9–16.   Egypt still abounds with vast monuments of its former grandeur: the ruins of it ancient cities and temples attest its magnificence, riches, and populousness.   The tombs of its kings, the stupendous pyramids alone, evince these things: the largest of three of them, situated a few leagues from Cairo, the site of the celebrated Memphis, according to the recent measurement of a French engineer, forms a square, each side of whose base is seven hundred and forty-six feet, covering more than thirteen acres of land: the perpendicular height of it is five hundred and forty-six feet; and it contains 6,000,000 of tons of stone, sufficient to build a wall ten feet high, and one foot thick, eighteen hundred miles in length!   These prodigious monuments of the ancient glory of Egypt, at once confirm and illustrate the truth and divinity of the Holy Scriptures.

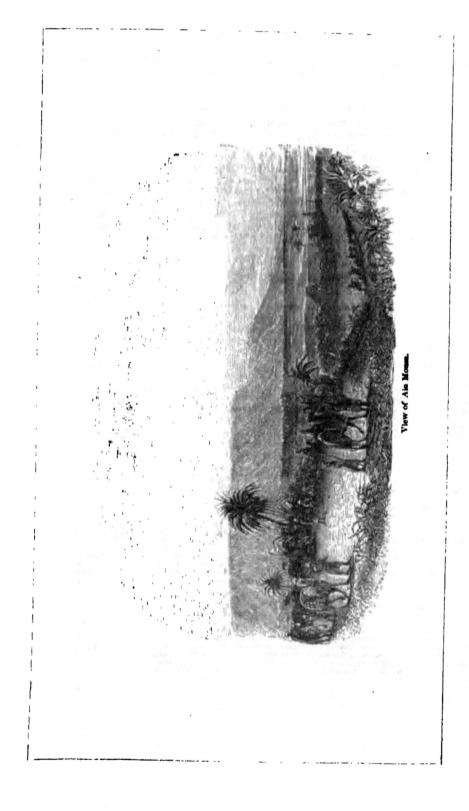

View of Aiu Monu.

CHAPTER IX.

THE Israelites, having acknowledged their thankfulness to God for his beneficent protection in delivering them out of Egyptian bondage, Moses conducted them from the Red sea into the desert of Shur or Etham. Here they travelled three days without finding any water, which, to so great a number of people, and in so hot a country, must have been very afflicting. At length, they came to a place called Marah, where they found some water; but, on tasting it, they could not drink it, on account of its being so exceeding bitter. This disappointment inflamed their thirst, and increased their dissatisfaction, insomuch that they began to murmur against Moses, asking him what they should drink? Moses was sensible of the calamity under which they labored; and, fearful lest they should, by their future murmurings, provoke the Almighty to punish them, he addressed himself to God in their behalf, who no sooner heard the complaint, than he was pleased to remove it. He ordered Moses to make use of the wood of a certain tree, which, as soon as it was thrown into the water, changed its offensive quality and became sweet.

From Marah the Israelites proceeded to Elim, where they found not only plenty of water, but also great numbers of palm or date trees,* the fruit of which being ripe supplied them with food. Here it may be supposed they made some stay; for when they left the place it was the fifteenth day of the second month, which was just a month from the day of their departure from Egypt.

On their removal from Elim they proceeded to the wilderness† of Sin, situated between Elim and Mount Sinai. Here again they fell into a general murmur against Moses and Aaron, on account of the barrenness of the place, and the scarcity of provisions. "Would to God," cried they, "we had died by the hand of the Lord in the land of Egypt, where we had plenty of bread and meat; for now ye have brought us into this desert, where we must perish with famine."

The Almighty, to convince these murmuring people of his divine power and protection, was pleased to inform them by the mouth of Moses, that he would take care to supply them with food from heaven, and it was not long before his beneficent promise was fulfilled. On that very evening he caused such a number of quails to fall among them, as almost covered their camp, by which they were plentifully supplied with the article of flesh. The next morning, as soon as the dew was gone, they found the surface of the earth covered with little white round things, resembling, in shape, the coriander seed. The Israelites, astonished at so singular a circumstance, said one to another, "What is this?" Upon which Moses answered, "It is the bread which the Lord hath given you to eat." And thence they gave it the name of *Manna.*

As this was the bread designed by the Almighty for the Israelites during their stay in the wilderness, and as they were strangers to its qualities, he was pleased to give them the following directions in what manner they were to manage it for the intended purposes.

That it was to be gathered by measure, an omer for every head, according to the number of each family; but this direction some persons slighting, and gathering above the portion allowed, found their quantity miraculously lessened, while the more moderate had theirs increased.

That it was to be gathered fresh every morning, all of which should be consumed the same day. This precept was likewise not observed by some, who, keeping a part till the next morning, found, upon examination, that it stunk, and was so putrefied as to be totally useless.

* PALM-TREE (see Engraving), a tall, fruit-bearing, shadowy tree, whose fruit is the date: it arrives at perfection in about thirty years, and thus continues about seventy years, bearing fifteen or twenty clusters of dates, each cluster weighing from fifteen to twenty pounds. Exod. xv. 27. The palm-tree is held in great estimation by the inhabitants of Arabia, Egypt, and Persia, on account of its adaptation to various valuable purposes. The Arabs celebrate its three hundred and sixty uses to which the different parts may be applied: they used the leaves for making ropes, sacks, mats, hats, sandals, and other things; and many people subsist almost entirely on its fruit. Palm-branches were carried as tokens of victory or joy (Lev. xxiii. 40, John xii. 13); and the beauty of this tree is made an emblem of the active virtues of a Christian. Ps. xcii. 12.

† WILDERNESS, a desert, or uncultivated tract of land. Exod. xiv. 3, 1 Kings xix. 15, Acts xxi. 38. The northwestern part of Arabia was almost wholly uncultivated; and hence Moses calls it "a terrible and a waste-howling wilderness." Deut. i. 19, xxxii. 10. Paran, Sin, and Sinai, were deserts in that dangerous country. Several wildernesses or small deserts existed in Canaan; as "the wilderness of Judea," famous for the ministry of John the Baptist. Matt. iii. 1

Palm Tree in the Sinai Mountains.

That, on the seventh day (which was the Sabbath) there could not be any found; and therefore, on the sixth, they should gather a double portion, which being laid up against the ensuing day, should be perfectly sweet and wholesome.

Such were the directions given by God to the Israelites for the use of this miraculous bread, on which they were chiefly supported for forty years. And in order to perpetuate the remembrance of it, and that their posterity might see on what God had fed them while in the wilderness, he appointed an omer of it to be put into a pot, and to be carefully preserved for that purpose.

Thus did the Almighty supply the wants of the discontented Israelites in the most ample manner; and farther to convince them of his peculiar favor and regard, directed their marches from place to place, and appointed their respective encampments.

Leaving the desert of Sin, and proceeding on their journey, they came to a place called Rephidim, where they struck their tents and encamped. Here they were again distressed for water, upon which they fell into their old way of distrusting God's providence, and murmuring against Moses; but on this occasion they were much more mutinous and desperate than ever. It was in vain for Moses to endeavor to persuade them to be patient, and wait the will of God: this only inflamed them the more, and at length their rage arose to such a height, that they threatened to stone him.

Moses, not knowing what to do in order to appease the rage of the people, addressed himself to God, who was pleased to dissipate his fear, by promising to signalize that place by a miraculous supply of water, as he had lately done another by a miraculous supply of food. "Go," said he, "on before the people, and take with thee of the elders of Israel: and thy rod wherewith thou smotest the river, take in thine hand and go. Behold I will stand before thee there upon the rock in Horeb; and thou shall smite the rock, and there shall come water out of it, and the people shall drink." Moses did as he was commanded, and no sooner had he smitten the rock with his rod, than water in abundance gushed out from several places at the same time, which joining in one common stream ran down to the camp at Rephidim, by which the people were immediately supplied, and their thirst being quenched, their rage against Moses instantly ceased.[*] This station, however, on account of the infamous mutiny of the people, and their distrust of God, Moses (as a caution and remembrance to them in future) called Massah and Meribah, which in the Hebrew language, signifies *temptation* and *contention.*

A short time after this singular circumstance happened, and while the Israelites were yet encamped at Rephidim, they were one day suddenly alarmed at the approach of an army of the Amalekites. Moses reflecting a little on this unexpected circumstance, ordered Joshua[†] (a valiant young man who was always about him) to draw out a party of the choicest men in the camp, and early the next morning, to give the enemy battle.

Joshua obeyed the command of Moses, who the next morning, accompanied by Aaron and Hur, went to the top of an eminence, whence they might have a view of the engagement. Moses took with him his rod, and while he held it up during the battle, the Israelites prevailed; but when, through weariness, his hand began to drop, the Amalekites had the better. Aaron and Hur, observing this, took a stone, on which they sat Moses, and, placing themselves on each side, supported his hands, in one of which was the rod, and the other uplifted to God. This they continued to do till the going down of the sun, in which time the Amalekites were routed, and every man put to the sword.

[*] PRETENDED ROCK OF MOSES.—We are indebted to Professor Robinson's invaluable work ("Biblical Researches in Palestine") for the following interesting extract: "We came to the rock which they say Moses smote, and the water gushed out. As to this rock, one is at a loss whether most to admire the credulity of the monks or the legendary and discrepant reports of travellers. It is hardly necessary to remark, that there is not the slightest ground for assuming any connexion between this narrow valley and Rephidim; but on the contrary, there is everything against it. The rock itself is a large isolated cube of coarse red granite, which has fallen from the eastern mountain. Down its front, in an oblique line from top to bottom, runs a seam of a finer texture, from twelve to fifteen inches broad, having in it several irregular horizontal crevices, somewhat resembling the human mouth, one above another. These are said to be twelve in number; but I could make out only ten. The seam extends quite through the rock, and is visible on the opposite or back side; where also are similar crevices, though not so large. The holes did not appear to us to be artificial, as is usually reported, although we examined them particularly. They belong rather to the nature of the seam; yet it is possible that some of them may have been enlarged by artificial means. The rock is a singular one; and doubtless was selected, on account of this very singularity, as the scene of the miracle."

[†] This is the first mention made of Joshua, who makes so distinguished a figure in the subsequent part of the sacred history; in which he is frequently styled *the servant of Moses.*

Summit of Mount Sinai.

This distinguished success, in their first martial enterprise, gave great encouragement to the Israelites; and that so remarkable an action might be transmitted to posterity, God commanded Moses to record it in a book, that Joshua, the general, might thereby be animated to future services; "for," said he, "I will utterly put out the remembrance of Amalek from under heaven."* As a memorial of this victory, Moses erected an altar on the spot, and offered sacrifice to the Lord. The name he gave it was JEHOVAH-*Nissi,* which signifies "*the Lord is my banner.*"

Soon after the defeat of the Amalekites, Moses left Rephidim, and proceeded with all his people toward Mount Sinai,† where God at first appeared to him in the burning bush, and not far whence dwelt Jethro, his father-in-law.

Jethro having heard of all that God had done for Moses and his people, and understanding they were now near him, he took his daughter Zipporah (Moses's wife) with their two sons, Gershom and Eliezar, and went to the Israelites' camp, where, after mutual salutations and embraces, Moses entertained his father-in-law with a particular account of everything that had happened to him during his absence. In return, Jethro offered up solemn praises to God, and joined with Moses and the rest of the elders of Israel in sacrifices, and such other rejoicings as were thought proper on the occasion.

During Jethro's stay in the camp, he took notice of the great weight of business under which Moses labored, in hearing the complaints, and determining the differences, of so great a body of people; and therefore, being a wise and experienced man himself, he advised his son-in-law to appoint certain subordinate officers, properly qualified, men of sincerity and abilities, such as feared God and hated covetousness, to be rulers; some over thousands, some over hundreds, some over fifties, and some over tens, who should hear and determine all trifling disputes among the people, and refer the greater and more weighty causes only to him; assuring him that if, with God's approbation, he followed this advice, it would prove advantageous both to him and the people.

Moses, highly approving of this salutary advice from his father-in-law, immediately put it in practice, soon after which Jethro took his leave, and returned to his own habitation.

It was three months after the departure of the Israelites from Egypt, when they encamped in the wilderness of Sinai, near the mount of God. They had not been long here before the Almighty summoned Moses to come up to him on the mount. Moses readily obeying the Divine command, the Almighty charged him to remind the Israelites of the many wonders he had wrought in their favor, and to assure them that (notwithstanding their frequent murmurings and distrust of his providence) if, for the future, they would become obedient to his laws, he would still look upon them as his peculiar people, a favorite nation, and a royal priesthood.

Moses having communicated this gracious message from the Almighty to the elders, and they to the people, they unanimously answered, that whatsoever the Lord had commanded, or should afterward command, they would strictly and obediently perform.

With this answer Moses ascended the mount, and after making it known to the Almighty, he commanded him to direct the people to cleanse and purify themselves two days, for that on the third he should come down upon the mountain and make a covenant with them. He likewise gave him a strict charge to set boundaries about the foot of the mount, which none should attempt to pass under the severest penalties.

These orders were strictly obeyed, and every preparation made conformable to the Divine injunctions. On the third day, early in the morning, the people saw the

* AMALEK, or AMALEKITES, a very ancient people, supposed to have descended from Ham, Gen. xiv. 7, Num. xxiv. 20; but especially the posterity of Esau's grandson: they were powerful in Arabia, and cherishing the hatred of Esau against Jacob, they endeavored to cut off Israel in the desert, but they were defeated by Joshua, Exod. xvii. 8-16. For this wickedness God doomed them to be extirpated, Num. xxiv. 20; 1 Sam. xv. 1-33; xxx. 1-18.

† A mountain of Arabia Petrea, famous for its being the supposed place round which the Israelites were assembled when God gave them his law by the ministry of Moses, Exod. xvi. 1, xix. 1, 2-20; Lev. xxvi. 46; Gal. iv. 25. Sinai is a summit of the rocky district of Mount Horeb, on the peninsula formed by the two arms or gulfs of the Red sea, about two hundred and sixty miles from Cairo in Egypt. There are two lofty peaks in this range from six to eight thousand feet high, Horeb and Sinai: but travellers are not able to determine which of them is Sinai proper: one is called El Tor, or the Mountain, and the whole mountain range is called Djebel Moussa, or the Mount of Moses, by the Arabs, Exod. iii. 1-12; Deut. iv. 10-15, v. 2. Superstition has determined that the more elevated is Sinai, on which is built a chapel dedicated to St. Catharine, and a monastery to the same saint, at the foot of the mountain: to visit these sacred places, travellers are obliged to submit to various impositions from the Arabs.

mountain surrounded with a thick cloud, out of which proceeded such dreadful peals of thunder and flashes of lightning, as filled them with horror and amazement.

The first sounding of the trumpet was the signal for the people to approach the mountain; upon which, as soon as it began, Moses brought them out of the camp, and conducted them as near to the mount as the barrier would permit. Here they beheld an alarming sight indeed: the whole surface of the mount was covered with fire and smoke, while the foundation of it seemed to tremble and shake under them. In the midst of this dreadful scene the trumpet was heard to sound louder and louder, and the claps of thunder and flashes of fire were more frequent and violent. At length, on a sudden, the most solemn silence took place; and, after a short pause, the Almighty was heard (from the midst of the fire and smoke which yet continued) to pronounce the Law of the Decalogue, or Ten Commandments;* which is, indeed, a complete system of the moral part of the Jewish institutes, and, in few but very significant words, comprehends the duty of mankind to God, themselves, and their neighbor.

When the Divine voice ceased, the people, astonished at what they saw and heard, removed farther from the camp: and, in the height of their fear and surprise, addressed themselves to Moses, beseeching him that, for the future, he would speak to them in God's stead, and whatever he enjoined they would obey, because, were they again to hear the dreadful voice of God, they should certainly die with horror and astonishment.

Moses was far from being displeased at this request, as it evinced the reverence and respect they entertained, first, to the Divine Being, and next to himself. To ease their minds from the great terror they had felt, he assured them that all this wonderful scene was not exhibited to them with a design to create in them any slavish fear, but a filial confidence and submission to such laws as the Divine wisdom should hereafter think fit to enjoin.

Having said this to the people, Moses again ascended the mountain, where (in addition to the Decalogue) he received from God several other laws, both ceremonial and political; the whole of which were calculated with a wise design to preserve the people in their obedience to God; to prevent their intermixture with other nations, and to advance the welfare of their commonwealth, by securing to all the members of it a quiet enjoyment of their lives and properties.†

When Moses had received these additional laws, he returned from the mount, and immediately erected an altar to God, on which he offered up burnt and peace offerings. Having written down the last laws delivered to him by God, he caused them to be read to all the people, and exacted a solemn promise from them that they would keep them faithfully. He then confirmed the covenant, by sprinkling the altar, the book, and the people, with the blood of the victims slaughtered on the occasion; and, to perpetuate the remembrance of this alliance between God and his people, he ordered twelve pillars to be raised near the altar, according to the number of the twelve tribes.

Having delivered these laws to the people, and offered sacrifices to God, Moses took Nadab, Abihu, and seventy of the elders of Israel, some part of the way toward

* THE TEN COMMANDMENTS.—Though the ten commandments were given to the Jews particularly, yet the things contained in them are such as all mankind from the beginning were bound to observe; and therefore under the Mosaic dispensation they, and the tables on which they were engraven, and the ark in which they were put, were distinguished from the rest of God's ordinances by a peculiar regard, as containing the covenant of the Lord. And though the Mosaic dispensation be now at an end, yet concerning these moral precepts of it, our Saviour declares, that "one jot or tittle shall in nowise pass from the law till all be fulfilled." To comprehend the full extent of these commandments it will be requisite to observe the following rules. Where any sin is forbidden in them, the opposite duty is implicitly enjoined: and where any duty is enjoined, the opposite sin is implicitly forbidden. Where the highest degree of any evil is prohibited, whatever is faulty in the same kind, though in a lower degree, is by consequence prohibited. And where one instance of virtuous behavior is commanded, every other, that hath the same nature, and the same reason for it, is understood to be commanded too. What we are expected to abstain from, we are expected to avoid, as far we can, all temptations to it, and occasions of it; and what we are expected to practise, we are expected to use all fit means that may better enable us to practise it. All that we are bound to do ourselves, we are bound on fitting occasions to exhort and assist others to do when it belongs to them; and all that we are bound not to do, we are to tempt nobody else to do, but keep them back from it as much as we have opportunity. The ten commandments, excepting two that required enlargement, are delivered in a few words: which brief manner of speaking hath great majesty in it. But explaining them according to these rules,—which are natural and rational in themselves, favored by ancient Jewish writers, authorized by our blessed Saviour,—we shall find that there is no part of the moral law but may be fitly ranked under them.

† These laws the reader will find in the Book of Exodus beginning at the twenty-first chapter, and ending at the twenty-third, both inclusive.

the mountain, where, without incurring the least hurt, they were vouchsafed a prospect of the divine presence. Here Moses, having committed the care of the people to these elders, left them, and taking only Joshua with him, proceeded toward the mount, on arriving at which he left Joshua, and ascended it alone.

No sooner had Moses reached the summit of the mount, than the whole was covered with a thick cloud, and the glory of the Lord appeared upon it, like a devouring fire, in the sight of the children of Israel. On the seventh day God called to Moses, upon which he entered the midst of the cloud, and there continued for the space of forty days and forty nights.

During this long stay of Moses in the mount, he received instructions from God in what manner the tabernacle should be made, wherein he intended to be worshipped. He described to him the form of the sanctuary, the table of the show-bread, the altar of frankincense, the altar of burnt-offerings, the court of the tabernacle, the basin to wash in, the ark, the candlestick, and all the other sacred utensils. He gave him the form of the sacerdotal vestments, and taught him how the priests were to be consecrated; what part of the oblation they were to take, and in what manner the perpetual sacrifice was to be offered. He appointed the two chief men who were to be the builders of the tabernacle, namely, Bezaleel, of the tribe of Judah, and Aholiab, of the tribe of Dan. Having done this, and recommended a strict observation of the sabbath, the Almighty gave Moses the two tables of stone, on which were written, with his own hand (at least by his own direction), the ten great Commandments, which were the sum and substance of their moral law.

The long absence of Moses during his stay in the mount occasioned great murmurings among the people in the camp, who, giving their ruler over for lost, assembled themselves in a riotous manner about Aaron's tent, demanding him to make some gods to go before them. Astonishing as this demand was, yet such was the weakness of Aaron, and such his want of courage, that, instead of expostulating the matter with them, he not only tamely submitted to their request, but even contributed to their idolatry. He ordered them to take the golden ear-rings from their wives and children and bring them to him: having done this, he converted them into the figure of a molten calf,* with which the people were so well pleased that they unanimously exclaimed, " This is thy God, O Israel, that brought thee out of the land of Egypt."

When Aaron saw with what satisfaction the people received their golden god (as if possessed with the same idolatrous spirit), he built an altar before it, and proclaimed a solemn feast to be held the succeeding day. But it proved rather a feast of revelling and luxury, than one arising from religious motives; for after they had made their oblations and peace-offerings, they sat down to eat and drink, and spent the whole day in feasting, dancing, and other imprudent amusements.

While the wanton Israelites were thus idolatrously revelling in the camp, Moses was in conversation with God on the mount, little suspecting so sudden a change in a people, who had so lately and solemnly entered into a covenant of obedience to all that God should command. But he from whom no secrets can be hid was instantly apprized of this sudden revolt: " Go, get thee down," said he: " for thy people, whom thou broughtest out of Egypt, have corrupted themselves. I know them to be an obstinate people, therefore intercede not for them, but see me express my resentment in their destruction; and to thee will I transfer the blessings I intended for them, and of thee will I make a great nation."

But so far was Moses from seeking his own interest in the destruction of the people, that he threw himself at the feet of the Lord, and interceded for their pardon with so much importunity, that the Almighty was at length, in some measure, appeased, and Moses had reason to imagine that he would not inflict on them the punishment he had intended.

Happy in having obtained this pardon for the Israelites, Moses, taking with him the two tables on which were written the laws, hastened from the mount, and at the bottom of it found Joshua, who had been waiting his return. As they proceeded on

---

* It is the opinion of most commentators, that the reason why they worshipped the figure of a calf rather than any other creature was, from the corruptions they had learned among the Egyptians. These people worshipped their idol Apis, or Serapis, in a living bull, as likewise an image made in the form and similitude of a bull with a bushel on his head, in memory as some say, of Pharaoh's dreams, and Joseph's wise management in measuring out the corn to the people during the seven years' famine.

toward the camp, Joshua, hearing the noise of people shouting, observed to Moses, that there was the sound of war in the camp. But Moses, who knew the cause of it, told him that the noise was not like that which was either common to victory, or those who cried for quarters; but like the noise of those who rejoiced on some other occasion.

As soon as they approached the camp Moses saw the golden calf, and the people dancing before it; at which he was so incensed, that, in the violence of his rage, he threw the tables on which the law was written against a stone on the ground, and they were broken to pieces. He then took the idol calf and melted it, after which, grinding it into a powder, and mixing it with water (in order to make them more sensible of their folly in worshipping that for a god which was to pass through their bodies), he obliged them to drink it.*

Having inflicted this punishment on the people, Moses proceeded to chastise Aaron for having suffered such idolatrous acts to be practised. But all the excuse he could make was, that the people became so turbulent that, for his own safety, he was compelled to comply with their demand.

But Moses's business was to take vengeance on the idolaters; and, therefore, leaving his brother Aaron, he went into the midst of the camp, and called such to his assistance as had not been concerned in the late rebellion: "Let those," said he, "who are for the Lord, join themselves with me." In consequence of this, all the sons of Levi (who were totally exempt from the general guilt) immediately repaired to Moses, who ordered them to take their swords, go through the camp, and kill all the ringleaders of this idolatrous defection, together with their adherents, without paying any respect to age or quality, friendship or consanguinity. The Levites strictly obeyed the orders of Moses, and the number slain on that day was about three thousand men. For this laudable zeal and ready obedience Moses blessed the family of Levi, assuring them that by thus shedding the blood of their idolatrous brethren, without favor or distinction, they had obtained the approbation of the Lord, who would certainly not fail of rewarding them for it hereafter.†

This severe punishment inflicted on the idolatrous delinquents struck a terror throughout the whole camp. The next day Moses, in a very solemn manner, reproved them for their ingratitude and folly; but at the same time promised them that he would go again up to the mount, and try how far his prayers would prevail with the divine mercy to avert the punishment which they had so justly deserved.

Moses, agreeably to his promise, returned to the mount, and acknowledged to the Lord the great sin committed by his people. At the same time he besought forgiveness for them with that earnestness and concern, that he prayed God to blot him out of his book rather than not pardon them. But this was inconsistent with the divine justice, and therefore God gave him this short answer: "Whosoever hath sinned against me, him will I blot out of my book."

The divine wrath being in a great measure appeased at the intercession of Moses, the Lord commanded him to lead the people to the place he had appointed; but at the same time let him know he was not willing to go with them, because, being a stiff-necked people, they might provoke him to consume them on the way. To show,

* DESTRUCTION OF THE GOLDEN CALF.—As there is not the least question but that all which was known to the Hebrews of the metallurgic arts at this early time, had been acquired in Egypt, the making of the golden calf may be taken in evidence, amply confirmed by their existing monuments, of the very great skill in those arts which the Egyptians had attained. But the *destruction* of the same image, in the manner described, is a still more striking evidence of this. The art of thus treating gold was a secret, probably but known to Moses, in virtue of his perfect acquaintance with all the sciences which the Egyptians cultivated. Goguet, remarking on the subject, observes that those who work in metal know that this is an exceedingly difficult operation. "Commentators have been much perplexed to explain how Moses burnt the golden image, and reduced it to powder. Most of them offer only vain and improbable conjectures. But an able chymist has removed every difficulty on the subject, and has suggested this simple process as that which Moses employed. Instead of tartaric acid, which we employ for a similar purpose, the Hebrew legislator used *natron*, which is very common in the East. (STAHLL. Vitull. aureus, in Opusc. Chym.. Phys., Medic., p. 565.) The Scripture in informing us that Moses made the Israelites drink this powder, shows that he was perfectly acquainted with all the effect of his operation. He wished to aggravate the punishment of their disobedience; and for this purpose no means could have been more suitable: for gold, rendered potable by the process of which I have spoken, is of a most detestable taste." ("Origine des Lois," epoq. ii. liv. ii. chap 14.)

To this, from Goguet, it may be well to add that the operation of the acid, which acts upon gold is much assisted by the metal being previously heated. In this we see the reason why Moses cast the golden image into the fire in the first instance.

† This prediction was afterward fulfilled: for, on the institution of the priesthood, the Levites were appointed to the honor and emoluments of that office, though in subordination to that of Aaron and his posterity.

however, that he had not quite forsaken them, he told Moses that he would send his angel before them to drive out the inhabitants of the promised land, that he might perform the oath which he had made to their forefathers, Abraham, Isaac, and Jacob.

This was very afflicting news to the Israelites, who now plainly perceived that God's withdrawing his immediate presence from them was the consequence of their rebellion; upon which they very grievously mourned, and, to show their humiliation, laid aside the ornaments they were accustomed to wear.

But Moses, still to humble them the more, and to show them how highly they had offended God by their wicked apostacy, took a tent, and pitching it at some distance without the camp, called it "the tabernacle of the congregation," intimating that the Lord was so highly offended with them for their idolatry that he had removed from them, and would no longer dwell among them, as he had hitherto done. Soon after Moses repaired to the tabernacle, which he had no sooner entered than it was surrounded by the cloudy pillar, which had so much assisted the Israelites in their departure from Egypt.

This additional token of the divine wrath made the people particularly attentive to the motions of Moses; and therefore when he went out of the camp to the tabernacle they rose up, and stood every man at his tent door, looking after him till he had got in. And when they saw the cloudy pillar, which they knew was a token of God's presence, they all fell down and worshipped.

While Moses was in the tabernacle he was visited by God, who permitted him, in a very familiar manner, to converse with him; which favor Moses improved to the advantage of the people, endeavoring, with the greatest importunity, to obtain a reconciliation between them and their justly offended God.

A short time after this the Almighty commanded Moses to prepare two new tables of stone, like the former which he had broken, and to come up alone with them in the morning to Mount Sinai; "and I," said he, "will write in those tables the words that were in the first."

Moses strictly obeyed this command, and, early in the morning, repaired to Mount Sinai with the two tables, where, prostrating himself before the divine Majesty, he with the greatest fervency besought him to pardon the sins of the people. The Almighty was pleased to listen to his request, at the same time promising that he would make a covenant with his people on these conditions: That they should keep his commandments; that they should not worship the gods of the Canaanites; that they should make no alliances with the people of that country; that they should have no strange gods; and that they should strictly keep the sabbath, the passover, and other festivals ordained by the law.

For forty days and nights did Moses at this time continue (as he had done before) on Mount Sinai, without either eating or drinking, at the expiration of which he returned to the people, bringing with him the two tables of the law. By the long converse he had held with God, his face had contracted such a lustre that the people were not able to approach him; and therefore whenever he talked with them he covered his face with a veil, but took it off when he went into the tabernacle to receive the divine commands.

Agreeably to the instructions Moses had received from God during his last stay on the mount, he called the people together, and informed them that it was the Lord's will to have a tabernacle built for the performance of religious worship; and that he had commanded him to speak to them to bring in their offerings, which were to consist of such articles as were necessary for accomplishing the work.* These offerings were not to be exacted, but the people were to present them voluntarily; and so desirous were they of making some atonement for their past sins, that they soon brought in more than was requisite, so that Moses was obliged to cause proclamation to be made to restrain their liberality.

Having thus obtained a sufficient collection of all kinds of materials, Moses placed them in the hands of Bezaleel and Aholiah, the two great artists in building, whom God had before made choice of; and so expeditious were they in executing the work,

* The directions given at this time were the same with those which Moses received on his first going up to the mount; but, by reason of the people's transgression in idolizing the calf, they were not then delivered to them.

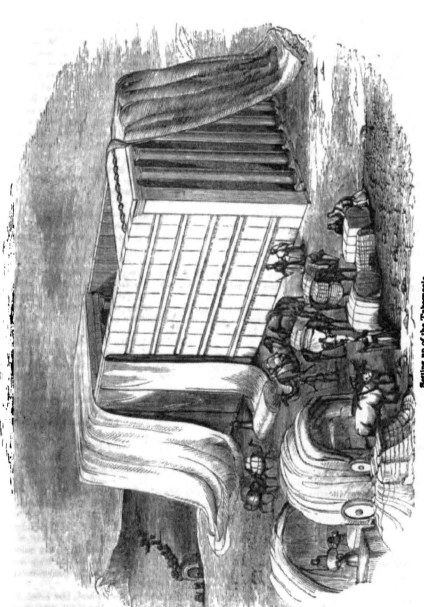

Setting up of the Tabernacle.

that, in less than six months, the tabernacle, with all its rich furniture, was entirely completed; and of which the following is an accurate description:

The tabernacle was formed somewhat like a tent, though much larger, and the whole was covered with curtains and skins. It was divided into two parts—the one covered, and properly called the tabernacle; and the other open, called the court. The covered part was again divided into two other parts, one of which was called the "holy of holies," and the curtains belonging to it were made of embroidered linen of several colors. There were ten curtains, twenty-eight cubits long and four broad: five curtains together made the two coverings, and the other five, being joined to these, covered the whole tabernacle. Above the rest were two other coverings, the one of goat's hair, the other of sheep-skins. These veils or coverings were laid on a square frame of planks resting on bases. There were forty-eight large planks, each a cubit and a half wide and ten cubits high, twenty of them on each side, and six at one end to the westward, and one on each corner: each plank was borne on two silver bases; they were let into one another, and held by bars running the length of the planks. The east end was open, and only covered with a curtain. The holy of holies was parted from the rest of the tabernacle by a curtain made fast to four pillars, standing ten cubits from the end. The whole length of the tabernacle was thirty-two cubits; the upper curtain which hung on the north and south sides was eight cubits in length, and that on the east and west four cubits.

The court was a spot of ground a hundred cubits long and fifty in breadth, enclosed by twenty columns, each of them twenty cubits high and ten in breadth, covered with silver, and standing on copper bases five cubits distant from each other, between which there were curtains drawn and fastened with hooks. At the east end was an entrance twenty cubits wide, covered with a curtain hanging loose.

The ark was in the sanctuary; it was a square chest made of shittim-wood, two cubits and a half long, and one cubit and a half wide and deep. It was covered with gold plates, and had a gold cornice which bore the lid. On the sides of it were rings, to put poles through to carry it. The covering was all of gold, and called the propitiatory or mercy-seat. There were two cherubims on it, which covered it with their wings; the tables of the law were in the ark, which was therefore called the ark of the testimony, or of the covenant.

The table was made of cedar covered with gold, two cubits long, one in breadth, and one and a half in height. About the edge of it was an ornament; it stood on four feet, and had wooden bars plated with gold to carry it on. On it was laid the offering or show-bread (which was changed every day), six loaves at each end, with incense over them. It was not lawful for any but the priests to eat of that bread.

The candlestick was of pure gold, had seven branches, three on each side and one in the middle: each branch had three knobs like apples, and three sockets in the shape of half almond-shells: that in the middle had four. On each branch was a gold lamp, and there were gold snuffers and nippers to dress them.

There were two altars: one for the burnt-offerings, five cubits long and wide, and three in height, with the figure of a seraphim at each corner. It was hollow, covered both within and without with brass plate, and open both at top and bottom. In the midst of it was a copper grate, standing on four feet, a cubit and a half high, and fastened with hooks and rings. On this grate were bound the offerings, for the performance of which there was every necessary article, such as kettles, ladles, tongs, hooks, &c.

The altar for incense was but one cubit in length and breadth, and two cubits high. It was plated with gold, and over it was a crown of the same metal. This altar was in the sanctuary with the ark, but that for burnt-offerings was placed on the north side of the tabernacle. On a pillar in the court was a large copper basin, with several cocks for the water to run out, that those who ministered might conveniently wash their hands previous to the discharge of their priestly function.

The vestments of the high-priest were, the breast-plate, the ephod, the robe, the close coat, the mitre, and the girdle. The ephod, the robe, and the close coat, were of fine linen, and covered the whole body from the neck to the heels. Over all was a purple tunic, a vestment larger and finer wrought, but not reaching so low, the bottom of which was ornamented with the representation of pomegranates and bells. The ephod consisted of two bands made of gold thread, and fastened to a kind of collar which hung down both before and behind from each shoulder, and, meeting,

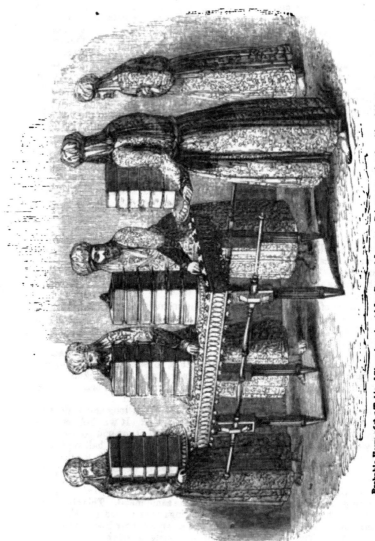

Probable Form of the Table of Shew-bread. (After Bernard Lamy.) Priests removing the old and placing the new.

served as a girdle to the tunic or vestment. On the shoulders were two large precious stones, which joined the front and hind parts of the ephod, and on them were marked the names of the twelve tribes of Israel, six on each. The breastplate was made of the same materials as the ephod, to which it was fastened with gold chains. It was a square ornament, very thick, and covered the whole breast. The girdle was likewise made of the same materials with the ephod. The mitre was made of fine flax, and covered the head; and in the front was a gold plate, on which were carved these words: HOLINESS TO THE LORD. These were the solemn ornaments belonging to the high-priest: the others were only a simple tunic or vestment, a linen mitre, and a girdle. They had all garments made of linen and cotton, which were fastened at the waist, whence they reached down to about the middle of the legs.

Such was the form of the tabernacle, and such the vestments appointed for the high-priest; the whole of which, as soon as completed, was presented to Moses for his inspection and approbation. Having viewed them attentively, and found that all was done as the Lord had commanded, he first praised God, and then bestowed his benediction on the people, for having so diligently attended to the divine injunction.

All things being now ready, on the first day of the first month,* in the second year

* MONTH, a space of four weeks, or the period of the revolution of the moon. Gen. xxix. 14. The Israelites reckoned their time by months, of which they had two series: one for civil purposes, commencing the year in their month Ethanim, the seventh of the sacred year (1 Kings viii. 2), computing from the creation of the world, and answering to our September; the other for their sacred purposes in their festivals, commencing the year in their month Abib, the seventh of the civil year, computing from the redemption from Egypt (Exod. xii. 2-18, xiii. 4), and answering to our March. The following table exhibits the order of the Jewish months, with the principal religious festivals of the Israelites and Jews:

HEBREW MONTHS.	Nearly corresponding with our months of	Months of the		Season.	SACRED FESTIVALS and Memorable Days.
		Sacred Year.	Civil Year.		
Abib, or Nisan, Exod. xii. 2-18, xiii. 4, Esth. iii. 7.	March.	1st.	7th.	Harvest.	14. Paschal Lamb killed. 15. PASSOVER. 16. First-fruits of barley harvest presented to the LORD. 21. Last day of the Passover.
Zif, or Iyar, 1 Kings vi. 1.	April.	2d.	8th.		
Sivan, Est. viii. 9.	May.	3d.	9th.	Summer.	6. PENTECOST. First fruits of wheat offered to the LORD.
Tammuz, Ezek. viii. 14.	June.	4th.	10th.		
Ab.	July.	5th.	11th.	Hot Season.	
Elul. Neh. vi. 15.	August.	6th.	12th.		9. Solomon's Temple taken by the Chaldeans; and the second Temple afterward by the Romans.
Ethanim, or Tisri, 1 Kings viii. 2.	September.	7th.	1st.	Seedtime.	1. Feast of Trumpets. 10. Day of Atonement. 15. FEAST OF TABERNACLES. 22. Last day of the feast.
Marchesvan, or Bul, 1 Kings vi. 38.	October.	8th.	2d.		
Chisleu, Zech. vii. 1.	November.	9th.	3d.	Winter.	25. Feast of the Dedication of the second Temple.
Tebeth. Est. ii. 16.	December.	10th.	4th.		
Sebat, Zech. i. 7.	January.	11th.	5th.	Cold Season.	
Adar, Est. iii. 7. Ve-Adar, or Second Adar, is here added when necessary.	February.	12th.	6th.		14 and 15. Feast of Purim, Est. ix. 18-21.

Costume of the High Priest.

after the departure of the Israelites from Egypt, the tabernacle was, by God's immediate command, set up, and all its rich furniture disposed in the proper places that had been appointed. But no sooner was this done, than the pillar of the cloud (which is called the Glory of the Lord) covered the whole, so that Moses himself, for some time, was not able to enter it.

The Almighty, at length, promising Moses to enter the tabernacle, gave him instructions (which he communicated to the people) in what manner (according to this new institution) he was to be worshipped by sacrifices and oblations; what festivals were to be observed, and how celebrated; what meats were forbidden; what the instances of uncleanness were; and what the degrees of consanguinity prohibited in marriage.

The creatures appointed to be offered in sacrifice were of five sorts, namely, oxen, lambs, goats, doves, and young pigeons, all of which were to be males and without blemish. The person who presented the offering was to do it at the altar, laying his two hands on the head of the creature, and then cutting its throat. The blood was to be received in a basin, and with it the priest was to sprinkle the vessels and corners of the altar, throwing the principal part at the foot of it. The victim was to be flayed, cut in pieces, and laid on the altar, where, either the whole, or some part of it (according to the several sorts of sacrifice), was to be burnt.

Libations were likewise added to the sacrifices. All the wine, or flour, offered with the victims, was called effusion, or pouring out. There was to be also a separate offering of fine flour and oil, baked on an iron, or in a pan, and sprinkled with oil and frankincense.

The sacrifices were of four sorts, namely,

1. The burnt-offering, every part of which was to be consumed by fire on the altar, after washing the feet and entrails.

2. The peace-offering, of which only the inward fat or tallow was to be burnt on the altar, made up with the liver and kidneys, and the tails of the lambs. The breast and the right shoulder belonged to the priests, the rest to him who offered the sacrifice.

3. The sacrifice of sin, committed either wilfully or ignorantly. In this the priest was to take some of the blood of the victim, dip his finger in it, and sprinkle seven times toward the veil of the sanctuary. The same parts of the victim were to be burnt on the altar in this as in the former sacrifice; the rest, if the sacrifice was offered for the sin of the high-priest, or for the people, was to be carried without the camp to be burnt there, with the skin, the head, the feet, and the bowels. If it was for a private person, the victim was to be divided, one half to the priest, and the other to him who offered the sacrifice.

4. The sacrifice of oblation was to consist either of fine flour, or incense, or cakes of fine flour and oil baked, or the first-fruits of new corn. With the things offered were always to be oil, salt, wine, and frankincense, the latter of which was to be thrown into the fire. Of the other things offered the priest was to take the whole, one part of which he was to burn, and the other to convert to his own use.

With respect to their festivals, the first and grand one to be observed was the Sabbath, which they were to keep in the strictest manner, dedicating it wholly to rest, and not doing any kind of business whatever.

The passover was likewise to be observed with great solemnity. It was to begin on the fourteenth day of the March moon; and for the seven days it lasted they were to eat only bread unleavened. The first day after the passover they were to offer new ears of corn; and on the fifteenth day was to be held another feast, called the harvest festival, on which they were to offer in thanksgiving two loaves made of new wheat, as the first-fruits of the harvest. The first day of the seventh month (which was the first of the civil year) was also to be held as a very solemn festival, in remembrance of the departure of the Israelites from Egypt. On the tenth of the same month was to be kept the feast of expiation, on which day the priests were to go into the sanctuary, and offer two goats, one of which was to be there given up as a solemn sacrifice for sin; but the other was to be carried, not only out of the tabernacle, but without the camp, also, and was therefore to be called the scape-goat. On the fifteenth of the same month was to begin the feast of tabernacles, which was to last eight days, being kept as a memorial that the Israelites had been accustomed to live in tents. The whole time was to be spent in mirth, and each day the people were to walk round the altar with boughs in their hands.

The High Priest on the Day of Atonement, and a Levite.

With respect to animal food they were to be very careful in making a proper distinction between beasts that were clean, and those that were otherwise, it being lawful for them to eat the first, but not the last. Two qualifications were required for reckoning a beast clean, which were, that it should have a cloven foot, and that it should chew the cud; so that it was unlawful for them to eat swine's flesh, or rabbits and hares, the former not chewing the cud, and the latter not having cloven feet. All birds of prey were forbidden; and it was unlawful for them to eat blood, or the flesh of beasts strangled.

Among the laws relative to uncleanness, leprosy was to be reckoned the greatest, of the nature and quality of which the priest was to judge, and to dispose of the party as he should think proper. Some uncleannesses were to be removed by washing their garments and bodies, and others by offering up sacrifices.

The laws relating to matrimony were principally these. They were forbidden to marry strange women. One man might have several wives; but the persons with whom it was not allowed to contract matrimony were, the father, mother, mother-in-law, sister by the father or mother's side, son's or daughter's daughter, father's wife's daughter, father or mother's sister, uncle, daughter-in-law, brother's wife, wife's sister or daughter, or grandson or granddaughter. It was, however, not only lawful, but a command enjoined, that the brother should marry the brother's widow, provided he died without issue.

Moses, having communicated these, and some other ordinances, to the people, proceeded next, agreeably to the divine command, to constitute his brother Aaron high-priest, and to fix the order of priesthood in his son and their posterity. In the execution of this ceremony Moses robed them, anointed their heads with oil, and made them offer sacrifices for sin. The function of the priests in general, was, to offer sacrifice to the Lord, but the high-priest's was of a particular nature. He was to go once a year, on the day of expiation, into the sanctuary, clad in his priestly garments, there to burn incense before the ark, and sprinkle the blood of the offering seven times with his finger. All the tribe of Levi were appointed to assist the priests in the services of the tabernacle; and to the whole were appointed particular allowances for their subsistence. But if any, either of the priests or Levites, had any bodily imperfection, they were to be excluded from the function, but, at the same time, permitted to enjoy the rights and privileges of their birth. The obligations they lay under were these: they were not to drink any wine, or any other intoxicating liquors, when they were to officiate in the tabernacle: they were not to marry a woman who had been divorced or prostituted; and lastly, they were not to attend funerals, unless those of their own fathers, mothers, sons, daughters, brothers, or maiden sisters.

On the eighth day after Aaron had been appointed to the office of high-priest, he offered his first burnt-offering for himself and the people. •This was very acceptable to the Almighty, who was pleased to testify his approbation by sending fire upon the altar, which consumed the offering in the sight of the people, who, with loud shouts and acclamations, expressed their joy for so singular a circumstance, and prostrated themselves on the ground in humble adoration before the Divine Majesty.

The fire thus miraculously kindled was, by the divine command, to be kept perpetually burning, and no other to be used in all the oblations to be made to God. But Nadab and Abihu, two of Aaron's sons, forgetful of their duty, took their censers, and putting common fire in them, laid incense thereon, and offered strange fire before the Lord. For this flagrant violation of the divine command, the Almighty was so offended, that, as a just punishment, he immediately struck them dead with lightning. To strike a terror into the rest of the priestly order, and deter them from disobedience to the commands of God, Moses ordered the people to take their dead bodies from the sanctuary, and carry them out of the camp in the same condition they found them. He likewise charged Aaron and the rest of his sons, not to mourn for Nadab and Abihu, in shaving their heads, or rending their clothes; but that they should leave those marks of mourning to the rest of the people, from whom they ought to distinguish themselves in this, as well as in other points, in reverence to that holy anointing, whereby they had been consecrated to the Lord, and thereby separated from their brethren.

A short time after the melancholy circumstance last related, another awful proof was given of the danger of incurring the displeasure of the Almighty. This was exemplified in the case of one, whose mother's name was Shelomith, an Israelitish

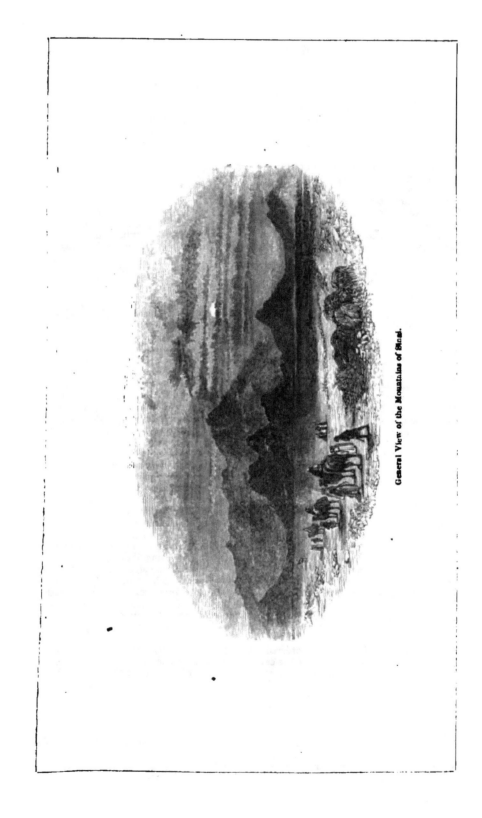

General View of the Mountains of Sinai.

woman of the tribe of Dan, but whose husband was an Egyptian, but supposed to have become a proselyte to the house of Israel. This young man quarreled with another, and a battle ensuing, Shelomith was worsted. Fired with resentment at being conquered, he in the height of his passion, cursed and blasphemed the name of the Lord; upon which being apprehended and brought before Moses, he ordered him into custody till he should know from the Lord what punishment to inflict on him for his transgression. Though the third command in the decalogue forbade the taking of God's name in vain, yet this blasphemous cursing being an offence of a higher nature, against which no positive law was yet provided, Moses had recourse to the Lord, who was pleased to tell him thus: "Bring forth," says he, "him that cursed without the camp, and let all that heard him lay their hands upon his head,* and let all the congregation stone him."

In obedience to the divine command, Moses ordered the sentence to be immediately put in execution; and a law was thereon made, that whosoever should, from that time, blaspheme the name of the Lord, whether he was an Israelite, or a stranger, should be stoned to death.

CHAPTER X.

WHILE the Israelites lay encamped in the wilderness of Sinai, the Almighty ordered Moses, assisted by Aaron, and the heads of the respective tribes, to make a general muster of the people, in order to ascertain the number of those who were able to carry arms. This was accordingly done, when the number of true born Israelites appeared to be 603,550 men,† exclusive of the tribe of Levi. These were, by the express command of the Almighty, exempted, being designed for the peculiar service of the tabernacle, not only to take charge thereof, and of all the vessels belonging to it, but likewise to take it down upon every remove, to guard it safe on the way, and to put it up again at such places as should be appointed for encampment.

The Israelites being thus mustered, Moses and Aaron, by the express command of God, appointed the manner of their encampment, which was not only to take place now, but to be continued ever after, as follows:

The whole body was divided into four grand camps, each consisting of three tribes, under one standard, and so placed as entirely to enclose the tabernacle.

The standard of the camp of Judah was first. It consisted of the tribes of Judah, Issachar, and Zebulon, (the sons of Leah), and was pitched on the east side of the tabernacle, toward the rising of the sun.

On the south side was the standard of the camp of Reuben, under which were the tribes of Reuben and Simeon (the sons of Leah likewise), and of Gad, the son of Zilpah, Leah's maid.

On the west side was the standard of the camp of Ephraim, under which were the tribes of Ephraim, Manasseh, and Benjamin.

On the north side was the standard of the camp of Dan, under which were the tribes of Dan and Naphtali (the sons of Bilhah, Rachel's maid), and of Asher (the son of Zilpah).

Between the four great camps and the tabernacle were four lesser camps, consisting of the priests and Levites, under whose immediate care and protection the tabernacle was placed.

On the east side were encamped Moses and Aaron, with Aaron's sons, who had the charge of the sanctuary.

* This way of laying hands on the heads of criminals may seem to arise from several causes. 1. That they were witnesses of the fact, and that the person condemned suffered justly; protesting, that if he were innocent they desired that his blood might fall on their own heads. 2. They put their hands on the head of the criminal in token of an expiatory sacrifice; for idolatry, blasphemy, and such grievous crimes, if they were not punished, they expected would attract a guilt, not only on the witness, but the whole nation, which by the death of the criminal, as by a victim, might be expiated. 3. That the criminal was the just cause of his own death.

† The ages of these men were, from twenty years old to fifty; and the exact number in each tribe was as follows:

In the tribe of Reuben, 46,500; Simeon, 59,300; Gad, 45,650; Judah, 74,600; Issachar, 54,400; Zebulon, 57,400; Ephraim, 40,500; Manasseh, 32,200; Benjamin, 35,400; Dan, 62,700; Asher, 41,500; Naphtali, 53,400; total 602,550.

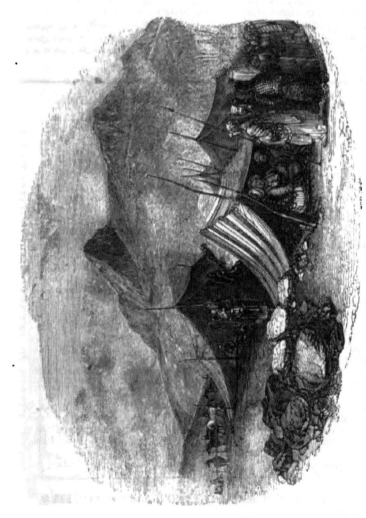

Bedouin Encampment in a Valley near Sinai.

On the south side were the Kohathites, a part of the Levites, descended from Kohath, the second son of Levi.

On the west side were the Gershonites, another part of the Levites, descended from Gershon, Levi's eldest son.

On the north side were planted the Merarites, the remaining part of the Levites, who descended from Merari, Levi's youngest son.

Such was the manner of the encampment of the Israelites, being the only regular description of one which the Bible contains; but, from incidental allusions, we may gather that the camps which the Hebrews in after-times formed in their military operations, differed in several respects from the present, the admirable arrangement of which is easily perceived, although some difference of opinion exists as to a few of the details.

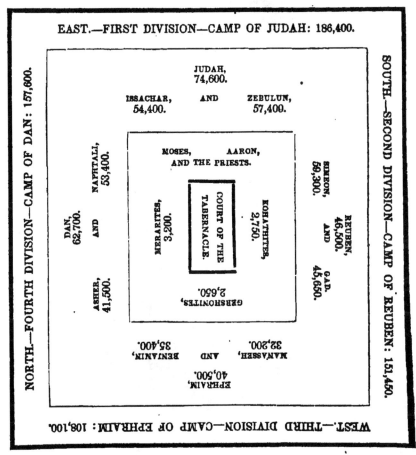

The diagram above will exhibit the apparent order better than a verbal description, however minute. It is thus seen that the camp was formed in a quadrangle, having on each side three tribes under one general standard. How these tribes were placed with regard to each other is not very clear; some fix the leading tribe in the centre, and the two others on each side; but the description seems rather to indicate that the leading tribe extended along the whole exterior line, and that the two other tribes pitched beside each other, within. The only other alternative seems to be, to suppose that the two minor tribes also extended in full line, the last tribe mentioned in each division, being the innermost. The collective encampment enclosed a

Valley in Sinai.

large open square, in the centre of which stood the tabernacle. The position which the tabernacle thus occupied still remains the place of honor in grand oriental camps, and is usually occupied by the tent of the king or general. The distance between it and the common camp was indicative of respect; what the distance was we are not told, except by the Rabbins, who say that it was two thousand cubits, and apparently ground this statement upon Josh. iii. 4. The interval was not however wholly vacant, being occupied by the small camps of the Levites, who had the charge and custody of the tabernacle, and pitched their tents around it; the tents of Moses, Aaron, and the priests, occupying the most honorable place, fronting the entrance to the tabernacle, or rather to the court which contained it. The Jewish writers say that the circumference of the entire encampment was about twelve miles; a statement which would seem sufficiently moderate when we recollect the hollow square in the centre, and consider the vast extent of ground required for the tents of two millions of people. This regular and admirable arrangement of so vast a host, under their ensigns, around the tabernacle, must have given a most striking and impressive appearance to the camp, as viewed from the hills. We know the effect which the view of it produced upon one person, who *did* view it from the hills, and then broke forth in rapture, exclaiming, " How goodly are thy tents, O Jacob! and thy tabernacles, O Israel! As the valleys are they spread forth, as the trees of lign-aloes which the Lord hath planted, and as cedar trees beside the waters." (Num. xxiv. 5, 6.)

The encampment being thus formed, the next consideration was, to regulate the mode of marching, which was accordingly done as follows:

Whenever they were to decamp (which was always to take place as soon as the pillar of the cloud left the tabernacle) the trumpet was to be immediately sounded, and, upon the first alarm, the standard of Judah being raised, the three tribes which belonged to it were to set forward. On the movement of these the tabernacle was to be taken down with all convenient expedition, and the Gershonites and Merarites were to attend the wagons with the boards and staves belonging to it. This being done, a second alarm was to be given by the trumpet, on which the standard of Reuben's camp was to advance with the three tribes belonging to it. After these were to follow the Kohathites, bearing the sanctuary, which, because it was more holy, and not so cumbersome, as the pillars and boards of the tabernacle, was not to be put into a wagon, but carried on their shoulders. Next was to follow the standard of Ephraim's camp, with the tribes belonging to it; and, last of all, the other three tribes, under the standard of Dan, were to bring up the rear.

A short time after these matters were adjusted, the pillar of the cloud gave the Israelites a signal to decamp. On their beginning to move, agreeably to the order prescribed, Moses addressed himself to God. " Rise," said he, " Lord, and let thine enemies be scattered; and let them that hate thee flee before thee. And when the ark of the covenant (by which they were directed when to stop) rested, he added "Return, O Lord, unto the many thousands of Israel."

After marching for three days in the wilderness of Sinai, the Israelites began to complain of the fatigues of their journey, and to relate their grievances, with great asperity, to Moses. This so offended the Almighty, that he sent down fire from heaven, which destroyed all those who were situated in the extreme parts of the camp. The rest were so terrified at this circumstance, that they immediately applied to Moses, at whose intercession the fire ceased, but, in remembrance of the incident, he called the place Taberah, which, in the Hebrew language, signifies *burning*.

But this instance of the divine power had little effect on the dissatisfied Israelites. They made heavy complaints for want of flesh for food; and intimated to Moses how much happier they were when in the land of Egypt, where, though in a state of bondage, they could possess a variety of articles necessary for the preservation of life.

Moses had often heard them murmur, and patiently borne with it, but now that they were grown so numerous, and the greatness of their numbers demanding still more care and vigilance to govern them than what came from the assistance of the magistrates appointed by the advice of his father-in-law Jethro, he became exceedingly uneasy, and, in an address to God, represented the great and heavy burdens under which he labored, in having the management of so numerous and dissatisfied a people.

No sooner did the Almighty hear the complaints of his faithful servant, than he immediately gave him relief, by ordering him to choose seventy men from among the elders of Israel, and to bring them with him to the tabernacle of the congregation.

"There," said he, "I will come down and talk with thee, and I will give them a portion of the same spirit with which I have inspired thee; and they shall bear the burden of the people with thee."

In conformity to the divine command, Moses selected seventy of the elders, sixty-eight of whom he conducted to the tabernacle, whither they had no sooner arrived, than the Almighty was pleased to fulfil his promise, by inspiring them with the like kind of spirit he had given to Moses, and by which they were enabled to prophesy. Nay, so extensive was this inspiration, that though the other two came not out with the rest to the tabernacle, but remained in the camp, yet they received the same impression of the spirit with the rest, and, in like manner, prophesied. This circumstance so surprised a certain young man in the camp, that he immediately hastened to the tabernacle, to acquaint Moses that Edad and Medad (which were the names of the two elders left behind) were prophesying in the camp. Joshua (who was totally unacquainted with the operations of the Lord by his spirit) was likewise greatly surprised, and, thinking it a derogation of his master, likewise ran to the tabernacle, and advised Moses to restrain them from that power which only belonged to himself. But Moses reproved him for his conduct in these words: "Dost thou," said he, "envy them on my account? Would to God that all the Lord's people were inspired, and that they might be endued with the spirit of prophecy!"

The murmurings of the people for want of flesh still continued, and to such a height did their fury arise, that they beset Moses's tent on all sides, and, in the most tumultuous manner, demanded of him to relieve their necessities. Thus circumstanced Moses applied himself to God, to whom he intimated the little probability there was of supplying so numerous a body of people with the article requested. The Almighty was pleased to promise that he would remove this evil; and at the same time gently rebuked Moses in these words: "Is the Lord's hand," said he, "waxed short? thou shalt see now whether my word shall come to pass unto thee or not."

It was not long before this divine promise was fulfilled; for the Almighty causing a south wind to arise, it drove prodigious quantities of quails from the seacoast to within a mile of the camp, which being taken by the people, they feasted on them in the most greedy manner.

But God soon called them to a dreadful account for their insolent demand of flesh, and their distrust of his providence: for while they were regaling themselves with these dainties, he visited them with a severe plague, of which great numbers died, and were buried on the spot where they fell. In consequence of this circumstance the place was called Kibroth-Hattaavah, which signifies *the graves or sepulchres of lust and concupiscence.*

From this place the Israelites marched to Hazeroth, where they had not been long before another circumstance occurred of a very disagreeable nature. Aaron and his sister Miriam, observing the great power their brother Moses had over the people, and that God chiefly made use of him in the delivery of his sacred oracles, began to look upon him with an eye of envy. To give some color to their conduct, they pretended to fall out with him, on account of his having married a foreigner, whom they contemptuously called an Ethiopian; and, to lessen his importance, and at the same time enlarge their own, they added, "What, hath the Lord spoken only to Moses? hath he not spoken also by us?"

Moses saw the discontent of his brother and sister; but considering it only as a personal pique, took no notice of it. The Almighty, however, being greatly offended at their conduct, thought proper to interpose, and convince them that such behavior to his faithful servant was of the most heinous nature, and should not pass unnoticed. Ordering, therefore, Moses, Aaron, and Miriam, to attend at the door of the tabernacle, he sharply rebuked the two latter for their insolence, asking them, how they durst speak against his servant Moses? "You," said he to Miriam, "have shared in the prophetic office, and to you have I declared my will in dreams and visions; but with Moses I have conversed more familiarly, and I will speak face to face with him, and show him as much of my glory as he is capable of seeing."

Thus Moses had the secret satisfaction of finding himself justified by his divine protector; but Aaron, to his great confusion, beheld his sister Miriam made a dreadful example of God's anger. She was suddenly afflicted with a most dreadful and inveterate leprosy; upon which Aaron, addressing himself to Moses, acknowledged the

11

sin they had committed, begged pardon, and solicited him to intercede with God in behalf of his sister, that the leprosy might be removed, and her former health restored.

Moses, who was naturally of a meek disposition, and ever ready to pardon an injury offered to himself, made no hesitation at complying with Aaron's request. His intercession had the desired effect: the Almighty was pleased to promise that the evil should be removed; but as the offence was of a public nature, he ordered her to be turned out of the camp for seven days, in the manner of a common leper, in order to deter others from committing the like seditious practices.

Soon after Miriam's return to the camp, the Israelites removed to the desert of Paran; whence, after several encampments, they reached Kadesh-Barnea, situated on the frontiers of the land of Canaan.

On their arrival at this place, Moses, by the divine command, selected twelve men, one from each tribe, whom he ordered to go as spies into the promised land, to take a view of the country. He charged them to make a diligent examination into the strength of its cities and inhabitants, the nature and fertility of its soil, and the principal articles it produced, some of the latter of which he told them to bring with them on their return.

With these instructions the twelve spies set forward on their journey, and proceeded from the entrance of the country on the north, to its extremity on the south. In their way back they passed through a valley remarkable for its fertility in vines, and therefore called the *valley of Eschol*, which signifies a *cluster of grapes*. Attracted by the beauty of the fruit, they determined to preserve some and carry it to the camp. They cut down a branch, on which was only one cluster of grapes, but of such an immoderate size, that they were obliged to lay it on a pole, and carry it between two of them. Nor was this the only product of this happy soil: the golden fig and beautiful pomegranate adorned the trees, and a variety of other fruits (of which they took samples with them) loaded the luxuriant branches.

The spies having, in the compass of forty days, taken a view of the whole country of Canaan, returned to the camp of the Israelites; and, after showing them the fruits of the land, gave them an account of the observations they had made in the course of their journey. "We have been," said they, "in the country to which you sent us. It is a fertile and plentiful land; but the inhabitants of it are powerful. There are great cities with strong walls. We have seen those men of the race of Anak, warlike men, and of a gigantic stature. The Amalekites inhabit the south part of the land; the Hittites, Jebusites, and Amorites, the mountains; and the Canaanites, the banks of the river Jordan."

The people were highly pleased with that part of the account relative to the fertility of the country; but when they reflected on its strength, with the size and number of its inhabitants, they were greatly alarmed, and expressed their fears at being brought to a place where they were in the most imminent danger. But Caleb and Joshua (two of the twelve who were sent to view the country) endeavored to remove their fears, by saying, "Let us make ourselves masters of the country, for we are strong enough to conquer the inhabitants."

This had the desired effect, and might have produced happy consequences, had it not been for the cowardly disposition of the other ten, who, perceiving that the account given by Caleb and Joshua had fired the people with a design of becoming the possessors of the country by a speedy conquest, began to retract from their former accounts, to paint matters in the worst light, and to represent it as a thing impossible, both by reason of the strength of its fortified towns, and the valor and gigantic stature of the inhabitants.

This cowardly representation defeated all the arguments used by Caleb and Joshua in favor of the enterprise. The Israelites, one and all, cried out they could never hope to overcome such powerful nations, in comparison of which they looked on themselves as mere grasshoppers and reptiles. In short, their murmurings grew to such a height by the next morning, that a return to Egypt was thought more advisable than to face such an enemy; and they went so far as to deliberate on a proper person who should reconduct them into the land of their former thraldom.

This perverseness of the people greatly afflicted Moses, who, finding them bent on their own ruin, and fearful that some dreadful consequence would follow, prostrated himself on the ground (as did also his brother Aaron) in the presence of the whole

Bedouins collecting Fruits in Palestine.

assembly, and besought of God that he would be merciful in his judgments on the people for their sin and ingratitude.

Caleb and Joshua expressed their grief by rending their clothes; and endeavored, in the most forcible manner, to convince the people that their fears were ill founded, and that they might, by putting their trust in God, overpower their enemies, and make themselves masters of the promised land. "The land" (said they) "that we pass through is indeed a rich and fertile land, abounding with all things necessary for life. If we please the Lord he will bring us into this land, and give it us. Do not, therefore, by rebelling against him, forfeit his promise and protection. Nor be afraid of the people of the land, whom we shall as surely conquer as we eat our food, and with as much ease. The Lord is with us, and we have nothing to fear."

But so far was this speech from making any impression on the perverse and obstinate Israelites, that, in a tumultuous manner, they called out to stone Caleb and Joshua; and which they would certainly have done, had not the glory of God at that instant visibly appeared before all the people, in the tabernacle of the congregation.

As soon as Moses saw this he prostrated himself before the Lord, who, being highly incensed against the Israelites for their perverse conduct, threatened to send a pestilence that should totally extirpate them, and at the same time told Moses that he would make him a prince of a more numerous and powerful nation.

The pious Moses (as he had several times done before) became again an intercessor for the people. He in the most earnest manner solicited the Almighty to pardon their offences, and represented the consequences that might follow should he totally destroy them: the substance of his solicitations and observations was in words to this effect: "O thou everlasting Jehovah, who appearedst to Abraham, to Isaac, and to Jacob, and who wast graciously pleased to promise that their children should inherit the land of Canaan, look in mercy on this people, whom neither promises will encourage, nor threatenings deter from disobeying thee. O Lord, turn away thy fierce anger, for thou art a God of mercy, and I will trust in thee to spare this wicked, this rebellious people."

These arguments and expostulations in some measure averted the divine vengeance, the Almighty promising Moses not to put his first design into execution. But as the ingratitude and infidelity of the people had become intolerable (notwithstanding God's constant care in providing against their wants, screening them from their enemies, and preserving them from all dangers), he declared that not one of those who had murmured, from twenty years old and upward, should ever enter the promised land; but that they should wander with their children about the wilderness for the space of forty years, in which time they should all pay the debt of nature, and that their children should have those possessions which, had they not been so disobedient, they might have enjoyed themselves.

As for the ten false spies, who were the immediate authors of this defection, they were all destroyed by a sudden death, and became the first instances of the punishment denounced against the body of the people.

Caleb and Joshua, who had not only done their duty in giving a faithful account of their observations, but also endeavored to remove the ill-concerted intentions of the people, were preserved. For this their conduct they received the divine approbation, as also a promise that they should live to enter and inherit the promised land.

When Moses related these particulars to the people their tempers were greatly altered, and they expressed their uneasiness for the offence they had committed by putting on the deepest mourning. Supposing that their forwardness now would make some atonement for their former cowardice, they assembled themselves together the next morning, and offered to go on the conquest. "We are ready," said they, "to go to the place whereof the Lord has spoken to us."

But this offer, instead of arising from any natural courage, took place only from a presumptuous rashness. This Moses well knew, and therefore endeavored all he could to dissuade them from so ill judged an enterprise. He told them it was contrary to God's express command, and therefore could not prosper; that by their late undutiful behavior they had forfeited his assistance and protection, without which it was impossible for them to succeed; and that, as the Amalekites and Canaanites had gained the passes of the mountains before them, every attempt must prove abortive.

But all this admonition had no weight with the obstinate Israelites. Notwithstanding the ark of the covenant was not with them; notwithstanding Moses, their general, was not at the head of them; yet out they marched to the top of the mountains, where, the enemy surprising them, they were immediately thrown into the greatest disorder, prodigious numbers were slain, and the rest obliged to save themselves by flight; nor did they stop till they came to a place called Hormah. Though it was but eleven days' journey hence to Kadesh-barnea, yet, for their disobedience, they were so interrupted as to be nearly two years in getting to the place whence they came.

Many remarkable circumstances occurred during the stay of the Israelites in the wilderness. The first recorded by the sacred historian is an instance of the divine severity on a man who, by a post-fact law, was adjudged to be stoned to death for violating the sabbath, by gathering sticks on that day. Though a particular injunction had been laid on the people to keep this commandment in the strictest manner, yet no penalty had been annexed to the violation of it. The people, therefore, who brought the offender before Moses, were ordered to keep him in custody till he should know the divine pleasure concerning sabbath-breakers. The Almighty was pleased to return for answer, that such transgressors should be stoned to death; upon which the offender was immediately conducted out of the camp, and the sentence executed.

The next material circumstance that occurred was a violent rebellion raised by Korah, great-grandson of Levi, and consequently one of the heads of that tribe. This ambitious person, having long envied Aaron, on account of him and his family being raised to the highest office in the priesthood, and to which he thought himself had an equal title, was always caballing against him, till at length he had brought over two hundred and fifty eminent persons to his interest, among whom were Dathan and Abiram, two of the chiefs of the tribe of Reuben.

As soon as Korah thought matters properly ripe for an open rupture, he appeared at the head of the faction, and publicly upbraided Moses and Aaron with an unjust ambition, in usurping that power to themselves of which he thought himself entitled to a part; and that the arbitrary measures they pursued were injurious to the people, by depriving them of their just and natural liberties.

This strange and unexpected address so surprised Moses, that he immediately prostrated himself on the ground, in which situation he lay for some time.* At length he arose, and, with great steadiness and magnanimity, informed them that the next day the Lord would decide the controversy, and would make it appear who were his servants, who were holy, and who the proper persons to be admitted into his divine presence. He then, with his usual calmness and serenity of mind, argued the matter with them, and, in the most mild manner, rebuked them for the impropriety of their conduct. He was rather more severe on Korah (who was the author of the defection) than the rest; and concluded with addressing them conjunctively in words to this effect: "Hear me" (says he), "ye sons of Levi. Is it a matter of so light concern, that the God of Israel hath distinguished you from the rest of Israel, to admit you to the more immediate service of the tabernacle, and to stand before the congregation and minister to them? Is not this an honor sufficient to satisfy your ambitious spirit, but that ye must aim at the priesthood too? This is the cause of your clamors; and for this ye have moved the people to sedition. But, be assured, whatever ye may pretend against Aaron, this insult is against the Lord, as it is against his dispensations that ye murmur and conspire."

Dathan and Abiram were at some distance when Moses thus talked with the rest of the conspirators; and therefore, supposing they had been drawn into the plot at the instigation of Korah, he sent for them privately, with a design of arguing the matter with them in the mildest terms. But instead of a civil answer, he received the following haughty message: "Is it" (said they) "a matter of so small moment, that thou hast brought us out of a land which flowed with plenty, to kill us in the desert? Thou affectest dominion, and wouldst make thyself prince over us also. Notwithstanding thy fair promises, thou hast not brought us into a land that flows with milk and honey, nor given us any inheritance of fields and vineyards; but when

---

* It is very reasonable to imagine, that Moses (who was well acquainted with the gracious and ready assistance of God in time of need) was, during the time of his being on the ground, applying himself to the Lord for protection against this mutinous body of people. And it is likewise reasonable to imagine, that while he lay in this humble posture God appeared to him, and gave him comfortable advice in what manner he should conduct himself; as he soon after spoke to them with great courage, and to vindicate himself, put the matter between him and them upon trial the next day.

we were ready to take possession of the promised land, thou didst turn us back into this barren desert, to repeat the fatigues and hardships we had before undergone. We will not come."

These unjust reproaches highly provoked Moses, but, instead of returning any ill language to them, he addressed himself to God, saying: "Respect not thou their offering: I have not taken one ass from them, neither have I hurt one of them." He then summoned Korah and all his companions to meet him and Aaron the next day at the tabernacle, and to bring with them their censers ready prepared with incense to appear before the Lord.

Accordingly, early the next morning, Moses and Aaron went to the tabernacle, whither Korah also repaired at the head of his party, with each man a censer in his hand, and attended by a prodigious multitude of people, who, in all probability, went as spectators of this singular contest.

The first thing that attracted their attention was the amazing splendor that issued from the cloud over the tabernacle, from which God called to Moses and Aaron, ordering them to withdraw, that he might inflict that punishment on the rebellious crew they justly deserved.

Moses and Aaron, knowing that the multitude who attended on this occasion did it only to gratify their curiosity, and at the same time lamenting that they should equally suffer with the wicked Korah and his party, prostrated themselves before God, and interceded for their protection. "O God" (said they), "thou God of the spirit of all flesh, shall one man sin, and wilt thou be angry with all?" Their prayers were no sooner offered than heard; and the Almighty, being pleased to listen to their solicitation, commanded them to tell the people to withdraw. Frightened at the amazing splendor that issued from the cloud, they readily obeyed this order, and retired at some distance from the tents of Korah and his two principal associates, Dathan and Abiram, who stood in a daring manner near their own tents, attended by their wives and families.

As soon as the multitude had retired to a proper distance, Moses addressed them in words to this effect: "By this" (said he) "you shall know that the Lord has commissioned me to do what I have done, and that I have undertaken nothing of my own head. If these men" (meaning Korah and his party) "die the common way of nature, or be visited as other men, then take it for granted the Lord hath not sent me; but if he deal with them after a strange and unusual manner, and the earth, opening her mouth, swallow them up alive, then shall ye understand that these men have provoked the Lord."

No sooner had Moses spoken these words than the earth was suddenly convulsed, and the surface of it opening, Korah and his two adherents, Dathan and Abiram, together with their families and substance, were all swallowed up alive, and, the ground closing on them, they perished. When the people who stood round them saw their dismal fate they were greatly frightened, and cried out, "Let us fly, lest the earth swallow us up also."

In the mean time God, to punish the rest of these rebellious people, who had profanely attempted to offer incense contrary to the law, sent down fire from heaven, and destroyed the whole two hundred and fifty men that had joined with Korah.

To perpetuate the memory of this judgment, as well as to deter, for the future, any but the sons of Aaron from presuming to burn incense before the Lord, Moses, by the divine command, ordered Eleazar, Aaron's son, to gather up the censers of the dead, and to have them beat into broad plates as a covering for the altar, assigning this as a reason: "That it might be for a memorial to the children of Israel, that no stranger, or any that was not of Aaron's family, should presume to offer incense before the Lord, lest he died the death of Korah and his company."

It might have been supposed that so dreadful a punishment would, at least for some time, have kept the Israelites within the bounds of their obedience; but no sooner were they recovered from their fright than they again began to murmur, and to accuse Moses and Aaron with having (as they called the late mutineers) murdered "the people of the Lord."

Moses and Aaron, well knowing the turbulent temper of the people, and fearing they might proceed to some violent outrage, took sanctuary in the tabernacle, which they had no sooner entered than the Almighty commanded them to withdraw from the rest of the congregation, for that in a short time he would destroy them.

In consequence of this, Moses and Aaron immediately prostrated themselves on the ground, and earnestly implored of God to spare the people; but, early as they were in their supplication, the divine vengeance was before them, for the Almighty, provoked by the repeated rebellions of the people, had already sent a pestilence among them.

As soon as Moses observed this, he ordered Aaron to take a censer, put fire and incense in it from the altar, and hasten to the congregation to make atonement for the sins of the people. Aaron did as Moses commanded, and standing between the dead and the living, he prayed for some time, and the plague ceased. But notwith-standing the very short time this calamity lasted, yet with such violence did it rage, that the number carried off by it amounted to fourteen thousand and seven hundred persons.

Though God had thus in two instances punished the people for their wickedness, yet, knowing that the minds of many of them were, by the insinuations of Korah and his accomplices, still prejudiced against Aaron and his family, on account of their being invested with the priesthood, he was pleased to put an end to all controversy on this head by the following miracle. He commanded Moses to take a rod from each tribe, and to write upon it the name of the prince of that tribe to whom it be-longed, and to write Aaron's name on that of the tribe of Levi; that, when this was done, he should lay up the twelve rods in the tabernacle, before the ark of the testi-mony, until the next morning, when some miraculous change should be seen that would determine in whose family the priesthood should be established.

Moses, who never failed paying an immediate obedience to the divine command, did as he was ordered; and going next morning to the tabernacle, brought out the twelve rods in the presence of all the people. Eleven of the rods were in the same state as when he put them into the tabernacle, but the twelfth (which belonged to Aaron) had a very different appearance, for it had not only budded, but likewise blossomed, and bore ripe almonds. A convincing proof to the people that God had singled out Aaron and his family to the priestly office.

In memory of this remarkable decision, God ordered Aaron's rod to be laid up in the ark of the covenant, that, by the people's seeing it, they might not again rebel, but remain satisfied with those whom he had been pleased, in so distinguished a manner, to appoint to the priestly office.

After the establishment of the high-priest's office in Aaron and his family, the Is-raelites moved about, from one place to another, in the wilderness, but chiefly about the mountains of Idumæa, until God, by shortening the period of human life, had taken away almost all that generation, "of whom he had sworn in his wrath," as the Psalmist expresses it, xcv. 2., "that they should not enter into his rest." And, in-deed, great reason had he to be angry with them, since, during the remainder of their peregrination, they were guilty of many more murmurings than Moses has thought proper to record, which, nevertheless, are mentioned, with no small severity, by other inspired writers. See Amos v. 26; Acts vii. 43.

As the time, however, of their entrance into the land of Canaan drew near, they advanced into the wilderness of Sin, and pitched their camp at Kadesh,* where Mir-iam,† sister to Moses and Aaron, died, and was buried.

The Israelites had not been long at Kadesh, before they were greatly distressed for water, upon which (as they had before done on similar occasions) they exclaimed, with great vehemence, against Moses and Aaron, saying, "Why have ye brought the Lord's people into the wilderness to kill them and their cattle? Why did you per-suade us to leave the fertile land of Egypt to bring us into this barren place, which affords neither water to quench our thirst, nor fruits to satisfy our hunger? Would to God we had perished with our brethren before the Lord."

The impatience and dissatisfaction of the Israelites greatly perplexed Moses and Aaron, who, as was their usual custom on such occasions, addressed themselves to God, beseeching him to remove the present distresses of the people. The Almighty

* This was not Kadesh-Barnea, the station or encampment of the Israelites on the confines of the northern part of Canaan; but another Kadesh, situated on the confines of Idumæa, and not far from the Red sea.

† Miriam was the eldest of the three, and was nearly a hundred and thirty years old. Eusebius assures us, that in his time her tomb was found at Kadesh, a small distance from Petrea, the capital of Arabia Petrea. Several of the ancients are of opinion that she died a virgin, and that she was the legislatrix and governess of the Israelitish women, as Moses was the legislator of the men.

was pleased to listen to their request: he ordered Moses to take his rod, and, with the assistance of Aaron, assemble the people together; which having done, he should speak to the rock in their sight, and it should immediately produce abundance of water.

Agreeably to these orders, Moses and Aaron assembled the people before the rock, who, no doubt, readily attended in expectation of having those grievances removed of which they had so greatly complained. Hitherto Moses had paid an *exact* and absolute obedience to all the commands God had enjoined him; but now (however it happened) he made some deviation from his instructions, and thereby committed the greatest miscarriage of his whole life. He was ordered to speak to the *rock* before the people; but, instead of so doing, he spoke to the *people*, saying, "Hear now, ye rebels; must we fetch you water out of this rock?" In doing this, he expressed impatience and heat of spirit, which were in direct opposition to that humility he had hitherto possessed.

This conduct of Moses was highly offensive to God, as appeared from his first striking the rock without its having the least effect. However, on striking it a second time, the water issued from it in great abundance, and not only the people, but likewise the cattle, were plentifully supplied with that necessary article they had so much wanted.

Though this was the first time that Moses had made the least deviation from the divine injunctions, yet it pleased the Almighty to make him sensible of his fault, and to inflict a punishment on him for his disobedience. Considering Aaron also as concerned with him in the transgression, he denounced this sentence against them conjunctively. "Because," said he, "ye believed me not, to sanctify me in the eyes of the children of Israel, therefore ye shall not bring this congregation into the land, which I have given them." From this unhappy accident, the place was called Meribah, which, in the Hebrew language, signifies, *chiding* or *strife*.

Though Moses had committed this offence, and received the divine chastisement, yet he still preserved the command and government of the people. Intending to decamp from Kadesh, as a necessary precaution in order to secure the safety of the people, he sent messengers to the king of Edom (upon whose borders they then were) requesting permission to pass through his territories, assuring him that they would not commit any hostilities, nor give the least molestation to any of his subjects. But the haughty Edomite was so far from granting his request, that he came out with a powerful army to oppose him; upon which Moses, after decamping from Kadesh, took another way, and marched to Mount Hor, near the borders of Edom, where they pitched their tents, and for some time encamped.

The time now drawing near, that the Israelites were to penetrate the promised land (into which the Lord had told Aaron he should not enter because of his transgression at Meribah), God gave Aaron notice that his dissolution was near at hand, that he might the more properly prepare himself for so awful an event. As a necessary introduction, the Almighty commanded Moses to take Aaron, and Eleazar his son (who was to succeed him in the office of high-priest), and conduct them to the top of the mount, where he should strip Aaron of his priestly garments, and put them upon Eleazar his son.

Moses having obeyed these commands, Aaron, in a very short time after, gave up the ghost;[*] and when the people heard that he was dead, they mourned for him thirty days.

CHAPTER XI.

WHILE the Israelites lay encamped near Mount Hor,[†] Arad, one of the kings of Canaan, who dwelt in the south, being informed of their situation, and that they in-

[*] He was buried on the spot where he died, it being the ancient custom to bury persons of eminence in high places. See Joshua xxiv. 30; Judges ii. 9. This event happened in the fortieth year after the Israelites left Egypt, on the first day of the fifth month, which answers to our July, at which time Aaron was one hundred and twenty-three years of age. See Numb. xxxiii. 38, 39.

[†] This name seems to have been anciently borne by the whole range of Mount Seir, and, when superseded by the latter denomination, continued to be preserved in the name of the particular summit on which Aaron died. Topographical probabilities concur with local traditions in identifying this Mount Hor

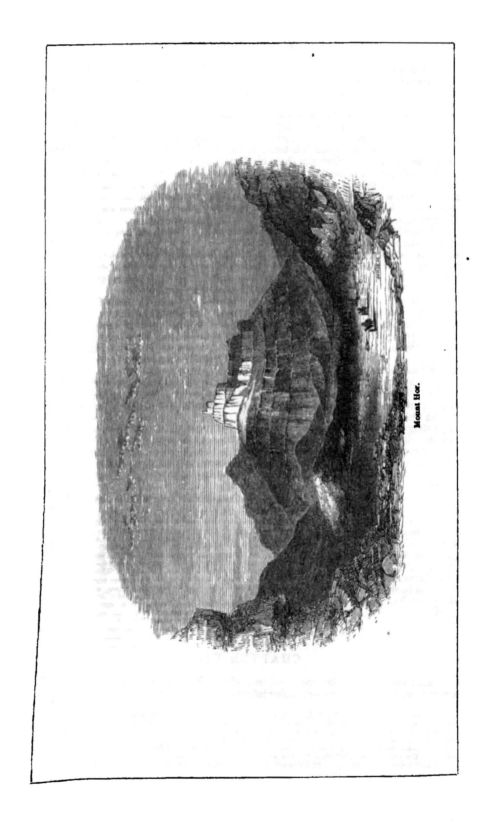

Mount Hor.

tended visiting his dominions, went out with a considerable army to interrupt their progress. Accordingly, coming up with them, an engagement took place, in which the Israelites were worsted, and some of them made prisoners.

In consequence of this repulse, the Israelites made a vow to God, promising, if he would deliver these people into their hands, they would utterly destroy their cities. Their divine protector was pleased to listen to their request; for, upon their engaging the Canaanites a second time, they obtained a complete victory, took possession of their cities, and put all the inhabitants to the sword.

Elated with this success the Israelites decamped from Mount Hor, and took their route by the Red sea, marching round Edom, through which they had been refused a passage by the king of the country. As the way was long, the passes difficult, and the country barren, they, forgetting their late success, and reflecting only on the present inconveniences, relapsed into their old humor of murmuring, and heavily complained both against God and Moses. "Wherefore," said they, "have ye brought us up out of Egypt to die in the wilderness? for there is no bread, neither is there any water, and our soul loatheth this light bread."

As a punishment to the Israelites for this fresh instance of their impiety and distrust, God sent among them prodigious numbers of fiery serpents, whose stings were so venomous, that those who were bit by them died; and by this plague, great numbers of the Israelites, in a very short space of time, were carried off.

This dreadful calamity so alarmed the people, that they flew to Moses for protection, acknowledging the offence they had committed, and beseeching him to intercede with God in their behalf. Moses, pitying their distress, readily complied with their request; upon which the Almighty was pleased to order him to make a serpent of brass resembling those by which they were afflicted, and to set it up on a high pole; telling him, at the same time, that such as were bitten, if they looked up to this serpent, should be healed.

Moses obeyed the divine command, and though the serpents did not cease biting, that the people might be more sensible of their transgression, yet, on looking up to the brazen serpent, the force of the sting lost its effect, and the person afflicted soon recovered.

The Israelites, after making various marches and encampments, between the countries of Moab and Ammon, without committing the least hostility, at length came to the borders of that part of the country inhabited by the Amorites. Hence Moses sent ambassadors to Sihon their king, requesting permission to pass through his country, and promising, at the same time, not to commit any depredation, or give him the least disturbance.

The Amorite prince, fearful of admitting so formidable a body into the heart of his

with the high mountain which rises conspicuously above the surrounding rocks in the vicinity of Petrea, the ancient capital of the Edomites or Nabathæans, which is in a valley (Wady-Mousa) that cuts the range of Seir about halfway between the Gulf of Akaba and the Dead sea, but rather nearer to the former than to the latter. This mountain, whose rugged pinnacle forms a very striking feature in one of the most interesting scenes in the world, is of very difficult and steep ascent, which is partly artificial, rude steps or niches being in some places formed in the rock. Dr. Macmichael, who visited the spot in 1818, in company with Mr. Bankes and Captains Irby and Mangles, says that it took his party one hour and a half to ascend its almost perpendicular sides. If this were really Mount Hor, as there seems little reason to doubt, the high-priest, before he lay down and died on that mountain, must have been able to mark out with his eye much of that wild region in which the Israelites had, for so many long years, wandered to and fro. From its summit, Mount Sinai might clearly be distinguished in the south; while the boundless desert, marked by so many wonderful transactions, in which he had borne a conspicuous part, spread its wide expanse before him on the west. The supposed tomb of Aaron is enclosed by a small modern building, crowned with a cupola, such as usually cover the remains of Moslem saints. At the time of the above visit, this spot formed the residence of an old Arab hermit, eighty years of age, the one half of which he had lived upon the mountain, from which he seldom descended, and where he chiefly subsisted through the charity of the native shepherds. He conducted the travellers into the building, and showed them the tomb, which lay at the further end of the building, behind two folding leaves of an iron grating. This monument, which is about three feet high, is patched together with fragments of stone and marble, and covered with a ragged pall. On the walls near the tomb are suspended beads, bits of cloth, leather, and yarn, with paras and similar articles, left as votive offerings by the Arabs. The old Arab lighted a lamp of butter, and conducted the travellers to a grotto or vault underneath, which is excavated in the rock, but contains nothing remarkable. The Arabs are in the habit of offering sacrifices to Haroun (Aaron), generally of a goat. When, however, they make a vow to slaughter a victim to him, they do not go to the top of the mountain, but think it sufficient to complete their sacrifice at a spot from which the cupola of the tomb is visible in the distance; where, after killing the animal, they throw a heap of stones over the blood that flows to the ground, and then feast on the carcase. The services thus rendered to the tomb of Aaron afford a striking picture of the debasing superstitions into which the Arabs have fallen. Burckhardt, who, in his Moslem character, sacrificed a goat, says, that while he did so his guide gave utterance to such exclamations as the following: "O, Haroun; look upon us! it is for you we slaughter this victim. O, Haroun, protect us and forgive us! O, Haroun, be content with our good intentions, for it is but a lean goat! O, Haroun, smooth our paths: and praise be to the Lord of all creatures!"

kingdom, positively denied the Israelites a passage; and thinking it better policy to attack than be attacked, gathered what force he could, and marched out to give them battle. They met near a place called Jahaz, when a desperate engagement ensued, in which the Amorites were totally defeated, and the whole body put to the sword. The Israelites pursuing their conquests made themselves masters of the most considerable places belonging to the Amorites, particularly Heshbon, which, with the villages about it, Sihon had before taken from the Moabites.

From Heshbon the Israelites marched toward Bashan (taking several other places in their way belonging to the Amorites, particularly a large city called Janzer) where the giant Og, another king of the Amorites, resided, and who, on the approach of the Israelites, drew out his gigantic troops in order to give them battle. Fearful lest the Israelites should be discouraged at the sight of this formidable army, Moses, by the command of God, bade them be of good spirits, and not entertain the least apprehensions of danger, for that God would deliver them into their hands, and they should make as easy a conquest over them as they had done over King Sihon.

Animated at this intelligence, the Israelites marched with all expedition against the Amorites, whom they attacked with such success as to obtain a complete victory, and not only the whole of the people, but likewise King Og and his sons, were put to the sword. They then seized on the principal parts of the country, and utterly destroyed the inhabitants, reserving only the cattle and spoil of the cities, as they had done before in the case of Sihon.

Encouraged by these successes, the Israelites marched to the plains of Moab, and encamped on the bank of the river Jordan, nearly opposite to Jericho. The approach of these victorious strangers struck a terror among the people wherever they went, and the fame of their late success against the Amorites threw Balak, the king of Moab, and all his people, into the most dreadful consternation.

Balak, knowing himself too weak to engage the mighty force of Israel himself, formed a strong alliance with his neighbors the Midianites, and a consultation was held between the heads of each, what steps should be taken to avoid the common danger, and to secure themselves against these bold invaders.

The result of this consultation was, that messengers should be sent to Balaam, a noted magician, who lived at Pethor, a city of Mesopotamia, to invite him by bribes to come to Moab, and, by cursing the Israelites, prevent their proving successful in that part of the country. In consequence of this determination, a select number of the principal people, both of Moab and Midian, were despatched to Balaam with many valuable presents, and with orders that they should, if possible, bring him with them to Moab, that, by his enchantments and curses, he might destroy the power of the Israelites, and thereby secure them from every kind of danger.

As soon as these deputies arrived at Pethor they delivered their message to Balaam, who desired them to tarry with him that night, for that he could not give them any answer till he had consulted the Lord. The Almighty, knowing the secrets of Balaam's heart, asked what men they were that were with him. To which he replied, "They are some whom the king of Moab hath sent to me, to let me know that there is a people come out of Egypt which cover the face of the earth; and to desire me to come to him and curse them, in hopes that he may then be able to overcome them and drive them away." To this God made answer, "Thou shalt not go with them; thou shalt not curse the people, for they are blessed."

Not daring to disobey the divine command, Balaam arose early in the morning, and going to the deputies, dismissed them, saying, "Be gone to your own country, for the Lord refuseth to give me leave to go with you."

The deputies, on their return to Moab, misrepresented Balaam's answer to the king; for, instead of telling him that God had refused to let him come, they told him that Balaam himself had refused to come. In consequence of this, Balak, suggesting that either the number and quality of his messengers did not answer Balaam's ambition, or the value of the presents his covetousness, resolved, if possible, to remove this obstacle by gratifying both. He accordingly despatched the chiefs of his nobility to Balaam, sending by them much more considerable presents than before, and at the same time this message: "Let nothing," said he, "hinder thee from coming to me; for I will promote thee to very great honor, and give thee whatsoever thou shalt ask, if thou wilt but come and curse this people."

Balaam, being naturally of a very avaricious disposition, accepted the presents from the deputies, but evaded complying with their request, by assuring them that he durst not, on any account whatever, counteract the divine will. However, in order to amuse and flatter them with expectations, he desired them to tarry a little while he made farther inquiries of the Lord, and, if he thought proper to admit his going, he would readily attend them.

The Almighty had at first given Balaam a positive answer, and it was certainly the highest disobedience and presumption to attempt the reversing it by a farther application. However, blinded by covetousness and ambition, he again addressed himself to God, who (provoked at his obstinacy and presumption) was pleased to give him this answer: "If the men," said he, "come to call thee, rise up and go with them; but yet the word which I shall say unto thee, that shalt thou do."

With this permission Balaam arose in the morning, and, saddling his ass, set forward with the messengers on their journey to Moab. On the road he was met by an angel with a drawn sword in his hand, whom, though he perceived not, his ass plainly saw, and being startled, turned aside in order to avoid him. With some difficulty Balaam beat his ass into the road again, soon after which the angel placed himself in a narrow passage between two walls which enclosed a vineyard. The ass, who was equally startled as before, not knowing how to avoid the angel, ran against one of the walls and crushed Balaam's foot, upon which he was so provoked that he beat him with great severity. At length the angel removed, and fixed himself in a place so very narrow that there was no possibility of passing him; upon which the ass made a full stop and fell beneath his rider. This enraged Balaam still more; and as he was beating the poor animal in the most unmerciful manner, God was pleased to give the ass the faculty of speech, who expostulated with his master on his severe treatment in words to this effect: "What," said he, "have I done to thee, that thou shouldst beat me these three times?"—"Because," said Balaam, "thou hast deserved it in mocking me: had I a sword in my hand I would kill thee." The ass replied, "Am I not thine ass, upon which thou hast been accustomed to ride ever since I was thine; did I ever serve thee so before?"

While Balaam was thus conversing with his ass, God was pleased to open his eyes, and let him see the angel standing in the way, with a naked sword in his hand. Terrified at so unexpected a sight, Balaam fell on his face, acknowledged his offence, asked pardon for it, and offered, if his journey was displeasing to God, immediately to return.

That his journey was displeasing to the Almighty he certainly could not be ignorant, because, in his first address, God had expressly interdicted his going. He was pleased, however, to suffer him to proceed, that some kind of advantage might be raised out of this man's wickedness, and to make him, who was hired to curse, the instrument of pronouncing a blessing on his people.

When Balak heard that Balaam was on the road, he went himself to receive him on the confines of his dominions. As soon as Balak saw him, he in a friendly manner blamed him for not coming at his first sending, which Balaam excused on account of the restraint that had been laid upon him by the Almighty. Balak then conducted him to his capital, where he that day publicly entertained him in the most sumptuous manner; and the next morning conducted him to the high places consecrated to the idol Baal, whence he might take an advantageous view of the camp of the Israelites.

After being here some short time, Balaam ordered seven altars to be erected, and seven oxen, together with the like number of rams, to be prepared for sacrifice. Balaam, having offered an ox and a ram on each altar, left Balak to stand by the sacrifices, while himself withdrew at some distance to consult the Lord. On his return he addressed the king, in the presence of the whole company, in words to this effect: "Thou hast caused me, O king," said he, "to come from out of the mountains of the east to curse the family of Jacob, and bid defiance to Israel. But how shall I curse those whom God hath not cursed? and how shall I defy those whom the Lord hath not defied? From the tops of the rocks I see their protector, and from the hills I behold him. Behold, this people shall be separated to God, and distinguished from all other people in religion, laws, and course of life: they shall not be reckoned among the nations." He then set forth the great prosperity and increase of the Israelites, and concluded by wishing that his lot, both in life and in death, might be like

View in the Land of Moab.

unto theirs. "Let me die," said he, "the death of the righteous, and let my last end be like his."

Balak, alarmed as well as incensed at these words, which were quite contrary to what he had expected, passionately said to Balaam, "What hast thou done? I sent for thee to curse mine enemies; but, instead thereof, thou hast blessed them." Balaam excused himself by urging the necessity of his instructions, from which, he said, it was not in his power at that time to make the least deviation.

Not discouraged at this rebuff, Balak, thinking that a change of place might produce a change of fortune, or better success, conducted Balaam to the top of Mount Pisgah, in order to try whether he could thence fulfil his wishes by cursing the Israelites.

Balaam, willing to please the king, had seven other altars erected here, and a bullock and ram offered on each. As soon as the sacrifices were ready he withdrew, as before, to consult the Lord, from whom he received fresh instructions. On his return to Balak and his attendants, the king, big with expectation of the result, asked what the Lord had spoken. Balaam, with the most serious countenance and solemn tone of voice, answered as follows: "Consider," said he, "O Balak, thou son of Zippor, consider that God, who hath already blessed Israel, and forbidden me to curse them, is not like a man that he should renounce his promise, or repent of what he does. Hath he promised, and shall he not perform? or hath he spoken, and shall he not make it good? Behold, I have received commission to bless, and he hath blessed, and I can not reverse it. He does not approve of afflictions or outrages against the posterity of Jacob, nor of vexation or trouble against the posterity of Israel. The Lord his God is with him, and the shout of a king is in him. God hath brought them out of Egypt; he hath, as it were, the strength of a unicorn. Surely no enchantment can prevail against Jacob, nor any divination against Israel. So that, considering what God will work this time for the deliverance of his people, all the world shall wonder and say, What hath God wrought, who hath put his people out of the reach of fraud or force, and turned the intended curse into a blessing! And to show their future strength and success, the people shall rise up as a great lion, and lift themselves up as a young lion. They shall not lie down until they eat of the prey, and drink of the blood of the slain."

Balak was so mortified at this speech that, in the height of his passion, he forbade Balaam either to bless or curse; but after his indignation was somewhat abated he changed his mind, and desired him to make a farther trial at another place. Accordingly, Balaam was conducted to the top of Mount Peor, where fresh altars were raised and fresh sacrifices offered; but all to no purpose. Balaam well knew the positive will of God in this case was to bless, and not to curse. He did not therefore, as before, retire for farther instructions, but, casting his eyes on the tents of the Israelites, thus exclaimed: "How goodly are thy tents, O Jacob, and thy tabernacles, O Israel!" He then, in proper and significant metaphors, foretold their extent, fertility, and strength, and that "those that blessed them should be blessed, and those that cursed them should be cursed."

Balak, enraged to hear Balaam, whom he had sent for to curse the Israelites, thus three times successively bless them, could no longer contain himself, but, clasping his hands together, bade him haste and be gone, since, by his folly, he had both abused God and defrauded himself. "I thought," said he, "to have promoted thee to great honor, if thou hadst answered my design in cursing Israel; but the Lord hath hindered thy preferment."

Balaam, in excuse, made use of the same arguments he had done before, namely, that he could not run counter to the divine commands, but must speak what the Lord had put into his mouth. He then, in expectation of obtaining some reward from the king, notwithstanding he had not answered the purposes for which he was sent, offered to advertise him of what the Israelites would do to his people in subsequent ages; which being accepted by Balak, he prophesied as follows: "That a star should come forth from Jacob, and a rod from Israel; that it should smite the chiefs of Moab, and destroy the children of Seth; that Edom should fall under its power; that the Amalekites should be totally destroyed, and the Kenites made captives."

Having said this Balaam left the king, but without receiving any reward, as he had expected, for his predictions. Vexed at this disappointment, and considering the Israelites as the occasion of it, he determined to wreak his vengeance on them. He knew that their prosperity depended on their strict observance of the divine laws and that there was no way to bring a curse on them but by seducing them from their duty. To accomplish, therefore, his wicked design, he advised both the Moabites and Midianites to send their daughters into the camp of the Israelites, that they might first entice the people into lewdness, and then into idolatry; by doing of which they would infallibly be deprived of that divine assistance that had hitherto protected them.

This wicked stratagem, being highly approved of by the Moabites and Midianites, was immediately put into execution, and in some measure attended with the wished-for success. Many of the Israelites were deluded by these strange women, not only to commit whoredom with them, but also idolatry, by assisting at their sacrifices, and worshipping their gods, even their god Baal-peor.

These offences were highly displeasing to God, who, as a punishment on the people, commanded Moses to take the chiefs of those who had worshipped Baal-peor, and hang them up in the sight of the people, without paying respect either to friendship or kindred. This was accordingly done, and the number that suffered was about one thousand. But the divine justice did not stop here, for those who had committed whoredom were visited with a dreadful plague, which in a short time carried off no less than twenty-four thousand persons.

These severe punishments opened the eyes of the sinful Israelites, who assembled at the door of the tabernacle, and, with the most expressive sense of affliction, bewailed their folly and wickedness in suffering themselves to have been deluded by a strange people who were their mortal enemies.

While the whole congregation were thus situated at the door of the tabernacle, they were surprised with an instance of the most unparalleled boldness and depravity in one of the chiefs of the tribe of Simeon, named Zimri, who, in the sight of Moses and all the people, brought with him a young Midianitish princess, named Cozbi, into the camp, and, with all the actions of gallantry, conducted her to his tent.

This impious as well as insolent behavior particularly engaged the attention of Phineas, the son of Eleazer the high-priest, who, fired with a just indignation, suddenly arose, and taking a javelin in his hand, ran to Zimri's tent, and put a period to their lives, by running them both through the body at the same instant.

After this zealous act of Phineas, the plague, which God had sent among the people for their lewdness and impiety, ceased. And Phineas not only received the highest commendation for his conduct among the people, but also from God, who was pleased to appoint a perpetual settlement of the priesthood on him and his posterity.

The disorders among the Israelites being thoroughly quelled, and the offenders punished, Moses by the direction of God, proceeded to take vengeance on the Midianites, who, by their conduct, had been the authors of the late calamities among the people. He ordered a detachment to be made out of 12,000 choice men, a thousand out of each tribe, whom he sent against the Midianites. Among them was the zealous Phineas, who took with him the ark, together with the sacred trumpets, the latter of which were to be blown, during the time of action, to animate the people.

The army of the Israelites was but small compared with the great numbers they had to oppose; but God, who put them on the expedition, was pleased to crown their attempts with such success, that conquest took place wherever they went. They vanquished five kings, whom, with their men, they put all to the sword. Among the slain was the wicked prophet Balaam,* who, though he had before escaped the sword of the angel, could not now avoid the common danger, but fell a victim to his own baseness.

In every city where the Israelites made a conquest, they destroyed not only the fortified places but likewise all the buildings, took all the women and children prisoners, and seized on their cattle, flocks, and goods.

The Israelites, having thus vanquished their enemies, and loaded themselves with the spoils of conquest, returned in triumph to the camp, where they were met by Moses, Eleazer the high-priest, and all the elders of the different tribes, who congratulated them on the occasion, and the people testified their joy by the loudest acclamations.

* It is evident, from this circumstance, that if Balaam did return to his own country when he left Balak, he did not continue long there; but it is much more probable that he never did return, but dwelt with the princes of Midian, in order to give them counsel.

But when Moses saw the women captives, remembering what damage they had done by alluring the Israelites into idolatry, he thought it unsafe that their lives should be spared. He therefore ordered that all those who had ever known man, together with all the male children, should be put to the sword, and none but virgins be saved alive. These orders were accordingly executed, and (as a proof of the importance of the victory) the number of virgin captives amounted to two and thirty thousand.

After this Moses gave orders that the conquerors should abide seven days without the camp, and that both the soldiers and spoils should pass through the ceremonies of a legal purification.

When the time of purification was expired, Moses, by the command of God, took an account of the whole booty that had been taken from the Midianites. This he divided into two equal parts, one of which he gave to the soldiers who had taken it, and the other half to the rest of the people who stayed at home. Out of the division given to the soldiers he ordered a five hundredth part to be paid as a tribute to Eleazer the high-priest, as a heave-offering to the Lord; and out of the other part allotted to the people, a fiftieth, both of persons and beasts, to be given to the Levites.

The plunder of cattle and flocks consisted of 670,500 sheep, 72,000 oxen, and 61,000 asses, besides a great quantity of rich goods and ornaments. And, what makes the victory still more miraculous is, that not one man among the Israelites was slain in the battle, as appeared from the report afterward made on a general muster of the whole that went out to war.

The officers of the army were sensible that, in saving the Midianitish women, they had committed a great transgression. They therefore presented a prodigious quantity of jewels, and other rich spoils, both as an expiatory offering to atone for their offence, and in gratitude to God's goodness for having given them so great and signal a victory.

The Israelites were now in possession of all that part of the country which lay on the east side of the river Jordan. It was a very fertile spot, and stored with good pasturage, in consequence of which the tribes of Reuben and Gad, together with the half-tribe of Manasseh, requested of Moses that they might be permitted to settle there, it being particularly commodious for the feeding of their flocks and cattle.

Moses, thinking this request arose from their pusillanimity, and that they were desirous of continuing in a country ready gained, and thereby avoid giving their assistance in farther conquests, was exceeding angry, and blamed them for offering a proposal so discouraging to the rest of the tribes. They told him they had no other reason for wishing to continue where they were than what they had already advanced, and that though they were desirous of settling there with their families, yet they wished not to decline the fatigues of war. They promised, in the most solemn manner, that a quota should go with the army into the land of Canaan, and contribute all the assistance they were able in reducing that country which had been so long promised, and that when these matters were accomplished, and not till then, would they desire to return to their families in the plains of Moab. On this reason, and on these promises, Moses told them their request should be granted.

As the Israelites were now in the neighborhood of Canaan, and the time very near of their entering that country to take possession of it, Moses called a general assembly of the people, to whom he enumerated the several stations and removes they had made from the time of their leaving the land of Goshen in Egypt, till their arrival in the plains of Moab. He then, by the direction of God, pointed out the limits of what they were to conquer, and appointed the distribution of the whole among the different tribes to be by lot, assigning the chief management of it to Eleazer the high-priest, and Joshua, the general of his army.

In the division of the country Moses assigned forty-eight cities, together with their suburbs, to be inhabited by the Levites, and withal ordered, that six of them should be made *cities of refuge*, whither the *innocent* manslayer, who had killed his neighbor by chance, might betake himself, and where he should remain in safety till the death of the high-priest, when he was at full liberty to go where he pleased with equal safety as when in the city of refuge. At the same time Moses made all proper provision that the *wilful* murderer should certainly be put to death. But in this, and all other capital cases, he made it a law that none should be convicted upon the evidence of any single person. A law was likewise made, that every daughter who should possess an inheritance in any tribe of the children of Israel should be married to one of the tribes of his father, that so the Israelites might every one enjoy the in-

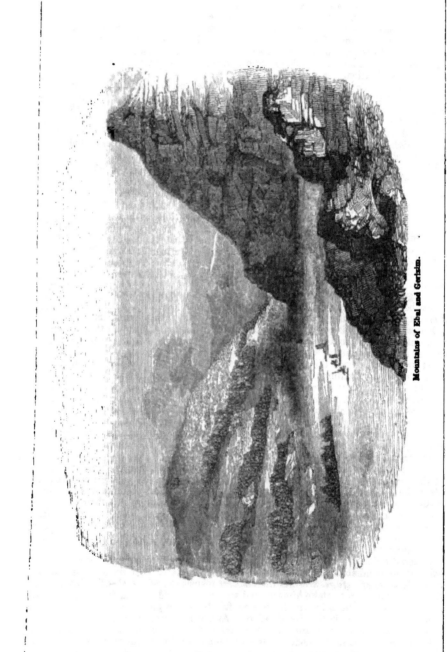

Mountains of Ebal and Gerizim.

heritance of his father; and the inheritance not to be transferred to another tribe. This was grounded on a law made before, which empowered daughters to inherit land where the heirs male should be deficient; and was the case of the daughters of Zelophehad (a descendant of Manasseh, the son of Joseph), who, by this additional law, were required to marry within the family of their father's tribe.

The forty years' travels of the Israelites being now nearly expired, Moses, considering that the then generation were either sprung up since the law was given at Mount Sinai, or too young to remember and understand it, thought proper to repeat the whole to them, that they might not be deficient in performing those duties so religiously enjoined. Accordingly, on the first day of the eleventh month, and in the fortieth year from their departure out of Egypt (being then encamped on the plains of Moab, by the banks of the river Jordan) Moses called all the people together, to whom he briefly related all that had befallen their fathers since the time of their leaving Egypt; the gracious dealings of God with them; their continual murmurings and rebellions against him; and the many severe judgments that followed thereupon, even to his own exclusion from the promised land. He then gave them a summary of all the laws which the divine goodness had calculated for their happiness; and, after repeating the decalogue almost word for word, he reminded them of the solemn and dreadful manner in which it was delivered from Mount Sinai, and of the manifold obligations they lay under to a strict observance of it. He encouraged them to be faithful to God, by assuring them, that, if they kept his commandments, they should not fail of having innumerable blessings heaped on them; but at the same time he threatened them with all manner of calamities if they departed from them. He then, in the name of the Lord, renewed the covenant which their fathers had made with God at Mount Horeb; commanded them to proclaim, on the mountains of Gerizim and Ebal,* beyond Jordan, blessings on such as observed the covenant, and curses on those who broke it: and to erect an altar there, on which should be written, in legible characters, the terms and conditions of the covenant.

These, and several other directions relative to their future conduct in the land of Canaan, did Moses not only deliver to the people by word of mouth, but likewise ordered them to be written in a book, which he committed to the care and custody of the Levites, who, by God's appointment, laid it up on the side of the ark, there to remain a witness against the people should they afterward rebel.

Such was the care and concern of Moses for the future welfare of the people: and that they might never want a proper fund of devotion, he composed a song, or poem, which he not only repeated to them, but likewise gave orders that they should all learn by heart. In this song he expressed, in a very elegant manner, the many benefits which God had bestowed on his people; their ingratitude and forgetfulness of him, the punishment wherewith he had afflicted them; and the threats of greater judgments, if they persisted in provoking him by a repetition of their follies. The whole of this beautiful song runs from the first verse of the thirty-second chapter of Deuteronomy to the forty-third.

The time was now near at hand when a period was to be put to Moses's earthly peregrinations. The Almighty had before told him, that he should not conduct the people into the promised land because of his error at the waters of Meribah: he therefore now commanded him to go up to the mountains of Abarim,† and there take a view of the land of Canaan, which he had promised to his forefathers, Abraham, Isaac, and Jacob; and farther told him, that after he had so done, he should die there, as his brother Aaron had done on Mount Hor.

Moses humbly submitted to the will of the Almighty, and, as a necessary prepara-

---

* These two mountains (of which we give a beautiful and correct representation, p. 177), are so near each other, that they are only separated by a valley of about two hundred paces wide, in which is situated the town of Shechem. They are much alike in length, height, and form: their figure is semicircular, and on the side of Shechem they are so steep that there is not the least shelving: they are at most about half a league in length. But notwithstanding they are so much alike in the particulars mentioned, they are very different in one instance; namely, Ebal is desolate and barren, whereas Gerizim is beautiful and fruitful.

† These mountains were situated in the country of the Moabites, between the two rivers Arnon and Jordan, and commanded a most extensive prospect of the land of Canaan. One part of these mountains was distinguished by the name of Nebo, as appears from Deut. xxxii. 49, but if we compare this with Deut. xxxiv. 1, we shall find that Nebo and Pisgah were one, and the same mountain. If, therefore, there was any distinction between the names it was probably this, that the top of the mountain was more peculiarly called Pisgah, which signifies to elevate or raise up, and, therefore, may very properly denote the top or summit, of any mountain. Not far from Nebo was Beth-peor, which was probably so called from some deity of that name worshipped by the Moabites.

Ancient Syrian Chief addressing the People.

tion to the execution of this last command, took a solemn farewell of the people, bestowing a prophetic blessing on each tribe, in like manner as Jacob had done a short time previous to his death.

The Almighty had before appointed Joshua to succeed Moses in his commission; and to prevent any disputes after his death, Moses first laid his own hands upon Joshua, and then presented him to Eleazer the high-priest, who, in a solemn form of admission, and in the presence of all the people, accepted him as leader and general of the Israelites; after which Moses gave Joshua some instructions relative to his office, and one more especially which concerned his consulting God, by way of Urim and Thummim,* on matters of emergency.

Having adjusted these matters, Moses, in conformity to the divine command, retired to Pisgah, the most elevated situation on Mount Nebo, directly opposite to Jericho, whence he might take a full view of the country, which God had promised to Abraham's posterity. At this time he was a hundred and twenty years of age, notwithstanding which, his natural strength and vigor were not abated, nor had his eyesight in the least failed him. He was, therefore, able to survey the beauteous prospect which the delightful plains of Jericho, and the fair cliffs and lofty cedars of Lebanon, afforded him; and having done this for some time, he at length resigned his soul into the hands of seraphim, who were waiting to convey it to a more happy Canaan than that which he had been surveying.

The Almighty was pleased to pay the funeral honors to the remains of this great prophet himself, by burying him in a valley in the land of Moab opposite to Beth-Peor, and that in so secret a manner, that the place of his interment was never yet discovered.

Thus died the illustrious and pious Moses, the most eminent servant of God, and the great conductor of his chosen people, who, as soon as they knew of his death, lamented the loss of him with the greatest solemnity, weeping and mourning for him in the plains of Moab for thirty days.

CHAPTER XII.

THE CONQUEST.

On the death of Moses, Joshua, being appointed to succeed him in the government of the Israelites, was installed into the kingly office by Eleazer, the high-priest, and with the universal approbation of the people. To encourage him in the great work he had to undertake, the Almighty expressly commanded him (as he had done his servant Moses) to lead the people over the Jordan, telling him that every place on which they should tread should be their own, and that no man should be able to stand against him: that in like manner as he had been with Moses, so he would be with him, and that he might be assured he would never forsake him.

Encouraged by these divine assurances, Joshua ordered the officers to proclaim throughout the camp, that within a few days they should pass the Jordan, in order to possess the land which the Almighty had promised them, and that therefore they should provide themselves with proper necessaries on the occasion. He then called together the leaders of the tribes of Reuben and Gad, and the half-tribe of Manasseh,

* Urim and Thummim, signifying *lights and perfections*, formed the oracle of God put into the sacred breastplate of judgment of Aaron, by which the Divine will was to be sought on solemn occasions: but while learned men have offered many and various conjectures, it is not agreed what they were, as it is not fully declared by Moses, Exod. xxviii. 30, Lev. viii. 8. Josephus supposes that they were the twelve precious stones of the breastplate, on which were engraven the names of several tribes of Israel, Exod. xxviii. 15-21; and that God gave answers to the high-priest inquiring before the most holy place, by an extraordinary glory illustrating the letters: but others are of opinion that they were given by an audible voice from the Shekinah, in the cloud of glory over the mercy-seat, Psal. lxxx. 1, xcix. 1. This oracle, it is believed, was not used during the life of Moses, as God spake to him directly, Exod. xxxiii. 11, Num. vii. 89; and afterward only in national difficulties, by the high-priest only, and not for any private person, Num. xxvii. 21, Josh. vii. 6-15. This sacred instrument is supposed to have been destroyed with the temple of Solomon, if not before: as the Jews acknowledge that it did not exist in the second temple, Ezra ii. 13, Neh. vii. 65. The rabbins indeed say, that it continued in use only under the tabernacle, 1 Sam. xxviii. 6: they have a maxim that the Holy Ghost spoke to Israel under the tabernacle by Urim and Thummim; under the first temple by prophets; and after the captivity of Babylon, by the Bath-kol, or Daughter of the voice; meaning a voice from heaven, as at the baptism, and transfiguration of Christ, Matt. iii. 17, xvii. 5; 2 Pet. i. 17.

† *See Engraving* (p. 179).—The costume is Egypto-Syrian—that is Egyptian, with such modifications as the Syrians appear to have given it in adopting it from the Egyptians. It has been very carefully studied.

whom he reminded of the promises they had made to Moses, and entreated them, not only for his sake, but also their own, to fulfil their engagements. They faithfully promised to comply with his request, and that they would be equally obedient to him as they had been to his predecessor.

Opposite to Joshua's camp stood the city of Jericho, which of course must be the first place he would have to attack after passing the river Jordan. As a necessary precaution, he sent two spies to take a view of the strength and situation of that city, and to learn the disposition of the inhabitants. They accordingly entered Jericho, and being considered as strangers come thither to gratify their curiosity, were permitted to perambulate the streets without the least molestation. On the close of the day they took up their residence in the house of a woman named Rahab, where, after refreshing themselves, they retired to rest.

In the meantime, information had been given the king that there were two spies in the city, and that they had concealed themselves in the house of Rahab. On this the king immediately despatched proper officers to seize them; but Rahab (who had been previously informed of it), before their arrival, had secreted the two spies under some stalks of flax on the roof of the house.

When the messengers arrived and related their business, Rahab told them there had been such people at her house, but she knew not who they were, nor whence they came; that a short time after dark, and before the gates of the city were shut, they departed; and, as they could not be got far, it would be no difficult matter to overtake them. The messengers, believing Rahab's story, left her, and immediately set out in pursuit of the spies.

As soon as they were gone, Rahab uncovered her guests, told them what had passed, and pointed out the great danger to which she had exposed herself and family for their protection. In return for this kindness, she exacted from them an oath, that when the city should be invested by the Hebrews, they should preserve her and her relations from the general destruction. To effect this, they told her that when she found the city attacked, to shut herself up with her family in her house, and that, in order to distinguish it from the rest, she must hang a scarlet thread to the door, which signal should be communicated to the general, who would, no doubt, give such such directions as to secure her from all danger. This being agreed on, Rahab, for the better security of her guests, let them down into the street by a rope fastened to the window, so that they made their escape unperceived. She advised them immediately to fly to the mountains, and there conceal themselves for three days, in which time the messengers, finding their endeavors ineffectual, would relinquish the pursuit.

The two spies took Rahab's advice, and the consequences turned out as she had predicted; for, after two days' search, the messengers, despairing of success, gave over the pursuit and returned to Jericho. At the close of the third day the two spies left the mountains, crossed the Jordan, and arriving safe at the camp of Joshua, gave him a faithful account of their expedition; adding, that for certain the Lord had delivered the country into their hands, for the people were quite dispirited at the name of the Israelites.

Pleased with this intelligence, Joshua, early the next morning, left Shittim, and conducted his army within a small distance of the place where it was intended they should cross the river Jordan. Here he communicated to every tribe the order to be observed in their march. He told them that when they saw the ark of the Lord carried by the priests, the whole army should then move and follow it, that they might know the way by which they were to go; and that they should leave a space of two thousand cubits between them and the ark. That when the priests were got into the middle of the channel, they should there stand still till the whole multitude were got safe on the opposite shore; and, to prepare themselves properly for this remarkable passage, they were all enjoined to sanctify themselves, by washing their clothes, avoiding all impurities, and abstaining from matrimonial intercourse the preceding night. He also, by the direction of the Almighty, appointed twelve men (one out of each tribe) to choose twelve stones from the middle of the river where the priests were to stand with the ark, and there to set them up (that they might be seen from each side of the river when the waters were abated) as a monument of this great miracle; and to take twelve others with them to be erected on the land for the like purpose.

Having given these necessary orders, early the next morning, which was the tenth day of the first month, the whole army proceeded on their march. The priests with the ark went first; and as soon as they touched the river with their feet, the rapidity of the stream abated; the waters above went back, and rose on heaps for a considerable distance, while those below continued their course the contrary way, so that there was a passage opened of about sixteen miles for the Israelites to pass. The priests stood with the ark in the middle of the channel till the whole multitude had got on the other side, when, having raised the twelve stones as Joshua had commanded, they left the bed of the river, on which the waters immediately returned, and resumed their natural course.

The Israelites, having by this miraculous passage gained the plains of Jericho, encamped in a place afterward called Gilgal,* where Joshua erected the twelve stones, which had been brought from the Jordan, as a monument to posterity of the Almighty's interposition in assisting them to pass that river.

This extraordinary event being soon circulated through the adjacent parts of the country, the people were filled with the greatest amazement; and when the kings of the Amorites (who were on the west side of the Jordan) and the kings of the Canaanites (who inhabited those parts next the sea) heard of it, their hearts sunk for fear, and their courage failed them.

Soon after Joshua had encamped his army, God commanded the rite of circumcision (which had been neglected for almost forty years) to be renewed, that the people might be properly qualified to partake of the ensuing passover.† This order being obeyed, the Lord said unto Joshua, "This day have I rolled away the reproach of Egypt [i. e. uncircumcision] from off you, wherefore the name of the place is called Gilgal [i. e. rolling] unto this day."

As the Israelites were now arrived in a country where there was a sufficiency of corn for unleavened bread, God insisted upon the observance of his ordinances, and resolved that all things should now go in a regular way. He therefore ceased to supply them any longer with manna, but left them for the future to enjoy the products of the promised inheritance.

Joshua, previous to his marching his army against Jericho, went from the camp alone, in order to reconnoitre the city, and to discover which would be the most advantageous way of approaching it. While he was making his observations, on a sudden there appeared before him a person resembling a man, but with a lustre in his face that indicated he was more than mortal. In his hand he held a flaming sword, and his whole appearance far surpassed anything of human nature. Undaunted at this unusual sight, Joshua advanced toward him, and demanding of what party he was, the vision replied, of the host of the Lord,‡ of which he was captain and guardian. On this answer, Joshua immediately threw himself prostrate on the ground, when the vision, after ordering him to loose the sandals from his feet, proceeded to instruct him in what manner he would have the siege carried on, that the Canaanites might see it was not the arm of flesh alone by which they would be defeated. The instructions Joshua received were these: that for six successive days the whole army should march round the city, with seven priests before the ark, having in their hands trumpets made of rams' horns. That on the seventh day, after the army had gone round the city seven times, upon signal given, the priests were to blow their trumpets as loud as possible, and the people, on a sudden, to set up a great shout; at which instant the walls of the city should fall to the ground, and they might walk into it without the least obstruction.

Having received these orders from the Divine messenger, Joshua returned to the camp, and early the next morning marched with his whole army against Jericho.‖

---

* This place received its name from the rite of circumcision, which had been long disused, being here renewed. It lay about two miles to the northeast of Jericho, and St. Jerome tells us, that in his time it was greatly venerated by the inhabitants.

† This was the third time of their celebrating that festival. The first was at their departure out of Egypt; and the second at their erecting the tabernacle at the foot of Mount Sinai.

‡ It is the opinion of the best commentators, both ancient and modern, that the person here called the captain of the Lord's host, was no other than an angel, or messenger from God, who was pleased in this manner to appear to Joshua, both to encourage and direct him.

‖ JERICHO, "the city of palm trees" (Deut. xxxiv. 3), derives all its importance from history. Though now only a miserable village, containing about thirty wretched cottages, which are inhabited by half-naked Arabs, it was one of the oldest cities in Palestine, and was the first place reduced by the Israelites on entering the Holy Land. It was rased to the ground by Joshua, who denounced a curse on the person who should rebuild it, Josh. vi. 20–26. Five hundred and thirty years afterward this malediction was literally

The Plain of Jericho.

The place was strong, well provided, and full of inhabitants, who had retired into it, and seemed resolved to make a vigorous defence.

But Joshua had an irresistible force on his side. He strictly obeyed the orders he had received, and the promises made him were amply fulfilled; for, on the seventh day, as soon as the people shouted, after going round the city seven times, the walls suddenly fell to the ground. In consequence of this, the Israelites immediately entered the place, and put every living creature to the sword, except Rahab and her relations, who, being preserved as had been directed by Joshua, agreeably to the promise made by the spies, were placed without the camp of the army.

In the city were found great quantities of gold, silver, and brass, the whole of which was of immense value, and being gathered together as Joshua had ordered, he presented it to the priests, to be deposited in the sacred treasury.

Having destroyed all the inhabitants, Joshua ordered the city to be set on fire, which was accordingly done, and the whole reduced to a heap of ashes. He likewise denounced a heavy curse on any person who should ever after attempt to rebuild it. That whoever should take upon him to lay the first stone might be punished by the loss of his eldest son; and whoever should finish the work, his youngest.

Notwithstanding Joshua had taken the greatest precaution to prevent private plunder in the taking of Jericho, yet one Achan, of the tribe of Judah, committed a violent depredation, by taking to himself the rich cloak of the king of the Canaanites, two hundred shekels of silver, and a wedge of gold of fifty shekels. He secreted these treasures in a pit he had dug in his tent, foolishly supposing the fact would be no more noticed by God than it was known by his companions. But in this he soon found himself mistaken.

About twelve miles from Jericho (to the east of Bethel) was a small city called Ai, which Joshua knowing to be neither populous nor well defended, he detached a small body of men to take it. But they did not find the conquest so easy as they had imagined; for no sooner did they approach the place than the inhabitants immediately sallied out upon them, and having slain some, the rest were so frightened that they betook themselves to flight, and were pursued by the enemy within a small distance of their own camp.

This defeat, though small, struck a universal damp on the spirits of the people; and Joshua, in particular, was so afflicted that he had recourse to the Almighty, who told him there was a latent cause of his displeasure among the people: that some of them had taken of the accursed thing, and also of those things which were devoted to the Lord, and, instead of bringing them to the treasury of God, had concealed

fulfilled upon Hiel of Bethel 1 Kings xvi. 34, who rebuilt the city, which soon appears to have attained a considerable degree of importance. There was a school of the prophets here in the days of Elijah and Elisha, both of whom seemed to have resided much here. In the vicinity of Jericho there was a large but unwholesome spring, which rendered the soil unfruitful, until it was cured by the prophet Elisha, 2 Kings, ii. 21. In Ezra ii. 34, and Neh. vii. 36, we read, that three hundred and forty-five of the inhabitants of Jericho, who had been carried into captivity, returned to Judea with Zerubbabel, and in Neh. iii. 2, we find them at work upon the walls of Jerusalem.

Jericho appears to have continued in a flourishing condition during several centuries. In the time of our Saviour it was inferior only to Jerusalem in the number and splendor of its public edifices, and was one of the royal residences of Herod misnamed the Great, who died there. It was situated in the hollow or bottom of the extensive plain called the "Great Plain," (which circumstance marks the propriety of the expression "going down to Jerusalem," in Luke x. 30), and is about nineteen miles distant from the capital of Judea. In the last war of the Romans with the Jews, Jericho was sacked by Vespasian, and its inhabitants were put to the sword. Subsequently re-established by the emperor Hadrian, A. D. 138, it was doomed at no very distant period to experience new disasters: again it was repaired by the Christians, who made it an episcopal see; but in the twelfth century it was captured by the Mohammedans, and has not since emerged from its ruins. Of all its magnificent buildings there remains part of only one tower, the dwelling of the governor of the district, which is seen in the middle of our engraving, and which is traditionally said to have been the dwelling of Zaccheus the publican, who dwelt at Jericho (Luke xix. 1, 2).

The steep mountainous ridge in the background of our engraving is called the mountain of Quarantania, and is supposed to have been the scene of our Saviour's temptation, Matt. iv. 1-10. Here Dr. Shaw is of opinion that the two spies of Joshua concealed themselves, Josh. ii. 16. This mountain commands a distinct and delightful view of the mountains of Arabia, and of the Dead sea, and of the extensive and fertile plain of Jericho. According to Mr. Maundrell, Quarantania is a most miserable, dry, and barren place, consisting of rocky mountains so torn and disordered, as if the earth had here suffered some great convulsion. On the left hand, looking down a steep valley, as he passed along, he saw ruins of small cells and cottages, the former habitations of hermits who had retired thither for penance and mortification; for which purpose a more comfortless and abandoned place could not be found in the whole earth. The particular mountainous precipice, whence "all the kingdoms of the world and the glory of them" were shown to Jesus Christ, is, as the evangelist describes it, "an exceeding high mountain" Matt. iv. 8, and in its ascent not only difficult but dangerous: it has a small chapel at the top, and another about half way down, founded on a projecting part of the rock. Near the latter are several caves and holes, excavated by the hermits, in which they kept their fast of Lent in imitation of that of Jesus Christ.

them for their own use. He likewise told Joshua that no success could attend the house of Israel till the accursed thing was removed; and discovered to him the means whereby the offender might be discovered and properly punished.

Agreeably to the Divine instructions, Joshua, early the next morning, set about the business of discovering the thief, who had brought so great an evil on the people. For this purpose, he ordered all the tribes to assemble before the altar, where, first casting lots among the tribes, it appeared the thief belonged to that of Judah. They then proceeded from tribe to family, from family to household, and from household to particular persons; when the criminal was at length discovered to be Achan, who, on Joshua's admonition, made an ample confession of the whole. "I have," says he, "sinned against the Lord God of Israel; for when I saw among the spoil a royal garment and two hundred shekels of silver, with a wedge of gold of fifty shekels weight, my covetousness prompted me to take them; which I did, and hid them in the earth in the midst of my tent."

On this frank confession, Joshua sent messengers to examine Achan's tent, who, finding the treasures, brought them away, and laid them before the people. The offender being thus fully convicted, they took him, together with his family (whom they considered as accomplices in his crime), his cattle, tent, and all his moveables, and conducted them to a neighboring valley (called from that time, in allusion to this man's name, the valley of Achor), where they were first stoned to death, and their bodies afterward reduced to ashes. They likewise burnt all their goods and utensils, and erected over the whole a pile of stones, to perpetuate the memory of the crime, and to deter others from committing the like offence.

The Divine vengeance being appeased by the sentence executed upon Achan, God commanded Joshua to make another attempt on the city of Ai, assuring him that he should be no less successful than he had been in the attack on Jericho. As an encouragement to the soldiers, he allowed them the plunder of the city and cattle, and, in order the more easily to facilitate the conquest, particularly enjoined Joshua to place a party of men in ambuscade near the city.

Agreeably to these instructions, Joshua selected thirty thousand men, out of which he sent away by night five thousand to conceal themselves between Bethel and Ai, who, on a signal given by him (which was to be the holding up of a spear with a banner upon it), were immediately to enter the city and set it on fire. Early the next morning, Joshua marched with his army before the north part of the city. As soon as the king of Ai perceived him, he immediately sallied out of the town with his troops, followed by the greater part of the inhabitants, all of whom had been so elated with their former success, that they did not doubt of soon making an easy conquest. They accordingly fell on the Israelites with great fury, who at the first onset gave way, and retreated a considerable distance from the city. But this was only a feint to draw the enemy into the plain; and therefore, as soon as Joshua saw that by this stratagem the city was pretty well emptied, he gave the signal to the ambuscade, who, finding it defenceless, immediately entered and set it on fire. The ascent of the smoke convinced Joshua that his men had got possession of the place; upon which he suddenly turned about and faced the enemy, who, little expecting the Israelites would rally, were so surprised that they began to think of retreating to the city. But when they saw it all in flames, and the party who had set it on fire just going to fall upon their rear, they were so dispirited that they could neither fight nor fly; in consequence of which they were all cut to pieces by the Israelites, who, immediately marching to the city, put all they found in it to the sword: the whole number, men, women, and children, slain that day, amounted to twelve thousand. The king of Ai being taken prisoner, was ordered to be hung on a gibbet till sunset; after which his body was taken down and buried under a great heap of stones near the entrance of the city. The cattle and spoil taken from the enemy were (according to the Divine appointment) divided among the soldiers, who so effectually destroyed the city as to leave it a mere heap of rubbish.

As Joshua was now but a small distance from the mountains of Gerizim and Ebal, he bethought himself of the command, which had been given him by Moses, relative to the reading of the law (with the blessings and curses thereunto annexed), from those two mountains. He accordingly went to Mount Ebal, where he erected an altar, on which he offered up sacrifices to God for his late victories. He likewise caused an abridgment of the law, or some of the most remarkable parts of it, to be engraven on stones; and afterward read the whole of it to the people, as had been commanded by Moses.

The great success of Joshua against the cities of Jericho and Ai, and the dreadful slaughter made among the inhabitants, had so alarmed the kings of the respective provinces on that side the river Jordan, that they confederated together, and entered into a league for their mutual defence. But the Gibeonites, foreseeing the destruction that awaited them, and being apprehensive that all resistance would be in vain, resolved to make a peace with the Israelites, which they effected by the following stratagem: They selected a certain number of artful men, who were instructed to feign themselves ambassadors come from a very distant country, in order to obtain a league with the people of Israel. To make this story appear plausible, they were dressed in tattered garments, with old clouted shoes on their feet; and their provision consisted of dry musty bread, which they carried in old sacks, with some wine in bottles, all tarnished and torn. In this woful-appearing plight they arrived at Gilgal, the place where the army of the Israelites was at this time encamped.

Being introduced to Joshua, they told him, that from the many miracles which God had wrought for the Israelites in the land of Egypt, and the wonderful successes wherewith he had blessed their arms against every power that had opposed them in coming to that place, their states and rulers had sent them, from a very remote country, to form a league of friendship with them, and that on such conditions as were customary with their forefathers. They then pointed to their garments, which they solemnly assured Joshua were quite new when they sat out on their journey, but that the length of it had reduced them to the state in which they then appeared.

This stratagem had the desired effect: The plausible story of these feigned ambassadors gained such credit with the Israelites, that they entered into an amicable alliance with them; and Eleazer, the high-priest, with the princes of the respective tribes, solemnly ratified the treaty, the whole multitude assenting to the oaths made by their leaders. When the business was over, the Gibeonites took their leave, and hasted home with the glad tidings of their successful expedition.

Three days after the departure of these ambassadors, the whole plot was discovered, when it appeared that the Gibeonites were inhabitants of Canaan, and that they resided at a small distance from Jerusalem. This discovery greatly alarmed Joshua, who immediately sent for their governors, and reproached them for having practised such a deception; to which they replied, that they were compelled to do it in their own defence, as they knew they should otherwise share a similar fate with the inhabitants of Jericho and Ai. Joshua was desirous of having the league cancelled; but as it was confirmed by a solemn oath, this could not be done, without incurring the divine displeasure. It was therefore resolved, in order to appease the people, that, as a punishment for the imposition, the Gibeonites should ever after be kept in a state of bondage, by being made hewers of wood and drawers of water. This sentence they received without the least murmur, humbly acquiescing in whatever was thought proper to be imposed upon them by the Israelites.

When the confederate princes (who were five in number, the principal of whom was Adonizedek, king of Jerusalem) heard of the separate treaty made by the Gibeonites, and the artful manner in which it was obtained, they resolved to be revenged on them for their desertion of the common cause. Accordingly they joined all their forces, and marched toward the city of Gibeon, with a firm resolution of totally destroying it. When they came within a small distance of the place, they pitched their tents, intending to begin the attack early the next morning. In the meantime the Gibeonites (not daring to trust to their own strength) despatched a messenger to Joshua, imploring his immediate assistance, as they must otherwise inevitably fall into the hands of the Canaanites.

Joshua lost no time in complying with their request. He immediately set out with his army, and after marching the whole night, arrived, the next morning, at the spot where the enemy were encamped. The appearance of so formidable an army, and so unexpected, had such an effect on the Canaanites, that on Joshua's making an attack they immediately gave way, and were entirely routed, many being killed, and the rest betaking themselves to a precipitate flight. God had all along encouraged Joshua by promising him success; and therefore, as the confederate forces were endeavoring to escape, there fell a most violent storm of hail, the stones of which were so large that more people were destroyed by them than what fell by the sword.

Joshua was so desirous of totally extirpating the Canaanites, and so elevated with the manifest interposition of the Almighty, that while he was in chase of them, he begged, in the most fervent manner, that the sun and moon might stand still till he had accomplished his wishes. Notwithstanding the singularity of this request, God was pleased to grant it; so that this was the most memorable day that ever happened, the Almighty condescending to alter the course of nature to answer the purposes of man.

The confederate kings, finding themselves closely pursued, and likely to be either slain, or made captives, concealed themselves in a cave, near Makkedah, a city belonging to the tribe of Judah; intelligence of which being given to Joshua, he ordered the mouth of the cave to be blocked up, and a guard placed over it, to prevent their escape. In this situation they remained till Joshua returned from pursuing the fugitives, when he ordered the cave to be opened, and the kings to be brought forth, and hung upon trees till the evening. This was accordingly done, when their bodies were taken down, and thrown into the cave; so that the place they had chosen for their sanctuary became their sepulchre.

After this signal victory, Joshua proceeded to the southern parts of Canaan; in which, having soon reduced the most considerable places, and put the inhabitants to the sword, he returned, with his victorious army, to the camp at Gilgal.

The great fame of Joshua being now spread throughout Canaan, several princes of the northern parts, at the instigation of Jabin, king of Hazor, confederated together, and raised a great army to engage the Israelites, which they encamped at Berotha, a city of the Upper Galilee, not far from the waters of Merom. This, however, did not in the least intimidate Joshua, who, in pursuance of the instructions which God had given him (namely, that he should not only destroy them, but also their horses and chariots), immediately took the field, marched toward the enemy, and fell so suddenly on them, that they were totally routed, and, except some few who escaped into the country, were all put to the sword; after which he ham-strung their horses and burnt their chariots. Jabin, king of Hazor, who had been at the head of the confederacy, and was taken prisoner, he put to death, and ordered his city to be burnt to the ground; but the other cities whose inhabitants were slain in the action, he left standing, and gave the cattle and plunder to the soldiers.

After defeating this powerful army, Joshua pursued his route to the most distant parts of Canaan; and, by degrees, subdued all the inhabitants of the country. He slew all their kings, who were thirty-one in number, together with the Anakims, or giants, of whom he left none remaining, except in Gaza, Gath, and Ashdod.

Joshua, having now extended his conquests as far as he thought necessary at present, resolved to divide the country he had taken among the nine tribes and a half who were yet unprovided for, and to dismiss the two tribes and a half (namely, those of Reuben, Gad, and the half-tribe of Manasseh) who had assisted him in the wars, and whose habitations had been settled by Moses on the east side of the river Jordan.

In consequence of this resolution, Joshua appointed commissioners to take a survey of the captured land, and ordered them to report the state of it with all expedition. These messengers having executed their commission, returned, at the expiration of seven months, to Joshua, to whom, having delivered their report, he, assisted by Eleazer the high-priest, the elders, and the princes of the respective tribes, divided the whole country into equal portions, for which (according to God's direction) each tribe cast lots; but as some of the tribes were larger, and some territories richer than others, he took care to adjust the proportion of land to the largeness of the tribe, and the number of families in each; so that, notwithstanding they cast lots, the divisions were all made as equal as possible.

As soon as Joshua had thus divided the country on the west side of the Jordan, he took up his residence at a small place near Shiloh, where after the wars the tabernacle was set up, that he might have the opportunity, as occasion should offer, of consulting the divine oracle.

After being here a few days, Joshua assembled together the auxiliaries (namely, the tribes of Reuben and Gad, with the half-tribe of Manasseh), and gave them an honorable dismission. "He acknowledged the great services they had done him in his wars with the Canaanites, and highly applauded their courage and fidelity. He exhorted them, as they were now going to be separated from the tabernacle, to be diligent in their duty to God, and to bear always in mind those laws which he had given them by his servant Moses. He advised them to distribute a share of the rich booty they had got among their brethren on the other side the Jordan; because, though they did not partake of the troubles of the war, they had nevertheless been of infinite service in protecting their families during their absence." With these acknowledgments and exhortations, together with many sincere wishes for their prosperity, Joshua dismissed them, and they immediately departed for their own country.

As soon as these two tribes and a half arrived on the opposite side of the river Jordan, they erected an altar near the place where they and their brethren had miraculously passed over, not for any religious use, but as a memorial to succeeding generations, that though they were parted by the river, they were of the same descent and religion, and held an equal right to the tabernacle at Shiloh, and to the worship of God performed there, as their brethren on the other side the Jordan. This had like to have proved of fatal consequences, for the latter, either from being misinformed, or misapprehending the intent of the altar being erected, fell into a violent rage, considering them as apostates from the true religion; and, in order to punish them, assembled their forces at Shiloh, with a resolution of immediately declaring war against them. But before they proceeded to these extremities, their rulers advised them to suspend the execution of their wrath till they had sent a deputation in order to know their reason for building such an altar. This being agreed to, they sent Phineas, the son of Eleazer, with ten princes, one out of each tribe, to expostulate with them on their conduct. On their arrival Phineas accosted them in very severe terms, charging them with idolatry and rebellion against the Lord.

He reminded them of the calamities which God had formerly sent upon them for their worship of Baal-peor; and that, if he had been so severe upon them for the offence of one man (namely, Achan only) what might they not expect, when two tribes and a half were going to make a general revolt? He then concluded by saying, "If ye have done this from any apprehension that the land ye possess on this side the Jordan is unclean, or less holy than ours, because the tabernacle is on our side, return and settle among us where the tabernacle resteth; but by no means rebel against the Lord, nor us, in building you an altar, besides the altar of the Lord."

The Reubenites, Gadites, and Manassites, concerned to hear the ill opinion which their brethren had conceived of them, protested their innocence of any idolatrous intention, and made a solemn appeal to God, that so far were they from setting up an altar in opposition to his, that the only design of the structure they had raised was, to perpetuate their right to the service of the tabernacle, and to secure it to their latest posterity.

From this answer the deputies were fully convinced that the accusation laid against their brethren was totally groundless, and instead of having committed a crime, that they had only given an instance of their sincere attachment to their religious duties. The deputies, therefore, after taking a friendly leave, returned to Shiloh, and having communicated the particulars of all that had passed to the people, they expressed the greatest satisfaction at the result of the embassy; and the angry thoughts of war were immediately changed into peace and brotherly affection. On the other hand, the Reubenites and their brethren, to prevent any future jealousy, or suspicion, called the altar they had erected Ed, intending it as a standing witness (for so the word signifies) that though they lived at a distance from the rest of their brethren, yet they had all but one origin, and one God, who was the common God and father of all Israel.

This matter being adjusted, and the Israelites quietly settled in the possession of their conquests on both sides the river Jordan, Joshua disbanded his forces, and retired to Shechem.

No particular occurrence took place from this period till the death of Joshua, which happened about twenty years after. He was at this time far advanced in years, and finding his dissolution near at hand, he convened a general assembly of the princes and magistrates, with as many of the common people as could be gathered together. As soon as they were met, he harangued them in a very pertinent discourse on the great benefits and protection they had received from the hand of Providence. He pointed out to them in what manner he had preserved them, even in the midst of dangers; and that he had not only relieved them in all their wants and distresses, but had removed them from the most abject, to the most prosperous situation in life. In gratitude to so great a protector and benefactor, he exhorted them to a faithful observance of his laws, and invited them to renew their covenant with God, which their forefathers had made. This being done in very ample and significant terms, he recorded the covenant in the book of the law, and set up a great stone under an oak, near a place of religious worship, as a testimony against them, should they ever after deny God's service.

A short time after this Joshua paid the debt of nature, in the one hundred and tenth year of his age. He was buried at Tinmathserah, in Mount Ephraim, which city, on the division of the land among the tribes, was given to him by the Israelites, as an acknowledgment for the great services they had received from his administration.

Much about the same time died Eleazer, the high-priest, who was likewise buried in one of the hills of Ephraim, which had been given him by the Israelites, and which afterward descended to Phineas, his son, and successor in the priesthood.

These two funerals, so near the same time and place, reminded the Israelites of the bones of Joseph, which, at his request, had been brought out of Egypt, but not yet interred. They therefore took this opportunity of performing the funeral obsequies of their great progenitor in Shechem, where Jacob had purchased a piece of ground of the sons of Hamor, and which afterward became the inheritance of Joseph's posterity.

CHAPTER XIII.

From Joshua to Samuel (a period of about four hundred and seventy-four years) the condition of the Israelites varied according as the fundamental law of the state was observed or transgressed, exactly as Moses had predicted, and as the sanctions of the law had determined.

The last admonitions of Joshua, and the solemn renewal of the covenant with Jehovah, failed to produce all the effect intended. That generation, indeed, never suffered idolatry to become predominant, but still they were very negligent with respect to the expulsion of the Canaanites. Only a few tribes made war upon them, and even they were soon weary of the contest. They spared their dangerous and corrupting neighbors, and, contrary to express statute, were satisfied with making them tributary. They even became connected with them by unlawful marriages, and then it was no longer easy for them to exterminate or banish the near relatives of their own families. The Hebrews thus rendered the execution of so severe a law in a manner impossible, and wove for themselves the web in which they were afterward entangled. Their Canaanitish relatives invited them to their festivals, where not only lascivious songs were sung in honor of the gods, but fornication and unnatural lusts were indulged in as part of the divine service. These debaucheries, then consecrated by the religious customs of all nations, were gratifying to the sensual appetites; and the subject of Jehovah too readily submitted himself to such deities, so highly honored by his connexions, and worshipped in all the neighboring nations. At first, probably, a symbolical representation of Jehovah was set up, but this was soon transferred to an idol, or was invoked as an idol by others. Idolatrous images were afterward set up, together with the image of Jehovah, and the Israelites fondly imagined that they should be the more prosperous if they rendered homage to the ancient gods of the land. The propensity to idolatry, which was predominant in all the rest of the world, thus spread itself among the chosen people like a plague. From time to time idolatry was publicly professed, and this national treachery to their king, Jehovah, always brought with it national misfortunes.

However, it does not appear that any form of idolatry was *openly* tolerated until that generation was extinct, which, under Joshua, had sworn anew to the covenant with Jehovah. After that the rulers were unable or unwilling any longer to prevent the public worship of pagan deities. But the Hebrews, rendered effeminate by this voluptuous religion, and forsaken by their king, Jehovah, were no longer able to contend with their foes, and were forced to bend their necks under a foreign yoke. In this humiliating and painful subjection to a conquering people, they called to mind their deliverance from Egypt, the ancient kindnesses of Jehovah, the promises and threatenings of the law: then they forsook their idols, who could afford them no help,—they returned to the sacred tabernacle, and then found a deliverer who freed them from their bondage. The reformation was generally of no longer duration than the life of the deliverer. As soon as that generation was extinct, idolatry again crept in by the same way, and soon became predominant. Then followed subjection and oppression under the yoke of some neighboring people, until a second reformation prepared them for a new deliverance. Between these extremes of prosperity and adversity, the consequences of their fidelity or treachery to their divine king, the Hebrew nation was continually fluctuating until the time of Samuel. Such were the arrangements of Providence, that as soon as idolatry gained the ascendency, some one of the neighboring nations grew powerful, acquired the preponderance, and subjected the Hebrews. Jehovah always permitted their oppressions to become sufficiently severe to arouse them from their slumbers, to remind them of the sanctions of the law, and to turn them again to their God and king. Then a hero arose, who inspired the people with courage, defeated their enemies, abolished idolatry, and reestablished the authority of Jehovah. As the Hebrews, in the course of time, became more obstinate in their idolatry, so each subsequent oppression of the nation was always more severe than the preceding. So difficult was it, as mankind were then situated, to preserve a knowledge of the true God in the world, although so repeatedly and so expressly revealed, and in so high a degree made manifest to the senses.*

After this general view of the whole period above referred to, we may proceed to the historical details from which that view is collected.

Soon after the death of Joshua, and while the contemporary elders still lived, the Israelites made some vigorous and successful exertions to extend their territory. The most remarkable of these exertions was that made by the tribe of Judah, assisted by that of Simeon. They slew ten thousand Canaanites and Perizzites in the territory of Bezek, the king of which, Adoni-bezek (literally, " my lord of Bezek"), contrived to make his escape; but he was pursued and taken, when the conquerors cut off his thumbs and great toes. Now this, at the first view, was a barbarous act. It was not a mode in which the Hebrews were wont to treat their captives; and the reason for it—that it was intended as an act of just retaliation, or, as we should say, of poetic justice—appears from the bitter remark of Adoni-bezek himself:—" Three score and ten kings, having their thumbs and great toes cut off, gathered their meat under my table: as I have done, so God hath requited me." This proves that, as we have already on more than one occasion intimated, the war practices of the Israelites—especially in the treatment of their captives—were not more barbarous, and, in many respects, less barbarous, than those of their contemporaries; and that even their polished neighbors, the Egyptians, were not in this respect above them. Adoni-bezek died soon after at Jerusalem, to which place he was taken by the conquerors. They at this time had possession of the lower part of that town, and soon after succeeded in taking the upper city, upon Mount Zion, which the Jebusites had hitherto retained. They sacked it and burned it with fire. But as we afterward again find it in the occupation of the Jebusites, down to the time of David, it seems they took advantage of some one of the subsequent oppressions of Israel to recover the site and rebuild the upper city.

Eleazer the high-priest, as we have seen, did not long survive Joshua; and the remnant of the seventy elders, originally appointed by Moses to assist him in the government of the nation, soon followed them to the tomb. While these venerable persons lived, the Israelites remained faithful to their divine King and to his laws. But soon after their death the beginnings of corruption appeared. A timely attempt was made to check its progress by the remonstrances and threatenings of a prophet from Gilgal. But although they quailed under the rebuke which was there administered, the effect was but temporary. The downward course which the nation had taken was speedily resumed; and it is strikingly illustrated by some circumstances which the author of the book of Judges has given in an appendix contained in the last five chapters of that book, but which we shall find it more convenient to introduce here in their proper chronological place.

The history of Micah furnishes a very interesting example of the extent to which even Israelites, well disposed in the main, had become familiarized with superstitious and idolatrous practices, and the curious manner in which they managed to make a monstrous and most unseemly alliance between the true doctrine in which they had been brought up, and the erroneous notions which they had imbibed.

A woman of Ephraim had, through a mistaken zeal, dedicated a large quantity of

* Jahn, b. iii. sect. 20.

silver (about five hundred and fifty ounces) to the Lord, intending that her son should make therewith a teraph, in the hope that by this means she might procure to her house the blessings of One who had absolutely forbidden all worship by images. Her son Micah knew not of this sacred appropriation of the money, and took it for the use of the house. But on learning its destination, and hearing his mother lay her curse upon the sacrilegious person by whom she supposed it had been stolen, he became alarmed, and restored her the silver; and received it again from her with directions to give effect to her intention. This he did. He provided a teraph, and all things necessary to the performance of religious services before it, including vestments for a priest. He set apart one of his own sons as priest, until he should be able to procure a Levite to take that character. He had not long to wait. It would seem that the dues of the Levites were not properly paid at this time; for a young Levite, who had lived at Bethlehem, felt himself obliged to leave that place and seek elsewhere a subsistence. Happening to call at Micah's house, he gladly accepted that person's offer to remain and act as priest for the recompense of his victuals, with two suits of clothes (one probably sacerdotal), and eleven shekels of silver. Micah was delighted at this completion of his establishment, and, with most marvellous infatuation, cried, " Now I know Jehovah will bless me, seeing I have a Levite to be my priest." Things went on tranquilly for a time. But it happened that the tribe of Dan could not get possession of more than the hilly part of its territory, as the Amorites retained the plain, which was the most rich and valuable part. They therefore sought elsewhere an equivalent territory which might be more easily acquired. Having ascertained that this might be found in the remote but wealthy and peaceable town and district of Laish, near the sources of the Jordan, a body of six hundred men was sent to get possession of it. From the persons they had previously sent to explore the country, they had heard of Micah's establishment; and so far from manifesting any surprise or indignation, they viewed the matter much in the same light as Micah did himself. They envied him his idol and his priest, and resolved to deprive him of both, and take them to their new settlement. They did so, notwithstanding the protests and outcries of the owner: and as for the Levite, he was easily persuaded to prefer the priesthood of a clan to that of a single family. His descendants continued long after to exercise the priestly office, in connexion with this idol, at Dan, which was the name the conquerors gave to the town of Laish: and it is lamentable to have to add, that there is good reason to suspect that this Levite was no other than a grandson of Moses.

It would seem that the tribe of Benjamin had much the start of the other tribes in the moral corruption, in the infamous vices, which resulted from the looseness of their religious notions, and from the contaminating example of the heathen, with whom they were surrounded and intermixed.

A Levite of Mount Ephraim was on his way home with his wife, whom he was bringing back from her father's house in Bethlehem; and, on the approach of night, he entered the town of Gibeah, in Benjamin, to tarry till the next morning. As the custom of the travellers was, he remained in the street till some one should invite them to his house. But in that wicked place no hospitable notice was taken of them until an old man, himself from Mount Ephraim, but living there, invited them to his home. In the night that house was besieged by the men of the place, after the same fashion and for the same purpose as that of Lot had been, when he entertained the angels in Sodom. The efforts of the aged host to turn them from their purpose were unavailing; and, as a last resource, the Levite, in the hope of diverting them from their abominable purpose, put forth his wife into the street. She was grievously maltreated by these vile people until the morning, when they left her. She then went and lay down at the door of the house in which her lord lay; and when he afterward opened it—she was dead. The Levite laid the corpse upon his beast and hastened to his home.

There was a rather mysterious custom, in calling an assembly, by sending to the different bodies or persons which were to compose it a portion of a divided beast (see 1 Sam. xi. 7); and it then became awfully imperative upon the party which received the bloody missive to obey the call which it intimated. To give a horrible intensity to the custom in this case, the Levite—a man of obviously peculiar character—divided his wife's body into twelve parts, and sent one portion to each of the tribes of Israel. The horror-struck tribes, on receiving their portion of the body, and hearing the statement which the messengers delivered, agreed that such a thing had not before been heard of in Israel, and hastened to the place of meeting, which was Mizpeh.

In the great audience there assembled, the Levite declared his wrongs; which when they had heard, the thousands of Israel vowed not to return to their homes until they had brought the offenders to condign punishment. And to express the earnestness of their purpose, they appointed one tenth of their whole number to bring in provisions for the rest, that the want of victuals might not, as often happens in Oriental warfare, oblige them to disperse before their object was accomplished. But, in the first instance, they sent messengers throughout the tribe of Benjamin, explaining the occasion of their assembling, and demanding that the offenders should be delivered up to justice. This the Benjamites were so far from granting that the whole tribe made common cause with the people of Gibeah, and all its force was called out to repel any attempt which the other tribes might make against them. Considering that the force of the eleven tribes amounted to four hundred thousand able men, whereas the Benjamites could bring together no more than twenty-six thousand, the hardihood of this resistance is well worthy of remark, if it does not make out the claim of the Benjamites to that character for indomitable courage which they appear to have acquired. Probably the influence of that acknowledged character upon their opponents, together with their own peculiar skill in the use of the sling, formed their main reliance. Among them were seven hundred left-handed men who could sling stones to a hair's breadth and not miss.

The Israelites committed one fatal oversight in this undertaking. Although the affair was of such grave importance, they neglected to consult their divine King, without whose permission they ought not to have supposed themselves authorized to act as they did. They first decided on war, and then only consulted him as to the manner it should be conducted. The consequence was that they were twice defeated by the Benjamites, who sallied from the town of Gibeah against them. Corrected by this experience, they applied in a proper manner to learn the will of their King; and then the victory was promised to them.

In their next attempt the Israelites resorted to the same familiar stratagem of ambuscade and of pretended flight, when the besieged sallied forth against them, as that whereby the town of Ai had been taken by Joshua, and with precisely the same result. Eighteen thousand Benjamites, "men of valor," were "trodden down with ease" by the vast host which now enclosed them. The rest endeavored to escape to the wilderness, but were all overtaken and destroyed, with the exception of six hundred who found shelter among the rocks of Rimmon. The conquerors then went through the land, subjecting it to military execution. They set on fire all the towns to which they came, and put to the sword the men, the cattle, and all that came to hand.

But when the heat of the conflict and execution had subsided, the national and clannish feelings of the Israelites were shocked at the reflection that they had extinguished a tribe in Israel. It was true that six hundred men remained alive among the rocks of Rimmon; but it was not clear how the race of Benjamin could be continued through them, as, at the very commencement of the undertaking, the Israelites had solemnly sworn that they would not give their daughters in marriage to the Benjamites. They had now leisure to repent of this vow; although, with reference to the vile propensities exhibited by the people of Gibeah, it was quite natural that in the first excitement such a vow should have been taken.

But now they were sincerely anxious to find means of repairing their error, and to provide the survivors with wives, that the house of Benjamin might not be wholly lost. It was found that the summons whereby the tribes had been assembled had been unheeded by the men of Jabesh-Gilead, whereby they had exposed themselves to the terrible doom which the very act of summons denounced against the disobedient. That doom was inflicted, save that all the virgins were spared to be wives for the Benjamites. But as these were still insufficient, the unprovided Benjamites were secretly advised to lie in wait in the vineyards near Shiloh, when they attended the next annual festival at the tabernacle; and when the young women of the place came out in dances, as at such times they were wont, they might seize and carry off the number they required. The men followed this advice. And when the fathers and brothers of the stolen maidens began to raise an outcry, the elders, by whom the measure had been counselled, interposed to pacify them, and persuaded them to over-look the matter, in consideration of the difficulties by which the case was surrounded.

The Benjamites then returned to their desolated cities, and rebuilt and re-occupied them as they were able. But from this time Benjamin was the least, although not the least distinguished, of all the tribes.

At length (B. C. 1572) the idolatries and demoralization of the Israelites had become so rank, that a fiery trial was judged necessary for their correction. A king named Cushan-rishthaim, reigning in Mesopotamia, had extended his power far on this side the Euphrates. He now advanced into Canaan, and, either by victory or menace, rendered the Hebrews tributary. They remained under severe bondage for eight years. At the end of that time, Othniel—that relative of Caleb who has already been mentioned—was incited to put himself at the head of the people and attempt their deliverance. The garrisons which the Mesopotamians had left in the country were suddenly surprised and slain; the armies of Israel again appeared in the field, and, although at first few in number, they fought at every point the troops opposed to them; and when their numbers were increased by the reinforcements which poured in from all quarters on the first news of probable success, they hazarded a general action, in which they obtained a complete victory over the Mesopotamians, and drove them beyond the Euphrates.*

Othniel remained the acknowledged judge, or regent, of the divine king for forty years. During his administration, the people remained faithful to their God and king, and consequently prospered. But when the beneficial control which Othniel exercised was withdrawn by his death, they fell again into idolatry and crime, and new afflictions became needful to them.

The instruments of their punishment, this time, were the Moabites. By a long peace, this nation had recovered from the defeats which they had suffered from the Amorites before the time of Moses; and, perceiving that the Israelites were not invincible, Eglon, the king of Moab, formed a confederacy with the Ammonites and Amalekites, and, with this help, made an attack upon them—probably under the same pretences which we shall find to have been employed on a subsequent occasion. He defeated the idolatrous Hebrews in battle, subdued the tribes beyond Jordan, and the southern tribes on this side the river, and established himself in Jericho, which he must have found a convenient post for intercepting, or at least checking, the communications between the eastern and western tribes. At that place the conquered tribes were obliged to bring him presents, or, in other words, to pay a periodical tribute. This subjection to a king who resided among them was still more oppressive than that from which they had been delivered by Othniel; and it continued more than twice as long—that is, for eighteen years. This oppression must have been particularly heavy upon the tribe of Benjamin, as it was their territory to which Jericho belonged, and which was therefore encumbered by the presence of the court of the conqueror. It was natural that those whose necks were the most galled by the yoke, should make the first effort to shake it off. Accordingly, the next deliverer was of the tribe of Benjamin. His name was Ehud, one of those left-handed men—or rather, perhaps, men who could use the left hand with as much ease and power as the right—for which this tribe seems to have been remarkable. He conducted a deputation which bore from the Israelites the customary tributes to the king. It seemed that men with weapons were not admitted to the king's presence: but Ehud had a two-edged dagger under his garment; but as he wore it on the right side, where it is worn by no right-handed man, its presence was not suspected. When he had left the presence and dismissed his people, Ehud went on as far as the carved images which had been placed at Gilgal. The sight of these images, which the Moabites had probably set up by the sacred monument of stones which the Israelites had there set up, seems to have revived the perhaps faltering zeal of the Benjamite, and he returned to Jericho and to the presence of the king, and intimated that he had a secret message to deliver. The king then withdrew with him to his "summer-parlor," which seems to have been such a detached or otherwise pleasantly-situated apartment as are still usually found in the mansions and gardens of the East, and to which the master retires to enjoy a freer air, and more open prospects, than any other part of his dwelling commands, and where also he usually withdraws to enjoy

* This paragraph is partly from Josephus, whose account is here in agreement with, while it fills up, the brief notice which the Book of Judges offers.

13

his siesta during the heat of the day. It is strictly a private apartment, which no one enters without being specially invited; and accordingly it is said of this, that it was an apartment "which he had for himself alone." As the king sat in this parlor, Ehud approached him, saying, "I have a message from God to thee." On hearing that sacred name, the king rose from his seat, and Ehud availed himself of the opportunity of burying his dagger in his bowels. The Benjamite then withdrew quietly, bolting after him the door of the summer-parlor; and as such parlors usually communicate by a private stair with the porch, without the *necessity* of passing into or through the interior parts of the mansion, there was nothing to impede his egress, unless the porters at the outer gate had seen cause for suspicion.

The scripture, as is frequently the case, mentions this as an historical fact, without commendatory or reprehensive remark; and we have no right to infer the approbation which is not expressed. No doubt Ehud's deed was a murder; and the only excuse for it is to be found in its public object, and in the fact that the notions of the East have always been, and are now far more lax on this point than those which Christian civilization has produced in Europe. There all means of getting rid of a public enemy, whom the arm of the law can not reach, are considered just and proper. No one can read a few pages of any oriental history without being fully aware of this; and it is by oriental notions, rather than by our own, that the act of Ehud must, to a certain extent, be judged.

The servants of Eglon supposed that their lord was taking his afternoon sleep in his summer-parlor, and hence a considerable time elapsed before his assassination was discovered.

In the meantime, Ehud was able to make known the death of the king, and to collect a body of men, with whom he went down to seize the fords of the Jordan, that the Moabites in Canaan might neither receive reinforcements from their own country nor escape to it. Confounded by the death of their king, they were easily overcome. All who were on this side the Jordan, ten thousand in number, were destroyed—not one escaped. This deliverance secured for Israel a repose of eighty years, terminating in the year B. C. 1426, being 182 years after the passage of the Jordan.

At or toward the end of this period of eighty years, a first attempt was made by the Philistines to bring the southern tribes under their yoke. But they were unable to accomplish their design, having been repulsed on their first advance, with the loss of six hundred men, by Shamgar and other husbandmen, who fought with ox-goads,* being then employed in the cultivation of the fields.

———

It is about this time that the story of Ruth, which occupies a separate book in the Hebrew scriptures, is placed by Usher and other chronologers. Being episodical, and only slightly connected with the historical narrative, we can not follow the details of this beautiful story; but the intimations of the state of society, and of the manners and ideas of the times, which it contains, are, even historically, of too much importance to be overlooked.

The scene of the principal part of the story is in Bethlehem of Judah.

A famine in the land drives an inhabitant of this town, with his wife and two sons, to the land of Moab, which, in consequence of the victories under Ehud, seems to have been at this time in some sort of subjection to the Israelites. The man's name was Elimelech, his wife's Naomi, and the sons were called Mahlon and Chilion. The woman lost her husband and two sons in the land of Moab, but the childless wives of her sons, who had married in that land, remained with her. One was called

* "At Khan Leban the country people were now everywhere at plough in the fields in order to sow cotton. 'Twas observable that in ploughing they used goads of an extraordinary size; upon measuring of several, I found them to be about eight feet long, and, at the bigger end, six inches in circumference. They are armed at the lesser end with a sharp prickle for driving the oxen; and at the other end with a small spade or paddle of iron, strong and massy, to clear the plough from the clay that encumbers it in working. May we not hence conjecture that it was with such a goad as one of these that Shamgar made that prodigious slaughter! I am confident that whoever should see one of these implements will judge it to be a weapon not less fit, perhaps fitter, than a sword for such an execution. Goads of this sort I always saw used hereabouts, and also in Syria: and the reason is because the same single person both drives the oxen and also holds and manages the plough, which makes it necessary to use such a goad as is described above to avoid the incumbrance of two instruments."—Maundrell, 110.

Summer Parlor on the Nile.

Orpah, and the other Ruth. At the end of ten years, Naomi determined to return home, but, with beautiful disinterestedness, exhorted the widows of her two sons to remain in their own land with their well-provided friends, and not go to be partakers of her destitution. Orpah accordingly remained: but nothing could overcome the devoted attachment of Ruth to the mother of her lost husband. To the really touching representations of Naomi, her still more touching reply was, "Entreat me not to leave thee, or to return from following thee: for whither thou goest, I will go; and where thou lodgest, I will lodge; thy people shall be my people, and thy God my God: where thou diest, will I die, and there will I be buried; the Lord do so to me, and more also, if aught but death part thee and me." This strong and unmistakable expression of most beautiful and true affections, could not be repelled by Naomi. They took their homeward way together.

It was barley harvest when Naomi and Ruth arrived at Bethlehem. Ruth, anxious to provide in any little way for their joint subsistence, soon bethought herself of going forth to seek permission to glean in some harvest field. It happened that the field where she asked and obtained this permission, from the overseer of the reapers, belonged to Boaz, a person of large possessions in these parts. Boaz himself came in the course of the day, to view the progress of the harvest. He greeted his reapers, "Jehovah be with you;" and they answered him, "Jehovah bless thee." His attention was attracted toward Ruth, and he inquired concerning her of his overseer, who told him that this was "The Moabitish damsel that came back with Naomi out of the land of Moab," and related how she had applied for leave to glean after the reapers. Boaz then himself accosted her, and kindly charged her not to go elsewhere, but to remain in his fields, and keep company with his maidens till the harvest was over. He had enjoined his young men not to molest her. If she were athirst she might go and drink freely from the vessels of water provided for the use of the reapers. Ruth was astonished at all this kindness, and fell at his feet, expressing her thanks and her surprise that he should take such kind notice of a stranger. But he said, "It has been fully shown me, all that thou hast done to thy mother-in-law, since the death of thy husband; and how thou hast left thy father and thy mother, and the land of thy nativity, and art come unto a people which thou knowest not heretofore. Jehovah recompense thy deed: and a full recompense be given to thee from Jehovah, the God of Israel, under whose wings thou art come to trust." She answered, "Let me find favor in thy sight, my lord, for that thou hast comforted me, and for that thou hast spoken friendly unto thine handmaid, though I be not like one of thine handmaidens."

When the meal-time of the harvest people came round, Boaz invited her to draw near and eat of the bread, and dip her morsel in the vinegar with them. He also handed her some new corn parched, which was considered rather a luxury, and therefore Ruth reserved part of it for Naomi.

All these little incidents, beautifully descriptive of the innocent old customs of harvest time, bring strongly before the mind of one who has studied the antiquities of Egypt, the agricultural scenes depicted in the grottoes of Eleithuias, in which so many of the usages of Egyptian agriculture are represented. There we see the different processes of cutting with the reaping hook, and of plucking up the stalks; gleaners; water refrigerating in porous jars (placed on stands) for the refreshment of the reapers; the reapers quenching their thirst; and women bearing away the vessels in which drink has been brought to them at their labor.

When Ruth returned home in the evening with the result of her day's gleaning—an ephah of barley—Naomi was anxious to know how it happened that her labors had been so prosperous: and when she heard the name of Boaz, she remarked that he was a near kinsman of the family; and advised that, according to his wish, Ruth should confine her gleaning to his fields. So Ruth gleaned in the fields of Boaz, until the end not only of the barley, but of the wheat harvest.

When the harvest was over, Naomi, who was anxious for the rest and welfare of the good and devoted creature who had been more than a daughter to her, acquainted her with what had lately engaged her thoughts. She said that Boaz was so near of kin that he came under the operation of the levirate law, which required that when a man died childless, his next of kin should marry the widow, in order that the first child born from this union should be counted as the son of the deceased, and inherit as his heir. It was, therefore, no less her duty than a circumstance highly calculated to promote her welfare, that Boaz should be reminded of the obligation which devolved

Market at Gaza.

upon him. But as it was not wished to press the matter upon him, if he were averse to it, it was necessary that the claim should, in the first instance, be privately made. In such a case, Ruth, a stranger very imperfectly acquainted with the laws and habits of the Israelites, could only submit herself to Naomi's guidance. She told Ruth that Boaz was engaged in winnowing his barley in the thrashing-floor; which, of course, was nothing more than a properly levelled place in the open air. Naomi conjectured he would rest there at night, and told Ruth to mark the spot to which he withdrew, and advance to claim the protection he was bound to render. All happened as Naomi had foreseen. Boaz, after he had supped, withdrew to sleep at the end of the heap of corn; and after he had lain down, Ruth advanced and placed herself at his feet: and when he awoke at midnight, and with much astonishment, asked who she was, she answered, "I am Ruth, thy handmaid: take therefore thy handmaid under thy protection, for thou art a near kinsman." Those who, measuring all things by their own small and current standards, regard as improper or indelicate this procedure of one

"Who feared no evil, for she knew no sin,"

need only hear the answer of Boaz to be satisfied. "Blessed be thou, of Jehovah, my daughter . . . , And now, my daughter, fear not: for all my fellow-citizens do know that thou art a virtuous woman." He added, however, that there was a person in the town more nearly related to her deceased husband; and on him properly the levirate duty devolved: but if *he* declined it, then it fell to himself, and he would certainly undertake it. It being too late for Ruth to return home, Boaz desired her to remain in the thrashing-floor for the night. Early in the morning he dismissed her, after having filled her veil with corn to take to Naomi.

In those times, and long after, it was customary to transact all business of a public nature and to administer justice in the gates. When there was little use of written documents, this gave to every transaction the binding obligation which the presence of many witnesses involved; and thus also justice was easily and speedily administered among the people, at the hours when they passed to and fro between the fields and the city. And such hours were, for this reason, those at which the judges and elders gave their attendance in the gates.—(See engraving, p. 197.)

Boaz therefore went up to the gate; and requested ten of the elders, there present, to sit down with him as witnesses of what was to take place. When the "near kinsman" passed by, he called him to sit down with them. He then questioned him as to his willingness "to raise up the name of the dead upon his inheritance." This he was not willing to do, "lest he should mar his own inheritance;" and therefore he was glad to relinquish his prior claim to Boaz, which he did by the significant action of drawing off his own shoe and giving it to him. This action was usual in all transactions of this nature, and it may well be interpreted by the familiar idiom which would express Boaz as being made, by this act and with reference to this particular question, *to stand in the shoes* of the person who had transferred to him his rights and duties. Boaz then declared all the people there present at the gate to be witnesses of this transfer, and they responded, "We are witnesses." After this Boaz took Ruth to be his wife; and the fruit of this union was Obed, the grandfather of David, of whom, according to the flesh, came the Saviour of the world.

From the repose which this narrative offers, one turns reluctantly to renewed scenes of war, oppression, and wrong.

It may be doubted that the authority—such as it was—of any of the judges extended over all the tribes. Hardly any of the oppressions to which the Israelites were subject appear to have been general, and in most cases the authority of the judge appears to have been confined to the tribes he had been instrumental in delivering from their oppressors. There is, for instance, not the least reason to suppose that the authority of Ehud extended over the northern tribes, which had not been effected by the oppression of the Moabites, from which he delivered the south and east. The eighty years of good conduct which followed this deliverance, is therefore only to be understood as exhibited by the tribes which were then delivered. The northern tribes, and in some degree those of the centre and the west, were meanwhile falling into those evil practices, from which it was necessary that distress and sorrow should bring them back. And therefore they were distressed.

The northern Canaanites had, in the course of time, recovered from the effects of that great overthrow which they sustained in the time of Joshua. A new Jabin, reigning like his predecessor in Hazor, by the lake Merom, rose into great power. His general, Sisera, was an able and successful warrior; and his powerful military force contained not fewer than nine hundred of those iron-armed chariots of war which the Israelites regarded with so much dread. With such a force he was enabled, for the punishment of their sins, to reduce the northern tribes to subjection, and hold them tributary. Considering the character of the power which now prevailed over them, there is reason to conclude that this was the severest of all the oppressions to which Israel had hitherto been subject. The song of Deborah conveys some intimations of their miserable condition. The villages and open homesteads, which were continually liable to be pillaged, and the inhabitants insulted and wronged by the Canaanites, were deserted throughout the land, and the people found it necessary to congregate in the walled towns. Travelling was unsafe; in consequence of which the high-ways were deserted, and those who were obliged to go from one place to another, found it necessary to journey in bye-roads and unfrequented paths. At the places to which it was necessary to resort for water, they were waylaid and robbed, wounded, or slain: and, to crown all, they were disarmed; among forty thousand in Israel, a shield or spear was not to be found. The details of this picture are exactly such as are offered by the condition of any oppressed or subjugated population, at this day, in the east. The government itself may be content with its tribute; but it will be obliged to wink at, because unable to prevent, the far greater grievances, the exactions, robberies, insults, woundings, deaths, to which the people are subjected by the inferior officers of government, by bands of licentious soldiers, and by an adverse and triumphant populace,—all of whom look upon them as their prey and spoil, as things made only to be trampled on. Such oppression the Israelites endured for twenty years. They then remembered that, to them, trouble was the punishment of sin; and that there was one able and willing to deliver them, if they would but turn themselves unto him. They did turn, and their deliverance was certain from that hour.

In those days a pious and able woman, well acquainted with the divine law, became an important person in Israel. Her name was Deborah, and she abode under a palm-tree in the southern part of Ephraim. Her high character for piety and wisdom occasioned the Israelites to resort to her for counsel and for justice; and it is not unlikely that her salutary influence contributed to move the people to that repentance which prepared the way for their deliverance. When their punishment had thus wrought its intended object, the divine king made known to the prophetess his intention to deliver the house of Israel from its bondage; but seeing that she, as a woman, could not personally lead the Israelites to battle, she sent to a person of the tribe of Naphtali, named Barak, and communicated to him the instructions she had received. These were, that he should bring together, at Mount Tabor, ten thousand men of the tribes of Naphtali and Zebulun, and with them give battle to the forces of King Jabin. Barak, being fully aware of the difficulty of assembling and arming a respectable force, and recollecting the greatness of that power he was to oppose, rather shrunk from the enterprise. He, however, offered to undertake it, if Deborah would afford him the benefit of her influential presence, but not else. She consented; but, to rebuke the weakness of his faith, she prophesied that Sisera—the redoubted captain of King Jabin's host—should not be slain in fight with him, or be taken captive by him, but should fall by a woman's hand.

They went into the north together, and the required number of men from Naphtali and Zebulun readily obeyed their call and marched to Mount Tabor. These two tribes had probably been selected on the ground that they were likely to engage more readily in this service, in consequence of their vicinity to the metropolitan seat of the oppressing power having rendered the yoke of servitude more galling and irritating to them than to the other tribes.

As soon as Jabin's general, Sisera, heard of the Hebrew force assembled on Mount Tabor, he brought forth his nine hundred chariots, and assembled his whole army, not doubting to surround and cut in pieces a body of men so comparatively small. The Hebrews were in general much afraid of war-chariots, to drawn battles in open plains they were unaccustomed, and the disparity of numbers was in this instance very great. Yet, encouraged by the assurances of victory which Deborah conveyed, Barak did not await the assault of Sisera, but marched his men down from the mountain into the open plain, and fell impetuously upon the adverse host. In Oriental warfare the result of the first shock usually decides the battle, and the army is lost which then gives way or has its ranks broken. So it was now. At the first shock the vast army of Sisera was seized with a panic terror. The soldiers threw away their arms, and sought only how they might escape; while the chariots, drawn by terrified horses, impeded the retreat of the fugitives, and added to the confusion and the loss. The carnage among the Canaanites was horrible; and, besides those who perished by the sword, vast numbers of them were swept away by the sudden overflow of the river Kishon. Sisera himself fled in his chariot across the plain of Esdraelon; but, fearing that his chariot rendered him too conspicuous, he dismounted and continued his flight on foot. At last he came to a nomade encampment, belonging to Heber the Kenite, one of the descendants of those of the family and clan of Jethro, who, with the brother-in-law of Moses, entered the land of Canaan with the Israelites, and enjoyed the privilege of pasturing their flocks in its plains. Heber was from home, but his wife knew the illustrious fugitive, and offered him the protection of her tent. This, as the Kenites had been neutral in the war, Sisera did not hesitate to accept. He knew that the tent of a Bedouin, and especially the woman's portion of it, was a sanctuary, which the owner would sooner perish than allow to be violated, and that infamy worse than death awaited him who allowed injury to befall the guest or fugitive who was admitted to its shelter. Being athirst, Sisera asked for water; but instead of this she gave him sour milk—the best beverage an Arab tent contains, and the refreshing qualities of which are well known to those who have travelled in the East. This, with his fatigue, disposed Sisera to sleep. As he slept, the thought occurred to Jael (that was the woman's name) that the greatest enemy of the now victorious Israelites lay helpless before her; and that it was in her power to win great favor from the victors, by anticipating the almost certain death which awaited the chief captain of Jabin's host. Having no weapon, she took a mallet and one of the long nails by which the tent cords are fastened to the ground, and stealing softly to the place where he lay, she smote the nail into his temple, pinning his head to the ground. Barak, passing that way soon after, in pursuit, was called in by Jael, and he beheld the redoubted Sisera dead at his feet— slain ignominiously by a woman's hand. He might then have pondered whether, had Sisera been the victor and himself the fugitive, the same fate might not have been his own. When we reflect that " there was peace between Jabin, king of Hazor, and the house of Heber the Kenite," and that it was in the knowledge that he deserved no wrong at *their* hands, that Sisera accepted the shelter which Jael offered; and when, moreover, we consider that the emir, Jael's husband, had no interest in the result, save that of standing well with the victorious party, it will be difficult to find any other motive than that which we have assigned—the desire to win the favor of the victors—for an act so grossly opposed to all those notions of honor among tentdwellers on which Sisera had relied for his safety. It was a most treacherous and cruel murder, wanting all those extenuations which were applicable to the assassination of King Eglon by Ehud.

The time is gone by when commentators or historians might venture to justify this deed. Our extended acquaintance with the East enables us to know that those Orientals whose principles would allow them to applaud the act of Ehud, would regard with horror the murder, in his sleep, of a confiding and friendly guest, to whom the sacred shelter of the tent had been offered. That Deborah, as a prophetess, was enabled to foretell the fall of Sisera by a woman's hand, does not convey the divine sanction of this deed, but only manifests the divine foreknowledge; and that the same Deborah, in her triumphant song, blesses Jael for this act, only indicates the feeling, in the first excitement of victory, of one who had far more cause to rejoice at the death of Sisera than Jael had to inflict it.

The triumphant song of Deborah has attracted great and deserved attention as a noble "specimen of the perfectly sublime ode." The design of this ode seems to be twofold, religious and political: first, to thank God for the recent deliverance of Israel from Canaanitish bondage and oppression; and, next, to celebrate the zeal and alacrity with which some of the tribes volunteered their services against the common enemy; and to censure the lukewarmness and apathy of others who stayed at home, and thus betrayed the public cause; and, by this contrast and exposure, to heal those fatal divisions among the tribes which were so injurious to the public weal. It consists of three parts:—first, the exordium, containing an appeal to past times, where Israel was under the special protection of Jehovah, as compared with their late disastrous condition; next, a recital of the circumstances which preceded and those that accompanied the victory; lastly, a fuller description of the concluding event, the death of Sisera, and the disappointed hopes of his mother for his triumphant return. The admired conclusion is thus:—

> " The mother of Sisera gazed through the window,
> Through the lattice she, lamenting, cried,
> ' Why is his chariot so long in coming ?"
> Wherefore linger the steps of his steeds ?'
> Her wise ladies answered their mistress,
> Yea, she returned answer to herself,—
> 'Have they not sped, and are dividing the spoil ?
> To every chief man a damsel or two ?
> To Sisera a spoil of various colors,
> A spoil of various-colored embroidery,
> A spoil of various-colored embroideries for the neck.'—
> So let thine enemies perish, O Jehovah !
> But let they who love thee become
> As the sun going forth in his strength."[†]

From the animadversions which this ode contains, it is easy to collect that only those tribes which were actually subject to the oppression, and even only those on which the oppression the most heavily fell, were willing to disturb themselves by engaging in warlike operations against the oppressor. It does not appear that the southern tribes and the tribes beyond Jordan were directly affected by the subjugation of the northern tribes; and even of those under tribute, the tribes more remote from the seat of King Jabin seem to have been more at ease than the others. All these were loath to come forward on this occasion; and, in general, we find that, among the Hebrews of this early period, there was little if any of that high-spirited and honorable abhorrence of a foreign yoke, which is, under God, the surest safeguard of a nation's independence. It was not the yoke itself they hated, but its physical weight upon their shoulders; and that weight must be very heavy before they could be roused to any great effort to shake it from them. The iron which entered their souls in Egypt still rusted there.

These sectional divisions—or rather this want of a general and sympathizing union among the several members of the house of Israel—were the obvious secondary cause of the miseries and oppressions under which different portions of that great body did from time to time fall; and this disunion itself was the natural and inevitable result of the neglect of the law, as a whole, and especially of those provisions which were, in their proper operation, admirably calculated to keep the tribes united together as one nation. It would be ridiculous to say that the theocratic policy was a failure. That which was not fairly and fully tried can not be said to fail. Ruin to the people did not come from the system itself: and that ruin did come from the neglect of its conditions, rather shows how well that system was calculated to form a happy and united people.

The victory of Deborah and Barak over Sisera gave to Israel a long repose from the aggressions of the nations west of the Jordan; for although their peace began again to be disturbed after forty years (in 1336 B. C.), the invasion was then from the *east*.

At the latter end of the forty years which followed the victory over Sisera, the

---

* The original is highly figurative; " Why is his chariot ashamed to come ?"

† " The first sentences exhibit a striking picture of maternal solicitude, and of a mind suspended and agitated between hope and fear. Immediately, impatient of delay, she anticipates the consolations of her friends ; and, her mind being somewhat elevated, she boasts with all the levity of a fond female,—

> 'Vast in her hopes and giddy with success.'

Let us here observe how well adapted every sentiment, every word, is to the character of the speaker. She makes no account of the slaughter of the enemy, of the valor and conduct of the conqueror, of the multitude of the captives, but

> ' Burns with a female thirst of prey and spoils.'

Nothing is omitted which is calculated to attract and engage the passions of a vain and trifling woman ; slaves, gold, and rich apparel. Nor is she satisfied with the bare enumeration of them, she repeats, she amplifies, she heightens every circumstance ; she seems to have the very plunder in her immediate possession ; she pauses and contemplates every particular. To add to the beauty of this passage, there is also an uncommon neatness in the versification ; great force, accuracy, and perspicuity in the diction ; and the utmost elegance in the repetitions, which, notwithstanding their apparent redundancy, are conducted with the most perfect brevity. In the end, the fatal disappointment of female hope and credulity, tacitly insinuated by the unexpected apostrophe,—

> ' So let thine enemies perish, O Jehovah !'

is expressed more forcibly by this very silence of the person who was just speaking, that it could possibly have been by all the powers of language."—LOWTH.

Israelites had again relapsed into their evil and idolatrous habits. This was particularly the case of the tribes beyond Jordan, whose repose had been of longer duration than that of the western tribes, for it does not appear that the oppressions of King Jabin had extended to them.

Their punishment was this time particularly heavy, and came from an unexpected quarter. The pastoral tribes dwelling on the borders of the land and in the eastern deserts—the Midianites, Amalekites, with other tribes of Arabia—came swarming into the land "like locusts," with countless flocks and herds, and pitching their tents in the plains and valleys. Arriving by the time the products of the soil began to be gathered in, they remained until the final ingatherings of the year, when the advance of winter warned them to withdraw into their deserts. Thus their cattle grew fat upon the rich pastures of the land, while those of Israel were starved; and the men themselves lived merrily upon the grain which the Hebrews had sowed, and upon the fruits which they had cultivated: and as, besides this deprivation of the sustenance for which they had labored, such lawless crews are always ready for any kind of great or small robbery and exaction, the Israelites were obliged to abandon the open country, and to resort to the walled towns, to intrench themselves in strongholds, and even to seek the shelter of the caves among the mountains. Even those who ventured to remain in occupation of their own allotments, were afraid to have it known that they had in their possession any of the produce of their own fields. All this while it does not appear that there was any open war, or any military operations. The invaders bore all before them, and had entirely their own way, by the mere force of the intimidating impressions which their numbers created. Countries or districts bordering on the desert are still subject to similar visitations, where the local government is not strong enough to prevent them, or where the preoccupation of the border soil by Arabs in the state of semi-cultivators, does not form an obstacle (as it does not so always) to the incursions of pure Bedouins. Down to a very recent date the very country east of the Jordan, which suffered the most on the present occasion, suffered much from the periodical sojourn and severe exactions of the Bedouin tribes,

These incursions of the Midianites were repeated for seven years. By this time the oppression had become so heavy that the Israelites, finding by bitter experience the insufficiency of all other help, cried to Him who had delivered them of old: their cry was heard. A prophet was commissioned to point out to them that their disobedience had been the cause of their sufferings, and to give to them the promise of a new deliverance.

The hero this time appointed to act for the deliverance of Israel, was Gideon of Manasseh. His family was exposed to the general suffering occasioned by the presence of the Bedouin tribes,—so much so, that having retained possession of some corn, they dared not thrash it out for use in the ordinary thrashing-floor, but, to conceal it from the knowledge or suspicion of the invaders, were obliged to perform this operation silently and secretly, in so unusual a place as the vineyard, near the wine-press. The thrashing-floors were watched by the Midianites at this time, when the harvests had been gathered in; but no regard was paid to the vineyards, as the season of ripe grapes was far off. Gideon was engaged in this service when " the angel of Jehovah" appeared to him standing under an oak which grew there. When apprized of his vocation to deliver Israel, the modest husbandman would have excused himself on the ground of his wanting that eminence of station which so important a service appeared to demand; and when silenced by the emphatic "I will be with thee" from his heavenly visitant, he still sought to have some certain tokens whereby he might feel assured, and be enabled to convey the assurance to others, that his call was indeed from God. Accordingly, a succession of signal miracles were wrought to satisfy his mind and to confirm his faith. The refection of kid's-flesh and bread, which the hospitable Gideon quickly got ready for the stranger, was, as he directed, laid upon a rock before him, and when he touched it with the end of his staff, a spontaneous fire arose by which it was consumed, as a sacrifice, and at the same time the stranger disappeared. After this, at the special desire of Gideon, " a sign" of his own choosing was granted to him. A fleece which he laid upon the thrashing-floor (in the open air) was saturated with dew, while the soil around was all dry; and again, condescending to his prayer, the Lord was pleased to reverse this miracle, by exempting the fleece alone from the dewy moisture which bespread the ground: Gideon was satisfied.

Yet the family from which the deliverer was chosen was not less tainted by the sins than visited by the punishments of Israel; for Joash, the father of Gideon, had erected an altar to Baal, at Ophrah, the town of his residence, at which the people of that place rendered their idolatrous services to that idol. This altar Gideon was directed to destroy, and in its place to erect, over the rock on which his offering had been consumed, an altar to Jehovah. It would seem that Joash himself was brought back to his fealty to Jehovah by the first of the miracles we have related, of which, probably, Gideon was not the sole witness: for when the men of Ophrah, early in the following morning, arose to render their worship to Baal, and, finding his altar overthrown, demanded the death of Gideon, his father stood forward to vindicate his conduct. He undauntedly retorted the sentence of death against the idolaters themselves, for their apostacy from Jehovah. By demanding the punishment of Gideon for his act against Baal, they recognised in fact the fairness of the punishments denounced by the law against those individuals or cities which turned away from Jehovah to serve other gods; and this, coupled with the derision of Joash at the impotency of Baal to vindicate or avenge his own cause, so wrought upon the people of that place, that they were among the foremost to gather to him when he sounded the trumpet of war. He then sent messengers throughout his own tribe of Manasseh (on both sides the Jordan), as well as through those of Asher, Naphtali, and Zebulon. And so cheerfully was the call obeyed, that Gideon soon found himself at the head of thirty-two thousand men. With this force Gideon marched to the mountains of Gilboa, where he found vast multitudes of the enemy encamped before him in the plain of Esdraelon. This fine plain had probably been before their favorite resort; but they seem to have congregated there in unusual numbers as soon as they heard of Gideon's preparations. And now that the people might have no cause to attribute their deliverance to their own numbers and prowess, it pleased the divine King of Israel to reduce this important army to a mere handful of spirited men. In the first place, Gideon was directed to proclaim liberty for all who now, in sight of the enemy, were fearful and faint-hearted, to return to their own homes. This proclamation, according to the law (Deut. xx. 8), ought in all cases to have been made; but it seems that from some reason or other (perhaps either from ignorance of the law, or from supposing that it was not intended to apply to such a case as the present), it would not have been made by Gideon without the special command which he received. Such a law, or practice, however inapplicable, or even ruinous, it might prove under the military systems and tactics of modern Europe, was well calculated to act beneficially in the warfare of those early times; for as everything then depended on the individual courage and prowess of those engaged, "the faint-hearted" were more likely to damage than assist those on whose side they appeared; as their conduct was tolerably certain to bring about results fatal to themselves, and discouraging to their more valorous companions. In the present instance the result was, that although the men composing the army of Gideon had come forward voluntarily, above two thirds of them were so intimidated in the actual presence of danger, that they took advantage of this permission to depart to their own homes. Of the thirty-two thousand, only ten thousand remained with Gideon. Yet as these were men of valor, as evinced by their determination to remain, room for vain-glorious boastings was still left, and therefore Gideon was informed that the number was still too large, and that a further reduction must be made. The process of this second selection was very curious. All those were dismissed who, in drinking at the watering-place, stooped down to drink in large draughts of water at the surface; but those who merely "lapped" the water, or took it up in the hollow of their hands to drink, were retained. The different methods of drinking have been supposed to have distinguished the self-indulgent from the more manly and active men. The latter—those who took up the water in their hollowed hands—were but three hundred out of the ten thousand; and these were declared sufficient for the enterprise.

The night after this, Gideon, with his faithful follower Phurah, went down to the camp of the enemy, in consequence of an intimation that he would there hear matter for his encouragement. What he heard was one soldier, just awakened, telling a dream to his companions. He had dreamed that he saw a barley-cake roll down from the hills to the Midianitish camp, where it overthrew the first tent to which it came. The interpretation which the other gave was—" This is none other than the sword of Gideon, the son of Joash, a man of Israel, into whose hand God delivereth Midian and the whole camp."

Several facts are indicated by this incident; such as the stress generally laid upon dreams in that age, as indicative of contingent results,—the honor attached to the office of spy, as one of danger, and which was therefore, as in the Mosaic age, assigned to, or undertaken by, the very chief persons in the army,—and the truly Oriental want of sentinels and pickets, even in the face of the enemy. This indeed may have been noticed on many former occasions; and to this astonishing neglect of a precaution which seems to us so obvious and so simple, may be attributed the facility and success of those sudden surprises of which we so often read in the military history of those early ages.

Gideon no sooner heard the dream and its interpretation than he understood and accepted the sign. He returned to his own small band, and proceeded to carry into immediate execution a remarkable stratagem which had already been suggested to him. He divided his three hundred men into three companies. Every man was provided with a trumpet in one hand, and in the other a pitcher containing a lighted lamp. They were then stationed in silence and darkness at different points on the outside of the enemy's camp. Then, on a signal given by Gideon, all the three companies, at the same instant, blew their trumpets, exposed their lamps, broke the pitchers which had concealed them, and then continued shouting, "The sword of Jehovah and of Gideon!"[*] The terrible din and crash which thus suddenly broke in upon the stillness of midnight, with the equally sudden blaze of light from three hundred lamps, which illumined its darkness, struck an instant panic into the vast host of Midian, suggesting to them that the lamp-bearing trumpeters (whose numbers must have been greatly magnified in the confused apprehension of men just awakened) were but the advanced guard of the Hebrew host whom they were lighting to the attack on the camp. They therefore fled in all directions, through the openings between the three companies. In their midnight flight, not doubting that the Hebrews had fallen upon them, they mistook friends for foes, and vast multitudes of them perished by each other's swords. The survivers, in their further flight, came up with the several parties which had been dismissed by Gideon to their homes, and these committed a terrible slaughter among the fugitives. Gideon also sent messengers desiring the Ephraimites to seize the various fords of the Jordan, between the two lakes, and thereby prevent the escape of any of the fugitives eastward, which was the direction they would naturally take. In this terrible overthrow no less than one hundred and twenty thousand of the various tribes of "the children of the east" perished; and so completely were the Midianites subdued, that from that time they were never able "to lift up their heads any more."

A remnant of fifteen thousand, headed by their emirs, Zebah and Zalmunna, managed to escape across the river (probably before the Ephraimites had seized the fords), and having reached a distance where they deemed themselves safe from further pursuit, they ventured to encamp. But Gideon himself, with his faithful three hundred, continued the pursuit even to that distance—even into the land of the tent-dwellers —and falling suddenly upon the camp, which lay carelessly secure, the already scared Midianites were completely overthrown. The two emirs themselves were taken alive and brought before Gideon. He had formed, for those times, the singularly generous intention to spare their lives; but when he gathered, from their own lips, that they had created a case of blood-revenge between himself and them, by putting to death, near Mount Tabor, his brethren, "the sons of his own mother,"[†] he, as the legal avenger of their blood, slew these emirs with his own hand.

Gideon seems to have been a man eminently qualified for the high and difficult station to which he was called. Firm even to sternness, where the exhibition of the stronger qualities seemed necessary, and in war "a mighty man of valor," we are called upon in his case, more frequently than in any other which has occurred, to admire his truly courteous and self-retreating character, and that nice and difficult tact—difficult, because spontaneously *natural*—in the management of men, which is a rarer and finer species of judgment, and by which he was intuitively taught to say

* The hint of this watchword was taken from the interpretation of the Midianitish soldier's dream, "the sword of Gideon," to which Gideon, with equal piety and modesty, prefixed, "the sword of Jehovah."
† The emphasis lies in the probability that his father had children by other wives than Gideon's mother. To be *her* children, therefore, constituted a far dearer tie than to be his *father's* children in the general sense.

the properest word, and do the properest deed at the most proper time. This is the true secret of his ultimate popularity and influence, which much exceeded that enjoyed by any judge before him. Some instances of the qualities which we have indicated have already appeared, and others will presently occur.

The Ephraimites who had guarded the Jordan, having performed all that their duty required, hastened to join Gideon in the pursuit of the Midianites. They met him on his return, and laid before him the heads of Oreb and Zeeb,* two emirs of Midian, whom they had taken and slain. This tribe of Ephraim, which was, after that of Judah, the most important in Israel, was exceedingly jealous of its superiority; and was, therefore, not a little annoyed that an obscure Abiezrite should have undertaken so great an enterprise as that now happily completed, without consulting them. They now took occasion to remonstrate with him sharply on the subject, but were soon pacified by his modest and good-tempered answer. "How little have I done now in comparison with you," he said. "Is not *the gleaning* of the grapes of Ephraim better than *the vintage* of Abiezer? God hath delivered up the princes of Midian, Oreb and Zeeb; and what have I been able to do in comparison with you?" Gideon knew what Solomon taught long after, "A soft answer turneth away wrath."

When he had crossed the Jordan in pursuit of the fugitives, he was anxious to obtain for his small band—"faint, yet pursuing"—refreshments from the town of Succoth, which he passed, and afterward from that of Peniel; but he was in both cases refused. The inhabitants seem to have been fearful of bringing upon themselves the vengeance of the Midianites, to whom they had for seven years been subject, and against whom they held it to be very unlikely that he would succeed with so small a force. They not only refused, but added insult to injury. Instead of chastising them on the spot, he coolly told both that he would do so on his return; and he now kept his promise. Coming upon Succoth by surprise, before the sun was up, he took the chief persons of Succoth, and, as he had threatened, scourged them to death with thorns and briars. Of Peniel he made a still severer example, for he beat down the fortress-tower of that city, and put to death the men belonging to it.

The Israelites, in the warmth of their gratitude, offered to make Gideon their king, and to continue the crown to his descendants. This proposal, which clearly shows how unmindful the Israelites had become of the great political principle of the theocracy with which they were so unwarrantably ready to dispense, was nobly rejected by Gideon, who replied to it in the true spirit of the theocracy: "I will not reign over you, neither shall my son reign over you; JEHOVAH, he shall reign over you." But while thus alive to the true political character of the Mosaic institutions, he was not equally cognizant of the religious obligations of that system. When he was called to his great work at Ophrah, he had been instructed to build an altar on the rock on which his offering had been accepted, and himself to offer sacrifices there. This probably led him to conclude that it would be right to form a religious establishment at that spot, for the worship of God by sacrifice. A more perfect acquaintance with the principles of the law would have taught him otherwise. However, to this object he applied the produce of the golden ear-rings of the Midianites, which, at his special request (not unlike that of Aaron, Exod. xxxii. 2), were cheerfully granted to him by the army as his share of the spoil. The weight being one thousand seven hundred shekels, the gold thus obtained must have been worth upward of fifteen thousand dollars of our money; and the "ephod" which he is described as having made with it, probably included not only "the priests' dress," as the word signifies, but a regular sacerdotal establishment in his own town, where sacrifices might be constantly offered. For this purpose such a sum as he applied to it must have been fully requisite. It has been disputed whether Gideon himself officiated as priest, or, like Micah, engaged a Levite for that purpose. The latter seems the more likely supposition, unless from having been once directed to offer sacrifice, Gideon concluded he had a superior claim to discharge that office.

However well intended this establishment may have been in the first instance, this was a most mistaken and dangerous step, resembling, in its principle, the establishment which the Danites had formed in the north. It infringed upon the peculiar claims of Shiloh, the seat of the Divine Presence; and the result of these and all attempts to form separate establishments affords ample illustration of the design with

* The names mean crow and wolf. It would seem that the chiefs of the Midianites (like the North American Indians) took the names of animals, as significant of qualities to which they aspired

which the formal worship of God by sacrifice was confined to one particular locality. It proved "a snare to Gideon and his family," in worshipping the true God in an improper manner. It became popular to "all Israel," who resorted to Ophrah to render that worship and service which was due only at the sacred tabernacle; and, with the predisposition to idolatry, it is not wonderful that, free at this place from the restraint and supervision which the worship at Shiloh imposed, the service at this place soon became associated with idolatrous ideas and objects, until at last it degenerated into rank idolatry after the death of Gideon. He survived and ruled Israel forty years after his victory over the Midianites, and during all this time the tranquillity of Israel appears to have been undisturbed.

CHAPTER XIV.

GIDEON left no less than seventy sons by his numerous wives, besides one spurious son called Abimelech, by a concubine (whom Josephus calls Drumah) who belonged to Shechem. A bastard among seventy legitimate sons was not likely to be pleasantly circumstanced when his father was dead, and it is not surprising that he soon withdrew from among them to his mother's relations at Shechem. They seem to have been persons of some consideration in that place.

After the death of Gideon, the history, without stating the fact, seems to require us to suppose that his sons had been invited to take the government, or to share it among them; and that they, actuated by the same noble, because disinterested regard for the principles of the theocracy which had influenced their father, had declined the offer. But Abimelech, "a bold, bad man," was of a different spirit. He soon saw the advantage which he might take of the existing posture of affairs. Prompted by him, his uncles and other maternal connexions suggested to the chief people of Shechem his willingness to undertake the charge which the people generally were anxious to see in the hands of a son, or some of the sons, of Gideon. They suggested whether it were not much better that one man should reign over them, than that they should be subject to all the sons of Gideon, seventy persons in number; and if the government of one man was to be desired, who had so strong a claim to *their* preference and attachment as one so closely connected with them as Abimelech? These suggestions had their weight upon the leading men of Shechem, particularly the consideration that he was "their brother." They supplied him with money out of the treasury of Baal-berith, whose worship seems to have been that to which the Israelites were at this time the most inclined. The sum was not large,[*] but it served him to hire a set of unprincipled men, prepared for any undertaking he might propose. And, with the usual short-sightedness of wicked men, thinking to concentrate in his own person the attachment of the Israelites to the house of Gideon, as well as to extinguish that which was likely to be the most active opposition he would have to encounter, Abimelech marched his troop to Ophrah, where he put to death all his brethren, the sons of Gideon, with the exception of the youngest, named Jotham, who managed to escape. This is the first example of a stroke of barbarous policy which has since been very common in the history of the East. In the first instance it had the effect he intended; for on his return to Shechem, the people of that place assembled and anointed Abimelech king, close to a pillar of stone that stood near that town—perhaps the same which Joshua had set up there as a memorial of the covenant with God.

When Jotham was made acquainted with this, he repaired secretly to the neighborhood of Shechem; and, taking advantage of some festival which brought the inhabitants together outside the town, he appeared suddenly on a cliff overlooking

---

[*] Seventy shekels of silver, about equal to forty dollars of our money. But proper allowance must be made for a great difference in the real value of money, although the precise amount of that difference can not be stated.

[†] GAZA, a principal city of the Philistines, given to Judah by Joshua, Josh. xv. 47, Judg. i. 18: it lay about sixty miles southwest of Jerusalem, three miles from the Mediterranean sea, and near to the confines of Egypt, Gen. x. 19. Gaza is famous for some of the exploits and the death of Samson, while in possession of the Philistines, Judg. xvi. 1–21. Being a border town, its changes were many in the course of ages. Alexander the Great made it desolate, as predicted; but it was rebuilt nearer to the sea; and in its vicinity, the Ethiopian nobleman was baptized by Philip, Acts viii. 26. Gaza as a sea-port, has been called the "Key of Syria:" it is now called Razza.

GAZA.

the valley in which they were assembled, and, in a loud voice, called their attention to his words. He then delivered that earliest and very fine parable which represents the trees as making choice of a king: The olive refused to leave its oil, the fig-tree its sweetness, and the vine-tree its wine, to reign over the trees (thus intimating the refusal of Gideon's sons); but the upstart bramble (representing Abimelech) accepts, with great dignity, the offered honor, and even proposes the conditions of its acceptance. These are exquisitely satirical, both in their terms and in their application;— "If ye truly intend to anoint me king over you, come, take shelter under my shadow; and if not, let fire come out of the bramble and devour the cedars of Lebanon." That they might be at no loss to understand his meaning, Jotham gave the obvious "moral," in which he included a bitter rebuke of the ingratitude of the people to their deliverer, all whose sons, save himself, they had slain; together with an intimation, which proved prophetic, of the probable result. He then fled with all haste, in fear of Abimelech; and ultimately settled beyond his reach, at Beer, in the tribe of Benjamin.

Abimelech reigned three years in Shechem, during which he so disgusted the men by whom he had been raised to that bad eminence on which he stood, that they expelled him from their city. In return, he, with the aid of the desperate fellows who remained with him, did his utmost to distress the inhabitants, so that at the season of vintage they were afraid to go out into their vineyards to collect their fruits. Hearing of these transactions, one Gaal went over to Shechem with his armed followers and kinsmen, to see how they might be turned to his advantage. We know not precisely who this person was, or whence he came; but there are circumstances in the original narrative which would suggest that he was a Canaanite, descended from the former rulers of Shechem, and that his people also were a remnant of the original Shechemites. He came so opportunely, that the people very gladly accepted his protection during the vintage. In the feats which followed the joyful labors of that season, Gaal, who seems to have been a cowardly, boasting fellow, spoke contemptuously of Abimelech, and talked largely of what he could and would do, if authority were vested in him. This was heard with much indignation by Zebul, one of the principal magistrates of the city, who lost no time in secretly sending to apprize Abimelech how matters stood, and advised him to show himself suddenly before the city, when he would undertake to induce Gaal to march out against him. Accordingly, one morning, when Zebul and other principal persons were with Gaal at the gate of the city, armed men were seen descending the hills. Zebul amused Gaal till they came nearer, and then, by reminding him of his recent boastings, compelled him to draw out his men to repel the advance of Abimelech. They met, and no sooner did Gaal see a few of his men fall, than, with the rest, he fled hastily into the city. Zebul availed himself of this palpable exhibition of impotence, if not cowardice, to induce the people of Shechem to expel Gaal and his troop from the town. Abimelech, who was staying at Arumah, a place not far off, was informed of this the next morning, as well as that the inhabitants, although no longer guarded by Gaal, went out daily to the labors of the field. He therefore laid ambushes in the neighborhood; and when the men were come forth to their work in the vineyards, two of the ambushed parties rose to destroy them, while a third hastened to the gates to prevent their return to the town. The city itself was then taken, and Abimelech caused all the buildings to be destroyed, and the ground to be strewn with salt, as a symbol of the desolation to which his intention consigned it. The fortress, however, still remained, and a thousand men were in it. But they, fancying that it was not tenable, withdrew to "the strong-hold of the temple of Baal-berith," which had the advantage of standing in a more elevated and commanding position. This, it will be noted, is the first temple which we read of in scripture. On perceiving this, Abimelech cut down the bough of a tree with his battle-axe, and bore it upon his shoulder, directing all his men to do the same. The wood was deposited against the entrance and walls of the strong-hold, and, when kindled, made a tremendous fire, in which the building and the thousand men it contained were destroyed.

To follow up this victory, Abimelech marched against Thebez, another revolted town. As before, he took the town itself with little difficulty, but all the people had shut themselves up in the tower or fortress, which offered a more serious obstacle. However, Abimelech advanced to the door with the intention of burning it down, when a woman threw a large stone from the battlements above. It fell upon him, and broke his scull; and mindful, even in that bitter moment, of that principle of military honor which counts death from a woman's hands disgraceful, he hastily called to his armor-bearer to thrust him through with his sword, that it might not be said a woman slew him. But the disgrace which he desired to avoid attached for ever to his name; for it was always remembered to his dishonor that a woman slew him.

After Abimelech, Tola, of the tribe of Issachar, but dwelling in Mount Ephraim, governed the people for twenty-three years.

He was succeeded by Jair, a Gileadite (of eastern Manasseh), who judged Israel twenty-two years. His opulence is indicated by his being the owner of thirty villages, which collectively bore the name of Havoth-Jair (Jair's villages), and that he had thirty sons, all of whom he could afford to mount on young asses. In those days horses and mules were not in use among the Hebrews. Their place was not unworthily substituted by the fine breed of asses which the country afforded; and to possess as many as thirty of these, young and vigorous, and fit for the saddle (implying the possession of many more, older and of inferior condition), was no questionable sign of wealth.

As the administration of these two judges was peaceable, the notice of them is confined to a few lines; the chief design of the sacred historian being to record the calamities which the Israelites drew upon themselves by their apostacies to the idolatries of the surrounding nations, and their providential deliverances upon their repentance and return to their God and king. After the calm of these administrations, they multiplied their idolatries; and in punishment for this, they were brought under a servitude to the Ammonites, which continued for eighteen years, and was particularly severe upon the tribes beyond Jordan, although the southern and central tribes on this side the river—Judah, Benjamin, and Ephraim—were also subdued.

Corrected by calamity, the Israelites put away their idols, and cried to God for pardon and deliverance. In reply to their suit, they were reminded of the deliverances which they had already experienced, notwithstanding which they had repeatedly turned to serve other gods. Their prayer was therefore refused, and they were told, " Go and cry to the gods that ye have chosen; let *them* deliver you in the time of your tribulation." Their reply to this was very proper: " We have sinned: do thou to us whatever seemeth good unto thee; only deliver us, we pray thee, this time." And forthwith they rooted out the remains of idolatry from among them, and worshipped Jehovah with such singleness and zeal that "his soul was grieved for the misery of Israel."

There was a man called Jephthah, who was, like Abimelech, the spurious son of a man who had a large family of legitimate children. When the father died, the other sons expelled Jephthah from among them, saying, " Thou shalt not inherit in our father's house, for thou art the son of a strange woman." As this last phrase generally denotes a foreigner, or one not of Israel, this treatment, although very harsh, was less unjust, under the peculiar circumstances of the Hebrew constitution, than might at the first view appear; for it was a strong point of the Mosaic policy to discourage all connexion with foreigners (necessarily idolaters); and nothing was better calculated to this end, for a people like the Hebrews, than the disqualification of the progeny of such connexions from receiving a share in the inheritance.

On this Jephthah withdrew into " the land of Tob," toward the borders of the desert : and as he had before this found opportunities of establishing a character for spirit and courage, he was soon joined by a number of destitute and idle young men, who were led by inclination, or more imperative inducements, to prefer the free life he led to the sober habits which a settling community requires. Besides, from pastoral societies, such as those beyond Jordan, the step into the free life of the desert is much shorter than it would be among a more agricultural people. It is really useless to attempt to consider Jephthah's troop otherwise than as a set of daring, careless fellows, acting as men do at the present day act in the east under similar circumstances, and similarly brought together. Being without any other means of subsistence, they unquestionably lived by a sort of robbery, as we should call it now, examples of which are found in all rude states of society, and to which, in such states of society, no one dreams of attaching disgrace. They lived doubtless by *raids*, or plundering excursions, into the neighboring small states, driving off the cattle, and taking whatever came to their hands; and we may from analogy conclude that they waylaid and levied

14

black-mail upon caravans, when composed of parties which they had no reason to treat with favor. Their point of honor probably was, to abstain from any acts against their own countrymen; and this exception existing, the body of the Israelites must have regarded the performances of Jephthah and his troop with favor, especially if, as is likely, they were thorns in the sides of the Ammonites, and took pleasure to annoy, in their own quarters, the enemies of Israel. However this may be, the courage and conduct of Jephthah became so well known by his successful enterprises, that when, after their repentance, the tribes beyond Jordan determined to make a stand against the Ammonites, but felt the want of a leader, they agreed that there was no known person so fit as Jephthah to lead them to battle. The chiefs of Gilead, his native district, therefore went in person to the land of Tob, to solicit this already celebrated person to undertake the conduct of the expedition. They were rather harshly received. "Did ye not hate me," said the hero, "and expel me from my father's house? and why do ye come to me *now*, when ye are in distress?" They, however, continued to press him, and intimated that, as had been usual in such cases, the government of, at least, the land of Gilead, would be the reward of his success. This was very agreeable to Jephthah, who forthwith accompanied them to Mizpeh, where this agreement was solemnly ratified, and all things necessary for conducting the war were regulated.

By the time Jephthah had organized his forces in Mizpeh, the Ammonites, taking alarm, had assembled a numerous army in Gilead. Although, from his previous habits of life, we should hardly have expected it from him, we find the Hebrew general commencing the war with much more than usual attention to those formalities which are judged necessary to render the grounds of quarrel manifest. He sent ambassadors to the king of the Ammonites, requiring to know why he had come to fight against the Hebrews in their own land. The king, in reply, alleged that he came to recover the land taken from his ancestors by the Israelites, on their way from Egypt, and of which he, therefore, required peaceable restitution. Jephthah in his reply gave a fair and clear recital of the whole transaction which had put these lands into the possession of the Hebrews, and he refused to surrender them on the following grounds: 1. He denied that the Ammonites had any existing title to the lands, for they had been driven out of these lands by the Amorites before the Hebrews appeared; and that they (the Hebrews) in overcoming and driving out the Amorites, without any assistance from, or friendly understanding with, the Ammonites, became entitled to the territory which the conquered people occupied; 2, that the title of the Israelites was confirmed by a prescription of above three hundred years, during which none of Ammon or of Moab had ever reclaimed these lands; and,—3, as an *argumentum ad hominem*, he alleged that the God of Israel was as well entitled to grant his people the lands which they held as was their own god Chemosh, according to their opinion, to grant to the Ammonites the lands which they now occupied. This admirable and well-reasoned statement concluded with an appeal to Heaven to decide the justice of the cause by the event of the battle which was now inevitable.

The result was such as might be expected. Jephthah defeated the Ammonites with great slaughter, and reduced the nation to subjection.

But not joy to exalt and gladden his heart, but a bitter grief to rend it deeply, awaited the victor on his return to Mizpeh. Feeling, perhaps, that he had not, like former deliverers, been expressly and publicly called and appointed by God to the work he had undertaken, he had sought to propitiate Heaven by a vow, that if allowed to return to his home in peace, whatsoever first came forth to meet him should be offered as a burnt-offering to Jehovah.

Jephthah had no child, save one daughter, a virgin, beautiful and young. And she, when the news came of his great victory, and of his return in triumph and peace, went forth at the head of her fair companions to meet her glorious father, dancing joyously to their timbrels as he drew nigh. Here, then, was the object of his vow— his cherished daughter—the only object in the world which could call forth those kindly sympathies and tendernesses which lurk deep within even those natures which have been the most scarred and roughened in the storms of life. The desolated father rent his clothes, crying, "Alas! my daughter, thou hast brought me low indeed!... for I have opened my mouth to Jehovah and I can not reverse it." Then, understanding the nature of his vow, that noble maiden, mindful only that Israel was delivered, and impressed with the solemn obligation which that vow imposed, sought not to

BUTLER. SC.

turn her father from his purpose, or encouraged him to seek those evasions which others have since discovered for him. With unexampled magnanimity she cried, " My father, if thou hast opened thy mouth to Jehovah, do with me according to that which thou hast spoken; for as much as Jehovah hath taken vengeance for thee upon thine enemies, upon the Ammonites." All she desired was that she might be allowed for two months to wander among the mountains, with her companions, to bewail that it was not her lot to be a bride and mother in Israel. At the end of that time Jephthah "did with her according to his vow."

It is much to be regretted that the reluctance of the sacred writer to express in plain terms the dreadful immolation which we believe to be thus indicated, has left the whole matter open as a subject of dispute. The early Jewish and Christian writers (including Josephus) made no question that Jephthah, under a most mistaken notion of duty, did, after the manner of the heathen, really offer his daughter in sacrifice; but the ingenuity of modern criticism has discovered the alternative that she was not immolated on the altar, but was devoted to perpetual virginity in the service of the tabernacle. It must be confessed that the subject is one of such difficulty, as to render it hard to reach a positive conclusion. But on anxiously considering the question, we are sorry to feel constrained to adhere to the harsher alternative.

There was no institution among the Jews under which practical effect could be given to the alternative which modern interpretation has provided; and even had not this been the case, there was, at the time that this devotement to the tabernacle must have taken place, no access to the tabernacle from the east; for Jephthah was about that time waging a bitter war with the tribe of Ephraim, in whose territory, at Shiloh, the ark was situated. This posture of affairs would preclude him from receiving from the priests those instructions and remonstrances which would have prevented that piteous immolation which he deemed his vow to require. We are persuaded that the more thoroughly any one makes himself acquainted with the spirit of the time, the state of religion, the nature of the ideas which then prevailed, the peculiarities of the ecclesiastical polity among the Hebrews, and the character of Jephthah himself,—the more strong will be his conviction that the infatuated hero really did offer his daughter in sacrifice, and the greater will the difficulty seem of providing any other alternative. The opinion of the Jews themselves is also entitled to some weight; and at a time when they abhorred the idea of human sacrifices, they not only state it as an unquestionable fact that this sacrifice did take place, but ascribe the deposition of the line of Eleazer from the high-priesthood, and the substitution of that of Ithamar, to the circumstance that the existing pontiff did not take measures to prevent this stain upon the annals of Israel.

We must consider how long the minds of the Israelites had been saturated with notions imbibed from the surrounding heathen, which implies the neglect, and consequent ignorance, of the divine law; and that among those ideas and practices that of the superior efficacy of human sacrifices occupied a prominent place. We may also reflect that a rough military adventurer, like Jephthah, had been even more than usually exposed to contaminating influences: such persons are also usually found to be superstitious, and are seldom capable of apprehending more than certain broad and hard features of such higher matters as are presented to their notice. Jephthah knew that human victims were generally regarded as in a peculiar degree acceptable to the gods; and as historical facts are in general more familiarly known than dogmas, it was probably unknown to him that human sacrifices were abhorrent to Jehovah, while he was certain to know that Abraham had been expressly commanded by God himself to offer his beloved Isaac upon the altar; and although the completion of this act was prevented, it would be remembered that the patriarch obtained high praise because he had not withheld even his only and well-loved son from God. That Jephthah made such a vow at all, corroborates the view we take of his character. It was superstitious; and it implies his imperfect knowledge of the law, which would have apprized him of various alternatives which would render the fulfilment of his vow incompatible with obedience to the law. But to such a mind the literal accomplishment of a vow—whatever its purport—will appear the first of duties; and in the fulfilment of such a vow as this, it would seem that the greater his own anguish, the more deeply the iron entered into his own soul, the more meritorious, and the more acceptable to God, the act of the offerer was deemed.

The virgins of Israel instituted an anniversary commemoration of four days, which they spent in celebrating the praises and bewailing the fate of Jephthah's daughter.

The misunderstanding with Ephraim, to which we have incidentally alluded, was similar to that which the tact of Gideon had averted on a former occasion. That haughty and overbearing tribe had been called to the war in the first instance, but refused to take part in the enterprise: but when that enterprise proved successful, they were astonished and mortified that Israel had been delivered by the Gileadites without their assistance. They then assembled tumultuously, and with many contemptuous and abusive expressions toward the Gileadites in general, and toward Jephthah in particular, they threatened to burn his house over his head, because he had not called them to the last decisive action. The conqueror stated the matter as it actually happened; for his rough nature would not permit him to smooth down their ruffled plumes, as Gideon had done on a similar occasion. And then, finding that they were still bent on mischief, he called out the Gileadites, who were highly exasperated at the reflections which had been cast upon them as "fugitives of Ephraim,"—"a base breed between Ephraim and Manasseh." A battle took place, in which the Ephraimites were signally defeated. They had crossed over to the eastern side of the Jordan, and, after the victory, the Gileadites hastened to seize the fords of that river, to intercept those of the fugitives who attempted to return to their homes. But as

Israelites of all the tribes were constantly passing the river, a test was necessary to distinguish the Ephraimites from the others. It is remarkable that the test chosen was that of pronunciation. When any man approached to cross the river, he was asked, "Art thou an Ephraimite?" If he answered "No," they said, "Then, say *Shibboleth*" (water-brooks); but if he were really an Ephraimite, he could not pronounce the *sh*, but gave the word as "*Sibboleth*;" and was slain on the spot. This incident is curious, as showing that lingual differences had already arisen by which particular tribes could be distinguished. In like manner a Galilean was, in the time of Christ, known at Jerusalem by his speech.

In this disastrous affair the loss of the Ephraimites amounted to forty-two thousand men. Such a success could be no matter of triumph to the unhappy Jephthah. His troubled life was not long protracted. He died after he had judged Israel six years. B. C. 1247.

After Jephthah follow the names of three judges, the silence of the record concerning whose actions may be understood to indicate a period of tranquillity and ease. These were Ibzan, of Bethlehem in Ephraim, for seven years; Elon, a Zebulonite, for ten years; and Abdon, an Ephraimite, for eight years. Under the repose of these administrations, however, the Hebrews again insensibly relapsed into idolatry. For this they were brought under a rigorous servitude to their western foes, the Philistines, which (in its full rigor) lasted for forty years. This people had so recruited their strength since the days of Shamgar, that they now take a very conspicuous place in the Hebrew history, forming by far the most powerful and inveterate enemies the Israelites had yet encountered. They continued much longer than any other power had done to wield the weapon by which the iniquities of Israel were chastised; for it was not until the time of David that the deliverance was completed.

When we read of the corrupt state of the nation at large, it would be a grievous error to infer that *all* had departed from God. There are various intimations that, in the worst times, not a few families were to be found religious and well regulated, and which maintained among themselves the faith of the one only God, and followed with exactitude all the requirements of the law. Thus, at a later day, when the prophet deemed that he was himself the only one by whom Jehovah was acknowledged, God himself knew that there were in Israel seven thousand persons whose knees had not been bowed to Baal. (1 Kings. xix. 18.) But although these were the salt of Israel, they could not preserve the mass from such putrefaction as required that it should be cast forth and trodden under foot.

And now, about the same time that the Israelites were cast forth to be trodden under foot by the Philistines, it pleased their offended King, while with the one hand he punished his revolted subjects, to provide with the other for the *beginnings* of their deliverance at a future day. For about that time the angel of Jehovah appeared to the wife of Manoah, a Danite, who had been barren, and promised her a son, who was to be a Nazarite (a person consecrated to God) from the womb, and that in time he should *begin* to deliver Israel from the yoke of the Philistines.

Accordingly, the woman gave birth in due season to a son, on whom the name of Samson was bestowed. As the child grew, it became manifest that the most extraordinary bodily powers had been given to him: while, to prevent undue exaltation of spirit from the consciousness of superior powers, it was known to him that his gifts had no necessary dependance on the physical complication of his thews and sinews, but on his condition as a Nazarite, and on the unshorn hair which formed the sign and symbol of that condition.

It is from the twentieth year of his age, which was also the twentieth of the bondage to the Philistines, that we are to date the commencement of Samson's vindictive administration. He proved to be a man of ungovernable passions; but, through the influence of his destiny to begin the deliverance of Israel, it was so ordered that even his worst passions, and even the sorrows and calamities which these passions wrought upon himself, were made the instruments of distress and ruin to the Philistines.

The fact that the territory occupied by the tribe of Dan, to which Samson belonged, immediately adjoined the country of the Philistines, in consequence of which he became well acquainted with that people, ministered occasion for most of his operations against them. And first—in the Philistine town of Timnath, Samson had seen a young woman with whom he was so well pleased that he resolved to obtain her for his wife. But as such matters were always adjusted between the parents of the respective parties, he went home and desired his father and mother to secure this woman for him. His parents would much have preferred that his choice had fallen on one of the daughters of his own people; but, seeing his determination was fixed, they yielded, and went back with him to Timnath. It was on this journey that Samson gave the first recorded indication of the prodigious strength with which he was endowed, by slaying, without any weapon in his hands, a young and fierce lion by which he was assailed.

At Timnath the proposals of his parents were favorably received by the parents of the damsel Samson sought in marriage. It was necessary, by the customs of the time and country, that at least a month should pass between such a proposal and the celebration of the marriage. At the expiration of this time, Samson, again accompanied by his parents, went down to Timnath to claim his bride. On the way he turned aside to see what had become of the carcass of the lion he had slain on the former journey. In that climate the carcasses of animals left dead upon the ground are speedily devoured by jackals and vultures, and other beasts and birds which feed on carrion. Even insects contribute largely to this service. Accordingly, Samson found only the clean skeleton of the lion, partially covered with the undevoured hide. In the cavity thus formed a swarm of bees had lodged and deposited their honey. At wedding-feasts it was at that time usual for the young men then assembled together to amuse themselves by proposing riddles—those who were unable to solve the riddle incurring a forfeiture to him by whom it was proposed, who himself was liable to a similar forfeiture if his riddle were found out. The adventure with the lion suggested to Samson the riddle which he proposed—"Out of the eater came forth food, and out of the fierce came forth sweetness." For three days they vainly tried to discover the meaning of this riddle; and at last, rather than incur the heavy forfeiture of "thirty shirts and thirty suits of raiment," they applied to the bride, and threatened destruction to her family if she did not extract from her husband the required solution, and make it known to them. He was very unwilling to tell her, declaring that even his father and mother were ignorant of it. But she put in practice all the little arts by which women have ever carried their points with men usually weak—as Samson was, with all his corporal strength—and by her tears, and reproaches of his want of love and confidence, she so wearied him that he at length gave her the information she desired. The guests were consequently enabled, within the given time, to answer—"What is sweeter than honey? What is fiercer than a lion?" But Samson was well convinced that the wit of man could never have discovered the true solution without a knowledge of the circumstances, which they could only have obtained by tampering with his wife. He exclaimed indignantly—"If ye had not ploughed with my heifer, ye had not found out my riddle!" He did not, however, as he might have done, refuse the payment of the forfeiture he had thus unexpectedly incurred; but to obtain it he went and slew thirty of the Philistines near Ascalon, and gave their raiment to the persons who had expounded his riddle. He then returned to his own home, without again seeing his wife, with whose conduct he was deeply disgusted.

But after some time his resentment subsided, and he went down to Timnath to revisit his wife, with a present of a kid. But he found that in the mean time she had been given in marriage to a man among the Philistines, who in former times had been his most dear and familiar friend, and whom, in that character, he had chosen to act as his paranymph, or brideman, at the wedding. The incensed hero rejected with indignation the offer of the father to give him his youngest daughter in lieu of the woman he had married; and regarding, probably, the treatment he had received as in some degree resulting from the insolence of superiority, and from the contempt in which the Philistines held the people they had so long held in subjection, he considered himself justified in avenging his own injuries upon the Philistine nation, as part and parcel of the wrongs his nation suffered. This mode of taking his revenge was no less remarkable than effective. He obtained three hundred jackals, and tying them together, with a firebrand between their tails, let them loose. The affrighted animals, being so bound as to be obliged to run side by side, hastened for shelter to the fields of standing and ripened corn, which, at that dry season, when the corn was ripe, was easily kindled into a blaze. As the tortured jackals took different directions, the conflagration was very extensive; nor was it confined to the standing corn, but wrought much damage among the olive-grounds and vineyards, and consumed the corn which had been cut down and heaped for the thrashing-floor.

When the Philistines understood the immediate cause of this act of hostility on the part of Samson, they went and burned his wife and her father's house with fire; thus punishing them for that breach of faith to which they were first led by the fear of this very punishment. If this act was intended to appease Samson, it had not that effect; for it did not prevent him from taking an opportunity which offered of discomfiting, with much slaughter, a considerable number of men belonging to that nation. He then withdrew to a strong rock called Etam, in the tribe of Judah. To that place he was pursued by a large body of Philistines, whose presence occasioned great alarm to the Judaites. But when they understood that Samson individually was the sole object of this incursion, they most shamefully undertook of themselves to deliver him up to his enemies. Accordingly, three thousand of them went up to him, feeling assured that he would not act against his own people. They told him they were come to bind him, and to put him into the hands of the Philistines. It strikingly illustrates the opinion Samson had of his own countrymen—an opinion which the circumstances justified—that before he consented to be bound, he obliged them to swear *that they would not kill him themselves.* He then allowed them to bind him securely with two new ropes, and to take him down to the Philistines. When he was led to their camp they raised a triumphant shout against him. As he heard that shout, "the Spirit of Jehovah came mightily upon him;" he burst his strong bands asunder as easily as if they had been tow burnt with fire, and seizing the jawbone of an ass which lay at hand, he flew upon the Philistines, and, with no other weapon, routed the whole thousands which had come against him, slaying many of their number. They only lived who fled. As Milton makes the hero observe—

> "Had Judah that day join'd, or one whole tribe,
> They had by this possess'd the towers of Gath,
> And lorded over them whom now they serve ;
> But what'more oft, in nations grown corrupt,
> And by their vices brought to servitude,
> Than to love bondage more than liberty,
> Bondage with ease than strenuous liberty ;
> And to despise, or envy, or suspect,
> Whom God hath of his special favor raised
> As their deliverer ! If he aught begin,
> How frequent to desert him, and at last
> To heap ingratitude on worthiest deeds."—SAMSON AGONISTES.

Proudly confident in his strength, Samson was not deterred from going again among the Philistines, as soon as a motive occurred in the indulgence of that blind passion which had already brought him into much trouble, and which was destined to be his ruin. He went to Gaza, to visit a harlot of that place. His arrival was soon known; and although this was a different state from that which had been the scene of his former exploits, the authorities of the place were too sensible of the importance of destroying this implacable enemy of their nation, to neglect the advantage which his folly had placed in their hands. The city gates were closed to prevent his escape; and a strong guard was placed there to surprise and kill him in the morning. Samson, however, anticipated their plan; and, rising at midnight, he went boldly to the gate, forced it from its place, and, by way of bravado, carried it off entire, posts, bars, and all, to the top of a hill on the way to Hebron. The guards were too much astonished and terrified to molest or pursue him.

After this Samson did not again venture into the territory of the Philistines, but sought at home the indulgence of those blinding passions which make the strongest weak. "He loved a woman in the vale of Serek," so celebrated for its vines. Her name was Delilah, and she was probably of Israel, although Josephus, to save the credit of his countrywomen, makes her a Philistine. The Philistines themselves took an anxious interest in all the movements of Samson, and were soon acquainted with this new besotment, of which they prepared to take advantage. A deputation, consisting of a principal person from each of the five Philistine states, went up the valley to the place where he was. And now, we observe, it was not their object to get possession of his person while he retained all his strength, but to ascertain how that strength might be taken from him. They were well persuaded that a strength so greatly exceeding all they knew or had ever heard of, and to which that possessed by the few descendants of Anak who lived among them could not for an instant be compared, must be supernatural—the result of some condition which might be neutralized, or of some charm which might be broken. They therefore offered Delilah the heavy bribe of eleven hundred shekels of silver from each of their number (amounting altogether to 687*l.*) to discover the secret of his great strength, and to betray him into their hands, that they might bind and afflict him. Samson amused her by telling her of certain processes whereby the weakness of other men would be brought upon him; but each time the imposition was detected, by her putting the process to the proof. Then she continued to worry him by such trite but always effective reproaches as, "How canst thou say 'I love thee,' when thy heart is not with me? for thou hast deceived me these three times, and hast not told me wherein thy great strength lieth." Thus day by day she pressed him and urged him, until "his soul was vexed unto death," and at last he told the whole truth to her—that he was a Nazarite from his birth, and that if he left that state by cutting off his hair, which had never yet been shorn or shaven, his extraordinary strength would depart from him. Delilah saw by his earnestness that he had this time told her the truth. Accordingly, she sent for a man, who, while the hero slept with his head upon her lap, shaved off the luxuriant tresses of his hair. His strength departed from him: but he knew it not; and when aroused from his sleep by the approach of the Philistines to seize him, he thought to put forth his wonted power and destroy them all; but his listless arms refused to render him their wonted service, and he knew, too late, that "Jehovah had departed from him."

The Philistines took and bound him; and, to complete his disablement, put out both his eyes—a mode of rendering a public enemy or offender incapable of further offence, of which this is the first historical instance, but which has ever since been much resorted to in the kingdoms of the East.* They then took him down to Gath, and binding him with fetters of brass, employed him to grind in the prison-house.

Nothing could more clearly than this deprivation evince the miraculous nature of the superhuman strength with which Samson had been for special purposes invested. Samson himself had *known* this before; but now, weak, blind, bound, "disglorified," and degraded to a woman's service,† he had occasion and leisure to *feel* it; and in his "prison-house" he probably learned more of himself than he had known in all his previous life. Nor was this knowledge unprofitable. He felt that although he had *begun* to deliver Israel, this employment of the gifts confided to him had rather been the incidental effect of his own insensate passions, than the result of those stern and steady purposes which became one who had so solemnly been set apart, even before his birth, to the salvation of his country. Such thoughts as these brought repentance to his soul; and as by this repentance his condition of Nazariteship was in some sort renewed, it pleased God that, along with the growth of his hair, his strength should gradually return to him.

Fatally for the Philistines, they took the view that, since the strength of Samson had been the gift of the God of Israel, their triumph over him evinced that their own god, Dagon, was more powerful than Jehovah. This raised the matter from being a case between Samson and the Philistines, to one between Jehovah and Dagon; and it thus became necessary that the divine honor should be vindicated. An occasion for this was soon offered under aggravated circumstances.

The Philistines held a feast to Dagon, their god, who, as they supposed, had delivered their enemy into their hands. In the height of their festivity they thought of ordering Samson himself to be produced, that the people might feed their eyes with the sight of the degraded condition of one who had not long since been their dread. The assembled multitude greeted his 'appearance with shouts of triumph, and praised their god who had reduced "the destroyer of their country" to be their bond-slave. After having been for some time exposed to their mockeries and insults, the blind hero desired the lad who led and held him by the hand, to let him rest himself against the pillars which sustained the chief weight of the roof of the temple, upon which no less than three thousand persons had assembled to view the spectacle, and celebrate Dagon's sacrifices. Thus placed, Samson breathed the prayer—

---

* This barbarous infliction is, however, now—under the operation of those humanizing influences which are insensibly pervading the East—in the course of being discontinued. It was formerly more common in Persia than in any other country; but it became comparatively rare under the late king; and we believe that no instance has yet occurred in which the present monarch has resorted to it.
† Grinding is almost invariably performed by women in the East.

Supporting Palace of Eastern Buildings.

"O Lord Jehovah, remember me, I pray thee, and strengthen me, I pray thee, *only this once*, O God, that I may at once be avenged of the Philistines for my two eyes!" Saying this, he grasped the pillars with his mighty arms, and crying, "Let me die with the Philistines!" he bowed himself with such prodigious force that the pillars gave way, and then the roof fell in, destroying with one tremendous crash all who were above it and below it.   Thus those whom Samson slew at his death were more in number than those he slew in his life.

"It is remarkable that the exploits of Samson against the Philistines were performed singly, and without any co-operation from his countrymen to vindicate their liberties: whether it was that the arm of the Lord might be the more visibly revealed in him, or that his countrymen were too much depressed by the severity of their servitude to be animated by his example.   They seem also to have feared him almost as much as they did the Philistines.   Else why should three thousand armed men of Judah have gone to persuade him to surrender himself to the Philistines, when, with such a leader, they might naturally expect to have been invincible? or why, when he destroyed [routed?] a thousand Philistines with so simple a weapon, did he not join in pursuit of the rest? So true was the prediction of the angel to his mother, that he should only *begin* to deliver Israel."[*]

It scarcely appears that Samson exercised any authority in the tribes; but to carry on the historical time, he is counted as one of the judges, and his administration is computed at forty years, ending by his death, in the year 1222 B. C.

CHAPTER XV.

SAMSON was the last of the military heroes stirred up to deliver Israel from its oppressors.   The two that followed, Eli and Samuel, were men of peace—the one a priest, and the other a Levite.

In the absence of a person specially called and appointed to deliver and judge the people, the civil government, by the principles of the theocracy, devolved on the high-priest, as the vizier of the great king, having access to his presence, and being the interpreter of his will.   It is not easy to see that Samson exercised the civil government over any of the tribes.   And although, therefore, in order to carry on the succession of times, it is convenient to say that at his death the government devolved on the high-priest, yet, in fact, there is little reason to question that the high-priest exercised as much authority before as after.   But, in such times as these, that authority was but small, and chiefly, as it would appear, judicial, particularly in adjusting disputes between persons of different tribes.   The heads of the several tribes seem to have considered themselves fully competent to manage their internal affairs; and their divided allegiance to Jehovah involved the political evil, that the authority of the general government was proportionably weakened, and the cohesion of the tribes in the same degree relaxed.   Subject to this preliminary observation, the high-priest may, for historical convenience, be considered the successor of Samson.

It is remarkable that functionaries so important, in the theory of the Hebrew constitution, as the high-priests, are scarcely noticed in the history of the Judges.   From Phineas, the grandson of Aaron, to Eli, a high-priest is not mentioned on any occasion, nor would even their names be known but for the list in Chronicles (1 Chron. vi. 4–16, 50–52), where the order is thus given:—Abishua, Bukki, Uzzi, Zerahiah, Meraioth.

In the person of Eli, a change in the line of succession to this high office took place, as he was the first of the race of Ithamar, the second son of Aaron.   But as the line of his elder son Eleazer was not extinct, and as the cause of the change is not assigned, some difficulty has been experienced in accounting for it.   The Jews, as we have seen, suppose that it was because the existing pontiff had not taken measures sufficiently active to prevent Jephthah from sacrificing his daughter.   But if, in the absence of all positive information, a conjecture might be hazarded, we would suggest the probability that the last pontiff of Eleazer's line died leaving no son old enough to take the office, and that it then (as afterward in the succession to the kingdom) devolved on his adult uncle or cousin of the line of Ithamar. Such a course resorted to in temporal successions, to avoid the evils of a minority and regency, must have been much more necessary in the case of the high-priesthood. That the change took place in some such natural and quiet way, seems to afford the most satisfactory explanation of the silence of the record of a matter of such importance.

Eli was a good and pious man, estimable in private life for his many virtues and the mildness of his character; but he was greatly wanting in those sterner virtues which became his public station, and which were indeed necessary for the repression of wickedness, and the punishment of the wrong doer. As he grew old, he devolved much of his public duty upon his sons Hophni and Phineas, two evil-disposed men, who possessed the energy their father lacked, without any of his virtues. Even in their sacred ministrations at the tabernacle, their conduct was so shamefully signalised by rapacity and licentiousness, that the people, through their misconduct, were led to abhor the offering of Jehovah. All this became known to Eli; but, instead of taking the immediate and decisive measures which became his station, he contented himself with a mild and ineffective remonstrance. This weakness of Eli was justly counted a sin in that venerable person; and a prophet was commissioned to warn him of the evil consequences, which were no less than the exclusion of his race from the pontificate to which he had been advanced. But even this could not rouse the old man to the exertion which became his station; but he seems rather to have acquiesced in this judgment as a thing not to be averted.

The next reproof which this remiss judge received was through an unexpected channel.

At the tabernacle, in personal attendance upon the high-priest, was a boy, a Levite, who having been the child signally granted in answer to the many prayers of Hannah, his previously barren mother, was by her consecrated from the womb, as a Nazarite, to Jehovah. In consequence of this, combined with his Levitical character, he had been left at the tabernacle as early as he could be separated from his mother's care, to render such services there as his tender years allowed. His name was Samuel: and as his pious mother came to Shiloh yearly with her husband to celebrate the passover (bringing with her a dress for her son), she had the delight of perceiving that he, growing up under the shadow of the altar, conducted himself with such propriety and discretion, that he stood very high in the favor of God and man. That he was thus, from his very infancy, constantly before the eyes of the people when they attended at the tabernacle, doubtless went far to prepare the way for that influence and station which he ultimately attained.

It was the thirty-first year of Eli's administration, when Samuel, then twelve years of age, lay on his bed at night, that he heard a voice calling him by his name. He supposed that it was Eli who had called; he hastened to him, but found that it was not so. This was repeated three times; and at the third time, Eli, concluding that it was the Lord who had called the lad, instructed him to answer, "Speak, Lord, for thy servant heareth." Samuel obeyed; and the Voice then delivered to him, as an irrevocable doom, the former denunciations against Eli's house, "because his sons had made themselves vile, *and he restrained them not;*" declaring that he would "do a thing in Israel at which both the ears of every one that heareth it shall tingle." In the morning, the lad, being pressed by Eli, delivered to him the message he had received. But even this only gave occasion for the further manifestation of the passive virtues of his character. "It is Jehovah," he said; "let him do what seemeth to him good."

After this, matters went on for some time much as they had done. Eli's sons pursued their old courses, making themselves still more vile; and their father, though now well aware of the doom which hung over himself and them, took no measures in the hope to avert it. But as Samuel grew, the word of the Lord again came to him from time to time, and all Israel knew that he was established to be a prophet of Jehovah.

Thus passed ten years, at the end of which the threatened judgments began to be inflicted upon the house of Eli. At that time the Israelites rashly, and without consulting their Divine King, embarked in a war with the Philistines. In the forty years since the death of Samson, this people had recruited their strength, and recovered the courage of which they appear to have been for a season deprived by the astounding calamity which swept away so many of their chiefs and nobles. In the first engagement the Israelites were defeated, with the loss of four thousand men. On this they sent to Shiloh for the ark of the covenant, not doubting of victory under its protection. The two sons of Eli, Hophni and Phineas, attended it to the camp. On its arrival there, "all Israel shouted with a great shout, so that the earth rang again." On hearing this, and being apprized of its cause, the Philistines were filled with consternation; and the manner in which their alarm was expressed affords a very clear intimation of the effect which had been produced on their minds, by the wonders which Jehovah had wrought for the deliverance and protection of Israel. "Wo unto us!" they cried; "who shall deliver us out of the hand of these mighty gods? These are the gods that smote the Egyptians with all the plagues of the wilderness." The procedure itself did not strike them as strange, for it was not unusual among ancient nations to take their gods to their wars; and the ark, with its cherubim, the Philistines supposed to be the god of the Hebrews. They did not question the existence of that God, or his special care for his people; neither did they deny his power, of which, indeed, they were afraid. They allowed Jehovah to be the god of the Hebrews, in the same sense in which they regarded Dagon to be their own god. It was his universal and exclusive power that they denied, or rather did not recognise.

Notwithstanding their alarm, the Philistines did not give way to despair; but like a brave people, which they were always, the imminence of the danger only stimulated them to the more strenuous exertions for victory. They cried to one another: "Be strong, and quit yourselves like men, O ye Philistines, that ye become not servants unto the Hebrews, as they have been to you! Quit yourselves like men, and fight!"

They fought: and the victory was given to them, to punish the Hebrews for their misdoings, and for having engaged in this war without consulting their King, as well as to teach them that undue confidence in the ark itself was a superstition, if not an idolatry, apart from a due reliance on God himself, whose footstool only the ark was. Thirty thousand men of Israel fell in the battle and pursuit; the guilty sons of Eli were among the slain, and *the ark itself was taken.*

Eli, blind and old, remained at Shiloh, anxiously expecting news from the camp; "for his heart trembled for the ark of God;" and that he might be in the way of receiving the earliest rumors from the war, he sat watching by the wayside. One day he heard an outcry in the town, which had been occasioned by the news brought by one of the fugitives from the battle. . This man, with his clothes rent and dust upon his head, soon came before the high-priest and gave to him the tidings, that Israel fled before the Philistines—that there had been a great slaughter—that his two sons, Hophni and Phineas, were slain—and that the ark of God was taken! No sooner had the last words passed the lips of the messenger, than the high-priest fell backward from off his seat; and being old and heavy, his neck was broken in the fall. Soon after the news of all these calamities was carried to the wife of Phineas; on hearing which she was taken with the pains of labor, and died, after she had looked upon the son to whom she gave birth, and given him the sad name of Ichabod (*Inglorious*); for she said, "The glory is departed from Israel; for the ark of JEHOVAH, the God of Israel, is taken." These incidents serve to evince the depth of that astonishment and grief with which the loss of the ark was regarded.

The Philistines soon found that they had small cause to rejoice in the glorious trophy they had won; and most convincingly was it made known to them that the Israelites had been defeated for the punishment of their sins, which rendered them unworthy of their God's protection, and not through his want of power to save. The Philistines certainly considered that they had taken captive the god of the Hebrews, and could, on the principles of pagan idolatry, hardly fail to attribute it to the superior power of Dagon, their own god. Yet they still must have had a very salutary dread of the God of Israel; and while they could not but regard the ark as the proudest of their trophies, it was probably more with the view of propitiating him, by associating him with their own god, than by way of insult, that they deposited the conquered ark in the temple of their Dagon at Azotus. But God disdained this dishonoring alliance; and twice the Philistines found their idol overthrown, and the second time broken to pieces, before the ark of God. And further to demonstrate his power in such a way as might include a punishment for their idolatry and for the abominations connected with it, the Lord smote the people of the place with

Ethiopian Car drawn by Oxen.

Indian Car drawn by Oxen.

hemorrhoids, or the piles, with a mortal destruction. The land also swarmed with jerboas, whereby the products of the fields were consumed. Attributing these calamities to the presence of the ark, they sent it to Gath, where it remained until the pressure of the same inflictions compelled them to send it from them. It was taken to Ekron, another of the five metropolitan cities of Philistia. The Ekronites received it with terror, crying, "They have brought round to us the ark of the God of Israel to slay us and our people." They therefore, in an assembly of "the lords of the Philistines," proposed that the ark should be sent back to its own place in the land of Israel. This was determined; nor was the determination too soon, for already the hand of God was so heavy upon Ekron, that "the cry of the city went up to the heavens." And that it might be sent away with all honor, the diviners, who were consulted as to the best means of giving effect to the intention which had been formed, counselled that five golden hemorrhoids, and five golden mice, one from each of the Philistine states, should be deposited in a coffer beside the ark, as a trespass-offering: for even thus early the custom had come into use of making votive offerings representing the instruments of affliction, or of the parts afflicted, to the god to whom the infliction or the cure was attributed. That they might give the glory to the God of Israel, and not harden their hearts as did the Egyptians, and thereby bring upon themselves the punishments of that people, were the reasons by which this course of conduct was enforced. And they are remarkable as showing the effect, even at this remote date, upon the neighboring nations, of the wonders of judgment and deliverance which had been wrought in the land of Egypt.

To testify all possible respect, the ark was placed in a new car,* to which were yoked two kine, whose necks had never before been subjected to the yoke. Their calves were tied up at home; and, by the advice of the priests, it was concluded to leave the cows free to take their own course: if the animals went away from their calves to the land of Israel, it was to be inferred that a right judgment had been formed of the cause from which their calamities proceeded; but if not, they might conclude that it had been the result of natural causes. From such incidents the heathen were even thus early accustomed to conjecture the will of their gods. In this case, no sooner were the kine set free than they turned their backs upon their young, and took the road toward the town of Bethshemesh in Judah, being the nearest city of the Levites toward the Philistine frontier. It was the time of the wheat-harvest, when the people of the town were abroad in the valley reaping the fruits of their fields. They beheld the ark advancing with great gladness; and when the kine stopped of their own accord, near a great stone, in a field belonging to one Joshua, the Levites who were present detached them from the car, and offered them up in sacrifice upon that stone before the ark. And the stone being thus consecrated by sacrifice, the ark was removed from the car and deposited thereon. The five lords of the Philistines, who

---

* CARS DRAWN BY OXEN.—That the Philistines thought of placing the ark on a car, to be drawn by oxen, shows that vehicles drawn by such animals were in use among them, at least in their sacred processions. There is nothing of the kind among the Egyptians. Their religious processions were walking processions, and by water: that is to say, as all their towns were along the Nile, their religious progresses from one place to another were by that river, the short distances to and from which they walked, bearing their arks, their idols, and their implements of religious service. The Jews had no religious processions after they became a settled people—unless it were in the removals of the ark; which removals resulted from circumstances, for it was intended to be stationary. It was indeed not unlawful to take the ark to the wars; but the only instance in which this is recorded to have been done, was when it was taken by the Philistines. In the wilderness the ark was carried on the shoulders of the Levites, as were the other more sacred utensils of the tabernacle; but the fabric itself, and its heavier furniture, were placed on cars or wagons drawn by oxen. The ark itself was never thus conveyed, except on the various stages of its return from the Philistines. For the Israelites, observing that those people had in this manner transported it safely, continued its removal in the same manner, until the consequences that ultimately ensued, reminded them of the more proper method.

Among the Egyptians, horses appear to have been invariably employed for draught, whether in chariots of war or peace. But, although they had not themselves the custom, their sculptures coincide with the scriptures in manifesting the use of oxen or kine for draught by other nations. All our examples adduced to illustrate the subjects of carts, apply to the present, since all the carts there represented, from one and modern sources, are drawn by oxen, equally with the more elegant class of vehicles represented in the present instance; and, taken together, they demonstrate the extensive use of oxen for draught in both the ancient and modern East. After Solomon, the Hebrews learned from the Egyptians and their nearer neighbors to have chariots of war drawn by horses; and kings and high military commanders appear to have had their private chariots also drawn by horses. To these and agricultural purposes, wheel-carriages seem to have been very much confined; but, as far as they were used, they appear, except in the cases specified, to have been drawn by oxen. The use of war-chariots has now nearly disappeared in the East, and with it the employment of horses for draught. Oxen are employed everywhere, from the Yellow sea to the Mediterranean. And in our present engravings, the elegance of the vehicles, and the cost and finish of the equipments, show that to ride in a car drawn by oxen is not, nor was, considered a mode of conveyance by any means so rude or ignoble as the illustrations at first sight might have suggested.

Monumental Pillars in Syria.

had followed the car to the borders of Bethshemesh (which was twelve miles distant from Ekron), and who had stood witnessing these proceedings, now returned home, well convinced that it was the hand of the God of Israel by which they had been smitten. The ark had been in their hands seven months.

The adventures of the ark, and its constant exposure to their sight, begat in the Bethshemites a familiarity toward it, inconsistent with the respect due to Jehovah, and which it was highly necessary to repress. When therefore their familiarity went so far that they ventured to raise the cover of the ark, to gratify their curiosity with a view of its contents, sixty of their number—principal persons of the place—were smitten with death. On this the people cried, with great consternation, "Who is able to stand before this holy God, Jehovah? and to whom shall he go from us?" They decided to invite the people of Kirjath-jearim to take the ark away. They did so, and deposited it in the house of Aminadab "upon the hill." This person set apart his son Eleazer to take the charge of it—to preserve it from pollution, and to keep all things clean and orderly about it. Thus it remained about eighty-two years. Why it was not returned to Shiloh does not very clearly appear. Probably no command on the subject was given; and from the experience which the Israelites now had of the jealousy with which its sanctity was guarded, they were afraid to remove it without express orders. Besides, at this time the people were again far gone into idolatrous practices, which made them comparatively indifferent about the ark; and it is not unlikely that the reaction of the sentiment of astonishment and grief with which its loss had been regarded, did much to impair that veneration of which it had been the object. Add to this that they had been without the ark for seven months, in the course of which they had accustomed their minds to the want of it, and had learned to regard it as less essential to them than it had before seemed. The tabernacle still remained at Shiloh, which continued to be the seat of the appointed ministrations, until it was removed, in the reign of Saul, to Nob, probably in consequence of the destruction of Shiloh in the Philistine war (1 Sam. xiv. 3; Jer. vii. 12–14, xxvi. 6–9).

For their idolatries and alienation, the Hebrews were punished by twenty years continuance (including the seven months of the ark's absence) of their subjection to the Philistines.

It is usually stated that Samuel succeeded Eli. He was then little more than twenty years of age; and although, as his years advanced, he doubtless acquired much authority among the people from the influence of his character and position, there is no evidence that it was any other than that which prophets usually exercised. It rather appears from the text that it was *after* the twenty years of further servitude to the Philistines, that Samuel was publicly called to assume the civil government.

At the end of these twenty years the people "lamented after the Lord," or repented of the sins by which they had alienated themselves from him, and were disposed to return to their allegiance. Samuel then came forward in his prophetic character, and promised them deliverance from the Philistines, if they would put away the strange gods—the Baals and Ashtaroths (representing the sun and moon), and devote themselves to the exclusive service of Jehovah. His directions were followed; and he then convened an assembly of all Israel at Mizpeh, where they held a solemn fast and humiliation for their sins, and poured out water before Jehovah, as expressive of their despondency or grief. And to testify their good intentions for the future, the prophet himself was there invested by them with the authority of a "judge."

The Philistines took umbrage at this great assembly in Mizpeh, which, they rightly judged, boded no good to the continuance of their dominion. They assembled their forces and marched to that place, to disperse the congregation. The people, not being prepared for war, were filled with alarm on the approach of their enemies, and besought Samuel to cry to Jehovah for them, that he might save them from the hand of the Philistines. Samuel did so with great earnestness; and he was in the act of offering up a lamb as a burnt-offering, when the Philistines drew near to battle. The prayers of the prophet were then answered by a terrible storm of thunder and lightning, by which the enemy were alarmed and confounded, while the Israelites, recognising the sign, were inspired with sudden and indomitable courage. They fell impetuously upon the force they had so lately dreaded, and slew vast numbers of them, chasing the remainder as far as Betchcar. In memory of this great victory, Samuel set up a memorial-stone, and gave it the name of Ebenezer (*the help-stone*), saying, "Hitherto Jehovah hath *helped* us."

This very brilliant victory broke the spirit of the Philistines for many years. They were obliged to restore all their conquests from the Israelites; and, for many years to come, they kept carefully within their own territories, and abstained from any hostile acts against the Hebrews. Their example was followed by the other neighbors of Israel, which hence enjoyed the felicity of a profound peace during the entire period of Samuel's sole administration.

This excellent judge administered justice regularly to the tribes in his annual circuit, which he took to the places of sacred stones at Bethel, Gilgal, and Mizpeh, and constantly at his own place of abode at Ramah, where he built an altar to Jehovah. This was probably by the divine permission or direction, at least for the present, as God had not yet given any declaration where the ark was to be fixed.

The sole administration of Samuel lasted twelve years, dating it, as we do, from the end of the Philistine servitude, and not from the death of Eli. Near the close of this period, when the prophet was "growing old and gray-headed," being sixty-four years of age, he appointed his sons, Joel and Abiah, to act for him at Bethel and Beersheba. But they walked not in the steps of their father. "They turned aside after lucre, and took bribes, and perverted judgment."

This misconduct of his sons, with his own advancing age, and the seemingly unsettled state in which the government would be left at his death, were among the causes which at this time induced the elders of Israel to resort to Samuel at Ramah, and to demand of him that a king should be appointed to reign over them, as in other nations.

The causes which we have just stated, together with the regular administration of justice to which Samuel had accustomed them, occasioned the demand, it would seem, *at this particular time;* but there were deeper causes which would unquestionably have brought them to this point ere long, if it had not now. These causes have been well discriminated by Jahn.

This able writer justly refers the frequent interruptions to the welfare of the Hebrew state under the judges to,—" 1. The effeminacy and cowardice of the people; and, 2, to the disunion and jealousy of the tribes, who never assisted each other with the requisite zeal and alacrity. But as this effeminacy arose from the vices of idolatry, and their cowardice from a want of confidence in Jehovah; so the disunion and jealousy of the tribes, though selfishness was the immediate cause, arose from a disposition to neglect their divine king, and not to consider themselves as the united and only people of Jehovah. This disposition, if it did not originate from, was at least very much heightened by the multiplication of deities. Thus both these causes of their misfortunes owed their origin to idolatry, that great cause of all their calamities, so often mentioned in the sanctions of the law. Thus the people, by increasing their gods, enervated themselves, and prepared for themselves those sufferings and chastisements by which they were again to be brought back to their King, Jehovah."

He proceeds to observe that " These causes of national misfortune were all in operation at the time of Samuel, and threatened to produce after his death still greater calamities. The tribes beyond the Jordan had formidable enemies in the Ammonites and the southern tribes in the Philistines, while the northern tribes stood aloof from the dangers of their more exposed countrymen. The latter seems to have been the principal reason why the rulers in general assembly requested a king. The tribes in southern Palestine and beyond the Jordan were the most earnest for this change in the government; they feared that the death of Samuel would leave them without a supreme magistrate, and that the nation being again disunited, they should be left to their fate. The degeneracy of Samuel's sons, who had been appointed subordinate judges, or deputies, increased their apprehensions. They, therefore, strenuously insisted on their demand, " Nay, but we will have a king over us, that we also may be like all the nations." They had reason to hope that a king invested with supreme authority might be able to unite the power of the whole nation and protect each tribe with the collected strength of all; that under him the affairs of government would be more promptly administered and necessary aid more readily afforded; that if he were a man devoted to Jehovah, he could more effectually repress or prevent idolatry, and thus place the welfare of the state on a more solid foundation. They might imagine themselves justified in this request as Moses had taken it for granted that the nation would eventually have a king, and the same thing had been promised to their great progenitor Abraham. It conduces greatly to the honor of the Hebrews that they attempted this change in their constitution, not by their own power, but in accordance with the principles of the theocracy; they requested it of their king, Jehovah, by the intervention of a prophet, and they effected it without bloodshed,—a manifest proof that the time of the judges was neither what is usually understood by a 'barbarous' nor an 'heroic age.'"

But as all the objects which they desired to realise were attainable under the theocracy, were they but faithful to its principles and engagements; and as the unseen king, Jehovah, would necessarily be obscured by a subordinate, visible monarch, he, by means of Samuel, gave the rulers to understand his disapprobation of their request; and at the same time represented to them the burdens they would have to bear under a king, especially how easily he might be led to imitate other oriental monarchs, and to disregard the law of Jehovah.

The picture which was then drawn by Samuel exhibits in a lively manner the character of the monarchies which at that time existed in the east, and enables us to ascertain that, whatever changes may have taken place in particular states, the monarchical principle as it then existed has been preserved to this day in its full vigor in the east. This is so true, that there is no royal usage mentioned by Samuel which may not be illustrated and explained from the modern sovereignties of that part of the world. The statement must have seemed the more effective from the implied contrast to the mild and gentle character of that service which the Lord, as king of Israel, had required. Samuel reminded them that their kings would soon fall into the state of other monarchs, to support which the heaviest exactions upon their persons and estates would become necessary. He would take their young men and employ them as charioteers and horsemen, and even (according to the Egyptian custom) as runners before and about his chariot.* A standing army would deprive them of the valuable services of their young men; and if this were not enough, the king of a future day would "take them to till *his* ground and to make *his* instruments of war and the furniture of *his* chariots. In like manner the daughters of Israel, who should marry and bring up children, would be largely taken to minister to the luxury of the court as "confectioners and bakers." Nor would he much scruple to take the chosen and best of their male and female slaves, as well as their laboring cattle, and "put them to his own work." And then to support his expenses, the heaviest exactions would be necessary; and although the kingly *tenth* were already appropriated to Jehovah, the divine king, not the less would their human king exact his kingly dues; thus, in fact, rendering their burdens greater than those of any other nation. A clear intimation was also given them of the danger to which their landed possessions would be ultimately exposed under the form of government which they so much desired. For the expression, "He will take the best of your fields, and of your vineyards, and of your olive-yards, and give them to his servants," manifestly refers to the fact that, inasmuch as their true king, Jehovah, was the sovereign proprietor of the soil, and as such had long before distributed the whole in inalienable estates among the people, whatever human king they might have, would necessarily stand in the, then and there, peculiar position, being only a civil governor, and not, like the neighboring king, also the territorial sovereign; and that hence, wanting the means of providing for his family and servants which other kings possessed, he would be tempted to avail himself of all kinds of pretences to dispossess them of the lands which they held from their divine king. "His servants ye will become," concludes the prophet. "And ye shall cry out in that day because of the king that ye have chosen: but Jehovah will not hear you in that day."

The purpose of the people was, however, too firmly fixed to be shaken even by this discouraging representation. An acquiescence in their demand was therefore reluctantly conceded, probably, as Jahn conjectures, "because the desired change was requested of the invisible King in a lawful manner, through the mediation of his prophet, and because, in the present disposition of the nation, it might be effected without bloodshed. If the remark of Polybius be in all cases true, that 'all aristocracies and democracies terminate at last in monarchy,'† this change must have taken place in some future time, and perhaps might have been attended with civil war.

"By this alteration of the constitution the theocracy was indeed thrown somewhat into the shade, as it was no longer so manifest that God was the king of the Hebrews. Still, however, as the principles of the theocracy were interwoven with the

* See engraving, page 227.   † Hist. lib. v. 6, 7.

Runners attending a Chariot.

fundamental and unchangeable laws of the state, their influence did not entirely cease, but the elected king was to act as the viceroy and vassal of Jehovah. On this account Moses had already established the following regulations (Deut. xvii. 14–20):

"1. That the Hebrews, whenever they adopted the monarchical form of government, should raise only those to the throne who were chosen by Jehovah himself. As monarchs (called kings of kings) were accustomed to appoint sub-kings, or viceroys, in the several provinces of their dominions, so was the king of the Hebrews to be called to the throne by Jehovah, to receive the kingdom from him, and in all respects to consider himself as his representative, viceroy, and vassal. On this occasion the will of Jehovah was to be made known by a prophet, or by means of Urim and Thummim, and the viceroy elect was to prove himself an instrument of God by protecting the commonwealth against its foes. The succession of the royal house was to depend on the will of God, to be made known by his prophets.

"2. Moses had likewise ordained that the new king should be a native Israelite. Thus foreigners were excluded from the throne, even though they should be proposed by false prophets; for, being heathens, they might transgress the fundamental law of the state by the introduction of idolatry; or, at least; it might be difficult for them to rule in all respects as the vassals of Jehovah. This regulation had reference merely to free elections, and was by no means to be understood, as it was explained by Judas of Galilee (Acts v. 37) and the Zealots during the last war with the Romans, that the Hebrews were not to submit to these foreign powers, under whose dominion they were brought by an all-directing Providence. On the contrary, Moses himself had predicted such events, and Jeremiah and Ezekiel earnestly exhorted their countrymen to surrender quietly to the Chaldeans."

Upon such conditions the choice of a king was permitted, according to law; and in the year 1110 B. C., 538 years after the exode, the first election took place.

Saul, the son of Kish, of the tribe of Benjamin, went forth about this time with a servant to seek some strayed asses belonging to his father. For three days the search was fruitless; and then finding himself near Ramah, the stated residence of Samuel, he resolved to go and consult him; for it was known to all Israel that nothing was hidden from the man of God. According to the still subsisting custom of the East, no one could, with the least propriety, present himself before a man in authority, and still less before a person of so sacred a character as Samuel bore, without some present, however small, in token of his respect and homage. But although the toil and travel-stained stranger who appeared before the prophet could only lay before him the worth of seven-pence halfpenny in silver, he was received with particular notice and honor; for it had been specially revealed to Samuel that on that day and at that hour the destined king of Israel would present himself before him. The prophet assured Saul that his father had found the asses, and began now to be anxious about his son. Nevertheless, he urged him to stay with him over the night, and partake of a feast which he had provided; at the same time conveying to him a slight intimation of the splendid fortunes which were in store for him; to which, with modest self-withdrawment, Saul replied, "Am not I a Benjamite, of the smallest of the tribes of Israel? and my family the least of all the families of the tribe of Benjamin? Wherefore then speakest thou so to me?" Part of this must be attributed to the Oriental forms of self-detraction; for although Benjamin was certainly the smallest of the tribes—as it had not recovered the serious blow inflicted by all the other tribes—it appears from the history that the family of Kish was of some consideration in Benjamin.

In consequence of the intimation he had previously received, Samuel had against this time prepared an entertainment, to which thirty principal persons of the place had been invited. Samuel conducted the stranger to the room in which these guests were assembled, and led him to the corner-seat of honor; and when the meat was served, directed the most honorable joint—the shoulder—to be set before him.

Being summer, the bed for Saul was made on the house-top; and before he lay down, Samuel communed with him there, probably to ascertain his sentiments and character, and to acquaint him with the true nature of that form of kingly government which he was destined to establish. Early in the morning the prophet called Saul to depart, and walked forth with him. After a time Samuel directed the servant to pass on before; and then the prophet, desiring Saul to stand still, that he might show him the purposes of God, produced a vial of oil, and poured it upon his

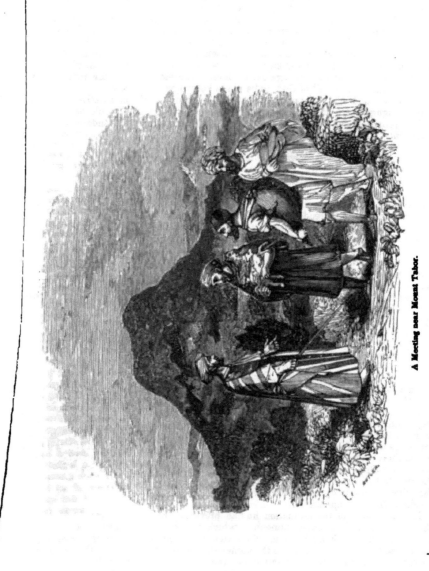

A Meeting near Mount Tabor.

head, thus anointing him "captain over the Lord's inheritance." He then kissed him, and to confirm his faith, proceeded to tell him all the incidents that would occur to him during his journey home, and to encourage him, under the sense he entertained of his own inferior claims to such a distinction, assured him that on the way, and through the divine influence, the needful qualifications should grow upon him, so that he should seem to receive another* heart and to become another man.

On his way home, all happened to Saul which the prophet had foreshown; and some of the incidents are too illustrative of the manners of the time to pass unnoticed. In the plain of Tabor he was met by three men who were proceeding to the place of sacred stones in Bethel, to worship God there. One of them carried three kids, intended as a sacrifice for each of their number; another had three loaves of bread; and the third a leather bottle of wine, all evidently intended to be used with the flesh of the kids in an offering-feast. They gave Saul the salutation of peace—such as travellers give each other by the way—probably the usual "Peace be unto thee!" which is no other than the common *Salam aleikoom* of the modern East; and they gave him two of the three loaves of bread which they had with them.

As Saul went on to Gibeah in Benjamin, which seems to have been called "the hill of God," either because there was here a "high-place" consecrated to the worship of God, or because it was the seat of a "school of the prophets," or a kind of college where young men were instructed in the duties of religion, in the knowledge of the law, in psalmody, and other religious exercises. Or it may have been so called for *both* these reasons, for both existed. As Saul drew nigh he perceived a company of these prophets returning from the high-place where they had been to worship; and as they went they sang the praises of God to the sound of the psaltery, the tabret, the pipe, and the harp. As they drew nigh the Spirit of God came upon him, as Samuel had predicted, and he became as another man. He joined the prophets, and sang the praises of God with them. And when those to whom he was known (for this was in his own tribe and neighborhood) witnessed this sudden endowment of the untaught husbandman they were much astonished, and said one to another, "What is this that is come unto the son of Kish? Is Saul also among the prophets?" Whence this last expression passed into a proverb, applied to one found in society with which his previous habits had not prepared him to mingle. It may be seen, however, that this incident would serve in a very conspicuous manner to direct attention to the person and character of Saul.

Samuel, in parting from Saul, had appointed a future meeting at Gilgal, to which place of sacred stones he convoked all Israel for the election of a king. As on other occasions, the choice of God was to be manifested by lot, which would also tend to prevent jealousies and the suspicion of partiality on the part of Samuel. In the usual manner of successive indications, the tribe of Benjamin was taken by the lot from the several tribes; then the family of Matri from the families of that tribe; then the house of Kish from the family of Matri; and, lastly, Saul from the household of Kish. But Saul was not to be found. Well assured of the result, he had not formed one in the assembly, but had, from modesty, kept himself apart among the baggage. When his retreat was discovered, he was led forward into the midst of the congregation; and the mass of the people observed with complacency that the elected king was of most noble presence, in the full prime of life, comely and tall, being higher by the head and shoulders than any of those among whom he stood. On such a man, in a rude age, when personal qualities are the most valued, the suffrages of all men would have centred, regarding him as pointed out by nature for rule and dominion. And so far did this feeling operate even on Samuel, that with evident pride that, since there must be a king, the divine choice had fallen on one who must seem in the eyes of all men so well qualified to dignify his high office, he thus proclaimed him to the people: "See ye him whom Jehovah hath chosen, *that there is none like him among all the people.*" And the people, responding to that feeling, raised at once the shout of recognition, "Long live the king!"

In concluding the present chapter, we are reluctant to withhold from the reader the very interesting survey which Jahn has taken of the office of the judges, and of

* *Another*, not *new*; a distinction which, from the Scriptural acceptation of the word *new*, together with the after conduct of Saul, it may be important to note.

† In this engraving (page 231) *ancient* musical instruments have been introduced (from Egyptian sources) for the sake of more effective illustration.

A Musical Procession.

the condition of Israel under their administration. This survey is imbodied in the ensuing paragraphs, but having modified several passages to suit them to the views which we have ourselves developed, we abstain from giving them the form of a direct quotation.

From what has been already said respecting the judges and their achievements, we can ascertain, with a tolerable degree of certainty, the nature of their office. Most of them, indeed, had been at the head of armies, and delivered their country from foreign oppression: Eli and Samuel, however, were not military men. Deborah was judge before she planned the war against Jabin; and of Jair, Ibzan, Elon, and Abdon, it is at least uncertain whether they ever held any military command. Judges are mentioned in the Mosaic law, in connexion with the high-priest, as arbiters of civil controversies, without any allusion to war. (Deut. xvii. 9.) In like manner, the judges who were appointed over Tyre after King Baal were certainly not military officers, for the city was at that time tributary to Babylon. The command of the army can therefore be scarcely considered as the peculiar distinction of these magistrates. But as in ancient times the duties of a judge were reckoned among the first and most important duties of a ruler, so the Hebrew judges appear to have been appointed for the general administration of public affairs, and the command of the army fell to them as the supreme executive officers. In many cases, it is true, military achievements were the means whereby men elevated themselves to the rank of judges; but our inquiry is, not how the office was obtained, but for what purposes it was instituted. It may, however, be proper to recollect that Jephthah and Samuel, and, for aught that appears, Jair, Elon, Ibzan, and Abdon, were raised to this office by the free, unsolicited voice of the people.

The office of these judges or regents was held during life, but it was not hereditary, neither could they appoint their successors. This arrangement might seem to be attended with the disadvantage that at the death of a judge the supreme executive authority ceased; but on consideration it will appear that these civil functions devolved on the high-priest, or rather were inherent to his high office, and were called into operation in the absence of any person more especially appointed to exercise them. And, without this, the apparent disadvantage would be more than counterbalanced by its preventing a degenerate heir or successor from giving to idolatry the support of his influence. This authority was limited by the law alone; and in doubtful cases they were directed by the sacred Oracle. (Num. xxvii. 21.) They were not obliged in common cases to ask advice of the ordinary rulers; it was sufficient that they did not remonstrate against the measures of the judge. In important emergencies, however, they convoked a general assembly of the rulers, over which they presided and exerted a powerful influence. They could issue orders, but not enact laws; they could neither levy taxes nor appoint officers, except perhaps in the army. Their authority extended only over those tribes by whom they had been elected or acknowledged; for, as has been before remarked, several of the judges presided over separate tribes. There was no salary attached to their office, nor was there any income appropriated to them, unless it might be a larger share of the spoils, and those presents which were made to them as testimonials of respect. (Judges viii. 24.) They had no external marks of dignity, and maintained no retinue of courtiers, though some of them were very opulent. They were not only simple in their manners, moderate in their desires, and free from avarice and ambition, but noble and magnanimous men, who felt that whatever they did for their country was above all reward, and could not be recompensed; who desired merely to promote the public good, and chose rather to deserve well of their country than to be enriched by its wealth. This exalted patriotism, like everything else connected with politics in the theocratical state of the Hebrews, was partly of a religious character; and those regents always conducted themselves as the officers of God; in all their enterprises they relied upon him, and their only care was that their countrymen should acknowledge the authority of Jehovah, their invisible King. (Judg. viii. 22, et seq.; comp. Heb. xi.) Still they were not without faults, neither are they so represented by their historians; they relate, on the contrary, with the utmost frankness, the great sins of which some of them were guilty. They were not merely deliverers of the state from a foreign yoke, but destroyers of idolatry, foes of pagan vices, promoters of the knowledge of God, of religion, and of morality; restorers of theocracy in the minds of the Hebrews, and powerful instruments of divine Providence in the promotion of the great design of preserving the Hebrew constitution, and by that means of rescuing the true religion from destruction.

By comparing the periods during which the Hebrews were oppressed by their enemies with those in which they were independent and governed by their own constitution, it is apparent that the nation in general experienced much more prosperity than adversity in the time of the judges:·their dominion continued four hundred and seventy-two years; but the whole period of foreign oppression amounts only to one hundred and thirty-one years, scarcely a fourth part of that period. Even during these years of bondage the whole nation was seldom under the yoke at the same time, but, for the most part, separate tribes only were held in servitude; nor were their oppressions always very severe; and all the calamities terminated in the advantage and glory of the people, as soon as they abolished idolatry and returned to their king, Jehovah. Neither was the nation in such a state of anarchy at this time as has generally been supposed. There were regular judicial tribunals at which justice could be obtained; and when there was no supreme regent, the public welfare was provided for by the high-priest and the ordinary rulers of the tribes. (Ruth iv. 1–11; Judg. viii. 22, xi. 1–11; 1 Sam. iv. 1, vii. 1, 2.) These rulers, it is true, were jealous of each other, and their jealousies not unfrequently broke out into civil war; but the union of the state was never entirely destroyed. They were not always provided with arms (2 Judg. v. 8; 1 Sam. xiii. 19); but yet, when united under their king, Jehovah, they gained splendid victories. They were not sufficiently careful to repress idolatry, but they never suffered it to become universally predominant. The sacred tabernacle was never entirely deserted and shut up, nor was it ever polluted by the rites of heathen superstition.

These times would certainly not be considered so turbulent as barbarous, much less would they be taken, contrary to the clearest evidence and to the analogy of all history, for an " heroic age,"* if they were viewed without the prejudices of preconceived hypothesis. It must never be forgotten that the book of Judges is by no means a complete history. It is, in a manner, a mere register of diseases, from which, however, we have no right to conclude that there were no healthy men, much less that there were no healthy seasons; when the book itself, for the most part, mentions only a few tribes in which the epidemic prevailed, and notices long periods during which it had entirely ceased. Whatever may be the result of more accurate investigation, it remains undeniable that the history of the Hebrews during this period perfectly corresponds throughout to the sanctions of the law; and they were always prosperous when they complied with the conditions on which prosperity was promised to them; it remains undeniable that the government of God was clearly manifested, not only to the Hebrews, but to their heathen neighbors, that the fulfilling of the promises and threatenings of the law were so many sensible proofs of the universal dominion of the divine King of the Hebrews; and, consequently, that all the various fortunes of that nation were so many means of preserving the knowledge of God on the earth. The Hebrews had no sufficient reason to desire a change in their constitution, since all that was necessary was that they should observe the conditions on which national prosperity had been promised to them.

CHAPTER XVI.

The election of Saul, though generally approved, did not meet with universal acceptance. In one point of view, the choice of a person belonging to a neutral and powerless tribe was calculated to obviate the rivalries of the two great tribes of Ephraim and Judah, who probably both thought that they had the better right to the distinction, but neither of whom were likely to agree that the other should have had it. But, on the other hand, Saul himself was not likely to derive the more respect from this neutral and politically insignificant position which prevented the mutual jealousies of these great rivals. But seeing that the tribe of Benjamin was, from its geographical position, closely connected with, and in some degree dependant on that of Judah, it is more probable that the dissentients, " the children of Belial," who despised Saul, and said, "How shall this man save us?" were of the haughty and tur-

* It is thus characterized by Heeren and other writers.

bulent tribe of Ephraim. Samuel left it to the people themselves to settle the money-price they were to pay for their new luxury; and, although he had foreshown the ex-actions which the regal state would in the end render necessary, it was not his object to give his sanction to that which he had announced as a contingent evil. Besides, the external organization of the new government was left to be developed by circum-stances, the prophet having only cared to secure the principles. Saul was left to grow into his position and its privileges, while Samuel continued to administer the civil government: for it is to be borne in mind that Samuel continued to judge Israel all the days of his life, which did not terminate until thirty-eight years after the election of Saul, who himself outlived the prophet but two years. The position of Saul was, therefore, for the greater part of his reign, chiefly that of a military leader, while Samuel continued to discharge the civil part of the regal office, to which it was prob-ably obvious that Saul was not competent. The *kingdom*, properly speaking, was not established, not developed under Saul, but only *begun* with him. And this it is necessary to understand, if we would clearly apprehend the *growth* of that monarchi-cal principle which was only *planted* with Saul.

After his election at Gilgal, the king returned to his own home at Gibeah, where such "presents" were brought him by the people as oriental kings usually receive, and which form no inconsiderable portion of their ordinary revenue. As the product of these offerings was probably more than adequate to the present wants and expecta-tions of the king, who as yet assumed no regal state, the question as to the permanent support of the kingly government was not yet pressed upon the attention of either the people or the king. The discontented parties, however, "brought him no presents." Saul took no notice of their insults, but wisely "held his peace."

Very soon after Saul's election, the Ammonites, under their king Nahash, marched into the old disputed territory beyond Jordan, and laid siege to the important city of Jabesh Gilead. The inhabitants, avowing their impotence, offered to submit to the condition of paying tribute to the Ammonites; but the insulting and barbarous king refused to receive their submission on any other terms than that the right eye of every one of them should be extinguished, that they might remain as so many living mon-uments of his victory. Here again was a barbarity of which the Israelites were never guilty, even in thought. The people of Jabesh Gilead were so distressed that they dared not absolutely refuse even these merciless conditions, but besought a grace of seven days for deliberation. This they did with the hope that the tribes on the other side the river might, in the interval, be roused by the news to appear for their deliv-erance. Nor was their hope in vain. Saul no sooner received the intelligence than he at once and decidedly stood up in his position of a hero and a king, claiming the obedience of the people, whom he summoned to follow him to the deliverance of Ja-besh Gilead. This call was readily obeyed; for it ran in the names of Saul *and Samuel*, and was conveyed in that imperative and compulsory form, which it was not, under any circumstances, judged safe to disobey. For he hewed a yoke of oxen in pieces, and sent the pieces by the hands of swift messengers to all Israel, calling them, by all the penalties of that well-known and dreaded sign, to follow him. All Israel obeyed with one consent. All the men, of age to bear arms, quitted their several la-bors, and hastened from all parts to the plain of Bezek, where Saul numbering his army, found it to consist of three hundred and thirty thousand men, of whom thirty thousand were of Judah, which seems rather an inadequate proportion for so large a tribe. It being already the sixth day, Saul sent to apprize the citizens of Jabesh Gil-ead of the help which was preparing for them, and which they might expect to re-ceive on the morrow, being the very day they were to surrender their eyes to the Ammonites.

Accordingly, in the morning, the king, having marched all night, appeared before Jabesh, at the head of his army, invested the camp of the Ammonites, and falling upon them on three different sides, overthrew them with a great slaughter. So com-plete was the rout, that those who escaped were so broken and dispersed, that no two could be found together.

Saul in this action displayed a large measure of those heroic qualities which the ancient nations most desired their monarchs to possess. Considering all the circum-stances, the promptitude and energy of his decision, the speed with which he collected an immense army and brought it into action, and the skill and good military conduct of the whole transaction, there are probably few operations of the Hebrew history which more recommend themselves to the respect and admiration of a modern soldier. Its effect was not lost upon the people, who joyfully recognised in their king the qualities which have generally been held most worthy of rule; and so much was their enthusiasm excited, that they began to talk of putting to death the small minority who had refused to recognise his sovereignty. But Samuel interposed to prevent an act unbecoming a day in which " God had wrought salvation in Israel." So harsh a proceeding would also have been rather likely to provoke than allay the disaffection of the leading tribes.

Samuel then invited the army, which comprehended in fact the effective body of the Hebrew people, to proceed to Gilgal, there solemnly to confirm the kingdom to Saul, seeing that now his claims were undisputed by any portion of the people. This was done with great solemnity, and with abundant sacrifices of peace and joy.

But lest this solemnity, which was obviously designed to remind the people of their continued dependance on Jehovah, should be construed into an approbation and sanction of all their proceedings, the prophet took this public occasion of reminding them that their proceeding had been most unpleasing to their Divine King; although, if they maintained their fidelity to him and to the principles of the theocracy, some of the evil consequences might be averted. He also neglected not the opportunity of justifying his own conduct and the purity of his administration. He challenged assembled Israel to produce one instance of oppression, fraud, or corruption, on his part, while he had been their sole judge; and in that vast multitude not one voice was raised to impugn his integrity and uprightness. He then proceeded to remind them of their past transgressions, in forgetting or turning astray from their God, with the punishments which had invariably followed, and the deliverances which their repentance had procured; showing them, by these instances, the sufficiency of their Divine Sovereign to rule them, and to save them from their enemies, without the intervention of an earthly king, whom they had persisted in demanding. And he assured them that, under their regal government, public sins would not come to be visited with public calamities. To add the greater weight to his words, and to evince the divine displeasure, the commissioned prophet called down thunder and rain from heaven, then at the usual season of wheat harvest, when the air is usually, in that country, serene and cloudless. On this the people were greatly alarmed at the possible consequences of the displeasure they had provoked, and besought Samuel to intercede for them. The prophet kindly encouraged them to hope that if they continued to trust faithfully in God, all would yet be well; and he assured them of continued intercession on their behalf, and of his services as a civil judge or teacher,—for that the omission would be a sin on his own part.

Saul, now fully established as king, dismissed his numerous army; but he retained three thousand of their number, two thousand of which he stationed at Michmash and Bethel, under his own immediate orders, while the other thousand were at Gibeah of Benjamin, under his eldest son Jonathan. Josephus says that these formed the body-guard of himself and his son. If so, he began very soon to act "like the kings of the nations," and to fulfil one part of the predictions of Samuel as to the course which the kingdom was likely to take. Even supposing (as we rather do) that he retained this force to be in readiness for the smaller military operations which he had in view, it is evident that he had already taken the idea of a standing army, the nucleus of which this body of three thousand men may be deemed to have formed. At all events, it may seem as an early indication of Saul's subsequently besetting public sin, of forgetting his properly vice-regal character, and his subordination to the Divine King. It was assuredly a new thing in Israel, and does savor somewhat of a distrust of God's providence, by which the peculiar people had hitherto been protected and delivered in every time of need; as well as of an affectation of that independent authority which " the kings of the nations" took to themselves. However, as the character of Saul seems to be held generally in more disesteem than the writers of his history intended, we shall not impute blame to him where the Scripture does not; but are ready to allow that, under all the circumstances, the measure was prudent and proper; for it appears that an enemy was then actually present in the country, whose expulsion the king had then in view. There were garrisons of the Philistines in the land. How this came to pass is not very clear. It would seem, however, that in resigning their conquests after their last defeat, they had retained some hill fortresses, from which they knew the Hebrews would find it difficult to dislodge them; and that when they recovered from the blow which was then inflicted upon their power, they contrived, by the help of this hold which they had in the country, to bring the southern tribes (at least those of Judah and Benjamin) under a sort of subjection. Thus when Saul was returning home after having been privately anointed by Samuel at Ramah, and met the sons of the prophets at Gibeah, we learn that at that place was "a garrison of the Philistines." And now we further learn that the Hebrews had in fact been disarmed by that people. According to that jealous policy of which other examples will ultimately be offered, they had even removed all the smiths of Israel, lest they should make weapons of war; in consequence of which the Hebrews were obliged to resort to the Philistines whenever their agricultural implements needed any other sharpening than that which a grindstone could give; and as this was an unpleasant alternative, even these important instruments had been suffered to become blunt at the time to which we are now come; and so strict had been the deprivation of arms that, in the military operations which soon after followed, no one of the Israelites, save Saul and his eldest son, was possessed of a spear or sword.

This was the state of southern Palestine, where Jonathan, acting doubtless by the orders of his father, attacked and overcame with his thousand men the Philistine garrison in Gibeah. Encouraged by this success, Saul caused open war to be proclaimed, by sound of trumpet, against the Philistines, and to assert his authority over the tribes beyond Jordan, who were but too apt to regard their interests as separate from those of the other tribes, and who might think themselves exempt from taking part in a war against a people whose oppressions had not extended to themselves,— Saul directed the proclamation to be made not only "throughout all the land," but in a special manner it included "those beyond Jordan." They did not disobey; but came with other Israelites, from all quarters, to the standard of the king at Gilgal. The people generally, though destitute of proper military weapons, were much inspirited by the success of Jonathan, and by their confidence in the now tried valor and military conduct of the king.

Meanwhile the Philistines were not heedless of this movement among the Israelites. No sooner did they hear of the defeat of their garrison in Gibeah than they assembled a formidable force, which seemed sufficient to overwhelm all opposition. It was composed of three thousand chariots of war, six thousand horsemen, and "people as the sand upon the seashore for multitude." The enthusiasm of the disarmed Israelites evaporated in the presence of this powerful force; and the army of Saul diminished every day, as great numbers of the men stole away to seek refuge in caves, in woods, in rocks, in towers, and in pits.

Saul had exhibited his inability of understanding his true position, or his disposition to regard himself as an independent sovereign, by entering upon or provoking this war without consulting, through Samuel or the priest, the divine will. Although not formally so declared, it was the well-understood practice of the Hebrew constitution, that no war *against any other than the doomed nations of Canaan* would be undertaken without the previous consent and promised assistance of the Great King. Yet Saul, without any such authority, had taken measures which were certain to produce a war with the Philistines. He probably thought that the aggressions of the Philistines, and their existing position as the oppressors of Israel, and their intrusion into the Hebrew territory, made his undertaking so obviously just and patriotic as to render a direct authorization superfluous, as its refusal could not be supposed: nor are we quite sure that in this he was mistaken. Be this as it may, Samuel was not willing that such a precedent should be established; and therefore he had appointed to meet Saul on a particular day at Gilgal, "to offer burnt-offerings and peace-offerings, and to show him what he should do," that is, both to propitiate the Lord, as on other occasions, and to advise Saul how to act in carrying on the war. On the appointed day Samuel did not arrive as soon as the king expected. The prophet probably delayed his coming on purpose to test his fidelity and obedience. Saul failed in this test. Seeing his force hourly diminishing by desertions; and in the pride of his fancied independence, considering that he had as much right as the Egyptian and other kings to perform the priestly functions, he ordered the victims to be brought, and offered them himself upon the altar. This usurpation of the priestly office by one who had no natural authority as an Aaronite, nor any special authorization as a prophet, was decisive of the character and the fate of Saul. If the principles of the theocracy were to be preserved, and if the political supremacy of Jehovah was at all to be maintained, it was indis-

Rome.

pensably necessary that the first manifestation by the kings of autocratic dispositions and of self-willed assumption of superiority to the law, should be visited by severe examples of punishment; for if not checked in the beginnings, the growth would have been fatal to the constitution. It will hence appear that the punishments which Saul incurred for this and other acts manifesting the same class of dispositions, were not so disproportioned to his offences, or so uncalled for by the occasions of the state, as some persons have been led to imagine.

Saul had scarcely made an end of offering his sacrifices before he was apprized of the approach of Samuel, and went forth to meet him. The apology he made to the prophet for what he had done,—that his force was diminishing, and that he was afraid that if he delayed any longer the Philistines would fall upon him before sacrifices had been offered to Jehovah—showed little of that reliance upon the Divine King, which every Hebrew general was expected to manifest; and but little anxiety to receive these prophetic counsels which Samuel had promised to deliver. Under nearly similar circumstances, how different was the conduct of Gideon, who gained immortal honor by these theocratic sentiments which enabled him to leave to his successors a memorable example of confidence in God! Samuel saw through the hollowness of Saul's apology, and warned him that by such sentiments as he entertained, and such conduct as he manifested, he was rendering himself unworthy to be the founder of a royal house, inasmuch as he could not become a pattern to his successors; and that by persevering in such a course he would compel the appointment of one more worthy than himself to reign over Israel, and to be the father of a kingly race. Samuel then retired from Gilgal, leaving Saul to carry on, as he saw best, the war he had undertaken.

On numbering his remaining force, Saul found that but six hundred men remained with him. With a less force than this, enemies as formidable as the Philistines had in former times been defeated. But Saul, entirely overlooking, or distrusting, that divine assistance which every Hebrew leader in a just war was entitled to expect, and regarding only the disparity of his force, felt that it would be imprudent to engage or oppose so vast an army with a mere handful of disheartened men. He therefore retired from the field, and threw himself into the reconquered fortress of Gibeah. On discovering his retreat, the Philistines sent three powerful detachments in different directions to ravage the country, while the main body of their army still remained encamped near Michmash.

In this extremity, an entire change was wrought in the aspect of affairs through the daring valor of Jonathan. Accompanied only by his armor-bearer, he withdrew secretly from the camp, and, by climbing, opened himself a passage to one of the outposts of the Philistines, upon the summit of a cliff, deemed inaccessible, and therefore not very strongly guarded; and penetrating to the enemy by so new and unexpected a path, he killed the advanced piquets, and, supported by his follower, slew all whom his hand encountered, and bore disorder and alarm into the camp of the Philistines, then much weakened by the detachments we have mentioned. The cries which arose from this part of the camp confounded and terrified the more distant parts; so that, aware of the presence of an enemy, which yet did not appear to them, they turned their arms against one another, and destroyed themselves with the blind fury of despairing men. The clamor which arose in the Philistine camp was heard by the Israelites. Saul at first was willing to go through the form of consulting the Lord by *urim;* but the confusion increasing in the Philistine camp, he deemed it a time for action rather than counsel; and directing the priest to forbear, he hastened to join his valiant son, whose absence was now known, and to whom this disorder was rightly attributed. The enemy were already flying in all directions, and Saul, with his small band, committed terrible havoc upon the fugitives. While thus engaged, his force increased with still greater rapidity than it had previously diminished: for not only did the Hebrew captives take the opportunity of making their escape and joining their king, but great numbers came forth from their lurking places to join in the pursuit; so that Saul soon found himself at the head of six thousand men. The rash and inconsiderate king, in his determination to make the most of his advantage, laid an interdictive curse upon any of his people who should taste food until the evening. Not only were the pursuers weakened and exhausted by the strict abstinence thus enjoined, but Jonathan, unaware of this interdict, unwittingly transgressed it by tasting a little wild honey which he met with in his way through a forest.

In the evening, the famished people, being then released from the interdict, flew ravenously upon the prey of cattle, and, in their impatience, began to devour the raw and living flesh. This being a transgression of the law which forbade meat not properly exsanguinated to be eaten, Saul, who was really rather zealous to observe the law when it did not interfere with his own objects, interposed, and ordered the meat to be properly and legally slaughtered and prepared for food.

The people being now refreshed, Saul proposed to continue the pursuit during the night, but deemed it prudent first to consult the Lord through the priest. No answer was given. This Saul interpreted to intimate that his solemn interdict had been transgressed; and, again unreasoning and rash, he swore that even were the transgressor his own son Jonathan, he should surely be put to death. It was Jonathan: the lot determined this. His father told him he must die; but the people, full of admiration of the young prince, protested that not a hair of his head should suffer damage, and thus saved his life.

This campaign, although concluded without a battle, was not the less productive of durable advantage. The glory which Saul acquired by it strengthened his authority among his own people, and henceforth no enemy to which he could be opposed seemed invincible to him. We see him, indeed, waging war, in turn, against Moab, Ammon, and Edom, and against the Amalekites and the Philistines; and in whatever direction he turned his arms, he obtained the victory and honor. Valiant himself, he esteemed valor in others; and whenever he discovered a man of ability and courage, he endeavored to draw him near to himself, and to attach him to his person. The qualities most prized by Saul were eminently possessed by his own cousin Abner, and he became "captain of the host," or generalissimo of the army of Israel.

The several expeditions of Saul against the enemies of Israel took up, at intervals, the space of five or six years. During these years, Samuel, without further interference in political affairs, continued to watch the civil interests of the people, and to administer justice between them. The authority which he still preserved in Israel was very great, and probably not considerably less than it had been at any former time.

About the tenth or eleventh year of Saul's reign, God made known to the prophet that the iniquity of the Amalekites had not reached its height, and that the time was fully come when the old sentence of utter extermination should be executed. Saul was charged with its execution; and his commission, as delivered to him by Samuel, was expressed in the most absolute terms, and left the king no option to spare aught that breathed. Under this supreme order, the king made a general call upon all the tribes, which brought together an army of two hundred thousand men, among whom there were but ten thousand men of Judah. The deficiency of that tribe in supplying its due proportion is probably not noticed by the historian on this and on a former occasion, without some object; and that object probably was to convey the intimation that since the sceptre had been of old promised to that tribe, it was discontented at the government of Saul, and less hearty than the other tribes in its obedience.

The king led his army into the territory of Amalek. There he made the most able disposition of his forces, seized the most favorable positions, and then turned his advantages against the enemy. A general action followed, in which the Israelites were victorious, and they pursued the Amalekites to their most distant and last retreats. Agag, the king, was taken alive with all his riches. Blinded by his ambition and his avarice to the danger of acting in defiance of a most positive and public command from God himself, Saul determined to spare the life of Agag, and to preserve the more valuable parts of all the booty from destruction; but with a most insulting or weak mockery of obedience, "all that was vile and refuse they utterly destroyed." He then led home his triumphant army, and paused in the land of Eastern Carmel,* where he erected a monument of the most important and distant expedition in which he had hitherto been engaged. He then passed on to Gilgal. Samuel came to him there soon after his arrival, and at once charged him with his disobedience. Saul behaved with a degree of confusion and meanness which we should scarcely have expected from him, and which the consciousness of wrong-doing only can explain. He affirmed and persisted that he *had* obeyed the Divine command, when everything before and around him evinced that he had not. In the end he confessed that he had acted

* On the southwestern borders of the Dead sea, and which we call "Eastern Carmel" to distinguish it from "Mount Carmel," which lies westward, on the Mediterranean.

wrong; but then excused himself by laying one part of it on the zeal of the people to sacrifice the best of the cattle to Jehovah, and part to his own fear of restraining them from it. It was a great grief to Samuel to hear the king of Israel betray such meanness of soul, in palliating an unjustifiable action; and, conceding the truth of the latter statement, he asked with severity, "Hath Jehovah as much delight in burnt-offerings and in sacrifices as in obedience to his voice? Behold, to obey is better than sacrifice; and to hearken than the fat of rams." He then continued authoritatively, as a prophet, to announce his rejection from being the founder of a royal house, as the fixed purpose of the Divine King whose imperative commands he had publicly disobeyed, or assumed a power of dispensing with, to such an extent as suited his convenience. It would be wrong to consider this as the sole act or omission for which this rejection was incurred. It was but one of many acts by which he indicated an utter incapability of apprehending his true position, and in consequence manifested dispositions and conduct utterly at variance with the principles of government which the welfare of the state, and, indeed, the very objects of its foundation, made it most essential to maintain. Unless the attempts at absolute independence made by Saul were checked, or visited with some signal mark of the divine displeasure, the precedents established by the first king were likely to become the rule to future sovereigns. And hence the necessity, now at the beginning, of peculiar strictness, or even of severity, for preventing the establishment of bad rules and precedents for future reigns.

Saul at first betrayed more anxiety about present appearances than ultimate results; and he entreated Samuel to remain, and honor him in the sight of the people, by joining with him in an act of worship to Jehovah. Samuel refused; and as he turned to go away, the king caught hold of the skirt of his robe to detain him, with such force, that the skirt was rent off. "So hath God," said the prophet, "rent from thee, this day, the kingdom of Israel, and given it to thy neighbor who is better than thee. Nor will *he who gives victory to Israel* lie or repent; for he is not a man, that he should repent." The expression which we have here particularly indicated was probably intended and understood as a further rebuke for the triumphal monument which Saul had erected in Carmel, and whereby he seemed to claim to himself that honor for the recent victory which, under the principles of the theocracy, was due to God only. Samuel, however, complied with the earnest wish of the king, and returned with him to the camp. There acting on the stern injunction which Saul had neglected, the prophet commanded the king of the Amalekites, by whose sword many mothers in Israel had been made childless, to be put to death. When the prophet and the king separated, the former proceeded to his usual residence at Ramah, and went no more to see Saul to the day of his death. Yet as he had a great regard for a man who, with all his faults, had many good natural qualities which would well have fitted him for rule in a simple human monarchy, and who, moreover, was faithful and even zealous for Jehovah, as his God, however deficient in obedience to him as his king, the prophet continued long to mourn greatly for him, and to bewail the doom which it had been his painful duty to declare.

After fifteen years, the Lord rebuked Samuel for this useless repining, and commanded him to proceed to Bethlehem, there to anoint the man worthier than Saul, whom he had chosen to fill his forfeited place, and to become the founder of a royal house. This was a delicate mission; for Samuel knew enough of Saul to fear that he would not scruple to put even himself to death if the fact came to his knowledge. He therefore veiled his real object under the form of a public sacrifice, which, in his prophetic character, he had a right to enjoin. That he still retained his authority as civil judge is evinced by the alarm which his unexpected visit occasioned to the elders of Bethlehem, who "trembled" at his coming, for fear it should be not "peaceably," but in judgment.

The family to which Samuel was sent was that of Jesse, the grandson of Boaz and Ruth, and, as such, a person of consideration in that place. Jesse was the father of eight sons, all of whom were present in Bethlehem, save the youngest, David by name, who was abroad with his father's flock. The whole family was invited by the prophet to be present at his sacrifice. Samuel knew that the destined king was to be found among Jesse's sons, but knew not as yet for which of them that distinction was intended. Still influenced by those general prepossessions in favor of such personal qualities as he had formerly beheld in Saul with complacency and admiration, Samuel no sooner beheld the commanding and stately figure of Jesse's eldest son, Eliab, than he concluded that "the Lord's anointed was before him." For this he received the striking rebuke, "Look not on his countenance, or on the height of his stature; because I have refused him: for Jehovah seeth not as man seeth; for man looketh on the outward appearance, but Jehovah looketh on the heart." It further appeared that no one of the other sons of Jesse then present was the object of the divine choice. On this, Samuel, with some surprise, asked Jesse whether he had other sons; and learning that the youngest, a mere youth of fifteen years old, was abroad in the fields, he caused him to be sent for. When he arrived, Samuel was struck by his uncommonly handsome appearance, especially by a freshness of complexion unusual in that country, and by the singular fire and beauty of his eyes. The divine choice was at once intimated to him, "Arise, anoint him, for this is he!" As in the case of Saul himself, this precious anointing was significant only of the divine intention and choice. As Saul had returned to his fields, so David returned to his flock. The path to the throne was to be opened by circumstances which did not yet appear. The anointing was the sign and seal of an ultimate intention. For the present David was not more a king, nor Saul less one, than before.

The doom of exclusion had been pronounced upon Saul at a time when he was daily strengthening himself on the throne, and increasing in power, popularity, and fame; and when his eldest son, Jonathan, stood, and deserved to stand, so high in the favor of all the people, that no man could, according to human probabilities, look upon any one else as likely to succeed him in the throne. But when the excitement of war and victory had subsided, and the king had leisure to consider and brood over the solemn and declaredly irrevocable sentence which the prophet had pronounced, a very serious effect was gradually produced upon his mind and character; for he was no longer prospered and directed by God, but left a prey to his own gloomy mind. The consciousness that he had not met the requirements of the high vocation to which, "when he was little in his own sight," he had been called, together with the threatened loss of his dominion and the possible destruction of his house, made him jealous, sanguinary, and irritable, and occasionally threw him into fits of the most profound and morbid melancholy. This is what, in the language of scripture, is called "the evil spirit that troubled him." That it was not a case of demoniacal possession, as some have been led by this form of expression to suppose, is obvious from the effects to which we shall presently advert. Nor was it needful; for, as acting upon the character of man, earth contains not a more evil spirit than the guilty or troubled mind abandoned to its own impulses.

Not long after David had been anointed by Samuel, the mental malady of Saul gathered such strength—the fits of his mad melancholy became so long and frequent, that some remedial measures appeared necessary. Remembering that Saul had always been remarkably sensible to the influence of sweet sounds, it occurred to his friends that it might be attended with good effects, were an able musician retained at court, to play before the king, when his fits of gloom and horror came upon him. Saul himself approved of this advice, and directed that a person with the suitable qualifications should be sought. This reminded one of the courtiers how skilfully and sweetly he had heard the youngest son of Jesse play upon the harp; and in mentioning this to the king he also took occasion to commend David as a young man of known valor, prudent in conduct, and very comely in his person. From this and other corroborative circumstances, it is easy to perceive that music was now, and much earlier, cultivated by the Hebrews as a private accomplishment and solace. It formed their most usual relaxation, and divided their time with the labors of agriculture and the care of flocks.

The report which he had heard engaged Saul to send to Jesse, demanding his son David. The old man accordingly sent him to court, together with such a present to the king as the customs of the age—and of the east in all ages, required as a homage. It consisted of a quantity of bread, a skin bottle of wine, and a kid.

Thus, in the providence of God, an opening was made for David, whereby he might become acquainted with the manners of the court, the business of government, and the affairs and interests of the several tribes, and was put in the way of securing the equally important advantage of becoming extensively known to the people. These were training circumstances for the high destinies which awaited him. Saul himself, ignorant that in him he beheld the "man worthier than himself," on whom the inheritance of his throne was to devolve, contributed to these preparations. He received the youthful minstrel with fervor; and, won by his engaging disposition and the beau-

16

ties of his mind and person, not less than by the melody of his harp, became much attached to him. The personal bravery of David, also, did not long remain unnoticed by the veteran hero, who soon elevated him to the honorable and confidential station of his armor-bearer—having obtained Jesse's consent to allow his son to remain in attendance upon him. His presence was a great solace and relief to Saul; for whenever he fell into his fits of melancholy, David played on his harp before him; and its soft and soothing strains soon calmed his troubled spirit, and brought peace to his soul.

In the twenty-six years which had passed since the signal overthrow of the Philistines at Michmash, that people had recruited their strength, and at last* deemed themselves able to wipe out the disgrace they then incurred, and to recover their previous superiority over the Israelites. They recommenced the war by invading the territory of Judah: Saul marched against them; and the two armies encamped in the face of each other, on the sides of opposite mountains which a valley separated. While thus stationed the Hebrews were astonished and terrified to behold a man of enormous stature, between nine and ten feet high, advance from the camp of the Philistines attended by his armor-bearer. His name was Goliah. He was arrayed in complete mail, and armed with weapons proportioned to his bulk. He stood forth between the hosts, and, as authorized by the Philistines, who were confident that his match could not be found, proposed, with great arrogance of language, that the question of tribute and servitude should be determined by the result of a single combat between himself and any champion which might be opposed to him. The Israelites were quite as much dismayed at the appearance of Goliah, and at the proposal which he made, as the Philistines could have expected, or as the Philistines themselves would have been under the same circumstances. No heart in Israel was found stout enough to dare the encounter with this dreadful Philistine; nor was any man then present willing to take on his single arm the serious consequences of the possible result. Then finding that no one of riper years or higher pretensions offered himself to the combat, David presented himself before Saul, whom he attended as his armor-bearer, and said, "Let no man's heart fail because of him; thy servant will go and fight with this Philistine." But Saul told him that he was unequal to such a contest, "For thou art but a youth, but he a man of war from his youth." The reply of David was equally forcible and modest:—"Thy servant tended his father's flock; and when there came a lion or a bear, and took a lamb out of the flock, then I pursued him and smote him, and snatched it from his mouth; and if he rose against me, I caught him by the beard, and smote him, and slew him. Both lions and bears hath thy servant smitten, and this uncircumcised Philistine shall be like one of them. Let me go and smite him, and take away the reproach from Israel; for who is this uncircumcised Philistine that he should defy the hosts of the living God?" He added, "Jehovah who delivered me from the power of lions and bears will deliver me from the hand of this Philistine." Saul had been too little accustomed to this mode of speaking and feeling not to be struck by it. Although he had himself not been prone to exhibit *military* confidence in God, he perceived that such a confidence now supplied the only prospect of success; he therefore said, "Go; and may Jehovah be with thee!" He would fain have arrayed him in his own complete armor; but David rejected this as an incumbrance, and stepped lightly forward in his ordinary dress, and without sword or shield, or spear, having only in his right hand a sling—with the use of which early pastoral habits had made him familiar—and in his left a little bag, containing five smooth pebbles picked up from the small brook that then meandered and still meanders through the valley of Elah.† The giant was astonished, and felt insulted that a mere youth should be sent forth to contend with so redoubted a champion as himself; and availing himself of the pause which the ancient champions were wont to take to abuse, threaten, and provoke each other, he cried, "Am I a dog, that thou comest against me with staves?" He then cursed him by his god, and, like the old Homeric heroes, threatened to give his flesh to the fowls of the air and to the beasts of the field. David's reply, conceived in the finest and truest spirit of the the-

* B. C. 1080, five years after the anointing of David.
† "We entered the famous Terebinthine vale, renowned for centuries as the field of the victory gained by David over the uncircumcised Philistine. Nothing has occurred to alter the face of the country. The very brook out of which David chose the five smooth stones has been noticed by many a thirsty pilgrim journeying from Jaffa to Jerusalem, all of whom must pass it in their way. The ruins of goodly edifices, indeed, attest the religious veneration entertained in later periods for this hallowed spot; but even there are now become so insignificant that they are scarcely discernible, and nothing can be said to interrupt the native dignity of this memorable scene."—CLARKE.

ocracy, at once satisfies us that we behold in him the man fit to reign over the peculiar people. "Thou comest to me with a sword, and with a spear, and with a shield; but I come to thee in the name of the Lord of hosts, the God of the hosts of Israel, whom thou hast defied. This day will Jehovah deliver thee into my hand; and I will take thy head from thee, and I will give thy carcass, and the carcasses of the host of the Philistines, this day to the fowls of the air and to the wild beasts of the earth, *that the whole earth may know that there is a God in Israel.* And all this assembly shall know that Jehovah can save without sword or spear; for the battle is Jehovah's, and he will deliver you into our hands." On this the enraged giant strode forward; and David hastened to fit a stone to his sling; and he flung it with so true an aim that it smote the Philistine in the only vulnerable part that was not cased in armor, his forehead, and buried itself deep in his brain. He then ran and cut off the monster's head with his own sword, thus fulfilling the prediction he had just uttered. A few minutes after he had gone forth, he returned, and laid the head and sword of the giant at the feet of Saul.

The overthrow of their champion struck a panic into the Philistines. They fled, and were pursued, with great slaughter, even to their own country, by the Israelites, who then returned and plundered their camp.

The honor which David won by this splendid achievement was too great for his safety. Saul could not but feel that the sort of spirit by which the youthful hero had been actuated was precisely that which on many preceding occasions he himself *ought* to have manifested, and for not doing which the doom of exclusion had been pronounced against him. The feeling that David was really the hero of the recent fight, was also not pleasant to one so jealous of his military glory. And when the women came forth from their towns to greet the returning conquerors with their instruments of music, and sang responsively to their tabrets and their viols,—

> "Saul has smitten his thousands,
> But David has his ten thousands slain,"

the indignation of the king was provoked to the utmost. "To me," he said, "they have ascribed but thousands, and to David tens of thousands: what more can he have but the kingdom?" It would therefore seem that this preference of David to him by the women in their songs first suggested to him the possibility that he was the man, worthier than himself, who was destined to succeed him and to supersede his descendants: and the notion having once occurred, he probably made such inquiries as enabled him to conclude or to discover that such was the fact. His knowledge of it appears soon after; and we know that from this time forward David became the object, not merely of his envy and jealousy, but of his hatred and dislike. Yet he was afraid, if he as yet wished, to do him any open injury; but as he could not bear him any longer in his former close attendance about his person, he threw him more into the *public* service, intrusting to him the command of a thousand men. From his subsequent expressions and conduct, it seems likely that the king expected that the inexperience of youth might lead David into such errors in this responsible public station as would either give him occasion to act against him, or would seriously damage his character with the people. But if such were his views, they were grievously disappointed. In his public station "David behaved himself wisely in all his ways, for Jehovah was with him;" and the opportunity which was given him only served to evince his talents for business and his attention to it; and, consequently, to increase and establish that popularity among the people which his character and exploits had already won. And so it was, that the dislike and apprehensions of Saul increased in proportion to the abilities and discretion which David evinced, and to the popularity which he acquired.

The king was under the full operation of those feelings, which as yet he durst not avow, when he happened to learn that his daughter Michal had become attached to David. This was far from displeasing him, as he thought it gave him an opportunity of entrapping the son of Jesse to his own destruction. He promised her to him; but on the condition of so difficult an enterprise against the Philistines, as he fully expected would ensure his death. But David, always victorious, returned in a few days with more numerous pledges of his valor than the king had ventured to demand; and he was then married to Michal, who could not with any decency be refused to him.

In some subsequent actions against the Philistines, with whom a desultory warfare was still carried on, David displayed such courage and military skill as greatly increased his renown in Israel, and increased in the same proportion the animosity of Saul. His hate became at last so ungovernable, that he could no longer confine the dark secret to his own bosom, or limit himself to underhand attempts against the life of Jesse's son. He avowed it to his son Jonathan and to his courtiers, charging them to take any favorable opportunity of putting him to death. He knew not yet of the strong attachment which subsisted between Jonathan and David,—that his noble son, rising far above all selfishness, pride, or envy, loved the son of Jesse even "as his own soul." He heard the command with horror, and apprized David of it, counselling him to hide himself until he should have an opportunity of remonstrating on the subject privately with the king. This he did with such effect, displaying the services and fidelity of David with such force, that the better reason of Saul prevailed for the time, and he solemnly swore to make no further attempt against his life.

But not long after, all the evil passions of Saul were again roused by the increased renown which David obtained, by a splendid victory over the Philistines. He had scarce returned to court before he had a narrow escape of being pinned to the wall by a javelin which the king threw at him in one of those fits of phrensied melancholy which the son of Jesse was at that moment endeavoring to sooth by playing on his harp.

David then withdrew to his own house. But the king had now committed himself, and henceforth threw aside all disguise or restraint. He sent some of his attendants to watch the house; and David would undoubtedly have been murdered the next morning, had not his faithful wife managed his escape during the night, by letting him down in a basket through one of the windows. In the morning, when the man demanded admittance with the intention of slaying her husband, Michal told them he was very ill and confined to his bed; and in proof of it showed them the bed, in which she had placed a figure made up so as to present the appearance of a body covered with the bedclothes. This news they carried to the king, who sent them back with orders to bring him alive in his bed. By this means Michal's artifice was discovered, and her father was so enraged, that, for her own safety, she made him believe that it was to save her own life she had consented to it.

As the only revenge then in his power, Saul took away Michal, and gave her in marriage to another; and the story which she had made up, that David had put her in fear of her life, probably precluded her from making that strenuous opposition which she might otherwise have done.

David himself escaped to Ramah, where he acquainted Samuel with all the king's behavior to him. Samuel took him to Naioth, which seems to have been a kind of school or college of the prophets, in the neighborhood of Ramah, over which Samuel presided. Saul soon heard where he was; and so reckless was he now become, and so madly bent on his murderous object, that he would not respect even this asylum, but sent messengers to bring David to him. These, when they beheld the company of prophets, with Samuel at their head, "prophesying," or singing hymns, fell into an ecstasy, and "prophesied" in like manner. The same happened to a second and a third party. At last Saul determined to go himself; and in his rage he probably intended to slay Samuel also for sheltering David. Indeed, that the youth had gone to Samuel, and was sheltered by him, must have confirmed his conviction that David was his appointed successor, if he did not yet know, as he probably did, that the son of Jesse had actually been anointed by the prophet. But no sooner had the king beheld what had so strongly affected his messengers, than he also, as had happened to him in his happier days, "prophesied," and lay in an ecstatic trance, divested of his outer garment, all that day and night.

This gave David an opportunity to leave the neighborhood; and he repaired to Gibeah, where the king resided, and where Jonathan then was, to seek a private interview with that valuable friend. Jonathan thought himself fully acquainted with all the intentions of his father, and would not believe that he really designed the death of David. But the latter was well assured of it; and thought that Saul, having become acquainted with their friendship, had concealed his full purpose from Jonathan. It was, however, agreed between them, that the conduct of the king on an approaching occasion should be deemed to determine his ultimate intentions; and that meanwhile David should keep himself concealed. The two friends then walked forth into the fields. Jonathan then avowed to David his conviction that he, and not himself, was the destined successor of Saul; and, with rare generosity of spirit and

Throwing a Javelin.

Escape from a Window.

abandonment of self, he expressed his cheerful assent to this, and only desired to receive the pledge of David that, if himself alive when he became king, protection should be granted to him from the designs which evil men might entertain; and that if not himself living, kindness should be extended to his family for his sake. This was a matter in which he might be allowed at this time to feel more than usual anxiety, as it appears, from a comparison of dates, that a son, Mephibosheth, had lately been born to him. Reciprocally, he would pledge himself to protect the life of David, to the extent of his power, from the designs of Saul and his other enemies. These things they swore before God to each other, and entered together into a covenant of peace and love.

It seems that by this time Saul lived in considerable state. At the recurrence of the new moons, he was accustomed to entertain his principal officers at meat. Such a feast was now near at hand; and it appears that Saul, who knew that David had returned to Gibeah, expected that, notwithstanding what had passed, he would make his appearance at this feast, as it would seem that non-attendance was regarded as an offensive neglect. Most probably the king thought that David might regard the attempt which had been made upon his life as mere phrenetic impulse, not indicative of any deliberate intention against him. The first day of the feast, the place which belonged to David at the king's table was vacant; but Saul then made no remark, thinking the absence might be accidental. But when the son of Jesse made no appearance on the second day, the king put some questions to Jonathan, who excused David's absence, alleging that it was by his permission and consent. On this Saul broke forth into the grossest abuse of Jonathan, and assuring him that his succession to the throne could never be secure while David lived, concluded with, "Wherefore now send for him; for he shall surely die." And when Jonathan ventured to remonstrate, "Wherefore shall he be slain? What hath he done?" the maddened king threw his javelin to smite him. That he could thus treat his own son, on whom, in fact, all the hopes that remained to him were centred, lessens our wonder at his behavior to David, and at the other acts of madness of which he was guilty. By this Jonathan knew that the king really intended to destroy his friend. He therefore took his bow and went forth, attended by a lad, as if to shoot in the field where David lay hid; for it had been agreed upon between them that the manner in which the arrows were shot, and the expressions used by the archer to the lad who collected the arrows after they had been discharged, was to be a sign intimating to David the course he was to take; thus preventing the danger which might accrue to both from another interview. But when the unfavorable sign had been given, which he knew would render his friend a fugitive, Jonathan could not resist the desire again to commune with him before he departed. He therefore sent away the lad, and as soon as he was gone " David arose out of a place toward the south, and fell on his face toward the ground, and three times did obeisance; and they kissed each other, and wept one with another, with great lamentation."

After taking leave of Jonathan, David took his journey westward, with the intention of putting himself beyond the reach of Saul, by going to the land of the Philistines, who were not at that time in actual hostilities with the Israelites, and with whom alone the enmity of Saul was not likely to operate to his disadvantage. In his way, attended by a few young men who were attached to him, he came to the town of Nob, belonging to the priests, about twelve miles from Gibeah, and in the neighborhood of Jerusalem and Anathoth. To this place the tabernacle had at this time been removed. We are not made acquainted with the precise occasion of its removal from Shiloh; but it was probably consequent upon the destruction of that town in the war with the Philistines. At this place he was received, as his rank and renown demanded, by the high-priest Ahimelech, whose surprise at seeing him he thought himself obliged to dispel, by the false and unseemly pretence that he had been sent by the king on private business of importance. But taking notice of the presence of one Doeg, an Edomite, the chief of Saul's shepherds, by whom he doubted not that he should be betrayed, he represented to Ahimelech that his business was urgent, and begged that he would supply some refreshment to himself and his men, after which he would continue his journey. The high-priest had nothing to offer but bread which had lain a week on the table of showbread in the sanctuary; and although by the priests only this might lawfully be eaten, he was induced by the alleged urgency of the occasion to give it to David and his men. David afterward

Eastern Forms of Obeisance.

inquired for weapons; and was told there were none but the sword of Goliah, which, as a pious memorial of the victory over that proud blasphemer, had been deposited in the tabernacle. This, at his desire, was brought to him, and having girded it on, he took leave of Ahimelech, and continued his journey till he reached the Philistine city of Gath, where he presented himself or was brought before Achish, the king of that place, or rather of the state of which that place was the denominating metropolis. It does not appear that David intended himself to be known; or if so, anticipated a more favorable reception: for when he found that he was recognised, and that the courtiers ominously represented him as that David to whom the maidens of Israel had in their songs ascribed the slaughter of tens of thousands of Philistines, and thousands only to Saul, dreading the result of such recollections, David feigned himself mad, with such success that Achish exclaimed, " Lo, ye see the man is mad; why have ye brought him to me? Have I need of madmen, that ye have brought this one to play the madman in my presence? Shall such a one come into my house?" He was therefore allowed to go where he pleased. He delayed not to avail himself of this advantage, and hastened into the territory of his own tribe of Judah, where he found shelter in the cave of Adullam. He was here joined by his parents and family, who probably deemed themselves unsafe in Bethlehem; and as soon as his retreat became known in the neighborhood, his reputation attracted to him a considerable number of men hanging loose upon society, as in the somewhat analogous case of Jephthah. To understand some of their future operations under David, it is quite necessary to give them just that character, and no other, which they bear in the Scriptural record, which states that "Every one in distress, every one in debt, and every one discontented, flocked to him; and he became chief over them, and there were with him about four hundred men."

From Adullam David took an opposite direction to that which he had first followed, and went into the land of Moab. Here he was well received; for the king consented to take the parents of the outcast under his protection, until the dawning of better days. They therefore remained among the Moabites until the troubles of their son ended with the life of Saul. But, although he might himself have found greater safety in that land, it was important to his future interests that he should return to his own country, that his conduct, adventures, and persecutions, there might keep him alive in the minds of the people. He did not himself plan anything with reference to the destination intended for him ultimately; but God, who best knew by what agencies to effect his purpose, sent the prophet Gad to command him to return into the land of Judah. He obeyed, and found shelter in the forest of Hareth.

Saul soon heard of David's return and the place of his retreat, and was greatly troubled; for, as his safety could not be the object of this move from the security which Moab afforded, he inferred that he had returned with the intention of acting offensively and vindictively against him when occasion or advantage offered. He therefore called together the officers of his court; and as there was not, as yet, any building or palace in which such assemblies could be held, the king sat upon a bank, under a tamarisk tree, with a spear in his hand.* It seems that the persons present were chiefly Benjamites; and Saul, speaking as one distrustful of their fidelity, appealed to their selfish interests, asking on what grounds they, as Benjamites, could hope to be bettered by the son of Jesse; and complained that there were plots between him and his own son Jonathan, of which they knew, but that they were not sorry for him, nor would give any information to him. On this Doeg, the Edomite, informed him of the assistance which David had received at Nob from the highpriest; but omitted to state, if he knew, the certainly false grounds on which that assistance had been claimed by David and given by the priest; and added (which was not true) that Ahimelech had " inquired of God" for him. On hearing this, Saul was highly enraged, and immediately sent for Ahimelech and all the priests of his family that were at Nob. When they arrived, the king fiercely charged him with his participation in what his jealous imagination tortured into a conspiracy of David against him. Ahimelech declared that he had entertained him merely as the king's son-in-law, and one employed on the king's business, and denied that he had consulted the sacred oracle on his behalf; but Saul, without listening to his statement, commanded his followers to slay them all. A dead stillness followed this

* The spear was obviously used by him not more as a weapon than as a sceptre. As such it is several times mentioned. The earliest sceptres were, in fact, spears in many ancient nations.

order; and, finding that no one moved to obey it, the frantic king turned to Doeg and commanded him to fall upon them. The unscrupulous Edomite was ready in his obedience; and although the Israelites then present had refused to stain their own hands with the blood of the most sacred persons in the land, they had not sufficient spirit or principle to interpose in their behalf, but stood by and saw them slaughtered by Doeg and his myrmidons. Not fewer than eighty-five priests fell in this horrid massacre; and immediately after, Doeg, by Saul's order, of course, proceeded to Nob, and slew all that lived in it—man, woman, child, and beast. This was a further development of that judgment upon the house of Eli which had been pronounced of old; this was that deed in Israel of which it had been predicted that "both the ears of every one that heareth it shall tingle." The only individual of the family of the high-priest who escaped was Abiathar, one of his sons. This person repaired to David, who was deeply afflicted at the intelligence which he brought, and desired him to remain with him.

Soon after this, David heard that a party of Philistines had come up against the border-town of Keilah, with the view of taking away the produce of the harvest which the people of that town had lately gathered in. He greatly desired to march his troop to the relief of that place; but his men, who, as might be expected from their character, were by no means distinguished for their courage or subordination, declined so bold an enterprise. At last, a distinct promise of victory from the sacred oracle, consulted by Abiathar, who acted as priest, encouraged their obedience. They went and obtained a complete victory over the Philistines, delivering Keilah from the danger by which it was threatened. This and other instances of David's readiness, in his own precarious situation, to employ his resources against the enemies of his country, must have tended much to raise his character among the people, and to keep him before the public eye.

He now entered and remained in the town he had relieved, which Saul no sooner understood than he exclaimed, "God hath delivered him into my hand; for he is shut in by entering into a town that hath gates and bars;" and he delayed not to call together a powerful force, which he marched to besiege that place. But David, being apprized by the oracle that the people of Keilah, unmindful of their obligation to him, would deliver him up to the king if he remained there until his arrival, withdrew from the place at the head of a force now increased to six hundred men. When Saul heard this, he discontinued his march against Keilah.

David now sought shelter in the eastern part of Judea, toward the Dead sea. There were strong posts and obscure retreats in that quarter, among the mountains and the woods, to which he successively removed, as the motions of Saul dictated; for the king, now openly bent on his destruction, hastened to every place to which he heard that the son of Jesse had retreated, hunting him "like a partridge in the mountains." He was for some time in different parts of the wilderness of Ziph. He was sheltered by a wood in that wilderness, when Jonathan, becoming acquainted with his place of retreat, went to him, "to encourage him to trust in God." He said to him, "Fear not, for the hand of Saul my father shall not find thee; and thou shalt be king over Israel, and I shall be next thee; *and that also Saul my father knoweth.*" Again the friends renewed their covenant before Jehovah, and parted—to meet no more. There is really nothing in all history finer than this love of Jonathan to David; it was, as the latter himself found occasion to describe it, "Wonderful, passing the love of women!" It was a noble spirit with which the son of the king held close to his heart, and admitted the superior claims of, the man destined to supersede him and his in the most splendid object of human ambition, which, on ordinary principles, he might have considered his just inheritance. But his were not ordinary principles, such as swayed the mind and determined the conduct of his father. His were the true principles of the theocracy, whereby he knew that Jehovah was the true king of Israel, and cheerfully submitted to his undoubted right to appoint whom he would as his regent, even to his own exclusion; and, with generous humility, was the first to recognise and admire the superior qualities of the man on whom it was known that his forfeited destinies had fallen. Yet lest, in our admiration of Jonathan's conduct, human virtue should seem too highly exalted, it may be well to remember that the hereditary principle in civil government was as yet without precedent among the Hebrews, with whom sons had not yet learned to look to succeed their fathers in their public offices. None of the judges had transmitted their authority to their sons or relatives: and the only instance in which an attempt had been made (by Abimelech) to establish this hereditary principle had most miserably failed. But the friendship of Jonathan and David is a passage in the history of the Hebrew kingdom from which the mind reluctantly withdraws. If it occurred in a fiction, it would be pointed out as an example of most refined and consummate art, that the author represents to us in such colors of beauty and truth the person he intends to set aside, and allows him so largely to share our sympathies and admiration with the hero of his tale.

Not long after this, some inhabitants of Ziph went to Gibeah and acquainted the king with the quarter in which David lay hid. Saul was so transported with joy at the news, that he heartily blessed them as the only people who had compassion upon him in his trouble; for by this time, if not before, it seems that his morbid fancy had fully persuaded him that David was really engaged in a conspiracy to take his life, and place the crown upon his own head. But David had timely intelligence that his retreat was betrayed, and withdrew southward into the wilderness of Moan. But Saul pursued him thither, and, with the design to surround him, was already on one side of the mountain, on the other side of which David lay, when he was providentially called off by intelligence of a sudden incursion into the country by the Philistines. He went and repulsed them; and then, at the head of three thousand men, returned to follow upon the tracks of Jesse's son—so inveterately was he now bent upon his fell purpose.

Meanwhile David had removed to the district of Engeddi, toward the southwestern extremity of the Dead sea, the caverns and rocky fastnesses of which offered many secure retreats. Saul pursued him into this region, and one day entered a large cave, to repose himself during the heat of the day. Now it happened that David and his men were already in this cave; but, being in the remote and dark inner extremity, were unperceived by the king; but he, being between them and the light which entered at the cave's mouth, was seen and recognised by them. As he lay asleep, David's men joyfully congratulated him that his enemy was now completely in his power. But they knew not what manner of spirit was in the son of Jesse. "Jehovah forbid," he said to them, "that I should do this thing to my master, the anointed of Jehovah, to stretch forth my hand against him; for the anointed of Jehovah is he;" and the men were with difficulty restrained by these words from putting the king to death. But that he might know how completely his life had been in the hands of the man whose life he sought, David went and cut off the skirt of his mantle. Saul at length arose, and left the cave, and went his way. David went out and called after him, "My lord, the king!" When Saul turned, David bowed himself reverently toward the earth, and proceeded in the most respectful terms to remonstrate against the injustice with which he had been treated, and the inveteracy with which he was pursued. He charitably imputed the designs laid to his charge to the suggestions of evil-minded men; and, in proof of their utter groundlessness, related what had happened in the cave, and produced the skirt to show how entirely the king's life had been in his power. Saul's naturally good feelings were touched by this generous forbearance from one who knew that his own life was then sought by him. "Is that thy voice, my son David!" he cried, and his softened heart yielded refreshing tears, such as he had not lately been wont to shed. That which had been in David a forbearance resulting from the natural and spontaneous impulse of his own feelings, seemed to the king an act of superhuman virtue, which forced upon him the recognition that he was indeed that "worthier" man to whom the inheritance of his crown had been prophesied. Rendering good for evil was a new thing to him; and now, in the regard and admiration which it excited, he freely acknowledged the conviction he entertained,—"And now, behold, I know well that thou wilt surely be king, and that the kingdom of Israel will be established in thy hand. Swear now, therefore, to me, by Jehovah, that thou wilt not cut off my seed after me, and that thou wilt not destroy my name out of my father's house." The anxiety of the king, and even of Jonathan, on this point, seems to show (what has already appeared in the case of Abimelech) that it was even then, as it ever has been until lately, usual for oriental kings to remove by death all those whose claims to the throne might seem superior or equal to their own, or whose presence might offer an alternative to the discontented: the intense horror with which the Hebrews regarded the prospect or fear of genealogical extinction, also contributes to explain the anxiety which both Saul and

Jonathan felt on this point more than on any other. David took the oath required from him; Saul then returned to Gibeah, and David, who had little confidence in the permanency of the impression he had made, remained in his strongholds.

Very soon after this, Samuel died, at the advanced age of ninety-two years (B. C. 1072), after he had judged Israel fifty years, that is, twelve years alone, and thirty-eight years jointly with Saul; for there is no doubt that he retained his authority as civil judge to the end of his life. The death of this good man was lamented as a common calamity by all true Israelites, who assembled in great numbers to honor his funeral. He was buried in the garden of his own house at Ramah.

As David immediately after removed much further southward, even " into the wilderness of Paran," it would seem that, having no confidence in Saul's fits of right feeling, he was fearful of the consequences of the absence of that degree of moral restraint upon him which had existed while the prophet lived. The southern country offers, in the proper season, excellent pastures, away to which those of Judah, who had " large possessions of cattle," were wont to send their flocks during a part of the year. The advantage offered by the free use of these open pastures was, however, in some degree counterbalanced by the danger from the prowling Arab tribes with which they sometimes came in contact. David probably supported his men during the eight months of his stay in this region by acting against those tribes, and making spoil of their cattle. And as their hand was against every man, it was natural that every man's hand should be against them; the rather, as we may be sure, from their general conduct, that they lost no occasions of oppressing or plundering the people inhabiting, or pasturing their flocks, along or near the southern frontier. Thus the presence of David's troop was, for that reason, a great advantage to the shepherds, as he had by this time secured sufficient control over his men to oblige them to respect the property of the Israelites. And this was, at least in the feelings of the people, no small thing in a body of men living abroad with swords in their hands, and obliged, as they were, to collect their subsistence in the best way they could. Among those who were advantaged by this, none were more so than the shepherds of Nabal, a man of large possessions in Carmel. When David returned northward, he heard that Nabal was making great preparations for the entertainment of his people during the shearing of his three thousand sheep; and being then greatly pressed for provisions, he sent some of his young men to this person to salute him respectfully in his name, and to request some small supply out of the abundance he had provided. Now in point of fact, according to all usage, Nabal ought to have anticipated this request, as soon as he learned that one who had protected his property in the wilderness was then in his neighborhood. But Nabal was "churlish and evil in all his manners, and irritable as a dog." This character, his insulting answer to the message fully supported:—" Who is David? and who is the son of Jesse? *There be many servants now-a-days that break away, every man from his master.* Shall I then take my bread, and my water, and my flesh, which I have killed for my shearers, and give it to men whom I know not whence they be ?" When this answer was brought back to David, he was highly enraged, and ordered his men to gird on their swords; and, with four hundred of them (leaving two hundred to protect the baggage), he set forth with the rash and cruel purpose of destroying the churl and all that belonged to him. The provocation, although very great, and not likely to be overlooked by a military man, was certainly not such as to justify this barbarous design. Its execution was, however, averted by Abigail, the wife of Nabal, who is described as " a woman of good understanding, and beautiful in form." Those shepherds who had been in the wilderness with the flocks, and were sensible of the value of that protection which David's troop had rendered, greatly disapproved of their master's conduct. They therefore reported the whole matter to their mistress, who appears to have had that real authority in the household which a woman of sense always has had in the house of even a brutal fool. She concurred in their apprehensions as to the probable consequences, and with a promptitude which bears out the character given to her, decided on the proper steps to avert them. While Nabal was eating and drinking, even to drunkenness, at the feast, she made up an elegant and liberal present, consisting of two hundred loaves of bread, two skin-bottles of wine, five measures of parched corn, five sheep ready dressed, two hundred clusters of raisins, and two hundred cakes of figs; and, having placed all this on asses, she set forth with suitable attendance to meet the enraged hero. She soon met him

Presents to a Bedouin Chief.

and his men, on full march to Carmel;
and after rendering him her most respectful homage, she spoke to him with such
fine tact and prudence, that his passion
grew calm under her hand; and she convinced him that the deed which he contemplated would cause the weight of innocent blood to lie heavy on his conscience
in after days. Being thus made to feel
that he had allowed the bitterness of "a
blockhead's insult" * to sink too deeply in
his soul, he felt really thankful that his fell
purpose had been interrupted:—"Blessed
be Jehovah, the God of Israel," he said,
" who sent thee this day to meet me; and
blessed be thy advice, and blessed be thou,
who hast kept me this day from coming
to shed blood, and from avenging myself
with mine own hand."

Abigail returned to her husband, and
the next day acquainted him with the
steps she had taken, and the imminent
danger into which his churlishness had
brought him and his. The view which
was presented to his mind of the evil
which had hung over his head struck him
with such intense dread and horror, that
in a few days he died of a broken heart.
When this came to the ears of David,
who had been much charmed by the good
sense and beauty of Abigail, he sent to
her, and she consented to become his wife.
He had previously married Ahinoam of
Jezreel, after Saul had given Michal to

* "Fate never wounds more deep the gen'rous heart,
'an when a blockhead's insult points the dart."
                                    JOHNSON.

another. Polygamy was not expressly forbidden by the law; neither did it receive any sanction therefrom. It was a matter of existing usage with which the law did not interfere; although it discouraged the formation, by the kings, of such extensive harems as the kings of the East have been wont to possess: and both David and his son Solomon had ample occasion to lament those besotting passions which led them to neglect this injunction, as well as to learn that there is in this matter an obvious social law which can not with impunity be transgressed.

Soon after this David removed to his former place of shelter, in the wilderness of Ziph. While he remained there, Saul justified the doubts which the son of Jesse, who well knew his character, entertained of the continuance of his good resolutions; for he again came to seek him at the head of three thousand men. But this only gave David another opportunity of evincing the true and generous loyalty of his own character. For one night, while the king lay asleep in the midst of his men, with his spear stuck in the ground at his head, to mark the station of the chief, David entered his camp, attended by Abishai (brother to the subsequently celebrated Joab), and, without being noticed, penetrated to the very spot where the king lay. Abishai thought this a fine opportunity of ending all their troubles with the life of their persecutor; and begged David to permit him to transfix the sleeping king with his spear. But, to the pious hero, "a divinely appointed king, although his enemy, was a sacred person. To lay violent hands on him, and to open a way to the throne by regicide, was a crime which he justly abhorred. What God had promised him he was willing to wait for, till He who had promised should deliver it to him in the ordinary course of his providence."[*] He therefore checked the misdirected zeal of Abishai, and withdrew with him, taking away the spear which was planted at Saul's head, and the vessel of water which stood there for his use. David then went and stationed himself at the edge of an opposite cliff overlooking the camp of Saul, and calling by name to Abner, the cousin and chief commander of the king, told him he was worthy of death for the careless manner in which he guarded the royal person. As he went on reproaching Abner, Saul, as he expected, recognised his voice, and guessing that he had again been spared when in his power, called out, "Is that thy voice, my son David?" and was answered, "It is my voice, my lord, O king!" David then proceeded with much energy, but in the most respectful language, to remonstrate against the treatment he received, and produced the evidence of the spear and water-jug, as evincing the value of the king's life in his eyes. The result was the same as it had been on a similar occasion before: Saul's heart was touched. He acknowledged that he had "acted foolishly, and erred exceedingly;" and after blessing David, returned to Gibeah.

David had before this formed the intention of again withdrawing to the Philistines; for in his remonstrance with Saul he had laid the responsibility of this measure upon his persecutors:—"If Jehovah hath stirred thee up against me, let him accept an offering; but if they be the children of men, accursed be they before Jehovah, for they now drive me out from abiding in the inheritance of Jehovah." He must not be allowed, however, thus easily to rid himself of the responsibility of so ill-advised and desperate an expedient, in which he neglected to ask counsel of God, but followed the impulse of his own apprehensions; and from the natural and obvious consequences of which he could only escape by acts of equivocation, hypocrisy, and ingratitude, which do no honor to his name. However, we are to regard David, in all this portion of his life, as a learner, as one who was in the course of being trained to rule wisely, by various disciplines, distresses, and errors;—for even the errors of conduct into which men fall, by having placed themselves in a false position through too confident a reliance on their own judgment, are not among the least profitable experiences which they obtain, and which go toward the ripening of their minds. But, undoubtedly, it had been better for David, and more becoming, had he remained in his own country, relying upon the protection of that good Providence by which he had hitherto been preserved.

On reaching Gath, with his six hundred men, David was well received by the king, who appears to have been the same Achish in whose presence he had formerly played the madman. The Hebrew chief soon took occasion to request the Philistine king to assign him some town in which he might reside apart with his people; and the king, with generous and unsuspecting confidence, made over to him, to his full

* Jahn, i. 102.

and exclusive possession, the small border town of Ziklag, which was situated not far from the brook Besor. Here he resided one year and four months, or until the death of Saul. From this place he undertook excursions against the ancient predatory enemies of Israel, the Amalekites, the Geshurites, and the Gezrites, who roved about in Arabia Petræa, on the seacoast as far as Pelusium, and on the southern frontier of the tribe of Judah. In all these excursions he utterly destroyed man, woman, and child, and took possession of the cattle and apparel, of which their wealth consisted. The exterminating character which he gave to this warfare was to prevent the Philistines from learning that he had been acting against their allies and friends; and he always pretended to Achish that his expedition had been against the Israelites and their allies, by which he established himself firmly in the confidence of that king. For the cool manner in which the son of Jesse poured out innocent blood to cover a deliberate and designing falsehood, we have no excuse to offer. He must bear the blame for ever.

In those days the Philistine states joined their forces for war against Israel; and David, having by his pretences impressed upon Achish the conviction that he now detested his own people, and was detested by them, was driven to the dreadful alternative of either taking the field with the Philistines and fighting against his brethren, or else of appearing ungrateful to Achish, and perhaps of occasioning the destruction of his family and himself. But from this difficulty he was extricated by the not unreasonable jealousy of the other Philistine princes, who expected he might turn against them in the battle in order to reconcile himself to his master. Achish was much hurt at such suspicions against one on whom he so perfectly relied, but was reluctantly obliged to dismiss him from the expedition.

On returning to Ziklag, David found the city pillaged and reduced to ashes. The Amalekites, Geshurites, and Gezrites, had taken the opportunity of his absence in another direction thus to avenge themselves for his former inroads upon them. They did not, however, retaliate to the full extent; for although " they took the men and women who were in it captive, they slew not any, either great or small, but carried them away." David's two wives were among the captives. His men were frantic at the loss of their families and substance, and at first talked of stoning their leader, whom they regarded as at least the remote cause of this calamity. But they were at last appeased, and set out in pursuit of the spoilers, notwithstanding the fatigue occasioned by their previous march. Two hundred of the men were unable to proceed· farther than the brook Besor; and David, leaving them there, continued the pursuit with the remaining four hundred. On their way they fell in with a man half dead with illness, hunger, and thirst. Having refreshed him with food and drink, they learned that he was an Egyptian, a slave to one of the party they pursued; but that having fallen ill three days before, his master had left him—to live or die, as might happen—and that since then no bread or water had passed his lips. He gave an account of the operations of the horde; and, when pressed, agreed to conduct the Hebrew party to the spot at which he knew that they intended to repose. When that spot was reached, the nomades were enjoying themselves in full security, as they supposed themselves beyond the reach of pursuit, and could not know that David would have returned to Ziklag so soon. They were thus easily overthrown; and not only did the Hebrews recapture all that they had taken, but gained besides so considerable a booty, that David was enabled to send presents to all the rulers in Judah who were favorable to his cause.

The four hundred men who had continued the pursuit were unwilling to share the additional spoil with the two hundred who had tarried by the brook Besor, although willing to restore their own property to them. But David took the opportunity of establishing the useful principle that all the persons engaged in an expedition should share equally, whatever part they took in it; or, in other words, that those whose presence protected the baggage should be equally benefited by a victory with those who went to the fight.

The present campaign of the Philistines against the Israelites was one of those large operations which nations can in general only undertake after long intervals of rest. There seems, indeed, during the reign of Saul, to have been always a sort of desultory and partial warfare between the two nations; but it had produced no measure comparable to this, which was intended to be decisive, and was calculated to tax to the utmost the resources of the belligerents. When Saul surveyed, from the

heights of Gilboa, the formidable army
which the Philistine had brought into the
plain of Esdraelon—that great battle-field
of nations—his heart failed him. Presenti-
ments of coming events cast deep shadows
over his troubled mind. He sought counsel of God. But God had forsaken him—
left him to his own devices—and answered
him not, "either by dreams, or by urim,
or by prophets."

The crimes of Saul arose from his disloyalty to Jehovah, in his reluctance to
acknowledge him as the true king of Israel. But as his God he worshipped him,
and had no tendency toward those idolatries by which so many subsequent kings
were disgraced. All idolatry and idolatrous
acts were discouraged and punished by
him. In obedience to the law (Deut. xviii.
10, 11), he banished from the land all the
diviners and wizards he could find. But
now, in his dismay, he directed his attendants to find out a woman skilful in necro-
mancy, that he might seek through her the
information which the Lord refused to
give. One was found at Endor, a town not
far from the camp in Gilboa; and to her
he repaired by night, disguised, with two
attendants, and desired her to evoke the
spirit of Samuel, that, in this dread emergency, he might ask counsel of him. Whatever might be the nature of the woman's
art, and her design in undertaking to fulfil
his wish—whether she meant to impose
on Saul by getting some accomplice to per-
sonate Samuel, who had only been dead
two years, and whose person must have
become well known to the Israelites during

Bedouins with Captives and Spoil.

his long administration—or whether she expected a demoniacal spirit to give him an answer; it appears from a close examination of the text, that, to the great astonishment of the woman herself, and before she had time to utter any of her incantations, the spirit of Samuel was permitted to appear, in a glorified form, and ominously clad in that mantle in which was the rent that signified the rending of the kingdom from the family of Saul. When the figure appeared, the king *knew* that it was Samuel, and bowed himself to the ground before him. From that awful and passionless form he heard that the doom declared long since was *now* to be accomplished;—to-morrow Israel should be given up to the sword of the Philistines—to-morrow Saul and his sons should be numbered with the dead. At these heavy tidings the king fell down as one dead, for he had touched no food that night or the preceding day, and was with difficulty restored to his senses, and refreshed by the woman and his attendants.

The next day all that had been foretold was accomplished. Israel fled before the Philistine archers; and Saul and his sons, unable to stem the retreating torrent, fled also. The three sons of the king, JONATHAN, Abinadab, and Melchi-shua, were slain. Saul himself was grievously wounded by the archers; and that he might not fall alive into the hands of the Philistines, and be subjected to their insults, he desired his armor-bearer to strike him through with his sword; and when that faithful follower refused, he fell upon his own sword: and the example was followed by the armor-bearer, when he beheld his lord lying dead before him. "So Saul died, and his three sons, and his armor-bearer, and all his men, that same day together."

The next day, when the Philistines came to collect the spoils of the slain, they found the bodies of Saul and his three sons. The indignity with which they treated the remains of these brave men has no previous example. They cut off their heads, and hung their bodies to the wall of the town of Bethshan, near the Jordan. Their heads and armor they sent into Philistia, as trophies of their triumph, by the hand of the messengers who were despatched to publish it in their temples and their towns. The bodies of Saul and his sons were soon stolen away by night from the wall of Bethshan, by some valiant men of Jabesh, on the opposite side of the river, where a grateful remembrance was cherished of the king's first military exploit, whereby the people of that town were delivered from the loss of their liberty and their eyes. To preclude any attempt at the recovery and continued insult of the bodies, the people burnt them, and buried the collected bones and ashes under a tamarisk-tree.

CHAPTER XVII.

On the third day of David's return to Ziklag a man arrived in haste, with his clothes rent, and earth upon his head, and laid at the feet of David the crown and armlet which Saul had worn. He told, truly, that Israel had fled before the Philistines, and that Saul and his sons were slain; but thinking to win royal rewards from the son of Jesse, he boasted that he had slain Saul with his own hand. The truth was probably that he had found the body of Saul in the night after the battle, and had taken from it the royal insignia which he brought to David. His expectations were grievously disappointed; for David, believing his statement, caused him to be put to death, as one who had not feared to slay the Lord's anointed. The man was an Amalekite. David mourned and fasted for the desolation of Israel, and he lamented the death of his beloved Jonathan, and even of Saul, in a most affecting and beautiful elegy, which we may here introduce as a specimen of the poetical compositions of one whose rank among the poets of the Hebrews is fully equal to that which he occupies among their kings :—*

"O, antelope of Israel! pierced on thy high place!
How are the mighty fallen!
 Tell it not in Gath;
Publish it not in the streets of Askelon;
Lest the daughters of the Philistines rejoice,
Lest the daughters of the uncircumcised triumph.

* The version now given is that of Boothroyd, altered in some of the lines.

> Ye mountains of Gilboa, on you be no dew,
> Nor rain, nor fields of first-fruits;
> Since there hath been vilely cast away,
> The shield of the mighty, the shield of Saul,
> The armor of him anointed with oil.
>   From the blood of the slain,
> From the fat of the mighty,
> The bow of Jonathan was not held back,
> Nor did the sword of Saul return in vain.
> Saul and Jonathan!
> In mutual love were they in life united,
> And in their death they were not separated.
> Swifter than eagles, stronger than lions were they!
>   Ye daughters of Israel weep over Saul,
> Who clothed you pleasantly in scarlet,
> And put golden ornaments upon your robes.
> How are the mighty fallen in the midst of battle!
>   O Jonathan, slain on thy own mountains!
> I am grieved for thee, O Jonathan, my brother!
> Very dear to me wast thou:
> Wonderful was thy love to me,
> Surpassing the love of women.
>   How are the mighty fallen!
> And the weapons of war perished!"

That he mourned even for Saul, will only be attributed to hypocrisy by those who are themselves incapable of such magnanimity, and are determined to forget that David, during the life of his persecutor, always respected him as a king appointed by God, and twice spared him when he had his life completely in his power.

With the approbation of the Lord, whom he consulted, David now removed, with his family and friends, to Hebron, where the rulers of the tribe of Judah, with views altogether theocratical, awarded the sceptre to him, as one whom God had already designated as king. David was at this time thirty years of age.

But no other tribe concurred with Judah in this important step. On the contrary, all the other tribes elected Saul's only surviving son, Eshbaal, as he was originally named (1 Chron. xiii. 33, ix. 39), but nicknamed Ishbosheth (*a man of shame*), from his weakness and incapacity, which, it would appear, saved his life, by precluding him from being present at the battle in which his brothers perished. This measure was probably promoted by that radical jealousy between the tribes of Judah and Ephraim, which prevented the latter (which took the lead among the other tribes) from concurring in the appointing a king of the rival tribe, or indeed from heartily sympathizing in any measure which that tribe originated. But the prime agent in this schism was Abner, the commander of the army, who had drawn off the remnant of the defeated army to the other side the Jordan, and there, at Mahanaim, proclaimed Ishbosheth king. Abner was a bold and able, but unprincipled man; and doubtless expected to govern in the name of his feeble nephew. And he did so.

For two years no hostile acts between the two kingdoms took place. But war was at length provoked by Abner, who crossed the Jordan with the intention to subdue the tribe of Judah to the authority of Ishbosheth. David sent Joab to meet him; and the opposing forces met near the pool of Gibeon. But the men on each side felt that they were all Israelites, and were reluctant to fight against each other. The two generals, therefore, thought of a device which has often been employed in the east, and elsewhere, to excite tribes or nations to battle, when relationship or other causes made them reluctant or wanting in zeal. Twelve men on each side were matched to fight against each other between the two armies; and so well were they matched that they no sooner came within reach of one another, than each man seized his antagonist by the head and sheathed his sword in his body, so that they were all killed upon the spot. This kindled the opposing forces, and a desperate and most sanguinary battle followed. It ended in the defeat of Abner, who was himself obliged to flee for his life. As he fled he was singled out by Joab's brother Asahel, "who was as swift of foot as any antelope of the field;" and he pursued him, without allowing himself to be drawn aside by other objects. He was close at the heels of Abner, when the latter looked back, and finding who it was, he became most anxious to avoid such a blood-feud as would arise between him and Joab, in case he slew his brother, even in his own defence. He therefore entreated Asahel to turn back that he might not be compelled to smite him to the ground. But finding that he was still pursued, and that it was impossible to outstrip his pursuer, he struck at him with the hinder point of

17

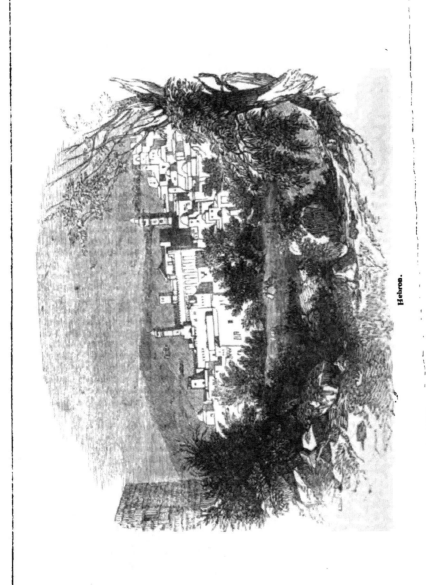

Hebron.

The Pursuer slain.

his spear,* and with such force tha, the weapon passed through him and came out behind. The pursuit of Abner and the other fugitives was continued by Joab and his other brother Abishai until sunset, by which time they were got as far as the hill of Ammah. Here the Benjamites (always valiant, and jealously attached to the house of Saul) rallied again under Abner, and posting themselves on the rising of the hill, stood prepared to make a stout defence; but their general, who was weary of fighting, called to Joab, and begged him to put a stop to the slaughter of his brethren, whose destruction could not but cause bitterness in the end. Although Joab had determined to continue the pursuit all night, he had the sense to hearken to his advice, and caused the trumpet to sound a retreat. After this, Abner and his men took the way to Mahanaim, and Joab returned to Hebron. Abner lost three hundred and sixty men in this action, while on David's side only nineteen were killed. The war having thus commenced was continued for several years; but it appears to have been a small irritating warfare, which never came to any important or decisive engagement between the opposing parties. It was, however, attended with this result, that the cause of David was gathering strength every day, while the house of Saul daily

_____

* The spear is armed at the lower end with a pointed iron, whereby it is stuck into the ground while the owner is in repose

became weaker and weaker. Indeed, it seems to have required all the great talents of Abner to keep the kingdom of Ishbosheth together.

Meanwhile David reigned prosperously in Hebron.* He increased the number of his wives to six, by all of whom sons were born to him in that place. In this small kingdom his good and prosperous government, together with the knowledge that he had been divinely appointed to reign over all Israel, appears insensibly to have inclined the other tribes toward him, by which, more even than by war, his cause gathered that strength which that of Ishbosheth lost. Abner was fully sensible that without himself the kingdom of his nephew would fall to pieces, or rather pass quietly into the hands of David. He rated his services at their full value; and although we do not ourselves see cause to suspect, as some have done, that he contemplated taking the crown to himself, it is certain that he was not disposed to consider himself responsible to the king for his conduct, or to allow any of his proceedings to be questioned by him. Now Ishbosheth had heard that Abner carried on a criminal intercourse with one of Saul's concubines, named Rizpah: and as, according to the usages of the East, the concubines of a deceased sovereign became the property of the successor in so strong and peculiar a sense, that such an act as that imputed to Abner might be interpreted into a design upon the crown,† or at least was an insulting encroachment upon the peculiar rights of royalty, even the timid Ishbosheth was roused to question Abner on the subject. It is not very clear whether the charge was true or false; but it is clear that this overbearing personage was astonished and disgusted that the king should dare to question any part of his conduct. He rose into a towering passion: "Am I, who, against Judah, have to this day shown kindness to the house of Saul, thy father, and to his brethren and to his friends, and have not delivered thee into the hands of David, such a dog's head that thou chargest me to-day with a fault concerning this woman? God do so to Abner, and more also, if, as Jehovah hath sworn to David, I do not so to him, by transferring the dominion of the house of Saul, and to set up the throne of David over Israel and over Judah, from Dan even to Beersheba." From this it seems that even Abner knew that he had acted against a higher duty, in setting up Ishbosheth in opposition to David; but this can not justify the grounds on which he *now* declared his intention to act against him.

---

* HEBRON is an ancient city of Palestine, situated in the heart of the hill-country of Judea, about twenty-seven miles southwest from Jerusalem. Originally it was called Kirjath-Arba, or the city of Arba, " which Arba was a great man among the Anakims." (Josh. xiv. 15.) In the vicinity of this place Abraham abode, after he parted with Lot (Gen. xiii. 18), and bought a field with a cave in which to bury his dead. (Gen. xxiii. 3-20.) Besides Abraham and Sarah, his son Isaac, his grandson Jacob, with their wives Rebekah and Leah, and his great grandson Joseph, were severally interred here. (Gen. xxiii. 19, xxv. 10, xlix. 29-33, l. 12, 13.) When the Hebrews invaded Palestine, Hebron was the residence of a king (Josh. xii. 10) named Hoham, who confederated with four other Canaanitish kings against Israel; but they were all discomfited and destroyed by Joshua. (Josh. x. 3, 4, 22-27.) After which the city, being taken, was assigned to Caleb (Josh. xix. 6-11) agreeably to a promise given him by Moses. (Numb. xiii. 30-33, xix. 5, 24.) Subsequently it was made a city of refuge, and given to the priests. (Josh. xxi. 11, xx. 7.) Afterward, when David succeeded Saul on the throne of Israel, he selected Hebron for his royal residence, and continued there until Jerusalem was captured from the Jebusites. (2 Sam. ii. 1, v. 4-9.; 1 Chron. xii. xiii.) On the division of the kingdom under Rehoboam, Hebron fell to the share of the king of Judah. (2 Chron. xi. 10.)

Hebrew, Habroun, or, according to the Arabic orthography followed by the moderns, El Hhalil, is a flourishing town, the flat-roofed houses of which are closely jammed together. It contains about four hundred families of Arabs. The hill above it is composed of limestone rock, partially covered with vines; and its end is clothed with a wood of olives. The hill beyond the mosque (which edifice forms a prominent object in our view) is more barren; and in the fore-ground there are masses of buildings thrown down and scattered in every direction, this portion of the town having been destroyed a few years since. The inhabitants are engaged in perpetual hostilities with those of Bethlehem, on which account it is less frequently visited by pilgrims. A splendid church was erected over the graves of the patriarchs by the emperess Helena: it has long been converted into a Turkish mosque. According to Ali Bey, who visited it in 1807, the ascent to it is by a large and fine staircase leading to a long gallery, the entrance to which is by a small court. Toward the left is a portico, resting upon square pillars. The vestibule of the temple contains two rooms, one of which is called the tomb of Abraham, the other that of Sarah. In the body of the church, between two large pillars on the right, is seen a small recess, in which is the sepulchre of Isaac, and in a similar one upon the left is that of his wife. On the opposite side of the court is another vestibule, which has also two rooms, respectively called the tombs of Jacob and his wife. At the extremity of the portico, on the right hand, is a door leading to a sort of long gallery, which still serves for a mosque; and passing thence, is observed another room, said to contain the ashes of Joseph. All the sepulchres of the patriarchs are covered with rich carpets of green silk, magnificently embroidered with gold; those of their wives are red, embroidered in like manner. The sultans of Constantinople furnish these carpets, which are renewed from time to time. Ali Bey counted nine, one over the other, upon the sepulchre of Abraham. The rooms also which contain the tombs are covered with rich carpets: the entrance to them is guarded by iron gates, and wooden doors plated with silver, having bolts and padlocks of the same metal. More than a hundred persons are employed in the service of this Mohammedan temple. The population of Hebron is considerable: the inhabitants manufacture glass lamps, which are exported to Egypt. Provisions are abundant, and there is a considerable number of shops.

† See instances of this in the case of Absalom (2 Sam. xx. 23) and Adonijah, 1 Kings, ii. 13-25.

What he had said was no vain threat, although he was probably willing afterward that the son of Saul should take it for an unmeaning outbreak of passion. He sent messengers to David to enter into a treaty with him, under which he would engage to use his great influence in bringing all Israel to acknowledge him as king; and after this he found a pretence for going himself unsuspectedly to Hebron to complete the agreement and arrange the steps to be taken. David had sent to Ishbosheth to desire him to restore to him his wife Michal, whom Saul had given to another. He had a perfect right to make this demand, if so inclined,—the rather as she had thus been disposed of against her own wish; but we may suppose that he was particularly induced to reclaim her at this juncture, in consideration of the satisfaction the measure was likely to give to those attached to the family of Saul. As this claim was doubtless supported by Abner, it was granted; and having obtained an order to demand her from her present husband, that personage himself undertook to escort her to David. From this transaction it would seem that the war had latterly been allowed to die away, although without any concession or treaty having been made on either side. That he was escorting the daughter of Saul to David, proved to Abner a favorable opportunity, on his way, of explaining his present sentiments to the elders of the tribes through which he passed; especially to those of Benjamin, which was naturally the most attached to the house of Saul, while his own influence in it was the greatest. He dwelt strongly on the public benefits which might be expected from the government of one who had been expressly nominated by Jehovah to the kingdom; and such a presentation, coming from such a quarter, coupled with the favorable dispositions toward David which had grown up during his reign in Hebron, was attended with such effect, that Abner was authorized to make overtures to him in behalf of the tribes which had hitherto adhered to the house of Saul.

Abner was received with great distinction and royally feasted by David; and after the business on which he really came had been settled to his satisfaction, he departed with the intention of inducing the tribes to concur in giving David a public invitation to take the crown of Israel.

Joab had been absent from Hebron during this visit of Abner; but he returned immediately after Abner had departed, and was deeply displeased when he learned what had occurred. Through the energy of his character, his abilities and experience in the affairs of peace and war, his influence and popularity with the army which was under his command, and his unquestioned devotion to the interests of David, this man had great authority with the king. His standing, indeed, in the kingdom of Judah, had much resemblance to that of Abner in the other kingdom; nor were their characters altogether unlike. In the points of difference, the advantage was on the side of Abner; for his experience in military and public affairs was larger, from which, together with his near relationship to Saul and his son, and the high stations he had occupied under them, his influence with the people was far greater than that which Joab or any other man in Israel could pretend to; and hence his greater power at this time of rendering essential services to the king of Judah. Abner and Joab also served very different masters; and thus it happened that while Abner was, in the public eye, the greatest man in the kingdom of Israel, Joab was in that of Judah only the greatest man next to David. Upon the whole, Abner was the only man in the country of whom Joab had cause to be afraid, and by whom it was likely that his own influence would be superseded in case the two kingdoms were united through his instrumentality. It was probably more from such considerations than any other that his displeasure at the intercourse between David and Abner arose. He went instantly to the king, and reproached him for allowing himself to be imposed upon by the able uncle of Ishbosheth, declaring his belief that the true object of his visit was to obtain such information concerning his state and resources as he might afterward employ against him. He then went out and sent a messenger after Abner to call him back in the name of the king. As he returned, Joab took care to meet him near the gate, and drew him aside as if to speak to him privately, and while he was entirely unguarded and unsuspicious, gave him a treacherous stab, of which he instantly died. The history describes this as an act of blood-revenge for the death of his brother Asahel by the hand of Abner; and while allowing him the full benefit of this motive, it is hard to believe that envy and jealousy sharpened not the dagger of the avenger. It must be conceded, nevertheless, that the existence of a blood-feud between them extenuated if it did not justify the act of Joab in the eyes of all Israel.

It was, in fact, according to the strict ideas of that barbarous institution, the imperative duty of Joab to shed the blood of Abner, who had slain his brother; and that Abner himself knew that the death of Asahel would be attended with this result, is evinced by his anxiety to avoid the fatal necessity of slaying his pursuer; for if the man-slayer is known, the avenger is not bound to make any distinction as to the circumstances under which his relative is slain: and at the present day, the one who slays another in battle is pursued by the avenger equally with the murderer. The extent to which the law of Moses had interfered with this custom only provided for the safety of the man-slayer while in a city of refuge. Hebron was a city of refuge; and if Joab had slain Abner *within* that city, the law would have allowed David to treat him as a murderer. This Joab knew; and hence his meeting Abner at the gate, and drawing him aside before he entered the city. These details we judge necessary, to show that those who most suffered from the death of Abner, and abhorred the manner in which it was inflicted, knew that his offence was not punishable by the king or by the law; and hence that it was *not merely* the rank and influence of Joab which prevented David from calling him to account for this barbarous deed. Perhaps *he could not* have punished Joab in any case; but it is important to know, that in the present case the law, custom, and public opinion, did not require or permit him to do so.

The resentment of David was nevertheless very great. Like other eastern sovereigns, he must have been impressed with the evils of this custom of blood-revenge, and the extent to which it interfered with good government; nor was he insensible to the insult offered to himself, in the present and other instances, by "the sons of Zeruiah," Joab and Abishai, and the high hand with which they wrought their own will. "I am this day weak," he said, "though an anointed king; and these men, the sons of Zeruiah, are too stubborn for me. Jehovah will reward the evil-doer according to his evil deeds." As it was of the highest importance to him that he should be clear of any suspicion of having had any part in the death of Abner, he publicly, "before Jehovah," declared himself guiltless of the blood which had been shed, and invoked the full burden of that blood on Joab and on his house. He ordered a public act of solemn mourning, in which he himself took a prominent part: and at the funeral he followed the body, as chief mourner, to the grave, where he stood weeping, and where he lamented, in elegiac verse, over the prince and great man who had that day fallen in Israel.

This conduct of David tended still further to satisfy and conciliate the tribes attached to the house of Saul; and by them the murder of Abner was never imputed to him. Indeed, the event must, at the time, have seemed to himself and others anything but advantageous for his cause. But we, who have his whole history before us, can see that the manner in which he ultimately became king over all Israel, by the free and unsolicited choice of the tribes, was more honorable and safe to him, and more becoming his divine appointment, than the same result brought about through the exertions of Abner, whose conduct, as between David and Ishbosheth, must have seemed very equivocal, and could, at the best, have been but "traitorously honest."*

When Ishbosheth heard of Abner's death (without being aware of the plot in which he was engaged), he felt that the right arm of his kingdom's strength was broken. Others felt this also: and the conviction that the son of Saul could not govern the troubled kingdom without Abner, grew stronger every day among the tribes, and directed their eyes to David as the only person under whom they could expect to realize the benefits the nation had expected to enjoy under a regal government. This feeling, this tendency of the nation toward David, was perceived, even in the court of Ishbosheth; and two of his officers, brothers, determined to anticipate the course which events were taking, by the assassination of their master, expecting by this act to deserve high rewards and honors from the king of Judah. Accordingly, they stole into his chamber, while, according to the universal custom of the East, he slept there during the mid-day heat. They pierced him as he slept, and then took off his head, with which they escaped unperceived, as at that time of the day most of the people were asleep. The murderers sped to Hebron, and laid the head of Saul's son at the feet of David, with the words, "Behold the head of Ishbosheth the son of Saul thine enemy, who sought thy life. Jehovah hath this day avenged my

* Bishop Hall

lord the king of Saul and of his seed." Astounding to them was the answer—"As Jehovah liveth, who hath redeemed my soul out of every distress! if, when one told me, saying, Behold, Saul is dead, thinking that he brought good tidings, I took hold of him and slew him at Ziklag, when he expected that I should have given him a reward for his tidings;—how much more when wicked men have slain a just person in his own house, upon his own bed, shall I not now require his blood from your hand, and destroy you from the earth?" And with these words he commanded his attendants to remove them to an ignominious death. The head of Ishbosheth he ordered to be deposited in the sepulchre of Abner.

The kingdom of Israel was now without even the appearance of a head, nor was there any remaining member of the family of Saul whom the most zealous adherents of that fallen house could dream of supporting in opposition to David. Saul had indeed left some sons by concubines, but they were living in obscurity, and even their existence was scarcely known to the people. Jonathan also had left one son, but he was a mere boy and lame. He was five years old when Saul and his sons perished in the battle of Gilboa, and he became lame from a fall which he received when his nurse fled with him, as soon as the tidings of that overthrow were brought to the house of Saul and Jonathan. His name was Mephibosheth.

David had reigned seven years and a half in Hebron, when, after the deaths of Abner and Ishbosheth, the crown of all Israel seemed to devolve upon him, as naturally as by an act of succession. It was probably the result of a unanimous decision in a great council of the eleven tribes, that those tribes sent an embassy to David in Hebron to invite him to assume the general government of the nation. This they did on the grounds of, 1, his military claim, as one who had often led them to victory in the days of Saul; and, 2, of his theocratical claim, as one who had been expressly nominated by God to govern Israel. By this we see that the people were on this occasion careful to recognise the theocracy, since they rested their preference of him on his having been nominated to the kingdom by Jehovah, and having proved himself worthy of it during the reign of Saul. The studious avoidance of all notice of the seven years in which the tribes had been separately ruled seems to intimate a desire that this measure should be formally regarded as following the death of Saul. David intimated his readiness to receive the honor designed for him, and to accede to the conditions on which the crown was to be held. The rulers of the eleven tribes, therefore, at the head of large bodies of the best trained men in the several tribes, described as "men that could keep rank," who were chosen to represent the whole of their several tribes in the great national act of inauguration, repaired to Hebron to make David king. The number amounted to not less than three hundred and forty thousand, and the enumeration in the book of Chronicles (1 Chron. xii. 23, *ad fin.*) is accompanied with several remarks, which the scantiness of our information concerning the *distinctive* character of the tribes makes interesting. It appears that many members of the tribe of Judah had adhered to the house of Saul, and abode within its dominions; for, on the present occasion, six thousand eight hundred men of that tribe, armed with shield and spear, came with the others to submit to David. There were seven thousand one hundred Simeonites of valor. The Levites sent four thousand six hundred; and there were three thousand seven hundred priests, headed by Jehoiada, the son of Benaiah; besides whom came Zadok at the head of twenty-two chiefs of his father's house. This Zadok, of the old pontifical line of Eleazer, is the same who was long after made sole high-priest by Solomon, to the final exclusion of the house of Eli; but, on the present occasion, he is particularly noticed as "a young man, mighty in valor," which shows—as indeed appears in the history—that the pursuits of the Levites, and even of the Aaronites, were not exclusively of an ecclesiastical and civil nature. From Benjamin came three thousand men; but the greater part of this tribe held back, still cherishing a lingering and futile attachment to the house of Saul, the rule of which had given to the tribe a flattering pre-eminence, which it was unwilling to relinquish. The half-tribe of Manasseh on this side the Jordan sent eighteen thousand men; and the proud tribe of Ephraim testified its concurrence by sending twenty-eight thousand. From Issachar came only two hundred men; but these were the chief persons in the tribe, the whole of which was at their beck, and would have been in attendance if required. To them is given the marked character of being men of political prudence and sagacity, who knew better than most men how Israel ought to act under the present and other circumstances, and whose support was therefore of great value to David. From Zebulon came not fewer than fifty thousand men, skilled in the use of all warlike weapons, and "not double-hearted," with respect to the object for which they came. Naphtali furnished one thousand captains, and with them thirty-seven thousand men, armed with shield and spear. Dan supplied twenty-eight thousand six hundred able warriors, and Asher forty thousand. The tribes beyond Jordan, Reuben, Gad, and the half-tribe of Manasseh, sent, collectively, one hundred and twenty thousand warlike men. One obvious remark, arising from the survey of these numbers, is the comparative largeness of the proportions furnished by the *remoter* tribes, to the north and beyond Jordan. This is, perhaps, explained by the absence in those tribes of any pretensions for themselves, and of any strong attachment for the house of Saul, which could interfere with the heartiness of their recognition of the claims of David; together with the operation of the principles which gives to a prophet and great man the least degree of honor in and near his own home.*

With this vast body, the flower of the Hebrew nation, and representing the whole of it, "David made a league before the Lord," which can be construed to have no other meaning than that which has already been indicated in the case of Saul, that he bound himself by oath to observe the conditions on which he received the sceptre, which are now unknown. He was then anointed king, and received the homage of his new subjects; and the whole was terminated by a feast to all the multitude assembled at Hebron, supplies for which were liberally sent in by all the neighboring tribes, "on asses, on camels, on mules, and on oxen," and consisted of meat, meal, figs, raisins, wine, oil, oxen, and sheep, in great abundance. "For there was great joy in Israel."

The first act of David's reign was to undertake the reduction of the fortress of Jebus, on Mount Zion, which had remained in the hands of the natives ever since the days of Joshua, and which, as Josephus reports,† had been, from its situation and its fortifications, hitherto deemed impregnable. The Jebusites, therefore, ridiculed the attempt, and appear to have placed the lame and the blind on the walls, in derision, as fully sufficient to keep him out. But from the lower city, which was already in the possession of the Israelites, there was "a gutter," or subterraneous communication, with the fortress, by which David introduced a party of men and took "the stronghold of Zion." In the operations of this seige such ability and conduct were displayed by Joab, that he was appointed to the same chief command of the armies of Israel which he had previously held in the separate kingdom of Judah. The fact that his rule was likely, under all circumstances, to find the most zealous supporters in his own tribe of Judah, probably disinclined him to remove from its borders; and he determined to make his new conquest the metropolis of his empire. A more central situation, with respect to all the tribes, would have placed him in the hands of the Ephraimites, whose cordiality toward a Judahite king might well be suspected, and in whom little confidence could be placed in times of danger and difficulty. Similar considerations have dictated the choice of a very inconveniently situated capital to the reigning dynasty of Persia. But although better sites for a metropolitan city might have been found in the largest extent of Palestine, there were not better within the limits to which, for the reasons indicated, the choice of David was confined. That the site is overlooked from the Mount of Olives, although a great disadvantage in the eyes of modern military engineers, was of little consequence under the ancient systems of warfare, and could not countervail the peculiar advantages which it offered in being enclosed on three sides by a natural fosse of ravines and deep valleys, and terminating in an eminence, which, while strong in its defences from *without*, commanded the town *within*, and was capable of being strongly fortified. The united influence of all these considerations appears to have determined the preference of David

* Of this Fuller seems to have given a satisfactory explanation. "How this comes to pass let others largely dispute. We may, in brief, conclude, it is partly because their cradles can be remembered, and those swaddling-clothes once used about them, to strengthen them while infants, are afterward abused against them, to disgrace them when men, and all the passages of their youth repeated to their disparagement; partly because all the faults of their family (which must be many in a numerous alliance) are charged on the prophet's account. Wherefore that prophet who comes at the first in his full growth from a far foreign place (not improving himself among them from a small spark to a fire, to a flame, but, sun-like, arising in perfect lustre), gains the greatest reputation among the people. Because, in some respects, he is like Melchisedek, 'without father, without mother, without descent,' while the admiring vulgar, transported with his preaching, and ignorant of his extraction on earth, will charitably presume his pedigree from heaven, and his breeding as well as calling to be divine."
† Antiq. v. 2. Josh. xv. 63.

for a site which was open to the serious objection, among others, of being so remote from the northern tribes as to render the legal obligation of resort to it three times every year a more burdensome matter to them than it need have been had a more centrical situation been chosen.

It is supposed that David first gave the name of Jerusalem ("the possession of peace") to the city, but this is not quite certain. On Mount Zion he fixed his residence, and erected a palace and other buildings, and it was on this account called "the city of David." This strong part of the whole metropolis ever after remained what may be called the royal quarter of the town.

The Philistines had good reason to dread the consequences of the consolidation of all the power of the Hebrew tribes in hands of such tried vigor as those of David, and they deemed it prudent to set upon him before he had time to establish himself firmly in his kingdom. Their measures were so well planned, and so secretly executed, that they appeared suddenly, in great force, in the heart of Judea, and took the king's native town of Bethlehem before he was able to make any resistance. Indeed, the danger of his position was so urgent, that he was obliged to withdraw, for present safety, with some attached followers, to his old retreat in the cave of Adullam. It was here that he happened to express a longing desire for a drink of water from that well of his native town at which the thirst of his younger days had often been assuaged. Hearing this, three of his most valiant and devoted men, Joab, Jashobeam, and Eleazer, secretly departed, and, breaking through the host of the Philistines, which was encamped along the valley of Rephaim, brought him the precious fluid for which they had perilled their lives. But when the king received it he would not drink, but poured it out as a libation to Jehovah.

Soon after this, David, encouraged by a favorable answer from God, fell upon the Philistines, and so effectually discomfited them in two different onsets, that they were never after able to make head against him or any of his successors. Thus was one of the most irritating thorns in the side of Israel most effectually removed.

And now, when David had a respite from war, about the tenth year of his reign,[*] he thought of the ark of God, which had so long remained in the house of Abinadab, at Kirjath-jearim, and contemplated its removal to Jerusalem, that the place which had now become the capital of the human kingdom, might also become the capital of the invisible King. The design being received with approbation by the elders and chiefs of Israel whom he consulted, the king prepared for its execution, by despatching messengers throughout all Israel, to summon all the priests and Levites, and to invite as many of the people as were so disposed to attend the solemnity. He also prepared a tabernacle[†] to receive the ark on its arrival. Accordingly, at the appointed time, the ark was removed from the house of Abinadab, upon a new cart, attended by David and his court, by a large body of priests and Levites, who sang and played on various instruments of music, and by a numerous concourse of people from all parts of the kingdom. On the irregularity of removing it on a cart, we have already had occasion to remark.[‡] This irregularity gave occasion to an accident, attended with such fatal consequences as threw an effectual damp upon the joy of the solemnity: for the cart being at one place much shaken by the oxen, the officious Uzzah, the son or grandson of Abinadab, was struck dead upon the spot for putting forth his hand to stay the ark, none but the priests being warranted to touch it under pain of death. (Num. iv. 15.) This event struck David and the people with such consternation, that the intention of taking the ark to Jerusalem was relinquished, and it was left in the house of a Levite named Obed-edom, near which the circumstance occurred. But about three months after, hearing that the blessing of Jehovah had very evidently rested on the house in which the ark lay, the king hastened to complete his design. He perceived the former improprieties, and directed that the priests should now bear the ark upon their shoulders; and the whole solemnity was placed under the direction of Chenaniah, the chief of the Levites, who was found to be best acquainted with the proper observances. This was a great day in Israel. Nothing was omitted by which the occasion could be honored. In the presence of that sacred symbol of

* Counting from his first becoming king over Judah only.

† The old tabernacle, made in the wilderness, with the altar, and all the sacred utensils, were, as it appears, at Gibeon; why David erected a new tabernacle, instead of removing the former, does not clearly appear; but it is probable that it was too large for the place within his new palace, which, for the present, he intended it to occupy.

‡ See the Note at p. 96.

the Divine King, David laid aside his royal mantle, and appeared in such a garb as the Levites wore, with and before whom he went, as one of them; and as they sang and played the triumphant song which he had composed for the occasion, he accompanied them with his renowned harp, and danced to the joyful sounds it gave forth. Michal, the daughter of Saul, beheld this from a window, when the procession was approaching its destination; and she, imbued with some of the royal notions which had been fatal to her father and his house, despised him in heart for acting so far beneath what she conceived to be the dignity of the king of Israel: and when he came home, she could not refrain from allowing vent to this feeling. The reply of David was spirited and proper, declaring that it was before Jehovah, the true king of Israel, that he had laid aside the king, and made himself one with the people. And if this were to be vile, as she deemed, "I will yet be more vile than thus, and will be base in mine own sight."

David now instituted a regular and orderly attendance upon the ark and its tabernacle. But the regular services of religion were still performed at Gibeon, where the old tabernacle and altar remained, and which was still therefore the place of concourse to the nation at their great festivals. Here the priests rendered their services, under Zadok. The solemn removal of the ark, and its dignified repose in the city of David, were well calculated to make an impression upon the multitudes who were present on that occasion, and awaken their slumbering zeal for Jehovah. These favorable and becoming dispositions the king wished to confirm and strengthen; and for that end made suitable regulations in the services of the priests and Levites, and this especially by animating and instructive psalms, which were composed partly by himself, and partly by other gifted persons. They were sung not only by the Levites at all the sacrifices, but also by the people while on their way to the national altar, to attend the feasts. A very precious collection of these compositions has been preserved to our own day in the book of Psalms, which has in all subsequent ages ministered much edification and comfort to a large portion of mankind. By such instructive means David, without coercive measures, brought the whole nation to forget their idols, and to worship Jehovah alone; and thus also their religion became honorable, even in the eyes of foreigners, and acceptable to many of them. The above is the first occasion on which Zadok is mentioned as high-priest. But after this, throughout the reign of David, he and Abiathar are often named separately or together, as *both* bearing that character—a singular innovation, resulting probably from circumstances over which the king had little control. It seems likely that after Saul had slain the priests of Ithamar's line at Nob he restored the pontificate to the line of Eleazer, in the person of Zadok; while David and his people, during his wandering and his reign in Judah, had been accustomed to look to Abiathar, the escaped son of Ahimelech, as the high-priest; and that, on his accession to the throne of Israel, he found the people so accustomed to regard Zadok as high-priest, that he thought it proper and prudent to recognise him in that character, without depriving Abiathar of the consideration he had previously enjoyed. If this explanation be correct, Zadok would have had this advantage over Abiathar, that he had actually discharged the regular functions of the high-priesthood at the tabernacle, which the other had never an opportunity of doing. It is probably on this account, that wherever the two names occur together, that of Zadok is placed first.

About five years after this, and the fifteenth of David's reign, when the king had finished and inhabited his palace of cedar, "and God had given him rest from his enemies round about," he meditated a design of building a temple to Jehovah, in place of the temporary tabernacle which he had provided. This design he mentioned to the prophet Nathan, to whom it seemed so obviously proper, that he gave it much commendation and encouragement. But the night following, a message from God to David was delivered to him. This message declared it seemly that the temple of God should be built by a man of peace; but his life had been spent in warfare, and he had shed much blood. He was therefore directed to leave the accomplishment of his plan to his son and successor, whose reign should be one of peace. Nevertheless, it was well for David that this intention had been formed; for the Lord, to testify his approbation of this and other evidences of his zeal, and of his attachment to the principles of the theocracy, promised to make his name "as great as the names of the great ones who are on the earth;" and, far beyond this, the Lord promised " to build *him* a house," by establishing the succession in his house, and by granting to his posterity an eternal kingdom. The gratitude with which this promise was received by David seems to show he had some conception of its extensive import. He went, and seating himself most reverently on the ground before the ark, poured forth the strong expression of his gratitude.

As the Israelites were always victorious in war while they were faithful to their God and to the principles of the theocracy, so now the arms of David prospered in whatever direction they were turned. Indeed, it is scarcely until his reign that the national character of the Hebrews can be deemed to have recovered of the wounds which it had received in Egypt; and we find among them little military skill, and as little valor or fortitude. But from this time forward, trained to war and victory by David, they may be recognised as a truly courageous people, possessing among them as much military skill, science, and discipline, as any other nation of the same rank and age could claim.

The neighboring and rival nations had soon cause to learn that a new king reigned in Israel. The time was come for the old enemies, who had so often inspired the Israelites with dread, to be afraid in their turn; and even the more distant foreign princes, whose assistance they procured, had cause to repent of provoking an enemy more puissant than themselves. It was now the turn of the Philistines to receive the yoke to which they had accustomed Israel. Attacked in their own country, and beaten on all hands, they were brought under tribute and subjection. The Moabites were more heavily dealt with: to secure his conquest, David thought it necessary to act with a severity not usual with him; for he put to death one half of those who were taken with arms in their hands: and although it was then, or had been not long previously, usual for the nations to put all the armed men to death, this deed strikes us as harsh, from comparison with the milder general character of David's own warfare, and can only be explained by reference to some peculiar circumstances with which we are unacquainted.

In the ancient promises to the Hebrews, the limit to which, in their palmy state, their victorious arms should extend, had been as clearly defined as the limit of their own proper territory. And the distinction here incidentally mentioned, between the limit of the *proper country* destined for their own occupation, and that of the *subject territory* which should be acquired, is of considerable importance, and should not be overlooked or confounded as it often has been. The *limit of conquest* was fully reached by David.

Eastward this limit was to extend to the Euphrates. Of the kings who reigned in the intermediate country, one of the most powerful was Hadadezer, king of Zobah. This sovereign, whose dominion extended eastward to the Euphrates, was defeated by David in the first battle, and lost twenty thousand infantry, seven thousand horsemen with their horses, and one thousand chariots of war. Of the chariots, the king of Israel preserved a hundred, with horses for them; but, mindful that the law of the kingdom forbade the accumulation of horses, all the others were destroyed. The Syrians of Damascus, who were allies (perhaps tributaries) of Hadadezer, and came to his assistance, shared his fate. Hadad, their king, was vanquished, with the loss of twenty-two thousand men, and David brought his territory under subjection to his sceptre. These two victories carried the eastern limit of his conquests to the Euphrates. Josephus adduces the testimony of a native historian, Nicolaus of Damascus, in confirmation of the testimony which the Hebrew writers have left. From this it seems that the kingdom, of which Damascus was the capital, had grown very powerful under this Hadad, who might, indeed, be considered as its actual founder; but after various engagements with King David, was finally overthrown in a great battle near the Euphrates, in which he performed deeds worthy of his high name. Josephus himself, in conformity with the Scriptural account, relates that after David had reduced to his obedience Damascus and all Syria, having strong garrisons in every place where they seemed necessary, he returned in triumph to Jerusalem, where he consecrated to God the golden shields which had been borne by the royal guard of Hadadezer, from whose cities he also brought much spoil of brass for the service of the future temple.

While David was engaged in these victories, the southern frontier of his conquests was, according to ancient promises, extended southward to the Red sea. This was the work of Joab's valiant brother, Abishai, who defeated the Edomites in "the Valley of Salt," at the southern extremity of the Dead sea, and then carried his victorious arms into the mountains, the enclosed valleys, and the rocky wildernesses of Mount Seir, leaving garrisons to secure the advantages he had gained.

David was too well acquainted with the law, to attempt to incorporate any of these conquests as integral parts of the Hebrew territory. He appears in most cases to have left the internal government of the conquered states in the hands of the native princes, who were required to render annually a certain amount of tribute, consisting, for the most part, of such articles as their country afforded in the most abundance, or which they had the best means of procuring or producing. The delivery of such tribute from subject states, under the name of presents, was anciently, as it is now, an occasion of great pomp and ceremony, which, on another occasion, we shall more particularly notice. The obedience of the more distant conquests was secured by garrisons, which do not seem to have been judged necessary in those nearer countries which the mere vicinity of the conquering power might sufficiently control.

Thus David literally became a "king of kings," and his fame extended into far countries. Some states which had been at hostilities with the states conquered by him sent splendid embassies, with valuable gifts, to congratulate him on his successes. Among these, Toi, the king of Hamah, upon the Orontes, who had been at war with Hadadezer, is particularly mentioned. He sent his own son Joram "to salute and bless" King David, and to deliver costly gifts, such as vessels and utensils of gold, silver, and fine brass. All the surplus wealth thus acquired from the states he conquered, or from those which sought his friendship and alliance, was treasured up by him for the great work which he had so much at heart, and which his son was destined to execute.

But of all David's foreign alliances, the earliest and most valuable was that with Hiram, king of Tyre. This had been formed very soon after David had taken Jerusalem and defeated the Philistines, and seems to have been sought by Hiram; for it will be remembered that David was famous in the closely neighboring states before he became king; and no doubt not only his eminent public qualities, but his remarkable personal history, was familiar not less to the Phœnicians than to the Philistines. And although an enterprising commercial and skilful manufacturing nation, like them, would be disposed to look down upon a people so inferior to themselves as the Hebrews in the finer and larger arts of social life, military talents and success, and such heroic qualities as the character of David offered, have never yet failed to be appreciated, wherever found. Hiram "was ever a lover of David," and the offered alliance must have been the more gratifying to him as it came before "David acquired a name, and [before] his fame went out into all lands, and the Lord brought the fear of him upon all nations." This alliance was one of mutual advantage. Tyre possessed but a narrow strip of maritime territory, the produce of which, if sedulously cultivated, would have been very inadequate to the supply of its teeming population and numerous fleets. But, besides this, the absorbing devotion of the Phœnicians to commerce and the arts rendered them averse to the slow pursuits of agriculture, the products of which they could so much more easily obtain by exchange against the products of their foreign traffic and their skill. To them therefore it was a most invaluable circumstance, that behind them lay a country in the hands of a people who had none of the advantages which were so much prized by themselves, but who had abundance of corn, wine, oil, and cattle, to barter for them. An alliance cemented by such reciprocal benefits, and undisturbed by territorial designs or jealousies, was likely to be permanent; and we know that it tended much to advance the Hebrews in the arts which belong to civilized life, and to promote the external splendor of this and the ensuing reign. In the present instance Hiram supplied the architects and mechanics, as well as the timber (hewn in Lebanon), whereby David was enabled to build his palace of cedar, and to undertake the other works which united the upper and lower cities, and rendered Jerusalem a strong and comely metropolis.

In the midst of his success and glory, the memory of Jonathan was still very dear to David. He caused inquiry to be made whether any of his family remained, "to whom he might show kindness;" he then first heard of his lame son Mephibosheth, and caused him to be conducted to Jerusalem. The afflicted young man was received with great kindness by the king; who restored to him the lands which had belonged to Saul for the support of his household, but desired that he would himself be a constant guest at the royal table, even as one of the king's own sons. This generous

Rocky Valley in Mount Sxir. The Entrance to a Tomb is shown on the left, and the Remains of an Amphitheatre in the distance

treatment, with the continued kindness which he afterward received, won entirely the open heart of Jonathan's son. He became strongly attached to the person and interests of David, whose higher qualities he regarded with admiration and reverence.

It was probably in the period of peace and glory which followed the victories of David over all the enemies of Israel, that he employed himself in the organization of the government. The very important part which he took in giving to all the departments of the government the form and character which he desired it to bear in future times, has, it seems to us, been rather overlooked and undervalued. For, in truth, David was the real founder of the Hebrew monarchy; and in that character his great abilities appear not less prominently than in the various other endowments by which he was so eminently distinguished from the mass of mankind.

During the days of his adversity, when persecuted by Saul, David had been treated by Nahash the king of Ammon with some kindness, of which he cherished a very grateful remembrance. When, therefore, he heard of his death, he sent an embassy to condole with the new king, Hanun, upon the loss of his father, and to congratulate him upon his peaceable succession. But this prince was led by his courtiers to regard the ambassadors as spies, and dared to give them such treatment as was then, and would be at this day in the East, regarded as the most ignominious which any men could receive. He caused their beards to be shaved, and their long garments to be cut short at their buttocks, and in this condition sent them away. When David heard of this grievous insult to him through his ambassadors, he was filled with indignation. He sent messengers to meet these personages, and to relieve them from the necessity of appearing at his court in their present degraded condition, by directing them to remain at Jericho until the renewed growth of their beards might enable them to appear without shame. As the insult was too gross to be allowed to pass unpunished, David ordered Joab to march with an imposing force against the Ammonites. Meanwhile that people had not been idle; but, fully aware of the probable effect of their ungenerous conduct, and not confiding in their own strength, they engaged the assistance of some of the neighboring princes of Syria—in fact, "hired" them as mercenaries, being the first example of the kind which history offers. The force thus obtained from four Syrian princes amounted to thirty-three thousand men, who came and encamped before Medeba in the land of Ammon. The force of the Ammonites themselves marched out of the town when the army of Israel appeared. Joab with his usual address hastened to prevent the junction of the two armies, and himself turned against the Syrians, while his brother Abishai kept the Ammonites in check. The Syrians were speedily put to flight by Joab; and when the Ammonites saw this, they also fled before Abishai, and hastened into the city.

In a second campaign, David himself marched against a powerful army, composed not only of the Syrians, but of Assyrians from beyond the Euphrates, whose assistance had been procured by Hadadezer, who seems now to have determined on a last and grand effort to recover and secure his independence. This formidable army was under the command of Shobach, the general of Hadadezer, and were encamped at Helam, near the Euphrates, where David found them. In the terrible battle which ensued the Israelites were victorious; and that day they destroyed 700 chariots, 7,000 horse, and 40,000 foot, being about half the force which the Syrians on both sides the river had been able to bring into the field. By this decisive victory the Syrian nations were completely subdued, and the Ammonites were henceforth left to their own resources.

The next campaign against that nation David left to the conduct of Joab, remaining himself at Jerusalem. Joab marched into the land of Ammon, and, after ravaging the country, laid siege to the metropolitan city of Rabbah, or Rabbath-Ammon,* which for some time held out against him.

* The site of the ancient capital of the Ammonites was first indicated by Seetzen, and has since been visited by various travellers. The original names of this town, which existed in the time of Moses, Ammon, and Rabbath-Ammon, was for a time observed by that of Philadelphia, which it took from Ptolemy Philadelphus, by whom it was rebuilt. That any portions of the ruins are of earlier date than this rebuilding by him, it would be absurd to expect; and most of them are obviously of later date, and may, for the most part, be referred to the period of the Roman domination in Syria. The present natives of the country now know nothing of the name of Philadelphia, but give to the site its original name of Ammon.
The very precise manner in which the prophecies applicable to the city have been fulfilled, gives to the place more interest than it could historically claim, although even that is not inconsiderable. The description which is the most available for our purposes is that which Lord Lindsay has given. In transcribing it, however, we omit the account of the ruins, which, although of high interest in themselves, are not such as the purpose of the present work requires us to describe:

Ruins of Ammon.

There was little in this war to occasion much anxiety in the king, who remained quiet at Jerusalem, where, in an evil and unguarded hour, his inordinate desires brought him very low, and entailed much anguish and sorrow on his future reign.

One afternoon the king arose from his mid-day sleep, and walked on the terraced roof of his palace,* from the commanding height of which he unhappily caught a view of a woman bathing. This was the beautiful Bathsheba, the wife of Uriah the Hittite, who was then serving under Joab at the siege of Rabbah. The king sent for her, and she became with child by him. Afflicted at this event, which was so calculated, by betraying the adulterous connexion, to bring upon the woman the ignominious death which the law demanded, if the husband should think proper to demand her punishment, David sent to desire Joab to send him to Jerusalem, as if with news of the war, hoping that his presence about this time would screen, or at least render doubtful, the effects of his own crime. But Uriah, either, as he professed, thinking the gratifications of home inconsistent with the obligations of his military service, or suspecting the fidelity of his wife, avoided her during his stay, and remained publicly among the king's attendants. Disappointed in this device by the proud honor or caution of Uriah, the king concluded that the life of Bathsheba and his own char-

"The scenery waxed drearier and drearier, as, at ten hours and a half from Jerash, we descended a precipitous stony slope into the valley of Ammon, and crossed a beautiful stream called Moiet Ammon. It has its source in a pond a few hundred paces from the southwest end of the town, and, after passing under ground several times, empties itself into the Zerka (Jabbok). The valley is bordered at intervals by strips of stunted grass, often interrupted; no oleanders cheered the eye with their rich blossoms; the hills on both sides were rocky and bare, and pierced with excavations and natural caves. Here, at a turning in the narrow valley, commences the antiquities of Ammon. It was situated on both sides the stream. The dreariness of its present aspect is quite indescribable. It looks like the abode of death. The valley stinks with dead camels. One of them was rotting in the stream, and, although we saw none among the ruins, they were absolutely *covered* in every direction with their dung. That morning's ride would have convinced a skeptic. How runs the prophecy? 'I will make Rabbah a stable for camels, and the Ammonites for flocks; and ye shall know that I am the Lord!'

"Nothing but the croaking of frogs and screams of wild birds broke the silence, as we advanced up this valley of desolation. Passing on the left an unopened tomb (for the singularity in these regions is where the tomb has *not* been violated), several broken sarcophagi, and an aqueduct, in one spot full of human sculls, a bridge on the right, a ruin on the left, apparently the southern gate of the town, a high wall and lofty terrace, with one pillar still standing, the remains probably of a portico, we halted under the square building supposed by Seetzen to have been a mausoleum, and, after a hasty glance at it, hurried up the glen in search of the principal ruins, which we found much more extensive and interesting than we expected, not certainly in such good preservation as those of Jerash, but designed on a much grander scale. Storks were perched in every direction on the tops of the different buildings; others soared at an immense height above us."

Then follows a more detailed account of the ruins, the predominant architectural character of which is indicated by the very fine specimen inserted in our text. By far the best and most ample description of the whole is that which has been given by Buckingham, in his "Travels among the Arab Tribes," 67-81. After his description, Lord Lindsay resumes:

"Such are the relics of the ancient Ammon, or rather of Philadelphia, for no building there can boast of a prior date to that of the change of name. It was a bright cheerful morning, but still the valley is a very dreary spot, even when the sun shines brightest. Vultures were garbaging on a camel, as we slowly rode back through the glen, and reascended the *akibe* by which we entered it. Ammon is now quite deserted, except by the Bedouins who water their flocks at its little river. We met sheep and goats by thousands, and camels by hundreds, coming down to drink, all in beautiful condition. How—let me again cite the prophecy—how runs it? 'Ammon shall be a desolation!—Rabbah of the Ammonites . . . shall be a desolate heap!—I will make Rabbah a stable for camels, and the Ammonites a couching place for flocks; and ye shall know that I am the Lord!'"

* There have been many grave remarks and sermons upon the consequences of *idleness,* as exemplified in this instance, and so forth. Now there is no idleness in the case, or anything to blame David for, but the sin into which he fell. It is quite true that, if he had not been at Jerusalem, and if he had not walked on the roof of his palace after sleep, this thing would not have happened to him; but this is no more than the obvious truth that if a man were doing one thing another thing would not have been done, which is as applicable to every human act as to that of David. *We are told that he ought not to have been at Jerusalem, but at the head of his army.* Now this is more than we know. It is, perhaps, rather creditable to David that he knew that a king had more important duties than to lead forth his armies in person on every occasion. He was doubtless ready, if there had been adequate occasion; but the result proved that Joab was fully equal to the service on which he was engaged; and the king could probably more easily find one to command the army, than to conduct the civil government in his own absence, according to his own plans and designs. Those must have singular notions of an oriental monarchy who suppose that David had grown indolent because he remained in his metropolis; for there are few men whose ordinary home duties are more arduous and laborious than those of most eastern kings; and we know, from a subsequent event, that David actually undertook in his own person more labor than he was able adequately to sustain. Then, *as to his afternoon sleep and subsequent walk:* the idleness of this has seemed unquestionable. But this is the ignorant inference of people who sleep outright by night for eight or nine hours, and then marvel to see others sleepful while they are wakeful, without considering that these others have slept but five hours at night, rose at daybreak, and have discharged half the duties of the day before they commence their own. In warm climates the cool morning hours are highly favorable to exertion, and therefore the orientals rise early to employ them; to compensate for which, and to obtain the total quantity of sleep which nature requires, they lie down again during the heat of the day, when, if they were awake, the relaxing warmth would make exertion difficult. Taken in all, the orientals do not sleep more, if as much, as we do; but they find it convenient and suitable to have two short sleeps instead of a single long one; and for this they do not deserve to be considered indolent. Joab doubtless slept as soundly in his camp this afternoon, as David in his palace.

acter could only be secured by his death. This therefore he contrived, in concert with the unprincipled Joab, in such a manner as to make him perish by the sword of the Ammonites, although this could not be effected without involving several other men in the slaughter. David concluded his complicated crime by sending back to Joab, through the messengers who brought this intelligence, a hypocritical message of condolence : " Let not this trouble thee, *for the sword devoureth one as well as another.*" And then, to fill up the measure of his successful guilt, he openly took Bathsheba to wife, after the days of her mourning were expired ; and she bore him a son.

But the deed which David had done with so much privacy, thinking to escape human detection, "displeased Jehovah; and he sent Nathan the prophet to reprove him." This he did with much tact, in a well-known and beautiful tale of oppression and distress,* so framed that the king did not at the first perceive its application to himself, and which worked so powerfully upon his feelings that his anger was kindled against the man "who had no pity," and he declared not only that he should, as the law required, make a fourfold restitution, but, with a severity beyond the law of the case, pronounced a sentence of death upon him. Instantly the prophet retorted, " *Thou* art the man !" In the name of the Lord, he authoritatively upbraided him with his ingratitude and transgression, and threatened him that *the sword* which he had privily employed to cut off Uriah should never depart from his own house, and that his own wives should be publicly dishonored by his neighbor.

Convicted and confounded, David instantly confessed his guilt—" I have sinned against JEHOVAH !" and for this speedy humiliation, without attempting to dissemble or cloak his guilt, the Lord was pleased to remit the sentence of death which he had pronounced on himself, and to transfer it to the fruit of his crime. The child died ; and the Rabbins remark that three more of David's sons were cut off by violent deaths; thus completing as it were the fourfold retaliation for the murder of Uriah, which he had himself denounced.

" The fall of David is one of the most instructive and alarming recorded in that most faithful and impartial of all histories, the Holy Bible. And the transgression of one idle and unguarded moment pierced him through with many sorrows and embittered the remainder of his life, and gave occasion for the enemies of the Lord to blaspheme on account of this crying offence of " the man after God's own heart." When he only cut off the skirt of Saul's robe, *his heart smote him* for the indignity thus offered to his master; but when he treacherously cut off a faithful and gallant soldier, who was fighting his battles, after having defiled his bed, his heart smote him not—at least we read not of any compunction or remorse of conscience till Nathan was sent to reprove him. Then, indeed, his sorrow was extreme ; and his Psalms, composed on this occasion, express in the most pathetic strains the anguish of a wounded spirit, and the bitterness of his penitence. (See Ps. xxxii., li., ciii.) Still the rising again of David holds forth no encouragement to sinners who may wish to shelter themselves under his example, or flatter themselves with the hope of obtaining his forgiveness; for though his life was spared, yet God inflicted upon him those temporal punishments which the prophet had denounced. The remainder of his days were as disastrous as the beginning had been prosperous.†

These things happened about the eighteenth year of David's reign, and the forty-eighth of his age.

Soon after this, Joab, always zealous for the honor and credit of his master, though not himself an unambitious man, sent to acquaint David that he had taken the royal quarter of the city of Rabbah ; and as this contained the sources from which the rest was supplied with water, it was not possible that it could much longer hold out. He therefore desired that the king would come with a suitable reinforcement and carry the town, that his might be the glory of bringing the war to a conclusion. David did so. The spoil taken in this metropolis was immense ; and among it was the crown of the king, of gold set round with jewels, and worth a talent of

* " There were two men in one city ; the one rich, and the other poor. The rich man had exceeding many flocks and herds : but the poor man had nothing but one little ewe lamb, which he had bought and nourished up ; and it grew up together with him and with his children ; and it ate of his own morsel, and drank of his own cup, and lay in his bosom, and was unto him like a daughter. Now a traveller came to the rich man, and he spared to take of his own flock and of his own herd to dress for the traveller that had come to him ; but took the poor man's lamb and dressed it for the man that had come to him."— 2 Sam. xii. 2–4.
† Hales, ii. 341–343.

gold, which may be reckoned at nearly thirty thousand dollars. This was "set upon David's head;" but whether as appropriating it to his own future use as king of Israel, or as the act of a conqueror to denote the transference to himself of that sovereignty over Ammon which the native princes had hitherto enjoyed, is not quite evident. It is certain that such of this cruel and arrogant people as were taken in Rabbah were treated with unusual severity—not, indeed, by their being put to torturing deaths, as the ambiguous terms of the text have suggested, but by their being reduced to personal servitude, and devoted to the most laborious employments which existed among the Hebrews, being such as those of sawing and cleaving wood, of harrowing the ground, and of laboring in the brick-fields.

This was prosperity; as was, not long after, the birth of another son from Bathsheba. This son was SOLOMON, who, long before his birth, and long before his mother was known to David, had been pointed out by name as "the man of peace," who was to succeed him in the throne, and through whom his dynasty was to reign in Israel.

But the commencement of the evils threatened upon the house of David was not long withheld. Amnon, the eldest of his sons, conceived a violent passion for his half-sister, Tamar, the full sister of Absalom. By a feigned sickness, he procured her presence in his house, and delayed not to declare to her his criminal desires; and finding that he could not persuade her to compliance, he by force effected her dishonor. Then, passing suddenly from a criminal excess of love to an equal excess of hate, he expelled her ignominiously from his house. Tamar, in her grief, rent her virginal robe and threw dust upon her head, and sought the asylum of her brother Absalom's house; for, according to the ideas of the East, the son of the same mother is, more than even the father, the proper person to protect a female and to redress her wrongs. No man could be more haughty and implacable than Absalom; but he was also deeply politic; and while he received the unhappy Tamar with tenderness, he desired her to conceal her grief, seeing that a brother was the cause of it, and to spend her remaining days in retirement in his house. He made no complaint on the subject, and, young as he was, so well concealed his deep resentment, that even Amnon had not the least suspicion of it. When the news of this villanous fact came to the ears of David, it troubled him greatly; but being greatly attached to Amnon, as being his eldest son and probable successor in the throne, he neglected to call him to account or to punish him for his transgression. This, we may be sure, increased the resentment of Absalom, and perhaps laid the foundation of his subsequent alienation from, and dislike to, his father.

Absalom waited two years before he found an opportunity of giving effect to his long and deeply-cherished purposes of vengeance. It seems that David allowed separate establishments to his sons very early. We find before that both Amnon and Absalom had separate houses, and now we learn that Absalom (and doubtless his brothers) had a distinct property to support his expenses. For at this time he was about to hold a grand sheep-shearing feast in Baal-hazor, to which he invited the king and all his sons. As Absalom had hoped, David declined, on the ground of the expense which his presence would occasion to his son; but all the princes went, and among them, and the chief of them, was the eldest, Amnon. Now Absalom felt that the day of his vengeance was come; and while he received his company with distinction, and royally entertained them, he gave secret orders to his servants to fall upon Amnon, and slay him, even at the table, on a given signal from himself. This was done. Amnon was slain while his heart was warm with wine; on which the other princes, expecting perhaps the same fate, made all haste to get to their mules, and fled to Jerusalem. Their arrival relieved the king from the horror into which he had been plunged by a rumor that *all* his sons had been slain; but still his indignation and grief were very great. Absalom himself fled the country, and found refuge with his maternal grandfather, Talmai, the king of Geshur, with whom he remained for three years.

During this time the grief of David for the murder of Amnon was gradually assuaged, and his heart insensibly turned with kindness toward Absalom, to whom he always had been much attached, and who was now his eldest son, and who might seem to have the more claim on his indulgence and sympathy on account of his exclusion from the succession to the throne, to which by birth he deemed himself entitled. Joab was not slow to perceive the turn which the king's feelings were

[Flight on Mules.]

taking, and was desirous of bringing about a reconciliation between David and Absalom; but not daring to speak openly to the king himself, in the first instance, he engaged a shrewd woman of Tekoah to come before the king with a fictitious tale of distress, which, as in the case of Nathan's story, might be made instructively applicable to the circumstances. The woman played her part to admiration; but when she began to make her application, the king at once guessed that she had been prompted by Joab; and this being admitted by the woman, the king turned to that personage, who was present all the time; and, glad that what was secretly his own desire was thus made to appear a concession to the urgent request of that powerful servant, he said, "Behold, now, I grant this request; go, then, and bring back the young man Absalom." He accordingly came back to Jerusalem; but his father declined to see him on his return; and he remained two years in Jerusalem without appearing before the king.

At the end of that time, Absalom was again, through the interference of Joab, admitted to the presence of his father, who embraced him and was reconciled to him.

It would seem that during his retirement Absalom had formed those designs, for the ultimate execution of which he soon after began to prepare the way: this was no less than to deprive his father of his crown. As David was already old, Absalom would probably have been content to await his death, but for peculiar circumstances. If David properly discharged his duty, he must have led his sons to understand, that although the succession to the throne had been assured to his family, the ordinary rules of succession were not to be considered obligatory or binding, inasmuch as the Supreme King possessed and would exercise the right of appointing the particular person who might be acceptable to him. In the absence of any contrary intimation, the ordinary rules might be observed; but, according to the principles of the theocratical government, no such rules could be of force when a special appointment intervened. It was already known to David, and could not but be known or suspected by Absalom, that not only he but some other of the king's sons were to be passed over by such an appointment, in favor of Solomon, to whom, by this time, the king probably began to pay attention as his successor. The fact that even the ordinary law of primogeniture, as applied to the government, had not yet been exemplified among the Hebrews, must have tended to increase Absalom's uncertainty of his own succession to his father. Besides, in contending for the crown while his father lived, he had but one competitor, and that one fondly attached to him; whereas, if he waited until his father's death, he might have many vigorous competitors in his brothers. These, or some of them, were probably the considerations in which the designs of Absalom originated. But these designs were not merely culpable as against his own father, but as an act of rebellion against the ordinations of the theocracy, since they involved an attempt to appropriate by force that which God had otherwise destinated, or which at least was to be left for his free appointment. The ultimate success of Absalom would, therefore, have utterly subverted the theocratical principle which still remained in the constitution of the Hebrew state.

At the first view, such an enterprise, against such a man as David, and by his own son, must have seemed wild and hopeless. But in the contest between youth and age—between novelty and habit—between the dignity and authority of an old king, and the ease and freedom of one who has *only* popularity to seek, the advantages are not all in favor of the old governor. Besides, it seems that there was much latent discontent among the people, arising in a considerable degree from that very confidence in the justice and wisdom of the king by which his throne ought to have been secured. It is the duty of an oriental king to administer justice in his own person, and that duty is not seldom among the heaviest of those which devolve upon him. This grew in time to be so sensibly felt, that ultimately among the Hebrews, as in some oriental and more European states, the king only undertook to attend to appeals from the ordinary tribunals. But under the former state of things, the people will rather bring their causes before a just and popular king than to the ordinary judges; and he in consequence is so overwhelmed with judicial business, that there remain only two alternatives—either to give up all his time to these matters, to the neglect of the general affairs of the nation, or else to risk his popularity by fixing a certain time every day for the hearing of causes, whereby some of the suiters must often wait many days before their causes can be brought under his notice. This hinderance to bringing a case immediately before the king is calculated to relieve him by inducing the people to resort to the inferior judges, from whom prompt justice might be obtained; but, on the other hand, it is well calculated to endanger his popularity with the unthinking multitude, who deem their own affairs of the highest importance, and attribute to his neglect or indolence the delay and difficulty which they experience. David made choice of the latter alternative, and suffered the inevitable consequences.

Absalom was not slow to perceive the advantage this was to him, or to neglect the use which might be made of it. He had other advantages: he was an exceedingly fine young man, admired by all Israel for his beauty, and particularly celebrated for the richness and luxuriance of his hair. This was no small matter among a people so open as were the Hebrews to receive impressions from the beauty, or tallness, or strength of their public men. It was also, probably, a great advantage to Absalom, as against David, and which would have availed him against any of his brothers, had any of them been older than himself, that he was maternally descended from a race of kings. When, even in our own day, we see the conventional rights of primogeniture set aside, in the East, in favor of the son of a nobly-descended mother,* we can not suppose this consideration without weight among the Israelites in the time of David.

Soon after the reconciliation with his father, Absalom began to live with great ostentation, taking upon him much more state than his station as the eldest son of the crown required, and more probably than his father exhibited as king. He had chariots, and a guard of horsemen, and never appeared in public but attended by fifty men. This, by contrast, the more enhanced the condescension and affability which his purposes required him to exemplify. It was his wont to make his appearance very early in the morning, in the way that led to the palace gate; and when any

* In Persia, Abbas Meerza, the father of the king, was, on account of the noble descent of his mother, nominated by his father to succeed him in the throne, in preference to an elder son whose mother was a merchant's daughter.

man who had a lawsuit came to the king for judgment, Absalom would call to him and inquire with much apparent interest from what town he came, and the nature of his suit before the king; he would then condole with him on the state of affairs which made it so difficult to obtain redress and justice, and would wind up with the passionate exclamation, " Oh that *I* were made judge in the land, that every man who hath any suit or cause might come unto *me*, and *I* would do him justice !" And then when any man passing by came to make his obeisance to the king's son, Absalom would put forth his arms, and take hold of him, and embrace him like a brother. "And after this manner," says the narrative, "did Absalom to all Israel who came to the king for judgment: *thus Absalom stole away the hearts of the men of Israel.*" And it is important to note, that the men whose hearts he thus "stole away," were inhabitants of all the different parts of the land, who would afterward carry to their several homes the impressions they had received.

At last, four years after his reconciliation to his father, Absalom judged his plans ripe for execution; he therefore obtained the king's permission to go to Hebron, under the pretence of offering there a sacrifice which he had vowed during his residence at Geshur. At this place he had appointed the chiefs of his party to meet him, while others, who were dispersed through all the tribes, were ordered to proclaim him king, as soon as they heard the signal given by the sound of the trumpet. At his arrival in Hebron, he sent for Ahithophel,* who readily came; and the defection of that great politician, who had been the chief of David's counsellors, and whose reputation for wisdom was so great that his opinion on most subjects was respected as that of an oracle, gave much strength to the cause of Absalom, and attracted to Hebron numbers of influential men from all quarters of the land.

Alarmed at this formidable rebellion so close to him, David hastily took flight with his family and servants, leaving ten of his concubine-wives in charge of the palace. He paused outside the town to survey the faithful few who were prepared to follow his fortunes. Among them were the high-priests, Zadok and Abiathar, with the priests and Levites bearing the ark. These David directed to return with the ark into the city: " If I shall find favor in the eyes of Jehovah, he will bring me back, and show me both it and his habitation. But if he thus say, ' I have no delight in thee,' behold, here am I, let him do to me as seemeth good unto him." From this and other expressions, similarly humbled and resigned to the dispensations of Providence, it appears that he recognised in this unnatural conspiracy against him a portion of the judgments which the prophet had been authorized to denounce against him for his iniquities in the matter of Uriah and Bathsheba. David also pointed out to the high-priests that they might render him much service by remaining in the city, from which they might secretly transmit intelligence and advice to him through their sons, Ahimaaz and Jonathan.

The whole of the two corps of body-guards (the Cherethites and Pelethites), as well as the six hundred Gathites, were ready to attend the king. The last-named body appear to have been native Philistines of Gath, whom David had attached to his service after the conquest of their country, and who had perhaps become proselytes.†

The king attempted to dissuade Ittai, their leader, from attending him with his men, apparently feeling that, as foreigners and mercenaries, they might be rather expected to attach themselves to the rising fortunes of Absalom. But the answer of Ittai was decisive: " As Jehovah liveth, and as my lord the king liveth, surely in what place my lord shall be, whether in death or life, there also will thy servant be."

Having taken this melancholy review of his followers, the king went on, " by the ascent of Mount Olivet, and wept as he went up, barefoot, and with his head covered; and all the people that were with him covered every man his head, weeping as they went up," in token of extreme sorrow and humiliation. They had scarcely reached the summit before David was joined by an old and attached friend named Hushai,

* The Jews suppose that Ahithophel was the grandfather of Bathsheba, and that he had been alienated from David by his conduct toward her, and by the murder of her husband. But this is doubtful.
† Some, however, think it was a band of native Israelites, called Gathites, in memory of the six hundred men who composed the band of followers who accompanied him when he sought refuge the second time in Gath, and in which indeed the members of that body had been incorporated, and were replaced as they died off. But there is no good reason why such a body should be named from Gath rather than from other places or circumstance in which their history connected them with David. Besides, he obviously speaks to Ittai, their leader, as to a foreigner, who, with "his brethren," could hardly be expected to incur distress for his sake.

who had been one of his council, and who came with his clothes rent and dust upon his head, resolved to share in the misfortunes of his king. But David, well convinced of his attachment, did not think it fit to take him with his train, but rather begged him to go and join himself to Absalom, where he might render much better service by thwarting the counsels of Ahithophel (of whose defection he had just heard), and by conveying to him, through the two high-priests, information of whatever resolutions the revolters might take. Hushai readily accepted this office, and acquitted himself in it with such consummate tact and zeal, as not a little contributed to the final overthrow of Absalom and his party.

In his further progress David was joined by Ziba, the steward of Mephibosheth, who brought with him some necessary refreshments, and falsely and treacherously reported that his master remained behind, in the expectation that the turn which affairs were taking might result in the restoration of the house of Saul in his person. David, sensibly hurt at this treatment from one who owed so much to his kindness and gratitude, hastily told Ziba henceforth to regard as his own property the lands he had hitherto managed for Mephibosheth. Immediately after, an incident occurred to confirm the impression he had thus received; for near Bahurim, a village not far on the eastern side of Olivet, he was encountered by one of Saul's family, named Shimei, who dared to throw at him and his people volleys of stones, accompanied by the grossest abuse and bitterest imprecations against David as the author of all the wrongs and misfortunes of the house of Saul, which he said were now in the course of being avenged. All this unexpected insult David bore with meekness and patience; for when Abishai desired permission to punish the man on the spot, the king refused: " Behold," he said, " my son, that came forth out of mine own bowels, seeketh my life, how much more now this Benjamite? Let him alone, and let him curse; for Jehovah hath bidden him. It may be that Jehovah will look upon mine affliction, and requite me good for his cursing this day."

Absalom delayed not to march to Jerusalem. He was surprised and gratified to find there Hushai, the old friend of his father, and gave him a place in his council. In that council the voice of Ahithophel was still paramount and decisive. Perceiving that many held back or wavered from the apprehension that Absalom would hardly go to the last extremities against his father, and that possibly they might become the victims of another reconciliation between David and his son, this wily and unprincipled statesman advised that Absalom should not delay to remove this apprehension by such an act as would, in the sight of all the people, commit him beyond all hope of a pardon or reconciliation to the bad cause in which he was engaged. This was, that he should rear a pavilion on the top of the palace (to render it conspicuous from afar), into which he should, "in the sight of all Israel," enter to the concubine-wives whom David had left in charge of the palace. This atrocious counsel was followed by Absalom, who thus unintentionally accomplished Nathan's prophecy.

The next advice of Ahithophel was that not a moment should be lost in crowning the success of the rebellion by the death of the king, without allowing him time to bring his resources into action. To this end he offered himself to pursue him at the head of twelve thousand men: "And I shall come upon him while he is weary and weak-handed, and terrify him; and while all the people who are with him flee, I will smite the king only. And I will bring back all the people unto thee, as a bride is brought to her husband (for only one man's life thou seekest); and the whole people shall have peace." This really sagacious advice was much approved by Absalom, who perhaps considered that the guilt would rest upon Ahithophel; and to the other counsellors it also seemed good. Hushai was absent: and as a high opinion of his prudence was entertained, Absalom sent for him, and then told him what Ahithophel had advised, and asked whether he thought that advice good. Hushai at once saw that David was lost, if this plan were not frustrated. He therefore, with great presence of mind, adduced several specious arguments against it, and in favor of delay; dwelling upon the known valor of David and his friends, and the serious consequence of any check or failure in the first attack. The least repulse at such a juncture might be fatal to the cause of Absalom. The awe in which they all stood of the military talents and courage of the old king gave such effect to these suggestions, that the counsel of Hushai was preferred to that of Ahithophel. Of all this Hushai apprized the high-priests, and desired them to convey the information to David through their sons, together with his advice that not a moment should be lost

Absalom's Sepulchre.

in passing to the country beyond Jordan. This message was conveyed to David with some danger and difficulty by Jonathan and Ahimaaz, who had remained in concealment at Ain Rogel, outside the city. Neither the information nor advice was lost upon the king, who instantly marched to the Jordan, and passed over with all his people, so that by the morning light not one was left in the plain of Jericho.

The far-seeing Ahithophel deemed the cause of Absalom to be lost, when he knew that the counsel of Hushai was to be followed. His pride also could little brook the neglect the advice which he had given, and which he had been used to see so reverently regarded. On both accounts, he abandoned the cause. He went to his own home; and while he was still wise enough to set his affairs in order, was mad enough to hang himself.

David established himself at the town of Mahanaim, which, it will be remembered, had been the royal seat of Ishbosheth, and which appears to have been chosen by him, and now by David, on account of the strength of its fortifications. To that place several principal persons of the country, who were well affected to the cause of David, brought a timely supply of provisions for himself and his men, together with tents, beds, and other necessary utensils. An aged person of Gilead, named Barzillai, particularly distinguished himself by his liberality on this occasion to the exiled king.

When Absalom heard that his father was at Mahanaim, he crossed the Jordan with an army, and encamped in the land of Gilead. His army was under the command of Amasa, his cousin.[*]

David, on his part, reviewed his force, which was but a handful of men as compared with the large host which Absalom brought into the field. He divided it into three battalions, the command of which he gave to Joab, Abishai, and Ittai the Gathite, intending himself to command the whole in person. But his people, aware that his valued life was principally sought, would not hear of it, but insisted on his remaining behind at Mahanaim, with a small reserved force. As the rest of his adherents marched out at the gate, David, who stood there, failed not to charge the commanders, in the hearing of the men, for his sake to respect the life of Absalom.

A most sanguinary action was soon after fought in the forest of Ephraim, wherein the rebel army was defeated, with the loss of twenty thousand men, slain in the battle-field, besides a great number of others who perished in the wood and in their flight. Absalom himself, mounted upon a mule,[†] was obliged to flee from a party of David's men toward the wood, where the boughs of a thick oak having taken hold of his bushy hair, in which he took so much pride, the mule continuing its speed, left him suspended in the air. The pursuing soldiers, seeing him in this state, respected the order of the king, and forbore to smite him; but Joab, who happened to learn what had occurred, ran and struck three darts through his body. " Whatever were Joab's crimes, among them disloyalty was not to be reckoned. And now he gave the most unequivocal proof of his unshaken fidelity, in knowingly incurring the king's displeasure, to rid him of an obstinate rebel against his own father, whom no forgiveness could soften and no favors could bind, for whom Joab himself had so successfully interceded, and was likely therefore to have been otherwise well disposed toward Absalom from the mere circumstance of having served him."[‡]

As the death of Absalom ended the cause of war, Joab caused the trumpet to sound a retreat, to stop the carnage. The body of Absalom was taken down, and cast into a large pit, and covered with a heap of stones. This was not the end or the sepulchre expected by this ambitious man, when he reared for himself a fair monument "in the king's dale," supposed the valley of Jehoshaphat, to keep his name in remembrance, because he had no sons, and therefore called it by his own name. In what manner we may venture to connect with Absalom the monument which now appears in the valley of Jehoshaphat bearing his name, is a matter on which a few words may be said in a note to this page.||

* Zeruiah, the mother of Joab and Abishai, was a sister of David; Abigail, the mother of Amasa, was another sister. Whence Joab, Abishai, and Amasa, were all nephews of David, and cousins of Absalom: whence also it happened that commanders of the opposite armies were sisters' sons. See 1 Chron. ii. 16, 17. But 2 Sam. xvii. 25, makes Abigail the grandmother of Amasa.

† As he had for civil state plenty of horses and chariots, this shows that the Hebrews had not yet come to use either in war.

‡ Hales, ii. 349.

|| ABSALOM'S SEPULCHRE, see p. 279.—Of the monument represented in the engraving, a very good and satisfactory account has been given by Mr. Wilde, whose description we shall here transcribe :—

"Descending to Gethsemane, we continued our course through the valley of Jehoshaphat by those remarkable monuments denominated the sepulchres of the patriarchs, which have been described, as well as

Race of Messengen.

The partisans of Absalom were no sooner acquainted with the death of their popular chief than they fled, every man to his own home.

Ahimaaz, the son of Zadok the high-priest, besought Joab to be allowed to bear
the tidings of the victory to the king. But as Joab knew that David would regard as
evil any tidings that included the death of his son, he, out of regard to Ahimaaz, refused his permission, but sent Cushi with the news. The other, afterward persisting
in his request, was allowed to go also; and he went with such speed that he outran
Cushi, and was first to appear before the king, who sat at the gate of Mahanaim,
anxiously awaiting tidings from the battle. The king and the father had struggled
hard within him; the father conquered; and now his absorbing desire was to know
that Absalom was safe. Aware of this feeling, Ahimaaz contented himself with re-
porting the victory, leaving to Cushi the less pleasant news; and he, when plainly
asked, " Is the young man Absalom safe?" answered, with much discretion, " The
enemies of my lord the king, and all that rise against thee to do thee evil, be as that
young man is." On hearing this, "the king was much moved, and went up to the
chamber over the gate; and as he went, thus he said, ' O my son Absalom! my son,
my son Absalom! would to God I had died for thee, O Absalom, my son, my son!'"
And thus he remained in the chamber over the gate, with his head covered like a
mourner, wailing for his son, and oblivious to all things else.

His faithful adherents, who, by venturing their lives for him against fearful odds,
had that day restored him to his throne, returning weary to the city, where they deserved to be greeted with thanks and praises, and triumphal songs, were quite confounded to learn this conduct of the king, and slunk into the town like guilty people—
even like defeated men rather than conquerors. As very serious consequences might
arise from this state of feeling, Joab went in to the king, and reproved him very
sharply for his unkingly conduct and untimely wailing, so calculated to discourage his
truest friends, and insisted that he should go forth and show himself to the people,
and speak kindly to them; " For," said he, " if thou go not forth, not a man will remain with thee this night; and this will be worse to thee than any evil that hath befallen thee from thy youth until now." The king could see the prudence of this
counsel; and, therefore, curbing his strong emotion, he went down to the gate and
sat there; on hearing which the people hastened to present themselves before him,
and all was well.

It might seem the obvious consequence of his victory, that David should repass the

drawn with great accuracy by most writers on Palestine. They are placed on the eastern side of Kedron,
nearly opposite the southern angle of the present wall, and are some of the rarest and most extraordinary
specimens of sepulchral architecture in existence. They are hewn out of the solid rock, with temple-like
fronts. Some of them are enormous masses separated from the rest of the rock, and left standing like so
many monolithic temples—monuments that record as well (if not more so) the labor and ingenuity of their
constructors as those to whose memory they have been erected. The names assigned to these tombs are
Jehoshaphat, James, Zechariah, and Absalom. This latter is the most elegant and tasteful piece of architecture in Judea, indeed, I might almost add, in the East, and viewed from the valley beneath, it is one of
the most beautiful tombs that I have ever seen in any country. It consists of a mass of rock twenty-four
feet square, separated from the rest, and standing in a small enclosure that surrounds three of its sides.
It has four pilasters with Ionic capitals on each front, the two outer ones being flat, while those in the centre are semicircular; the frieze is ornamented with triglyphs. The upper part is composed of several pieces,
and surmounted by a small spire terminating in a bunch of leaves. There is a hole in the back immediately beneath the architrave through which I was enabled to climb into its interior. As the door by which
it was entered was concealed, this opening was formed, in all probability, for the purpose of rifling the sepulchre of its contents. Within, it presents the usual form of eastern tombs, having niches at the sides
for bodies. The general opinion of antiquaries is, that the Grecian architecture exhibited on the exterior
of this rock is no test of the date of its construction; and that it was added in later times, and a similar
workmanship is visible in the other neighboring tombs. To it may be referred that rebuke of our Lord to
the Pharisees, regarding their garnishing the sepulchres of the prophets. The tradition is, that this pillar,
of which we have an account in the book of Samuel, was erected by Absalom. ' Now Absalom in his lifetime had taken and reared up for himself a pillar, which is in the *king's dale*; for he said, I have no son to
keep my name in remembrance; and he called the pillar after his own name; and it is called unto this day
Absalom's Place.' Josephus also informs us that ' Absalom had erected for himself a stone marble pillar
in the *king's dale*, two furlongs distant from Jerusalem, which he named Absalom's Stand, saying, that if
his children were killed, his name would remain by that pillar.' I see no reason to doubt the tradition regarding this monument, although the historian has stated it to be a greater distance from the city than we
now find it; but this is an error into which he often falls. In confirmation of its supposed origin I may add,
that it has ever been a place of detestation to the Hebrews; and every Jew who passes it by throws a
stone at it to this day, so that a large cairn has formed round its base.

" The style of the whole of these four sepulchres, but especially the two I have more particularly noticed,
is very peculiar, and is totally different from other tombs in this neighborhood. An inspection of them
would lead us to believe that, at the time of erection, the Hebrews had not quite forgot the lessons on
architecture which their forefathers had learned in Egypt. Around these mausolea, upon the sides of the
rocks, and the slopes of Mount Olivet, there are hundreds of plain flat gravestones belonging to the Jews.
All these have Hebrew inscriptions, some of which a Hebrew scholar resident in the city informed me
'ere dated a short time subsequent to the Christian era."—*Wilde's* " *Narrative of a Voyage*," p. 325-7.

Jordan at the head of his conquering army, and resume his throne at Jerusalem. But the mass of the people had chosen another for their king, and by that act had virtually, to the extent of their power, deposed himself; and in such a case it would appear that the civil principles of the constitution required that he should, in a certain sense, be re-elected to the crown by the people, before he was entitled to regard himself as king over any but such as had continued to recognise him in that character. He therefore remained beyond Jordan until the tribes should decide to recall him. It seems there was a general disposition among the people to do this; they blamed one another for their rebellion against the king, and their remissness in recalling him; but all seemed to shrink from taking the first step in the matter. Judah, from its more intimate relations with David, might be expected to give the example; but Judah had been the headquarters of the rebellion; and it appears that Jerusalem was in the occupation of Amasa, who, from the extent to which he had committed himself in Absalom's rebellion, might judge his case desperate, and hence use all his influence to prevent the king's return. This state of affairs being understood by David, he sent to the high-priests, who were still in Jerusalem, charging them to remind the elders of Judah of the obligation which seemed peculiarly to devolve upon them, and also to gain over Amasa by the offer to make him captain of the host in the place of Joab. This was attended with the desired result; and the elders of Judah sent back the answer, "Return thou, and all thy servants." On receiving this invitation, the king marched to the Jordan; and the men of Judah, on their part, assembled at Gilgal, to assist him over the river, and to receive him on his arrival. Among these, and foremost among them, were a thousand men of Benjamin, *headed by Shimei*, and including Ziba with his fifteen sons and twenty servants. No sooner had the king passed the river in a ferry-boat,* than Shimei threw himself at his feet, acknowledged his former crime, but trusted that it would be forgiven in consideration of his being the first in all Israel (except Judah) to come forward with a powerful party, to promote his restoration. In consideration of this circumstance, and, what was a greater merit and benefit—that his party was from the tribe of Benjamin—it would have been a most ungracious act had the king been inexorable. He therefore pardoned him freely, although some of his officers were for putting him to death. For the like reason, probably,—that is, for fear of disgusting the valuable party to which he belonged, and in which he had much influence,—the king dared not entirely recall from Ziba the grant of Mephibosheth's lands which he had hastily made to him. When the son of Jonathan came to the Jordan to meet the king, he made it clear to him that he had been slandered by his steward, who had purposely neglected to provide him with the means of escape from Jerusalem when he purposed to join the king in his exile; so that, in consequence of his lameness, he had been obliged to remain behind; but, during his stay, had remained in retirement, and, as a mourner, had neither dressed his feet, trimmed his beard, nor changed his clothes. Under the circumstances, the king could only say, "Thou and Ziba divide the land;" to which the reply of Mephibosheth was worthy of the son of the generous Jonathan, "Yea, let him take all, since my lord the king is come again to his own house in peace."

The rich old man of Gilead, Barzillai, who had so liberally ministered to the wants of David during his exile, came down to the Jordan to see him over. The king would fain have persuaded him to accompany him to Jerusalem, that he might have an opportunity of rewarding his services; but Barzillai returned the touching reply, "How long have I to live that I should go up with the king to Jerusalem? I am this day eighty years old, and can I discern between good and evil? Can thy servant taste what I eat, or what I drink? Can I hear any more the voice of singing-men and singing-women? Why then should thy servant be yet a burden to my lord the king? Let thy servant just go over Jordan with the king; and then let thy servant, I pray thee, return, *that I may die in my own city, near the grave of my father and my mother.*" He, however, recommended the fortunes of his son Chimham to the care of the king, who accordingly took that person with him to Jerusalem.

From the result, we may doubt the wisdom of the separate appeal which David

---

* The first and only time we ever read of a ferry-boat on the Jordan. The interpretation is, however, rather doubtful. Some make it a *bridge of boats*. Many interpreters prefer the sense of the Septuagint and Syriac, which, instead of, "And there went over a ferry-boat to carry over the king's household, and to do what he thought good," read, "And these (the men of Judah and Benjamin) went over the Jordan before the king, and performed the service of bringing over the king's household, and in doing what he thought good"

had made to his own tribe of Judah, inasmuch as his more intimate connexion with that tribe, by birth and by having reigned over it separately for seven years, required the most cautious policy on his side, to prevent his appearing to the other tribes as the king of a party. Now, when he had crossed the Jordan, people from all the tribes flocked to him to join in the act of recall and restoration. But when they came to consider of it, the other tribes were not willing to forgive Judah for having been beforehand with them; or, in other words, that, instead of inviting them to join with themselves in the act of recall, the elders of Judah, by acting independently had enabled themselves to exhibit the appearance of more alacrity and zeal in the king's behalf, putting the other tribes in an unfavorable position by comparison. They alleged also their claim to be considered, on the ground that the ten tribes had tenfold the interest in the kingdom to that which the single tribe of Judah could claim. The answer of that tribe was the most impolitic and provoking that could be made. They alleged that seeing the king was of their own tribe, "their bone and their flesh," they had a right to take a peculiar and exclusive interest in his recall. This quarrel grew so hot, as to strengthen the natural disposition of the tribes to regard David as the king of the Judahites; and but a slight impulse was wanting to induce them to leave him to his own party. This impulse was supplied by one Sheba, of the discontented tribe of Benjamin, who, perceiving the state of feeling, blew the trumpet, and gave forth the Hebrew watchword of revolt, "To your tents, O Israel!" and, in the name of the tribes, disclaimed all further interest in David, and bade defiance to his adherents. The effect of this move, perhaps, exceeded his expectation. On a sudden he saw himself at the head of all the tribes, except that of Judah, which had occasioned this defection, and which was left almost alone to conduct the king from the Jordan to Jerusalem.

This circumstance, perhaps, supplied to David an additional motive for performing his secret promise of making Amasa captain of the host; as that person appears to have been high in favor with the tribes. But most readers will feel displeased that Joab should at this juncture—after the brilliant displays which he had so lately afforded of his loyalty, courage, and prudence—be displaced in favor of the rebel leader; and even if judged by the principles of the East, that every stroke of policy by which something may be gained, is a good stroke, whatever interests or honor it sacrifices,— even judged by this rule, the policy of this operation may very much be doubted, as, indeed, David himself had soon occasion to suspect. In fact, we agree with Hales, that in this David "seems to have acted rather ungratefully and unwisely, justifying Joab's reproach (on a former occasion), 'thou lovest thine enemies and hatest thy friends.' But the old grudge and jealousy which he entertained against 'the sons of Zeruiah,' who were above his control, and too powerful to be punished, as in Abner's case, combined with Joab's disobedience of orders in killing Absalom, which he could never forget, nor forgive, to the day of his death, seem to have got the better of his usual temporizing caution and political prudence."

Amasa, the new captain of the host, failed to assemble the forces of Judah, to act against Sheba, within the time which the king had appointed. Whether this arose from want of zeal or ability in him, or from the disgust of the Judahites at the removal of Joab from an office which he had filled with great distinction for twenty-seven years, we know not. The king was in consequence obliged to order Joab's brother, Abishai, to take the command of the royal guards, and pursue Sheba without delay, before he could get into the fenced cities; for that otherwise he might raise a rebellion more dangerous than Absalom's. On this occasion Joab went with Abishai as a volunteer, followed by the company which formed his private command, for his zeal for his king and country rose paramount above his sense of the disgrace which had recently been inflicted on him. But when Amasa, with the force he had collected, joined them at Gibeon to take the command, Joab, under the pretext of saluting him as his "*brother*," slew him, just as in a former time he had slain Abner. He then took the command himself, causing proclamation to be made,—"He that favoreth Joab, and he that is for David, let him follow Joab." He then pursued Sheba, besieged him in a town to which he had fled, demanded his head from the inhabitants, and crushed the rebellion. He then returned triumphant to Jerusalem, self-reinstated in his former station, of which David dared no more to deprive him.

About the thirty-fourth year of David's reign* commenced a grievous famine, which

* So Hales; but some think that although the history *relates* the event in this place, it actually occurred in the early part of David's reign. And there are some very probable reasons for this conclusion.

continued for three successive years. When the sacred oracle was consulted, it declared that this was on account of the unatoned blood of the Gibeonites, whom Saul, in despite of the ancient treaty between that people and the Israelites, had cut off. This circumstance is not mentioned in the history of Saul; but, from the circumstances, it may perhaps be collected that Saul, finding the difficulty, to which we have adverted more than once, of forming a landed property for his family, where the land was already inalienably parcelled out among the people, had, under pretence of zeal for the interests of his own people, formed the design of utterly destroying the Gibeonites, and, as far as he was able, executed that design, giving their lands and wealth to his relatives, by the survivors of whom they were still possessed. As it therefore appeared that the calamity which punished this breach of national faith could only be averted through satisfaction being rendered to the remnant of the Gibeonites, David sent to learn what satisfaction they required. They, actuated by the powerful principles of revenge for blood, to which we had such frequent occasion to advert, refused to take "silver or gold," that is, a blood-fine, from the house of Saul, but demanded that execution should be performed upon seven members of that house. Seven members of Saul's family were accordingly sought out and given up to them. These were, two sons of Saul by his concubine Rizpah, and five grandsons by his eldest daughter Merab; Mephibosheth (who appears to have been the only other member of the family) was held back by David, on account of the covenant between him and Jonathan. The Gibeonites took these persons, and, after having slain them, hanged up their bodies upon a hill. This was against the law, which forbids that a body should be kept hanging after the going down of the sun on the first day. How long they thus remained, is not stated; but the famine had been occasioned by drought, and they hung there until the rains of heaven fell upon them. It was then made known to David that Rizpah, the mother of two of them, had spread sackcloth for herself upon the rock, and had there remained to protect the bodies from the birds of the air and the beasts of the field. Touched by this striking instance of the tenderness of maternal affection, David not only directed the bodies of these persons to be taken down, but he went (or sent) to Jabesh Gilead, to remove from under the oak in that place, the bones of Saul and Jonathan, and deposite them, with all respect, in the family sepulchre at Kelah in Benjamin, together with the remains of these unhappy members of their house.

David has been censured by some writers for consenting to the demand of the Gibeonites; but the reader must perceive that the demand of the Gibeonites was one which the king could not refuse. *They* might have accepted the blood-fine; but this was optional with them, and they were perfectly entitled to refuse it, and to demand blood for blood. That the persons who were slain had themselves no hand in the crime for which they were punished, is more than we know; it is most likely that they were active parties in it, and still more that they reaped the profits of it. But even were this not the case, it is a well-known principle of blood-avengement that the heirs and relatives of the blood-shedder are responsible for the blood in their own persons, in case the avenger is not able to reach the actual perpetrator. That David had any interest in getting rid of these persons is equally absurd and untrue, for they made no pretensions to the crown themselves, nor did others make such pretensions for them. Even when the cause of Saul's house was most in want of a head, none of these persons appeared to advance their claims, nor did the warmest partisans of the cause dream of producing any of them in opposition to David.

Now that the Israelites had been weakened by two rebellions and three years of famine, the Philistines deemed the opportunity favorable for an attempt to shake off their yoke. They therefore renewed the war about the thirty-seventh year of David's reign, but were defeated in four engagements, and finally subdued. In all these engagements the Philistines exhibited their old passion for bringing gigantic champions into the field. In the first of these engagements, David himself, notwithstanding his years, shrunk not from the combat with the giant Izbi-benob; but he waxed faint, and was in danger of being slain, had not the brave and trusty Abishai hastened to his relief, and killed the gigantic Philistine. After this the people would no more allow David to go forth in person to battle, "lest he should quench the light of Israel." This war completely extinguished the gigantic race to which Goliah had belonged.

The numbering of the people was one of the last and most reprehensible acts of the reign of David. In itself, an enumeration of the population might be not only inno-cent but useful; it was the motive by which the deed was rendered evil. This mo-tive, so offensive to God, was obviously supplied by the design of forcing all the Is-raelites into military service, with a view to foreign conquests; a design not only pitiable in so old a man, but in every way repugnant to both the internal and exter-nal polity of the theocratical government. That the census was not, as in former times, taken through the priests and magistrates, but by Joab, as commander-in-chief, assisted by the other military chiefs, sufficiently indicates the military object of the census; and if they were accompanied by the regular troops under their command, as the mention of their "encamping" leads one to suspect, it may seem that the ob-ject was known to and disliked by the people, and that the census could only be taken in the presence of a military force. Indeed the measure was repugnant to the wishes of the military commanders themselves, and was in a peculiar degree abhorrent to Joab, who saw the danger to the liberties of the people, and gave it all the opposition in his power, and undertook it reluctantly, when he found the king adhered to his purpose with the obstinacy of age.

At the end of nine months and twenty days, Joab brought to the king the return of the adult male population, which was 900,000 men in the ten tribes of Israel, and 400,000, in round numbers, in the tribe of Judah alone; being, together, 1,300,000. But the tribes of Levi and Benjamin were not included in this account; for Joab did not finish the enumeration, probably in consequence of some indications of the Divine displeasure in the course of it. According to usual proportions, the entire population of Israel at this time (without including these two tribes) could not well have been less than 5,200,000. The same marks of the Divine displeasure which prevented the completion of the census were probably those which awakened the slumbering con-science of David when the return was presented to him. He confessed before God that he had sinned, and prayed to be forgiven. The next morning it was made known to him, through the prophet Gad, that he had sinned indeed, and that his sin was not of such a nature as, with a due regard to the public principles of the govern-ment, could be allowed to pass without signal punishment. The choice of punish-ment was offered to him: seven years of famine, three months to be pursued by his enemies, or three days of pestilence. The humbled monarch confessed the choice to be hard, but fixed on the latter alternative, as the more equal punishment, and such as seemed more immediately under the direction of Heaven. Accordingly, Jehovah sent a pestilence, which in the course of two days destroyed 70,000 men, from Dan to Beersheba. It was then beginning to visit Jerusalem, when God was pleased to put a stop to it, at the earnest prayer of David. He beheld the commissioned angel stand in the thrashing-floor of Araunah, a chief person among the Jebusites, as one preparing to destroy. And then he and the elders of Israel, all clad in sackcloth, fell upon their faces, and the king cried—"Is it not I that commanded the people to be numbered? Even I it is that have sinned and done evil indeed; but as for these sheep, what have they done? Let thy hand, I pray thee, O Jehovah, my God, be on me, and on my father's house; but not on thy people that they should be plagued." This noble prayer was granted as soon as uttered. Through the prophet Gad, he was commanded to erect an altar, and offer sacrifices on that spot of ground where he had seen the destroying angel stand. The king accordingly bought the thrashing-floor from Araunah (who would willingly have given it free of cost) for fifty shekels of silver.* He then hastened to erect an altar, and to offer thereon burnt-offerings, and peace-offerings; and a miraculous fire which descended from the heavens and consumed the victims gave manifest proof of the Divine complacency, and so sanc-tified the spot as to point it out for the site of the future temple. The plague was stayed.

David was now advancing toward seventy years of age, and it appeared, from the declining state of his health, that his latter end could not be far off. This made

* As this was little more than thirty dollars of our money, and paid not only for the thrashing-floor, but for all that was upon it—cattle and implements—it seems to show that the value of the precious metals among the Hebrews at this time was much higher than it is now with us. It is, however, possible that Araunah merely set a nominal price to satisfy the delicacy of the king, who would not sacrifice to God at the cost of other people. There is an apparent contradiction between the account in 2 Sam. xxiv. 24, and 1 Chron. xxi. 25, which says that David gave Araunah 600 shekels of gold by weight (which would be no less than $6,000 of our money); but this may be removed by the very probable supposition that after Da-vid knew, by the acceptance of the altar erected on the spot, that the temple was to be built in this place, he made a further purchase of a sufficient site for the additional and much larger sum just named.

Adonijah, his eldest surviving son, determine to take measures to secure the throne, which, had it been hereditary, would naturally have devolved to him. He doubtless knew that the crown had been assigned to his younger brother Solomon, and felt that this was perhaps his only opportunity of asserting what he conceived to be his natural rights. Adonijah was a very handsome man, and he had not at any time been balked or contradicted by his father, many of whose sorrows arose from his excessive indulgence of his children. He now, in apparent imitation of Absalom, set up a splendid retinue, and courted popularity among the people; and he succeeded in drawing over to his party Joab, who now at last forsook his old master, and Abiathar the high-priest, who had shared all his fortunes. One day, when matters seemed ripe for the further development of his designs, he made a grand entertainment at Ain Rogel, the fountain in the king's garden, to which he invited all the king's sons, with the significant exception of Solomon, and the principal persons in the state, with the exception of those who were known to be in Solomon's interest. There he was proclaimed king in the usual form—" Long live the king Adonijah !"—by the powerful party assembled.

In this important emergency, Nathan the prophet sent Bathsheba to inform the king of these proceedings, and afterward came in himself and confirmed her account. By both he was reminded of his previous declarations that Solomon was to be his successor in the throne. The old king was roused to his wonted energy by this intelligence. He instantly appointed Nathan the prophet, Zadok the priest, Benaiah, and his own guards the Cherithites and Pelethites, who continued faithful, to take Solomon, and conduct him, mounted on the king's own mule, to the fountain of Gihon, and there to anoint and proclaim him king. The ceremony was thus attended with every circumstance which could give it authority in the eyes of the people, as indicating the intention of the king, which, it was now well known, was according to the will of God. There was the mule, which none but David had ever been seen to ride, and which, he having habitually ridden, none but a king might ride; there was the prophet who could only sanction that which he knew to be the will of God; there was Zadok, with the holy anointing oil from the tabernacle; and there were the guards, whom the people had been accustomed to see in attendance only on the king. The whole ceremony was also directed to take place on one of the most public and frequented roads leading from Jerusalem. The people were adequately impressed by all these considerations and circumstances; they heartily shouted, " Long live King Solomon !" The earth was, as it were, rent with the rejoicing clamor, mixed with the sounds of trumpets and of pipes. The party of Adonijah heard the noise; and when informed of the cause, they were all so struck with consternation at the promptitude and effect of this counter-move, that they dispersed immediately, and slunk away every man to his own house. Adonijah, seeing himself thus forsaken, and dreading nothing less than immediate death, fled to the refuge of the altar (erected on the tharshing-floor of Araunah). Solomon, being informed of this, sent to tell him that, if by his future conduct he proved himself a worthy man, he would not hurt a hair of his head, but at the same time assured him that any future instance of a disloyal intention would be fatal to him. On leaving the altar, Adonijah went and rendered his homage to the new king; after which he was ordered to retire to his own house.

The waning spark of David's life gleamed up once again before it finally expired. He availed himself of this to call a general assembly of the nation to ratify the coronation of Solomon, and to receive the declaration of his views and designs. The aged king was able to stand up on his feet as he addressed the assembly at considerable length. Perceiving from the revolts of Absalom and Adonijah, into which last some of his own stanchest friends had been drawn, that the principle of primogeniture was likely to interfere very seriously with the true doctrine of the theocracy, he was careful to point out how the sceptre had been assigned to Judah, not the first-born of Jacob; and in the tribe of Judah, to the family of Jesse, not the first or most powerful of that tribe; and of the eight sons of Jesse, to David the youngest; and of the sons of David, to Solomon, at a time when there were living three (if not four[*]) older than he. He then proceeded to state the reasons which had prevented him from building to the Lord that temple which he had designed; and since this great work had been reserved for the peaceable reign of his son, he solemnly ex-

* Chileab, the son of Abigail, is not historically named. The probability is that he died early.

horted him and the nation to erect that temple according to the model which he had himself supplied, and to contribute liberally themselves toward it, in addition to the ample stores and materials which in the course of his reign he had been enabled to provide. He concluded with a most noble and devout thanksgiving to the Lord for all the mercies which he had shown to himself and to his people: and this, with the rest of his conduct on this occasion, shows that, whatever were now the bodily infirmities of the aged king, his better faculties were still in their prime.

Solomon was now again anointed king in the presence, and with the sanction of the assembly, by Zadok, who himself was now declared and recognised as sole high-priest, Abiathar being deposed from his participation in that dignity on account of his having gone over to Adonijah. It is impossible not to see in all this a strenuous assertion by David of the theocratical principles of the constitution, which rendered conclusive and final any appointment which the Divine King had made, or might make; and for this he deserves the more honor, as there is good reason to think that, for himself merely, as a father, he would quite as soon have seen Absalom or Adonijah on the throne as Solomon. Of Abiathar it was quite necessary to make an example; for, as high-priest, he of all men ought to have been sensible of the obligation of the divine appointment, the maintenance of which had now become one of the most marked and grand prerogatives of Jehovah as king of the Hebrews, and the one which was calculated to keep his superiority present to the minds of the people. If this prerogative were allowed to be contemned by the high-priest, who should be its most strenuous supporter, the people would not be likely to hold it in much respect.

The enthusiasm manifested by the king for the object which for many years past he had so much at heart, kindled a corresponding zeal in the people, who presented liberal offerings for the great work which Solomon was destined to execute.

The following day was spent as a high festival. Holocausts of numerous steers, and rams, and lambs, were offered to Jehovah, and also abundant peace-offerings, on which the people feasted with great gladness, before they departed to their homes. This was, in fact, the coronation-feast of Solomon. He, being now twice anointed, and formally recognised by the people, mounted the throne of his father, and administered the government while David still lived.

It was not, however, long before David felt that his last hour approached. He then sent for his son, to give to him his last counsels. He first of all recapitulated the gracious promises which God had made to him and his posterity, and then reminded Solomon that these promises were only, in their first and obvious sense, to be understood as conditional, and depending upon their observance of the divine law; so that they might expect their prosperity to rise and fall in proportion to their obedience. He then proceeded to advise him as to the course he should take with reference to certain persons whom his own history has brought conspicuously under the notice of the reader. The predominating influence of the sons of Zeruiah had, throughout his reign, been very galling to himself, and he advised his son not to incur the same grievance, or to submit to it. As to Joab, he had, through policy, been pardoned for his part in Adonijah's rebellion, as David himself had, from like reasons, been compelled to overlook the crimes of which he had been guilty—such as the murders of Abner and Amasa; yet, should he again offend, Solomon was advised to bring him to condign punishment, by which he would strike terror into evil doers, and, more than by any other act, evince the strength and firmness of his government.

The pardon which Shimei had asked, beside the Jordan, with a thousand men at his back, could not well have been refused, and David had no wish to annul it; but, aware of the character of this disaffected and dangerous Benjamite, he cautioned Solomon against him, and advised to keep him under his eye in Jerusalem, and watch him well that he might have no opportunity of stirring up seditions among the tribes; and should his conduct again offer occasion, David counselled the young king not to spare him, but at once rid his kingdom of so suspicious and malevolent a character.

David appears to have survived the coronation of Solomon about six months; for, although he reigned seven years and six months over Judah, and thirty-three years over all Israel, yet the whole duration is reckoned only forty years in 2 Sam. v. 4, 5; 1 Chron. xxix. 27. The interval he seems to have employed in the development, for the benefit of his son, of those plans and regulations which had long before been formed and considered in his own mind, and to which the due effect was afterward given by his son. These are fully stated in the first five chapters of the second book of Chronicles.

David was seventy years of age when "he slept with his fathers." At that time certainly the period of human life was reduced to the present standard; for, in recording his death at this age, the historian says, "He died in a good old age, full of days, riches, and honor." He was buried in a stately tomb, which, according to a touching custom, still prevalent in the East, he had *prepared for himself*, in that part of the city (on Mount Zion) which he had covered with buildings, and which was called after him, "the city of David."

CHAPTER XVIII.

On the death of David, his son Solomon, who had been declared by him king of Israel, with the divine approbation, succeeded to the throne, to the universal satisfaction of the people. This event took place when he was about twenty years of age, and in the year 1030 B. C. Never monarch ascended the throne with greater advantages, or knew better how to secure and improve them. Under David the kingdom had been much extended, and brought under good regulations. The arms of the Hebrews had for so many years been feared by all the neighboring nations, so that the habit of respect and obedience on their part offered to the new king the reasonable prospect, confirmed by a divine promise, that his reign should be one of peace. *Now*, the predominant tribe of Judah lay as a lion and as a lioness, which no nation ventured to rouse up. (Gen. xlix. 9; Num. xxiii. 24, xxiv. 9.) The Hebrews were the ruling people, and their empire the principal monarchy of Western Asia. From the Mediterranean sea and the Phœnicians to the Euphrates, in its nearer and remoter bounds—from the river of Egypt and the Elanitic gulf to Berytus, Hamath, and Thapsacus, all were subject to the dominion of Solomon; nor were the tribes which wander in northern Arabia, eastward to the Persian gulf, unconscious of his rule. At home the Canaanites had not, as we have seen, been either entirely expelled or annihilated; but they had become obedient and peaceable subjects, and, which was of importance to an eastern king, liable to services which no king dared to impose upon the Israelites themselves. Jahn calculates that their whole number may have been about four or five hundred thousand, since ultimately one hundred fifty-three thousand were able to render soccage to the king. The warlike and civilized Philistines, the Edomites, Moabites, and Ammonites, the Syrians of Damascus, and some tribes of the nomadic Arabians of the desert, were all tributary to him. The revenues derived from the subject states were large; and the wealth in the royal treasures great beyond calculation: and the king had the enterprise and talent to open new sources through which riches were poured into the country from distant lands. Nor were the prospects and promises with which this reign opened frustrated in its continuance. "Peace gave to all his subjects prosperity; the trade which he introduced brought wealth into the country, and promoted the sciences and arts, which there found an active protector in the king, who was himself distinguished for his learning. The building of the temple and of several palaces introduced foreign artists, by whom the Hebrews were instructed. Many foreigners, and even sovereign princes, were attracted to Jerusalem, in order to see and converse with the prosperous royal sage. The regular progress of all business, the arrangements for security from foreign and domestic enemies, the army, the cavalry, the armories, the chariots, the palaces, the royal household, the good order in the administration, and in the service of the court, excited as much admiration as the wisdom and learning of the viceroy of Jehovah. *So much was effected by the single influence of David, because he scrupulously* conformed himself to the theocracy of the Hebrew state."[*]

Such is the *argument* to the history of Solomon's reign, to the details of which we now proceed.

Although Solomon was not the first-born, nor even the eldest living son of David, but succeeded to the throne through the special appointment of the Supreme King,

Jehovah, there was one circumstance which, from the usual notions of the Orientals, could not but be highly favorable to him, even had *all* his elder brothers been alive. Amnon had been born before his father became king, and Absalom and Adonijah while he was king of Judah only; while Solomon was born when his father was king over all Israel, and lord over many neighboring states. And in the East there is a strong prejudice in favor of him who is the son of *the king* and of *the kingdom,* that is, who is born while his father actually *reigns* over the states which he leaves at his death. Thus, therefore, if at the death of David, Amnon and Absalom had been alive, as well as Adonijah and Solomon, there might have been a contest among them on these grounds:—Amnon would have claimed as the eldest son of David; Absalom would probably have disputed this claim on the ground, first, that he was the first-born *after David became a king;* and, secondly, on the ground that his mother was of a royal house: this claim could not have been disputed by Adonijah; but he would have considered his own claim good as against Amnon, on the one hand, and as against Solomon on the other. But Solomon might have claimed on the same ground as the others against Amnon; and against Absalom and Adonijah, on the ground that their father was only king of Judah when they were born, but king of all Israel at the time of his own birth. And this claim would, in fact, have been but a carrying out of the principle on which Absalom and Adonijah are supposed to oppose Amnon; and in this claim there would have seemed so much reason to an Oriental, that, apart from all other considerations, we doubt not it would have found many adherents in Israel; and we *have* no doubt that it did operate in producing a more cheerful acquiescence in the preference given to Solomon.

Soon after the death of his father, Solomon discovered a new plot of Adonijah's, so deeply laid and carefully veiled, that he even ventured to make the king's own mother, Bathsheba, an acting though unconscious party in it. And here it may be proper to observe, that in eastern countries, where polygamy is allowed, or not forbidden, by the law, and where the kings have numerous wives and concubines, there is no dignity analogous to that which the sole wife of a sovereign occupies in Europe. In fact, there is no *queen,* in the proper sense of the word, as applied to the consort of a king. But the *mother* of the king (and, next to her, or instead of her, the mother of the heir apparent) is the woman of the greatest influence and highest station in the state, and the one whose condition is the most queenly of any which the East affords. According to this view, Bathsheba—during the latter part of David's reign, as mother of the heir apparent, and during at least the early portion of Solomon's reign, as mother of the king—was, in fact, queen of Israel; whence in both periods we find her taking a part in public affairs, which, however slight, is such as none but a woman so placed could have taken.

The first manifestation of Adonijah's design was to endeavor to procure permission to espouse Abishag, one of the wives of his father, whom he had taken in his last days and had left a virgin. He had the address to interest Bathsheba in his object, and to get her to propose the subject to the king, although part of what he said to her as an inducement was well calculated to awaken her suspicions: " Thou knowest," said he, " that the kingdom was mine, and that all Israel set their faces on me, that I should reign; howbeit, the kingdom is turned about, and is become my brother's, for it was his from the Lord."

The king was seated on his throne when Bathsheba appeared before him to urge the suit of Adonijah. He rose when he beheld her, and bowed to her; after which he caused a seat to be brought and placed at his right hand for her. She then made "the one small petition" with which she was charged. The king instantly saw through the whole; and knew enough of the several parties to feel assured (or actually knew) that the measure had been prompted by Joab and Abiathar, or that at least they were parties to the ulterior design. According to what we have already stated respecting the widows of a deceased king, it is obvious that Solomon recognised in this insidious demand a plan formed to accredit the former pretensions of Adonijah. He therefore answered warmly, "And why dost thou ask Abishag, the Shunammite, for Adonijah? Ask for him the kingdom also; for he is mine elder brother, even for him, and for Abiathar the priest, and for Joab the son of Zeruiah." By this he clearly intimated that he considered Joab and Abiathar as parties in this new plot, and, as such, liable to the punishments which he proceeded to inflict. Adonijah he ordered to be put to death, as one whom it was no longer safe

Great Mogul on his Throne.

Howdah of an Indian Prince.

to pardon. On receiving this news, Joab justified the suspicions (if not more) of the king, by fleeing for refuge to the·sanctuary of the altar—a plain act of a guilty conscience. When this was told to Solomon, he ordered Benaiah to go and put him to death. Benaiah went, and ordered him, in the king's name, to come forth. This he refused, saying, "Nay, but I will die here!" either in the hope that Solomon would so far regard the altar as not to slay him, or that he would die there in the hope that God, whose altar it was, would be gracious to him. This being a new case, in which Benaiah liked not to act on his own responsibility, he returned to report the matter to the king, who, with great firmness, and with a freedom from superstition which shows how well he understood the letter and spirit of the law, said, "Do as he hath said, and slay him there, and bury him, that thou mayest take away the innocent blood, which Joab shed, from me and from the house of my father." So Joab was slain at the altar, and buried in the garden of his own house in the wilderness. Benaiah, who had been his executioner, was made commander-in-chief in his room. It appears that in the Hebrew kingdom, as in some other ancient and in some modern states, it was the duty of the king's chief officer to execute his sentence upon high offenders.

As to Abiathar, who had before joined Adonijah, and was no stranger to the more recent intrigue, he had shared the fate of Joab, if the king had not been mindful of his early and long-continued attachment to David, and respected the sacred character he bore. He was commanded to withdraw to his estate in Anathoth, and no longer presume to exercise his sacerdotal functions. Thus was the house of Eli finally degraded in the person of Abiathar, and the house of Eleazer completely restored in the person of Zadok.

This affair reminded Solomon of the necessity of keeping watch over another disaffected person, Shimei, as counselled by David. He therefore ordered him to fix his residence in Jerusalem, which he engaged him by oath not to leave, forewarning him that the breach of this engagement would be at the expense of his life. Of this Shimei was properly mindful for two years; but then he was induced to leave the city, and went as far as Gath (a suspicious quarter) in pursuit of two runaway slaves. He was therefore, on his return, consigned to the sword of Benaiah.

By the removal of these dangerous persons, Solomon felt his throne secured to him. He then sought an alliance worthy of the rank to which his kingdom had attained. The nearest power, from an alliance with which even he might derive honor, was that of Egypt. He therefore demanded and received the daughter of the reigning Pharaoh in marriage. His new spouse was received by the king of Israel with great magnificence, and was lodged in "the city of David," until the new and splendid palace, which he had already commenced, should be completed. That Solomon should thus contract an alliance, on equal terms, with the reigning family of that great nation which had formerly held the Israelites in bondage, was, in the ordinary point of view, a great thing for him, and shows the relative importance into which the Hebrew kingdom had now risen. The king is in no part of Scripture blamed for this alliance, even in places where it seems unlikely that blame would have been spared had he been considered blameworthy; and as we know that the Egyptians were idolaters, this absence of blame may intimate that Solomon stipulated that the Egyptian princess should abandon the worship of her own gods, and conform to the Jewish law. This at least was what would be required by the law of Moses, which the king was not likely (at least, at this time of his life) to neglect. Nor need we suppose that the royal family of Egypt would make much difficulty in this; for, *except among the Israelites*, the religion of a woman has never in the East been considered of much consequence.

Solomon, soon after, sought by his example to restore the proper order of public worship. At Gibeon was the tabernacle and altar of Moses, and there, notwithstanding the absence of the ark, the symbol of the divine presence, the Shechinah, still abode. This therefore was, according to the law, the only proper seat of public worship, and the place to which the tribes should resort to render homage to the Great King. Therefore, at one of the religious festivals, the king repaired to Gibeon, accompanied by all his court, the officers of his army, and the chiefs and elders of his people, with a vast multitude of the people. There, in the midst of all the state and ceremony of the holy solemnities, the king presented, to be offered on the brazen altar, a thousand beasts, as a holocaust. This solemn act of homage from the young

Solomon returning to Jerusalem.

king was acceptable to God, who in the following night manifested himself to him in a dream, and promised to satisfy whatever wish he might then form. Instead of expressing the usual desires which animate kings, as well as others, for wealth, and glory, and length of days, Solomon expressed his sense of the difficulties, to one so young, of the high station to which he had been called; and, humbly conscious of his lack of the experience required to conduct well the affairs of his large empire and numerous people, he prayed for wisdom—nothing but wisdom: "I am but a youth: I know not how to go or to come in. And thy servant is in the midst of thy people, whom thou hast chosen, a great people, that can not be numbered nor counted for multitude. Give, therefore, thy servant an understanding heart to judge thy people, that I may discern between good and evil: for who is able to judge this thy so great a people?" This request which Solomon had made was highly pleasing to God. That which he *had* asked was promised to him in abounding measure—wisdom such as none before him had ever possessed, or should possess in future times: and since he had made so excellent a choice, that which he *had not* asked should also be given to him—riches and honors beyond all the kings of his time, and, beside this, length of days, if he continued in obedience. Solomon awoke; and feeling within himself that illumination of mind and spirit which assured him that his dream had indeed been oracular and divine, he returned with great joy to Jerusalem.

Soon after this, the discharge of those judicial duties which engage so much of the attention of eastern kings, gave him an opportunity of displaying so much discernment as satisfied the people of his uncommon endowments, and his eminent qualifications for his high place. This was his celebrated judgment between the two harlots who both claimed a living child, and both disclaimed one that had died; in which he discovered the rightful owner of the living child by calling forth that self-denying tenderness which always reigns in a mother's heart.* This produced the very best effect among all the people; for, generally, nothing is better understood and appreciated, popularly, than an acute and able judicial decision of some difficult point in a case easily understood, and by which the sympathies are much engaged.

The preparations for the temple had from the first engaged the attention of Solomon. Among the first who sent to congratulate him on his succession was Hiram, king of Tyre, who has already been named as an attached friend and ally of David. The value of the friendship offered by this monarch was fully appreciated by Solomon, who returned the embassy with a letter, in which he opened the noble design he entertained, and solicited the same sort of assistance in the furtherance of it, as the same king had rendered to his father David, when building his palace. Hiram assented with great willingness, and performed the required services with such fidelity and zeal, as laid the foundation of a lasting friendship between the kings, and to the formation of other mutually beneficial connexions between them. The forests of the Lebanon mountains only could supply the timber required for this great work. Such of these forests as lay nearest the sea were in the possession of the Phœnicians; among whom timber was in such constant demand that they had acquired great and acknowledged skill in the felling and transportation thereof, and hence it was of much importance that Hiram consented to employ large bodies of men in Lebanon to hew timber, as well as others to perform the service of bringing it down to the seaside, whence it was to be taken along the coast in floats to the port of Joppa, from which place it could be easily taken across the country to Jerusalem. This portion of the assistance rendered by Hiram was of the utmost value and importance. If he had declined Solomon's proposals, all else that he wanted might have been obtained from Egypt. But that country was so far from being able to supply timber, that it wanted it more than almost any nation.

Solomon also desired that Phœnician artificers of all descriptions should be sent to Jerusalem, particularly such as excelled in the arts of design, and in the working of gold, silver, and other metals, as well as precious stones; nor was he insensible of the value and beauty of those scarlet, purple, and other fine dyes, in the preparation and application of which the Tyrians excelled. Men skilled in all these branches of art were largely supplied by Hiram. He sent also a person of his own name, a Tyrian by birth, who seems to have been a second Bezaleel; for his abilities were so great, and his attainments so extensive and various, that he was skilled not only in

* See the original narrative in 1 Kings iii. 16-28.

the working of metals, but in all kinds of works in wood and stone, and even in embroidery, in tapestry, in dyes, and the manufacture of all sorts of fine cloth. And not only this, but his general attainments in art, and his inventive powers, enabled him to devise the means of executing, and to execute, whatever work in art might be proposed to him. This man was a treasure to Solomon, who made him overseer not only of the men whom the king of Tyre now sent, but of his own workmen, and those whom David had formerly engaged and retained in his employment.

In return for all these advantages, Solomon engaged on his part to furnish the king of Tyre yearly with 2,500 quarters of wheat, and 150,000 gallons of pure olive oil, for his own use, beside furnishing the men employed in Lebanon with the same corn quantities, respectively, of wheat and barley, and the same liquid quantities of wine and oil.

Josephus informs us that the correspondence on this subject between Solomon and Hiram, copies of which are given by him as well as in the books of Kings and Chronicles, were in his time still preserved in the archives of Tyre.

Three years were spent in preparation; but at last all was ready, and the foundation of this famous temple was laid in the fourth year of Solomon's reign (1027 B. C.), in the second month, and finished in the eleventh year and eighth month; being a space of seven years and six months.

Many elaborate treatises have been written on this magnificent structure, but no satisfactory result has been obtained therefrom. This may arise from a mistaken reference to classical ideas and models, and from the scanty knowledge we possess of ancient and modern oriental architecture. Hence it is that modern commentators and illustrators of Scripture have generally shrunk from the subject; and hence the many conjectural plans which have been exhibited as illustrative of this far-famed building, must be looked upon as inconclusive. The only safe ground we have to go upon is Scripture, whence our account shall be derived, and, for the most part, in the sacred historian's own language.

We learn, from the history of David, that when he was raised to the throne of Israel, he piously resolved to erect a temple to the honor of Jehovah. Thus, in one of his beautiful psalms, he says: "Lord, remember David, and all his afflictions: how he sware unto the Lord, and vowed unto the mighty God of Jacob; surely I will not come into the tabernacle of my house, nor go up into my bed; I will not give sleep to mine eyes, or slumber to mine eyelids, until I find out a place for the Lord, a habitation for the mighty God of Jacob," Psa. cxxxii. 1-5. Because, however, David was a man of war, God, by his prophet Nathan, intimated to him that while he approved of his design, he nevertheless should not be permitted to build him a house; but, at the same time, he gave him a promise that his son and successor should fulfil his pious intention: see 1 Chron. xvii.

The good monarch acquiesced in the Divine will; and, to enable his son to perform so glorious a work, he himself commenced preparations, and we find him, in his last moments, instructing Solomon in God's promises, and in his duty in building the temple, at the conclusion of which he states what material he had prepared for the undertaking: "Now, behold, in my trouble I have prepared for the house of the Lord a hundred thousand talents of gold, and a thousand thousand talents of silver; and of brass and iron without weight, for it is in abundance: timber also and stone have I prepared; and thou mayest add thereto. Moreover there are workmen with thee in abundance, hewers and workers of stone and timber, and all manner of cunning men for every manner of work. Of the gold, the silver, and the brass, and the iron, there is no number. Arise, therefore, and be doing, and the Lord be with thee."—1 Chron. xxii. 14-16. David, moreover, gave to Solomon "the pattern of the porch, and of the houses thereof, and of the treasuries thereof, and of the upper chambers thereof, and of the inner parlors thereof, and of the place of the mercy-seat, and the pattern of all that he had by the spirit, of the courts of the house of the Lord, and of all the chambers round about, of the treasuries of the house of God, and of the treasuries of the dedicated things; also for the courses of the priests and the Levites, and for all the work of the service of the house of the Lord, and for all the vessels of service in the house of the Lord. He gave of gold by weight for things of gold, for all instruments of all manner of service; silver also for all instruments of silver by weight, for all instruments of every kind of service: even the weight for the candlesticks of gold, and for their lamps of gold, by weight for every candlestick, and for the lamps thereof: and for the candlesticks of silver by weight, both for the candlestick, and also for the lamps thereof, according to the use of every candlestick. And by weight he gave gold for the tables of showbread, for every table; and likewise silver for the tables of silver: also pure gold for the flesh-hooks, and the bowls, and the cups; and for the golden basins he gave gold by weight for every basin; and likewise silver by weight for every basin of silver: and for the altar of incense refined gold by weight; and gold for the pattern of the chariot of the cherubim, that spread out their wings, and covered the ark of the covenant of the Lord. All this, said David, the Lord made me to understand in writing by his hand upon me, even all the works of this pattern. And David said to Solomon his son, Be strong and of good courage, and do it: fear not, nor be dismayed, for the Lord God, even my God, will be with thee; he will not fail thee, nor forsake thee, until thou hast finished all the work for the service of the house of the Lord. And, behold, the courses of the priests and the Levites, even they shall be with thee for all the service of the house of God: and there shall be with thee for all manner of workmanship every willing skilful man, for any manner of service: also the princes and all the people will be wholly at thy commandment." 1 Chron. xxviii. 11–21.

The youthful monarch was not unmindful of his royal parent's charge. No sooner was he seated peaceably on his throne, than we find him addressing Hiram king of Tyre in these words: "Thou knowest how that David my father could not build a house unto the name of the Lord his God for the wars which were about him on every side, until the Lord put them under the soles of his feet. But now the Lord my God hath given me rest on every side, so that there is neither adversary nor evil occurrent. And, behold, I purpose to build a house unto the name of the Lord my God, as the Lord spake unto David my father, saying, Thy son whom I will set upon thy throne in thy room, he shall build a house unto my name. Now therefore command thou that they hew me cedar-trees out of Lebanon; and my servants shall be with thy servants: and unto thee will I give hire for thy servants according to all that thou shalt appoint: for thou knowest that there is not among us any that can skill to hew timber like unto the Sidonians." 1 Kings v. 3–6.

In this request, as we have already stated, Hiram, who was the friend of Solomon, complied, and the building was commenced, in the four hundred and eighteenth year after the children of Israel were come out of the land of Egypt. There were employed, in the construction of this building, one hundred and eighty-three thousand men, including Hebrews and Canaanites; and though everything was made ready ere it came to the spot, so that, in the language of Holy Writ, "there was neither hammer nor axe nor any tool of iron heard in the house, while it was in building." 1 Kings vi. 7.

The site on which the temple was built was Mount Moriah, "where the Lord appeared unto David his father, in the place that David had prepared in the threshing-floor of Ornan the Jebusite." 2 Chron. ii. 1.

The description which the sacred historian gives of the building is as follows: "And the house which King Solomon built for the Lord, the length thereof was threescore cubits, and the breadth thereof twenty cubits, and the height thereof thirty cubits. And the porch before the temple of the house, twenty cubits was the length thereof, according to the breadth of the house; and ten cubits was the breadth thereof before the house. And for the house he made windows of narrow lights" (or windows broad within and narrow without). "And against the wall of the house he built chambers round about, against the walls of the house round about, both of the temple and of the oracle: and he made chambers round about: the nethermost chamber was five cubits broad, and the middle was six cubits broad, and the third was seven cubits broad: for without in the wall of the house he made narrowed rests round about, that the beams should not be fastened in the walls of the house. The door for the middle chamber was in the right side of the house: and they went up with winding stairs into the middle chamber, and out of the middle into the third. So he built the house and finished it; and covered the house with beams and boards of cedar. And then he built chambers against all the house, five cubits high: and they rested on the house with timber of cedar. And he built the walls of the house within with boards of cedar, both the floor of the house, and the walls of the ceiling: and he covered them on the inside with wood, and covered the floor of the house with planks of fir. And he built twenty cubits on the sides of the house, both the floor and the walls with boards of cedar: he even built them for it within, even for the oracle, even for the most holy place. And the house, that is the temple before it, was forty cubits long. And the cedar of the house within was carved with knops [gourds] and open flowers: all was cedar; there was no stone seen. And the oracle he prepared in the house within, to set there the ark of the covenant of the Lord. And the oracle in the forepart was twenty cubits in length, and twenty cubits in breadth, and twenty cubits in the height thereof: and he overlaid it with pure gold; and so covered the altar which was of cedar. So Solomon overlaid the house within with pure gold: and he made a partition by the chains of gold before the oracle; and he overlaid it with gold. And the whole house he overlaid with gold, until he had finished all the house; also the whole altar that was by the oracle he overlaid with gold. And within the oracle he made two cherubim of olive-tree, each ten cubits high. And five cubits was the one wing of the cherub, and five cubits the other wing of the cherub: from the uttermost part of the one wing unto the uttermost part of the other were ten cubits. And the other cherub was ten cubits: both the cherubim were of one measure and one size. The height of the one cherub was ten cubits, and so was it of the other cherub. And he set the cherubim within the inner house: and they stretched forth the wings of the cherubim, so that the wing of the one touched the one wall, and the wing of the other cherub touched the other wall; and their wings touched one another in the midst of the house. And he overlaid the cherubim with gold. And he carved all the walls of the house round about with carved figures of cherubim and palm-trees and open flowers within and without. And the floor of the house he overlaid with gold, within and without. And for the entering of the oracle he made doors of olive-tree: the lintel and side-posts were a fifth part of the wall. The two doors also were of olive-tree; and he carved upon them carvings of cherubim and palm-trees and open flowers, and overlaid them with gold, and spread gold upon the cherubim, and upon the palm-trees. So also made he for the door of the temple-posts of olive-tree, a fourth part of the wall. And the two doors were of fir-tree: the two leaves of the one door were folding, and the two leaves of the other door were folding. And he carved thereon cherubim and palm-trees, and open flowers: and covered them with gold fitted upon the carved work. And he built the inner court with three rows of hewed stone, and a row of cedar-beams." 1 Kings vi.

In the next chapter we read of two remarkable pillars connected with the porch. Speaking of Hiram, whom Solomon had caused to be fetched from Tyre, to aid in the erection of the temple, the sacred historian says: "He was a widow's son of the tribe of Naphtali, and his father was a man of Tyre, a worker in brass; and he was filled with wisdom, and understanding, and cunning, to work all works in brass. And he came to King Solomon, and wrought all his work. For he cast two pillars of brass, of eighteen cubits high apiece; and a line of twelve cubits did compass either of them about. And he made two chapiters of molten brass, to set upon the tops of the pillars: the height of the one chapiter was five cubits, and the height of the other chapiter was five cubits: and nets of checkerwork and wreaths of chain-work, for the chapiters which were upon the top of the pillars; seven for the one chapiter, and seven for the other chapiter. And he made the pillars, and two rows round about upon the one network, to cover the chapiters that were upon the top, with pomegranates: and so did he for the other chapiter. And the chapiters that were upon the top of the pillars were of lily-work in the porch four cubits. And the chapiters upon the two pillars had pomegranates also above, over against the belly which was by the network: and the pomegranates were two hundred in rows round about upon the other chapiter. And he set up the pillars in the porch of the temple: and he set up the right pillar, and called the name thereof Jachin" (which may be read, "it shall stand"); "and he set up the left pillar, and called the name thereof Boaz" (which may be read, "in strength," thus forming a kind of sentence, "It shall stand in strength"). 1 Kings vii. 14–21. The reader will find other interesting details concerning the temple in the concluding verses of this chapter, and in the parallel chapters, 2 Chron. iii.–vi.; 1 Chron. xxii.–xxix.; and 1 Kings vii., viii.

The temple, with all things destined for its service, and every arrangement connected with it, being completed, its dedication was celebrated the year after, with a magnificence worthy of the object and the occasion. All the chief men in Israel were present—the heads of tribes, and paternal chiefs, together with multitudes of people from all parts of the land. The priests, if not the Levites, also attended in full force, the succession of the courses being *afterward* to commence. God himself was pleased to manifest his presence and his complacency by two striking miracles:—

At the moment when the ark of the covenant, having been brought in high procession from its former place in "the city of David," was deposited in the holy of holies, the numerous Levitical choirs thundered forth their well-known song,—sent to the heavens by their united voices, and by the harmonious concord of a thousand instruments,—"Praise Jehovah! for he is good; for his mercy endureth for ever!" Suddenly, as at the consecration of the first tabernacle, the house of God was covered with a thick cloud, which filled it, and which enveloped all the assistants in such profound obscurity that the priests were unable to continue their services. This was a manifest symbol that God had accepted this as his house, his palace; and that his Presence had entered to inhabit there. It was so understood by Solomon, whose voice rose amidst the silence which ensued. "Jehovah said that he would dwell in the thick darkness. I have assuredly built for thee a house to dwell in, a settled place for thee to abide in for ever!" The king stood on a brazen platform which had been erected in front of the altar; and now, turning to the people, he explained the origin and object of this building. After which "he spread forth his hands toward the heavens" to address himself to God. The prayer he offered on this occasion is one of the noblest and most sublime compositions in the Bible. It exhibits the most exalted conceptions of the omnipresence of God, and of his superintending providence; and dwells more especially on his peculiar protection of the Hebrew nation, from the time of its departure from Egypt, and imploring pardon and forgiveness for all their sins and transgressions in the land, and during those ensuing captivities which, in the same prophetic spirit that animated the last address of Moses, he appears to have foreseen. Nothing can be finer than that part of his long and beautiful address, in which, recurring to the idea of *inhabitance* which had been so forcibly brought before his mind, he cries, "But will God indeed dwell on the earth? Behold the heaven, and the heaven of heavens can not contain thee; how much less this house that I have builded!"

The king had no sooner concluded his prayer than a fire from the heavens descended upon the altar and consumed the burnt-offerings. All the Israelites beheld this prodigy, and bent their faces toward the earth in adoration, and repeated with one voice the praise which was the most acceptable to him: "He is good; his mercy endureth for ever!"

By these two signs the sanctuary and the altar received the same acceptance and consecration which had been granted in the wilderness to the tabernacle and the altar there.

After this the sacrifices were resumed, and countless victims were offered. During two consecutive weeks the people celebrated this great solemnity with unabated zeal. It was the year of jubilee, which had probably been chosen as a season of general joy and leisure; and hence the unusually great concourse to Jerusalem. In this year the jubilee feast was followed by that of tabernacles, which explains the duration of this great festival beyond the seven days in which public festivals usually terminated. On the last day of the second feast, the king blessed the people, and dismissed them to their homes, to which they repaired, "joyful and glad of heart for all the good which Jehovah had done for David his servant, and for Israel his people."

Solomon having thus worthily accomplished the obligation imposed upon him by his father, felt himself at liberty to build various sumptuous structures, and undertake various works suited to the honor of his crown and the dignity of his great kingdom. All that can be said with reference to these will be little more than an amplification of his own statement on the subject: "I raised magnificent works; I built for myself houses; I planted for myself vineyards; I made for myself gardens and groves, and planted in them fruit-trees of every kind; I made also *pools of water*,[*] to water therewith the growing plantations. I bought men-servants and

---

[*] SOLOMON'S POOLS (see *Engraving*, p. 299).—The pools of Solomon are situated about one hour's distance to the south of Bethlehem: and to them the king of Israel is supposed to refer in Eccles. ii. 4–6, where, among other magnificent works executed by him, he enumerates vineyards, gardens, orchards, and pools. These pools are three in number, of an oblong quadrangular form, cut out of the native rock, and are covered with a thick coat of plaster in the inside, and supported by abutments: the workmanship through-

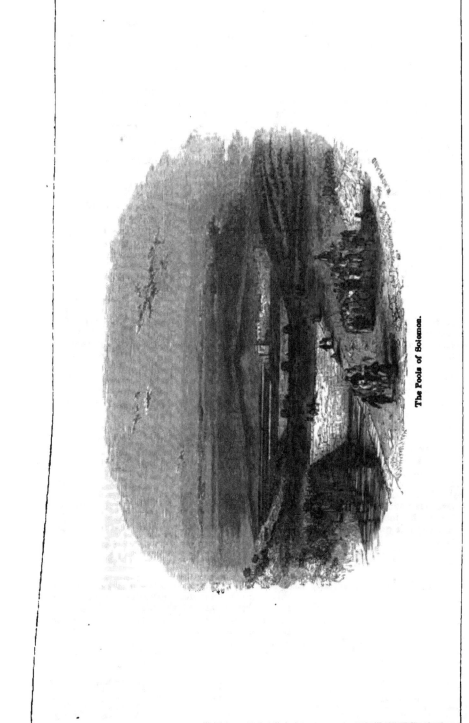

The Pools of Solomon.

women-servants, and had servants born in my house; I possessed also herds and flocks in abundance, more than any had before me in Jerusalem; I collected also silver and gold, and precious treasure from kings and provinces; I procured men-singers and women-singers, and the sweetest instruments of music, the delight of the children of men. Thus I became great, and possessed more than any who had been before me in Jerusalem." (Eccles. ii. 3–9.)

Of the royal buildings to which allusion has been made, our more particular information is respecting the palace which the king built for himself, another for "Pharaoh's daughter," and "the house of the forest of Lebanon." It is difficult, from the brief intimations which the scriptural history offers, to form a clear or connected idea of these buildings. The description of Josephus, although more precise, does not supply this deficiency; but by its assistance we may make out that the two palaces, for himself and the princess of Egypt, were not separate buildings, but, as the existing arrangements in oriental palaces would suggest, a distinct part, or wing, of the same building. It may assist the matter to understand that an oriental palace consists, for the most part, of a series of open quadrangles, with distinct appropriations, and each surrounded with buildings suitable to its appropriation. In fact, they are distinct buildings, connected only by communicating doors, similar in their general plan to each other, but differing much in size and workmanship. The quadrangle into which the gate of entrance opens usually contains the state apartments and offices, principally the hall in which the sovereign gives audience, sits in judgment, and transacts all public business. Hence the court is very often called *"the gate,"* of which we have a familiar instance in the Ottoman *Porte,* and of which examples are found in scripture with reference to the courts of the Hebrew, Babylonian, and Persian kings.* Now, from the description of Josephus, it would appear that the palace, as a whole, consisted of three quadrangles, of which that in the centre contained the hall of audience and justice, and other state apartments, while that on the right hand formed the king's palace of residence, and that on the left was the palace of the Egyptian princess. The only point on which we are in doubt, is, whether the three quadrangles were on a line with each other, or that the one which contained the public halls was in advance of the others; for in this way, equally with the other, the palaces of the king and queen might be respectively described as to the right and left of the public building. There are some who think that "the house of the forest of Lebanon" was the same as this front or public portion of the whole

out, like everything Jewish, is more remarkable for 'strength than beauty. They are situated in a most secluded situation, at the south end of a small valley, in the midst of mountains; and are so disposed on the sloping hill, that the water in the uppermost pool flows into the second, and thence into the third. That on the west is nearest to the source of the spring which supplies it with water, and is stated by Dr. Richardson to be 480 feet long; the second is about 600 feet, and the third about 660 feet in length. The breadth of them all is nearly the same; but no traveller, ancient or modern, has ascertained their depth. The pools communicate freely with each other, and are capable of containing a great quantity of water, which they discharge into a small aqueduct that conveys it to Jerusalem. This aqueduct was constructed all along on the surface of the ground, and framed of perforated stones let one into another, with a fillet round the cavity, so framed as to prevent leakage, and united to each other with so firm a cement that they will sometimes sooner break than endure a separation. These pipes were covered, for greater security, with a case or layer of smaller stones, which were laid over them in a very strong mortar. "The whole work," says Maundrell, "seems to be endued with such absolute firmness, as if it had been designed for eternity. But the Turks have demonstrated, in this instance, that nothing can be so well wrought but they are able to destroy it. For of this strong aqueduct, which was carried formerly five or six leagues with so vast expense and labor, you now see only here and there a fragment remaining."

The fountain whence these pools principally derive their waters is at the distance of about one hundred and forty paces from them. This, the friars of Bethlehem are fully persuaded, is the "sealed fountain" to which Solomon compares his bride. (Sol. Song, iv. 12.) In confirmation of their opinion, they pretend a tradition, that King Solomon shut up these springs, and kept the door of them sealed with his signet, in order that he might preserve the waters for his drinking in their natural freshness and purity. Nor was it difficult thus to secure them, as they rise under ground, and there is no avenue to them but by a little hole, like the mouth of a narrow well. Through this hole you descend directly, though not without some difficulty, for about four yards, when you arrive in a vaulted room, forty-five feet in length and twenty-four in breadth, adjoining to which there is another room of the same kind, but somewhat less. Both these rooms are covered with handsome stone arches, of great antiquity, which Maundrell thinks may be the work of Solomon.

Below these pools, at the distance of more than half a mile, is a deep valley, enclosed on each side by lofty mountains, which the monks of Bethlehem affirm to be the "enclosed garden" alluded to in Sol. Song, iv. 12. Whether this conjecture (for it is no more than a conjecture) be well founded or not, Maundrell thinks it probable enough that the pools may be the same with Solomon's, there not being the like supply of excellent spring water to be met with anywhere else throughout Palestine. But if Solomon made the gardens in the rocky ground now assigned for them, it may be safely affirmed, that he demonstrated greater power and wealth in finishing his design than he did wisdom in selecting the place for it.

* 2 Sam. xv. 2; Est. ii. 19, 21; iii. 2, 3; Dan. ii. 49. Compare Matt. xvi. 18; see also Xenop. Cyrop. i. 3; viii. 3.

pile; nor should we like absolutely to deny this, although it seems more probable that it was a royal residence in the neighbborhood of Jerusalem, deriving its name either from the number of cedar pillars which supported its galleries and halls, or from the plantations by which it was surrounded. These structures were, for the most part, built with immense blocks of squared stones, and the whole was fitted up with cedar; while the nobler rooms and galleries were lined with slabs of costly polished marble to the floor, and were above enriched with sculptures (on the wall), and apparently with paintings (on the plaster), especially toward the ceiling, all of which we may conclude to have been very much in the style of similar things among the Egyptians, whose palaces were decorated after the same style. And if we have rightly interpreted Josephus to intimate that there were three ranges of ornaments in the principal rooms—polished slabs at the bottom, sculpture above, and painting toward the top, it would be very easy to show how the same ideas and distributions are retained in the palaces of the modern East, where, above basement slabs of *looking-glass*, are wrought recesses, and carvings, and arabesques, and ornaments of stucco (sculpture being interdicted); while toward the ceiling much highly-colored painting is displayed. If we may credit Josephus, "barbaric pearl and gold" were not wanting among the materials which contributed to the decoration of the more splendid apartments. The historian is at a loss for words to express the full conception, which the traditions of his fathers had conveyed to his mind, of the splendors of Solomon's palatial buildings: "It would be an endless task," he says, "to give a particular survey of this mighty mass of building; so many courts and other contrivances; such a variety of chambers and offices, great and small; long and large galleries; vast rooms of state, and others for feasting and entertainment, set out as richly as could be with costly furniture and gildings; besides, that all the service for the king's table were of pure gold. In a word, the whole palace was in a manner made up, from the base to the coping, of white marble, cedar, gold and silver, with precious stones here and there intermingled upon the walls and ceilings."

The descriptions in the Greek writers of the Persian courts in Susa and Ecbatana; the tales of the early travellers in the East about the kings of Samarcand or Cathay; and even the imagination of the oriental romancers and poets, have scarcely conceived a more splendid pageant than Solomon, seated on his throne of ivory, receiving the homage of distant princes who came to admire his magnificence, and put to the test his noted wisdom. This throne was of pure ivory, covered with gold; six steps led up to the seat, and on each side of the steps were twelve lions carved. All the vessels of his palace were of pure gold—silver was thought too mean : his armory was furnished with gold; two hundred targets and three hundred shields of beaten gold were suspended in the house of Lebanon. Josephus mentions a body of archers who escorted him from the city to his country palace, clad in dresses of Tyrian purple, and their hair powdered with gold dust. But, enormous as this wealth appears, the statement of his expenditure on the temple, and of his annual revenue, so passes all credibility, that any attempt at forming a calculation on the uncertain data we possess, may at once be abandoned as a hopeless task. No better proof can be given of the uncertainty of our authorities, of our imperfect knowledge of the Hebrew weights of money, and, above all, of our total ignorance of the relative value which the precious metals bore to the commodities of life, than the estimate, made by Dr. Prideaux, of the treasures left by David, amounting to eight hundred millions— nearly the capital of the national debt of England.

Our inquiry into the sources of the vast wealth which Solomon undoubtedly possessed, may lead to more satisfactory, though still imperfect, results. The treasures of David were accumulated rather by conquest than by traffic. Some of the nations he subdued, particularly the Edomites, were wealthy. All the tribes seem to have worn a great deal of gold and silver in their ornaments and their armor; their idols were often of gold, and the treasuries of their temples perhaps contained considerable wealth. But during the reign of Solomon, almost the whole commerce of the world passed into his territories. The treaty with Tyre was of the utmost importance; nor is there any instance in which two neighboring nations so clearly saw, and so steadily pursued, without jealousy or mistrust, their mutual and inseparable interests. On one occasion only, when Solomon presented to Hiram twenty inland cities which he had conquered, Hiram expressed great dissatisfaction, and called the territory by the opprobrious name of Cabul. The Tyrian had perhaps cast a wistful eye on the noble bay and harbor of Acro, or Ptolemais, which the prudent Hebrew either would not or could not—since it was part of the promised land—dissever from his dominions. So strict was the confederacy, that Tyre may be considered the port of Palestine, Palestine the granary of Tyre. Tyre furnished the ship-builders and mariners; the fruitful plains of Palestine victualled the fleets, and supplied the manufacturers and merchants of the Phœnician league with all the necessaries of life.

This league comprehended Tyre, Aradus, Sidon, perhaps Tripolis, Byblus and Berytus; the narrow slip of territory which belonged to these states was barren, rocky, and unproductive. The first branch of commerce, into which this enterprising people either admitted the Jews as regular partners, or at least permitted them to share its advantages, was the traffic of the Mediterranean. To every part of that sea the Phœnicians had pursued their discoveries; they had planted colonies, and worked the mines. This was the trade to Tarshish, so celebrated, that ships of Tarshish seem to have become the common name for large merchant vessels. Tarshish was probably a name as indefinite, as the West Indies in early European navigation; properly speaking, it was the south of Spain, then rich in mines of gold and silver, the Peru of Tyrian adventure. Whether or not as early as the days of Solomon,—without doubt in the more flourishing period of Phœnicia; before the city on the mainland was destroyed by Nebuchadnezzar, and insular Tyre became the emporium—the Phœnician navies extended their voyages beyond the pillars of Hercules, where they founded Cadiz. Northward they sailed along the coast of France to the British isles: southward along the African shore; where the boundaries of their navigation are quite uncertain, yet probably extended to the gold coast. The second branch of commerce was the inland trade with Egypt. This was carried on entirely by the Jews. Egypt supplied horses in vast numbers, and linen yarn. The valleys of the Nile produced flax in abundance; and the yarn, according to the description of the prudent housewife in the Proverbs, was spun and woven by the females in Palestine. The third, and more important branch, was the maritime trade by the Red sea. The conquests of David had already made the Jews masters of the eastern branch of this gulf. Solomon built or improved the towns and ports of Elath and Ezion-geber. Hence a fleet, manned by Tyrians, sailed for Ophir, their East Indies, as Tarshish was their West. They sailed along the eastern coast of Africa, in some part of which the real Ophir was probably situated. When the Egyptians under Necho, after the declension of the Israelitish kingdom, took possession of this branch of commerce, there seems little reason to doubt the plain and consistent account of Herodotus, that the Tyrians sailed round the continent of Africa. The whole maritime commerce, with eastern Asia, the southern shores of the Arabian peninsula, the coasts of the Persian gulf, and without doubt some parts of India, entered, in the same manner, the Red sea, and was brought to Elath and Ezion-geber.

Besides this maritime traffic the caravan trade by land engaged a full share of Solomon's attention. By the possession of a southern frontier stretching across from the Elanitic gulf to the Mediterranean, the land traffic between Egypt and Syria lay completely at his mercy. He felt this, and through some arrangement with his father-in-law the king of Egypt, he contrived to monopolize it entirely in his own hands. It appears that what Syria chiefly required from Egypt were *linen fabrics* and *yarn*, for the manufacture of which that country had long been celebrated; also *chariots*, the extensive use of which in Egypt has already been pointed out; and *horses*, of which that country possessed a very excellent and superior breed, if we may judge from the numerous fine examples which the paintings and sculptures offer. All this trade Solomon appears to have intercepted and monopolized. He was supplied by contract, at a fixed price, with certain quantities adequate to the supply of the Syrian market, which, after retaining what he required for himself, his factors sold, doubtless at a high profit, to the different kings of Syria. The price was doubtless arbitrary, and dependant on times and circumstances; but the contract price at which the chariots and horses were supplied by the Egyptians to the Hebrew factors happens to be named,—six hundred silver shekels for a chariot, and one fourth of that sum, or one hundred and fifty shekels, for a horse.

This was not the only land traffic which engaged the notice of Solomon. His attention was attracted to the extensive and valuable caravan trade which, from very remote ages, coming from the farther east, and the Persian gulf, proceeded to Egypt, Tyre, and other points on the Mediterranean, by the Euphrates and across the great

Tadmor, (Palmyra.)

Syrian desert. The habitable points of that desert, even to the great river, were now under the dominion of the Hebrew king, and even the Bedouin tribes by whom it was chiefly inhabited were brought under tribute to him, and were kept in order by the dread of his great name. Under these circumstances, Solomon was in nearly as favorable a position for taking a part in this trade as in the land traffic between Egypt and Syria. But the measures which he took were different, and more specially adapted to the circumstances of the case. They were less coercive, and dealt more in the offer of inducements and advantages. And the reason is obvious; for although the ordinary track of the great caravans lay through his territories, it was in the power of its conductors to alter that tract so as to pass northward beyond the limits of his dominion; but this would have produced such expense, trouble and delay, that it would have been preferable to maintain the old route even at the expense of some check and inconvenience. Whether the measures of Solomon were felt to be such, we do not know; they were possibly deemed by the caravan merchants and by the Hebrews, as mutually advantageous, although the ultimate purchasers, who could be no parties in this arrangement, possibly regarded them in a different light. The plan of Solomon was to erect in the very heart of the desert an emporium for this important trade. The route of a caravan is so directed as to include as many as possible of the places at which water may be found. At the most important of these stations, where water, and by consequence palm-trees, was found in the most abundance, the Hebrew king built a city and called it Tadmor* (a palm-tree), whence its Greek name of Palmyra. But Greek and Roman names never fixed themselves in the soil of Syria, and the ruins of the city bear, to this day, among the natives, the primitive name of *Tadmor.* Here the caravans not only found water as before, but every advantage of shelter and rest, while by this establishment Solomon was enabled more effectively to overawe the tribes, and to afford protection to the caravans from the predatory attempts and exactions of the Bedouins. Here the caravan merchants would soon find it convenient to dispose of their commodities, and leave the further distribution of them, to the nations west of the desert, either to the factors of Solomon, or to private merchants,—for we do not know to what extent the king found it advisable to have this trade free to his own subjects. It may be that private persons among his subjects, or even foreigners from the west, were not prevented from here meeting and dealing with the eastern merchants; but from the general—and with our present lights, we must say short-sighted—policy of Solomon's commercial doings, it may be inferred that he monopolized such advantages in this trade as he deemed safe or prudent. At the least, it must be presumed that he derived a considerable revenue, in the way of customs, from such merchandise as did not pass into the hands of his own factors; and this, however advantageous to the king, may have been felt by the caravan merchants but as a reasonable equivalent for the protection they enjoyed, and their freedom from the exactions of the Bedouins. Much of this, which we have stated as probably connected with the foundation of this city of the desert, is not stated in scripture: but it is deducible from the improbability that without strong inducements a city would have been founded in such a situation, and from the detection of these inducements in the commercial enterprises of Solomon, with the illustration applied to the particular instance, which is derivable from the fact that the wealth and glory in which the Palmyra of a later day appears, was due entirely to the circumstance that its position made it an emporium for the caravan trade of the desert. In fact, that it was such at a long subsequent date, and that its very existence depended on its being such, illustrates and justifies that intention in its foundation which, on the strongest circumstantial evidence, we have ventured to ascribe to Solomon.

Besides these branches of commerce, "the traffic of the *spice* merchants" is mentioned among the sources from which wealth accrued to Solomon. In what form this profit was derived is not distinctly intimated. From the analogy of his other operations, we might conclude that he bought up the costly spices and aromatics brought by the spice caravans of southernmost Arabia, which must needs pass through his territories; and that after deducting what sufficed for the large consumption of his own nation, he sold the residue at an enhanced price to the neighboring nations. As it is certain that, from his own wants merely, an act of trade must have taken place between him and these caravans, this seems the more obvious conclusion, although,

---

* In the Ketib of 1 Kings ix. 18 it is put *Tamar*, the proper word for a palm-tree, showing that *Tadmor* has the same meaning, and probably that the *d* is merely introduced for euphony.

without this, he may have derived an important item of profit from this trade by levying customs upon it in its passage through his dominions.

Such, as far as they can be traced, were the commercial operations of Solomon. It is quite easy *now*, and in a commercial country like our own, to see that these operations were, for the most part, based on wrong views and principles, inasmuch as however they might tend to the aggrandizement of *the king*, they could confer little solid and enduring benefit on *the nation*. But in the East, where the king is the state, and becomes himself the centre of most public acts, he is seldom found to take interest in commerce, but from regarding it as a source of emolument to the state, by his direct and personal concern therein. The king himself is a trader, with such advantages resulting from his position, as inevitably exclude the private merchant from the field in which he appears. He is inevitably a monopolist; and a sovereign monopoly is, if not an evil, at least not a benefit to the people, whatever wealth it may seem to bring into the country. The river, however noble, gives fertility only to the banks which hem it in; and it is only when its waters are drawn off in their course, and exhausted into a thousand channels, that they bless and glorify the wide country around. Solomon, in his book of Ecclesiastes, acquaints us with many "vanities" and "sore evils" which he saw "under the sun;" but from this statement we do not learn that he ever became conscious of the very great vanity and most sore evil of a rich king over a poor people, or of the system which makes the king rich while the people remain comparatively poor.

Large revenues were derived from the annual tributes of the foreign states, which were now subject to the Hebrew sceptre, or over which it exercised a more or less stringent influence. The kings and princes of such states appear to have sent their tribute in the form of quantities of the principal articles which their country produced, or was able to procure; as did also the governors of the provinces not left under the native princes. Besides the regular tax or tribute derived from countries more or less closely annexed to the Hebrew kingdom, there were more distant states which found it good policy to conciliate the favor of Solomon, or to avert his hostility by annual offerings, which, under the soft name of "presents," formed no contemptible item of the royal revenue. Of that revenue one item is mentioned in rather singular terms: "All the earth sought to Solomon to hear his wisdom, which God had put into his heart. And they brought every man his *present*, utensils of silver, and utensils of gold, and garments, and armor, and spices, horses and mules, *a rate year by year*." Here the terms "presents," and "a rate year by year," have a degree of opposition at the first view, which seems to require us to suppose either that those great men who had once resorted to Jerusalem to hear the wisdom of Solomon, and to behold the manifestation of it in the ordering of his court and kingdom, not only brought with them the presents which the usages of the East rendered the necessary accompaniments of such visits, but that they continued to send from their several lands yearly gifts of compliment to him. Or else, that the desire of thus complimenting the monarch whom God had so eminently gifted, furnished a decent pretence to those who had other reasons for rendering a real tribute to him. The latter interpretation is that which we prefer. And it is certain that in the case of the only royal visit which is particularly described—that of the queen of Sheba—only such presents as she brought with her are named, and no "rate year by year" is intimated. Ethiopia was too remote to be within reach of the influences which may have determined the monarchs of nearer nations to make their "presents" to Solomon a yearly payment.

The articles mentioned in the extract just given, together with those named in other places, enable us to form some idea of the display which these annual or occasional renderings of tributes and of traffics must have offered. It has been the fashion of the East to make a show of such offerings by their being taken in procession to the palace of the king by the persons, arrayed in their varied costumes, by whom they were brought to the country. To this custom we have more than once had occasion to allude in the course of the present work. Many were the spectacles of this sort which must have delighted the eyes of the Israelites during the splendid reign of Solomon. There are paintings of Egypt, and sculptures of Persia, which enable us to form some idea of these imposing exhibitions, which indeed are in strict correspondence with those which the courts of the East have still preserved. Of the representations to which we allude, the former is no less interesting and instructive from the details which it offers, than venerable from its high antiquity. It is at Thebes; and

20

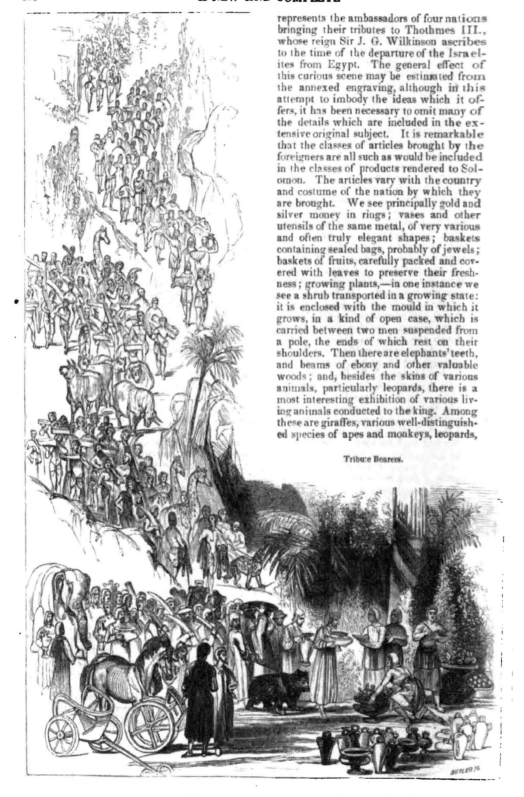

represents the ambassadors of four nations bringing their tributes to Thothmes III., whose reign Sir J. G. Wilkinson ascribes to the time of the departure of the Israelites from Egypt. The general effect of this curious scene may be estimated from the annexed engraving, although in this attempt to imbody the ideas which it offers, it has been necessary to omit many of the details which are included in the extensive original subject. It is remarkable that the classes of articles brought by the foreigners are all such as would be included in the classes of products rendered to Solomon. The articles vary with the country and costume of the nation by which they are brought. We see principally gold and silver money in rings; vases and other utensils of the same metal, of very various and often truly elegant shapes; baskets containing sealed bags, probably of jewels; baskets of fruits, carefully packed and covered with leaves to preserve their freshness; growing plants,—in one instance we see a shrub transported in a growing state: it is enclosed with the mould in which it grows, in a kind of open case, which is carried between two men suspended from a pole, the ends of which rest on their shoulders. Then there are elephants' teeth, and beams of ebony and other valuable woods; and, besides the skins of various animals, particularly leopards, there is a most interesting exhibition of various living animals conducted to the king. Among these are giraffes, various well-distinguished species of apes and monkeys, leopards,

Tribute Bearers.

Baalbec.

and even bears. There were also oxen, of a different breed to that common in the country, as were probably the horses, which also figure in the procession, and which, with chariots, form perhaps the most remarkable objects of the whole, as being brought to a country which itself abounded in horses and chariots; but the horses were probably desirable to the Egyptians as of a foreign breed, and the chariots as a curious foreign manufacture. Upon the whole, a more striking and appropriate illustration of this part of Solomon's glory can not well be imagined.

The wealth which flowed into the royal treasury from these various sources appears to have been freely disbursed by Solomon in enriching his buildings, in extending their number, and in the ordering of his court and kingdom. Besides the buildings which have already been pointed out, various public structures were built by him in Jerusalem, which city he also enclosed by new walls, fortified with strong towers. Other important towns (as Gaza) were fortified, and new ones built in different parts of the country. Besides Tadmor, which has already engaged our notice, Baalath is named among the towns built by him; and this is supposed by many to be no other than the afterward celebrated city of Baalbec, in the great valley of Cœle-Syria.

It was from these various sources of wealth, that the precious metals and all other valuable commodities were in such abundance—that, in the figurative language of the sacred historian, *silver was in Jerusalem as stones, and cedar-trees as sycamores.*

Solomon was not less celebrated for his wisdom than his magnificence. The visits of the neighboring princes, particularly that of the queen of Sheba (a part of Arabia Felix), were to admire the one, as much as the other. Hebrew tradition, perhaps the superstitious wonder of his own age, ascribed to Solomon the highest skill in magical arts, and even unbounded dominion over all the invisible world. More sober history recognises in Solomon the great poet, naturalist, and moral philosopher of his time. His poetry, consisting of one thousand and five songs, except his epithalamium, and perhaps some of the Psalms, has entirely perished. His natural history of plants and animals has suffered the same fate. But the great part of the book of Proverbs and Ecclesiastes (perhaps more properly reckoned as a poem) have preserved the conclusions of his moral wisdom.

The latter book, or poem, derives new interest, when considered as coming from the most voluptuous, magnificent, and instructed of monarchs, who sums up the estimate of human life in the melancholy sentence—*Vanity of vanities! vanity of vanities!* It is a sad commentary on the termination of the splendid life and reign of the great Hebrew sovereign. For even had not this desponding confession been extorted by the satiety of passion, and the weariness of a spirit, over-excited by all the gratifications this world can bestow—had no higher wisdom suggested this humiliating conclusion—the state of his own powerful kingdom, during his declining years, might have furnished a melancholy lesson on the instability of human grandeur. Solomon, in his old age, was about to bequeath to his heir, an insecure throne, a discontented people, formidable enemies on the frontiers, and perhaps a contested succession. He could not even take refuge in the sanctuary of conscious innocence, and assume the dignity of suffering unmerited degradation; for he had set at defiance every principle of the Hebrew constitution. He had formed a connexion with Egypt—he had multiplied a great force of cavalry—he had accumulated gold and silver—he had married many foreign wives. His seraglio was on as vast a scale as the rest of his expenditure—he had seven hundred wives, and three hundred concubines. The influence of these women, not merely led him to permit an idolatrous worship within his dominions, but even Solomon had been so infatuated, as to consecrate to the obscene and barbarous deities of the neighboring nations, a part of one of the hills, which overlooked Jerusalem—a spot almost fronting the splendid temple, which he himself had built to the one Almighty God of the universe. Hence clouds on all sides gathered about his declining day. Hadad, one of the blood-royal of the Edomite princes, began to organize a revolt in that province, on which so much of the Jewish commerce depended. An adventurer seized on Damascus, and set up an independent sovereignty, thus endangering the communication from Tadmor. A domestic enemy, still more dangerous, appeared in the person of Jeroboam, a man of great valor, supported by the prophet Ahijah, who foretold his future rule over the ten tribes. Though forced to fly, Jeroboam found an asylum with Shishak, or Sesac, the Sesonchosis of Manetho, who was raising the kingdom of Egypt to its former alarming grandeur; and, notwithstanding his alliance with Solomon, made no scruple against harboring his rebellious subject. Above all, the people were oppressed and dissatisfied; either because the enormous revenues of the kingdom were more than absorbed by the vast expenditure of the sovereign; or because the more productive branches of commerce were interrupted by the rebellions of the Edomites and Damascenes. At this period likewise, Solomon departed from the national, though iniquitous policy of his earlier reign, during which he had laid all the burdens of labor and taxation on the strangers, and exempted the Israelites from every claim but that of military service. The language held to Rehoboam, on his accession, shows that the people had suffered deeply from the arbitrary exactions of the king, who, with the state and splendor, had assumed the despotism of an oriental monarch. Hence the decline of the Jewish kingdom, supported rather by the fame of its sovereign, than by its inherent strength, was as rapid as its rise. Solomon died after a reign of forty years, and with him expired the glory and the power of the Jewish empire.

CHAPTER XIX.

THE effects of the arbitrary policy and inordinate expense which had prevailed in the court of Solomon during the last years of his reign, began to appear as soon as his death was announced. The rulers of the tribes assembled at the city of Shechem, in the tribe of Ephraim,—which tribe, it will be remembered, was always disposed to regard with strong jealousy the superiority of Judah. Here they wished to enter into a new stipulation with the heir to the throne—a precaution which had been neglected under the excitement and extraordinary circumstances which attended the accession of Solomon. If Rehoboam had been wise, the place which had been chosen for this congress, and the presence of Jeroboam,—who had hastened from Egypt when he heard of Solomon's death, and took a prominent part in the present matter— were circumstances, which among others, might have apprized him that the occasion was one of no ordinary moment, and required the most careful and skilful management. Rehoboam was not equal to this crisis; for when the rulers demanded, as the condition of their submission, that he should abrogate a portion of the burdens which his father had imposed upon them, he failed to discern what might be gained by a ready and cheerful concession, and required three days on which to deliberate on their demand. In this time he decided to reject the counsel of the older and more prudent counsellers, who enforced the necessity of compliance with this demand, and chose rather to adopt the advice of the young and headstrong courtiers—warm advocates of the royal prerogative,—who exhorted him to overawe the remonstrants by his majesty, and to drive them back like yelping dogs to their kennels. Accordingly when the three days had expired, his fatal and foolish answer was, that his little finger should be heavier upon the nation than his father's loins; and that whereas his father had only chastised them with whips, he would chastise them with scorpions. Nothing could more clearly than this answer evince the unfitness of Rehoboam for the crisis which had now occurred, and his utter ignorance of the spirit which was in Israel; while it at the same time indicates the arbitrary notions of the royal prerogative which he found occasion to imbibe during the later years of his father's reign.

On receiving this answer ten of the tribes instantly renounced their allegiance to the house of David, and chose Jeroboam for their king. Two of the tribes, Judah and Benjamin, alone adhered to Rehoboam,—Judah had the good reason that the family of David was of their tribe; and both these tribes were advantaged by the presence of the metropolis on their respective borders, and had necessarily derived peculiar benefits from that profuse expenditure of the late king of which the other tribes had cause to complain.

Thus was the great and powerful empire which David had erected, and which Solomon had ruled, already divided into two very unequal parts. Jeroboam had ten of the tribes, and his dominion extended over the tributary nations eastward, toward the Euphrates; while Rehoboam only retained the tribes of Judah and Benjamin, which are henceforth, from their strict identity of interest, to be regarded as one tribe, under the name of Judah. To this division belonged also the subject territories of Philistia and Edom. But notwithstanding the more than equal figure which this kingdom makes in the further history of the Hebrew nation, it may be well to bear in mind that what is henceforth to be called the kingdom of Judah, ruled by the house of David, formed not above a fourth part of the dominions of Solomon.

Rehoboam was not disposed to submit quietly to this proceeding. At first, affecting to suppose that his authority over the ten tribes would still be recognised, he sent, at the usual season, the officer who was "over the tribute" to collect the taxes which had been exacted in the last years of his father's reign. But the people rose, and testified their indignation and defiance by stoning this obnoxious personage to death. On this Rehoboam resolved to attempt to reduce the revolted tribes to his obedience by force of arms, and collected a large army for that purpose. But when the prophet Shemaiah announced to him the Lord's command to relinquish this enterprise, he manifested some sense of his true position by disbanding his army. This, it must be allowed, was a signal example of submission, and may intimate that when thus reminded of it he became sensible of the propriety of the requisition. No definite treaty of peace was, however, concluded, and the frontiers of the two kingdoms continued to present a hostile aspect.

In the preceding history we have seen that Jehovah, from the time of Moses to the death of Solomon, always governed the Hebrews according to the promises and threatenings which he delivered from Mount Horeb. If they deviated from the principle of worshipping Jehovah as the only true God, that is, if they revolted from their lawful king, he brought them by suitable chastisements, to reflect on their obligations, to return to Jehovah, and again to keep sacred the fundamental law of their church and state. The same course we shall find pursued in the government of the two kingdoms. If the monarchs of both had viewed the late great revolution, the sundering of the empire, as a consequence of the idolatrous and unlawful practices of Solomon's court, as a warning (for such it really was) to them not to break the fundamental law of the state, but to govern their subjects according to the law, and to treat them as the subjects of Jehovah; then both kingdoms might have enjoyed uninterrupted prosperity. Even Jeroboam, though he had received no promise of an eternal kingdom, as David had, yet the assurance was given him that if he obeyed the law as David did, the throne should long continue in his family. (1 Kings xi. 37, 38, xii. 21-24: 2 Chron. xi. 1-4, xii. 15.) But as the kings of both kingdoms often disregarded the fundamental laws of the commonwealth—by idolatry rebelled against their divine sovereign, carried their disorders so far, and treated their subjects in such a manner, that they are aptly described by Isaiah and Ezekiel (Isa. lvi. 9; Ezek. xxxiv.) under the image of wicked shepherds—there arose a succession of prophets, who, by impressive declarations and symbolic actions, reminded both rulers and subjects of their duties to Jehovah, and threatened them with punishment in case of disobedience.

Even the rebellious backslidings from God which more particularly distinguished the kingdom of Israel, did not prevent Jehovah from governing the kingdom according to his law. We shall see in the sequel how he exterminated, one after another, those royal families who not only retained the arbitrary institutions of Jeroboam, and tolerated and patronised idolatry, with its concomitant vices, but even introduced and protected it by their royal authority. The extermination of the reigning family he announced beforehand by a prophet, and appointed his successor. We shall see that the higher their corruptions rose, so much the more decisive and striking were the declarations and signs made to show the Israelites that the Lord of the universe was their Lord and King, and that all idols were as nothing when opposed to him. Even Naaman, the Syrian, acknowledged, and the Syrians generally found to their sorrow, that the God of the Hebrews was not a mere national god, but that his power extended over all nations. The history represents a contest between Jehovah, who ought to be acknowledged as God, and the idolatrous Israelites; and everything is ordered to preserve the authority of Jehovah in their minds. At last, after all milder punishments had proved fruitless, these rebellions were followed by the destruction of the kingdom, and the captivity of the people, which had been predicted by Moses, and afterward by Ahijah, Hosea, Amos, and other prophets. (Deut. xxviii. 36; 1 Kings xiv. 15; Hosea ix; Amos v.)

We shall also find that the divine Providence was favorable or adverse to the kingdom of Judah, according as the people obeyed or transgressed the law; only here the royal family remained unchanged, according to the promise given to David. We shall here meet indeed with many idolatrous and rebellious kings, but they were al-

Ancient Egyptian Worship.

ways succeeded by those of purer mind, who put a stop to idolatry, re-established theocracy in the hearts of their subjects, and, by the aid of prophets, priests, and Levites, and the services of the temple, restored the knowledge and worship of God. Judah, therefore, although much smaller than Israel, continued her national existence one hundred and thirty-four years longer; but at last, as no durable reformation was produced, she experienced the same fate as her sister kingdom, in fulfilment of the predictions of Moses and several other prophets.

The following account of the two kingdoms, therefore, should be viewed as that of a real theocracy; and thus, as a continued execution of the determination of God, that the true religion should be preserved on the earth. In this view it certainly deserves our most attentive study.*

Shechem being one of the most important towns in his own tribe of Ephraim, was made by Jeroboam the metropolis of the new kingdom. He had also a summer residence at Tirzah,† in the tribe of Manasseh, which, therefore, seems in the history to share the metropolitan dignity with Shechem.

The new king, little regarding the unconditional promises which had been made to him, applied himself to such operations of human policy as might tend to establish his kingdom, and confirm its separation from that of Judah. Viewing them as measures of policy in the abstract, the praise of much political sagacity and foresight need not be denied to their author; and it is certain that they were successful in promoting the object he had in view. But they were, in his peculiar position, as a king in Israel—that is, a vicegerent of Jehovah, not only improper, but in the highest degree criminal; for they involved an interference with matters far above the prerogative of Jehovah's vassal, and the abrogation of institutions which the Supreme King had established as essential to the good government and subordination of *his* kingdom, with the introduction of other institutions of a nature abhorrent to the Mosaic law, and of a tendency against which that law had most jealously guarded the people. Jeroboam is therefore to be regarded, not as gratuitously and from abstract preference of evil, leading the people into wrong courses; but as being careless whether the course he took were good or evil, so that it tended, in his judgment, to the security of his kingdom; for he had failed to learn that hard truth—that implicit obedience to the behests of his Almighty superior, not tortuous courses of political expediency, offered the true security of his peculiar kingdom.

Jeroboam was much annoyed at the obligation which the law imposed, of the resort of all the Israelites three times a year to Jerusalem. He clearly perceived that this concourse and frequent meeting of all the tribes to the same place, and for the same object, was a strong uniting circumstance among them; and he feared that the continuance of this usage might ultimately tend to the reunion of the several kingdoms under the house of David. Undoubtedly it was an awkward circumstance that the subjects of one king should be obliged thus often to resort to the metropolis of a neighboring and unfriendly monarch; and still more, that his own kingdom should be drained of a considerable portion of its wealth for the support of a service which was exclusively confined to the now adverse metropolis, and for the maintenance of priests and Levites whose services were rendered at Jerusalem, in the presence and under the authority of the rival sovereign. This was a state of things for which, it must be allowed, Jeroboam was under strong and natural inducements to seek a remedy. His duty was to have trusted that God, who had promised to continue his kingdom if he were obedient, and who had, indeed, already interposed his authority to prevent Rehoboam from warring against him, would provide a remedy for these difficulties, or take measures to prevent the consequences which he apprehended. But Jeroboam wanted that trust in God which it behooved the vassal of Jehovah to exhibit; and he applied himself to devise measures of his own to meet these exigencies. The measures which he took were so bold and decisive, that they at once took root, and became in their development so interwoven with the political constitution of the country, that even the more pious successors of this king in the throne of Israel did not venture to abolish them, or re-establish the authority of the fundamental law.

* The above, is adopted, with some abridgment, from Jahn, book v. sect. 35.
† From the manner in which it is mentioned, Tirzah must have enjoyed a very fine situation, and have made a fair appearance; but even its site is not now known, and that it was in Manasseh is little more than a conjecture. It had been one of the royal cities of the Canaanites (Josh. xii. 24).

Under the pretence that Jerusalem was too distant for the resort of his subjects, he established two places of resort at the opposite extremities of his kingdom, the one in the north, at Dan, and the other in the south, at Bethel. Both of these places, it will be remembered, had been previously places of public resort,—Bethel as a place of sacred stones, and Dan on account of the ephod and teraphim which the Danites had reft from Micah and established at that place. Then, to give this resort an object, he established at these places golden or gilded calves, in unquestionable imitation of the Apis and Mnevis of the Egyptians, among whom he had spent the years of his exile. We are not at all to suppose that he intended to introduce the worship of other gods. These images were doubtless intended as symbols of Jehovah; and the worship rendered before them was held to be in his honor. But on account of the danger of idolatry, the use of all such symbols had been interdicted by the fundamental law of the state; and the use in particular of this very symbol of a golden calf, to which, from Egyptian contaminations, the Israelites were (as Jeroboam must have known) more attached than to any other, had in former times brought signal punishment upon the Hebrews in the wilderness. It was, then, not the worship of other gods, but the worship of the true God in an irregular, dangerous, and interdicted manner, which constituted the crime of Jeroboam, who "sinned and made Israel to sin."

Nor did the irregularities end here. Jeroboam made his system a complete one. He not only changed the *place* of concourse to the people, but also altered the *time*, directing that all the festivals should be observed a month later than the law commanded, an alteration by which considerable confusion must have been at first produced, as the law had appointed these festivals with a reference to the seasons of the year. For this new worship, temples and altars were erected at Dan and Bethel, and to its support the tithes and other sacerdotal dues accruing within the ten tribes were directed; thus at once cutting off the greater part of the income of the establishment of Jerusalem. It is probable that this wealth might still have been retained by the Levites whose cities were within the limits of the kingdom, and by such of the Aaronic priests as might have chosen to conform to the new order of things. But to the eternal honor of this much-calumniated body, they all refused to sanction these proceedings, or to take any part in such violation of the Divine law; in consequence of which they not only forfeited the dues which had afforded them subsistence in the ten tribes, but found it prudent and necessary to abandon also the cities which belonged to them in those tribes, and withdraw into the kingdom of Judah. There they were cheerfully received, although the two tribes forming that kingdom, thus became burdened with the whole charge which had hitherto been shared among twelve tribes. This fact is very valuable, as showing that the Levitical tribe had conciliated, and was entitled to, the esteem and respect of the people. In the end many persons belonging to the other tribes, who disapproved of Jeroboam's innovations, and were disposed to maintain their own fidelity to the spirit of the Mosaical institutions, followed the example of the Levites, and withdrew into the kingdom of Judah. It is not necessary to point out how seriously these migrations lessened the true strength of Jeroboam's kingdom, and increased that of his rival.

Jeroboam was thus left to establish a new priesthood for his new worship. Priests were accordingly appointed from all the tribes indiscriminately; but as to the important office of high-priest, his prudence and ambition suggested its annexation to the crown, as was the case in Egypt and some other heathen countries.

Jehovah was not slow in manifesting his displeasure at these proceedings. At one of the periodical feasts (that of tabernacles) the time for which had been altered by him, Jeroboam was discharging the priestly act of offering incense on the altar at Bethel, when a prophet of God from Judah appeared on the spot, and denounced destruction upon this altar, to be executed by a future king of Judah, Josiah by name: and, in proof of his mission, announced that it should even now receive such a crack that its ashes should be scattered abroad. Hearing this, the king stretched forth his hand to seize the prophet, when his arm stiffened in the act, and could not be again drawn back, until the prophet himself interceded with God for him. At the same time the altar was rent, and the ashes strewed abroad, as the prophet had said.

This message seems to have produced no good effect either on the king or the people; and this may have been partly owing to the misconduct of the prophet himself; for after having publicly declared that he was forbidden to eat or drink in Bethel, or to make any stay there, he allowed himself, after having departed, to be imposed upon and brought back, and to be feasted in Bethel, by a sort of Balaamite prophet; for which he was slain by a lion on his return home, and his body was brought back and buried in Bethel. As the prophet had thus acted against his own avowed orders, and had in consequence been destroyed with manifest marks of the Divine displeasure, the occasion was doubtless taken to diminish the credit and effect of the mission with which he had been charged.

Jeroboam lived to see three kings upon the throne of Judah. There arose a skirmishing warfare between the two kingdoms in the latter years of Rehoboam; and in the reign of his successor the war was brought to a great pitched battle, the result o: which was adverse to Jeroboam. In the latter years of his reign, the prophet Ahijah who had originally communicated the Divine appointment to him, was commissioned to denounce the death of his most hopeful son, Abijah, about whose sickness the wife of Jeroboam went to consult him in disguise. The prophet, though blind with age, knew her by the prophetic impulse which came upon him; and he not only told her this, but declared the approaching destruction of Jeroboam's race by a succeeding king of Israel, and also announced the ultimate captivity of the tribes of Israel beyond the Euphrates for their manifold iniquities.

Jeroboam himself died in the year 968, B. C., after a reign of twenty-two years.

His son Nadab ascended the throne in the second year of Asa, king of Judah. He reigned two years, during which he adhered to the system of his father, and at the end of which an intimate of his own, named Baasha, of the tribe of Issachar, conspired against him and slew him as he was laying siege to Gibbethon, a fortress which the Philistines retained in their possession. According to the policy of the East, Baasha having slain the head of the house of Jeroboam, hastened to destroy all its other members, who might prove disturbers of his safety in the throne. Thus was the denunciation of the prophet Ahijah against the house of Jeroboam speedily accomplished.

The government of Baasha proved not only offensive to God, but oppressive to the people, on both which grounds great numbers of the subjects of this kingdom sought repose in that of Judah. It was probably partly in consequence of the alarm which this constant migration of his people produced, that Baasha entered into a skirmishing warfare with Asa, king of Judah, and ultimately laid siege to, and took the town of Ramah, seven miles to the north of Jerusalem, which he began to rebuild and fortify, with the view of leaving a garrison in it to check the communication with Jerusalem, and to become a point from which excursions might be made into the kingdom of Judah. This bold proceeding occasioned much alarm in Judah; but instead of opposing it by force of arms, King Asa collected all the gold he could find in his own treasury, *and that of the temple*, and sent it to Ben-Hadad, the king of Syria, to induce him to make a diversion in his favor. Accordingly the Syrians fell upon the north of Israel, and took all the fenced cities of Naphtali; which obliged Baasha to relinquish his enterprise in the south, and march to the defence of his own territories.

Time only confirmed Baasha in the evil courses which had proved the ruin of the house of Jeroboam; in consequence of which a prophet, named Jehu, the son of another prophet called Hanani, was sent to declare for his house the same doom which he had himself been the agent of inflicting upon that of Jeroboam.

Baasha died in 966, B. C., after a reign of twenty-three years.

After the death of Baasha, Israel became the prey of a series of sanguinary revolutions. His son Elah remained only two years on the throne, at the expiration of which he was assassinated during a feast by one of his generals, of the name of Zimri, who then assumed the crown. Zimri, during the few days of his reign, found time to extirpate the whole family of his predecessor, thus accomplishing upon the house of Baasha the doom which the prophet had declared.

The army, which was engaged against the Philistines, no sooner heard of the murder of their king than they declared in favor of Omri, their own commander, and proclaimed him king. This new king immediately marched with all his forces against his rival, and used such diligence that he shut him up in the summer capital of Tirzah. Zimri made no resistance, but fled to his harem, which he set on fire, and perished in the flames. He had reigned only seven days; and this signal and speedy

Samaria.

end gave occasion to the proverb in Israel, "Had Zimri peace, who slew his master?" Omri had another competitor: for while the army had elected him, a portion of the people, equally disgusted at the deed of Zimri, had made Tibni king. The kingdom was thus split into factions, and it was only after a civil war of six years that the faction of Omri prevailed, and Tibni was put to death. Omri reigned above five years after this. He was more guilty before God than any of his predecessors, for he appears to have taken measures to turn into actual idolatry that which under the former kings had only been an irregular and interdicted form of worship and service. Finding some disadvantages in the situation of Tirzah, however pleasant, for a metropolis, Omri purchased a hill of a person called Samar for two talents of silver ($3,750), and built thereon a city, which, after the name of the previous owner of the site, he called SAMARIA,* and made it the capital of his dominion. So well was the situation chosen, that the city remained the metropolis of the kingdom while the kingdom endured, and was still a place of importance when the Hebrews ceased the second time to be a nation. There are some respects in which its site is deemed by travellers preferable to that of Jerusalem.

After his reign of eleven completed years, counted as twelve in the Scriptures, because he had entered on the twelfth, Omri died in the year 931 B. C., being the thirty-ninth year of Asa king of Judah.

JUDAH, FROM B. C. 990 TO B. C. 929.

Except in its first act, the commencement of Rehoboam's reign was not blameworthy, nor, as it respects his separate kingdom, unprosperous. In those days the wealth and welfare of a state were deemed to consist in a numerous population; and of this kind of strength the kingdom of Judah received large additions by migration from that of Israel, through the defection of the Levitical body, and the discontent with which a large and valuable portion of the population regarded the arbitrary innovations of Jeroboam. It may indeed be, in a great degree, imputed to this cause, that, although so much inferior in territorial extent, the kingdom of Judah appears throughout the history of the two kingdoms to be at least equal to that of Israel.

Rehoboam, seeing that he had an adverse kingdom so near at hand, employed the first years of his reign in putting his dominions in a condition of defence. He built and fortified a considerable number of places in Judah and Benjamin, which he stored well with arms and victuals, and in which he placed strong garrisons. For three years he remained faithful to the principles of the theocracy, and received a full measure of the prosperity which had been promised to such obedience. But when he beheld himself, as he deemed, secure and prosperous in his kingdom, his rectitude,

---

* SAMARIA.—The text to which this note is appended sufficiently indicates the origin of Samaria. It remained the capital of Israel until the ruin of that kingdom by the Assyrians, after which it became the chief seat of the people whom the king of Assyria planted in the desolated country, and who are hence, in the subsequent history, known by the name of Samaritans. Between them and the restored Jews there was always a bitter and not always bloodless enmity, which subsisted down to the extinction of the Hebrew commonwealth. The town was utterly destroyed by Hyrcanus, the king-priest of the Jews, in the year 129 B. C.; and in this state it remained until the time of Herod the Great, who, being much pleased with its situation, rebuilt it in a very beautiful manner, and gave it the name of Sebaste, a Greek word equivalent to the Latin Augusta, in honor of the Emperor Augustus. Under this name it continued to flourish until the Jews were finally expelled from Palestine by the Emperor Adrian, after which the place went gradually to decay; and at present the inhabited part of the site forms a mean and miserably poor village, named Subusta, containing not more than thirty dwellings.

"The situation," says Dr. Richardson, "is exceedingly beautiful, and strong by nature—more so, I think, than Jerusalem. It stands on a fine large insulated hill, compassed all round by a broad deep valley; and when fortified, as it is stated to have been, by Herod, one would have imagined that in the ancient system of warfare nothing but famine could have reduced such a place. The valley is surrounded by four hills, one on each side, which are cultivated in terraces to the top, sown with grain, and planted with fig and olive trees, as is also the valley. The hill of Samaria itself, likewise, rises in terraces to a height equal to any of the adjoining mountains."

The first view of the place, even in its present state, is highly imposing. And there are sufficient remains of Herod's city to enforce the impressions which the history of the site has prepared the mind to receive. These, however, consist chiefly of numerous limestone columns, still standing, on the upper part of the hill, but without their capitals. Hardy counted eighty that were standing, besides many that lay prostrate. There are also some remains of fortifications; but the most conspicuous ruin is that which appears in the cut on page 315. This was a large church, attributed to the Emperess Helena, and said to have been built over the dungeon in which John the Baptist was confined and afterward beheaded by order of Herod. This cave or dungeon is still pointed out; besides which there are under the church several vaults, which probably opened into the sides of the hill. The building itself is in a very elaborate but fantastic style of architecture; the columns used in which are of no known order, although the capitals approach nearer to the Corinthian than to any other. The east end, with its pentagonal projection, is nearly perfect, confirming a remark of Maundrell, that if any portion of a church is left standing in these parts it is sure to be the eastern end.

The Walls of Jerusalem, and part of the Valley of Jehosaphat.—2 Sam. xv. 23–30. 2 Kings, xviii. 17, 18.

which appears never to have been founded on very strong principles, gave way. It was not long before the acts which stained the later years of his father were more than equalled by him. Not only was idolatry openly tolerated and practised, but also the abominable acts, outrageous even to the mere instincts of morality, which some of these idolatries sanctioned or required. Thus the abominations of Judah very soon exceeded those of Israel. And we shall, throughout the historical period on which we have entered, observe one very important distinction in the religious (which, according to the spirit of the Hebrew institutions, means also the political) condition of the two kingdoms. Israel rested with tolerable uniformity in a sort of intermediate system between the true religion and idolatry, with enough of elementary truth to preserve some show of fidelity to the system, and enough of idolatry and human invention to satisfy the corrupt tendencies of the age and country. Hence, while on the one hand it never, under its best kings, reached that purity of adherence to the Mosaical system which was sometimes exemplified in the sister kingdom, so, on the other, it never, or very rarely, fell to those depths of iniquity to which Judah sometimes sunk under its more wicked and weak kings. For Judah, resting on no such intermediate point as had been found in Israel, was in a state of constant oscillation between the *extremes* of good and evil.

In the case of Rehoboam, the loose principles which prevailed at the latter end of his father's reign, together with the fact that the mother, from whom his first ideas had been imbibed, was an Ammonitess, may partly account for the extreme facility of his fall. Indeed, with reference to the latter fact, it may be observed that among the kings there is scarcely one known to be the son of a foreign and consequently idolatrous mother, who did not fall into idolatry; a circumstance which is sufficient alone to explain and justify the policy by which such connexions were forbidden.

The chastisement of Rehoboam and his people was not long delayed. It was inflicted by the Egyptians, who, in the fifth year of Rehoboam, invaded the land under Shishak their king, in such strong force as intimated the expectation of a more formidable resistance than was encountered; or rather, perhaps, was designed to shorten the war by overawing opposition. There were twelve hundred chariots, sixty thousand horsemen, and a vast body of infantry, the latter composed chiefly from the subject nations of Lybia and Ethiopia. Shishak took with ease the fenced cities on which Rehoboam had placed so much reliance; and when he appeared before Jerusalem, that city appears to have opened its gates to him. Here he reaped the first-fruits of that rich spoil, from the gold of the temple and of the palace, which supplied so many subsequent demands. In the extremity of distress, while the city was in the hands of an insulting conqueror, who stripped the most sacred places of their costly ornaments and wealth, the king of Judah and his people turned repentingly to God, and implored deliverance from his hand. He heard them, and inclined Shishak to withdraw with the rich spoil he had gained, without attempting to retain permanent possession of his conquest. Astonished himself at the facility with which that conquest had been made, this king despised the people who had submitted so unresistingly to his arms, and, according to the testimony of Herodotus,* cited by Josephus himself, he erected, at different points on his march home, triumphal columns, charged with emblems very little to the honor of the nation which had not opposed him.

Although it is difficult to assign a specific reason, beyond a conqueror's thirst for spoil, for this invasion of the dominions of the son by a power which had been so friendly to the father, it does not strike us, as it does some writers, that the difficulty is increased by the fact of the matrimonial alliance which Solomon had formed with the royal family of Egypt. Rehoboam was born before that alliance was contracted, and he and his mother were not likely to be regarded with much favor by the Egyptian princess or her family. Indeed it would seem that *she* had died, or her influence had declined, or her friends deemed her wrong, before the latter end of Solomon's reign; for it is evident that the king of Egypt, this very Shishak, was not on the most friendly terms with Solomon, since he granted his favor and protection to the fugitive Jeroboam, whose prospective pretensions to divide the kingdom with the son of Solomon forms the only apparent ground of the distinction with which he was treated. This circumstance may direct attention to what appears to us the greater

* Herodotus, i. 105.

probability, that the expedition was undertaken at the suggestion of Jeroboam, who had much cause to be alarmed at the defection of his subjects to Rehoboam, and at the diligence which that king employed in strengthening his kingdom. The rich plunder which was to be obtained would, when pointed out, be an adequate inducement to the enterprise.

The severe lesson administered by this invasion to Rehoboam and his people was not in vain, for we read no more of idolatrous abominations during the eleven remaining years of this reign. In consequence, these were rather prosperous years for the kingdom; and, save a few skirmishes with the king of Israel, we learn of no troubles by which it was, during these years, disturbed. But, like his father, Rehoboam "desired many wives." His harem contained eighteen wives and sixty concubines,—a number which, we can not doubt, was much opposed to the notions of the Hebrew people, although it seems rather moderate as compared with the establishment of Solomon, or those which we still find among the kings of the East. Of all his wives, the one Rehoboam loved the most was Maachah, a daughter (or grand-daughter*) of Absalom. Her son, Abijah, he designed for his successor in the throne: to ensure which object, he made adequate provision for his other sons while he lived, and prudently separated them from each other, by dispersing them through his dominions as governors of the principal towns. This policy was successful; for although this king had twenty-eight sons, besides three-score daughters, his settlement of the crown was not disputed at his death. This event took place in the year 973 B. C., in the eighteenth year of his reign.

Abijah, otherwise called Abijam, succeeded his father, and the first public act of his short reign appears to justify the preference which had been given to him. Jeroboam, whose policy it was to harass and weaken the house of David, and to render the two kingdoms as inimical to each other as possible, thought the succession of the new king, young and inexperienced, a favorable opportunity for an aggressive movement. He seems therefore to have made a general military levy, which amounted to the prodigious number of eight hundred thousand men. Abijah when he heard of this formidable muster was not discouraged, but, although he could raise only half the number of men, took the field against his opponent. They met near Mount Zemarim, on the borders of Ephraim. The armies were drawn out in battle array, when Abijah, who was posted on an elevated spot, finding the opportunity favorable, beckoned with his hand, and began to harangue Jeroboam and the hostile army. His speech was good, and to the purpose; but it does not seem to us entitled to the unqualified praise which it has generally received. He began with affirming the divine right of the house of David to reign over all Israel, by virtue of the immutable covenant by which Jehovah had promised to David that his posterity should reign for ever. Consequently he treated the secession of the ten tribes as an unprincipled act of rebellion against the royal dynasty of David, and against God—an act whereby the crafty Jeroboam, with a number of vain and lawless associates, had availed themselves of the weakness and inexperience of Rehoboam to deprive the chosen house of its just rights. This statement doubtless imbodies the view which the house of David, and the party attached to its interests, took of the recent event. They regarded as a rebellion what was truly a revolution; and which, although, like other revolutions, it had its secret springs (as in the jealousy between the tribes of Ephraim and Judah), was not only justifiable in its abstract principles, but on the peculiar theory of the Hebrew constitution: for it had the previous sanction and appointment of Jehovah, as declared to both parties; and, in its immediate cause, sprung from a most insulting refusal of the representative of the dynasty to concede that redress of grievances which ten twelfths of the whole nation demanded, and which it had a right to demand and obtain before it recognised him as king. However, a king of Judah could not well be expected to take any other than a dynastic and party view of this great question: and that such, necessarily, was the view of Abijah is what we have desired to explain, as the generally good spirit

* This lady is mentioned in three places, and in all of them the name of her father is differently given. In 1 Kings xv. 2, it is "Maachah, the daughter of Abishalom;" in 2 Chron. xi. 20, "Maachah, the daughter of Absalom;" and in 2 Chron. xiii., "Michaiah, the daughter of Uriel of Gibeah." The Jews believe that Absalom the son of David is intended. This does not appear quite certain; but if so, we may take their explanation that Maachah was the daughter of Tamar, the daughter of Absalom; in which case, the comparison of texts will intimate that Uriel married Tamar, and Maachah was their daughter, which consequently makes her the grand-daughter of Absalom and daughter of Uriel. This, upon the whole, seems more probable than that the several names, Abishalom, Absalom, and Uriel, all point to the same person as the father of Maachah.

of his harangue has disposed hasty thinkers to take the impression which he intended to convey.

With more justice, Abijah proceeded to animadvert on the measures—the corruptions and arbitrary changes—by which Jeroboam had endeavored to secure his kingdom; and, with becoming pride, contrasted this with the beautiful order in which, according to the law of Moses, and the institutions of David and Solomon, the worship of Jehovah was conducted by the Levitical priesthood in that "holy and beautiful house" which the Great King honored with the visible symbol of his inhabitance. He concluded: " *We* keep the charge of Jehovah our God; but *ye* have forsaken him. And, behold, God himself is with us for our captain, and his priests with sounding trumpets to cry alarm against you. O children of Israel, fight not against Jehovah the God of your fathers; for ye shall not prosper." (2 Chron. xiii. 11, 12.)

By Jeroboam this harangue was only viewed as an opportunity for executing a really clever military operation. He secretly ordered a body of men to file round the hill, and attack the Judahites in the rear, while he assailed them in front. This manœuvre was so well executed, that Abijah, by the time he had finished his speech, perceived that he was surrounded by the enemy. The army of Judah raised a cry of astonishment and alarm, and a universal panic would in all likelihood have ensued. But the priests at that instant sounded their silver trumpets, at which well-known and inspiriting signal the more stout-hearted raised a cry for help to Jehovah, and rushed upon the enemy; and their spirited example raised the courage and faith of the more timid and wavering. The host of Israel could not withstand the force which this divine impulse gave to the arm of Judah. Their dense mass was broken and fled, and of the whole number it is said not fewer than five hundred thousand were slain,—a slaughter, as Josephus (Antiq. viii. 2, 3) remarks, such as never occurred in any other war, whether it were of the Greeks or the barbarians.* This would still be true if the number had been much smaller. "In numbers so large," Jahn (book v., sect. 36) remarks, "there may be some error of the transcribers; but it is certain that after this defeat the kingdom of Israel was considerably weakened, while that of Judah made constant progress in power and importance. We must here mention, once for all, that, owing to the mistakes of transcribers in copying numerals, we can not answer for the correctness of the great numbers of men which are mentioned here and in the sequel. *When there are no means of rectifying these numbers, we set them down as they occur in the books.*" Such also is our own practice.

This great victory was pursued by Abijah, in the re-taking and annexation to his dominion of some border towns and districts, some of which had originally belonged to Judah and Benjamin, but which the Israelites had found means to include in their portion of the divided kingdom. Among these towns was Bethel; and this being the seat of one of the golden calves, the loss of it must have been a matter of peculiar mortification to Jeroboam, and of triumph to Abijah.

The reign of Abijah was not by any means answerable to the expectations which his speech and his victory are calculated to excite. We are told that " he walked in all the sins of his father," and that " his heart was not perfect with Jehovah his God;" by which it would appear that he did not take sufficient heed to avoid and remove the idolatries and abominations which Solomon and Rehoboam had introduced or tolerated. He died in 970 B. C., after a reign of three years, leaving behind him twenty-two sons and sixteen daughters, whom he had by fourteen wives.

· The son who succeeded him was named Asa. He was still very young, and the affairs of the kingdom appear for sometime to have been administered by his grandmother, Maachah, whose name has already been mentioned. Asa, for his virtues, his fidelity to the principles of the theocracy, and the prosperity and victory with which he was in consequence favored, takes place in the first rank of the kings of Judah. He enjoys the high character that " his heart was perfect with Jehovah all his days: and he did that which was right with Jehovah, as did his father David." His first cares were directed toward the utter uprooting of the idolatries and abomina-

---

* With reference to the high numbers which occur here, Dr. Hales observes: " The numbers in this wonderful battle are probably corrupt, and should be reduced to forty thousand, eighty thousand, and fifty thousand (slain), as in the Latin Vulgate of Sixtus Quintus, and many earlier editions, and in the old Latin translation of Josephus: and that such were the readings in the Greek text of that author originally, Vignoles judiciously collects from Abarbanel's charge against Josephus of having made Jeroboam's loss no more than fifty thousand men, *contrary to the Hebrew text*." See Kennicott's " Dissertations," vol. i., p. 533, and vol. ii., p. 201, &c., 564. To this we may add the remark of Jahn, in which we more entirely concur.

tions which had been suffered to creep in during the preceding reigns. He drove from his states the corrupters of youth, and with an unsparing hand he purged Jerusalem of the infamies which had long harbored there. The idols were overthrown and broken in pieces, and the groves which had sheltered the dark abominations of idolatry were cut down: even his grandmother, Maachah, he deprived of the authority—removing her from being queen—which she had abused to the encouragement of idolatry; and the idols which she had set up he utterly destroyed. By thus clearing them from defiling admixtures, the pure and grand doctrines and practices of the Mosaical system shone forth with a lustre that seemed new in that corrupt age. Again the priests of Jehovah were held in honor by the people; and again the temple, its past losses being in part repaired by the royal munificence, was provided with all that suited the dignity of the splendid ritual service there rendered to God; for Asa was enabled to replace with silver and gold a portion of the precious things which Shishak had taken from the temple, and which Rehoboam had supplied with brass.

Ten years of prosperity and peace rewarded the pious zeal of the king of Judah. In these years much was done by him to strengthen and improve his kingdom, especially in repairing and strengthening the fortified towns, and in surrounding with strong walls and towers many.which had not previously been fortified. We are also informed that "Asa had an army of three hundred thousand out of Judah, who bore shields and spears; and of two hundred and eighty thousand out of Benjamin, who bore shields and spears: all these were men of valor." This and other passages of the same nature, describing the immense military force of the small kingdoms of Judah and Israel (even setting aside those which labor under the suspicion of having been altered by the copyists), appear to intimate that the general enrolment for military service which David contemplated, but was prevented from completely executing, was accomplished by later kings. It is always important to remember, however, that the modern European sense of the word *army*, as applied to a body of men exclusively devoted to a military profession, is unknown to the history of this period; and in the statement before us we are to see no more than that the men thus numbered were provided with weapons (or that the king had weapons to arm them), and were, the whole or any part of them, bound to obey any call from the king into actual service.

An occasion for such a call occurred to Asa after ten years of prosperity and peace. His dominions were then exposed to a most formidable invasion from "Zerah the Cushite," with a million of men and three hundred chariots.* It is beyond the range of probability, from the state of Egypt at this time, in the reign of Osorkon I.,† who succeeded Sheshonk (or Shishak), that an army under Zerah should have marched through Egypt from the Ethiopia south of the cataracts of the Nile. It must therefore be concluded that the army was composed of the Cushites (or Ethiopians) of Arabia, the original seat of all the Cushites; and as the army was partly composed of Lybians, who, if this supposition be correct, could not well have passed from Africa through the breadth of Egypt on this occasion, it may, with very sufficient probability, be conjectured that they formed a portion of the Libyan auxiliaries in the army with which Shishak invaded Palestine, twenty-five years before, and who, instead of returning to their own deserts, deemed it quite as well to remain in those of Arabia Petræa, and in the country between Egypt and Palestine. And this explanation seems to be confirmed by the fact, which appears in the sequel, that they held some border towns (such as Gerar) in this district. The flocks und herds, and the tents of the invading host, sufficiently intimate the nomade character of the invasion.

This emergency was met by Asa in the true spirit of the theocracy. Fully conscious of the physical inadequacy of his force to meet the enemy, he nevertheless went forth boldly to give them battle, trusting in Jehovah, who had so often given his

---

* Josephus gives nine hundred thousand infantry and one hundred thousand cavalry, which some would reduce by striking off a cipher from each number. A merely conjectural emendation is, however, so difficult and hazardous, that it is better to retain the original numbers, even when doubtful. In the present instance we may refer to what has just been said as to the distinction between the armies of that time and our own. And if Asa in his contracted territory was able to call out above five hundred thousand men, there is no solid reason why it should be impossible to the Cushite nomades, among whom every man was able to use arms, to bring double that number together. There must always be a vast difference in numbers between the army that must be kept and paid permanently, and that which may be raised by a general call upon the adult male population to a warlike enterprise, and only for the time of that enterprise. The army of Tamerlane (as we call him) is said to have amounted to one million six hundred thousand men, and that of his antagonist Bajazet to one million four hundred thousand. *Laonic. Chalcocond. de rebus Turc* l. iii. p. 96, 102.

† His name is so given in the monuments, but in ancient writers it is *Osorthon.*

21

people the victory against far greater odds, and to whom he made the public and becoming appeal:—"O Jehovah, it is nothing with thee to help, whether with many or with them that have no power: Help us, O Jehovah, our God; for we rest on thee, and in thy name we go against this multitude. O Jehovah, thou art our God; let not man prevail against thee." The consequence of this proper manifestation of reliance upon their Omnipotent King was a very splendid victory over the Cushites. They were defeated in the great battle of Mareshah,* in the valley of Zephathah, and fled before the army of Judah, which commenced a vigorous pursuit, attended with great slaughter. The Ethiopians and Lybians fled toward their tents and to Gerar and other towns, which some of them (we have supposed the Lybians) occupied on the border land toward Philistia. Here the conquerors found a rich spoil of cattle from the camps of the nomades, and of goods from the towns. On their triumphal return, they were met by the prophet Obed, who excited the piety and gratitude of the king and his army by reminding them to whom the victory was really due, even to Jehovah; and he called to their remembrance the privilege they enjoyed, as contrasted with the kingdom of Israel, in the marked and beneficent protection and care of their Great King, and hinted at the duties which resulted from the enjoyment of such privileges. This was attended with very good effects; and in the warmth of his gratitude for the deliverance with which he had been favored, Asa prosecuted his reforms with new vigor. He rooted out every remnant of idolatry, and engaged the whole people to renew their covenant with Jehovah.

It appears that the effect of the manifest tokens of the divine favor which Asa received, especially in the great victory over Zerah, was felt in the neighboring kingdom, and induced large numbers of the subjects of Baasha to migrate into his dominions. A constant and large accession of men, induced by such considerations, and by revived attachment to the theocracy, was calculated to give, and did give, a vast superiority of moral character to the kingdom of Judah. It was probably, as intimated in the last chapter, this tendency of his most valuable subjects to migrate into Judah, which induced Baasha to take the town of Ramah, and fortify it for a frontier barrier. The measure which Asa took on this occasion, of hiring the king of Syria to forego his previous alliance with Baasha, and cause a diversion in his own favor by invading the kingdom of Israel, was effectual as to the recovery of Ramah; for the death of Baasha, the following year, prevented him from resuming his designs. Asa availed himself of the materials which Baasha had brought together for the fortification of Ramah, to fortify the towns of Geba and Mizpeh. This advantage was, however, dearly purchased by the treasure of the temple and the palace which he was obliged to squander, to secure the assistance of the Syrians; and still more, by the displeasure of God, who denounced this proceeding as not only wrong in itself, but as indicating a want of that confidence in him through which he had been enabled to overthrow the vast host which the Cushites brought against him. This intimation of the Divine displeasure was conveyed to the king by the prophet Hanani, and was received by Asa with such resentment that he put the messenger in prison. Indeed, he appears to have grown increasingly irritable in the later years of his reign, in consequence of which he was led to commit many acts of severity and injustice. But for this some allowance may be made in consideration of his sufferings from a disease in his feet, which appears to have been the gout. With reference to this disease, Asa incurs some blame in the Scriptural narrative for his resort to "the physicians instead of relying upon God;" the cause of which rather extraordinary censure is probably to be found in the fact that those physicians who were not priests or Levites (in whose hands the medical science of the Hebrews chiefly rested) were foreigners and idolaters, who trusted more to superstitious rites and incantations than to the simple remedies which nature offered. With all these defects, for which much allowance may be made, Asa bears a good character in the Scriptural narrative, on account of the general rectitude of his conduct, and of his zealous services in upholding the great principles of the theocracy.

Asa died in the year 929 B. C., in the second year of Ahab, king of Israel, and after a long and, upon the whole, prosperous reign of forty-one years. He was sincerely lamented by all his subjects, who, according to their mode of testifying their final approbation, honored his remains with a magnificent funeral. His body, laid on a bed of state, was burned with vast quantities of aromatic substances: and the ashes,

---

* This was a town fortified by Rehoboam (2 Chron. xi. 8). It was the birthplace of the prophet Micah.

collected with care, were afterward deposited in the sepulchre which he had prepared for himself on Mount Zion. The burning of the dead, as a rite of sepulture, had originally been regarded with dislike by the Hebrews. But a change of feeling in this matter had by this time taken place; for the practice is not now mentioned as a new thing, and had probably been some time previously introduced. Afterward burning was considered the most distinguished honor which could be rendered to the dead, and the omission of it, in the case of royal personages, a disgrace. (See 2 Chron. xvi. 14, xxi. 19; Jer. xxxiv. 5; Amos vi. 10.) But in later days the Jews conceived a dislike to this rite; and their doctors endeavored, in consequence, to pervert the passages of Scripture which refer to it, so as to induce a belief that the aromatic substances alone, and not the body, were burnt.

ISRAEL, from b. c. 931 to b. c. 895.

Ahab, the son of Omri, mounted the throne of Israel in the year 931 B. C., being the thirty-eighth year of Asa, king of Judah. This king was, throughout his reign of twenty-two years, entirely under the influence of his idolatrous and unprincipled wife, Jezebel, a daughter of Ethbaal, or Ithobalus, king of Tyre. Hitherto the irregularities connected with the service before the golden calves, as symbols of Jehovah, had formed the chief offence of Israel. But now Ahab and Jezebel united their authority to introduce the gods of other nations. The king built a temple in Samaria, erected an image, and consecrated a grove to Baal, the god of the Sidonians. Jezebel, earnest in promoting the worship of her own god, maintained a multitude of priests and prophets of Baal. In a few years idolatry became the predominant religion of the land; and Jehovah, and the golden calves as representations of him, were viewed with no more reverence than Baal and his image. It now appeared as if the knowledge of the true God was for ever lost to the Israelites; but Elijah the prophet boldly stood up, and opposed himself to the authority of the king, and succeeded in retaining many of his countrymen in the worship of Jehovah. The greater the power was which supported idolatry, so much the more striking were the prophecies and miracles which directed the attention of the Israelites to Jehovah, and brought disgrace upon the idols, and confusion on their worshippers. The history of this great and memorable struggle gives to the narrative of Ahab's reign an unusual prominence and extent in the Hebrew annals; and although a writer studious of brevity might at the first view be disposed to omit, as episodical, much of the history of Elijah the Tishbite,* a little reflection will render it manifest that the prominence given to the history of this illustrious champion for the truth, was a designed and necessary result from the fact that the history of the Hebrew nation is the history of a church; and that although the history of this great controversy might be omitted or overlooked by those who erroneously regard the history of the Hebrews merely as a *political* history, in the other point of view it becomes of the most vital importance.

The first appearance of Elijah is with great abruptness to announce a drought, and consequent famine, for the punishment of the idolatry into which the nation had fallen; and that this calamity should only be removed at his own intercession. He apprehended that the iniquities of the land would bring down upon it destruction from God; and he therefore prayed for this lesser visitation, which might possibly bring the king and people to repentance.

After such a denunciation, it was necessary that the prophet should withdraw himself from the presence and solicitations of the king, when the drought should commence, which it did, probably about the sixth year of Ahab. Accordingly, obeying the directions of the divine oracle, he withdrew to his native district beyond Jordan, and hid himself in a cave by the brook Cherith; where the providence of God secured his support by putting it into the hearts of the Arabs encamped in the neighborhood, to send him bread and meat every morning and evening; and the brook furnished him with drink, until "the end of the year," or beginning of spring, when it was dried up from the continued drought.

It was probably under the irritation produced by the first pressure of the calamity, that Jezebel induced the king to issue orders for the destruction of all the prophets

---

* He is introduced as "Elijah the Tishbite, of the inhabitants of Gilead." It is probable therefore that the designation of "Tishbite" is from some town in Gilead, which can not now be clearly ascertained.

of Jehovah.* Many of them perished: but a good and devout man, even in the palace of Ahab,—Obadiah, the steward of his household,—managed to save a hundred of the number by sheltering them in caverns, where he provided for their maintenance until, probably, an opportunity was found for their escape into the kingdom of Judah.

When the brook of Cherith was dried up, the prophet was then directed by the Divine Voice to proceed westward to Sarepta,† a town of Sidon, under the dominion of Jezebel's father; where he lodged with a poor widow, and was miraculously supported with her and her family for a considerable time, according to his own prediction—"that her single barrel of meal should not waste, nor her single cruse of oil fail, until that day when Jehovah should send rain upon the earth." While he remained at this place, the prophet, by his prayers to God, restored to life the son of the widow with whom he lodged. Here he stayed until the end of three years from the commencement of the drought, when he was commanded to go and show himself to Ahab. That king had meanwhile caused the most diligent search to be made for him in every quarter, doubtless with the view of inducing him to offer up those intercessions through which alone the present grievous calamity could terminate. But at this time, having probably relinquished this search as hopeless, the attention of the king was directed to the discovery of any remaining supplies of water which might still exist in the land. He had, therefore, for the purposes of this exploration, divided the country between himself and Obadiah; and both proceeded personally to visit all the brooks and fountains of the land. Obadiah was journeying on this mission, when Elijah, who was returning from Sarepta, met him, and commissioned him to announce his arrival to Ahab. The king, when he saw the prophet, reproached him as the cause of the national calamities—"Art thou he that troubleth Israel?" But the prophet boldly retorted the charge upon himself and his father's house, because they had forsaken Jehovah and followed Baal. He then secured the attention of the king by intimating an intention of interceding for rain; and required him to call a general assembly of all the people at Mount Carmel, and also to bring all the prophets or priests of Baal,† and of the groves.

There, in the audience of that vast assembly, Elijah reproached the people with the destruction of the prophets of Jehovah, of whom, he alleged, that he alone remained, while the prophets of Baal alone were four hundred and fifty, fed at the table of Jezebel; and then he called them to account for their divided worship—"How long halt ye between two opinions? If JEHOVAH be the God, follow him; but if Baal, then follow him." The people intimated their uncertainty by their silence to this appeal; on which the prophet, fully conscious of his unlimited commission, proposed a solemn sacrifice to each, and "the God that answereth by fire (to consume his sacrifice) let him be the God." As this was a fair trial of Baal's supposed power in his own element, the most zealous of his worshippers could make no objection to it, and the proposal was approved by all the people. Accordingly, when Baal answered not the earnest and ultimately maddened invocations of his prophets—but Jehovah instantly answered the prayer of Elijah, by sending fire (as on former occasions) to consume the victim on the altar, although it had previously been inundated with water by the direction of the prophet—then the people, yielding to one mighty impulse of conviction, fell upon their faces, and cried, "JEHOVAH, HE IS THE GOD! JEHOVAH, HE IS THE GOD!"—thus also expressing that Baal was *not* the God, and rejecting him. To ratify this abjuration of Baal, Elijah commanded them to destroy his priests; and this, in the enthusiasm of their re-kindled zeal for Jehovah, they immediately did, at the brook Kishon, which had been the scene of Barak's victory over the Canaanites.

Immediately after this sublime national act of acknowledgment of Jehovah and rejection of Baal, the prophet went up to the top of Carmel, and prayed fervently for rain seven times; the promise of which (speedily followed by fulfilment) at last appeared in the form of "a little cloud like a man's hand," rising out of the Mediterranean sea—a phenomenon which, in warm maritime climates, is not the unusual harbinger of rain.

This remarkable transaction may be ascribed to the tenth year of Ahab's reign.

Elijah was now compelled to fly for his life, to avoid the threatened vengeance of Jezebel for the destruction of her prophets. He fled southward, and when he had

* There were probably "students in the schools of the prophets," or persons who devoted themselves to the study of the divine law, and on whom the spirit of prophecy occasionally came.
† Now called *Surphen*, about three hours' journey from Sidon on the way to Tyre.
‡ It may assist the comprehension of the narrative to know that Baal was an impersonation of the sun.

travelled nearly 100 miles, from Samaria to Beersheba, he left his servant and went alone a day's journey into the wilderness. There he sat, for rest and shelter, under the scanty shade which a broom-tree offered, the mighty spirit by which he had hitherto been sustained, gave way, and he prayed for death to end his troubles. "It is enough:" he cried, "now, O Jehovah, take away my life; for I am not better than my fathers!" To strengthen his now sinking faith, and reward his sufferings in the cause of the God of Israel, whose honor he had so zealously vindicated, the prophet was encouraged by an angel to undertake a long journey to "the mount of God," Horeb, where the Divine presence had been manifested to Moses, the founder of the law; and of which a further manifestation was now probably promised to this great champion and restorer of the same law. On this mysterious occasion the angel touched him twice, to rouse him from his sleep, and twice made him eat of food which he found prepared for him. In the strength which that food gave, the prophet journeyed (doubtless by a circuitous route) forty days, until he came, it is supposed, to the cave where Moses was stationed, when he saw the glory of Jehovah in "the cleft of the rock."

There he heard the voice of Jehovah calling to him, "What doest thou here, Elijah?" The prophet, evidently recognising that voice, said, "I have been very zealous for Jehovah, the God of Hosts; for the children of Israel have forsaken thy covenant, thrown down thy altars, and slain thy prophets with the sword, and I only am left; and they seek my life to take it away." Then the voice commanded him to go forth, for Jehovah was about to pass by. The first harbinger of the Divine presence was a great and strong wind, which rent the mountain and brake the rock in pieces; but Jehovah was not in that wind. Then followed an earthquake; but Jehovah was not in the earthquake. This was succeeded by a fire; but Jehovah was not in the fire. After this, came "*a still, small Voice;*" and when the prophet heard it, he knew the Voice of God, and, reverently hiding his face in his mantle, he stood forth in the entrance of the cave. The Voice repeated the former question, "What doest thou here, Elijah?" to which the same answer as before was returned. The Voice, in reply, gently rebuked the prophet for his crimination of the whole people of Israel, and his discouraging representation of himself as the only prophet left. "I have yet left to me *seven thousand* men, in Israel, who have not bowed the knee to Baal." He was further instructed to return by a different route, by the way of Damascus; and, by the way to anoint or appoint Elisha to be his own successor, and (either by himself or Elisha), Hazael to be king of Damascene-Syria, and Jehu to be king of Israel —as the chosen ministers of Divine vengeance upon the house and people of Ahab.

Of the three, Elisha was the only one to whom Elijah himself made known this appointment. Elisha was the son of Shaphat, an opulent man of Abel-maholah, in the half-tribe of Manasseh, west of the Jordan. The prophet found him ploughing with twelve yoke of oxen, when, by a significant action, still well understood in the East, that of throwing his own mantle upon him, he conveyed the intimation of his prophetic call. That call was understood and obeyed by Elisha; and after having, with the prophet's permission, taken leave of his parents, he hastened to follow Elijah, to whom he ever after remained attached.

It is singular that the first formal alliance between the kingdoms of Israel and Judah took place during the reigns of two princes of such opposite characters as Ahab in Israel, and Jehoshaphat in Judah. But it was so: and in forming it, and in cementing it by the marriage of his eldest son Jehoram to Athaliah the daughter of Ahab and Jezebel, he doubtless acted from very ill-considered policy, and laid in a great store of disasters for himself and his house. It is unfortunate that we are unacquainted with the motives which led to this most unhappy connexion. A close and intimate union between the two kingdoms could not but be, *in itself,* a political good; and the error of Jehoshaphat probably lay in considering this fact by itself, without taking due account of that evil character of Ahab and his house, and that alienation of his people from God, which were calculated to neutralize, and actually did far more than neutralize, the natural advantages of such alliance. The marriage took place in the fifteenth year of Ahab's, and the thirteenth of Jehoshaphat's reign.

Not long after this, Ahab had cause to be alarmed at the designs of Ben-hadad, the king of Damascene-Syria, which kingdom had been gathering such strength, while that of the Hebrews had been weakened by divisions and by misconduct, that even the subjugation of Israel did not seem to Ben-hadad an enterprise to which his ambition might not aspire. To this end he made immense preparations: he claimed the united aid of all his tributary princes, thirty-two in number, and ultimately appeared with all his forces before Samaria, to which he laid seige. He first summoned Ahab to deliver up all his most precious things; and, compelled by dire necessity, the king of Israel consented. But Ben-hadad was only induced by this readiness of yielding, to enhance his terms, and sent further demands, which were so very hard and insulting, that the spirit of Ahab was at last roused, and, supported by the advice of his council, he determined to act on the defensive. Soon after a prophet came with the promise of victory over the vast host of the Syrians, by means of a mere handful of spirited young men who were particularly indicated.

The confidence of the Syrians was so great that they led a careless and jovial life, thinking of little but of indulgence in wine and good cheer, of which the king himself set the example. In the midst of these feasts, a body of two hundred and thirty-two men was seen to leave the city, and advance toward the camp. Ben-hadad, when he heard of it, quietly ordered them to be taken alive, whether they came for peace or for war. But suddenly these men fell upon the advanced sentinels, and upon all who were near them; and the cries and confusion of so many persons, taken as it were by surprise, were instrumental in creating a general panic among the vast Syrian host. Drawn himself by the irresistible movement, Ben-hadad fled on horseback, with all his army; and the troops of Israel (7,000 in number), which attended the motions and watched the effect of the sally of the brave two hundred and thirty-two, closely pursued the flying Syrians, and rendered the victory complete.

The prophet who foretold this victory now apprized Ahab that Ben-hadad would renew his attempt the ensuing year. This took place accordingly. The Syrians came in equal force as before, and, as they thought, with wiser counsels. The kingdom of Damascene-Syria was mostly a plain; whereas the kingdom of Israel, and the site of Samaria, in particular, was mountainous. Rightly attributing their defeat to the God (or, as they chose in their idolatrous ignorance, to say the *gods*) of Israel, they reasoned that he was a god of the hills, and therefore among the hills more powerful than their gods, who were gods of the valleys and the plains. Instead therefore of going among the hills as before, they would now fight in the plains, where they could not doubt of success. This reasoning, however absurd it now seems to us and did then seem (such were their privileges) to all enlightened Israelites, was in strict and philosophical accordance with the first principles of idolatry, and the general system of national and local deities. But such a view being taken by them, it became necessary to Jehovah to vindicate his own honor and assert his omnipotence by their overthrow. *For this reason* he delivered this vast host that covered the land into the hands of the comparatively small and feeble host of Israel. The Syrians were cut in pieces; 100,000 of their number were left dead upon the field of battle, and the rest were entirely dispersed. Ben-hadad, with a large number of the fugitives, sought refuge in Aphek; but by the sudden fall of the wall of that fortified town, 27,000 of his men were crushed to death, and the place was rendered defenceless. Nothing was now left to him but to yield himself up to Ahab. That monarch, weak and criminal by turns, received the Syrian king into his friendship, and formed an impious alliance with him, regardless not only of the law, but of the honor of God, who had given him the victory, and had delivered for punishment into his hands this blasphemer and enemy of his Great Name. For this he was, in the name of Jehovah, severely rebuked and threatened by one of "the sons of the prophets," by the way-side; in consequence he withdrew to his palace "heavy and displeased."

The history of Ahab affords one more, and the last, interview between him and Elijah. This was about nine years after the grand solemnity at Mount Carmel, and the nineteenth of Ahab's reign.

At that time the king took a fancy to enlarge his own garden by taking into it an adjoining vineyard which formed part of the patrimonial estate of a person named Naboth. He made him the fair offer of its value in money, or to give him some other piece of land of equal value. But Naboth, considering it a religious duty to preserve "the inheritance of his fathers," declined on any terms to alienate it. The reason was good, and ought to have satisfied the king. But he received the refusal like a spoiled child; he lay down upon his bed, and turned away his face to the wall, and refused to take his food. When his wife heard this she came to him, and having learned the cause of his grief, she said indignantly, "Dost thou not now govern the

Terrace Cultivation.

kingdom of Israel; Arise, eat food, and let thine heart be cheerful; the vineyard of Naboth, the Jezreelite, *I will give to thee.*" Accordingly, she procured Naboth to be put to death under the form of law. At a public feast he was accused by suborned witnesses of blasphemy, for which he was stoned to death, and his estates confiscated to the king. Jezebel then went to Ahab, apprized him of what had happened, and told him to go down and take possession of the vineyard. It is clear that if he did not suggest, he approved of the crime, and proceeded with joy to reap the fruits of it. But in the vineyard of Naboth, the unexpected and unwelcome sight of Elijah the prophet met his view. Struck by his own conscience, he cried, "Hast thou found me, O mine enemy?" To which Elijah replied, "I have found thee, because thou hast sold thyself to work evil in the eyes of Jehovah." He then proceeded to denounce the doom of utter extermination upon himself and his house for his manifold iniquities; and then, with reference to the immediate offence, he said, "Hast thou slain and also taken possession? Thus saith Jehovah, In whatsoever place the dogs licked up the blood of Naboth, shall dogs lick up thy blood, even thine. And concerning Jezebel, Jehovah hath also spoken, saying, The dogs shall eat Jezebel under the wall of Jezreel. Him who dieth of Ahab in the city shall the dogs eat; and him that dieth in the fields shall the fowls of the air eat." We are immediately reminded, however, that this terrible doom, although now denounced, as following this crowning deed of guilt, was really a consequence of this *and all the other* iniquities of Ahab's reign; for it is added, "Now there had been none like to Ahab, who, stirred up by Jezebel his wife, sold himself to work wickedness in the eyes of Jehovah. And he committed great abominations by going after vile idols, according to all that the Amorites did, whom Jehovah cast out before the Israelites."

When Ahab heard the heavy doom pronounced against him by the prophet, "he rent his clothes (in token of extreme grief), and put sackcloth upon his flesh, and fasted, and lay in sackcloth, and went mournfully." This conduct found some acceptance with God, who said to Elijah, Seest thou how Ahab humbleth himself before me? Because he humbleth himself before me, I will not bring the evil in his days, but in his son's days will I bring this evil upon his house." From the judicial sentence specially applicable to the case of Naboth, there was, however, no dispensation; as it behooved the Divine king to demonstrate that he still possessed and exercised the authority of supreme civil governor, and that the kings were responsible to him and punishable by him. This was signally shown in the sequel.

Israel was now at peace with Syria, but it had not recovered possession of all the places which had at different times been lost to that power. Of these, Ramoth Gilead, beyond Jordan, was one which, from its proximity and importance, Ahab was particularly anxious to regain possession. He therefore resolved to expel the Syrian garrison from that place; and as he was aware that the attempt would be opposed by the whole power of the Syrian kingdom, he claimed the assistance of Jehoshaphat, the king of Judah, which that prince, with the facility of disposition which formed the chief defect of his excellent character, very readily granted. Nevertheless, when the preparations were completed, Jehoshaphat, unsatisfied by the assurances of success which Ahab's own "prophets" had given, desired that some other prophet of Jehovah should be consulted. This request was more distasteful to Ahab than he liked to avow. "There is yet one man," he said, "Micaiah,* the son of Imlah, but him I hate, because he prophesieth not good concerning me, but evil." He was, however, sent for; and although the messenger had strongly inculcated upon him the necessity of making his counsel conformable to the wishes of the king and the predictions of his own prophets, the undaunted Micaiah boldly foretold the fatal result of the expedition. At this the king was so much enraged, that he ordered him to be kept in confinement, and fed with the bread and the water of affliction until he returned in peace. "If thou return at all in peace," rejoined the faithful prophet, "then Jehovah hath not spoken by me."

Ben-hadad, the king of Syria, repaid the misplaced kindness of Ahab by the most bitter enmity against his person; and he gave strict orders to his troops that their principal object should be his destruction. Ahab seems to have had some private information of this; for he went, himself, disguised to the battle, and treacherously persuaded Jehoshaphat to appear in all the ensigns of his high rank.† In consequence of

---

* Josephus and other ancient Jews understood that this Micaiah was the same prophet who had rebuked Ahab for his alliance with Ben-hadad.

† Josephus, supported by the Septuagint, says he wore the royal robes of Ahab.

this the king of Judah was nearly slain, being surrounded by the Syrians, who pressed toward the point in which one royally arrayed appeared. But they discovered their mistake in time, and turned their attention in another direction. Ahab, with all his contrivance, could not avoid his doom. A Syrian archer* sent forth from his bow an arrow at random. Guided by the unseen Power which had numbered the days of Ahab, that arrow found the disguised king, penetrated between the joints of his strong armor, and gave him his death-wound. He directed his charioteer to drive him out of the battle; but perceiving that a general action was coming on, he remained, and was held up in his chariot until the evening, animating his friends by his voice and presence. After the fall of night had terminated the combat, the king died, and the army was directed to disperse. The body of Ahab was taken to Samaria, to be deposited in the family sepulchre; and to mark the literal fulfilment of Elijah's prophecy, the historian acquaints us that his chariot was washed, and his armor rinsed in the pool of Samaria, where the dogs licked up the blood that he had lost. Thus signally, in the mysterious dispensations of Divine providence, were reconciled the seemingly discordant declarations of the two prophets, one of whom had foretold his death at Ramoth Gilead, and the other that dogs should claim his blood in Samaria.

The history of Ahab is almost exclusively occupied with the record of his guilt, and we are referred for information concerning his other public acts to a chronicle which no longer exists. But it transpires that he built several cities in Israel, and also a palace, which, from the quantities of ivory with which it was ornamented, was distinguished as "the ivory palace."

Ahab's death took place in the year 909 B. C., after a reign of twenty-two years.

He was succeeded in his throne and in his sin by his son AHAZIAH. The chief event of his short reign was the revolt of the Moabites, who, since their subjection by David, had continued to supply Israel with a rich tribute of flocks and fleeces.† Ahaziah himself having received serious injuries by a fall through a lattice in an upper chamber of his palace, sent messengers into the land of the Philistines, to consult Baal-zebub, the fly-god of Ekron, whether he should recover. But they were met on the way by the prophet Elijah, who sent them back to the king with a denunciation of death, for his impiety in forsaking the God of Israel and resorting to strange gods. The messengers knew not the prophet; but when they described him to the king as a man clad with a hairy garment, and with a leathern girdle about his loins, he recognised Elijah, and sent an officer with fifty men to apprehend him. But the prophet, whom they found sitting upon a hill, called down fire from heaven, which consumed this party, and also a second; but he went voluntarily with the third, the officer in command of which humbled himself before him, and besought him. The prophet confirmed to the king himself his former denunciation of speedy death; and, accordingly, Ahaziah died, after a short reign of two years, leaving no son to succeed him. This king maintained the alliance which his father had established with King Jehoshaphat, and even persuaded that monarch to admit him to share in his contemplated maritime expedition to the regions of Ophir, of which there will be occasion to speak in the next chapter.

Ahaziah was succeeded by his brother JEHORAM. This king, like his predecessors, " did evil in the sight of Jehovah," yet not to the same extent of enormity as they; for although the loose and irregular service of the golden calves was maintained by him, he overthrew the images of Baal, and discouraged the grosser idolatries which his father and brother had introduced.

The first and most urgent care of the new king was to reduce to obedience the Moabites, who, as just mentioned, had revolted on the death of Ahab. As the king of Judah had himself been troubled by the Moabites, he readily undertook to take a very prominent part in this enterprise, to which he also brought the support of his own tributary, the king of Edom. The plan of the campaign was, that the allied army should invade the land of Moab in its least defensible quarter, by going round by " the wilderness of Edom," southward of the Dead sea; which also offered the advantage that the forces of the king of Israel could be successively joined by those of the kings of Judah and Edom on the march. This circuitous march occupied seven days; and toward the end of it the army and the horses suffered greatly from

* Josephus says this was Naaman, who will soon come again before us.
† The annual tribute rendered by the Moabites had been 100,000 lambs and 100,000 wethers, with their wool.

thirst, probably occasioned by the failure of the wells and brooks, from which an adequate supply of water had been expected. Much loss had already been incurred through this unexpected drought, and nothing less than utter ruin seemed to impend over the allies when they lay on the borders of Moab, within view of the enemy, which had advanced to meet them. In this emergency the very proper course occurred to Jehoshaphat of consulting a prophet of Jehovah. On inquiry it was discovered that Elisha, "who had poured water on the hands of Elijah"—a proverbial expression from the most conspicuous act of service in a personal attendant—was the only prophet to be found in that neighborhood. Full of the faith of his illustrious master, this faithful disciple of Elijah had beheld the Jordan divide before that prophet, and had been with him when, upborne by the whirlwind, he was taken gloriously away from the earth, in the chariot and horses which glowed like fire, and who had substituted himself in his mission to work marvels and reprove kings in the name of Jehovah. Already had the " spirit and power of Elias," which abode in him, been manifested to all Israel by the prodigies he had wrought. The waters of the Jordan had divided before him, the second time, when smote by the fallen mantle of Elijah;—the bad waters of Jericho had become permanently wholesome at his word;—and to evince the power of his curse, bears from the woods had destroyed forty-two young men belonging to idolatrous Bethel, who, joining unbelief to insult, had bade him, in terms of mockery and derision,—" Go up, thou bald head ! Go up, thou bald head !" —ascend after his master.

The prophet, thus already distinguished, was sought in his retreat by the three kings. His greeting of Jehoram was severe, " What have *I* to do with *thee ?* Get thee to the prophets of thy father and to the prophets of thy mother." Nevertheless, but avowedly on the sole account of the good Jehoshaphat, he interested himself for the salvation of the army, which was in such imminent danger : and, having consulted the Lord, he promised that on the morrow there should be such an abundance of water, that the bed of the torrent, near which the army was encamped, should not be able to contain it ; and, more than this, he also indicated that this should be but the prelude of a signal victory over and complete ruin of the enemy.

All things happened as he had said. In the morning, at the time of offering sacrifice, the waters descended in such full-flood from the heights of Edom, that the camp would have been submerged, had not the army, by the direction of the prophet, previously dug large ditches to receive the redundant waters. All this was unknown to the Moabites, who, when they arose in the morning, and, on looking toward the camp of the allies, beheld the lurid rays of the rising sun reflected from the waters, which now covered the arid sands of yesterday, doubted not that it was blood which they saw, and formed the not by any means improbable conclusion that the armies of Israel and Judah had quarrelled with and destroyed each other. They therefore rushed without the least care or order to the pillage of the camp ; but so far from finding it deserted, they were surrounded and cut in pieces by the armed and now invigorated allies. The remnant of the army was pursued into the interior of the country by the conquerors, whose course was blackened by the fire and crimsoned by the sword. Ultimately they invested the metropolitan city of Kir-haraseth,* in which the king, Mesha, had taken refuge. One part of the walls had already been destroyed, and the king, seeing he could no longer defend the place, attempted to break through the besieging host at the head of seven hundred swordsmen. But failing in this desperate effort, he sought to propitiate his cruel gods by offering up the frightful sacrifice of his eldest son, the heir of his throne, in the breach. Seized with horror at this spectacle, the conquering kings abandoned the siege, withdrew from the country, and returned to their own states. In taking this step they did not consider, or, perhaps, not care, that they gave to the horrible act of the Moabite the very effect which he desired, and enabled him to delude himself with the persuasion that his sacrifice had been successful, and well-pleasing to the powers of Heaven.

In the remaining history of Jehoram's reign, the prophet Elisha occupies nearly as conspicuous a place as Elijah did in that of Ahab. The wonders wrought by his hands were numerous ; but they were less signal, and less attended with public and important results—less designed to effect public objects, than those of his master. Indeed his national acts were less considerable than those of Elijah ; and although he possessed great influence, and was undoubtedly the foremost man of his age, he

* The same place which is otherwise called Rabbath-Moab, and, classically, Areopolis.

wanted those energies of character, and that consuming zeal which his predecessor manifested; or, perhaps more correctly, the exigencies of the times were not such as to call for the exercise of such endowments as had been possessed by Elijah. But although those of his successor were different in their kind, we know not that, with regard to the differing time, they were less useful or eminent. In this, and in a thousand other historical examples,—more especially in the history of the Hebrews,—we see men raised up for, and proportioned to, the times in which they live, and the occasions which call for them. The most eminent of the prophets, since Moses, was given to the most corrupt time; in which only a man of his indomitable, ardent, and almost fierce spirit, could have been equal to the fiery and almost single-handed struggle for God against principalities and powers. Elisha fell in milder times, and was correspondingly of a milder character, although he was not found unequal to any of the more trying circumstances which arose during the period of his prophetic administration. Indeed his conduct on such occasions was such as to suggest that it was only the milder spirit of the time on which he fell, precluding occasion for their exercise, that prevented the manifestation in him of that grander class of endowments which his predecessor displayed. As it was, Elisha, instead of being like his master, driven by persecution from the haunts of men to the deserts and the mountains, and reduced to a state of dependance on the special providence of God, for the bread he ate, and the water he drank,—enjoyed a sufficiency of all things, and lived in honor and esteem among his countrymen; and even among the purple and fine linen of king's courts, the rough mantle of the prophet was regarded with respect.

In such a history as the present it is only necessary to report those of his acts which were connected with, or bore upon, the public history of the nation; yet his more private acts may be also briefly indicated for the sake of the illustration which they afford of the spirit and manners of the time.

The first of his operations which we read of, after that which connected him with the deliverance of Israel and the defeat of the Moabites, was an act of benevolence toward the widow of one of those "sons of the prophets" who had now come under his supervision. He had died without having the means of satisfying a debt he had incurred,* in consequence of which the creditor was disposed to indemnify himself by making bondsmen of her two sons; but on her complaint to Elisha, he multiplied a small quantity of oil which she possessed, until the price it brought more than sufficed to pay the implacable creditor.

The occasions of the prophet frequently led him to visit the city of Shunem, which being observed by a benevolent woman, she suggested to her husband that they should prepare a small separate apartment,† and furnish it with a bed, a table, a seat, and a lamp; and that this should be reserved for his use when he visited Shunem. This was accordingly done, and the prophet accepted the hospitalities of these good Shunemites. Elisha was very sensible of their kind attention, and wished to repay it by some substantial benefit. He sent for the woman, and offered to speak to the king or to the captain of the host on her behalf. This she declined; and the prophet felt at a loss what to do for them, until it was suggested by his servant Gehazi that the woman had long been childless, on which Elisha again sent for her, and as she stood respectfully at the door, he conveyed to her the astonishing intimation that, nine months thence, her arms should embrace a son. Accordingly, the child was born, and had grown up, when one day he received a stroke of the sun on his head, and died very soon. The mother laid him on the prophet's bed, and actuated by an undefinable, but intelligible impulse, sought and obtained the permission of her husband to go to Elisha, who was known to be then at Carmel. Accordingly an ass was saddled, on which, driven by a servant on foot,‡ she sped to that place. Elisha saw her afar off, and said to Gehazi, "Behold, yonder is the Shunamite! Run now, I pray thee, and say to her,—Is it well with thee? well with thy husband? well with the child?" The bereaved mother answered, "Well," but pressed on toward the man of God. On approaching him she alighted from her beast, and threw herself at his feet, on which

* The Jews think the person was Obadiah, and that his debt was contracted on account of the expense of maintaining the hundred prophets whom he concealed in caverns.
† Called in our version "a little chamber in the wall." It denotes doubtless what the Arabs still call by the same name (Oleah), which is a small building, generally at some distance from the house, like a summer-house in our gardens.
‡ It is still the usual practice in the East for a man on foot to lead or drive the ass on which a woman rides.

she laid hold. The officious Gehazi drew nigh to thrust her away, but Elisha checked him,—" Let her alone; for her soul is troubled within her: although Jehovah hath hidden from me the cause, and hath not told me of it."   When, in a few broken exclamations, she had made known the cause of her grief, the prophet gave his staff to Gehazi, with instructions to go and lay it on the face of the child. But the mother refused to leave the prophet, and he was induced to rise and return with her. They met Gehazi on his way back, who told them, " The child is not awaked!" They hasted on, and the prophet shut himself up with the child. It was not long before he directed the mother to be called, and presented to her the *living* boy.

Another time, when there was a dearth in the land, Elisha was at the school of the prophets at Gilgal; and at the proper time, gave the order to the servants, " Set on the great pot, and seeth pottage for the sons of the prophets." When this was dressed, it was found that a wild and bitter gourd had been gathered and shred into the pot by mistake. " O man of God! there is death in the pot!" cried the sons of the prophets, when they began to eat. But Elisha directed a handful of meal to be cast into the pot, and it was found that all the poisonous qualities of the pottage had disappeared.

In the kingdom of Damascene-Syria, the chief captain of the host, high in the favor and confidence of the king, was a person called Naaman, who had the misfortune of being a leper. This, which would have been a disqualification for all employment and society in Israel, could not but be a great annoyance and distress to a public man in Syria. When therefore a little Hebrew girl, who in a former war had been taken captive, and was now a slave in the household of this personage, was heard to say, " Would to God my lord were with the prophet, that is in Samaria, for he would recover him of his leprosy!" she was eagerly questioned on the matter, and the result was that the king of Syria sent Naaman, with a splendid retinue and camels laden with presents* to Samaria, with a sufficiently laconic letter to the King Jehoram. " When this letter cometh to thee, thou must recover from his leprosy Naaman, my servant. Behold, I have sent him with it." The king of Israel was utterly confounded when he read this epistle. He rent his clothes, and cried, " Am I a god, to kill and to make alive, that this man sendeth to me to recover a man of his leprosy? Consider, I pray you, and see how he seeketh an occasion of quarrelling with me." Intelligence of this affair, and of the king's vexation, was brought to Elisha, who desired that the Syrian stranger might be sent to him. Accordingly Naaman came with his chariot and horses and imposing retinue, and stood before the door of Elisha's house. The prophet did not make his appearance; but sent out a message directing him to go and bathe seven times in the river Jordan. The self-esteem of the distinguished leper was much hurt at this treatment. He expected that Elisha would have paid him personal attention and respect, and would have healed him by an appeal to his God, Jehovah, and by the stroking of his hand. He therefore turned and went away in a rage, exclaiming, " Are not Abana and Pharpar, rivers of Damascus, better than all the waters of Israel? May I not wash in them and be clean?" His attendants, however, succeeded in soothing him, and persuaded him to follow the prophet's directions; and when he rose, perfectly cleansed, from the Jordan, his feelings turned to conviction and gratitude; he returned to Samaria, and presented himself to the prophet, declaring his belief that Jehovah was the true and only God, and that henceforth he would offer burnt-offerings and sacrifices to no other. He would also have pressed upon his acceptance a valuable present, but this was firmly declined by Elisha; and when his covetous servant Gehazi, compromised the honor of God and of his own master, by following the Syrian, to ask a gift in the name of the prophet, the leprosy from which Naaman had been cleansed was declared by the prophet to be the abiding portion of him and of his race.

These and other miracles wrought by this prophet, fixed upon him *personally* the regard and veneration of the people; and while there is reason to think that the state of manners and of religion was not altogether so bad as it had been under Ahab, the practices and ideas of their corrupt system of religion was now too closely interwoven with their habits of life and mind to be easily shaken off. They rested on their intermediate system. Habit had reconciled even their consciences to it; and in general, to fall back upon it, after having strayed into *foreign* idolatries, was in their sight a com-

* The presents included ten talents of silver, equal to fifteen thousand dollars, six thousand shekels of gold, equal to sixty thousand dollars, and ten dresses of honor.

plete and perfect reformation. And as to the race of Ahab, *that* was hastening with rapid strides to its doom. The famine which about this time desolated the land, and the new war with the Syrians, which was carried on under the very walls of the capital, was met by the king without any fixed faith, or any determinate rule of conduct ; sometimes he attributed his calamities to Elisha, and vowed his destruction ; and at others he resorted to that same prophet as to his only friend and deliverer.

In this war the Syrians had laid an ambuscade, in which the king would undoubtedly have perished had not Elisha ensured his safety by discovering the plan of the enemy to him. This happened more than once ; and the Syrian king at first suspected treachery in his own camp; but being assured that it was owing to Elisha, "who could tell the king of Israel the words he spoke in his bed-chamber," he was much irritated, and, with singular infatuation, despatched a column of his best troops to invest the town of Dothan, where the prophet then abode, in such a manner that his escape seemed impossible to his own terrified servant. "Fear not," said Elisha, "for they that are with us are more than they that are with them ;" and then, praying that his eyes might be opened to the view of "things invisible to mortal sight," he beheld the mountain full of chariots and horses, glowing like fire, round about the prophet. At his request, the Syrian troop was then smitten with blindness, and in that condition he went among them, and conducted them to the very gates of the hostile metropolis, Samaria, where their eyes were opened, and he dismissed them in peace, after inducing Jehoram to give them refreshment, instead of slaying them, as was his own wish. This generous conduct seems to have had such good effect that the Syrian hordes for the present abandoned their enterprise, and returned to their own country.

After this came on a severe famine, of seven years' continuance, and the evils of it were aggravated by war, for the Syrian king deemed this season of weakness and exhaustion too favorable for his designs to be neglected. He marched directly to Samaria, and formally invested that strong place, which, seemingly, he hoped less to gain by force of arms than by so blockading it as ultimately to starve it into a surrender; which work, he knew, was already more than half accomplished to his hands. The siege was protracted until the inhabitants were driven to the most horrible shifts to prolong their miserable existence. We are told that an ass's head was sold for eighty silver shekels, equal to thirty dollars of our money, and the fourth part of a cab* of vetches for five shekels, equal to three dollars of our money. In this case the extremity of the famine is shown not merely by the cost of the articles, but by the fact that the flesh of an ass, for which such an enormous price was now paid, was forbidden by the law,† and could not be touched by a Hebrew under ordinary circumstances.

One day as the king was passing along the ramparts, two women importunately demanded justice at his hands. They had between them slain, boiled, and eaten the son of one of them, with the understanding that the son of the other was next to be sacrificed to satisfy their wants. But the mother of the living son relented, and refused to yield him to so horrible a fate. This was the injustice of which the mother of the slaughtered child complained, and for which she clamored for redress. When the king heard this shocking case, he rent his clothes, which gave the people present occasion to observe that his inner dress was the sackcloth of a mourner. He might have remembered that such calamities had been threatened, ages back, by Moses, as the suitable punishment of such iniquities as those into which Israel had actually fallen (Deut. xxviii. 52-57). His indignation, however, turned against Elisha (who had, perhaps, encouraged him to hold out by promises of deliverance), and he swore that he should lose his head that day, and instantly despatched an officer to execute an intention so worthy of the son of Jezebel. But the messenger was no sooner gone than he relented, and went hastily after him, to revoke the order, and to excuse himself to Elisha. This moment of right feeling was the moment in which deliverance was announced. "Thus saith Jehovah," said the prophet, when the king stood in his presence, "to-morrow about this time shall a seah‡ of fine flour be sold for a shekel, and two seahs of barley for a shekel, in the gate of Samaria." This appeared so utterly

* The fourth part of a cab was less than a pint of our measure.
† No animal food was allowed but that of animals which ruminate and divide the hoof. The ass does neither ; and was therefore for food more unclean than even the hog, which does divide the hoof although it does not ruminate.
‡ Somewhat more than a peck.

incredible to the courtier "on whose arm the king leaned," that he said, "Behold, were Jehovah to open windows in heaven, then this thing might be." To which the prophet severely retorted, "Behold, *thou* shalt see it with thine eyes, but shalt not eat thereof."

In fact, during the following night, Jehovah caused the Syrians to hear a great noise of chariots and horses, which led them to conclude that Jehoram had contrived to obtain assistance from the king of Egypt and other neighboring princes; and this infused into them such a panic terror, that they precipitately raised the siege; and, in the belief that they were pursued by a puissant army come to the relief of Israel, they abandoned the camp with all their baggage and provisions. Toward the morning, some lepers, who, as such, abode without the town, made up their minds to go to the camp of the Syrians seeking food; for they concluded that it was better to risk death by the Syrian sword than to die of famine where they were.' On reaching the camp they found it deserted; and after satisfying their present wants, and appropriating to their own use some good things from the spoil, they proceeded to bear their glad tidings to the city. The king was slow to believe them, and suspected the whole to be a stratagem of the Syrians. Men were therefore mounted on two of the five only horses now remaining, and sent to make observations. The report with which they returned was quite conformable to that of the lepers. The people then left the city, and hastened to pillage the camp of the Syrians, in which provisions were found in such abundance that a market was established at the gate of Samaria,* where, as the prophet had predicted, a seah of wheat was sold for a shekel, and two seahs of barley for the same. The officer who refused to believe this prediction was placed by the king to preserve order at the gate; but so great was the press of the famishing multitude to obtain corn, that he was thrown down and trodden to death. Thus was accomplished the other prediction, that he should see the truth of the first prophecy without enjoying its benefits.

We know not precisely how long after this the seven years of famine terminated. Of these years the hospitable Shunemite had been warned by Elisha, and had withdrawn to a neighboring country; on which the state assumed the possession of her lands. After the famine was over, she returned, and came before the king to petition for the restoration of the property. At that time the servant of Elisha was engaged in giving the king an account of the various miracles wrought by his master, and when the woman appeared, he was relating how her son had been restored to life. The relater then said, "My lord, this is the woman, and this is her son whom Elisha restored to life." The king was struck by this coincidence, and proceeded to question her on the subject, and ended with directing that not only should the lands be restored to her, but the value of their produce during the years of her absence. This was a very becoming act, and, like several other recorded acts of Jehoram, worthy of commendation; but it is not by particular acts, however laudable, that the sins of a criminal life can be covered: and the fulfilment of the doom pronounced upon the house of Ahab was now near at hand.

Jehoram was desirous of pursuing his recent advantage over the Syrians to the extent of taking from them the city of Ramoth in Gilead, which still remained in their possession. Fortified by an alliance with his nephew Ahaziah, king of Judah, he therefore declared war against Hazael, whom a revolution, predicted by Elisha, had placed upon the throne of Damascene-Syria, in the room of Ben-hadad. Ramoth was invested by the two kings; and before that place, where Ahab had received his death-wound, Jehoram was also wounded by an arrow—not mortally, but so seriously that he withdrew to Jezreel to be healed, leaving the conduct of the siege to Jehu, the son of Nimshi. The king of Judah also returned to Jerusalem, but afterward proceeded to Jezreel to visit his wounded relative.

At this juncture Elisha sent one of the sons of the prophet to execute the commission, long since intrusted to Elijah, of anointing Jehu as king of Israel. He arrived at the time when the chief officers of the army besieging Ramoth were together. He called out Jehu, and anointed him in an inner chamber, delivering at the same time the announcement of his call to the throne of Israel, and to be Jehovah's avenger upon the house of Ahab. No sooner had he done this than he opened

---

* It is still not unusual in the East for the wholesale market for country produce and cattle to be held (for a short time in the early morning) at the gates of towns. Manufactured goods are sold and fruits retailed in the bazars within the towns.

the door and fled. Jehu returned to his companions, as if nothing had happened. But they had noticed the prophetic garb of the person who had called him out, and it being the fashion of those days to speak contemptuously of the prophetic calling, they asked, "On what business came this mad fellow to thee?" Jehu affected some reluctance to tell them; but this made them the more urgent; and when he made the fact known to them, it was so agreeable to their own wishes, that they instantly tendered him their homage, and proclaimed him king by sound of trumpet, and with cries of "Jehu is king!" At his desire, measures were taken to prevent this intelligence from spreading for the present; in consequence of which, King Jehoram and King Ahaziah remained at Jezreel, quite unsuspicious of what had occurred. But one day the watchman announced the distant approach of a large party; and the king of Israel sent, successively, two messengers to ascertain whether it came with peaceable designs or not. But as they did not return, and the watchman having in the meantime ascertained, from his manner of driving his chariot, that the principal person was Jehu, the two kings went forth themselves to meet him. They met in the fatal field of Naboth. "Is it peace, Jehu?" the king inquired of the general; who answered, "What peace as long as the idolatries of thy mother Jezebel and her sorceries are so many?" On hearing which, Jehoram cried to the king of Judah, "There is treachery, O Ahaziah!" and turned his chariot to escape. But Jehu drew his bow with all his force, and the arrow which he discharged smote the king between the shoulders, and went through his heart. Jehu directed the body to be taken from the chariot and left on that ground, reminding Bidkar, his captain, to whom he gave this order, that they were together in attendance upon Ahab in that very place, when the prophet Elijah appeared and denounced that doom upon his house, and the bloody requital in that spot, which was now being accomplished.

Ahaziah also attempted to escape; but Jehu directed some of his followers to pursue and smite him in his chariot. They did so, and wounded him: but he continued his flight till he reached Megiddo, where he died of his wounds. His body was removed to Jerusalem for sepulture.[*]

Jehu entered Jezreel. The news of what had happened preceded him: and Jezebel tired her head and painted her eyes, and looked out of a window; and this she did, we should imagine, not with any view of trying the power of her allurements upon Jehu—for she was by this time an aged woman—but for state, and to manifest to the last the pride and royalty of her spirit. As Jehu drew nigh, she called to him, "Had Zimri peace, who slew his master?" But this was the day of vengeance and of punishment, and not of relentings; and Jehu looked up and cried, "Who is on my side, who?" On which two or three eunuchs of the harem looked out to him. "Throw her down!" was the unflinching command of Jehu. So they threw her down, and some of her blood was sprinkled upon the wall, and upon the horses that trod upon her. After this, Jehu went into the palace, and ate and drank; and he then said, "Go, look after this accursed woman, and bury her; for she was a king's daughter." But it was then found that all the body, except the scull, the feet, and the palms of her hands, had been devoured by such ravenous dogs as those by which eastern cities are still infested. "This," said Jehu, "is the word of Jehovah, which he spake by the mouth of Elijah the Tishbite, saying, In the district of Jezreel shall dogs eat the flesh of Jezebel; and the carcass of Jezebel shall be as dung upon the face of the field in the district of Jezreel; so that they shall not say, This is Jezebel."

Ahab had left not fewer than seventy sons, and these were all in Samaria,[†] which was not only the metropolis but one of the strongest places in the kingdom; and Jehu, reflecting, probably, on what happened after the death of Zimri,—when two kings reigned, one like himself, a military leader upheld by the arm, whom a

---

[*] This is the account given in the Book of Kings (2 Kings ix. 27-29); but another account (2 Chron. xxii. 9) says he hid himself in Samaria, where he was discovered and put to death. From this difference it may seem that some circumstances are omitted, by which the two accounts might be reconciled. But as we do not know with certainty how to reconcile them, we have given one of the accounts only in the text, and have preferred that in Kings, solely because it is that which Josephus has followed.

[†] From the expression that they were "with the great men of the city, who brought them up," we infer that, as is still usual in some eastern countries, the king relieved himself from the charge of their maintenance, by consigning one young prince to this great person, and another to another, to be maintained and educated as became their station. This charge is to be received as an honor and distinction, and is sometimes of ultimate benefit; but on account of the great expense and inconvenience, it is often received with dissatisfaction, and many would decline it if they dared.

portion of the nation refused to acknowledge, and adhered to another,—apprehended that something similar might again occur. He therefore wrote to the chief
persons of Samaria, and to those who had the charge of Ahab's children, to sound
their intentions. He told them that they were in a well-fortified city, with troops,
chariots, and arms; and that, being thus circumstanced, they had better set up one
of Ahab's sons for king, and fight for him, letting the crown be the prize of the
conqueror. And this, really, was the only course which men faithful and attached to
the dynasty of Omri could have taken. This the chief persons and guardians of the
princes in Samaria were not,—or not to the extent of risking the consequences of civil
war, and of opposition to Jehu. In fact, they were intimidated by his promptitude
in action, and at the manner in which the two kings and Jezebel had been disposed
of; and there was something calculated to damp their spirits (if they had any) in a
message which showed that Jehu was prepared for the most resolute course they
could take. They replied, "We are thy servants, and will do all that thou shalt bid
us; we will not make any man king: do thou what is good in thine eyes." Jehu's
reply was prompt and horribly decisive: "If ye be for me, and will hearken to my
voice, take off the heads of your master's sons, and come to me to Jezreel by this
time to-morrow." When this letter arrived, the seventy princes were instantly
decapitated, and their heads sent in baskets to Jezreel. When Jehu heard of their
arrival, he, according to a barbarous eastern custom not yet extinct, directed them to
be piled up in two heaps at the entrance of the city-gate until the morning. In the
morning he went out to the assembled people, and with the evident design of pointing out the extent to which the house of Ahab wanted any hearty adherents, even
among those who might be supposed most attached to its interests, he said, "Ye are
righteous. Behold, I conspired against my master, and slew him: but who hath
slain all these? Now know, that nothing of the word of Jehovah, which he spoke
concerning the house of Ahab, shall fall to the ground; for Jehovah will do what
he spoke by his servant Elijah."

Jehu delayed not to go to Samaria, and in his way encountered some of the brothers
of Ahaziah, the king of Judah, who, ignorant of the late occurrences, were on their
way to visit the sons of Ahab. Regarding their connexion by blood and friendship
with the house of Ahab, Jehu considered them included in his commission to exterminate that house root and branch. He therefore commanded them to be arrested
and slain. Their number was forty-two.

In his further progress, Jehu met with Jonadab, the son of Rechab, a pastoral
religionist held in high esteem by the people, and whose influence with them was
very great. Jehu, with his usual tact, at once felt the advantage which the countenance of this person might be to his cause. He therefore accosted him: "Is thy
heart as right with my heart, as my heart is with thine?" Jonadab answered, "It
is."—"If it be," said Jehu, "give to me thy hand." And he gave him his hand,
and Jehu took him up into his chariot, saying, "Come and see my zeal for Jehovah!"
They thus entered Samaria together, where Jehu completed the destruction of the
house of Ahab by cutting off all its remaining members.

In Samaria Ahab had erected a celebrated temple to the idol Baal. On entering
the town Jehu declared an intention to aggrandize the worship of that god, and render to him higher honors than he had yet received in Israel. He was therefore
determined to celebrate a great feast in honor of Baal, to which he convoked all the
priests, prophets, and votaries of that idol. The concourse was so great that the
temple was filled from one end to another; and while they were in the midst of their
idolatrous worship, Jehu sent in a body of armed men who put them all to the sword.
The idols, and the implements and ornaments of idol worship, were then overthrown, broken, or reduced to ashes; and the temple itself was demolished and
turned into a common jakes. But the worship of Baal was far from being confined
to Samaria, and Jehu sought for it in all quarters of the land, and rooted it out
wherever it was found. His conduct in this matter was so well pleasing to God, that
the throne of Israel was, by a special promise, assured to his posterity unto the
fourth generation.

Defile in Idumea, (Mount Seir,) in the road from Palestine to Egypt.

CHAPTER XX.

JUDAH, from b. c. 929 to b. c. 725.

Jehoshaphat, the son of Asa, began to reign over Judah in the year 929 B.C., being the second year of Ahab in Israel. The alliance which he formed with Ahab has brought him forward, in the preceding chapter, sufficiently to intimate to the reader the excellent character which he bore. He indeed takes rank among the most faithful, and *therefore* most illustrious and wise of the Hebrew kings. Direct idolatry had been put down by his father, and the first acts of his own reign were to root out the remoter incentives thereto and instruments thereof. He destroyed the high places and the groves which his father had spared. Other kings before him had been satisfied with external operations; but to his enlightened mind it appeared that effects more deep and permanent might be secured by acting upon the inner sense of the people, by instructing them fully in the principles and distinguishing privileges of their theocratical system, and by rendering those principles operative, as the standards of public and judicial action, throughout the land. The land had already been purged, as by fire, from the noxious weeds by which it had been overgrown; and now the king made it his business to occupy the cleared soil with corn—the staff of life—and with fruits " pleasant to the eye, and good for food."

To these ends the king sent out a number of " princes," whose rank and influence secured attention and respect to the priests and Levites who were with them to instruct the people. They had with them copies of the law : and, in their several bands, visited all the towns of the country—thus bearing instruction to the very doors of a people who had become too indolent or too indifferent themselves to seek for it. So earnest was the king in this object, that he went himself throughout the land to see that his orders were duly executed.

The attention of this able king was also directed to the reform of abuses in other departments of the state, and to the cultivation of the financial and military resources of his kingdom. The people, rendered happy by his cares, grew prosperous, and increased in numbers; in the same degree the real power of the government was strengthened, and was such as inspired the people with confidence, and their enemies with fear. Edom continued firm in its obedience, Philistia regularly remitted its presents and tribute-silver, and several of the Arabian tribes sought his favor, or acknowledged his power, by large yearly tributes of sheep and goats from their flocks. The men enrolled as fit to bear arms, and liable to be called into action, was not less than 1,160,000, which is not far short of the number in the united kingdom in the time of David. Of these a certain proportion were kept in service. The best of the troops were stationed at Jerusalem, and the remainder distributed into the fortress and walled towns; and a strong force was concentrated on the northern frontier, especially in those lands of Ephraim which Asa had taken from Baasha. New fortresses were constructed in different parts of the country, and were well garrisoned and supplied with all the munitions of war.

The capital error of this monarch, the alliance he contracted with Ahab in the thirteenth year of his reign, has already been noticed in the preceding chapter, as well as the part he took in the battle of Ramoth Gilead, in which Ahab was slain, but his own life was preserved, notwithstanding the very imminent danger into which he had fallen. On his return to Jerusalem after this escape, the Divine dissatisfaction at his conduct was announced to him by the prophet Jehu.

After this he engaged himself in his former peaceful and honorable undertakings; and gave particular attention to the administration of justice in his dominions. He established a supreme tribunal (of appeal probably) at Jerusalem, and placed judges in all the principal cities of the country. This great improvement relieved the king from the fatigue and great attention which the exercise of the judicial functions of royalty had exacted from the earlier kings, while it secured to the suiters more prompt attention than they could by any other means receive. The king was very sensible of the importance of this step; and, in his anxiety that it should work well, gave an admirable charge to the judges; the force of which can only be well appreciated by those who perceive that the counteracting evils which he feared were precisely those by which the administration of justice in the East is at this day corrupted and disgraced. "Take heed what ye do: for ye judge not for man, but for Jehovah, who is with you in the judgment. Wherefore now, let the fear of Jehovah be upon you; take heed and act uprightly; for with Jehovah our God there is no injustice, no respect of persons, no taking of bribes." This was addressed to the judges appointed to the cities. In the address to the judges of the supreme tribunal at Jerusalem, it is not supposed, by any implication, that they could be partial or corrupt; and they are only reminded of the duty of judging according to the Divine law, the causes that came before them. This tribunal was composed of the most distinguished men among the priests, the Levites, and the family chiefs. In matters pertaining to religion, this tribunal was presided over by the high-priest Amariah, but in civil matters, or those in which the crown was interested, by Zebadiah, "the ruler," or hereditary chief, of the tribe of Judah—an interesting indication that the forms of the patriarchal were not, even yet, entirely lost in those of the regal government.

About the same time the king made another tour through his dominions, from Beersheba in the south, to Mount Ephraim in the north, seeking to bring back the people more entirely "to Jehovah the God of their fathers." In the northern districts which had been recovered or taken from Israel, the high places of the Ephraimites were not taken away, because they had not as yet "prepared their hearts unto the God of their fathers," as had the Judahites, whose high places had been taken away at the beginning of this reign.

The unfortunate expedition with Ahab against Ramoth Gilead being unsuccessful, tended much to lower Jehoshaphat in the estimation of the neighboring nations; and thus the alliance with the king of Israel brought its own punishment. The Ammonites and Moabites, who had been brought into a state of subjection by David, now began to conceive hopes of deliverance from the yoke under which they lay. It was their policy, however, not in the first instance to revolt from the kingdom to which they were immediately subject—that of Israel, but first to try their strength against the lesser kingdom of Judah. They therefore invaded that country from the south, by the way of Edom, supported by some Arabian hordes, which they had engaged in their cause, and who indeed are seldom loath to engage in any cause by which good prospects of spoil are offered. The expedition assumed the character of an Arabian invasion, and, as such, was so expeditious that the invaders had rounded the southern extremity of the Dead sea, and came to a halt in the famous valley of Engedi, before Jehoshaphat had the least intimation of their design. Taken thus by surprise, he was much alarmed in the first instance; but by throwing himself unreservedly upon the protection and help of the Divine King, he ensured the safety of his kingdom, and took the most becoming step which it was possible that a king of the chosen nation could take. He proclaimed a general fast throughout Judah, and the people gathered together from all quarters to Jerusalem, and stood there in and around the temple, to cry to God for help. And he heard them: for the spirit of prophecy fell upon one of the Levites, named Jahaziel, and in the name of Jehovah he directed that they should march to meet the enemy, whose station he indicated, not to fight, but to witness their extirpation and to seize the spoil. As they went forth early in the morning toward the wilderness of Tekoah, Jehoshaphat exerted himself to keep up the confidence of the people in the sufficiency of the Divine protection; and as they proceeded, he directed that the Levitical singers should march in front, and "in the beauty of holiness" (or in the same habits, and after the same manner as in the temple-service), should sing the praises of God, saying, "Praise Jehovah! for he is good; for his mercy endureth for ever." Surely never, from the beginning of the world, was there such a march as this against an army of hostile invaders. The event was such as the prophet had foreshown. It seems that the children of Lot had quarrelled and fought with their Arabian allies; and when they had succeeded in destroying them, they turned their arms against each other, and fought with unextinguishable fury until none remained alive on the battle-field. So that when the Hebrews arrived at the place which the prophet had indicated, many a beating heart among them was relieved, and all were inconceivably astonished, to see the wilderness covered with the bodies of the slain—not one had escaped. The Judahites were three days in collecting an immense spoil of precious metals and stones, and valuable arms and raiment; and in the end it was found that more was collected than could be taken away. On the fourth day they returned home to Jerusalem, before entering which they held a solemn thanksgiving in the valley of Shaveh, or the King's dale, hence called the valley of Berachah (*blessing*), and also the valley of Jehoshaphat. After this they entered the city in triumphal procession, with music and with singing. The neighboring nations rightly ascribed this signal deliverance to the God of the Hebrews; and were for some time inspired with a salutary fear of molesting a people so highly favored.

The next undertaking of Jehoshaphat was an attempt to revive the ancient traffic of Solomon, by the Red sea, to the region of gold. For this purpose he built a navy at his port of Ezion-geber, at the head of the Elanitic gulf. But, in an evil day, he consented to allow Ahaziah, the king of Israel, to take part in the enterprise, in consequence of which, as a prophet forewarned him, his ships were wrecked soon after they left the port. Another expedition was proposed by the king of Israel: but Jehoshaphat declined, and appears to have relinquished all further designs of this nature. Josephus informs us that the ships which had been built were too large and unwieldy; and we may infer that Jehoshaphat discovered that he could not accomplish an enterprise of this nature in the want of such skilful shipwrights and able mariners as those with which the Phœnicians had constructed and manned the ships of Solomon.

One of the last public acts of Jehoshaphat's reign was that of taking part with Jehoram, king of Israel, in an expedition against the Moabites, who had revolted after the death of Ahab. Jehoshaphat was probably the more induced to lend his assistance by the consideration of the recent invasion of his own dominions by the same people. The circumstances and result of this expedition have been related in the preceding chapter. The success which was granted to it is entirely ascribed to the Divine favor toward the king of Judah.

Soon after this Jehoshaphat " slept with his fathers," after he had lived sixty years, and reigned twenty-five.

His eldest son, JEHORAM, ascended the throne of Judah in the year 904 B. C., in the thirty-second year of his own age, and in the third year of the reign of his namesake and relative, Jehoram, the son of Ahab, in Israel. This, it will be remembered, was the prince who was married to Athaliah, the daughter of Ahab and Jezebel. The evil effects of this connexion began now very manifestly to appear, and preponderated over the good example which the reign of Jehoshaphat had offered. In fact, Athaliah proved her descent by rivalling her mother, Jezebel, in idolatry, in pride, and in the part she took in public affairs after the death of Jehoshaphat. And, to complete the resemblance, she appears to have rendered her husband, as the mere instrument of her will and purposes, quite as effectual as Jezebel rendered Ahab.

It was undoubtedly through her influence that the first act of Jehoram's reign was to destroy his six brothers, whom Jehoshaphat had amply provided for, and stationed (as governors, probably) in as many fenced cities of Judah. With them perished several of the first persons in the state, who had enjoyed the confidence of the late king, and had been active in promoting his laudable designs. This evidence of her power redoubled the audacity of the proud queen; and soon after, idolatry, which had been banished from Judah during the two preceding reigns, was restored, by public authority, to honor; and the sedulous endeavors made in the two former reigns to reform the religion and morals of the people gave place to the efforts of new men to corrupt and ruin all. High places, similar to those in Israel, again appeared upon the hills of Judah; and the people were seduced and urged into idolatry and its concomitant abominations.

For these things heavy calamities were denounced against Jehoram, early in his reign, by the prophet Elisha* in a letter: and thus did that great prophet take cognizance of the affairs of Judah also. The evils that he threatened followed soon.

The king of Edom, who assisted the kings of Judah and Israel in the war against Moab, had, according to Josephus, been slain by his revolted subjects, and the new sovereign desired to signalize his accession, and to propitiate his subjects, by freeing them from the tribute to which his father had submitted. This essay was not at first successful; but although once defeated by Jehoram, who still had his father's army under his command, the Edomites succeeded in throwing the yoke of Judah from off

---

* The Masorete text here reads *Elijah* (2 Chron. xxi. 12) instead of *Elisha*: for Elijah had been translated in the time of Jehoshaphat. 2 Kings iii. 11.

their necks, according to the prophecy of Isaac to the founder of that nation.* Emboldened by this, the Philistines also rebelled, and, assisted by the Arabs who bordered on the Cushites, they invaded Judah, plundered and ravaged the whole country, and even Jerusalem and the royal palace. They led away into slavery all the women of the king's harem, except Athaliah, who was spared in anger, and made captive all the royal princes, except Ahaziah, otherwise called Jehoahaz, the youngest of them all. To consummate all, the king himself was smitten with an incurable disease in the bowels, from which he suffered for two years the most horrible torments, and at last, after a reign of eight years, died without being regretted. The voice of the people denied to his remains the honors of a royal burial, and a place in the sepulchre of the kings.

Ahaziah, his youngest son, was twenty-two years old when he succeeded his father. He reigned only one year; for following the evil counsels of his mother and the house of Ahab, he foolishly joined Jehoram of Israel in the war against Hazael king of Syria, the result of which, with his death, inflicted by Jehu, has been recorded in the preceding chapter.

Not Jehu in Israel thirsted more after the blood of Ahab's house, than did Athaliah, in Judah, for the blood of her own children. She had long been the virtual possessor of the supreme power in Judah; but now she disdained an authority so precarious and indirect, and would reign alone. As even the most wicked persons seldom shed blood from absolute wantonness of cruelty, it may be considered that her spirit may have been rendered unusually savage at this time by the sanguinary proceedings of Jehu in Israel against the house to which she herself belonged, and in which she had lost, at one fell swoop, a mother, a brother, and a son, with many other of her near relatives. It must also have appeared to her that the sort of authority she had hitherto exercised, first as queen-consort and then as queen-mother, was now in very great danger; as it might be expected that whichever of her grandsons succeeded to the throne, he would prefer the counsels and guidance of his mother to her own. Here then were two powerful motives,—dread of losing her power, and jealousy of being superseded by another woman,—bringing her to the atrocious resolution of destroying all the children of her own son Ahaziah. She little considered that by this she was fulfilling a part of the mission against the house of Ahab which Jehu himself could not execute; for through herself the taint of Ahab's blood had been given to the house of David. Her fell purpose was promptly executed. All her grandsons were slain in one day, with the exception of Joash, an infant, who was stolen away by his aunt Jehoshebad, the wife of the high-priest Jehoiada and daughter of the late king Ahaziah, and hidden with his nurse in one of the chambers of the temple. Thus, in the providence of God, the royal line of the house of David was preserved from utter extinction. No retreat could have been more secure than that which was chosen for the infant prince; for not only were the apartments of the temple under the sole direction of the priests, and to the innermost of which no others had access; but Athaliah had put herself out of the way of obtaining information of the fact by her entire neglect of the temple and the institutions connected with it. And although she did not, indeed could not, actually put down the temple-worship, her preference and favor was given to the temple of Baal, and his high-priest, Mattan, was upheld by her as of equal rank and importance with the high-priest of Jehovah.

Now although the Judahites were but too prone to fall into idolatry, the good effects of the reforms of Asa and Jehoshaphat, and of the principles which the latter had been so careful to inculcate, did not so soon evaporate as to dispose the people generally to approve or concur in the rapid and decisive measures which Athaliah had taken in establishing the worship of Baal; and when to this was added their natural abhorrence of the barbarous massacre which rooted her throne in blood, and their dislike, in common with all orientals, at the public rule of a woman, we have a sufficient explanation of the fact that the public feeling was not with queen Athaliah, and that, indeed, her rule was regarded with such disgust as disposed the people to hail with joy the advent of their hidden king.

Joash remained six years concealed in the secret chambers of the temple, his existence even, much more his presence there, being unknown and unsuspected by Athaliah and others, as it was supposed he had perished in the slaughter of his father's

* To Esau Isaac said,—"Thou shalt serve thy brother; and it shall come to pass when thou shalt have the dominion, that thou shalt break his yoke from off thy neck." Gen. xxvii. 40.

sons. In the seventh year the high-priest Jehoiada judged that the fit time had arrived for the disclosure. He therefore made known the secret to some of the chiefs and military commanders on whom he could depend, and received from them the promise to concur in the bold act of proclaiming and crowning the rightful king. Joash was now only seven years of age; but good reason was seen to prefer the regency of such a man as Jehoiada to the reign of such a woman as Athaliah. The persons whom Jehoiada had admitted to his confidence went about the country gaining over the paternal chiefs, and inducing them, as well as the Levites not on duty, to repair to Jerusalem. When all the adherents thus acquired had come to the metropolis, the high-priest concerted with them the plan of operations. According to this it was determined that the partisans of the young prince should be divided into three bodies, one of which was to guard the prince in the temple, the second to keep all the avenues, and the third was placed at the gate leading to the royal palace. The people were to be admitted as usual to the outer courts. Then the armories of the temple were opened, and the spears, bucklers, and shields of King David were distributed to these parties, as well as to the Levites, who were to form an impenetrable barrier around the king during the ceremony. When all was disposed in this order, the high-priest appeared, leading by the hand the last scion of the royal house of David. He placed him by the pillar where the kings were usually stationed, and having anointed him with the sacred oil, he placed the crown upon his head, arrayed him in royal robes, and gave into his hands the book of the law, on which the usual oaths were administered to him. He was then seated on a throne which had been provided, in doing which he was hailed and recognised by the acclamations of "Long live the king."

By this time Athaliah had observed some indications of an extraordinary movement in the temple; and when these rejoicing clamors broke upon her ear, she hastened thither, and penetrated even to the court of the priests, where the sight met her view of the enthroned boy, crowned, and royally arrayed, while the hereditary chiefs, the military commanders and the Levites, stood at their several stations as in attendance on their king,—the latter, as was their wont in the temple, blowing their trumpets, and playing on their various instruments of music. No sooner did Athaliah behold this, than she rent her clothes, crying, "Treason! treason!" Jehoiada fearing that the guards would kill her on the spot, and thus pollute the holy place with human blood, which was most abhorrent to God, directed them to take her outside the temple courts, and there she was put to death. The king was then conducted with great pomp to the palace, escorted by all his guard, and there took possession of the throne of his fathers.

Jehoiada, without any formal appointment, appears to have been recognised, with one consent, as the guardian of the king and regent of the kingdom. He availed himself of the favorable dispositions which now existed, to induce the people to renew their ancient covenant with Jehovah. This precaution had become necessary from the long continuance of an idolatrous government. Actuated by the impulse thus received and the enthusiasm thus excited, and led by the priests and Levites of Jehovah, the people proceeded once more to extirpate the idolatries of Baal. They hastened to his temple, where they slew the high-priest Mattan before the altars, and then pulled the whole fabric to the ground. And not only at Jerusalem, but everywhere throughout the land, the temples, altars and monuments of Baal were utterly destroyed.

Jehoiada, being now at the head of affairs, both religious and civil, applied himself with great diligence in bringing into an orderly and efficient condition the administrations of both the court and temple. Those who had signalized their zeal in the restoration of the king, or were otherwise distinguished for their abilities, were appointed to high posts in the state, while the services of the temple were brought back to the models of David and Solomon. The glory of restoring the fabric of the temple he reserved for the king, who accordingly, in the twenty-third year of his reign, thoroughly repaired that famous structure, after it had been built nearly one hundred and sixty years; and made numerous vessels of gold and silver for the sacred services, and presented burnt-offerings continually during the lifetime of Jehoiada, who died at the great age of one hundred and thirty-seven years. He was honored with a sepulchre among the kings of the family of David, "because he had done good in Israel."

We may estimate the merits of Jehoiada's administration from the evil consequences that followed his death. It then appeared that the good qualities which the king had seemed to manifest were the effects rather of the right counsels under which he had acted, than of any solid principles of good. As we have before seen stronger and older men than Joash yielding to the witcheries of idolatry, which seem so strange to us, we are the less surprised at the fall of this king. It now appeared what deep root idolatry had taken in the land during the years of its predominance under Jehoram, Ahaziah, and Athaliah: and the men of station who had imbibed or had been brought up in its principles, now reared themselves on high, as soon as the repressive power of God's high-priest was withdrawn. They repaired to the royal court, and by their attentions and flatteries so won upon the king that he was at length induced to give first his tolerance, and then his sanction, to the rank idolatries by which the two kingdoms had often been brought very low. Against this, Zechariah, the son of the late high-priest and a near relation to the king, raised his voice, and predicted the national calamities which would too surely follow; on which the people rose upon him, and, having received a consenting intimation from the king, stoned him to death in the very court of the temple. Thus did Joash repay the deep obligations, for his life and throne, which he owed to the house of Jehoiada. "The Lord look upon it and require it!"* was the prayer of the dying martyr. And HE did require it. That very year, Hazael of Syria, who was then in possession of Gilead, advanced against Jerusalem, and, although his force was but small, defeated a large army which opposed him, and entered the city, from which he returned with abundant plunder to his own country. The chiefs who had seduced Joash were slain in the battle; and the king himself, who had been grievously wounded, was soon after murdered by his own servants, and the public voice refused the honors of a royal burial to his remains. He reigned forty years.

Joash was succeeded on the throne by his son AMAZIAH, then twenty-five years of age. The first act of his reign was to punish the murderers of his father: but it is mentioned that he respected the law of Moses by not including their children in their doom; and this seems to show that a contrary practice had previously prevailed.

About the twelfth year of his reign, Amaziah took measures for reducing to their former subjection the Edomites, who had revolted in the time of Jehoram. Not satisfied with the strength he could raise in his own kingdom, the king of Judah hired a hundred thousand auxiliaries out of Israel for a hundred talents of silver. But these were tainted with idolatry: on which account a prophet was commissioned to exhort Amaziah to forego their assistance, and dismiss them. By a memorable act of faith, the king at once yielded to this hard demand, and sent home the Israelites, for whose services he had already paid. He then gained a decisive victory over the Edomites in the Salt valley, at the southern extremity of the Dead sea. Ten thousand of the Edomites fell; and ten thousand more were cast down from the cliffs of their native mountains, and dashed in pieces.†

This victory was the ruin of Amaziah, whose conduct had been hitherto praiseworthy. The idols of Edom, which he brought home among the spoil, proved a snare to him; and, in the end, he fell to the worship of "the gods who could not deliver their own people:" for which he was, without effect, upbraided by a prophet, and threatened with destructions from God.

The Israelites whom the king of Judah had dismissed from his army were filled with resentment at the indignity cast upon them, and probably disappointed in their hope of a share in the spoils of Edom. To testify their resentment, and to obtain compensation, they smote and plundered several of the towns of Judah, on their homeward march, and destroyed many of the inhabitants. It was probably on this account that Amaziah, elated by his victory over the Edomites, determined to make war upon Israel. It is singular that, instead of commencing, as usual, by some aggressive movement or overt act of warfare, Amaziah sent a formal challenge to the king of Israel, inviting a pitched battle, in the phrase, "Come, and let us look one another in the face." The truly oriental answer of Joash seemed designed to dissuade him from this undertaking, but was conceived in terms not well calculated

* May not one of the essential differences of the Jewish and Christian dispensations be illustrated by the last words of two men respectively eminent in each, and dying under very similar circumstances? "Lord, lay not this sin to their charge!" was the last cry of the dying Stephen.

† This was probably at or in the neighborhood of Petra, of Mount Seir, of which see our engraving, p. 75.

to accomplish the object: "A thistle that was in Lebanon, sent to the cedar of Lebanon, saying, 'Give thy daughter to my son to wife:' and a wild beast of Lebanon passed by and trod down the thistle. Thou sayest, 'Lo! I have smitten the Edomites,' and thy heart is lifted up. Abide now at home: why shouldst thou meddle to thy hurt, so that thou shouldst fall, and Judah with thee?"

But Amaziah was not to be thus deterred. The two kings met in battle. Amaziah was defeated and taken prisoner, and his army routed at Beth-shemesh. Joash then pursued his triumphant march to Jerusalem, which he plundered, and spared not to lay his hands upon the sacred things of the temple. He also broke down four hundred cubits of the city wall. He however restored Amaziah to his throne, but took hostages with him on his return to Samaria.

The life of Amaziah ended in a conspiracy, which may have been induced by the disgrace which he had brought upon the nation. This conspiracy was discovered by him, and he hastened to the fortified town of Lachish. But he was pursued and slain by the conspirators, who brought back his body "upon horses to Jerusalem," where a place in the sepulchres of his fathers was not denied him. He reigned twenty-nine years.—B. C. 809.

Uzziah, otherwise called Azariah, was only five years old when his father was slain. The Judahites were in no haste to tender their allegiance to an infant. They waited until he was sixteen years of age, and he was then formally called to the throne.* Much favorable influence upon the character of Uzziah is attributed to the early instruction and subsequent influence of the wise and holy Zechariah.† His adhesion to the principles of the theocracy secured him prosperity and honor. He paid equal attention to the arts of peace and of war; and he throve in all the undertakings, whether of war or peace, to which he put his hand. In the arts which belong to both, he encouraged and promoted various improvements; and it may be pardoned in an oriental king, if, in his improvements and undertakings, his own interest and glory was the inciting motive. It is rare, and in fact difficult, for an oriental monarch (considering the institutions by which he is surrounded, and the ideas which press upon him) to contemplate the interests of his people otherwise than as a contingent effect of undertakings in which *his own* interests and glory are the *primary* motives. So Uzziah performed the good deed of building towers and digging wells in the desert; but the reason immediately follows: "*For* he had many cattle both in the valleys and in the plains." He also "loved husbandry," and planted vineyards; and, accordingly, "*he* had ground-tillers and vine-dressers‡ in the mountains and in Carmel." These were laudable things; for the people could not but be benefited by them, even though their benefit were less the immediate intention than the indirect effect.

The same may even less doubtfully be said of this king's military organizations and improvements. New fortifications were built and the old repaired. At Jerusalem not only were the injuries which the walls had sustained repaired, but the gates and angles were strengthened with towers; and on these were mounted engines invented by skilful men, and made under the king's encouragement and direction, for the purpose of discharging arrows and great stones. It may be doubtful whether these engines were invented by Hebrew engineers, or successfully copied by them from foreigners. We have certainly no opinion that the Hebrews had much genius for mechanical invention; but we are bound to say the antiquities of Egypt, in the numerous warlike scenes which they represent, do not, as far as we know, contain any examples of projectile engines: and it must be admitted that *in the art of war* many ingenious devices originate with nations not otherwise distinguished for their inventive faculties.

Uzziah provided ample stores of weapons and armor—spears, shields, helmets, breastplates, bows, and stone-slings—for the numerous body which he enrolled as ready to be called into action, and which consisted of not less than 307,500 men un-

* "This naturally accounts for the length of the interregnum. (2 Kings xv. 1, 2; 2 Chron. xxvi. 1.) Amaziah was slain fifteen years current after the death of Jehoash, king of Israel (2 Kings xiv. 17), or fourteen years complete from the accession of Jeroboam II., his son: and Azariah, or Uzziah, did not begin to reign till the twenty-fifth of Jeroboam (according to the foregoing correction, instead of the twenty-seventh year, 2 Kings xv. i.), which gives the length of the interregnum eleven years complete."—*Hales.*

† No one will, of course, confound this person with the prophet of the same name, who lived long after. It is not, in fact, *known* who he was. Some conjecture that he was the son of the Zechariah who was slain in the time of Joash. But we know of no other foundation for this but the name. The distance of *time* does not favor the conjecture which identifies him with the Zechariah of Isaiah viii. 2.

‡ See page 345.

Egyptian Vintage and Vine-dressers.

der 2,600 paternal chiefs. This form-ed a sort of militia, divided into bands, liable to be called into actual service by rotation, according to the number required.

With this force, and under these arrangements, Uzziah was enabled to establish and extend his power. He recovered possession of the port of Elath on the Red sea; he got posses-sion of the principal Philistine towns, Gath, Jabneh, and Ashdod. The Arab hordes on the borders were subdued; and the Ammonites were reduced to tribute.

Elated by all this prosperity, the king of Judah saw not why he should be precluded from a distinction which other monarchs enjoyed, and which his neighbor of Israel probably exer-cised —that of officiating on particular occasions at the incense-altar, as high-priest. He made the attempt. He went into the holy place, which none but the priests might lawfully enter, to offer incense on the altar there; but was followed by the high-priest, Aza-riah, and by eighty other priests, who opposed his design, and warned him of his trespass. The king, made wrathful by this opposition, seized the censer to offer incense; but in that moment he was smitten with leprosy, the marks of which appeared visibly on his forehead. On perceiving this, he priests thrust him forth as a pollution; nay, confounded and conscience-smitten, he hastened to leave the place.* From that day he was obliged to live apart as a leper, and his son Jotham administered the affairs of the government in his father's name. The year in which this happened is not well determined; but the whole duration of his reign was fifty-two years. This is the longest reign of any king of Judah, with the sole exception of Manasseh. Isaiah received his appointment to the prophetic office in the year that King Uzziah died (B.C. 757); and Amos, Hoshea, and probably Joel, began to prophecy in his reign.

The death of Uzziah left the kingdom under the same actual ruler, but exchanged his regency for the sovereignty. Jotham was twenty-five years old when he began to reign. He was a good and prosperous prince, and during the sixteen years of his separate reign continued the improvements and plans of his father. He built several fortresses, and confirmed the subjection of the Ammonites to his sceptre. It was in this reign† that the city of Rome was founded, with the destinies of which the Hebrews were in the end to be so intimately connected. Jotham died in the year B. C. 741.

Ahaz succeeded Jotham when he was twenty years of age. He proved the most corrupt monarch that the house of David had as yet produced. He respected neither Jehovah, the law, nor the prophets; he broke through all the salutary restraints which law and usage imposed upon the Hebrew kings, and regarded nothing but his own depraved inclinations. He introduced the Syrian idolatry into Jerusalem, erected altars to the Syrian gods, altered the temple in many respects, according to the Syrian model, and finally caused it to be entirely shut up. For these things, adversities and punishments came soon upon him.

Pekah king of Israel, and Rezin king of Syria, had formed an alliance against Judah in the last year of Jotham, which began to take effect as soon as Ahaz had evinced the unworthiness of his character. The object of this alliance appears to have been no less than to dethrone the house of David, and to make "the son of Tabeal" king in the room of Ahaz.‡

In this war Elath was taken from Judah by the king of Syria, who restored it to the Edomites. He also defeated Ahaz in battle and carried away large numbers of his subjects as captives to Damascus. Pekah on his part was equally successful. He slew in one day 120,000 men of Judah, and carried away captives not fewer than 200,000 women and children, together with much spoil, to Samaria. But on his arrival there he was met by the prophet Obed, and by some of the chiefs of Ephraim. The former awakened the king's apprehensions for the consequences of the Divine anger on account of the evil already committed against the house of Judah, and exhorted him not to add to this evil and to their danger, by reducing the women and children of that kindred state to bondage. The prophet was vigorously seconded by the chiefs, who positively declared to the troops, "Ye *shall not* bring in hither these captives to increase our guilt before Jehovah. Intend ye to add to our sin and to our trespass? for our trespass is great, and fierce is the wrath of Jehovah against Israel." On hearing this the warriors abandoned their captives, and left them in the hands of the chiefs, who, with the concurrence and help of the people, "took the captives, and from the spoil clothed all that were naked among them, and arrayed and shod them, and gave them to eat and drink, and anointed them, and carried all the feeble of them upon asses, and brought them to Jericho, the city of palm-trees, to their brethren." This beautiful incident comes over our sense as might some strain of soft and happy music amid the bray of trumpets and the the alarms of war. It also proves that, even in the worst of times, a righteous few were found, even in Israel, who honored the God of their fathers and stood in dread of his judgments.

The narrative in Isaiah records an unsuccessful attempt of the confederates against Jerusalem, the proper place of which in the history is not easily found, but which may appear to have been posterior to the occurrences which have been related. At the same time, the Edomites and Philistines invaded the south of Judah, and took possession of several cities of the low country, with their villages, and occupied

* To this prodigy Josephus adds an earthquake, which, he says, shook the earth with such violence that the roof of the temple was rent; and one half of a mountain on the west of Jerusalem fell, or rather slipped, into the valley below, covering the royal gardens.
† B.C. 748, or according to others, 750 or 752, all which dates fell in this reign.
‡ Isa. vii. 5, 6. Of this "son of Tabeal" nothing is known, although much has been conjectured. Some make it to be Pekah himself, but the interpretation on which it is founded is not very sound, although the thing itself might not be unlikely.

them. Thus harassed on every hand, the besotted king rejected a token of deliverance which Isaiah was commissioned to offer him from God, under the pretext that he "would not tempt Jehovah," but in reality, because he had already chosen another alternative. This was to induce Tiglath-Pileser, the king of Assyria, to make a diversion in his favor by invading the kingdoms of Syria and Israel.

Pul, the father of this king, was the first Assyrian monarch who took part in the affairs of the West. By invading Israel, he had made known the power of that monarchy to Syria and Palestine. Tiglath-Pileser, for his own objects, lent a willing ear to the suit of Ahaz, who professed himself his vassal, and sent him a subsidy of all the sacred and royal treasures. He marched an army westward, defeated and slew Rezin the king of Syria, took Damascus, and sent the inhabitants away into Assyria—thus putting an end to that monarchy of Damascene-Syria, which has so often come under our notice. At the same time he carried away the tribes beyond Jordan—Reuben, Gad, and half Manasseh—captives to Media, where they were planted in Halah, Habor, and on the River Gozan; and to them he added the other half of the tribe of Manasseh which was seated in Galilee.

Syria, with the countries of Gilead and Bashan, were thus annexed to the dominions of the Assyrian king, who remained some time at Damascus, settling his conquests. Ahaz had small cause to rejoice in this alteration, for although he was delivered from his immediate fears, the formidable Assyrian had now become his near neighbor, and was not likely to treat him with much consideration; and in fact the result was that "he distressed Ahaz, and strengthened him not." The king of Judah, however, found it prudent to visit Tiglath-Pileser at Damascus, to congratulate him on his victories, and to tender his homage. This visit only taught him new fashions of idolatry and sin; which on his return home he continued to practise apparently until his death, which took place in B.C. 725, after a disgraceful reign of sixteen years. He was allowed a grave in Jerusalem; but no place in the sepulchre of the kings was granted to him.

CHAPTER XXI.

ISRAEL, from b. c. 895, to b. c. 719.

Jehu, having executed his avenging mission upon the house of Ahab, and overthrown the idolatries of Baal, ascended the throne of Israel in the year B. C. 895.

There was a point beyond which Jehu was not prepared to go in his boasted zeal for Jehovah. He was ready to punish and discountenance all foreign worship; but it was no part of his policy to heal the schism between Judah and Israel, by abolishing the separate and highly irregular establishment, for the worship of Jehovah, before the symbolic golden calves, which Jeroboam had established, and which all his successors had maintained. The vital root therefore remained in the ground, although the branches had been lopped off. It also appeared, ere long, that the foreign idolatries of Ahab and Jezebel had acquired too much prevalence to be entirely extirpated by any coercive reformation. As soon as the heat of that reformation had cooled, such idolatries again gradually stole into use, although no longer with the sanction or favor of the government.

For these things the kingdom of Israel was in the latter days of Jehu allowed to be shorn of the provinces beyond Jordan. That fair country was ravaged, and its fortresses seized by Hazael, king of Syria, who, without any recorded opposition from the king of Israel, appears to have annexed it to his own dominions.

Jehu died in B. C. 867, after a reign of twenty-eight years.

He was succeeded by his son Jehoahaz, who reigned seventeen inglorious years. He followed the latter course of his father, and the people followed their own course. The same kind of punishment was therefore continued. The Syrians were still permitted to prevail over Israel, until, at length, Jehoahaz had only left, of all his forces, ten chariots, fifty horsemen, and ten thousand infantry; for "the king of Syria had destroyed the rest, and trampled on them like dust." By these calamities the king was at last awakened to a sense of his position and his danger: he made supplication to

Jehovah with tears; and therefore his latter days were favored with peace. He died in 850 B. C.

Joash, his son, began to reign in the thirty-seventh year of his namesake, Joash king of Judah. Josephus gives this king a good character, which the sacred historian does not confirm. From looking at the few incidents of his life which it has been deemed worth while to preserve, we may reconcile these statements by discovering that he was in his private character a well-disposed, although weak man; while as a king he made no efforts to discourage idolatry or heal the schism which the establishment of the golden calves had produced. In his days Elisha the prophet fell sick of that illness of which he died. When the king heard of his danger, he went to visit his dying bed, and wept over him, crying, "O my father! my father!—the chariot of Israel, and the horsemen thereof!" As the idolatrous generation was now becoming extinct, and the good dispositions of Joash himself were recognised, the dying prophet was enabled to assure him, by a significant symbol, of three victories over the Syrians. Accordingly, Joash was enabled to keep them in check, and in the end to gain the ascendency over them, so as to recover from Ben-hadad the possessions of which his own father had been deprived by the father of that Syrian king.

Joash reigned seventeen years.

In the year 234 B. C., Jeroboam II. succeeded his father, whom he appears to have much resembled in character and proceedings. He began badly; and Josephus says that he engaged in various absurd foreign undertakings which proved very injurious to the nation. He was probably improved by ripening years; for the prophet Jonah was commissioned to promise him the complete recovery of the former dominions of the state. A great victory over the Syrians accordingly restored to him all the ancient divisions of Israel, from Hamath to the borders of the Dead sea. His signal success over Amaziah the king of Judah has been recorded in the preceding chapter. Upon the whole, the reign of Jeroboam II. may be regarded as a brilliant one, considering the evil days on which the history has now fallen. In fact, it would not be easy to point to any king of the separate kingdom of Israel whose reign was more prosperous.

The prophet Jonah, named in the preceding paragraph, is the same whose reluctant mission to Nineveh, the capital of the Assyrian empire, is related in the book which bears his name. "The king of Nineveh," whose humiliation with that of his people averted the doom impending over "that exceeding great city," is supposed to have been the predecessor of Pul, whom the history will speedily bring before us. Jonah's remarkable mission appears to have taken place about the year 800 B. C., at the latter end of the reign of Jeroboam, who died in 793 B. C., after a reign of forty-one years.

There was a delay in calling his son Zechariah to the throne. Jeroboam II. began to reign in the fifteenth year of Amaziah king of Judah, and reigned forty-one years (2 Kings xiv. 43); he died, therefore, in the sixteenth year of Uzziah king of Judah; but his son Zechariah did not succeed him until the thirty-eighth of Uzziah (2 Kings xv. 8), which produces an interregnum of not less than twenty-two years. During this period great internal commotions prevailed, which more than compensated the absence of foreign war. Kings were suddenly raised to the throne, and as suddenly removed, agreeably to the representation which the prophet Hoshea gives of the state of the kingdom. The same representation also proves that at this period very gross corruptions of religion and of morals prevailed. Even the ultimate call of Zechariah to the throne had scarcely any effect in allaying these disturbances, and he was himself slain by Shallum in the sixth month of his reign. He was the last king of the house of Jehu: and thus was fulfilled the prediction that the family of Jehu should only retain the throne to the fourth generation.

Shallum, whose deed in slaying Zechariah was performed with the sanction and in the presence of the people, ascended the vacant throne in the year 771 B. C. But on receiving intelligence of this event, Menahem, the general of the army, marched against the new king, and having defeated and slain him in battle, after a reign of but thirty days, mounted the throne himself: and through his influence with the army, he was enabled not only to retain his post, but to subdue the disturbances by which the country had of late years been distracted. In doing this he proceeded with a degree of barbarity which would have been scarcely excusable in even a foreign conqueror (Joseph. Antiq. ix. 11, sec. 1).

It was in the time of Menahem that the Assyrians under Pul made their first appearance in Syria. Their formidable force precluded even the show of opposition from the king of Israel, who deemed it the wiser course to purchase peace from the Assyrian king at the price of a thousand talents of silver.* This sum he raised by the unpopular measure of a poll tax of fifty shekels each upon sixty thousand of his wealthiest subjects. This is the first instance in either kingdom of money raised by taxation for a public object. In the kingdom of Judah such exigencies were met from the treasury of the temple, or of the crown; and probably there were, in ordinary times, analogous resources in Israel, but which we may readily conclude to have been exhausted in the recent troubles and confusions in that kingdom. Professor Jahn considers that the government of Israel had by this time become wholly military, in which conclusion we are disposed to acquiesce, although from other intimations than those to which he adverts.

After a reign of ten years Menahem died in 760 B. C., and was succeeded by his son Pekahiah, who, after a short and undistinguished reign of two years, was slain by Pekah, the commander of the forces, who placed himself on the throne.

The alliance of Pekah with Rezin the king of Syria, against the house of David, has been recorded in the preceding chapter, as well as the consequences which resulted from the resort of Ahaz king of Judah to the protection of Tiglath-pileser, the new king of Assyria, who overran Gilead and Galilee, and removed the inhabitants to Assyria and Media. After a reign of twenty years, Pekah received from Hoshea the same doom which he had himself inflicted upon his predecessor. This was in 738 B. C., being in the third year of the reign of Ahaz in Judah.

It appears that although Hoshea is counted as the next king, he was not immediately able to establish himself on the throne, but that an interregnum, or period of anarchy, of ten years' duration, followed the murder of Pekah.† Thus, although the kingdom of Israel was now enclosed within very narrow boundaries, and surrounded on the north and east by the powerful Assyrians, it could not remain quiet, but was continually exhausting its strength in domestic conspiracies and broils.

From this struggle the regicide Hoshea emerged as king. He proved a better ruler than most of his predecessors. He allowed the king of Judah (Hezekiah) to send messengers through the country inviting the people to a great passover which he intended to celebrate at Jerusalem, nor did he throw any obstacles in the way of the persons disposed to accept the invitation. He had a spirit which might have enabled him to advance the power and interests of the country under ordinary circumstances; but now, doomed of God, the kingdom was too much weakened to make the least effort against the Assyrian power. When therefore Shalmaneser, the new Assyrian king, invaded the country, he bowed his neck to receive the yoke of a tributary. This yoke, however, he found so galling that ere long he took measures for shaking it off. He made a treaty with "So," or Sabaco‡ king of Egypt, and on the strength of it ventured to seize and imprison the Assyrian officer appointed to collect the tribute. Upon this, Shalmaneser laid siege to Samaria, and after three years gained possession of that city and destroyed it. During all this time the king of Egypt made no attempt to come to the assistance of Israel, as Isaiah had from the beginning predicted, in language of strong reprehension against this alliance (Isaiah xxx. 1–7). The fall of Samaria consummated the conquest of the country by the Assyrians. Hoshea was himself among the captives, and was sent in chains to Nineveh; but what afterward became of him is not known. Considerable numbers of the principal Israelites, during the war, and at its disastrous conclusion, fled the country, some to Egypt, but more into Judea, where they settled down as subjects of Hezekiah, whose kingdom must have been considerably strengthened by this means.

According to a piece of oriental policy of which modern examples have been offered, Shalmaneser removed from the land the principal inhabitants, the soldiers, and the artisans to Halah, to the river Habor (Chebar in Ezekiel), to Gozan, and to

---

* Almost one million eight hundred thousand dollars, by the present value of this quantity of silver.

† "Pekah, king of Israel, began to reign in the fifty-second year of Uzziah (2 Kings xv. 27; 2 Chron. xxvi. 3); and in the twentieth year of his reign was slain by Hoshea (xv. 30) In the third year of the reign of Ahaz king of Judah (2 Kings xvi. 1); but Hoshea did not begin to reign until the twelfth year of Ahaz (xvii. 1), or the thirteenth current (2 Kings xvi. 10); consequently the second interregnum in Israel lasted 13—3 = 10 years."—Hales.

‡ This So, or Sabaco of profane authors,—Sabakoph on the monuments,—was an Ethiopian who ruled in Egypt, and whose right to the crown of which may have been (in part, at least) derived from marriage, although Herodotus represents him solely as an intrusive conqueror. His name occurs at Abydus; and the respect paid to his monuments by his successors may be considered to imply that his reign was not a wrongful usurpation.

the cities of the Medes. On the other hand, colonists were brought from Babylon, Cuthah, Ava, Hamath, and Sepharvaim, and seated in Samaria. It appears also that other colonists were afterward sent into the country by Esarhaddon. These people mingled with the Israelites, who still abode in the land, and were all comprehended under the general name of SAMARITANS, which was derived from the city of Samaria. At first all of them were worshippers of idols; but as wild beasts increased in their depopulated country, they were much disturbed by lions. According to the notions respecting national and local gods which then prevailed in the world, it is not strange that they attributed this calamity to the anger of the god of the country on account of their neglect of his worship. Accordingly, an Israelitish priest was recalled from exile, in order to instruct these idolaters in the worship of Jehovah as a national Deity. He settled at Bethel, where one of the golden calves had formerly stood; and afterward the Samaritans united the worship of Jehovah with the worship of their own gods.

We will follow the expatriated Israelites into the places of their captivity; but, first, it is necessary that our attention should be turned to the affairs of Judah, which the mercy and long-suffering of God still continue to spare.

JUDAH, FROM B. C. 725, TO B. C. 586.

Hezekiah was twenty-five years of age when he succeeded his father, Ahaz, in the kingdom of Judah. He was a most pious prince, and thoroughly imbued with the principles of the theocracy. He testified the most lively zeal for the service and honor of Jehovah; while, as a king, he was disposed to manifest the most unreserved reliance on him, and subserviency to him, as Sovereign Lord of the Hebrew people. He therefore won the high eulogium that "there was none like him among all the kings of Judah after him, nor any that were before him."[*]

---

[*] 2 Kings xviii. 1-5. Such, however, must be understood as popular forms of describing superior character; for the same is said, in the same terms, of his own great grandson, Josiah.

[†] THE SEPULCHRE OF THE KINGS.—It would be rather difficult to prove that the ancient sepulchre which now bears this name is really that to which there are such frequent allusions in the history of the kingdom of Judah. But it would be equally difficult to disprove it. The situation is not unsuitable, nor the internal arrangements unbecoming such a distinction. And if any difficulty were to be started with reference to the architectural character of the sculptured exterior, it might very easily be answered that this was added at a period long subsequent to the original construction of the tomb. It might also be added, that if this be not the Sepulchre of the Kings, no other sepulchre now existing near Jerusalem is entitled to compete that distinction with it. Upon the whole, this is a matter on which one would not like to give a decided opinion; but apart from this matter, the sepulchre in question is of great interest from the very complete example which it offers of the ancient sepulchres.

The Sepulchre of the Kings, so called, is situated nearly a mile to the north of the northwestern gate (Damascus-gate) of the present city, but appears to have been only just outside the northwestern angle of the ancient wall.

These splendid remains differ from most other rock-carved sepulchres in not being cut in the side of a hill, but beneath a level spot of ground approached by a narrow path, which leads to a square enclosure, hewn out of the limestone stratum, of about fifteen or twenty feet deep. A wall of the natural rock separates this from an inner square court, which opens into it by a round arch. On the southern side of this court (which is covered with rubbish and brambles) is a very handsome square portico, with a beautifully-carved architrave—forming probably the most complete specimen of Hebrew sculpture that now exists. The frieze is adorned with a regulus, triglyphs, vine-leaves, and other floral embellishments, while the centre is charged with an immense cluster of grapes. A pilaster at either end still remains, and in all probability there were anciently two columns in the centre, now destroyed. The face of the rock within the portico is smooth, and presents no appearance of openings, but a low doorway on the left hand leads into a large square antechamber, hewn out of the solid rock. There are no niches, or places for sarcophagi in this apartment, but a series of small chambers branch off on each of its three sides. These are, for the most part, oblong crypts, with ledges on either side for holding the bodies or coffins.

The doors of those chambers have attracted much and deserved attention; they are made of single stones or slabs, seven inches thick, sculptured in panels, so as exactly to resemble doors made by a carpenter at the present day, the whole being completely smoothed and polished, and of the most accurate proportions. These doors turned on pivots, of the same stone, which were inserted in sockets above and below.

There are no troughs or soroi in any of the chambers, but simply ledges on the sides, for bodies or coffins.

A low door and a flight of steps lead down into another suite of chambers, of similar form and construction. In these are found some fine sarcophagi of unsurpassed elegance in form and ornament. Each of them consists of two half cylinders of white marble, excavated within, and which, when placed together, resemble the shaft of a beautiful pillar. The bottom part is comparatively plain; but the lid, or upper part, is covered with the most elaborately carved foliage in basso relievo, traced in vines, roses, and lily-work. The groove, or cavity, for the body, which is principally hollowed out from the bottom part, is about two feet broad, and a foot deep—a sufficiently large space to contain the body of an ordinary-sized person. The ends also of these sarcophagi are carved; and the general form and appearance might suggest a resemblance to the large carriage-trunks of former days. The niches for the sarcophagi form the segment of a dome, being somewhat differently shaped from some of those in the upper chambers. Above the place of each coffin is a small niche, apparently designed to contain a lamp.

This account of the Royal Sepulchres is abridged and slightly altered from a longer description in Dr. Wilde's "Narrative," ii. 298-301. The Rev. J. D. Paxton is another recent traveller, who has given a very clear description of these sepulchres, the exterior of which is represented in our engraving, at page 351, from a drawing by Mr. Arundale.

Sepulchre of the Kings.†

He began his reign by the restoration of the true religion and the abolishment of idolatry throughout his dominions. In the very first month he opened the doors of the temple, which his father had closed, and restored the worship and service of God in proper order and beauty. In extirpating idolatry he was not content, with the abolition of its grosser forms, but sought out the more *native* and intimate superstitions which were incentives thereto. The altars illegally erected to Jehovah, which former kings had spared, were by him overthrown. .The brazen serpent, which Moses had made in the wilderness, and which was preserved in the temple, came in time to be regarded as a holy relic, to which at last a sort of superstitious worship was paid, and incense burned before it. This was not unnatural, considering the history of this relic, combined with the fact that ophiolatry was then, and before and after, a very common superstition in Egypt and other countries. It nobly illustrates the vigor of Hezekiah's character, and of an entire freedom from superstition, of which it is difficult *now* to appreciate the full merit, that he spared not even this certainly interesting relic, but broke it in pieces, and instead of *nahash*, "a serpent," called it contemptuously *nehushtan*, "a brazen bauble."

Much attention was also paid by Hezekiah to the dignified and orderly celebration of the festivals, which formed so conspicuous a feature in the ritual system of the Hebrews. The passover in particular, which had fallen into neglect, was revived with great splendor, and, as noticed in the last chapter, Hezekiah sent couriers through the kingdom of Israel to invite the attendance of the Israelites. His object was so obviously religious only, without any political motives, that the last king of Israel offered no opposition: and indeed a kingdom so nearly on the point of being absorbed into the great Assyrian empire, had small occasion to concern itself respecting any possible designs of Hezekiah. The Israelites were therefore left to act as their own dispositions might determine. The couriers went on from city to city proclaiming the message, and delivering the letters with which they were charged. In these the king of Judah manifested great anxiety to induce the Israelites—" the remnant who had escaped out of the hands of the kings of Assyria"—to return to Jehovah, and by that return avert that utter destruction which seemed to impend over them. The great body of the Israelites received the invitation with laughter and derision; but in Zebulon and Asher some were found "who humbled themselves and came to Jerusalem."

Like David, his great model, Hezekiah made provision for the instruction and moral improvement of the people, by the public singing of the Psalms in the temple, and by a new collection of the moral maxims of Solomon.

For his righteous doings the Lord was with Hezekiah, and prospered him in all his reasonable undertakings. He extended the fortifications and magazines throughout the country; he supplied Jerusalem more plentifully with water by means of a new aqueduct; and the Philistines, who had penetrated into the southern parts of Judea in the reign of his father, were conquered by his arms.

The possession of the kingdom of Damascene-Syria, and the entire conquest of Israel, rendered the kings of Assyria all-powerful in those countries. Phœnicia was the next to experience the force of their arms. The Tyrians only (according to the citation which Josephus adduces from their own historian Menander) refused to receive the Assyrian yoke. They fought and dispersed the fleet which the subjugated Phœnicians had furnished for the ulterior objects and remoter enterprises of Shalmaneser. To avenge this act, the Assyrian king left his troops for five years in the Tyrian territory, where they grievously distressed the citizens of Tyre, by cutting off all access to the river and aqueduct from which the town obtained its water. It was the death of Shalmaneser, apparently, which induced the Assyrians to abandon the siege.

It was probably the same occasion, together with an undue reliance upon his fortifications, and too much confidence derived from the success which had attended the small wars in which he had been engaged, which led Hezekiah into the same temerity which had been the ruin of Hoshea. He discontinued the tribute to the Assyrians which had been imposed upon his father, and by that act threw off the yoke which Ahaz had voluntarily taken on himself.

In the fourteenth year of Hezekiah, the new king of Assyria, named Sennacherib, came a large army to reduce the kingdom of Judah to obedience, as well as to invade Egypt, on account of the encouragement which "So," the king of that country, had given to Hoshea to revolt, by promises of assistance, which he proved unable to render. Such promises appear to have been renewed to Hezekiah, to induce him to give trouble and employment to a power of which the Egyptians had good cause to be jealous. But the new king Sethos (Se-pthah, priest of Pthah), who had been a priest, considering the services of the soldiers unnecessary to the security of a kingdom intrusted to the protection of the gods, treated the military caste with much indignity, and much abridged their privileges, in consequence of which they refused, when required, to march against the Assyrians.

Hezekiah, disappointed of the assistance which he had expected from Egypt,* and observing the overwhelming nature of the force put in action, delayed not to make his submissions to Sennacherib, humbly acknowledging his offence, and offering to submit to any tribute which the king might impose upon him. The desire of the Assyrian not to delay his more important operations against Egypt, seems to have inclined him to listen favorably to this overture. He demanded three hundred talents of silver, and thirty talents of gold; and this was paid by Hezekiah, although to raise it he was compelled to exhaust the royal and sacred treasures, and even to strip off the gold with which the doors and pillars of the temple were overlaid.

Sennacherib received the silver and gold; but after he had taken Ashdod, one of the keys of Egypt, he began to think it would be unsafe in his invasion of that country to leave the kingdom of Judah unsubdued in his rear. He therefore determined to complete the subjugation of Judah in the first place,—the rather as his recent observations, and the humble submission of Hezekiah, left him little reason to expect much delay or difficulty in this enterprise. He soon reduced all the cities to his power except Libnah and Lachish, to which he laid siege, and Jerusalem, to which he sent his general Rabshakeh with a very haughty summons to surrender. Many blasphemous and disparaging expressions were applied to Jehovah by the heathen general. By this he was, as it were, bound to vindicate his own honor and power; and, accordingly, the prophet Isaiah was commissioned to promise the king deliverance, and to foretell the destruction of the Assyrian host: "Lo! I will send *a blast* upon him, and he shall hear *a rumor*, and shall return to his own land, and I will cause him to fall by the sword in his own land." 2 Kings xix. 7.

The *rumor* by which Sennacherib was alarmed and interrupted, was no other than the report which was spread abroad that Tirhakah the Ethiopian, king of Upper Egypt, was marching with an immense army to cut off his retreat. He then determined to withdraw; but first sent a boasting letter to Hezekiah, defying the God of Israel, and threatening what destructions he would execute upon the nation on his return. But that very night an immense proportion of the Assyrian host, even one hundred and eighty thousand men, were struck dead by "the BLAST" which the prophet had predicted, and which has, with great probability, been ascribed to the agency of the *simoom*, or hot pestilential south wind, which we may have another occasion to notice.

Sennacherib returned to Nineveh, and in the exasperation of defeat he behaved with great severity to the captive Israelites. But his career was soon closed. Fifty-two days after his return he was slain, while worshipping in the temple of the god Nisroc, by his two eldest sons. Thus the prophecy of Isaiah was in every point accomplished. The parricides fled into Armenia, leaving the steps of the throne clear for the ascent of the third son, whose name was Esarhaddon. This great blow so weakened the Assyrian monarchy as not only to free the king of Judah from his apprehensions, but enabled the Medes and Babylonians to assert their independence.

The same year Hezekiah fell sick—apparently of the plague,—and he was warned by the prophet Isaiah to prepare for death. The king was afflicted at these tidings; and turning his face to the wall (as he lay in his bed), to be unnoticed by his attendants, he besought the Lord, with tears, to remember him with favor. His prayer was heard; and the prophet, who had not yet left the palace, was charged to return and acquaint Hezekiah that, on the third following day, he should resume his customary attendance at the temple; and not only that, but that fifteen years should be added to his life. In confirmation of this extraordinary communication, the king desired some miraculous sign; and accordingly the shadow of the style upon the dial of Ahaz went backward ten degrees. The event corresponded to these intimations.

* That he had expectations from that quarter, and that such expectations were known to the Syrians. appears from Rabshakeh's advice to him,—"Not to trust upon the staff of that bruised reed, Egypt (upon which if a man lean it will break and pierce his hand);" 2 Kings xviii. 17-35

The prolongation of life was the more important and desirable to Hezekiah, as at that time there was no direct heir to the crown. These circumstances, together with the signal deliverance from Sennacherib, not only cured the people of the idolatry which Ahaz had introduced, and retained them for some time in their fidelity to Jehovah, but excited the curiosity and admiration of the neighboring nations. Merodach-Baladan, the king of Babylon, sent an embassy to congratulate the king on his deliverance from the Assyrians (through which Merodach himself had been enabled to establish his independence in Babylon), and upon his recovery from his illness, as well as to make particular inquiries respecting the miracle by which it was accompanied, and which must have been of peculiar interest to a scientific people like the Babylonians. Hezekiah appears to have been highly flattered by this embassy from so distant a quarter. The embassadors were treated with much attention and respect, and the king himself took pleasure in showing them the curiosities and treasures of his kingdom. That he had treasures to show, seems to signify that he had recovered his wealth from the Assyrians, or had enriched himself by their spoil.

The sacred historian attributes Hezekiah's conduct on this occasion to "his pride of heart," involving an appropriation to himself of that glory which belonged only to Jehovah. Although, therefore, his conduct did not occasion the doom, it gave the prophet Isaiah occasion to make known to him that the treasures of his kingdom were the destined spoil, and his posterity the destined captives of the very nation whose present embassage had produced in him so much unseemly pride. This was in every way a most remarkable prediction; for Babylon was then an inconsiderable kingdom, and the people almost unknown by whom the prediction was to be fulfilled. Hezekiah received this announcement with true oriental submission—satisfied, he said, if there were but peace and truth in his own days.

The remainder of Hezekiah's reign, through the years of prolonged life which had been granted to him, appears to have been prosperous and happy. To no other man was it ever granted to view the approach of death with certain knowledge, through the long, but constantly shortening, vista of years that lay before him. At the time long before appointed, Hezekiah died, after a reign of twenty-nine years, B. C. 725.

Manasseh was but twelve years of age when he lost his father, and began to reign. The temptations which surrounded him, and the evil counsels which were pressed upon him, were too strong for his youth. He was corrupted; and it seemed the special object of his reign to overthrow all the good his father had wrought in Judah. The crimes of all former kings seem light in comparison with those which disgraced his reign. He upheld idolatry with all the influence of the regal power, and that with such inconceivable boldness, that the pure and holy ceremonies of the temple service were superseded by obscene rites of an idol image set up in the very sanctuary; while the courts of God's house were occupied by altars to "the host of heaven," or the heavenly bodies. He maintained herds of necromancers, astrologers, and soothsayers of various kinds. The practice which was, of all others, the most abhorrent to Jehovah, the king sanctioned by his own atrocious example; for he devoted his own children, by fire, to strange gods, in the blood-stained valley of Ben-Hinnom. Wickedness now reigned on high, and as usual persecuted righteousness and truth; so that, by a strong but significant hyperbole, we are told that innocent blood flowed in the streets of Jerusalem like water.

While these things were transacting in Judah, Esarhaddon, the king of Assyria, was consolidating his power, and endeavoring to reunite the broken fragments of his father's empire. It was not until the thirtieth year of his reign that he recovered Babylon, the affairs of which appear to have fallen into great disorder after the death of Merodach-Baladan, if we may judge from the occurrence of five reigns and two interregnums of ten years, all in the course of the twenty-nine years which preceded its reduction again under the Assyrian yoke.

When Esarhaddon had sufficiently re-established his authority, and settled his affairs in the east, he turned his attention westward, and determined to restore his authority in that quarter, and to avenge the disgrace and loss which the Assyrians had sustained in Palestine. This intention constituted him Jehovah's avenger upon the king and nation of Judah, for the manifold iniquities into which they had by this time fallen.

Esarhaddon entered Judah in great force, defeated Manasseh in battle, took him alive, and sent him in chains to Babylon, together with many of his nobles and of the people. They were sent to Babylon probably because Esarhaddon, to prevent another defection, made that city his chief residence during the last thirteen years of his reign. It was probably on the same occasion that he removed the principal remaining inhabitants of Israel, and replaced them by more colonists from the East.

In the solitude of his prison at Babylon, Manasseh became an altered and a better man. The sins of his past life, and the grievous errors of his government were brought vividly before him; and humbling himself before the God of his fathers, he cried earnestly for pardon, and besought an opportunity of evincing the sincerity of his repentance. The history makes mention of his prayer, as having been preserved; and the Apocrypha contains a prayer which purports to be that which he used on this occasion. This it would be difficult to prove; but the prayer itself is a good one, and suitable to the occasion.

His prayer was heard, and the opportunity which he sought was granted to him. Esarhaddon gave way to the suggestions of a more generous policy than that by which he had been at first actuated. He released the captive from his prison, and after having, we may presume, won him over to the interests of Assyria, and weaned from the national bias in favor of an Egyptian alliance, sent him home with honor. Unquestionably, he remained tributary to the Assyrian monarch, and his territory was probably considered as forming a useful barrier between the territories of Assyria and of Egypt. On his return, Manasseh applied himslf with great diligence to the correction of the abuses of his former reign. He also fortified the city of Zion on the west side by a second high wall (or, perhaps, he only rebuilt and carried to a greater height the wall which the Assyrians had thrown down), and endeavored as far as possible to restore the weakened kingdom to a better state. He died in B. C. 696, after a protracted reign of fifty-five years; and, mindful of the first iniquities of his reign, a place in the Sepulchre of the Kings was denied him, but he was buried in his own garden.

AMON the son of Manasseh was twenty-five years of age when he ascended the throne of Judah. He had been born after the repentance and restoration of his father; yet the first ways of Manasseh, and not the last, were those which he chose to follow. He revived the idolatries which had been suppressed; but the full development of his plans and character was interrupted by a conspiracy, in which he perished after a short reign of two years. B. C. 639.

Josiah was but eight years old at the death of his father; and during his minority the affairs of the government were administered by the high-priest Joachim and a council of elders at Jerusalem. The young king profited well by the excellent education he received under the tutelage of the high-priest. After a minority of eight years he assumed the government, and proceeded to act with far greater vigor against the idolatries of the land than the regent had ventured to exercise. He not only destroyed every form of idolatry which he was able to detect, but overthrew the altars illegally erected to Jehovah, and corrected the other irregularities which had in previous times been tolerated. In the course of these purgations, which were conducted by the king in person, he came to Bethel, and there (according to the prediction made nearly four centuries before, which had mentioned him *by name*) he defiled the altar which Jeroboam had erected before the golden calf in that place, by burning thereon the disinterred bones of dead men—the bones of the worshippers. And it was thus *that the* idolatrous altars were defiled by him throughout the land.

The zeal of the king took him beyond the limits of his own kingdom into the land of Israel, which he traversed even to its remoter parts, uprooting idolatry and all its adjuncts, wherever he came. For this rather remarkable proceeding out of his own kingdom there are different ways of accounting. The most probable seems to be that in restoring Manasseh to his throne, the king of Assyria had extended his authority (for the purpose of internal government) over the neighboring territory. His favor and confidence, continued to Josiah, agrees with and helps to explain some other circumstances.

When these operations were completed, measures were taken for a thorough repair of the temple. While this was in progress, the high-priest, Hilkiah, discovered the autograph copy of the Law, written by the hand of Moses, which had been deposited in or beside the ark of the covenant in the sanctuary. By his direction Shaphan, the chief scribe, read therefrom in the audience of the king, who no sooner heard that part which contains the prophecies of Moses against the nation, foretelling the captivities and destructions which should befall it for its iniquities, than Josiah knew by signs not to be mistaken, that the predicted calamities were imminent, for the iniquities had been rife, and the doom could not but soon follow; already, indeed, by the captivity of Israel, it had been half accomplished. It was for this that the king rent his garments.* He delayed not to send to Huldah the prophetess, " who dwelt in the college at Jerusalem," to learn from her the real intentions of Jehovah, and the sense in which these alarming denunciations were to be understood. She confirmed the obvious interpretation—that the unquenchable wrath of God would ere long be poured out upon Judah and Jerusalem, consuming, or bringing into bondage, the land, the city, the temple, the people, the king:—but adding, for the king himself, that because of the righteousness which had been found in him, he should be gathered to his grave before those evil days arrived.

By these disclosures new zeal for the Law was kindled in the heart of Josiah. The very same year, he caused the passover to be celebrated with great solemnity, in which not only the people of Judah, but the remnant of the Hebrew race which the Assyrians had left in the land of Israel, joined. There had been no such passover since the foundation of the kingdom.

To understand the circumstances which led to the death of King Josiah, it is necessary to view correctly the position of his kingdom, as a frontier barrier between the two great kingdoms of Assyria and Egypt, whose borders, by the conquests of the former power were, and had for some time been, in close and dangerous approximation. It is obvious that, from the first, the political game of Western Asia in that age lay between Egypt and Assyria, the former power being the only power west of the Euphrates which could for an instant be expected to resist or retaliate the aggressive movements of the latter. There was little question that the rich and fertile valley of the Nile might tempt the cupidity or the ambition of the Assyrians. It was therefore the obvious policy of the kings of Egypt to maintain the kingdoms of Israel and Judah, as a barrier between their country and the Assyrians, and it was the equally obvious policy of the latter to break that barrier down. Hence Hoshea in Israel had been encouraged by Sabaco to assert his independence, with a promise of support, which there is reason to believe that the Egyptian king was less unwilling than unable to render. The fall of Israel, as it weakened the barrier, could not but be a matter of regret to the Egyptians, and it would still be their desire to strengthen the hands of the kings of Judah. In this position it became a question at Jerusalem, as it had been in Samaria, whether the forbearance of the Assyrians should be purchased by submission, or that reliance should be reposed on the support of Egypt in opposition to that great power. The kings and people seem to have been generally well disposed " to lean upon Egypt," not more from habit and ancient intercourse, than from the perception that it was clearly the interest of that country to support them against the Assyrians. But when it had happened more than once that Egypt, after having encouraged them to shake off the Assyrian yoke, was unable (we can not believe unwilling) to render the stipulated assistance at the time it was most needed, and left them exposed to the tender mercies of the provoked Assyrians, the prophets raised their voice against a confidence and an alliance by which nothing but calamity had been produced, and encouraged unreserved and quiet submission to the Assyrian yoke. Even Hezekiah however, as we have seen, was induced by the prospect of support from Egypt, to throw off his dependance on Assyria. The consequent invasion of Judah by Sennacherib was so obviously threatening to Egypt, that Sethos (the king who then reigned in Lower Egypt) could only have been prevented by the state of affairs in his own dominion from rendering the assistance which he had led the king of Judah to expect. But, as already stated, this very unwarlike person—a priest by education and habit—had so offended the powerful military caste by abridgments of their privileges, that they refused to act, even in defence of the country. But when Tirhakah, the Ethiopian, who ruled in Upper Egypt, heard of

* It is quite evident that the king had never before read or heard these denunciations of the law, which seems hard to account for, when we consider that copies of the law do not appear to have been scarce, the rather as, no great while before, many copies had been made under the direction of Hezekiah. It has been suggested that the book in common use, and even that used by kings and priests, was some abstract, like our abridgment of the statutes, which contained only matters of positive law, omitting the promises and threatenings. The king being impatient to know the contents, the scribe begins to read immediately; and as the books of the times were written upon long scrolls, and rolled upon a stick, the latter part of Deuteronomy would come first in course; and there the scribe would find those terrible threatenings whereby the king was so strongly affected. See Deut. xxviii.

the threatened invasion by Sennacherib, he marched against him; and the Scriptural account would imply that the mere rumor of his approach sufficed to induce the Assyrians to contemplate a retreat, which was hastened by the singular destruction in his army by the pestilential simoom.* This solitary example of assistance from Egypt, although from an unexpected quarter, may be supposed to have strengthened the predilection of the king and people of Judah toward the Egyptian alliance; and it was almost certainly with the concurrence of Egypt that Manasseh allowed himself to incur the wrath of the Assyrians. But during his imprisonment at Babylon he would seem to have acquired the conviction that it was his best policy to adhere to his Assyrian vassalage; and we may conclude he was not released without such oaths and covenants as his awakened conscience bound him to observe. He was probably restored to his throne as a sworn tributary, or as being bound to keep the country as a frontier against Egypt. The conduct of Josiah renders this the most probable conclusion.

The Assyrian power got involved in wars with the Medes and Chaldeans, by which its attention was fully engaged and its energies weakened. Egypt, on the other hand, united under one king, had been consolidating its strength. Pharaoh-Necho, the king of that country, thought the opportunity favorable to act aggressively against the Assyrians, and to that end resolved to march and attack this old enemy on his old frontier. Carchemish, an important post on the Euphrates, and the key of Assyria on the western side, was the point to which his march was directed. He passed along the seacoast of Palestine, northward, the route usually followed by the Egyptian kings when they entered Asia. Josiah being apprized of this, and mindful of his relation to Assyria, and of his obligation to defend the frontier against the Egyptians, assembled his forces and determined to impede, if he could not prevent, the march of Necho through his territories. When the Egyptian king heard that Josiah had posted himself on the skirts of the plain of Esdraelon—that great battle-field of nations—to oppose his progress, he sent messengers to engage him to desist from his interference, alleging that he had no hostile intentions against Judah, but against an enemy with whom he was at war, and warning Josiah that his imprudent interference might prove fatal to himself and his people. But these considerations had no weight with Josiah, against what appeared to him a clear case of duty. He resisted the progress of the Egyptian army with great spirit, considering the disproportion of numbers. He himself fought in disguise; but a commissioned arrow found him out, and inflicted a mortal wound in the neck. He directed his attendants to remove him from the battle-field. Escaping from the heavy shower of arrows with which their broken ranks were overwhelmed, they removed him from the chariot in which he was wounded, and placing him in "a second one that he had," they conveyed him to Jerusalem, where he died. Thus prematurely perished, at the age of thirty-nine, one of the best and most zealous kings who ever sat upon the throne of David. His zeal in his vocation, as the overturner of idolatry, must have been much stimulated by the knowledge that he had been pre-ordained, by name, to this service, many centuries before his birth. We know not why the last act of his life should be deemed blameworthy by many who in other respects think highly of his character and reign. Was it not rather noble and heroic in him to oppose the vast host of Necho, in obedience to the obligation which his family had incurred to the Assyrian kings, and in consideration of which his grandfather, his father, and himself, had

* Sir J. G. Wilkinson alleges, we know not on what authority, that Sennacherib was fought and beaten by Tirhakah, and attributes to the jealousy of the Memphites the version of the affair given to Herodotus, by which he considers the truth to be disguised and the glory of Tirhakah obscured. This version is, that the Assyrians actually invaded Egypt; and Sethos being unsupported by the military, was induced by a dream to march against the enemy at the head of an undisciplined rabble of artisans and laborers. While the two parties were encamped opposite each other, near Pelusium, a prodigious number of field mice visited the Assyrian camp by night and gnawed to pieces their quivers and bows, as well as the handles of their shields; so that, in the morning, finding themselves without arms, they fled in confusion, losing great numbers of their men. This is the story which Sir J. G. Wilkinson regards as invented by the Memphites to withdraw from Tirhakah the credit of the Assyrian overthrow, which was really his work. But from the cast given the story, we are very much more disposed to believe that it is rather a version of the extraordinary overthrow which the Assyrians sustained by night in Palestine, and which the Egyptians desired to appropriate to their own country and their own gods. Or may it not be that, seeing the Hebrews alleged their God to be the Creator of the world, the Egyptians considered him the same as Phtah, the creator in their mythology, and whose priest Sethos had been? This seems to us very likely, the rather as it is difficult without this supposed identity to account for a circumstance in a following reign, when Necho expected to influence the pious Josiah by telling that God had sent him (Necho) to war against the Syrians.

been permitted to exercise the sovereign authority in the land? The death of Josiah was lamented by the prophet Jeremiah in an elegiac ode, which has not been preserved.

Intent upon his original design, Necho paused not to avenge himself upon the Judahites for the opposition he had encountered, but continued his march to the Euphrates.

Three months had scarcely elapsed, when, returning victorious from the capture of Carchemish and the defeat of the Assyrians, he learned that the people had called a younger son of Josiah, named JEHOAHAZ or Shallum, twenty-three years old, to the throne, overlooking his elder brother. Displeased that such a step had been taken without any reference to the will of their now paramount lord and conqueror, he sent and summoned Jehoahaz to attend on him at Riblah, in the land of Hamath; and having deposed him and condemned the land to pay in tribute a hundred talents of silver and a talent of gold, he took him as a prisoner to Jerusalem. On arriving there, Necho made Eliakim, the eldest son of Josiah, king in the room of his father, changing his name to Jehoiakim, according to a custom frequently practised by lords paramount and masters toward subject princes and slaves. The altered name was a mark of subjection. Then taking the silver and gold which he had levied upon the people, Necho departed for Egypt, taking with him the captive Jehoahaz, who there terminated his short and inglorious career, according to the prophecy of Jeremiah.—Jer. xxii. 10–12.

JEHOIAKIM, the eldest son of Josiah, was twenty-five years old when he began to reign. He reigned eleven years, and by his idolatries and misgovernment proved himself worthy of the throne of Ahaz and Manasseh. Early in his reign he was called to repentance by the prophet Jeremiah, who publicly, at the feast of tabernacles, in the ears of the assembled nation, denounced, in the name of Jehovah, the severest judgments against king and people, including the destruction of the city and the temple. For this he was seized as a seditious person, worthy of death; but he was acquitted by the nobles, and on this and other occasions screened by some persons of influence, who had been in power in the good times of Josiah.

Meanwhile the war in the east approached its termination. The allied Medes and Babylonians—the former under Cyaxares, and the latter under Nabopolassar—besieged the last Assyrian king in Nineveh. The siege was turned into a blockade; and Nabopolassar, already assuming the government of the empire which had fallen from the enfeebled hands of the Assyrians, despatched his son Nebuchadnezzar westward, with an adequate force, to chastise the Egyptians for their late proceedings, and to restore the revolted Syrians and Phœnicians to their obedience. In these different objects he completely succeeded.* Carchemish (Jer. xlvii. 2) he recovered from the Egyptians, and Jehoiakim was compelled to transfer his allegiance from Necho to the Babylonian. This was in the first year of his reign; in the second Nineveh was taken and destroyed by the allies. The conquering Medes were content to have secured their independence and avenged their wrongs, and left to the conquering Chaldeans the lion's share of the spoil. Babylon now became the imperial capital; but Nabopolassar himself, the founder of the great Chaldæ-Babylonian empire, died almost immediately after the fall of Nineveh, and the young hero in the west was called to fill the glorious throne which his father had set up.

The absence of Nebuchadnezzar in another quarter seemed to the king of Egypt a favorable opportunity of recovering his foreign conquests. He therefore undertook another expedition against Carchemish (Jer. xlvi. 2); and as Jehoiakim, in Judea, renounced, about the same time, his sworn allegiance to Nebuchadnezzar, there is much reason to conclude that he was encouraged to this step by the Egyptian king. This measure was earnestly but ineffectually reprobated by the prophet Jeremiah, who foretold the consequences which actually followed.

Nebuchadnezzar, who was certainly the greatest general of that age, did not allow the Egyptian king to surprise him. He met and defeated him at Carchemish, and then, pursuing his victory, stripped the Egyptian of all his northern possessions, from the river Euphrates to the Nile, and this by so strong an act of repression that he dared "come no more out of his own land."

The king of Judah now lay at the mercy of the hero whose anger he had so unadvisedly provoked. Nebuchadnezzar laid siege to Jerusalem, and took it. He com-

---

* Berosus in Egypt. 'Antiq.' x. 11, 1.

mitted no destructions but such as were the direct effect of his military operations; and, with a leniency very rare in those days, he refrained from displacing Jehoiakim from his throne. He was content to indemnify himself by the spoils of the temple, part of the golden ornaments and vessels of which he took away; and with removing to Babylon some members of the royal family, and sons of the principal nobles. These would serve as hostages, and at the same time help to swell the pomp and ostentation of the Babylonian court. Among the persons thus removed was Daniel and his three friends, whose condition and conduct will soon engage our notice, as part of the history of the captivity. It must be evident that the leniency exhibited on this occasion by Nebuchadnezzar, may be ascribed to his desire to maintain the kingdom of Judah as a barrier between his Syrian dominions and Egypt; for since Egypt had become aggressive, it was no longer his interest that this barrier should be destroyed.

The court at Jerusalem soon again fell into much disorder. The king turned a deaf ear to all wise counsel and all truth, as delivered by the prophet Jeremiah, and listened only to the false prophets, who won his favor by the flattering prospects which they drew, and by the chimerical hopes which they created. The final result was, that this prince again had the temerity to renounce his allegiance to the Babylonian, to whose clemency he owed his life and throne.

This occurred in the fourth year of Jehoiakim, B. C. 604, which it is important to note, as it is from this date that the "seventy years" of the Babylonish captivity is with the greatest apparent propriety dated. (Jer. xxv. 11; 2 Chron. xxxvi. 21–23.) This period of seventy years of exile was foretold by Jeremiah;[*] and it is most remarkable, that, from whichever of the more marked points these seventy years be commenced, we are brought at the termination to some one equally marked point in the history of the restoration and re-settlement of the nation.

Jehoiakim was not at all reformed by the calamity which had befallen his house and country. It only served to increase the ferocity of his spirit. This reign, therefore, continued to be cruel, tyrannical, and oppressive, and, still more and more, "his eyes and his heart were intent on covetousness, oppression, and the shedding of innocent blood." Of this an instance is found in the case of the prophet Urijah, "whom he slew with the sword, and cast his dead body into the graves of the common people," because he prophesied of the impending calamities of Judah and Jerusalem. (Jer. xxii. 13–16, xxvi. 20–23.) For these things the *personal* doom of Jehoiakim was thus pronounced by Jeremiah :—

"——Thus saith JEHOVAH,
Concerning Jehoiakim, son of Josiah, king of Israel,— .
They shall not lament for him, saying,
Ah, my brother! nor [*for the queen*], Ah, sister!
They shall not lament for him, saying,
Ah, Lord! nor [*for her*], Ah, her glory!
With the burial of an ass shall he be buried,
Drawn forth and cast beyond the gates of Jerusalem."—(Jer. xxii. 18, 19.)

For this prophecy the prophet was cast into prison, in the fourth year of Jehoiakim. The following year, acted upon by that strong *constraint* to deliver the word intrusted to him, which he himself so forcibly describes,[†] Jeremiah dictated to

* Dated from this point, the seventy years expired in B. C. 536, the year that Cyrus took Babylon, and issued a decree for the return of such of the Jews as chose, throughout his dominions, to their own land (Ezra iii. 1, v. 13); and this agrees with the account of Josephus, "in the first year of Cyrus, which was the seventieth (τὸ ἑβδομηκοστὸν) from the day of the removal of our people from their native land to Babylon," &c. (Ant. xi. 1, 1); for from B. C. 605 to B. C. 536 was sixty-nine years complete, or seventy years current. Hales, to whom we are indebted for this conclusion, thinks that it affords a satisfactory adjustment of the chronology of this most intricate and disputed period of the captivity, and that in it "all the varying reports of sacred and profane chronology are reconciled and brought into harmony with each other."

† "Thou didst persuade me, JEHOVAH, and I was persuaded;
Thou wast stronger than I, and didst prevail.
I am every day the object of laughter;
Every one of them holdeth me in derision.
For whensoever I speak,—
If I cry out of violence, and proclaim devastation,
The word of Jehovah is turned against me,
Into reproach and disgrace continually.
But when I say, I will not make mention of it,
Neither will I speak any more in his name;
Then it becomes in my heart as a burning fire,
Being pent up in my bones:
I am weary with refraining, and CAN NOT [*be silent*]."—Jer. xx. 7-9.

his friend and follower, the scribe Baruch, another prophecy, to the same effect as the former, but couched in stronger language, declaring the ruin which impended, through the Babylonian king, unless speedy and strong repentance intervened to avert the doom.   The roll, thus written, Baruch was sent to read publicly to the people assembled from all the country on account of a solemn fast for which public opinion had called.   Baruch accordingly read it in the court of the temple, in the audience of all the people assembled there.   He afterward, at their request, read it more privately to the princes.   They heard it with consternation, and determined to make its contents known to the king.   Baruch was directed to go and conceal himself, and the roll was taken and read to the king, who was then sitting in his winter apartment, with a brazier of burning charcoal before him.   When he had heard three or four sections, the king kindled into rage, and taking the roll from the reader, he cut it with the scribe's knife, and threw it into the fire, where it was consumed.   He also ordered the prophet and his friend to be put to death; but this was averted by the kind providence of the Almighty Master whom they served.

The undaunted prophet directed Baruch to rewrite the prophecy which had been burnt, with additional matter of the same purport; while to Jehoiakim himself the terrible message was sent:

> "Thus saith JEHOVAH,
> Concerning Jehoiakim, king of Judah,—
> He shall have none to sit upon the throne of David;
> And his dead body shall be cast out,
> In the day to the heat, and in the night to the frost."—Jer. xxxvi. 30.

The end of this miserable man doubtless corresponded with these predictions, although the historical narrative of that event is involved in some obscurity and apparent contradiction.   The statement we shall now give appears to be the only one by which, as it appears to us, all these difficulties can be reconciled.   It is evident that if Jehoiakim did not again revolt, his conduct was at least so unsatisfactory to the king of Babylon, that he sent an army against Jerusalem, containing some Chaldean troops, but composed chiefly from the surrounding subject nations, as the Syrians, Moabites, and Ammonites.   *In what manner* they performed their mission we know not, but according to the figurative description which Ezekiel (ix. 5–9) gives of Jehoiakim as a rapacious "lion's whelp," we learn that "the nations from the provinces set about him on every side, and spread their net over him, and he was taken in their pit; and they secured him with chains, and brought him to the king of Babylon."   Nebuchadnezzar was then probably at Riblah, at which place the eastern conquerors appear to have usually held their court when in Syria.   He bound the captive king "with fetters [intending] to carry him to Babylon" (2 Chron. xxxvi. 6); but took him first to Jerusalem, where he appears to have died before this intention could be executed; and the prophecies require us to conclude that his body was cast forth with indignity, and lay exposed to the elements and beasts of prey, which is what is intended by "the burial of an ass."

The preceding invaders appear to have been contented with securing the person of Jehoiakim, and taking him to Nebuchadnezzar; for when they had departed with their royal captive, the people made his son JECONIAH (otherwise Jehoiachim and Coniah) king in the room of his father.   He was then (B. C. 597) eighteen years of age, and had barely time to manifest his bad disposition, when Nebuchadnezzer himself, who was displeased at this appointment, appeared before Jerusalem.   It would seem that he was admitted without opposition; but Jeconiah was, nevertheless, held a close prisoner.   The money which remained in the royal treasury, and the golden utensils of the temple, were collected and sent as spoil to Babylon; and the deposed king, and his whole court, seven thousand soldiers, one thousand artisans, and two thousand nobles and men of wealth, altogether, with wives and children, amounting probably to 40,000 persons, were sent away into captivity to the river Chebar (Chaboras) in Mesopotamia.   Thus only the lower class of citizens and peasantry were left behind.   The future prophet, Ezekiel, was among the captives; and Mattaniah, the remaining son of Josiah, and brother of Jehoiakim, was made king of the impoverished land by Nebuchadnezzar, who, according to the custom in such cases, changed his name to ZEDEKIAH, and bound him by strong and solemn oaths of allegiance.

The Hebrews who remained in Judah continued however to cherish dreams of independence from the Chaldeans—impossible under the circumstances in which West-

Sidon.

ern Asia was then placed, or possible only through such special interventions of Providence as had glorified their early history, but all further claim to which they had long since forfeited. Even the captives in Mesopotamia and Chaldea were looking forward to a speedy return to their own land. These extravagant expectations were strongly discouraged by Jeremiah in Jerusalem, and by Ezekiel in Mesopotamia; but their reproofs were not heeded, nor their prophecies believed. Accordingly, Zedekiah, who seems not to have been ill-disposed, otherwise than as influenced by evil counsellors, was led openly to renounce his allegiance, in the ninth year of his reign. The temerity of this act would be astonishing and unaccountable, were it not that, as usual, the renunciation was attended by an alliance with the king of Egypt, Pharaoh-Hophra—the Apries and Vaphres of profane authors—who indeed had acquired a prominence in this quarter which might make the preference of his alliance seem a comparatively safe speculation. Apries, in the early part of his reign, was a very prosperous king. He sent an expedition against the Isle of Cyprus; besieged and took Gaza (Jer. xlvii. 1) and the city of Sidon; engaged and vanquished the king of Tyre; and, being uniformly successful, he made himself master of Phœnicia, and part of Palestine; thus recovering much of that influence in Syria which had been taken from Egypt by the Assyrians and Babylonians.

From the result it is evident that, on receiving the news of this revolt of one who owed his throne to him, and whose fidelity to him had been pledged by the most solemn vows, Nebuchadnezzar resolved no longer to attempt to maintain the separate existence of Judah as a royal state, but to incorporate it absolutely, as a province, with his empire. An army was, with little delay, marched into Judea, and laid immediate siege to Jerusalem. Jeremiah continued to counsel the king to save the city and temple by unreserved submission to the Chaldeans, and abandonment of the Egyptian alliance; but his auditors, trusting that the Egyptians would march to the relief of the place, determined to protract the defence of the city to the utmost. The Egyptians did, in fact, march to their assistance; but when Nebuchadnezzar raised the siege of Jerusalem and advanced to meet them, they retreated before him into Egypt, without hazarding a battle.

The withdrawl of the Chaldean forces from Jerusalem, with the confident expectation that they would be defeated by the Egyptians, filled the inhabitants with the most extravagant joy, and quite reversed—and so evinced the hollowness of—the slight acts of repentance and reformation which the apparent urgency of danger had produced. Their short-lived joy was terminated by the reappearance of the Chaldeans before the city. They prepared, however, to make a vigorous, or at least a protracted defence, for they well knew that, after so many provocations, little mercy was to be expected from Nebuchadnezzar, and they were probably acquainted with the fell purpose which that great monarch appears to have formed.

In the account of this siege much notice is taken of the respective works, the forts, the towers, &c., of the besiegers and the besieged. This may throw some light on the state to which the art of attacking and defending towns had then attained.

The siege was continued until the eleventh year of Zedekiah (B. C. 586), eighteen months from the beginning, when the Chaldeans stormed the city about midnight, and put the inhabitants to the sword, young and old, many of them in the very courts of the temple. The king himself, with his sons, his officers, and the remnant of the army, escaped from the city, but were pursued by the Chaldeans, and overtaken in the plain of Jericho, and carried as prisoners to Nebuchadnezzar, who was then at Riblah in the province of Hamah. The Babylonian king upbraided Zedekiah for his ingratitude and breach of faith, and ordered a terrible punishment to be inflicted on him. To cut off all future hope of reigning in his race, he ordered his sons to be slain before his eyes; and then, to exclude him from all hope of ever again reigning in his own person, he ordered that the last throes of his murdered children should be his last sight in this world. His eyes were put out—a barbarous mode of disqualifying a man for political good or evil, with which the governments of the East still continue to visit those whose offences excite displeasure, or whose pretensions create fear. The blind king was then led in fetters of brass to Babylon, where he died. Thus were fulfilled two prophecies, by different and distant prophets, which by their apparent dissonance had created mirth and derision in Jerusalem. Jeremiah had told the king, after the return of the Chaldean army to the siege, that he should surely be taken prisoner; that his eyes should see the king of Babylon, and that he should be carried captive to Babylon, and that he should die there, not by the sword, but in peace, and with the same honorable "burnings" with which his fathers had been interred;[*] while Ezekiel had predicted that he should be brought captive to Babylon, yet should never see that city, although he should die therein.[†]

Nebuchadnezzar appears to have been dissatisfied at the only partial manner in which his purposes against Judah had been executed. He therefore sent Nebuzaradan, the captain of his guard, with an army of Chaldeans to Jerusalem. The temple and the city were then burnt to the ground, and all the walls demolished, while all the vessels of brass, silver, and gold, which had been left before, and all the treasure of the temple, the palace, and the houses of the nobles, were taken for spoil; and of the people none were left but the poor of the land to be vine-dressers and husbandmen. This was about a month after the city was first taken.

Thus was the land made desolate, that "she might enjoy her sabbaths," or the arrearage of sabbatic years, of which she had been defrauded by the avarice and disobedience of the people. That these sabbatic years, being the celebration of every seventh year as a season of rest, even to the soil which then lay fallow, amounted to not less than seventy, shows how soon, and how long, that important and faith-testing institution had been neglected by the nation. The early predictions of Moses,[‡] and the later one of Jeremiah,[§] that the land should enjoy the *rest* of which it had been defrauded, is very remarkable, when we consider that, as exemplified in Israel, it was not the general policy of the conquerors to leave the conquered country in desolation, but to replenish it by foreign colonists, by whom it might be cultivated.

Nebuchadnezzar made Gedaliah, a Hebrew of distinction, governor of the poor remnant which was left in the land. Gedaliah was a well-disposed man, of a generous and unsuspecting nature, who was anxious to promote the well-being of the people by reconciling them to the Babylonian government. In this design he was assisted by Jeremiah, who had been released from prison when the city was taken, and was treated with much consideration by the Babylonian general, to whose care he had been recommended by Nebuchadnezzar himself. Nebuzaradan indeed offered to take him to Babylon and provide for him there; but the prophet chose rather to remain with his friend Gedaliah, who fixed his residence at Mizpeh beyond Jordan.

As soon as the Babylonian army had withdrawn, those nobles and warriors returned who had saved themselves by flight in the first instance. Among these was Ishmael, a prince of the royal family, who, jealous of the possession by Gedaliah of the government to which he considered that his birth gave him the best right, formed a conspiracy to take away his life. This was intimated to the governor, but he treated it as an infamous calumny upon Ishmael, which generous confidence was rewarded by his being murdered, with all the Hebrews and Chaldeans at Mizpeh who were attached to him, by that bad man and his dependants. The vengeance of the Chaldeans was now to be dreaded, and therefore Ishmael and all his followers fled toward the country of the Ammonites (who had promoted the designs of Ishmael). They attempted to take with them the king's daughter and the residue of the people; but these were recovered by Johanan and other officers, who pursued them, so that Ishmael escaped with only eight men to the Ammonites. Johanan and the others were fearful of the effects of the resentment of the Chaldeans for the massacre of which Ishmael had been guilty. They therefore determined to take refuge in Egypt with all the people. This intention was earnestly opposed by Jeremiah, who, in the name of Jehovah, promised them peace and safety if they remained; but threatened death by pestilence, famine, and sword, if they went down to Egypt. They went, however, and compelled Jeremiah himself to go with them; and it is alleged by tradition that they put him to death in that country for the ominous prophecies he continued to utter there.

Nebuzaradan soon after arrived in the country with the view of avenging the murder of Gedaliah and the massacre of the Chaldeans who were with him: but the country was so thin of inhabitants, in consequence of the secession to Egypt, that he could find no more than seven hundred and forty-five persons in the land, whom he sent into captivity beyond the Euphrates. Thus signally was the long predicted depopulation of the land completed; and although nomadic tribes wandered through the country, and the Edomites settled in some of its southern parts, yet the land remained,

---

* Jer. xxxii. 4, 5; xxxiv. 3, 5.   † Ezek. xii. 13.   ‡ Lev. xxvi. 34.   § 2 Chron. xxxvi. 21.

on the whole, uninhabited, and ready for the Hebrews, whose return had as much been the subject of prophecy as their captivity had been.

For the clearer apprehension of the facts which have been stated, it will be desirable to trace the further operations of the Babylonians in those quarters.

The year after the conquest of Judea, Nebuchadnezzar resolved to take a severe revenge upon all the surrounding nations which had solicited the Judahites to a confederacy against him, or had encouraged them to rebel, although they now, for the most part, rejoiced in their destruction. These were the Ammonites, Moabites, Edomites, Arabians, the Sidonians, Tyrians, and Philistines; nor did he forget the Egyptians, who had taken a foremost part in action or intrigue against him. This had been foretold by the prophets. It had been foretold that all these nations were to be subdued by Nebuchadnezzar, and were assigned to share with the Hebrews the bondage of seventy years to that power. Some of them were conquered sooner and some later; but the end of this period was the common term for the deliverance of them all from their bondage to Babylon.

After Nebuchadnezzar had subdued the eastern and western states in his first campaign, he commenced the siege of the strong city of old Tyre, on the continent, in the year B. C. 584, being two years after the destruction of Jerusalem. This siege occupied thirteen years, a fact which illustrates, perhaps, not so much the strength of the place as the vitality of a commercial state. This is, however, only to intimate that during this period the city was invested by a Chaldean army; for many other important enterprises were undertaken and accomplished during the same period. It was during the siege that Nebuzaradan marched into Judea to avenge the murder of Gedaliah and the Chaldeans, as was just related.

Before Tyre was taken, the inhabitants, having the command of the sea, fled with all their effects to the insular Tyre in its neighborhood; so that the Chaldean army found but little spoil to reward their long toil and patience in the siege. This had been foretold by the prophet Ezekiel (Ezek. xxix. 18–20), but although Nebuchadnezzar and his army were to obtain "no wages for the great service they had served against Tyre," in the long course of which "every head was made bald and every shoulder peeled," yet as a compensation they were promised the plunder of " the land of Egypt, her multitude, her spoil, and her prey." Accordingly, in the spring of the year B. C. 570, after the war with Tyre was finished, Nebuchadnezzar invaded Egypt, and, from a concurrence of weakening circumstances in that country, was enabled to overrun the whole country from Migdol, its northern extremity, near the Red sea, to Syene, the southern, bordering upon Ethiopia. This he also subdued, together with the other auxiliaries of the Egyptians. The reigning king was the same Pharaoh-Hophra, or Apries, who was on the throne at the time Jerusalem was besieged, and whose faint and abortive motion to relieve his allies has been recorded. This proud and haughty tyrant was reduced to vassalage; and so wasted and depopulated was the land by the invaders, that it lay comparatively desolate for forty years. The king was himself soon after defeated and captured by his discontented and revolted subjects, under Amasis, who was made king, and who was reluctantly compelled by the clamors of the soldiers to inflict death upon his predecessor. Amasis was confirmed in the throne by the Assyrian king.

CHAPTER XXII.

THE CAPTIVITY:

BEFORE we enter upon the historical details of the period which now opens, it is proper to take a rapid survey of the principles developed in the history through which we have passed, and to indicate the consequences which are exhibited in the portion that lies before us.

In the commencement of the work, we have stated, in general terms, the leading design of the selection of the Hebrew race, and of their settlement in the land of Canaan as a distinct and peculiar people, and separated from all other nations by the peculiar institutions which were given to them. That they were appointed to be "stewards of the mysteries of God," is the substance of the considerations stated there and

Collecting Dung for Fuel.

enforced in subsequent passages. The history itself shows under what forms and obligations the stewardship was imposed, and how unfaithfully its duties were discharged; and we are come to the punishments which that unfaithfulness incurred.

And did that unfaithfulness render the promises and designs of God of no effect? Nay, much otherwise; but rather tended to illustrate the more strongly his Almightiness, by the accomplishment of all his designs, in spite of, *and even through*, the reluctance, the improbity, and the treachery of the instruments he employed. They might have worked his high will with great happiness and honor to themselves; but since they did not choose this, they were compelled to work that will even by their misery and dishonor. It was not in the power of the instruments to frustrate the intentions of Jehovah; they only had power to determine whether that will should be accomplished with happiness or with misery to themselves, and, in consequence, somewhat to vary *the mode* in which those designs were exhibited and fulfilled.

The main cause of the personal and national failure of the Israelites, as instruments of a design which was accomplished notwithstanding their misdoings, is by no means of difficult detection. Politically considered, it may be resolved into what has been in all ages and countries the leading cause of calamity and miscarriage—a reliance upon men and upon individual character, which at best is but temporary and fluctuating, rather than upon institutions which are permanent and unchanging. In *these*, every needful amelioration is an abiding good; whereas the existence of a good king, or judge, or priest, is at the most but " a fortunate accident," contingent on that most feeble thing, the breath of man. Nothing had been wanting to fortify their peculiar position by institutions admirably suited to their destined object, and made more impregnable by numerous sanctions and obligations than any other institutions ever were, or ever can, indeed, with any propriety, be made, by any authority short of that infinite wisdom by which the Hebrew institutions were established. Thus the nation was placed in the peculiarly advantageous position—which many enlightened nations have struggled for and sought after in vain—that their happiness, their prosperity, their liberties, were not dependant on the will of any men or set of men, but rested on firm institutions which were as obligatory upon the chiefs of the land as upon the meanest of the people.

But this was a new thing on the earth, and the Hebrew nation seemed utterly incapable of appreciating its value; and, indeed, what oriental nation is there, at this advanced day, by which the value of so precious a gift would be duly appreciated? They rested always on men; they always wanted leaders. And as they were led they followed: if their leaders were good and just men, they did well; if evil men, not well. They turned their back upon institutions, and threw themselves upon the accidents of human character:—and they fared accordingly. This preference occurs everywhere in the history of this people, and is with peculiar prominence evinced in their determination to have " a king to rule them like the nations;" in the ease with which Jeroboam was enabled to establish a schismatical worship in ten of the tribes; and in the facility with which, even in Judah, the people followed the examples offered by their kings.

With reference to this point, the character so frequently given to Jeroboam when the sacred writers have occasion to mention his name, as "Jeroboam, the son of Nebat, who sinned, *and made Israel to sin*," has always seemed to us frightfully emphatic and significant.

Had the ancient Hebrews adhered to their institutions, it was impossible for them, as a political body, not to have fulfilled their special vocation in the world. But having, by the neglect of those institutions (which, among other benefits, secured the absence of idolatry and its concomitant vices), done all that in them lay to frustrate the very objects for the promotion of which existence had been given to them, they made it necessary that God should accomplish his own objects, not, as desired, by their welfare and by the confusion of their enemies, but by their misery and destitution. It was left him to demonstrate his almightiness—his supreme power over all the " gods" which swarmed the world, not by overthrowing with his strong hand all the enemies who rose against them, and by maintaining them in the land he had given them, against the old conquerors by whom great empires were thrown down, but by making these very nations the instruments of his punishments upon the chosen people. And this was accomplished under such peculiar circumstances of manifest intention and instrumentality, that the conquerors themselves were brought to acknowledge the supremacy of Jehovah, and that they had been but the blind agents of his will. The strong and marked interference to prevent " the great kings" from engrossing to themselves the merit or glory of their victories, and from despising the God of the people who, for their sins, had been abased at *their* footstool, even extorted from these proud monarchs the avowal that they had received *all* their crowns and *all* their kingdoms from " the most high God," whom the Hebrews worshipped. Now this and other results of the destitution of the Hebrews as strongly, and perhaps more strikingly, subserved the great object of keeping alive in the world the knowledge of a supreme and *universal* governor and creator, as by maintaining the Hebrews in Palestine. Indeed, that this great truth was diffused among, and impressed upon, the conquering nations by the captivity of the Hebrews,—that " the Lord's song" was not sung utterly in vain in a strange land, by the captives who wept when they remembered Zion under the willows and beside the waters of Babylon,—in short, that they received some salt which kept them from utter putrefaction, some leaven which wrought vitally in them and prepared them for the revelations which the " fulness of times" produced—is evinced by the history of Daniel, by the edicts of Nebuchadnezzar, of Darius, and, above all, of Cyrus, and may even be traced in the tradition which ascribes the doctrines and important reforms of Zoroaster to his intercourse with the Jewish captives and prophets at Babylon.

Thus, although they had forfeited the high destiny of preserving and propagating certain truths as an independent and sovereign people, the forfeiture extended only to their own position, for the truths intrusted to them were still preserved and diffused through the instrumentality of their bondage and punishment. This was true even in the times posterior to their restoration to their own land.

We have been anxious to make these remarks, lest the facts of the history should seem to intimate that the divine intention in the establishment of the Hebrew commonwealth was *frustrated* by the perversity of the people which rendered the subversion of that commonwealth necessary. Having, as we trust, shown that there is no room for this conclusion, it may seem better to reserve such further remarks as may tend to develop the spirit of the ensuing history, for the natural connexion with the record of the circumstances in which they are involved. We now therefore proceed to record the captivities of Israel and of Judah.

When Jerusalem was destroyed, one hundred and ninety-four years had elapsed since the Israelites of Galilee and Gilead had been led away captive into Assyria; one hundred and thirty-three years since Shalmaneser had removed the ten tribes to Halah, and Habor by the river Gozan, and to Hara and other cities of Media; and ten years since Nebuchadnezzar had banished some of the inhabitants of Jerusalem to the river of Chebar. The determination of the sites to which the Israelites were removed is a matter of some interest, but one which, in a work like the present, does not require any large investigation. The interest lies in the means thus given of determining the district to which the Israelites were expatriated; and it is sufficient for us to state that all the investigations which have yet been instituted, and all the information which has yet been acquired, concur in referring all these names (excepting, of course, the river Chebar) to that northwestern part of the present Persian empire which formed the ancient Media. It is, indeed, remarkable that the only other cities whose names occur in the history of the captivity of the ten tribes, are Rhages and Ecbatana, which we know to have been important cities of Media, in both of which it appears that the expatriated Israelites were settled in considerable numbers.

Even this much it is important to learn; because of itself it throws much light upon the policy of the Assyrian conquerors, and upon the position which the removed Israelites ultimately occupied. Media was then subject to the Assyrian empire, although still chiefly *occupied* by the native Medes; it seems, therefore, to have been the policy of the Medes to remove the inhabitants of one conquered country to another conquered country with the view of weakening the separate interest or nationality of both, and of promoting such a fusion of races and nations as might tend to realize tranquillity and permanence to the general empire. From this allocation of the expatriated Israelites in Media results the important fact that, whereas Judah was always subject to the conquering nation, Israel was only so for a short time, as the Medes, among whom they were placed, were not long in asserting their independence of Assyria, which empire they (with the Babylonians) ultimately subverted, and continued independent of the great Babylonian empire which succeeded, and to which the captives of Judah were subject. So, then, the relations of the ten tribes were with the Medes, not with the Assyrians or Babylonians; and their relations with the Medes were not, and were necessarily far better than, those between captives and conquerors. It does not appear how the Medes could regard them, or that they did regard them, otherwise than as useful and respectable colonists whom the common oppressor had placed among them, and whose continued presence it was desirable to solicit and retain. It is hard to call this a captivity; but since it is usually so described, it is important to remark that the captivity of the ten tribes and that of Judah was under different, and independent, and not always friendly, states. There is a vague notion that since the Babylonians subverted and succeeded the Assyrians, the Israelites, who had been captives to the Assyrians, became such to the Babylonians, and were afterward joined in that captivity by their brethren of Judah; but this, as we have seen, was by no means the case.

The information we possess respecting the condition of the ten tribes, before and after the fall of Jerusalem, is exceedingly scanty. It is certain that during the long years which passed before Judah also was carried into captivity, the expatriated Israelites fully participated in all the extravagant hopes of their brethren in Judah, and were looking with sanguine expectations for a speedy restoration to their own land; and the adverse prophecies and declarations of Ezekiel were as little heeded by them as those of Jeremiah were at Jerusalem.

The apocryphal book of Tobit is the only source from which any information can be obtained as to the social position of the expatriated Israelites. We are certainly not among those who would like to repose much belief in "the stupid story of Tobias and his dog;" yet the *framework* of that story is so much in agreement with what we do know, and is so probable and natural in itself, that it would seem to have been "founded on facts," and to have been concocted by one who was intimately acquainted with the condition and affairs of the Israelites under the Assyrians.

From this it would appear, that many of the captives were stationed at Nineveh itself, where they would seem to have lived much like other citizens, and were allowed to possess or acquire considerable wealth. Among these was Tobit, of the town and city of Naphtali, a man who feared God, as doubtless many other of the captives did, and who, as far as in his power, squared his conduct by the rules and observances of the Mosaical law, and acquired such a character for probity, that the conqueror himself, Shalmaneser, took notice of him, and appointed him his purveyor. This promotion of one of the expatriated Hebrews is significant in its indications, as it shows that, as afterward with their brethren in Babylon, offices of importance and profit were, under the Assyrians, open to the ambition, or rewarded the good conduct of the Israelites. Tobit availed himself of his position to visit his brother Israelites in other cities, to cheer them and to encourage their reasonable hopes and enterprises. He must have acquired considerable wealth, as he was enabled to deposite ten talents of silver in the hands of Gabel of Rhages, in Media. That he did this may seem to imply that the captives stationed in Media were considered more securely circumstanced than those directly under the eye of the Assyrians. When Sennacherib returned from his signal overthrow in Palestine, he vented his ill-humor upon the Hebrew captives, and caused many of them to be put to death, and their bodies were cast forth to remain unburied beyond the walls of Nineveh. This was very shocking to the pious Tobit, who made it a practice to inter by night the bodies of his brethren whom he found unburied. The absence of the bodies occasioned inquiry, and the truth came to the knowledge of the tyrant, who would have put him to death; but the good man received timely warning, and made his escape from Nineveh. The tyrant himself was soon slain by his own sons; and (another marked instance of promotion) his successor, Esarhaddon, appointed Achiacharus, Tobit's nephew, to be his "cupbearer, and keeper of the signet, and overseer of the accounts." Through this person Tobit received permission to return to Nineveh. But he was reduced to comparative poverty, and total blindness was soon after added to his misfortunes. His nephew, Achiacharus, was kind to the family under these circumstances, until Tobit thought proper to remove into Elymais. There poverty was still their lot; and they were supported chiefly by the wife, Anna, who took in "woman's work," and sometimes obtained presents from her employers above her actual earnings.

At last Tobit, who had returned to Nineveh, bethought him of the valuable property he had left with Gabel at Rhages, and he sent his son to reclaim it, after giving him such instructions as shows that travelling was then, as almost ever since, dangerous in those countries. The romantic adventures of young Tobias on the journey form the most suspicious part of the book—perhaps the only suspicious part; for which reason, as well as because it affords none of the illustration we require, we willingly pass it by. It may suffice to state that Tobias prospered in his journey. Tobit lived in Nineveh to the good old age of 158 years, and before his death foretold the approaching troubles of Assyria and the destruction of Nineveh, and that "for a time peace should rather be in Media," to which country he advised his son to withdraw. Tobias was mindful of his counsel, and withdrew to Ecbatana, where, in due time, he heard of the destruction of Nineveh by the combined forces of the Medes and Babylonians.

We have already stated the inferences, as to the condition of the expatriated Israelites, which this narrative opens, although we have no information as to their condition after the fall of Nineveh and during the contemporary captivity of Judah. But there is every reason to conclude that their position under the Medes, when Media became an independent and well-governed state, was even less disadvantageous and unequal than it had been when that country was part of the Assyrian empire.

We have brought the history of the kingdom of Judah down to the destruction of Jerusalem and the desolation of the country. But the history of the captivity must take us back to an earlier date, even to the time when Nebuchadnezzar spoiled the temple of its costly utensils, and sent away to Babylon a number of young princes and nobles as hostages for the fidelity of the people and their new king. This was eleven years before the fall of Jerusalem.

Among these captives were Daniel, and his three friends, Hananiah, Mishael, and Azariah. These, as tokens of their enslaved condition, received Chaldean names, more familiar than their own to the organs of the conquering people. Daniel was called Belteshazzar; Hananiah, Shadrach; Mishael, Meshach; and Azariah, Abednego. These were, among others of the most promising of the youths, selected to be educated in the palace for three years, under the charge of the chief of the eunuchs, in the learning and language of the Chaldeans, to qualify them for holding offices about the court and in the state. At the end of that time they were brought before the king to be examined as to their proficiency, when the young persons named were " found to be ten times better informed in all matters of wisdom and understanding than all the magi or astrologers that were in the whole realm." They were accordingly admitted to a place in that learned body.

Seventeen years after the destruction of Jerusalem, and the second year after the devastation of Egypt, when all his enemies were subdued on every side, and when his rule extended over many nations, Nebuchadnezzar had a dream, which left a profound impression upon his mind, but the details of which he was unable to recover when he awoke. He therefore sent for all the magi and astrologers, requiring that by their occult skill and pretended influence with the gods, they should not only interpret but recover the dream he had lost. This they avowed themselves unable to do; whereupon the enraged and disappointed king commanded them to be massacred. Daniel and his friends were sought for, to be included in this doom; but Daniel, being informed of the cause, repaired to the royal presence, and promised that if further time were allowed, he would undertake that the dream and an interpretation should be found. To this the king willingly agreed; and the pious youths betook themselves to fasting and prayer, in the hope that God would enable them to satisfy the king's demand. Nor was their expectation disappointed. The matter was made known to Daniel in a vision. He was then enabled to remind the king that he had seen in his dream a compound image, and to inform him that this image represented " the things that should come to pass thereafter." In this compound image, the *head of pure gold* denoted Nebuchadnezzar himself, and the succeeding kings of the Babylonian dynasty; *the breast and arms of silver*, indicated the succeeding but inferior empire of the Medes and Persians; *the belly and thighs of brass*, the next following empire of the Macedonians and the Greeks, whose arms were brass; *the legs of iron*, and *the toes partly iron and partly clay*, refer to the Roman empire, which should be strong as iron, but the kingdoms into which it would ultimately subdivide, composed of heterogeneous materials, which should be partly strong and partly weak; and, lastly, *the STONE smiting the image and filling the whole earth*, denoted the kingdom of Christ, which was to be set up upon the ruins of these temporal kingdoms and empires, and

24

was destined to fill the whole earth, and to stand or continue for ever. "Thou art this head of gold," said the prophet to the king; but he did not indicate the names and sources of the succeeding and then non-existing empires with equal distinctness. But we know them, not only from the order in which they succeed, and from the characters ascribed to them; but from the subsequent visions of Daniel himself, in which these empires are distinctly named, and by which the meaning of this primary vision is gradually unfolded, and which form, together, one grand chain of prophecy, extending to the end of time, and so clear and distinct, that as much of them (nearly the whole) as is already fulfilled, and which was once a shadowing forth of the future, reads like a condensed history of past ages.

From the first, Daniel had disclaimed any peculiar pretensions to wisdom. "There is," he said, "a God in heaven who revealeth secrets;" and to him he not only referred all the credit of the interpretation, but plainly told the king that it was to the appointments of this "God in heaven," who had the supreme disposal of all events, that *he* owed all the kingdoms which he ruled. Here was a grand instance of that testimony for Jehovah to which, when introducing this chapter, we had occasion to advert. The king was much struck by it, so that, while he prostrated himself before Daniel as before a superior, he acknowledged that the God who could enable him to reveal this great secret was indeed the God of gods and Lord of kings. Who does not see that it was for the purpose of impressing this conviction that the dream was given to him, the forgetfulness inflicted, and the interpretation bestowed on Daniel?

Nebuchadnezzar was not slow in rewarding the distinguished qualities which the prophet exhibited. He appointed him ruler over the whole province of Babylon, and, at the same time, "chief governor over all the wise men of Babylon" (*Rab-Mag*, or *Archimagus*, Jer. xxxii. 3), two of the highest civil and scientific offices in the state. At his request, also, his three friends were appointed to conduct under him in the affairs of his provincial government, while he himself took a high place, if not the first place, in the civil councils of the king.

The services of Daniel and his friends proved too valuable to be dispensed with; but mature deliberation disgusted the king at his dream and its interpretation; and his pride disposed him to retract the acknowledgment he had made of the supremacy of the God of a conquered people. It was, as we apprehend, under this influence that he erected a great image, of which not the head only, but the whole figure was of gold,* to denote the continuance of his empire, in opposition to his dream; and it was dedicated to the tutelary god Bel, or Belus, whose power he now considered superior to that of the God of the Hebrews; whereby, in the most offensive manner, he revoked his former concession. All men were commanded to worship this, and no other god, on pain of death: in consequence of which, the three friends of Daniel, who continued their worship of Jehovah, with their faces turned toward Jerusalem, and took no notice of the golden image, were seized, and cast into an intensely heated furnace. But by the special and manifest interposition of the God they served, they were delivered without a hair of their heads being injured: by which fact the king, who was present, was constrained to confess that the God of the Hebrews, who could after this sort deliver his people, was unquestionably superior to all others.

Nebuchadnezzar manifestly was endowed with many great and generous qualities; but he was spoiled by prosperity, while, by the very aggrandizement which exalted his pride, he had been fixed into a position which made it necessary to the Divine glory that he should be brought to, and kept in, the acknowledgment that in all his acts he had been but an instrument in the hands of the God worshipped by one of the nations which had received his yoke, and whose superiority at least, if not his unity, he was required to acknowledge.

In another dream he was forewarned of the consequences of his excessive pride. This dream Daniel unflinchingly interpreted; but whatever effect it might produce was of no long duration. Twelve months after, while contemplating his extensive dominion and the splendor to which he had raised the great city of Babylon, his

---

* This was probably the statue of solid gold, twelve cubits high, which, according to Herodotus, stood in the temple of Belus, until it was taken away by Xerxes. The height mentioned by Daniel, sixty cubits, probably included the pedestal or pillars on which it stood, as otherwise its height would have been disproportionate to its breadth, six cubits.

heart swelled with kingly pride, and he exclaimed, "Is not this great Babylon, which I have built for the capital of the kingdom, by the might of my power, and for the honor of my majesty?" While these words were in his mouth, there fell a voice from heaven, saying, "O king Nebuchadnezzar, to thee it is spoken: The kingdom is departed from thee. And they shall drive thee from men, and thy dwelling shall be with the beasts of the field; they shall make thee to eat grass as oxen, and seven times [years] shall pass over thee, until thou know that the Most High ruleth in the kingdom of men, and giveth it to whomsoever he will." The thing was accomplished that very hour; and in this state he remained until "his hairs were grown like eagles' feathers, and his nails like birds' claws." The meaning of which seems to be that his proud mind was in that instant shattered, and fell into a kind of monomania, which made him fancy himself some animal; in consequence of which it was judged necessary by his physicians to humor his fancy by treating him as such, and by allowing him within certain limits to act as such. The sequel can not be more emphatically told than in his own words, as found in an edict, recounting these circumstances, which he issued on his recovery. "At the end of the days, I, Nebuchadnezzar, lifted up mine eyes unto heaven, and mine understanding returned unto me, and I blessed the Most High, and I praised and honored him that liveth for ever and ever, whose dominion is an everlasting dominion, and his kingdom from generation to generation. And all the inhabitants of the earth are reputed as nothing; and he doeth according to his will in the army of heaven, and among the inhabitants of the earth; and none can stay his hand, or say unto him, What doest thou? At the same time my reason returned; and for the glory of my kingdom, mine honor and brightness returned unto me; and my counsellors and lords sought unto me; and I was established in my kingdom, and excellent majesty was added unto me. Now I, Nebuchadnezzar, praise, and extol, and honor the King of heaven, all whose works are truth, and his ways judgment; and those that walk in pride he is able to abase." This noble acknowledgment demonstrates our former argument, that care was taken by Jehovah to maintain his own honor, and to secure his own great objects, notwithstanding, and indeed *through*, that bondage to which sin had reduced his people.

After a long reign of forty-three years, Nebuchadnezzar died in 561, and was succeeded by his son, Evil-Merodach. A Jewish tradition* reports that this prince behaved so ill, by provoking a rupture with the Medes, during the distraction of his father, that Nebuchadnezzar, on his recovery, threw him into prison; and that he there became acquainted with, and interested in, Jehoiachim, the imprisoned king of Judah. However this may be, it is certain that one of the first acts of his reign was to release Jehoiachim from his long imprisonment of thirty-seven years; and during the remainder of his life he treated him with much distinction and kindness, giving him a place at his court and table above all the other captive kings then in Babylon. As, however, the text implies that he died before his benefactor, who himself survived but three years, the Hebrew king could not long have outlived his release. Evil-Merodach was slain in a battle against the united Medes and Persians, who by this time had become very powerful by their junction and intermarriages. The combined force was on this occasion commanded by young Cyrus, who had already begun to distinguish himself, and who had been appointed to this command by his uncle and father-in-law, Cyaxares—"Darius the Mede" of scripture—king of the Medes. This was in B. C. 558.

Evil-Merodach was succeeded by his son Belshazzar. The *end* only of this monarch's reign is noticed in scripture; but Xenophon† gives instances of his earlier conduct in the throne, of which only a barbarous and jealous tyrant could have been capable. His last and most heinous offence was the profanation of the sacred vessels belonging to the Jerusalem temple, which his illustrious grandfather, and even his incapable father, had respected. Having made a great feast "to a thousand of his lords," he ordered the sacred vessels to be brought, that he and his wassailers might drink wine from them. That there was an intentional insult to the Most High in this act transpires in the narrative: "They praised the gods of gold, silver, brass, iron, and stone; but THE God in whose hand was their breath, and whose were all their ways, they praised or glorified not." Indeed, to appreciate fully this act and its conse-

* Noticed by Jerome on Isaiah xiv.   † Cyrop. l. 4.

quences, it is indispensably necessary that the mind should revert to the operations by which the supremacy of Jehovah was impressed upon Nebuchadnezzar—operations not hid in a corner; and which, together with the public confessions and declarations of this conviction which were extorted from that magnanimous king, must have diffused much formal acquaintance with the name and claims of Jehovah among the Babylonians, with which also the royal family must have been in a peculiar degree familiar, not only through these circumstances, but through Daniel, who had occupied high rank at court in the still recent reign of Nebuchadnezzar, and whose mere presence must constantly have suggested the means to which his advancement was owing. From this it will be seen, that, on the principle of operation which we have indicated in the early part of this chapter, the time was now come for another act whereby Jehovah might vindicate the honor of his own great Name, and enforce his peculiar and exclusive claims to the homage of mankind.

Suddenly a mysterious hand appeared, writing conspicuously upon the wall words of ominous import, but which no one could understand; for, although they were in the vernacular Chaldean language, the character in which they were written was the primitive old Hebrew, which differed totally from the Chaldee; and was the original from which that which is called the Samaritan character was formed. The king himself was greatly agitated, and commanded the instant attendance of the magi and astrologers. They came, but were utterly unable to divine the meaning of the portentous words upon the wall. This increased the terror of the impious king, which was at its height when the queen-mother, or rather grandmother* made her appearance. She soothed the troubled monarch, and reminded him of the services and character of Daniel; indicating him as one " in whom is the spirit of the holy God; and in the days of thy grandfather light, and understanding, and wisdom, like the wisdom of the gods was found in him;" and therefore one who was likely to afford Belshazzar the satisfaction which he sought. It was probably the custom at Babylon (as with respect to the corresponding officer in other oriental courts) for the archimagus to lose his office on the death of the king to whose court he was attached; and that, consequently, Daniel had withdrawn into private life on the death of Nebuchadnezzar. This will explain how the king needed to be reminded of him, and how the prophet was in the first instance absent from among those who were called to interpret the writing on the wall.

Daniel was sent for: and when he appeared, the king repeated what he had heard of him; stated the inability of the magicians to interpret the portentous words; and promised him as the reward of interpretation, that he should be clad in scarlet,† with a chain of gold about his neck, and that he should rank as the third person in the kingdom. The venerable prophet modestly waived the proffered honors and rewards, as having no weight to induce his compliance:—" Thy gifts be to thyself, and give thy rewards to another; nevertheless I will read the writing to the king." But, first, he undauntedly reminded the king of the experience, and resulting convictions of his renowned grandfather—adding, with emphasis, " And thou, his grandson, O Belshazzar, hast not humbled thy heart, although thou knewest all this." He then read the inscription :—

" MENE,   MENE,   TEKEL,   [PERES],   UPHARSIN."
Number,   Number,   Weight,   [Division]   and Divisions,
and proceeded to give the interpretation :—

" Mene, God hath *numbered* thy reign, and
" [Mene], hath *finished* it.‡
" Tekel, Thou art *weighed* in the balance and found wanting.
" Peres, Thy kingdom is *divided*.
" Upharsin, *And* given to the Mede and the Persian [Darius and Cyrus]."

The king heard this terrible sentence: but made no remark further than to command that Daniel should be invested with the promised scarlet robe and golden chain, and that the third rank in the kingdom should be assigned to him.

The sacred historian adds, with great conciseness, " That same night was Belshaz-

---

* So she is called by Josephus, ἡ μαμμη αυτου; indeed, the part she took on this occasion is so probable of no one as of the widow of Nebuchadnezzar.

† It is singular that in Persia *scarlet* is at this day the distinctive color of nobility. A khan, or noble, is known by the scarlet mantle which he wears on occasions of ceremony.

‡ The repetition merely giving emphasis to the signification, indicating its certainty and speedy accomplishment

zar, king of the Chaldeans, slain." *How*, we are not told: but we may collect from Xenophon (Cyrop. lib. vii.) that he was slain through the conspiracy of two nobles, on whom he had inflicted the greatest indignities which men could receive. This was in 553 B. C., in the fifth year of his reign.

He was succeeded by his son, a boy, named Laborosoarchod (Joseph. cont. Apion, i. 20); but as he was put out of the way in less than a year, he is passed over in Ptolemy's Canon, as well as in the sacred history, which relates that, as following the death of Belshazzar, " Darius the Mede took the kingdom." In fact, the family of Nebuchadnezzar being extinct, Cyaxares, or (to give him his scriptural name) Darius, who was brother to the queen-mother, and the next of kin by her side to the crown, had the most obvious right to the vacant throne; and while his power was so great as to overawe all competition, the express indication of him by the prophet in his interpretation of the inscription was calculated to have much weight with all concerned, and indeed with the whole nation.

Daniel, naturally, came into high favor with Darius, to whose accession he had so materially contributed. On making out new appointments of the governors of provinces, the prophet was set over them all: and the king contemplated a still further elevation for him. This excited the dislike and jealousy of the native princes and presidents, who determined to work his ruin. In his administration, his hands were so pure, that no ground of accusation could be found against him. They therefore devised a plan by which Daniel's known and tried fidelity to his religion should work his destruction. They procured from the careless and vain king a decree, that no one should for thirty days offer any prayer or petition to any god or man save the king himself, under pain of being cast into the lion's den. The king at once became painfully conscious of his weak and criminal conduct, when his most trusted servant, Daniel, was accused before him as an open transgressor of this decree, and his punishment demanded. Among the Medes and Persians there was a singular restraint upon despotism—which while at the first view it seemed to give intensity to the exercise of despotic power, really tended to deter the kings from hasty and ill-considered decisions, by compelling them to feel the evil consequences with which they were attended. The king's word was irrevocable law. He could not himself dispense with the consequences of his own acts. Of this Darius was reminded: and he saw at once that he was precluded from interfering in behalf of his friend. It is a beautiful illustration of the great truth, which appears as the main argument of this chapter, namely, that the glory of God was promoted among the heathen by the captivity of his people,— that the king himself was already so well acquainted with the character and power of Jehovah, that he spontaneously rested himself upon the hope, that, although unable himself to deliver him from this well-laid snare, the God whom Daniel served would certainly not suffer him to perish. The prophet was cast into the lion's den; and the mouth thereof was closed with a sealed stone. The king spent the night sleepless and in sorrow. Impelled by his vague hopes, he hastened early in the morning to the cavern, and cried in a doleful voice, " O Daniel, servant of the living God, hath thy God, whom thou servest continually, been able to deliver thee from the lions?" To the unutterable joy and astonishment of the king, the quiet voice of Daniel returned an affirmative answer, assuring the king of his perfect safety. Instantly the cavern was opened, the servant of God drawn forth ; and his accusers were cast in, and immediately destroyed by the savage inmates of the den. This striking interposition induced the king to issue a proclamation, to the same ultimate effect as that which Nebuchadnezzar had issued in a former time. He wrote unto " all peoples, nations, and languages, that dwell in all the earth," charging them to " tremble and fear before the God of Daniel; for he is the God that liveth, and is steadfast for ever, and his kingdom shall not be destroyed, and his dominion shall be even unto the end." It would not be easy to overrate the importance of the diffusion of such truths as these through the length and breadth of the Median empire.

It was the established policy of the Medes and Persians to conciliate the good will of the subject states, by leaving the practical government in the hands of native princes. Darius, therefore, as we may collect from Berosus, appointed Nabonadius, a Babylonian noble, unconnected with the royal family, to be viceroy, or king under him. This appointment was confirmed or continued by Cyrus, when he succeeded to the general empire on the death of his uncle, in B. C. 551.

During the first years of his reign, Cyrus was too much occupied in foreign wars to pay much attention to Babylon; and this gave Nabonadius an opportunity to assert his independence, and to maintain it until the hero was at leisure to call him to account. This was not until B. C. 538, when this great prince marched against Babylon, with the determination to crown his many victories by its reduction. Nabonadius, on his part, seems to have been encouraged by his diviners (Isa. xliv. 25), to repose much confidence in his own resources, and in the stability of the kingdom he had established. He ventured to meet the Persian army on its advance toward the city; but was defeated in a pitched battle, and driven back to abide a siege within the walls of Babylon. Still all was not lost; for not only was the city strongly fortified, but a siege by blockage was likely to be indefinitely protracted, as the town not only possessed immense stores of provisions, but the consumption of them would be greatly lessened by means of the large open spaces within the city, in which all kinds of produce could be raised to a considerable extent. In fact, the siege continued for two years, and Babylon was then only taken by a remarkable stratagem. Cyrus observed that the town lay the most exposed on the side of the river, and therefore he caused a new bed to be dug for its waters; and at an appointed time, by night, the dikes were cut, and the Euphrates rolled its humbled stream into this new channel; and the old one, left dry, offered a free passage to the exulting Persians. Even yet, however, their condition, in the bed of the river, might have been perilous, and a vigilant enemy might have surprised them as in a net; but that night a public festival was celebrated in Babylon, and all there was confusion and drunkenness. From this, as well as from the little reason to apprehend danger on that side, the gates leading from the quays into the city were that night left open, so that an easy and unopposed access was offered to the army of Cyrus, and the king was horror-struck and paralyzed, as successive messengers arrived in haste from the various distant quarters of the city, to inform him that the Persians had entered there, and thus to learn, that, at both extremities at once, great Babylon was taken, B. C. 536.

Daniel was still alive, and there is evidence that Cyrus knew and valued his character. The apocryphal history of Bel and Dragon says that Cyrus conversed much with him, and honored him above all his friends. But we have better evidence in *effects* which, seeing Daniel still lived, may very safely be, in some degree, referred to the instruction and counsel which the now very aged prophet was able to give.

There is an important and most striking prophecy by Isaiah (xliv. 24, to xlv. 6) in which Cyrus is mentioned by name, and his exploits predicted, *more than a century before his birth*. To him it is expressly addressed, and in terms of tenderness and respect, which was never, in any other instance, applied to a heathen—if it be just to apply that name to Cyrus. In this splendid prophecy Jehovah calls Cyrus " my shepherd, who shall perform all my pleasure;" and, " mine anointed." His victories are foretold, and ascribed to Jehovah; and, in a particular manner, the taking of Babylon by him is foreshown, even to the indication of the very peculiar manner in which that conquest was achieved.* And the *object* of all this—of his existence, of

---

* " Thus saith Jehovah of his anointed,
Of Cyrus, whose right hand I hold fast,
That I may subdue nations before him,
And ungird the loins of kings;
That I may open before him the valves,
And the gates shall not be shut;
I myself will march on before thee,
And will make the crooked places straight,
The valves of brass will I break asunder,
And the bars of iron will I hew down.
And I will give to thee the treasures of darkness,
And stores deeply hid in secret places;
That thou mayest know that I, JEHOVAH,
That call thee by name, am the God of Israel
For the sake of Jacob my servant,
And of Israel my chosen one,
I have even called thee by name:
I have surnamed thee, yet Me thou knowest not.
I am JEHOVAH, and there is none else;
There is no God besides me.
I girded thee though thou hast not known me;
That they may know, from the rising of the sun,
And from the west, that there is none beside me.
I am JEHOVAH. and there is none else:
I form the light, and create darkness,
I make peace, and create evil
I, JEHOVAH, do all these things."

his acts, and even of this prophecy concerning him and them—is declared, with marked emphasis, to be, that he may be in a condition to restore the captivity of Judah, and that such convictions might be wrought in him as might incline to fulfil this his vocation, and to become acquainted with the supreme and sole power of Jehovah. And the careful reader will not fail to note in this sublime address to one destined to live in a future generation, not only a clear assertion of the unity of God, and his universal power and providence, but a distinct blow at the peculiar superstition of Cyrus and his people—which consisted in the adoration of two principles—the good and evil, represented by light and darkness. Hence the emphasis of—

> "I form the light, and create darkness;
> I make peace, and create evil."

We can easily imagine the impression which the perusal of these prophecies would make upon the ingenuous mind of this great man, accompanied by the explanations which Daniel could pour into his willing ears, and with the further intimation, collected from the prophecies of Jeremiah respecting the seventy years of the captivity, that the time of the restoration was then arrived, and himself the long pre-determined instrument of giving effect to the Divine intention. His consciousness of all this is evinced in the proclamation, which he issued the same year that Babylon was taken. This proclamation is to be regarded as the final acknowledgment from the conquering foreign kings of the supremacy of Jehovah, and it was most interesting from the distinctness with which this acknowledgment is conveyed—" Thus saith Cyrus king of Persia—JEHOVAH, the God of the heavens, hath given me all the kingdoms of the earth; and he hath charged me to build for himself a temple in Jerusalem, which is in Judah." In this he manifestly alludes to the charge conveyed in the prophecy—

> "Who [JEHOVAH] saith of Cyrus, He is my shepherd!
> And he shall perform all my pleasures;
> Even saying to Jerusalem, Thou shalt be built;
> To the temple, Thy foundation shall be laid."

Accordingly, the proclamation proceeded not only to grant free permission for such of the seed of Abraham as thought proper to return to their own land, but also commanded the authorities of the places in which they lived to afford every facility to their remigration.

Before accompanying them on their return, it may be well to contemplate the results of the circumstances which have been related, as affecting the position of the captive Jews *during* the period through which we have passed.

There is certainly nothing to suggest that their condition was one of abject wretchedness. This is in some degree shown by the high offices enjoyed by Daniel and his three friends; and by the distinction conferred upon King Jehoiachin by Evil-Merodach. He not only enjoyed the first rank over all the kings then at Babylon, but ate at the table of the monarch, and received allowances corresponding to his rank. While these circumstances of honor must have reflected a degree of dignity on the exiles, sufficient to protect them from being ill-treated or despised; we see that there was always some person of their nation high in favor and influence at court, able to protect them from wrong, and probably to secure for them important and peculiar privileges. They, most likely, came to be considered as respectable colonists, enjoying the peculiar protection of the sovereign. Although Jehoiachin did not long survive his release from prison, his son Salathiel, and his grandson Zerubbabel undoubtedly partook in and succeeded to the respect which he received. If the story in the apocryphal book of Esdras (1 Esd. iii., iv.) of the discussion before Darius, in which Zerubbabel won the prize, be a mere fiction, it is still at least probable that the young prince, although he held no office, had free access to the court; which privilege must have afforded him many opportunities of alleviating the condition of his countrymen. It is even not improbable that (as is implied in the apocryphal story of Susannah, and as the tradition of the Jews affirm) the exiles had magistrates and a prince from their own number. Jehoiachin, and after him Salathiel and Zerubbabel, might have been regarded as their princes, in the same manner as Jozadak and Jeshua were as their high-priests.

At the same time it can not be denied that their humiliation, as a people punished by their God, was always extremely painful, and frequently drew on them expressions of contempt. The peculiarities of their religion afforded many opportunities for the ridicule and scorn of the Babylonians and Chaldeans,—a striking example of which is given in the profanation of the sacred vessels by Belshazzar. By such insults they were made to feel so much the more sensibly the loss of their houses, their gardens, and fruitful fields; the leaving of their capital and temple, and the cessation of the public solemnities of their religion. (See Jahn, theil ii. band 1, sect. 45, ' Zustand der Hebraer in dem Exilium.)

———

CHAPTER XXIII.

THE RESTORATION.

WE consider the great argument of the preceding chapter to have been, that the honor of Jehovah was as adequately maintained, and that the knowledge of his claim to be the supreme and *only* God, to have been even more diffused by the destitution of the Hebrews, than it would even have been by their continuance in their own land. It also appears very clearly to us, that by a succession of such operations as those which elicited the public acknowledgments of Nebuchadnezzar, Darius and Cyrus, and by acts which could not but be known to many nations, these objects might have been promoted as well without as by the restoration of the Hebrew people to their own land, and the re-establishment of the temple service. It may then be asked, why it was expedient that Judah should be at all restored; and, being restored, why Israel—the ten tribes—were not? These interesting questions we can not discuss in the extent which they deserve; but we may suggest, that since, by immutable promises, the privilege had been secured to the seed of Abraham of upholding the standard of divine truth in the world, until " the fulness of times," and since the nationality of Judah, *until then*, had been anciently secured by the guarantee of the Lord's promise,— it was necessary that a restricted restoration, after punishment and correction, should for these purposes take place. This was all the more necessary, as it was from Judah and from the royal house of David that, as was well known, *he* was to spring who was to enlighten and redeem the world, and to bring in that new creation for which the moral universe groaned as the times advanced to their completion. For his identity, as the ransomer promised of old, it was necessary that the dying struggles of the Hebrew nationality should not be yet permitted to terminate. And further, inasmuch as the bondage of the Hebrews east of the Euphrates, had tended in no small degree to advance in that quarter the knowledge of the great preparatory principles of which the Jews were the commissioned conservators, it remained for the west to be in like manner allowed to catch such glimmerings of light, as might make the nations impatient of their blindness, and prepare them to hail with gladness the future " day-spring from on high." And this was, in fact, accomplished by the intercourse of the Hebrews with the western nations—Egypt, Syria, Asia-Minor, Greece, Rome—in subjection, in conflicts, or in commerce.

That Judah was preferred to this vocation, and that the ten tribes were not nationally or formally restored, must be accounted for by the further development of a consideration to which the reader's attention was called in the preceding chapter. The political sins of Judah were there traced to the disposition to lean rather upon men than upon institutions. The sin of Israel was even greater, and merited greater severity of punishment. *There*, not only was the same disposition exhibited, but the institutions themselves were corrupted, alienated, tortured from the objects for which they were expressly framed, and, with most culpable ingenuity, made subservient to the very circumstances against which they were designed to operate. In Judah, the building of God was indeed often neglected, often allowed to run to ruin; but it was not, as in Israel, made the abiding habitation of unclean and evil things. In Judah, a good king could purge out abuses and correct evils; but in Israel the tampering with institutions was so effective, that the best kings were unable to lay an improving finger on them. For these things Israel was thrown loose from the mercies of God, much sooner than Judah; and the evil had been so heinous and deeply rooted, that no promise or hope of restoration was held forth, nor did any take place.

By the attention which, through the captivity and consequent dispersion of the Jews among what was then (if we except Egypt) the most civilized nation of the world, had been directed to the majesty and providence of Jehovah, we consider that a very important part of the mission confided to the Hebrews was accomplished; for an impression was made, the effects of which may without difficulty be traced to the time of Christ, and, therefore, we are thus brought to a sort of *end* in the national history of the Hebrew people. Undoubtedly, the real fall of Jerusalem was that which was wrought by the hand of Nebuchadnezzar; the real destruction was that which the Assyrians worked in the north, and the Babylonians in the south; and the real dispersion of the race was that which took place in consequence of the Assyrian and Babylonian captivities. A remnant only was preserved, as necessary for the remaining objects which have just been indicated; and it is the history of that remnant which forms the subject of the present chapters.

It is unquestionable that this remnant was highly fitted for its vocation. The large mass of the Israelites were natives of the land of their exile, in which they were for the most part so comfortably situated that only those whose religious zeal and sentiments were above the average warmth, would be likely, or did, encounter the dangers of the desert and the inconveniences and anxieties of an unsettled country. The circumstances of the remigration were in fact such as to attract only those who were in the soundest state of moral health. They were also cured of all danger of idolatry, and of all disposition to make light of their own institutions. That the Hebrews as a body profited largely by the correction which they had received, is unquestionable—so largely indeed that under temptations as great as any to which they had in former times yielded, idolatry was ever after their abhorrence. And indeed if, during the period of the captivity, the proudest heathen were made so seriously attentive to the God of Israel, much more were the Hebrews likely to be awakened by the same events to be true to their own God. On this point we copy the remarks of Professor Jahn:—

"Among the Hebrews who, agreeably to the sanctions of the law, were punished for idolatry by total banishment from their native land, there were certainly many who did not worship idols; and probably not a few, in consequence of this national judgment, so often predicted, were brought to reflect on and to abhor the superstition which had been the cause of so great a calamity. Others, not wholly relinquishing idolatry, still retained a reverence for Jehovah. They never, like other transplanted nations, intermingled with the people among whom they were settled, but continued a peculiar race. There were doubtless individual exceptions; but the nation as such remained distinct. The intermingling with pagans, and that entire extinction of the Hebrews as a peculiar people which must have resulted from it, was promoted by the rite of circumcision, by the prohibition of many kinds of food allowed among other nations, by ceremonial impurities, and by various other institutions, designed to segregate and consequently to preserve the nation. These usages had by time become a second nature, so that any intimate connexion with Gentiles was a matter of considerable difficulty. The ancient favors of Jehovah, the miraculous deliverances which he had vouchsafed exclusively to them, and the promises he had given them for futurity, were not easily forgotten. The fulfilment of so many prophecies respecting the fall of the Assyrian empire and of the city of Nineveh, respecting the Babylonian captivity and the destruction of Jerusalem, must have raised Jehovah in their eyes far above all idols; and the very punishment they were then suffering was well calculated to awaken reflection, and thus become a bitter but powerful antidote to their propensity to idolatry. Many Israelites, therefore, in Assyria and Media (as the book of Tobit testifies) persisted in the sincere worship of Jehovah; neither could the Jews in Babylon, and those by the river Chebar, fall easily into idolatry, while such men as Ezekiel and Daniel were constantly and earnestly reminding them of the God whom they were bound to serve.

"The prophecies of Ezekiel, relating for the most part to events near at hand, were accomplished before the eyes of the unbelieving exiles; and every fulfilment was a new proof that Jehovah, the author of these predictions, was the God and ruler of the world. Thus there were repeated opportunities to remind this superstitious people of Jehovah their God. The remarkable prophecy respecting the conquest and destruction of the powerful city Tyre, which was so speedily accomplished, is particularly worthy of notice. By such striking accomplishments of the prophecies respecting occurrences near at hand, the belief of predictions of more distant events was strengthened, and the eyes of the Hebrews were eagerly directed toward the future."

Thus, and through the deliverance which Jehovah wrought in behalf of his persecuted servants,—and through the acknowledgments which were extorted from the
pagan monarchs under whose yoke the necks of Israel and Judah were placed,—" God
pursued them (so to speak) with the efficacious dealings of his providence, with miracles and prophecies, in order to compel them to preserve the true religion, and to
place them in a situation in which it would hardly be possible for them to exchange
the worship of the creator and governor of the world for the worship of idols.   By
the prophet Ezekiel (Ezek. xx. 32-44), Jehovah declares in so many words that even
if the Hebrews desired to become united with the heathen, it should not be done; and
that he would himself find means effectually to prevent the execution of such a design" (Jahn, ii. 1, sect. 53, Ruckker der zehen Stamme).

That the restoration to Palestine, which now took place, is, at least primarily, that
of which the prophets delivered such glowing predictions, very few who carefully examine the subject will find reason to doubt.   The more closely the matter is examined,
the more clearly the details of the prophecy will be found to agree with *this* fulfilment.
We are quite aware that the large terms and forcible expressions employed by the
prophets have led all the Jews and many Christians into the expectation of a more
brilliant and complete restoration than on this occasion took place.   Our undertaking
is however to record past events rather than to undertake the development of prophecies which may be deemed unfulfilled.   That these prophecies have a further
meaning beyond the literal and primary purport, we take to be evinced not only by the
glowing language employed, but by the present condition of the Hebrew nation, "like
a column left standing amid the wreck of worlds and the ruins of nature" (' Trans. of
the Parisian Sanhedrim,' p. 68, 1807), in which they manifestly remain awaiting destinies yet to come; but that these destinies include the restoration and independent
and happy settlement of the nation in Palestine, we hold to be considerably less certain *and less important* than has of late years been made to appear.

Now, by the decree of Cyrus, the mountains were made low and the valleys filled
for the return of the Hebrews to their own land.   But seeing that only the two tribes
of Judah and Benjamin—conventionally regarded as one tribe—formally returned to
Palestine, it becomes an interesting question, What became of the other ten tribes?

As the invitation of Cyrus was directed to all the people of Jehovah, and proclaimed throughout his empire, there is every reason to conclude that not a few of
the ten tribes returned to Palestine.   Those who supposed they could improve their
condition by removing, would attach themselves here and there to a caravan of merchants, and proceed to the land of their fathers.   But as they arrived one after another,
and in small companies, their return is not particularly noticed in a history so concise.   There might even have been many Israelites in the first great caravan under
Zerubbabel; but, however this may be, it is highly probable that the Israelites returned in considerable numbers, as soon as they heard of the settlement of the prosperity of their brethren in Palestine.   Most of these arrivals were probably subsequent to the close of the Old Testament canonical history, and when the restored
nation had acquired a somewhat settled form.   But whether their return were early
or late, it is certain that at least a portion of them did return, for the history of later
periods mentions Israelites as settled in Galilee and Peræa (1 Mac. v. 9-24) long
before the time of Christ.   But connecting themselves with the tribe of Judah, they
finally lost the name of Israelites, and all Hebrews were indiscriminately designated
as Jews.

But since many of the tribe of Judah chose to remain in the land of their exile, it
is reasonable to suppose that still greater numbers of the Israelites who had lived in
those countries 200 years longer, would feel little inclination to exchange the comforts
they there enjoyed for the uncertain advantages of Palestine.   But as the jealousy
between Judah and Israel had now ceased, according to the predictions of the prophets, those Israelites also who remained in exile joined themselves to the tribe of
Judah, which was in the possession of the temple, and, consequently, they too received the denomination of Jews.

On these grounds Professor Jahn conceives that all questions and investigations for
the purpose of ascertaining what has become of the ten tribes, and whether it is
likely they will ever be discovered, are superfluous and idle.   We are not ourselves
quite so clear that this is the case.   We grant indeed that there is no good reason
for expecting to find the remnant of the ten tribes *as distinct* from the remnant of

Judah; but that traces of the Hebrews of *both* captivities, without distinction of tribes, may be found in the countries in which they were so long located, there is much reason to conclude. We say *in* those countries, for the reasons which prevented them from returning to Palestine were as operative in preventing their migration in any other direction. Indeed, while the second temple stood, one would expect that such of them as were disposed to migrate at all, would return to the land of their fathers, as many of them, no doubt, did. But, apart from this preference, there was much reason for their remaining in Media; for the empire which comprehended that country, continued long to be possessed by a nation which was quite able to protect them and make their homes secure; while the religion which it professed was more in agreement with that of Moses, and less revolting to the peculiar notions of the Hebrews, than any other they could find in the world. It is certain also, that for a long course of ages a large remnant of the captivity of Judah remained in Babylonia, and this so much composed of the *elite* of the nation, as to secure the respect of the Jews who returned to Palestine and multiplied there—all traces of which estimation of the Babylonian Jews is not even at this day wholly obliterated; and this fact would suggest the probability of a similar local fixity of the ten tribes in Media and Assyria. Indeed the probability is the greater, from the fact that in those countries, as history proves, they would be much less liable to be disturbed by wars and troubles than the Jews of Babylonia. It is probably under such a class of impressions, that the Jews themselves have generally been disposed to look for traces of the ten tribes in that direction. Nor, as it would appear, has the search been quite abortive.

In the twelfth century of Christ, the district referred to at page 367 was visited by the Spanish Jew, Benjamin of Tudela. After speaking of large congregations of Jews in this quarter, he comes to Amaria [which Major Rawlinson regards as the same as Halah, now Holwan], where he found 25,000 Jews. "This congregation forms part of those," says Rabbi Benjamin, "who live in the mountains of Chaphton, which amount to more than 100, extending to the frontiers of Media. These Jews are descendants of those who were originally led into captivity by King Shalmaneser. They speak the Syriac language, and among them are many excellent talmudic scholars."[*] Benjamin then gives the history of the false Messiah, David El Roy, who sprang from the city of Amaria, and whose romantic history has lately been made familiar to the English public.

Recently, the Rabbi David D'Beth Hillel has much obscure and dispersed talk about the fragments of the tribes which he found in the same quarter. But the following statement by Major Rawlinson will give more satisfaction to the reader:—

"If the Samaritan captives can be supposed to have retained to the present day any distinct individuality of character, perhaps the Kalhurs, who are believed to have inhabited from the remotest antiquity those regions around Mount Zagros, preserve in their name the title of Calah [Halah]. They state themselves to be descended from Roham, or Nebuchadnezzar, the conqueror of the Jews,—perhaps an obscure tradition of their real origin. They have many Jewish names among them, and, above all, their general physiognomy is strongly indicative of an Israelitish descent. The Iliyat of this tribe now mostly profess Mohammedanism; but a part of them, together with the Gurans, who acknowledge themselves to be an offset of the Kalhurs, and most of the other tribes of the neighborhood, are still of the 'Ali-Ilahi persuasion—a faith which bears evident marks of Judaism, singularly amalgamated with Sabæan, Christian, and Mohammedan legends. The tomb of Baba Yadgar, in the pass of Zardah, is regarded as their holy place; and this, at the time of the Arab invasion of Persia, was regarded as the abode of Elias. The 'Ali-Ilahis believe in a series of successive incarnations of the godhead, amounting to a thousand and one. Benjamin, Moses, Elias, David, Jesus Christ, Ali, and his tutor Salman, a joint development, the Imam Husein, and the Haf-tan (the seven bodies), are considered the chief of these incarnations. The Haf-tan were seven Pirs, or spiritual guides, who lived in the early ages of Islam, and each, worshipped as the Deity, is an object of adoration in some particular part of Kurdistan—Baba Yadgar was one of these. The whole of the incarnations were thus regarded as one and the same person, the bodily form of the Divine manifestation being alone changed; but the most perfect development is supposed to have taken place in the persons of Benjamin, David, and

* The Itinerary of Rabbi Benjamin of Tudela. Translated and edited by A. Asher. Berlin, 1840.

Ali." Referring to the passage already adduced from Rabbi Benjamin, the major notices that he appears to have considered the whole of these 'Ali-Ilahis as Jews, and remarks, "It is possible that in his time their religion was less corrupted."[*]

Abandoning this subject for the present, we may now be allowed to return to the historical narrative.

All obstacles being removed, and every facility afforded, Zerubbabel, the grandson of King Jehoiachim, and Jeshua, a grandson of the high-priest Jozadak, with ten of the principal elders, prepared themselves for the journey home. The number of the remnant who joined these heads of the nation was, in round numbers, 50,000, including 7,337 male and female servants.[†] This large body was composed chiefly, it would seem, of members of the tribes of Judah, Benjamin, and Levi, although the comparatively high number of the remigrants supports the probability that a considerable proportion were of the ten tribes. The prophet Daniel, who must at this time have been about ninety years old, remained at the court of Cyrus, where he could probably render much more service to his nation than by returning to Palestine.

Those who were to return assembled from all quarters at an appointed place, according to the usual method of collecting a caravan, furnished with provisions and other things necessary for the journey. Their camels, horses, and beasts of burden, amounted to eight thousand one hundred and thirty-six. Zerubbabel, on whom devolved the serious responsibility of directing this immense caravan, received from Cyrus the sacred vessels of the temple, and was intrusted with the very large contributions toward the rebuilding of the sacred edifice made by those of the Hebrew race who chose to remain behind. Zerubbabel was not only appointed leader or sheikh of the caravan, but the office of governor of Judea was intrusted to him. This appointment may probably be attributed not more to the circumstance which inclined Cyrus to show peculiar favor to the nation, than to the general policy of the Persian kings in leaving the governments of conquered provinces to native governors, whenever this could be done with safety. Several months were consumed in preparations for the journey; and encumbered as they were with baggage and young children, and therefore obliged to travel slowly, the journey itself occupied four months.

The "seventy years" of the captivity were completed by the time they arrived; and they were now to settle in their own land, governed by their own laws, and forming a distinct commonwealth. The Persian sovereignty was not a calamity, but a benefit, from the protection and security which it gave to a colony as yet too weak for independence.

The people dispersed themselves on their arrival in search of their native cities and of necessaries for their families. But in the following month, being the seventh of the Jewish year, they all assembled at Jerusalem to celebrate the feast of tabernacles. On this occasion an altar was reared upon the ruins of the temple, and the customary sacrifices were offered; and on this altar the daily morning and evening sacrifices were afterward continued.

In the second month of the second year of their return, the people again assembled at Jerusalem, to lay the foundation of the temple, the preparations for which, through the voluntary contributions of the people and the elders, were now completed. This was a most joyful occasion to all but the old people; and very loud were the shouts of gladness which were raised: but, loud as were the sounds of rejoicing, they were neutralized by the wailings of the old people, who had seen "the holy and beautiful house" in which their fathers praised Jehovah; and who wept bitterly and loudly at the comparison: for they could perceive that the edifice would neither be so large, so magnificent, nor so richly ornamented as the temple of Solomon. It is true, as appears from the record found at Ecbatana in the time of Darius Hystaspes, that Cyrus had directed that the temple should be twice as large as that of Solomon, and that the expense should be defrayed from the royal treasury. But either the proper officers had neglected to give effect to these orders, or the Jews were backward to avail themselves of the full extent of the monarch's bounty, lest they should awaken the envy of the worshippers of Ormuzd, and expose themselves to their persecutions. From whatever cause, it is certain that they did not build the temple so large as the decree of Cyrus allowed. (Ezra iv. 1–5.)

* 'Geographical Journal,' vol. ix. part 1, p. 26.
† The number of the congregation was 42,680, which, with 7,337 servants, makes 49,697.

The Persian governors of Syria and Palestine offered no opposition to the settle ment of the Jews in their own country or to their proceedings there. No doubt, therefore, orders corresponding to the tenor of the decree under which the restora tion took place, had been forwarded to them. This indeed is stated by Josephus; although such orders, being sent direct to the Persian magistrates, are not noticed by Ezra. But opposition, persevering and venomous, came from another and probably unexpected quarter. This was from the colonists whom the Assyrian kings had planted in the land of Israel, and who had intermarried with the remaining Israelites, and now formed one people with them under the name of Samaritans. It does not appear that the Samaritans were, at this time, completely purged of the idolatries which their fathers had brought from foreign lands; yet the measures employed to enlighten them with the knowledge of the true God seem gradually to have produced a considerable effect. The return of the Jews from their seventy years' captivity so clearly evinced the over-ruling providence of Jehovah, that the Samaritans were extremely desirous to join in rebuilding his temple and celebrating his worship: "They said unto the chief of the fathers, 'Let us build with you; for we seek your God, as ye do; and we have done sacrifice to him since the days of Esarhaddon, king of Assyria, who brought us up hither.'" This proposal was steadily rejected by the Jews: and, whatever their motives may have been, it is easy to discern important reasons in consequence of which this rejection appears to have been subservient to the purposes of the Divine economy.[*]

Finding they could not prevail, the Samaritans used every means in their power to thwart the enterprise. Their influence at the Persian court appears to have been considerable, owing perhaps, as Josephus suggests, to their claiming to be of Median and Persian origin. Through this influence they managed, during the latter days of Cyrus, who was either absent in foreign wars or not at leisure to attend to such pro vincial matters, to oppose such obstacles to the progress of the work that the people got disheartened, and discontinued the building. This discouragement continued during the succeeding reigns of Cambyses and of Smerdis the magian; nor was the work resumed until the second year of Darius Hystaspes.

The proceedings of the Samaritans in this matter naturally excited the enmity of the Jews; and thus was laid the foundation of the hatred between the two nations, which new provocations continually increased, until, at last, all friendly intercourse between them was entirely discontinued.

Cyrus died seven years after the restoration of the Jews. The reigns of Cam byses his son, and of the usurping magian Smerdis (seven months), occupied together eight years. Darius Hystaspes, one of the seven nobles who slew the intrusive magian, was elected king, B. C. 521.

At Jerusalem, the people had by this time lost their zeal in a work which had been so much obstructed, and, counting from the destruction of the former temple instead of from the commencement of the captivity, they argued that the time for the rebuild ing of the sacred edifice had not yet arrived. But while they erected fine buildings for their own use, and bestowed much expense and labor on the mere ornamental parts of their own dwellings, this was obviously a mere pretence, and provoked the severe reproaches of the prophet Haggai, who attributed to this neglect the drought, and consequent failure of crops, which had then occurred; and was authorized to promise the blessings of plenty from the time they should recommence the building of the temple. And, to neutralize the discouragements arising from the detractive or sorrowful comparisons of the old men who had seen the temple of Solomon, he was commissioned to deliver the celebrated prophecy:—

> "Thus saith the Lord of hosts:
> Yet once more, and in a little while,
> And I will shake the heavens and the earth,
> And the sea and the dry land;

[*] "The intermixture of the Samaritans with the Jews might have rendered the accomplishment of the prophecies concerning the family and birth of the Messiah less clear—might have reintroduced idolatry among the restored Jews, now completely abhorrent from it, and in various ways defeated the grand objects of Providence in selecting and preserving a peculiar people. In consequence of this rejection and the alienation it produced, the Jews probably became more vigilant in preserving the strictness, and the Samaritans more jealous in emulating the purity, of the Mosaic ritual. They became hostile, and there fore unsuspected guardians and vouchers of the integrity of the sacred text, particularly of the Penta teuch. And while the Jews in general, blinded by their national prejudices, could see in the promised Messiah only a national and temporal deliverer, the Samaritans appear to have judged of his pretensions with more justice and success."—(Dean Graves's "Lectures on the Pentateuch," p. 347. 5th Ed. 1839.

> And I will shake all the nations,
> And the Desire of all nations shall come,
> And I will fill this house with glory, saith the Lord of hosts.
> The silver is mine, and the gold is mine, saith the Lord of hosts.
> The glory of this latter house shall be greater than of the former, saith the Lord of hosts.
> And in this place will I give peace, saith the Lord of hosts."—Hag. ii. 6–9.

The prophecies of Zechariah tended to the same objects as those of Haggai; and in consequence of their forcible representations, the building of the temple was resumed with rekindled zeal. To this resumption of the work, after so long a suspension, the Samaritans succeeded in drawing the attention of Tatnai, the Persian general-governor of Syria, who, being a man of impartial justice, determined to go himself to Jerusalem to investigate the matter. He there demanded the authority of the Jewish chiefs for their operations, and was referred by them to the edict of Cyrus. Tatnai sent a clear and rigidly unbiased report of the matter to the king, and did not deem it necessary to direct the present suspension of the work. The reference to the Persian court could not have been made under more favorable circumstances; for Darius was of a mild and just character; and, still more, was a devoted admirer of Cyrus, and disposed to pay the highest respect to his acts and intentions.* The king, on receiving the report of Tatnai, directed a search to be made among the archives of the kingdom. It was naturally sought at first among the records kept in the treasure house at Babylon. It was not found there; but a roll containing the edict was ultimately discovered in the record chamber of the palace at Achmetha (Ecbatana). It directed not only that the temple should be rebuilt, and of larger dimensions than before, but that the expenses should be defrayed out of the royal treasury. The king directed a copy of this edict to be-forwarded to Tatnai, together with a letter, in which he was enjoined not to obstruct the building, but zealously to forward it, to defray the expenses out of the royal revenues accruing within his government, and also to furnish the priests with such animals as were necessary for the sacrifices, with wheat, salt, wine, and oil, from day to day, for the divine service. "That they may offer sacrifices of a sweet savor to the God of heaven, and pray for the life of the king and of his sons." The letter concluded with an order (apparently levelled at the Samaritans), that whosoever obstructed the execution of the decree should be hanged, and their houses demolished: and an imprecation was added on all kings and people who should attempt to destroy the house of God.

This transaction gives a very favorable idea of the good order and efficient administration of the Persian government; while the concluding direction affords another and very important illustration of the honor which Jehovah had obtained for his name among the heathen through the eastward dispersion of the Hebrews. Indeed, the edict of Cyrus, which was on this occasion brought to light, contained such a declaration of reverence for, and dependance on, Jehovah, as alone could not but have had great weight upon the mind of Darius. It may be remarked, indeed, that Darius himself was a disciple and supporter of Zoroaster, the reformer of the magian religion, who is supposed to have profited largely by his intercourse with the Hebrew captives and prophets in Babylon.

Under these favoring auspices, the work proceeded with renewed spirit; and four years after, being the sixth of Darius (B. C. 516), the temple was completed. It was dedicated with great solemnity, of which there has ever since been an annual commemoration in "The Feast of Dedication." In the following month the Passover was celebrated in a regular and solemn manner, for the first time since the restoration. The temple service was then re-established as before the Captivity; Jeshua, the high-priest, encouraging the other priests and the Levites by his example to attend to their peculiar duties.

The Jews appear to have been undisturbed during the remainder of the thirty-six years in which Darius reigned. It is possible, indeed, that some difficulty arose in

---

* Hystaspes, the father of Darius, was high in the confidence and favor of Cyrus, and he (and very probably his son) could not but have known so eminent a person as Daniel when at the court of Susa. Indeed, the wisdom of Daniel appears to have been a proverb (Ezekiel xxviii. 3). It is remarkable that Hystaspes ultimately succeeded (under his son) to the very office of archimagus, or master of the magians, which Daniel had formerly occupied.

† The cut (page 383) actually represents the library at Constantinople, but it is applicable to the present subjects, as showing the manner in which records, books, &c., are (and probably were anciently) kept by the orientals.

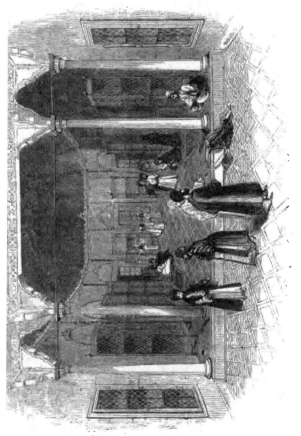

Record Chamber.

the latter years of that reign from their relation to the Persian empire. Darius, whose whole reign was occupied in foreign and generally successful war, had then extended his operations westward. After the Persians had lost the battle of Marathon in B. C. 490, Darius made immense preparations for renewing the war, which kept all Asia in a ferment for three years: in the fourth Egypt revolted, which occasioned the division of the army into two, one to act against Greece and the other against Egypt. But just as all preparations were completed, Darius died, B. C. 485. Now, as the rendez-vous of the army in this expedition against Egypt was in the neighborhood of the Hebrew territory, it is in every way likely that the Jews were obliged to participate in its operations; or it is possible that they obtained an exemption from personal service on condition of supplying the army with provisions.

Xerxes completed the intentions of his father as to Egypt, which he succeeded in again bringing under the Persian yoke. His subsequent gigantic plans and operations against Greece, however important, claim no notice in this place. As the resources of the empire were on this occasion taxed to the uttermost, there is no reason to suppose that the Jews were able to avoid contributing toward this vast undertaking, either by their property or personal service, or by both. At the commencement of his reign the Samaritans made some attempt to prejudice him against the inhabitants of Judah and Jerusalem. But the king confirmed in every particular the grants made by his father. Xerxes is the Ahasuerus of Ezra iv. 6. (See also Joseph. Antiq., xi. 4, 8; xi. 5. 1.)

He was succeeded in B. C. 464 by his son Artaxerxes Longimanus, whose protract-ed reign was replete with incidents most important and interesting to the Jews. At the beginning of it they began regularly to rebuild Jerusalem, and to surround it by a wall. But they were stopped in their work by an order from the king, in conse-quence of a letter of complaint from the principal Samaritan officers, who described Jerusalem, truly enough, as " a rebellious and bad city;" and warned him that if the city were rebuilt and fortified, the inhabitants were sure to prove seditious as in for-mer times, and would be likely to raise up troubles, and endanger the Persian do-minion in that quarter. They appealed to the archives of the empire to prove that the town had been demolished and dismantled on account of its rebellion and sedi-tions. The records were accordingly consulted, and the fact being found as thus stated, the king delayed not to send a letter authorizing the Samaritan chiefs to stop the work until further orders. This they forthwith did, and with no gentle hand.* This opposition of the Samaritans was remarkably well-timed, and hence, in all prob-ability, its success. Immediately on the death of Xerxes, Egypt had again revolted from the Persian yoke (Diod. lib. iii.); the Samaritans therefore could not have chosen a fitter opportunity to carry their point, or a stronger argument to work upon the king's fears, than the danger that might result from allowing the Jews to fortify their city. For, strengthen and increased as they were in the seventy-two years since their return, it might be apprehended that, as in former times, they would not only them-selves follow the example of Egypt by refusing to pay tribute, but that they might offer serious obstruction to the Persian army to be employed in the reduction of Egypt, in going or returning through Palestine.

After he had subdued all his domestic foes and competitors for the crown, Artax-erxes, in the third year of his reign, celebrated at Susa the general and protracted re-joicing which usually attended the settlement of a new king on the throne. At a public banquet, the king, in his cups probably, had the folly to send for the queen, Vashti, that the banqueters might be witnesses of her extreme beauty. An order so repugnant to the customs of women, the queen was under the necessity of disobey-ing, and disobedience, whatever were the cause, could not be allowed to pass un-punished. All the sages of Persia held that, to prevent the evil effects of this exam-ple, it was necessary that the queen should be deposed, and that the act of deposi-tion should be accompanied by a decree *that every man should bear rule in his own house!* So Vashti was deposed; and, ultimately, a beautiful Jewish damsel named Esther was promoted to her place, in the fourth year of Artaxerxes.

The king had now leisure to turn his attention to Egypt, and in the course of the expedition to bring that country back to its subjection, which was happily concluded

* Ezra iv. 6-23. The whole passage is referred to this reign in the text (after Howe and Hales), under the impression that where it stands in the original narrative it is an historical anticipation, and not in its proper chronological place.

An Encampment.

Tartar or Turkish Courier.

in the sixth year of his reign. He had probably sufficient opportunity to become acquainted with the present character and position of the Jews, and with the claims to his favor which they derived from the edicts of Cyrus and Darius. At all events, in the seventh year of his reign, he indicated his knowledge of those edicts and his willingness to enforce them, by authorizing " Ezra the priest, and a scribe of the Law of the God of Heaven" to proceed to Jerusalem " to beautify the house of Jehovah," and to establish the ecclesiastical and civil institutions with greater firmness and order than they had yet acquired. His powers were very large. He was commissioned to appoint judges, superior and inferior, to rectify abuses, to enforce the observance of the law, to punish the refractory with fines, imprisonment, banishment, or even with death, according to the degree of their offences. He was also permitted to make a collection for the service of the temple among those Hebrews who chose to remain in the land of their exile; and the king and his council not only largely contributed toward the same object, but the ministers of the royal revenues west of the Euphrates were charged to furnish Ezra with whatever (within certain limits) of silver, corn, wine, oil and salt (without limit) which he might require for the service of the temple. Such persons of the Hebrew race as thought proper to return with Ezra to their own land, were permitted and invited to do so. From the whole tenor of this commission it is evident that the God of the Hebrews was still held in high respect at the Persian court; and, by a new concession, all his ministers, even to the lowest *nethinim*, were exempted from tribute, and thus put on an equality with the Persians and the Medes. For these favors some writers would assign " the solicitations of Esther" as the motive. But it is not clear that the king knew she was a Jewess. It was certainly perfectly competent for Esther to make the king better acquainted with the claims of the God she served and of the people to whom she belonged; nor should she be blamed for employing, or the king for receiving, such influence. But there were other and adequate means through which " the great king" might acquire this knowledge, at which he certainly arrived. To the series of splendid acknowledgments extracted from these illustrious monarchs through the captivity and vassalage of the Jews, let us add that of Artaxerxes, whose commission to Ezra orders: " Whatsoever is commanded by THE GOD OF HEAVEN let it be diligently done for the house of THE GOD OF HEAVEN; *lest there be wrath* [from Him] against the realm of the king and his sons."

It is worthy of remark however, that the decree of Artaxerxes was limited to the same object—the temple—as the edicts of former kings; and that no mention is made of the walls, from which it appears that the king was not yet prepared to concede that Jerusalem should be fortified.

The rendezvous of the party gathering for this second caravan was by the river Ahava, where the number assembled was found to consist of sixty "houses," containing one thousand seven hundred and fifty-four (adult ?) males, so that, with women and children, there were probably not less than six thousand persons. When Ezra surveyed this party it was with much chagrin that he found not one of the tribe of Levi among them, notwithstanding the exemption from tribute; and it was not without difficulty that two families of priests were induced to join the emigrants.

Considering the treasure with which they were charged, and the number of helpless women and children of the party, there was much ground to apprehend danger from the Arabs infesting the desert over which the caravan must pass, and who then, as now, were wont to assault, or at least to levy large contributions on caravans too weak or too timid to resist them. Ezra therefore appointed a special season for fasting and prayer beside the river, that they might, as it were, throw themselves upon the special protection and guidance of Jehovah: for, as Ezra ingenuously confesses, " I was ashamed to require of the king a band of soldiers and horsemen to defend us against the enemy by the way; because we had spoken unto the king, saying, ' The hand of our God is upon all them for good that seek him, but his power and his wrath is against all that forsake him.' "

Their confidence was not in vain, for they all arrived safely at Jerusalem after a journey of four months. They set out on the first month of the seventh year of the king's reign, and reached their destination on the first day of the fifth month, B. C. 457.

Of all the improvements and regulations which Ezra introduced into Judea, the book which bears his name only records his exertions in removing the heathen women

Ancient Persian Cupbearers.

with whom matrimonial connexions had very generally been formed by the Jews—
to such an extent indeed that even the sons of the high-priest Jeshua, and many of
the other priests, had fallen into this grievous error. To annul these marriages, was
a measure, however harsh to the natural affections, indispensably necessary as a security against a relapse into idolatry.

While Ezra was thus, and by other means, laboring to raise the character and improve the condition of the Hebrews in Judea, all the Jews in the Persian dominions
were suddenly threatened with entire extermination. Haman, an Amalekite, and as
such, an inveterate foe of the Hebrew nation, occupied the chief place in the confidence and service of the Persian king. His paltry pride being irritated by the apparent disrespect of a Jewish officer, named Mordecai (the uncle of Queen Esther, but
not known as such), he laid a plot for the massacre of the whole nation and the spo-
liation of their goods. The book of Esther, to which we must refer the reader, relates at large the particulars of the plot, and shows how the machinations of the
Amalekite were defeated by the address and piety of Queen Esther, and turned upon
the unprincipled contriver himself, who was destroyed with all his family, and Mordecai (by virtue of an old and neglected service) promoted to his place.

In the narrative of this transaction, the attention is arrested by the further illustration, offered in the case of Haman and afterward of Mordecai, of the distinction and
wealth which foreigners and captives—or, at least, persons of foreign and captive
origin—were enabled to attain. The *rank* is obvious; and as to the *wealth* they were
allowed to acquire, no more striking illustration can be afforded than by the fact that
Haman, to gratify his barbarous whim, was in a condition to offer the king a gratuity
of ten thousand talents of silver, to defray the probable deficiency of the royal revenue
by the proscription of the Jews throughout the empire. This the king declined accepting. The amount, computed by the Babylonish talent, would be upward of two
millions sterling; and this, it appears, was considerably short of the full amount of
the Jewish tribute.

On this occasion, we also have another example of the mischievous consequences
which might result from the king being unmindful of the heavy responsibility of caution, which was designed to be imposed by the well-meant law which precluded his
decrees from being changed or repealed. For when Artaxerxes became convinced of
the grievous wrong into which he had been led in decreeing the massacre of the
Jews, it was beyond his power to recall the order he had issued. All he could do
was to despatch swift couriers with a counter decree, empowering the Jews to stand
upon their defence when assaulted, with the aid of whatever moral advantage they
might derive from this indication of the present intentions of the king. On the appointed day, which had been destined to sweep the race of Israel from the face of the
earth, the Jews were by no means wanting to themselves. They repelled their
assailants by force of arms, and that with such effect, that in Susa itself eight hundred men fell by their hands, and in the different provinces seventy-five thousand.
The slaughter among the Jews themselves is not stated, but must have been considerable.

This great deliverance has ever since been commemorated by the annual feast of
Purim, or of Lots,—so called from the lots which were superstitiously cast by Haman
to find a propitious day for the massacre.

It was not until the twentieth year of his reign that Artaxerxes granted the long-
delayed permission to build the walls of Jerusalem. It was then obtained at the instance of a Jew named Nehemiah, who held at the Persian court the high and confidential office of cup-bearer, or butler. He had become acquainted with the mortifica-
tions and insults to which the inhabitants of Jerusalem were exposed through the
defenceless condition of their city; and the depression of his spirits, in consequence,
was too strongly marked on his countenance to pass unnoticed by the king, who demanded the cause of his sadness. As it was no ordinary misdemeanor to exhibit sadness in the presence of "the king of kings," Nehemiah was much alarmed, but
answered, "Let the king live for ever: why should not my countenance be sad when
the city, the place of my fathers' sepulchres, lieth waste, and the gates thereof are
consumed with fire?" The king encouraged him to declare his wishes freely, and
the result was that Artaxerxes consented to dispense with his services at court for a
few years, and gave him the appointment of *tirshata*, or civil governor, of Judea, in
succession to Zerubbabel, whose death about this time might furnish an additional

Modern Oriental Gate.

reason for the appointment (Neh. xii. 47). This would not interfere with the commission of Ezra, which was chiefly of an ecclesiastical nature, and who, by the discharge of his proper function of teaching the law to the people, would give the new governor important co-operation.

Nehemiah was commissioned to build walls and gates to the town, to erect a palace for himself and future governors, and afterward to rebuild the city. All this he accomplished with singular zeal, ability, and disinterestedness, in the course of his administration of twelve years, to which his leave of absence from the Persian court extended. He had to encounter much opposition and many threats from the chiefs of the surrounding nations,—Sanballat the Samaritan, Tobiah the Ammonite, the Arabians, and the remnant of the Philistines. But Nehemiah piously encouraged the people to rely on JEHOVAH, and " to fight for their brethren, their sons and their daughters, their wives and their homes." And he divided them into two parts, one to fight and the other to labor and build; and even the builders " with one hand wrought in the work, and with the other held a weapon." Thus, by the most noble exertions, the whole wall, which was distributed in lots among the priests and chiefs of the people, was finished, with all the towers and gates, in the short space of fifty-two days.

On the commission of Nehemiah, Hales, following the acute observations of Howes, remarks :—

" This change in the conduct of Artaxerxes, respecting the Jews, may be accounted for upon sound political principles, and not merely from regard to the solicitations of his cup-bearer or the influence of his queen.

" Four years before, in the sixteenth year of his reign, Artaxerxes, who, after the reduction of Egypt, had prosecuted the war against their auxiliaries, the Athenians, suffered a signal defeat of his forces by sea and land, from Cimon the Athenian general, which compelled him to make an inglorious peace with them, upon the humiliating conditions, 1, that the Greek cities throughout Asia should be free and enjoy their own laws; 2, that no Persian governor should come within three days' journey of any part of the sea with an army ; and 3, that no Persian ships of war should sail between the northern extremity of Asia Minor and the boundary of Palestine, according to Diodorus Siculus (lib. xii). Thus excluded from the whole line of sea-coast, and precluded from keeping garrisons in any of the maritime towns, it became not only a matter of prudence but of necessity to conciliate the Jews ; to attach them to the Persian interest, and detach them from the Grecians by further privileges ; that the Persians might have the benefit of a friendly fortified town like Jerusalem, within three days' journey of the sea, and a most important pass to keep up the communication between Persia and Egypt ; and, to confirm this conjecture, we may remark that in all the ensuing Egyptian wars, the Jews remained faithful to the Persians ; and even after the Macedonian invasion :—and surely some such powerful motive must have been opposed in the king's mind to the jealousy and displeasure this measure must unavoidably excite in the neighboring provinces hostile to the Jews, whose remonstrances had so much weight with him formerly. It was necessary, therefore, to intrust the important mission to an officer high in former trust and confidence, such as Nehemiah, whose services at court Artaxerxes reluctantly dispensed with, as appears from his appointing a set time for Nehemiah's return, and afterward, from his return again to Persia in the thirty-second year of his reign."

While the city remained unwalled the mass of the people had chosen rather to dwell in the country than in a place so conspicuous and yet so insecure. The walls were built on the old foundations; and Nehemiah found that although as enclosed within the walls " the city was large and great," yet " the people were few therein, and the houses were not builded." He therefore caused the people to be registered, and required that one family in ten (to be chosen by lot) should come to reside in Jerusalem. Those who, without waiting the decision of the lot, voluntarily offered themselves to dwell in Jerusalem, were received with peculiar favor. The city was thus replenished with inhabitants, and the walls with defenders. The walls were dedicated with great solemnity and joy. And while the governor was thus heedful of the stone-and-mortar framework of the social system which he desired to establish, he was by no means negligent of the inhabiting and animating spirit. He applied himself diligently (assisted by Ezra) to the organization of the temple-service, and of the civil government ; while various abuses, which the unsettled condition of affairs had engendered, were corrected by him with a firm and unsparing hand. And to strengthen his authority and influence, and that he and his government might not be burdensome to the people, this fine-spirited man declined to receive the usual dues of a governor; but while he travelled with a great retinue, maintained a large number of servants, and kept open table at Jerusalem, the heavy charges were entirely borne from his own private fortune, which must have been very considerable. That he, a foreigner and a captive, was enabled to accumulate such a fortune, affords another illustration of the liberality of the Persian government; which also was unquestionably, as far as the Hebrews at least were concerned, the best and most generous of the foreign governments, to which they were at any time subjected.

It was during the government of Nehemiah that Ezra, his ecclesiastical coadjutor, completed his collection and revisal of the sacred books. Traces of his careful hand may still be detected throughout the historical books of scripture; and the settlement of the Old Testament canon in nearly its present shape, may be ascribed to him. Among his labors was the exchange of the old Hebrew character of writing—with which the people had now become unacquainted—for the more shapely and generally known Chaldean character, with which alone the people were now familiar. The difference thus created is not so great as that which would take place were the Germans to exchange their peculiar (and not very elegant) character of print for that (the Roman) which prevails among nearly all other European nations. The Samaritans did not adopt or need this change in their copies of the Pentateuch; they retained the original character, which, therefore, has since been known as the Samaritan character.

It was not alone the old Hebrew *character* of writing, but the language itself, which had become unintelligible to the mass of the people, who had been born beyond the Euphrates, and had imbibed the East-Aramæan or Chaldee dialect as a mother tongue. The old Hebrew was still well known to, and spoken by, educated persons in their intercourse with each other; but the Chaldee was used in all the common intercourse of life, since that only was understood by all. It was not, however, until the time of the Maccabees, that the old Hebrew was completely displaced by the Chaldee. This last language is but a dialect of the Hebrew, which fact accounts for the ease with which the Jews fell into the use of it during the captivity. It however assigned to words essentially the same such additional or new meanings, and such differing terminations and pronunciation; that the old Hebrew could be but imperfectly intelligible to those who understood only the Chaldee.

Accordingly, when Ezra had finished his revision of the sacred books, and the people thronged to Jerusalem to hear the authentic law from his lips, it was necessary that some of the Levites should interpret to the multitude what this excellent person read in Hebrew from the book. This was a very solemn and interesting occasion. The people assembled in the open street; and Ezra, raised above the people on a kind of pulpit made for the occasion, read from the book of the law to an immense audience, who listened with most rapt attention to the interpretations which the surrounding Levites gave. It is manifest that the copies of the law had been scarce, and that it had not been publicly read to the people, for it is manifest that they heard much on this occasion with which they were not previously acquainted; and the consciousness of the extent to which the injunctions which they heard had been neglected by them, filled them with grief, and occasioned much and loud lamentation, which the Levites allayed with difficulty. Among other things, they heard of the feast of tabernacles, and found that the time of its celebration was close at hand. They therefore proceeded forthwith to manifest their obedience to this law, and they celebrated the feast in a manner so distinguished that nothing like it had been known since the time of Joshua.

Nehemiah and Ezra availed themselves of the favorable disposition which at this time existed to induce the people to enter into one of those solemn covenants which we have had frequent occasion to notice in the past history. This was, however, more specific in its obligations; for the people pledged themselves: 1, to walk in God's law as given to Moses; 2, not to intermarry with the people of the land; 3, to observe the sabbath day, and not to buy or to sell goods thereon; 4, to keep the sabbatical year, and to remit all debts therein; 5, to pay a tax of a third of a shekel yearly for the service of the temple; 6, and to render their first-fruits and tithes as required by the law.

At the expiration of his twelfth year of office, when his leave of absence expired, Nehemiah returned to resume his station at the Persian court.

When he departed, no person with adequate authority appears to have been left to carry on or complete his measures. His salutary regulations, and even the solemn covenant into which the people had entered, were gradually infringed and violated. The general laxity of principle and conduct may be estimated from the proceedings of the persons who might have been expected to offer the brightest examples of knowledge and faithfulness. Thus the high-priest himself, Eliashib, gave Tobiah the Ammonite (the grand opponent of Nehemiah) for lodging, even in the temple itself, a large chamber, which had been used as a store room for the tithes and offerings. This Tobiah, as well as his son Johanan, had married Jewish women and became allied to the high-priest. One of the grandsons of Eliashib was also son-in-law to Sanballat the Horonite, another of Nehemiah's great adversaries. The temple service was neglected; the tithes, appointed for the support of the Levites and the singers, were abstracted by the high-priest and his agents, or withheld by the people; the sabbath was profaned in every possible way ;* and marriages with strange women were frequent among the people. In accounting for the demoralization of this period, it may not be improper to connect it with the frequent march of Persian troops through the territory in passing to and from Egypt, which was frequently in a state of revolt. By this Judea was made to share in the evils of war, than which nothing is more relaxing of the bonds by which the order of civil society is maintained.

The tidings of this relapse occasioned much grief to Nehemiah at the Persian court, and he ultimately succeeded in obtaining permission to return to Judea. He returned in his former capacity as governor, and applied himself most vigorously to the correction of the evils which had gained ground during his absence.† His exertions appear to have been continued for four years, or until the third year of Darius Nothus, whom Nehemiah designates as Darius the Persian. The end, therefore, of this eminent person's second reform, which may be taken as the final act in the restoration and settlement of the Jews in their own land, may be ascribed to the year B. C. 420. With this year, therefore, the canon of the Old Testament concludes; for Malachi, the last of the prophets, is alleged by tradition, supported by every probability of internal evidence, to have prophesied during this later administration of Nehemiah. Malachi is supposed by many to be the same as Ezra.

One of the measures of Nehemiah was to expel the grandson of the high-priest, who had wedded the daughter of Sanballat, from whom he declined to separate. This act was attended with important consequences. Josephus informs us that this person's name was Manasseh; and that, on being expelled from Jerusalem, he went to his father-in-law Sanballat, who, by his interest with the Persian king, obtained permission to build a temple upon Mount Gerizim like that at Jerusalem, and in which Jehovah was to be worshipped with similar services. Of this establishment he made Manasseh the high-priest. This, in future, attracted numbers of Jews who had married strange wives from whom they could not bring themselves to part, or who had rendered themselves amenable to punishment by other transgressions of the law. And this, while it tended in a very serious degree to aggravate the enmity between the two nations, served ere long to correct the remaining idolatrous practices, and tendencies to idolatry among the Samaritans. Receiving the account of these matters through Josephus, and other prejudiced writers, it behooves us to be cautious of receiving all the impressions they intend to convey. The temple of Gerizim was undoubtedly a schismatical establishment. But seeing that, on the one hand, the Samaritans were anxious to worship Jehovah according to the regulations of Moses, while, on the other, the Jews, whether right or wrong, pertinaciously refused to receive their adhesion to the temple of Jerusalem, it is difficult to see what other course was left them than to build a temple for themselves. Besides, the obligation of adhesion to one temple was imposed only on the seed of Abraham; and the law made no provision for the case of a people who desired to worship Jehovah, but were repelled by the Jews. And this very fact may suggest that this repulsion was in itself not legal, whatever good effects may ultimately have resulted from it.

* One of the profanations consisted in the practice of the Tyrians bringing fish to the city for sale on the sabbath day. A curious fact.
† The time is uncertain and conjectures vary. Hales makes it B. C. 424, six years after his return to Persia.

Tomb of Ezra.

CHAPTER XXIV.

FROM B. C. 420, TO B. C. 163.

AFTER Nehemiah, no more separate governors of Judea were sent from Persia. The territory was annexed to the province of Cœle-Syria, and the administration of Jewish affairs was left to the high-priests, subject to the control of the provincial governors. This raised the high-priesthood to a degree of temporal dignity and power, which very soon made it such an object of worldly ambition, as occasioned many violent and disgraceful contests among persons who had had the least possible regard for the religious character and obligations of the sacerdotal office.

The history of this period is obscure and intricate. Facts are few, and some of those which we possess are hard to reconcile. But there is enough to acquaint us with the unholy violence and unprincipled conduct of the competitors for the priesthood, and the sufferings arising from this, as well as from the arbitrary proceedings of those who succeeded in obtaining that high office.

Jeshua, the high-priest who returned with Zerubbabel, was succeeded by his son Joachim, and he by his son Eliashib, who obtains unfavorable notice in the history of Nehemiah's second administration. He was then old, and died in B. C. 413. He was succeeded by his son Joiada or Judas, who held the office for forty years, B. C. 413–373.

Artaxerxes, who died in 423 B. C., left one son by his queen, and seventeen sons by his concubines. The first was named Xerxes, and, among the latter, history only knows Sogdianus, Ochus, and Arsites. Xerxes, the only legitimate son, succeeded; but, after forty-five days, he was slain by Sogdianus, who mounted the throne. On this, Ochus, who was governor of Hyrcania, marched thence with a powerful army to avenge the deed. Sogdianus submitted, and was put to death.* Ochus, in ascending the vacant throne, took the name of Darius, and was surnamed Nothus, or "bastard," to distinguish him from others of the name.

Of the events of this troubled reign, it is perhaps only necessary to notice that the Egyptians again shook off the Persian yoke, and made Amyrtæus of Sais their king, 413 B. C. With the aid of the Arabians, they drove the Persians out of Egypt, pursued them as far as Phœnicia, and maintained their independence sixty-four years. Ochus sent an army against them without success. The Persian forces marched to Egypt along the coast, through Judea. This event could not fail to act to the serious detriment and disquiet of the Jews; but we possess no precise information on the subject. The Persian army while on its march might have laid waste Idumea, because the Idumeans had perhaps taken part with those Arabs, who, in conjunction with the Egyptians, had pursued the Persians into Phœnicia, while the Jews continued faithful to the Persian government, with which they certainly had no reason to be dissatisfied. The prophet Malachi appears to allude to these circumstances. (Mal. i. 2–5.)

Darius Nothus died in 404 B. C., and was succeeded by his eldest son Arsaces, who, on his accession, took the name of Artaxerxes, and was surnamed Memnon, on account of his astonishing "memory." The long reign of this monarch was full of striking and important events; but our notice must be confined to the circumstances connected with Egypt and Phœnicia, with which the Jews could not but be in some way involved.

Artaxerxes determined to make a vigorous effort to restore the Persian power in Egypt, and to this end made most extensive preparation, continued for three years. At last, in 473 B. C., he had equipped a most formidable expedition by land and sea, which, he confidently expected, would speedily reduce the strongholds, and firmly establish his authority throughout the country. But the jealousy between the commanders of the land and sea forces, prevented that union of purpose and action which was essential to success. Pelusium was found to be impregnable, and all the fortified towns were placed in a state of defence. The Persian general, Pharnabazus, therefore, despaired of making any impression upon them, and advanced into the interior; but being opposed by the Egyptian king (Nectanebo) with a considerable force, and in consequence of the want of boats, being constantly impeded in his movements by

---

* He was smothered in ashes. Ochus had sworn not to kill him by sword, poison, or hunger; and therefore invented this novel kind of death to observe the letter while he infringed the spirit of his oath.

the various channels of the rising Nile, he was obliged to retreat and relinquish the hope of subjecting Egypt to the Persian yoke.

The Egyptian king, by whom the Persians were thus repelled, was succeeded in 369 B. C. by Teos or Tachos, who formed large designs, and made extensive preparations for acting offensively against the Persian power. He made an alliance with the Lacedæmonians, and received from them 10,000 auxiliaries under the command of Agesilaus their king. Both the person and counsels of this consummate general were treated with considerable disrespect; and the king persisted in leading his army in person into Phœnicia against the Persians. But his absence was immediately followed by a powerful conspiracy in favor of his relative Nectanebo, for whom the army also declared, so that the infatuated Tacho had no resource but to flee from his own people and throw himself under the protection of the great and generous king of Persia, whose dominions he had invaded.

The Idumeans again suffered much from being mixed up in the contest between the Persians and Egyptians. Nor can it be supposed that the Jews escaped without much moral, if not physical injury. It will be considered that they were exposed to the burdens of a military rendezvous from 377 to 374 B. C.; for at that time there were assembled in their vicinity 200,000 barbarian soldiers, besides 20,000 Greeks; and 300 ships of war, 200 galleys of thirty rowers, and a great number of store-ships were collected at Acco (Acre). The invading army of Persia, both in going and returning, took its route along their coasts, as did afterward the Egyptian army in its invasion of Phœnicia. These circumstances could not but be attended with very injurious effects; but upon the whole the Jews may be considered to have enjoyed peace and comfort during most of the reign of Artaxerxes Memnon, who was a prince of mild and humane character, and governed with much moderation and prudence, and with considerable political wisdom. However, in all the provinces, much depended on the character of the governor or satrap, whose powers, within his province, were almost regal. Artaxerxes died in 358 B. C., after a long reign of forty-six years. The pen of Xenophon has immortalized the revolt of his younger brother Cyrus, by which the early part of his reign was much troubled. The retreat of the 10,000 Greeks—who had fought for Cyrus and survived his overthrow and death—under the conduct of the historian himself, has been more admired and celebrated than most ancient or modern victories.

It was between the periods of disturbance which have been indicated, namely, in 373 B. C., that the high-priest Joiada died, and was succeeded by his son Jonathan or Jochanan (John). About the time of the Egyptian invasion, this person occasioned much trouble to his nation. His brother Jesus had become so great a favorite with the Persian governor Bagoses, that he nominated him to the priesthood. When Jesus came to Jerusalem in that capacity, he was slain by Jonathan in the very temple. Bagoses no sooner heard of this outrage than he hastened to Jerusalem; and when an attempt was made to exclude him from the temple as a gentile, and consequently unclean, he replied with vehemence, "What! am not I as clean as the dead carcase that lies in your temple?" The punishment which Bagoses imposed for the murder of Jesus was a heavy tax upon the lambs offered in sacrifice. This onerous impost was not remitted until the succeeding reign; and it must have been the more sensibly felt, as the priests had for many years been accustomed to receive large contributions from the Persian kings toward defraying the expense of the sacrifices.

Artaxerxes Memnon was succeeded in the throne of Persia by his son Ochus. In his reign, among many other disturbances which we need not mention, the Sidonians, Phœnicians, and Cyprians revolted, and made common cause with the Egyptians, who still maintained their independence. After repeated failures of his generals to reduce them, Ochus himself took the command of the expedition against them. He besieged Sidon, which was betrayed to him by the king Tennes; on which the Sidonians in despair set fire to the city, and burned themselves with all their treasures. Terrified by this catastrophe of Sidon, the other Phœnicians submitted on the best terms they could obtain; and among them we may include the Jews, who seem to have joined the common cause. Being anxious to invade Egypt, Ochus was not unreasonable in his demands. After having also received the submission of Cyprus, the king marched into Egypt 350 B. C., and completely reduced it, chiefly by the assistance of Mentor the Rhodian, and 10,000 mercenary Greeks whom he had drawn into his service. The Egyptians were treated with a severity more congenial to the savage disposition of Ochus than was the moderation to which policy had constrained him in Phœnicia:—he dismantled the towns; he plundered the temples of their treasures and public records; and the ox-god Apis he sacrificed *to an ass*—a severe practical satire upon the animal-worship of Egypt, and not less significant as an act of revenge upon the Egyptians for their having nicknamed himself *The Ass*, on account of his apparent inactivity and sluggishness. Ochus returned in triumph to Babylon, laden with spoil of gold and silver, and other precious things from the kingdoms and provinces he had conquered. From this decisive war the humiliation of Egypt may be dated. Nectanebo II., the last of her native kings, now fled with all the treasures he could collect into Ethiopia. Thenceforth, even to this day, it has been the destiny of Egypt only to change masters, as Ezekiel the prophet had foretold (Ezek. xxix. 13–16).

That the Jews were involved in the revolt of the Phœnicians has been already intimated. This appears from the fact that Ochus went from Phœnicia to Jericho, subdued that city, took some of the inhabitants with him into Egypt, and sent others into Hyrcania to people that province. But that the disaffection of the Jews was not general, or that, at least, it was not shared by the inhabitants of Jerusalem, may be inferred from the fact that this city was not disturbed. Indeed, the Jews owed some gratitude to Ochus for remitting at his accession the heavy tax* which Bagoses had in the preceding reign imposed.

It was in the eighteenth year of Ochus (B. C. 341) that the high-priest Jonathan, whose murder of his brother Jesus had given occasion for the imposition of this tax, died, and was succeeded by Jaddua or Jaddus.

Ochus, after having re-established his dominion over all the provinces which had newly or in former times revolted, abandoned himself to luxurious repose, leaving the government in the hands of Bagoas, an Egyptian eunuch, and of his general Memnon, from both of whom he had received important services during the Egyptian war. But Bagoas could not forgive the ruin of his country, although that had been the basis of his own fortunes. He poisoned Ochus and destroyed all his sons, except Arses the youngest. This horrid act was followed by his sending back to Egypt such of the plundered archives as he could collect. Arses, whom he had spared, he placed on the throne, expecting to reign in his name. But finding that the young king contemplated the punishment of the murderer of his father and his brothers, Bagoas anticipated his intention, and in the third year of his reign destroyed him and all the remaining members of his family. The eunuch, whose soul was now hardened to iron by the concurrent and repeated action of grief and crime, tendered the sceptre to Codomanus, the governor of Armenia, a descendant of Darius Nothus,† and who on his accession assumed the name of Darius, and is known in history as Darius Codomanus, B. C. 335. Bagoas soon repented of his choice, and plotted the death of this king also; but Darius, having discovered his design, returned to his own lips the poisoned chalice which he had prepared for the king.

Few kings ever enjoyed greater advantages than Darius at their accession. He had no competitors or opponents; his treasures, increased under Ochus by the plunder of many lands, seemed exhaustless; his dominion appeared well established over all the nations which abode from the Indus to the isles of Greece, and from the cataracts of the Nile to the Caucasian mountains; and with all this, the personal bravery of Darius and his acknowledged merits made him universally respected and admired throughout his empire. But bright as appeared his star, another had risen before which his own grew pale and became extinct.

Alexander, the son of Philip king of Macedon, ascended the throne when he was only twenty years of age, in B. C. 335, being the very same year that Darius Codomanus became king of Persia. It is not necessary in a work of this nature to record the exploits of this celebrated hero, unless as far as necessary to carry on the history of Palestine and the Jews.

---

* Jahn estimates that it must have produced 50,000l., perhaps rather too high an estimate.

† His grandfather was the brother of Darius Nothus, and his father was the only one of the family who escaped the massacre with which Ochus commenced his reign. He afterward married and had a son, who was this Codomanus. The young man lived in obscurity during most of the reign of Ochus, supporting himself as an *astanda*, or courier, by carrying the royal despatches. He at last had an opportunity of distinguishing his valor by slaying a Cadusian champion, who, like another Goliah, defied the whole Persian army. For this gallant exploit he was rewarded by Ochus with the important government of Armenia.

In the spring of B. C. 334, Alexander arrived at Sestos on the Hellespont, at the head of little more than thirty thousand foot and five thousand horse, and had them conveyed to Asia by his fleet of one hundred and sixty galleys, besides transports, without any opposition from the enemy on their landing. He had with him only seventy talents, or a month's pay for his army, and before he left home he disposed of almost all the revenues of the crown among his friends. When asked "what he left for himself?" he answered, "*Hope*." Such was the spirit with which Alexander invaded Asia.

On the fifth day after the passage of the Hellespont, Alexander met the Persians at the river Granicus in the Lesser Phrygia, where the governor of the western provinces had assembled an army of one hundred thousand foot and twenty thousand horse to oppose his passage. By defeating this great army, Alexander gained possession of the Persian treasury at Sardis, the capital of the western division of the Persian empire; several provinces of Asia Minor then voluntarily submitted to him, and in the course of the summer others were subjugated. In the campaign of the following year (B. C. 333) Alexander subdued Phrygia, Paphlagonia, Pisidia, Cappadocia, and Cilicia.

Darius, meanwhile, was not remiss in making preparations for a vigorous resistance to the most formidable enemy the empire had ever seen. His admiral, whom he had sent with a fleet to make a diversion by a descent upon Macedonia, died in the midst of the enterprise; and, in an age where so much depended upon individuals, his death spoiled the undertaking. Darius then assembled a vast army, which some accounts make four hundred thousand, others six hundred thousand men, in Babylonia, and led them in person toward Cilicia to meet Alexander. That hero, on hearing of this movement, hastened forward to seize the passes of Cilicia. In this he succeeded, and stationed himself at Issus, where not more than thirty thousand men could march up to the attack. In this position his flanks were protected, and he could bring his whole army into action, while the Persians could only bring a number of men equal to his own into conflict. Darius saw too late how much wiser it had been for him to await the Greeks in the plains of Damascus. He lost the battle. The vast number of his soldiers was worse than useless; for the retreat was thus so obstructed, that more were crushed to death in the eagerness of flight than had been slain by the weapons of the Greeks. Darius himself escaped with difficulty, leaving his whole camp, with his own rich baggage, and his mother, wife, and sons, in the hands of the victor. These last were treated with tenderness and respect by the generous conqueror. To him this victory opened Syria, Phœnicia, and Egypt. Immediately after the battle he sent to Damascus, and took all the heavy baggage, equipage, and treasures of the Persian army, with their wives and children, which had been left behind in the disastrous expedition to the Syrian straits.

For the present, Alexander did not follow Darius, who withdrew beyond the Euphrates; but, according to his original plan of reducing first all the maritime provinces of the empire, he marched in the spring of B. C. 332 into Phenicia. All the states of that country tendered their submission to him, except Tyre, which, however, was willing to render him barren testimonials of respect, had he been content with these. The siege of this place was one of the most splendid of Alexander's operations, and is even at this day regarded with admiration by military men. Tyre, which since the destruction of the ancient city by Nebuchadnezzar had been rebuilt upon an island about four hundred fathoms from the shore, relied upon the aid of Carthage (which was promised by the Carthaginian ambassadors there present in the city) and still more upon its situation, Alexander being destitute of shipping,* and on its walls, which were high and strong, and which were now additionally strengthened. The city was plentifully supplied with provisions, and fresh supplies could be brought by sea without any difficulty. But Alexander, with the rubbish of the ancient city, constructed a causeway from the shore to the island, and in seven months took the place by storm, although the Tyrians defended themselves bravely. Many of them fled to Carthage by sea; but of those who remained, eight thousand were

* Alexander, after the battle of the Granicus, had discharged and dismissed his fleet, which was too small to cope with that of the Persians (collected from Egypt and Phœnicia), and yet too large for his slender treasury to maintain. He declared that he would render himself master of the sea by conquering on land—that is, by getting the ports and harbors of the enemy into his possession. It was in consequence of this large idea that he persevered in reducing Phœnicia and Egypt before he advanced into the interior

put to the sword, thirty thousand were sold into slavery, and two thousand were crucified, while the city was plundered and laid in ashes. These barbarities were committed under the policy of deterring other places from offering resistance to the conqueror. Thus the prophecy of Zechariah respecting new Tyre was literally accomplished, as the previous prophecy of Ezekiel against the old city had been fulfilled in the time of Nebuchadnezzar. Alexander had, however, enlarged views of commercial policy, which induced him to re-people Tyre from the neighboring countries; and, improved in its harbors and basins by the very isthmus which he had made, and by which, consolidated by time, the island has ever since been connected with the shore, this maritime city was not long in recovering much of its former greatness.

There is every reason to conclude that Alexander, when he invaded Syria, summoned all the cities to surrender, to pay to him their customary tribute, and to furnish his army with provisions. Josephus affirms that during the siege of Tyre, a written order of this description came to Jerusalem, addressed to Jaddua, the high-priest, as the chief magistrate of the nation. Jaddua replied that he had sworn fealty to Darius, and could not violate his oath as long as that monarch was living. Alexander, naturally of a furious and impetuous temper, was highly irritated by this reply, and threatened that as soon as he had completed the conquest of Tyre, he would, by the punishment of the Jewish high-priest, teach all others to whom they were to keep their oaths.

Accordingly, on his progress to Egypt, after the destruction of Tyre (B. C. 332) he turned aside from Gaza, which he reduced, to chastise Jerusalem. But he was met at Sapha—an eminence near Jerusalem, which commanded a view of the city and temple—by a solemn procession, consisting of the high-priest arrayed in his pontifical robes, attended by the priests in their proper habits, and by a number of the citizens in white raiment. This course Jaddua had been commanded to take, in a vision, the preceding night. When Alexander beheld the high-priest he instantly advanced to meet him, adored the sacred NAME inscribed on his mitre, and saluted him first. This singular conduct the hero accounted for by observing to those around him— "I adore not the high-priest, but the God with whose priesthood he is honored. When I was at Dios in Macedonia, and considering in myself how to subdue Asia, I saw in a dream such a person, in his present dress, who encouraged me not to delay, but to pass over with confidence, for that himself would lead my army and give me the Persian empire. Since therefore I have seen no other person in such a dress as I now see, and recollect the vision and the exhortation in my dream, I think that having undertaken this expedition by a Divine mission, I shall conquer Darius, overthrow the Persian empire, and succeed in all my designs." Having thus spoken (to Parmenio) he gave his right hand to the high-priest, and going into the temple, he offered sacrifice according to the high-priest's directions, and treated the pontiff and the priests with distinguished honors. The book of Daniel was then shown to him, in which it was foretold that one of the Greeks should overthrow the Persian empire, pleased at which, and believing himself to be the person intended, he dismissed the multitude. The day after, he caused the people to be assembled, and desired them to ask what favors they desired; on which, at the suggestion of the high-priest, they asked and obtained the free enjoyment of their national laws, and an exemption from tribute every seventh year. He also, by a bold anticipation of his fortunes, promised that the Jews in Babylon and Media should enjoy their own laws; and he offered to take with him in his expedition any of the people who chose to share his prospects. (Joseph. Antiq. xi. 8, 4, 5.)

This story has been much questioned by many writers, as they were at perfect liberty to do. Nevertheless, as these questioners are of the same class as those who doubt on the unusual or supernatural details of the sacred history itself, it is impossible not to see that the *animus* of objection is essentially the same. We are therefore disposed to declare our belief in this statement, 1. Because Alexander had been a clear and conspicuous object of prophecy; and that an operation upon his mind by dream or vision, was as natural and necessary as in the cases of Nebuchadnezzar and Belshazzar. 2. Because it was as necessary that the God of the Hebrews should be made known to him as the bestower of empires, as to the other great conquerors— all of whom had been brought to avow it. 3. Because an operation upon the mind of Alexander was a natural and necessary sequel to the operations upon the minds of

City of Alexandria.

those former conquerors. 4. Because the impression described as being made by this dream upon Alexander, and the conduct which resulted from it, are perfectly in unison with his character and conduct as described by other historians. 5. Because the Jews actually did enjoy the privileges which are described as the result of this transaction, and which it would not otherwise be easy to account for, or to refer to any other origin.

The Samaritans had early submitted to Alexander, and sent him auxiliaries at the siege of Tyre; and now seeing the favor with which the Jews had been treated, they were not at all backward to claim the same privileges which had been conceded to them; for, as Josephus (with some asperity) remarks, the Samaritans were always ready to profess themselves to be Jews, when the sons of Abraham were in prosperous circumstances, and equally ready to disavow the connexion when the Jews were in distress or difficulty. They also met Alexander in solemn procession, and as they were graciously received, they also requested exemption from tribute on the sabbatical year, since they, as well as the Jews, then left their lands uncultivated. But as, when pressed, they could not give a direct and satisfactory answer to the question whether they were Jews, Alexander told them he would take time to consider the matter, and let them know his decision when he returned from Egypt. It was not his policy to encourage such applications, as others, under the same or other pretences, might make similar claims of exemption, to the great injury of the public revenues. The eight thousand Samaritans who had assisted him at the siege of Tyre he took with him to Egypt, and assigned them lands in the Thebaid.

When Alexander reached Egypt, he met with no opposition. The Persian garrisons were too weak to resist him, and the natives everywhere hailed him as their deliverer from the Persian bondage. In fact the Egyptians abhorred the Persians, and liked the Greeks as much as any foreigners could be liked by them. And the reason is very obvious. The Persians hated and despised image and animal worship as thoroughly as it was possible for the Jews to do, and the power of their arms gave them much opportunity for the exercise of the iconoclastic zeal by which they were actuated. They lost no opportunity of throwing contempt and ignominy upon the idols and idolaters of Egypt. But the pliable Greek regarded the same objects with reverence, and had no difficulty of so adopting them into his own system, or of identifying them with his own idols, as it enabled him to participate in the worship which the Egyptians rendered to them.

From Egypt Alexander went to visit the temple of Ammon, in an oasis of the western desert; and at this celebrated temple got himself recognised as the son of the god (commonly known as Jupiter Ammon) worshipped there.* It is better (with Plutarch) to attribute this to political motives, than to admit that impression of Alexander's understanding which the affair is calculated to convey. Alexander had much good sense, as yet uncorrupted by the extraordinary prosperity which had attended his undertakings; but he knew that there were millions in the world who would receive the belief of his heavenly origin as a discouragement to resistance, and as a consolation in defeat.

After his return from Libya, Alexander wintered at Memphis, and appointed separate and independent governors of the several garrisoned towns, in order to prevent the mischief so often experienced by the Persians in intrusting too much power to a single hand. He prudently separated the financial, judicial, and military functions, to prevent the oppression of the people by their union; and his enlightened and comprehensive policy chose the site of a new city, Alexandria, to be the emporium of commerce for the eastern and western worlds by its two adjacent seas, the Red sea and the Mediterranean. The great prosperity which the city ultimately reached, and a considerable share of which it has ever since retained, affords the best illustration of the large and sagacious views with which it was founded.

Early in the spring of B. C. 331 Alexander prepared to seek Darius beyond the Euphrates. The rendezvous of his army was appointed at Tyre; in advancing to which Alexander once more passed through Palestine. During his absence in Egypt, some Samaritans (perhaps enraged that they had not obtained the same privileges as the Jews) set fire to the house of Andromachus, whom Alexander had appointed their governor, and he perished in the flames. The other Samaritans delivered up the col-

* This god was worshipped under the form of a ram: hence the ram's horns which appear on the head of Alexander in many figures of him.

prits to Alexander, now on his return from Egypt; but they could hardly dare at this time to remind him of their previous claim (respecting the sabbatic year), which he had promised to consider, as the conqueror was so highly enraged that, not satisfied with the punishment of the actual culprits, he removed the Samaritans from their city, and transferred thither a Macedonian colony. (Curtius, iv. 21. Comp. Euseb. Chron.) The Samaritans, thus excluded from Samaria, thenceforth made Shechem their metropolis. This, it will be remembered, was at the foot of Mount Gerizim, on which the Samaritan temple stood.

The operations and victories of Alexander beyond the Euphrates are not so connected with the history of Palestine as to require to be traced in this work. We therefore abstain from particular notice of the battle of Arbela, in Assyria (fought Oct. 1, B. C. 331), which gave Alexander possession of the Persian throne; the flight of Darius into Media, with the view of raising new levies there; the prevention of this intention by the speedy pursuit of Alexander; the further flight of Darius, and his murder by the conspirators, into whose hands he had fallen, and whom Alexander ultimately overtook and punished. As little need our attention be detained by his northern and Indian expeditions, full as they are of interesting circumstances on which it might be pleasant to expatiate.

He returned to Persia in B. C. 324, with a character still great, and adequate to great occasions; but, upon the whole, very much damaged in its finer traits, by the intoxication of mind which, but too naturally, his inordinate successes produced. On his return he inquired into and punished the mal-administrations of his generals and governors of provinces during his long absence eastward. The last year of his life he spent in a circuit through the imperial cities of Persepolis, Susa, Ecbatana, and Babylon, and in forming the noblest plans for the consolidation and improvement of his mighty empire. These plans we can not recapitulate; but they are well worth the most attentive study of those who would realize a just impression respecting one of the most remarkable men the world has produced. The grasp of his mind was perhaps as large as that of his ambition: and while we regard his plans of universal conquest, and the sacrifice of human life and happiness which his causeless wars involved, with the most intense dislike, we have no desire to conceal our admiration of the many illustrious qualities which his mind exhibited.

Alexander arrived at Babylon in B. C. 324, intending to make that city his future residence, and the capital of his gigantic empire. Hence he was full of projects for restoring that city to its ancient beauty and magnificence. This included the rebuilding of the temple of Belus, which the Jewish prophecies had devoted to destruction, *never to be rebuilt.* Alexander, nevertheless, actually commenced this work. The soldiers were employed in turn to remove the rubbish. The Jews alone refused to render any assistance, and suffered many stripes for their refusal, and paid heavy fines, until the king, astonished at their firmness, pardoned and excused them. "They also," adds their historian (Hecatæus, in Joseph. contra Apion, i. 22), "on their return home, pulled down the temples and altars which had been erected by the colonists in their land, and paid a fine for some to the satraps, or governors, and received a pardon for others."

The death of Alexander at Babylon,—in the midst of his prosperity, his excesses, his large plans, and also during his ominous attempt to rebuild the temple of Belus, and at the early age of thirty-two years,—was calamitous to the Jewish nation. For amid the contests that prevailed among Alexander's successors,—each striving for the mastery, and celebrating his death, as he himself foretold, with funeral games the most bloody,—"evils were multiplied in the earth" (1 Macc. i. 19), and the Jews, from their intermediate situation, lying between the two powerful kingdoms (as they speedily became) of Syria northward, and of Egypt southward, were alternately harassed by both. According to the imagery of Josephus, "They resembled a ship tossed by a hurricane, and buffeted on both sides by the waves, while they lay in the midst of contending seas." (Antiq. xii. 3, 3. See Hales, ii. 537.)

Every one is acquainted with the scramble for empire which took place among the generals and principal officers of Alexander upon his death. It is useless to enter into the details and trace the results of this struggle in the present work. It is only necessary that we should disentangle from the complicated web which history here weaves, such threads as may be found useful in leading on the history of the Jews and Palestine.

26

It was determined that Aridæus, an illegitimate brother of Alexander, a man of no capacity, should be made king under the name of Philip, and that a posthumous son of Alexander's, called Alexander Ægus, should be joined to him, Perdiccas being regent and guardian of the two kings, who were both incapable of reigning. After some deliberation Perdiccas distributed the governments among the generals and ministers. Some who had been appointed by Alexander were confirmed in their provinces. The rest are named below.*

It was scarcely possible that the authority of two such kings, vested in a regent, should hold in check the powerful and ambitious governors of the provinces. Indeed the latter paid them the least possible regard and attention, and immediately after the assignment of the provinces, wars broke out not only between the governors themselves, but between them and the regent.

Our plan of confining our notices to the circumstances which more immediately affected Palestine, leads us first to notice the combination against the regent Perdiccas, which was formed in B. C. 322 by Antigonus, Antipater, Leonatus, and Ptolemy, on account of the design which Perdiccas betrayed of appropriating the crown of Macedonia, of which Antigonus was himself desirous. Perdiccas, who kept the young kings constantly with him, was then in Cappadocia. The next spring he, accompanied by the two kings, marched a large army *through Syria* into Egypt, to subdue Ptolemy in the first place, while Eumenes was left in Asia Minor to prosecute the war against Antipater and his allies. The result of this expedition was, that Perdiccas was slain by his own soldiers, who went over to Ptolemy, who was a very able and popular man, and natural brother to Alexander. Eumenes was proclaimed an outlaw, and, ultimately, the regency was undertaken by Antipater, who made some changes in the governments, appointing Seleucus governor of Babylonia; Antigonus to be general of Asia, to prosecute the war against the outlawed Eumenes; and the command of the cavalry he gave to his own son Cassander, who was then with Antigonus.

The passage of a part of the royal army, through Judea, in going to and from Egypt, as just related, could not fail to involve the Jews in some of the miseries of war. But when the same royal army, under Antigonus, was otherwise employed against Eumenes, Ptolemy, who had become very powerful, embraced the opportunity to take possession of Judea, Samaria, Phœnicia and Cœle-Syria, which were all easily subjugated by Nicanor his general. Laomedon the governor was taken prisoner, but contrived to make his escape. Thus Palestine was partly the theatre of this short war; but as Laomedon could make but a faint resistance, little injury was probably sustained by the inhabitants; and, since it was their destiny to be a subject people, the inhabitants were well rewarded for what they then suffered, by passing under the dominion of so benevolent a prince as Ptolemy Lagus. He went himself to Jerusalem, as Josephus says, for the purpose of sacrifice in the temple after the example of Alexander, and on this occasion declared himself master of the country. To secure his dominions he took a number of the people with him to Egypt. Among these were several of the Samaritans and several thousand Jews; but their condition could not be very calamitous, as many of their countrymen soon followed them of their own accord.

Ptolemy was soon made acquainted with the fidelity with which the Jews had maintained their allegiance to the Persian kings. This was a rare quality in those times: and wishing to attach such a people to himself, he restored the privileges they had enjoyed under Alexander; he employed a part of them to garrison his fortresses; others he sent to Cyrene, that he might have some faithful subjects in that newly-acquired territory; and many more were assigned a residence in Alexandria, with the grant of the same privileges as Alexander had bestowed on the Macedonian inhabitants of that city.

In 316 the puppet-king Aridæus was privately put to death, by Olympias, the mother of Alexander the Great, and in the same year Alexander Ægeus was imprisoned with his mother Roxana, by Cassander, governor of Caria; and he also was murdered

---

* Porus and Taxiles had India; Sebyrrius, Arachosia and Gedrosia; Tleopolemus, Caramania; Peucestes, Persia; Python, Media; Phrataphernes, Parthia and Hyrcania; Stanasor, Aria and Drangiana; Philip, Bactria and Sogdiana; Arcesilaus, Mesopotamia; Archon, Babylonia: *Ptolemy Lagus, Egypt; Laomedon, Syria and Palestine*; Philotas, Silicia; Eumenes, Paphlagonia and Cappadocia; *Antigonus, Pamphylia, Lycia, and Greater Phrygia*: Cassander, Caria; Meleager, Lydia; Leonatus, Lesser Phrygia, and the country around the Hellespont; Lysimachus, Thrace; *Antipater, Macedonia: Seleucus*, afterward destined to be the greatest of these names, received the important office of commander of the cavalry.

in B. C. 310. Even this, however, did not quite put an end to the mockery of dependance and deference; for it was not until the death of Hercules, the remaining son of Alexander the Great, by his wife Barsine, that the satraps put on crowns and took the name of kings.

By the year B. C. 315 the turbulent and ambitious Antigonus had acquired such power as excited the alarm of Seleucus, Ptolemy, Lysimachus, and Cassander (then governor of Macedonia), who entered into an allegiance against him. Antigonus himself was not idle, for the year following he wrested from the grasp of Ptolemy, Palestine, Phœnicia, and Cœle-Syria. In consequence of this Palestine and its vicinity became for three years the theatre of war between Ptolemy and Antigonus, and during that time the Jews must have suffered much, as their country frequently changed masters. The consequence was, that many of the inhabitants voluntarily withdrew to Egypt, where, and particularly at Alexandria, they could enjoy freedom and peace under a mild government. During these wars Jerusalem does not, however, appear to have been molested, and was spared when Ptolemy gave up Samaria, Acco (Acre), Joppa, and Gaza, to pillage.

It was at the last-mentioned city, Gaza, that the great battle was fought between Ptolemy and Demetrius (B. C. 312), which, by the defeat of the latter, threw the country again into the hands of the satrap of Egypt. In this battle Demetrius had a large force of elephants, mounted by native Indian riders. But notwithstanding the alarm which they inspired, they contributed to his defeat through the confusion they produced, when annoyed and harassed by the prudent measures which Ptolemy took against them. They were all taken, and most of the Indians slain.

Seleucus had a joint command in this action. He was soon after furnished by Ptolemy with an inconsiderable force of two hundred horse and eight hundred foot, with which he might prosecute his own interests, and at the same time annoy Antigonus in the east. With this handful of men he crossed the desert and the Euphrates, and paused at Haran to increase his army in Mesopotamia. His entrance into Babylonia was like a triumphal procession, for the people, mindful of the justice of his previous administration, and the great qualities of character and conduct which he had displayed, flocked to his standard in crowds, and he recovered with the utmost ease not only the city and province of Babylon, but the whole of Media and Susiana; and he was enabled to establish his interest in this quarter upon so solid a foundation that it could no more be shaken, notwithstanding the momentary appearance of success which next year attended an attempt made by Demetrius to recover Babylon for his father Antigonus. It is from this recovery of Babylon by Demetrius in October B. C. 312, twelve years after the death of Alexander, that the celebrated "Era of the Seleucidæ" commences. It is also called the "Greek" and the "Alexandrian Era;" while the Jews, because obliged to employ it in all their civil contracts, called it the "Era of Contracts." Some nations compute from the spring of the ensuing year: but that, as some suppose, this arose from the fact that Seleucus was not fully established until then in the possession of Babylon (after the attempt of Demetrius) may very well be doubted. It is more natural to resolve the difference into an adjustment of the era to the different times at which the year was commenced by different nations—some at the autumnal, and others at the vernal equinox.*

Meanwhile Demetrius gained an important advantage over the general (Cilles) whom Ptolemy had despatched to drive him out of Upper Syria, where he remained with the remnant of his army; and on this occasion the victor, following the example which had lately been set by Ptolemy, directed the prisoners which were taken to be restored. It is interesting to note the introduction of such civilized amenities into transactions so essentially savage, and so humiliating to the just pride of reason, as those which warfare involve and produce. When the news of this success reached Antigonus (then in Phrygia) he hastened to join his son; and the aspect of their joint forces was so formidable, that Ptolemy judged it prudent to evacuate his recent con-

* It may be doubted whether the Era in its origin had any real reference to the taking of Babylon, although that event happened to occur in the year to which its commencement is referred. This Era long continued in general use in Western Asia. The Arabians, who called it the "Era of the two-horned" (Dilkerneia), meaning Alexander, did not relinquish it till long after the Era of the Hegira had been adopted. It is still retained by the Syrian Christians under the name of the Era of Alexander. Even the Jews, who in the first instance had been obliged to adopt it from its general use in civil contracts, employed no other epoch until A. D. 1040, when, being expelled from Asia by the califs, and scattered about in Spain, England, Germany, Poland, and other western countries, they began to date from the creation, although still without entirely dropping the Era of the Seleucidæ.

quests in Syria. Having therefore caused most of the fortifications of the places he relinquished to be demolished, he withdrew into Egypt, laden with spoil, and attended by great numbers of Jews, who were weary of continuing in what seemed likely to become the troubled battle-ground between the great ruling powers of Egypt and Syria, and chose rather to avail themselves of the security and ample privileges by which the wise policy of Ptolemy invited them to settle in Egypt.

Elated by his successes, Antigonus conceived the design of reducing to his yoke the Nabathæan Arabs, who at this time inhabited the mountains of Seir. Availing himself of the absence of the active population of Petra at a great and distant fair in the desert, the general Athenæus sacked that remarkable metropolis, and departed with immense booty. But overcome with fatigue, the army halted on the way, and lay carelessly at rest, when it was surrounded and cut in pieces by the hosts of the returning Nabathæans. Sixty only escaped. Antigonus afterward sent Demetrius to avenge this loss. But he, advancing to Petra, and perceiving the hazard and delay of the enterprise, was glad to compound with the people on terms which bore a show of honor to his father, without being disgraceful to them. Petra, which was the chief scene of these enterprises, was doubtless the city, in a valley of Mount Seir, which, after the oblivion of ages, has been brought to our knowledge and abundantly described by Burkhardt, Mangles, Laborde, and other travellers. We notice this expedition chiefly for the sake of recording, that Demetrius on his return by way of the Dead sea, took notice of the asphaltos of that lake, and gave such an account of it to Antigonus as led him to desire to render it a source of profit to his treasury. He therefore despatched the aged historian Hieronymus, with men to collect the asphaltos for the benefit of the government. The Arabs looked on quietly, and offered no interruption until a large quantity had been collected and preparations were made for carrying it away; then they came down with six thousand men, and surrounding those who were employed in this business, cut them in pieces. Hieronymus escaped. Thus we perceive that the Asphaltic lake, otherwise useless, had become a source of wealth and object of contention on account of its bitumen.

We need not enter into the treaties and wars between the satraps, during the succeeding years. Antigonus remained in possession of Syria. In 306 B. C., Demetrius, who had been highly successful in Greece, invaded the island of Cyprus, and made the conquest of it after repelling Ptolemy, who came with a fleet to the assistance of his allies. This conquest was so pleasing to Antigonus that he thereupon assumed the title of king, and had such confidence in the duty and affection of his excellent son, that he saluted him (by letter) with the same title, thus making him the associate of his government. When this was heard in Egypt, the people, out of their attachment to Ptolemy, saluted him also as king, whereupon Lysimachus in Thrace, Seleucus in Babylon, and even Cassander in Macedonia, were hailed by the regal title, by the nations under their rule. This none of them strenuously forbade or opposed; and although they did not immediately call themselves kings on their coins and in their edicts, they all did so ere long, with more or less show of decent reluctance and delay. In those times, however, the kingly title was very common, and much less of special significance was connected with it than it has since acquired.

Elated by this and his other great successes, Antigonus cast his eyes upon Egypt. In 305 B. C. he collected in Syria an army of eighty thousand foot, eight thousand horse, and eighty-three elephants, and marched along the coast of Palestine to Gaza; to which point Demetrius also repaired by sea, with a fleet of one hundred and fifty ships of war, and one hundred storeships. This formidable expedition failed through mismanagement on their side, met by excellent management and preparation on the part of Ptolemy. Antigonus retired from the Egyptian frontier in disgrace, not a little heightened by the avidity with which his own soldiers embraced the opportunity of escaping from his austere rule to the mild and paternal sway of the Egyptian king.

Meanwhile Seleucus had been consolidating in the east that power which ultimately made him the greatest of the successors of Alexander. By 303 B. C. he had established his dominion over all the eastern provinces to the borders of India, and in that year was preparing for the invasion of that country, when affairs called his attention to the west, and he concluded a treaty with the Indian king, from whom he received five hundred elephants,—a fact which we particularly notice as explaining the frequent presence of that noble beast in the subsequent warfares in Syria and

[Use of Elephants in War.]

Palestine. Subsequent supplies were afterward obtained from the same source, in order to keep up this favorite force in the armies of the Syrian kings.*

At last the several kings, wearied out with troubles and conflicts which the insatiable and turbulent ambition of Antigonus occasioned, made common cause against him, Seleucus taking the lead, and bringing the largest force into the field. The belligerants met and fought a battle, intended by all to be decisive, at Ipsus in Phrygia, in the year B. C. 301. Antigonus brought into the field between seventy and eighty thousand foot, ten thousand horse, and seventy elephants; and Seleucus and his confederates had sixty-four thousand infantry, ten thousand five hundred cavalry, above one hundred chariots armed with scythes, and four hundred elephants. The courageous old man, Antigonus, now fourscore and upward, behaved with his usual valor and conduct, but not with his usual spirit. Seleucus, by an adroit interposition of his elephants, managed to prevent Demetrius from properly supporting his father with the cavalry, which he commanded; and the final result was, that Antigonus fell on the field of battle pierced by many arrows, while Demetrius managed with a poor remnant of the army to escape to Ephesus. He sur-

* The ancient Egyptians do not appear to have known the elephant, although quantities of the teeth were brought to the country and to Palestine. We do not remember to have met with a single instance in which this animal is described as being figured on the old monuments of that country.

vived seventeen years, and took an active part in the affairs of that time, but not so as to bring him under our future notice.

This great victory was followed by a treaty between the four potentates who had weathered the storm which had raged since the death of Alexander, being Seleucus, Ptolemy, Lysimachus, and Cassander. Each was formally to assume the royal dignity, and to govern his provinces with imperial power. The distribution was made on the principle of each retaining what he already had, and taking his due share of the empire which Antigonus had lost with life. To Cassander was allotted Macedonia and Greece; to Lysimachus Thrace, Bithynia, and some of the adjacent provinces; to Ptolemy, Libya, Egypt, Arabia Petræa, Palestine, and Cœle-Syria; to Seleucus, all the rest, being in fact the lion's share—including many provinces in Syria, Asia-Minor, Mesopotamia, Babylonia, and the East as far as the frontiers of India.

This settlement must have been highly satisfactory to the Jews, whom it restored to the dominion of Ptolemy, with whose generally beneficent government, and particular favor to themselves, they had every reason to be satisfied. The prospects of durable peace, under the shadow of so great a king, must also have been contemplated with peculiar satisfaction by a people who suffered so much of the horrors and penalties, without sharing in the contingent honors and benefits of war.

They were not disappointed. Ptolemy, now relieved from his long conflict, and settled firmly upon his throne, applied himself with great and laudable diligence to the improvement of his dominions. One great point of his policy was really to attach to his rule the several nations which had become subject to it. From this policy sprang the favors which he showered upon the Jews, and the indulgence with which, notwithstanding their peculiarities, they were on all occasions treated. The most perfect religious toleration was established by this eminent monarch, whose interest it was to harmonize the differences of religious practice and opinion which existed between his Greek and Egyptian subjects: the religion of the Jews was comprehended in this indulgence; and their synagogue was as much tolerated and respected as the temples of Isis and of Jupiter. Ptolemy made Alexandria the metropolis of his empire, and gave full effect to the intention of its great founder by taking such measures as ere long rendered it the first commercial city in the world.—This, among others, was a circumstance calculated to attract the Jews to that city; as, first their long absence from their native land—during the captivity, and then the troubles of war in that land—troubles peculiarly unfavorable to the peaceful pursuits and hopes of agriculture—had already turned their attention toward commerce.

Seleucus, between whose territories and those of Ptolemy, Palestine was now situated, saw the wisdom of the policy followed by the king of Egypt, and applied himself with great vigor to work it out in his own dominions. In those dominions many fine cities had been entirely destroyed, and others greatly injured by the ravages of war. To repair these losses, Seleucus built many new cities, among which are reckoned sixteen which he, from his father, called Antiochia or Antioch; nine to which he gave his own name; six on which he bestowed that of his mother Laodicea; six which he called Apamea after his first wife, and one after his last wife Stratonice. Of all these towns the most celebrated was the city of Antioch, on the Orontes in Syria, which became the metropolitan residence of all the succeeding kings, and in a later day, of the Roman governors; and which has ever since survived, and which still exists, and retains some relative consequence by virtue of the corresponding decline of all prosperity and population in the country in which it is found. Its name will occur very often in the remainder of our narrative. Next to Antioch in importance was Seleucus on the Tigris, which may in fact be considered the capital of the eastern portion of the empire. It was situated about fifty miles north-by-east of Babylon, twenty-three miles below the site of the present city of Bagdad, and just opposite to the ancient city of Ctesiphon. This city (founded in B. C. 293) tended much to the final ruin and desolation of Babylon. Great privileges were granted to the citizens; and on this account many of the inhabitants of Babylon removed thither; and after the transfer of the trade to Seleucia, these removals became still more frequent. It was in this manner that Babylon was gradually depopulated; but the precise period when it became entirely deserted can not now be ascertained. It may be interesting to note this, as many of the eastern Jews were involved in whatever transactions took place in this quarter, which, from the time of the captivity to this day, has never been destitute of a large and often influential Jewish population. But now Babylon itself

Antioch.

is not more desolate—is even less desolate—has more to mark it as the site of a great city of old times, than the superseding Selucia, which only received existence in the last days of Babylon. " I have," says a late traveller, " walked over the ground it occupied, and found the site of the royal city only marked by the parallel embankments of ancient aqueducts, and by the consolidated grit and debris which devote to utter barrenness, in this primeval country, the spots which towns once occupied, as if man had branded the ground by the treading of his feet."

In his newly-founded towns, it was the policy of Seleucus to induce as many as possible of the Jews to settle by important privileges and immunities, such as those which Ptolemy had extended to them. The consequence was that the Jews were attracted to these spots in such numbers, and especially to Antioch, that in them they formed nearly as large a proportion of the inhabitants as at Alexandria itself.

In all this, we think it is not difficult to perceive a further development of the divine plan, which now, as the times advanced, dictated the dispersion of numerous bodies of Jews among the Gentile nations,—while the nation still maintained in its own land the standards of ceremonial worship and of doctrine—with the view of making the nations acquainted with certain truths and great principles, which should work in their minds as leaven until the times of quickening arrived.

During the time of Ptolemy Soter, the prosperity of the Jews was much strengthened by the internal administration of the excellent high-priest Simon the just. In 300 he succeeded Onias I., who had in 321 succeeded Jaddua, the high-priest in the time of Alexander the Great. Simon repaired and fortified the city and temple of Jerusalem, with strong and lofty walls; and made a spacious cistern, or reservoir of water, " in compass as a sea."* He is reported to have completed the canon of the Old Testament by the addition of the books of Ezra, Haggai, Zechariah, Nehemiah, Esther, and Malachi. This is not unlikely, as also that the book of Chronicles was completed in its present state; for the genealogy of David in the first book comes down to about the year B. C. 300; and it may also be remarked that in the catalogue of high-priests as given in Nehemiah, Jaddua is mentioned in such a manner as to intimate that he had been for some time dead. The Jews also affirm that Simon was " the last of the great synagogue:" which some ingeniously paraphrase into " the last president of the great council, or Sanhedrim, among the high-priests" (Hales, ii. 538); whereas it seems clear that no Sanhedrim at or before this time existed. And from the fact that this " great synagogue" is not (like the Sanhedrim) described as being composed of seventy members, but of one hundred and twenty, among whom were Ezra, Haggai, Zechariah, Nehemiah, and Malachi—it would appear that it rather denoted the succession of devout and patriotic men who distinguished themselves after the captivity, by their labors toward the collection and revision of the sacred books, and the settlement and improvement of the civil and religious institutions of their country; and of whom Simon, by completing the sacred canon, became the last. Simon died in B. C. 291, and was succeeded by his son Eleazer.

Not long after this (B. C. 285), the king of Egypt, having conceived just cause of displeasure against his eldest son Ptolemy Keraunus, took measures to secure the succession to his youngest son Ptolemy Philadelphus. His advanced age warned him that he had no time to lose; he therefore resigned the diadem to Philadelphus (" the brother-loving"), and enrolled himself among the royal life-guards. He died two years after (B. C. 283) at the age of eighty-four, forty years after the death of Alexander.

As for Ptolemy Keraunus, he ultimately sought refuge at the court of Seleucus, by whom he was most kindly received and entertained: but he justified the ill opinion of him on which his own father had acted by destroying his benefactor. This was in B. C. 280, only seven months after Seleucus had consummated the greatness of his empire by the overthrow of Lysimachus, who had himself previously added the kingdom of Macedonia to his own of Thrace. Thus Seleucus became the possessor of three out of the four kingdoms into which the empire of Alexander had, in the defeat of Antigonus, been divided. After his death, Ptolemy Keraunus managed to seat himself on the Macedonian throne; but the very next year he was taken prisoner and cut in pieces by the Gauls, who had invaded Macedonia.

Seleucus was succeeded in what may be called the throne of Asia by his son Antiochus Soter. This prince, after he had secured the eastern provinces of the empire,

---

* Ecclus. i. 1–3. The whole chapter, entitled " The praise of Simon the son of Onias," is devoted to a splendid eulogium on his deeds and character.

endeavored to reduce the western, but his general Patrocles was defeated in Bithynia, and the loss of his army disabled him from immediately prosecuting the claims upon Macedonia and Thrace. Meanwhile the sceptre of Macedonia was seized by the vigorous hands of Alexander Gonatus, a son of Demetrius Poliorcetes, and consequently a grandson of Antigonus, and to him Antiochus at length felt himself constrained to cede that country; and the family of Antigonus reigned there until the time of Perseus, the last king, who was conquered by the Romans. Antiochus Soter died in B. C. 261 after nominating as his successor his second son Antiochus Theos ("the God"). This prince was his son by his mother-in-law Stratonice, whom his too indulgent father had divorced to please him.

The accession of Antiochus II. took place about the middle of the reign of Ptolemy Philadelphus in Egypt. This last-named monarch was quite as tolerant and as friendly to the Jews as his father had been. He was a great encourager of learning and patron of learned men. Under his auspices was executed that valuable translation of the Hebrew scriptures into Greek, called the Septuagint, from the seventy, or seventy-two, translators said to have been employed thereon. Eleazer was still the high-priest, and appears to have interested himself much in this undertaking, and was careful to furnish for the purpose correct copies of the sacred books. The date of B. C. 278 is usually assigned to this translation. Thus the Jewish scriptures were made accessible to the heathen. It is unquestionable that copies of this version, or extracts from it, found their way in process of time into the libraries of the learned and curious of Greece and Rome; and there is no means of calculating the full extent of its operation in opening the minds of the more educated and thoughtful class among the heathen to the perception of some of the great truths which they could learn only from that book, and which it was now becoming important that they should know. It was even a great matter that they should have the means of knowing clearly what the Jews believed, whatever they may themselves have thought of that belief. This version soon came into common use among the Jews themselves everywhere, even in Palestine, the original Hebrew having become a learned language. Indeed, the quotations from the Old Testament made by the evangelists and apostles, and even by Christ himself, are generally, if not always from this version.

In the third year of Antiochus a long and bloody war broke out between him and Ptolemy Philadelphus. The latter king, bending under the weight of years, commanded by his generals, while Antiochus, in the vigor of youth, led his armies in person. Neither monarch appears to have gained any very decided advantages over the other; while we know that much was lost by Antiochus; for while his attention was engaged by wars in the west the eastern provinces of his vast empire—Parthia, Bactria, and other provinces beyond the Tigris—revolted from his dominion; this was in B. C. 250, from which the foundation of the Parthian empire *may* be dated; but it is perhaps better, with the Parthians themselves, to date it from the ensuing reign, when they completely established their independence. It is here however we are to seek the real beginning of the Parthian empire, which was ultimately destined to set bounds to the conquests of the Romans, and to vanquish the vanquishers of the world. The immediate result was that Antiochus was obliged, in the year B. C. 249, to make peace with Philadelphus on such terms as he could obtain. These were, that he should repudiate his beloved queen, who was his half-sister, and marry Berenice, a daughter of Philadelphus, and that the first male issue of the marriage should succeed to the throne.

As Philadelphus on his part gave for the dower of his daughter half the revenues of Palestine, Phœnicia and Cœle-Syria, the Jews may seem to have come partly under the dominion of Antiochus. But as the king retained the other half in his own hands, and as the revenues of Judea were always farmed by the high-priest, the circumstance made no change in their condition. Besides, the arrangement was too soon broken up to produce any marked effect. These were the important nuptials between "the king of the north," and "the daughter of the king of the south," which the prophet Daniel had long before predicted (Dan. xi. 6). It was only two years after this (B. C. 247) that Philadelphus died; immediately on which he put away Berenice and restored his beloved Laodicea; but she, fearing his fickleness, poisoned him, and set her son SELEUCUS CALLINICUS ("illustrious conqueror") upon the throne (B. C. 246). On this Berenice sought shelter with her son (the heir by treaty) in the sacred groves of Daphne (near Antioch); but at the instigation of his mother, Callinicus tore her from that sanctuary, and slew her, with her infant son.

Now Berenice was full sister to the new king of Egypt, PTOLEMY III., surnamed EUERGETES,* who immediately placed himself at the head of his army to avenge her wrongs. He was eminently successful. He entered Syria, slew the queen Laodicea, and overran the whole empire, as far as the Tigris on the east and Babylon on the south.† On he marched, from province to province, levying heavy contributions, until commotions in Egypt obliged him to abandon his enterprise and return home. On his way he called at Jerusalem, where he offered many sacrifices, and made large presents to the temple. There is little doubt but that the high-priest took the opportunity of pointing out to him those prophecies of Daniel (xi. 6–8) which had been accomplished in the late events and his recent achievements; and this may probably have been the cause of his presents and offerings.

The high-priest of the Jews was then Onias II. Eleazer, the high-priest at the time the Greek translation of the Scriptures was made, died in B. C. 276, and was succeeded, not by his own son Onias, but by Manasses, a son of Jaddua. He died in B. C. 250, and Onias III. then became high-priest. As usual, Onias farmed the tribute exacted from Judea by the Egyptians. But, growing covetous as he advanced in years, he withheld, under one pretence or another, the twenty talents which his predecessors had been accustomed to pay every year to the king of Egypt as a tribute for the whole people. This went on for twenty-four years, and, the arrears then amounting to four hundred and eighty talents, the king deemed it full time to take energetic measures to secure the payment of this portion of the royal revenues. He sent an officer named Athenion to demand the payment of what was already due, and to require a more punctual payment in future, with the threat that unless measures of compliance were taken, he would confiscate all the lands of Judea, and send a colony of soldiers to occupy them. The infatuated priest was disposed to neglect the warning and brave the danger, which filled all the people with consternation. But the evils which might have been apprehended were averted through the policy and address of Joseph, the high-priest's nephew; who generously borrowed the money upon his own credit, paid the tribute, and so ingratiated himself at the Egyptian court that he obtained the lucrative privilege of farming the king's revenues not only in Judea and Samaria, but in Phœnicia and Cœle-Syria.

Seleucus Callinicus, in his emergencies, had promised to his younger brother Antiochus Hierax, who was governor of Asia Minor, the independent possession of several cities in that province, for his assistance in the war with P. Euergetes. But when he had (B. C. 243) obtained a truce of ten years from the Egyptian king, he refused to fulfil this engagement. This led to a bloody war between the two brothers, in which Seleucus was so generally unsuccessful that it would appear as if the title of Callinicus (*illustrious conquerer*) had been bestowed upon him in derision. He was however ultimately successful through the losses and weakness which other enemies brought upon Antiochus Hierax ("the Hawk"—from his rapacity), who was in the end obliged to take refuge in Egypt, where he was put to death in B. C. 240. Toward the end of this war, Mesopotamia appears to have been the scene of action; for in that quarter occurred the battle in which eight thousand Babylonian Jews (subjects of Seleucus) and four thousand Macedonians defeated one hundred and twenty thousand Gauls whom Antiochus had in his pay (Macc. viii. 20).

S. Callinicus being now relieved from the western war, turned his attention to the recovery of the eastern provinces which had revolted in the time of his father. Renewed troubles in Syria prevented any result from his first attempt in B. C. 236; and in his second, in 230, he was defeated and taken prisoner by the Parthians, whose king, Arsaces, treated the royal captive with the respect becoming his rank, but never set him at liberty. He died in B. C. 226 by a fall from his horse. On this event Seleucus III. inherited the remains of his father's kingdom. This prince was equally

---

* We may add in a note that this title (*the Benefactor*) was conferred on Ptolemy by his Egyptian subjects on his return from his eastern expedition. He recovered and brought back, with other booty to an immense amount, 2,500 idolatrous images, chiefly those which Cambyses had taken away from the Egyptians. When he restored the idols to their temples, the Egyptians manifested their gratitude by saluting with this title. They were less prone than the Greeks of Asia to *deify* their kings.

† The inscription found at Adule by Cosmas gives a more extensive range to his operations, affirming that after having subdued the west of Asia, ultimately crossed the Euphrates, and brought under his dominion, not only Mesopotamia and Babylonia, but Media, Persia, and the whole country as far as Bactria. As this needs more collateral support than it has received, we adopt a more limited statement in the text.

weak in body and mind, and therefore most unaptly surnamed Keraunus ('thunder'). When a war broke out in B. C. 223, his imbecile conduct so provoked his generals, that he was poisoned by their contrivance.

Of these troubles and dissensions in Syria, Ptolemy Euergetes, in Egypt, took due advantage in strengthening and extending his own empire. In B. C. 222, the year after the murder of Seleucus III., his reign was terminated through his murder by his own son Ptolemy, who succeeded him, and who, on account of this horrid deed, was ironically surnamed PHILOPATOR ("father-loving"). P. Euergetes is popularly considered the last good king of Egypt, which is true in the sense that the succeeding Ptolemies governed far worse than the first three of that name—all of whom were just and humane men, and whose reigns were glorious and beneficent. If Euergetes was inferior in some respects to Lagus and Philadelphus, he was more than in the same degree superior to his own successors.

At this time the Jews had for about sixty years enjoyed almost uninterrupted tranquillity under the shadow of the Egyptian throne. During this period circumstances led them into much intercourse with the Greeks, who were their masters and the ruling people in Egypt, Syria, Asia Minor—and, in fact, in all the country west of the Tigris. A predominance of Greeks and of Grecian ideas, which has dotted the surface of westernmost Asia with frequent monuments of Grecian art, was not without much effect upon the Jews in this period. Among other indications, the increasing prevalence, in and after this period, of Greek proper names among the Jews, may be taken. There is ample evidence that the more opulent classes cultivated the language, and imbibed some of the manners of the Greeks. It is also apparent that some acquaintance with the Greek philosophers was obtained, and made wild work in Jewish minds. Nothing manifests this more clearly than the rise of the SADDUCEES, whose system was nothing more than a very awkward attempt to graft the negations of Greek philosophy upon the Hebrew creed. It confirms this view, that the sect of the Sadducees was never popular with the mass of the nation—but was always confined to those whose condition in life brought them the most into contact with the notions of the Greeks—the wealthy, noble, and ruling classes. Priests—even high-priests—sometimes adopted the views of this sect.

It has already been stated that the high-priest Simon the Just was counted as the last of " the great synagogue," who had applied themselves to the great work of collecting, revising, and completing the canon of the Old Testament. To this followed " a new synagogue," which applied itself diligently to the work of expounding and commenting upon the completed canon. This school lasted until the time of Judah Hakkadosh, who to prevent these comments or " traditions" (which were deemed of equal authority with the text) from being lost, after the dispersion, committed them to writing, in the Mishna—which, with its comments, has since constituted the great law-book of the Jews, from which, even more than from the Scriptures, they have deduced their religious and civil obligations. The founder and first president of this school, or synagogue, was Antigonus Socho, or Sochæus. He (or, according to some accounts, his successor Joseph) was fond of teaching that God was to be served wholly from disinterested motives, of pure love and reverence, founded on the contemplation of his infinite perfections, without regard to the prospects of future reward, or to the dread of future punishment. This was either misunderstood or wilfully perverted by some of his scholars, and in particular by Sadoc and Baithos, who declared their disbelief that there was any future state of reward or punishment. Perhaps *they* stopped at this; but the views ultimately imbodied in the creed of the sect which took its name from the first of these persons, inculcated that the soul was mortal like the body, and perished with it, and consequently that there was not, nor could be, any resurrection. They also held that there was no spiritual being, good or bad. (Matt. xxii. 23; Acts xxiii. 8.) They rejected the doctrine of an overruling Providence, and maintained that all events resulted from the free and unconstrained actions of men. That, like the Samaritans, they rejected all the sacred books save the Pentateuch, is inferred from the unsupported authority of a passage of doubtful interpretation in Josephus.* And as there is some evidence to the contrary, it is safer to conclude that they admitted the authority of the other books, but ascribed to them an inferior value and importance than to the Pentateuch. But it is certain that they rejected absolutely the " traditions," to which such supreme importance was attached

* Antiq. xiii 10, 6.

by the mass of the nation. This was a good thing in them; and in this they agreed with Jesus Christ and his apostles, who were opposed to them and by them on every other point. In fact, it would seem as if this sect in its beginning was intended merely as an opposition to the tradition party, which was likely to be regarded with apprehension by the more open and thinking minds. The doctrinal errors had no necessary connexion with the anti-tradition zeal of the party, and were probably grafted on it through the speculative tendencies of some of its original leaders.

After the murder of Seleucus Keraunus, who left no son, the kingdom of Syria fell to his brother ANTIOCHUS III., who had been brought up at Seleucia on the Tigris. He came to Antioch; and his reign was so productive in great events that he ultimately acquired the surname of "THE GREAT." He carried on the wars against the revolted provinces with such success that he soon recovered almost all Asia-Minor, Media, Persia, and Babylonia. The effeminate character of Ptolemy Philopator—who was a mean voluptuary, abandoned to the most shameful vices, and entirely governed by the creatures and instruments of his pleasures—led Antiochus to contemplate the feasibility of obtaining possession of the valuable provinces of Cœle-Syria, Phœnicia, and Palestine. Great part of the first of these provinces, with the city of Damascus, he easily acquired, through the defection of Theodotian the governor—a brave man rendered a traitor by the desire of revenge, and by contempt for the character of his master. The campaign was terminated by a truce for four months, which circumstances made desirable for both parties before prosecuting the war. Negotiations for a peace were indeed entered into; but as both parties claimed Cœle-Syria and Palestine in virtue of the treaty by which the empire of Alexander was divided after the fall of Antigonus, the truce expired without anything having been concluded.

The war was therefore resumed in 219 B. C. Antiochus marched into the disputed territory and carried all things before him:—forcing the passes of Lebanon, he penetrated into Phœnicia, and after securing the coast, marched into the interior, and brought under his power all the cities of Galilee; after which he passed beyond Jordan, and won the ancient territory of the tribes beyond that river, with the metropolis Rabbath-Ammon, which Ptolemy Philadelphus had fortified, and named after himself Philadelphia. At the same time, Antiochus subjugated some of the neighboring Arabs; and on his return threw garrisons into Samaria and some of the adjacent towns; and at the close of this brilliant campaign, he took up his winter quarters in Ptolemais (afterward Cæsarea).

These large and repeated losses at length roused all the energies which Ptolemy was capable of exerting. He forsook his drunken revels, and placing himself at the head of an army of seventy thousand infantry, five thousand cavalry, and seventy-three elephants, he marched from Pelusium through the desert, and encamped at Raphia, a place between Rhinoculura (El Arish) and Gaza. Antiochus, with the confidence of victory which his recent successes inspired, advanced to meet him at that place, with an army of sixty-two thousand infantry, six thousand cavalry, and one hundred and twenty elephants. He was totally defeated, with such loss that he made no attempt to repair it, but abandoned all his conquests and withdrew to Antioch. By a peace, concluded soon after, he relinquished all pretension to the disputed territories. Philopator now recovered all the former possessions of his crown without striking a blow; for the cities hastened to emulate each other in renewing their homage to him by their ambassadors. Among these the Jews, always partial to the Egyptian rule, were the most forward: and the king was induced to pay a visit to Jerusalem, as well as to the other principal cities. There he offered sacrifices according to the Jewish law, and presented gifts to the temple. But, unhappily, the beauty of the building, and the peculiar order and solemnity of the worship, excited the curiosity of the king to see the interior. Simon II., who had but lately succeeded Onias II. in the high-priesthood, remonstrated against this intention, intimating that it was unlawful even for the priests to enter the inner sanctuary. Philopater answered haughtily, that although *they* were deprived of that honor, *he* ought not; and pressed forward to enter the sacred place. But while he was passing through the inner court for that purpose, he was "shaken like a reed, and fell speechless to the ground," overcome either by his own superstitious fears, or, as the historian seems to intimate, by a supernatural dread and horror cast on him from above. He was carried out half dead, and speedily departed from the city full of displeasure against the Jewish people. He therefore commenced a most barbarous persecution against

Execution by Elephants.

the Jews in Egypt on his return home. In the first place he caused a decree to be inscribed on brazen pillars at the palace-gate, that none should enter there who did not sacrifice to the gods he worshipped—which effectually excluded the Jews from all access to his person. Then he deprived the Jews in Alexandria of the high civil privileges they had enjoyed, degrading them from the first to the third or last class of inhabitants. He also ordered them to be formally enrolled, and that at the time of their enrolment, the mark of an ivy-leaf (one of the insignia of *his* god, Bacchus) should be impressed upon them with a hot iron: if any refused this mark they were to be made slaves; and whoever opposed the decree was to be put to death. Again, they were tempted to apostacy by the promise of restoration to the rank of citizens of the first class; but of the many thousands of Jews then at Alexandria, only three hundred appear to have submitted to the humiliating condition, and these were held in such abhorrence by the majority of their countrymen, and were so pointedly shunned, and excluded from the society of their old associates, that the king, when acquainted with it, was highly enraged, and regarded this as an opposition to his authority; he vowed to extirpate the whole nation. To begin with the Jews in Egypt, he ordered them all to be brought in chains to Alexandria. Having thus brought them all together, they were shut up in the hippodrome, which was a large enclosure outside the city, built for the purpose of horse-racing and other public amusements, where he intended to expose them as a spectacle, to be destroyed by elephants. At the appointed time, the people assembled in crowds, and the elephants were on the spot; but the effects of a drunken bout, the preceding night, prevented the attendance of the king, and caused the postponement of the show. The next day, a similar *disappointment* proceeded from the same unseemly cause. But on the third, the king managed to be present, and the elephants were brought out after they had been intoxicated with wine and frankincense to render them more ferocious. But they spent their fury, not on the unhappy Jews, but turned upon the spectators, of whom they destroyed great numbers. This, connected with some unusual appearances in the air, appeared to the king and his attendants so manifest an interposition of a Divine Power in behalf of the Jews, that he instantly ordered them to be set at liberty; and fearful of having provoked the vengeance of Heaven, he hastened to restore the Jews to their former privileges by rescinding all the decrees he had issued against them. Now also, his better reason gaining sway, considering that those who had so signally evinced their fidelity to their God were not likely to be unfaithful to their king, he bestowed upon them many marks of his munificence and confidence. Among other things, he abandoned to their disposal the three hundred apostates, who were speedily put to death by their offended brethren.*

Ptolemy Philopator died in B. C. 205, leaving his crown to PTOLEMY EPIPHANES, then a child five years of age. Meanwhile Antiochus III. had won the surname of Great, by his eminent successes in the East, where he restored the ancient supremacy of the Seleucidæ. At the death of Philopator, he had but recently returned from his eastern wars. He was not slow in perceiving the advantage which he might take of the infancy of the new king in accomplishing what had been one of the first objects of his reign. This design again exposed unhappy Palestine to all the horrors of war. The first campaign put Antiochus in possession of the standing bone of contention, Cœle-Syria and Palestine. It is remarkable that on this occasion the Jews relinquished their usual attachment to the Egyptian yoke, and took a very decided part with Antiochus. For this many reasons may be conceived, but none are distinctly known; we have however no doubt that one of them may be found in the indulgent consideration with which the Jews of Babylonia and other eastern provinces had been treated

* It is right to apprize the reader that the whole of this account of the visit of Philopator to Jerusalem and its consequences, down to this point, is not in Josephus, but is given on the sole authority of the author of the *third* book of Maccabees. In all, there are *five* books of Maccabees, of which *two* only are included in our Apocrypha. The *third*, which relates solely to this persecution of the Jews by Ptolemy Philopator, exists in Greek, and is found in some ancient manuscripts of the Greek Septuagint, particularly in the Alexandrian and Vatican manuscripts. There is also a Syriac version of it from the Greek; but it has never been inserted in the Vulgate, or in our English Bibles, but English translations of it exist. It appears to have been the work of an Alexandrian Jew; and while we admit that the book is full of absurdities, and that the authority is of very little value in itself, yet we think that in the outline facts, as related in the text, there is so much appearance of probability, and so many small agreements with the accounts which history has preserved of the manners and ideas and circumstances of the times, as well as with the character of the king, that we are disposed to regard it as substantially true. The silence of Josephus is indeed a suspicious circumstance to which we are willing that due weight should be given; but it will be noticed by every reader that the history of Josephus is remarkably brief at this period

by Antiochus—a fact which could not fail to be known in Palestine and at Jerusalem. The next year, however, Antiochus having been called away into Asia Minor, Palestine was speedily recovered by Scopas, the Egyptian general, who did not fail to make the Jews aware of his consciousness of the favor to Antiochus which they had manifested. The Egyptians were, however, soon again driven out of the country by Antiochus, and on this occasion such important services were rendered him by the Jews, and when he came to Jerusalem (B. C. 198), so lively were their demonstrations of joy, that the king, to confirm their attachment to his government, and to reward their services, granted them many important favors; and aware that there were no points on which they were more anxious than in what concerned their city and temple, he declared his intention to restore the city to its ancient splendor and dignity, and thoroughly to repair the temple at his own cost; he guarantied the inviolability of the sacred place from the intrusion of strangers; and by liberal grants, he made ample provision for the due and orderly performance of the sacred services. Antiochus also expressed his confidence in the attachment of the Jews by establishing colonies of them, on very advantageous terms, in Phrygia, Lydia, and other districts of doubtful fidelity—a circumstance which accounts for the great number of Jews scattered through those countries at the preaching of the gospel. (1 Pet. i. 1; James i. 1.) But it was the destiny of Antiochus to come into contact with the iron power which was ere long to break in pieces all the kingdoms of the earth, and to make their glory a vain thing. The ROMANS had already become great, and began to interfere with their usual haughtiness in the affairs of the East. The successful termination of the second Punic war had covered them with renown, and spread their fame far and wide; and already they had indicated to sagacious persons, by the reduction of Macedonia to the state of a subject kingdom, the ultimate tendencies of their great and still increasing power. Antiochus regarded this phenomenon with some apprehension, and perceiving, at the same time, what appeared advantageous opportunities of recovering in the north all that had belonged to the first Seleucus, he felt disposed to bring his southern contest to a conclusion. He therefore temporized with the Egyptians, whose power he had greatly underrated, and made an offer of his beautiful daughter Cleopatra in marriage with the young king of Egypt, as soon as he should become of age; promising, as her dower, to restore the provinces of Cœle-Syria and Palestine, which he had wrested from Egypt. The princess was accordingly betrothed to ·P. Epiphanes; but the marriage did not actually take place until B. C. 192, when the young monarch reached the eighteenth year of his age.

Antiochus availed himself of this settlement of affairs to prosecute his other plans. He reduced the maritime Greek cities of Asia Minor, and crossing the Hellespont, wrested the Chersonese from the weakened hands of the Macedonian king. This brought him into direct and fatal collision with the Romans. And here it may be observed that long before this the political sagacity of Ptolemy Philadelphus had detected the nascent greatness of the Roman state, and had anxiously cultivated its friendship. This also had been the policy of his successors; and the guardians of the young king, when apprehensive of the danger of Antiochus, had placed him under the guardianship of the republic.

When Antiochus had passed into Europe and taken possession of Thrace, the Romans sent an embassy to require restitution not only of all he had taken from Philip of Macedon, but of all that he had taken from their ward the king of Egypt. The Syrian king answered the requisition as haughtily as it was made; and it was manifest that an appeal to arms could not be far distant. What brought on the actual conflict was the passage of Antiochus into Greece, at the invitation of the Ætolians, who made him their commander-in-chief. In Greece his proceedings were not taken with that ability which distinguished the earlier part of his career, and in 191 B. C., he was utterly routed at Thermopylæ, and compelled to withdraw from Europe, by the consul Acilius Glabrio. The marriage of his daughter with Ptolemy had been completed the year before this at Raphia, but he still retained possession of the provinces to be ceded,* and endeavored to corrupt his daughter to betray the interests of her husband. But he was disappointed. She was more attached to

---

* Jerome and Appian say that Antiochus did surrender these provinces; and Josephus appears to concur with them, intimating that the revenues were paid to the Egyptian king. (Ant. xii. 4. 1.) But Polybius denies it; and this denial is confirmed by the fact that they still remained in the possession of the sons and successors of Antiochus.

Ptolemy than to her father; and, being probably dissatisfied at his breach of promise, she joined her husband in an embassy to Rome in 191 B. C., to congratulate the Romans on driving Antiochus out of Greece, and to assure the senate of the readiness of the king and queen to conform themselves to its directions.

Antiochus was now driven to seek peace with Rome; but the terms which they offered were so hard, that he could not bring himself to accept them. In all human probability he had brought himself into this condition by his inability to appreciate the value of the advice tendered to him by Hannibal, who, expelled from Carthage, had in 195 B. C., sought refuge at his court; and who, while he encouraged his enmity to the Romans, had exhorted him to make Italy the seat of the war. In 190 B. C., Cornelius Scipio (consul), assisted by his brother Africanus, passed over into Asia to conduct the war against Antiochus. Under their able management, it was soon brought to a conclusion, and the Syrian king was compelled from his capital of Antioch to sue for peace, which he obtained on very humiliating terms, but not essentially harder than those which he had at first refused. He relinquished all Asia Minor west of the Taurus: he agreed to pay all the expenses of the war, estimated at eighteen thousand Euobic talents, by regulated instalments; he was to deliver up his elephants and his ships-of-war (excepting twelve) to the Romans; and he was to give into their hands Hannibal and other eminent foreigners, who had sought protection at his court. The aged Carthaginian and another contrived to make their escape; but the rest were given up, together with the twelve hostages, for the observance of the treaty, among whom the king's younger son, Antiochus, surnamed Epiphanes was one. After this Antiochus withdrew to the eastern provinces of his empire, where he endeavored to collect the arrears of tribute due to him, to defray his heavy engagements to the Romans. There he was slain, two years after, by the natives of Elymais in Persia, when he attempted to seize the treasures contained in their rich temple. This was in B. C. 187, in the fifty-second year of his age, and the thirty-seventh of his reign. The leading events of his reign had been foreshown by Daniel (xi. 13–19).

SIMON II., who was high-priest of the Jews at the time of the unhappy visit of Ptolemy IV. to Jerusalem, died in B. C. 195, after an administration of twenty-two years. He was succeeded by his son ONIAS III. Onias was a person of great piety, and of mild and amiable disposition—and well worthy of better times than those in which he lived, and of a better end than it was his lot to experience. During the first years of his administration, when his excellent intentions received full effect under the favorable auspices of Antiochus and his successor, "the holy city was inhabited in all peace, and the laws were kept very well." The nation was also at this time held in such high estimation that the sovereigns of the neighboring countries courted its friendship, and made magnificent offerings to the temple. And we are persuaded that this was not merely on account of the Jews, but with the design of honoring and with the hope of propitiating their God, JEHOVAH, whose fame was by this time widely extended among the nations, and his power acknowledged and feared by many of them.

SELEUCUS IV., surnamed PHILOPATOR, the eldest son of Antiochus the Great, succeeded to the throne of his father, and to the heavy obligations under which he lay to the Romans. He was as well disposed toward the Jews as his father had been; and notwithstanding his embarrassments, gave orders that the charges of the public worship should continue to be defrayed out of his own treasury. But subsequently, upon the information of Simon—a Benjamite, who was made governor of the temple, and had quarrelled with Onias—that the treasury of the Jerusalem temple was very rich, and abundantly more than sufficient to supply the sacrifices and oblations,—the king, who was greatly straitened for money, to raise the money required by the Romans, sent his treasurer Heliodorus to seize and bring him the reported treasure. Heliodorus concealed the object of his journey until he reached Jerusalem, when he made it known to the high-priest, and demanded the quiet surrender of the money. Onias informed him in reply, that there was indeed considerable treasure in the temple; but by no means of such large amount as had been reported. Great part of it consisted of holy gifts, and offerings consecrated to God, and the appropriation of which could not be disturbed without sacrilege. The rest had been placed there by way of security, for the relief of widows and orphans, who claimed it as their property; and a considerable sum had been deposited there by Hyrcanus (the son of that Joseph who obtained the farming of the revenues from Ptolemy Euergetes, as before related), a person of great opulence and high rank. He added, that being by virtue of his office the guardian of this wealth, he could not consent to its being taken from the right owners, and thereby disgrace his office and profane the sanctity of that holy place which was held in reverence by all the world. Determined to fulfil his mission, whatever impression this statement may have made upon his mind, Heliodorus marched directly to the temple, and was there vainly opposed by the high-priest and the other ministers of the sacred services. The outer gates were ordered to be demolished; and the whole city was in the utmost agonies of apprehension. But when Heliodorus was about to enter, at the head of his Syrians, he was struck with a panic terror, similar to that which Ptolemy Philopator had before experienced, and, falling to the ground, speechless, he was carried off for dead by his guard. Onias prayed for him and he recovered, and made all haste to quit the city. His plan being thus frustrated, the guilty Simon had the effrontery to charge Onias himself with having procured this visit from Heliodorus: some believed it; and in consequence there arose hostile conflicts between the parties of Onias and Simon, in which many lives were lost. At last, Onias resolved to proceed himself to Antioch and lay the whole matter before Seleucus. He was favorably received by the king, who heard and credited his statements, and, in consequence, decreed the banishment of Simon from his native country. This was in B. C. 176. In the year following, Seleucus was induced to send his son Demetrius as a hostage to Rome, to relieve his own brother Antiochus, who had now been twelve years in that city. Demetrius had departed, and Antiochus was not come; and the absence of the two who stood next the throne afforded Heliodorus an opportunity of conspiring against his master, whom he removed by poison, and himself assumed the government. Antiochus was visiting Athens, on his way home, when he heard of this. He immediately applied himself to the old enemy of his father, Eumenes, king of Pergamos* (to whom the Romans had consigned the greater part of the territory in Asia Minor, which they compelled Antiochus the Great to cede) who, with his brother Attalus, was easily induced to assist him against the usurper. They succeeded, and their success placed the brother instead of the son of Seleucus upon the throne of Syria, with the concurrence of the Romans.

Antiochus IV. was scarcely settled on the throne before Jesus, or, by his Greek name, Jason,† repaired to Antioch, and, availing himself of the penury of the royal treasury, tempted the new king by the offer of four hundred and forty talents of silver to depose the excellent Onias III. from the high-priesthood, and to appoint himself in his place. He also obtained an order that Onias should be summoned to Antioch, and commanded to dwell there. Finding how acceptable money was to the king, Jason offered one hundred and fifty talents more for, and obtained, the privilege of erecting at Jerusalem a gymnasium, or place for such public sports and exercises as were usual among the Greeks, as well as for permission to establish an academy in which Jewish youth might be brought up after the manner of the Greeks; and also the important privilege of making what Jews he pleased free of the city of Antioch. The obvious object of all this was as opposite as possible to that of the Mosaic institutions. It was intended to facilitate the commixture of the Jews with foreigners, and to lessen the dislike with which the Greeks were disposed to regard a people so peculiar and so exclusive. This might have been a good design under general considerations of human policy, but was calculated to be most injurious and fatal as respected the Jews, whose institutions designedly made them a peculiar people, and whatever tended to make them otherwise must needs have been in counteraction of the great principle of their establishment. The effects which resulted from the exertions of Jason, after he had established himself in the high-priesthood, were such as might have been foreseen. The example of a person in his commanding position drew forth and gave full scope to the more lax dispositions which existed among the people, especially among the younger class, who were enchanted with the ease and freedom of the Grecian customs, and weary of the restraints and limitations of their own. Such as these abandoned themselves with all the phrensy of a new excitement, from which all restraint had been withdrawn, to the license which was offered to

* The founder of the celebrated library at Pergamos, and the reputed inventor of parchment.
† Most persons of consequence had now two names; one native Hebrew name, used among their own countrymen, and another Greek (as much as possible like the other in sound or meaning), used in their intercourse with the heathen.

them. The exercises of the gymnasium seem to have taken their minds with the force of a fascination. The priests neglected their service in the temple to be present at these spectacles. It is well known that some of these exercises were performed naked; and it is related that many of the Jewish competitors found means to efface the marks of circumcision, that they might not be distinguished from other people. In the Greek cities of Asia, in which Jews were settled, this became a common practice among those young men who wished to distinguish themselves in the sports of the gymnasium.[*] We allude to this as a striking illustration of the extent in which this rite operated in fulfilling its design of separating the Jews from other people. The year after his promotion, Jason sent some young men, on whom he had conferred the citizenship of Antioch, to assist at the games which were celebrated at Tyre (in the presence of Antiochus) in honor of Hercules. They were intrusted with a large sum of money, to be expended in sacrifices to that god. But even the least scrupulous of the high-priest's followers were not prepared to go to this extent with him, and instead of obeying their instructions, they presented the money to the Tyrians as a contribution toward the repair of their fleet.

Jason only enjoyed his ill-gotten dignity for three years. His younger brother Onias, or, by his Greek name, Menelaus, having been sent to Antioch with tribute, took advantage of the opportunity to ingratiate himself with Antiochus, and by offering three hundred talents more than Jason had paid, succeeded in getting himself appointed to the high-priesthood in his room. But he was repulsed in his attempt to assume that high office, and returned to Antioch, where he induced the king to establish him by force, by professing for himself and his associates an entire conformity to the religion of the Greeks. Jason was in consequence expelled by an armed force, and compelled to retire to the land of the Ammonites, leaving the pontificate to his still less scrupulous brother.

Menelaus found that he had over-taxed his resources in the payment he had agreed to make for his promotion, and in consequence of the non-payment he was summoned to Antioch by the king. Antiochus was absent when he arrived, and he soon learned that there was no hope of his retaining the favor of the king unless the payment was completed. Having exhausted his own coffers as well as credit, he privately sent to his brother Lysimachus (whom he had left as his representative at Jerusalem) to withdraw some of the sacred vessels of gold from the temple, to sell them at Tyre and the neighboring cities, and send him the amount. This disgraceful affair was not managed with such secrecy but that it came to the knowledge of his elder brother, the deposed high-priest, Onias III., who was still residing at Antioch, much respected by the numerous Jews of that city, before whom he spoke of this sacrilege in such strong language as threw them into such a state of ferment and displeasure as was likely to prove dangerous to Menelaus. He therefore, by bribery, prevailed on Andronicus, the king's deputy at Antioch, to put him to death. Onias, apprized of these intrigues, had taken refuge in the sanctuary of Daphne;[†] but was induced to quit it by the assurances and promises he received from Andronicus, and was barbarously murdered as soon as he had passed the sacred bounds. This atrocious deed raised a terrible outcry among the Jews at Antioch, who hastened to make their complaints to the king on his return to that city. Antiochus, to do him justice, was much affected, and shed tears, when he heard them. He promised justice, and performed it; for, after proper investigation, Andronicus was stripped of his purple, and put to death on the very spot where Onias had been murdered. Menelaus, the more guilty of the two, found means to escape the storm which destroyed the agent of his crime. But the sums of money which were necessary to enable him to maintain his credit, obliged his brother Lysimachus to resort to such repeated and unheard-of exactions, violence, and sacrilege, that the people of Jerusalem rose against him, scattered like chaff the three thousand men he had got to defend him, and, when he himself fled to the treasury of the temple, pursued and slew him there.

Antiochus having soon after come to Tyre, the Jewish elders sent three venerable deputies thither to justify this act, and to accuse Menelaus as the author of all the troubles which had happened in Judea and Antioch. The case which they made out was so strong, and was heard with so much attention by the king, that Menelaus

---

* To this practice allusions are made by St. Paul: Rom. ii. 25; 1 Cor. vii. 18.
† This was a grove about three miles from Antioch, which had been made a sanctuary for criminals and a place of pleasure. In the end the place became so infamous that no man of character could visit it.

felt greatly alarmed for the result. He therefore applied himself to. the king's favorite, Ptolemy Macron, and promised him so large a sum that he was induced to watch the inconstant temper of the king, and availed himself of an opportunity of getting him not only to absolve Menelaus, but to condemn the three Jewish deputies to death. This most unjust and horrid sentence was immediately executed. This terrible crime shocked the whole nation, and was abhorrent even to foreigners, for the Tyrians ventured to express their sense of the wrong, by giving an honorable burial to the murdered men. The ultimate effect was to make Antiochus himself a sharer in the aversion with which Menelaus was regarded by the nation : but, at the same time, the paramount influence of that guilty person with the king seemed to be so clearly manifested, that all further notion of resisting his authority was abandoned, and he was enabled to resume his station at Jerusalem. This was greatly facilitated by the presence of the king himself with a powerful army in the country, for which circumstance we must now proceed to account.

It will be remembered that the king of Egypt, Ptolemy Epiphanes, had been married to Cleopatra, daughter of Antiochus the Great, and sister of the present Antiochus. Ptolemy was taken off by poison in B. C. 181, after a profligate and troubled reign of twenty-four years. He left three children: Ptolemy Philometor, Ptolemy Physcon, and Cleopatra, who was successively married to her two brothers.

Ptolemy VI., surnamed Philometor ("mother-loving"), was but a child at the death of his father, and the government was conducted with ability by his mother Cleopatra. But she died in B. C. 173, on which the regency devolved on Eulæus the eunuch, and Lennæus, the prime minister—the tutors of the young prince. They immediately advanced a claim to the possession of Cœle-Syria and Palestine, on the ground that they had been secured to Ptolemy Lagus by the partition-treaty of B. C. 301; and that they had again been given by Antiochus the Great in dowry with his daughter Cleopatra on her becoming queen of Egypt. Antiochus refused to listen to such demands; and both parties sent deputies to Rome to argue their respective claims before the senate.

When Philometor had completed his fourteenth year, he was solemnly invested with the government, on which occasion embassies of congratulation were sent from all the neighboring nations. Apollonius, the ambassador of Antiochus, was instructed to take the opportunity of sounding the dispositions of the Egyptian court; and when this person informed Antiochus that he was viewed as an enemy by the Egyptians, he immediately proceeded to Joppa, to survey his frontiers toward Egypt, and to put them in a state of defence. On this occasion he paid a visit to Jerusalem. The city was illuminated, and the king was received by Jason (who was then high-priest) with every demonstration of respect. Afterward he returned to Antioch through Phœnicia.

Having completed his preparations for war, Antiochus, in B. C. 171, led his army along the coast of Palestine, and gave the Egyptians a signal overthrow at Pelusium. He then left garrisons on the frontier and withdrew into winter-quarters at Tyre. It was during his stay there that the deputies arrived to complain of Menelaus, and were put to death, as just related. In the spring of the next year (B. C. 170) Antiochus undertook a second expedition against the Egyptians, and attacked them by sea and land. He defeated them on the frontiers and took Pelusium. After his victory he might have cut the Egyptian army in pieces, but he behaved with such humanity as gained him great favor with the Egyptians. At length all surrendered to him voluntarily; and with a small body of troops he overran all the country except Alexandria, and obtained possession of the person of the young king, whom he treated with apparent consideration and regard.

While Antiochus was thus employed, a rumor of his death before Alexandria reached Palestine, on which the deposed high-priest, Jason, quitted the land of the Ammonites, and with a party, assisted by friends within, surprised Jerusalem, massacred the citizens, drove his brother Menelaus into the castle, and possessed himself of the principality. But he was speedily compelled to quit the city and country, at the news that Antiochus was alive, and marching with a powerful army against Jerusalem. After wandering from one place to another, a fugitive and a vagabond, Jason at last perished miserably, a refugee in the strange land of Lacedæmonia. The news of this movement had been reported to Antiochus with such exaggeration as led him to conclude that Judea had revolted; and being further provoked by hearing that the Jews had made public rejoicings at the news of his death, he marched in great wrath from Egypt, took Jerusalem by assault, destroyed eighty thousand persons, plundered the temple of all its treasures, vessels, and golden ornaments, and carried away one thousand eight hundred talents to Antioch.

Ptolemy Philometer being now actually under the power of Antiochus, the people of Alexandria proclaimed his brother king under the name of Ptolemy Euergetes II.; but who was afterward nick-named Physcon ("big-belly") on account of his corpulency. This afforded Antiochus a pretext for returning the next year (B. C. 169) to Egypt with the declared intention of supporting Ptolemy Philometor in the throne, but with the real purpose of bringing the whole country under his power. At the end, however, perceiving that the conquest of Alexandria would be an undertaking of great difficulty, he withdrew to Memphis, and affected to deliver up the kingdom to Philometor, and returned to Antioch. But as he retained in his own hands Pelusium, the key of the kingdom on the side of Syria, his ulterior designs were transparent to Philometor, who therefore made an agreement with Physcon that they should share the government between them and resist Antiochus with their united power; and also that a joint embassy should be sent to Rome to implore the protection of the republic against their uncle.

This brought on a fourth invasion of Egypt by Antiochus (B. C. 168), who now threw off the mask he had hitherto chosen to wear, and declared himself the enemy of both the brother kings. He took possession of all the country as far as Alexandria, and then advanced toward that city. He was within four miles thereof, when he was met at Eleusis, by the ambassadors which the Roman republic had sent to adjust these differences. And this they did in the usual summary manner of that arrogant people. At the head of the ambassadors was Popilius Lænas, whom Antiochus had known during his thirteen years' residence at Rome. Rejoiced to see him, Antiochus stretched forth his arms to embrace him. But the Roman sternly repelled the salute, demanding first to receive an answer to the written orders of the senate, which he delivered. The king intimated that he would confer on the matter with his friends, and acquaint the ambassadors with the result: on which Popilius drew with his staff a circle around the king on the sand, and said, " I require your answer before you quit this circle." The king was confounded; but after a moment of rapid and condensed deliberation, he bowed his proud head, and said, falteringly, " I will obey the senate !" On which Popilius, who had hitherto seen only the *king* of Syria, recognised the *friend*, and extended to him his hand. Perhaps this conduct in either party would not have occurred the year, or even the month before; but the Romans had just concluded their war with Perseus, and made Macedonia a Roman province, and the ambassadors had waited at Delos to learn the issue of this war before they sailed for Egypt.

Antiochus obeyed the senate, by immediately withdrawing his forces from Egypt. On his way homeward, he marched along the coast of Palestine; and he despatched Apollonius, his general, with twenty-two thousand men to vent his mortification and fury upon the inhabitants of Jerusalem, which, as well as the rest of the province, had for two years been groaning under the tyranny and rapacity of Philip, the Phrygian governor, " more barbarous than his master;" and of Menelaus the apostate highpriest, " worse than all the rest." Apollonius came to Jerusalem, and as his men remained quiet, and he was himself known as the collector of the tribute in Palestine, and as such usually attended by an armed force, his hostile intentions were not suspected by the Jews. All things remained quiet until the sabbath, on which day, it was known, the Jews of that age would not fight even in self-defence. The soldiers were then let loose, and scoured the streets, slaughtering all they met—who suffered themselves meekly to be slain, none being found who attempted to stand on their defence. The women and children were spared, to be sold for slaves. All the streets of Jerusalem, and the courts of the temple flowed with blood; the houses were pillaged and the city wall thrown down. Apollonius then demolished all the buildings near Mount Zion, and with the materials strengthened the fortifications of the citadel, which he furnished with a garrison and held under his own command. This castle was so situated as to give the garrison complete command of the temple, and the remains of the people would no longer visit the sanctuary, or the priests perform the public services of religion. Accordingly, in the month of June, B. C. 167 the daily sacrifice ceased, and Jerusalem was soon completely deserted, as the surviving inhabitants fled to the cities of the neighboring Gentiles.

An edict was now issued at Antioch, and proclaimed in all the provinces of Syria, commanding the inhabitants of the whole empire to worship the gods of the king, and to acknowledge no religion but his—with the declared object " that all should become one people." Antiochus was unquestionably a madman. This is not doubted by any one who has studied the whole of his history, which it has been no part of our duty to relate: and it is surely not very necessary to analyse the interior motives of a madman's acts. Hales fancies that "this general persecution seems to have been raised by Antiochus, not from any regard to his own religion, but from a regular plan and deep-laid scheme of plundering the temples throughout his dominions, after he had suppressed their worship. For the temples were not only enriched by the offerings of the votaries, but from their sanctity were the great banks of deposite, and the grand magazines of commerce." But there was no general persecution, although the edict was general in its terms. The cities containing the wealthiest temples already worshipped the gods of Greece; and it must have been known, as proved the fact, that none of the other pagan nations would make much difficulty in complying with the royal edict. It must have been known, in fact, that none but the Jews were likely to oppose themselves to the operation of this decree; and we are therefore not disposed to look for any deeper cause than the insane abhorrence which Antiochus had conceived against that people, and which he could not safely manifest without bringing them into a condition of apparent contumacy, which might, in some degree, excuse, in the eyes of the heathen, his contemplated severities against them.

The pagan generally, as we have intimated, found no difficulty in complying with the royal edict. The Samaritans, who were anxious to claim a Jewish origin in the time of Alexander, now wrote to Antiochus to inform him that they were Sidonians, and offered to dedicate their temple on Mount Gerizim to Jupiter Xenius, "the defender of strangers." Even many Jews submitted to the edict for fear of punishment, and a still greater number, long attached to the customs of the Greeks, were glad to avail themselves of the apparent compulsions under which they were now placed. But the better part of the people fled, and kept themselves concealed. An old man of the name of Athenæus was sent to Jerusalem to instruct the Jews in the Greek religion, and to compel the observance of its rites. He dedicated the temple to Jupiter Olympius, and on the altar of Jehovah he placed a smaller altar to be used in sacrificing to the heathen god. This new altar, built by order of the desolater Antiochus, is what Daniel alludes to when he speaks of the "abomination that maketh desolate," or "abomination of desolation."* This altar was set up on the fifteenth day of the month Cisleu (November—December), and the heathen sacrifices were commenced on the twenty-fifth of the same month. Circumcision, the keeping of the sabbath, and every peculiar observance of the law was made a capital offence; and all the copies of the law which could be found were taken away, defaced, torn in pieces, burned. The reading of it was forbidden; and it is said to have been at this time that the Jews first took to the public reading in the synagogues, of the other books of Scripture, as substitutes for the interdicted Pentateuch, which usage they afterward retained, when the reading of the law was restored. Groves were consecrated, and idolatrous altars erected in every city, and the citizens were required to offer sacrifices to the gods, and to eat swine's flesh every month on the birth-day of the king; and on the feast of Bacchus, the Jews were compelled to join in the celebration, and to walk in procession crowned with ivy. Instant death was the penalty of refusal. Among other instances of cruel punishment at Jerusalem, two women, with their infant children, whom they had circumcised with their own hands, were thrown from the battlements on the south side of the temple, into the deep vale below. Officers were sent into all the towns, attended by bands of soldiers, to enforce obedience to the royal edict.

It seems that ultimately Antiochus came into Palestine to observe that his orders had been duly executed; and the history relates that he commanded and superintended the most horrible tortures of the recusants:—particular mention is made of the martyrdom of Eleazer, in his ninetieth year, for refusing to eat swine's flesh (2 Macc. vi. 18–31); and of the heroic matron and her seven sons, who nobly set the royal

---

* This is from Jahn, who remarks further, "This interpretation agrees much better with the literal meaning of the words than that adopted by those who apply this expression to the erecting of an image to Jupiter Olympius; a mode of explanation which is at variance with the authority of Josephus and the first book of Maccabees. Undoubtedly there was an image erected to Jupiter Olympius, for the pagan religion required it; but this is not the circumstance referred to by the prophet, in the words which have been quoted."

madman at defiance and professed their belief that "The King of the World would raise up to everlasting life those who died for his laws;" and threatening their tormentor that "he should have no resurrection to life, but receive the just punishment of his pride through the judgment of God." Never before were the Jews exposed to so furious a persecution—indeed it is the first time in which they can be said to have been persecuted on account of their religion. It was undoubtedly made instrumental in the then great mission of the Jews in calling the attention of the heathen to the great principles of doctrine of which they had been the special conservators. The mere fact of this conspicuous persecution for opinion, which was a new thing to the heathen, and still more the historical results of this persecution, were calculated to draw the attention of every reflecting mind among the heathen to those religious peculiarities on behalf of which such numbers of the Jewish people were willing to peril their lives.

The persecution had lasted about six months, when God raised up a deliverer for a people whom he had not yet abandoned, in the noble family of the Asamoneans. MATTATHIAS was the son of John, the son of Simon, the son of Asamonias, from whom the family took its name. He was a priest of the course of Joarib, the first of the twenty-four courses appointed by David (1 Chron. xxiv. 7), descended from Phineas, the son of Eleazer, the elder branch of the family of Aaron (1 Macc. ii. 55). He had five sons, whose names were JOHANAN (John), SIMON, JUDAS, ELEAZER, and JONATHAN. He was one of the principal inhabitants of Modin, a town near the seashore, about a mile from Joppa (Jaffa), and four miles from Lydda or Diospolis. To this city a royal officer named Appelles was sent to enforce the edict. With many fair promises, he endeavored to induce Mattathias, as a leading man in the place, to set the example of sacrificing to the idol. But the undaunted priest repelled his offers with indignation and abhorrence, and with a loud voice, in the hearing of the whole assembly, proclaimed his refusal to sacrifice. At this juncture a certain Jew passed toward the altar with the intention of sacrificing, when Mattathias, in obedience to the law, struck him down with his own hand, as a rebel against Jehovah. This was the earnest-blood of the great war which followed. Kindled by his own act, the zealous priest and his sons, assisted by the citizens, whom their daring act emboldened, rushed upon the commissioner and his retinue, slew them on the spot, and tore down the idolatrous altar. Alive to the consequences of this deed, Mattathias proclaimed through the city, "Whosoever is zealous for the law, and a maintainer of the covenant, let him follow me!" Thus he and his sons fled to the mountains of Judea. They were only *ten* in number at first, but were soon joined by many Jews who were determined to maintain the religion of their fathers.

These conscientious persons were disposed to construe the obligations of the law all the more rigidly and literally, out of opposition to the loose principles of those who had joined the Greeks—it being the tendency of all great struggles to produce extreme parties. They hence held it to be imperative to abstain from the use of arms on the sabbath day. In consequence of this a thousand persons, who had taken refuge in a large cave not far from Jerusalem, allowed themselves to be slaughtered on that day without the least resistance. This event opened the eyes of Mattathias and his adherents; who, after mature deliberation, determined that it was not only lawful, but their duty, to stand on their defence on the sabbath day; although they still thought themselves bound from voluntarily becoming on that day the assailants. They took every means of making this resolution known throughout the country, so that from that time no scruples on the subject were entertained.

Meanwhile the party of Mattathias went on steadily increasing, until it amounted to a considerable body of men, who were prepared to hazard everything in defence of their religion. This ardor could not long be restrained, and Mattathias, emerging from his concealment, went with them throughout the Jewish cities, and everywhere demolished the idolatrous altars, circumcised the children, slew the apostate Jews and the officers appointed to execute the decree of Antiochus, recovered many of the copies of the law which the oppressors had taken away, and gained several important advantages over the enemy. While engaged in these expeditions the heroic priest died, in the year B. C. 167. Before his death he appointed his third and bravest son, Judas, to be military leader; associating with him Simon, his second and most prudent son, as counsellor. Judas is supposed to have derived his celebrated surname of *Maccabeus* from a cabalistic word formed of M. C. B. I., the initial letters of the He-

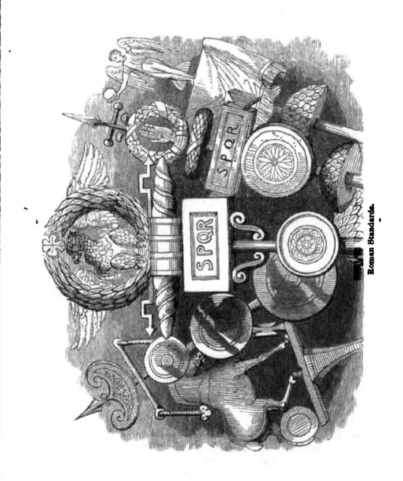

Roman Standards.

brew text *Mi Chamoka Baalim Jehovah*, "Who is like unto thee among the gods, O Jehovah!" (Exod. vi. 11), which letters *might* have been displayed on his sacred standard: like the S. P. Q. R. for *Senatus populus que Romanus* on the Roman ensigns.

The noble war for the rights of opinion commenced by Mattathias was carried on for twenty-six years by his illustrious sons—counting from the first stroke at Modin—with five successive kings of Syria. Within this period Judas and his brothers established the independence of their country and the aggrandizement of their family, after destroying above two hundred thousand of the best troops of the Syrian kings. "Such a triumph of a petty province over a great empire is hardly to be paralleled in the annals of history." (Hales ii. 551.)

The first enterprise of Judas, and his comparatively small but resolute band, was against Apollonius, whose barbarous exploits at Jerusalem have lately been recorded. He was at the head of a large army, but was defeated and slain by Judas, who took his sword, with which he afterward fought all his life long.

The next exploit of Judas was the defeat of Seron, a Syrian general, with a large host of Græcising Jews and apostate Samaritans. The small force with which he achieved this victory was encouraged by the hero in the words of Jonathan, the son of Saul, "With the God of Heaven it is all one to deliver with a great multitude or a small company:" adding the emphatic words, "*We fight for our lives and our laws.*" This battle was fought near Betheron.

Antiochus was filled with rage and indignation at these successes of an adversary which seemed so contemptible, but whose fame had now spread into all the neighboring nations. He formed large plans of vengeance, but finding these checked by the exhausted state of his treasury—for he had squandered wealth like a madman, as he was—he resolved to proceed into the eastern provinces to recruit his finances. His son, the heir of his crown, then about seven years old, he committed to the care of Lysias, "a nobleman, and one of the blood royal," and appointed him regent of all the western provinces, from the Euphrates to Egypt, and commissioned him to raise and march an army to extirpate the Jews, and to plant a foreign colony in their room, B. C. 166.

The next year Lysias was able to send a large army of forty thousand foot and seven thousand horse into Judea, under the command of Nicanor and Gorgias. So confident were they of victory that Nicanor proclaimed a sale of the captive Jews beforehand, at the rate of ninety for a talent, or about two pounds sterling a head. This drew a crowd of merchants from the coast to the Syrian camp at Emmaus, near Jerusalem, to make a cheap purchase of slaves. This was *not* a peculiar circumstance; for it was then usual (according to Polybius) for the march of armies to be attended by slave-dealers. Under these alarming circumstances Judas and his party assembled at Mizpeh—that ancient place of concourse—where they fasted and prayed; after which Judas, in obedience to the law, dismissed all such of his men as had in the course of the preceding year built houses, betrothed wives, or were planting vineyards, or were fearful; and this strong act of faith reduced his small army from six thousand to three thousand men.

The Syrian generals deemed it superfluous to employ their large force against so small a body. Gorgias, therefore, with a chosen army of five thousand foot and one thousand horse, marched by night to surprise the army of Judas. But that vigilant commander was apprized of the design, and determined to take advantage of the separation of the two generals. He marched therefore early in the evening, and fell by night upon the camp of Nicanor. Not the least expectation of an attack being entertained, the whole camp was thrown into confusion, and the soldiers fled. Three thousand Syrians were slain, and many soldiers and slave-dealers made prisoners. Early in the morning Gorgias, returning from his abortive march to Mizpeh, beheld the Syrian camp in flames, which threw his soldiers into such a panic that they betook themselves to instant flight; but were pressed upon so vigorously by the conquering Jews, that in all they destroyed that day nine thousand of their enemies, and wounded many more. Nicanor escaped in the disguise of a slave to Antioch, declaring his conviction that a mighty God fought for the Jews. In the camp of the Syrians the latter found great quantities of gold and silver, including the money which the slave-dealers had brought to purchase their persons. This victory was celebrated by a feast of thanksgiving.

On the news of this defeat, the regent Lysias assembled a larger army of sixty thousand choice infantry, and five thousand horse, and marched himself at their head, to invade Judea in the south. He entered Idumea, which name must be understood as distinguishing the more modern territory of the Edomites, from their older and more southern territory of Edom, in Mount Seir, which the Nabathæans now occupied. Idumea was now, then, confined to the region west and southwest of the Asphaltic lake, which had in former times belonged to the tribes of Simeon and Judah. But after the Captivity it had been occupied by Edomites from Arabia Petræa, the ancient Edom, who made Hebron their capital, and rebuilt, on their northern frontier, the strong fortress of Bethsur, or Bethsura, which had been originally built by Rehoboam. (2 Chron. xi. 7.) At this last-named very advantageous post, Lysias encamped, and was there set upon by the dauntless Judas, who, with only ten thousand men, gained a most important victory, slaying five thousand men on the spot, and putting the rest to flight. Observing that the Jews fought like men who were determined to conquer or die, Lysias did not venture to renew the engagement, and indeed his soldiers were so disheartened that he was soon obliged to return to Antioch, and there issue orders that recruits for a new expedition should be raised in distant countries, B. C. 165.

This victory made Judas master of Judea; and he determined to return to Jerusalem, to repair and beautify the temple, which was then deserted and dilapidated. In the neglected courts of the Lord's house shrubs were growing "as in the forest or on the mountain." The whole host cast ashes on their heads, and cried toward heaven, when they beheld the desolation of that holy place. The work of restoration was commenced with ardor; new utensils were provided for the sacred services; the old altar, having been defiled by idolatrous sacrifices, was taken away, and a new one erected in its place; and the sacrifices were recommenced precisely three years after the temple had been dedicated to Jupiter Olympius. A feast of eight days celebrated this new dedication, and an annual festival was instituted in honor of the event.

The castle on Mount Zion soon, however, proved a serious annoyance to the people, as it was still in the hands of the Syrians, who lost no opportunity of disturbing the services of the temple. The army of Judas was too small to allow him to blockade the castle, but he fortified the temple-mount against their aggressions with high walls and towers. He also strengthened the important fortress of Bethsura, to protect the frontier toward Idumea, as it lay about mid-way between Jerusalem and Hebron.

When Antiochus Epiphanes received intelligence of the success of the Jewish arms, and the defeat of the Syrian hosts, he was at Élymias in Persia, detained by an insurrection occasioned by his plundering the celebrated temple in which his father Antiochus the Great had lost his life. Transported with ungovernable passion at the news, he hastened his homeward march to Antioch, devoting the Jewish nation to utter destruction. But while his mouth uttered the deep curses and fell purposes of his heart, he was smitten with sore and remediless torments in his inner parts. Yet on he went, until he fell from his chariot, and suffered much from the fall. He was then carried on a litter, but his disease acquired such a loathsome character that his person became an abhorrence to himself and to all who had occasion to be near him. In a disease so timed and so peculiar, the proud monarch was led to perceive the hand of God, and to acknowledge that his barbarities and sacrileges were justly punished by the torments which he endured and by the death which lay before him. He died early in the year 164 B. C., and in him perished a man whose wild extravagances dissolute and undignified character, savage cruelties, and capricious alternations of temper, abundantly justified the nickname of Epimanes, "madman" by which in his later years his assumed title of Epiphanes "illustrious" was ridiculed.

Antiochus V., surnamed Eupator "well-fathered", then a child nine years of age, was set up for king by his guardian Lysias, and his succession received the important sanction of the Romans; for although Demetrius (the son of Seleucus Philopator), still a hostage at Rome, and then twenty-three years of age, failed not to urge his claims upon the attention of the senate, that sage body decided that it was more for the interests of Rome that a minor should occupy the throne of Syria, than the ardent and able Demetrius.

In the year 164 B. C.; the war against the Maccabees was renewed by the regent Lysias. He invaded Judea with an army of eighty thousand foot, eighty elephants, and a large body of cavalry. He laid siege to Bethsura, but was repulsed by Judas, with the loss of eleven thousand foot, and one thousand six hundred horse, and his whole army was broken up. This defeat convinced Lysias that the Jews could not be overcome, because of the almightiness of the God by whom they were helped. He therefore offered them peace, on the condition of their being loyal to the state; on their acceptance of which, he issued a decree in the name of the king, which allowed them the free exercise of their own customs and worship, and permitted them to live according to their own laws. The apostate high-priest Menelaus, who had been all this while with the Syrians, and had exerted himself in promoting this peace, was now sent back to the Jews to be reinstated in his pontificate. It is of some importance to note that the Roman ambassadors at the Syrian court used their efficient aid in obtaining this treaty for the Jews.

The peace thus afforded was of no long continuance: for although, formally, the war with the kingdom had ceased, the governors of the Syrian provinces were not backward in giving the Jews all the molestation in their power, and in encouraging such of the neighboring nations as were, from old or new enmities, disposed to disturb them—such as the Joppites, the Jamnites, the Arabians, and the Idumeans, all of whom were successively reduced by Judas, after a bloody warfare, the particulars of which are recorded in 2 Macc. x. 14–38; xi. 1–38.

All this time the citadel on Mount Zion, garrisoned by Syrians and renegade Jews, continued to prove a great annoyance to the temple worship, which at last proved so intolerable, that Judas was induced to lay siege to it, after his return from the defeat of Gorgias the governor of Idumea. But some of the besieged, forcing their way through in a sally, hastened to the court at Antioch, and complained of the continued hostility of the Jews to the Syrian government, as evinced by this attempt upon the Syrian garrison; and by dwelling on this and other matters, contrived to stir up Lysias to undertake a new war against them. The Syrian army which was raised for this war in B. C. 163, consisted of one hundred thousand foot, twenty thousand horse, thirty-two elephants, and three hundred chariots armed with scythes—a prodigious force in that age, when, on account of the extravagant wages which soldiers received, it was difficult to keep more than eighty thousand men in the field. The young king was present in the camp, but of course Lysias was the actual commander. The Jews did not venture to attack the royal army in the open field. But while the Syrians laid seige to Bethsura, Judas fell upon them in the night, slew four thousand of them before they well knew who was among them, and drew off safely by break of day. The day after, a battle took place, in which the Syrians lost six hundred men; but Judas, fearing to be surrounded by the numbers of the enemy, thought proper to retire to Jerusalem, the fortifications of which he now strengthened and put in a state of defence. In this battle Judas lost his brother Eleazer. That valiant man perceiving one of the elephants more splendidly caparisoned than the others, mistakenly supposed it to be that of the king, and fought his way to it, got under it, stabbed it in the belly, and was crushed to death by the fall of the huge beast upon him.

It being a sabbatic year of rest to the land, Bethsura soon after surrendered for lack of provisions; and Jerusalem, which was next besieged, must have shared the same fate, and all the advantages which had been gained appeared now to be on the point of being lost for ever; when providentially the young king and his guardian were re-called by a civil war at home, commenced by Philip, who had been appointed regent by Antiochus Epiphanes before his death, to the exclusion of Lysias, whose ill success in the former war with the Jews had been highly displeasing to him. When this intelligence reached the camp, the king and council hastily concluded a peace with the Jews on the former terms—that they should be allowed to live according to their own laws. The siege was then broken up, but the treaty was violated by the Syrians in the demolition of the strong walls of the mount on which the temple stood. The royal army was then marched against Philip, who had gotten possession of Antioch, the metropolis, but who was defeated and slain.

Now at last the traitor and apostate Menelaus met the fate he had long deserved. At the approach of the Syrian army he had abandoned his countrymen, and had stimulated the operations against them by his advice and counsel, in the secret hope of being made governor of the province, if Judas and his party were destroyed. But the intended mischief recoiled on his own wicked head. On the conclusion of the peace, he was viewed by the king and regent as the author of all these unhappy wars, and was sentenced to be suffocated in the ash-tower at Berea;* while the office to which he aspired was given to Judas himself, who was appointed to be chief governor " from Ptolemais unto the Gerrhenians."

In the room of Menelaus, Jachimus, or Alcimus, was nominated to the high-priesthood, to the exclusion of the rightful claimant, Onias, the son of that Onias who had been slain at Antioch at the instigation of Menelaus. Upon this disappointment, Onias retired in disgust to Egypt, where his military and political talents procured him high favor from Ptolemy Philometor, and he was ultimately empowered to build a temple and establish a priesthood, for the numerous Jews of Egypt and Cyrene, at Heliopolis; and which subsisted nearly as long as that of Jerusalem, both being destroyed in the reign of Vespasian. There can be no question of the irregularity of this establishment; and although Onias justified it to the Jews by reference to the text Isa. xix. 18, 19, the temple at Jerusalem was always held in much superior estimation by the Jews even of Egypt, who frequently repaired thither to worship.

CHAPTER XXV.

WITH the promotion of Judas Maccabeus to be chief governor of Judea, the rule of the Asamonian dynasty may be conveniently taken to commence, and the period which that rule embraces may be suitably introduced in a new chapter.

Alcimus, the new high-priest, did not long enjoy his dignity, for his profligacy, and his attempts to revive the heathenish rites, so offended the Jews, that they expelled him.

We have already noticed the refusal of the Roman senate to support the claim of Demetrius to the crown of Syria, or to allow him to depart for that country. Subsequently, acting by the advice of his friend Polybius, the historian, he made his escape from Rome, and landed with a few men, only eight friends and their servants, at Tripolis in Phœnicia. Here he had the art to make it believed that his wild enterprise was sanctioned by the Romans; under which persuasion he was joined by several of his adherents, with whom he advanced toward Antioch. Here the army declared for him, and secured the persons of Antiochus Eupator and Lysias, and, in proof of their sincerity, brought them to Demetrius; but he said, "Let me not see their face!" on which hint they were slain by the soldiers, B. C. 162.

In the preceding year one of the Roman ambassadors at the court of A. Eupator had been slain, while enforcing the treaty with Antiochus the Great, by destroying all the elephants, and all but twelve of the ships-of-war. Demetrius, anxious to have his claims recognised by Rome, sent the murderer thither, together with a present of a crown of gold. The present was accepted by the senate; but they dismissed the murderer, resolving to take some future occasion of making the whole Syrian empire responsible for the act.

When Demetrius was established on the throne of Syria, the apostate Jews, with Alcimus at their head, gathered around him, and filled his ears with reports and insinuations injurious to Judas and the party of which he was the leader. As people naturally listen with pleasure to those who express conformity of views, it is not wonderful that these traitors gained the attention of the king, who could as yet know but little of the real state of affairs in his kingdom. He reappointed Alcimus as high-priest, and sent a considerable military force, under the command of Bacchides, governor of Mesopotamia, to reinstate him, and to take vengeance upon those whom he had represented as equally the enemies of himself and the king. As Bacchides, accompanied by the high-priest, entered the country with professions of peace, many Jews, relying thereon, put themselves in his power, and were treacherously slain. After this Bacchides reinstated Alcimus; and intrusting the province to his charge, and leaving a force that seemed sufficient to support him, he returned to the king. Judas, who had not appeared in the field against Bacchides, came forward after he withdrew; and Alcimus, unable to offer any effectual resistance, again repaired with

* This punishment was borrowed by the Syrian-Greeks from the Persians. A place was enclosed with high walls and filled with ashes. A piece of timber was made to project over the ashes, and on this the criminal was placed. He was liberally supplied with meat and drink, until overcome with sleep, he fell into the deceitful heap, and died an easy death. Only criminals of high rank were thus punished, it being considered a sort of privileged death.

his complaints to the king. On this Demetrius, resolving on the utter destruction of the Maccabees, sent a large army into Judea, under the command of the same Nicanor whom Judas had defeated five years before. At first he endeavored to entrap the Jewish chief with friendly professions, but finding Judas too wary to be thus caught, hostilities commenced, and in a battle fought at Capharsalama, Nicanor was defeated with the loss of fifty thousand men. He was then forced to seek refuge in the castle of Mount Zion, until the reinforcements, for which he sent, should arrive from Syria. These were promptly supplied, and then he hazarded another battle, in which he was himself slain, and his army cut in pieces. B. C. 160.

Now Judas, having heard of the already extensive conquests of the Romans, and having become sensible of the great controlling power which they exercised in the affairs of Western Asia and of Egypt, took the opportunity of the respite which this victory procured, to send an embassy to Rome, to solicit an alliance with that great people, and therewith protection from the Syrian government. It was part of the systematic plan of subjugation practised by that most politic body, the Roman senate, to grant liberty to those who were under foreign dominion, that they might detach them from their rulers, and afterward enslave them when fit opportunity offered.* The Jewish ambassadors were therefore very graciously received; an offensive and defensive alliance was readily concluded with the Jews; and a letter was immediately after written to Demetrius, commanding him to desist from persecuting them, and threatening him with war if he persisted. But before the ambassadors returned, or this letter had been received, Judas had fallen in a furious conflict with Bacchides, whom (with Alcimus) the king had sent to avenge the defeat of Nicanor and his host. With only eight hundred men, the rest having deserted him, Judas charged the Syrians, defeated their right wing and pursued them to Azotus: but the left wing, being unbroken, pursued him closely in turn; and after a most obstinate engagement the greatest of the later Jewish heroes lay dead upon the field. This was not far from Modin, his native town; and his brothers Simon and Jonathan, having concluded a truce, were enabled to deposite his remains in the family sepulchre at that place.

The death of Judas restored the ascendency to the apostate Jews, and was followed by a merciless persecution of his adherents. They were thus made strongly sensible of the want of a head, and therefore they elected Jonathan, the valiant younger brother of Judas, to be their chief and leader. He led them into the wilderness of Tekoah, and encamped at the cistern of Aspher. After some skirmishes with the Arabs in that quarter, Jonathan deemed it advisable to send the wives and children, and the most valuable property of his party, to the safe keeping of the friendly Nabathæans of Mount Seir, under a convoy commanded by his brother John. This party was attacked on the way and plundered by the Arabs, and John himself was killed. For this, Jonathan soon after took a severe revenge upon the bridal procession at the marriage of one of the princesses of this same tribe, which he attacked, and slew the greater part, and took their spoils.

After this, Jonathan, the more effectually to secure to himself from his enemies, withdrew into the marshes formed by the overflowings of the Jordan, access to which was very difficult. Bacchides, however, made an attack on the sabbath-day upon the pass leading to the camp, and carried it by storm. The Jews defended themselves with great valor; but being oppressed by numbers, they leaped into the overflowing Jordan and swam to the other side, whither the enemy did not venture to pursue them.

It was not without difficulty that Jonathan roused his adherents to the exertions which they made on this occasion. In fact there are several indications, at and before this time, that the people were becoming tired of this long struggle for their religion and liberties, and disposed to submit to circumstances, for the sake of the quiet of which they had been so many years deprived. Besides, by this time the original character of the war, as one of resistance against religious persecution, had somewhat changed. There was more of politics mixed in it; and with that change, the ardor of the orthodox Jews appears to have abated. The Syrian government had also become much more mild since the time of Antiochus Epiphanes, and under favoring circumstances, it might have been expected that the Jews would without difficul-

* This is the drift of Justin's remark with reference to this very transaction: "A Demetrio cum defecissent Judæi, amicitia Romanorum petita, primi omnium ex Orientalibus libertatem receperunt: facile tunc Romanis de alieno largientibus." Lib. xxxvi. cap. 2.

The River Jordan.

ty have obtained what they sought. It was probably the knowledge of this, as well as from the consciousness that the breach was not likely to be healed by continued warfare, that latterly produced so great a reluctance to support the Maccabees, and so strong a disposition to submit to the Syrians. We may thus account not only for the circumstance which occasions this remark, but for the readiness of some of the best supporters of the Maccabees to listen to the fair promises of the Syrian generals; for the desertion of Judas, before his last action, by the great body of his adherents; and for his comparative inaction on several recent occasions. To the operation of these circumstances we are also disposed to refer the anxiety of Judas to conclude a treaty with the Romans. For this step he has been blamed by some persons, who appear to have inadequately considered the circumstances. It is not clear to us that if Judas had been aware that the step he took was likely to lead to the future subjection of the country to the Romans, he would have been deterred from seeking their alliance. He did not fight for national independence, which was a moral impossibility, but for the liberty of conscience. If that had been conceded by the Syrian kings, the Jews would readily have returned to their political subjection, and were indeed anxious to do so. If therefore Judas had known the ultimate contingency of subjection to the Romans instead of the Syrians, there was nothing in that to deter him, if he felt that the Romans were likely to be more tolerant of the religious peculiarities of his nation. It is quite true that by the skilful use of circumstances which ultimately arose, the Jews were enabled to establish a modified independence —which independence the Romans destroyed. But these circumstances were not foreseen in the time of Judas, and independence was not among the objects originally contemplated. It is only in forgetfulness of those facts that any one can impute blame to Judas for the measure which he took—which measure, indeed, we can not trace to have had any grave effect upon ultimate results. Whether the Jews had offered themselves to the notice of the Romans at this time or not, they certainly could not long have escaped the attention of that people, nor, unless events had taken an entirely different course to that which they actually took, could their subjection to the Roman yoke have been long postponed.

From the Jordan, Bacchides returned to Jerusalem, and was employed for some time in strengthening the fortresses of Judea, particularly the citadel at Jerusalem and the important fortresses of Gazara.[*] The sons of some of the principal persons among the Jews he took and detained in the citadel as hostages for the good conduct of their friends. But in the same year Alcimus was seized with a kind of cramp, and died in much agony, while giving orders for the demolition of the wall which separated the court of the Gentiles from that of the Israelites, so as to give the former free access to the privileged part of the temple; and Bacchides, having nothing to detain him in Judea after the death of the man on whose account the war was undertaken, withdrew from the country, and allowed the Jews two years of repose. To what extent this may have been due to the interposition of the Romans, we have no means of knowing; but the results of the application to the senate must by this time have been known both at Antioch and in Judea. Probably the death of Judas, before the return of his ambassadors, went far to neutralize the immediate effects which might have been expected from this treaty.

This tranquillity was not favorable to the designs of the Græcising Jews, who laid a plot to surprise and seize Jonathan and his adherents, all in one night, throughout the land, and prevailed on Bacchides to return with the force under his command to give effect to their design (B. C. 158). A timely discovery of the plot enabled Jonathan to damp the ardor of the conspirators by putting to death fifty of the principal of them. Not, however, feeling himself in a condition to oppose Bacchides in the field, Jonathan, with his friends and his brother Simon, withdrew to the wilderness, where they so strongly repaired the dilapidated fortress of Bethbasi, that they were enabled to maintain a

---

[*] There is some doubt respecting this place, which is so often named in the history of the Maccabees. Some think it the same as Gaza, which indeed is still called Gazara, and that is certainly a strong circumstance in its favor. Upon the whole, however, there are several passages in which the place is named which seem to refer it to the neighborhood of Joppa, and others which can not without much straining and difficulty be made to apply to Gaza. In one of a set of unpublished maps by Professor Robinson (for which we are indebted to his kindness) we find that a site named Yasur occurred in his line of route, three miles and a half to the east of Jaffa, and we much more than suspect that this marks the site not only of the Gazara in question, but also (believing the names identical) of the Gazer which was one of the royal cities of the old Canaanites, and the same which the king of Egypt took from the Canaanites, and gave, for a dowry with his daughter, to Solomon. All circumstances appear to agree with this allocation

long siege against Bacchides, and at length to defeat him. This affair wonderfully enlightened the Syrian general, who now perceived that he had been but the tool of a faction; and, in his resentment, he put to death several of the persons who had the most actively stimulated his enterprise. At this juncture, Jonathan sent to him a deputation with proposals of peace, and Bacchides readily acceded to the terms which were offered. The treaty being concluded and sworn to by both parties, an exchange of prisoners took place, and Bacchides withdrew from the land, B. C. 156. Peace being thus happily restored, Jonathan fixed his residence at the strong post of Michmash, six miles north-by-east from Jerusalem, where he governed according to the laws of Moses, and to the extent of his power reformed the public abuses which had sprung up during the past troubles.

About the year B. C. 154, Demetrius Soter retired to a new palace which he had built near Antioch, and there abandoned himself entirely to luxury and pleasure. All business and all care was refused admission, and consequently all the responsibilities and duties of his high office were utterly neglected. Hence arose great administrative abuses, and these led to discontents, and discontents to conspiracies, which were eagerly fostered by different neighboring kings, especially by Ptolemy Philometor, king of Egypt,* from whom the island of Cyprus had been taken by Demetrius. They availed themselves of the services of Heraclides, who had been banished by Demetrius, and who had since lived at Rhodes; and now, at the instigation of these kings, he persuaded a young man of obscure birth, named Balas, to announce himself as the son of Antiochus Epiphanes, and as such lay claim to the throne of Syria. As soon as he had been sufficiently tutored in the part he was to act, he publicly advanced his pretensions, which were acknowledged at once by Ptolemy Philometor, by Ariarathes, king of Cappadocia, and by Attalus, king of Pergamus (B. C. 153). He was then sent to Rome, together with a true daughter of Antiochus; and although the senate soon detected the imposture, their old grudge against Demetrius, for having taken the throne of Syria without their consent, led them to recognise him, and empower him to raise forces for the recovery of a kingdom in which he could have had no just pretensions to supersede Demetrius (the son of the elder brother), even had his alleged birth been true. Balas now assumed the name of Alexander, and the title of king of Syria. He delayed not to levy troops, and sailed to Ptolemais (previously Accho), now Acre, in Palestine, where he was joined by numbers who had become disaffected to Demetrius. That infatuated person was now fairly roused from his lethargy, and came forth from his disgraceful retreat—but it was too late.

This conjuncture of affairs was highly favorable to the interests of the Jews, as, from the high military character they had now acquired, the rivals vied with each other in the honors and immunities which they offered for the assistance of Jonathan and the Jews. First, Demetrius sent a letter appointing Jonathan his general in Judea, empowering him to levy forces, and promising to release the hostages. When the contents of this letter were made known, the hostages were restored by the garrison of the citadel, and the fortresses throughout the country were given up to him by the Syrian garrisons which Bacchides had left in them. The citadel and Bethsura indeed still held out, as they were garrisoned by apostate Jews who had no other resource. Jonathan now removed from Michmash and fixed his residence at Jerusalem, which he occupied himself in repairing, and in rebuilding those walls of the temple-mount which Antiochus Eupator had cast down.

On the other hand, Balas, acting probably by the advice of Ptolemy Philometor (who was well acquainted with the affairs and interests of the Jews), sent also a letter to Jonathan, in the very commencement of which he styled him "Brother," gave him the title and rank of "Friend of the King," appointed him to the high-priesthood, and sent him a purple robe and diadem, thereby creating him Ethnarch, or Prince of Judea. It was in the seventh month of this same year (B. C. 153) that Jonathan put

* As the transactions in Egypt, since they were last noticed, have not, up to this point, been necessarily involved in the current of our history, we have not allowed them to engage our notice. It may however be briefly indicated in a note, that, after their junction against Antiochus Epiphanes, quarrels arose between the two brother kings, Philometor and Physcon, which the Romans endeavored to adjust in B. C. 162, by arranging that Philometor should retain Egypt and Cyprus, and that Physcon should reign in Libya and Cyrene. But they soon again were at variance respecting Cyprus, which Physcon wanted, but which Philometor resolved to retain according to the terms of the agreement. Meanwhile, as often happens in such cases, a third party (Demetrius) stepped in, and appropriated to himself the disputed island. Hence the enmity of Philometor to the king of Syria.

on the holy robe of the high-priest, after that high office had been vacant for seven years.

Demetrius did not yet despair of outbidding Balas in this struggle to gain the favor and assistance of Jonathan. The list of the exemptions, immunities, and privileges which he offered is exceedingly curious, as showing the extent and minute ramifications of the previous exactions of the Syrian government; and we have therefore introduced it entire in a note below.* The extravagant generosity of these offers made Jonathan and the patriots suspicious of their sincerity, and, mindful of the past sufferings they had experienced through Demetrius, they agreed to espouse the cause of Alexander.

Next year (B. C. 152) both the kings took the field with their armies, and Demetrius, who, when sober, wanted neither courage nor conduct, defeated his rival in the first battle; but Alexander Balas, being reinforced by the kings who had put him forward, was more successful in a great battle fought the year after, in which Demetrius himself was slain.

The successful impostor now mounted the throne of Syria, and married Cleopatra, a daughter of his great friend Ptolemy Philometor of Egypt, who himself conducted the bride to Ptolemais in Palestine, where the nuptials were celebrated with great magnificence (B. C. 150). Jonathan was present on this occasion, and, mindful of the services he had rendered during the war, both Ptolemy and Alexander treated him with distinguished honors. He was again presented with a purple robe, and appointed commander or Meridarch of Judea.

Alexander Balas, who had manifested considerable ability during this contest, was no sooner firmly settled on the throne, than he lapsed into the same errors which had been fatal to his predecessor. He abandoned the cares of government to his favorite Ammonius, that he might enjoy a luxurious life undisturbed. This minister put to death all the members of the royal family he could get into his power. But there still lived in Cnidus two sons of Demetrius, the elder of whom, Demetrius II., surnamed Nicator, landed at Cilicia in B. C. 148, and soon collected a great army with which to assert his right to the crown. He also gained over to his interest Apollonius the governor of Cœle-Syria, whose first proof of attachment to his new master was to invade Judea, which still adhered to the cause of Alexander. Jonathan came down from the mountains into the plain of the coast, and after taking Joppa, before his eyes, defeated Apollonius with terrible loss. Ashdod he then subdued, and Ascalon opened wide her gates to receive the conqueror. For this essential service he received from Alexander a golden clasp or buckle, such as only members of the royal family might wear; and the town and territory of Ekron, near the coast, was also

---

* "King Demetrius unto the people of the Jews sendeth greeting. Whereas ye have kept covenant with us, and continued in our friendship, not joining yourselves with our enemies, we have heard thereof, and are glad. Wherefore now continue ye still to be faithful unto us, and we will well recompense you for the things ye do in our behalf, and will grant you many immunities, and give you rewards. And now do I free you, and for your sake I release all the Jews from tributes, and from the customs of salt, and from crown taxes. And from that which appertaineth unto me to receive for the third part of the seed, and the half of the fruit-trees, I release it from this day forth, so that they shall not be taken of the land of Judea, nor of the three governments which are added thereunto out of the country of Samaria and Galilee, from this day forth for ever more. Let Jerusalem also be holy and free, with the borders thereof, both from tenths and tributes. And as for the tower which is at Jerusalem, I yield up my authority over it, and give it to the high-priest, that he may set in it such men as he shall choose to keep it. Moreover, I freely set at liberty every one of the Jews that were carried captives out of the land of Judea into any part of my kingdom, and I will that all my officers remit the tributes even of their cattle. Furthermore, I will that all the feasts, and sabbaths, and new moons, and solemn days, and the three days before the feast, and the three days after the feast, shall be all days of immunity and freedom for all the Jews of my realm. Also no man shall have authority to meddle with them, or to molest any of them in any matter. I will further, that there be enrolled among the king's forces about thirty thousand men of the Jews, unto whom pay shall be given, as belongeth to all the king's forces. And of them shall be placed in the king's strongholds, of whom also some shall be set over the affairs of the kingdom, which are of trust; and I will that their overseers and governors be of themselves, and that they live after their own laws, even as the king hath commanded in the land of Judea. And concerning the three governments that are added to Judea from the country of Samaria, let them be joined with Judea, that they may be reckoned to be under one, nor bound to obey other authority than the high-priest's. As for Ptolemais, and the land pertaining thereto, I give it as a free gift to the sanctuary. Moreover, I give every year fifteen thousand shekels of silver out of the king's accounts to the places appertaining. And all the overplus, which the officers payed not in as in former time, henceforth shall be given toward the use of the temple. And beside this, the five thousand shekels of silver, which they took from the uses of the temple out of the accounts year by year, even those things shall be released, because they appertain to the priests that minister. And whosoever they be that flee unto the temple at Jerusalem, or be within the liberties thereof, being indebted unto the king, or for any other matter, let them be at liberty, and all that they have in my realm. For the building also and the repairing of the works of the sanctuary expenses shall be given out of the king's account. Yea, and for the building of the walls of Jerusalem, and the fortifying thereof round about, expenses shall be given out of the king's account, as also for the building of the walls of Judea."

Ascalon.

bestowed upon him. The king himself remained shut up in Antioch, awaiting the succors which he expected from his father-in-law of Egypt. Philometor came indeed; but having discovered a plot formed against his life by the favorite Ammonius, and the infatuated Balas refusing to deliver up that guilty minister, Ptolemy testified his resentment by taking away his daughter, and bestowing her on Demetrius, whose cause he thenceforth espoused. This decided the contest. Ammonius was slain by the citizens, and A. Balas only avoided a similar fate by flight. The character which Ptolemy Philometor bore among the Syrians for justice and clemency was so high, that they pressed him to accept the vacant crown. But this he prudently declined, and recommended the rightful heir to their choice. The next year Alexander appeared again, in a condition to make one more struggle for the crown. He was defeated, and fled into Arabia, where an emir, with whom he sought shelter, rendered his name, Zabdiel, infamous by the murder of his guest, whose head he sent to the king of Egypt. That monarch himself died the same year (B. C. 146). He left one son, a child, who was put to death by Physcon, who now reigned sole king of Egypt.

In Judea, Jonathan now employed himself in besieging the citadel of Jerusalem, which still remained in the hands of the apostate Jews and the Syrians, and which had so long proved a serious annoyance to the inhabitants of the city. Complaint of this operation having reached Demetrius. he cited Jonathan to Ptolemais to answer for his conduct. He went; but left orders that the siege should be vigorously prosecuted in his absence. He took with him valuable presents for the king, by which and other means he so won his favor, that he not only confirmed him in the high-priesthood and all his other honors, but also ratified the offers of his father, which Jonathan had once declined for the friendship of Balas. As the citadel still held out, Jonathan urged the king to withdraw the garrisons from it and from Bethsura; which Demetrius promised to do, provided the Jews would send a reinforcement to put down a dangerous disturbance which had broken out at Antioch; for the new king had already managed, by his gross misconduct and cruelty, to alienate the affections of both his Syrian subjects and Egyptian allies. The Jews rendered the required service. But when Demetrius deemed himself secure, and without further need of them, he behaved with great ingratitude. He demanded all the taxes, tolls, and tributes which he had promised to remit, and thus succeeded in alienating the Jews as much as his other subjects.

Alexander Balas left a son called Antiochus, whom the Arabian emir Zabdiel had retained in his hands when he slew the father; and he was persuaded by Tryphon (the former governor of Antioch under A. Balas) to send the young prince with him to lay claim to the throne of Syria. Antiochus was joyfully received by the malecontents, and by the numerous soldiers whom the false economy of Demetrius had disbanded. In a pitched battle, Demetrius was defeated, his elephants were taken, and Antioch was lost, B. C. 144.

As soon as Antiochus VI., surnamed Theos, had been crowned, his guardian Tryphon (for Antiochus was but a child) wrote in his name to invite the adhesion of Jonathan; and offered in return to observe faithfully all the promises which Demetrius had broken, and to appoint his brother Simon the royal governor of the district extending from the mountains between Tyre and Ptolemais to the borders of Egypt. These conditions were accepted by Jonathan, who, with the assistance of the Syrian forces, expelled the hostile garrison from Gaza, Bethsura, and Joppa; but the citadel of Jerusalem still held out for Demetrius.

With due regard to the past and the future, Jonathan deemed it advisable at this time to seek a renewal of the alliance with the Romans. The ambassadors were received at Rome with favor, and dismissed with assurances of friendship. On their return they (as the ambassadors of Judas had formerly done) visited the Spartans, and concluded a league with them, under some notion which the Jews entertained that the Spartans were of the stock of Abraham.

Tryphon had contemplated the advancement of the son of Alexander Balas, merely as a means of intruding himself into the throne of Syria. Things were now, in his judgment, ripe for the removal of the young king, and for his own intrusion, when he found that Jonathan was likely to prove an obstacle to the execution of his design. He therefore invaded Palestine, and had advanced as far as Bethshan, when, being intimidated by the appearance of Jonathan with forty thousand men, he pretended that his mission was entirely of a friendly nature—and that he had entered the country to put him in possession of Ptolemais. He played this part so naturally that the Jewish hero was deceived, and dismissed his army, saving three thousand men, two thousand of whom he left in Galilee, and advanced with the other thousand to take possession of Ptolemais. He had no sooner entered that city than the gates were shut, his men cut in pieces, and himself laden with chains. Not long after he was put to death by the perfidious Tryphon, who next slew his young master and set on his brows the Syrian crown.

The Jews, whose prospects had lately been so fair, were filled with consternation when they heard of the captivity and subsequent murder of Jonathan. But Simon, the brother of Jonathan, who had already been enabled to prove himself a true Maccabee, called them together in the temple, encouraged them to make a vigorous defence, and offered to become their high-priest and leader in the room of his brother. He said:—"Since all my brethren are slain for Israel's sake, and I alone am left, far be it from me to spare my own life in any time of trouble." The offer was gladly accepted by the people, and he was unanimously elected to succeed Jonathan: and, seeing he had sons of high promise, it was decided that the honors to which Simon was called should be inherited by his descendants. The form of expression is however remarkable, as showing that some doubts were entertained as to the strict legality of this procedure. It is said, "The Jews and the priests were well pleased that Simon should be their governor and priest [he and his sons] for ever, until there should arise a faithful prophet to show them what they should do."

We are free to express our own opinion that the three brothers, Judas, Jonathan, and Simon, were men of great ability and unquestionable courage; and we believe they sincerely desired the welfare of their country, and to preserve the purity of religious worship, to promote which objects they would at any time have shed their last blood. But we think also that Judas is the only one of the brothers of whose high moral principle or disinterestedness much can be said. From the time that Jonathan accepted the high-priesthood, and various personal honors, from Alexander Balas, it is easy to detect in most of the alternations of policy a leaning to that course which included the aggrandizement of the family and the promotion of its chiefs. We do not say or think that they would knowingly have sacrificed any public object to their own aggrandizement. But the disposition to seek or prefer that particular good to our country which comprehends honor or power to ourselves, belongs to a lower class of minds and principles than that which refuses wealth or power in connexion with any public service, lest the motive of that service might be suspected. It must also be said, that the disposition of the later Maccabees to play fast and loose between the competitors for the Syrian crown, and equally to accept the favors which rival kings offered, when it was impossible to perform equally to both the conditions which were expected in return, is not entitled to much praise.

Had Jonathan and Simon been perfectly disinterested men, the obvious duty imposed upon them by the Law would have been to direct the attention of the Jews and of the Syrian king to Onias, then in Egypt, as the rightful high-priest, of the elder branch of the family of Aaron, who was unsuspected of any idolatrous taint, and whose abilities were of no common order: and the promises of the continuance of the sceptre of Judah to the house of David, should have induced Simon, at least, when affairs were taking a turn favorable to the independence of the nation, to direct the hopes of Israel toward some able member of that illustrious house. But it is time to return to follow the course of our narrative.

Simon removed the corpse of his illustrious brother from Bascana, in Gilead, where he was slain, to the family sepulchre at Modin, where he subsequently erected a noble mausoleum, which was still standing in the time of Eusebius and Jerome.

At the first opportunity, Simon sent an embassy to Rome and Lacedæmon to announce to the senate the death of his brother, and his own succession to his dignities, and to seek a renewal of the alliance. Both nations received the ambassadors with honor, expressed the usual regret, and the usual congratulations, and readily renewed the treaty, with the terms of which graven on brass the deputation returned.

The first care of Simon was to put the country in a state of defence, by repairing the fortresses and furnishing them with provisions. As the conflict between Tryphon and Demetrius still continued, and it was the unhappiness of the Jews that their position did not allow them to remain neutral, there were many sufficient causes to induce them to prefer the side of Demetrius, notwithstanding the ill-treatment they had formerly received from him. This personage, although nearly the whole of Syria was lost to him, remained in luxurious repose at Laodicea, whither Simon sent ambassadors to him, with a crown of gold, to treat about the renewal of the former terms of accommodation. To this Demetrius, in his fallen estate, most gladly agreed, confirming solemnly all the immunities and privileges specified in his father's letter to Jonathan, with an act of amnesty for all past offences. These privileges were so great that they may be said to have raised the nation to a state of independence. The Jews themselves certainly considered that they were by this act delivered from the Syrian yoke ; and therefore this first year of Simon's reign (B. C. 143), as high-priest and ethnarch, or, in short, as Prince of the Jews, they signalized by making it an epoch from which to compute their times. This era is used on the coins of Simon, as well as by Josephus and the author of the first book of Maccabees.

The next care of Simon was to reduce the strong fortresses that still held out. Gaza he took, and expelled the idolatrous inhabitants; and the citadel of Jerusalem, which had so long been a thorn in the sides of the Maccabees, was compelled by the famine which a rigorous blockade produced, to surrender in B. C. 142. Aware of the valor of his son John, Simon made him captain-general of his forces, and sent him to reside in Gazara on the sea-coast ; while he made the temple-mount at Jerusalem his own residence. This he strongly fortified; and his palace probably stood on the site which the castle of Antonia afterward occupied.

Having thus gained complete possession of the country, and the rights and liberties of the nation being established, a great council of the nation was held at Jerusalem, which testified its gratitude by confirming to Simon all his honors, and, in more distinct terms than before, entailed them on his descendants. This decree of the assembly was graven on brass, and fixed to a monument which was erected in the temple-court.

Anxious to have the independence conceded, by Demetrius recognised by the Romans, another embassy was sent to the senate, with a present of a shield of gold, weighing one thousand minæ, equal, at the lowest computation, to fifty thousand pounds sterling. The deputation was well received, and the present graciously accepted. Their suit was granted, and missions were sent by the senate to the kings of Egypt, Pergamus, Cappadocia, Syria (Demetrius), and Parthia, and to all the cities and states of Greece, Asia Minor, and of the isles in alliance with the Romans, to engage them to treat the Jews as their friends and allies, B. C. 141.

In the same year Demetrius, whose cause appeared to be lost in the west, was invited to the east by large promises of support in any attempt he might make to bring back the Parthians to their allegiance. He was at first successful, but was in the end surprised and made prisoner by the Parthians. In this war he was assisted by a body of Jews under the command of John the son of Simon, whose exploits in Hyrcania procured him the honorary surname of Hyrcanus. As for Demetrius, he was well treated by the Parthian king, Arsaces V., otherwise called Mithridates ; who indeed first took care to exhibit him in different parts of his empire, but afterward sent him into Hyrcania, where he treated him with the respect due to his rank, and even gave him his daughter Rhodoguna in marriage. Meanwhile his cause in Syria was maintained against Tryphon by his wife Cleopatra, who had shut herself up, with her children, in Seleucia on the Orontes ; and a powerful force, composed of persons discontented with the government of Tryphon, was gathering around her, when she heard that her captive husband had married Rhodoguna. This offended her pride, and was also calculated to weaken her party. Therefore, from both policy and revenge, she sent to Antiochus, the brother of Demetrius, who was then at Rhodes, and made him the offer of her hand and of the kingdom. Antiochus VII., who, from his passion for hunting, received the surname of Sidetes (" the hunter"), eagerly accepted the proposal, and delayed not to assume the title of king of Syria, although as yet unable to proceed to the continent, B. C. 141.

The next year (B. C. 140) Antiochus wrote "from the isles of the sea," being still at Rhodes, " to Simon the high-priest and ethnarch, and to the people of the Jews," announcing his intention of coming speedily to recover the dominions of his father from the usurper Tryphon; and, to secure their assistance, confirming all the privileges granted by former kings, together with the royal privilege of coining money, which seems the only one which former kings had withheld, or which seemed wanting to complete the sort of secondary independence which they had by this time acquired.

The year after (B. C. 139) Antiochus landed in Syria to attack Tryphon, with whose tyrannies the people and even the soldiers had become completely weary. On the appearance of Sidetes he was deserted by most of his forces, and he therefore fled to Dora (south of Carmel) on the coast of Palestine. Antiochus pursued and besieged him there; but he fled by ship to Orthosia, a maritime town of Phœnicia; and, again, thence to Apamea, where he was taken and put to death.

Finding with how much more facility than he had been prepared to expect, the kingdom fell to him, Antiochus, very soon after his landing, formed the intention of reducing to their former complete subjection to the Syrian crown, the provinces and cities which had availed themselves of the troubled reigns of his predecessors to acquire such independence as the Jews had established. This was an intention which any king in those times was likely to have formed with reference to privileges so recent, and so much extorted by temporary emergencies, and by which the power and dignity of the crown were so seriously impaired. Antiochus probably considered his own acts more binding than the treaties obtained from the usurper Balas, or from the distressed Demetrius; yet even his own letter, written in the expectation of needing the aid which the event proved that he did not require, was not likely to be considered by him any strong bar to the execution of his design.

His intentions were indicated on his first arrival in Palestine, to besiege Tryphon in Dora. Simon then sent two thousand men to assist him in the siege, with a good supply of warlike stores and engines, but the king declined to receive them, and sent over to Jerusalem one of his generals, named Athenobius, with a requisition for the surrender of Joppa, Gazara, and the citadel of Jerusalem, which belonged to the Syrian crown, or else to pay five hundred talents for each of the former, and five hundred more for the arrears of tribute from those cities beyond the limits of Judea, of which the Jews had gained possession, and on account of ravages which they had committed in his dominions. This demand was skilfully framed to steer clear of any points comprehended in the treaties or in the letter of Antiochus himself, and the demand seems upon the whole as moderate as could be framed consistently with the intention of retaining some hold upon the country. Writers call the answer of Simon "wise." It appears to us rather feeble. He denied that the Jews held any possessions but what belonged to their fathers, and which they had found opportunity to recover. With regard to the fortified towns of Joppa and Gazara, he called attention to the injuries which the people had been continually receiving from those places, as justifying the measures he had taken; but he was willing to give the king one hundred talents for the right of possession. Athenobius returned with this answer to the king, to whom also he gave a very flaming account of the state and splendor in which Simon lived, and of the large quantities of gold and silver plate which appeared in his house and at his table. At this the king was so moved, that he sent an army under Cendebeus to invade Judea: but he was met and defeated by John Hyrcanus and Judas, the two sons of Simon; and the Syrians were expelled the country.

The peace purchased by this victory was not of long duration. Simon availed himself of it to make a tour of inspection through the country, in the course of which he arrived at Jericho, where he took up his abode in the castle of his son-in-law Ptolemy, who was governor there. This Ptolemy, desiring to secure the government to himself, caused the old man and his two sons, Mattathias and Judas, to be treacherously murdered at an entertainment. He also sent a party to destroy John Hyrcanus at Gazara; but John had timely warning, and fled to Jerusalem, where he was readily recognised by the people as the successor of his father in the high-priesthood, and in the principality of Judea. Then Ptolemy, against whom the people of Jerusalem shut their gates, fled to a fortress near Jericho, and thence to Zeno, the prince of Philadelphia (Rabbath-Ammon), probably to await there the arrival of Antiochus, to whom he had sent, desiring the assistance of an army to reduce Judea again to the Syrian yoke. But his name occurs in history no more; whence it is probable that although Antiochus may have liked the crime, he hated the criminal, and would afford him no countenance. However, the king marched a large army into Judea in B. C. 135, and having ravaged the country, advanced to besiege Hyrcanus in Jerusalem, which was soon reduced to great extremities for want of provisions, which had been scarce that year. On the approach of the feast of Tabernacles in autumn, Hyrcanus besought a week's truce for the celebration of the feast; and this was not only granted by Antiochus, but he furnished the victims required for sacrifice, which could not be procured within the city. Finally, he concluded a peace with the Jews, when it was in his power to extirpate them from the country, and he was exhorted by many to do so, but generously refused. He was content to dismantle Jerusalem, and to bind them to pay tribute (not for their proper country, but) for Joppa and other towns beyond the limits of Judea, which they had either taken by arms, or held by the grants of his predecessors.

Four years after (B. C. 131), Antiochus Sidetes marched with a great army against the Parthians, under the pretence of delivering his brother Demetrius. Hyrcanus accompanied him in this expedition, and left him victorious in three battles over the Parthian king Phraates, which put A. Sidetes in possession of Babylonia, Media, and the other revolted provinces, and confined the Parthians within the original limits of their own kingdom. But while the Syrian army was dispersed in winter quarters, the Parthians, assisted by the natives, conspired against them, and slew them all in one whole day; Antiochus himself perished in the massacre, and scarcely a man remained to bear back to Syria the report of the catastrophe.

Upon this Phraates sent to re-take Demetrius, whom, after having been vanquished in the former campaign, he had liberated, and sent back to Syria, to create such a diversion there as might induce Antiochus to relinquish his enterprise. But Demetrius made such speed that he escaped the pursuit, and, on his re-appearance in Syria, coupled with the news of the death of his brother, he was enabled to recover his throne without much difficulty.

Hyrcanus neglected not to avail himself of the confusion into which the Syrian empire fell, and the loss of strength which it sustained after the downfall of A. Sidetes. He got possession of several towns on the sea-coast, and beyond Jordan, and annexed them to his territories. He also rendered himself more completely independent; for after this neither he nor his descendants paid any more tribute, service, or homage to the kings of Syria. Next Hyrcanus invaded Samaria. He took Shechem, the chief seat of the Samaritans, and demolished the temple which they had built on mount Gerizim. However, they continued to have an altar on the spot, on which they have offered sacrifices, according to the Levitical law, even to this day. After this, Hyrcanus invaded and subdued the Idumeans, to whom he offered the alternative of either relinquishing their idolatries and embracing the Jewish religion, or else of leaving the country into which they had intruded, and seeking a settlement elsewhere. They preferred the former alternatives, and as proselytes, gradually became so incorporated with the Jews as to be counted one people with them; and at length the name itself was lost, or absorbed in that of the Jews.*

The course of events now again calls our attention to Egypt. That country was still ruled by Ptolemy Physcon, whose gross and beast-like person bore the very impress of that cruel and voluptuous character which belonged to him. We gladly hurry over the revolting theme which his character and conduct offer, merely to mention that Cleopatra, the sister of the late Philometor and himself, became the wife of the former, by whom he had a son, and two daughters, both of the name of Cleopatra. After the death of Philometor, his young son was slain by Physcon, who also married the widow, his own sister. Of the two daughters, one was that Cleopatra who was married to Alexander Balas, king of Syria, then to Demetrius Nicator, then to Antiochus Sidetes, and after the return of Demetrius became his wife again. Her sister, the other Cleopatra, was defiled by her uncle Physcon, who afterward repudiated his wife (her mother and his own sister), and married this young princess. His oppressions and cruelties toward his subjects were so severe, that at last they could bear them no longer, but rose against him, and compelled him to flee to Cyprus. The people then intrusted the government to his sister and divorced wife, the elder Cleopatra. Her son by him was with his father at Cyprus, and Physcon, fearing that the son's name might be used to strengthen Cleopatra on the throne, slew him, and sent his head, feet, and hands to her, directing that they should be given her in the midst of an entertainment. In the war which followed, Physcon was victorious, and Cleo-

* The rabbins indeed have long spoken and still speak of Edom and the Edomites as existing. But these are merely feigned and well understood names for denoting, not Edom, but Rome and Christendom, and not the Edomites, but the Christians of the Roman empire, and of the states into which that empire broke up, for fear of incurring the displeasure of the nations among which they dwelt, if they said of them, without disguise, all they wished to say.

patra in her despair sent to Demetrius of Syria, the husband of her eldest daughter, offering him the crown of Egypt if he would come with an army to her aid. Allured by the splendid bribe, Demetrius immediately marched an army through Palestine into Egypt. But, while he was engaged in the siege of Pelusium, Antioch and several other of his own cities revolted from him, and he was obliged to abandon the prospect before him and return the way he came. Cleopatra then fled to seek protection with her daughter the queen of Syria, who then resided at Ptolemais in Palestine. Physcon then regained possession of his throne, which he retained until his death in B. C. 117.

The passage and return of the Syrian through Palestine could not but be attended with much annoyance to the Jews, and it may be proper to regard it as in some measure the cause of the embassy which Hyrcanus sent to Rome the same year (B. C. 128), to solicit the renewal of the treaties into which the senate had entered with his predecessors, and to complain of the small attention which Antiochus and Demetrius had paid to its former mandates. The ambassadors were received with the usual favor by the senate, which readily consented to renew the treaty which had been concluded with Simon, and which moreover took upon itself to abrogate the disadvantageous treaty which the Jews had been compelled to make with A. Sidetes. It also decreed that Hyrcanus should hold the towns of Joppa, Gazara, and others beyond the limits of Judea, without paying tribute for them to the Syrian kings; and that the latter should not presume to march armies through Palestine without permission. This last clause was doubtless intended to check the enterprises of the kings of Syria against Egypt. Ambassadors were appointed to see all this executed; and the Jewish deputation were furnished with money to bear their expenses home. Hyrcanus was too sensible of the importance of these favors to neglect the expression of his gratitude; and the next year another embassy was sent to Rome with a present of a cup and shield of gold, which the senate accepted, and passed another decree confirming the former. By these treaties, as well as by the unquiet state of the Syrian kingdom, Hyrcanus was much strengthened in what we may now call his dominions.

Demetrius was one of those men whom even adversity could not improve. After his restoration, he fell into the same misconduct which had before occasioned him the loss of his kingdom. His subjects again were alienated from him; and readily joined a competitor who was brought forward and supported by P. Physcon, in revenge for the recent attempt of Demetrius to take possession of his kingdom. The young man put forward on this occasion was the son of a merchant of Alexandria, and claimed to be the adopted son of Antiochus Sidetes, or (according to some) of Alexander Balas. He assumed the name of Alexander, but was nicknamed in derision, Zebinas ("the bought one"). Notwithstanding the weakness of his pretensions, he easily succeeded in depriving the universally disliked Demetrius of his kingdom and life, B. C. 126.

Zebinas was an equitable and popular ruler; but he did not obtain the whole of the kingdom, as part was retained by Cleopatra—that wife of many husbands who has so often been named. To strengthen her cause, she caused Seleucus, her son by Demetrius, to be proclaimed king of Syria, but retained all power in her own hands; and when in the twentieth year of his age (B. C. 124) he manifested a desire really to reign, she slew him by a javelin with her own hands. A. Zebinas, on the other hand, strengthened his cause by an alliance with John Hyrcanus, who skilfully availed himself of all these troubles to confirm his independence, and to enlarge his dominion. Zebinas could not, however, long maintain his position. A very proper and spirited refusal to do homage to P. Physcon for the crown of Syria, lost him the support and procured him the enmity of that monarch, who immediately came to terms with Cleopatra, and furnished her with an army whereby Zebinas was defeated, and ultimately fell into the hands of Ptolemy, who put him to death. Thus Cleopatra became mistress of all Syria, her younger son by Demetrius, Antiochus VIII., surnamed Gryphus ("hook-nosed," from γρυψ, a vulture), being seated on the throne. Soon after (B. C. 120), finding that Gryphus was also disposed to claim the power as well as name of king, she prepared poison for him; but she was detected, and the king compelled his murderous mother to drink the poisoned cup herself.

Ptolemy Physcon died in B. C. 117, twenty-nine years after his brother Philometor. He left all power in the hands of Cleopatra, his wife and daughter-in-law—sister of the Syrian queen whose doom concluded the last paragraph. Physcon had by her two sons, Lathyrus and Alexander, and left to Cleopatra the choice of a king from them. She would have preferred the youngest, Alexander; but the voice of the people compelled her to appoint Ptolemy Lathyrus.

Antiochus Gryphus had a half-brother, whom his mother Cleopatra had borne to Antiochus Sidetes. This young prince was sent by his mother to be brought up at Cyzicus on the Propontis, and hence his name of Antiochus Cyzicenus. He soon appeared as a competitor for the Syrian throne, and after various conflicts the brothers agreed in B. C. 112 to divide the empire between them. A. Cyzicenus obtaind Cœle-Syria and Phœnicia, and fixed his residence at Damascus. Both the kings were heartless libertines; and their relatively uneasy position gave them too much employment, in watching and annoying each other, to permit them to interfere much with the Jews, whose princes well knew how to avail themselves of such opportunities to aggrandize the power of the nation.

There is one exception. In B. C. 110 Hyrcanus ventured to besiege Samaria, the inhabitants of which were not Samaritans, properly so called, but were descended from the Syro-Macedonian colony, which Alexander planted there when he rooted out the former inhabitants. The siege was conducted by Hyrcanus himself, with his two sons Aristobulus and Antigonus. They enclosed the city by a wall and a ditch, and all supplies being thus completely cut off, the place was soon reduced to the last extremity from scarcity of food. In this emergency, the besieged sent to A. Cyzicenus, supplicating his aid. He marched himself to afford it; but was met on the way by a detachment of the Jewish army under the command of Aristobulus. In a bloody engagement the Syrians were totally routed, and A. Cyzicenus himself escaped with difficulty. In the next year (B. C. 109) Samaria was taken and totally demolished. This victory, with its results, made Hyrcanus master of all Judea, Samaria, and Galilee, and of several places beyond their limits; and raised the glory of the Asamonean princes to its height. Hyrcanus spent the rest of his reign without foreign wars, and respected by all the neighboring potentates. He died in B. C. 106, after a reign of thirty years.

Hyrcanus left the principality to his wife; but Aristobulus, his eldest son, soon possessed himself of the government; and as his mother refused to lay down her authority, he committed her to prison, where she perished of hunger. Having established himself in the principality and high-priesthood, Aristobulus ventured on the very questionable step of assuming the diadem and regal title. And thus (as seems to have been predicted by Zechariah, vi. 9—15) was brought about that state of things, which early existed in Egypt and other countries, in which the offices of the king and high-priest were united in the same person. Aristobulus availed himself of the disagreements between the two kings of Syria to extend his dominions. He subdued Iturea beyond Jordan, and offered the inhabitants the alternative of circumcision or expatriation. They preferred the former, and accordingly became Jews, and were incorporated with the Jewish nation. Aristobulus fell sick during this campaign, leaving his brother Antigonus to complete the subjection of the country, and the settlement of its affairs. On the return of the latter to Jerusalem, the king was taught to regard him as one who aimed at his life and kingdom, and under that mistaken impression, ordered his death. Discovering his error, he fell sick and died after a reign of only one year, B. C. 105.

He was succeeded by his brother, the third son of Hyrcanus, Alexander Jannæus, whose Hebrew name was probably Jonathan; as the name of "Jonathan" or "King Jonathan," occurs on some coins in the Hebrew, while the reverse has the legend "King Alexander" in Greek. He had been brought up in Galilee, and from early childhood he had not been admitted to the presence of his father. Alexander pursued the policy of his predecessors, of turning to his own advantage the divisions in the Syrian empire. Nor was he singular in this, for many cities (Tyre, Ptolemais, Gaza, Dora, and others) had contrived to make themselves independent. The three last of the cities we have named, A. Jannæus desired to subdue to his own power; which seems to us a very unprincipled design; but it is difficult to find anything like principle in any public transactions of any parties in this most unprincipled age. In B. C. 104 he took the field against Ptolemais, and detached a part of his army against Dora and Gaza. Before this time (namely, in B. C. 107), Ptolemy Lathyrus had been expelled from Egypt by his mother, and withdrew to Cyprus, where he reigned up to the date to which we have now come. To him the beleaguered cities now applied for aid. This he readily granted, and landed in Palestine with an army of 30,000 men. He was very successful, defeating Alexander in a pitched battle on the banks of the Jordan, in which the Jews lost 30,000 men, and then overrunning and furiously ravaging the country, so that the Asamonean cause seemed on the brink of utter ruin, when Cleopatra, the queen of Egypt, fearing that the conquest of Palestine by Lathyrus would be but a step toward the invasion of Egypt, sent an army to the assistance of Alexander. By this means he recovered his footing, and Lathyrus was compelled to withdraw to Cyprus, B. C. 101. Alexander had gained none of the original objects of the war he had so unjustly commenced, and the nation had suffered greatly. The king soon after paid a visit to the Egyptian queen, to whom he had been so much indebted. This visit had nearly proved fatal to him. This ambitious and unscrupulous woman was advised to put him to death and unite Judea to Egypt: and she was inclining to such suggestions, when the interposition of Ananias, the Jewish cammander of her forces, inclined her to a more just and generous policy, and she concluded an alliance with Jannæus at Bethshan (Scythopolis).

After Cleopatra had returned to her own country, Alexander began to resume his former projects of reducing to his yoke the towns and fortresses on his borders—pursuing, in short, the same needlessly aggressive policy which had well nigh been his ruin. Gadara he took after a ten months' siege. He also took the strong fortress of Amathus beyond Jordan; but on his return he was surprised and defeated with the loss of ten thousand men, by the prince of Philadelphia, whose treasures had been deposited there, and returned with disgrace to Jerusalem. He was a Sadducee: this, and his other humiliations, were therefore matters of high satisfaction to the Pharisees, who had great influence with the mass of the people, which they employed with much success, to alienate their affections from Alexander. The king, nothing discouraged, turned his attention to the towns on his southern border. Raphia and Anthedon he took: the conquest of Gaza was more difficult; but at last he won it by treachery, burned it, and massacred the inhabitants, but with so much loss to his own troops, that he returned with little honor and less spoil to Jerusalem.

The long cherished hatred of the Pharisees, and dislike of the people toward the king, broke out openly in the year B. C. 95. He was officiating as high-priest at the feast of tabernacles, and was offering sacrifice upon the great altar, when the people began to pelt him furiously with the citrons which they bore in their hands at that celebration, at the same time assailing him with the most opprobrious expressions. In accordance with the severe principles of the Sadducees, which he had on so many occasions exemplified, he let loose his guard upon the insurgents, by whom six thousand of them were cut down, and thus the disturbance was, for the time, allayed with blood. To prevent such insults in future, he enclosed the priests' court, which contained the altar and sanctuary, by a wooden partition, which excluded the approach of the people, and for his greater security, he took into his pay a body of six thousand foreign mercenaries, who soon became almost his only support.

After this, A. Jannæus turned his attention to the countries beyond Jordan. In B. C. 94 he made the Arabs of Gilead, and the inhabitants of Moab, tributary. In B. C. 93 he destroyed the strong fortress of Amathus, his former enterprise against which had been followed by his defeat, as lately mentioned. In the next year, while in a campaign against Obodas, the Emir of the Arabs of Gaulonitis, he fell into an ambush in the mountains near Gadara, where his army was driven over the precipices and utterly destroyed, and he himself escaped with difficulty. This disaster imbittered the feelings of the already discontented Pharisees, who were at all times jealous even to madness of the national honor. A successful and glorious Sadducee they might have borne; but an unsuccessful one was intolerable. They took up arms, supported by the masses, and broke out into open rebellion, which they maintained for six years, and in which, although repeatedly defeated, their refractory spirit remained unsubdued. At last, after fifty thousand of the malecontents had been destroyed, besides the loss on the other side, the king, although successful, became weary of slaughter and intestine turmoil, and made every effort and declared his readiness to make any sacrifice for the sake of peace. He sent some of his friends to the assembled people, to know what he could do to satisfy them—" Die!" was the answer, given with such vehemence and fury as showed him that there was no hope of accommodation. The malecontents, on their part, sought the help of the Moabites and the Arabians of Gilead, whom Alexander had made tributary, and whose tribute he was now obliged to remit, to prevent their hostilities. The invitation was then sent to Demetrius Eucerus, king of Damascus. He gladly accepted the call, and entered Judea with an army of forty thousand foot and three thousand horse, with which he overthrew Alexander with the loss of all his Greek mercenaries to a man, B. C. 89. His utter ruin was inevitable, had it not been that six thousand of the Jews themselves, taking compassion upon his distress, deserted from the Syrians, and joined him. This so much alarmed Demetrius, fearing lest the defection should extend, that he withdrew his forces from the country to employ them against his brother Philip. The indomitable spirit of Alexander Jannæus, and the large resources which he found in himself, now very conspicuously appeared; for no sooner had the Syrians departed, than he again got together his broken army, and recommenced operations with increased vigor and success against his own discontented subjects. In one great action, fought in B. C. 87, he utterly cut off the greater part of the insurgent army, and shut up the remainder in Bethone, which he besieged and took the year after. On this occasion he was guilty of a most barbarous act, for which the nickname of "Thracian" was justly given to him. He sent eight hundred of the principal captives to Jerusalem, and there crucified them all in one day and in one place, and put their wives and children to death before their eyes, as they hung dying on the crosses; while he sat, feasting with his wives and concubines, within view of the horrid scene, to glut his eyes with their torments. Certainly, the existence of a man who could do this was an evil upon the earth; and it seems alone sufficient to induce a suspicion that there was good cause for the intense dislike with which he was regarded by the people.

After this Alexander had no more disturbance, and he was enabled to spend three years in recovering the fortresses which had revolted, and in reducing the provinces beyond Jordan which had got loose from his dominion, during the civil war. Returning victorious to Jerusalem in B. C. 82, he abandoned himself to luxury and revelling, which speedily brought on a quartan ague, under which he languished for three years, and of which he died in B. C. 78, at the siege of Ragaba beyond Jordan, in the country of the Gergesenes, in the forty-ninth year of his age, and the twenty-seventh of his eventful reign. That reign might be deemed successful in its ultimate results, if judged only by the enlarged dominion which he left to his successors; for at his death the Jewish kingdom included Mount Carmel and all the coast as far as Rhinocolura; it embraced on the south all Idumea; northward it extended to Scythopolis (Bethshan) and Mount Tabor; and beyond Jordan it comprehended Gaulonitis, and all the territory of Gadara, including the land of the Moabites on the south, and extending as far as Pella on the east.

Alexander Jannæus left the government in the hands of his Queen Alexandra, influenced doubtless by the recent example of the female reigns in Egypt and Syria. She was to enjoy the government while she lived, and was to determine which of her two sons, Hyrcanus and Aristobulus, should succeed her. On the approach of death, Alexander gave her such counsels as he judged best calculated to insure her a peaceable reign. Sensible that most of his own troubles had been produced through the agency of the great control which the Pharisees had acquired over public opinion, he exhorted her above all things to cultivate their favor, and to attempt no public measure without their approval. This advice may have been good; but the motive claims no high commendation. He wished his wife to reign after him; and to secure that private object he was willing that all the energies of the government should be sacrificed, and that all the powers of the state should be thrown into the hands of men whom, whether justly or not, he despised and hated. He also instructed the queen what course to take in throwing herself into the hands of the Pharisees. He counselled her to conceal his death until the capture of the fortress, and then, on the triumphant return to Jerusalem, she was to convene the heads of the Pharisees, and offer to be guided entirely by their counsels in the administration of the government; she was also to lay his dead body before them, and leave it wholly to their discretion whether to treat it with ignominy or honor. "If thou dost but this," concluded the king, "I shall be sure of a glorious funeral, and thou wilt rule in safety." Alexandra followed all his directions to a letter; and the event answered to his prediction. The Pharisees were suddenly appeased, as by a miracle; they spoke with profound reverence of the king, whose death they had so often invoked; they lauded to the skies his heroic achievements; and none of all his predecessors had a funeral nearly as magnificent as that of Alexander Jannæus.

The Pharisees, having now the upper hand in the state, proceeded to do what any successful party would have done in the same circumstances. They released all the prisoners and recalled all the exiles of their own party; and being thus strengthened by the recovery of the ablest men of their body, they delayed not to demand justice against the advisers of the crucifixion of the eight hundred; and certainly, if there were any persons active in advising that dreadful enormity, they richly deserved punishment. Diogenes, the chief confidant of the late king, was the first to feel the wrath and vengeance of the Pharisees, and after he had been cut off, they proceeded to the more obnoxious of Alexander's advisers. The queen, sore against her will, submitted to all their demands, to avoid the worse evils of a civil war.

Queen Alexandra appointed to the high-priesthood her eldest son Hyrcanus, a person of mild and inactive disposition, ill qualified to take part in the turmoils of the troubled days in which he was cast. The other son, Aristobulus, was of a different spirit—with the same impulsive energies of character, and nearly as unscrupulous, as his father. He burned with indignation at the degraded, although safe, position which his mother occupied; and in the seventh year of her reign (B. C. 72) he appeared before her at the head of a large party of friends of congenial sentiments, and solicited permission either to leave the country, or to be permitted to retire to the frontier garrison towns, where they might be secure from the malice of the Pharisees. The queen agreed to the latter proposal, and put them in possession of all the fortresses, except Hyrcania, Alexandrium, and Machærus, where she kept her treasures. Next year Aristobulus was intrusted with the command of an army sent against Damascus, but he returned without doing anything memorable, although he was mindful not to neglect the opportunity of ingratiating himself with the troops.

In the year B. C. 69 some attempts made by Selene (reigning in Ptolemais) to extend her dominions in Cœle-Syria, drew the attention of Tigranes, the Armenian king whom, as already related, the Syrians had called to reign over them. He came against her with a large army, subdued Ptolemais, took Selene prisoner, and ultimately ordered her to be put to death at Seleucia on the Tigris. Her sons were at Rome. While Tigranes was engaged before Ptolemais, Alexandra sent an embassy with valuable presents, to obtain his friendship. The rapid progress which the Romans were at this time making in Asia Minor so strongly called his attention to that quarter, that he returned a more favorable answer than might have been expected, and hastened back to his own country. Queen Alexandra died in the same year.

On the death of his mother, the mild and feeble Hyrcanus took possession of the throne. He reigned only three months. His more enterprising and able brother, Aristobulus, had obtained possession of most of the fortresses in the kingdom during the sickness of his mother: the people, also, had by this time grown weary of the tyranny of the Pharisees, and greatly fearing the possible results of their ascendency over such a person as Hyrcanus, readily declared themselves in favor of his brother: and as the soldiers also deserted to him, Hyrcanus had no alternative but to resign his crown and mitre to Aristobulus; and he agreed, with little reluctance, to lead a private life under his protection. "So," as Josephus expresses it, "Aristobulus went to the palace, and Hyrcanus to the house of Aristobulus."

An Idumean originally called Antipas, but better known by the name of Antipater, had by this time become a great man in Judea. He was high in the confidence of Alexander Jannæus, and of Queen Alexandra, who had intrusted him with the government of his native province of Idumea. He had amassed considerable wealth, and formed connexions with the Arabs in the east, and with the Gazites and Ascalonites in the west. Such a man might expect, under a weak ruler like Hyrcanus, to benefit largely by the distractions of the country; whereas the firm rule of a man like Aristobulus was calculated to nip all his budding hopes. This consideration decided him to take up the cause of the deposed Hyrcanus, whom he gradually drew into the belief that his brother had designs against his life, and after much solicitation persuaded him to flee to Petra, and claim the protection of the Arabian king Aretas. That prince readily espoused his cause, and brought him back to Judea, with an army of fifty thousand men: and being there joined by such of the Jews as favored the cause of the elder brother, he gave battle to Aristobulus, defeated him, and compelled him with the heads of his party, to take refuge in the temple-mount, and besieged him there, B. C. 66.

So great was the hatred of the besiegers against Aristobulus and his party, that at the feast of the passover, they would allow no animals for sacrifices to be carried into the temple, although Aristobulus had given to them over the walls the full sum they demanded for such permission.

The great war of the Romans in Asia Minor against Mithridates, king of Pontus, is of importance from its result of bringing all Western Asia under the power of the Romans; but the circumstances of that war have no such connexion with our history as to require their exhibition in this place. Tigranes was soon involved in this war; and in B. C. 69 he was obliged to withdraw his forces from Syria to make head against the Romans nearer home.

This gave an opportunity to ANTIOCHUS ASIATICUS, the son of Selene and A. Eusebes, to seize the government; and, having contracted an alliance with the Roman general, Lucullus, he contrived to retain a part of the empire, until the arrival of Pompey in the East. He arrived to take the command of the Roman armies in the year B. C. 66. While himself employed in the north against Mithridates and Tigranes, Pompey sent Scaurus into Syria. While that general was at Damascus, he received from Aristobulus (then besieged in the temple) an application, with the offer of four hundred talents if he would come to his aid. The offer of a similar sum soon after came from Hyrcanus; but the Roman, considering that it would be easier to frighten away the besieging Nabathæans for Aristobulus than to take so strong a fortress for Hyrcanus, determined to accept the offer of the former. He accordingly received the money; and three hundred talents were also given to Gabinius. Scaurus then commanded Aretas to abandon the siege and quit the country, or expect that the Roman arms would be turned against him. Awed by this threat, the Arabian king immediately obeyed; but he was pursued and overtaken in his homeward march by the active Aristobulus, and defeated with great slaughter.

In B. C. 65, Pompey came into Syria, all the princes of which were prepared to look to him as the arbiter of their fate. Antiochus Asiaticus humbly sued to be confirmed in his kingdom; but he was refused, on the pretext that he was too weak to defend the country against the Jews and Arabs; and that the Romans having overcome Tigranes, Syria became theirs by right of conquest, and they were not disposed to forego the rewards of their toils. In the person of Antiochus XI. was deposed the last of a regal dynasty, descended from Seleucus, which had ruled Syria for two hundred and forty-seven years. His dominions, together with Phœnicia, then passed into the condition of a Roman province.

Twelve kings and many ambassadors repaired to Damascus to render their homage to the illustrious Roman, or to receive from him the award of their fate. Aristobulus, to whom the recognition of his title by the Romans was at this time of great importance, sent an embassy with the present of a golden vine, valued at five hundred talents. But as those who saw this vine subsequently in the capitol at Rome declare that it bore the name of Alexander Jannæus, it would seem that he was not successful in his application, unless, as some imagine, the vine had been made by Alexander Jannæus and placed in the temple, from which it was taken by his son to be presented to the Romans.

The next year, B. C. 64, Pompey again returned to Damascus from Asia Minor, with large designs for the southward extension of the Roman power, which had already been established as far as the Caspian in the north. At that place, the competing Jewish princes produced their cause before him: Hyrcanus through Antipater, and Aristobulus through Nicodemus. The delegates were heard, and dismissed in a friendly manner, with orders that the two brothers should appear in person. Unfortunately for Aristobulus, his cause was much prejudiced by the allusion of Nicodemus to the bribes which Scaurus and Gabinius had received, whereby he provoked the resentment of two persons whose influence with Pompey was very great. As ordered, Hyrcanus and Aristobulus appeared at Damascus in the spring of B. C. 63, to plead their own cause before Pompey, and each attended by multitudes of witnesses to prove the justice of their respective claims. A third Jewish party, uninvited and undesired by either of the others, also appeared, in the persons of many Jews of high consideration, who were prepared to plead, and did plead, against *both* the brothers, that in order to enslave a free people they had changed the form of government from pontifical to regal, contrary to established usage and precedent. Hyrcanus, on his part, rested on his rights as the elder brother, and complained of the usurpation of Aristobulus: the latter pleaded the necessity which the imbecile character of Hyrcanus had imposed upon him. This was precisely the worst plea he could have made; for imbecility of character was, for their own selfish ends, far from being esteemed a disqualification by the Romans, in the princes under their control. However, Pompey did not openly declare his sentiments, but left the matter undecided, until he should have leisure to come in person to Jerusalem and settle it there. But Aristobulus, perceiving clearly that the decision would not be in his favor, withdrew without taking leave, in order to make the requisite preparations, and he thus rendered his case still more desperate.

Pompey was occupied for a time in reducing Aretas and his Nabathæans to subjection. This being effected, he marched against Aristobulus, of whose hostile preparations he was well apprized. He found him in the frontier fortress of Alexandrium (which was situated upon the top of a high rock), and well prepared for an attack. On his arrival, Pompey summoned the Jewish prince to his presence; and Aristobulus, afraid of irritating him by a refusal, and relying on his honor, came down and had several interviews with the Roman general, who, in the end, refused to let him go until he had signed an order for the surrender of all the fortresses to the Romans. But, resenting deeply this imposition, Aristobulus was no sooner dismissed than he fled to Jerusalem, and there prepared for a siege. But, when Pompey approached with his army, his resolution forsook him, as well it might; and he went forth to meet the Roman, to whom he tendered his submission, and offered a sum of money to prevent a war. His proposal was accepted; and Gabinius, one of Pompey's lieutenants, whom there has been previous occasion to name, was sent with a body of troops to recover the city and receive the money. But when Aristobulus returned with the Romans, his own party shut the gates against him and them; on which the captive prince was put in chains. Pompey then himself marched to Jerusalem, and the party of Hyrcanus, being the most numerous in the city, and well aware of his favorable dispositions toward them, opened the gates to him. The party of Aristobulus now withdrew into the temple, which was by this time a strong fortress, fully resolved to abide the result of a siege. They held out for three months, and might have done so much longer, but for the remaining superstition respecting the Sabbath. Pompey being apprized that, although on that as on any other day they would stand on their defence if actually attacked, they would not on that day act on the offensive, or disturb any operations short of actual assault, he sagaciously made use of every Sabbath in filling up the ditch and planting his engines, in which he experienced not the least opposition, and this enabled him to make his attacks with more effect on the other days of the week. At last the temple was taken by assault in the first year of the 179th Olympiad, ending in B. C. 63, the same year in which C. Antonius and M. Tullius Cicero were consuls, and on the very day observed with fasting and humiliation on the conquest of Jerusalem by Nebuchadnezzar. These dates fix the year from which the direct rule of the Romans over Judea may be dated.

Pompey violated the sanctity of the temple, by intruding with his principal officers into the holy of holies. He was not stricken as Ptolemy Philopator and Heliodorus had been, but it has been remarked by some that he never prospered in any of his subsequent undertakings. By the Jews, of course, this act was deeply resented. Pompey, however, spared the sacred treasury, although it contained two thousand talents; and the sacred utensils, and other articles of great value, were left for the sacred uses to which they had been devoted. But he ordered the walls of Jerusalem to be demolished. Hyrcanus he appointed to be high-priest and prince of the country, on condition that he should submit to the Romans, pay tribute, not assume the crown, nor seek to extend his territory beyond the ancient limits of Judea. All the places beyond those limits which the Jews had conquered were also restored to Syria, which was made a Roman province, and left under the rule of Scaurus as prefect, with two legions to preserve tranquillity. Thus the Jews, from being old allies of the Romans, were at once reduced to the condition of a subordinate principality, and were compelled to pay large tribute to the conquerors.

Pompey returned to Rome laden with the spoils of conquered nations, and with a long train of royal and illustrious captives to grace his triumph. Among them were Aristobulus, his two daughters, and his two sons, Alexander and Antigonus. Alexander escaped by the way, and returned to Judea. The rest were among the three hundred and twenty-four noble prisoners who graced the triumph of Pompey in B. C. 61. Pompey was the first to discontinue the barbarous custom of putting the captives to death in the capitol after this public exhibition.   They were all liberated and sent home at the public expense, with the exception of Tigranes and Aristobulus, who were detained lest they should excite disturbances in their respective countries.

CHAPTER XXVI.

ALTHOUGH Hyrcanus II. had again become the nominal head of the reduced and dependant princedom of Judea, Antipater was the actual governor, and managed all things as he would.

In the year 57 B. C., Alexander, the eldest son of Aristobulus, who had escaped on the way to Rome, reappeared in Judea, and soon succeeded in collecting an army of ten thousand foot and fifteen hundred horse.   He seized and garrisoned the strong fortresses of Alexandrium, Machærus, Hyrcania, and several others, and thence ravaged the whole country.   Hyrcanus was not in a condition to make head against him: but for the protection of Jerusalem he was desirous of rebuilding the walls of that city; but this was forbidden by the jealousy of the Romans, and the prince was then obliged to apply to them for assistance.   Gabinius (the same who had before been in the country with Pompey), who had lately become proconsul of Syria, sent some troops into Judea under the command of Mark Anthony, the commander of the cavalry—who afterward took so conspicuous a part in the affairs of Rome, while he prepared to follow himself with a larger army.   The Roman general, being joined by Antipater with the forces of Hyrcanus, defeated Alexander near Jerusalem, with the loss of three thousand men, and compelled him to seek refuge in Alexandrium, to which siege was immediately laid.   Gabinius, who had now arrived, perceiving that the reduction of so strong a place would require time, left a sufficient force to invest it, and with the rest made a progress through the country.   Many cities which he found in ruins, he directed to be rebuilt, according to the intentions of Pompey:*   among these was Samaria, which, after his own name, he called Gabiana, which was not long after changed by Herod to Sebaste.   When he returned to the camp at Alexandrium he was visited by the mother of the besieged Alexander, who had already offered to capitulate, and now, by her address and mediation, was allowed to depart on condition that the fortresses which he held in his power should be demolished, that they might give no occasion for future revolts.

Gabinius then went to Jerusalem, and confirmed Hyrcanus in the high-priesthood; but he took upon him to change the government to an aristocracy, undoubtedly at the request of the Jews themselves, who had formerly much desired such a change from Pompey.   Hitherto the administration of public affairs had been managed, under the prince, by two councils, or courts of justice; the lesser, consisting of twenty-three persons, was instituted in every city, and each of these lesser councils was subject to the control of the great council, or Sanhedrim,† of seventy-two members, sitting at

---

*. Those were—Scythopolis (Bethshan), Samaria, Dora, Azotus or Ashdod, Jamnia, Gaza, Anthedon, Raphia, Gamala, Apollonia, Marissa, and some others.

† This is the first historical notice of such a council.   The Jews deem that the council of seventy elders appointed to assist Moses was afterward constantly maintained, and that with it we are to identify the Sanhedrim of their later history.   But if such a body had existed, it is impossible but that its presence must have been indicated, in the long intervening period, on some of the many occasions which would have called for the exercise of its functions.   That the Sanhedrim was intended as an imitation of the council of the seventy elders, is very possible and likely; but scarcely any one who has examined the matter closely imagines that it had any earlier existence than the time of the Maccabees.

The high-priest was usually the president of this tribunal, and there were two vice-presidents who sat the one on his right hand and the other on his left.   The members were—1. Those who were called "chief priests" in the Gospels.   These were partly priests, who had previously exercised the office of high-priests, and partly of the heads of the twenty-four classes of priests, who were called honorarily, high or chief priests.   2. Elders, being the heads of tribes and of large groups of allied families.   3. The scribes, or men of learning.   It is to be understood, however, that although all the chief priests had a seat in the Sanhedrim, only those of the elders and scribes sat there who were elected to fill up vacancies.

There is no reason to doubt the assertion of the Talmudists, that the Sanhedrim had secretaries and apparitors.   The place in which this great council sat in Jerusalem can not with any certainty be determined.   The Talmudists inform us that the council sat so as to form a semi-circle, of which the president and two vice-presidents occupied the centre.   We learn from other sources that they either sat upon the floor, carpets being spread under them, or upon cushions slightly elevated, with their knees bent and legs crossed, as is still the fashion in the East.

Appeals from the municipal councils and other matters of importance, were brought before this high council.   Its powers were much limited by the Romans; but in the time of Christ it still possessed the

Roman Consul.

Jerusalem. Both were suppressed by Gabinius, who divided the country into five districts, appointing in each an executive council for its government. These districts will be sufficiently indicated by the names of the cities in which the respective councils sat:—Jerusalem, Jericho, Gadara, Amathus, and Sepphoris. This, in fact, changed the government into an aristocracy, for all real power rested in the hands of the several councils, composed of the principal persons of each district, and the power of the prince was completely nullified. This form of government continued to the year 44 B. C., when Hyrcanus was restored to his former power by Julius Cæsar.

About this time Aristobulus contrived to escape from his captivity at Rome, with his younger son Antigonus, and returned to Judea, where his presence excited a revolt. But he was ere long defeated, taken captive with his son, and sent back to his former prison. The report which Gabinius sent, however, of the services which the wife of Aristobulus had rendered in suppressing her son Alexander's insurrection, procured the release of all the family except Aristobulus himself.

In 56 B. C. Gabinius undertook to restore Ptolemy Auletes to the throne of Egypt. He and Mark Anthony succeeded in this object, in which they received no slight assistance from Hyrcanus, or rather from Antipater, who eagerly laid hold of every opportunity of serving and ingratiating himself with the Romans, through whose favor alone could he hope that his ambitious designs would ever be realized. By his means the Roman army was most bountifully furnished with provisions, arms, and money; and measures were taken to dispose the Jews of Egypt to forward their cause, which they had large means of doing. While the substantial force of the Romans was absent on this expedition, Alexander, the son of Aristobulus, got together a large army, with which he contrived to make himself master of Judea, and massacred all the Romans who had the misfortune to fall in his way. Several fled to Mount Gerizim, and were there besieged by Alexander, when Gabinius returned victorious from Egypt. The proconsul endeavored, through Antipater, to make peace with him; but as, although many had abandoned him on the approach of the Romans, he was still at the head of thirty thousand men, he refused to listen to any terms of accommodation. In a battle, which soon followed, near Mount Tabor, ten thousand of his men were slain, and the rest dispersed. Gabinius then went to Jerusalem, and settled affairs there according to the views of Antipater, who had much influence both with him and Anthony.

In the year 55 the proconsul Gabinius was recalled, to answer for the venality and extortion of his government. Yet he is regretted by Josephus as one who was friendly to the Jews; who, however, had to pay a high price for his friendship. They certainly gained nothing by the exchange for the new proconsul, who was no other than the wealthy and avaricious Crassus (the colleague of Pompey and Julius Cæsar in the triumvirate), who procured himself to be invested with unusually large powers, and who, being consul for that year, embarked for Syria before his consulship expired. Crassus was bent on an expedition against the Parthians; and he failed not, before his departure, to plunder the temple at Jerusalem of all the treasures which Pompey had spared. He took everything that he deemed worth taking, and the value of his plunder is estimated at ten thousand talents. In the war against the Parthians, which was entirely unexpected and unprovoked, Crassus was at first successful; but in the end, he and his son were slain, and the Roman army disgraced, B. C. 53.

Cassius, who had commanded a wing of the Roman army in the battle, conducted a body of five hundred horse safely back to Syria, the government of which devolved on him until a successor to Crassus should be appointed. Having, with much ability, so organized the broken resources of the province as to defend it successfully against the Parthian invasion of 52 B. C., he afterward marched into Judea, and forced Alexander, who began raising fresh disturbances as soon as the news of the defeat of Crassus arrived in Syria, to terms of peace.

In the civil war which broke out between Pompey and Cæsar, Syria and Palestine were variously involved. When Cæsar passed the Rubicon in 49 B. C., and made himself master of Rome, he thought that Aristobulus might be useful to his cause against that of Pompey, which was strong in the east; and therefore sent him into Palestine, with two legions under his command, to keep Syria in awe. But

power of trying offenders and of passing sentence; although when the penalty was high or capital, it was necessary that it should be confirmed by the Roman governor, who also assumed the right of executing as his own the sentence which he had confirmed.

Pompey's party contrived to poison him on the way, and thus frustrated the design. His always-active son, Alexander, had raised forces in expectation of his father's arrival; but Pompey sent orders to his son-in-law, Q. Metellus Scipio, whom he had promoted to the government of Syria, to put him to death. He was accordingly taken, brought to Antioch, tried, and beheaded.

In the midst of all the causes of agitation in Judea—from the contests of the Asamonean princes—from the different characters of the governors of Syria—from the march of armies—from the intrigues which divided courts and people in the quarrel between Pompey and Cæsar—Antipater never slept, was never found wanting to himself. He had availed himself of his power over the feeble Hyrcanus to make for himself a personal influence and reputation, through the services he was thereby able to render to the various parties and persons whose friendship might be useful to him. He was moreover the father of four sons, who understood and concurred in his views —all of them brave, ambitious, magnificent, full of spirit and high hopes. One of them, Phasael, was already governor of Jerusalem, and another, Herod, was governor of Galilee. These, it will be perceived, were two of the five districts into which the country had been divided by Gabinius. Thus the family went on gathering strength from day to day, while the Asamonean family—through the imbecility of Hyrcanus, and the reverses of Aristobulus and his sons—sustained a daily loss of power and influence. In the contest between Pompey and Cæsar, Antipater, who was under obligations to the former, was in a critical and difficult position. But such men as he are never wrong. Their felicitous instincts enable them to discover the falling cause in sufficient time to make the abandonment of it a merit with him whose star is rising. Thus Antipater turned in good time to the side of the new master; and in the Egyptian campaign rendered important services to Cæsar by bringing to his aid the forces concentrated in Judea, Idumea, and part of Arabia; while in action he displayed great abilities and courage, which no one knew better than Cæsar how to appreciate and respect. On his return from Egypt, the crown of which he had fixed on the head of the too-celebrated Cleopatra, the eldest daughter of Ptolemy Auletes, he went to Jerusalem, and there employed the absolute power he possessed quite in subservience to the views and wishes of Antipater. In vain did Antigonus, the surviving son of Aristobulus, appear, and plead that the lives of his father and brother had been lost in his cause: he was heard coldly, and dismissed as a troublesome person. Cæsar abrogated the aristocratical government which Gabinius had established ten years before, and confirmed Hyrcanus in his full powers as high-priest and ethnarch. He ordered the remission every sabbatic year of the annual tribute payable to the Romans: he further conceded that the Jews should not, as formerly, be obliged to provide winter quarters for the Roman troops, or to pay an equivalent in money; and he granted such further privileges and immunities to the Jews throughout the empire, that the Roman yoke became very light upon them for a time. Antipater himself was appointed procurator of Judea for the Romans. The decree in which these privileges were imbodied was engraved on brass, and laid up in the capitol at Rome, and in the temples of Zidon, Tyre, and Ascalon. Hyrcanus afterward ventured, by ambassadors sent to Rome, to solicit permission to fortify Jerusalem, and to rebuild the walls which Pompey had thrown down. This was granted by Cæsar, and immediately executed by Antipater.

Julius Cæsar left the government of Syria in the hands of Sextus Cæsar, his relative, who was also well disposed toward the family of Antipater. The promotion of his son Herod to be governor of Galilee has already been noticed. He displayed great activity and daring in clearing his province of the robbers by which it had been infested. But having put the leader of these banditti, with several of his associates to death, by his own mere authority, without any form of trial, the jealousy of several of the leading Jews was awakened, and they obliged Hyrcanus to cite him to Jerusalem to answer for his conduct before the Sanhedrim. He came arrayed in purple, with a numerous retinue, and presented to Hyrcanus a letter from Sextus Cæsar, commanding him to acquit Herod under pain of his highest displeasure. The prince, who liked Herod, was well enough inclined to this before, and the accusers were so damped by the young man's audacity, as well as by the letter, which also intimidated the Sanhedrim, that they all sat in awkward silence until one firm and honest voice, that of Sameas, was heard rebuking the members of the council for their cowardice, and predicting that the day would come when Herod would refuse them the pardon

29

which they were then all too ready to extend to him. This was verified in the end. When Sameas had spoken, the Sanhedrim exhibited some inclination to act; but Hyrcanus adjourned the sitting, and gave Herod a hint to quit Jerusalem. He repaired to Sextus Cæsar at Damascus, and not only obtained his protection, but received from him the government of all Cœle-Syria, on condition of paying a stipulated tribute. On this Herod collected a small army, and was with difficulty persuaded by his father and his brother Phasael from marching to Jerusalem, to avenge himself for the insult he considered he had received in being summoned before the Sanhedrim.

The assassination of Sextus Cæsar in Syria, by Bassus, and of Cæsar himself at Rome, by Brutus, Cassius, and their confederates, rekindled the flames of civil war, and might have prostrated the hopes of one less ductile than Antipater. Cassius passed over into Syria to secure that important province for the republic, and was compelled to exact heavy contributions to maintain the large army he had raised. Judea was assessed at seven hundred talents, one half of which Antipater commissioned his sons Phasael and Herod to raise, and intrusted the collection of the other half to Malichus, a Jew, one of the chief supporters of Hyrcanus. Herod won the favor of Cassius by the promptitude with which he produced his quota; but Malichus, being more dilatory, would have been put to death, had not Hyrcanus redeemed him by paying one hundred talents out of his own coffers. There was something in this affair to kindle the smouldering jealousy with which Malichus and the heads of the Jewish nation were disposed to regard the concentration of all the real power of the government in the hands of an Idumean and foreigner, as they regarded Antipater; and they plotted to destroy him and all his family. Antipater was poisoned by a glass of wine given to him at the very table of Hyrcanus: in revenge for which Phasael and Herod procured Malichus to be put to death by the Roman garrison at Tyre, in obedience to an order which they obtained from Cassius.

The influence of Antipater over Hyrcanus being now withdrawn, the adverse party soon succeeded in bringing him over to their views, by directing his fears toward the overgrown and increasing power of the sons of Antipater. Felix, the commander of the Roman forces at Jerusalem, was also led into the same views; for by this time (42 B. C.) Cassius and Brutus had been defeated and slain at Philippi by Anthony and Octavius. This party was, however, soon mastered by the brothers, who recovered Massada and all the fortresses of which it had obtained possession, and even dared to expel Felix from Jerusalem, as the change of affairs produced by the battle of Philippi, rendered it unlikely that the now dominant avengers of Cæsar would resent the insult offered to one employed by his slayers. They upbraided Hyrcanus for favoring a party which had always sought to curb his power, which had been on all occasions supported by the sagacious and firm counsels of Antipater. A reconciliation was, however, soon effected, as Herod greatly wished to strengthen his pretensions by a marriage with Miriam or Miriamne, the beautiful granddaughter of the high-priest, to whom he was accordingly espoused.

But although the adverse party had been repressed, it was not extinguished; and it soon found a new head in the person of Antigonus, the surviving son of Aristobulus, whose unsuccessful application to Cæsar has lately been noticed. Nothing less was now professed than an intention to restore him to the throne of his father, his claims to which were strongly supported by some neighboring princes, and even by the Roman governor of Damascus, who had been won by a sum of money. But when he arrived in Judea with his army, he was totally defeated by Herod, and compelled for the present to relinquish his purpose.

This was the state of affairs (B. C. 41) when, after the battle of Philippi, Mark Anthony passed into Syria, to secure that important province for the conquerors. The discontented party sent a deputation to him soon after his arrival, to complain of the sons of Antipater. But Anthony who had been already joined by Herod, and had accepted presents from him, was indisposed toward them, especially when Herod reminded him of the services, well known to himself, which Antipater had rendered to Gabinius in the expedition to Egypt. About the same time Anthony received an embassy from Hyrcanus, touching the ransom of the inhabitants of Gophna, Emmaus, Lydda, Thamna, and some other places, whom Cassius had sold for slaves because they refused to pay their portion of the seven hundred talents which he exacted. Anthony granted the application, and notified his determination to the Tyrians, who had probably purchased most of these persons, Tyre being a great mart for slaves.

Nothing discouraged by the former neglect, one hundred Jews of the first consideration repaired to Anthony at Daphne near Antioch, to renew their complaints against Herod and Phasael. Anthony gave them an audience, and then turning to Hyrcanus, who was present, asked him, in their hearing, whom *he* esteemed most able to conduct the affairs of the government, under himself. Influenced, probably, by the recent contract of marriage between his grand-daughter and Herod, he named the two brothers, on which Anthony conferred upon them the rank and power of Tetrarchs, committed the affairs of Judea to their management, imprisoned fifteen of the deputies, and would have put them to death, had not Herod interceded for them. So things were managed in those times. With the usual pertinency of the nation, the discontented Jews renewed the complaint at Tyre in a body of a thousand deputies; but Anthony thought proper to treat this as a tumultuous assembly, and ordered his soldiers to disperse it, which was not done without bloodshed. Anthony was then on his way to Egypt. Summoned, on his first arrival in Syria, to appear before him to account for the part she was alleged to have taken in assisting Cassius, Cleopatra had not in vain exercised upon him the fascinations by which Cæsar had before been subdued. The story of Anthony's thraldrom to this charming but most unprincipled woman, is too familiar to need more than the slight allusions which the connexion of this history requires. Lost in luxurious ease and dalliance, Anthony wasted much time at Alexandria, leaving the affairs of Syria and Asia Minor to get into a state of confusion, satisfying himself that by-and-by he would rouse himself to some great effort which would set all right.

In the spring of the year B. C. 40 the news from both Syria and Italy compelled the warrior to break off the enchantment by which he was bound, and to look closely to his affairs. In Syria, the people disgusted and exhausted by the successive exactions of Cassius and Anthony, refused to bear them any longer. The people of Aradus kindled the flame of opposition, by openly resisting the collectors of tribute, which example was soon followed by others. They united themselves with the Palmyrenes, and the princes whom Anthony had deposed, and called to the Parthians for aid. They gladly responded to the call, and entered the country in great numbers under the command of their king's son Pacorus, and of a Roman general (Labienus) who had belonged to the party of Pompey. The king with one division of the army took possession of Syria, while Labienus with another performed the same service in Syria. Anthony was made perfectly acquainted with this when he reached Tyre; but the news which he also received from Italy so much more nearly concerned his personal prosperity, that he immediately embarked for that country. On his arrival, affairs between him and Octavius wore, for a time, a threatening aspect. But the opportune death of Anthony's wife Fulvia allowed an opening for intermarriages ·between Anthony, Octavius, and Lepidus, and peace between the triumvirs was for a time restored. They then divided the Roman empire among themselves. Anthony received Syria and the East, Lepidus obtained Africa, and Octavius all the West. B. C. 40.

Meanwhile the Parthians, having made themselves masters of Syria, as related, began to take part in the affairs of Palestine. Pacorus was induced by the offer of one thousand talents in money, *and five hundred women*, to undertake to place Antigonus on the throne of Judea. To put this contract in execution he furnished a body of soldiers, under the command of his cup-bearer, who also bore the name of Pacorus, to assist the operations of Antigonus. The united force found no effectual resistance until it reached Jerusalem, where the struggle was protracted without any decisive results. But at length it was agreed between the real belligerants to admit the Parthian commander within the city, to act as umpire between them. Phasael (the governor of Jerusalem) invited him to his own house, and allowed himself to be persuaded that the best course that could be taken would be for him and Hyrcanus to go and submit the matter in dispute to the arbitration of Barzapharnes, the Parthian governor of Syria. They went notwithstanding the dissuasions of the less confiding Herod. Barzapharnes treated them with great attention and respect, until he supposed that sufficient time had elapsed to enable Pacorus to secure Herod at Jerusalem, when he immediately put them in chains, and shut them up in prison. But Herod, suspecting the treachery of the Parthians, withdrew with his family by night from Jerusalem, and repaired to the strong fortress of Massada, situated upon a high mountain west of the Dead sea. On finding that Herod had escaped, the Parthians plundered the country, made Antigonus king according to their contract, and departed, leaving Hyrcanus and Phasael in his hands. Phasael, feeling assured that he was doomed to death, dashed out his brains against his prison walls. The life of his aged uncle was spared by the nephew; but he cut off his ears to disqualify him from ever again acting as high-priest, and thus mutilated, sent him back to the safe keeping of the Parthians, who sent him to Seleucia on the Tigris.

In this seemingly desperate state of his affairs, for to the great body of the Jews themselves Antigonus appears to have been more acceptable than he, Herod repaired to Egypt, and took ship at Alexandria for Rome. He was warmly welcomed by Anthony, by whom he was introduced to Octavius, who was induced to notice him favorably by the report of the very great services which Antipater had rendered to his grand-uncle (and adoptive father) Cæsar, in the Egyptian expedition. The object of Herod's journey was to induce the Romans to raise to the throne of Judea Aristobulus, the brother of his espoused Miriamne. This Aristobulus was the son of Alexandra, the·daughter of Hyrcanus, by Alexander the eldest son of Aristobulus, so that he seemed to unite in his person the claims of both branches of the Asamonean family. For himself, Herod proposed to govern the country under Aristobulus, as his father had governed it under Hyrcanus. But Anthony suggested the startling idea of making Herod himself king of Judea; and noticing the eagerness with which he grasped at the glittering bait, he undertook, on the promise of a sum of money, to secure this object for him. He easily induced Octavius to concur with him; and their joint representations secured the appointment from the senate. Accordingly, during the consulship of Demetrius Calvinus and Asinius Pollio, in the one hundred and eighty-fourth Olympiad, in the year B. C. 40, the man who had a few weeks before been on the point of destroying himself from sheer despair of his fortunes, was conducted to the Capitol between the two foremost men in the world, Anthony and Octavius, and there consecrated king, with idolatrous sacrifices. All this was so soon accomplished, that Herod departed from Rome seven days after his arrival, and landed at Ptolemais only three months after his flight from Jerusalem. If the Parthians had still been in possession of Syria, it would have availed him little to have been made a king at Rome; but by the time of his return they had already been driven out of Syria by the Romans, and had withdrawn beyond the Euphrates.

Herod diligently applied himself to the collecting such a force as might enable him to relieve the friends he had left in Massada, who had all the while been closely besieged by Antigonus, and were at one time reduced to such extremities for want of water, that they had fully intended to surrender the next day, when an abundant fall of rain during the intervening night filled all the cisterns and enabled them to hold out until Herod came to their relief.

Three years elapsed before Herod can be said to have obtained possession of the throne which the Romans had given to him. The assistance which the Romans themselves rendered is of questionable value, as at first the generals appointed to assist him would only act just as money induced them; and under pretence that the forces wanted provisions, ravaged the country in such a manner as was well calculated to render his cause odious to the Jews. One good service to the land was performed in the extirpation of the numerous bands of robbers which infested Galilee, dwelling chiefly in the caverns of the hill country, and which were so numerous as sometimes to give battle to the troops in the open field. They were, however, pursued with fire and sword, in all their difficult retreats, and after great numbers had been slain, the rest sought refuge beyond Jordan.

The arrival of Anthony in Syria enabled Herod to obtain more efficient assistance than before; and, after having subdued the open country, he, with his Roman auxiliaries, sat down before Jerusalem. During this siege he consummated his marriage with Miriamne, to whom he had four years before been betrothed. He was not only passionately attached to this lady, but he hoped that the affinity thus contracted with the Asamonean family, which was still very popular among the Jews, would conciliate the people to his government. The city held out for six months, whereby the Romans were so greatly exasperated that when at last (B. C. 27) they took it by storm, they plundered the town and massacred the inhabitants without mercy. Herod complained that they were going to make him king of a desert; and paid down a large sum of money to induce them to desist. Antigonus surrendered himself in rather a cowardly manner to the Roman general 'Sosius), and, throwing himself at his feet, besought his clemency with so much abjectness, that the Roman repelled him with contempt, addressing him by the name of Antigona, as if unworthy a man's name. He sent him to Anthony, who at first intended to reserve him for his triumph; but, being assured by Herod that while Antigonus lived the Jews generally would not acknowledge himself as king, or cease to raise disturbances on his behalf, and this representation being backed by a sum of money, Anthony put him to death at Antioch, by the rods and the axe of the lictor—an indignity which the Romans had never before inflicted upon a crowned head. Thus ignominiously ended the dynasty of the Asamoneans, one hundred and twenty-six years after its glorious commencement.

Herod commenced his reign by cutting off all the heads of the Asamonean party, not only to secure himself in the throne, but, by the confiscation of their property, to enrich his coffers, which were well exhausted by his profuse expenditure, and by the rapacity of the Romans. In this process all the members of the Sanhedrim perished, except Pollio and Sameas, which last, it will be remembered, had predicted this result. The ground on which they were spared was, that they alone had counselled submission to the course of events, by surrendering the city to Herod; whereas the others were constantly encouraging each other and the citizens in the now vain expectation that Jehovah would, as of old, interpose for the deliverance of his temple.*

Herod, sensible that the Jews would not tolerate his own assumption of the high-priesthood in the room of Antigonus, designed to render that office politically insignificant, and therefore appointed it to Ananel of Babylon, an obscure priest, although descended from the ancient high-priests, and who was entirely without influence or connexions to render him dangerous (B. C. 36). This appointment occasioned confusion in his own family; for Miriamne his wife, and Alexandra her mother, took umbrage at the exclusion of her brother Aristobulus—the same youth for whose brows he had originally designed the diadem which he had himself been induced to assume. Miriamne was constantly harassing him on the subject; and her mother Alexandra, a woman of great spirit, went much further, for she complained to Cleopatra, queen of Egypt, by letter, and had begun to engage the interest of Anthony himself in the matter, when Herod saw that it was necessary to his domestic peace and public safety that he should depose Ananel and promote Aristobulus to his office, who was then but seventeen years of age. He was, however, so seriously displeased at the bold step which Alexandra had taken, that he ordered her to be confined in her own palace, and placed around her some of his confidential servants to watch all her movements. She wrote to Cleopatra, complaining of this treatment, and in reply was advised to make her escape to Egypt. Accordingly she arranged that herself and Aristobulus should be placed in two coffins, and carried by attached servants to the seacoast, where a ship was waiting to receive them. But their flight was intercepted by Herod, whom, however, the fear of Cleopatra prevented from treating them with harshness. He, however, secretly resolved to put Aristobulus out of the way, as a person whose influence he had great reason to dread.

This intention was strengthened when he perceived how dangerously the discharge of his functions brought under the admiring notice of the Jews this beautiful fragment of the Maccabean race, in which they were delighted to trace out the noble qualities

* This Pollio and Sameas of Josephus are the famous Hillel and Shammai of the Rabbinical writers—two of the most eminent of the ancient doctors of the nation. Hillel was of the royal line of David, being descended from Shephatiah, David's son by Abital (1 Chron. iii. 2). He was born in Babylonia, and came to Jerusalem in the fortieth year of his age; and for his eminence in the study of the law, he was appointed president of the Sanhedrim, forty years after, in the eightieth year of his age, and held that high station for forty years more; and it continued in his family to the tenth generation. He was succeeded by Simeon, supposed to be the same who took Christ in his arms when he was presented in the temple (Luke ii. 22-35). His son Gamaliel was president of the Sanhedrim when Peter and the apostles were summoned before them (Acts v. 34); "at whose feet" the Apostle Paul was "brought up," or educated, in the sect and discipline of the Pharisees (Acts xxiii. 3). He lived until within eighteen years of the destruction of Jerusalem, and in the Jewish writings is distinguished by the title of Gamaliel the Old. He was succeeded by Simeon II., who perished in the destruction of Jerusalem. His son was Gamaliel II., and his again Simeon III. He was succeeded by his son, the celebrated R. Judah Hakkadosh, or "the holy," who committed the traditional law to writing, in the Mishna. His son and successor was Gamaliel III.; after him Judah Gemaricus; after him Hillel II., the ingenious compiler of the present Jewish Calendar, A. D. 358.

Shammai had been a disciple of Hillel, and approached the nearest to him in learning and eminence of all the Mishnical doctors. He was vice-president of the Sanhedrim, and disagreed in several points with his master. Hillel was of a mild and conciliatory temper; but Shammai of an angry and fierce spirit. Hence proceeded violent disputes and contests between the two schools, which at length ended in bloodshed. At last they were allayed by a fictitious Bath Col, or voice from heaven, deciding in favor of Hillel, to which the school of Shammai submitted. See Hales, ii. 593. Persons acquainted with the matters in controversy between the schools of Hillel and Shammai will find various marked allusions to them in the Gospels, and, although less frequently, in the Epistles.

and lineaments by which that race had been distinguished. At the feast of tabernacles, Aristobulus officiated at the altar in the splendid robes of the high-priest, which set off to such advantage the angelic grace and beauty of his youthful person, that the Jews could not contain themselves, but gave vent to the most lively demonstrations of their admiration and love. This sealed his doom. Soon after, Herod engaged Aristobulus, with suitable companions of his own age, in a variety of sports and entertainments at Jericho. Among other things they bathed in a lake, where the young men kept immersing Aristobulus, as if in sport, until he was drowned. Loud were the lamentations of Herod at this most unhappy "accident." By these, and by the grand funeral with which he honored the remains of Aristobulus, and by the trophies with which he surcharged his tomb, he sought to disguise from the people the real character of this transaction. But they were not deceived. The deed inspired the whole nation with hatred and horror, which even his own family shared. As to Alexandra, her emotions were so overpowering that only the hope of vengeance enabled her to live.

Old Hyrcanus was at this time in Jerusalem. He had been, and might have remained, very happily situated at Seleucia, where he was treated by the Jews in that quarter, who were more numerous and more wealthy than those of Judea, as their king and high-priest; in which point of view he was also considered and respected by the Parthian king. But when the fears and suspicions of Herod extended even to him, and, desiring to get him into his power, he sent, and invited him to come and spend the evening of his days in his own land, and with his own family, and engaged the Parthian king to permit him to do so,—Hyrcanus, who liked Herod, and had great confidence in his gratitude, could not be dissuaded by the earnest remonstrances and entreaties of his eastern friends; but returned to Jerusalem, where he was well received, and until a more convenient season, treated by Herod with attention and respect.

Anthony was now again in Syria, and on his arrival had invited Cleopatra to join him at Laodicea. Alexandra again applied to Cleopatra; and she took much interest in the matter—not from any strong natural feelings—for she had herself committed crimes as great, but in the hope of inducing Anthony to add Judea to her dominions if Herod were disgraced. She therefore brought the affair under the notice of Anthony; and as he could not but remember that Herod had originally sought for the murdered youth the crown he now wore himself, he was induced to summon him to Laodicea to answer for his conduct. Herod was obliged to obey, and was not without anxiety for the result. He however took care so to propitiate Anthony beforehand, by the profusion of his gifts, that on his arrival he was immediately acquitted, and the avarice of Cleopatra was in some degree appeased by the assignment of Cœle-Syria to her, in lieu of Judea, of which she had always been, and soon again became covetous, B. C. 34.

Before his departure from Jerusalem, Herod, uncertain of the result, had left private instructions with his uncle Joseph (who had married his sister Salome) to put Miriamne to death in case he was condemned, for he knew that Anthony had heard much of her extreme beauty, and feared that he might take her to himself, after his death. Joseph had the great imprudence to divulge this secret to Mariamne herself, representing it, however, as resulting from the excess of her husband's love to her. But she rather regarded it as a proof of so savage a nature, that she conceived an unconquerable repugnance toward him. Soon after a rumor came that he had been put to death by Anthony; on which Alexandra, who was now also acquainted with the barbarous orders left with Joseph, was preparing to seek protection with the Roman legion stationed in the city, when letters from Herod himself, announcing his acquittal and speedy return, induced them to relinquish their design. The firebrand of the family was Salome, the sister of Herod, and she failed not to apprize her brother of this intention, as well as to insinuate that too close an intimacy had subsisted between Mariamne and Joseph. Salome had been, it seems, provoked to hatred of this high-born lady, by the hauteur with which she had been looked down upon and treated as an inferior by her. Although struck with jealousy, the king allowed his deep love for Mariamne to subdue him, when all her beauty shone once more upon him. He could only bring himself to question her gently, and was satisfied from her answers, and from the conscious innocence of her manner, that she had been maligned. Afterward, while assuring her of the sincerity and ardor of his love toward her, she tauntingly reminded him of the proof of that which he had given in his orders to Joseph. This most imprudent disclosure rekindled all the jealousy of Herod. Convinced that the charge which he had heard was true, he flung her from his arms; Joseph he ordered to be put to death, without admitting him to his presence; and although his love for Mariamne at this time restrained his rage against her, he put her mother Alexandra into custody, as the cause of all these evils.

The disgraceful history of Anthony in Egypt is familiar to the reader; and it is only needful to advert to one or two points in which Herod and Palestine were more or less involved.

In B. C. 33 Jerusalem was "honored" with a visit from Cleopatra, on her return from the banks of the Euphrates, whither she had accompanied Anthony on his Armenian expedition. Before this she had succeeded in persuading Anthony—although he steadily refused wholly to sacrifice Herod to her ambition—to give her the fertile territories around Jericho, the celebrated balsam afforded by which, together with the palm-trees in which it abounded, furnished a considerable revenue, the deprivation of which could not but have given great offence to Herod. The means which this abandoned woman used, during her stay at Jerusalem, to bring the king under the spell of those fascinations for which, more than for her beauty, she was celebrated, added, in his mind, disgust and contempt to the sense of wrong; and although he received and entertained her with the most sedulous attention and apparent respect, he had it seriously in consideration whether, seeing she was wholly in his power, he could safely compass the death of one who had more than once endeavored to accomplish his own. The dread of Anthony's vengeance deterred him, and he conducted the queen with honor to the frontiers of her own kingdom, after having endeavored to propitiate her cupidity by ample gifts. But nothing could satiate her thirst for gain and aggrandizement, and her plots to gain possession of Judea were continued, and could hardly have been defeated by a less accomplished master in her own arts than Herod "the Great." One time she engaged Anthony to commit to him a hazardous war on her account with the Arabian king reigning in Petra, calculating that the death of either of them would enable her to appropriate his dominions. Herod gained one battle; but he lost another through the defection of the Egyptian general at a critical moment of the conflict. Herod was, however, ultimately successful, and won great honor by a signal and effective victory, which brought the Arabians of Seir under his dominion.

The same year (B. C. 31) had opened with an earthquake so tremendous as had never before been known in Judea: it is said that not fewer than thirty thousand persons were either swallowed up in the chasms which opened in the earth, or destroyed by the fall of their houses. The confusion and loss which this calamity occasioned greatly troubled the king, and not long after he found (as far as his own interests were concerned) a more serious matter of anxiety in the result of the battle of Actium (Sept. 2d., B. C. 31), when Octavius obtained a decided victory over Anthony, who fled to Egypt, as his last retreat. Herod did not exhibit any blameworthy alacrity in abandoning the patron of his fortunes. He sent by a special messenger to exhort him to put to immediate death the woman who had been his ruin, seize her treasures and kingdom, and thus obtain means of raising another army, with which either once more to contend for empire, or at least to secure a more advantageous peace than he could otherwise expect. But finding that Anthony paid no heed to this proposal, and neglected his own offers of service, he thought it was high time to take care of himself, by detaching his fortunes from one whose utter ruin he saw to be inevitable. Therefore when Octavius, early in B. C. 30, had come to Rhodes, on his way to Egypt, he went thither to him.

But before his departure he made such arrangements as showed, after his own peculiar manner, the sense he entertained of the serious importance of the present contingencies. He placed his mother, sister, wives, and children, in the strong fortress of Massada, under the care of his brother Pheroras. But seeing that Mariamne and her mother Alexandra could not agree with his mother and sister, he placed them separately in the fortress of Alexandrium, under the care of a trusty Idumean named Sohemus, with secret orders to put them both to death, if Octavius should treat him harshly; and that, in concurrence with Pheroras, he should endeavor to secure the crown for his children. And, fearful that the existence and presence of Hyrcanus might suggest the obvious course of deposing himself and restoring the original occupant of the throne, he was glad of the opportunity of putting him to death, with the faint show of justice which might be derived from the detected design of the old man (instigated by his daughter Alexandra) to make his escape to the Arabian king Malchus, the most active of Herod's foreign enemies, and the son of that king Aretas who had formerly invaded Judea for the purpose of restoring Hyrcanus to the throne which his brother had usurped. Hyrcanus was eighty years of age when he was thus made to experience the heartless ingratitude of the man who owed life and all things to his favor.

On his arrival at Rhodes, Herod conducted himself with the tact of no common man. When admitted to an audience he frankly acknowledged all he had done for Anthony, and all he would still have done had his services been accepted. He even stated the last counsel which he had given to that infatuated man; and having thus enabled Octavius to judge how faithful he was to his friends, he offered him that friendship which the conduct of Anthony left him free to offer. Octavius was charmed by this manly frankness; and, mindful of Antipater's services to Julius Cæsar, and of the part which he had himself taken in placing Herod on the throne, his overtures were received with pleasure, and he was directed again to take up and wear on his head the diadem which he had laid aside when he entered the presence. By this significant intimation he was confirmed in his kingdom; and then and after he was treated with a degree of consideration not usually paid to tributary kings.

Meanwhile Mariamne had, by her address, managed to extract from Sohemus the acknowledgment of the last directions concerning her which he had received from Herod. The consequence was that although she concealed her knowledge of the fact, she received him on his return with coldness and dislike, which offended him highly; and, presuming on the depth of his affection for her, she continued long to maintain a degree of haughtiness and reserve which greatly aggravated his displeasure. After Herod had been fluctuating for a whole year between love and resentment, Mariamne one day brought matters to a crisis by her pointed refusal to receive his love, and by her upbraiding him with the murder of her grandfather and brother. Enraged beyond further endurance, Herod immediately ordered her confidential eunuch to be put to the torture, that he might discover the cause of her altered conduct; but the tortured wretch could only say that it probably arose from some communication which Sohemus had made to her. This hint sufficed; as he concluded that Sohemus must have been too intimate with her, or that he would not have revealed the secret with which he had been intrusted. Sohemus was immediately seized and put to death; Mariamne herself was then accused by Herod of adultery before judges of his own selection, by whom she was condemned, but with a conviction that their sentence of death would not be executed. Neither would it, probably, but for the intervention of Cypros the mother of Herod, and Salome his sister, who, fearing he might relent, suggested that by delay occasion for a popular commotion in her favor might be given. She was therefore led to immediate execution, and met her death with the firmness which became her race, although assailed on the way by the violent and indecent reproaches of her own mother Alexandra, who now began to be seriously alarmed for her own safety. She, however, did not long escape; for when Herod fell sick the next year (B. C. 28), from the poignancy of his remorse and anguish at the loss of Mariamne, she laid a plot for seizing the government; but it was disclosed to Herod by the officers whose fidelity she endeavored to corrupt, and he instantly ordered her to be put to death.

We must return to an earlier year, to notice that Octavius passed through Syria on his way to Egypt, and that Herod went to meet him at Ptolemais, where he entertained him and his army with the most profuse magnificence. Besides this he presented the emperor with eight hundred talents, and furnished large supplies of bread, wine, and other provisions, for the march through the desert, where the army might have been much distressed for the want of such necessaries. He accompanied the army himself through the desert to Pelusium. On the return of Octavius the same way, after the death of Anthony and Cleopatra, and the reduction of Egypt to the condition of a Roman province, he was received and entertained with the same truly royal liberality and magnificence, by which he was so gratified that, in return, he presented Herod with the four thousand Gauls who had formed the body-guard of Cleopatra, and also restored to him the districts and towns of which the principality had been divested by Pompey and Anthony.

In B. C. 27, four years after the battle of Actium, Octavius received from the flattery of the senate the name—or rather the title which became a name—of Augustus, and with it all the powers of the state. That he might not, however, seem to assume all the authority to himself, he divided the empire into two parts, the quiet and peaceable portions he assigned to the senate, to be governed by consular and prætorian officers; these were called *senatorial;* but the turbulent and insecure provinces which lay on the outskirts of the empire, he reserved for himself; these were called *imperial,* and were governed by presidents and procurators. This was one of the strokes of deep statesmanship which distinguish the history of Augustus Cæsar, for under the appearance of leaving to the senate the most settled and easily governed provinces, he secured in his own hands the whole military power of the empire, which was necessarily stationed in the comparatively unsettled imperial provinces to retain them in subjection—such as Egypt, *Syria,* Phœnicia, Silicia, and Cyprus, in the east, and Spain in the west.

In the year B. C. 25, Herod found an opportunity of cutting off the last branch of the Asamonean race. His turbulent sister Salome, having fallen out with her second husband Costabarus, the governor of Idumea and Gaza, she took the liberty of sending him a bill of divorce, in conformity with the Roman customs, but contrary to the Mosaical law and usage, which confined that privilege to her husband (Deut. xxiv. 1, 2, &c.; Mat. v. 31; xix. 7); and she then returned to her brother, before whom she cunningly ascribed her conduct to the fact that Costabarus, in conjunction with some chiefs of the Asamonean party, had entered into a conspiracy against him. In proof of this, she stated that he kept in concealment the sons of Babas, whom Herod had, at the taking of Jerusalem, intrusted to him to be destroyed. The sons of Babas were found in the retreat indicated by Salome, and put to death; and, taking all the rest for granted, the king ordered Costabarus and his alleged associates to be immediately executed.

The Asamonean family being now extirpated, root and branch, and no person being in existence whose claims to the throne could be considered superior to his own, Herod ventured to manifest a greater disregard for the law of Moses, and more attachment to heathenish customs than he had previously deemed safe. He began by abolishing some of the ceremonies which the former required, and by introducing not a few of the latter. He then proceeded to build a magnificent theatre in the city, and a spacious amphitheatre in the suburbs, where he instituted public games, which were celebrated every fifth year in honor of Augustus. In order to draw the larger concourse on these occasions, proclamation of the approaching games were made, not only in his own dominions, but in neighboring provinces and distant kingdoms. Gladiators, wrestlers, and musicians, were invited from all parts of the world, and prizes of great value were proposed to the victors. These games, and more especially the combats between men and wild beasts, were highly displeasing to the Jews; who also viewed with a jealous eye the trophies with which the places of public entertainment were adorned, regarding them as coming within the interdiction of idolatrous images by the Mosaical law. In vain did Herod endeavor to overcome their dislike. Connected with other causes of discontent, old and new, it increased daily, and at last grew to such a height that ten of the most zealous malecontents, including one blind man, formed a conspiracy, and assembled, with daggers concealed under their garments, for the purpose of assassinating Herod when he entered the theatre. They had brought their minds to a state of indifference to the result; for they were persuaded that if they failed, their death could not but render the tyrant more odious to the people, and thus equally work out the object they sought. Nor were they quite mistaken. Their design *was* discovered; and they were put to death with the most cruel tortures. But when the mob indicated their view of the matter—their hatred of himself, and sympathy with the intended assassins—by literally tearing the informer in pieces, and throwing his flesh to the dogs, Herod was exasperated to the uttermost. By torture, he compelled some women to name the principal persons who were concerned in this transaction, all of whom were hurried off to instant death *together with their innocent families.* This crowning act of savageness rendered the tyrant so perfectly detestable to his subjects, that he began very seriously to contemplate the possibility of a general revolt, and to take his measures accordingly. He built new fortresses and fortified towns throughout the land, and strengthened those that previously existed. In this he did more than the original inducement required;

for Herod was a man of taste, and had quite a passion for building and improvements, so that in the course of his long reign the country assumed a greatly improved appearance, through the number of fine towns and magnificent public works and buildings which he erected. In this respect there had been no king like him since Solomon; and if *he could* have reigned in peace, if domestic troubles, opposition from his subjects, and the connexion with the Romans, had not called into active operation all the darker features of his character, it is easy to conceive that his reign might have been very happy and glorious.

He rebuilt Samaria, or rather completed the rebuilding of it which Gabinius had begun. His attention seems to have been drawn to its excellent site, and strong military position; and, from the magnificent scale on which it was restored, we conceive that he contemplated the possibility of withdrawing his court to it, in the very likely contingency of being unable to maintain himself at Jerusalem. He gave the completed city the name of Sebaste—the name, in Greek, of his great patron Augustus. He also built Gaba in Galilee, and Heshbon in Perea; besides many others which he called by the names of the different members of his own family—as, Antipatris, from the name of his father Antipater; Cypron, near Jericho, after his mother Cypros (who was descended from an Arabian family, although born at Ascalon in Palestine); and Phasaelis, in the plains of Jericho, after his brother Phasael. In most of these cities he planted colonies of his foreign soldiers, to hold the country in subjection.

To extend his fame, Herod even built numerous splendid edifices, and made large improvements in cities beyond the limits of his own dominion—such as gymnasiums at Ptolemais, Tripolis, and Damascus; the city walls at Bibulus; porticoes, or covered walls, at Tyre, Beyrutus, and Antioch; bazars and theatres at Zidon and Damascus; an aqueduct at Laodicea on the sea; and baths, reservoirs, and porticoes, at Ascalon. He also made groves in several cities; to others he made rich presents, or furnished endowments for the support of their games; and by such means his fame was widely spread in the Roman empire.

At Jerusalem Herod built himself a splendid palace, on Mount Zion, the site of the original fortress of Jebus, and of the citadel which had so much annoyed the Jews during the Maccabean wars. It was in the Grecian style of architecture, and two large and sumptuous apartments in it Herod named Cæsareum, in honor of the emperor, and Agrippeum, after his favorite Agrippa.

We receive a better idea of the largeness of Herod's views, however, by his building the town and forming the harbor at what he named Cæsarea. The site had formerly been marked by a castle called Strato's tower, on the coast between Dora and Joppa. Here he made the most convenient and safest port to be found on all the coast of Phœnicia and Palestine, by running out a vast semi-circular mole or breakwater, of great depth and extent, into the sea, so as to form a spacious and secure harbor against the stormy winds from the south and west, leaving only an entrance into it from the north. This soon became a noted point of departure from, and entrance into, Palestine; and, as such, is often mentioned in the Acts of the Apostles. It also acquired a new importance as the seat of government after Judea became an imperial province; Cæsarea being then the usual residence of the procurator.

In the year B. C. 22, the want of the usual rains in Syria and Palestine produced a severe famine, which was followed by a pestilence that carried off great multitudes of the people. Herod behaved nobly on this occasion. He exhausted his treasury and even the silver plate of his table in purchasing provisions from Egypt, and in buying wool for clothing, as most of the sheep of the country had been slaughtered in the dearth. This bounty was not confined to his own dominions, but extended to the neighboring Syrians. By this conduct so much of gratitude and kind feeling toward him was produced, as only the continued and growing tyranny of his subsequent reign could obliterate.

The next year Herod contracted a marriage with another Mariamne, the daughter of the priest Simon. To pave the way for this alliance, the king removed the existing high-priest, Jesus the son of Phabet, and invested the father of Mariamne with that once high office. Herod next began to build a castle, which he called Herodium, on a small round hill, near the place where he repulsed the Parthians, under the cupbearer Pacorus, when they pursued him on his flight from Jerusalem. The situation and the protection which the castle offered were so inviting, that numbers of

Oriental Builders.

opulent people began to build themselves houses around, so that in a short time the spot was occupied by a fair city.

About this time Herod might be deemed to have attained the summit of all his wishes. Strong in the favor of the emperor, he was feared, if not loved, by the people under his rule, and respected by the Roman governors and by the neighboring princes and kings. Of the favor and confidence of Augustus he received proofs which were of high value to him. As a reward for his services in clearing the country of robbers, the valuable districts of Trachonitis, Auranitis, and Batanea, beyond Jordan, were added to his dominion; and, what was perhaps more for his personal influence and honor, he was soon after named the emperor's procurator in Syria, and orders were given to the governor of that great province to undertake nothing of importance without his knowledge and advice. Herod also procured from the emperor the dignity of a tetrarch for his only surviving brother, Pheroras; for Herod himself had given him a territory in Perea beyond Jordan, with a revenue of one hundred talents, in order that he might live in a style suitable to his birth, without being dependant on the king's successor. As some acknowledgment for all these favors, Herod built a temple of white marble at Paneas (Banias, the sources of the Jordan), and dedicated it to Augustus. But this act, and others of a similar character, were so highly offensive to the Jews, that, to pacify them, Herod was obliged to remit a portion of their tribute.

It seems likely that the reflections made upon his conduct in building heathen temples first drew his attention to the condition of JEHOVAH's temple at Jerusalem, which in the lapse of time had gone much out of repair, and had sustained great damage during the civil wars. He was then led to form the bold design of pulling it down and rebuilding it entirely on a more magnificent scale. To this he was induced not only from the magnificence of his ideas, his love of building, and the desire of fame, but also to conciliate the good opinion of his discontented subjects, and create a new interest in the continuance of his life and welfare.

Herod made his proposal in a general assembly of the people at Jerusalem, probably at the passover, in the year B. C. 19, the eighteenth of his reign. The people were much startled by the offer. They recognised the grandeur of the undertaking, and the need and benefit of it; but they were fearful that, after he had taken down the old building, he might be unable or unwilling to build the new. To meet this objection, Herod undertook not to demolish the old temple until *all* the materials required for the new one were collected on the spot; and on these terms his offer was accepted with as much satisfaction as the Jews were capable of deriving from any of *his* acts. Herod kept his word. A thousand carts were speedily at work in drawing stones and materials; ten thousand of the most skilful workmen were brought together; and a thousand priests were so far instructed in masonry and carpentry as might enable them to expedite and superintend the work. After two years had been spent in these preparations, the old temple was pulled down, and the new one commenced in the year B. C. 17. And with such vigor was the work carried on, that the sanctuary, or, in effect, the proper temple, was finished in a year and a half, and the rest of the temple, containing the outer buildings, colonnades, and porticoes, in eight years more, so as to be then fit for divine service, according to the king's intention, B. C. 7. But the expense of finishing and adorning the whole continued to be long after carried on from the sacred treasury, until the fatal government of Gessius Florus, in the year A. D. 62. . Hence, during the ministry of Christ (A. D. 28), the Jews said to him, "Forty and six years hath this temple been in building, and wilt thou erect it in three days?" (John ii. 20.)

By the first Mariamne, Herod had two sons, Alexander and Aristobulus, whom he sent to be educated at Rome, where they remained three years, under the immediate inspection of Augustus, who had kindly lodged them in his own palace. Two years after the foundation of the temple, Herod went to Rome himself, to pay his respects to the emperor, and take back to Judea his sons, whose education was now complete. He was received with unusual friendliness by Augustus, and was entertained with much distinction during his stay. Soon after his return he married the elder of the brothers to Glaphyra, the daughter of Archelaus, king of Cappadocia, and the younger to Berenice, the daughter of his own notorious sister Salome. Now it happened that both the young men inherited a full share of the pride and hauteur of their mother Mariamne, and were disposed to look down upon all the connexions of their father.

That they ever entertained any designs against him is not probable, but it is very probable, from their conduct, that apart from their respect for him, they deemed their right to the crown irrefragable, derived from their mother rather than from him, and, in point of fact, much greater than his own. By corrupting her own daughter, who was married to one of the brothers, Salome made herself acquainted with their more private sentiments, and learned that their sympathies leaned all to the side of their murdered mother, and that in their own domestic circles they spoke with strong abhorrence of the authors of her undeserved and untimely death, and lamented the various acts of cruelty of which their father had been guilty. This was enough to determine Salome to accomplish their ruin, as she saw clearly that if ever they possessed power, she was likely to suffer for the part she had taken in compassing the death of Mariamne. She was also envious of their popularity; for the very same feeling which inclined them to rest upon their connexion with the Asamonean dynasty, inclined the Jews to regard them with peculiar interest and favor as the last relics of that illustrious house. Salome therefore took every occasion of prejudicing Herod against his sons, and of turning his paternal love and pride into jealousy and dislike. To this end indeed, little more was needed than to make known to him, with some exaggeration, the true state of their feelings.

The first measure which Herod took to check the pride of the two brothers was, three years after his return (B. C. 13), to bring to court his eldest son Antipater, whom he had by his first wife Doris, while he was in a private station, and whom he had divorced on his marriage with Mariamne. But this measure, intended to teach them wholesome caution, only operated in provoking Alexander and Aristobulus to greater discontent and more intemperate language than before. In fact, they had almost insensibly become the heads of the Asamonean party, still very powerful in the country, and were urged on by the necessities of that position, and by the conviction that the popular feeling was entirely on their side. As to Antipater, he had all the ambition of his father with all the artfulness of his aunt. Openly, he seemed to advocate the cause of the brothers, and to extenuate their indiscretions, while he took care to surround the king with persons who reported to him all their sayings with the most invidious aggravations. By this means the affection with which Herod had regarded the brothers, not only for their own noble qualities, but for their mother's sake, was alienated from them, and fixed upon Antipater. Him, the father at length recommended to Augustus as his successor, and obtained from him authority to leave the crown to him in the first instance, and afterward to the sons of Mariamne, B. C. 11.

The curious reader will find in Josephus a full account of all the various plots which were laid by Antipater, assisted by his aunt Salome and his uncle Pheroras, to bring about the destruction of the young princes. This they at last effected by a false charge that they designed to poison their father. On this, he brought them to trial before a council held at Beyrutus, at which the Roman governors Saturnius and Volumnius presided, and where Herod pleaded in person against his sons with such vehemence that he, with some difficulty, procured their condemnation, although nothing could be clearly proved against them but an intention to withdraw to some foreign country, where they might live in peace. The time and the mode of putting the sentence into execution were left to the king's own discretion. This was not until he came to Sebaste, where, in a fit of rage, produced in the same manner, and through the same agencies as his previous treatment of these unfortunate young men, he ordered them to be strangled, B. C. 6. In these two unfortunate brothers the noble family of the Asamoneans may be said to have become utterly extinct.

It was somewhat before this time that Herod, being greatly in want of money, bethought himself of opening the tomb of David, having probably heard the story of the treasure which the first Hyrcanus was reported to have found there. As might be expected, he discovered nothing but the royal ornaments with which the king had been buried.

In the spring of the year B. C. 5 the birth of the great harbinger, John the Baptist, announced the approach of One greater than he, whose sandal-thong he, thereafter, declared himself unworthy to loose.

At and for some time before the date to which we are now arrived, the relations of Herod with Rome had become more unpleasant than at any former period. Not long before he put Alexander and Aristobulus to death, Herod had a quarrel with Obadas king of Arabia, which led him to march some troops into that country, and to the defeat of the banded robbers, against whom chiefly he acted, and of a party of Arabs who came to their relief. This affair was reported to Augustus in such a manner as raised his wrath against Herod; and attending only to the fact that Herod *had* march-ed a military force into Arabia, which Herod's friends could not deny, he, without inquiring into the provocation and circumstances, wrote to Herod a very severe letter, the substance of which was, that he had hitherto treated him as a friend, but should henceforth treat him as a subject. Herod sent an embassy to clear himself; but Augustus repeatedly refused to listen to them; and so the king was obliged for a time to submit to all the injurious treatment which the emperor thought proper to inflict. The chief of these was the degrading his kingdom to a Roman province. For soon after, Josephus incidentally mentions, that "the whole nation took an oath of fidelity to Cæsar and to the king jointly, except six thousand of the Pharisees, who, through their hostility to the regal government, refused to take it, and were fined for their refusal by the king; but the wife of his brother Pheroras paid the fine for them." As this was shortly before the death of Pheroras himself, it coincides with the time of this decree for the enrolment of which St. Luke (ii. 1) makes mention; and we may therefore certainly infer that the oath was administered at the same time, ac-cording to the usage of the Roman census, in which a return of persons' ages and properties was required to be made upon oath, under penalty of the confiscation of the goods of the delinquents. And the reason for registering ages was, that among the Syrians, males from fourteen years of age and females from twelve, until their sixty-fifth year, were subject to a capitation or poll-tax, by the Roman law. This tax was two *drachmæ* a head, or half a *stater*, equal to thirty cents of our money.[*]

Cyrenius, a Roman senator and procurator, or collector of the emperor's revenue, was employed to make the enrolment. This person, whom Tacitus calls Quirinus, and describes as " an active soldier and rigid commissioner,"[†] was well qualified for an employment so odious to Herod and to his subjects, and probably came to execute the decree with an armed force. By the wary policy of the Romans, to prevent in-surrection as well as to expedite business, all were required to repair to their own cities. Even in Italy the consular edict commanded the Latin citizens not to be enrolled at Rome, but all in their own cities. And this precaution was of course more necessary in such turbulent provinces as Judea and Galilee.[‡]

The decree was peremptory, and admitted of no delay: therefore, in the autumn of the year 5 of the popular era Before Christ,[§] a carpenter of Nazareth in Gali-lee, by name Joseph, journeyed with his wife Mary, although she was then large with child, to Bethlehem in Judea, that being their paternal city, as they were both "of the race and lineage of David." They were not among the first comers, and the place was so thronged that they could not find room even in the lodging-rooms of the caravanserai of Bethlehem, but were obliged to seek shelter in the stables of the same. Here the woman was taken in labor, and gave birth to a male child. That child, thus humbly born, was the long-promised "Desire of Nations," the "Saviour of the World"—JESUS CHRIST. Nor did he come sooner than he was expected. The Jews expected anxiously, and from day to day, the Great Deliverer of whom their prophets had spoken; and the precise fore-calculations of the prophet Daniel had given them to know that the time of his coming was near. This indeed partly ex-

---

[*] See the case of Christ, and Peter afterward, where "*a stater*," the amount for *both*, was procured by miracle. Matt. xvii. 24–27.

[†] *Impiger militiæ et scribus ministeriis.*

[‡] For this clear view of the somewhat perplexed subject of the *Census* alluded to by St. Luke, we are in-debted to Dr. Hales, from whose excellent "Analysis of Chronology" we have, indeed, obtained much and various aid in the present history.

[§] That the birth of Christ is thus given to the autumn of the year five *before* Christ, is an apparent anom-aly, which may require a few words of explanation. The Era of the Birth of Christ was not in use until A. D. 532 in the time of Justinian, when it was introduced by Dionysius Exiguus, a Scythian by birth, and a Roman abbot; and which only began to prevail in the West about the time of Charles Martel and Pope Gregory II., A. D. 730. It has long been agreed by *all* chronologers that Dionysius made a mistake in pla-cing the birth of Christ some years too late; but the amount of the difference has been variously estimated, at two, three, four, five, or even eight years. The most general conclusion is that which is adopted in our Bibles, and which places the birth of Christ four years before the common era, or more probably a few months more, according to the conclusion of Hales, which we have deemed it proper to adopt. The grounds of this conclusion are largely and ably stated in the "Analysis," vol. i., p. 83–93. As to the day—it appears that the 25th of December was not fixed upon till the time of Constantine, in the fourth century, although there was an early tradition in its favor. It is probable that it really took place about or at the Feast of Tabernacles (say the autumnal equinox) of B. C. 5, or at the Passover (say the vernal equinox) of B. C. 4. The former is the opinion of Hales and others, and the latter of Archbishop Usher and our Bibles.

plains the uneasy relations between Herod and his subjects; and the distaste of the latter to the kingship which he had taken. For they wanted no king, until their king Messiah should come to take the throne of his father David, and lead them forth, conquering and to conquer, breaking the nations in pieces as an iron rod breaks the vessels of the potter, and bringing all the Gentiles to their feet. Full of these magnificent ideas of their king Messiah, they failed to recognise the promised Deliverer, in One who came to deliver them, not from the Romans—but from their sins; whose kingdom was not to be of this world—and whose reign, not over lands and territories, but in the hearts of men.

Nor was he expected only by the Jews. He was the "Desire of *Nations*." There were strong pulsations of the universal heart, in expectation of some great change, of the advent of some distinguished personage who should bring in a new order of things, of some kind or other, and who should work such deeds and establish such dominion as never before existed. It was even expected that this great personage should issue from Judea; an expectation which was probably derived from the more distinct anticipations of the Jews, if not partly from a remote glimpse at the meaning of those prophecies which referred to Messiah, and which many educated persons must have read in the Greek translation of the Hebrew Scriptures. But the expectations which the nations entertained were, like those of the Jews, connected with dreams of a universal temporal empire, which the expected Messiah was to establish. As, however, they had not the strong national interest in the expectation of a conquering king, they clung with less tenacity than the Jews to this notion of his functions, although, blinded by it, they were for a while as unable as the Hebrews to recognise the ANOINTED OF GOD in the infant of Bethlehem.

The prevalence and character of this expectation account for the watchfulness of Herod, and for the horrible promptitude with which he ordered the massacre of *all* the infants of Bethlehem as soon as the inquiries of the Parthian magi gave him cause to suspect that THE KING OF THE JEWS had been born there.

The census, which was begun by Cyrenius, was not completed to the extent originally contemplated, for Herod found means to disabuse Augustus of the impression under which he had acted, and was restored to the imperial favor and confidence. To make him some amends the emperor was disposed to have consigned to him the forfeited kingdom of the Nabathæans; but the painful disagreements and atrocities in the family of Herod were about the same time brought so conspicuously under his notice, that, with his usual sagacity, he doubted the wisdom of committing the conquest and government of a new kingdom to an old man who had proved himself incapable of ruling his own house.

We have before incidentally mentioned the part which was taken by the wife of Pheroras, in paying the fines of the Pharisees, who refused to take the oath required of all the people. In consequence of this, many of that powerful body began to whisper that God would give the kingdom to Pheroras; on which account Herod caused several Pharisees and some members of his own family to be executed. Further, regarding the wife of Pheroras as the cause of all this trouble, he very peremptorily required him to divorce her. His brother replied that nothing but death should separate him from his wife, and retired in disgust to Perea, in his own territory beyond Jordan. Thus was quite destroyed the good understanding which had for so many years subsisted between the two brothers. Blinded by resentment, Pheroras readily came into the plans of Antipater: and between them it was settled that Herod should be taken off by poison; that Antipater should sit on his throne; and that meanwhile he should contrive to be sent to Rome, to preclude any suspicion of his part in the transaction. This plot would probably have succeeded but for the death of Pheroras himself, which led to the discovery of the whole, and even made known to Herod the part which Antipater had taken in compassing the death of the two sons of the first Mariamne. It appeared also that the second Mariamne was a party in this conspiracy, in consequence of which she was divorced, the name of her son was struck out of the king's will, and her father, the high-priest Simon, was deposed from his office, which was given to Matthias the son of Theophilus. On these disclosures, Herod managed to get Antipater back from Rome, without allowing him to become acquainted with what had transpired. On his arrival he was formally accused before Quintilius Varus, the prefect of Syria, who was then at Jerusalem, and was imprisoned until the affair should have been submitted to the judgment of Augustus.

Meanwhile Herod, then in the sixty-ninth year of his age, fell ill of that grievous disease of which he died, and which, by some singular dispensation of Providence, appears to have been the peculiar lot of tyrannous and proud sovereigns, and which rendered him wretched in himself and a terror to all around him. A report got into circulation that his disease afforded no chance of his recovery, in consequence of which a dangerous tumult was excited by two celebrated doctors, named Judas and Matthias, who instigated their disciples to pull down and destroy a golden eagle of large size and exquisite workmanship, which had been placed over one of the gates of the temple. Scarcely had this rash act been completed, when the royal guards appeared and seized the two leaders and forty of their most zealous disciples. Some of them were burnt, and others executed in various ways by Herod's order. Being suspected of having privately encouraged the tumult, Matthias was deprived of his high-priesthood, and the office given to Joazar, the brother of his wife.

In the meantime the disease of Herod became more loathsome and intolerable. It appears to have been an erosion of the bowels and other viscera by worms, which occasioned violent spasms and the most exquisite tortures, until he at length became a mass of putrefaction. Experiencing no benefit from the warm baths of Calirrhoe beyond Jordan, he gave up all hopes of recovery, and after having distributed presents among his attendants and soldiers, he returned to Jericho. His sufferings were not likely to humanize his naturally savage disposition. He was convinced, by the recent outbreak, that his death would occasion no sorrow in Israel, and therefore, to oblige the nation to mourn at his death, he sent for the heads of the most eminent families in Judea, and confined them in prison, leaving orders with his sister Salome and her husband Alexas to put them all to death as soon as he should have breathed his last. This sanguinary design was, however, not executed by them.

At length Herod received full powers from Rome to proceed against his son Antipater. At this intelligence, the dying tyrant appeared to revive; but he soon after attempted suicide, and although prevented, the wailing cries, usual in such cases, were raised throughout the palace for him, as if he were actually dead. When Antipater, in his confinement heard these well-known lamentations, he attempted by large bribes to induce his guard to permit his escape; but he was so universally hated for procuring the death of the sons of Mariamne, that the guard made his offers known, and Herod ordered his immediate execution. On the fifth day after, Herod himself died, shortly before the Passover, in the seventieth year of his age, and the thirty-seventh from his appointment to the throne. Before his death was announced, Salome, as if by his order, liberated the nobles confined in the hippodrome, whose death she had been charged to execute, but dared not, had she been so inclined. His corpse, under the escort of his life-guard, composed of Thracians, Germans, and Gauls, was carried with great pomp to Herodium, and there buried.

Herod had ten wives, two of whom bore him no children, and whose names history has not preserved. As it is of some importance to understand clearly the combinations of relationship among his descendants by these different wives, the details in the note below will not be unacceptable to the reader.*

---

* The wives of Herod "the Great" were:—
I. Doris, the mother of Antipater.
II. Mariamne, the daughter of Alexandra. She had—
1. Alexander, who married Glaphyra, the daughter of the king of Cappadocia, by whom he had—Tigranes, king of Armenia, and Alexander, who married a daughter of Antiochus king of Comagene.
2. Aristobulus, who married Berenice the daughter of Salome, the sister of Herod, by whom he had—Herod, king of Chalcis, who married, first, Mariamne, the daughter of Olympias (sister of Archelaus the ethnarch); and afterward his niece Berenice, by whom he had Aristobulus, Berenicicus, and Hyrcanus. The eldest of these, Aristobulus, married Salome (she whose dancing cost John the Baptist his head), then the widow of the tetrarch Philip, by whom he had Agrippa, Herod, and Aristobulus. *Agrippa* I., king of the Jews, who married Cypros the daughter of (Mariamne's daughter) Salampso, by whom he had Drusius; Agrippa II., who was at first king of Chalcis, and afterward tetrarch of Trachonitis; Berenice, whose second husband was her uncle Herod, king of Chalcis; Mariamne, married first to Archelaus son of Chelcias, and afterward to Demetrius, alabarch of the Jews at Alexandria, by whom she had Berenice and Agrippa; Drusilla, who was first married to Aziz, king of Emesa, and afterward to Felix the Roman procurator of Judea, by whom she had a son named Agrippa, who, with his wife, perished in the flames of Vesuvius. The third son of Aristobulus the son of Mariamne, was *Aristobulus*, who married Jotape, daughter to the king of Emesa: and there were two daughters. *Herodias*, who married, first, Herod (called Philip in the Gospels), son of Herod the Great by the second Mariamne, by whom she had Salome (the dancer), and afterward to his half-brother Herod Antipas, the tetrarch of Galilee,—both her uncles. *Mariamne*, who married her uncle Antipater.
3. The third son of Mariamne was Herod, who died young while at his studies in Rome.
Mariamne had also two daughters:—
4. Salampso, who married her cousin Phasael, after having been promised to Pheroras.

Herod was succeeded in the kingdom of Judea by his son Archelaus, whose evil conduct so displeased the Romans, that they reduced Judea to the form of a Roman province, ruling it by procurators or governors, sent and recalled at their pleasure; the power of life and death was taken out of the hands of the Jews, and vested in Roman governor; and the taxes being gathered by the publicans, were paid more directly to the emperor.

As there are several Herods mentioned in the New Testament, it may not be amiss here to distinguish them, according to the best authority which can be obtained. 1. Herod the king of Judea (already noticed), who died while Christ was an infant. (See Matt. ii. 19.) 2. His son, Herod Antipas, the tetrarch* of Galilee, who took away his brother Philip's wife, and beheaded John the Baptist. (See Matt. xiv. 3-10.) 3. That Herod who put the Apostle James to death, and was afterward smitten by the angel of the Lord with a strange and sudden death. (See Acts xii. 2, and ver. 20-23.) Historians consider him the grandson of the first Herod, and the father of King Agrippa, before whom Paul made his defence. The almighty Disposer of all events, at whose nod empires rise and fall, and nations flourish or decay, marks with undeviating attention, and a retributive hand, not only the sins of a people, but the turpitude of those who profess to govern.

CHAPTER XXVII.

HAVING, in the preceding pages, given an accurate account of every material occurrence related in the sacred Scriptures, from the creation of the world to the death the prophet Nehemiah, and thence to the rebuilding of the temple of Jerusalem by Herod, we shall conclude the OLD TESTAMENT HISTORY by devoting a few pages here to the prophecies concerning CHRIST and the Christian Religion.

The coming of a Saviour, which was the hope of Israel and the expectation of the Jews in every age, is frequently foretold throughout the Old Testament scriptures. They represent it as announced by the voice of God to the first human pair, and as forming, from the first to the last, the theme of all the prophets. And, however imperfect a summary view of such numerous prophecies must necessarily be, a few remarks respecting them shall be prefixed to the more direct and immediate proofs of the inspiration of scripture, derived from existing facts, in order that the reader may be rather induced to search the scriptures to see how clearly they testify of Jesus, than contented to rest satisfied with the mere opening of the subject.

A few of the leading features of the prophecies concerning Christ, and their fulfilment, shall be traced as they mark the time of his appearance, the place of his birth, and the family out of which he was to arise, his life and character, his sufferings and his death, the nature of his doctrine, and the extent of his kingdom.

5. Cypros, who married Antipater, the son of Salome, sister of Herod the Great.
III. Herod's third wife was Pallas, by whom he had a son, Phasael.
IV. Phædra, who had a daughter called Roxana, married to a son of Pheroras.
V. Mariamne, daughter of the high-priest Simon. Herod had by her—Herod-Philip, the first husband of Herodias, by whom he had Salome (the dancing lady), whose first husband was Philip, and her second Aristobulus, the son of Herod king of Chalcis.
VI. Malthace, a Samaritan woman, who was mother to Archelaus the ethnarch of Judea, and Herod Antipas, the tetrarch of Galilee, who married first a daughter of the Arabian king Aretas, whom he put away, and took Herodias, the wife of his brother Herod-Philip, who was still living. Malthace had also a daughter, Olympias, who married Joseph, a nephew to Herod the Great.
VII. Cleopatra, who was the mother of Herod and Philip, tetrarch of Trachonitis, which last married the noted Salome, daughter of Herod-Philip and Herodias.
VIII. Elphis had a daughter called Salome, married to a son of Pheroras.
* The title and office of *tetrarch* had its origin from the Gauls, who having made an incursion into Asia Minor, succeeded in taking from the king of Bithynia that part of it which from them took the name of Galatia. The Gauls who made this invasion consisted of three tribes; and each tribe was divided into four parts, or tetrarchates, each of which obeyed its own tetrarch. The tetrarch was of course subordinate to the king. The appellation of tetrarch, which was thus originally applied to the chief magistrate of the fourth part of a tribe, subject to the authority of the king, was afterward extended in its application, and given to any governors, subject to some king or emperor, without regard to the proportion of the people or tribe which they governed. Thus Herod Antipas and Philip were denominated tetrarchs, although they did not rule as much as the fourth part of the whole territory. Although these rulers were dependant upon the Roman emperor, they nevertheless governed the people within their jurisdiction according to their own choice and authority. They were, however, inferior in point of rank to the ethnarchs, who, although they did not publicly assume the name of king, were addressed with that title by their subjects, as was the case, for instance, with respect to Archelaus. (Matt. ii. 22; Jos. Antiq. xvii. 11, 4.)

The time of the Messiah's appearance in the world, as predicted in the Old Testament, is defined by a number of concurring circumstances that fix it to the very date of the advent of Christ. The sceptre was not to depart from Judah, nor a lawgiver to cease from among his descendants, till Shiloh should come. (Gen. xlix. 10.) The desire of all nations, the messenger of the covenant, the Lord whom they sought, was to come to the second temple, and to impart to it, from his presence, a greater glory than that of the former. (Hag. ii. 7–9; Mal. iii. 1.) A messenger was to appear before him, the voice of one crying in the wilderness, to prepare his way. (Isa. xl. 3; Mal. iii. 1; iv. 5.) A specified period,—marked, according to similar computations in the Jewish scriptures, by weeks of years, each day for a year,—was set, from the going forth of the command to restore and to build Jerusalem, after the Babylonish captivity, unto Messiah the prince. (Dan. ix. 25.) A period somewhat longer was determined upon the people and upon the holy city. (Isa. ix. 24.) After the Messiah was to be cut off, the people of the prince that should come were to destroy the city and the sanctuary; desolations, even to the consummation, were determined, and the sacrifice and oblation were to cease. (Dan. ix. 26, 27.) A king did reign over the Jews in their own land, though the ten tribes had long ceased to be a kingdom; their national council, the members of which, as Jews, were lineally descended from Judah, exercised its authority and power—the temple was standing—the oblation and sacrifice, according to the law of Moses, were there duly and daily offered up—and the time prescribed for the coming of the Messiah had drawn to its close—at the commencement of the Christian era. Before the public ministry of Jesus, a messenger appeared to prepare his way; and Josephus, in the history of that time, speaks of the blameless life and cruel death of "John that was called the Baptist," and describes his preaching and baptism. (Josephus's Antiquities, b. 18, c. 5, sec. 2.) But every mark that denoted the fulness of the time, and of its signs, when the Messiah was to appear, was erased soon after the death of Christ, and being fixed to that single period, those marks could no more be restored again than time past could return. The time determined on the people and on the holy city, seventy weeks or four hundred and ninety years, passed away. The tribe of Judah were no longer united under a king. Banished from their own land, and subjected to every oppression, there was no more a lawgiver of the tribe of Judah, though Judah was he whom his brethren were to serve. Of the temple one stone was not left upon another. The sacrifice and oblation, which none but priests could offer, altogether ceased when the genealogies of the tribe of Levi were lost, and when the Jews had no temple, nor country, nor priest, nor altar. Ere Jerusalem was destroyed, or desolation had passed over the land of Judea, the expectation was universal among the Jews that their Messiah was then to appear; and heathen as well as Jewish historians testify of the belief then prevalent over the whole East that the ancient prophecies bore a direct and express reference to that period. And the question might now go to the heart of a Jew, however loth to abandon the long-cherished hope of his race, how can these prophecies be true, if the Messiah be not come? or where, from the first words of Moses to the last of Malachi, can there be found such marks of the time when Shiloh was to come, or Messiah the prince to be cut off, as pertained to the period when their forefathers crucified Jesus—a period which closed over the glory of Judah, and which, in the continued unbelief of the Jews, has not heretofore left, for nearly eighteen centuries, a bright page in their history beyond it?

Though the countrymen of Christ when he came would not receive him, yet it was of the Jews that Jesus was to come; and the human lineage of the Messiah is as clearly marked in the prophecies as the time of his appearance. The divinity of the person of the Messiah, and his taking upon himself the likeness of sinful flesh, is declared in the Old Testament as well as in the new. He whose name was to be called the wonderful, the counsellor, the mighty God, was to become a child that was to be born, a son that was to be given. (Isa. ix. 6.) It was the seed of the woman that was to bruise the serpent's head. (Gen. iii. 15.) The line of his descent, according to the flesh, and the place of his birth, were expressly foretold. It was in the seed of Abraham that all the nations of the earth were to be blessed. (Gen. xxii. 18.) It was from the midst of the Israelites, of their brethren, that a prophet like unto Moses was to arise. (Deut. xviii. 15.) And he was to be not only of the tribe of Judah, (Gen. xlix. 8, &c.), but also of the house or family of David. From the root of Jesse a branch was to grow up, on which the spirit of the Lord was to rest, and to which the Gentiles would seek. (Isa. xi. 1–10.) It was unto David that a righteous branch was to arise, a king, whose name was to be called *the Lord our righteousness.* (Jer. xxiii. 5, 6.) And it was in Bethlehem Ephratah, in the land of Judah, little as it was among the thousands of Israel, that he was to come, whose goings forth had been of old, from everlasting. (Micah, v. 2.) And Jesus is he alone of the seed of the woman, of the descendants. of Abraham, of the tribe of Judah, of the house of David, in whom all the families of the earth can be blessed; to whom the Gentiles seek, and who, ere the family genealogies of the Jews were lost, was shown by them to be born of the lineage of David, and in the town of Bethlehem.

The history of the life of Christ by the four evangelists is simply a record of what he said and did, and his character is illustrated by his words and actions alone. Christians have often tried to delineate it; and if in the attempt their thoughts have harmonized with the divine records, their hearts may well have then felt as it were the impression of that divine image after which man was at first created. Even some who never sought to be the champions of the Christian faith, have been struck with irresistible admiration of the life of its author. Rousseau acknowledges that it would have been nothing less than a miracle that such a character, if not real, could ever have been thought of by fishermen of Galilee. And Lord Byron not only called Christ diviner than Socrates, but he he has no less truly than nobly said, that "if ever God was man, or man God, he was both." But the divine character is such that none but a divine hand could draw; and seeking in the prophecies what the Messiah was to be, we read what Jesus was while he dwelt among men.

"Thou art fairer than the children of men; grace is poured into thy lips, therefore God hath blessed thee for ever. The sceptre of thy kingdom is a right sceptre—thou lovest righteousness and hatest iniquity. (Psalm xlv. 2, 6, 7.) The spirit of the Lord shall rest upon him, the spirit of knowledge and of the fear of the Lord. He shall not judge after the sight of his eyes, neither reprove after the hearing of his ears. But with righteousness shall he judge the poor, and reprove with equity for the meek of the earth. And righteousness shall be the girdle of his loins, and faithfulness the girdle of his reins. (Isa. xi. 2–5.) He shall feed his flock like a shepherd, he shall gather the lambs with his arm, and carry them in his bosom. (Isa. xl. 11.) He shall not cry, nor lift up, nor cause his voice to be heard in the streets. A bruised reed shall he not break, and the smoking flax shall he not quench. (Isa. xlii. 2, 3.) Thy king cometh unto thee: he is just, and having salvation, lowly, and riding upon an ass. (Zech. ix. 9.) He hath done no violence, neither was there any deceit in his lips. (Isa. liii. 9.) He was oppressed and afflicted, yet he opened not his mouth; he was brought as a lamb to the slaughter, and as a sheep before her shearers is dumb, so he opened not his mouth. (Isa. liii. 7.) I gave my back to the smiters, and my cheek to them that plucked off the hair; I hid not my face from shame and spitting. (Isa. l. 6.) He shall not fail nor be discouraged, till he have set judgment in the earth. (Isa. xlii. 4.) I have set my face as a flint, and I know that I shall not be ashamed. (Isa. l. 7.) He shall deliver the needy when he crieth, the poor also, and him that hath no helper. He shall redeem their soul from deceit and violence, and precious shall their blood be in his sight. Men shall be blessed in him—all nations shall call him blessed." Psalm lxxii. 12, 14, 17.

The death of Christ was as unparalleled as his life, and the prophecies are as minutely descriptive of his sufferings as of his virtues. His growing up as a tender plant (Isa. liii. 2); his riding in humble triumph into Jerusalem; his being betrayed for thirty pieces of silver (Zech. xi. 12), and scourged, and buffeted, and spit upon; the piercing of his hands and of his feet, and yet every bone of him remaining unbroken; the last offered draught of vinegar and gall; the parting of his raiment, and casting lots upon his vesture (Psalm xxii. 69); the manner of his death and of his burial (Isa. liii. 9), and his rising again without seeing corruption (Psalm xvi. 10), were all as minutely predicted as literally fulfilled. The last three verses of the fifty-second and the whole of the fifty-third chapter of Isaiah,—written above seven hundred years before the Christian era, and forming, word for word, a part of the Jewish as well as of the Christian scriptures,—prophetically describe, like a very history of the facts, the sufferings and the death of Christ; his rejection by the Jews; his humility, his meekness, his affliction, and his agony; how his words were disbelieved; how his state was lowly; how his sorrow was severe; how his visage and his form were marred more than the sons of men; and how he opened not his mouth but to make

intercession for the transgressors. In direct opposition to every dispensation of Providence which is registered in the records of the Jews, this prophecy represents spotless innocence suffering by the appointment of Heaven—death as the issue of perfect obedience—God's righteous servant as forsaken by him—and one who was perfectly immaculate bearing the chastisement of many guilty, sprinkling many nations from their iniquity by virtue of his sacrifice, justifying many by his knowledge, and dividing a portion with the great, and the spoil with the strong, because he had poured out his soul unto death.

The prophecies concerning the humiliation, the sufferings, and the cutting off of the Messiah, need only to be read from the Jewish scriptures, to show that the very unbelief of the Jews is an evidence against them, and the very scandal of the cross a strong testimony to Jesus. For thus it is written, and thus it behooved Christ to suffer, according to the scriptures. And those things which God before had showed by the mouth of all his prophets that Christ should suffer, he hath so fulfilled.

That the Jews still retain these prophecies, and are the means of preserving them and communicating them throughout the world, while they bear so strongly against themselves, and testify so clearly of a Saviour that was first to suffer and then to be exalted, are facts which give a confirmation to the truth of Christianity, than which it is difficult to conceive any stronger. The prophecies that testify of the sufferings of the Messiah need no forced interpretation, but apply, in a plain and literal manner, to the history of the sufferings and of the death of Christ. In the testimony of the Jews to the existence of these prophecies, long prior to the Christian era; in their remaining unaltered to this hour; in the accounts given by the evangelists of the life and death of Christ; in the testimony of heathen authors, and in the arguments of the first opposers of Christianity, from the mean condition of its author and the manner of his death,—we have now more ample evidence of the fulfilment of all these prophecies than could have been conceived possible at so great a distance of time.

But if there be any truth, the perception and acknowledgment of which should lead to a sense of its importance, or a feeling of its power, it is surely that of the cutting off of the Messiah, as making reconciliation for iniquity, or the death of Christ as a sacrifice for the sins of men. It is not merely the knowledge of his righteous life, and of his ignominious death, in confirmation of the word of prophecy, but an interest also in them that every sinner needs. There exists not the man, except he be alike ignorant of the spirit within him and of the father of spirits, who could think of standing for himself, to answer for his sins, in the immediate presence of an all-holy God, and to abide the scrutiny of omniscience, and the awards of strict unmitigated justice enforced by almighty power. Nor could man of himself, in whom sin has once dwelt, be ever meet, whatever his thoughts of immortality might be, for participating in the holiness or partaking of the happiness of Heaven. And who is there that, even in the search after divine truth, can pass by Calvary, or cast but a glance toward it, and there behold in the sufferings of Christ a clear prophetic mark of his messiahship, without pondering deeply on the guiltiness of sin, which nothing less than the voluntary death of the Son of God could expiate, and on that infinite goodness and love which found and gave the ransom, whereby, though guilt could not be unpunished, the guilty might be saved. And if he reflect upon the manner in which this vision and prophecy were sealed up, who that has a heart within him, or that can be drawn with those cords of love which are the bands of a man, can refrain from feeling the personal application to himself of the words of Jesus—"I, if I be lifted up from the earth, will draw all men unto me?"

But the prophecies further present us with the character of the Gospel as well as of its author, and with a description of the extent of his kingdom as well as of his sufferings. That he was to make a full and clear revelation of the will of God, and establish a new and perfect religion, was frequently and explicitly foretold. (Deut. xviii. 18, 19. Isa. ix. 6, 7; xlii. 6; xi. 1–5; lv. 3, 4. Jer. xxxi. 31–34. Ezek. xxxiv. 23, 24.) The words of God were to be put into his mouth, and whoever would not hearken unto him, God would require it of them. He was to be given for a covenant of the people, for a light of the Gentiles, to open the blind eyes. His law was to be put in the inward parts, or to be written not in tables of stone, but in the heart. And the religion of Jesus is pure, spiritual, perfect, and adapted alike to all. It is a revelation of the whole counsel of God; it is a law which has to be written on the heart; a kingdom which is established within. The doctrine of the gospel is altogether a doctrine according to godliness. This its enemies will not deny, for it is the cause why they hate it. Its very excellence and perfection is a stumbling-block to them. There is not a sin which it does not reprobate, nor a virtue which it does not inculcate. And too pure and perfect it would indeed be for man, were not reconciliation made for iniquity, and redemption to be found from its bondage.

But the complete revelation of the will of God, which of itself would have pointed out a highway of holiness that men could never have reached, was to be accompanied with a revelation also of the grace and mercy of God, which might well suffice to show that the light was indeed light from Heaven. And while Jesus gave new commandments unto men, he announced tidings of great joy, which it never entered into the heart of man to conceive. In fulfilment of the prophetic character and office of the Messiah, he published salvation. Never was any anointed like Christ to preach good tidings to the meek; to bind up the broken-hearted; to proclaim liberty to the captive, the opening of the prison to them that are bound; to comfort them that mourn in Zion; to give to those who mourn for sin, or who seek for true consolation amid the bereavements or any of the evils of life, beauty for ashes, the oil of joy for mourning, and the garment of praise for the spirit of heaviness. And none like him ever proclaimed either the acceptable year of the Lord, or the day of judgment of our God. (Isa. lxi. 1–3.) What many wise men of old sought to know, Jesus taught. What they desired to see, he hath revealed. All that he taught, as well as all that he did and suffered, bore witness of him as the promised Messiah; and that kingdom has now come nigh which the prophets saw afar off.

That the gospel emanated from Judea—that it was rejected by a great proportion of the Jews—that it was opposed at first by human power—that kings have acknowledged and supported it—that it has already continued for many ages—and that it has been propagated throughout many countries—are facts that were clearly foretold, and have been literally fulfilled. " Out of Zion shall go forth the law; and the word of the Lord from Jerusalem. (Isa. ii. 3, 4. Micah, iv. 2.) He shall be for a sanctuary, but for a stone of stumbling and for a rock of offence to both the houses of Israel; for a gin and for a snare to the inhabitants of Jerusalem. Who hath believed our report, and to whom is the arm of the Lord revealed? (Isa. viii. 14; liii. 1.) The kings of the earth set themselves, and the rulers take counsel together against the Lord and against his anointed. (Psalm ii. 2. Matt. x. 17; xvi. 18; xxiv. 9–14.) To a servant of rulers, kings shall see and arise, princes also shall worship. The Gentiles shall come to thy light, and kings to the brightness of thy rising. (Isa. xlix. 7–23.) The Gentiles shall see thy righteousness; a people that know me not shall be called after my name. Behold thou shalt call a nation that thou knowest not, and nations that know not thee shall run unto thee." (Isa. xi. 10; lv. 5.) No one is now ignorant of the facts, that a system of religion which inculcates piety, and purity, and love,— which releases man from every burdensome rite and from every barbarous institution, and proffers the greatest of blessings,—arose from the land of Judea, was rejected by the Jews, persecuted by Jews and Gentiles, and yet has subsisted for many ages, and has been spread into many countries, and is outwardly owned by kings and by people as the faith of the civilized world.

The final extension of the gospel over all the earth is the theme of many prophecies (Isa. xxv. 7; ii. 2; xxxv. 1; xl. 5; xlii. 4; lii. 10; liv. 1–5; lx. 5; lxv. 1. Psalm lxxii. 8–17; ii. 8; xxii. 27, 28. Hosea, l. 10. Micah, iv. 1), while it is also clearly implied in others, that a long period was to elapse before the reign of darkness was to cease, or the veil to be taken off all nations. After the Messiah was to be cut off, and the city of Jerusalem and the sanctuary to be destroyed, desolations, even to the consummation, and until judgment should come upon the desolator, were determined; the children of Israel were to abide many days without a king, or ephod, or sacrifice; desolations of many generations were to pass over the land of Judea; Jerusalem was to be trodden down of the Gentiles, and blindness in part was to happen to Israel, till the times of the Gentiles should be fulfilled; and a great apostacy was to arise, and to prevail for a long, but limited period, before the stone that was to be cut out without hands was to become a great kingdom and fill the whole earth, or the last days should arrive, wherein the mountain of the Lord's house would be finally established and exalted above all, and all nations flow into it. (Dan. ix. 27. Hosea, iii. 4. Isa. lxi. 4. Luke, xxi. 24. Rom. xi. 25. 2 Thess. ii. 1–12. Dan. ii. 45. Isa. ii. 2. Micah, iv. 1.) But already, far beyond the conception of man to have harbored the thought, hath the light which has come out of Judea enlightened the nations; already have the scriptures been made known in a tenfold degree more than any other book; long has he been a light to the Gentiles, and long have kings seen and arisen, and princes rendered worship to him whom man despised, and whom the Jewish nation abhorred. The Christian faith made at first its bloodless way throughout the world. And though many a conspiracy has been formed, and many a bloody warfare waged against it, it not only stands unsubdued and unshaken after every assault, but the vain rage of its adversaries has been subservient to its extension and its triumphs. As a matter of history, the progress of Christianity is at least astonishing; as the fulfilment of many prophecies, it is evidently miraculous.

In closing even this brief and very imperfect summary of the prophecies relative to the Christian faith and to its author, are we not authorized to consider ancient prophecy, as bearing testimony to Jesus as the Saviour; the time and the place of the birth of Christ; the tribe and family from which he was descended; his life, his character, his sufferings, and his death; the nature of his doctrine, and the fate of his religion;— that it was to proceed from Jerusalem; that the Jews would reject it; that it would be opposed and persecuted at first; that kings would nevertheless acknowledge its divine authority; and that it would spread throughout many a nation, even to the uttermost parts of the earth.

Why, then, were so many prophecies delivered? Why, from the calling of Abraham to the present time, have the Jews been separated, as a peculiar people, from all the nations of the earth? Why, from the age of Moses to that of Malachi, during the space of a thousand years, did a succession of prophets arise, all testifying of a Saviour that was to come? Why was the book of prophecy sealed for nearly four hundred years before the coming of Christ? Why is there still, to this day, undisputed, if not miraculous evidence of the antiquity of all these prophecies, by their being sacredly preserved, in every age, in the custody and guardianship of the enemies of Christianity? Why was such a multitude of facts foretold that are applicable to Christ and to him alone? Why?—but that all this mighty preparation might usher in the gospel of righteousness, and prepare the way for the kingdom of God; and that Christians also, in every age, might add to their "peace and joy in believing" the perfect trust, that however great the promises of God may be, they still are sure; and that he who spared not his own Son, but gave him up for us all, will with him also, if his we be, freely give us all things. And if we ever read a book for any object, ought we not diligently to search the scriptures, to see how they testify of Christ? And ought not every word of such testimony to be, like all scripture besides, profitable for doctrine and for instruction in righteousness? And may it not be profitable "for reproof and for correction" to all who mind only earthly things—who are eager to seek after unprofitable knowledge—who could talk, with all volubility, of the temporal concerns of others or their own—who could expatiate freely, perhaps, on the properties of a beast, the quality of their food, or the beauty of a garment— and who, although they have had the Bible constantly beside them, have, for many a year, remained ignorant of the value of the treasure it contains, or of the fulness of the testimony which God has given of his son? None surely would any longer wilfully refrain from searching the scriptures to see how they testify of Jesus, or from seeking the words of eternal life which may be found in them, were they to lay to heart the thought that the second coming of Christ to judge the quick and the dead, is as certain as that the prophetic tidings of his first advent—once heard afar off— have already proved true.

———

END OF THE OLD TESTAMENT HISTORY.

"AND HE BEARING HIS CROSS WENT FORTH " JOHN XIX. 17

"AND HE BEARING HIS CROSS WENT FORTH" — JOHN XIX. 17

A
NEW AND COMPLETE
HISTORY OF THE BIBLE.

PART II.

CONTAINING THE HISTORY OF THE NEW TESTAMENT.

CHAPTER I.

THE historical part of the New Testament is contained in the four Gospels of Matthew, Mark, Luke, and John; and, in a very particular manner, claims the most serious attention of every person, as it conveys to us the blessed tidings of our recovering that happy state which our first parents forfeited in paradise. Indeed, the New Testament is the best commentary on the Old. By a diligent comparison of both together, with all the parallel passages marked only in the margin of our common bibles, an infinitely greater knowledge of Scripture will generally be acquired than is commonly either thought of or believed. The truth is, there is so great a unity in all the parts of the Bible—such an intimate connexion in its matter, phraseology, doctrines, facts, and the like—so many allusions made from one passage to another, that there is scarcely a question connected with biblical interpretation that may not, by this means only, be very safely and satisfactorily determined.

In passing from the contemplation of Jewish affairs to the glorious objects presented to our notice in the New Testament, we seem to emerge from dreary and uncomfortable shades, into the cheerful light of day; and leave, without regret, a road rendered tedious by Jewish ceremonies, crowded with human traditions, and encumbered with heathen altars, to pursue the open path marked out by the reforming hand of the SON OF GOD.

From an early period after the fall of man, a gracious intimation had been given of God's intention to visit the world by a Divine Person, who should restore sinners from their ruined condition, destroy the power of death and hell, and lead his followers to eternal felicity. Promises to this effect were, from season to season, given to God's chosen people; this great object held a place in all the predictions of the prophets, and was shadowed forth in all the types and ceremonies of the Jewish law. The character of this sacred Messenger was drawn with sufficient clearness, to render him desirable with all the truly pious, and to distinguish him, when come, to the view of every humble and earnest inquirer.

It was about four thousand years after the creation of the world, and when the Roman empire having gained the ascendency over all nations, a universal peace had taken place; while Augustus Cæsar was emperor at Rome, and Herod, by Cæsar's authority, had been made king of Judea; that the period arrived for the fulfilment of these gracious promises, in the birth of " the Prince of Peace." A general expectation seems to have prevailed among the Jews, that about this time the great Deliverer was to make his appearance; nor are there wanting evidences, that such an event was looked for, even in the gentile or heathen world.

But though the train of divine providence had all along tended to this object, the appearance of the expected Redeemer, as we shall see, was not to be marked by earthly pomp. On the contrary, as if God would show his utter disregard of what poor depraved mortals so highly esteem, " the King of glory" was to be ushered into the world in the most obscure condition; while divine honor and heavenly attention were to supply the place of vain and empty worldly grandeur: the carnal and the high-minded were to be disappointed in their calculations, while humble, pious souls were to rejoice in his salvation.

As an introduction to the event about to take place, an angel appeared to a priest named Zacharias (while offering incense in the temple), informing him that he should have a son, who was to be called John: that this child should be filled with the Holy Ghost from his birth; and that he should be the forerunner of the Lord from heaven, in order to prepare his way. Zacharias, though a righteous man, being, with his wife Elisabeth, far advanced in years, seemed to hesitate through unbelief; whereupon the angel, declaring his name to be Gabriel, assured the priest that he should be "dumb, and not able to speak," till the fulfilment of this prediction; thus at once confirming the truth of the message, and chastizing the unbelief of Zacharias.

In the sixth month from this period of time, the angel Gabriel was sent to a virgin of the house of David, whose name was Mary; a poor young woman, promised in marriage to Joseph, a carpenter, who was likewise of the house of David; that royal family being, at this time, reduced to a low condition. Saluting the highly-favored virgin, the angel made known to her that she should bear a son, whose name should be called Jesus;* that God would give him the throne of David, and a kingdom without end; and that this holy child should be produced by the power of the Divine Spirit; on account of which he should be called " the Son of God."

Shortly after this wonderful occurrence, Elisabeth was honored by a visit from Mary, who was her near relation, and both of them, in a divine rapture, rejoiced and praised God, on account of the approaching visitation of mercy and grace toward his people. Nor was it long before Zacharias witnessed, in the birth of John, the fulfilment of the angel's prediction; and having his tongue loosed, he straightway employed it in divine praises, and in prophesying the dawn of the gospel-day.

In the meantime the angel of the Lord appearing to Joseph in a dream, removed from his mind all suspicion with respect to the character of Mary his espoused wife; shortly after which, in consequence of a decree from the Roman emperor, for the taxing (or enrolling) of all his subjects, in the several cities of their respective families, Joseph and Mary repaired together to Bethlehem,† the city of David, to whose family they both belonged. The inn at this place being crowded with strangers, there was found no other accommodation for this humble pair, than a stable; and here the long-promised infant was born, and, being wrapped in swaddling clothes, was laid in a manger.‡

* The name *Jesus*, in Greek, corresponds with *Joshua*, in Hebrew; both of them signifying a *Saviour*: and *Christ* is the same in Greek, with *Messiah* in Hebrew, *i. e.* the *anointed*. This title is given to our Saviour, in allusion to the custom of anointing kings, priests, and sometimes prophets, with oil; Jesus being anointed to the great office of Redeemer, by the holy Spirit, which was given him without measure.

† A city of Judah, situated on an eminence overlooking Tekoah, at the distance of nine miles south, and about six miles southwest of Jerusalem. It was also called Ephrath (Gen. xxxv. 16-19), and Ephraiah, Ruth iv 11. Though a city of no great note, it was celebrated as the birth-place of David (1 Sam. xvi. 1), and it became famous as the birth-place of the Messiah (Mic. v. 2, Matt. ii. 5-8). The village of Bethlehem, in 1784, was supposed to contain six hundred men capable of bearing arms; but war and tyrannical government have reduced it to a miserable condition. Mr. Whiting, an American missionary, visited it in 1834, when it had just suffered severely from oppressive despotism; and he passed over the ruins of houses and fields that had just then been demolished, and parks of olive and fig-trees which had been cut down by order of the pacha, for alleged rebellion and flight. It is now called Beet-la-hm, and contains about 1,000 professing Christians.

‡ There has been much misconception both as regards the "inn" and the "manger:" for although it has been rightly apprehended by some recent writers, that the inn must be understood to answer to the still existing "caravansary" of the East, they have wanted that practical acquaintance with details, which could alone enable them to apply their general information effectively to the illustration of the present passage.

In the East there is not, and we have no information or probability that there ever were, such places of entertainment as we understand when we speak of "inns." A person who comes to a town, where he has no friends to receive him into their houses, seeks accommodation at the *caravansary* or *khan*, where he may stay as long as he pleases, generally without payment; but is only provided with lodging for himself and beast, if he has any, and with water from a well on the premises. The room or cell which he obtains is perfectly bare. He may procure a mat, perhaps, but nothing more: and hence every one who travels, provided he has a beast, takes with him a rug, a piece of carpet, or even a mattress (that is, a thick quilt, padded with wool or cotton), or something of the sort, to form his bed wherever he rests, whether in a town or country caravansary: but one who travels on foot can not thus encumber himself, and is well content to make the cloak he had worn by day serve for bed and bedding at night. It is the same with respect to food: he purchases what he needs from the town or village in or near which the khan may be situated; and if he requires a cooked meal, he dresses it himself, for which purpose a traveller's baggage also contains one or more pots and dishes, with a vessel for water. A foot traveller dispenses with warm meals; unless he may sometimes be enabled to procure something ready dressed, in the markets of the more considerable towns to which he comes. In those parts where towns are widely asunder, khans are more or less dis-

Bethlehem.

Such were the lowly circumstances under which the divine Saviour made his appearance in our world! But though disregarded by men, his birth passed not unnoticed nor unsung by angels. The event was made known to a company of shepherds, by one of these celestial messengers, who was suddenly joined by a multitude of the heavenly hosts, praising God, and saying, "Glory to God in the highest, and on earth peace, good will toward men." This intelligence, thus wonderfully communicated, carried the shepherds in haste to view the infant, and produced a report which struck with astonishment all who heard it.

In conformity with the Jewish law, the child Jesus was circumcised, at eight days old, and, some time afterward, presented before the Lord, in the temple at Jerusalem. On this occasion two memorable testimonies were borne to his character, as the Messiah. Old Simeon, a devout man, who waited for the consolation of Israel, took the holy infant in his arms, and blessing God, said, "Lord, now lettest thou thy servant depart in peace, according to thy word; for mine eyes have seen thy salvation!"—while Anna, an aged widow of great piety, coming into the temple at the same time, "gave thanks likewise unto the Lord, and spake of him to all them that looked for redemption in Jerusalem."

persed over the open country; and in these, or wherever they are not, the traveller lives upon the victuals which he has brought with him from the last inhabited town, in the knowledge that these remote khans offer nothing but shelter, and that no provisions can be obtained in their neighborhood. These facts may be found usefully to illustrate those passages of Scripture which allude to travelling, and to the accommodation of travellers.

As to the khans themselves, they vary considerably in their arrangements and importance; and it would here answer no illustrative purpose to particularize them all. We shall therefore merely mention the plan and arrangement which most generally prevail in such establishments, and of which the others are merely variations: the rather, as it so happens, that it is from these that we are ourselves best able to collect what seems a clear understanding of the present text.

A khan, then, usually presents, externally, the appearance of a square, formed by strong and lofty walls, with a high, and often handsome gateway, which offers an entrance to the interior. On passing through this, the traveller finds himself in a large open quadrangle, surrounded on all sides by a number of distinct recesses, the back walls of which contain doors leading to the small cells or rooms which afford to travellers the accommodation they require. Every apartment is thus perfectly detached, consisting of the room and the recess in front. In the latter the occupant usually sits till the day has declined, and there he often prefers to sleep at night. Besides these private apartments, there is usually in the centre of one or more of these sides of the quadrangle, a large and lofty hall, where the principal persons may meet for conversation or entertainment. The floor of all these apartments—the recesses, rooms, and halls, are raised two or three feet above the level of the court which they surround, upon a platform or bank of earth faced with masonry. In the centre of the court is a well or cistern, offering to the travellers that most essential of conveniences in a warm climate—pure water.

Many caravansaries are without stables; the cattle being accommodated in the open area. But the most complete establishments have very excellent stables, in covered avenues which extend behind the ranges of apartments—that is, between the back walls of these ranges of building, and the external wall of the khan; and the entrance to it is by a covered passage at one of the corners of the quadrangle. The stable is on a level with the court, and consequently below the level of the buildings, by the height of the platform on which they stand. Nevertheless, this platform is allowed to project behind into the stable, so as to form a bench, to which the horses' heads are turned, and on which they can, if they like, rest the nose-bags, of hair-cloth, from which they eat, to enable them to reach the bottom, when its contents get low. It also often happens that not only this bench exists in the stable, but also recesses corresponding to those in front of the apartments, and formed by the side walls, which divide the rooms, being allowed to project behind into the stable, just as the projection of the same walls into the great area forms the recesses in front. These recesses in the stable, or the bench, if there are none, furnish accommodation to the servants or others who have charge of the beasts: and when persons find on their arrival that the apartments usually appropriated to travellers are already occupied, they are glad to find accommodation in the stable, particularly when the nights are cold or the season inclement.

Now, in our opinion, the ancient or the existing usages of the East supply no greater probability than that the Saviour of the world was born in such a stable as this. Not knowing that there were stables to oriental caravansaries, some recent writers of great information and ability have concluded that our Lord was born in a place distinct from and unconnected in any way with the "inn"—probably in a shed or outhouse—perhaps in a cave.

The word rendered "manger" has given occasion to some discussion. The most eminent scholars, since Salmasius, have held that it means a stable or stall for cattle. The same thing is implied, if it be understood to mean a manger. This being the case, it is evident from our description, that the part of the stable could not reasonably have been other than one of those recesses, or at least a portion of the bench, which we have mentioned as affording accommodation to travellers under certain circumstances. If we will have the word to mean "a manger," with Campbell and others, then we are to consider that the Orientals have no mangers, but feed their cattle from hair-bags; a fact which led Bishop Pearce to entertain the strange idea that the infant Jesus was cradled in such a bag. It can not even be shown that the classical ancients, although they fed their horses differently from the Orientals, had any such mangers as ours; but either nose-bags or vessels of stone or metal. Therefore, if we would retain the word "manger," we must needs understand it in the large sense of an eating place, not an eating thing—that is, the place to which the horses' heads were turned when they ate, or on which the thing from which they ate rested while they did eat. And this brings us to the same conclusion as before; for, in the above description, we have shown that, in the stable, their heads are turned toward the same bench or recesses. We therefore think that we are fairly entitled to the conclusion which we have stated. The explanation here given was strongly suggested to the present writer's mind while himself finding accommodation in a recess of such stables, when there was "no room" for him in the proper lodging apartments of caravansaries: and he is disposed to hope that it may be found to obviate the difficulties which have been discovered in the case before us.

In the meantime a new and uncommon star had appeared in the heavens, which served as a signal that the star of Jacob had arisen upon the world, and as a guide to certain persons called "wise men," who came from the east to Jerusalem, to inquire after him who was "born king of the Jews." When Herod the king had received information of these things, he determined, if possible, to crush at once the child whom he considered as the rival of his family. Accordingly, he requested of the wise men, that when they had found the object of their search, they should bring him word, that he also might join in paying him adoration.

On leaving Jerusalem, the eastern sages found, to their joy, that the star which they had seen before they set out on their journey, had again appeared! It now became their guide to Bethlehem, and stood over the house where the holy family at this time resided. Having worshipped the wonderful babe, and, according to the eastern custom, made an offering of gold, frankincense, and myrrh; and being warned in a dream of Herod's bloody intention, " they departed into their own country another way." The tyrant, thus baffled in his purpose, caused all the children to be destroyed in Bethlehem and the neighboring country, "from two years old and under;" but Joseph had received timely notice by an angel, and the heaven-protected infant was now in Egypt.

The death of Herod (who was succeeded by his son Archelaus) being made known to Joseph, by an angel, he returned with Mary and the young child, and dwelt in Nazareth, a city of Galilee, where "the child grew and waxed strong in spirit, filled with wisdom; and the grace of God was upon him." From this place Joseph, the supposed father, and Mary, the mother of Jesus, went yearly to Jerusalem, to the feast of the passover. On one of these occasions, when he was twelve years old, having accompanied them to the feast, he was left behind, on the return of his parents, who travelled a day's journey under the supposition that Jesus was in company with some of their relations.

When, however, after discovering their mistake, they returned to the city to make inquiry, he was found in the temple, "sitting in the midst of the doctors, both hearing them, and asking them questions," while the uncommon wisdom of his youthful mind astonished all who heard him. "Wist ye not," said he to his parents, when they had thus found him, "that I must be about my father's business?" He then went down with them to Nazareth, and was subject to them; "increasing in wisdom and stature, and in favor with God and man."

While thus the early part of the life of Jesus was spent at Nazareth in Galilee, John, who was designed as his forerunner in the ministry, was raised to maturity in that part of Judea which was called the desert, or the wilderness. In this retired situation, in the reign of Tiberius Cæsar, Pontius Pilate being governor of Judea, Herod, tetrarch of Galilee, and Annas and Caiaphas being high-priests, John received a divine commission; in consequence of which, he went forth into the country about Jordan, preaching the necessity of repentance for the remission of sins; exhorting the people to the practice of righteousness; directing their attention to the Messiah, who was shortly to follow him; and baptizing all who gave evidence of the power of his doctrine on their hearts; hence he was called "John the Baptist."

The appearance of this preacher, who was clothed in raiment of camel's hair, with a leathern girdle about his loins; the doctrines which he so earnestly inculcated; and the strict sanctity and self-denial of his life, excited great attention among the people, and drew crowds to his baptism. In the meantime, to the multitudes who attended his ministry, he failed not to declare the superiority of the approaching Messiah; informing the people, that while he himself baptized with water only, a mightier One would come after him, who should baptize with the Holy Ghost.

While John was thus employed, Jesus, who had hitherto lived in retirement, being now about thirty years of age, made his appearance at the river Jordan, and claimed the ordinance of baptism at the hands of his servant. On this occasion God was pleased to introduce his Son to the world; for upon his being baptized, and going up out of the water, the heavens were opened, the Holy Ghost descended upon him like a dove, and the voice of the eternal Father proclaimed, " This is my beloved Son, in whom I am well pleased."

Immediately after this solemnity, Jesus was conducted, by an impulse of the Holy Spirit, into the wilderness, where, in a state of seclusion from the world, he spent forty days in fasting and communion with God, as a preparation for the great work of the ministry, which he was about to undertake. Here he was assaulted with three powerful temptations from the devil, each of which was repelled by an appeal to the written word of God.

First, he was tempted to turn stones into bread, that he might thus at once prove his power, as the Son of God, and allay his hunger. But he answered, "It is written, Man shall not live by bread alone, but by every word that proceedeth out of the mouth of God." Secondly, the devil requested that he would prove himself to be under the protection of Heaven, by casting himself down from the pinnacle (or battlements) of the temple; but Christ showed the wickedness of tempting, or rashly presuming on divine providence, by answering, "It is written, Thou shalt not tempt the Lord thy God." Thirdly, he was promised, by this impudent tempter, all the kingdoms of the world, if he would fall down and worship him to which, with holy indignation, Jesus answered, "Get thee hence, Satan; for it is written, Thou shalt worship the Lord thy God, and him only shalt thou serve."

The infernal enemy, thus baffled in all his attempts, was compelled to leave the conqueror; angels came and ministered to his wants; and Jesus went forth from his retirement, to enter on the glorious work of blessing, reforming, and redeeming lost man.

While the Redeemer was thus secluded from the world, the report of John's ministry and baptism having excited the notice of the Jewish council, messengers were sent from that body to learn who this strange character might be. To their inquiry on this point, John answered, that he was not the Christ, nor the prophet Elijah (who in their opinion was to revisit the earth); but that he was come as "the voice of one crying in the wilderness, make straight the way of the Lord"—according to the prophecy of Isaiah; declaring, at the same time, that there was one who had appeared among the people, the latchet of whose shoes he was not worthy to loose.

On the next day, Jesus having now returned from the desert, John saw him approaching, and took occasion to point him out to the people, under the character of "the Lamb of God, which taketh away the sin of the world;" announcing him as the person of whose coming he had before given notice, and testifying, in plain and positive terms, that he was the Son of God. Again, on the following day, looking on the divine Saviour as he was walking at some little distance, he repeated his former expression, "Behold the Lamb of God!" in consequence of which, two of John's disciples attached themselves to Christ, and became his followers.

One of these disciples was Andrew; the other, though not named, was probably John, who afterward wrote one of the gospels, and is distinguished by the title of "the beloved disciple." Shortly afterward they were joined by three others, viz., Simon Peter (who is called Cephas); Philip, of Bethsaida; and Nathanael, of whom Jesus testified that he was an Israelite indeed, in whom was no guile. With these disciples our Lord attended a marriage in Cana* of Galilee, where he wrought his

* Cana of Galilee (see engraving, page 481), is a village, consisting of a few miserable huts. The ground rises gently toward the village: it is stony, and partially covered with short grass: olive trees grow here. The hills in the distance are gray and barren. The ruins of a church are shown to the traveller: it is said to have been erected by the Emperess Helena on the spot where the nuptial feast was celebrated, of which we have an account in John, ii. 1-10; and there is also exhibited a stone vessel, which is gravely said to have been one of those used on that occasion. When Dr. Clarke visited Cana, in walking among the ruins, he observed large massy pots of stone, answering to the description given by the evangelist. They were not preserved or exhibited as relics, but were lying about, disregarded by the modern inhabitants, as antiquities with the use of which they were unacquainted. From their appearance, and the number of them, it is quite evident that the practice of keeping water in large stone pots, each holding from eighteen to twenty-seven gallons, was once common in this country.

About a quarter of a mile from the village is a spring of delicious water, close to the road, whence all the water is taken for the supply of the inhabitants. Here pilgrims usually halt, as the source of the water which our Saviour, by his first miracle, converted into wine. At such places it is usual to meet, either shepherds reposing with their flocks, or caravans halting to drink. There being a few olive trees near the spot, travellers alight, spread their carpets, and, having filled their pipes, generally smoke tobacco and take coffee; always preferring repose in those places to the accommodations which are offered in the villages. While Mr Rae Wilson was sitting upon the shattered wall which enclosed "the well of Cana, six females, having their faces veiled, came down to the well, each carrying on her head a pot for the purpose of being filled with water." "These vessels are formed of clay, hardened by the heat of the sun, and are of a globular shape and large at the mouth, not unlike the bottles used in our country for holding vitriol, but not so large. Many of them have handles attached to the sides: and it was a wonderful coincidence with Scripture, that the vessels appeared to contain much about the same quantity as those which, the evangelist informs us, were employed on occasion of the celebration of the marriage which was honored by the Saviour's presence; viz., three firkins, of about twelve gallons, each. It is a further remarkable circumstance, that, in the Holy Land, it rarely happens that men are employed for the purpose of drawing water; but it is a duty entirely devolving on the females, and shows strongly that such a practice has been continued from the earliest ages." (Gen. xxi. 31, xxiv. 11-30. Exod. ii. 16.) The female figures seen in the foreground of our engraving were barefooted, and very miserable. They were all veiled with a large calico sheet which they wrapped in folds around them.

Cana of Galilee.

first public miracle, by turning water into wine; thus supplying the need of the guests, and confirming the faith of his disciples.

From Cana, Jesus went to Capernaum, a city of Galilee; and thence, after a short stay, to Jerusalem, where he attended the feast of the passover, for the first time after his entrance into the ministry. On this occasion he found the temple occupied as a place of traffic by some who sold oxen, sheep, and doves, for the sacrifices, and by others who accommodated the traders by changing money. Filled with holy indignation to see the house of God thus profaned, he drove them forth from the temple with a scourge of small cords, pouring out the money of the exchangers, and overturning the tables at which they were sitting.

The miracles which were performed by our Lord, during this feast of the passover, induced numbers to believe in him, and excited the attention of many others. Among these was Nicodemus, a ruler of the Jews, who made a visit to Jesus by night, in order to have a private conference with him on the subject of his doctrines and the nature of that kingdom which had been lately spoken of.

In answer, therefore, to his first address, the great Teacher assured him that it was absolutely necessary, in order to the enjoyment of the kingdom of God, that a man should be "born again;" or that such a renewal of the heart should be experienced as might be termed "a new birth." Having further informed him that this divine change was to be effected by the influence of the Holy Spirit, our Lord went on to instruct him in the doctrine of salvation, by faith in the Son of God; and closed his discourse by showing the difference between the follower of evil and the follower of truth—a discourse which, eventually, appears to have made a salutary impression on the mind of Nicodemus.

The passover being ended, Jesus left Jerusalem and went into other parts of Judea, where he employed his disciples in baptizing, and was followed by great numbers of people; and when an account of this was brought to John the Baptist, that faithful herald, so far from being displeased at the rising glory of his Master, rejoiced in the prospect, and again took the occasion to set forth the superior excellence of the person and ministry of the Son of God.

The course of John was now near its close; for about this time, having reproved Herod for taking away his brother Philip's wife, he was imprisoned by the tetrarch, and not long after was, by his order, put to death. A more particular account of this event will be given hereafter. In the meantime, Jesus departed from Judea on a journey to Galilee; and passing in his way through the country of Samaria, he held a conversation with a woman of that country, which produced a happy change in her character, and through her means many of the Samaritans were brought to hear his word, and to believe in him as the promised Messiah.

Arriving in Galilee, he proclaimed "the gospel of the kingdom of God" to the people, many of whom were disposed to receive the heavenly message; and being humbly and earnestly applied to by a nobleman in behalf of his son, who was sick at Capernaum, the compassionate Saviour gave the healing word, and the young man was restored.

While in the country of Galilee (where, we are told, he had come "in the power of the spirit"), Jesus enterrd into a synagogue at Nazareth, and stood up to read. The book of the prophecy of Isaiah was delivered to him, and he opened to a prediction which pointed immediately to himself. This passage, he declared to the congregation, was that day fulfilled. But some of his remarks gave such offence to the Nazarenes, that they violently thrust him out, and led him to the brow of the mountain on which the city stood, designing to cast him down headlong from the precipice. This, however, he miraculously avoided, by passing through the midst of them and going his way.

Leaving Nazareth* after this outrage, Jesus took up his abode in Capernaum, where he went on to preach the necessity of repentance as a preparation for that divine kingdom which was now at hand. Here, as he walked by the sea of Galilee, he saw Simon Peter, and Andrew his brother, who were fishermen, and who it seems had

* A city of Zebulon in Galilee, about seventy miles north of Jerusalem: it stood low in public estimation for the character of its inhabitants (John i. 46), yet it became famous as the residence of Jesus until he entered on his ministry (Matt. i. 23, Luke ii. 51, iv. 16). Nazareth still exists with a population of from 5,000 to 7,000, some of whom are Mohammedans, but mostly of several sects of ignorant and superstitious professors of Christianity. The Roman Catholics have a church here, called the "Church of the Annunciation," the most magnificent of any in the land, except that at Jerusalem.

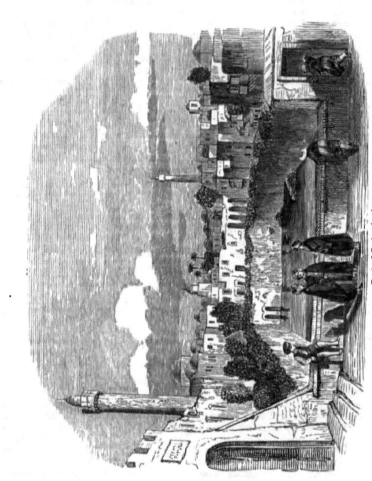

Pool of Bethesda. †

returned for awhile to their former employment. These he now called to become his constant attendants, as well as James and John, the sons of Zebedee, whom he found engaged in the same occupation.

These fishermen (who were henceforward to be employed in catching *men*) let down their nets at the direction of Christ, and enclosed such a multitude of fish as struck them with astonishment and awe; and having brought their vessels to the land, they forsook all and followed their Master.

The ministry of our Lord at Capernaum was marked with signal and wonderful instances of his power and goodness. While he was in the synagogue, there appeared a man in the congregation possessed with the spirit of a demon, who cried out in a fearful manner, and acknowledged him to be "the Holy One of God." At the word of Jesus the man was straightway released from the fury of this foul spirit. Coming from the synagogue into the house of Simon Peter, he found the mother of Peter's wife lying ill of a fever, and taking her by the hand "he rebuked the fever," which immediately left her, and she arose restored to health.

The fame of these miracles drew together in the evening great numbers of people, who thronged the house where Jesus had taken up his lodging, bringing with them those that "were sick with divers diseases," and "many that were possessed with devils," toward all of whom the gracious Saviour manifested the kindness of his heart by delivering them from their various maladies. The voice of fame, however, did not occasion our Lord to forget the exercises of devotion, nor did his labors cause him to neglect them; for we are told that, rising up early the next morning, "he departed into a solitary place, and there prayed."

The blessings of the ministry and miracles of Christ were not confined to Capernaum. "He went about all Galilee, teaching in their synagogues, and preaching the gospel of the kingdom, and healing all manner of sickness and all manner of disease among the people." His fame also went throughout the country of Syria, whence they brought the afflicted to experience the effects of his healing power. "And there followed him," we are told, "great multitudes of people, from Galilee, and from Decapolis, and from Jerusalem, and from Judea, and from beyond Jordan."

But though our Redeemer was thus compassionate to the *bodies* of men, to heal their souls and to reform their conduct was his great object. He availed himself, therefore, of the opportunity which the vast crowd collected together now afforded to deliver a discourse, which is generally termed "the sermon on the mount,"—a discourse replete with those heavenly doctrines and precepts which form so distinguishing a character of his holy religion.

On coming down from the mountain, he was addressed by a man afflicted with the leprosy, in compliance with whose humble petition Jesus put forth his hand and healed him. Afterward he entered again into Capernaum, where he was attended by crowds, who came to hear him and to be cured of their diseases. Among others, a man sick of the palsy was brought forward, but because of the multitude about the door he was let down on his bed through the roof of the house. This remarkable instance of faith met the approbation of our Lord, who pronounced the cure of the sick man by saying, "Son, be of good cheer; thy sins be forgiven thee."

Some of the scribes and Pharisees who were present on this occasion considered this declaration as blasphemy; but, to show them that he had indeed the power to forgive sins, Jesus addressed the paralytic man, saying, "Arise, and take up thy bed, and go thy way into thine house." The word of Christ was immediately obeyed, and "he departed to his own house, glorifying God." Shortly after this wonderful event, Matthew (otherwise called Levi), a publican, or tax-gatherer, was called by Christ to become his disciple and attendant; and such was the influence of this call that he immediately left his employment and followed Jesus.

The time of the passover* being now again near at hand, Jesus went up to Jerusalem, in order to be present at the feast. Here he performed a remarkable cure on a poor afflicted man, who had labored under an infirmity for thirty-eight years. This helpless creature was lying near a pool, called Bethesda,† to which numbers of dis-

---

* This is simply called, by the evangelist, "a feast of the Jews;" though it seems probable that it was the feast of the passover.

† No pool named Bethesda is noticed by the Jewish writers; but it is thought by some that it may have been the great pool of which they say, that, between Hebron and Jerusalem was the fountain Etham, from which the waters were conducted in pipes to *is the great pool in Jerusalem*. Benjamin of Tudela speaks

eased persons resorted, on account of a supernatural virtue produced in the water by the going down of an angel, at certain seasons, into the pool. The first who stepped in after the stirring of the water was healed of his disorder: but this poor man, having no one to assist him at such seasons, still missed the opportunity of a cure. The compassionate Jesus, however, found him, and administered to him that relief which he sought in vain at the pool of Bethesda.

It was the sabbath-day when this act of mercy was performed; and as the Jews saw the man who had been healed carrying his bed, they took occasion to find fault, and to persecute Jesus as a breaker of the Sabbath. This produced a defence on the part of Christ, in which we find him declaring himself the Son of God—asserting his authority over the living and the dead—and appealing to undeniable evidences to prove and establish the divine character to which he laid claim.

Not long after this, our Lord again incurred the censure of the Pharisees for healing on the Sabbath. In a synagogue in Galilee, he found a man whose right hand was withered: he restored the hand to soundness, and defended his conduct; but his arguments, though they confounded his adversaries, served to incense them the more, and they communed together and took counsel how they might destroy him.

In consequence of these malicious designs, Jesus retired to the sea of Tiberias,[*] where he continued to teach the multitudes that resorted to him, and to heal all who were diseased. Here too, after having spent a whole night in prayer on a mountain, he called together his disciples, from among whom he chose twelve, ordaining them as apostles, or special messengers, who were to hold the highest offices in the

of a pool, as existing in his time, at which the ancients were supposed to have slain their sacrifices; and he very probably had in view the pool which is at present considered to represent the "pool of Bethesda" of our text. Many, from the mention of sheep in connexion with the pool, surmise that here the sheep destined for sacrifice were washed. If so, the washing was either before or after the victims were slaughtered. but it was not required that they should be washed *before* being slaughtered; and for the washing of the victims *after* they had been slain, there was in the temple a chamber with a proper supply of water. It is perhaps best, therefore, to take the word κολυμβήθρα, rendered "pool," in its more definite acceptation of "bath," and understand that the pool was a bath for unclean persons, for whose accommodation the "five porches" or cloistered walks were erected.

Bethesda means "house of mercy, grace, or goodness;" doubtless because many miserable objects there received mercy and healing. Athanasius speaks of the pool itself as still existing in his time, although the surrounding buildings were, as we might expect, in ruin. The place to which the name of the pool of Bethesda is now given, is very possibly the same thus mentioned. Chateaubriand thinks it offers the only example now left of the primitive architecture of the Jews at Jerusalem. In conformity with other travellers, he states that it is still to be seen near St. Stephen's gate. It was situated near the temple, on the north; and is a reservoir one hundred and fifty feet long, and forty wide. The sides are walled, and these walls are composed of a bed of large stones, joined together by iron cramps; a wall of mixed materials runs upon these large stones; a layer of flints is stuck upon the surface of this wall; and a coating laid over these flints. The four beds are perpendicular to the bottom, and not horizontal; the coating was on the side next to the water, and the large stones rested, as they still do, against the ground. The pool is now dry and filled up. Here grow some pomegranate-trees and a species of wild tamarind of a bluish color; the western angle is quite full of nopals. On the west side may also be seen two arches, which probably led to an aqueduct that carried the water into the interior of the temple. Chateaubriand considers that this pool is at the same time the Bethesda of Scripture and the *Stagnum Salomonis* of Josephus; and presumes that it offers all which now remains of the Jerusalem of David and Solomon.

[*] REFLECTIONS AT TIBERIAS.—The composure which came over my feverish spirits at this hour was inexpressibly refreshing: I laid myself down upon the ground, and, resting my head upon a stone near me, drew a little coolness from the soil: while the simple train of reflections which naturally sprung up from the scene around me added much to my enjoyment. At a great distance to the north was the mountainous horizon, on the summit of which stands Safet, glistening with its noble castle. It is not improbably supposed that our Saviour had this spot in his eye, and directed the attention of his disciples to it, when he said, "A city that is set on a hill can not be hid;" for it is in full view from the Mount of Beatitudes as well as from this place; and, indeed, seems to command all the country round to a great extent. Tracing, at a glance, the margin of this simple lake, on the opposite or eastern side, the eye rests on the inhospitable country of the Gadarenes—inhospitable to this day. But that which awakens the tenderest emotions in viewing a scene like this, is the remembrance of One who, formerly, so often passed this way; and never passed without leaving, by his words and actions, some memorial of his divine wisdom and love. Here, or in this neighborhood, most of his mighty works were done: and in our daily religious services we have read. with the most intense interest, those passages of the gospel which refer to these regions. However uncertain other traditional geographical notices may be, *here* no doubt interrupts our enjoyment in tracing the Redeemer's footsteps. This, and no other, is the sea of Galilee—in its dimensions, as I should judge, resembling exactly the size of the Isle of Malta, about twenty miles in length, twelve in breadth, and sixty in circumference. Here Jesus called the sons of Zebedee, from mending their nets, to become "fishers of men." Here he preached to the multitudes crowding to the water's edge, himself putting off a little from the shore in Simon Peter's boat. But there is not now a single boat upon the lake to remind us of its former use. Yonder, on the right must have been the very spot where, in the middle of their passage from this side toward Bethsaida and Capernaum, the disciples were affrighted at seeing Jesus upon the water—when he gently upbraided the sinking faith of Peter; when he said to the winds and waves, "Be still!"—and the sweet serenity which now rest upon the surface is the very same stillness which then succeeded. Here, finally, it was that Jesus appeared, the third time after his resurrection, to his disciples (John xxi.), and put that question to the zealous, backslidden, but repentant Peter, "Simon, son of Jonas, lovest thou me?"—one question thrice repeated; plainly denoting what the Saviour requires of all who profess to be his; and followed up by that solemn charge, "Feed my lambs—feed my sheep."

church, and to whom he gave authority not only to preach in his name, but to heal diseases and to cast out devils.

The names of these twelve apostles were Simon, surnamed Peter, and Andrew his brother; James and John, the sons of Zebedee; Philip and Bartholomew; Matthew the publican, and Thomas, surnamed Didymus; James, the son of Alpheus, and Judas (or Jude) his brother;* Simon the Canaanite, surnamed Zelotes; and Judas Iscariot, who proved the betrayer of his Master.

CHAPTER II.

HAVING appointed the twelve apostles to their high office, our Lord, attended by the whole company of his disciples and a great multitude from different parts, stood in a plain, and repeated, in substance, a considerable part of his sermon on the mount, after which he entered into Capernaum, where he restored to health the servant of a Roman centurion,† and then, leaving Capernaum, he entered into the city of Nain.

Hitherto we have seen the great Saviour of men displaying his power in healing diseases and expelling demons: we are now to behold him exercising his authority over DEATH! At the gate of the city of Nain he met a train of mourners, attending the corpse of a young man, who was the only son of his mother, and she a widow. Jesus had compassion on the disconsolate parent: he spoke to her a word of encouragement; and, addressing the corpse as it lay on the bier, commanded the young man to arise. His word was attended with life: " he that was dead sat up and began to speak, and he delivered him to his mother."

This astonishing miracle struck the multitude with awe, and a rumor concerning this great prophet " went forth throughout all Judea, and throughout all the region round about." In the meantime, the disciples of John resorting to their master in prison and giving him an account of these miracles, he sent two of his disciples to Jesus, with an inquiry whether he was indeed the expected Messiah. It does not seem probable that this step was taken in consequence of any doubt in the mind of John; but, for whatever purpose it might have been intended, our Lord returned an appropriate answer, and then bore his testimony to the character of this faithful and eminent servant of God.

After an awful warning to the cities of Chorazin, Bethsaida, and Capernaum—where most of his mighty works had been done—and a gracious invitation to laboring and heavy-laden sinners, to come and find rest in his service, our Lord entered into the house of Simon, a Pharisee, being invited by the owner to eat with him; and here an occurrence took place, which served further to manifest the abundant grace of the Redeemer's heart.

A woman who had been a notorious sinner, but who was now a real penitent, humbly approached with an alabaster-box of ointment, stooped, weeping, at the feet of Jesus, and, washing them with her tears, wiped them with the hairs of her head, and anointed them with the ointment. The condescension of Christ in suffering this freedom from a person of her character, met the disapprobation of the Pharisee; but Jesus showed him by a striking parable, the impropriety of his censure, and pronounced the sins of the penitent woman forgiven.

After this, accompanied by his twelve apostles, " he went throughout every city and village, preaching and showing the glad tidings of the kingdom of God." Certain women also, " who had been healed of evil spirits and infirmities," attended him, and assisted in supplying his wants. Among these was Mary Magdalene, out of whom, we are told, he had cast seven devils.

Having healed a poor creature who was blind and dumb, and possessed by a demon, Jesus was accused by the Pharisees, of casting out devils through Beelzebub, the prince of devils. This wicked and absurd charge he clearly confuted; and warned them that their sinful malice in thus sinning against the Holy Ghost, would never be forgiven. Some of the scribes and Pharisees then required of him a sign from heaven; but he refused to gratify their vain curiosity; and having delivered many solemn admonitions, and much divine instruction, he departed to the seaside, where

* Called also Lebbeus, whose surname was Thaddeus.
† A captain over a hundred soldiers.

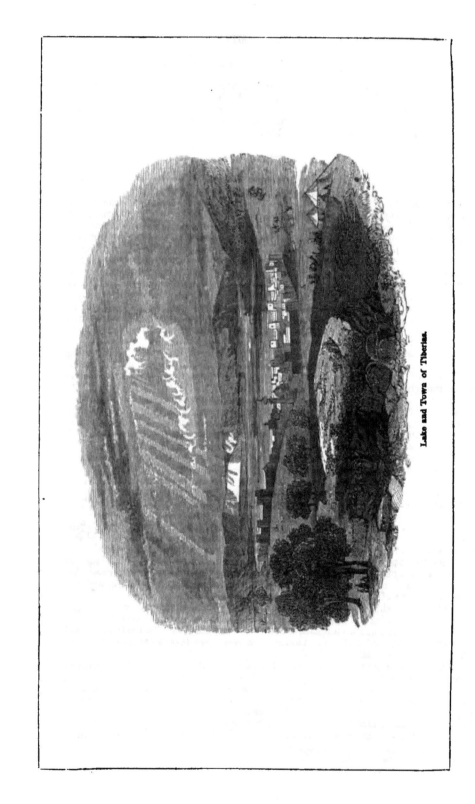

Lake and Town of Tiberias.

he taught the people in a series of parables, which he afterward expounded more fully to his disciples.

He who had power over demons, diseases, and death, could also control the winds and the seas. An instance of this occurred, when going on board a vessel with his disciples, in order to pass over the lake of Tiberias,* there arose a great tempest, and the ship was covered with the waves. In the midst of the storm, Jesus was asleep in the hinder part of the vessel; but the disciples, overwhelmed with fear, broke in upon his slumber, crying out, " Master, master, we perish !" He arose from his pil-

---

* Tiberias, one of the principal cities of Galilee, was erected by the tetrarch Herod Antipas, who gave it this appellation in honor of the emperor Tiberius. It was this Herod who beheaded John the Baptist (Matt. xiv. 3–11), and who sought the life of Christ himself (Luke xiii. 31). He probably resided in Tiberias; which may be the reason why the Saviour never visited this place. It was situated near the sea of Galilee, on a plain of singular fertility, which was greatly increased by assiduous cultivation. Josephus describes this region as a perfect paradise, blessed with a delicious temperature, and producing the fruits of every climate under heaven, not at stated periods merely, but in endless succession throughout the year. The neglect of agriculture in modern times has, of course, made it less productive; but the mildness of the climate, and the richness of the soil, are still extolled by travellers. When the Romans made war upon the Jews, Tiberias surrendered without waiting for a siege: on this account the Jews remained unmolested; and after the destruction of Jerusalem, this city became eminent for its academy, over which a succession of Jewish doctors presided until the fourth century. In the early ages of Christianity, Tiberias was an episcopal see; in the seventh century it was taken by the Saracens under the calif Omar; and though it passed into the hands of the Christians during the crusades, the Mahometans regained the possession of it toward the close of the fourteenth century. Widely scattered ruins of walls and other buildings, as well as fragments of columns, indicate the ancient extent of Tiberias. The stone of these ruins is described by the Rev. William Jowett as being " very black, so that there is nothing about them of the splendor of antiquity—nothing but an air of mourning and desolation. In this circumstance they differ so greatly from the magnificent antiquities of Egypt and Greece, as to leave the most sombre impression on the fancy: they are perfectly funereal."

The modern town of Tiberias, which is delineated in our engraving, is, by the natives, called Tabaria, or Tabbareeah; it occupies part of the site of the ancient city, and is situated at a short distance to the east from the sea of Galilee. It is surrounded with walls and towers, which at first view are very imposing: on a nearer approach, however, their insignificance is apparent. A few cannon would put them down in an instant, though to an assault from the natives they would present, probably, a very long and effectual resistance. One fourth of the space within the walls is stated by Dr. Richardson to be unoccupied by house or building; and many parts of the town are in a ruined and filthy condition. The population has been computed at one thousand five hundred or two thousand persons; eighty houses are occupied by Christians, and one hundred and fifty by Turks, but the largest portion (amounting to two hundred) is tenanted by Jews of all nations, who come here to spend the rest of their days. On the north side of the town, not far from the lake, there is a Greek church, the architecture of which exhibits much of the character of those sacred edifices which were erected by the Emperess Helena: it is said to occupy the identical spot on which stood the house of the apostle Peter, who, previously to his becoming a disciple of Jesus Christ, had been a fisherman on the lake.

To the south of Tiberias lie the celebrated hot baths, the water of which contains a strong solution of muriate of soda (common salt), with a considerable intermixture of iron and sulphur; it emits a powerful sulphurous smell. A thermometer placed in different spots where the water gushes out, rose to the various heights of 131, 132, 138, and 139 degrees of Fahrenheit; in the bath, where it cools after standing some time, its temperature was 110. An humble building is erected over the bath, containing mean apartments, on one side for men, on the other for women: it is much frequented, as a cure for almost every complaint, particularly by the Jews, who have a great veneration for a Roman sepulchre excavated in a cliff near the spot, which they imagine to be the tomb of Jacob. About a mile from the town, and exactly in front of the lake, is a chain of rocks, in which are distinctly seen cavities or grottoes that have resisted the ravages of time. These are uniformly represented to travellers as the places referred to in the gospel history, which were the resort of miserable and fierce demoniacs, upon one of whom Jesus Christ wrought a miraculous and instantaneous cure (Matt. viii. 28; Mark v. 2, 3; Luke viii. 37).

The sea of Galilee, which is seen in the back ground of our engraving, derives its name from its situation on the eastern borders of the province of Galilee; it was anciently called the sea of Chinnereth, or Chinneroth (Numb. xxxiv. 11; Josh. xii. 3), from its vicinity to a town of that name. In I Mac. xi. 67, it is called the water of Gennesar, and in Luke v. 1, the lake of Gennesaret, from the neighboring land of that name. Its most common appellation is the sea of Tiberias, from the contiguous town of Tiberias, which has been described in the preceding paragraphs.

This capacious lake is from twelve to fifteen miles in length, and from six to nine in breadth; along the shore its depth varies, and in some parts it may be sixty feet. The water is perfectly fresh, and is used by the inhabitants of Tiberias to drink, and for every culinary purpose. The waters of the northern part of this lake abound with delicious fish. It is remarkable that there is not a single boat of any description on the sea of Tiberias at present, although it is evident from the gospel history that it was much navigated in the time of Jesus Christ. The fish are caught partly by the fishermen going into the water up to their waists, and throwing in a hand-net, and partly with casting-nets from the beach; the consequence is, that a very small quantity only is taken, in comparison of what might be obtained if boats were employed. This accounts for the circumstance of fish being so dear at Tiberias, as to be sold at the same price per pound as meat. Viewed from a height, the water looks, amid the surrounding mountains, like an immense reservoir; and from the northern part being covered with volcanic remains, it has been conjectured that this lake was at one period the crater of a volcano. It has been compared by travellers to Loch Lomond in Scotland; and, like the lake of Windermere in Westmoreland, it is often greatly agitated by winds. A strong current marks the passage of the Jordan through this lake; and when this is opposed by contrary winds, which blow here with the force of a hurricane from the southeast, sweeping into the lake from the mountains, a boisterous sea is instantly raised, which the small vessels of the country (such as were anciently in use) were ill qualified to resist. Such a tempest is described in Matt. viii. 24–26, which was miraculously calmed by Jesus Christ with a word. The broad and extended surface of this lake, " covering the bottom of a profound valley, surrounded by lofty and precipitous eminences, when added to the impression under which every Christian pilgrim approaches, gives to it a character of unparalleled dignity."

low, and gently reproving their want of faith, "rebuked the winds and the sea, and there was a great calm!"

Arriving in the country of the Gadarenes (or Gergesenes), on the other side of the lake, he was met by two men, coming out from among the tombs, who, though possessed with devils, and raging with madness, cried out, acknowledging Jesus to be the Son of God. From these unhappy creatures he expelled the infernal spirits, suffering them, at their own request, to take possession of a herd of swine, which were feeding near the seaside; whereupon the whole herd ran violently down into the sea, and perished.

The loss of the swine, and probably the fear of some other calamity, induced the wicked Gadarenes earnestly to request that Jesus would leave their country; and thus they lost the benefits and blessings of his ministry; for he accordingly departed from the coast of Gadara, and returned to the city of Capernaum.

While in the house of Matthew, who had made an entertainment for his master, he received an application from the ruler of the synagogue, by the name of Jairus, who fell at his feet, begging that he would come and heal his little daughter, then lying at the point of death. Before he arrived at the ruler's house, the spirit of the damsel had fled; but Jesus, taking her by the hand, awoke her from the sleep of death, and restored her to the astonished and rejoicing parents.

After several other miracles of mercy and goodness, and a considerable time spent in proclaiming the good news of salvation, in different parts of the country, where he observed the multitudes as sheep without a shepherd, Jesus determined that the gospel should be more diffusively published. Accordingly, having called together his twelve apostles, and addressed them with a discourse filled with suitable instruction, advice, and encouragement, he sent them forth, by two and two, to preach the kingdom of God among "the lost sheep of the house of Israel," and to work miracles through his power.

Thus commissioned, the apostles went forward into the work; nor did their master remain inactive: "He departed thence, to teach and to preach" in the different cities of the Jews.

In the meantime John the Baptist had ended his mortal race, having fallen a sacrifice to the pride of Herod, and the cruelty of his unlawful wife Herodias. At Herod's birth-night feast, the daughter of this Herodias so pleased the king, by her expertness in dancing, that he promised, with an oath, to give her whatsoever she might ask. The occasion was seized by the wicked Herodias, who instructed her daughter to ask the head of John the Baptist. This was accordingly done; and the bloody gift was presented to the damsel in a charger.

On the return of the twelve apostles, and their report to Christ, he took them with him to a desert place, there to spend some little time in retirement. Thither, however, the people quickly followed him; and in this wilderness, the situation of the multitude drew forth a new instance of the Redeemer's power and goodness. They were without food, and likely to suffer for the want of it. But a lad present having five barley loaves and two small fishes, these were so increased, under the wonder-working hands of Christ, that five thousand men, besides a number of women and children, were amply supplied, and twelve baskets were filled with the fragments which remained.

This miracle, so pleasing to the multitude, produced a determination, on their part, to make Christ a temporal king; but, far from acceding to these views, he dismissed the crowd, and sending his disciples on before him, in a vessel, he retired to a mountain, and spent the evening in prayer.

While Jesus was thus engaged in secret devotion, the disciples were tossed on the water by a tempestuous wind. But about the fourth watch of the night (or three o'clock in the morning), they saw him approaching the vessel, walking on the waves. Struck with the sight of what appeared to them to be a spirit, "they cried out for fear." But Jesus quickly removed their apprehensions; and Peter, in the forwardness of his heart, obtained leave to meet him on the water. Soon, however, his fear overpowered his faith, and, beginning to sink, he was dependant on the hand of his master for deliverance from death.

Landing on the coast of Gennesareth, Jesus was, in a little time, surrounded by numbers bringing the sick in beds, to be healed. In the meantime, many of the people who had been miraculously fed by Christ, followed him to the city of Capernaum. But Jesus taking occasion to reprove their selfish motives, directed their attention to that food which would nourish the soul; declaring himself to be the bread of God which came down from heaven, to give life to the world. The heavenly discourse which he delivered, gave offence to some of his carnal followers, while it exhibited the only means of restoring lost sinners to spiritual life and eternal felicity.

After reproving the Pharisees for their hypocritical attention to mere external ceremonies, while they overlooked inward purity and a righteous conduct, we find our Lord departing into the borders of Tyre and Sidon. Here, at the humble entreaty of a Syrophenician woman, in behalf of her daughter, who was grievously distressed by a demon, he delivered the afflicted creature from her calamity; and then, leaving these coasts, came near to the sea of Galilee, where, for a while, he rested himself on a mountain.

To this place the multitudes quickly resorted, bringing with them the lame, the blind, the dumb, the maimed, and many others, and laying them at the feet of Jesus to be healed. Here, too, his power and compassion were again manifested, in a miraculous supply of food; the fainting multitude, to the number of four thousand, beside women and children, being fed from seven loaves and a few small fishes; and seven baskets-full of the fragments being afterward gathered up.

From the place above mentioned, Jesus passed over to Dalmanutha, in the coasts of Magdala, where he was beset by the Pharisees and Sadducees, who demanded of him a sign from heaven, but met as they deserved, with a refusal and reproof. Going thence to the city of Bethsaida, he restored a blind man to sight; after which, we find him visiting the towns of Cæsarea Philippi. In this journey our Lord entered into a private conversation with his disciples, on the subject of his own person and character; and from that time began to give them some intimation concerning his approaching sufferings, and his resurrection from the dead.

The disciples had heretofore seen their Lord, great indeed in power, but lowly in appearance. It remained for some of them to witness a splendor in his person, infinitely transcending the pomp of the greatest earthly king. Taking with him three of his chosen followers, Peter, James, and John, and ascending a high mountain, for the purpose of private devotion, it came to pass, while engaged in prayer, that he was suddenly, and in a glorious manner, transfigured in their presence. His face shone as the sun, and his raiment became white and dazzling. At the same time also, appeared two glorified saints, Moses and Elijah, who entered into a conversation with Jesus, concerning his approaching death, which was to be accomplished at Jerusalem.

It seems to have been the night-season when this wonderful event took place. The three disciples, fatigued with the labors of the day, had sunk down to sleep, but awakened with the splendor of the light, they beheld the glorious scene; while, as it passed off, a bright cloud overshadowed them, and a voice from the cloud proclaimed, " This is my beloved Son, in whom I am well pleased; hear ye him!"

On coming down from the mountain, the next day after the transfiguration, we find Jesus healing a youth, who from his childhood had been afflicted with lunacy and a dumb spirit; and some time afterward, at Capernaum, directing Peter to go to the sea, and take from the mouth of the first fish which should come to his hook, a piece of money, for the purpose of paying tribute to the tax-gatherers.

In the way to Capernaum, the disciples, not yet fully acquainted with the spiritual nature of their Master's kingdom, had held some dispute among themselves, who should be the greatest. Jesus, therefore, knowing what had passed, took occasion to warn them against a vain ambition; inculcating on their minds a spirit of genuine humility, as the proper temper to be possessed by his servants, and pointing out the necessity of renouncing all objects which might be inconsistent with the service of God, though dear to the feelings, as the hand, the foot, or the eye, to the body.

After discourse of this sort, and much more, in which our Lord instructed his disciples in the proper manner of dealing with each other, as members of his church, and pressed on them a ready disposition toward the forgiveness of injuries; we find him appointing, in addition to the twelve apostles, seventy disciples, whom " he sent two and two before his face, into every city and place, whither he himself would come."

In the meantime, going up to Jerusalem, to the feast of tabernacles, Jesus entered into the temple and taught. On this occasion much division and contention ensued

Defile between Jerusalem and Jericho.

among the people. Some, offended at his faithful dealing, "sought to take him ;" "but his hour was not yet come." Some believed in him, as the promised Messiah, and others rejected him. At length the Pharisees sent chief-priests and officers to apprehend him ; but, overpowered with the force of his words, they returned without him, declaring, "Never man spake like *this* man."

After another instructive lecture, on the following day, and a disputation with the Jews, we have an account of the return of the seventy disciples to their master, with the report of their success. While engaged in discourse with these disciples, a certain lawyer (or expounder of the Jewish laws), came forward, and with much self-consequence and secret contempt of Jesus, proposed a plausible question, but with a design to involve him in a difficulty. He begged to be informed what he must do, for the attainment of eternal life. Had the question been proposed with an humble and teachable disposition, our Lord would doubtless have given a direct and explicit answer; but knowing the proud and captious temper of the scribe, he replied in a way which might tend to humble or silence him. He therefore referred him to the demands of the law, upon obedience to which the scribe placed his dependance, assuring him a complete compliance with those claims, of perfect love to God and man, would secure to him the blessing desired. " This do, and thou shalt live ;" as if he had said " Perform, punctually and perpetually, without interruption or imperfection, all the injunctions of the holy and spiritual law of God, and eternal life shall be thine; but, remember, that the least deviation or defect will ruin thee for ever."[*]

The scribe, willing to stand on his own defence, and to evade conviction, proposed another question—"Who is my neighbor ?" It should seem that he, like all others who seek salvation by their own doings, was desirous of narrowing the demands of the law as much as possible, and reducing the number of those to whom the duties of love were owing. Our Lord wisely took this occasion of confuting the prevalent notion that neighbors were only such persons as lived near each other, or were connected by the ties of blood or religion. He therefore showed, by a parable, that we ought to extend our kindness to all our fellow-creatures in distress, of whatever nation or profession, even to those who have been separated from us by party quarrels and distinctions.

" A certain traveller," said our Lord, " going from Jerusalem to Jericho,[†] was set

[*] In this manner, St. Paul speaks (Gal. iii. 10), " For as many as are of the works of the law," that is, who seek justification by it, " are under the curse ;" for it is written, " Cursed is every one that continueth not in all things which are written in the book of the law *to do them.*"

[†] Jericho was at this time a very important city ; indeed it would seem from Josephus to have been next in consequence to Jerusalem itself. At this place also twelve thousand priests and Levites were stationed, with a view to the rotation of service at Jerusalem. Hence the peculiar propriety with which our Lord introduces the priest and Levite as passing this way. The road to Perea, beyond Jordan, also passed this way, whence it was one of the most frequented roads of Palestine. How fitly the road from Jerusalem to Jericho was made the scene of this interesting story, will appear when it is understood that this road has always been infested by numerous daring and desperate robbers ; and its character is so notorious, even at the present day, in this respect, that travellers are rarely allowed by the governor of Jerusalem to proceed to Jericho and the Dead sea without an escort. Josephus intimates, and Jerome says, that the savage mountainous wilderness through which this road passed had acquired the name of *the bloody way.* The monks however have restricted this name, or rather that of the " Valley of Abdonim" (blood), to a small round, grassy valley, which they have fixed upon as the place where the supposed facts of this parable took place. That the region is well suited for a scene of robbery and murder will appear by the following, from Mr, Buckingham :

" The whole of this road from Jerusalem to Jericho is held to be the most dangerous about Palestine ; and, indeed, in this portion of it, the very aspect of the scenery is sufficient, on the one hand, to tempt to robbery and murder, and, on the other, to occasion a dread of it in those who pass that way. It was partly to prevent any accident happening to us at this early stage of our journey, and partly perhaps to calm our fears on that score, that a messenger had been despatched by our guides to an encampment of their tribe near, desiring them to send an escort to meet us at this place. We were met here accordingly by a band of about twenty persons, on foot, all armed with matchlocks, and presenting the most ferocious and robber-like appearance that could be imagined. The effect of this was heightened by the shouts which they sent forth from hill to hill, and which were re-echoed through all the valleys ; while the bold projecting crags of rock, and the dark shadows in which everything was buried below, the towering height of the cliffs above, and the forbidding desolation which everywhere reigned around, presented a picture that was quite in harmony throughout all its parts. It made us feel most forcibly the propriety of its being chosen as the scene of the delightful tale of compassion which we had before so often admired for its doctrine, independently of its local beauty. In these gloomy solitudes, pillage, wounds, and death, would be accompanied with double terror from the frightful aspect of everything around. Here the unfeeling act of passing by a fellow-creature in distress, as the priest and Levite are said to have done, strikes one with horror, as an act almost more than inhuman. And here, too, the compassion of the Good Samaritan is doubly virtuous, from the purity of the motive which must have led to it, in a spot where no eyes were fixed on him to draw forth the performance of any duty, and from the courage which was necessary to admit of a man's exposing himself, by such delay, to the risk of a similar fate to that from which he was endeavoring to rescue a fellow-creature."

If space allowed, we should also be glad to transcribe the account which Sir F. Henniker gives of his

upon by thieves, who not only rifled him of his clothes and money, but so dangerously wounded him, that they left him almost expiring on the ground. By chance a priest came that way, and saw the poor wretch weltering in his blood: but the sight did not affect him, he passed along unconcerned. Next came a Levite, as void of tenderness and humanity as the priest. At last the groans of the poor wretch stirred up the curiosity of a Samaritan to see the cause, which he no sooner discovered, but, moved with compassion, he went to him, raised his head, recalled his fainting spirits, and closed his gaping wounds with healing balsams; then mounting him on his own beast he gently conveyed the man to the first inn, where at his own cost he entertained him while he stayed with him, and at his departure promised the host to be at whatever further expense should be incurred." Our blessed Saviour applying this parable to the lawyer, asked him which he thought was neighbor to the poor traveller. The lawyer replied, "Undoubtedly he that was kind, and careful of him." Then says he to the lawyer, "Go thou and do likewise." Hereby plainly intimating, that no distance of country or religion destroyed the true notion of neighborhood, but every person with whom we converse in peace and charity is that neighbor, whom we are to love as ourselves.

Two sisters, Martha and Mary, who make a considerable figure in the sacred history, now present themselves to our notice. While, at a certain time, Jesus was entertained at the house of these pious women, Mary took her seat at the feet of the divine teacher, in order to receive instruction; while Martha, suffering herself to be over-anxious in making provision, complained of her sister's neglect, in not rendering her assistance. It was on this occasion that Christ gave to Martha that memorable admonition, so worthy of attention from the human family in general: "Martha, Martha, thou art careful and troubled about many things. But *one* thing is needful. And Mary hath chosen that good part which shall not be taken away from her."

A great part of the gospel records, which yet remain to be noticed, consist in a detail of the discourses delivered by Christ to his disciples, together with reproofs to the hypocritical scribes and Pharisees, and a number of interesting parables. A brief notice of the most remarkable of these objects, as we pass on, is all that the limits of our history will allow.

In answer to the request of his disciples, we find our Lord giving them instructions on the subject of prayer, and encouraging them to the exercise of this sacred privilege. When a certain Pharisee, with whom Jesus dined, found fault because he did not use the ceremony of the elders, by first washing, he took occasion to expose the vain pretences and hypocrisy of these people, who, while they were superstitiously nice in small matters, passed over judgment and the love of God: and warning his disciples against such principles, he exhorted them not to fear the displeasure of man, but to stand in awe of him who has power to cast into hell, as well as to kill the body.

Occurrences which, in a religious light, might appear unimportant, afforded occasion to this heavenly teacher, for the most important religious instruction. Thus, when one of the company desired him to interfere in the settlement of an inheritance, Jesus cautioned him, as well as the congregation in general, to "beware of covetousness;" and, in an impressive parable, represented the folly and final wretchedness of those who feel secure of happiness in the possession of earthly plenty, and are disposed to "eat, drink, and be merry," while they are "not rich toward God."

Our Lord was now, it seems, on another circuit through Galilee; where, in one of the synagogues, he released from her affliction, a woman who had been bowed together with her infirmity for eighteen years; after which, we are informed of his returning toward Jerusalem, teaching in the different cities and villages on the way.

Being at the table of one of the Pharisees, in the course of this journey, Jesus improved the season by the parable of the *Wedding Supper;* setting forth, under figures, the rich provision of the gospel, and representing the various success of his ministers in delivering the gracious invitation to sinners. On leaving the house, multitudes followed him; and the publicans and sinners drawing near to hear him, the self-righteous scribes and Pharisees murmured at his condescension to these people. Our Lord defended his conduct on this occasion, in three parables, the last of which,

---

being stripped naked by the Arabs, and left severely wounded, on this road, in the year 1820. As this traveller states, a similar circumstance happened to the monk Brocard (not indeed two hundred years ago, as he says, but) toward the end of the thirteenth century. Many other testimonies might be collected of the dangerous character of the road from Jerusalem to Jericho.

called the parable of *the Prodigal Son*, is so very interesting and important, that we must not omit a brief sketch of its contents.

A certain man is represented as having two sons; the younger of whom, having received his portion, went into a distant country, where he "wasted his substance with riotous living." Reduced by poverty and famine to a state of wretchedness, he became a keeper of swine, to a citizen of that country; but happily, in this situation, "he came to himself," and took the resolution to try once more the kindness of a father. Accordingly, he returned, with an humble and penitent confession, to his injured parent, who received him with joy and feasting, while the elder brother, murmuring at his reception, refused to unite in the pleasure and festivity of the day.

This parable, which seems evidently to represent, in the person of the younger brother, the publicans and sinners, and in that of the elder, the scribes and Pharisees, contains also important instruction for *us*. In the younger brother we may see the sad fruits of sin and dissipation, both in a temporal and spiritual point of view, as well as the happy result of a return to God; while the disposition and conduct of the elder, still serve to mark the character of the self-righteous, wherever they are found.

The parable of the unjust steward, which follows that of the prodigal, is intended to admonish us, so to use the possessions of this world (called "the mammon of unrighteousness") as to secure the friendship of the distressed, especially among the friends of Christ; in other words, to use these worldly things to the glory of God and the good of men. And in the next parable which comes under our notice, two characters are represented, in their different states, both in this world and in that beyond the grave.

This is the parable of the rich man and Lazarus the beggar: the former living in splendor and plenty, but forgetful of God and religion; the latter lying, an afflicted outcast, at the rich man's gate, but blessed with the favor of Heaven. Such was the state of things in this world; but greatly was it reversed in the other! The beggar dying, "was carried by the angels into Abraham's bosom," while, in hell, the rich man lifting up his eyes in torment, saw the blessedness of the once-afflicted Lazarus.

After just mentioning the healing of the ten men who were diseased with leprosy; the parable of the importunate widow, which was designed to encourage us to perseverance in prayer; and that of the Pharisee and publican, showing the contrast between proud self-righteousness and humble penitence,—we hasten on to the feast of the dedication, at Jerusalem, where we find our Lord restoring to sight a man who had been blind from his birth.

This miracle, though attested in the clearest manner, had no effect toward removing the prejudice and enmity of the Pharisees. It was wrought on the sabbath day, and this, in their esteem, afforded some pretext for opposition. They accused Jesus of profaning the sabbath, and cast the man (who had now become his disciple) out of the synagogue. This opposition became still more violent, when Christ, in a discourse held with the Jews, in the porch of the temple, declared, "I and my Father are one." They even took up stones to stone him; "but he escaped out of their hands, and went again beyond Jordan," where many resorted to him, and believed on him.

We must not omit to mention here, among other instances of his goodness, the gracious regard shown to helpless infancy, by the Redeemer; who, when some persons present brought young children to him, that they might share in his favor, "took them up in his arms, put his hands upon them, and blessed them." Then, departing thence, he went on to some other place which he had designed to visit.

In the way, he was accosted by a young ruler, who, in an earnest manner, desired to know what he should do to inherit eternal life. The result of the conversation showed, that this amiable youth, with all his morality, was incapable of renouncing the world for Christ, and Jesus improved the serious occasion, by delivering a general caution against setting the heart on the perishing riches of this world; assuring his disciples, that those who had forsaken all for him, should, in some sense, be great gainers, even in *this* life; and that in the world to come, they should have life everlasting.

The next event to which we shall here pay attention, is the resurrection of Lazarus. This man was the brother of Martha and Mary, who have been already introduced to our notice. Of this little family (who resided in the town of Bethany), it is testified, that they were all beloved of Jesus. Yet Lazarus, though loved of his

Jerusalem, with its walls. A north-west view.

Lord, was sick, and eventually died of his illness. In the meantime a message from the two sisters had reached the Saviour, mentioning the sickness of his friend; but continuing some time where he was, he did not reach the house of mourning till four days after the death and burial of Lazarus.

This circumstance, however, offered no difficulty to him who was "the Resurrection and the Life." Accompanied by a train of mourners, and the sisters of the deceased, with whom he wept on this occasion, he came to the sepulchre; and the stone which covered the mouth being removed, Jesus, after addressing his heavenly Father, "cried with a loud voice, Lazarus, come forth!" His word was attended with life-giving power: the grave resigned its prisoner; "and he that was dead came forth," bound with grave-clothes, and his head wrapt with a napkin. "Loose him," said Christ, "and let him go."

From that day forth, the Jews, convinced of his miraculous power, but still cherishing their enmity against him, "took counsel together to put him to death." On this account "Jesus walked no more openly among the Jews," till the time appointed for his suffering; but went, with his disciples, into the country near the wilderness, to a city called Ephraim.

CHAPTER III.

THE passover, which now drew near, was the season appointed in the divine purpose for the death of Jesus Christ—himself the great passover, the atoning sacrifice for the sins of men. He departed, therefore, from the place of his retreat, in order to meet the fate which he well knew awaited him, and of which he informed his disciples in the journey to Jerusalem.*

* JERUSALEM (Northwest View).—"Beautiful for situation, the joy of the whole earth, was mount Zion." to the heart of every devout Israelite: for thither "the tribes of the Lord went up to give thanks unto the name of the Lord;" and "there" also were "set thrones of judgment, the thrones of the house of David." (Psalm xlviii. 2, cxxii. 4, 5.) Jerusalem is situated near the centre of Palestine, among the mountains, about thirty-seven miles from the Mediterranean sea, and twenty-three from the river Jordan. The most ancient name of this city was Salem (Gen. xiv. 18); and it was afterward called Jebus, from one of the sons of Canaan (Josh. xviii. 28). Being a very strong position, it resisted many attempts of the Israelites to subdue it, until at length it was reduced by David (2 Sam. v. 6-9), after which it received its present name, and was also called the city of David.

After its destruction by the Chaldæans, Jerusalem was rebuilt by the Jews on their return from the Babylonish captivity, about the year B. C. 536. They exerted themselves much, in order to restore its former splendor; and Herod the Great expended vast sums in its embellishment. At length it was taken, A. D. 71, by the Romans under Titus, who ineffectually endeavored to save its celebrated temple; the foundations of which were ploughed up by the Roman soldiers. Thus, agreeably to the predictions of the prophets, "Zion was ploughed as a field, and Jerusalem became heaps" (Jer. xxvi. 18, Mic. iii. 12); and, conformably to the prophecy of Jesus Christ, not one stone was left upon another which was not thrown down (Matt. xxiv. 2). As, however, the Jews continued to return, the emperor Hadrian planted a Roman colony there, and erected a city on part of the former site of Jerusalem, which he called Ælia Capitolina, and exerted himself to obliterate all traces both of Judaism and Christianity. But in the reign of Constantine, the first Christian emperor, it resumed its ancient name, which it has retained to the present day. Julian the apostate, who, after his father, succeeded to the throne of his uncle Constantine, endeavored to rebuild the temple; but his design (and that of the Jews whom he patronised) was frustrated, A. D. 363. An earthquake, a whirlwind, and a fiery eruption, compelled the workmen to abandon their design.

The subsequent history of Jerusalem may be narrated in few words. In A. D. 613 it was taken by Cosrhoes, king of Persia, who slew ninety thousand of the inhabitants; and, to the utmost of his power, demolished whatever the Christians had venerated. In A. D. 627 the emperor Heraclius defeated Cosrhoes, and Jerusalem was recovered by the Greeks. The calif Omar, the third in succession from Mohammed, was its next conqueror; A. D. 636 he captured it from the Christians after a siege of four months; and it continued under the califs of Bagdad until A. D. 868, when it was taken by Ahmed, a Turkish sovereign of Egypt. During the space of 220 years it was subject to several masters, Turkish and Saracenic; and in 1099 it was taken by the crusaders under Godfrey of Bouillon, when the standard of the cross was triumphantly displayed upon its walls, and it again became the capital of a kingdom. The Christian monarchy of Jerusalem was of short duration.

Godfrey was succeeded by his brother Baldwin, who died in 1118. In the year 1186 Saladin, sultan of the East, captured the city, which was restored to the Latin princes by Saleh Ismael, emir of Damascus, and fifty years afterward they lost it to the sultans of Egypt, who held it until 1382. Selim the Turkish sultan, reduced Egypt and Syria, including Jerusalem, in 1517; and it still continues under the Turkish dominion, "trodden down of the Gentiles," in literal fulfilment of our Lord's prediction.

Our engraving (page 495) exhibits a general view of Jerusalem with the walls. This city occupies an irregular square between two miles and a half and three miles in circumference. The walls by which it is surrounded are flanked, at irregular distances, by square towers, and have battlements all around on their summits, with loop-holes for arrows or musketry close to the top. The walls appear to be about fifty feet in height, but are not surrounded by a ditch: within them are seen crowded dwellings, remarkable in no respect, except being terraced by flat roofs, and generally built of stone. The large building, with a cupola toward the left, is the mosque of Omar, the most elegant edifice of the Turks in Jerusalem. It occupies the site of the great temple of Solomon, and is held in such profound veneration by the Mussulmans, as

On leaving Jericho, where they called on the way, Jesus was addressed by two blind men (one of whom was known by the name of Bartimeus, the son of Timeus), who cried out to him, "Jesus, thou son of David, have mercy on us!" The compassionate Saviour restored their sight, and they followed him with thankful hearts, glorying God.

In the crowd which gathered around Jesus, in passing through Jericho, was a man by the name of Zaccheus, a chief man among the publicans, and rich. Being low of stature, he ran before the multitude, and climbed a sycamore-tree, in order to have a sight of this great prophet. He was not, however, concealed from the eye of Christ, who called him down from the tree, and graciously declared, that salvation had come to his house; while Zaccheus, under a divine influence, professed his intention to give half his goods to the poor, and his readiness to restore fourfold to any person who might have been defrauded by his dealings.

Six days before the passover, Jesus came to Bethany,* where, being at supper in the house of Martha, with his disciples and Lazarus, Mary expressed her holy affection by pouring on his head an alabaster-box of precious ointment, anointing his feet also, and wiping them with her hair; and this act Jesus declared, was the anointing of his body to his approaching burial.

Having come to the mount of Olives, he sent two of his disciples to procure a colt (the foal of an ass) on which, though never before ridden by man, he made his entry into the city of Jerusalem; thus fulfilling a prophecy respecting the Messiah, in Zech. ix. 9. In the meantime, the multitude that surrounded him spread their garments in the way, and cutting branches from the trees, strewed them in the road, according to the usual custom of expressing joy, on the arrival of a great prince. Many also from Jerusalem met him with branches of palm-trees; while all his disciples and followers united in crying, "Hosanna to the Son of David!"

The heart of Jesus, however, was far from being elated with this triumph. "When he was come near, he beheld the city, and wept over it!" He saw the approaching doom of this devoted place, when God, in righteous indignation, would give it up to the power of the Roman armies; and, in a prophecy directed to the city, he foretold that doom.

Having entered into the temple, and again expelled the profane rabble of traders and money-changers, who, it seems, had resumed their seats,† he healed the blind

to have become forbidden ground to any Jew or Christian, who, if detected entering its precincts, must either adopt the Mussulman faith or forfeit his life. Two modern travellers, however (the late Mr. Burckhardt, and M. Badhia under the assumed name of Ali Bey), succeeded in obtaining a view of the interior of this building, in the garb of Moslems; and subsequently it was visited and examined in detail, four several times, by Dr. Richardson, whose skill as a physician had procured for him that extraordinary privilege. The elevated platform or terrace upon which it stands is bounded by embankment-walls, and others of ancient construction, forming a level area of 795 feet in length by 750 feet in breath. The two low cupolas toward the right of our plate indicate the church of the Holy Sepulchre, of the interior of which a view has been given at page 503. It is erected on the site of the magnificent ancient church which was destroyed by fire some years ago: it has been rebuilt by various sects of Christians, who have separate portions of the building allotted to them for the performance of their respective services. The general plan of the former building is stated to have been preserved with such exactness, that the descriptions of it given by former travellers are equally applicable to the modern edifice. The Greek, Armenian, and Latin Christians, severally have their convents: the principal is that of Saint Salvador, which is occupied by monks of the Franciscan order, who hospitably entertain pilgrims of all Christian nations. It will accommodate about two hundred persons, and is so completely enclosed by lofty walls as to resemble a fortress.

The population, ordinarily resident in Jerusalem, may be stated at 12,000; but it is considerably increased by the pilgrims who flock thither at certain seasons of the year, particularly at Easter, when they are crowded into the several convents.

* BETHANY, as we are informed (John xi. 18), was "nigh unto Jerusalem, about fifteen furlongs off." The place is not mentioned, at least under this name, in the Old Testament; but it occurs several times in the Talmudical writings. It is situated to the east of the Mount of Olives, on the road to Jericho. Its situation is pleasant and somewhat romantic, being sheltered by the Mount of Olives on the north, and abounding with trees and long grass. It is now a poor village, inhabited by Arabs; and the cultivation of the adjacent soil is much neglected. It seems, however, about our Saviour's time to have enjoyed some kind of trade (perhaps in olives, figs, and dates, which abounded in this neighborhood), as the Jewish writers mention "the shops of Bethany," which were, as they inform us, destroyed three years before Jerusalem. Bethany is at present chiefly noticed on account of its mention in the gospels; and in consequence of which, it contains a full proportion of the sort of objects to which the attention of pilgrims is usually directed: these are the tomb of Lazarus, with the ruins of the house he is supposed to have occupied, and also the houses of his sisters, and of Simon the leper. That which is shown as the house of Lazarus is a ruin, the stones of which are very large, and of a solid and sombre cast of architecture; and which the Rev. V. Monroe ("Summer's Ramble in Syria," vol. i., p. 189) conjectures to have formed part of the convent built by Fulco, king of Jerusalem. Near these ruins is the alleged tomb of Lazarus, thus noticed by the same writer: "The exterior doorway of the tomb of Lazarus is formed artificially of stone-work; but the steep, narrow, and winding staircase which leads below, is cut in the living rock, as well as the grave itself."

† It does not appear probable, that this transaction, recorded so late in two of the evangelists, is the same with that mentioned by John, so early in the public ministry of Christ.

and the lame, who came to him there; though his wonderful works, and the shoutings of the children in the temple, crying, "Hosanna to the Son of David," sorely displeased the chief priests and scribes, who "sought to destroy him, and could not find what they might do; for all the people were very attentive to hear him."

In the course of his public exercises, Jesus having addressed his heavenly Father, praying that God would glorify his own name, a voice from heaven declared, "I have both glorified it, and will glorify it again." This voice was mistaken by some for thunder; others said an angel had spoken to him; but Jesus assured them that this voice had come, not on his account, but for their sakes, that they might profit by this divine testimony.

After many discourses and admonitions delivered to the scribes and Pharisees, who endeavored, but in vain, "to entangle him in his talk," as well as several parables, which we here pass over, we find our Lord, in a prophetic way, informing his disciples on the subject of the destruction of Jerusalem; the certainty of that calamitous event, and the circumstances which would attend it. He foretels also the spread of the gospel; represents, in the parable of the five talents, and in that of the ten virgins, the state of the visible church on earth; and closes his discourse with an account of the great day of judgment; when he, as the king, will sit upon the throne of his glory, and pass on the righteous and the wicked their final sentence.

We next take a view of our divine Saviour, preparing to eat the last passover with his disciples; while Judas Iscariot, one of the twelve apostles, makes a bargain with the chief priests and captains, to betray him into their hands. Thirty pieces of silver were the price of his master's blood; and from that time "he sought opportunity to betray him in the absence of the multitude."

At the supper of the passover, which Jesus informed his disciples was the last he should eat with them on earth, he made a declaration that one of them would betray him; and intimating to Judas that he was acquainted with his design, the traitor went out, in order to accomplish his purpose. On this memorable night, Jesus instituted what is termed the Lord's Supper; giving to his disciples the bread, in token of his body, broken for his people; and then the wine, representing his blood, shed for the remission of sins. At this passover too, our Lord gave a notable example of humble condescension, by girding himself with a towel, and washing the feet of his disciples.

Judas being now gone, Jesus entered on a long discourse fitly adapted to the situation of his disciples under the melancholy prospect of parting with their Lord. This was closed by a fervent prayer in their behalf; and then he went out with his disciples, and, crossing the Brook Kedron, entered into a garden called Gethsemane,* where

* OLIVE TREES NOW STANDING IN THE GARDEN OF GETHSEMANE (see engraving, p. 499).—The Garden of Gethsemane is one of those sacred places in the vicinity of Jerusalem, which is visited by every Christian pilgrim. This deeply interesting spot is situated between the foot of the Mount of Olives and the brook Kedron: it was a place frequently resorted to by Jesus Christ and his Apostles. Thither Judas proceeded, accompanied by a number of officers, to betray him; and here the Saviour endured his "agony and bloody sweat." (Luke, xxii. 39–49. Matt. xxvi. 36–56. Mark, xiv. 32–46. John, xviii. 1–12.) This garden is surrounded by a coarse low wall, of a few feet in height, and about the third part of an acre in extent. When Mr. Catherwood was here in 1834, taking the drawings for his beautiful panorama of Jerusalem, it was planted with olive, almond, and fig trees. Eight of the olive trees are so large, that they are said to have been in existence ever since the time of Jesus Christ. Although we are informed by Josephus that Titus cut down all the trees within one hundred furlongs of the city; yet it is not improbable that these trees (which are unquestionably of very remote antiquity) may have arisen from the roots of the ancient trees; because the olive is very long-lived, and possesses the peculiar property of shooting up again, however frequently it may be cut down. The trees, now standing in the Garden of Gethsemane, are of the species known to botanists as the *Olea Europæa*: they are wild olives, and appear pollarded from extreme age, and their stems are very rough and knarled: they are highly venerated by the members of the Roman communion here, who consider any attempt to cut or injure them as an act of profanation. Should any one of them, indeed, be known to pluck any of the leaves, he would incur a sentence of excommunication. Of the stones of the olives, beads are made, which the monks of the Latin convent regard as one of the most sacred objects that can be presented to a Christian traveller.

At the upper end of the garden is a naked ledge of rock, where Peter, James, and John, are said to have slept during the Redeemer's agony; and a few paces thence a grotto is shown, in which it is reported that he underwent the bitterest part of his agony, and "his sweat was as it were great drops of blood falling down to the ground." (Luke, xxii. 44.) A small plot of ground, twelve yards long, is separated as accursed ground, being the reputed spot where Judas betrayed his master with a kiss.

The ridiculous gravity with which the precise places are shown, where the most affecting and important incidents in our Saviour's history occurred, can not entirely destroy the interest we feel, when we imagine ourselves to be near the spot where the disciples and their Lord so often met to converse about the things pertaining to his kingdom, and to receive instruction in the mysterious plan of redemption which was then opening so gloriously upon a ruined world.

The prospect from the Garden of Gethsemane is one of the most pleasing in the vicinity of Jerusalem. The walls of the city are very distinctly seen hence, at the extreme edge of a precipitous bank.

Olive Trees standing in the Garden of Gethsemane.

he had often before retired. Here he gave his disciples notice of his being about to be taken, even on that night, when they would all be scattered from him, as sheep when the shepherd is smitten (Zech. xiii. 7).

This declaration roused the zeal of Peter, who, too full of confidence, avowed his determination never to forsake his master; but Christ assured him, that before the cock should crow twice on that night, Peter would thrice deny that he knew him. The event, as we shall see, proved the knowledge which Jesus had of Peter's weakness, and served as a warning to him ever afterward.

And now, taking with him three of his disciples, Peter, James, and John, and retiring from the rest, Jesus began to feel that severe anguish of mind, which was the consequence of his taking our sins, and standing in the place of transgressors. Nor was this all. Having withdrawn a small distance from the three disciples, he fell on his face in prayer, and being in an agony, "his sweat was as it were great drops of blood falling down to the ground." In this conflict of soul, there appeared an angel from heaven, strengthening him; after which he returned and joined the company of his disciples.

In the meantime, Judas, with a band of armed men, approached, with lanterns and torches; and giving them the appointed token, by kissing his master, they took hold on the unresisting Jesus, and having bound him, they led him away to Caiaphas, the high-priest. After a mock trial before the Jewish council—where he suffered the most shameful treatment—he was pronounced worthy of death; but, as the Jews had not now the power of life and death in their hands, he was sent to Pontius Pilate, the Roman governor, in order that this sentence might be confirmed.

We must not, however, omit to take notice of Peter, while his master stood arraigned before the council. While all the other disciples, except John, had fled, Peter, following at a distance, obtained admittance into the palace of the high-priest. Here he was three times charged, by some present, with being a disciple of Jesus, and three times he denied the charge. But when, on the third denial, the cock crew a second time, "Jesus turned and looked on Peter." His heart was immediately smitten; he remembered his Lord's prediction, and "he went out and wept bitterly."

In the case of Peter there was hope; but in that of Judas there was none. When the traitor saw that his master was condemned, his guilty soul was stung with remorse; "he brought again the thirty pieces of silver to the chief priests and elders," and declaring that he had "betrayed the innocent blood," he cast them down in the temple, and departing in despair, went and hanged himself.

———

CHAPTER IV.

From the bar of Pilate, Jesus was passed to Herod, the tetrarch of Galilee—who happened at that time to be in Jerusalem—and from Herod he was returned to Pilate. His trial then proceeded; and, notwithstanding the persuasion of the governor that Jesus was innocent, the voice of the multitude and of the chief priests prevailed; and Pilate, having scourged him, delivered him up to their fury. The most cruel indignities followed. They crowned him with thorns, mocked him, spit upon him, smote him on the head, and ultimately led him away to be crucified.

Pilate had, indeed, shown a desire to deliver Christ from the sentence of condemnation, and, as it was the custom at the passover, to release a prisoner, he proposed him as the object of favor on this occasion; but such was the malice of his enemies, that they cried out for the death of Jesus, and for the release of Barabbas, who was a murderer and a robber; and such was the time-serving spirit of Pilate, that he could not resist the wishes of the multitude.

The place of execution was called Calvary, a little without the city of Jerusalem; and thither Jesus was conducted, bearing his cross. It was the third hour of the day (or nine o'clock in the morning) when, arriving at the place, they crucified Jesus Christ, nailing his hands and feet to the cross, and raising him up between the heavens and the earth; while, full of divine compassion on his murderers, he prayed, "Father,

Through the trees, the bridge over the Kedron is clearly perceptible; and the Turkish burial-ground is a marked point, from the tombs being mostly white, with turbans on the top, to indicate the Moslem faith of the individuals whose remains are there interred.

forgive them, for they know not what they do!" At the same time, also, they crucified two thieves—who had been brought along with Jesus—the one on his right hand, and the other on his left.

The cross of Christ is one of the most interesting objects which can be presented to the Christian reader. An eminent divine says of it: "Let it be to the Jews a scandal, or offensive to their fancy, prepossessed with expectations of a Messiah flourishing in secular pomp and prosperity; let it be folly to the Greeks, or seem absurd to men puffed up and corrupted in mind, with fleshly notions and maxims of worldly craft, disposing them to value nothing which is not grateful to present sense or fancy, that God should put his own beloved Son into so very sad and despicable a condition; that salvation from death and misery should be procured by so miserable a death; that eternal joy, glory, and happiness, should issue from these fountains of sorrow and shame; that a person in external semblance devoted to so opprobrious usage should be the Lord and Redeemer of mankind, the King and Judge of all the world; let, I say, this doctrine be scandalous and disdainful to some persons tainted with prejudice; let it be strange and incredible to others blinded with self-conceit; let all the inconsiderate, all the proud, all the profane part of mankind, openly with their mouth, or closely in heart, slight and reject it: yet to us it must appear grateful and joyous; to us it is a faithful and most credible proposition, worthy of all acceptation, that Jesus Christ came into the world to save sinners, in this way of suffering for them." In such a light as this must every true Christian look upon the cross of his blessed Redeemer.

The cruel mode of punishment by crucifixion appears to have been in use from the earliest recorded period of history. Possibly it was the invention of some barbarous tribe to prevent the escape of a captive, by fastening him to a tree; or used to inflict death on an enemy, by leaving him exposed upon a tree, to be a prey to birds and beasts, or to die of hunger. In time, however, it was adopted by the most civilized nations of antiquity. Among the Carthaginians, persons of all ranks, even commanders of armies, were subject to it: among the Romans, however, it was considered as the punishment of slaves, and inflicted on that class only. With reference to the Hebrews, it seems doubtful whether crucifixion was a mode of punishment practised by them in ancient times. The putting the sons of Saul to death, as recorded 2 Sam. xxi., has been adduced as an argument that it was; and the term "hanged on a tree," which is used, Acts x. 39, to describe crucifixion, seems to favor such a view.

Whatever the original form of crosses may have been, we can not tell; but in the course of time they were made of two pieces of wood, and they have been divided by antiquaries into three kinds: 1, the *crux decussata*, or cross divided like the letter X, and usually called St. Andrew's cross; 2, the *crux commissa*, or joined cross, consisting of an upright piece of timber, with a transverse piece on the extreme top, at right angles with the first, like the letter T; and 3, the *crux immissa*, or let-in cross, in which the transverse piece of timber is let into the upright, but placed somewhat below the top of the upright, in this form †. It is the latter cross on which our Saviour is usually represented to have suffered, and though there may not be any absolute authority for ascertaining the precise form of the cross used on this occasion, yet the circumstance of an inscription being placed over his sacred head renders the conjecture probable.

It is said by St. John, (xix. 17), that Jesus went forth "bearing his cross." Accordingly, we find painters representing our Saviour bearing the entire cross on which he suffered. This, however, if we take into consideration the great weight the cross is thought to have been, from its size, and from its being made of the hardest wood, generally of oak, could scarcely be possible; and painters themselves have also been practically sensible of this; for the same painter who represents Christ bearing his cross, gives a representation of one shorter and more portable, than that which he exhibits in a painting of the crucifixion. But this, some imagine, may be correct. They think that the cross which our Saviour carried was a representation of the cross of actual crucifixion; and that it was usual for prisoners to bear such, to suggest to the people in the streets through which they were conducted the kind of punishment they were about to undergo. Lipsius, on the contrary, explains that the heaviest part of the cross, the perpendicular beam, was either fixed in the ground before, or was ready to be set up when the condemned person arrived; and he contends, that the

32

part which the prisoner carried was the large cross-beam to which the arms of the crucified were fastened. There are others, again, who think that the crosses of the ancients were not so lofty, large, and massive, as those depicted by painters; and certainly instruments of such dimensions would be unnecessary for the purpose. *Pone crucem servo*, "Put the cross to the slave," is an expression used by Juvenal. It is probable, therefore, that it was the real cross which our Saviour carried, and that he was nailed to it before it was raised and fixed in the ground; which is in accordance with the general opinion.

The manner in which this was done has been thus graphically described: "When the malefactor had carried his cross to the place of execution, a hole was dug in the earth in which it was to be fixed; the criminal was stripped; a stupefying potion was given him; the cross was laid on the ground; he was distended upon it, and four soldiers, two on each side, at the same time were employed in driving four large nails through his hands and feet. After they had deeply fixed and riveted these nails in the wood, they elevated the cross with the sufferer upon it; and in order to infix it the more firmly and securely in the earth, they let it violently fall into the cavity they had prepared to receive it. This vehement precipitation of the cross must have occasioned a most dreadful convulsive shock, and agitated the whole frame of the malefactor in a dire and most excruciating manner. These several particulars were observed in the crucifixion of our Lord. Upon his arrival at Calvary, he was stripped; the medicated cup was offered to him; he was fastened to the cross; and while they were employed in piercing his hands and his feet, it is probable that he offered to Heaven that most benevolent and affecting prayer for his murderers, 'Father, forgive them, for they know not what they do.'"

Of whatever size the cross on which our Redeemer paid the penalty of our transgressions might have been, we learn from St. Mark that it was of great weight. He intimates to us, in a parallel passage to that of St. John, that the soldiers, finding that Jesus, exhausted by his sufferings, was no longer able to bear his cross, laid hold of one Simon, a Cyrenian, who happened to be passing, and compelled him to bear it for the sufferer (Mark xv. 21). The practice of a prisoner bearing his own cross, at least among the Romans, very probably arose from the deep disgust and horror with which they looked upon this instrument of punishment; the prisoner, accordingly, was condemned to bear his own instrument of torture.

Previous to crucifixion, it was the custom to scourge the sufferer, after which he was stripped naked; and it is probable, as we have seen, that he was laid down on the cross for the purpose of having the nails driven into his hands and feet; or, as was sometimes the case, of being fastened to the cross with ropes. The cross was then elevated, and afterward the legs were broken, and wounds were inflicted with a spear or other sharp instrument, to hasten death. But this was not invariably done; and as, in the case of its omission, death would not ensue for a length of time, guards were placed to prevent the relations and friends from giving them any relief, taking them away while alive, or removing their bodies after they were dead. Sometimes crucifixion took place with the head downward; and St. Peter is said to have suffered death in this way, at his own express desire, deeming himself unworthy to suffer in the same position with his beloved master.

In leading to his death a person condemned to crucifixion, it was usual to carry an inscription before him, stating the crime for which he suffered. To the charge of Jesus, no crime could be laid; but to his cross they fastened this inscription: "This is the King of the Jews," Luke xxiii. 38. This was written in three different languages, and the reason which has been given for this is, that none might be unapprized of its contents. It was written in Greek, which was the general language of commerce in western Asia, and which would be familiar to many Jews from Europe, Egypt, and elsewhere; it also was written in the Syriac, called "Hebrew," the vernacular language of Palestine; and it was written in Latin, probably for the use of the Romans, many of whom would assemble at Jerusalem during the paschal week.

To advert to the many passages of holy writ which point to the cross of Christ as the foundation of a sinner's hope, would extend our work beyond the assigned limits. It must suffice, therefore, to say, that it is the sum and substance of the Bible, and that, if we would be saved by it, we must look to it with an eye of faith, as eagerly

Interior of the Church of the Holy Sepulchre, at Jerusalem.

and fixedly as the Israelites of old, when bitten by the fiery serpents, looked to the brazen serpent—which prefigured the cross—erected by Moses to effect their cure. There alone is our hope of redemption.

The punishment of crucifixion, it has been said, was so common among the Romans, that, by a very usual figure, pains, afflictions, troubles, &c., were called crosses. Hence, our Saviour says, that his disciples must take up their cross, and follow him (Matt. xvi. 24). The cross, therefore, is the sign of ignominy and suffering, yet it is the badge and glory of the Christian. Christ is the way we are to follow; and there is no way of attaining that glory and happiness which are promised in the gospel, but by the cross of Christ.

While under the agonies of the cross, the Redeemer manifested his filial affection, by committing his mother to the care of the beloved John; and in the same situation, he gave a signal instance of the power and freeness of his grace, toward one of the thieves, who hung beside him. The heart of this poor creature was smitten with conviction and repentance, and, addressing a prayer to the dying Saviour, he received the soul-cheering answer, " To-day shalt thou be with me in paradise."

About the sixth hour (or middle of the day) a supernatural darkness covered the whole land, which continued till the ninth hour (or three o'clock in the afternoon), when Jesus cried with a loud voice, " Eloi, Eloi, lama, sabachthani !"—that is, " My God, my God, why hast thou forsaken me !"—thus showing that his soul was in pangs, as well as his body. After a little space, he cried again with a loud voice, and commending his spirit into the hands of his Father, " he bowed his head, and gave up the ghost."

At this awful event, the veil of the temple was rent in twain from the top to the bottom; the earth quaked, and the rocks were torn asunder; the graves, too, of many of the saints were opened, and the dead, arising, appeared to many in the city of Jerusalem. These fearful tokens gave a solemn check to the feelings of the multitude that attended, and produced on the minds of several a conviction that Jesus was the Son of God.

Thus expired this wonderful Sufferer !—a ransom for sinners, a Saviour to all who truly believe in his name. And now, as the next day was the sabbath of the Jews, as the bodies were not to remain on the cross on that day, and as they were making preparation for its approach, they petitioned Pilate that the legs of the crucified might be broken, and that they might be taken away. The soldiers, therefore, having broken the legs of the two malefactors, when they came to Jesus and found that he was already dead, forebore to perform the operation on him; but one of them, to insure his death, pierced his side with a spear, whence there issued blood and water.

When the evening was come, Joseph of Arimathea, a rich man and a counsellor, and one who " waited for the kingdom of God," having begged of Pilate the body of Jesus, took it down from the cross, and, assisted by Nicodemus, wrapped it in fine linen, with a quantity of spices, after the Jewish mode of burying. Thus prepared, they laid the sacred body in Joseph's own new tomb, which was hewn out of a rock, in a garden near at hand, and rolling a large stone to the door of the sepulchre, they departed.

At the same time, several pious women who followed Jesus from Galilee, and who from a distance had beheld the mournful scene of his sufferings, being present at his burial, and seeing how the body was deposited, " returned and prepared spices and ointments," intending after the Sabbath to visit the sepulchre for the purpose of embalming the body of their Lord. The chief priests and Pharisees, on their part, took a different course. By the authority of Pilate, they sealed the stone at the mouth of the tomb, setting around it a guard of soldiers, to prevent any attempt by the disciples of Jesus to steal him away, and thus pretend that their Master was risen.

Such was the state of things, till the commencement of the third day, being the first day of the week. Early in the morning of that day, Mary Magdalene, with Salome, and another female disciple by the name of Mary, coming to the sepulchre for the purpose (as before mentioned) of embalming the body of Christ, found the stone removed from the door. Scenes the most awful and glorious had just before been exhibited. A great earthquake shook the place; the angel of the Lord descending from heaven, rolled away the stone and sat upon it; and while the keepers, struck with terror, became as dead men, Jesus, awaking from the sleep of death, arose and left the tomb.*

His first appearance after this great event was to Mary Magdalene, who stood weeping at the sepulchre when Peter and John, who had made a visit to the place, had departed. Afterward he appeared to a company of women on their return from the sepulchre; then to two of the disciples on their way to a village called Emmaus, a few miles from Jerusalem. The reports, however, of these witnesses of the resurrection met with but little credit with the rest of the disciples, till Jesus, on the evening of the same day, presented himself among them, and confirmed their faith by appealing to his lately wounded hands and feet.

In the meantime, the affrighted guards had fled from the sepulchre and related their tale of wonder to the chief priests, who, alarmed at the consequences that might follow, hired these wretched creatures to say that the disciples came by night, and stole away the body of Jesus while they were asleep. This absurd report was accordingly propagated, and prevailed among the Jews as a fact.

It is proper we should here take notice of the case of Thomas, called Didymus, who, not being with the disciples when Jesus made his appearance among them as above mentioned, declared that he would not believe in the reality of his resurrection unless he should see and feel the print of the nails in his hands, and the effect of the wound in his side. Accordingly about eight days after, when the disciples were all together, Jesus again appearing among them presented his hands and his side to Thomas, with a reproof for his unbelief; while the astonished disciple, overpowered with conviction, exclaimed, "My Lord and my God."

"After these things, Jesus showed himself again to his disciples at the sea of Tiberias," where several of them were employed in fishing, and then, by appointment, he met the eleven apostles on a mountain in Galilee, where he delivered to them the great gospel commission, to go forth and "teach all nations, baptizing them in the name of the Father, and of the Son, and of the Holy Ghost;" pronouncing at the same time, "He that believeth, and is baptized, shall be saved; but he that believeth not shall be damned."

Forty days was the time pre-ordained for our Lord's continuance upon earth after his resurrection. These days being now almost expired, the apostles, according as they had been ordered, with some of their select friends, returned to Jerusalem, and there assembled themselves in a private place, as they had always done after the crucifixion of their Master. Here our blessed Lord appeared to them for the last time; and after instructing them in many particulars concerning the kingdom of God, and the manner in which they were to behave themselves in propagating the doctrine of the gospel, he put them in mind that, during his abode with them in Galilee, he had often told them that all things written in the law, the prophets, and the Psalms, concerning him were to be exactly accomplished. At the same time "he opened their understandings;" that is, he removed their prejudices by the operation of his Spirit, cleared their doubts, improved their memories, strengthened their judgments, and enabled them to discern the true meaning of the Scriptures. He then reminded them that both Moses and the prophets had foretold that the Messiah was to suffer in the very same manner he had suffered; that he was to rise from the dead on the third day as he had done; and that repentance and remission of sins was to

---

* THE RESURRECTION.—Twice had the sun gone down on the earth, and all as yet was quiet at the sepulchre: Death held his sceptre o'er the Son of God; still and silent the hours passed on; the guards stood by their posts; the rays of midnight moon gleamed on their helmets and on their spears; the enemies of Christ exulted in their success; the hearts of his friends were sunk in despondency and sorrow; while the spirits of glory waited with anxious suspense to behold the event—wondering at the depth of the ways of God. At length, the morning star, arising in the east, announced the approach of light: the third day began to dawn on the world, when on a sudden the earth trembled to its centre, and the powers of Heaven were shaken; an angel of God descended; the guards shrunk back from the terror of his presence, and fell prostrate on the ground. His countenance was like lightning, and his raiment was white as snow; he rolled away the stone from the door of the sepulchre, and sat on it.

But who is this that cometh from the tomb, with dyed garments from the bed of death! He that is glorious in his appearance, walking in the greatness of his strength! It is thy Prince, O Zion! Christian, it is your Lord! He hath trodden the winepress alone; he hath stained his raiment with blood; but now, as the firstborn from the womb of nature, he meets the morning of his resurrection. He arises, a conqueror from the grave; he returns with blessings from the world of spirits; he brings salvation to the sons of men. Never did the returning sun usher in a day so glorious! It was the jubilee of the universe! The morning stars sang together, and all the sons of God shouted aloud for joy! The Father of Mercies looked down from his throne in the heavens with complacency; he beheld his world restored—he saw his work, that it was good. Then did the desert rejoice; the face of nature was gladdened before him, when the blessings of the Eternal descended, as the dews of heaven, for the refreshing of the nations.

be preached in the Messiah's name among all nations, beginning with the Jews. He told them that they were to testify unto the world the exact accomplishment in him of all things foretold concerning the Messiah; and closed his instructions to them by giving them a particular charge, that they should not depart from Jerusalem until they had received that miraculous effusion of the Holy Ghost which he had promised and would shortly send down upon them. He likewise gave them to understand, that after the descent of the Holy Ghost upon them they would have juster notions of those matters, and be sufficiently enabled to be the authentic witnesses of his life and actions throughout the world.

After our blessed Lord had thus fortified his apostles for the important work they were going to undertake, he led them out of the city to that part of the mount of Olives which was nearest to Bethany. On their arrival there, he gave them some farther instructions relative to the measures they were to follow in order to propagate his gospel, after which he lifted up his hands and blessed them. While he was doing this, and his apostles were placed in an adoring posture, he was parted from them in the midst of the day, being gradually taken up in a shining cloud, and triumphantly carried into heaven, where he now sitteth at the right hand of God his Father, "to whom be honor, glory, and power, for ever and ever. Amen."

In this illustrious manner did the GREAT REDEEMER of mankind depart, after having finished the grand work about which he was sent into the world; a work which angels with joy described was to happen, and which through all eternity to come, at periods the most immensely distant from the time of its execution, will be looked back upon with inexpressible delight by every inhabitant of heaven; for though the minute affairs of time may vanish together and be lost when they are removed far back by the endless progression of duration, yet this object is such that no distance, however great, can lessen it. The kingdom of heaven is erected on the incarnation and sufferings of the Son of God, and therefore no mortal whatever can forget the foundation on which his happiness stands established; nor will any fail of obtaining a seat in those mansions, provided he preserves a proper subjection to Him who reigneth for ever and ever, and whose favor is better than life itself.

It may not be improper, in this place, to admit a few reflections on the life of the blessed Jesus—a life the greatest and best that was ever led by man, or was ever the subject of any history, since the universe was called from its original chaos by the powerful word of the Almighty.

The human character of the blessed Jesus is entirely different from that of all other men whatever; for whereas they have selfish passions deeply rooted in their breasts, and are influenced by them in almost everything they do, Jesus was so entirely free from them, that the most severe scrutiny can not furnish one single action, in the whole course of his life, wherein he consulted his own interest only. No; he was influenced by very different motives: the happiness and eternal welfare of sinners regulated his conduct; and while others followed their respective occupations, Jesus had no other business than that of promoting the happiness of the sons of men. Nor did he wait till he was solicited to extend his benevolent hand to the distressed: "he went about doing good," and always accounted it "more blessed to give than to receive;" resembling God rather than man. He went about doing good; benevolence was the very life of his soul: he not only did good to objects presented to him for relief, but he industriously sought them out, in order to extend his compassionate assistance.

It is common for persons of the most exalted faculties to be elated with success and applause, or dejected by censure and disappointments; but the blessed Jesus was not elated by the one nor depressed by the other. He was never more courageous than when he met with the greatest opposition and cruel treatment; nor more humble than when the sons of men worshipped at his feet.

He came into the world inspired with the grandest purpose that ever was formed, that of saving from eternal perdition, not a single nation, but the whole world; and in the execution of it, went through the longest and heaviest train of labors that ever was sustained, with a constancy and resolution, on which no disadvantageous impression could be made by any accident whatever. Calumny, threatenings, bad success, with many other evils constantly attending him, served only to quicken his endeavors in this glorious enterprise, which he unweariedly pursued even till he finished it by his death.

The generality of mankind are prone to retaliate injuries received, and all seem to take a satisfaction in complaining of the cruelties of those who oppress them; whereas the whole of Christ's labors breathed nothing but meekness, patience, and forgiveness, even to his bitterest enemies, and in the midst of the most excruciating torments. The words, "Father, forgive them, for they know not what they do," uttered by him when his enemies were nailing him to the cross, fitly express the temper which he maintained through the whole course of his life, even when assaulted by the heaviest provocations. He was destined to sufferings here below, in order that he might raise his people to honor, glory, and immortality, in the realms of bliss above; and therefore patiently, yea joyfully, submitted to all that the malice of earth and hell could inflict. He was vilified, that we might be honored; he died, that we might live for ever and ever.

To conclude: the greatest and best men have discovered the degeneracy and corruption of human nature, and shown themselves to have been nothing more than men; but it was otherwise with Jesus. He was superior to all the men that ever lived, both with regard to the purity of his manners, and the perfection of his virtues. He was holy, harmless, undefiled, and separated from sinners.

Whether we consider him as a teacher, or as a man, "he did no sin; neither was guile found in his mouth." His whole life was perfectly free from spot or weakness; at the same time it was remarkable for the greatest and extensive exercises of virtue. But never to have committed the least sin, in word or in deed, never to have uttered any sentiment that could be censured, upon the various topics of religion and morality, which were the daily subjects of his discourses, and that through the course of a life filled with action, and led under the observation of many enemies, who had always access to converse with him, and who often came to find fault, is a pitch of perfection evidently above the reach of human nature; and consequently he who possessed it must have been divine.

Such was the person who is the subject of the evangelical history. If the reader, by reviewing his life, doctrine, and miracles, as they are here represented to him, united in one series, has a clearer idea of these things than before, or observes a beauty in his actions thus linked together, which taken separately do not appear so fully; if he feels himself touched by the character of Jesus in general, or with any of his sermons and actions in particular, thus simply delineated in writing, whose principal charms are the beauties of truth: above all, if his dying so generously for men strikes him with admiration, or fills him with joy in the prospect of that pardon which is thereby purchased for the world: let him seriously consider with himself what improvement he ought to make of the divine goodness.

Jesus, by his death, hath set open the gates of immortality to the sons of men; and by his word, spirit, and example, graciously offers to make them meet for the glorious rewards in the kingdom of the heavenly Canaan, and to conduct them into the inheritance of the saints in light. Let us, therefore, remember, that being born under the dispensation of his gospel, we have, from our earliest years, enjoyed the best means of securing to ourselves an interest in that favor of God, which is life; and that loving-kindness, which is better than life.

We have been called to aspire after an exaltation to the felicity of the heavenly mansions exhibited to mortal eyes in the man Jesus Christ, to fire us with the noblest ambition. His gospel teaches us that we are made for eternity; and that our present life is to our future existence, as infancy is to manhood. But as in the former, many things are to be learned, many hardships to be endured, many habits to be acquired, and that by a course of exercises, which in themselves though painful, and possibly useless to the child, yet are necessary to fit him for the business and enjoyments of manhood. So while we remain in this infancy of human life, things are to be learned, hardships to be endured, and habits to be acquired, by a laborious discipline, which, however painful, must be undergone, because necessary to fit us for the employments and pleasures of our riper existence, in the realms above, always remembering that whatever our trials may be, in this world, if we ask for God's assistance, he has promised to give it. Inflamed, therefore, with the love of immortality and its joys, let us submit ourselves to our heavenly teacher, and learn of him those graces, which alone can render life pleasant, death desirable, and fill eternity with ecstatic joys.

We can not close the solemn scene of the life of our dear Lord and Saviour with greater propriety than by making a few observations on the nature of his religion, and considering the great benefits which will infallibly result to all, who shall, by faith, receive and embrace his holy doctrine.

The religion of Christ is the perfection of human nature, and the foundation of uniform, exalted pleasure: of public order, and private happiness. Christianity is the most excellent and the most useful institution, having "the promise of the life that now is, and of that which is to come." It is the voice of reason; it is also the language of scripture: "the ways of wisdom are ways of pleasantness, and all her paths are peace." And our blessed Saviour himself assures us, that his precepts are easy, and the burden of his religion light.

The Christian religion comprehends all we ought to believe, and all we ought to practise: its positive rights are few, and perfectly intelligible to every capacity; and the whole is manifestly adapted to establish in us a proper sense of the great obligations we lay under both to God and Christ.

The gospel places religion not in abtruse speculation, and metaphysical subtleties; not in outward show, and tedious ceremony; not in superstitious austerities and enthusiastic visions; but in purity of heart and holiness of life. The sum of our duty (according to our great master himself) consists in the love of God, and of our neighbor. According to St. Paul, in denying ungodliness, and worldly lusts; and in living soberly, righteously and godly in this present world. According to St. James, in visiting the fatherless and widow in affliction, and in keeping ourselves unspotted from the world. This is the constant strain and tenor of the gospel. This it inculcates most earnestly, and on this it lays the greatest stress.

It may be asked if the Christian religion is only a view of the law of nature, or merely a refined system of morality? To which we answer, that it is a great deal more than either. It is an act of grace, a stupendous plan of Providence, for the recovery of mankind from a state of degradation and ruin, to the favor of the Almighty, and to the hopes of a happy immortality through a mediator.

Under this dispensation, true religion consists in a repentance toward God, and in faith in the Lord Jesus Christ, as the person appointed by the supreme Authority of heaven and earth, to reconcile apostate man to his offended Creator. And what hardship is there in all this? Surely none. Nay, the practice of religion is much easier than the servitude of sin.

It certainly must be allowed by all that our rational powers are impaired, and the soul weakened by sin. The animal passions are strong, and apt to oppose the dictates of the spirit of God: objects of sense make powerful impressions on the mind. We are, in every situation, surrounded with many snares and temptations. In such a disordered state of things, to maintain an undeviating path of duty, can not be effected by poor weak man. There are, however, generous aids afforded us to persevere in the ways of the Lord.

The gracious author of nature has planted in the human breast a quick sense of good and evil; a faculty which strongly dictates right and wrong; and though by the strength of appetite and warmth of passion, men are often hurried into immoral practices, yet in the beginning, especially when there has been the advantage of a good education, it is usually with reluctance and opposition of mind. What inward struggles precede! What bitter pangs attend their sinful excesses! What guilty blushes and uneasy fears! What frightful prospects and pale reviews! "Terrors are upon them, and a fire not blown consumeth them." To make a mock at sin, and to commit iniquity without remorse, requires great length of time, and much painful labor; more labor than is requisite to attain that habitual goodness which is the glory of the man, the ornament of the Christian, and the chief of his happiness.

The soul can no more be reconciled to acts of wickedness and injustice, than the body to excess, but by suffering many bitter pains, and cruel attacks.

The mouth of conscience may, indeed, be stopped for a time, by false principles: its secret whispers may be drowned by the noise of company, and stifled by the entertainments of sense; but this principle of conscience is so deeply rooted in human nature, and, at the same time, her voice is so clear and strong, that the sinner's arts will be unable to lull her into a lasting security.

When the hour of calamity arrives, when sickness seizeth, and death approaches the sinner, conscience now constrains him to listen to her accusations, and will not suffer the temples of his head to take any rest. "There is no peace to the wicked;"

the foundations of peace are subverted, they are at utter enmity with their reason, with their conscience, and with their God.

Not so is the case of true religion. For when religion, pure and genuine, forms the tempers, and governs the life, conscience applauds, and peace takes his residence in the breast. The soul is in its proper state. There is order and regularity both in the faculties and actions. Conscious of its own integrity, and secure of divine approbation, the soul enjoys a calmness not to be described. But why do we call this happy frame calmness only? It is far more than mere calmness. The air may be calm, and the day overcast with thick mists and clouds. The pious and virtuous mind resembles a serene day, enlightened and enlivened with the brightest rays of the sun. Though all without may be clouds and darkness, there is light in the heart of a pious man. "He is satisfied from himself, and is filled with peace and joy in believing." In the concluding scene (the awful moment of dissolution) all is peaceful and serene. The immortal part quits its tenement of clay, with the well-grounded hopes of ascending to happiness and glory.

Nor does the gospel enjoin any duty but what is fit and reasonable. It calls upon all its professors to practise reverence, submission, and gratitude to God; justice, truth, and universal benevolence to men: and to maintain the government of our own minds. And what has any one to object against this? From the least to the greatest commandment of our dear Redeemer, there is not one which impartial reason can find fault with. "His law is perfect; his precepts are true and righteous, altogether." Not even those excepted, which require us to love our enemies, to deny ourselves, and to take up our cross. To forgive an injury is more generous and manly than to revenge it; to control a licentious appetite than to indulge it; to suffer poverty, reproach, and even death itself, in the sacred cause of truth and integrity, is much wiser and better, than, by base compliances, to make shipwreck of faith and a good conscience.

Thus in a storm at sea, or a conflagration on the land, a man with pleasure abandons his lumber to secure his jewels. Piety and virtue are the wisest and most reasonable things in the world; vice and wickedness the most irrational and absurd.

The all-wise Author of our being hath so framed our natures, and placed us in such relations, that there is nothing vicious but what is injurious; nothing virtuous but what is advantageous to our present interest, both with respect to body and mind. Meekness and humility, patience and universal charity, and grace, give a joy unknown to transgressors.

The divine virtues of truth and equity are the only bands of friendship, the only supports of society: Temperance and sobriety are the best preservatives of health and strength; but sin and debauchery impair the body, consume the substance, reduce us to poverty, and form the direct path to an immature and untimely death.

To render our duty easy, we have the example, as well as the commands, of the blessed Jesus. The masters of morality among the heathens gave excellent rules for the regulation of men's manners; but they wanted either the honesty, or the courage to try their own arguments upon themselves. It was a strong presumption that the yoke of the scribes and Pharisees was grievous, when they laid " heavy burdens upon men's shoulders," which they themselves refused to touch with one of their fingers. Not thus our great law-giver, Jesus Christ the righteous. His behavior was in all respects conformable to his doctrine. His devotion toward God, how sublime and ardent!—benevolence toward men, how great and diffusive! He was in his life an exact pattern of innocence; for he "did no sin; neither was guile found in his mouth." In the Son of God incarnate is exhibited the brightest, the fairest resemblance of the Father, that heaven and earth ever beheld, an example peculiarly persuasive, calculated to inspire resolution, and to animate us to use our utmost endeavors to imitate the divine pattern, the example of "the Author and Finisher of our faith," of him "who loved us and gave himself for us." Our profession and character as Christians oblige us to make this example the model of our lives. Every motive of decency, gratitude, and interest, constrain us to tread the paths he trod before us.

We should also remember that our burden is easy; because God, who " knoweth whereof we are made, who considereth that we are but dust," is ever ready to assist us. The heathens themselves had some notion of this assistance, though guided only by the glimmering lamp of reason. But what they looked upon as probable, the gospel clearly and strongly asserts. We there hear the apostle exhorting, "Let us come boldly to the throne of grace, that we may obtain mercy, and find grace to help in time of need." We there hear the blessed Jesus himself arguing in this convincing manner: "If ye, being evil, know how to give good gifts unto your children, how much more shall your heavenly Father give the holy spirit to them that ask him ?"

We would not here be understood to mean, that the agency of the spirit is irresistible, and lays a necessitating bias on all the faculties and affections. Were this the case, precepts and prohibitions, promises and threatenings, would signify nothing; and duty and obligation would be words without a meaning. The spirit assisteth in a manner agreeable to the frame of human nature; not controlling the free use of reason, but by assisting the understanding, influencing the will, and moderating the affections. But though we may not be able to explain the mode of his operations, the Scriptures warrant us to assert, that when men are renewed and prepared for heaven, it is "through sanctification of the spirit," and "belief of the truth." How enlivening the thought!—how encouraging the motive! We are not left to struggle alone with the difficulties which attend the practice of virtue, in the present imperfect state. The merciful Father of our spirit is ever near to help our infirmities, to enlighten the understanding, to strengthen good resolutions, and, in concurrence with our own endeavors, to make us conquerors over all opposition. Faithful is he to his promises, and will not suffer the sincere and well disposed to be tempted above what they are able to bear. What can be desired more than this ? To promote the happiness of his people, everything is done that is requisite, his grace is all-sufficient, his spirit is able to conduct us through this vale of tears, to never-fading bliss.

We should also remember, that the great doctrine of the gospel, concerning the propitious mercy of God to all penitents, through Christ Jesus, greatly contributes to the consolation of Christians. Let it be granted, that the hope of pardon is essential to the religion of fallen creatures, and one of its first principles, yet, considering the doubts and suspicions which are apt to arise in a mind conscious of guilt, it is undoubtedly a great and inestimable favor, to be relieved in this respect, by the interposition of Divine assistance. This is our happiness. We are fully assured, that upon our true repentance, we shall, "through the mediation of Christ," receive the "full remission of sins," and be restored to the same state and favor with our Maker, as if we had never transgressed his laws. Here the gospel triumphs. With these assurances it abounds. Upon this head the declaration of our blessed Saviour and his apostles are so express and full, that every one who believes them, and knows himself to be a true penitent, must banish every doubt and fear, and rejoice with joy unspeakable. "Come unto me all ye that labor, and are heavy-laden, and I will give you rest" (Matt. xi. 28). "All manner of sin and blasphemy shall be forgiven unto men" (Matt. xii. 31). "Be it known unto you therefore men and brethren, that through this man is preached unto you the forgiveness of sins; and by him all that believe are justified from all things, from which we could not be justified by the law of Moses." (Acts xiii. 38, 39.) What grace and favor is this! Who can dwell upon the transporting theme too long! Now our way is plain before us, and the burden we are to bear is made comfortably easy. No sins are unpardonable, if repented and forsaken.

Consider this, all ye who have never yet regarded religion, but pursued a course of vice and sensuality all your lives long. Though your conduct has been base to the last degree, your case is not desperate. Far from it. The God whom you have so highly offended commiserates your errors, is ever ready to extend his pardoning mercy to his most degenerate creatures, upon their faith and repentance, and " is in Christ Jesus reconciling the world to himself, not imputing unto [penitent] sinners their trespasses. Let the wicked [therefore] forsake his way, and the unrighteous man his thoughts; and let him return unto the ·Lord, and he will have mercy upon him ; and to our God, for he will abundantly pardon." (Isaiah lv. 7.)

Another particular, which renders the Christian religion delightful is, its leading us to the perfect, eternal life of heaven. It can not be denied but that we may draw from the light of nature strong presumptions of a future state. The present existence does not look like an entire scene, but rather like the infancy of human nature, which is capable of arriving at a much higher degree of maturity; but whatever solid foundation the doctrine of a future state may have had, in nature and reason, certain it is, through the habitual neglect of reflection, and the force of irregular passions, this doctrine was, before the coming of our blessed Saviour, very much disfigured, and in a great measure lost, among the sons of men.

In the heathen world, a future state of rewards and punishments was a matter of mere speculation and uncertainty, sometimes hoped for, sometimes doubted of, and sometimes absolutely denied. The law of Moses, though of divine original, is chiefly enforced by promises of temporal blessings; and, even in the writings of the prophets, a future immortality is very sparingly mentioned, and obscurely represented, but the doctrine of our Saviour hath "brought life and immortality to light." In the gospel we have a distinct account of another world, attended with many engaging circumstances; about which the decisions of reason were dark and confused. We have the testimony of the Author of our religion, who was raised from the dead, and who afterward, in the presence of his disciples, ascended into heaven. In the New Testament it is expressly declared, that good men, "when absent from the body, are present with the Lord." Here we are assured of the resurrection of the body in a glorious form, clothed with immortal vigor, suited to the active nature of the animating spirit, and assisting its most enlarged operations and incessant progress toward perfection. Here we are assured that "the righteous shall go into life everlasting," that they shall enter into the heavenly Canaan, where no ignorance shall cloud the understanding, no vice disturb the will. In these regions of perfection, nothing but love shall possess the soul; nothing but gratitude employ the tongue; there the righteous shall be united to an innumerable company of angels, and to the general assembly and church of the first-born. There they shall see their exalted Redeemer, at the right-hand of Omnipotence, and sit down with him on his throne; there they shall be admitted into the immediate presence of the supreme Fountain of life and happiness, and, beholding his face, be changed into the same image, from glory to glory.

Here language—here imagination fails us! It requires the genius, the knowledge, the pen of an angel, to paint the happiness, the blissful scene of the New Jerusalem, which human eyes can not behold, till this mortal body shall be purified from its corruption, and dressed in the robes of immortality: "Eye hath not seen, nor ear heard, neither hath it entered into the heart to conceive, the joys which God hath prepared for them that love him."

What is the heaven of the heathens when compared with the heaven of the Christians? The hope, the prospect of this, is sufficient to reconcile us to all the difficulties that may attend our progress, sweeten all our labors, alleviate every grief, and silence every murmur.

But why, says the libertine in the gayety of his heart, should there be any difficulties, or restraint, at all? God hath made nothing in vain. The appetites he hath planted in the human breast are to be gratified. To deny or restrain them, is ignominious bondage; but to give full scope to every desire and passion of the heart, without check or control, is true manly freedom.

In opposition to this loose and careless way of reasoning, let it be considered, that the liberty of a rational creature doth not consist in an entire exemption from all control, but in following the dictates of reason, as the governing principle, and in keeping the various passions in due subordination. To follow the regular notion of those affections which the wise Creator hath implanted within us, is our duty; but as our natural desires, in this state of trial, are often irregular, we are bound to restrain their excesses, and not indulge them, but in a strict subserviency to the integrity and peace of our minds, and to the order and happiness of human society established in the world. Those who allow the supreme command to be usurped by sensual and brutal appetites, may "promise themselves liberties," but are truly and absolutely the "servants of corruption." To be vicious, is to be enslaved. We behold with pity those miserable objects that are chained in the galleys, or confined in dark prisons and loathsome dungeons; but how much more abject and vile is the slavery of the sinner! No slavery of the body is equal to the bondage of the mind; no chains press so closely, or gall so cruelly, as the fetters of sin, which corrode the very substance of the soul, and fret every faculty.

It must, indeed, be confessed, that there are some profligates, so hardened by customs, as to be past all feeling; and, because insensible of their bondage, boast of this insensibility as a mark of their native freedom, and of their happiness.

Vain men! They might extol with equal propriety the peculiar happiness of an apoplexy, or the profound tranquillity of a lethargy.

Thus have we endeavored to place, in a plain and conspicuous light, some of the peculiar excellences of the Christian religion; and hence many useful reflections will naturally arise in the mind of every attentive reader. It is the religion of Jesus that hath removed idolatry and superstition, and brought immortality to light, when concealed under a veil of darkness almost impenetrable. This hath set the great truths of religion in a clear and conspicuous point of view, and proposed new and powerful motives to influence our minds, and to determine our conduct. Nothing is enjoined to be believed but what is worthy of God, nothing to be practised but what is friendly to man. All the doctrines of the gospel are rational and consistent; all its precepts are truly wise, just, and good. The gospel contains nothing grievous to an ingenuous mind; it debars us from nothing but doing harm to ourselves, or to our fellow-creatures; and permits us to range anywhere but in the paths of danger and destruction. It only requires us to act up to its excellent commands, and to prefer to the vanishing pleasure of sin, the smiles of a reconciled God, and "an eternal weight of glory."

Surely no man who is a real friend to the cause of virtue, and to the interest of mankind, can ever be an enemy to Christianity, if he truly understands it, and seriously reflects on its wise and useful tendency. It conducteth us to our journey's end, by the plainest and securest path; where the "steps are not straitened, and where he that runneth stumbleth not."

We ought daily to adore the God of nature for lighting up the sun, that glorious, though imperfect image of his own unapproachable lustre; and appointing it to gild the earth with its various rays, to cheer us with its benign influence, and to guide and direct us in our journeys and our labors. But how incomparably more valuable is that "day-spring from on high which hath visited us, to give light to them that sit in darkness, and in the shadow of death, and to guide our feet into the way of peace?" Oh Christians, whose eyes are so happy to see, and your ears to hear, what abundant reason have you to give daily and hourly praise to your beneficent Creator! When, therefore, your minds are delighted with contemplating the riches of the gospel; when you reflect (as you certainly must do) with wonder and joy on the happy means of your redemption; when you feel the burden of your guilt removed, the freedom of your address to the throne of grace encouraged, and see the prospect of a fair inheritance of eternal glory opening upon you; then, in the pleasing transports of your souls, borrow the joyful anthem of the psalmist, and say, with the humblest gratitude and self-resignation, "God is the Lord who showeth us light; bind the sacrifice with cords, even to the horns of the altar." Adore "God, who first commanded the light to shine out of darkness," that by the discoveries of his word, and the operations of his spirit, he hath "shined in your hearts, to give you the knowledge of his glory, as reflected from the face of his Son."

Let us, therefore, who live under the gospel, the most gracious dispensation bestowed by God to mankind, "count all things but loss, for the excellency of the knowledge of Christ Jesus our Lord;" and not suffer ourselves, by the slight cavils of unbelievers, to be "moved away from the hope of the gospel." Let us demonstrate that we believe the superior excellency of the Christian dispensation, by conforming to its precepts. Let us show that we are Christians in deed and in truth; not by endless disputes about trifles, and the transports of a blind zeal, but by abounding in those "fruits of righteousness, which are, through Christ, to the praise and glory of God."

From what has been said, we may clearly perceive how groundless all those prejudices are which some conceive against religion, as if it were a peevish, morose thing, burdensome to human nature, and inconsistent with the true enjoyment of life. Such sentiments are too apt to prevail in the heat of youth, when the spirits are brisk and lively, and the passions warm and impetuous; but it is wholly a mistake, and a mistake of the most dangerous tendency. The truth is, there is no pleasure like that of a good conscience; no real peace but what results from a sense of the Divine favor. This enables the mind, and can alone support it under all the various and unequal scenes of the present state of trial. This lays a sure foundation of an easy, comfortable life, of a serene, peaceful death, and of eternal joy and happiness hereafter: whereas vice is ruinous to all our most valuable interests; spoils the native beauty, and subverts the order of the soul; renders us the scorn of man, the rejected of God, and, without timely repentance, will rob us of a happy eternity. Religion is the health, the liberty, and the happiness of the soul; sin is the disease, the servitude, and destruction of it.—It will perhaps be said, that the sons of vice and riot have pleasure in sensual indulgences. This we allow; but must observe, that it is altogether of the lowest kind—empty, fleeting, and transient; "like the crackling of thorns under a pot, so is the mirth of the wicked." It makes a noise and a blaze for the present, but soon vanishes away into smoke and vapor.

On the other hand, the pleasure of religion is solid and lasting, and will attend us through all, even the last stages of life. When we have passed the levity of youth, and have lost all relish for gay entertainments; when old age steals upon us, and stoops toward the grave, this will cleave fast to us, and give us relief.

Clad in this immortal robe, we need not fear the awful summons of the king of terrors, nor regret our retiring into the chambers of the dust. Our immortal part will wing its way to the arms of its Redeemer, and find rest in the heavenly mansions. And though our earthly part, this tabernacle of clay, returns to its original dust, and is dissolved,—our joy, our consolation, our confidence is, that "we have a building of God, a house not made with hands, eternal in the heavens."

Such will be the happy consequences attendant on all those who strictly adhere to the Christian religion, and diligently, through the course of their lives, follow the precepts laid down by their divine Master, the great Saviour and Redeemer of the world.

MIRACLES, PARABLES, AND DISCOURSES OF JESUS.

OUR Saviour's miracles were exceedingly numerous, various, and benevolent, in their character, but only a very small number of them are specifically mentioned. The following is, therefore, only a list of those more particularly noted of the miracles of Christ:—

MIRACLES.	PLACES.	RECORD.
Water turned into wine	Cana.	John ii. 1–11.
The Capernaum nobleman's son cured	Cana	John iv. 46–54.
Surprising draught of fishes	Sea of Galilee.	Luke v. 1–11.
Demoniac cured	Capernaum.	Mark i. 22–28.
Peter's mother-in-law healed	Capernaum.	Mark i. 30, 31.
Leper healed	Capernaum.	Mark i. 40–45.
Centurion's servant healed	Capernaum.	Matt. viii. 5–13.
Widow's son raised from the dead.	Nain	Luke vii. 11–17.
Tempest calmed	Sea of Galilee.	Matt. viii. 23–27.
Demoniacs of Gadara cured	Gadara	Matt. viii. 28–34.
Man sick of the palsy cured	Capernaum.	Matt. ix. 1–8.
Jarius's daughter raised to life	Capernaum.	Matt. ix. 18–26.
Sight restored to two blind men	Capernaum.	Matt. ix. 27–31.
Dumb demoniac cured	Capernaum.	Matt. ix. 32, 33.
Woman diseased with issue of blood healed	Capernaum.	Luke viii. 43–48.
Diseased cripple at Bethesda cured	Jerusalem.	John v. 1–9.
Man with a withered hand cured	Judea	Matt. xii. 10–13.
Demoniac cured	Capernaum	Matt. xii. 22, 23.
Five thousand fed	Decapolis	Matt. xiv. 15.–21.
Canaanite woman's daughter cured	Near Tyre	Matt. xv. 23–28.
Man deaf and dumb cured	Decapolis	Mark vii. 31–37.
Four thousand fed	Decapolis	Matt. xv. 32–39.
Blind man restored to sight	Bethsaida	Mark viii. 22–26.
Boy possessed of a devil cured	Tabor	Matt. xvii. 14–21.
Man born blind restored to sight	Jerusalem	John ix.
Woman of eighteen years' infirmity cured	Galilee	Luke xiii. 11–17.
Dropsical man cured	Galilee	Luke xiv. 1–6.
Ten lepers cleansed	Samaria	Luke xvii. 11–19.
Lazarus raised from the grave to life	Bethany	John xi.
Two blind men restored to sight	Jericho	Matt. xx. 30–34
Fig-tree blasted	Olivet	Matt. xxi. 18–21.
The ear of Malchus healed	Gethsemane	Luke xxii. 50–51.
Wondrous draught of fishes	Sea of Galilee.	John xxi. 1–14.

Parable, a comparison or similitude, ingeniously and impressively representing moral or religious truth (Matt. xiii. 3, 10, 18, 23). Jotham's parable is the most ancient on record (Judg. ix. 7–15). Our Saviour's parables are most instructive (Matt. xiii. 53, 54); and the following are the principal recorded:—

SUBJECT OF PARABLE.	PLACE.	RECORD.
1. Building on rock and sand	Galilee	Matt. vii. 24.
2. Blind leading the blind	Galilee	Luke vi. 39.
3. Two debtors	Galilee	— vii. 41.
4. Evil spirit returning	Galilee	Matt. xii. 43
5. Sower and the seed	Galilee	— xiii. 3.
6. Tares in the field	Galilee	— — 25.
7. Growth of seed	Galilee	Mark iv. 26.
8. Grain of mustard-seed	Galilee	Matt. xiii. 31.
9. Leaven in meal	Galilee	— — 33.
10. Treasure hid in the field	Galilee	— — 44.
11. Pearl of great price	Galilee	— — 45.
12. Net cast into the sea	Galilee	— — 47.
13. Good householder	Galilee	— — 52.
14. Who need a physician	Galilee	— ix. 12.
15. Bridegroom's attendants	Galilee	— — 15.
16. New cloth on an old garment	Galilee	— — 16.
17. New wine in old bottles	Galilee	— — 17.
18. Bread of life	Galilee	John vi. 32.
19. What defiles a man	Galilee	Matt. xv. 11.
20. Lost sheep	Galilee	— xviii. 12.
21. The lord and unmerciful servant	Galilee	— — 23.
22. Good Samaritan	Jerusalem	Luke x. 30.
23. Rich fool	Galilee	— xii. 16.
24. Lord and his servants	Galilee	— — 36.
25. Barren fig-tree	Galilee	— xiii. 6.
26. Ambitious guests	Galilee	— xiv. 7.
27. Great supper	Galilee	— — 16.
28. Hating father and mother	Galilee	— — 26.
29. Building a tower	Galilee	— — 28.
30. King going to war	Galilee	— — 31.
31. Lost sheep, with additions	Galilee	— xv. 3.
32. Lost piece of silver	Galilee	— — 8.
33. Prodigal son	Galilee	— — 11.
34. Unjust steward	Galilee	— xvi. 1.
35. Rich man and Lazarus	Galilee	— — 19.
36. Master and servant	Galilee	— xvii. 7.
37. Unjust judge and widow	Jerusalem	— xviii. 1.
38. Pharisee and publican	Jerusalem	— — 9.
39. Sheepfold	Jerusalem	John x. 1.
40. Good shepherd	Jerusalem	— — 11
41. Laborers in the vineyard	Beyond Jordan	Matt. xx. 1
42. Ten pounds for trading	Jericho	Luke xix. 11.
43. Two sons	Jerusalem	Matt. xxi. 28.
44. Husbandmen and vineyard	Jerusalem	— — 33.
45. Haughty builders	Jerusalem	— — 42
46. Marriage feast	Jerusalem	— xxii. 1.
47. Wedding garment	Jerusalem	— — 11.
48. Budding of trees	Jerusalem	— — 29.
49. Wicked servant	Jerusalem	— xxiv. 44.
50. Ten virgins	Jerusalem	— xxv. 1.
51. Talents for trading	Jerusalem	— — 14.
52. Sheep and goats	Jerusalem	— — 31.
53. True vine	Jerusalem	John xv. 1.

The following list of the remarkable discourses of Christ will illustrate his wisdom and his doctrine:—

DISCOURSES.	PLACE.	RECORD.
Conversation with Nicodemus	Jerusalem	John iii. 1–21.
——————the Samaritan woman	Sychar	John iv. 1–42.
Discourse in the synagogue	Nazareth	Luke iv. 16–31.
Sermon on the mount	Near Nazareth	Matt. v., vi., vii.
Ordination charge to the apostles	Galilee	Matt. x.
Denunciations against Chorazin	Galilee	Matt. xi. 20–24.
Discourse concerning healing the infirm man at Bethesda	Jerusalem	John v.
——————on his disciples plucking ears of corn on the sabbath	Judea	Matt. xii. 1–8.
Refutation of charge of working miracles by agency of Beelzebub	Capernaum	Matt. xii. 22–37.
Discourse on the bread of life	Capernaum	John vi.
——————concerning internal purity	Capernaum	Matt. xv. 1–20.
——————against giving or taking offence and forgiving of injuries	Capernaum	Matt. xviii.
——————at the feast of tabernacles	Jerusalem	John vii.
——————on occasion of the adulteress	Jerusalem	John viii. 1–11.
——————concerning the sheep	Jerusalem	John x.
Denunciation against the scribes and Pharisees	Perea	Luke xi. 37–45.
Discourse on humility and prudence	Galilee	Luke xiv. 7–14.
Directions how to attain heaven	Perea	Matt. xix. 16–30.
Discourse on the sufferings of Christ	Jerusalem	Matt. xx. 17–19.
Denunciations against the Pharisees	Jerusalem	Matt. xxiii.
Predictions of the ruin of Jerusalem	Jerusalem	Matt. xxiv.
Discourse of consolation	Jerusalem	John xiv–xvi.
——————on the way to Gethsemane	Jerusalem	Matt. xxvi. 31–36.
——————with Peter after his resurrection	Galilee	John xxi. 5–22.
——————with his disciples before his ascension	Mount Olivet	Luke xxiv. 50–53.

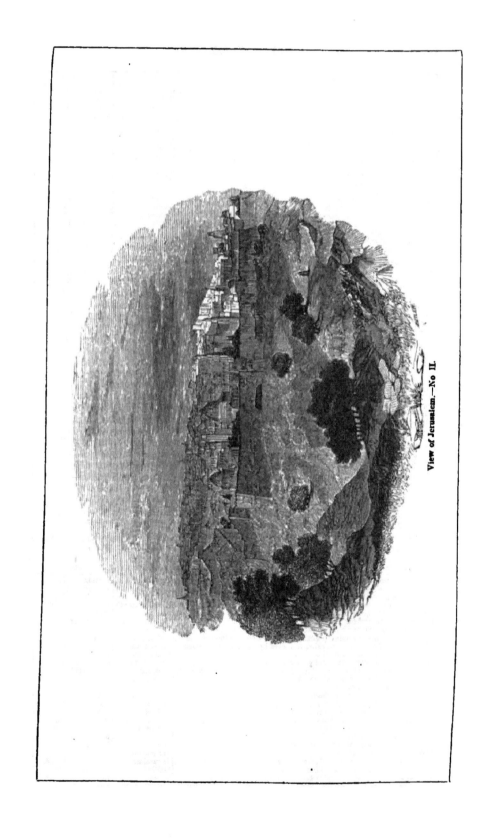

View of Jerusalem.—No II.

CHAPTER V.

FROM THE ASCENSION OF OUR BLESSED LORD INTO HEAVEN TO THE FULL ESTABLISHMENT
OF CHRISTIANITY BY HIS APOSTLES, AND OTHER PROPAGATORS OF HIS GOSPEL.

The blessed Saviour of the world having fulfilled all things prophesied of his mission here on earth, and having, in a most solemn manner, taken leave of his disciples, visibly retired before their eyes to eternal rest in his Father's kingdom. With hearts full of grief and admiration they deplored the loss of the presence of their dear-loved Lord; and, with longing eyes, paid their last attendance till he disappeared. They continued, for some time, fondly looking toward the place where their Lord was gone, till at length two angels in the shape of men, and gloriously apparelled, appeared before them, and delivered a message of consolation to this effect: " Forbear, O Galileans, your further admiration: your gracious Lord, whom even now you beheld ascending to heaven, shall one day come to judge the world in as glorious a manner as he now departed from you. He hath not absolutely left you, but is gone to take possession of that kingdom which he will continue to govern to the end of the world."

The apostles and disciples of our Lord (among whom was Mary the mother of Jesus, and some other pious women who had attended him in his ministry) being greatly comforted by this divine message, immediately returned to Jerusalem, where they spent their time in acts of religious worship, assembling daily in a certain upper room, which they had made choice of for that purpose.

Peter had thought it necessary that a proper person should be chosen to supply the place of the perfidious Judas, that the number of the apostles might be twelve, as was originally appointed by their Master. To effect this, in one of their assemblies (which consisted of one hundred and twenty) Peter addressed himself to his fellow-apostles in a speech which he had made for the purpose, the substance of which was to this effect: " Ye know, brethren, what the royal prophet David (Psal. xli. 9) foretold, and which has been punctually fulfilled, concerning Judas, who was of our society, a fellow-disciple, and an apostle chosen with us. For a sum of money he betrayed his Master to his enemies, after which, being troubled for what he had done, he returned the money to the priest, who, not daring to put it into the treasury, bought a field with it for the interment of strangers. This fact, and the fate of Judas, were universally known to all that dwelt in Jerusalem, and therefore the field that was bought with that money was vulgarly known by the name of the Field of Blood. To Judas, therefore, belongs that which is mentioned by the holy psalmist (Psal. lxix. 25, and cix. 8), not by way of execration, but of prediction: that, as he should come to a desperate miserable end, so the office which he had held with the rest of the twelve, should be bestowed on another. It is then our duty, according to this prophecy, to make choice of some one of these persons that are present (and who have continued with us ever since our Lord undertook the charge and care of us, till his ascension into heaven) that he may succeed Judas in the apostleship."

The proposition made by Peter was unanimously approved of by the assembly; upon which two candidates were immediately nominated, namely, Jonas, surnamed Barnabas, and Matthias, one of the seventy disciples. The choice of one of these two was to be determined by lot, previous to which the apostles solemnly invoked the divine direction in the following words: " Thou, Lord, which knowest the hearts of all men, show whether of those two thou hast chosen, that he may take part of this ministry and apostleship, from which Judas, by transgression, fell" (Acts i. 24, 25). Having said this, they proceeded to draw lots, which happening to fall on Matthias, he was accordingly elected into the number of the twelve apostles.

The number of the apostles being now complete, on the day of Pentecost,* they

---

* This word is derived from the Greek, and signifies the *fiftieth*, because the feast of Pentecost was celebrated the *fiftieth* day after the sixteenth of the month Nisan, which was the second day of the feast of the Passover (Levit. xxiii. 15, 16). And for the same reason it is called the *feast of Weeks*, because it was observed seven weeks after the Passover (Deut. xvi. 9). It was at first instituted in order to oblige the Jews to repair to the temple of the Lord, there to acknowledge his dominion and sovereignty over all their labors, and there to render thanks to him for the law, which he gave them on the *fiftieth* day after their departure out of Egypt. In like manner, the Christian Church celebrates the feast of Pentecost fifty days, or seven weeks, after the Passover, or resurrection of our blessed Saviour, to put us in remembrance, that the *Gifts of the Spirit* were then poured out in a plentiful manner, as the *first-fruits* of our Saviour's ascension into heaven, and that the *Gospel* began to be published by the apostles on the like day that the ancient *Law* was given to the Hebrews.

all assembled together at their accustomed place, in order to perform their religious duties. While they were thus employed, a prodigious noise (much like the rushing of a loud impetuous wind) suddenly filled all the house in which they were, and a kind of fiery vapor, or exhalation, formed in the figure of a man's tongue, but divided a little at the tip, sat on the head of each; whereupon they were all immediately filled with the Holy Ghost, and, by its divine inspiration, were enabled to speak in several different languages.

At this time there were at Jerusalem many Jews and proselytes, who had come thither from different parts of the world, to the celebration of the feast. When these, therefore, were informed of the great miracle which had taken place with the apostles, and were convinced of the truth of it by hearing them speak the languages of their respective countries, they were greatly astonished, and knew not what to make of so singular an event. Some of them argued among themselves to this effect: "How have these men, who are natives of Galilee, and have continued all their lives there, acquired this knowledge? For in our respective languages we hear them preaching the doctrine of Christ, and the wonderful things God hath wrought by him. This certainly must imply something of very great moment." But others were of a different opinion, and, in a scoffing manner, ridiculed the miracle, attributing the powers possessed by the apostles to arise from inebriation: "These men," said they, "are full of new wine."

To destroy this calumny, and to open the eyes of the yet-deluded and perverse Jews, Peter, in the name of the rest, addressed the multitude in a most admirable speech, the substance of which was to the following effect: " Ye men of Judea, and all that at this time see and hear what the Lord hath done, be assured these things are not the effect of wine: ye know in your consciences it can not be so, since it is but the third hour of the day.* But this is the completion of a famous prophecy of Joel, who saith, In the last days I will pour out my spirit upon all flesh; your sons and your daughters shall prophesy, your young men shall see visions, and your old men shall dream dreams. (See Joel ii. 28.) All ranks and qualities of men shall receive the effusion of the Spirit of God, and those who were never brought up in the schools of the prophets, shall be enabled to preach the gospel of Christ wherever they go. And after that there shall be fearful and astonishing sights and prodigies, and many great slaughters in Judea, as forerunners and prognostics of the destruction which shall befall this people for their crucifying Christ, and from which the only way to rescue yourselves is, to repent and acknowledge him, which is the design of this miraculous descent of the Holy Ghost. Observe and attend, ye men of Israel, for you are chiefly concerned in this great affair. This Jesus of Nazareth being demonstrated to be sent from God by the mighty works he did among you, all which you know to be true; him, I say, being permitted to fall into your hands, you apprehended and barbarously crucified; him, whom God, by his determinate council, had given to retrieve you from your lost condition, ye, with profane hands, have slain. This same Jesus, whom ye thus treated, hath God raised again, delivering him from the power of death; and, besides many other things, the prophecies concerning him required that he should not long lie under death. Hear what David the royal psalmist says: I have set the Lord always before me; because he is at my right hand, I shall not be moved. Therefore my heart is glad, and my glory rejoiceth; my flesh also shall rest in hope. For thou wilt not leave my soul in hell, neither wilt thou suffer thine holy one to see corruption. Thou wilt show me the path of life; in thy presence is fulness of joy, at thy right hand there are pleasures for evermore. Give me leave, brethren, to speak freely concerning David, who thus prophesied. He died like other men, had a solemn interment, and we have his monument this day to show, and whence he never arose. Therefore, he spake not of himself, but by way of prediction of the Messiah, whom he knew would infallibly spring from his loins, and be a prince and ruler of his church. These words of his were prophetic, and literally verified in the resurrection of Jesus, whose soul did not continue so long in a state of separation as that his body should be corrupted; and accordingly God raised him up in three days, of which all we apostles were eye-witnesses. He having, therefore, assumed his regal state and office in heaven, and God having given him power to send the Holy Ghost, he hath now punctually fulfilled his promise in sending it on us in the

* That is, nine o'clock, the time of morning prayers, to which the Jews generally went fasting.

most extensive manner; one great effect of which yourselves can testify, by having heard us speak languages which, a short time before, we did not understand. This great and important truth, therefore, I now proclaim to you, that God the Father hath raised up that Christ, whom ye Jews have crucified, and that he now sits on the right hand of him in the kingdom of heaven."

This speech, or rather sermon, of Peter's, so wrought upon the minds of the people, that they called out most passionately to him, and the rest of the apostles, requesting their advice what measures they should pursue, in order to shake off that guilt with which they had been so long loaded. Peter readily complied with their request, and in a most tender and affectionate address, told them, that in order to lay aside their infidelity, they must, with true contrition, acknowledge their sins, enter upon the Christian profession with a firm resolution of never falling from it; and that they must receive baptism from the apostles, who were thereby empowered to convey remission of sins to all true penitents. "Repent and be baptized every one of you in the name of Jesus Christ for the remission of sins, and ye shall receive the gift of the Holy Ghost. For the promise is unto you and to your children, and to all that are afar off, even as many as the Lord our God shall call." (Acts ii. 38, 39.)

In consequence of this affectionate address, those who were really touched with what Peter had said immediately renounced their former course of life, and proved the sincerity of their hearts by receiving baptism. On that day about three thousand people were converted to the faith of Christ, who continued assiduous in hearing the apostles teach, and in bringing their goods liberally for the relief of the distressed. Nor were the converts only impressed with fear and reverence, but a general surprise took place among all that saw these strange and early operations of the Holy Ghost, which were still farther confirmed by several miracles performed by the apostles.

The gospel thus gaining ground, those that received it assembled together for the service of God, constantly observing the times of public prayers, and receiving the sacrament of the Lord's supper; they distributed to the necessities of the poorer sort as freely as God had given them ability, spending their time in acts of devotion and charity, and exercising works of mercy to all. By the pious examples of these many others were induced to join them, which gave the apostles a fruitful harvest of their ministry, and by their repeated exhortations, others were daily rescued from the wicked and dangerous converse of the perverse Jews, and heartily embraced the doctrine of Christ.

. After this wonderful reformation among the people in consequence of Peter's discourses, that apostle, accompanied by John, went one day to the temple about three o'clock in the afternoon, which was one of the times generally set apart for prayer. As they entered in at the gate of the temple toward the east in Solomon's porch, which was called the *beautiful gate*, they saw a poor cripple, who had been lame from his birth, lying there, and begging alms of those who passed him. As soon as the cripple saw Peter and John, he looked up in their faces and earnestly begged charity of them; upon which Peter, looking steadfastly at him, said, "Silver and gold have I none, but such as I have give I thee; in the name of Jesus Christ of Nazareth, rise up and walk." No sooner were these words spoken than the poor cripple was made whole. His joints became straight and his nerves strong, so that he went with the apostles into the temple, "walking, and leaping, and praising God."

The poor man, who had sat daily, for a long time, asking alms at the door of the temple, was universally known by the people, who seeing him walking and praising God, were amazed at the greatness of the cure; they therefore flocked in great numbers round the apostles, by whom the poor man kept close, being unwilling to part with those from whom he had received so distinguished a benefit. Peter, observing the astonishment of the multitude, and thinking it a convenient opportunity of increasing the number of his followers, addressed himself to them in a long and very pertinent harangue, the substance of which was to this effect: "Ye men of Israel, why do you look upon this cure as a thing strange? Or why do you attribute anything to us in this matter, as if it were in our power to perform so great a miracle? The God of our fathers gave this power to Jesus, whom you delivered to Pilate to be crucified, releasing a known murderer and a thief, and putting to death him, who came to give life to the world; whom God hath been pleased to raise from the dead, and make us witnesses thereof. Be assured, it is by belief in him that this man hath been recovered from his lameness. The man you all well know, having, for many years, seen him a begging cripple; and the faith we have in the power of him on whom we believe, hath wrought the remarkable cure at which you all so greatly wonder. I do imagine, brethren, that such among you who rejected Christ did it through ignorance, not knowing him to be the Messiah; and that the like was the case with your rulers. But by these means the many prophecies in the scriptures, that the Messiah should be put to death, have been fulfilled. Do you, therefore, amend your lives, that your past offences may be pardoned, and that, at the second coming of Christ for the delivery and rescue of the faithful, you may, by repentance, be admitted into the number of the elect. The Christ you have persecuted, and of whose resurrection we have been eye-witnesses, hath now entered upon his sovereignty in Heaven, whereby hath been fulfilled all the prophecies concerning him, particularly that of Moses, who truly said unto the fathers, A prophet shall the Lord your God raise up unto you of your brethren, like unto me, and him shall ye hear in all things whatsoever he shall say unto you. And it shall come to pass, that every soul which shall not hear that prophet, shall be destroyed from among the people. And not only Moses, but all the prophets, from Samuel, as many as have spoken,* have foretold the coming of the Messiah, with the destruction of those who should reject, and the especial mercies to them that should believe in him. Ye are the particular persons of whom the prophets foretold, and to whom the promise and covenant which God made with Abraham (that in his seed all the nations of the earth should be blessed) did primarily belong. Ye are the heirs of this covenant, and God hath been pleased to make the first overtures of mercy to you, that ye might receive the gospel of his beloved Son, and repent of the iniquities which ye have done unto him." This was the purport of St. Peter's speech on this occasion; and such was its efficacy, that it converted so many of his hearers, as to make the whole number amount to no less than five thousand.

While Peter was instructing the people, " the captain of the temple," at the instigation of the priests and Sadducees, came with an armed force, suddenly seized the two apostles, and conducted them to prison. The next morning the great sanhedrim met, and having ordered the apostles to be brought before them, demanded by what power they had wrought that miracle upon the lame man, and who it was that gave them authority to preach to the people? In answer to these questions, Peter, being endued with an extraordinary presence of mind and elocution of tongue, spoke to this effect: " Ye rulers of the people, and elders of Israel, we are this day examined before you concerning an action, which is so far from being criminal, that it is an act of special mercy. Be assured, that the miraculous cure performed on the lame man was wrought by no other means than by invoking the name of Jesus of Nazareth, whom ye crucified, and God most miraculously raised again. This is he that was prophecied of under the title of a refuse stone, rejected by you, the chief of the Jews, and treated with contempt; but is now, by his resurrection, enthroned in power, and is indeed become the ruler and king of the church, the prime foundation-stone of the whole fabric. In him alone must salvation now be hoped for by all; nor can ye expect to be saved unless you readily receive and heartily embrace his doctrine."

The council, seeing with what courage and freedom of speech the apostles behaved themselves, and withal considering that their education alone could not have raised them above the capacity of other men (being neither skilled in the learning of the Jews, nor, as men of distinction, instructed in their laws), they were greatly astonished; and still more so when they recollected that the two apostles were of those who had attended Jesus in his lifetime, and saw the man on whom they had wrought the miraculous cure stand by them ready to attest the truth of it. From these considerations, they knew not for some time how to act, till at length they resolved to hold a private conference among themselves, and for that purpose ordered the apostles to withdraw. As soon as they were gone, the council entered into debate on the subject, arguing with one another to this effect: " As to the men, we have nothing to accuse them of; for that they have performed a great miracle is apparent to many, and the man that was healed is a living witness of the truth of it. Since, therefore,

* The account of the prophets is here begun from Samuel, because the schools of the prophets were first instituted and erected by him; and not that there was no prophet before him. The sons of the prophets spent the greater part of their time in studying the law, and praising and serving God, and some were sent on messages to the people (for all were not called to the prophetic office) and therefore it is added, *as many as have spoken*; that is, as many out of the schools of the prophets as were Divinely called to the prophetic office.

they have not been guilty of any breach of our laws, to prevent their further seducing the people (who are too apt to be led away by them) we will call them in and forbid them, upon severe penalties, to preach Christ and his gospel any more." In consequence of this resolution, the two apostles were called in, and commanded not to talk privately or teach publicly anything concerning the faith of Christ. But the Christian heroes, whose commission was from a higher power than any on earth, slighting this interdict and all their threats, made answer, "That since they had received a command from Heaven to declare to all nations what they had heard or seen, it was certainly their duty to obey God rather than them." This was a fair appeal to the consciences of their very judges; but their judges, instead of being satisfied with it, would probably have proceeded to some greater violence, had not the people's veneration for the apostles put a restraint upon their malice. All, therefore, that they dared to do was to repeat and enforce their menaces; having done which, they ordered them to be discharged.

As soon as the two apostles were dismissed, they returned with great joy to their brethren, who with infinite satisfaction heard the report of all that had passed. They then unanimously glorified God, who by his holy prophet David had foretold what was now come to pass: that the Jews should oppose Christ, say false things of him, deny and crucify him first, and, when God had raised him from the dead, oppose the preaching of him; that the princes and governors, Herod and Pontius Pilate, should combine against him, and the rulers should, in council, endeavor to suppress the propagation of his doctrine. "And now, Lord," said they, "behold their threatenings, and grant unto thy servants that with all boldness they may speak thy word, by stretching forth thy hand to heal, and that signs and wonders may be done by the name of thy holy child Jesus." No sooner had they concluded their prayer than the house in which they were was shaken with a mighty wind, in like manner as it had been before on the day of Pentecost; whereupon they were instantly replenished with fresh measures of the Holy Ghost, and, notwithstanding all the threats of the Jewish rulers, found themselves invigorated to preach the gospel of Christ with more boldness and resolution than ever.

The charity at this time among believers was very large and extensive. Such as had houses, or possessions of any kind, sold them, and deposited the money in the hands of the apostles, to be by them distributed in due proportions according to the necessities of their brethren. This a certain Levite (a native of Cyprus, called Joses, but by the apostles surnamed Barnabas, or "the Son of Consolation") did with great readiness and singleness of heart, selling the estate of which he was possessed, and giving the whole produce to the apostles. In imitation of this good man, one Ananias, with his wife Sapphira, resolved to devote all they had to the service of the church; in consequence of which they sold their estate: but afterward altering their minds, jointly agreed to keep some part of the money, intending thereby to impose upon the apostles. Ananias going first into the presence of the apostles, with great assurance and seeming cheerfulness, produced the money and laid it at their feet. But Peter, who by Divine inspiration knew the cheat, in a holy indignation and abhorrence of so vile an act of sacrilege, reprehended him in words to this effect: "How, O Ananias, hath Satan persuaded thee thus to attempt to deceive the Holy Ghost, in purloining part of that which thou hadst consecrated to God's service and the use of his church? Before thy land was sold, was it not wholly thine? And when it was sold, didst thou not receive the full price for it? Was it not then in thy full power to perform thy vow? Thy iniquitous conduct in concealing a part of the money is not only an injury to the church, but to God, who knew thy private vow, that it was consecrating of all, and not this part only which thou hast brought to us." These piercing words, together with the horrors of conscious guilt, so impressed the mind and heart of Ananias, that he fell down dead on the spot, to the great astonishment and terror of all present, and his body was immediately taken away for interment. About three hours after, his wife Sapphira went to the assembly, not in the least suspecting what had happened to her sacrilegious consort. Peter asked her whether the sum which her husband had brought was the whole for which their estate was sold. To this she answered in the affirmative; upon which Peter reprehended her in words to this effect: "How durst you both combine to provoke God, to try whether he will punish this your impious fraud or not? That you may see how highly God resents your sacrilegious intentions, behold the men are coming in who have buried your dead husband, and now they shall do as much for you." No sooner had he spoken these words than Sapphira fell dead at his feet, and the same persons that had buried Ananias carried her out from the assembly, and laid her by him. These remarkable instances of the Divine wrath filled all the converts with fear and trembling, and prevented, in a great measure, that hypocrisy and dissimulation by which others might have flattered themselves with deceiving the church.

Miracles of severity were not, however, much practised by the apostles. Acts of mercy were their proper province, and healing the diseased and freeing the possessed, a great part of their employment. In the execution of this business the divine power so far attended them, that even the shadow of Peter passing by cured the sick, who, in the open streets, were laid on beds and couches, on purpose to receive the benefit of his salutary influence. Nor were these marvellous cures confined to the inhabitants of Jerusalem only, but the people of several neighboring towns and villages brought thither their sick, their lame, and possessed, all of whom were, by the apostles, relieved from their respective infirmities.

The fame of these cures, and the great success which Christianity gained by the miracles and preaching of the apostles, reaching the ears of the high-priest, and some others of the Sanhedrim (who were of the sect of the Sadducees), they were highly incensed against the apostles, and therefore caused them to be apprehended, and thrown into the common prison. But that very night they were released from their confinement. The prison-doors, though fastened with the utmost caution, opened of themselves at the approach of a messenger from the courts of heaven, who commanded the apostles to leave the dungeon, repair to the temple, and preach the glad tidings of the gospel to the people.

Early the next morning the council again assembled, and, thinking the apostles were in safe custody, despatched their officers to the prison, with orders to bring them immediately before them. The officers accordingly went to obey their orders, but, behold, when they came to the prison, they could not find the apostles. In consequence of this they returned to the council, telling them, that the doors of the prison were shut, indeed, and the keepers all upon their guard, but as for the persons whom they were sent for, there was not one of them to be found. This intelligence greatly surprised the council, who wondered how it could be, that, the prison being shut, and the guard at the doors, the prisoners should escape. But, while they were in this state of perplexity, a messenger arrived with news, that the men, whom they had the night before committed to prison, were then in the temple, preaching and instructing the people. In consequence of this, the captain of the guard, with some other officers, immediately went to the temple, and entreated the apostles to go before the council, not daring to offer any violence to them, for fear of being stoned by the people.

As soon as the apostles appeared before their judges, the high-priest demanded how they durst presume to preach a doctrine, which so lately had been interdicted them. To which Peter, in the name of the rest, returned them an answer to this effect: "We certainly ought to obey God rather than man. And though you have so barbarously and contumeliously treated the blessed Jesus, yet God hath raised him up to be a prince and Saviour, to give both repentance and remission of sins. And of these things both we, and the miraculous power which the Holy Ghost hath conferred on all Christians, are witnesses."

This answer greatly exasperated the council, and they began to consult among themselves in what manner they should punish them. Their first resolution was, to put them to death, but this was over-ruled by the wise advice of a certain Pharisee, named Gamaliel, a man of the most distinguished reputation, and universally respected. After ordering the apostles to withdraw, he advised the council to proceed in the affair with great caution, lest bad consequences might attend their resolutions. He told them that several persons had formerly raised parties, and drawn great numbers of people after them; but that all their schemes had miscarried, and their designs rendered abortive, without the interposition of that court. That they would, therefore, do well to let the apostles alone; for, if their doctrines and designs were of human invention, they would come to nothing; but if they were of God, all their powers and policies would be of none effect, and sad experience would too soon convince them that they had themselves opposed the counsels of the Most High.

This speech so far diverted the indignation of the council, that they changed the sentence (at first designed against the apostles' lives) into a corporal punishment. They therefore, after remanding them into court, ordered them to be immediately scourged, which being done, they strictly charged them not to preach any more in the name of Jesus, and, with this charge, gave them their liberty.

But this punishment and injunction had little effect on the disciples of the blessed Jesus. They returned home in triumph, rejoicing that they were thought worthy to suffer in so righteous a cause, and to undergo shame and reproach for so kind and powerful a Master. Nor could all the opposition of man, blended with the malice of the power of darkness, discourage them from performing their duty to God, or lessen their zeal for preaching, both in public and private, the doctrine of the gospel.

The great increase of believers, and the ready access to the common fund for the relief of the poor, made the institution of another order of men in the Christian church highly necessary. Among the great number of converts were some Jews, who, by having been long in foreign countries, had disused the Hebrew, and spoke only the Grecian tongue, so that they were considered by the common Jews as if they had been foreigners. These people complained to the apostles, that, in the distribution of the charity-money, an undue preference was given to the Hebrew widows, while theirs were too frequently neglected. In consequence of this complaint the apostles assembled together the whole multitude of their disciples, when Peter, in the name of the rest, addressed them in words to this effect: " It is not reasonable that we should neglect the preaching of the gospel, by undertaking the care of looking after the poor. Therefore, brethren, do you nominate to us seven men, who have shown themselves to be faithful, trusty persons, eminent among you for wisdom, and other good gifts, that we may appoint (that is, consecrate, or ordain) to the office of deacons in the church, and intrust them with the care of distributing to those who want out of the public stock. In the choice of these, let it be observed, that they be person well versed in the knowledge of divine matters, that they may give assistance to us occasionally in preaching the word, and receiving proselytes to the faith, by baptism. And by these means we shall be less interrupted in our daily employment of praying, and preaching the gospel."

This proposal was highly satisfactory to the whole assembly, who immediately nominated seven persons, namely, Stephen, Philip, Prochorus, Nicanor, Timon, Pharmenas, and Nicolas. These seven they presented to the twelve apostles, who, by prayer, and laying their hands on them, ordained them to the office of deacons.* Of these seven, the most eminent for the gifts and graces of the Holy Spirit was Stephen. He preached the gospel with a noble courage and resolution, and confirmed it with many public and unquestionable miracles among the people, insomuch, that by his means the Christian religion gained ground abundantly. Converts came in apace; and great numbers of the priests themselves laid aside their prejudices and embraced the gospel.

The great zeal of Stephen for propagating the gospel, and the success that attended his endeavors, soon awakened the malice of his adversaries, who procured some members† of the most learned synagogues, then in Jerusalem, to dispute with him.

* The names of these seven deacons are all of Greek extract, whence we may infer, that, very probably, they were all natives of Greece, and that, consequently, by their designation, the church was desirous to give full satisfaction to the complaint of those, whose widows had been before neglected. Of the first two of these, viz., Stephen and Philip, the sacred history has given us a sufficient account, but of the rest we have nothing certain, except we will admit of what the Latins tell us of Prochorus, viz., that on the 9th of August he suffered martyrdom at Antioch, after having made himself famous for his miracles : of Nicanor, that on the 10th of January he suffered in the Isle of Cyprus, after having given great demonstrations of his faith and virtue: of Timon, that on the 19th of April, he was first thrown into the fire, and, when he had miraculously escaped thence, he was fixed upon a cross at Corinth: of Parmenas, that on the 23d of January he suffered at Philippi, in Macedonia: and of Nicolas, that, either by design or indiscretion, he gave rise to the infamous sect of Nicolaitans, and therefore no Christian church has ever yet paid any honor to his memory.

† As there were people of all nations, proselytes to the Jewish religion, dwelling at Jerusalem, it is reasonable to imagine, that they had synagogues, or places appointed for prayer, for hearing the law, and pious exhortations in their own languages. The Jews tell us, that there were no less than four hundred and eighty of these in Jerusalem, which were so many inferior churches, and subordinate to the temple, as their cathedral. These synagogues very probably were built, and maintained by the several nations, or degrees of people that resorted to them, and from these they had their names, as the synagogue of Libertines, that is, of such as were denizens of Rome, of the Cyrenians, the Alexandrians, &c. But it is to be observed of these synagogues, that they were not only places of religious worship, but a sort of colleges or schools likewise, where persons were instructed in the law and traditions of the Jews. The Jews at this time were dispersed in several foreign parts, and from these they sent their youth to Jerusalem to be educated in the synagogue, or college, peculiar to their respective countries. St. Paul was of the province of Cilicia, and, as it is reasonable to think that he studied in a college, either belonging to the country where

But when they found their disputants baffled, and unable to withstand the force of those arguments with which the divine wisdom had inspired Stephen, they betook themselves to vile practices. Having procured some profligate men to accuse him of blasphemy, they caused him to be apprehended, and, in a tumultuous manner, took him before the Sanhedrim, in order to obtain a formal sentence against him.

While Stephen stood before the council, the judges, and all the people then present, beheld a lustre and radiancy in his countenance, not unlike the appearance of an angel. This, however, did not so far intimidate the Sanhedrim as to prevent them from listening to the accusation of the false-witnesses, who charged him with blasphemy, in foretelling the destruction of the temple, and the change of the Mosaic rites and ceremonies. "This man," said they, "ceaseth not to speak blasphemous words against this holy place and the law. For we have heard him say, Jesus of Nazareth shall destroy this place, and shall change the customs which Moses delivered us.

The high-priest, having heard the accusation against Stephen, asked him, whether or not he was guilty of thus prophesying the destruction of the temple, and change of the Jewish religion? In answer to this question, Stephen made a very grave and severe oration, the substance of which was to the following effect:

"Hearken unto me, ye descendants of Jacob; the Almighty, whose glory is from everlasting, appeared to our father Abraham, before he sojourned in Charran, even while he dwelt in Mesopotamia, commanding him to leave his country and relations, and retire into a land which he would show him.

"Abraham obeyed the divine mandate; he left the land of the Chaldeans and pitched his tent in Charran; whence, after his father was dead, he removed into Canaan, even the land you now inhabit; but he gave him no inheritance in this country, not even so much as to set his foot upon. He promised, indeed, he would give it him for a possession, which should descend to his posterity, though at this time he had no child.

"God also indicated to him that his seed should sojourn in a strange land; the people of which should make them bondmen, and treat them cruelly four hundred years. After which, he would judge that nation, bring out his people, who should serve him in this place, as an earnest of which he gave him the covenant of circumcision; and afterward a son, whom Abraham circumcised the eighth day, calling his name Isaac, who begat Jacob, and Jacob begat the twelve patriarchs.

"But these, moved with envy, sold their brother Joseph into Egypt, where the Almighty protected him, delivered him from all his afflictions, endued him with wisdom, and gave him favor in the sight of Pharaoh, the monarch of Egypt, who made him governor both of his house and kingdom.

"Soon after this exaltation of Joseph, the countries of Egypt and Canaan were afflicted with a terrible famine, and our fathers found no sustenance, either for themselves or flocks. But as soon as Jacob heard the welcome tidings that there was corn in Egypt, he sent our fathers thither to purchase bread for the people of his household. And in their second journey thither, Joseph made himself known to his brethren, and also informed Pharaoh of his country and relations. After which Joseph's father, with his whole house, consisting of threescore and fifteen souls, went down into Egypt, where both Jacob and our fathers died, and were carried to Sychem, and deposited in the sepulchre purchased of the sons of Emmor, the father of Sychem.

"But as the time for fulfilling the promise made to Abraham approached, the people multiplied in Egypt, till another king arose, who was not acquainted with the merits of Joseph, and the great things he had done for that country. This prince used our fathers with cruelty, and artfully attempted to destroy all the male children. At this time Moses was born, and being exceeding fair, was nourished three months in his father's house; but as it was dangerous to conceal him there any longer, he was hid among the flags on the bank of the river; when the daughter of Pharaoh found him, and educated him as her own son.

"Thus Moses became acquainted with all the learning of Egypt, and was mighty both in word and deed; but when he was forty years old he thought proper to visit

he was born, or proper to his quality, as a freeman of Rome; there seems to be no incongruity in supposing, that he might possibly be one, either of those Libertine or Cilician disputants, who entered the lists with St. Stephen.

his brethren, the children of Israel; and seeing an Egyptian smite a Hebrew, he assisted the suffering person, and slew the Egyptian; supposing that his brethren would have been persuaded that from his hand, with the assistance of the Almighty, they might expect deliverance; but they conceived no hopes of this kind.

"The next day he again visited them, and seeing two of them striving together, he endeavored to make them friends: 'Ye are brethren,' said he to them, 'why do ye injure one another?' But he who did his neighbor wrong, instead of listening to his advice, thrust him away, saying, 'By what authority art thou a judge of our actions? Wilt thou kill me as thou didst the Egyptian yesterday?'

"Moses, at this answer, fled from Egypt, and sojourned in the land of Media, where he begat two sons. And at the end of forty years, the angel of the Lord appeared unto him in the wilderness of Mount Sinai, out of the middle of a bush burning with fire: this was a sight which surprised Moses; and as he drew near to view more attentively so uncommon a thing, God called unto him, saying, 'I am the God of thy fathers, the God of Abraham, the God of Isaac, and the God of Jacob.' At which Moses trembled, and turned aside his face. But the Lord said to him, 'Put off thy shoes from thy feet, for the place where thou standest is holy ground. I have long seen the afflictions of my people, which are in Egypt; I have heard their cries, and am now descended from heaven to deliver them. Come, therefore, I will send thee into Egypt.'

"Thus was that Moses whom they refused sent by God to be ruler and deliverer, by the hand of the angel who appeared to him in the bush. Accordingly he brought them out after he had showed signs and wonders in the land of Egypt, in the Red sea, and in the wilderness, forty years. It is this Moses that told our fathers, 'A prophet shall the Lord your God raise up unto you, and your brethren, like unto me. Him shall ye hear.'

"And this prophet is the same who was in the church in the wilderness, with the angel which spake unto Moses in Mount Sinai, and with our fathers; the same who received the lively oracles to give unto us; he whom our fathers would not obey, but thrust him from them, and were desirous of returning to their state of bondage—commanding Aaron to make them gods to go before them, and pretending that they knew not what was become of Moses, who delivered them from the slavery of Egypt. They now made a calf, offered sacrifices to it, and rejoiced in the work of their own hands. From these idolatrous proceedings they lost that divine protection which had hitherto attended them as the prophets have recorded. 'O ye houses of Israel! have you offered unto me slain beasts and sacrifices, by the space of forty years in the wilderness? Yea, ye took up the tabernacle of Moloch, and the star of your god Remphan: figures which ye made to worship them: I will carry you away beyond Babylon.'

"Our fathers were possessed of the tabernacle of witness in the wilderness, being made according to the pattern Moses had seen in the mount. This tabernacle our fathers brought in with Jesus into the possession of the Gentiles, who were driven out by the Almighty, till the days of David, a favorite of the Most High, and who was desirous of finding a tabernacle for the God of Jacob; but Solomon built him a house.

"We must not, however, think that the Almighty will reside in temples made with hands, as the prophet beautifully observed: 'Heaven is my throne and earth is my footstool: what house will ye build me, saith the Lord, or where is the place of my rest? Hath not my hand made all these things?'

"Ye stiff-necked, ye uncircumcised in heart and ears, will ye for ever resist the Holy Ghost? Ye tread in the paths of your fathers; as they did, so do you still continue to do. Did not your fathers persecute every one of the prophets? did not they slay them who showed the coming of the Holy One, whom ye yourselves have betrayed and murdered? Ye have received the law by the disposition of angels, but never kept it."

This speech, but particularly the conclusive part of it, incensed the council to such a degree against Stephen, that they made use of the most bitter invectives, and resolved to chastise him by no less a punishment than death. But Stephen was totally regardless of what they said or did, having his mind employed in the delightful prospect of heaven, and the appearance of the blessed Jesus standing at the right hand of God. The visionary prospect of this heavenly scene so enraptured his soul, that he could not help communicating it to the council. "Behold," said he, "I see the heavens opened, and the Son of Man standing at the right hand of God." On saying these words, the resentment of the council against him was so ungovernably increased, that raising a loud clamor, and stopping their ears against all cries for mercy, they immediately dragged him away without the city, and stoned him to death. While Stephen was undergoing this punishment, he first devoutly recommended his soul to God, and then earnestly prayed for his murderers, that the sin they were committing " might not be laid to their charge;" having done which, he quietly resigned his soul into the hands of Him who gave it. His remains were decently interred by devout men (proselytes to the Christian faith) who made great lamentation over him.

Among the many that were enraged against Stephen, one particular person who had but too great a hand in his death, was a young man of Cilicia, named Saul. This person, out of his great officiousness to have Stephen executed, undertook to look to the clothes of the witnesses, who usually stripped themselves to throw the first stones (as the law directed) at the person who was to suffer by their evidence. Not satisfied with this, Saul, out of his passionate concern for the traditions of the ancients, and his natural inveteracy on that account, against the advocates of the gospel, resolved to persecute all he could who professed the new religion. He accordingly applied to the sanhedrim for a commission for this purpose, which was no sooner granted than he immediately proceeded to carry it into execution. Having proper assistance, he broke open houses, seized upon all who looked like the disciples of Jesus, and unmercifully dragged them to prison, where he caused them to be scourged and otherwise ignominiously punished. These acts of cruelty he exercised wherever he went; so that most of the believers, except the apostles, were forced to leave Jerusalem, and disperse themselves in the regions of Judea and Samaria, Syria and Phœnicia, Cyrus and Antioch, &c.

In consequence of this, the glad tidings of the gospel (which had till now been confined to Judea, and many professors of it obliged to hide themselves in secret places) was preached to the Gentile world, and an ancient prophecy was fulfilled which says, " Out of Sion shall go forth the law, and the word of the Lord from Jerusalem." Thus did the Almighty bring good out of evil, and cause the malicious intentions of the wicked to redound to his honor and praise.

CHAPTER VI.

Among those who fled from Jerusalem in consequence of the violent persecution by Saul, was Philip the deacon, the next in order after Stephen. He directed his course toward Samaria, preaching the gospel at various places in his way, and at length took up his residence in that city. His labors here were crowned with success; he confirmed the doctrine he preached by the performance of many distinguished miracles, and in a short time was attended by a prodigious number of converts. In the city lived a person named Simon, who, by his sorcery and magical arts, had so strangely gained the veneration of the people, that they considered his diabolical illusions as real operations of the power of God. Simon, seeing great numbers of his admirers fall off from him, and embrace the doctrine preached by Philip, pretended to be a convert likewise, and (in hopes of obtaining some share of the miraculous gifts, which he could not but admire in Philip) was baptized by him with some others who had embraced the doctrine of Christ.

The great success which attended Philip at Samaria being made known to the apostles at Jerusalem, they sent Peter and John to confer the gifts of the Holy Ghost on the new converts. Simon, the magician, perceiving that a power of working miracles was consequent to all those on whom the apostles laid their hands, offered to give them money if they would invest him with a like power. But Peter, knowing the insincerity of his heart, rejected his offer with scorn and detestation; and severely rebuked him in words to this effect: " Thy money (said the great apostle) perish with thee. As thy heart is full of hypocrisy and deceit, thou shalt never be invested with any part of this divine privilege, for thy design in desiring these gifts is to advance thy own credit and esteem among men, and not to enlarge the kingdom of Christ. Repent, therefore, and humble thyself before God for this wicked and impious proposal, that the thoughts of thy heart may be forgiven thee; for I perceive that thy temper and disposition of mind is still vicious and corrupt; that thou art yet bound by the chains of iniquity, and in a state displeasing to God, and dangerous to thyself."

This severe rebuke from Peter greatly affected the mind of Simon; his conscience flew in his face, and he earnestly entreated the apostles to make intercession for him to the throne of grace, that the Almighty might pardon his sins, and not inflict on him those heavy judgments which Peter had intimated were likely to fall on him for his enormous transgressions.

The two apostles, having confirmed the doctrine preached by Philip in Samaria, left that city and returned to Jerusalem, in their way to which they expounded the doctrine of Christ in several considerable villages, and were so successful, as to bring over a prodigious number of sincere proselytes.

Soon after Peter and John left Samaria, Philip received orders from a heavenly messenger to quit that city, and go southward into the road which led from Jerusalem to Gaza. Philip immediately obeyed the divine mandate; but he had not travelled far before he espied a chariot with a splendid retinue, which, on inquiry, he found belonged to a eunuch, the treasurer of Candace, queen of Ethiopia, who being a proselyte to the Jewish religion had been to pay his devotions at Jerusalem, and was then upon his journey home. When Philip approached the chariot he was directed by the spirit of God to stop and speak to the person within it. This he accordingly did, and found the treasurer commendably employed in reading a passage of the prophet Isaiah. Philip, after apologizing for interrupting him, asked if he clearly understood what he was reading; upon which the treasurer candidly acknowledged he did not, and besought him to get into the chariot and instruct him. Philip readily obeyed, and when he came to examine the passage which had so much perplexed, and engaged the attention of the treasurer, he found it to be the following: " He was led as a lamb to the slaughter, and like a sheep dumb before the shearer he opened not his mouth; in his humiliation his judgment was taken away, and who shall declare his generation? For his life was taken from the earth." This text the treasurer desired Philip to explain, asking him whether the prophet spoke this of himself, or of some other person? Philip took this opportunity of preaching to him the gospel of Jesus Christ, and clearly pointed out to him that not only the sense of the passage in question, but likewise several others in the ancient prophets, was fully accomplished in his person, and the transactions that had taken place during his stay on earth.

While Philip was expounding the doctrine of Christ to the Ethiopian, they happened to come unto a certain water; and the eunuch said, "See, here is water; what doth hinder me to be baptized?" And Philip said, "If thou believest with all thy heart, thou mayest." And he answered and said, "I believe that Jesus Christ is the Son of God." And he commanded the chariot to stand still, and they went down into the water, both Philip and the eunuch, and he baptized him. "And when they were come up out of the water, the spirit of the Lord caught away Philip, that the eunuch saw him no more, and he went on his way rejoicing. But Philip was found at Azotus; and passing through he preached in all the cities, till he came to Cesarea."* (Acts viii. 36-40.)

In the meantime Saul was very active in persecuting the believers of Christ in Jerusalem and its neighborhood; but such was his fiery zeal against the faithful, that he resolved to carry his cruelty and resentment still farther. He therefore applied to the sanhedrim, and obtained a commission from that court to extend his persecution to Damascus, and to bring such believers as he might find in that city bound to Jerusalem.

Saul, pleased with the horrid power with which he was invested by the sanhedrim, left Jerusalem, and prosecuted his journey toward Damascus,† being fully resolved to

---

* A city and port of Palestine, on the Mediterranean sea, seventy-five miles northwest from Jerusalem. The tower of Strato was erected here for the defence of the harbor; but Herod the Great improved the port by a breakwater, and built the city, which he called Cesarea, in honor of his patron Augustus, to whom also he erected a superb temple, adorned with the statue of that emperor. It soon rose to an extraordinary height of magnificence, and became the residence of the Roman proconsul; hence the fact of Paul being kept a prisoner for two years at Cesarea, and that so many things are mentioned as having occurred in relation to Christians in this great city. (Acts viii. 40; x. 1; xii. 19; xxiii.; xxiv.; xxv. 4-14.) Our engraving represents the present condition, merely ruins of Cesarea.

† The ancient capital of Syria, supposed to be the oldest city existing in the world: it is situated on the river Barrady, and lies about 160 miles northeast of Jerusalem. (Gen. xv. 2; 1 Kings xi. 24; xv. 18.) Tradition says that Abel was murdered here; and that Abraham was king of Damascus; it is, however, celebrated in the apostolic history for the conversion of the apostle Paul. (Acts ix. 1-22.) This city is now call-

Ruins of Cesarea.

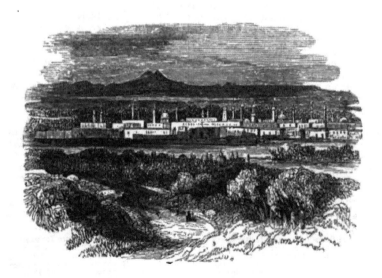

View of the present city of Damascus.

execute his commission with the strictest severity. But it was the divine will, in mercy to him as well as those he went to persecute, to frustrate his intentions. When he came near Damascus, a refulgent light, far exceeding the brightness of the sun, darted upon him, at which he was greatly amazed and confounded, falling, together with his horse, prostrate on the ground. This light was accompanied with a voice, in the Hebrew language, saying, "Saul, Saul, why persecutest thou me?" To which Saul replied, "Who art thou, Lord?" He was immediately answered, "I am Jesus whom thou persecutest. It is hard for thee to kick against the pricks." As if he had said, "All thy attempts to extirpate the faith in me will prove abortive, and, like kicking against the spikes, wound and torment thyself."

Saul was now sufficiently convinced of his folly in acting against Jesus, whom he was now assured to be the true Messiah. He therefore, trembling with fear, said, "Lord, what wilt thou have me to do?" On which a voice replied, "Arise, and go into the city, and it shall be told thee what thou must do." Those who accompanied Saul were struck with fear and amazement, wondering that they should hear a voice, and yet see no man speak, while Saul himself was so dazzled and overpowered by the light, that he quite lost his eyesight. His companions, therefore, led him by the hand into the city of Damascus, where he continued three days totally blind, nor did he, in the whole time, take the least refreshment.

At this time there dwelt in the city a certain disciple, named Ananias, whom the Lord, in a vision, commanded to go and find out one Saul of Tarsus (then lodging at the house of one Judas, a Jew), and, by laying his hands on him, to remove his blindness. Ananias was startled at the name of the man, and, to excuse himself, alleged his violent persecutions of the church, and with what a wicked intent he was then come to Damascus. But to this the vision told him, that he was appointed, by the Divine Being, to be a powerful instrument in the propagation of the gospel, both among the Jews and Gentiles, and that, how much soever he had persecuted Christianity heretofore, he was now to become a zealous defender of it, and even to die in testimony of its truth.

Encouraged with this assurance, Ananias repaired to the house where Saul was, and, laying his hands on him, delivered a message to this effect: "That the Lord Jesus, who had appeared to him in his journey, had sent him not only to restore his eyesight, but likewise to bestow upon him the gifts and graces of the Holy Spirit, such as might qualify him for the ministry to which he was then appointed." No sooner had Ananias finished his speech, than thick films, like scales, fell from Saul's eyes, and he received his sight; immediately after which he was baptized, and continued some days with the disciples at Damascus, preaching in the synagogues, and proving that Jesus was the Messiah.

After staying some time at Damascus, Saul retired into the neighboring parts of Arabia Petrea, where he first planted the gospel; and, in the beginning of the next year, returned to Damascus. Here he applied, with the utmost assiduity, to the great work of the ministry, preaching Christ daily in the synagogues, and confuting all those who argued against his doctrine. He was, indeed, remarkably zealous in his preaching, and blessed with a very extraordinary method of reasoning, whereby he undeniably proved the fundamental points of Christianity. This irritated the Jews to the highest degree; and at length, after about three years' continuance in the city, they found means to prevail on the governor of Damascus to have him apprehended, and confined. But they knew it would be difficult to take him, as he had so many friends in the city; they therefore kept themselves in continual watch, searching all the houses where they thought he might conceal himself, and likewise obtained a guard from the governor, to attend the different gates of the city, in order to prevent his escape. In this distress his Christian friends were far from deserting him; they tried every method that offered to procure his escape; but finding it impossible for him to pass through either of the gates of the city, they let him down from one of their houses in a basket over the wall, by which means the cruel designs of his enemies were rendered abortive.

ed Demesek, and contains a population of about 80,000, or, as some reckon, 150,000, mostly Mohammedans; but about 3,000 are Jews, and about 10,000 are of several denominations of professing Christians. Damascus is a city of great trade, and therefore important as a missionary station, especially for the circulation of the Scriptures through a vast district of Asia. Seventy or eighty minarets, rising above the houses give a pleasing appearance to the city of Damascus, as represented in our second engraving on page 527.

Saul having thus escaped from his malicious persecutors in Damascus, repaired to Jerusalem, where, at first, he was but coolly received among many of the disciples. They were not insensible of his former conduct, and were therefore doubtful of the sincerity of his heart, till at length Barnabas, who was privy to the circumstances that had attended him both before and after his conversion, introduced him to the apostles, and, having clearly related to them every particular that had passed, they admitted him into their communion. He continued some time at Jerusalem, during which he preached with great boldness to the people; and his sermons were so powerful, and disputations with his opponents so unanswerable, that they, like the Jews at Damascus, formed designs against his life. But as soon as this was known to the brethren, they conducted him to Cesarea, whence he set sail to his own city, Tarsus, and continued, for some years, preaching the gospel with great success in various parts of Cilicia and Syria.

The church, at this time, was free from persecution, and flourished exceedingly; upon which Peter took the opportunity of making a general visitation to all the reformed places in Judea, Galilee, and Samaria. In his progress he arrived at a town called Lydda, where he cured one Æneas of a paralytic disorder, which had confined him to his bed for eight years; and from this miracle all the inhabitants of Lydda, as well as a neighboring town called Saron, were prevailed on to embrace the doctrine of Christ. From Lydda he was entreated by two messengers to go over to Joppa,* on account of one Tabitha, a Christian woman, venerable

* This place occurs, under the name of Japhe, in Josh. xix. 46; and which is still preserved in the present name of Jaffa, or Yaffa. It is situated about forty miles west of Jerusalem, on the shore of the Mediterranean. Its fame, as a seaport, ascends to the remotest times in history, sacred and profane. In the former we find it the principal port of Palestine, and the peculiar port of Jerusalem; being, in fact, the only port in Judea. Hence we find that the materials obtained from Tyre, for the building of Solomon's temple, were brought to this port, to be conveyed thence by land to Jerusalem. But although Joppa was long the port of Judea—as its distance afforded an easy communication with the capital, while its geographical position opened an extensive trade to all the coasts and islands of the Mediterranean—it was never a safe or commodious harbor; and those travellers are mistaken who attribute its present condition to the neglect of ages. Josephus repeatedly explains its natural unfitness for a good haven, in nearly the same terms which are employed by modern travellers in describing its present condition ("Antiq." xv. 9, 6; "De Bello Jud." iii. 9, 3). This similarity is noticed by Mr. Buckingham, who himself says: "The port is formed by a ledge of rocks, running north and south before the promontory, leaving a confined and narrow space between the rocks and the town. Here the small trading-vessels of the country find shelter from the south and west winds, and land their cargoes on narrow wharfs, running along before the magazines. When the wind blows strong from the northward, they are obliged to warp out, and seek shelter in the small bay to the northeast of the town, as the sea breaks in here with great violence; and there is not more than three fathoms of water in the deepest part of the harbor: so accurately do the local features of the place correspond with those given of it by Josephus." Clarke also describes the harbor as one of the worst in the Mediterranean; so that ships generally anchor about a mile from the town, to avoid the rocks and shoals of the place. From this account it will appear that Joppa afforded the only port, though a bad one, for the important district behind it, inland. The bad state of the ancient roads, or rather perhaps the absence of any roads, made a near harbor, however incommodious, of more immediate consequence than a good one at any greater distance.

The coast of Joppa is low; but the town itself is seated on a conical promontory, jutting out into the sea, and rising to the height of about one hundred and fifty feet above its level; having a desert coast to the north and south, the Mediterranean on the west, and fertile plains and gardens behind it, on the east. The base of the hill is surrounded by a wall, which begins and ends at the sea, and is fourteen or fifteen feet high, and two or three feet thick: with towers at certain distances, alternately round and square: being of stone, it was of sufficient strength to oblige the French army under Bonaparte, to break ground and erect batteries against it, before a breach could be made. At present it is in a bad condition, many parts having given way from the violent rains of about seven years since; so that, if Ibrahim Pacha had been obliged to besiege it, he would have found the walls ready breached to his hands.

On the land side the town is approached through extensive and richly productive gardens, by which it is surrounded; the light, sandy soil being very favorable to the production of various kinds of fruits. These gardens are fenced with hedges of the prickly-pear, and are abundantly stocked with orange lemon, pomegranate, and fig-trees, and with water-melons. The oranges and lemons grow to a prodigious size; the pomegranate have also a great reputation; and the water-melons are celebrated over all the Levant for their delicious flavor. The town itself is thus noticed by Buckingham:—

"The town, seated on a promontory, and facing chiefly to the northward, looks like a heap of buildings, crowded as closely as possible into a given space; and, from the steepness of its site, these buildings appear in some places to stand one on the other. The most prominent features of the architecture from without, are the flattened domes, by which most of the buildings were crowned, and the appearance of arched vaults. There are no light and elegant edifices, no towering minarets, no imposing fortifications, but all is mean and gloomy aspect. . . . The walls and fortifications have a weak and contemptible appearance, compared even with those of Accho (Acre); and, as at that place, the entrance is prepossessing, but its interior disappoints the expectations raised. After passing a gate crowned with three small cupolas there is seen, on the right, a gaudy fountain, faced with marble slabs, and decorated with painted devices, and Arabic sentences in characters of gold. Passing within, however, the town has all the appearance of a poor village, and every part of it that we saw was of corresponding meanness." Many of the streets are connected by flights of steps. The Mussulman part of the town is very much dilapidated, but the street by the sea-wall is clean and regular.

Beside the citadel on the top of the hill, there is a small fort, near the sea, on the west, another on the north, and a third near the eastern gate of entrance; mounting, in all, from fifty to sixty pieces of cannon. The religious structures are, three mosques, and the Latin, Greek, and Armenian convents. The popula-

for her piety and diffusive charity, who was lately dead. Peter complied with the request of the messengers, and immediately accompanied them to Joppa. On his arrival at the house he found the body in an upper chamber ready prepared for interment, and surrounded by a number of mournful widows, who showed him the coats and garments wherewith she had clothed them, the monuments of her liberality. They durst not, however, request him to raise her from the dead, but by their tears, and great commendations of her charity, sufficiently testified their wishes that he would do it. Peter was not insensible of their meaning, and was willing to grant what he knew would give them general satisfaction. Having, therefore, ordered them to withdraw, he first knelt down, and prayed for some time, with great fervency; after which, turning himself to the body, he said, " Tabitha, arise." Upon this, the good woman instantly opened her eyes, and Peter, taking her by the hand, raised her up, and presented her alive to her friends and relations. This miracle gained Peter a prodigious number of converts, and encouraged him, for a considerable time, to continue his abode at Joppa, during which he resided in the house of one Simon, a tanner.

During his stay at Joppa, he one day retired to the top of the house, about noon, to pray. After he had finished his devotions he found himself hungry, and called for meat; but, while the people were preparing his dinner, he fell asleep, and beheld, in a vision, a large sheet, or table-cloth, let down, as it were, by the four corners from heaven, wherein were creatures of all kinds, clean and unclean; and, at the same time a voice said to him, " Arise, Peter, kill and eat." But the apostle, being tenacious of the rites and institutions of the Mosaic law, declared his aversion to such a proceeding; upon which the voice rejoined, that what God had pronounced clean, he ought by no means to account common or unclean. This representation was made to him three several times, after which the sheet was taken up, and the vision disappeared.

When Peter awoke he could not help seriously reflecting on the vision he had beheld; and while he was wondering within himself what might be the event, he was interrupted by three messengers, who, knocking at the gate, desired to speak with him. They were accordingly admitted, and as soon as they saw Peter they acquainted him with their business, which was to the following purport: that " Cornelius, a Roman, captain of a company in the Italian legion,[*] then at Cesarea, a person of eminent virtue, piety, and charity, had, by an immediate command from God, sent to him, begging that he would return with them to give him some instructions on so important and singular an occasion." Peter detained the messengers that night; but the next day he set out with them accompanied by some of his brethren, and the day following arrived at Cesarea.

Cornelius, being in expectation of his coming, had invited his friends and relations to his house, and as soon as Peter entered, he fell down at his feet to worship him; but the apostle, rejecting that honor as being due to God alone, raised him up, and then told the company that, " though they must know it was not lawful for a Jew to converse (more especially on the duties of religion) with those of another nation; yet since God had taught him to make no distinction, he very readily attended their pleasure, and desired to know the occasion of their sending for him."

The reply Cornelius made in answer to this was to the following effect: " Four days ago, being fervently employed in the duties of fasting and prayer, an angel from

---

tion may be from four to five thousand, mostly Turks and Arabs : the Christians not being estimated at more than six hundred. Joppa still enjoys a traffic, which, considering the state of the country, may be called considerable, with the neighboring coasts. In the way of manufacture it is chiefly noted for its soap, which is an article of export to Damascus and Cairo, and is used in all the baths of the principal cities. The delicious fruits of the vicinity are also largely exported, particularly the melons. There are no antiquities at Joppa, nor can any be expected in a town which has been so often sacked and destroyed— five times by the Assyrians and Egyptians, in their wars with the Jews ; three times by the Romans ; and twice by the Saracens, in the wars of the Crusades.

[*] The cohort of the Romans, which we call band, was a body of infantry, consisting of five hundred men, ten of which bands made a legion ; and the manner in which the Romans distinguished and denominated their bands and legions was very various. Sometimes it was from the order of places, and so they were called the first or second band, according to their rank and precedency ; Sometimes from the commanders they were under, as the Augustan and Claudian band, &c., because persons of that name did lead them ; Sometimes from their own behavior, as the Victrix, the Ferrea, the conquering, the iron band, &c., by reason of the great valor, which, in some sharp engagements, these had shown ; Sometimes from the countries they were chiefly quartered in, as the German and Pannonian band, &c., and sometimes from the parts whence they were gathered, as this of Cornelius, is called the Italian band, because it was raised out of that country, and was a body of forces well known for their gallantry and great exploits, among the writers of the Roman history.

Joppa.

the courts of heaven appeared to me, declaring that my prayers and alms were come up as a memorial before the throne of the Most High; and at the same time ordered me to send to Joppa for one Simon Peter, who lodged in the house of a tanner near the seaside, and would give me further information in the mysteries of salvation. Accordingly I made no hesitation to obey the heavenly messenger; I sent immediately for thee, and now thou art come, and we are met together, I desire to hear what instructions thou hast to communicate."

From this relation of the Roman officer Peter delivered a discourse to the assembly, which he began by declaring that he perceived plainly God had made no distinction of persons and people, but that the pious and godly of all nations were to meet with acceptance. He told them, that peace and reconciliation between God and man was a doctrine published by the prophets of old, and of late, since the time of John the Baptist, preached through Galilee and Judea; that of this peace Jesus of Nazareth was the only Mediator between God and man, as appeared by the divine powers and graces wherewith he was invested, and which he constantly exercised in doing good to mankind; that of his life and actions, more especially of his crucifixion by the Jews, and resurrection from the dead, of his appearing to his disciples, and even eating and drinking with them after his resurrection, he and the rest of the apostles were chosen witnesses; that from him they had received, before his ascension, a command and commission to publish to all nations, that he was the person, whom God had ordained to be the great Judge of the world; that all the prophets, with one consent, bore witness of him; and that whoever believed in his name would certainly receive the remission of sins.

While Peter was thus speaking, the Holy Ghost came down upon the whole audience, and inspired them with gifts and graces, fitting them for several conditions in the church. The Jews who accompanied Peter, were greatly astonished to see that the gifts of the Holy Ghost were poured upon the Gentiles; which being observed by Peter, he told them he knew no reason why those persons should not be baptized (having received the Holy Ghost) as well as they. He accordingly gave orders that they should be baptized, which being done, he stayed with them several days, in order to confirm them in the holy faith they had so happily and earnestly embraced.

The conduct of Peter on this occasion was considered in various lights by the brethren at Jerusalem, who being but lately converted to the Christian faith, were zealously attached to the religious ceremonies of the Mosaic institution, and therefore most of them severely charged Peter, on his return to Jerusalem, as being too familiar with the Gentiles. How powerful is the prejudice of education! The Jews had, for many ages, conceived an inveterate hatred to the Gentiles, considering them as persons not approved of by the Almighty, who had chosen the Jews for his peculiar people. The law of Moses, indeed, enjoined them to be kind to their own nation, in preference to all others; and the rites and institutions of their religion, and the peculiar form of their commonwealth rendered them very different from the inhabitants of other countries; a separation which in after ages they contracted into a much narrower compass. They were also tenaciously proud of their external privileges in being the descendants of Abraham; and therefore looked upon the rest of the world as reprobates, refusing to hold any conversation with them, or even to treat them with common civility.

It is therefore no wonder that they were highly displeased with Peter; nor would he, in all probability, have been able to defend his conduct in a satisfactory manner, had he not been charged with a peculiar commission from God for extending the privileges of the gospel to the Gentile world. To satisfy them, however, of the propriety of his conduct, he first gave them a plain and minute narrative of the whole affair, together with the occasion of it; and then took occasion from the whole, to draw this inference: that, "since God had been pleased to bestow on these Gentiles the same privileges, and marks of conversion, that he had done on his select disciples, it would have been direct disobedience in him to the divine will, had he denied them admission into the church, or refused them his instructions and conversation."

From this representation the whole audience were perfectly satisfied; and their displeasure against Peter was turned into praise and thanksgiving to God, for having communicated the same mercy to the Gentiles as he had done to the Jews; namely, " repentance unto life eternal."

CHAPTER VII.

AFTER the general dispersion which took place in consequence of the martydom of Stephen, and the persecutions that followed, some disciples, who were born in Cyprus and Cyrene,* having travelled through several countries, and hitherto preached to the Jews only, at length came to Antioch,† where, hearing of the conversion of Cornelius and others, they applied themselves to the Greeks who lived in that city, and, by the blessing of God, daily made great numbers of converts. Intimation of this being given to the apostles at Jerusalem, they despatched one Barnabas, a pious man, and endued with many excellent gifts, to assist the disciples, and confirm the believers in that city.

The success of the gospel in so large a place as Antioch, gave great satisfaction to Barnabas, who, after continuing there some time, and exhorting the people to hold fast the possession of that faith they had newly embraced, departed thence to Tarsus, in order to find out Saul, whom he considered, from the fame he had heard of him as a necessary person to assist him in facilitating the further promulgation of the gospel. Having found out Saul, he returned with him, in a short time, to Antioch, where, for the space of a whole year, they daily resorted to the most public places, preaching and expounding the doctrine of their great Master; by means of which they soon gained over such a prodigious number of converts, that in this city the disciples of Jesus were first distinguished by the honorable name of Christians.‡

The extensive circulation of the gospel at Antioch opened an intercourse between the Christians of that city and those of Jerusalem. Many people resorted from the latter place to the former, and among them was one person named Agabus, who foretold, that there would shortly be a great famine in many parts of the Roman empire, which accordingly happened in the fourth year of the reign of the emperor Claudius. In consequence of this prophecy, the Christians of Antioch determined to make a collection for their brethren in Judea, which, on the approach of the dearth, they accordingly did, and sent it to the elders at Jerusalem by the hands of Barnabas and Saul.

About this time Herod Agrippa, the grandson of Herod the Great, in order to ingratiate himself with the heads of the obstinate Jews, raised a most violent persecution against the Christians, in the commencement of which he ordered James, the son of Zebedee, and brother of John, commonly called "the Great,"‖ to be put to death. Finding this cruel act was acceptable to the chief-priests and rulers, he resolved to extend his cruelty to Peter. He accordingly caused him to be apprehended and put into prison, designing, immediately after the feast of the passover, to bring him forth to the Jews, and, if they desired it, to have him executed. But the Christians were incessant in their prayers to God for his safety; nor were their prayers and solicitations in vain. Herod was persuaded in his own mind, that he should soon accom-

* This was a city of great note, and once of such power, as to contend with Carthage for some pre-eminences. It stood on the western parts of Lybia (properly so called), and, as it was the principal city, it sometimes gave the name of Cyrenaica to the whole country, which by the sacred writer is paraphrastically called Lybia about Cyrene (Acts ii. 10). The city itself is famous in Holy Writ for being the birthplace of that Simon, whom the Jews compelled to bear our Saviour's Cross.

† This Antioch (to distinguish it from sixteen other cities, which, in Syria, and other countries, bore that name) was frequently called Antiochia Epidaphne, from its neighborhood to Daphne, a village where the temple of Daphne stood. It was built, as some say, by Antiochus Epiphanes; as others, by Seleucus Nicanor, the first king of Syria after Alexander the Great, in memory of his father Antiochus, and was, after that, the royal seat of the kings of Syria. In the flourishing times of the Roman empire it was the ordinary residence of the prefect, or governor of the eastern provinces, and was also honored with the residence of many of the Roman emperors, especially of Verus and Valens, who spent here the greatest part of their time. As to its situation, it lay on both sides the river Orontes, about twelve miles distant from the Mediterranean sea; was, in former times, adorned with many sumptuous palaces and stately temples, and both by Nature and Art fortified even to admiration; but, being taken by the Saracens, and afterward by the Turks, it began to grow into decay, and has ever since been in a desolate and ruinous condition (see engraving, page 407).

‡ Before this they were called among themselves *brethren, saints, disciples, believers,* and *those that called on the name of Christ:* and among their enemies, *Galileans, Nazarenes,* and *men of the sect:* but now by the conversion of so many heathens, both in Cesarea and Antioch, the believing Jews and Gentiles being all made one church, this new name was given them, as being more expressive of their common relation to Christ, their great Lord and Master.

‖ He is commonly called *the Great* to distinguish him from another of the same name, who was bishop of Jerusalem, and called *the Less.* He had his first instruction, together with John, from the Baptist; but how he disposed of himself after our Lord's ascension does not appear. That he was very zealous and industrious in propagating the gospel, appears evident from Herod's making choice of him for the first sacrifice (after the death of Stephen) to the fury of the people.

34

plish his design, and sacrifice Peter to the insatiable cruelty of the Jews. But the night before this intended execution, a messenger from the courts of Heaven visited the gloomy horrors of the dungeon, where he found Peter asleep between two of his keepers. The angel raised him up, and taking off his chains, ordered him to gird on his garments, and follow him. Peter obeyed, and having passed through the first and second watch, they came to the iron gate leading to the city, which opened to them of its own accord. The angel also accompanied him through one of the streets, and then departed. On this Peter, who had hitherto been confused, thinking all that had passed was no more than a dream, came to himself, and perceived that it was no vision, but that his great and beloved Master had really sent a messenger from above, and released him from prison. He therefore repaired to the house of Mary, the mother of John, surnamed Mark, where several disciples were met together, and sending up their prayers to Heaven for his deliverance. As he stood knocking without, a maid-servant of the house, named Rhoda, knowing his voice, ran in, and acquainted the company that Peter was at the door. At first they would not pay any attention to what she said; but on her persisting in the truth of what she asserted, they concluded that it must have been his angel. Their doubts, however, were soon removed by the entrance of Peter, at the sight of whom they were all greatly astonished. Peter beckoning them to hold their peace, related the whole particulars of his miraculous escape from prison, and, after ordering them to acquaint James, and the other brethren, with this good news, withdrew himself to a place of more retirement and security.

Early the next morning the officers went from Herod to the prison, with orders to bring Peter out to the people, who were gathered together to behold his execution. But when they came to the prison, they were informed by the keepers that Peter had made his escape. The officers immediately returned with this intelligence to Herod, who was so irritated at his being disappointed in his wicked design, that he commanded the keepers to be put to death, as supposing them accessary to his escape; after which he left Jerusalem, and retired to Cesarea.

While Herod was in Cesarea, a misunderstanding took place between him and the inhabitants of Tyre and Sidon, against whom he was about to declare war. But they, dreading his power (and knowing that in this time of scarcity their country was in a great measure dependant on Herod's dominions for its support), sent ambassadors to Blastus, Herod's chamberlain, requesting him to intercede in their behalf, and, if possible, to bring about an accommodation. Though Herod was highly displeased with them, yet he so far listened to his chamberlain as to appoint a day for holding a public conference with the ambassadors; at which time, being dressed in his royal robes, and seated on a throne, he made a long harangue on the occasion. The fawning multitude, thinking to ingratiate themselves in his favor, and please the tyrant's pride with flattering applause, shouted out, " It is the voice of a god, and not of a man." This gratified the pride of Herod, who, assuming to himself that praise which belonged only to God, was instantly struck by an angel with a mortification in his bowels, which, in a short time, put a period to his existence.

The tyrant Herod being thus removed, the gospel greatly flourished and increased, new converts daily thronging to be admitted to the faith.

About this time Barnabas and Saul, having discharged their trust in disposing of the contributions raised in Antioch for the benefit of the Christians in Jerusalem and Judea, returned to that city, taking with them John, surnamed Mark,* a person well calculated to assist them in the propagation of the gospel.

Barnabas and Saul had not been long returned to Antioch, when God, by some particular inspiration, gave them to understand, that he had appointed them to carry his word into other places. This was likewise revealed to the members of the church then at Antioch, who, in consequence thereof, betook themselves to fasting and prayer; and Simeon, Lucius, and Manaen (all of whom were endued with the spirit of prophecy), having laid their hands on them, sent them away to preach the gospel wherever they might be directed by divine inspiration.

On their departure from Antioch they went first to Seleucia,† whence they took

* This person, who is sometimes called John-Mark, and at other times simply Mark, or John, is very frequently confounded with the Evangelist St. Mark. He was a cousin and disciple of Barnabas, and the son of a Christian woman called Mary, at whose house in Jerusalem the apostles and disciples often assembled.
† This city lay on the west, or rather a little northwest of the city of Antioch, upon the Mediterranean sea, and was so called from Seleucus its founder.

shipping for Cyprus, and began their ministerial office in the city of Salamis,* where they preached in the synagogues, and employed Mark, who was of their company, in several offices of the church which they could not conveniently attend themselves.

From Salamis they proceeded to Paphos,† the residence of Sergius Paulus, the pro-consul, or governor of the island, a man of great wisdom and prudence, but unhappily seduced by the wicked artifices of Bar-Jesus, an impostor, who styled himself Elymas, or the magician. The governor being informed of the doctrine preached by Saul and Barnabas, was desirous of hearing it, and therefore sent to them for that purpose. They accordingly attended, but while Saul was delivering a discourse to him and the company present, the sorcerer (who stood by the pro-consul) used all the arguments he could to prevent his being converted to the faith. This being observed by Saul, he turned himself to the sorcerer, and severely chastised him in words to this effect: ' O thou vile sorcerer ! Like the devil, by whom thou workest, thou art an enemy to all goodness. Wilt thou persist in sorcery, in defiance of the faith of Christ, which comes armed with a much greater power of miracles than those to which thou falsely pretendest ? Thou shalt soon feel the vengeance of Heaven ; for thou that perversely holdest out against the light of the gospel, shalt lose thy sight, which, by the power of God, shall, for a time be taken from thee." No sooner had Saul uttered these words than the sorcerer was struck blind, and implored some of the company to conduct him to his habitation. This miracle convinced the pro-consul of the truth of the doctrine he had heard, and he immediately became a convert to the faith. And from this event it is supposed, by some, that Saul changed his name to that of Paul,‡ which he ever after retained.

After staying some time in the island of Cyprus, Paul and his companions went to Perga in Pamphylia,‖ where Mark (not choosing any longer to prosecute so wandering a course of life) took his leave, and returned to Jerusalem.

From Perga they went to Antioch in Pisidia,§ where, going into the synagogue on the sabbath-day, they sat themselves down to hear the performance of divine worship. After the lessons, one out of the law, and the other out of the prophets (it being the custom for the Jewish doctors to expound some part of the scripture for the instruction of the people) the chief persons of the assembly sent to Paul and his companions, to know whether either of them would preach a sermon of exhortation to the audience. This was an offer highly satisfactory to Paul, who, after intimating his acceptance of it, arose, and delivered a discourse to the people in words to this effect :—

"Hearken, all ye descendants of Jacob, and ye that fear the Almighty, to the words of my mouth. The God of Israel made choice of our fathers, and loved them, when they had no city of their own to dwell in, but were strangers and slaves in Egypt, bringing them thence with a mighty hand, and a stretched-out arm ; fed them in the wilderness forty years, and would not suffer his anger to rise against them, though they often provoked him in the desert. On their arrival in the land he promised their fathers, he destroyed the nations that inhabited it, and placed them in that fruitful country, dividing it to them by lot.

" When they were settled in the land, he gave them judges during four hundred

* This was once a famous city in the isle of Cyprus, opposite to Seleucia, on the Syrian coast ; and, as it was the first place in these parts where the gospel was preached, it was, in the primitive times, made the see of the primate, or metropolitan of the whole island. In the reign of the emperor Trajan, it was destroyed by the Jews, and rebuilt, but, after that, being in the time of Herodius, sacked, and razed to the ground by the Saracens, it never recovered its former splendor, though out of its ruins is said to have arisen Famagusta, which was the chief place of the isle, when the Turks took it from the Venetians, in the year 1570.

† Paphos was another city of Cyprus, lying on the western (as Salamis did on the eastern) track of the island. It was once famous for having in it a celebrated temple dedicated to Venus, who, thence, is called, by ancient writers, the Paphian Queen.

‡ It is very observable, that all along, before this circumstance of the apostle's life, St. Luke calls him by the name of Saul, but ever after by that of Paul. Hence some imagine, that he assumed that name to himself, in memory of his converting Sergius Paulus ; just as the ancient Roman generals were accustomed to adopt the names of the provinces which they conquered. St. Austin more than once asserts, that he took it from a principle of humility, by a small variation changing his former name (whereby a proud haughty king of Israel was called) into that of Paulus, which signifies *little* ; and that, in conformity to this, he calls himself " less than the least of the apostles." But the most rational account of the matter seems to be that of Origen, namely, that he, being of Jewish parentage, and born in Tarsus, a Roman city, had, at his circumcision, two names given him, Saul, a Jewish, and Paul, a Roman name, and that when he preached to the Jews, he was called by his Jewish, and when to the Gentiles (as he did chiefly after this time) by his Roman name.

‖ Pamphylia was a province of the lesser Asia, not far from Cyprus.

§ This lay a little to the north of Pamphylia.

and fifty years, till Samuel the prophet. But on their desiring a king, he placed over them Saul the son of Cis, a Benjamite, who reigned about forty years. After his death he placed David on the throne of Israel, giving him this testimony : I have found David the son of Jesse, a man after mine own heart, which shall fulfil all my will. And according to his promise the Almighty hath raised up to the sons of David a Saviour Jesus, which is Christ the Lord ; the baptism of repentance having been preached before his coming by John. And as his forerunner executed his office, he asked his followers, Whom think ye that I am ? You must not mistake me for the Messiah ; he will soon follow me ; but I am not worthy to perform the meanest office for him.

" To you, therefore, ye descendants of Abraham, and all others who fear the Almighty, is this word of salvation sent. For the inhabitants of Jerusalem, and rulers of Israel, being ignorant of him, and the voices of the prophets, though read every sabbath in their synagogues, fulfilled their predictions by condemning the immaculate Son of the Most High. They found, indeed, no fault in him, though they earnestly desired Pilate that he might be slain.

" When everything that had been written by the prophets concerning him was fulfilled, they took him from the tree, and deposited his body in the chambers of the grave. But death had no power to detain him ; his almighty Father raised him from the habitations of the dead. After which he was seen during many days by his disciples who attended him from Galilee, and were the witnesses chosen by Omnipotence, of these great and miraculous works. And we now declare unto you glad tidings, namely, that the promise made by the Almighty to our forefathers, he hath performed to us their children, by raising Jesus from the dead. The prophet David also said, Thou art my son, this day have I begotten thee. He also foretold that he should return from the chambers of the dust, and no more be subject to corruption : I will give you (said he) the sure mercies of David. And again, Thou shalt not suffer thine holy one to see corruption. Now this prophecy must relate to the Messiah, for David himself, after he had swayed the sceptre of Israel a certain time, died, was deposited in the chamber of the grave, and his flesh saw corruption ; but the great Son of David, whom the Almighty raised from the dead, never saw corruption.

" Be it therefore known unto you, men and brethren, that through this Saviour is preached unto you the forgiveness of sins. It is by his merits we are justified from all things, which was impossible by the law of Moses. Be careful, therefore, lest what was foretold by the prophets come upon you : ' Behold, ye despisers, and wonder and perish ; for I work a work in your days, a work which you shall in no wise believe though a man declare it unto you.' "

This discourse was so well received by great numbers of the people, that when they got out of the synagogue, they besought Paul that he would deliver it again on the next Sabbath. Paul promised to comply with their request, which he accordingly did, and on that day almost all the inhabitants of the city flocked to hear him. This irritated such of the Jews as were strong enemies to the gospel ; nor could they refrain from showing their malice on the occasion. They several times not only interrupted, but peremptorily contradicted Paul while he was preaching, and at length uttered many blasphemous expressions against the name of Jesus of Nazareth. But their opposition could not daunt the apostles, who boldly answered them as follows : " It was necessary that the word of God should first have been spoken to you ; but seeing ye put it from you, and judge yourselves unworthy of everlasting life, lo, we turn to the Gentiles. For so hath the Lord commanded us, saying, I have set thee to be a light of the Gentiles, that thou shouldst be for salvation unto the ends of the earth."

When the Gentiles heard this, they were greatly rejoiced, and glorified the name of God for his beneficent mercy revealed in the gospel ; and all who had any care or thought of the life to come immediately embraced the doctrine of Christ. This increased the malice and fury of the Jews, who, by false and artful insinuations, prevailed on some of the more bigoted and honorable women to bring over their husbands to their party : the consequence of this was, that Paul and Barnabas were driven out of the city, on leaving which they shook the dust off their feet, in testimony of the sense they had of the ingratitude and infidelity of their oppressors.

From Antioch Paul and Barnabas went to Iconium, where they entered into the synagogue of the Jews, and, according to their usual custom, preached to the people; the consequence of which was that many, both Jews and Greeks, became proselytes to the Christian religion. From this success the two apostles continued some time at Iconium, during which the number of converts daily increased, and, to confirm them in the faith, God added his testimony to their preaching, by enabling them to work miracles. But though they had gained a considerable numoer of inhabitants to the faith, yet there were many who continued in their infidelity: the whole leaven of Jewish malice began again to show itself, and the unbelieving Jews, having stirred up the Gentiles against the apostles, at length prevailed on the multitude to stone them. But the apostles, having timely notice of their designs, fled from the city to Lystra and Derbe (two other cities in the province of Lycaonia), where they preached the gospel to the inhabitants, as also to those who dwelt in the countries adjoining.

While they were at Lystra, a happy circumstance occurred both for the promulgation of the gospel, and the conversion of a people who had greatly been devoted to paganism. As Paul was one day preaching to the multitude, he saw among them a man who had been lame from his mother's womb, and had never walked. From the earnest attention which the cripple gave to the discourse, Paul (who had for some time taken particular notice of him) perceived that he had faith, and therefore thought proper to add the cure of his body to that of his soul, knowing that it would not only be beneficial to him, but would likewise confirm the faith of all who should believe in his doctrine. And that the miracle might be wrought in the most conspicuous manner, Paul, in the midst of the congregation, said in an audible voice to the man, "Stand upright on thy feet;" which words were no sooner pronounced than he arose, "and leaped and walked."

The people who beheld this miracle well knew that it could not be wrought by any human power; but having been initiated in the superstitious customs of the heathens, they cried out, "The gods are come down to us in the likeness of men." Accordingly they called Barnabas Jupiter, on account of his venerable gravity, and Paul they named Mercurius, "because he was the chief speaker."

It was not long before the fame of this miracle was spread throughout the city; in consequence of which almost all the inhabitants gathered themselves together, and preceded by the priest of Jupiter, and oxen dressed in garlands, went to the house where the apostles resided, intending to offer sacrifice before them. But as soon as Paul and Barnabas understood their intentions, they were greatly affected at their superstitious design; and rending their clothes to express their grief and abhorrence of the action, ran out to the multitude, whom Paul addressed in words to this effect: "Ye men of Lystra, ye are mistaken in the object of your worship; for though we have done many miracles in the name and by the power of Christ, yet we are no more than men, and subject to the same passions with yourselves, and preach unto you the glad tidings of salvation, that ye may forsake the vanities of this world, and return to the living God, who created the heaven and the earth, the sea, and all the creatures they contain. This Omnipotent Being suffered all nations formerly to walk in their own ways, though he never left himself without witness, doing the greatest good to the children of men; it is he that sendeth rain from heaven, and crowneth the year with fruitful seasons, filling our hearts with joy and gladness."

This argument had the desired effect, the people, though with some difficulty, being persuaded to lay aside their idolatrous intentions. And surely no argument could be more properly adapted to answer the wishes of the inspired preacher. Is it possible that any human being can survey the several parts of the creation, and not discover in every place evident traces of an Infinite wisdom, power, and goodness? Who can survey universal nature, and not at once see and admire its great Author, who has disposed of all created things with such order and regularity as to display in the clearest manner his own power and glory? Behold the sun! how justly is that source of light and heat placed in the centre of the planetary choir, that each may enjoy its destined share of its prolific beams; so that the earth is not burnt by a too near approach, nor chilled by the northern blasts from too great a recess, but impregnated with fruits and flowers by the happy influence of a vital heat, and crowned with luxuriant plenty by the benign influences of the season. Who can contemplate the wonderful properties of the air, and not reflect on the Divine wisdom that formed it? If we survey the earth, we there discover the footsteps of an Almighty Being, who hath filled it with a great variety of admirable and useful creatures, all of which are maintained by the bounty of his hand. It is he that clothes the grass with a delightful verdure, that crowns the year with his loving kindness, and causes the valleys to stand thick with corn. It is he that maketh the grass to grow upon the mountains, and herbs for the service of man. He adorns the lilies of the field, that neither toil nor spin, with a glory that excels the pomp and grandeur of Solomon's court. He "shut up the sea with doors," and said, "Hitherto shalt thou come and no farther, and here shall thy proud waves be stayed." It is the Almighty Being that arrests the storm, and smooths the tempestuous billows of the deep; that delivereth the mariner from all his troubles, and bringeth his ship into the desired haven of safety. How reasonable, therefore, is it that we should worship and adore this Omnipotent, this kind Creator, and not transfer the honors due to him alone to frail mortals, much less to dumb idols, the work of men's hands!

After Paul had performed the miracle on the lame man, he and Barnabas continued to persevere in the execution of their important commission, declaring, wherever they went, the glad tidings of salvation to all who believed in the doctrine of Christ. But the malice of their enemies still pursued them: some inveterate Jews, who had come from Antioch and Iconium, so exasperated and stirred up the multitude against them, that they took Paul, whom, just before, they would have adored, and stoned him; after which they dragged him out of the city, supposing him to be dead. But when the disciples went to the place where he was (probably to inter his body) he rose up, and went into the city for that night, and the next day departed, with Barnabas, to Derbe, where they preached the gospel, and converted many to the faith.

They did not, however, continue long at Derbe, but returned to Lystra, Iconium, and Antioch, confirming the Christians of those places in the faith, earnestly persuading them to persevere, and not to be discouraged at those troubles and persecutions which they must expect would attend the profession of the gospel. And that the affairs of the church might be conducted with more regularity, they ordained elders and pastors, to teach, instruct, and watch over them; having done which, they left them to the protection of the Almighty, to whose care they recommended them by prayer and fasting.

From Antioch they passed through Pisidia, and thence went to Pamphylia; and, having preached to the people at Perga, they went down to Attalia, and returned, by sea, to Antioch in Syria, whence they had set out on this holy expedition. On their arrival here, they immediately assembled the church together, and, having given an account of their success, what miracles God had wrought by their hands, and a large "door of faith," he, by their ministry, had opened to the Gentiles, they suspended their further travels for the present, and for a considerable time, took up their abode with the disciples in that city.

During their stay here, the church was greatly disturbed by means of some persons coming from Judea, who taught the people that there was no salvation without circumcision, and the observance of other legal ceremonies. This doctrine was strongly opposed by Paul and Barnabas; in consequence of which, after many conferences and disputations, it was at length proposed, that the decision of the matter should be referred to the general assembly of the apostles at Jerusalem. This the whole church readily agreed to; and having deputed Barnabas and Paul, together with some others, to go with the message, they conducted them part of the way, and the two apostles, in passing through Phœnicia and Samaria, took care to relate what success they had met with in the conversion of the Gentiles, to the great joy and comfort of all the brethren in those parts.

On their arrival at Jerusalem they were kindly received by the apostles and elders of the church, to whom, after reciting the great success they had met with in the propagation of the gospel, they delivered the message on which they were sent. They told them, that when the Gentile proselytes, or others uncircumcised, came in to the faith, some Jewish converts, of the sect of the Pharisees, said that such could not be admitted into the church of Christ without circumcision; that great disputes had arisen on this head, and that the matter was referred to the church at Jerusalem.

In consequence of this intelligence a council was immediately summoned to deliberate on the matter, and great disputes took place on the occasion. At length Peter, rising from his seat, addressed the audience in words to this effect: "It is well known to you all, that some time since God made choice of me first to preach the gospel to the Gentiles; and God, who knew the sincerity of their hearts, testified that they were acceptable to him and fit to be baptized, bestowing on them the gift of the Holy Ghost, as he had before upon us, making no difference between us and them. By this one act the matter is already sufficiently determined. Why then do ye press this thing so contrary to the will of God? And why would ye wish to impose on the Gentile converts the performance of the Mosaic law, which belonged not to them, and which we Jews were so far from being able to perform, that our conduct could not be justified? It is from the gospel that we expect salvation and justification, through faith and obedience to Christ, and not by an observation of the Mosaic law: whence it is plain, that if the Gentiles believe, they have the same way to salvation as ourselves."

When Peter had concluded his observations, Paul and Barnabas, in confirmation of what he had said, declared what miracles God had done by them in the conversion of the Gentiles, which they said was another argument and testimony from heaven, that no difference ought to be made between them and the Jews.

Upon this James stood up, and spoke to this effect: "Men and brethren, Peter hath sufficiently demonstrated that it was the will of God the Gentiles should, without scruple, have the gospel preached to them, and be baptized. And this is agreeable to what hath been foretold by the old prophets, particularly Amos: 'In the later days I will return, and will build again the tabernacle of David which is fallen down; and I will build again the ruins thereof, and I will set it up: that the residue of men might seek after the Lord, and all the Gentiles upon whom my name is called, saith the Lord, who doeth all these things.' Wherefore it is my conclusion and determination, that we should not compel those to be circumcised, who from Gentiles turn Christians, but content ourselves if they believe. We who are Jews need not fear that this will bring a contempt upon Moses or the laws of the Jews, since the contrary appears by the Christian practice; for even where those proselytes of the Gentiles are, the books of Moses are continued among them, being read in the synagogues every sabbath-day, to signify their respect to the law."

This determination being unanimously agreed to, it was next resolved to send some proper persons with Paul and Barnabas to Antioch, in order that they, having been present, might give a satisfactory account of the result of the apostles' embassy. They accordingly made choice of two, namely, Judas, surnamed Barsabas, and Silas, men of distinguished reputation, and well respected by all Christians. These, accompanied by Paul and Barnabas, proceeded to Antioch, taking with them a decree drawn up by the council, which was to this effect: "Forasmuch as we have heard, that certain which went out from us, have troubled you with words, subverting your souls, saying ye must be circumcised and keep the law; to whom we gave no such commandment: it seemed good unto us, being assembled with one accord, to send chosen men unto you, with our beloved Barnabas and Paul: men that have hazarded their lives for the name of our Lord Jesus Christ. We have sent therefore Judas and Silas, who shall also tell you the same things by mouth. For it seemed good to the Holy Ghost, and to us, to lay upon you no greater burden than these necessary things; that ye abstain from meats offered to idols, and from blood, and from things strangled, and from fornication: from which if ye keep yourselves, ye shall do well. Fare ye well." (Acts xv. 24–29.)

With this decree they immediately repaired to Antioch, whither they they had no sooner arrived, than the Christian converts, both Jews and Gentiles, assembled together in order to know the issue of their embassy. As soon as they were met, Paul and Barnabas presented to them the decretal epistle, which they caused to be read in the hearing of the whole congregation. The contents of the decree, which were ultimate, gave the highest satisfaction to the Gentile converts, who greatly rejoiced at finding themselves discharged from the burden of the law, and confirmed in their Christian liberty.

While Judas and Silas were at Antioch (being both men of excellent gifts in the interpretation of the Scriptures), they employed their time in confirming believers in the truth of Christianity, and, after a short stay, were, with all kindness and civility, dismissed by the church, in order to return to Jerusalem. But Silas, for some reasons, was unwilling to depart so soon, choosing rather to tarry with Paul and Barnabas. This he accordingly did, and those three, together with several others of the brethren, employed themselves in instructing such as had already received the Christian faith, and in preaching to others who had not yet embraced it.

Soon after the determination of the council at Jerusalem, Peter went thence to Antioch, where, using the liberty which the gospel had given him, he for some time conversed familiarly with the Gentile converts, eating with them, and living with them in the same manner they did. This he had been taught to do by the vision of the sheet let down from heaven; this had been lately decreed at Jerusalem; this he had before practised with regard to Cornelius and his family, and justified the action to the satisfaction of his brethren; this he had likewise done after his arrival at Antioch, till some Jewish Christians (still tenacious of the ceremonial law) coming thither from Jerusalem, Peter, fearful of offending or displeasing them, withdrew himself from the Gentiles, as if it had been unlawful for him to hold conversation with uncircumcised persons; notwithstanding he knew, and was fully satisfied that our blessed Saviour had broken down the wall of partition between the Jew and Gentile.

Peter, by thus acting against the light of his own mind and judgment, condemned what he had approved, and destroyed the superstructure he had before erected: at the same time he confirmed the Jewish zealots in their gross errors, filled the minds of the Gentiles with scruples, and their consciences with fears.

Paul, who was not ignorant of what pernicious influence the example of so great an apostle might be, especially when he saw Barnabas carried away with the stream of his indiscretion, was greatly irritated at his conduct, and, in the presence of the whole church, severely rebuked him, for endeavoring to impose that yoke on the Gentiles, which he, though a Jew, thought himself at liberty to shake off.

A few days after this Paul and Barnabas resolved to leave Antioch, and visit those places in which they had some time before planted Christianity among the Gentiles. In this intended excursion Barnabas proposed taking with them John Mark; but the proposition was highly disapproved by Paul, on account of Mark's having deserted them at Pamphylia. In consequence of this, a warm dispute took place between them, the issue of which was, that they determined to separate.* Accordingly Barnabas, accompanied by Mark, went to Cyprus, which was his native country; and soon after Paul, having chosen Silas for his companion, set out on his intended visitation of the several places in which he had before propagated Christianity.

CHAPTER VIII.

WHEN Paul left Antioch, after his separation from Barnabas, he and his companion Silas travelled over the provinces of Syria and Cilicia, confirming the churches, and leaving with each a copy of the decree, which a short time before had been passed by the council at Jerusalem. From these parts they sailed to Crete,† where Paul propagated the gospel, and constituted Titus pastor of the island, leaving him to settle those affairs of the church, which time would not permit the apostle to do.

From Crete Paul and Silas returned to Cilicia, and thence went to Lystra. Here they met with a young man named Timothy, whose father was a Greek, but his mother a Jewish convert, by whom he had been brought up under all the advantages of a pious and religious education, especially with regard to the holy Scriptures, which he had studied with the greatest assiduity and success. This person Paul designed as a companion of his travels, and a special instrument in the ministry of the

---

* Hence we may learn not only that these great lights in the Christian church were men of the like passions with us, but that God, upon this occasion, did most eminently illustrate the wisdom of his providence, by rendering the frailties of two such eminent servants instrumental to the benefit of his church, since both of them thenceforward employed their extraordinary industry and zeal, singly and apart, which till then had been united, and confined to the same places.

† This was one of the richest and best islands in the whole Mediterranean sea. It is said at one time to have contained no less than a hundred considerable towns or cities, whence it had the name of Hecatompolis. From the goodness of the soil, and temperature of the air, it was likewise styled Macorios, or the Happy island. At present it is commonly called Candia, from its principal town, which bears that name. It is situated opposite the mouth of the Ægean sea, or Archipelago; and while it continued in the hands of the Venetians was an archbishop's see; great, rich, and populous: but since it came into the possession of the Turks (which was in the year 1669) it has lost all marks of its former grandeur.

Thyatira.

gospel. But knowing that his being uncircumcised would prove a stumbling-block to the Jews, he caused him to be circumcised; being willing, in lawful and indifferent matters, to conform himself to the tempers and dispositions of all, that he might thereby further succeed in his ministry, and the sooner establish that doctrine he was sent to propagate.

After staying a short time at Lystra, they passed through Phrygia* and Galatia,† where the apostle Paul was entertained with the greatest kindness and veneration by the people, who looked upon him as an angel sent immediately from heaven. Hence he intended to have continued his progress through the proconsular Asia, but was prohibited from so doing by a particular revelation. In consequence of this he went to Mysia,‡ and after attempting in vain to go into Bithynia,‖ proceeded to Troas,§ where, soon after his arrival, he had a vision, commanding him to direct his course for Macedonia.¶ Paul made immediate preparations for obeying these orders, being fully assured it was the Lord who had called him to preach the gospel in that country.

Paul and his companions, having embarked at Troas, sailed to the island of Samothracia,** and the next day, landed at Neapolis,†† a port in Macedonia, whence they travelled to Philippi,‡‡ a Roman colony, where they continued some days.

At a small distance from Philippi the Jews had a *proseuche*, or place of devotion, which was much frequented by the devout women of their religion, who met there to pray and hear the law. In this place Paul and his companions preached the glad tidings of the gospel, and, by the influence of the Holy Spirit, made many converts. Among these was a certain woman named Lydia, a seller of purple in Philippi, but a native of Thyatira,‖‖ whom they baptized, with her household; in return for which she invited them to lodge in her house during their abode in that city.

As Paul and his companions were one day going, as usual, to the before-mentioned place of devotion, they were met by a certain damsel, who was possessed with a spirit of divination, by means of which her masters acquired considerable advantage.

* Phrygia is a province of Asia Minor, having Bithynia to the north, Galatia to the east, Lycia to the south, and Mysia to the west. The inhabitants of this country, who are said to have been the inventors of augury, and other kinds of divination, were anciently more superstitious than the other Asiatics, as appears from the rites which they used in the sacrifice of Cybele, and other heathen goddesses.

† Galatia is a province of Asia Minor, bounded on the west by Phrygia, on the east by the river Halys, on the north by Paphlagonia, and on the south by Lycaonia.

‡ Mysia is another small province of Asia Minor, bounded on the east by Phrygia, on the west by Troas, on the north by Bithynia, and on the south by the river Hermus.

‖ Bithynia is likewise a region of Asia Minor, and received its name from one of its kings, named Bythinus; but in what age he reigned we are not informed.

§ Troas was a small country belonging to Phrygia Minor, and situated to the west of Mysia, upon the Hellespont. It took its name from its principal city, which was a seaport, and situated about four miles from old Troy.

¶ This is a large province in Greece, and was anciently called Emmathia, but, from the kings of Macedon, it was afterward called Macedonia, which name it has ever since retained.

** Samothracia is a small island in the Ægean sea, lying to the west of Troas, opposite the coast of Thrace, whence it received its name.

†† Neapolis was a seaport, and stood very near to Thrace. At first it belonged to that province, but was afterward taken into Macedonia.

‡‡ Philippi was one of the chief cities of Macedonia, lying to the west of Neapolis. It was originally called Dathos, but afterward took its name from Philip, the famous king of Macedon, who repaired and beautified it. In process of time it became a Roman colony, and the inhabitants enjoyed the privileges of Roman citizens, and were governed by the Roman laws. These indulgences were conferred on them both by Julius and Augustus Cæsar, very probably, in memory of the two great battles that were fought in the plains adjacent, the first between Julius and Pompey the Great, and the second between Augustus and Mark Antony on the one side, and Cassius and Brutus on the other.

‖‖ This ancient city still survives as an inhabited site, under the Turkish name of Ark-hissar, or the White castle. It can not however compare with the two other inhabited sites, being greatly inferior to Pergamos, and immeasurably so to Smyrna. In ancient remains it is poorer than any of the seven. It is situated about twenty-seven miles to the north of Sardis, and is thus noticed by Pliny Fisk, the American missionary: "Thyatira is situated near a small river, a branch of the Caicus, in the centre of an extensive plain. At the distance of three or four miles it is almost completely surrounded by mountains. The houses are low; many of them of mud or earth. Excepting the motsellim's palace, there is scarcely a decent house in the place. The streets are narrow and dirty, and everything indicates poverty and degradation. We had a letter of introduction to Economo, the bishop's procurator, and a principal man among the Greeks of this town. . . . He says the Turks have destroyed all remnants of the ancient church; and even the place where it stood is now unknown. At present there are in the town one thousand houses for which taxes are paid to the government." (Memoir of the Rev. P. Fisk. Boston, Mass. 1828.) It appears, from Hartley, that the Greeks occupy three hundred houses, the Armenians thirty. Each of them has a church. The town is embosomed in poplars and cypresses. The traveller last named observes: "The sacred writer of the Acts of the Apostles informs us that Lydia was a seller of purple in the city of Thyatira; and the discovery of an inscription here, which makes mention of 'the dyers,' has been considered important in connexion with this passage. I know not if other travellers have remarked, that even at the present time, Thyatira is famous for dying. In answer to inquiries on the subject, I was informed that the cloths which are dyed scarlet here, are considered superior to any others furnished by Asia Minor; and that large quantities are sent weekly to Smyrna, for the purposes of commerce."

This woman followed Paul and his companion, crying out, "These men are the servants of the Most High God, which show us the way of salvation." Paul, at first took no notice of her, not being willing to multiply miracles without necessity. But when he saw her following them several days together, he began to be troubled; and therefore, in imitation of his great Master (who would not suffer the devil to acknowledge him, lest his false and lying tongue should prejudice the truth in the minds of men), commanded the spirit, in the name of Jesus, to come out of her. Accordingly the evil spirit obeyed, and at that instant left the damsel.

This miraculous cure proving a great loss to her masters, who had acquired large sums from her soothsaying, they were vehemently incensed against the apostles. They therefore caused Paul and Silas to be apprehended and carried before the magistrates of the city, to whom they accused them of introducing many innovations, which were prejudicial to the state, and unlawful for them to comply with, as being Romans.

The magistrates, being concerned for the tranquillity of the state, and fearful of all disturbances, were very forward to punish the offenders, against whom the multitude testified; and therefore they commanded the officers to strip them, and scourge them severely as seditious persons. This was accordingly done, after which they were committed to close custody, and the jailer, having received a strict charge to keep them in the utmost security, not only thrust them into the inner prison, but likewise made their feet fast to the stocks.

But neither the obscure dungeon, nor the pitchy mantle of the night, can intercept the beams of divine joy and comfort from the souls of pious men. Their minds were all serenity; and at midnight they prayed, and sung praises to God so loud, that they were heard in every part of the prison. Nor were their prayers offered to the throne of grace in vain: an earthquake shook the foundations of the prison, opened the doors, loosed the chains, and set the prisoners at liberty.

This convulsion of nature roused the jailer from his sleep; and concluding, from what he saw, that all his prisoners were escaped, he was going to put a period to his life, which being observed by Paul, he hastily called out, "Do thyself no harm, for we are all here." The keeper was as much surprised at this as he had been before terrified at the thoughts of their escape; and calling for a light, he went immediately into the presence of Paul and Silas, fell down at their feet, took them from the dungeon, brought them to his own house, washed their stripes, and then besought them to instruct him in the knowledge of that God who was so mighty to save. Paul readily granted his request, telling him, that if he believed in Jesus Christ, he and his whole house might be saved. Accordingly the jailer, with all his family, were, after a competent instruction, baptized, and received as members of the Christian church.—How happy a change does the doctrine of the gospel make in the minds of men! How does it smooth the roughest tempers, and instil in their minds the sweetest principles of civility and good-nature! He, who put a few moments before tyrannized over Paul and Silas with the most cruel usage, now treated them with the greatest respect, and showed them the highest marks of kindness.

Early the next morning the magistrates (either, having heard what had happened, or reflecting on what they had done as too harsh and unjustifiable) sent their sergeant to the jailer, with orders immediately to discharge Paul and Silas. The jailer joyfully delivered the message, and bade them depart in peace; but Paul, in order to make the magistrates sensible what injury they had done them, and how unjustly they had punished them without examination or trial, refused to accept of their discharge, alleging, "that they were not only innocent persons, but denizens of Rome; that, as they had been illegally scourged and committed to prison, their delivery should be as public as was the injury, and attended with a solemn retraction of what they had done."

The magistrates were greatly terrified at this message, well knowing how dangerous it was to provoke the formidable power of the Romans, who never suffered any freeman to be beaten uncondemned. They therefore went to the prison, and very submissively entreated them to depart without any further disturbance. This small recompense for the cruel usage they had received was accepted by the meek followers of the blessed Jesus: they accordingly left the prison, and retired to the house of Lydia, in which were a great number of converts. To those they related all that had passed, and after some conference with them, they took their leave and departed.

From Philippi Paul and his companions travelled toward the west, till they arrived at Thessalonica,* the metropolis of Macedonia. Here Paul preached in the synagogues of the Jews three sabbath-days successively, proving, from the predictions of the Old Testament, that the Messiah was to suffer, and to rise again; and that the blessed Jesus was the Messiah spoken of by the prophets. Some of his hearers, among whom were several women of rank and quality, believed, and were converted to the faith, but the greater part of the Jews disapproved of his doctrine.

During their stay at Thessalonica, they lodged in the house of a certain Christian named Jason, who entertained them very courteously. But the Jews, in general, were so incensed against them, that they would not suffer them to continue at rest. They refused to embrace the gospel themselves, and therefore envied its success, and determined to oppose its progress. Accordingly they gathered together a great number of lewd and wicked people, who beset the house of Jason, intending to take Paul, and deliver him up to an incensed multitude. But in this they were disappointed, he with his companions being removed thence by the Christians, and concealed in some other part of the city. This disappointment increased their rage, and they determined to be revenged on Jason, who had concealed them. Accordingly they seized him, with some others of the brethren, and carried them before the magistrates of the city, accused them with disturbing the peace of the empire, and setting up Jesus as a king, in derogation of the emperor's dignity and authority. In consequence of this accusation, both the people and magistrates became their enemies; and though Jason was only accused of harboring Paul and his companions, yet the magistrates could not be prevailed on to dismiss Jason and his brethren till they had given security for their future appearance.

As soon as the tumult was over, those Thessalonians who had been converted sent away Paul and his companions, by night, to Berœa, a city about fifty miles to the south of Thessalonica. Here also Paul's great love for his countrymen the Jews, and his earnest wishes for their salvation, excited him to preach to them in particular. Accordingly, he entered into their synagogue, and explained the gospel to them, proving, from the scriptures of the Old Testament, the truth of the doctrine he advanced. The Jews here were of a more ingenuous and candid temper than those of Thessalonica; and as they heard him, with great reverence and attention, expound the Scriptures, so they searched diligently, whether his proofs were proper and pertinent, and consonant to the sense of the text to which he referred. Having done this, and found everything agreeable to what Paul had advanced, many of them believed; and some Gentiles (among whom were several women of quality) following their example, became obedient to the faith. The news of this remarkable success being carried to Thessalonica, the Jews of that place were so incensed, that great numbers of them went to Berœa, and raised tumults in that city; in consequence of which Paul, to avoid their fury, was obliged to leave the place, but Silas and Timothy, who, perhaps, were either less known, or less envied, remained behind.

Paul, leaving Berœa under the conduct of certain guides, it was imagined that he designed to retire by sea out of Greece, that his restless enemies might cease their persecution; but the guides, in conformity to Paul's direction, conducted them to Athens,† where they left him, after receiving orders to tell Silas and Timothy to repair to him as soon as possible.

While Paul continued at Athens, expecting the arrival of his companions, he walked up and down to take an accurate survey of the city, which he found wretchedly overrun with superstition and idolatry. The inhabitants were remarkably religious and devout, they had a great number of gods whom they adored; false, indeed, they were, but such as they, being destitute of revelation, accounted true; and so very careful were they that no deity should want due honor from them, that they had an altar inscribed, "to the unknown God."‡

* Thessalonica was anciently called Thesma, from the sea to which it adjoins. It is the opinion of some that it received the latter name in memory of the victory which Philip king of Macedon obtained over the Thessalonians; but others think it took its name from Thessalonica, the wife of Cassander, and daughter of Philip. It is at present called Salonichi, has a safe harbor for the benefit of commerce, and is an archbishop's see of the Grecian church.

† Athens was once the most celebrated city for learning of any in the world. It was situated on a gulf of the Ægean sea, which comes up to the isthmus of the Peloponnese, or Morea, in that district of Greece called Attica, and was the parent of that dialect which was esteemed the purest and finest Greek. Cicero calls it the fountain whence civility, learning, and laws, were derived to other nations.

‡ That the Athenians had altars in their public places, without names on them, and others to unknown gods, is evident from the testimony of Laertius, who informs us, that when a great plague raged at Athens,

Athens.—The Areopagus.

These superstitious practices greatly afflicted Paul, in consequence of which he exerted all his endeavors to convert the people. He disputed on the sabbath-day in the synagogues of the Jews; and, at other times, took all opportunities of preaching to the Athenians the coming of the Messiah to save the world.

This doctrine was equally new and strange to the Athenians; and though they did not persecute Paul as the Jews had done, yet his preaching Jesus was considered, by the Epicurean* and Stoic philosophers, as a fabulous legend. The generality of the people, however, considered it as a discovery of some new gods, which they had not yet placed in their temples; and though they were not unwilling to receive any new deities, yet, as the Areopagus†. was to judge of all gods, to whom public worship might be allowed, they took him before the members of that court to give an account of his doctrine.

Paul, being placed before the judges of this high assembly, explained the nature of the doctrine he taught in a very grave and elegant speech, the substance of which was to this effect: " Ye men of Athens, I am here brought as a prisoner into your supreme tribunal, as one who sets forth strange doctrines; and yet, from the observations I have made since I arrived in your city, I find you so much attached to superstition, that you know not what you worship, nay, that you even have such a number of idols, that you can not find names for them; for one of your altars has upon it an inscription to the unknown God. That the true God of heaven and earth is, in a great measure unknown to you is very evident, and *that* is the Being whose works I now publish to you. By him was all nature created; and as he fills immensity with his presence, so he can not be circumscribed by temples made with hands. Our worship, as men, can add nothing to his perfections; for all we have, and all we enjoy, is the unmerited gift of his inexhaustible bounty. When he created us out of nothing, he appointed that we should consider ourselves as children of the same common parent; and in the course of his providence he has so ordered it, that either by nature or revelation we should use such means as may, in the end, lead us to the knowledge of himself, and promote our eternal happiness, for he is everywhere present, and none of our thoughts can be hidden from him. Nay, be not surprised, for one of your own poets has expressly declared, that we are the offspring of the Supreme Being, and therefore, we are not to form carnal notions of his perfections, as if he could be represented in a human shape. It is true, God, in his infinite mercy, drew a veil over those ages of ignorance; but now he hath made his will known, and, therefore, those who have been long slaves to their lusts and passions, are commanded to turn from the evil of their ways, in order to obtain the divine favor. And this is the more necessary, because he hath fixed, by an unalterable decree, that when the universal frame of nature shall be dissolved, he will raise mankind from the grave, and reward or punish them according to their works here below. As a proof of this he has already raised up Christ from the dead, and, as he has become the first fruits of those who still sleep, so he has ordered that by him all mankind shall be judged. Such is the doctrine I deliver unto you, and I leave you to judge whether or not I have acted as an impostor."

That part of Paul's discourse in which he mentioned the resurrection, gave great offence to some of the philosophers, who mocked and derided him; while others, more modest, but not satisfied with the proofs he had given, gravely said, " We would hear thee again of this matter." After this Paul left the court, but not without some success, for a few of his auditors (among whom were Dionysius, one of the senators, and Damaris, a lady of considerable rank) believed his doctrine, and attended his instructions. Thus boldly did this intrepid servant and soldier of Jesus Christ assert the cause of his divine Master among the great, the wise, and the learned; and thus did he reason, with the most distinguished strength and eloquence, on the

and several means had been attempted for the removal of it, they were advised by Epimedies, the philosopher, to build an altar, and dedicate it to the proper and peculiar god to whom sacrifices were due; and the Athenians, not knowing by what name to call him, erected an altar with this inscription : " To the gods of Asia, Europe, and Africa, to the strange and unknown god ;" by which, as some imagine, they intended the God of the Jews, who had given such wonderful deliverances to his own people.

* The Epicureans among the Greeks and Romans were much the same as the Sadducees among the Jews ; for both denied a divine providence and a future state.

† The Areopagus was a celebrated court or senate, where justice was administered to all ranks of people by judges learned in the law. It was situated on Mars' hill, an eminence without the city, and many of the inhabitants of Athens spent much of their time in it, disputing with each other on speculative points, and asking news concerning the progress of the Roman arms in different parts of the world.

B J LOSSING. Sc.

Corinth.—View of the Acropolis.

nature of God, and the manner in which he has commanded his creatures to worship him even in spirit and in truth.

During Paul's stay at Athens, Timothy and Silas (according to the orders they had received) came to him from Thessalonica, with an account that the Christians there had been under persecution from their fellow-citizens ever since his departure. This gave great uneasiness to Paul, and at first inclined him to visit them in person, in order to confirm them in the faith they had embraced. But reflecting on the consequences that might ensue if he went himself, he sent Timothy and Silas to comfort them, and put them in mind of what he had before told them, namely, that persecution would be the constant attendant on their profession.

After the departure of Timothy and Silas, Paul left Athens, and went to Corinth,* where he met with a certain Jew, named Aquila, lately come from Italy, with Priscilla his wife, because Claudius had made an edict for banishing all the Jews from Rome. Paul having instructed these two in the Christian faith, took up his lodgings with them (and made their house his principal place of residence) during his stay at Corinth. Every sabbath-day he preached in the synagogues, laboring to convince both Jews and Greeks, that Jesus was the true Messiah.

A short time after Paul had been at Corinth, Timothy and Silas arrived thither from Thessalonica, with the joyful news of the steadfast adherence of the Christians in that city to the truth of the gospel. This was a matter of great consolation to Paul, who thereupon wrote his first epistle to the Thessalonians. In this epistle " he highly applauds their courage and zeal in the belief of the Christian religion, and exhorts them to a noble constancy and perseverance amidst their afflictions: he commends them for their charity to the believers in Macedonia, and gives them many instructions concerning conversation, and leading a good life: he exhorts them to the practice of all purity and holiness; to avoid idleness; to be diligent in their callings, and not immoderate in their grief for the dead; and concludes with instructions to them concerning the doctrine of the resurrection, the manner of Christ's coming to judge the world, and the obligation all were under to make a timely preparation for so solemn an event."

After the arrival of Timothy and Silas at Corinth, Paul preached the doctrine of Christ with fresh ardor to the Jews; but they, instead of attending to what he said, opposed him, and what they could not conquer by fair argument, and force of reason, they endeavored to carry by noise and clamor, blended with blasphemous and opprobrious language. In consequence of this, Paul, to testify his abhorrence of their be-

* The large and wealthy city of Corinth was the metropolis of Achaia, and situated upon the isthmus of the same name, which joins the Peloponnesus to the continent. Its situation was highly favorable for that commerce which ultimately rendered it one of the most wealthy and luxurious cities of the world. For, being between two ports, the one of which was open to the eastern and the other to the western navigator, while its geographical situation placed it, as it were, in the centre of the civilized world, it became the point where the merchants from the three quarters of the globe met and exchanged their treasures. It was also celebrated for the Isthmian games, to which the apostle makes some striking and remarkably appropriate allusions, in his Epistles to the Corinthians. Nor should it be unnoticed that in the centre of the city there stood a famous temple of Venus in which a thousand priestesses of the goddess ministered to licentiousness, under the patronage of religion. From such various causes Corinth had an influx of foreigners of all descriptions, who carried the riches and the vices of all nations into a city, in which the merchant, the warrior, and the seaman, could enjoy them for his money. Devoted to traffic, and to the enjoyment of the wealth which that traffic secured, the Corinthians were exempt from the influence of that thirst for conquest and military glory by which their neighbors were actuated; hence they were seldom engaged in any war, except for the defence of their country, or in behalf of the liberties of Greece: yet Corinth furnished many brave and experienced commanders to other Grecian states, among whom it was common to prefer a Corinthian general to one of their own or any other state. As might be expected, Corinth was not remarkably distinguished for philosophy or science; but its wealth attracted to it the arts, which assisted to enrich and aggrandize it, till it became one of the very finest cities in all Greece. The Corinthian order of architecture took its name from that rich and flowery style which prevailed in its sumptuous edifices—its temples, palaces, theatres, and porticoes.

The Corinthians having ill-treated the Roman ambassadors, their city fell a prey to the Romans, with all its treasures and works of art, and was totally destroyed by Mummius. It lay a long while desolate, till it was rebuilt by Julius Cæsar, by whom it was peopled with a colony of Romans; and, favored by its admirable situation, it was soon restored to a most flourishing condition. "The ancient manners," says Hug, "abundantly returned: Acro-Corinth was again the Isthmian Dione, and an intemperate life was commonly called the Corinthian mode of life. Among all the cities that ever existed this was accounted the most voluptuous; and the satirist could only jocularly seem to be at a loss whether, in this respect, he should give the preference to Corinth or to Athens."

Corinth still exists as an inhabited town, under the name of Corantho. It is a long straggling place, which is well paved, and can boast of some tolerably good buildings, with a castle of some strength, which is kept in a good state of defence. There are still some considerable ruins, to attest the ancient consequence of Corinth, and the taste and elegance of its public buildings. The extensive view from the summit of the high mountain which commands the town, and which was the Acropolis (Acro-Corinth) of the ancient city, is pronounced by travellers to be one of the finest in the world.

Ruins of the Temple of Diana at Ephesus.

The Modern City of Corinth, viewed from the Bay.

havior, shook his garments, and told them, that since they were determined to draw down the vengeance of Heaven upon their own heads, he was absolutely guiltless and innocent, and would thenceforth address himself to the Gentiles. Accordingly he left them, and repaired to the house of one Justus, a religious proselyte, where, by his preaching and miracles, he converted great numbers to the faith, among whom were some few Jews, particularly Crispus, the chief ruler of the synagogue, and two others of considerable distinction, who, with their families, were baptized, and admitted members of the Christian church.

Paul was greatly perplexed in his mind on account of the perverseness and obstinacy of the Jews, and began to despair of being able to convince them of the impropriety of their behavior, or to bring them to an effectual discernment of the truth of his doctrine. But he was encouraged to persevere in the attempt by a heavenly vision, in which he was told, that notwithstanding the bad success he had hitherto met with, there was a large harvest to be gathered in that place: that therefore he should not be afraid of his enemies, but preach the gospel boldly, for that he might be assured of the divine protection in all his undertakings. In consequence of this, and in certain hopes of success, Paul continued at Corinth for the space of one year and six months, teaching the word of God with various success to the people.

Some time after Paul had received encouragement from the heavenly vision, the Jews made a general insurrection against him, and having taken him into custody, carried him before Gallio, who at that time was pro-consul of Achaia. The accusation they laid against him was, that he had attempted to introduce a new religion, contrary to what was established by the Jewish law, and permitted by the Roman powers. But, as Gallio apprehended that this was a controversy which did not fall under the cognizance of the civil judicature, he would not have any concern in it, and therefore ordered his officers to drive them out of the court. Upon this the Gentiles took Sosthenes, a ruler of the synagogue, and one of Paul's chief accusers, and beat him publicly before the tribunal; but this did not give the pro-consul the least disturbance.

Paul continued at Corinth some time after this incident, and before his departure thence, wrote his second epistle to the Thessalonians. In this epistle " he endeavors to confirm their minds in the faith, and to animate them courageously to endure persecution from the unbelieving Jews, a lost and undone race of men, whom the divine vengeance was ready to overtake: he rectifies the misinterpretation which false teachers had made of some passages in his former epistle, relative to the day of judgment, as if it was just at hand, and shows what events (especially that of the coming and destruction of the man of sin) must precede the approach of that day. Having craved their prayers in his behalf, and made his request to God in theirs, he concludes with divers precepts, especially to shun idleness and ill company, and not to be weary in well doing."

After Paul had planted the church of Corinth, he left that city, and taking with him Aquila and Priscilla, embarked at Cenchrea, whence they sailed to Ephesus. Here he preached some time in the synagogue of the Jews; but being resolved to attend the celebration of the passover at Jerusalem, he set sail for Cesarea, leaving behind him Aquila and Priscilla, to whom he promised to return (if God would permit) as soon as possible. From Cesarea Paul proceeded to Jerusalem, and after having visited the church there, and kept the feast of the passover, went to Antioch. Here he stayed some time, and then traversed the countries of Galatia and Phrygia, taking his course toward Ephesus, and confirming the new-converted Christians in every place through which he passed.

During the time Paul spent in this large circuit, Providence took care of the churches of Ephesus and Corinth by means of one Apollos, an eloquent Jew of Alexandria, and well acquainted with the law and writings of the prophets. This man, going to Ephesus, though he was only instructed in the rudiments of Christianity, and John's baptism, yet taught with great courage, and a most powerful zeal. After being fully instructed in the faith by Aquila and Priscilla, he passed over into Achaia, being furnished with recommendatory letters by the churches of Ephesus and Corinth. He was of great service in Achaia, by watering what Paul had planted, confirming the disciples, and powerfully convincing many others of the Jews that Jesus was the true and only Messiah promised in the sacred writings.

" While Apollos was thus employed, Paul returned to Ephesus, where he took up his abode for a considerable time. The first thing he did after his return was, to examine certain disciples (in number about twelve) whether they had received the Holy Ghost since they believed? And they said unto him, We have not so much as heard whether there be any Holy Ghost. And he said unto them, Unto what then were ye baptized? And they said, Unto John's baptism. Then said Paul, John verily baptized with the baptism of repentance, saying unto the people, that they should believe on him which should come after him, that is, on Christ Jesus. When they heard this, they were baptized in the name of the Lord Jesus." (Acts xix. 3–6. After the apostle had prayed and laid his hands on them, they received the gift of tongues and other miraculous powers.

After this Paul entered into the Jewish synagogues, in which (for the first three months) he daily contended and disputed with the Jews, endeavoring, with great earnestness and resolution, to convince them of the truth of the Christian religion. But when, instead of meeting with success, he found they were inflexible in their obstinacy and infidelity, he left the synagogue, and taking those with him whom he had converted, instructed them, and others who resorted to him, in the school of one Tyrannus. Here he continued to preach the gospel two years, by which means the Jews and proselytes had an opportunity of hearing the glad tidings of salvation; and as miracles were the clearest evidence of a divine commission, God was pleased to testify the truth of the doctrine Paul preached, by a variety of miraculous operations, many of which were of the most peculiar and extraordinary nature; for he not only healed those diseased persons that came to him, but if handkerchiefs or aprons were only touched by him, and applied to the sick, or those possessed with evil spirits, they were instantly cured.

In the city of Ephesus and its neighborhood were many vagabond Jews, who went about from one place to the other, pretending to cure diseases, and cast out devils by their exorcisms. Among these were seven brothers (the sons of one Sceva, a Jewish priest) who observing with what facility Paul effected his miraculous cures and dispossessions of evil spirits, attempted themselves to do the like; and, to add greater force to their proceedings, instead of the usual form of incantation (which was in the name of the God of Abraham, Isaac, and Jacob), they invoked the name of Jesus over a demoniac. But here it pleased God to make a most distinguished and visible difference between those who applied this powerful name regularly and with commission, and others, who, of their own heads, and for ill designs, dared to usurp it; for the demoniac, falling upon the exorcists, tore off their clothes, wounded their bodies, and scarce suffered them to escape with their lives.

When this singular event came to be known among the Jews and Gentiles in Ephesus, they were filled with such a reverential fear, that none dared to mention the name of Jesus, but with the most profound respect; and many, who had addicted themselves to the study of magic, acknowledged their sins, and publicly burnt their books, the value of which was estimated at no less than fifty thousand pieces of silver. So efficacious was the gospel of Christ in these parts.

While Paul was diligently pursuing his ministry at Ephesus, Peter was preaching the gospel to the Jews in several provinces of the lesser Asia; whence, travelling eastward, he at length came to the ancient city of Babylon in Chaldea. Here he stayed some time, and hence wrote his first epistle (which is called a catholic or general epistle) to the converted Jews who were dispersed in various parts of Chaldea. Peter introduces this admirable epistle with a solemn thanksgiving to God for their call to Christianity, whereby they had obtained a lively hope of an eternal inheritance in heaven; after which he recommends them to the practice of several virtues, as a means to make their calling and election sure, namely, "that they should live in a constant worship and fear of God, and imitate their master Jesus Christ, in holiness and purity; that they should be diligent hearers of the gospel, and grow up to perfection by it; that they should lead exemplary lives among the Gentiles, abstaining from carnal lusts, and behaving themselves with modesty, thereby to convince their enemies that calumnies would be unreasonable; that they should behave themselves well under their respective relations, submitting themselves to their governors, whether superior or inferior to themselves in point of circumstances; that servants should obey their masters, wives be subject to their husbands, and husbands honor their wives; that they should all love one another fervently and unfeignedly, bear afflictions patiently, live in union, and sympathize with each other in their afflictions.

And lastly, that the ministers and pastors of the several churches should take special care of the flocks committed to their charge; teach them diligently, and govern them gently, not seeking their own gain and profit, but the salvation of the souls of the people."—This is the purport of Peter's epistle to the converted Jews; and the whole is written with a fervor and zeal truly consistent with the sentiments and abilities of so great an apostle. The language is simple, and every expression so formed, as to convey a thorough idea of his meaning to the weakest capacity. All the arguments he makes use of to teach them patience are drawn from the sacred writings, and are consistent with the doctrines of true religion.

CHAPTER IX.

PAUL, having been at Ephesus* about two years, resolved to return into Macedonia, and after going thence to Jerusalem, in order to celebrate the feast of pentecost, to proceed in his journey, which he had long intended, to Rome. In consequence of these resolutions, and as a necessary preparation to carry them into execution, he sent Timothy and Erastus before him into Macedonia, while himself stayed behind at Ephesus, in order to settle some matters that were necessary to be adjusted previous to his departure.

Soon after Timothy and Erastus had left Ephesus, Paul received information of some disturbances at Corinth, hatched and fomented by a number of false teachers crept in among the converts of that city, who endeavored to draw them into parties and factions, by persuading some to be for Paul, and others for Apollos, the different persons from whom they had received instructions relative to the Christian faith. In consequence of these disturbances they committed great disorders, and celebrated the holy sacrament very irreverently. They were addicted to fornication, and one in particular, had run into incest, by marrying his father's wife. They were unjust and fraudulent in their dealings; they went to law at heathen tribunals, and among them were found some, who were bold and profligate enough to deny the resurrection.

* EPHESUS.—RUINS OF THE TEMPLE OF DIANA (*see Engraving*).—Ephesus was a celebrated city on the coast of Asia Minor, situated between Smyrna and Miletus, on the sides and at the foot of a range of mountains which overlooked a fine plain watered and fertilized by the river Cayster. Among other splendid edifices which adorned this metropolis of Ionia, was the magnificent temple of Diana, which was two hundred and twenty years in building; and was reckoned one of the seven wonders of the world. This edifice having been burnt by the incendiary Herostratus, B. C. 356, in the foolish hope of immortalizing his name, it was afterward rebuilt with increased splendor at the common expense of the Grecian states of Asia Minor. The remains of ancient Ephesus have been discovered by learned modern travellers, at the Turkish village of Ayasaluk. The ruins delineated in our engraving comprise all that is supposed now to exist of this far-famed structure, which in the time of St. Paul had lost nothing of its magnificence. Here was preserved a wooden statue of Diana, which the credulous Ephesians were taught to believe had fallen from heaven (Acts xix. 35), and of this temple small silver models were made, and sold to devotees. (Acts xix. 24.) Nero is said to have plundered this temple of many votive images, and great sums of gold and silver. This edifice appears to have remained entire in the second century; though the worship of Diana diminished and sunk into insignificance, in proportion to the extension of Christianity. At a later period "the temple of the great goddess Diana, whom Asia and all the world" worshipped (Acts xix. 27), was again destroyed by the Goths and other barbarians; and time has so completed the havoc made by the hand of man, that this mighty fabric has almost entirely disappeared.

During three years' residence in this city (Acts xx. 31), the great apostle of the Gentiles was enabled, with divine assistance, to establish the faith of Christ, and to found a flourishing Christian church. Of his great care of the Ephesian community strong proof is extant in the affecting charge which he gave to the elders, whom he had convened at Miletus on his return from Macedonia (Acts xx. 16-35); and still more in the epistle which he addressed to them from Rome. Ecclesiastical history represents Timothy to have been the first bishop of Ephesus, but there is greater evidence that the apostle John resided here toward the close of his life; here also he is supposed to have written his Gospel, and to have finally ended his life.

The Ephesian church is the first of the "apocalyptic churches" addressed by the apostle John in the name of Jesus Christ. "His charge against her is declension in religious fervor (Rev. ii. 4); and his threat in consequence (ii. 5), is a total extinction of her ecclesiastical brightness. After a protracted struggle with the sword of Rome, and the sophisms of the Gnostics, Ephesus at last gave way. The incipient indifference censured by the warning voice of the prophet, increased to a total forgetfulness; till at length the threatenings of the Apocalypse were fulfilled; and Ephesus sunk with the general overthrow of the Greek empire, in the fourteenth century." The plough has passed over this once celebrated city: and, in March, 1826, when it was visited by the Rev. Messrs. Arundell and Hartley, green corn was growing in all directions amid the forsaken ruins; and one solitary individual only was found, who bore the name of Christ, instead of its once flourishing church. Where assembled thousands once exclaimed "Great is Diana of the Ephesians!" the eagle now yells, and the jackal moans. The sea having retired from the scene of desolation, a pestilential morass, covered with mud and rushes, has succeeded to the waters, which brought up the ships laden with merchandise from every country. The surrounding country, however, is both fertile and healthy: and the adjacent hills would furnish many delightful situations for villages, if the difficulties were removed which are thrown in the way of the industrious cultivator by a despotic government, oppressive agas, and wandering banditti.

Ephesus.

To quell these schisms and factions which had taken place, and to chastise them in a proper manner for their misconduct, Paul wrote his first Epistle to the Corinthians, in which he "shows the inequality of Christ's ministers, and their insufficiency for the work to which they are ordained, without the Divine assistance; orders the incestuous person to be excommunicated, lest his example should infect others; blames their litigious law-suits, as thinking it much better to refer their differences to some of their own body; propounds the first institution of the sacrament, and a previous examination of their lives to bring them to a right use of it; and having added several things concerning a decent behavior both of men and women in their churches—concerning the gifts of the Holy Ghost, the excellence of charity, the gift of tongues, and prayer in an unknown language, he proves the truth of the gospel, and the certainty of a future resurrection, almost to a demonstration.

It was about this time also that Paul wrote his Epistle to the Galatians. He had received information that, since his departure thence, several impostors had crept in among them, who strongly insisted on the necessity of circumcision and other Mosaic rites, and greatly disparaged his authority. Paul therefore, in this epistle, reproves them with some necessary warmth and severity for suffering themselves so easily to be imposed upon by the crafty artifices of seducers. He largely refutes these judaical opinions wherewith they were infected, and, by several arguments, proves that the slavery of the law brought a curse with it; was destructive of their Christian liberty, and incapable of procuring their justification in the sight of God. Among these reproofs and arguments, however, he intermixes several exhortations full of paternal and apostolic charity; and, toward the conclusion, gives them many excellent rules and directions for the conduct of their lives and conversations.

A short time before Paul left Ephesus, a circumstance occurred which occasioned a general disturbance thoughout the city, and had nearly proved fatal to him and his adherents. In the celebrated temple of Diana was an image of that goddess, which the idolatrous priests persuaded the people was made by Jupiter himself, and dropped down from heaven; for which reason it was held in great veneration, not only at Ephesus, but throughout all Asia. In consequence of this, the people procured silver shrines, or figures of the temple and Diana, of such a size as to carry in their pockets, either for curiosity or to stir them up to devotion. This proved the source of a great deal of business to the silversmiths of Ephesus, of whom one Demetrius was the chief. This man plainly perceiving that Christianity tended to the subversion of idolatry, and consequently to the ruin of their gainful employment, called all the artists together, and pathetically represented to them how inevitably they must be reduced to a state of poverty, if they suffered Paul to bring their temple and goddess into contempt, by persuading people, as he did, that they were no gods which were made with hands.

This speech of Demetrius fired them with a zeal which they could no longer contain; so that they cried out with one voice, "Great is Diana of the Ephesians." They should, indeed, have considered that if their goddess was able to defend herself against the doctrines preached by Paul, neither she nor the temple was in any danger; whereas if Paul was able to destroy their gods, it was in vain for them to resist him. But interest and superstition, meeting in the minds of a bigoted multitude, admitted of no reason. They were all fired with a zeal for their goddess, and determined, if they could find Paul, to expose him to the beasts in the theatre, it being customary in those days, at the celebration of their public games and festivals, to expose such as they deemed criminals to the ravage of wild beasts for the diversion of the spectators. The whole city was filled with the tumult; and the crowd, missing Paul, laid hold on Gaius and Aristarchus, two Macedonians of Paul's company, and hurried them into the theatre, with a design to throw them to the wild beasts. Paul, who was at this time in a place of security, hearing of the danger to which his brethren were exposed, was very desirous of venturing after them, in order to speak in their behalf; but he was at last dissuaded from it not only by the Christians, but also by the Gentile governors of the theatrical games, who were his friends, and who assured him that he would only endanger himself without rescuing his friends.

The noise and confusion of the multitude was now prodigious, most of them not knowing the reason for which they were come together; and therefore some said one thing, and some another. In this distraction, Alexander, a Jewish convert, was singled out by the multitude, and by the instigation of the Jews was going to make his defence, in which doubtless he would have laid the whole blame upon Paul; but the multitude perceiving him to be a Jew, and therefore suspecting he was one of Paul's associates, raised another outcry for near two hours together, wherein nothing could be heard but "Great is Diana of the Ephesians." This confusion brought the town-clerk, or recorder of the city, who kept the register of the games, into the theatre, to suppress, if possible, so uncommon a tumult. Having with great difficulty obtained silence, he calmly and discreetly told them, "that it was sufficiently known to all the world what a mighty veneration the inhabitants of Ephesus had for their great goddess Diana, and the famous image which fell down from Jupiter, so that there needed not any disturbance to vindicate and assert it; that they had seized on persons who were not guilty either of sacrilege or blasphemy against their goddess; that if Demetrius and his company had any just charge against them, the courts were sitting, and they might enter their accusation; or if the controversy was about any other matter, there were proper judicatures to determine it in; that therefore they would do well to be pacified, having done more already than they could answer, and being in danger of incurring a severe punishment, if they should be called to an account (as very likely they might be) for that day's riotous assembly."

This speech had the desired effect: the multitude were convinced that they had acted very improperly, and therefore repaired to their respective habitations; and Gaius, Aristarchus, and Alexander, were released without any hurt. But the escape of Paul was so remarkable that he mentions it as a remarkable deliverance. "We had," says he, "the sentence of death in ourselves, that we should not trust in ourselves, but in God, who raised the dead, who delivered us from so great a death." And in another place he tells us, "he fought with beasts at Ephesus;" alluding either to the design of the enraged multitude of throwing him to the wild beasts in the theatre, though their intention was not executed, or to the manners of the people, who justly deserved the character of being savage and brutal to the highest degree.

Soon after the tumult was suppressed at Ephesus, Paul, having called the church together, and constituted Timothy bishop of the place, took his leave, and departed by Troas to Macedonia, where, having instructed some and confirmed others in the principles of a sound faith and holy life, he continued his preaching all over the country, even as far as Illyricum.* During this journey Paul met with many troubles and dangers; "without were fightings, and within fears:" but God, who comforteth those that are cast down, revived his spirits by the arrival of Titus, who gave him a pleasing account of the good effects his epistle had produced at Corinth, and what great reformation it had wrought among the converts of that city. But, as several vain-glorious teachers still persisted in their contumacy, vilifying his authority, and misrepresenting his words and actions; charging him particularly with levity, in not going there according to his promise; with severity in his dealings with the incestuous person; with imperiousness in his writings, abjectness in his person, and some small tincture of irreligion in overthrowing the Mosaic law (all which he understood from Titus), he thought it necessary to write a second epistle to the Corinthians. In this epistle "he excuses his not going directly to Corinth, for fear of occasioning them sorrow, and giving himself uneasiness, in being obliged to treat with severity those who had not yet amended their faults. He commends their zeal against the incestuous person, but now that he had suffered enough for his transgression, allowed them to be reconciled to him. He justifies his own conduct, vindicates the dignity and ministry of the gospel, and proves its great excellence above the law. He declaims against those false teachers who made it their business to traduce and vilify him, and threatens them with his apostolic authority whenever he shall arrive among them. He then speaks of himself with some advantage, and though he mentions his supernatural gifts and revelations, yet seems to glory most in his extraordinary laborings and sufferings for the gospel. And lastly, he exhorts them all to the works

* This is a province of Europe, lying to the north or northwest of Macedonia, along the Adriatic sea, now called the gulf of Venice. It was commonly distinguished into two parts; Lyburnia to the north, where now lies Croatia: and Dalmatia to the south, which still retains its name. St. Paul tells us, that "from Jerusalem, and round about unto Illyricum, he had fully preached the gospel of Christ. (Rom. xv. 19.) So that he must have travelled into Syria, Phœnicia, Arabia, Cilicia, Pamphylia, Pisidia, Lyaconia, Galatia, Pontus, Paphlagonia, Phrygia, Troas, Asia, Caria, Lysia, Ionia, Lydia, the isles of Cyprus and Crete, Thracia, Macedonia, Thessalia, and Achaia. So, justly and without ostentation might he say, that in relation to the other apostles, "he labored more abundantly than them all." (1 Cor. xv. 10.)

of penance and mortification, lest when he arrived thither he should be obliged to exert his authority against offenders; and particularly cautions them to have their alms in readiness, that they may not be a hinderance to him when he shall arrive at Corinth."

After Paul had travelled through the principal places in Macedonia and Achaia, confirming those who had been converted, and bringing over others to the faith, he proceeded to Corinth, where he took up his residence for the space of three months. During his abode here he wrote his famous Epistle to the Romans, which he sent by Phebe, a deaconess of the church of Cenchrea, near Corinth. In this epistle "he states and determines the great controversy between the Jews and the Gentiles, relative to the obligation of the rites and ceremonies of the Mosaic law, and those main and material doctrines of Christianity which depend on it, such as that of Christian liberty, the use of different things, &c. He also points out the effects of original sin, and the power it has even among the regenerate; and, through the whole of the epistle, intermixes many admirable instructions and exhortations to the duties of a holy and religious life such as the Christian doctrine doth naturally tend to produce."

Paul, having gathered considerable alms both in Macedonia and Achaia, resolved to leave Corinth, in order to carry them into Judea for the relief of the Christians in those parts. His first intention was to go through Syria, as being by far the nearest way; but having received information that the Jews of that country had formed a conspiracy against his life, he altered his course, and determined to go through Macedonia. Accordingly, leaving Corinth, he proceeded to Philippi, where he stayed some time, in order to celebrate the feast of the passover. Hence he took shipping, and in five days landed at Troas, where he continued a week. On the sabbath, which was the last day of his staying there, he preached to the Christians of the place, who had assembled together in order to receive the sacrament; and, as he intended leaving them the next morning, he continued his harangue till midnight. The length of his discourse, and the time of night, caused some of his hearers to be so fatigued as to fall asleep. Among these was a young man named Eutychus, who, sitting in a higher window, so forgot himself that he fell thence to the ground, and was taken up dead. This circumstance being made known to the apostle, he stopped his discourse, and going to the young man, by prayers to the throne of grace, restored him to life and health. How indefatigable was this great apostle in doing good! how closely did he tread in the steps of his great Master, who "went about doing good!" He preached and wrought miracles wherever he went. Like a master-builder, he either laid a foundation or raised the superstructure. He was "instant, in season and out of season," and spared no pains in endeavoring to secure the eternal welfare of his fellow-creatures.

After performing this miracle, Paul resumed his discourse, and, having spent the whole night in these holy exercises, early the next morning he took his leave, and travelled on foot to Assos,* whither he had before sent his companions (among whom was Luke) by sea. From Assos they sailed to Mitylene;† then, passing by Chios,‡ arrived at Samos,§ and proceeded to Trogyllium,‖ whence, after staying one day,

* Assos is a seaport-town, situate on the southwest part of the province of Troas, and over against the island Lesbos. By land it is a great deal nearer Troas than it is by sea, because of a promontory that runs a great way into the ocean, and must be doubled before we can come to Assos, which was the reason that the apostle chose rather to walk it.
† Mitylene was one of the principal cities of the isle of Lesbos, seated in a peninsula, with a commodious haven on each side, and soon became so considerable, as to give name to the whole island (at present called Metelin) many years ago. The island (which is one of the largest in the Archipelago) was, in former times, renowned for the many eminent persons it had produced; such as Sappho, the inventress of Sapphic verses; Alcæus, a famous lyric poet; Pittacus, one of the seven wise men of Greece; Theophrastus, the noble physician and philosopher; and Arion, the celebrated musician; and the Turks, who have it now in possession, think it still a place of consequence enough to deserve a fortress and garrison to defend it.
‡ Chios is an island in the archipelago, next to Lesbos, or Metelin, both in its situation and bigness. It lies over against Smyrna, and is not above four leagues distant from the Asiatic continent. It is celebrated by Horace and Martial, for the wine and figs that came thence; but at present its renown is that it produces the most excellent mastic in the world, wherein the people pay their tribute to the grand seignior. Nor is it less remarkable for what Sir Paul Ricaut, in his Present State of the Greek Church, tells us of it, viz.: that there is no place in the Turkish dominions, where Christians enjoy more freedom in their religion and estates than in this isle, to which they are entitled by an ancient capitulation, made with Sultan Mahomet II., which to this day is maintained so faithfully, that no Turk can strike or abuse a Christian without severe correction.
‖ Trogyllium is a cape, or promontory, on the Asiatic coast, opposite to Samos, and much below Ephesus, having a town of the same name.
§ Samos is another isle in the Archipelago, lying southeast of Chios, and about five miles from the Asiatic continent. It is famous among the heathen writers for the worship of Juno; for one of the sybils,

they went to Miletus,* not putting in at Ephesus, because the apostle was resolved, if possible, to be at Jerusalem at the feast of Pentecost.

Soon after Paul arrived at Miletus he sent to Ephesus, to assemble together the pastors and elders of the churches in that city. On their arrival, he delivered to them a very long and pathetic discourse, wherein he reminded them with what uprightness and integrity, with what affection and humility, and with what great danger and trouble, he had been conversant among them, and preached the gospel to them, ever since his coming into those parts: that he had not failed to acquaint them both publicly and privately, with whatsoever might be profitable to their souls, urging both Jews and Gentiles to repentance and reformation, and a hearty reception of the faith of Christ: that now he was determined to go to Jerusalem, where he did not know what particular sufferings would befall him, only that he had been foretold by those who were endued with prophetic gifts of the Holy Ghost, that in every city bonds and afflictions would attend him; but that he was not concerned at this, being willing to lay down his life whenever the gospel required it, and fully determined to serve, with the strictest fidelity, his great Lord and Master. Here he made a short pause, and then resumed his discourse in words to this effect: "I well know that you will see my face no more; but for my encouragement and satisfaction, ye yourselves can bear me witness, that I have not, by concealing any part of the Christian doctrine, betrayed your souls. And as for yourselves, whom God hath made bishops and pastors of his church, you should be careful to feed, guide, and direct those Christians under your inspection, and be infinitely tender of the welfare of souls, for whose redemption the blessed Jesus laid down his own life. All the care, therefore, possible for you to use is no more than necessary; for after my departure heretical teachers will appear in the church, to the great danger of the souls of men, seeking, by every crafty method and pernicious doctrine, to gain proselytes to their party, and, by those means, fill the church of Christ with schisms and factions. Watch ye, therefore, and remember with what tears and sorrow I have, during three years, warned you of these things. And now I recommend you to the Divine favor and protection, and to the rules and instructions of the gospel, which, if properly adhered to, will undoubtedly dispose and perfect you for that state of happiness which the Almighty hath prepared for good men in the mansions of eternity. Ye well know that I have from the beginning dealt faithfully and uprightly with you; that I have not had any covetous designs, or ever desired the riches of other men; nay, I have labored with mine own hands, to support myself and my companions: you ought, therefore, to support the weak and relieve the poor, rather than be yourselves chargeable to others, according to that incomparable saying of the great Redeemer of mankind, 'It is more blessed to give than to receive.'" If we minutely attend to the whole of this apostle's preaching and writing, we shall find that he strenuously inculcates not only points of faith, but also practical duties, without which our faith would be in vain.

After Paul had finished his farewell discourse to the bishops and pastors of Ephesus, he knelt down, and, by way of a final conclusion, joined with them fervently in prayer; which being over they all melted into tears, and with the greatest expression of sorrow attended him to the ship, grieving in the most passionate manner on account of his having told them that they should see his face no more.

After Paul had taken this affecting farewell of the pastors and elders of Ephesus, he with his attendants left Miletus, and going on board a ship sailed with a fair wind to Coos.† The day after their arrival here, they proceeded to Rhodes, and from

called Sybilla Samia; for Pherecydes, who foretold an earthquake that happened there, by drinking of the waters; and, more especially, for the birth of Pythagoras, who excelled all the seven wise men, so renowned among the Greeks. It was formerly a free commonwealth, and the inhabitants were so powerful, that they managed many prosperous wars against their neighbors: but at present the Turks have reduced it to such a mean and depopulated condition, that a few pirates dare land and plunder as they please; so that ever since the year 1676, no Turk has ventured to live upon it, for fear of being carried into captivity by those rovers.

* Miletus was a port-town on the continent of Asia Minor, and in the province of Caria, memorable for being the birthplace of Thales, one of the seven wise men in Greece, and father of the Ionic philosopher; of Anaximenes, the scholar; Timotheus the musician, and Anaximenius the philosopher. At present it is called, by the Turks, Melas: and not far distant from it is the true Meander, which, though it encircles all the plain it runs through with many pleasing mazes and innumerable windings, yet, in some places, it goes with such a current as stirs up the earth and gravel from the bottom, which makes its water not so clear and crystalline as might be expected.

† This was an island in the Archipelago, lying near the southwest point of Asia Minor, and having a city of the same name. It was formerly celebrated for the birth of Hippocrates the famous physician, and Apelles the famous painter; for a stately temple dedicated to Apollo, and another to Juno; for the richness of its wines, and for the fineness of a stuff made here, which was perfectly transparent, and called vestimenta cos.

Rhodes* to Patara,† where meeting with a ship bound for Phœnicia they went on board, and, passing Cyprus, sailed to Syria, and landed at Tyre, the place where the ship was to unlade her burden.

Paul stayed at Tyre seven days, in the course of which he was advised by some Christians of the place not to go up to Jerusalem. But this advice Paul would by no means take; upon which the disciples, accompanied by their wives and children, attended him out of the city, and when they came to the seashore Paul knelt down and prayed for them in the same manner he had done before at Miletus.

From Tyre Paul and his companions sailed to Ptolemais,† where they stayed one day, spending their time in conversation with the disciples of that place. The next day they went to Cesarea, and visited Philip, one of the seven deacons, who had been sent by the apostles to preach the gospel in Samaria and other places. This Philip had four virgin daughters, all of whom were endued with the gift of prophecy; and on this account, together with Paul's great regard for Philip, he resided at his house during his stay at Cesarea.

While Paul was at Philip's house, there came thither a prophet, named Agabus, from Judea. This person, after the manner of the old prophets (who often prophesied by symbols or significant expressions), took Paul's girdle, and binding it about his own hands and feet, said, in the presence and hearing of the whole company, "Thus saith the Holy Ghost, so shall the Jews at Jerusalem bind the man who owneth this girdle, and shall deliver him into the hands of the Gentiles." On the prophet's saying these words, not only the companions of Paul, but likewise all the Christians present, were greatly troubled, and earnestly besought him that he would not go up to Jerusalem. To which Paul replied, "What mean ye to weep, and to break mine heart? for I am ready not to be bound only, but also to die at Jerusalem for the name of the Lord Jesus."   •

When the disciples found that Paul's resolution was not to be shaken, they did not importune him any farther; in consequence of which he and his companions left Cesarea, and prosecuting their journey arrived safe at Jerusalem, where they were kindly and joyfully received by the Christians of that city.

The day after Paul and his companions arrived at Jerusalem, they went to the house of James the apostle, where the rest of the bishops and governors of the church were assembled together. After mutual salutations, Paul gave them a particular account of the success with which God had blessed his endeavors in propagating Christianity among the Gentiles. for which they all joined in glorifying God. Having done this, they told Paul that he was now come to a place in which there were many thousands of Jewish converts, who were all zealous for the law of Moses, and who had been informed that he taught the Jews whom he converted to renounce circumcision and the ceremonies of the law: that as soon as the multitude heard of his arrival, they would all assemble together to see how he behaved himself in this matter; and therefore, to prevent any disturbance, they thought it advisable for him to join himself with four men who were then going to discharge a vow; to perform the usual rites and ceremonies with them; to be at the charge of having their heads shaved; and to provide such sacrifices as the law directed: whereby it would appear that the reports spread of him were groundless, and that himself was an observer of the Mosaic institutions.

Paul readily agreed to follow the advice given him by his brethren; in consequence of which, taking with him the four persons who were to discharge their vows, he went into the temple, and told the priests, that, as the time of their vow was now expired and their purification regularly performed, they were come to make their oblation according to law.

The time of offering these oblations was seven days, near the close of which certain Jews from Asia (who had there been strong opposers to Paul's doctrine), finding him

---

* Rhodes lies south of the province of Caria in lesser Asia; and, among the Asiatic isles, was accounted for dignity next to Cyprus and Lesbos. It was remarkable among the ancients for the expertness of its inhabitants in the art of navigation; for a college, in which the students were eminent for eloquence and mathematics; for the clearness of its air; for its pleasant and healthy climate, which induced the Roman nobility to make it a place of their recess; and, more especially, for its prodigious statue of brass, consecrated to Apollo, or the sun, and called his Colossus. This statue was seventy cubits high, and stood astride over the mouth of the harbor, so that the ships sailed between its legs.

† This is a seaport of Lycia, formerly beautified with a good harbor, and many temples, whereof one was dedicated to Apollo.

‡ A seaport of Syria, between Tyre and Cesarea:

in the temple, began to raise a tumult, and, seizing on him, called to their brethren the Jews to assist them, declaring that he was the person who had preached doctrines derogatory to the Jewish nation, and destructive to the institutions of the law of Moses. This accusation, though absolutely false, occasioned such a universal disgust among the people to Paul, that they immediately fell on him and dragged him out of the temple, shutting the doors to prevent his returning into that holy place. After they had got him out of the temple they treated him with great indignity, and would certainly have killed him, had not Claudius Lysias, the commander of the Roman garrison in the castle of Antonia, come with a considerable force to his assistance. Lysias conducted him to the castle, in the way to which Paul begged permission to speak to him; but the governor (supposing him to be an Egyptian, who not many years before had raised a sedition in Judea, and headed a party of four thousand profligate wretches) seemed to refuse him that favor, until Paul informed him that he was a Jew of Tarsus, and a freeman of a rich and honorable city, and therefore humbly hoped that he would not deny him the privilege of vindicating himself. The governor consenting to this request, Paul, standing upon the stairs that led into the castle, after making signs for the multitude to be silent, made a speech to them in the Hebrew language, the substance of which was to the following effect:

"Listen, ye descendants of Jacob, to a person of your own religion, and like yourselves a child of Abraham; born in Tarsus, and brought up in this city, at the feet of Gamaliel, and fully instructed in the law delivered by Moses to our forefathers, and formerly as zealous for the temple worship as ye are at present.

"Nay, I persecuted unto death all who believed in Jesus, seizing on all I could find, both men and women, and casting them into prison.

"But as I was pursuing my journey to execute this commission, and was arrived near Damascus, there appeared, about midday, a light from heaven shining round about me.

"Terrified at so awful an appearance, I fell to the ground, and heard a voice saying unto me, 'Saul, Saul, why persecutest thou me?' To which I answered, 'Who art thou, Lord?' And the voice replied, 'I am Jesus of Nazareth whom thou persecutest.'

"After recovering from the terror with which my mind was filled, I answered, 'What shall I do, Lord?' And the Lord said unto me, 'Arise, and go into Damascus, and there it shall be told thee of all things which are appointed for thee to do.'

"The brilliancy of the glory deprived me of sight; so that my companions led me by the hand to Damascus, where one Ananias, a person well respected by all the Jews of that city, visited me, and said, 'Brother Saul, receive thy sight.' And in a moment my eyes were opened, and I saw him standing before me. When he saw that my sight was restored, he said to me, 'The God of Abraham, Isaac, and Jacob, hath appointed thee to know his will, to see the great Messiah, the Holy One of God, and hear the voice of his mouth; for thou art chosen to be a witness to all the nations of the earth for those surprising things thou hast seen and heard. Why, therefore, tarriest thou here any longer? 'Arise, and be baptized, and wash away thy sins, calling on the name of the Lord.'

"After this glorious vision and miraculous power of the Most High, when I was returned from Damascus to Jerusalem and offering up my prayers in the temple, I fell into a trance, and again saw the Great Son of David, who said unto me, 'Depart quickly from Jerusalem, for the descendants of Jacob will refuse to believe thy testimony concerning me.' And I answered, 'Lord, they know how cruelly I used thy saints and followers; that I imprisoned and beat them in every synagogue whither I went. Nay, when they shed the blood of thy holy martyr Stephen, I was also one of the spectators; I consented to his death; I even kept the raiment of those that slew him.' But the Lord replied, 'Depart, for I will send thee far hence unto the Gentiles.'"

The Jews had been very quiet, and paid great attention to Paul's speech till he came to this part of it: his mentioning the commission he had received to preach the gospel to the Gentiles, threw them into the most violent outrage, and they cried out with one voice, "Away with such a fellow from the earth; for it is not fit that he should live." And, the more to express their indignation, they threw off their clothes and cast dust into the air, as though they intended that moment to stone him.

When Lysias, the captain of the guard, found to what a violent degree the people were incensed against Paul, he ordered him to be taken within the castle, and that he should be examined by scourging till he confessed the reason of the uncommon rage shown against him by the people.* Accordingly the lictor bound him, and was going to put the orders he had received into execution, when Paul asked the centurion who stood by whether or not it was lawful to scourge a citizen of Rome before any sentence had been passed upon him. But the centurion, instead of answering his question, immediately repaired to Lysias, beseeching him to be careful how he proceeded against the prisoner, because he was a Roman. On this information Lysias went immediately into the prison, and asked Paul whether he was really a free citizen of Rome. Being answered in the affirmative, Lysias said he had himself procured that great privilege by a large sum of money; upon which Paul answered, "But I was freeborn."† On receiving this account, Lysias commanded the centurion not to scourge him, being terrified at what he had already done, namely, his causing to be bound with chains a free denizen of the Roman empire. The next day he ordered his chains to be taken off; and that he might thoroughly satisfy himself of the cause of so unusual a tumult, convened the members of the sanhedrim, before whom he conducted Paul in order to undergo an examination by that tribunal.

Paul was not in the least terrified at the sight of so considerable and powerful an assembly. Without waiting for any questions being asked him, looking earnestly at the council, he coolly said, "Men and brethren, I have lived in all good conscience before God until this day."‡ But, however this expression might tend to show the true state of his mind, Ananias the high-priest was so offended at it that he commanded those who stood next him to strike him on the face; at which Paul replied, "God shall smite thee, thou whited wall."‖ On this, some of the spectators, looking sternly at Paul, cried out, "Revilest thou God's high-priest?" In answer to this, Paul told them he did not know that Ananias was high-priest, not supposing it possible that a person who can give such unjust orders could be invested with so sacred a character. But, since it was so, he confessed it was very wrong to revile him, God himself having commanded that "no man should speak evil of the rulers of the people."

Paul, perceiving that the council consisted partly of Sadducees and partly of Pharisees (in order to elude the malice of his enemies), made open declaration that he was a Pharisee, even as his father was before him, and that the great offence taken against him was his belief of a future resurrection. This declaration threw the whole court in confusion, by exciting the regard of the Pharisees, who favored the doctrine of the resurrection, and incurring the resentment of the Sadducees, who strongly opposed it.

The dissensions between these two sects on this occasion arose to such a violent degree, that Lysias, fearing lest Paul should be torn in pieces between them, com-

---

† As Lysias did not understand Hebrew, he could not tell what the purport of St. Paul's speech to the people was; but, by their mad and outrageous behavior, he guessed that he must have said something very provoking, either against the law or the dignity of their nation, and therefore was willing to know the truth of it from himself. Scourging was a method of examination used by the Romans, and other nations, to force such as were supposed guilty to confess what they had done, what were their motives, and who were accessaries to the fact.

† It is probable that Paul's father might have been rewarded with the freedom of the city for his fidelity and bravery in some military service, emoluments being then conferred, not on those who had most interest with men in power, but on those who had most merit from their actions.

‡ The apostle, by here using the words "a good conscience," does not mean a conscience void of all error and offence, because he owns himself to have been guilty of a great sin in persecuting the church of Christ. (1 Tim. i. 13.) His meaning, therefore, is such a conscience as was consistent with the ideas he entertained at different periods of his life, namely, before and after his conversion. The sense, therefore, of this passage may be thus explained: "While I was persuaded that the Christian religion was false, I persecuted it with the utmost vigor; but, as soon as I came to perceive its divine institution, I declared for it, and have ever since maintained it, even to the hazard of my life. The religion of the Jews I did not forsake out of any hardships that it required, or any prejudice I had conceived against its precepts; nor did I embrace that of the Christians upon any other account, than a full conviction of its truth and veracity. I was a good Jew, in short, as long as I thought it my duty to be so; and when I thought it my duty to be otherwise, I became a zealous Christian; in all which God knows the sincerity of my heart, and is witness of my uprightness."

‖ "A whited wall" was a proverbial expression denoting a hypocrite of any kind, and the propriety of it appears in this: that as the wall had a fair outside, but nothing but dirt, or sticks and stones, within, so the high-priest had the outward appearance of a righteous judge, sitting as one that would pass sentence according to law, and yet commanding him to be punished for speaking the truth, and so condemning the innocent, contrary to the law of nature, as well as that of Moses. Our blessed Saviour makes use of a comparison of the same nature, when he calls the scribes and Pharisees "whited sepulchres." It should be observed, in vindication of St. Paul, that his words, "God shall smite thee," are a prediction, not an imprecation; and a prediction which Josephus tells us was fulfilled in a short time; for he was murdered in a mutiny.

manded the soldiers to take him from the bar, and re-conduct him to the castle. This was accordingly done, and to comfort him after all his frights and fears, God was pleased to appear to him that night in a vision, encouraging him to constancy and resolution, and assuring him that, as he had borne testimony to his cause at Jerusalem, so, in despite of all his enemies, he should live to do the like at Rome. "Be of good cheer, Paul: for as thou hast testified of me in Jerusalem, so must thou bear witness also at Rome."

The next morning the Jews, whose envy and malice were increased against Paul by the dilatory proceedings of the sanhedrim, determined to use a quicker method of putting a period to his life. In order to this, about forty of the most turbulent among them entered into a wicked conspiracy, which they ratified with an imprecation never to eat or drink until they had killed Paul. Having formed this inhuman resolution, they went to the sanhedrim and acquainted them with their design, to effect which they advised, that some of the members should solicit Lysias to bring Paul again before them, under pretence of inquiring more accurately into his case, and that, before he reached the court, they would not fail to waylay and despatch him.

This wicked plot was readily approved of by the sanhedrim, but its execution was happily frustrated by Paul's nephew, who, having discovered their intentions, went immediately to his uncle, to whom he related the whole affair. Paul communicated the intelligence to Lysias, who immediately commanded two parties of foot and one of horse, to be ready by nine o'clock, in order to conduct him to Cesarea, where Felix, the Roman governor, then resided. At the same time Lysias despatched a letter to Felix, the substance of which was, "that the person whom he had sent to him was a freeman of Rome; that the Jews had ill treated him, and conspired against his life; that the measures he had taken were designed to secure him from the violence of the multitude; and that he had ordered his enemies to appear before him at Cesarea, that he might judge what was the cause of their being so incensed against the person whom he had sent to him under military protection."

The guards, having received these orders from Lysias, conducted Paul the same night to Antipatris,* and the next morning to Cesarea. On their arrival there, they immediately gave Lysias's letter to Felix, who, after having read the contents, asked Paul some questions relative to the place of his birth, and the manner of his life. Finding, by his answers, that Paul was a native of Cilicia, Felix told him that as soon as his accusers came thither from Jerusalem, he would give him a fair and candid hearing; and in the meantime gave orders that he should be secured in that part of his palace called Herod's hall,† where he should be supplied with every article that was necessary during his confinement.

CHAPTER X.

AFTER Paul had been confined five days at Cesarea, by order of Felix, there came thither Ananias the high-priest, and several other members of the sanhedrim, together with Tertullus, a man of great elocution, and an inveterate enemy to Paul. Being all assembled before Felix, Tertullus made a long speech, in which he made use of all the insinuating arts that could arise from human invention to prepossess the governor in his own favor; having done which he accused Paul "of being a seditious person, and a disturber of the public peace, who had set himself at the head of the sect of Nazarenes, and made no manner of scruple to profane even the temple itself." This accusation was altogether false, notwithstanding which it was confirmed by all the members of the sanhedrim, who had come from Jerusalem on this occasion.

Tertullus having finished his accusation against Paul, Felix told him that he was now at liberty to make his defence; upon which Paul addressed himself to the court in words to this effect:—

"I answer this charge of the Jews with the greater satisfaction before thee, because

* Antipatris was a city on the borders of Samaria, near the Mediterranean sea; and situated about thirty-eight miles from Jerusalem.
† This was a magnificent palace built by Herod the Great for his own habitation, whenever he went to Cesarea: and was afterward used by the Roman governors for the place of their residence, and for the confinement of some particular persons.

thou hast for many years been a judge of this nation. About twelve days since, I repaired to Jerusalem to worship the God of Jacob. But I neither disputed with any man, or endeavored to stir the people in the synagogues or the city. Nor can they prove the charge they have brought against me.

"This, however, I readily confess, that after the way which they call heresy, so worship I the God of my fathers; and according to this faith, I am careful to maintain a clear and quiet conscience, both toward God and man.

"After I had spent some years in distant countries, I repaired to Jerusalem, with the alms I had collected in other provinces, for the poor of mine own nation, and offerings to the God of Jacob. And while I was performing the duties of religion, certain Asiatic Jews found me in the temple, purified according to law; but neither attended with a multitude of followers, or the least tumultuous assembly. It was therefore necessary that these Jews should have been here, if they had anything to allege against me. Nay, I appeal to those of the sanhedrim here present, if anything has been laid to my charge, except the objections of the Sadducees, who violently opposed me for asserting the doctrine of the resurrection."

Felix, having thus heard both parties, refused to make any final determination till he had more fully advised about it, and consulted Lysias, the governor of the castle, who was the most proper person to give an account of the cause of the controversy. In the meantime Felix gave orders that, though Paul should be kept under a guard, yet his confinement should be so free and easy, that none of his friends should be hindered from visiting, or doing him any offices of kindness.

A few days after this, Felix, being desirous that his wife Drusilla (who had been a Jewess) should hear Paul, he ordered him to be brought before them, and gave him permission to speak freely concerning the doctrines of Christianity. In his discourse he particularly pointed out the great obligation which the laws of Christ laid on mankind to preserve justice and righteousness, sobriety and chastity, both toward themselves and others, more especially from this consideration, namely, the strict and impartial account that must be given, in the day of judgment, of all the actions of their past lives, and the consequences that would inevitably follow, either to be rewarded or eternally punished.

This discourse had such an effect on Felix, that he could not help trembling as he sat on his throne; and as soon as he had a little recovered his spirits, he abruptly interrupted Paul, by saying, "Go thy way for this time; when I have a convenient season, I will call for thee."

Felix, no doubt, had sufficient reason to tremble, and his conscience to be sensibly alarmed at Paul's discourse; for he was a man notoriously infamous for rapine and violence. He made his own will the law of his government, practising all manner of cruelty and injustice. To these bad qualities he added bribery and covetousness; and therefore often sent for Paul to discourse with him, expecting he would have given him a considerable sum for his release, having, in all probability, heard that Paul had taken with him a large quantity of money to Jerusalem. But finding that no offers were made him, either by the apostle or his friends, he kept him prisoner two years; when himself being discharged from his office by Nero, he left Paul in prison, in order to gratify the malice of the Jews,* and engage them to speak the better of him, after his departure from Judea.

On the deposition of Felix the government of Judea was invested in Portius Festus, who, after staying three days at Cesarea, went to Jerusalem. On his arrival thither, the high-priest, and other members of the sanhedrim, exhibited fresh accusations against Paul, and, in order to his trial, desired that he might be sent for up to Jerusalem, intending to have him assassinated in the way. But Festus, being unwilling to grant their request, told them, that he was shortly going himself to Cesarea, and that if they had any complaint against Paul, they must come thither and accuse him, when he would not fail to do them justice.

In consequence of this the Jews followed Festus to Cesarea, and when he was

* Felix had greatly exasperated the Jews by his unjust and violent proceedings while he continued in the government: and therefore, upon his dismission, he thought to have pacified them in some measure, by leaving Paul (whom he might have discharged long before) still in custody, and consequently still liable to become a prey to their greedy malice. But herein he found himself greatly mistaken; for no sooner was he removed from his office, than several of the principal Jews of Cesarea took a journey to Rome on purpose to accuse him, and would certainly have wrought his ruin, had not his brother Pallas (who was in very distinguished favor with Nero) interceded for his pardon.

seated on his throne, they renewed their charge, and produced their articles against Paul, which were much the same as what they had accused him of before Felix. But Paul defended himself so well, by making it appear that he had neither offended against the Jewish laws, nor against the temple, nor against the emperor, that their charge, for want of sufficient proof, fell to the ground. Festus, however, being willing to procure the favor of the Jews at his entrance on the government, asked Paul if he would go and be tried before him at Jerusalem? But the apostle, well knowing the malice of his enemies, and being unwilling to trust himself in their power, boldly declared, "as he then stood at the emperor's judgment-seat, when he ought to have a final trial, if he had done anything worthy of death, he did not wish to avoid punishment; but that, as he had not injured any of the Jews, and they could not prove anything against him, he ought not to be made a victim to their fury; and therefore, as he was a Roman, he appealed to the emperor himself."* Festus, finding Paul resolute in maintaining his privilege, conferred for some time with his council, and then, with some seeming emotion, told him that since he "had appealed unto Cæsar, unto Cæsar he should go."

A few days after this, King Agrippa (who succeeded Herod in the tetrarchate of Galilee), with his sister Bernice, went to Cesarea, in order to pay a visit to the new governor. Festus took this opportunity of mentioning Paul's case to Agrippa, with the remarkable tumult that had been occasioned by him among the Jews, and the appeal he had made to Cæsar, the whole of which he related in words to this effect: "That Felix, upon his parting with the government of Judea, had left a certain prisoner, against whom some of the chief of the Jews had brought an information, and immediately demanded judgment, which, according to the Roman law, could not be done without first hearing the case and bringing the parties together. That to this purpose he had ordered his accusers to come to Cesarea, but, upon the result, found that the dispute between them was about matters of religion, and whether a person called Jesus was really dead or alive. That being himself unacquainted with such kind of controversies, he had referred the prisoner to the Jewish sanhedrim, but that he, declining their judgment, had appealed to Cæsar: and that therefore he kept him still in prison, until he could meet with a convenient opportunity to send him to Rome."

This account given of Paul by Festus greatly excited the curiosity of King Agrippa, who intimated his desire of hearing himself what Paul had to say in his own defence. Accordingly the next day the king and his sister, accompanied by Festus the governor, and several other persons of distinction, went into the court with a pompous and splendid retinue, where the prisoner was brought before them. As soon as Paul appeared, Festus informed the court "how greatly he had been importuned by the Jews, both at Cesarea and Jerusalem, to put the prisoner to death as a malefactor; but having, on examination, found him guilty of no capital crime, and the prisoner himself having appealed unto Cæsar, he was determined to send him to Rome. That he was willing, however, to have his cause again discussed before so judicious a person as Agrippa, that he might be furnished with some material particulars to send with him, as it would be highly absurd to send a prisoner without signifying the crimes alleged against him."

Festus having finished his speech, King Agrippa told Paul he was at full liberty to make his own defence; upon which, after silence being called, Paul, chiefly addressing himself to Agrippa, spoke to this effect:—

"I consider it as a peculiar happiness, King Agrippa, that I am to make my defence against the accusations of the Jews, before thee, because thou art well acquainted with their customs, and the questions commonly debated among them: I therefore beseech thee to hear me patiently. All the Jews are well acquainted with my manner of life, from my youth, the greatest part of it having been spent with mine own countrymen at Jerusalem. They also know that I was educated under the institutions of the Pharisees, the strictest sect of our religion, and am now arraigned for a tenet believed by all their fathers; a tenet sufficiently credible in itself, and plainly revealed in the Scriptures, I mean the resurrection of the dead. Why should

* This manner of appealing was very common among the Romans, and introduced to secure the lives and fortunes of the people from the unjust encroachments and over-rigorous severities of the magistrates. Paul well knew he should not have fair and equitable dealings from the governor, when swayed by the Jews, his sworn and inveterate enemies, and therefore appealed from him to the emperor; nor could Festus deny his demand.

any mortal think it either incredible or impossible, that God should raise the dead ?

" I indeed thought myself indispensably obliged to oppose the religion of Jesus of Nazareth. Nor was I satisfied with imprisoning and punishing with death itself, the saints I found at Jerusalem; I even persecuted them in strange cities, whither my implacable zeal pursued them, having procured authority for that purpose from the chief priests and elders.

" Accordingly, I departed for Damascus with a commission from the sanhedrim; but as I was travelling toward that city, I saw at midday, O king, a light from heaven, far exceeding the brightness of the sun, encompassing me and my companions. On seeing this awful appearance, we all fell to the earth; and I heard a voice, which said to me, in the Hebrew language, Saul, Saul, why persecutest thou me ? It is hard for thee to kick against the pricks. To which I answered, Who art thou, Lord ? And he replied, I am Jesus whom thou persecutest. But be not terrified, arise from the earth; for I have appeared unto thee, that thou mightest be both a witness of the things thou hast seen, and also of others which I will hereafter reveal unto thee; my power, delivering thee from the Jews and Gentiles, to whom now I send thee to preach the gospel; to withdraw the veil of darkness and ignorance; to turn them from falsehood unto truth, and from the power of Satan unto God.

" Accordingly, King Agrippa, I readily obeyed the heavenly vision; I preached the gospel first to the inhabitants of Damascus, then to those of Jerusalem and Judea, and afterward to the Gentiles; persuading them to forsake their iniquities, and, by sincere repentance, turn to the living God.

" These endeavors to save the souls of sinful mortals exasperated the Jews, who caught me in the temple, and entered into a conspiracy to destroy me. But by the help of Omnipotence, I still remain a witness to all the human race, preaching nothing but what Moses and all the prophets foretold, namely, that the Messiah should suffer, be the first that should rise from the chambers of the grave, and publish the glad tidings of salvation, both to the Jews and Gentiles."

This discourse was conceived in such a light by Festus, that he thought Paul was delirious, and therefore abruptly told him, that his too much learning had made him mad. The reply Paul made to this was to the following purport : " I am far, most noble Festus, from being transported with idle and distracted ideas; the words I speak are dictated by truth and sobriety; and I am persuaded that King Agrippa himself is not ignorant of those things; for they were transacted openly before the world. I am confident, King Agrippa, that thou believest the prophets; and therefore must know that all their predictions were fulfilled in Christ." To this Agrippa answered, " Thou hast almost persuaded me to become a Christian." Paul replied, " I sincerely wish, that not only thou, but also all that hear me, were not *almost*, but *altogether*, the same as myself, except being prisoners." Upon this the assembly broke up; and when Agrippa and Festus had conferred together about Paul's case, they freely owned that the accusation laid against him amounted neither to a capital offence, nor anything deserving imprisonment; and that, had he not appealed unto Cæsar, he might have been legally discharged.*

It being now finally determined that Paul should be sent to Rome, he, and some other prisoners of note, were committed to the charge of one Julius, a centurion, or captain of a legion called Augustus's band. Accordingly they went on board a ship of Adramyttium,† and coasting along Asia, arrived at Sidon, where Julius (who all along treated Paul with great civility) gave him leave to go ashore and refresh himself. From Sidon they set sail, and came within sight of Cyprus, and having passed over the seas of Cilicia and Pamphylia, landed at Myra, a port in Lycia, where the ship finished its voyage. Hence they embarked on board a ship of Alexandria bound for Italy; and having passed by Cnidus,‡ with some difficulty made for Salome, a promontory on the eastern shore of Crete, whence, after many days slow sailing,

* It was the custom of the Romans that, after a prisoner had appealed unto the emperor, no inferior judge could either condemn or acquit him.
† Adramyttium was a seaport in Mysia, a province of Asia Minor, lying opposite to the isle of Lesbos, and not far from Troas.
‡ Cnidus was a city which stood on a promontory, or foreland of the same name, in that part of the province of Caria which was more particularly called Doris. This city was remarkable for the worship of Venus, and for the celebrated statue of that goddess made by the famous artificer Praxiteles.

they arrived at a place called the Fair Havens, on the coast of the same island. As the season of the year was far advanced, and sailing in those seas exceedingly dangerous, Paul advised the centurion to put in here, and winter. But Julius, preferring the judgment of the master of the ship, and the wind, at that time blowing gently at south, they put again to sea, in hopes of reaching Phenice, another harbor of Crete, where there was safe riding, and there to winter. It was not long, however, before they found themselves disappointed; for the calm southerly gale which blew before, suddenly changed to a stormy and tempestuous northeast wind, which bore down all before it, so that they were forced to let the ship drive; but, to secure it from splitting, they undergirt it, and to prevent its running aground on the shallows, threw out a great part of its lading and tackle.

In this wretched and dangerous situation did they continue for the space of fourteen days, during which they saw neither sun nor stars, so that the whole company (except Paul) began to give themselves up as lost. This being observed by the apostle, he addressed himself to them in words to this effect: "Had you taken my advice, and stayed at Crete, you would not have been in this danger; but take comfort, for we shall suffer no loss but that of the ship. This I can assure you has been made known to me by a divine messenger, who, appearing to me in the night, said, Fear not, Paul, for thou must be brought before Cæsar, and God hath, for thy sake, granted life and safety to all them that are with thee in the ship. Wherefore be of good cheer, for I am confident this vision will be made good, coming from God, as it certainly doth. But one passage more I received in this vision, namely, that after shipwreck we shall be cast on a certain island."

On the fourteenth night, the sailors, thinking they were near land, sounded, and found themselves in twenty fathoms water, soon after which they were convinced, by a second sounding, that they were near some coast. But apprehending that they might strike upon some shelves in the dark, they thought proper to come to an anchor, till the morning might give them better information. In the meantime the weather continuing exceedingly boisterous, they altered their intentions, and not staying for daylight, attempted to save themselves by getting into the boat. On this Paul told Julius, "that though he had said no person in the ship should perish, it was upon condition that they believed and trusted in God for their preservation: that therefore the seamen should continue in the ship and do their duty, and not endeavor to effect their escape by the boat; which if they did, they would be all in danger of their lives." Upon this the soldiers, to prevent the seamen's design, cut the ropes that fastened the boat, which was soon driven away by the impetuosity of the waves.

A little before daybreak Paul advised all the people on board the ship to take some refreshment, because, during the time of their danger, which had been fourteen days, they had taken but very little sustenance; and to encourage them to do this, he assured them again, that "not a hair of their heads should perish." Having said this, Paul "took bread, and gave thanks to God in the presence of them all; and when he had broken it, he began to eat. Then were they all of good cheer, and they also took some meat."

In the morning they discovered land, and discerning a creek which seemed to make a kind of haven, they resolved, if possible, to put in there; but in their passage unexpectedly fell into a place where two seas met, and where the forepart of the ship striking upon a neck of land that ran out into the sea, the hinder part was soon beaten in pieces by the violence of the waves. When the soldiers saw what was likely to be their fate, they proposed putting all the prisoners to the sword, lest any of them should swim to land, and make their escape; but the centurion, who was willing to save Paul, not approving of this design, gave orders that every one should shift for himself; the issue of which was, that some by swimming, others fastening to planks, and others on pieces of the broken ship (to the number of 276 persons) all got safe on shore.

The country on which they were cast was (as Paul had foretold) an island called Melita,* now called Malta, situated on the Lybian sea, between Syracuse and Africa.

* It is well known that the ancient name of Malta was Melita. This island, being situated midway, as it were, between the continents of Europe and Africa, has been reckoned sometimes as belonging to the one, and sometimes to the other. It is, however, rather nearer to Europe than to Africa, being one hundred and ninety miles from Cape Spartivento, in Calabria, the nearest point on the continent of Europe: and two hundred miles from Calipia, the nearest part of Africa; it is, however, only sixty miles from Cape Passaro, in Sicily. The island is sixty miles in circumference, twenty long, and twelve broad. Near it, on the west,

The natives of the place received them with great civility and kindness, made fires to dry their wet clothes, and entertained them with every necessary that was requisite for their distressed situation.

As Paul was laying a few sticks upon the fire, a viper, enlivened by the heat, came out of the bundle of wood from which he had taken them, and fastened upon his hand. When the natives saw this, they concluded that he must certainly be some notorious murderer, who, though Providence had suffered to escape the dangers of the sea, had been reserved for a more public and solemn execution. But when they saw him shake off the venomous creature into the fire, and no harm ensue, they changed their sentiments, and cried out that "he was a god."*

At a small distance from that part of the island on which Paul and his company were shipwrecked, lived Publius the governor, who received and entertained them with great civility and hospitality for three days. During this time, Paul, being informed that the governor's father lay dangerously ill of a fever and bloody flux, in acknowledgment for the favors received from Publius, went to his apartment, and, after praying some time, laid his hands upon him and healed him. The news of this miraculous cure was soon spread throughout the island, in consequence of which such as were afflicted with any disease were brought to Paul, who restored them to their former health and strength. This increased Paul's fame, and was of considerable advantage to his companions and fellow-sufferers, who on his account were highly caressed and entertained; and when they left the island they received many marks of esteem from the inhabitants, who furnished them with all necessaries proper for their voyage.

After staying three months at Miletus, they embarked on board the Castor and Pol-

is another and smaller island, called Goza, about thirty miles in circumference. Malta has no mountains, nor any very high hills; and it therefore makes no very conspicuous figure from the sea. There are no ports or bays on the African side of the island: but several very deep ones on the coast facing Sicily. The most important of these are the Calle della Melleha, the Porto di S. Paolo, and the two which are separated by the tongue of land on which stands the modern capital, Citta Valetta. The more ancient capital, in which, as appears from his intercourse with the governor, St. Paul remained during his stay, is situated about the centre of the island, upon a hill of moderate elevation, between which and the bay of St. Paul the ground is more low and level than in most other parts of the island. The cathedral church of St. Paul, upon the top of the hill, is supposed by the inhabitants, from old traditions, to occupy the site on which the palace of Publius, the governor. stood at the time of St. Paul's visit. There are in this city numerous alleged memorials of the apostle's sojourn; the process of identifying the spots where St. Paul lodged, and where he did this and this, being pushed to an extreme, is calculated to annoy even those who are disposed to acquiesce in the conclusion that the town was really visited by the apostle of the Gentiles.

Malta is naturally a barren rock; but where some soil has been found, or has been artificially laid, the productive power is very great, and the produce of a very superior description. The island does not, however, produce nearly sufficient corn for the sustenance of its inhabitants, who are obliged to import from abroad the greater part of that which they consume. But this is partly owing to the extreme populousness of the island, which, in proportion to its extent, contains more inhabitants than any other country of Europe.

The island was originally colonized by the Phœnicians, from whom it was taken, about 736 years B. C., by the Greek colonists in Sicily, to whom the island owed the name of Melita, perhaps on account of the excellent honey for which it has been at all times noted. An island of so much importance as a maritime and commercial station, was not overlooked by the Carthaginians, who, about 528 B. C., began to dispute its possession with the Greeks, and after for a time dividing it with them, made themselves entire masters of it. The inhabitants of Greek descent, however, remained, and the Punic, or Phœnician, and the Greek languages were equally spoken. Malta flourished greatly under the dominion of Carthage; but ultimately partook of the disasters which befell that power. In the first Punic war it was ravaged and seized by the Romans, who however lost it again, and only became masters of it under the treaty which placed in their hands (B. C. 242) all the islands between Italy and Africa. The Romans treated the inhabitants well. They made Melita a *municipium*, allowing the people to be governed by their own laws. The government was administered by a pro-prætor, who depended on the prætor of Sicily, and this office appears to have been held by Publius at the time of the shipwreck. When the Roman empire was divided, Malta fell to the lot of Constantine. About the middle of the fifth century it was seized by the Vandals, and ten years after by the Goths, who had obtained possession of Sicily. But about a century later (A. D. 553) the island was united to the lower empire by Belisarius, when sent to wrest Africa from the Vandals. The inhabitants were not allowed to enjoy the same privileges they had possessed under the Roman emperor, nor was the Greek government popular; hence the inhabitants willingly received the Arabs, who about the end of the ninth century, took the island from the Greeks, and established in it a government dependant on the emir of Sicily. The Arabs must have become largely mixed with the population to impress upon it, to the extent they did, their own language and customs. The present inhabitants have an Arabian aspect, and their language is an Arabian dialect, easily understood by the native Arabians, and by the Moors of Africa. Malta was taken from the Arabs by the Normans, in the year 1090. Its subsequent changes of masters need not here be stated, till 1530, when the emperor Charles V., who had annexed it to his empire, transferred it to the knights of St. John of Jerusalem, whom the Turks had recently dispossessed of Rhodes. The glory which Malta acquired in 1583, by the defeat of thirty thousand invading Turks—the continued distinction which it enjoyed, as a sovereign state, under the knights—the attention which it engaged, at the commencement of this century, from its surrender to Bonaparte on his way to Egypt—from its recovery by the English—and from its being the alleged ground of the memorable war which terminated at Waterloo: all these are circumstances, in the history of this celebrated island, too notorious to require more than this brief indication-

* Hercules was one of the gods whom the people of this island worshipped; and to him they ascribed the power of curing the bite of serpents.

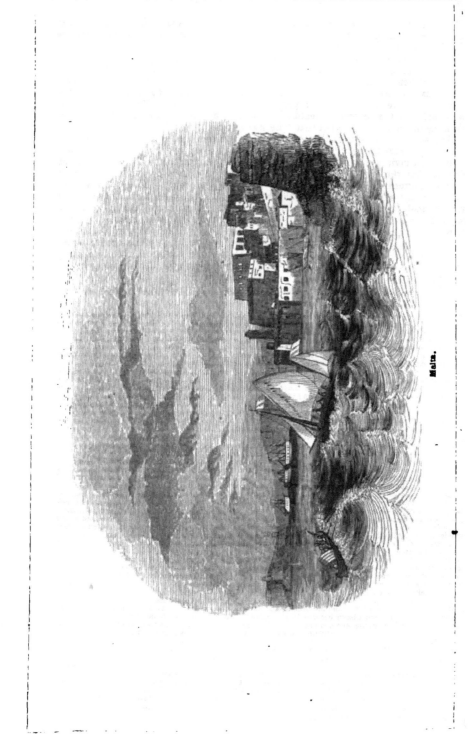

Malta.

lux, a ship of Alexandria bound for Italy. On their arrival at Syracuse,* they cast anchor, and went on shore to refresh themselves. Here they stopped three days, when they again embarked and sailed for Rhegium,† and thence to Puteoli,‡ where they landed. Finding in this place some Christians, at their earnest solicitation they continued with them a week, and then set forward on their journey to Rome.

When the Christians of Rome|| heard that Paul was on his journey to that city, great numbers of them went to meet him, some as far as Apiiforum, and others as far as a place called the Three Taverns. As soon as Paul saw them he was greatly rejoiced, and thanked God and took courage. They all conducted him in a kind of triumph to the city, on their arrival at which Julius delivered the rest of his prisoners over to the captain of the guard; but Paul was permitted to take up his residence in a private house, with only one soldier to guard him.

After Paul had been at Rome three days, he sent for the heads or rulers of the Jews in that city, who being assembled, he addressed himself to them in words to this effect: "Men and brethren, though I have done nothing contrary to the laws and customs of the Jews, yet was I by them apprehended and accused before the Roman governor, who, when he had examined me and found no capital accusation laid by my enemies, would have discharged me. But the Jews opposing it, I was forced to appeal to Cæsar to get out of their hands, not that I had any complaint to make to him against my countrymen. And this is the cause of my desiring to speak with you; for I am imprisoned, as you see, for teaching the belief and expectation of a future resurrection, which is the result of all the promises of God to the Jews, and that on which every true Israelite depends." The answer the rulers made to this was to the following purport: "We have no letters from Judea that mention

* This was a city of Sicily, seated on the east side of the island, with a fine prospect from every entrance, both by sea and land. Its port, which had the sea on both sides of it, was almost all of it environed with beautiful buildings, and all that part of it which was without the city, was on both sides banked up, and sustained with very fair walls of marble. The city itself, while in its splendor, was the largest and richest that the Greeks possessed in any part of the world; for, according to Strabo, it was twenty-two miles in circumference; and both Livy and Plutarch inform us, that the spoil of it was equal to that of Carthage. It was called quadruplex, as being divided into four parts, Acradino, Tyche, Neapolis, and the island of Ortygia. The first of these contained in it the famous temple of Jupiter; the second, the temple of Fortune; the third, a large amphitheatre, and a wonderful statue of Apollo, in the midst of a spacious square; and the fourth, the two temples of Diana and Minerva, and the renowned fountain of Arethusa. About two hundred and ten years before the birth of Christ, this city was taken and sacked by Marcellus, the Roman general, and, in storming the place, Archimedes, the great mathematician, who is esteemed the first inventor of the sphere, and who, during the siege, had sorely galled the Romans with his military engines, was slain by a common soldier, while he was intent upon his studies. After it was thus destroyed by Marcellus, Augustus rebuilt that part of it which stood upon the island, and, in time, it so far recovered itself, as to have three walls, three castles, and a marble gate, and to be able to send out twelve thousand horse, and four hundred ships. But it was totally destroyed by the Saracens, in 884, and scarcely any vestiges of it are now to be seen.

† Rhegium, now called Reggio, was a port-town in Italy, opposite to Messina in the island of Sicily; it is thought to have this name given it by the Greeks, who suppose that about this place Sicily was broken off from the continent of Italy by the sea.

‡ Puteoli was a noted town for trade, which lay not far from Naples; it was famous for its hot baths; and from these baths, or pits of water, called in Latin putei, the town is said to have taken its name.

|| A city of Italy, the most celebrated upon earth, and for several centuries the mistress of the world: it had been a station of the Etrurians, but it was founded by Romulus, at the head of a banditti, in the reign of King Hezekiah, about A. M. 3251, and B. C. 753. It gradually increased until it extended over seven hills, and ultimately to cover thirteen; and at the advent of Christ, its inhabitants were supposed to amount to about two millions. Christianity triumphed at Rome in the apostolic age, when a flourishing church was formed in that city, whose pastor was regarded with great respect by other churches, on account of the importance of his station, the metropolis of the world, and so near to the palace of the Cæsars. And such was the enmity of the idolatrous priests against the gospel, that many of the early pastors of the Christian church at Rome suffered martyrdom for the faith of Christ. Constantine, the emperor, about A. D. 313, professed his belief in Christianity, and afterward showed his zeal by building many churches, granting large honors to their ministers, especially dignifying the senior pastor at Rome. Multitudes now embraced the religion of the emperor; and ungodly men, for the sake of emolument, aspired to be its ministers: ceremonies were multiplied, to be performed by prayerless ministers, who thus daily corrupted its doctrines. Constantine removing the seat of his government to his new city Constantinople, a path was opened for the ambition of the Roman bishop, who, by progressive steps, advanced to the predicted elevation, on which he claimed to be the head of a hierarchy, as pope, or father of the church on earth, and vicar of Christ—but in the expressive language of apostolic prophecy, the "man of sin," the "mystery of iniquity," and "a beast." (2 Thess. ii. 3–8; Rev. xiii. 1–18.) Rome has greatly declined from its former glory, having now only about a hundred and fifty thousand inhabitants; but it abounds with vast monuments of its former grandeur. St. Peter's cathedral, far larger than St. Paul's cathedral, London, is believed to be the most magnificent place of worship in the world; and the Vatican, or winter-palace of the pope, is reckoned to contain twelve thousand five hundred chambers, halls, and closets. Roman catholics regard the pope, or bishop of Rome, as the visible head of the whole Christian church, and his decisions in religion as infallible: but every succeeding pope has been an enemy to the circulation of the Bible. Scarcely anything of pure scriptural Christianity can be discovered among the mass of superstitions observed in public worship at Rome; and, as the consequence, the morals of the people are the grossest opprobrium to the name of Christ.

Colossæ. The houses of the modern village of Khonas.

Roman Officers.

thee, neither have the converted Jews made any complaint against thee. But we desire to hear thy opinion more at large; for as concerning this profession and doctrine of Christianity, we know it is generally opposed by our brethren the Jews."

Paul readily complied with this request, and a day being appointed, not only the rulers, but many others of the Jews assembled at his house, to whom he preached from morning till night, explaining the doctrine of the gospel, and proving, from the promises and predictions of the Old Testament, that Jesus was the true Messiah. But his discourse was attended with different success, some of his hearers being convinced of the truth of what he asserted, while others persisted in their infidelity. In consequence of this, warm disputes took place between them; upon which, as they were about to depart, Paul, addressing himself to those who opposed his doctrine, told them that their unbelief was a strict fulfilment of what had been predicted by the prophet Isaiah: "Well," said he, "spake the Holy Ghost by Isaiah the prophet unto our fathers, saying, Go unto this people, and say, Hearing ye shall hear, and shall not understand; and seeing ye shall see, and not perceive. For the heart of this people is waxed gross, and their ears are dull of hearing, and their eyes have they closed; lest they should see with their eyes, and hear with their ears, and understand with their hearts, and should be converted, and I should heal them. Be it known, therefore, unto you, that the salvation of God is sent unto the Gentiles, and that they will hear it." After Paul had said this, the whole company departed, disagreeing among themselves on the subject which had been propounded to them.

Paul continued to reside in the house he had hired for the space of two years, during which he employed himself in expounding the doctrine of the gospel to all who came to him. He preached daily without the least molestation, and with such success that many people of distinction, some of whom were of the emperor's court, were converted, and became his constant disciples.

Among others of the apostle's converts at Rome was one Onesimus, who some time before had been servant to Philemon, a person of distinction at Colossæ.* Onesimus, having committed some indiscretion, left his master, and rambled as far as Rome, where, hearing Paul preach, he conceived such an idea of the truth of his doctrine that he became a most serious convert. Paul, however, understanding that he was another man's servant, advised him to return to his master, which he readily agreeing to, Paul sent an epistle by him to Philemon, in which he "earnestly requests that he will pardon him, and, notwithstanding his former faults, treat him as a brother; promising withal, that if he had wronged or owed him anything, he himself would not fail to repay it." This epistle may be considered as a masterpiece of eloquence in the persuasive way; for the apostle has therein had recourse to all the considerations which friendship, religion, piety, and tenderness, can inspire, to reconcile an incensed master to an indiscreet servant.

The Christians of Philippi having heard of Paul's imprisonment at Rome, and not knowing to what distress he might be reduced, raised a contribution for him, and sent it by Epaphroditus their bishop. This gave great satisfaction to Paul, not so much on account of the money they had sent, but from its being a proof that they still retained Christian principles. To encourage them, therefore, to persevere in the faith of Christ, and to withstand all opposition that might be made against them by the enemies of the gospel, he returned them an epistle, "wherein he gives some account of the state of his affairs at Rome; gratefully acknowledges their kindness to him; and warns them against the dangerous opinions which the Judaising teachers might vent against them. He likewise advises them to live in continual obedience to Christ; to

* Colossæ was situated in the southern part of Phrygia. Though a town of considerable note, it was by no means the principal one of Phrygia; for when that great province was ultimately divided into Phrygia Pacatiana and Phrygia Salutaris, it ranked but as the sixth city of the former division. The town was seated on an eminence to the south of the Meander, at a place where the river Lycus began to run under ground, as it did for five furlongs, after which it again rose and flowed into the Meander. This valuable indication of the site of Colossæ, furnished by Herodotus (lib. vii. cap. 30) establishes the truth of the received conclusion, that the ancient city is represented by the modern village of Khonas. This village is described by Mr. Arundell as being situated most picturesquely under the immense range of Mount Cadmus, which rises to a very lofty and perpendicular height behind the village, in some parts clothed with pines, in others bare of soil, with vast chasms and caverns. The immense perpendicular chasm, seen in the view, affords an outlet to a wide mountain-torrent, the bed of which is dry in summer. The approach to Khonas, as well as the village itself, is beautiful, abounding in tall trees, from which vines of most luxuriant growth are suspended. In the immediate neighborhood of the village are several vestiges of an ancient city, consisting of arches, vaults, squared stones, while the ground is strewed with broken pottery, which so generally and so remarkably indicates the sites of ancient towns in the east. That these ruins are all that now remain of Colossæ, there seems no just reason to doubt.

avoid disputations, delight in prayer, be courageous under affliction, united in love, and clothed in humility, in imitation of the blessed Jesus, who so far humbled himself as to ' become obedient unto death, even the death of the cross.' "

Paul had lived three years at Ephesus, preaching the gospel to the numerous inhabitants of that city, and was therefore well acquainted with the state and condition of the place; so that taking the opportunity of Tychicus's going thither from Rome, he wrote his Epistle to the Ephesians, wherein " he endeavors to countermine the principles and practices both of the Jews and Gentiles; to confirm them in the belief and practices of the Christian doctrine; and to instruct them fully in the great mysteries of the gospel; their redemption and justification by the death of Christ; their gratuitous election; their union with the Jews in one body, of which Christ is the head, and the glorious exaltation of that head above all with creatures both spiritual and temporal; together with many excellent precepts, both as to the general duties of religion and the duties of their particular relations."

Paul himself had never been at Colossæ; but one Epaphras, who was at that time a prisoner with him at Rome, had preached the gospel there with good success; and from him he learned that certain false teachers had endeavored to corrupt the minds of the Christians in that city. In opposition to this, and to secure the converts is their faith, he wrote his Epistle to the Colossians, wherein he beautifully sets forth the Messiah, and all the benefits that will be bestowed on such as believe in him, as being the image of his Father, the Redeemer of all mankind, the reconciler of all things to God, and the Head of the Church, which gives life and vigor to all its members. He commends the doctrine preached to them by Epaphras, and exhorts them not to be led away by the reasonings of human philosophy; and concludes with giving them a list of many chief and principal duties of a Christian life, especially such as respect the relations of husbands and wives, parents and children, masters and servants.

During the time Paul was thus laudably employed at Rome, James the apostle, and bishop of Jerusalem, was dedicating his time, as much as in him lay, to the propagation of the gospel within his provinces. Considering within himself that it belonged to him to take care of all the converted among the twelve tribes of Israel, wherever dispersed, he wrote an epistle to them, the design of which was, " to confute and suppress a dangerous error then growing up in the church, viz., that a bare ' naked faith' was sufficient to secure men's salvation, without any attention to good works; to comfort Christians under the persecutions which were going to be raised against them by worldly powers; and to awaken them out of their stupidity when judgments were ready to overtake them." To this purpose he inserts in his epistle many excellent exhortations, such as, to bear afflictions, to hear the word of God, to mortify their passions, to bridle their tongues, to avoid cursing and swearing, and to adorn their Christian profession with a good conversation, with meekness, peaceableness, and charity."

It was not long after James had written this epistle, before a period was put to all his labors. The governing part of the Jews, being highly enraged at the disappointment they had met with in Paul's appealing to Cæsar, were now resolved to revenge it upon James; accordingly, taking the opportunity of the death of Festus (before the arrival of Albinus his successor) Ananias the high-priest summoned James, and some others, before the sanhedrim, who required them to renounce their Christian faith. Their desire more especially was, that James should make his renunciation in the most public manner, and therefore they carried him up to the battlements of the temple, and threatened to throw him down thence in case he refused complying with their request. But James, instead of gratifying their desires, began himself to confess, and to exhort others to confess, the faith of Christ, in the presence of those who came to hear his recantation; upon which the members of the sanhedrim were so incensed that they ordered him to be thrown down headlong from the place where he stood. By this fall he was greatly bruised, but not quite killed; and therefore having recovered himself so far as to be able to rise on his knees, he prayed fervently to Heaven for his persecutors, in the manner of the protomartyr Stephen. But malice is too diabolical to be pacified with kindness, or satisfied with cruelty. Accordingly, his enemies, vexed that they had not fully accomplished their work, poured a shower of stones upon him while he was imploring their forgiveness at the throne of grace, and one of them, more cruel and inveterate than the rest, put an end to his misery, by dashing out his brains with a fuller's club.*

Thus did this great and good man finish his course in the 96th year of his age, and about twenty-four years after our blessed Saviour's ascension into heaven. His remains were deposited in a tomb which he had caused to be made on the Mount of Olives; and his brother Simon was, by the general voice of the Christians, appointed his successor in the bishopric of Jerusalem.

The apostle James was a man of exemplary piety and devotion. Prayer was his daily business and delight: so constant was he at his devotions that his knees became hard and callous; and so prevalent in his petitions to Heaven, that, in a time of great drought, he prayed for rain and obtained it. Nor was his charity to his fellow-creatures less than his piety toward God; he did good to all, watched over the souls of men, and made their eternal welfare his constant study. He was of a remarkably meek and humble temper, honoring what was excellent in others, but concealing what was valuable in himself. The dignity of the place he so worthily filled, could not induce him to entertain lofty thoughts of himself above his brethren: on the contrary, he strove to conceal whatever might place him in a higher rank than the other disciples of the Lord of Glory. He was the delight of all good men, and so much in the favor and estimation of the people, that they used to flock after him, and strive who should touch even but the hem of his garment. In short, he was a man of so amiable a temper, as to be the wonder of the age in which he lived; and from the reputation of his holy and religious life, was styled James the Just.

CHAPTER XI.

AFTER Paul had continued at Rome upward of two years in a state of confinement, he obtained his liberty, but by what means we have not any account in history.† It may be presumed, that the Jews not having sufficient proof of the accusation they had laid against him, or being informed that what they alleged was no violation of any Roman law, they durst not implead him before the emperor; and therefore, of course, he was permitted to go at large.

Paul, having obtained his liberty, left Rome, and travelled into various parts of Italy, preaching the gospel with different success. In some places he made many converts, but in others he met with great opposition. Before he left Italy, he wrote

* The perpetrators of this barbarous act were considered in the most detestable light by the sober and just persons among the Jews themselves. Even their own historian Josephus could not but condemn it, and, as himself testifies, all the honest and conscientious people of the city remonstrated against it, both to their king Agrippa, and to the Roman governor Albinus; insomuch that the high-priest by whose authority it was committed was, in a few months after, degraded, and another placed in his stead.

† During St. Paul's first imprisonment he was allowed to remain "in his own hired house, with a soldier that kept him." How he was circumstanced in his second imprisonment, during which this epistle appears to have been written, we have no means of knowing with certainty; but the probability seems to be that his treatment was then much less favorable than in the first instance it had been. The old ecclesiastical traditions state that, just before the end of their lives, the apostles Peter and Paul were together confined in the Mamertine prison at Rome. Of this joint imprisonment we shall say nothing, nor of that of St. Peter in particular. But since it seems that St. Paul was kept as a prisoner at Rome, and since it is probable that his treatment was not very favorable, we are inclined to consider it probable that he was kept in a prison; and, if so, we are induced to think the Mamertine prison the more likely to have been the place of his confinement, from finding it frequently mentioned in the old martyrologies as the place in which many of the early martyrs were imprisoned.

The Mamertine prisons date from the earliest times of Rome; being constructed, according to Livy, by Ancus Martius, and enlarged by Servius Tullius. The lower prison, however, assigned to the latter king, is supposed by some to have been a quarry, and by others, one of those subterranean granaries which were used in very ancient times. Be this as it may, these prisons, which still exist, offer a striking instance of the durability of Roman works. They occur on the descent of the Capitoline mount toward the Forum; and near the entrance were the Scalæ Gemoniæ, by which the culprits were dragged to the prison, or out of it to execution. They consist of two apartments, one above the other, built with large uncemented stones. There is no entrance, except by a small aperture in the upper roof, and by a similar hole in the upper floor, leading to the cell below, without any staircase to either. The upper prison is twenty-seven feet long by twenty wide; and the lower one, which is elliptical, measures twenty feet by ten. The height of the former is fourteen feet, and of the latter eleven. In the lower dungeon is a small spring, which is said at Rome to have arisen at the command of St. Peter, to enable him to baptize his keepers, Processus and Martinianus, with forty-seven companions, whom he had converted. They also show the pillar to which it is alleged that this apostle was bound. The prison itself, with a small chapel in front, is now dedicated to him: and over it is the church of S. Giuseppe de' Falegnami, built in 1539. Dr. Burton says that a more horrible place for the confinement of a human being can scarcely be conceived; and Sallust, in a passage adduced by him, says that, from uncleanness, darkness, and foul smells, its appearance was disgusting and terrific. See Burton's Description of the Antiquities of Rome, 1821.

The Mamertine Prison, Rome—the subterranean cell in which St. Paul and St. Peter are said to have been confined.

his famous and most elaborate epistle to the Hebrews, that is, to the converted Jews who dwelt in Jerusalem and its neighborhood. His main design in this epistle is, " to magnify Christ and the religion of the gospel above Moses and the Jewish economy, that, by this means, he may the better establish the converted Jews in the belief and profession of Christianity. To this purpose he represents our Saviour, in his divine nature, far superior to all angels, and all created beings ; and in his mediatorial capacity, a greater lawgiver than Moses, a greater priest than Aaron, and a greater king and priest than Melchizedec. He informs them, that the ceremonies, the sacrifices, and the observances of the law, could have no virtue in themselves, but only as they were types of Jesus Christ ; and being now accomplished in his person, and by his ministry, were finally and totally abolished. He insists upon the necessity of faith, and, by the examples of the patriarchs and prophets, proves that justification is to be had no other way, than by the merits of a dying Saviour. And lastly, he lays before them many excellent precepts for the regulation of their lives ; exhortations to trust and confidence in Christ, in all their sufferings ; and strict cautions against apostacy from his religion, even in the hottest persecutions."

A short time after Paul had written this epistle to the Hebrews, he left Italy, and, accompanied by Timothy, prosecuted his long-intended journey into Spain ; and, according to the testimony of several writers, crossed the sea, and preached the gospel in Britain.* What success he had in these western parts is not known ; however, after going from one place to another for the space of eight or nine months, he returned again eastward, visited Sicily, Greece, and Crete (at the latter of which places he constituted Titus bishop of the island), and then went into Judea, where we shall for the present leave him, in order to take some notice of Peter, his fellow-laborer in the cause of Christ.

In what manner Peter employed his time after his escape out of prison, we have not any certain account. It is, however, generally agreed, that about the second year of the emperor Claudius, he went to Rome, and there continued for some time, till at length that emperor, taking advantage of some seditions and tumults raised by the Jews, published an edict for banishing all the Jews from that city ; in consequence of which Peter returned to Jerusalem. After staying some time in the capital of Judea, he visited the several churches which he had planted in the east, and carried the glad tidings of the gospel into Africa, Sicily, Italy, and even as far as Britain, in all which places he brought over great numbers to the Christain faith.

Having thus propagated the gospel in the western, as well as the eastern parts of the world, Peter, toward the latter end of the reign of Nero, returned to Rome, the Jews, after the death of Claudius, being permitted to reside in that city with the same freedom as before that emperor issued his edict for their banishment. On Peter's arrival at Rome, he met with his fellow-laborer Paul, who had just returned thither from Judea. The two apostles found the minds of the people strangely bewitched, and hardened against the doctrines of the gospel, by the subtleties and magical arts of Simon Magus, whom Peter had severely chastised for his wickedness at Samaria. This monster of impiety not only opposed the preaching of the apostles, but likewise did all in his power to render them and their doctrine odious to the emperor. Peter, foreseeing that the calumnies of Simon and his adherents would be injurious to the cause of his great Master, thought himself obliged to oppose him with all his might ; and having discovered the vanity of his impostures in several remarkable instances, he at length worked him up to such a pitch of madness and desperation, that to give the people an evident demonstration of his having those supernatural powers he had pretended, he promised that, on such a day, he would ascend visibly up into heaven. Accordingly, at the time appointed, when prodigious numbers of people were assembled to behold so extraordinary a sight, he went up to the summit of a mount, whence he raised himself, and, by the assistance of some magic arts, seemed as if he was flying toward the regions of heaven. Peter and Paul, beholding the delusion, had recourse to prayers, and obtained their petitions of the Almighty, namely, that the impostor should be soon discovered, for the honor of the

* Clemens, in his famous epistle to the Corinthians, expressly tells us, that being a preacher both to the east and west, he taught righteousness to the whole world, and went to the utmost bounds of the west ; and Theodoret and others inform us, that he preached not only in Spain, but went to other nations, and brought the gospel into the isles of the sea, by which he undoubtedly means Britain ; and therefore he elsewhere reckons the Gauls and Britons among the people whom the apostles, and particularly Paul, persuaded to embrace the doctrine of Christ.

blessed Jesus. Accordingly, he fell headlong to the ground, and was so bruised by the fall, that in a short time he expired.

The emperor Nero was a professed patron of magicians, and therefore, when he heard of this event, he was greatly irritated. He had a particular dislike to the doctrine of Christianity, as being totally repugnant to the lusts and passions which he indulged; and was highly offended at Peter for having made so many converts, among whom were several persons of distinction. In consequence of this, he ordered him and Paul to be apprehended and cast into prison, soon after which an event* occurred, whence he took the opportunity of showing his resentment to the Jews, and that in the most severe manner. He issued out an edict, ordering Christian Jews to be persecuted in every part of his empire; in consequence of which, all orders and degrees of that people were treated with the greatest contempt and cruelty that could be invented.

But before the burning of the city, and the persecution commenced against the Christians, in consequence of Nero's edict, both Peter and Paul made their escape from confinement. Peter continued at Rome, but Paul left it, and went into Judea, where he stayed some time, after which he went into Asia, and met Timothy at Ephesus. Hence he paid a visit to the Colossians, whom he had never before seen, and after staying with them some time, returned to Ephesus, and excommunicated Hymeneus and Alexander, for denying the resurrection of the dead, and other articles of the Christian faith. From Ephesus he went into Macedonia, but previous to his departure, enjoined Timothy, whom he had constituted bishop of Ephesus (see 1 Tim. i. 3), constantly to reside in that city, and to take the charge of all the pro-consular Asia.

After Paul had visited several places in Macedonia, he went to Philippi (see Philip. i. 25, 26), where he stayed some time, during which he daily preached to the people, made many new converts, and farther established those who had before embraced the faith in the principles of Christianity. Before he left Macedonia, he wrote his first epistle to Timothy, in which "he lays down the duties and qualifications of a bishop, as well in respect of his ministry, as of his private conversation, and instructs him in the office of a true Christian pastor."

Leaving Macedonia, Paul directed his course to Nicopolis, a populous city situated on the banks of the Danube, where he took up his winter quarters. During his stay here he wrote his epistle to Titus at Crete; wherein "he describes to him (as he had done to Timothy) the qualifications which a bishop ought to have, and more especially a bishop of Crete, where some sharpness and severity were necessary amidst a people of their perverse and obstinate tempers. He admonishes him not to suffer the flock, committed to his charge, to be led away by the delusions of Judaism; and lastly, lays down precepts for people in all conditions of life, even not forgetting servants, because our blessed Saviour has poured out his grace upon all men."

In the beginning of the spring Paul left Nicopolis, and went to Corinth. After staying a short time here, he crossed the sea into Asia, and went to Ephesus, and thence proceeded to Miletum. From Miletum he travelled northward to Troas, and lodged with Carpus, one of his disciples, where he left his cloak (see 2 Tim. iv. 13), some books, and other articles. From Troas he went to Antioch, Iconium, and Lys-

---

* The emperor Nero, in the former part of his reign, governed with tolerable credit to himself; but in the latter part he gave way to the greatest extravagance of temper, and to the most atrocious barbarities. The event above alluded to is this. Among other diabolical whims he took it into his head to order that the city of Rome should be set on fire, which was done by his officers, guards, and servants, accordingly. While the imperial city was in flames, he went up to the tower of Mæcenas, played upon his harp, sung the song of the burning of Troy, and openly declared that he wished the ruin of all things before his death. Among the noble buildings burnt was the Circus, or place appropriated to horse-races: it was half a mile in length, of an oval form, with rows of seats rising above each other, and capable of receiving, with ease, upward of a hundred thousand spectators. Beside this noble pile, many other palaces and houses were consumed; several thousands perished in the flames, were smothered with the smoke, or buried beneath the ruins.

This dreadful conflagration continued nine days; when Nero, finding that his conduct was greatly blamed, and a severe odium cast upon him, determined to lay the whole upon the Christians, at once to excuse himself, and have an opportunity of glutting his sight with new cruelties. This was the occasion of the first persecution; and the barbarities exercised upon the Christians were such as even excited the commiseration of the Romans themselves. Nero even refined upon cruelty, and contrived all manner of punishments for the Christians that the most infernal imagination could design. In particular, he had some sewed up in the skins of wild beasts, and then worried by dogs till they expired; and others dressed in shirts made stiff with wax, fixed to axle-trees, and set on fire in his gardens in order to illuminate them. This persecution was general throughout the whole of the Roman empire; but it rather increased than diminished the spirit of Christianity.

tra, where he suffered those persecutions and afflictions, of which he makes mention to Timothy, and thanks God for his deliverance from them (2 Tim. iii. 4).

After visiting these and many other places, Paul went again to Rome, knowing that the persecution which had taken place in that city, in consequence of the edict issued by Nero, was somewhat abated. Meeting with Peter, they conjunctively used their utmost endeavors to instruct the Jews in their synagogues, and to convert the Gentiles in all public places and assemblies. This, however, soon raised the malice and indignation of the magistrates, who were still inflamed against the Jews. Nero was at that time in Greece, and had left Helius to supply his place during his absence, investing him with exorbitant powers, which he exercised with the most unbounded rigor. It was a crime sufficient for these two apostles (in the eyes of Helius) that they were Christians. The particular prejudice he took against Peter was, his having defeated Simon Magus; and that against Paul, his having converted one of the emperor's concubines. He therefore ordered them both to be apprehended and committed to prison, where they spent their time in the most solemn acts of devotion, and, as opportunity offered, preached the gospel to their guards and fellow-prisoners, among whom it is said they converted Processus and Martinian, two principal officers of the army.

While they were in prison, Peter wrote his second general epistle to the converted Jews, who were dispersed in the several provinces of Asia. In this epistle "he endeavors, by earnest exhortations, to prevail with them to persevere in the doctrine which they had received, and to testify the soundness and sincerity of their faith by a Christian life. He forewarns them of the false teachers that would shortly spring up among them, foretells their sad and miserable destruction, and describes them by their odious characters, that they may avoid them. He vindicates the doctrine of Christ's coming to judgment, which the heretics of those times denied, that thereby they might encourage men the more securely to pursue their lewd courses. And lastly, he describes the great and terrible day of the Lord, when the elements shall melt, and the whole frame of nature be dissolved, thereby to excite them to become circumspect and diligent, in order to be found of him in peace, without spot, and blameless."

Much about the same time that Peter wrote this epistle to the converted Jews in Asia, Paul wrote his second epistle to Timothy, wherein "he informs him of the near approach of his death, and desires him to come to him before winter, because most of his companions, upon one affair or other, were departed from him. He exhorts him to discharge all the duties of a bishop and pastor, suitable to those excellent gifts he had received, and with a generous contempt of the world, and worldly things. He admonishes him not to forget the doctrine which he had taught him, not to be surprised or disturbed at the apostacy of some from the faith, but to preach the more zealously against such opposers as placed their confidence in those teachers who left the truth to turn unto fables. And lastly, he informs him, how, at his first appearing before Helius, all his companions, for fear of being involved in his punishment, forsook him, but that the Lord stood by him and strengthened him, to make his preaching more conspicuous and effectual to the Gentiles."

When the two apostles had been in confinement about eight months, the cruel Nero returned from Greece, and entered his palace at Rome in great triumph.* Soon after his return it was ultimately resolved, that the two apostles should be put to death. Peter, as a Jew and foreigner, was sentenced to be crucified; and Paul, as a Roman citizen, to be beheaded. On the 29th of June (as it is generally supposed) these sentences were put in execution. Peter, after being first scourged, according to the Roman custom, was taken from the prison, and led to the top of the Vatican mount, near the Tiber, where he was sentenced to surrender up his life on the cross. On his arrival at the place of execution, he begged the favor of the officers that he might not be crucified in the common manner, but with his head downward,

* Subsequently to the burning of Rome, Nero built himself a glorious palace on Mount Palatine, which was named the Golden Palace. When the emperor saw it finished, he said, "Now I am going to be lodged like a man!" This splendid fabric was burnt and rebuilt in the reign of Commodus; and of the palace so rebuilt, in its present ruined condition, fringing the mount with its broken arches, a representation is given in our present engraving, on page 577. It still bears the name of Nero's Palace; and although of somewhat later origin than the time of St. Paul, it will be considered interesting from its approximation to his time, and from its furnishing the only idea attainable from actual remains of the palaces in which the Roman emperors abode.

Ruins of the Palace of Nero.

thinking himself unworthy to suffer in the same posture in which his Lord and Master had suffered before him. This request was accordingly complied with; and in this manner did the great apostle Peter resign his soul into the hands of Him who came down from heaven to ransom mankind from destruction, and open for them the gates of the heavenly Canaan.

While Peter was suffering on the top of the Vatican mount, his fellow-apostle Paul was conducted to a place called Aquæ Salviæ, about three miles from Rome, in order to undergo the punishment denounced against him by the cruel Nero. In his way he converted three of the soldiers who were sent to guard him to his execution, and who, within a few days after, died martyrs themselves. As soon as Paul arrived at the place of execution, he knelt down, and after praying for some time with the greatest fervency, cheerfully gave up his neck to the fatal stroke; quitting this vale of misery in hopes of passing to the blissful regions of immortality, to the kingdom of his beloved Master, the great Redeemer of the human race.

Thus died these two most eminent apostles of Jesus Christ, after they had, with indefatigable labor, reaped a glorious harvest of infinite numbers of souls, and triumphantly propagated salvation through the then most considerable parts of the world.

The body of Peter, being taken from the cross, was embalmed after the Jewish manner by Marcellinus the presbyter, and buried in the Vatican near the Triumphal way. Over his grave a small church was afterward erected, which being in the course of time destroyed, his body was removed to the cemetery in the Appian way, two miles distant from Rome. Here it continued till the time of Pope Cornelius, when it was reconveyed to the Vatican, where it abode in some obscurity till Constantine the Great, from the profound reverence he had for the Christian religion, having rebuilt and enlarged the Vatican to the honor of St. Peter, enriched it with gifts and ornaments, which in every age increased in splendor and beauty, till it became one of the wonders of the world, and in that light was considered for many years after.

The remains of Paul were deposited in the Via Ostiensis, about two miles from Rome. Constantine the Great, at the instance of Pope Sylvester, built a stately church over his grave, which he adorned with a hundred marble columns, and beautified with the most exquisite workmanship.

It may not be improper, before we part with these two great apostles, to mention some particulars relative to their persons and characters. And first,

St. Peter (according to the description given of him by Nicephorus) was of a middle size, but somewhat slender, and inclining to tallness: his complexion was very pale; his hair thick and curled; his eyes black; his eyebrows thin; and his nose large, but not sharp. With respect to his disposition, if we consider him as a man, there seems to have been a natural eagerness predominant in his temper, which animated his soul to the most bold and sometimes rash undertakings. It was this, in a great measure, that prompted him to be so very forward to speak, and to return answers sometimes before he had well considered them. It was this that made him expose his person to the most imminent dangers, promise those great things in behalf of his master, resolutely draw his sword in his quarrel against a whole band of soldiers, and wound a servant of the high-priest; nay, he had in all probability attempted greater things, had not his Lord restrained his impetuosity, and given a reasonable check to his fury.

If we consider him as a disciple of the blessed Jesus, we shall find him exemplary in the great duties of religion. His humility and lowliness of mind were remarkable. With what a passionate earnestness on the conviction of a miracle, did he beg of our blessed Saviour to depart from him, thinking it unworthy the Son of God to come near so vile a sinner!

When the great Redeemer of mankind, by that amazing condescension, stooped so low as to wash the feet of his disciples, Peter could not be persuaded to admit his performing it, thinking it highly improper that so great a person should submit to such a servile office toward a person so mean as himself; nor could he be induced to admit of it till his great Master threatened to deprive him of his favor.

When Cornelius the Roman centurion would have treated him with more than ordinary marks of esteem and veneration, he was so far from complying with it, that he declared he was nothing more than a mortal like himself.

His love and zeal for his master were remarkable; he thought he could never express either at too high a rate; venturing on the greatest perils, and exposing his life to the most imminent dangers. His forwardness to own his great Master for the Messiah and Son of the Most High, was remarkably great; and it was this that drew from his Lord that honorable encomium, "Blessed art thou, Simon Bar-jona."

But his distinguished courage and constancy in confessing Christ, even before his most inveterate enemies, was still greater after he had recovered himself from his fall. How plainly does he tell the Jews that they were the murderers and crucifiers of the Lord of Glory? Nay, with what an undaunted courage, with what a heroic greatness of soul, did he tell the very sanhedrim, who had sentenced and condemned him, that they were guilty of his death, and that they had no other way of escaping the vengeance of the Almighty, but by the merits of that very Jesus whom they had crucified and put to death.

Lastly, if we consider him as an apostle, as a pastor, or shepherd of the souls of men, we shall find him faithful and diligent in his office, zealously endeavoring to instruct the ignorant, reduce the erroneous, strengthen the weak, confirm the strong, reclaim the vicious, and turn the children of men into the paths of righteousness. He never omitted any opportunity of preaching to the people, and spreading the glad tidings of the gospel among the human race; and so powerful were his discourses, that he brought over many thousands of converts. How many painful journeys and dangerous voyages did he undertake! With what unconquerable patience did he endure the greatest trials, surmount every difficulty, and remove every disposition, that he might circulate and establish the gospel of his beloved Master! never refusing even to lay down his life to promote it. Nor was he assiduous only to perform these duties himself; but was also careful to animate others to do the like, earnestly pressing and persuading the pastors and governors of the church "to feed the flock of God," to labor freely for the good of the souls of men, and not to undertake those offices to acquire advantages to themselves; beseeching them to treat the flock committed to their care with lenity and gentleness, and to be themselves shining examples of piety and religion, the surest method of rendering their ministry successful. And because it was impossible for him to be always present, to teach and warn the children of men, he endeavored, by letters, to imprint in their minds the practice of what they had been taught—a method he tells us he was resolved to pursue as long as he continued an inhabitant of this world; "thinking it meet, while he was in this tabernacle, to stir up, by putting them in mind of these things; that so they might be able, after his decease, to have them always in remembrance."

Thus lived, thus died Simon Peter, called to be an apostle of Jesus Christ, and at length to offer up his life in ratification of the doctrine he delivered and the faith he maintained and propagated.

St. Paul was in person of a low and small stature, somewhat stooping: his complexion was fair; his countenance grave; his head small; his eyes sparkling; his nose high and bending; and his hair thick and dark, but mixed with gray. His constitution was weak, and he was often subject to distempers; but his mind was strong, and he possessed a solid judgment, quick discernment, and prompt memory, all which were improved by the advantages of a liberal education. His humility and self-abasement were wonderful; his sobriety and temperance singularly strict; and his contempt for the world great and generous. His kindness and charity were remarkable: he had a quick sense of the wants of others, and a most compassionate tenderness for all who were in distress. To what place soever he went, it was always one of his first cares to make provision for the poor, and to stir up the bounty of the rich and wealthy in their behalf. But his charity to the souls of men was infinitely greater, fearing no dangers, refusing no labors, going through good and evil report, that he might gain men over to the knowledge of the truth, take them out of the crooked paths, and place them in the straight way that leadeth to life eternal.

Nor was his charity to men greater than his zeal to God, laboring, with all his might, to promote the honor of his Master. When he was at Athens, and saw the people of that city involved in the grossest superstition and idolatry, and giving that honor which was due to God alone, to statues and images, his zeal was fired, and he could not help letting them know the resentment of his mind, and how greatly they dishonored God, the great Maker and Preserver of the world.

Through the course of an extensive ministry, he never suffered himself to be interrupted in his endeavors for propagating the gospel by the dangers and difficulties he met with, or the troubles and oppositions that were raised against him. This will evidently appear if we take a survey of the trials and sufferings he underwent; some part whereof are thus briefly summed up by himself: "In labors abundant, in stripes above measure, in death oft; thrice beaten with rods, once stoned, thrice suffered shipwreck, a night and a day in the deep. In journeying often, in perils of water, in perils by his countrymen, in perils by the heathens, in perils in the city, in perils in the wilderness, in perils in the sea, in perils among false brethren; in weariness and painfulness, in watchings often, in hunger and thirst; in fastings often; in cold and nakedness, and besides those things that were without, which daily came upon him, the care of all the churches." (2 Cor. xi. 23, &c.) An account, though very great, yet far short of what he endured. He did not want for solicitations both from Jews and Gentiles; and might, doubtless, in some measure, have made his own terms, would he have been false to his trust, and quitted that way which was then everywhere spoken against. But alas! those things weighed little with our apostle, who "counted not his life dear unto him, so that he might finish his course with joy, and the ministry which he had received of the Lord Jesus." And therefore, when he found himself under the sentence of death, he could triumphantly say, "I have fought a good fight, I have finished my course, I have kept the faith."

THE EPISTLES OF PAUL.

EPISTLE.	WHERE WRITTEN.	FOR WHOSE USE.	A. D.
1. Thessalonians I.	Corinth	Gentile Christians	52
2. Thessalonians II.	Do.	Do. Do.	52
3. Galatians	Do.	Do. Do.	53
4. Corinthians I.	Ephesus	Do. Do.	57
5. Romans	Corinth	Do. Do.	58
6. Corinthians II.	Macedonia	Do. Do.	59
7. Ephesians	Rome	Do. Do.	62
8. Philippians	Do.	Do. Do.	62
9. Colossians	Do.	Do. Do.	62
10. Philemon	Do.	Philemon of Colosse	62
11. Hebrews	Italy	Hebrew Christians	63
12. Timothy I.	Macedonia	Timothy the Evangelist	65
13. Titus	Do.	Titus the Evangelist	65
14. Timothy II.	Rome	Timothy the Evangelist	66

CHAPTER XII.

IN the preceding chapters we have given a minute detail of the transactions of those two great apostles, Peter and Paul, as related by the evangelist St. Luke, together with an account of the persecutions and sufferings of St. Stephen, and St. James the Less, bishop of Jerusalem. We shall therefore in this chapter proceed to relate the particulars concerning their fellow-laborers in the cause of Christ; in doing which we shall begin with the Apostle

ST. ANDREW.

After the ascension of our blessed Lord into heaven, and the descent of the Holy Ghost on the apostles, to qualify them for the great business they were about to undertake, St. Andrew was appointed to preach the gospel in Scythia and the neighboring countries. Accordingly, he departed from Jerusalem, and first travelled through Cappadocia, Galatia, and Bithynia, instructing the inhabitants in the faith of Christ, and continued his journey along the Euxine sea, into the deserts of Scythia. On his arrival at a place called Amynsus, he was received with great civility by a distinguished Jew of that town; upon which he went into the synagogue, preached to them concerning Jesus, and, from the prophecies of the Old Testament, proved him to be the Messiah and Saviour of the world. During his stay here he converted many to the true faith, having done which, previous to his departure, he ordained them priests, and settled the times of their public meetings for the performance of divine worship.

Leaving Amynsus, he proceeded to Trapezium, a maritime city on the Euxine sea; whence, after visiting many other places, he went to Nice, where he stayed two years, preaching and working miracles with great success. From Nice he proceeded to Nicomedia, and thence to Chalcedon, where he took shipping, and sailing through the Propontis, passed the Euxine sea to Heraclea, and afterward to Amastris; in all which places he met with very great difficulties, but overcame them by an invincible patience and resolution.

From Amastris, Andrew went to Sinope, a city situated on the Euxine sea, and famous both for the birth and burial of King Mithridates. The inhabitants of this city were chiefly Jews, who, partly from a zeal for their religion, and partly from their barbarous manners, were exasperated against Andrew, and entered into a confederacy to burn the house in which he lodged. But being disappointed in their design, they treated him with the most savage cruelty, throwing him on the ground, stamping upon him with their feet, pulling and dragging him from place to place: some beating him with clubs, and others pelting him with stones, till at length, apprehending they had entirely deprived him of life, they cast him out into the fields. But he miraculously recovered, and returned publicly into the city; by which, and other miracles he wrought among them, he converted many from the errors of their ways, and induced them to become disciples of the blessed Jesus.

Departing from Sinope, he returned to Jerusalem, and after staying a short time in his own country, went again into the province allotted for the service of his ministry, which greatly flourished through the power of the Divine grace that attended it. He travelled over Thrace, Macedonia, Thessaly, Achaia, and Epirus,* preaching the gospel, propagating Christianity, and confirming the doctrine he taught with signs and miracles. At length he arrived at Patrea,† a city of Achaia, where he gave his last and greatest testimony to the gospel of his Divine Master, by cheerfully sealing it with his blood.

It happened that Ægenas, the pro-consul of Achaia, came at this time to Patrea, where, knowing that many of the people had abandoned the heathen religion and embraced the gospel of Christ, he had recourse to every method, both of favor and cruelty, to reduce the people to their old idolatry. The apostle, whom no difficulties or dangers could deter from performing the duties of his ministry, addressed himself to the pro-consul, calmly putting him in mind that, being only a judge of men, he ought to revere Him who was the supreme and impartial Judge of all, pay him the divine honors due to his exalted majesty, and abandon the impieties of his idolatrous worship; observing to him, that if he would renounce his idolatries, and heartily embrace the Christian faith, he might, with him and the members who had believed in the Son of God, receive eternal happiness in the Messiah's kingdom.

The pro-consul told St. Andrew he would never embrace the religion he had mentioned, and that if he did not sacrifice to the gods (in order that all those whom he had seduced might, by his example, be brought back to the ancient religion they had forsaken) he would cause him to be immediately put to death. The apostle replied, that he saw it was in vain to endeavor to persuade a person incapable of sober counsels, and hardened in his own blindness and folly, to forsake his evil ways; and that, with respect to himself, he might act as he pleased, and if he had any torment greater than another, he might inflict it upon him; as the stricter constancy he showed in his sufferings for Christ, the more acceptable he should be to his Lord and Master after his departure from this wicked world.

This so irritated Ægenas, that he immediately condemned him to death. Accordingly, after being scourged in the most unmerciful manner by seven lictors, he was led away to be crucified. As soon as he approached the cross, he knelt down and saluted it in words to this effect: "I have long desired and expected this happy hour. The cross has been consecrated by the body of Christ hanging on it, and adorned with his members as with so many inestimable jewels. I therefore come joyfully and triumphantly to it, that it may receive me as a disciple and follower of him who once hung upon it, and be the means of carrying me safe to my Master, being the instrument on which he redeemed me."

After offering up his prayers to the throne of grace, and exhorting the people to

* Epirus was a province of Greece, lying along the coast of the Ionian sea, and having for its bounds, Albania on the north, Thessaly on the south, Achaia on the southeast, and the ocean on the west.
† Patrea was situated on a hill near the sea, about ten miles from the mouth of the gulf Lepanto. The goddess Diana was worshipped here in the most diabolical manner, having a most beautiful young man and maid, every year, sacrificed to her, till, by the preaching of St. Andrew, one Eurypilus, a great man of the place, being converted to Christianity, occasioned that barbarous custom to be totally laid aside.

constancy and perseverance in the faith he had delivered to them, he was fastened to the cross, on which he hung two whole days, teaching and instructing the people. In the meantime, great interest was made with the pro-consul to save his life; but the apostle earnestly begged of God that he might then depart, and seal the truth of his religion with his blood. His prayers were heard, and he soon after expired on the last day of November, but in what year is not certain.

The cross on which he was fixed was made of two pieces of timber, crossing each other in the middle, in the shape of the letter X (which has ever since been known by the name of "St. Andrew's Cross"), and to this he was fastened, not with nails, but cords, to make his death more painful and lingering.

His body being taken down from the cross, was decently and honorably interred by Maximilla, a lady of great quality and estate, and whom Nicephorus tells us was wife to the pro-consul. Constantine the Great afterward removed his body to Constantinople, and buried it in the great church he had built to the honor of the apostles. This structure being taken down some hundred years after by the emperor Justinian, in order to be rebuilt, the body of St. Andrew was found in a wooden coffin, and again deposited in the same place it had been before, which was afterward reverenced by all true professors of the Christian religion.

ST. JAMES, the Great.

This apostle was surnamed the Great, to distinguish him from that James (another of the apostles) who was bishop of Jerusalem. After the ascension of the blessed Jesus he preached to the dispersed Jews; that is, to those converts who were dispersed after the death of Stephen. He first preached the gospel in several parts of Judea and Samaria, after which he visited Spain, where he planted Christianity, and appointed some select disciples to perfect what he had begun.

After this he returned to Judea, where he continued preaching in different parts for some time, with great success; till at length Herod (who was a bigot to the Jewish religion, and desirous of acquiring the favor of the Jews) began a violent persecution against the Christians, and to such a degree did his zeal animate him, that, after a short trial, he ordered James to be put to death.

As he was led to the place of execution, the officer that guarded him to the tribunal, or rather his accuser, having been converted by that remarkable courage and constancy shown by the apostle at the time of his trial, repented of what he had done, came and fell down at the apostle's feet, and heartily begged pardon for what he had said against him. The holy man, after recovering from his surprise, tenderly embraced him. "Peace," said he, "my son, peace be to thee and the pardon of thy faults." Upon which the officer publicly declared himself a Christian, and both were beheaded at the same time.

Thus fell the great apostle St. James, taking cheerfully that cup of which he had long before told his Lord and Master he was both ready and willing to drink.

ST. JOHN, the Evangelist.

Though this apostle was by much the youngest of the whole, yet he was admitted into as great a share of his Master's confidence as any. He was one of those to whom our Lord communicated the most private passages of his life; one of those whom he took with him when he raised the daughter of Jairus from the dead; one of those to whom he gave a specimen of his divinity in his transfiguration on the mount; one of those who were present at his conference with Moses and Elijah, and heard that voice which declared him "the beloved Son of God;" and one of those who were companions in his solitude, most retired devotions, and bitter agonies in the garden.

These instances of particular favor our apostle endeavored in some measure to answer, by returns of particular kindness and constancy; for though he at first deserted his Master on his apprehension, yet he soon discovered the impropriety of his conduct: he therefore went back to seek his Saviour; confidently entered the high-priest's hall; followed our Lord through the several particulars of his trial; and at last waited on him at his execution, owning him, as well as being owned by him, in the midst of armed soldiers, and in the thickest crowds of his inveterate enemies. Here it was that our Great Redeemer committed to his care his sorrowful and disconsolate mother with his dying breath. And certainly our blessed Lord could not have

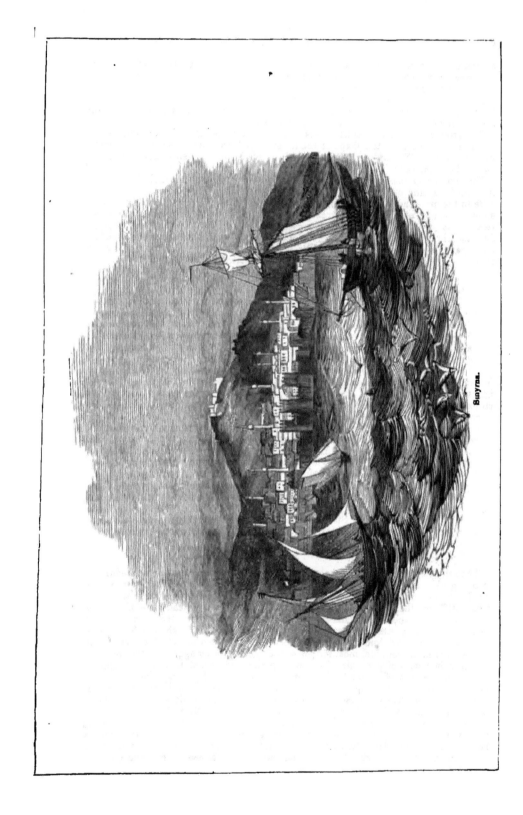

Smyrna.

given a more honorable testimony of his particular kindness and respect to John, than by leaving his own mother to his trust and care, and substituting him to supply that duty he himself paid her while he resided in this vale of sorrow.

When the apostles made a division of the provinces among them after our Saviour's ascension into heaven, in order to circulate the doctrine of their Lord and Master, that of Asia fell to the share of St. John, though he did not immediately enter upon his charge, but continued at Jerusalem till the death of the blessed Virgin, which happened about fifteen years after our Lord's ascension.

After being thus released from the trust committed to his care by his dying Master, he went into Asia, and industriously applied himself to the propagation of Christianity, preaching where the gospel had not then been known, and confirming it where it was already planted. Many churches of note and eminence were founded by him, particularly those of Smyrna,* Philadelphia, Laodicea, and others; but his chief place of residence was at Ephesus, where St. Paul had founded a church, and constituted Timothy its pastor.

After John had spent several years at Ephesus, an accusation was laid against him before the emperor Domitian (who had then begun a persecution against the Christians) as being an asserter of false doctrine and impiety, and a public subverter of the religion of the empire. In consequence of this, and in conformity to the orders of Domitian, the pro-consul of Ephesus sent him bound to Rome, where he met with that treatment which might have been expected from so barbarous a prince, being thrown into a caldron of boiling oil. But the Almighty, who reserved him for farther service in the vineyard of his Son, restrained the heat, as he did in the fiery furnace of old, and delivered him from this seemingly unavoidable destruction. And surely one would have thought that so miraculous a deliverance might have been sufficient to have persuaded any rational man that the religion he taught was from God, and that he was protected from danger by the hand of Omnipotence. But miracles themselves were not sufficient to convince this cruel emperor, or abate his fury. He ordered St. John to be transported to a disconsolate island in the archipelago, called Patmos,† where he continued several years, instructing the poor inhabitants in the knowledge of the Christian faith; and here, about the end of Domitian's reign, he wrote his book of Revelation, exhibiting, by visions and prophetical representations, the state and condition of Christianity that would take place in the future periods and ages of the church.

On the death of Domitian, and the succession of Narva (who repealed all the odious acts of his predecessors, and by public edicts recalled those whom the fury of Domitian had banished), St. John returned to Asia, and again fixed his residence at Ephesus, on account of Timothy, their pastor, having some time before been put to death by the people of that city. Here, with the assistance of seven other bishops or pastors, he took upon himself the large diocess of Asia Minor, spending his time in an indefatigable execution of his charge, travelling from one part to another, and

---

* A city of Asia Minor, about forty miles south of Ephesus, famous for its having been thought the birth-place of Homer, but more so as having contained one of the seven churches of Asia specially addressed by Jesus Christ. (Rev. i. 11 ; ii. 8.) Polycarp is supposed by some to have been the angel or bishop of this Christian congregation addressed by John, as he sustained that office some years afterward, and was martyred here, A. D. 160, at the age of ninety-five. Smyrna is now the principal emporium of trade in the Levant; it is called by the Turks Ismir, and the population is estimated to include 70,000 Turks, 30,000 Greeks, 15,000 Armenians, 10,000 Jews, 5,000 Franks, &c.

† This is a small island in the Icarian sea, about thirty miles from the nearest point on the western coast of Asia Minor, being the Posidium promontory in Caria. The island does not exceed fifteen miles in circumference, and is nothing but a continued rock, very mountainous, and very barren. The only spot in it which has now any cultivation, or is indeed worth any, is a small valley on the west, where the richer inhabitants have a few gardens. Its coast is high, and consists of a collection of capes, which form so many ports, some of which are excellent. The only one in use, however, is a deep gulf on the northeast of the island, sheltered by high mountains on every side but one, where it is protected by a projecting cape. The island produces almost nothing, being furnished from abroad with nearly every article of subsistence. The town is situated upon a high rocky mountain, rising immediately from the sea. It contains about four hundred houses, which, with fifty more at the Scala, form all the habitations in the island. In the middle of the town, near the top of the mountain, is the large and strong monastery of St. John the Evangelist, built by Alexius Commenes. About half-way down the mountain from the town to the Scala, there is a natural grotto in the rock, in which it is believed by the natives that St. John abode and wrote the Apocalypse. They have built a small church over it, decked out in the usual tawdry style of the Greek churches.

The island is now called the Patmo. On account of its stern and desolate character, the Roman emperors thought it a suitable spot to which criminals might be confined. To this island, accordingly, the apostle John was banished by the emperor Domitian, toward the end of his reign, or about the year 95 or 96. It is usually stated, after Tertullian, that his banishment took place after the apostle had been miraculously delivered, unhurt, from a vessel of flaming oil, into which he had been cast.

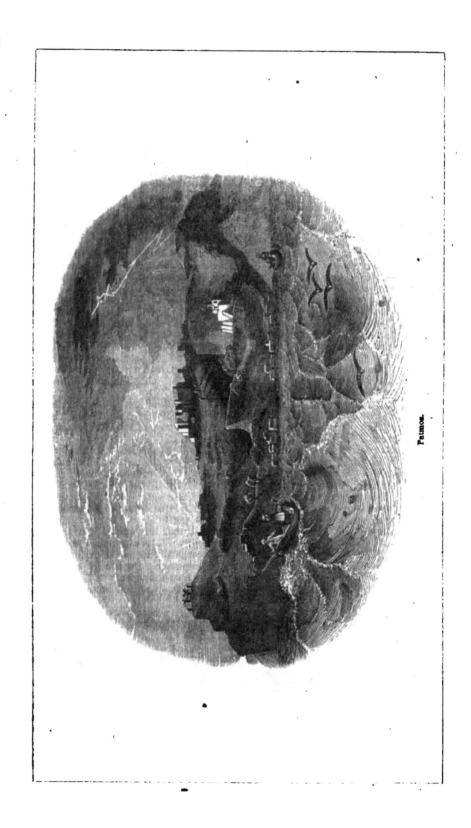

Patmos.

instructing the people in the principles of that holy religion he was sent to propagate. In this manner did John continue to spend his time, till death put a period to his labors, which happened in the beginning of the reign of the emperor Trajan. His remains were deposited in the city of Ephesus, where several of the fathers observe that his tomb, in their time, was remaining in a church, which was built to his honor and called by his name. He was the only apostle who escaped a violent death; notwithstanding which he is deemed a martyr on account of his having undergone the mode of an execution, though it did not take effect. He lived the longest of any of the apostles, being nearly a hundred years of age at the time of his death.

St. John, having been brought up to the business of a fisherman, never received a liberal education; but what was wanting from human art was abundantly supplied by the excellent constitution of his mind, and that fulness of Divine grace with which he was adorned. His humility was admirable, always studiously concealing whatever tended to his own honor. In his epistles he never styles himself either apostle or evangelist; the title of "presbyter," or "elder," is all he assumes, and probably as much in regard to his age as his office. In his Gospel, when he speaks of "the disciple whom Jesus loved," he conceals his own name, leaving the reader to discover who he meant. He practised charity to the utmost extent, and affectionately recommended it to all mankind. This, and the love of our neighbor, is the great vein that runs through all his writings, more especially his epistles, wherein he urges it as the great and peculiar law of Christianity, and without which all pretensions to our blessed Saviour are vain and frivolous, useless and insignificant. When age and the infirmities of nature had rendered him so weak that he was unable to preach to the people any longer, he was led, at every public meeting, to the church at Ephesus, where he generally addressed himself to the people in these words: "Little children, love one another." When his hearers, tired with the constant repetition of the same thing, asked him the reason of it, he told them that to love one another was the command of our blessed Saviour.

The greatest instance of our apostle's care for the souls of men is displayed in the inimitable writings he left to posterity; the first of which in point of time, though placed last in the sacred canon, is his Apocalypse, or book of Revelation, which he wrote during his banishment in the island of Patmos.

Next to the Apocalypse, in order of time, are his three epistles, the first of which is catholic, calculated for all times and places, containing the most excellent rules for the conduct of a Christian life, pressing to holiness and pureness of manners, and not to be satisfied with a naked and empty profession of religion—not to be led away with the crafty insinuation of seducers; and cautioning them against the poisonous principles and practices of the Gnostics. The apostle here, according to his usual modesty, conceals his name, it being of more consequence to a wise man what is *said* than who *says it*. It appears from St. Augustine that this epistle was anciently ascribed to the Parthians, because in all probability St. John preached the gospel in Parthia. The other two epistles are but short, and directed to particular persons; the one to a woman of honorable quality, encouraging her and her children to charity, to perseverance in good works, and to show no countenance to false teachers and deceivers. The other epistle is directed to the charitable and hospitable Gaius, the kindest friend and the most courteous entertainer of all indigent Christians.

Before he undertook the task of writing his gospel, he caused a general fast to be kept in all the churches throughout Asia, to implore the blessing of Heaven on so great and momentous an undertaking. When this was done, he set to work and completed it in so excellent and sublime a manner, that the ancients generally compared him to an eagle soaring aloft among the clouds, whither the meek eye of man was not able to follow him.

St. Paul, in speaking of the writings of this apostle, says, "Among all the evangelical writers, none are like St. John for the sublimity of his speech, and the height of his discourses, which are beyond any man's capacity fully to reach and comprehend." This is corroborated by Epiphanius, who says, "St. John, by a loftiness and speech peculiar to himself, acquaints us, as it were out of the clouds and dark recesses of wisdom, with the divine doctrine of the Son of God."

Such is the character given of the writings of this great apostle and evangelist, who was honored with the endearing title of being the beloved disciple of the Son of

God; a writer so profound as to deserve, by way of eminence, the character of St. John the Divine.

ST. PHILIP.

In the distribution made by the apostles of the several regions of the world in which they were to preach the gospel after our Lord's ascension, the upper Asia fell to Philip, where he labored with the most indefatigable diligence to propagate the doctrine of his Master in those parts. From the constancy and power of his preaching, and the efficacy of his miracles, he gained numerous converts, whom he baptized in the Christian faith, curing at once their bodies of infirmities and distempers, and their souls of errors and idolatry. Here he continued a considerable time, and, before he left the place, settled the churches and appointed Christian pastors over those whom he had converted.

After Philip had for several years successfully exercised his apostolic office in upper Asia, he went to Hierapolis in Phrygia, a city remarkably rich and populous, but at the same time overrun with the most enormous idolatry. Philip was greatly grieved to see the people so wretchedly enslaved by error and superstition; he, therefore repeatedly offered up his prayers to Heaven in their behalf, till, by his prayers, and often calling on the name of Christ, he procured the death, or at least the vanishing of a dragon, or enormous serpent, to which they paid adoration.

Having thus demolished their deity, Philip clearly demonstrated to them how ridiculous and unjust it was to pay divine honors to such odious creatures: he told them that God alone was to be worshipped as the great parent of all the world, who, in the beginning made men after his glorious image, and when fallen from that innocent and happy state, sent his own Son into the world to redeem them. That, in order to perform this glorious work, he died on the cross, and rose again from the dead, and at the end of the world would come again to raise all the sons of men from the chambers of the dust, and either sentence them to everlasting punishment, or reward them with everlasting felicity.

This discourse roused them from their lethargy, insomuch that great numbers, being ashamed of their idolatry, immediately forsook it, and embraced the doctrine of the gospel. But the success attending Philip's endeavors proved fatal to him. The magistrates were so incensed at his having obtained such a number of converts, that they resolved to put an effectual stop to his proceedings. They accordingly ordered him to be seized, and thrown into prison, whence, after being severely scourged, he was led to execution, and put to death, the manner of which, according to some, was by being hanged against a pillar, and, according to others, by crucifixion.

As soon as he was dead, his body was taken down by Bartholemew, his fellow-laborer in the gospel, and Mariamne his sister, the constant companion of his travels, and decently interred in a private place near the city, both of whom, for performing this friendly office, barely escaped with their lives.

The martyrdom of St. Philip happened about eight years after that of St. James the Great.

ST. BARTHOLEMEW.

This apostle is mentioned among the immediate disciples of our Lord, under the appellation of Bartholemew, though it is evident, from divers passages in Scripture, that he was also called Nathaniel.*

After our Lord's ascension into heaven, Bartholemew visited different parts of the world, in order to propagate the gospel of his Master, and at length penetrated as far

---

* That Nathaniel and Bartholomew were only two names for one and the same person, the one his proper and the other his relative name, is beyond all doubt; but then the question is, upon what account it was that he had his relative name conferred on him. That several sects in the Jewish church denominated themselves from some famous person of that nation (as the Essenes did from Enoch, and the Sadducees from Sadoc), can not be denied; and therefore, if we may suppose that there were others who called themselves Tholmæans, from Tholmai, scholar to Heber, the ancient master of the Hebrews, who flourished in Debir and Hebron, it will be no hard matter to make Nathaniel of this order and institution, and thereupon to give him the name of Bartholemew, i. e., a scholar of the Tholmæans, and so create him, as he is said to have been, a doctor of the Jewish law. But an easier explanation of this matter will appear from the following observations. That, as the first syllable of his name signifies a son, the word Bar-tholomew will import no more than the son of Tholomew, or Tholmai, which was no uncommon name among the Jews. And, that it was a usual thing among them for the son thus to derive his name, is evident from the instance of Bar-timæus, which is interpreted the son of Timæus (Mark x. 46), and that of Bar-jona (Matt. xvi. 17), which St. John makes the same with Simon, son of Jonas. (John xxi. 15.)

as the Hither India. Here he remained a considerable time, and then went to Hiera-polis in Phrygia, where he labored (in conjunction with Philip) to plant Christianity in those parts; and to convince the blind idolaters of the evil of their ways, and direct them in the paths which lead to eternal salvation. This enraging the bigoted magis-trates, they sentenced Bartholemew to death, and he was accordingly fastened to a cross; but their consciences staring them in their faces for the iniquity they were about to commit, they ordered him to be taken down and set at liberty.

In consequence of this our apostle left Hierapolis, and went to Lycaonia, where he obtained a great number of converts, whom he instructed and trained up in the prin-ciples of the Christian religion. From Lycaonia he went to Albania, a city on the Caspian sea, a place miserably overrun with idolatry, from which he labored hard to reclaim the people. But his endeavors to "turn them from darkness unto light, and from the power of Satan unto God," instead of proving effectual, only procured his destruction. The magistrates were so incensed against him, that they prevailed on the governor to order him to be put to death, which was accordingly done with the most distinguished cruelty. It is the general opinion of most writers, that he was first severely beaten with sticks, then crucified, afterward flayed while still alive, and lastly, that his head was severed from his body.

ST. MATTHEW.

During the first eight years after our blessed Lord's ascension into heaven, Matthew continued to preach the gospel with great assiduity in different parts of Judea; after which he left the country of Palestine in order to convert the Gentile world. But before his departure, at the earnest solicitation of the Jewish converts in Judea, he wrote the history of the life and actions of the blessed Jesus, which he left among them as a standing monument of what he had so often delivered to them in his sermons.

After Matthew left Judea, he travelled into various parts, but the particular places he visited are not certainly known. However, after laboring indefatigably in the vineyard of his Master, he suffered martyrdom at a city called Nadabar in Ethiopia; but the particular manner of his death is not certainly known, though it is the gen-eral conceived opinion that he was slain with a halberd. His martyrdom is com-memorated by the church on the 21st day of September.

St. Matthew was a remarkable instance of the power of religion, in bringing men to a proper temper of mind. If we reflect upon his circumstances while he continued a stranger to the great Redeemer of mankind, we shall find that the love of the world had possessed his heart. But notwithstanding this, no sooner did Christ call him, than he abandoned, without the least scruple or hesitation, all his riches; nay, he not only renounced his lucrative trade, but ran the greatest hazards of displeasing the masters who employed him, for quitting their service without giving them the least notice, and leaving his accounts in confusion. Had our blessed Saviour appeared as a secular prince, clothed with temporal power and authority, it would have been no wonder for him to have gone over to his service; but when he appeared under all the circumstances of poverty, when he seemed to promise his followers nothing but misery and sufferings in this life, and to propose no other rewards than the invisible encouragements of another world, his change appears truly wonderful and surprising. But divine grace can subdue all opposition.

His contempt of the world was fully manifested in his exemplary temperance and abstemiousness from all delights and pleasures; insomuch that he even refused the ordinary conveniences and accommodations of life. He was remarkably modest in the opinion he entertained of himself, always giving the preference to others, even though their abilities were not so conspicuous as his own. The rest of the evangel-ists are careful to mention the honor of his apostleship, but speak of his former sor-did, dishonest, and disgraceful course of life, only under the name of Levi; while he himself sets it down with all its circumstances, under his own proper and common name; a conduct which at once commends the prudence and candor of the apostle, and suggests to us this useful reflection, that the greatest sinners are not excluded from divine grace; nor can any, if penitent, have just reason to despair, when publi-cans and sinners find mercy at the throne of grace.

The Gospel which St. Matthew wrote at the entreaty of the Jewish converts, before he left Judea, was penned in the Hebrew language, but soon after translated into Greek by one of his disciples. After the Greek translation was admitted, the Hebrew copy was chiefly owned and used by the Nazaræi, a middle sect between Jews and Christians; with the former, they adhered to the rites and ceremonies of the Mosaic law, and with the latter, they believed in Christ, and embraced his religion; and hence this Gospel has been styled, "The Gospel according to the Hebrews," and "The Gospel of the Nazarenes."

ST. THOMAS.

The apostle Thomas, after our Lord's ascension, continued to preach the gospel in various parts of Judea; till at length, being interrupted by the dispersion of the Christian church in Jerusalem, he repaired into Parthia, the province assigned him for his ministry. He afterward preached the gospel to the Medes, Persians, Carmans, Hyrcani, Bractarians, and the neighboring nations. During his preaching in Persia, he is said to have met with the magi, or wise men, who had taken that long journey at our Saviour's birth to worship him, whom he baptized, and took with him, as his companions and assistants in propagating the Gospel.

Leaving Persia, he travelled into Ethiopia, preaching the glad tidings of the gospel, healing the sick, and working other miracles, to prove he had his commission from on high.

After travelling through these countries, he entered India, and went first to Socotora, an island in the Arabian sea, and then to Cranganor, whence, having converted many from the error of their ways, he travelled farther into the east. Having successfully preached the gospel here, he returned back to the kingdom of Coromandel, where, at Malipur, the metropolis of the kingdom, not far from the mouth of the Ganges, he began to erect a place for divine worship, but was interrupted by the idolatrous priests, and Sagamo, prince of the country. However, after he had performed several miracles, he was suffered to proceed in the work, and Sagamo himself embraced the Christian faith, whose example was soon followed by great numbers of his friends and subjects.

This remarkable success alarmed the Brachmans, who plainly perceived that their religion would be soon extirpated unless some method could be found of putting a a stop to the progress of Christianity; they therefore resolved to put the apostle to death. At a small distance from the city was a tomb, whither St. Thomas often retired for private devotion. Hither the Brachmans and their armed followers pursued him; and while he was at prayer, they first threw at him a shower of darts, after which one of the priests ran him through the body with a lance. His corpse was taken up by his disciples, and buried in the church he had caused to be erected, and which was afterward improved into a fabric of very great magnificence.

St. Chrysostom says, that St. Thomas, who at first was the weakest and most incredulous of all the apostles, became, through Christ's condescension to satisfy his scruples, and the power of the divine grace, the most active and invincible of them all; travelling over most parts of the world, and living without fear in the midst of barbarous nations, through the efficacy of that Almighty power, which can make the weakest vessels to perform acts of the greatest difficulty and moment.

ST. SIMON, COMMONLY CALLED THE ZEALOT.

This apostle, in the catalogue of our Lord's chosen disciples, is styled "Simon the Canaanite," whence some are of opinion that he was born at Cana, in Galilee; and it is generally thought that he was the bridegroom mentioned by St. John, at whose marriage our blessed Saviour turned the water into wine.

The name of this apostle is derived from the Hebrew word *knah*, which signifies *zeal*, and denotes a warm and sprightly disposition. He did not, however, acquire this name from his ardent affection to his Master, and the desire of advancing his religion in the world, but from his zealous attachment to a particular sect of religion before he became acquainted with his great Lord and Master.

In order to explain this matter more clearly to the understanding of our readers, it is necessary to observe, that as there were several sects and parties among the Jews, so there was one, either a distinct sect, or at least a branch of the Pharisees, called the sect of the Zealots. This sect took upon them to inflict punishments in extraordinary cases; and that not only by the connivance, but with the leave both of the rulers and people, till, in process of time, their zeal degenerated into all kinds of licentiousness and wild extravagance; and they not only became the pests of the commonwealth in their own territories, but were likewise hated by the people of those parts which belonged to the Romans. They were continually urging the people to shake off the Roman yoke and assert their natural liberty, taking care, when they had thrown all things into confusion, to make their own advantage of the consequences arising therefrom. Josephus gives a very long and particular account of them, throughout the whole of which he repeatedly represents them as the great plague of the Jewish nation. Various attempts were made, especially by Ananias, the high-priest, to reduce them to order, and oblige them to observe the rules of sobriety; but all endeavors proved ineffectual. They continued their violent proceedings, and, joining with the Idumeans, committed every kind of outrage. They broke into the sanctuary, slew the priests themselves before the altar, and filled the streets of Jerusalem with tumults, rapine, and blood. Nay, when Jerusalem was closely besieged by the Roman army, they continued their detestable proceedings, creating fresh tumults and factions, and were indeed the principal cause of the ill success of the Jews in that fatal war.

This is a true account of the sect of the Zealots; though, whatever St. Simon was before, we have no reason to suspect but that after his conversion he was very zealous for the honor of his Master, and considered all those who were enemies to Christ as enemies to himself, however near they might be to him in any natural relation. As he was very exact in all the practical duties of the Christian religion, so he showed a very serious and pious indignation toward those who professed religion, and a faith in Christ, with their mouths, but dishonored their sacred profession by their irregular and vicious lives, as many of the first professing Christians really did.

St. Simon continued in communion with the rest of the apostles, and disciples at Jerusalem, and at the feast of Pentecost received the same miraculous gifts of the Holy Ghost; so that he was qualified with the rest of his brethren for the apostolic office. In propagating the gospel of the Son of God, we can not doubt of his exercising his gifts with the same zeal and fidelity as his fellow-apostles, though in what part of the world is uncertain. Some say he went into Egypt, Cyrene, and Africa, preaching the gospel to the inhabitants of those remote and barbarous countries; and others add, that after he had passed through those burning wastes, he preached the gospel to the inhabitants of the western parts, and even in Britain, where, having converted great multitudes, and sustained the greatest hardships and persecutions, he was at last crucified, and buried in some part of that island, but the exact place where is unknown.

ST. JUDE.

It is very observable of this apostle that the evangelists commonly call him, not Jude, but either Thaddæus or Labbæus; the reason of which, in all human probability, is from the particular dislike they had to the name, which was so nearly similar to that of the base and perfidious Judas Iscariot, who treacherously sold and betrayed his Master.

Jude was brother to James the Less, afterward bishop of Jerusalem, being the son of Joseph by a former wife. It is not known when or by what means he became a disciple of our blessed Saviour, there not being anything said of him till we find him in the catalogue of the twelve apostles; nor afterward till Christ's Last Supper, when discoursing with them about his departure, and comforting them with a promise that he would return to them again, meaning after his resurrection from the dead.

The sacred records are so very short in their accounts of this apostle, that we must be beholden to other ecclesiastical writers for information relative to his conduct after the ascension of our blessed Lord into heaven. Paulinus tells us that the part which fell to his share in the apostolic division of the provinces was Lybia; but he does not tell us whether it was the Cyrenian Lybia which is thought to have received the gospel from St. Mark, or the more southern parts of Africa. But, however that be, in his first setting out to preach the gospel, he travelled up and down Judea and Galilee; then through Samaria into Idumea, and to the cities of Arabia and the neighboring countries, and afterward to Syria and Mesopotamia. Nicephorus adds, that he came at last to Edessa, where Agabarus governed, and where Thaddeus, one of the seventy, had already sown the seeds of the gospel. Here he perfected what the other had begun; and having by his sermons and miracles established the religion of Jesus, he died in peace: but others say that he was slain at Berites, and honorably buried there. The writers of the Latin church are unanimous in declaring that he travelled into Persia, where, after great success in his apostolical ministry for many years, he was at last, for his freely and openly reproving the superstitious rites and customs of the Magi, cruelly put to death.

St. Jude wrote only one epistle, which is placed the last of those seven styled catholic in the sacred canon. It has no particular inscription, as the other six have, but is thought to have been primarily intended for the Christian Jews in their several dispersions, as were the epistles of the apostle Peter. In it he informs them that he at first intended to have wrote to them concerning the "common salvation," in order to confirm them in their belief; but, finding the doctrine of Christ attacked on all sides by heretics, he thought it more necessary to exhort them to stand up manfully in defence of the "faith once delivered to the saints," and to oppose those false teachers who so earnestly labored to corrupt them; and that they might know these the better, he describes them in their proper colors, and foretells their future if not impending danger; but, at the same time, he endeavors to exhort them, by all gentle methods to save them, and to take them "out of the fire" into which their own folly had cast them.

It was some time before this epistle was generally received in the church. The author indeed, like St. James, St. John, and sometimes St. Paul, does not call himself an apostle, but only "the servant of Christ." But he has added what is equivalent, Jude "the brother of James," a character which can only belong to himself: and surely the humility of a follower of Christ should be no objection to his writings.

ST. MATTHIAS.

Matthias was one of the seventy disciples whom our blessed Lord made choice of to assist him in the discharge of his public ministry. After his death, Matthias was elected into the apostleship, to supply the place of Judas, who was so struck with remorse at having betrayed his Master, as to put a period to his existence.

After our Lord's ascension into heaven, Matthias spent the first year of his ministry in Judea, where he was so successful as to bring over a prodigious number of people to the Christian faith. From Judea he travelled into other countries, and, proceeding eastward, came at length to Ethiopia. Here he likewise made many converts, but the inhabitants in general being of a fierce and untractable temper, resolved to take away his life, which they effected by first stoning him, and then severing his head from his body.

ST. MARK.

In the dispersion of the apostles for propagating the gospel in different parts of the world, after our Lord's ascension into heaven, St. Mark was by Peter sent into Egypt, where he soon planted a church in Alexandria, the metropolis; and such was his success, that he converted prodigious multitudes of people, both men and women, to the Christian religion.

St. Mark did not confine himself to Alexandria and the oriental parts of Egypt, but removed westward to Lybia, passing through the countries of Marmarcia, Pentapolis, and others adjacent, where, though the people were both barbarous in their manners and idolatrous in their worship, yet by his preaching and miracles he prevailed on them to embrace the tenets of the gospel; nor did he leave them till he had confirmed them in the faith.

After this long tour he returned to Alexandria, where he preached with the greatest freedom, ordered and disposed of the affairs of the church, and wisely provided for a succession by constituting governors and pastors of it. But the restless enemy of the souls of men would not suffer our apostle to continue in peace and quietness; for while he was assiduously laboring in the vineyard of his Master, the idolatrous inhabitants, about the time of Easter, when they were celebrating the solemnities of Serapis, tumultuously seized him, and, binding his feet with cords, dragged him through the streets and over the most craggy places to the Bucelus, a precipice near the sea, leaving him there in a lonesome prison for that night; but his great and beloved Master appeared to him in a vision, comforting and encouraging him under the ruins of his shattered body.

Early the next morning the tragedy began afresh; and they dragged him about in the same cruel and barbarous manner till he expired. But their malice did not end with his death, for they burnt his mangled body after they had so inhumanly deprived it of life; but the Christians gathered up his bones and ashes, and decently interred them near the place where he used to preach. His remains were afterward, with great pomp, removed from Alexandria to Venice, where they were religiously honored, and he was adopted the titular saint and patron of that state.

He suffered martyrdom on the 25th of April, but the year is not absolutely known; the most probable opinion is that it happened about the end of the reign of Nero.

His Gospel, the only writing he left behind him, was written at the entreaty and earnest desire of the converts at Rome, who, not content with having heard St. Peter preach, pressed St. Mark, his disciple, to commit to writing an historical account of what he had delivered to them, which he performed with equal faithfulness and brevity, and being perused and approved by St. Peter, it was commanded to be publicly read in their assemblies. It was frequently styled St. Peter's gospel, not because he dictated it to St. Mark, but because the latter composed it from the accounts St. Peter usually delivered in his discourse to the people. And this is probably the reason of what St. Chrysostom observes, that in his style and manner of expression he delights to imitate St. Peter, representing a great deal in a few words.

ST. LUKE.

The Evangelist St. Luke was a native of Antioch in Syria, and by profession a physician; and it is the general opinion of most ancient historians, that he was also well acquainted with the art of painting.

After our Lord's ascension into heaven, he spent a great part of his time with St. Paul, whom he accompanied to various places, and greatly assisted in bringing over proselytes to the Christian faith. This so endeared him to that apostle, that he seems delighted with owning him for his fellow-laborer, and in calling him "the beloved physician," and the "brother whose praise is in the gospel."

St. Luke preached the gospel with great success in a variety of places, independent of his assisting St. Paul. He travelled into different parts of Egypt and Greece, in the latter of which countries the idolatrous priests were so incensed against him that they put him to death, which they effected by hanging him on the branch of an olive-tree. The anniversary of his martyrdom is held on the 18th of October.

St. Luke wrote two books for the use of the church; namely his Gospel, and the Acts of the Apostles. Both these he dedicated to Theophilus, which many of the ancients suppose to be a feigned name, denoting a lover of God, a title common to all sincere Christians. But others think it was a real person, because the title of "most excellent" is attributed to him; which was the usual form of address, in those times, to princes, and other distinguished characters.

His Gospel contains the principal transactions of the life of our blessed Redeemer; and in his Acts of the Apostles, which it is probable he wrote at Rome about the time of Paul's imprisonment, are recorded the most material actions of the principal apostles, especially St. Paul, whose activity in the cause of Christ made him bear a very great part in the labors of his Master; and St. Luke, being his almost constant attendant, and privy to his most intimate transactions, was consequently capable of giving a more full and satisfactory account of them than any other of the apostles.

In both these treatises his manner of writing is exact and accurate; his style noble and elegant, sublime and lofty, and yet clear and perspicuous, flowing with an easy and natural grace and sweetness, admirably adapted to an historical design. In short, as an historian he was faithful in his relations, and elegant in his writings; as a minister, careful and diligent for the good of souls; as a Christian, devout and pious; and to crown all the rest, he laid down his life in testimony of the gospel he had both preached and published to the world.

ST. BARNABAS.

After our Lord's ascension into heaven, Barnabas continued for a considerable time with St. Paul, being his constant attendant wherever he went. He travelled with nim to a great variety of places in different parts of the world, and was of the most infinite service in helping him to propagate the gospel of his great Lord and Master. At length, however, a dispute arose between them while they were at Antioch, the issue of which was, that Barnabas left Paul at Antioch, and retired to Cyprus, his native country.

After this separation from St. Paul, the sacred writings give us no account of St. Barnabas; nor are the ecclesiastical writers agreed among themselves with regard to the actions of our apostle, after his sailing for Cyprus. This, however, seems to be certain, that he did not spend the whole remainder of his life in that island, but visited different parts of the world, preaching the glad tidings of the gospel, healing the sick, and working other miracles among the Gentiles. After long and painful travels, attended with different degrees of success in different places, he returned to Cyprus, his native country, where he suffered martyrdom in the following manner: certain Jews coming from Syria and Salamis, where Barnabas was then preaching the gospel, being highly exasperated at his extraordinary success, fell upon him as he was disputing in the synagogue, dragged him out, and after the most inhuman tortures, stoned him to death. His kinsman, John Mark, who was a spectator of this barbarous action, privately interred his body in a cave; where it remained till the time of the emperor Zeno, in the year of Christ 485, when it was discovered, with St. Matthew's Gospel, in Hebrew, written with his own hand, lying on his breast.

TIMOTHY.

This great assertor of the cause of Christ was a disciple of St. Paul, and born at Lystra in Lyaconia. His father was a Gentile, but his mother was a Jewess. Her name was Eurice, and that of his grandmother Lais. These particulars are taken notice of, because St. Paul commends their piety, and the good education which they had given Timothy.

When St. Paul came to Derbe and Lystra, about the year of Christ 51 or 52, the brethren gave such an advantageous testimony of the merit and good disposition of Timothy, that the apostle took him with him, in order to assist him in propagating the doctrine of his great Lord and Master. Timothy applied himself to labor with St. Paul in the business of the gospel, and did him very important services, through the whole course of his preaching. St. Paul calls him not only his dearly beloved son, but also his brother, the companion of his labors, and a man of God.

This holy disciple accompanied St. Paul to Macedonia, to Philippi, to Thessalonica, to Berea; and when the apostle went from Berea, he left Timothy and Silas there, to confirm the converts. When he came to Athens, he sent for Timothy to come thither. to him: and when he was come, and had given him an account of the churches of Macedonia, St. Paul sent him back to Thessalonica, whence he afterward returned with Silas, and came to St. Paul at Corinth. There he continued with him for some time, and the apostle mentions him with Silas, at the beginning of the two Epistles which he then wrote to the Thessalonians.

Some years after this, St. Paul sent Timothy and Erastus into Macedonia; and gave Timothy orders to call at Corinth, to refresh the minds of the Corinthians with regard to the truths which he had inculcated in them. Some time after, writing to the same Corinthians, he recommends them to take care of Timothy, and send him back in peace; after which Timothy returned to St. Paul into Asia, who there stayed for him. They went together into Macedonia; and the apostle puts Timothy's name with his own before the second Epistle to the Corinthians, which he wrote to them from Macedonia, about the middle of the year of Christ 57. And he sends his recommendations to the Romans in the letter which he wrote from Corinth the same year.

When St. Paul returned from Rome, in 64, he left Timothy at Ephesus to take care of that church, of which he was the first bishop, as he is recognised by the council of Chalcedon. St. Paul wrote to him from Macedonia the first of the two letters which are addressed to him. He recommends him to be more moderate in his austerities, and to drink a little wine, because of the weakness of his stomach, and his frequent infirmities. After the apostle came to Rome in the year 65, being then very near his death, he wrote to him his second letter, which is full of marks of kindness and tenderness for this his dear disciple; and which is justly looked upon as the last will of St. Paul. He desires him to come to Rome to him before winter, and bring with him several things which he had left at Troas. If Timothy went to Rome, as it is probable he did, he must have been an eyewitness of the martyrdom of Paul, which happened in the year of Christ 66.

After Timothy had visited Paul at Rome, he returned to Ephesus, where he continued to govern the church as its bishop, without the least interruption, for a considerable time, till at length he fell a victim to the malice of the pagans, who were his most inveterate enemies. These heathens made a great feast, in the celebration of which they carried in procession the images of their idols, being all masked, and armed with clubs and other offensive weapons. Timothy, seeing the procession, was so irritated at their idolatry and superstition, that he rushed in among them in order to stop their proceedings; upon which they immediately fell upon him, and, with their clubs, beat him in so unmerciful a manner that he soon expired. They left the body on the spot where they had murdered him, which was removed thence by some of his disciples, and decently interred on the top of a mountain at a small distance from the city. The Greeks commemorate his martyrdom on the 22d of January, the day on which it is supposed he gave up his life in defence of the doctrine he had long labored to propagate; and during which time he had brought over great numbers of people to embrace the truth of the Christian religion.

TITUS.

Titus was a native of Greece, and a Gentile by birth; but was converted to the Christian faith by the apostle Paul, who, in consequence of his strict adherence to the doctrine of Christ, calls him his son. St. Jerome tells us that he was St. Paul's interpreter; and that, probably, because he might write what Paul dictated, or translate into Greek what he had written in Latin.

Soon after the conversion of Titus, the apostle Paul took him with him to Jerusalem; which was at the time when he went thither about deciding the dispute then in agitation relative to the converted Gentiles being made subject to the ceremonies of the Mosaic law. On their arrival there, some of the people were desirous that Titus should be circumcised; but this was not only refused by Titus, but totally objected to by Paul.

After this controversy was ended at Jerusalem, Paul sent Titus thence to Corinth, in order to adjust some disputes which had taken place in the church of that city. Titus was received by the people with the greatest marks of respect; and, from the various discourses he preached on the occasion, was so successful as effectually to discharge the business on which he was sent.

After staying some time at Corinth, Titus went thence into Macedonia, in order to inform Paul of the state of the church in that city. Paul was well pleased with the account he gave, and the success of his embassy; and intending himself to go to Corinth, desired Titus to return thither, to make some necessary preparations previous to his departure for that city. Titus readily undertook the journey, and immediately set off, carrying with him St. Paul's second epistle to the Corinthians.

Titus was made bishop of the island of Crete, about the sixty-third year after Christ, when St. Paul was obliged to quit that island, in order to take care of the other churches. The following year, Paul wrote him to desire, that as soon as he should have sent Tychicus to him for supplying his place in Crete, he would come to him to Nicopolis, in Epirus, where the apostle intended to pass his winter.

The subject of this epistle is to represent to Titus what are the qualities that a bishop should be endued with. As the principal function which Titus was to exercise in the isle of Crete was to ordain priests and bishops, it was highly incumbent on him to make a discreet choice. The apostle also gives him a sketch of the advice and instructions which he was to propound to all sorts of persons: to the aged, both men and women; to young people of each sex; to slaves or servants. He exhorts him to keep a strict eye over the Cretans; and to reprove them with severity, as being a people addicted to lying, wickedness, idleness, and gluttony. And, as many Jews were in the churches of Crete, he exhorts Titus to oppose their vain traditions and Jewish fables; and at the same time to show them that the observation of the law ceremonies is no longer necessary; that the distinction of meat is abolished; and that everything is pure and clean to those that are so themselves. He puts him in mind of exhorting the faithful to be obedient to temporal power; to avoid disputes, quarrels, and slander; to apply themselves to honest callings, and to shun the company of a heretic, after the first and second admonition.

Titus was deputed to preach the gospel in Dalmatia, where he was situated when the apostle wrote his second epistle to Timothy. He afterward returned into Crete, from which it is said he propagated the gospel into the neighboring islands. He died at the age of ninety-four, and was buried in Crete. The Greeks keep his festival on the 25th of August, and the Latins on the 4th of January.

JOHN MARK.

John Mark, cousin to St. Barnabas and a disciple of his, was the son of a Christian woman named Mary, who had a house in Jerusalem, where the apostles and the faithful generally used to meet. Here they were at prayers in the night, when St. Peter, who was delivered out of prison by the angel, came and knocked at the door; and in this house the celebrated church of Sion was said to have been afterward established.

John Mark, whom some very improperly confound with the Evangelist St. Mark, adhered to St. Paul and St. Barnabas, and followed them in their return to Antioch. He continued in their company and service till they came to Perga, in Pamphylia; but then, seeing that they were undertaking a longer journey, he left them and returned to Jerusalem. This happened in the year 45 of the common era.

Some years after, that is to say in the year 51, Paul and Barnabas preparing to return into Asia, in order to visit the churches which they had formed there, the latter was of opinion that John should accompany them in this journey: but Paul would not consent to it; upon which occasion these two apostles separated. Paul went to Asia, and Barnabas with John Mark to the isle of Cyprus. What John Mark did after this journey we do not know, till we find him at Rome in the year 63, performing signal services for St. Paul during his imprisonment.

The apostle speaks advantageously of him in his epistle to the Colossians: "Marcus, sister's son to Barnabas, saluteth you. If he cometh unto you, receive him." He makes mention of him again in his epistle to Philemon, written in the year 63, at which time he was with St. Paul at Rome; but in the year 65 he was with Timothy in Asia. And St. Paul, writing to Timothy, desires him to bring Marcus to Rome, adding that he was useful to him for the ministry of the gospel.

In the Greek and Latin churches, the festival of John Mark is kept on the 27th of September. Some say that he was bishop of Biblis, in Phœnicia. The Greeks give him the title of apostle, and say that the sick were cured by his shadow only. It is very probable that he died at Ephesus, where his tomb was very much celebrated and resorted to. He is sometimes called simply John, or Mark. The year of his death we are strangers to, and shall not collect all that is said of him in apocryphal and uncertain authors.

CLEMENT.

Clement is mentioned by St. Paul in his epistle to the Philippians, where the apostle says that Clement's name is written in the book of life. The generality of the fathers and other interpreters make no question but that this is the same Clement who succeeded St. Paul, after Linus and Anaclet, in the government of the church of Rome; and this seems to be intimated when, in the office for St. Clement's day, that church appoints this part of the Epistle to the Philippians to be read.

We find several things relating to Clement's life in the recognitions and constitutions called apostolic; but as those works are not all looked upon as authentic, though there may be truths in some of them derived from the tradition of the first ages, little stress is to be laid upon their testimony. St. Chrysostrom thinks that Clement, mentioned by St. Paul in his Epistle to the Philippians, was one of the apostle's constant fellow-travellers. Irenæus, Origin, Clemens of Alexandria, and others of the ancients, assert that Clement was a disciple of the apostles; that he had seen them and heard their instructions. St. Epiphanius, Jerome, Rufinus, Bede, and some others, were of opinion, that as the apostles St. Peter and St. Paul could not be continually at Rome, by reason of the frequent journeys which they were obliged to make to other places, and it was not proper that the city of Rome should be without a bishop, there was a necessity to supply the want of them by establishing Linus, Anaclet, and Clement, there. The constitutions inform us that Linus was ordained by St. Paul; Tertullian and Epiphanius say that St. Peter ordained Clement. Rufinus tells us that this apostle chose St. Clement for his successor. But Epiphanius believes, that after he had been made bishop of Rome by St. Peter, he refused to exercise his office till, after the death of Linus and Anaclet, he was obliged to take upon him the care of the church; and this is the most generally-received opinion. St. Peter's immediate successor was Linus; Linus was succeeded by Anaclet, and Anaclet by Clement, in the year of Christ 91, which was the tenth of the reign of Domitian.

During his government over the church of Rome, that of Corinth was disturbed by a spirit of division, upon which Clement wrote a letter to the Corinthians, which is still extant, and was so much esteemed by the ancients that they read it publicly in many churches, and some have been inclined to range it among the canonical writings.

In what manner Clement conducted himself, and how he escaped the general persecution under the emperor Domitian, we have not any certain accounts; but we are very well assured that he lived to the third year of the emperor Trajan, which is the hundredth of the Christian era. His festival is set down by Bede, and all the Latin martyrologists, on the 23d of November, and the Greeks honor him on the 24th and 25th of the same month. Rufinus and Pope Zozimus give him the title of martyr; and the Roman church, in its canon, places him among the saints who have sacrificed their lives in the cause of Christ.

Thus have we given the most ample account of the followers of the blessed Jesus; the persons who spread, and caused to be spread, the light of the gospel over the whole world, removed the veil of ignorance and superstition drawn over the kingdoms of the earth, and taught us the method of attaining eternal happiness in the courts of the New Jerusalem.

May we all follow their glorious examples! May we imitate their faith, their piety, their charity, and their love! Then shall we "pass through things temporal in such a manner that we shall finally gain the things eternal," and, through the merits of an all-perfect Redeemer, be admitted as worthy guests at the marriage supper of the Lamb.

CHAPTER XIII.

THE SEVEN CHURCHES OF ASIA.

THE sure word of prophecy has unfolded many a desolation which has come upon the earth; but while it thus reveals the operation, in some of its bearings, of the "mystery of iniquity," it forms itself a part of the "mystery of godliness:" and it is no less the testimony of Jesus, because it shows, as far as earthly ruins can reveal, the progress and the issue of the dominion of "other lords" over the hearts of the children of men. The sins of men have caused, and the cruelty of men has effected, the dire desolations which the word of God foretold. Signs and tokens of his judgments there indeed have been, yet they are never to be found but where iniquity first prevailed. And though all other warnings were to fail, the sight of his past judgments and the sounding of those that are to come, might teach the unrepenting and unconverted sinner to give heed to the threatenings of his word, and to the terrors of the Lord, and to try his ways and turn unto God while space for repentance may be found, ere, as death leaves him, judgment shall find him. And may not the desolations which God has wrought upon the earth, and that accredit his word, wherein life and immortality are brought to light, teach the man whose God is the world, to cease to account it worthy of his worship and of his love, and to abjure that "covetousness which is idolatry," till the idol of mammon in the temple within shall fall, as fell the image of Dagon before the ark of the Lord in which "the testimony" was kept?

But naming, as millions do, the name of Christ without departing from iniquity, there is another warning voice that may come more closely to them all. And it is

Pergamos.

not only from the desolate regions where heathens dwelt, which show how holy men of old spake as they were moved by the Holy Ghost; but also from the ruins of some of the cities where churches were formed by apostles, and where the religion of Jesus once existed in its purity, that all may learn to know that God is no respecter of persons, and that he will by no means clear the guilty. "He that hath an ear let him hear what the Spirit saith unto the churches."

What church could rightfully claim or ever seek a higher title than that which is given in Scripture to the seven churches of Asia, the angels of which were the seven stars in the right hand of Him who is the first and the last—of Him that liveth and was dead, and is alive for evermore, and that hath the keys of hell and of death; and which themselves were the seven golden candlesticks in the midst of which he walked? And who that hath an ear to hear, may not humbly hear and greatly profit by what the Spirit said unto them? (Rev. ii. and iii.)

The CHURCH OF EPHESUS, after a commendation of their first works, to which they were commanded to return, were accused of having left their first love, and threatened with the removal of their candlestick out of its place, except they should repent. (Ch. ii. 5.) Ephesus is situated nearly fifty miles south of Smyrna. It was the metropolis of Lydia, and a great and opulent city, and (according to Strabo) the greatest emporium of Asia Minor. It was chiefly famous for the temple of Diana, "whom all Asia worshipped," which was adorned with 127 columns of Parian marble, each of a single shaft, and sixty feet high, and which formed one of the seven wonders of the world. The remains of its magnificent theatre, in which it is said that twenty thousand people could easily have been seated, are yet to be seen. (Acts xix. 29.) But "a few heaps of stones, and some miserable mud cottages, occasionally tenanted by Turks, without one Christian residing there,* are all the remains of ancient Ephesus." It is, as described by different travellers, a solemn and most forlorn spot. The epistle to the Ephesians is read throughout the world; but there is none in Ephesus to read it now. They left their first love, they returned not to their first works. Their candlestick has been removed out of its place, and the great city of Ephesus is no more.

The CHURCH OF SMYRNA was approved of as "rich," and no judgment was denounced against it. They were warned of a tribulation of ten days (the ten years' persecution by Diocletian), and were enjoined to be faithful unto death, and they would receive a crown of life. (Ch. ii. 8–11.) And, unlike to the fate of the more famous city of Ephesus, Smyrna is still a large city, containing nearly one hundred thousand inhabitants, with several Greek churches, and an English and other Christian ministers have resided in it. The light has indeed become dim, but the candlestick has not been wholly removed out of its place.

The CHURCH OF PERGAMOS is commended for holding fast the name of the Lord, and not denying his faith, during a time of persecution, and in the midst of a wicked city. But there were some in it who held doctrines and did deeds which the Lord hated. Against them he was to fight with the sword of his mouth; and all were called to repent. But it is not said, as of Ephesus, that their candlestick would be removed out of its place. (Ch. ii. 12–16.) This city, the capital of Hellespontic Mysia, was situated on the right bank of the river Caicus, nearly sixty-four miles to the north of Smyrna. Its ancient consideration may be inferred from its possessing a library of two hundred thousand volumes, which Anthony and Cleopatra transferred to Alexandria. It is also noted as the birthplace of the physician Galen. It still, in its decline, retains some part of its ancient importance; and, under the name of Bergamo, contains a population which Mr. Macfarlane estimates at fourteen thousand, of which there are about three thousand Greeks, three hundred Armenians, and not quite three hundred Jews; the rest are Turks. The town consists of small and mean wooden houses, among which appear the remains of early Christian churches, showing, "like vast fortresses amid barracks of wood."

In the CHURCH OF THYATIRA, like that of Pergamos, some tares were soon mingled with the wheat. He who hath eyes like unto a flame of fire discerneth both. Yet, happily for the souls of the people, more than for the safety of the city, the general character of that church, as it then existed, is thus described: "I know thy works, and charity, and service, and faith, and thy patience, and thy works; and the last to be more than the first." (Ch. ii. 19.) But against those, for such there were among

* Arundel's Visit to the Seven Churches of Asia, p. 27.

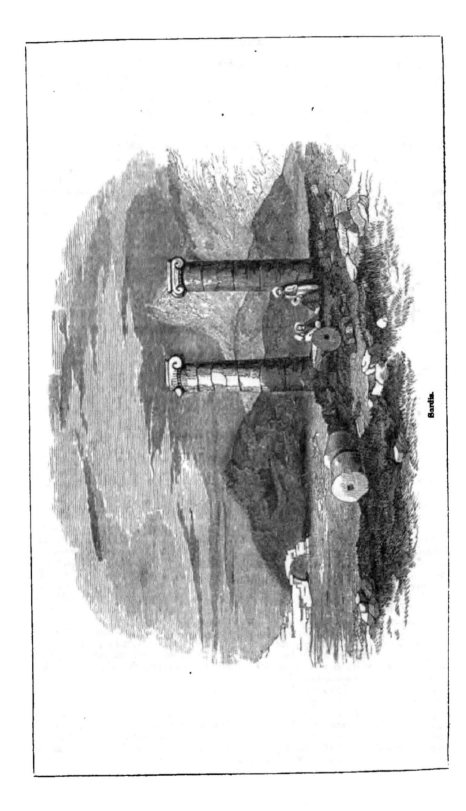

Sardis.

them, who had committed fornication, and eaten things sacrificed unto idols, to whom the Lord gave space to repent of their fornication, and they repented not, great tribulation was denounced; and to every one of them was to be given according to their works. These, thus warned while on earth in vain, have long since passed, where all are daily hastening, to the place where no repentance can be found and no work be done. "But unto the rest in Thyatira (as many as have not known the depths of Satan) I will put upon you, saith the Lord, none other burden." (Ver. 24.) There were those in Thyatira who could save a city. It still exists, while greater cities have fallen. Mr. Hartley, who visited it in 1826, describes it as "embosomed in cypresses and poplars. The Greeks are said to occupy three hundred houses, and the Armenians thirty. Each of them has a church."

The CHURCH OF SARDIS differed from those of Pergamos and Thyatira. They had not denied the faith, but the Lord had a few things against them, for there were some evil doers among them, and on those, if they repented not, judgment was to rest. But in Sardis, great though the city was, and founded though the church had been by an apostle, there were only a few names which had not defiled their garments. And to that church the Spirit said, "I know thy works, that thou hast a name that thou livest, and art dead." But the Lord is long-suffering, not willing that any should perish, but that all should come to repentance. And the church of Sardis was thus warned: Be watchful, and strengthen the things which remain, that are ready to die; for I have not found thy works perfect before God. Remember, therefore, how thou hast received and heard, and hold fast and repent. If therefore thou shalt not watch, I will come on thee as a thief, and thou shalt not know what hour I will come upon thee." (Ch. iii. 2, 3.)

Sardis, whose ruins now bear the modified name of *Sart*, is situated about sixty miles north-northwest from Ephesus, at the foot of mount Tmolus, and on the river Pactolus, so renowned for its fabled golden sands. This great and ancient city was the capital of the kingdom of Lydia, whose monarch, Crœsus, when defeated in the plain before this city of Cyrus, was master of all the nations within the river Halys. This dominion then passed to the Persians, and Sardis became the residence of the satrap to whom the government was committed; and being at this time one of the most splendid and opulent cities of the east, was the chosen resort of the Persian kings when in this part of their empire. It surrendered quietly to Alexander, after he had defeated the Persians in the battle of the Granicus. Sardis continued a great city under the Romans, until the terrible earthquake which happened in the time of Tiberius. It was, however, rebuilt by order of that emperor: but subsequent calamities of the same description, with the ravages and spoliations of the Goths, Saracens, and Turks, have made it an utter desolation, reducing it to little better than a heap of ruins, in which, nevertheless, some remains of its ancient splendor may be detected.

"And to the angel of the CHURCH IN PHILADELPHIA write, These things saith He that is holy, He that is true, He that hath the key of David, He that openeth and no man shutteth, and shutteth and no man openeth:—I know thy works: behold, I have set before thee an open door, and no man can shut it; for thou hast a little strength, and hast kept my word, and hast not denied my name.—Because thou hast kept the word of my patience, I also will keep thee from the hour of temptation, which shall come upon all the world." (Ch. iii. 9, 10.) The promises of the Lord are as sure as his threatenings. Philadelphia alone long withstood the power of the Turks, and, in the words of Gibbon, "at length capitulated with the proudest of the Ottomans. Among the Greek colonies and churches of Asia," he adds, "Philadelphia is still erect: a column in a scene of ruins." (Ch. 64.) "It is indeed an interesting circumstance," says Mr. Hartley, "to find Christianity more flourishing here than in many other parts of the Turkish empire: there is still a numerous Christian population; they occupy 300 houses. Divine service is performed every Sunday in five churches." Nor is it less interesting in these eventful times, and notwithstanding the general degeneracy of the Greek church, to learn that the present bishop of Philadelphia accounts "the Bible the only foundation of all religious belief;" and that he admits that "abuses have entered into the church, which former ages might endure, but the present must put them down."—It may well be added, as stated by Mr. Hartley, "The circumstance that Philadelphia is now called Allah-Shehr, the city of God, when viewed in connexion with the promises made to that church, and especially

Philadelphia.

with that of writing the name of the city of God upon its faithful members, is, to say the least, a singular concurrence." From the prevailing iniquities of men many a sign has been given how terrible are the judgments of God. But from the fidelity of the church in Philadelphia of old in keeping his word, a name and memorial of his faithfulness has been left on earth, while the higher glories promised to those that overcame, shall be ratified in heaven; and toward them, but not them only, shall the glorified Redeemer confirm the truth of his blessed words, " Him that overcometh will I make a pillar in the temple of my God ;" even as assuredly as Philadelphia, when all else fell around it, " stood erect," our enemies themselves being judges, " a column in a scene of ruins."

"And unto the angel of the CHURCH of the LAODICEANS write, These things saith the Amen, the faithful and true Witness, the beginning of the creation of God ; I know thy works, that thou art neither cold nor hot: I would thou wert cold or hot. So then because thou art lukewarm, and neither cold nor hot, I will spew thee out of my mouth. Because thou sayest, I am rich and increased with goods, and have need of nothing ; and knowest not that thou art wretched, and miserable, and poor, and blind, and naked: I counsel thee to buy of me gold tried in the fire, that thou mayest be rich ; and white raiment, that thou mayest be clothed, and that the shame of thy nakedness do not appear ; and anoint thine eyes with eye-salve, that thou mayest see." (Rev. iii. 14, &c,) All the other churches were found worthy of some commendation, and there was some blessing in them all. The church of Ephesus had labored and not fainted, though she had forsaken her first love ; and the threatened punishment, except she repented, was the removal of her candlestick out of its place. A faithless and wicked few polluted the churches of Pergamos and Thyatira by their doctrines or by their lives ; but the body was sound, and the churches had a portion in Christ. Even in Sardis, though it was dead, there was life in a few who had not defiled their garments ; " and they shall walk with me in white, said the Lord, for they are worthy."

But in what the Spirit said to the church in Laodicea, there was not one word of approval ; it was lukewarm without exception, and therefore it was wholly loathed. The religion of Jesus had become to them as an ordinary matter. They would attend to it just as they did to other things which they loved as well. The sacrifice of the Son of God upon the cross was nothing thought of more than a common gift by man. They were not constrained by the love of Christ more than by other feelings. They could repeat the words of the first great commandment of the law, and of the second, that is like unto it ; but they showed no sign that the one or the other was truly a law to them. There was no Dorcas among them, who, out of pure Christian love, made clothes for the poor. There was no Philemon, to whom it could be said, " The church in thy house," and who could look on a servant as " a brother beloved." There was no servant who looked to the eye of his Father in heaven more than to that of his master on earth, and to the recompense of eternal reward more than to the hireling wages of a day ; and who, by showing all good fidelity, sought to adorn the doctrine of God his Saviour in all things. There was nothing done, as everything should be, heartily, as to the Lord, and not unto men. The power of the world to come, and of that which now is, hung, as it were, even balanced in their minds ; each had its separate influence and weight, even to a scruple; and they were kept distinct, as if there should never be any interference between them, or as if they were to hang in separate scales.

This was given unto the world, and that unto God, as if these Christian men had been full of the faith, that the revealed will of the Most High had no title to a supreme ascendency over them, that all " the deeds done in the body would never be brought into judgment, and that lukewarmness was requital enough for redeeming love. Their only dread seemed to be lest they should be righteous overmuch. And for fear of that, which would have been inconsistent with their character, though not with their profession, they disregarded the words of one who was wiser than Solomon, and of that which now had laid down his life for their sakes: they did not strive to enter in at the strait gate ; to be perfect was no purpose of theirs ; there was no fight in their faith, no running in their race, no wrestling in their warfare, no victory in their work. Yet they could show a goodly form or framework of religion, on which they had raised many a high hope.

They trusted to redemption through Christ, while they were not redeemed from

Laodicea.

sin, nor actuated by the love of God. They used the means of grace, but neglected the end for which that grace had appeared. They were rich, they thought, and increased with goods, and had need of nothing. But they wanted zeal; and all they had was nothing worth. Whatever they vainly imagined themselves to be, the Spirit knew them truly, and told them what they were, even wretched, and miserable, and poor, and blind, and naked. They had done no evil, they thought, but they did little good. And they neither felt nor lived as if they knew that whatsoever is not of faith is sin. Their lukewarmness was worse, for it rendered their state more hopeless than if they had been cold. For sooner would a man in Sardis have felt that the chill of death was upon him, and have cried out for life, and called to the physician, than would a man of Laodicea, who could calmly count his even pulse, and think his life secure, while death was preying on his vitals. The character of lukewarm Christians, a self-contradicting name, is the same in every age. Such was the church of the Laodiceans. But what is that city now, or how is it changed from what it was?

Laodicea was the metropolis of the Greater Phrygia; and, as heathen writers attest, it was an extensive and very celebrated city. Instead of then verging to its decline, it arose to its greatest eminence only about the beginning of the Christian era. "It was the mother-church of sixteen bishoprics." Its three theatres, and the immense circus, which was capable of containing upward of thirty thousand spectators, the spacious remains of which (with other ruins buried under ruins) are yet to be seen, give proof of the greatness of its ancient wealth and population, and indicate too strongly, that in that city where Christians were rebuked without exception for their lukewarmness, there were multitudes who were lovers of pleasure more than lovers of God. The amphitheatre was built after the Apocalypse was written, and the warning of the Spirit had been given to the church of the Laodiceans to be zealous and repent; but whatever they there may have heard or beheld, their hearts would neither have been quickened to a renewed zeal for the service and glory of God, nor turned to a deeper sorrow for sin, and to a repentance not to be repented of. But the fate of Laodicea, though opposite, has been no less marked than that of Philadelphia. There are no sights of grandeur nor scenes of temptation around it now. Its own tragedy may be briefly told. It was lukewarm, and neither cold nor hot; and therefore it was loathsome in the sight of God. It was loved, and rebuked, and chastened in vain. And it has been blotted from the world. It is now as desolate as its inhabitants were destitute of the fear and love of God; and as the church of the Laodiceans was devoid of true faith in the Saviour, and zeal in his service. It is, as described in his Travels by Dr. Smith, "utterly desolated, and without any inhabitant, except wolves, and jackals, and foxes." It can boast of no human inhabitant, except occasionally when wandering Turkomans pitch their tents in its spacious amphitheatre. The "finest sculptured fragments" are to be seen at a considerable depth, in excavations which have been made among the ruins. (Arundel's Travels, p. 85.) And Col. Leake observes, "There are few ancient cities more likely than Laodicea to preserve many curious remains of antiquity beneath the surface of the soil; its opulence, and the earthquakes to which it was subject, rendering it probable that valuable works of art were often there buried beneath the ruins of the public and private edifices." A fearful significancy is thus given to the terrific denunciation, "Because thou art lukewarm, and neither cold nor hot, I will spew thee out of my mouth."

"He that hath ears to hear, let him hear what the Spirit saith unto the churches." The Spirit searcheth all things, yea, the deep things of God. Each church, and each individual therein, was weighed in the balance of the sanctuary, according to their works. Each was approved of according to its character, or rebuked and warned according to its deeds. Was the church itself pure, the diseased members alone were to be cut off. Was the church itself dead, yet the few names in which there was life, were all written before God, and not one of those who overcame would be blotted out of the book of life. All the seven churches were severally exhorted by the Spirit according to their need. The faith delivered to the saints was preached unto them all; and all, as Christian churches, possessed the means of salvation. The Son of man walked in the midst of them, beholding those who were, and those who were not his.

By the preaching of the gospel, and by the written word, every man in each of the churches was warned, and every man was taught in all wisdom, that every man might be presented perfect in Christ Jesus. And in what the Spirit said unto each and all of the churches which he that hath ears to hear was commanded to hear, the promise of everlasting blessedness, under a variety of the most glorious representations, was given, without exception, restriction, or reservation, to him that overcometh. The language of love, as well as of remonstrance and rebuke, was urged even on the lukewarm Laodiceans. And if any Christian fell, it was from his own resistance and quenching of the Spirit; from his choosing other lords than Jesus to have dominion over him; from his lukewarmness, deadness, and virtual denial of the faith; and from his own wilful rejection of freely-offered and dearly-purchased grace, sufficient, if sought, and cherished, and zealously used, to have enabled him to overcome and triumph in that warfare against spiritual wickedness to which Christ hath called his disciples; and in which, as the finisher of their faith, he is able to make the Christian more than conqueror.

But if such, as the Spirit described them and knew them to be, were the churches, and Christians then, what are the churches and what are Christians now? Or rather, we would ask of the reader, what is your own hope toward God, and what the work of your faith? If, while Christianity was in its prime, and when its divine truths had scarcely ceased to reach the ears of believers from the lips of apostles, on whose heads the Spirit had visibly descended, and cloven tongues, like as of fire, had sat; if, even at that time, one of the seven churches of Asia had already departed from its first love; if two others were partially polluted by the errors in doctrine, and evils in the practice, of some of their members; if another had only a few names that were worthy, and yet another none; and if they who formed the last and worst of these, thought themselves rich and increased with goods, and that they had need of nothing; and knew not that, being lukewarm, they were wretched, and miserable, and poor, and blind, and naked; have you an ear to hear or a heart to understand such knowledge? and do you, professing yourself a Christian, as they also did, see no cause or warning here to question and examine yourself, even as the same Spirit would search and try you, of your works, and charity, and service, and faith, and patience?

What is your labor of love, or wherein do you labor at all for his name's sake, by whose name you are called? What trials does your faith patiently endure? what temptations does it triumphantly overcome? Is Christ in you the hope of glory, and is your heart purified through that blessed hope? To a church we trust you belong; but whose is the kingdom within you? What principles ever actuate you which Christ and his apostles taught? Where, in your affections and life, are the fruits of the Spirit—love, joy, peace, long-suffering, gentleness, goodness, meekness, temperance? Turn the precepts of the gospel into questions, and ask thus what the Spirit would say unto you, as he said unto the churches.

What the Spirit said unto primitive and apostolic churches, over which "the beloved disciple" personally presided, may suffice to prove that none who have left their first love, if ever they have truly felt the love of Jesus—that none who are guilty of seducing others into sin and uncleanness—that none who have a name that they live, and are dead—and that none who are lukewarm, are worthy members of any Christian communion; and that while such they continue, no Christian communion can be profitable to them. But unto them is " space to repent" given. And to them the word and Spirit speak in entreaties, encouragements, exhortations, and warnings, that they may turn from their sins to the Saviour, and that they may live and not die. But were there one name in Sodom, or a few in Sardis, that are the Lord's, he knows and names them every one; and precious his sight is the death of his saints. Some, on the other hand, may be sunk into the depths of Satan, though in outward fellowship with a church, were such to be found, as pure as once was that of Thyatira. Whatever, therefore, the profession of your faith may be, seek the kingdom of God and his righteousness; that kingdom which is righteousness and peace and joy in the Holy Ghost, and that righteousness which is through faith in Christ, who gave himself for the church, that he might sanctify and cleanse it. And whatever dangers may then encompass you around, fear not—only believe; all things are possible to him that believeth.

It was by keeping the word of the Lord, and not denying his faith, by hearing what the Spirit said, that the church of Philadelphia held fast what they had, and no man took their crown, though situated directly between the church of Laodicea, which ,was lukewarm, and Sardis, which was dead. And dead as Sardis was, the Lord had a few names in it which had not defiled their garments—Christians, worthy of the name, who lived, as you yourself should ever live, in the faith of the Lord Jesus—dead unto sin, and alive unto righteousness; while all around them, though naming the name of Jesus, were dead in trespasses and sins. Try your faith by its fruits; judge yourself that you be not judged; examine yourself whether you be in the faith; prove your own self; and with the whole counsel of God, as revealed in the gospel, open to your view, let the rule of your self-scrutiny be what the Spirit said unto the churches.

Many prophecies remain which are not here noticed. But were any gainsayers to ask for more obvious facts and some demonstration of the truth of prophecy, which your own ears might hear and your eyes see, you have only to hear how they speak evil of the things that they understand not—how they speak great swelling words of vanity to allure others, promising them liberty while they themselves are the children of corruption; you have only to look on these scoffers, and mockers, and false teachers, who have come in the last times; who walk after their own lusts, who despise government, who are presumptuous and self-willed, and who foam out their own shame, to hear and to see the loud and living witnesses of the truth of God's holy and unerring word. (2 Pet. iii. 3; Jude xiii.) Such have been, and such are, the enemies of the Christian faith. Yet it calls them from darkness to light, and from death to life. Turn ye, turn ye: why, it asks of these boasters of reason, why will ye die?

If you have seen any wonderful things out of the law of the Lord, and have looked, though from afar off, on the judgments of God that have come upon the earth, lay not aside the thought of these things when you lay down this book. Treat them not as if they were an idle tale, or as if you yourself were not to be a witness—and more than a witness—of a far greater judgment, which shall be brought nigh unto you, and shall be your own.

If, in traversing some of the plainest paths of the field of prophecy, you have been led by a way which you knew not of before, let that path lead you to the well of living waters, which springeth up into everlasting life to every one that thirsts after it and drinks. Let the words of our Lord and Saviour Jesus Christ be to you this wellspring of the Christian life. Let the word of God enlighten your eyes, and it will also rejoice your heart. Search the Scriptures, in them there are no lying divinations; they testify of Jesus, and in them you will find eternal life. Pray for the teaching and the aid of that Spirit by whose inspiration they were given. And above all Christian virtues, that may bear witness of your faith, put on charity, love to God and love to man, the warp and woof of the Christian's new vesture without a seam; even that charity, or love, by which faith worketh, which is the fruit of the Spirit, the end of the commandment, the fulfilling of the law, the bond of perfectness, and a better gift and a more excellent way than speaking with tongues, or interpreting, or prophesying, and without which you would be as nothing, though you understood all mystery and all knowledge. From the want of this the earth has been covered with ruins. Let it be yours, and however poor may be your earthly portion, it will be infinitely more profitable to you than all the kingdoms of the world, and all their glory. Prophecies shall fall; tongues shall cease; knowledge shall vanish away; the earth and the works that are therein shall be burned up; but charity never faileth.

If you have kept the word of the Lord, and have not denied his name, hold that fast which thou hast, that no man take thy crown. But if heretofore you have been lukewarm, and destitute of Christian faith, and zeal, and hope, and love, it would be vain to leave you with any mortal admonition; hear what the Spirit saith, and harden not your heart against the heavenly counsel, and the glorious encouragement given unto you by that Jesus of whom all the prophets bear witness, and unto whom all things are now committed by the Father. "I counsel thee to buy of me gold tried in the fire, that thou mayst be rich; and white raiment, that thou mayst be clothed, and that the shame of thy nakedness do not appear; and anoint thine eyes with eyesalve, that thou mayest see. As many as I love I rebuke and chasten; be zealous, therefore, and repent. Behold, I stand at the door and knock: if any man hear my voice, and open the door, I will come in to him, and will sup with him, and he with me. To him that overcometh will I grant to sit with me in my throne, even as I also overcame, and am set down with my Father in his throne. He that hath an ear to hear, let him hear what the Spirit saith unto the churches."

CHAPTER XIV.

CONTAINING AN ACCOUNT OF THE FINAL DESTRUCTION OF JERUSALEM BY THE ROMANS, AS FORETOLD BY OUR BLESSED REDEEMER A SHORT TIME BEFORE HIS DEATH.

THE Jews remain to this day not only the guardians of the Old Testament scriptures, but living witnesses of the truth of many prophecies, which, in the first ages of their history, unfolded their fate until the latest generations. Jewish and heathen historians fully describe the dreadful miseries which they suffered when all their cities were laid waste, when Jerusalem itself was destroyed in the seventieth year of the Christian era, and the remnant of their race, after an almost uninterrupted possession of Judea by their forefathers for fifteen hundred years, were driven from their country and scattered throughout the world. A brief detail of the unparalleled miseries which they then endured may serve to connect their former history with their subsequent alike unparalleled fate, and to show that the prophecies respecting the destruction of Jerusalem are as circumstantial and precise, and were as minutely fulfilled, as those in which their more recent and present history may be read.

The Israelites were chosen to be a peculiar people. The worship of the only living and true God was maintained among them alone for many ages, while idolatry and polytheism (or the worship of many gods) otherwise universally prevailed. But the Father of the universe is no respecter of persons. A divine law was given to the descendants of Abraham, and blessings and curses were set before them, to cleave to their race in every age, according as they would observe and obey the commandments of the Lord, or refuse to hearken unto his voice, and to do all his commandments and statutes. Their history, and their continued preservation as a people, is thus an express record and manifestation of the doings of Providence. To read of their calamities is to see the judgments of God; and to compare them with the prophecies is to witness the truth of his word. There were intermingled seasons of prosperity and triumph, or of oppression and misery, as they enjoyed or forfeited their promised blessings, throughout the long period that they dwelt in the land of Canaan. But their punishments were to rise progressively with their sins; and so awfully sinful were the inhabitants of Jerusalem after the time of their merciful visitation had passed, and when the dark unbroken era of their miseries began, that Josephus, their great historian, and the greatest of their generals in their wars with the Romans, has recorded his opinion that, had they delayed their coming, the city would have been swallowed up by an earthquake or overflowed by water, or, as it was worse than Sodom, would have been destroyed by fire from heaven.* The vial of wrath was not poured out till the measure of their iniquities was full.

Instruments are never wanting for the execution of the purposes of God; nor, when needful for the confirmation of his word, is there any want of full testimony that his declared purposes have been fulfilled. There is nothing similar in history to the siege and destruction of Jerusalem, and to the miseries which its inhabitants inflicted and brought upon themselves by their savage barbarity and unyielding obstinacy; nor was there ever any other city or country of whose destruction, devastation, and misery, there is so clear and authenticated a detail. Josephus, himself a Jew and an eye-witness of the facts he relates, gives a circumstantial account of the whole war, which furnishes complete evidence, not only of the truth of what Moses and the prophets had foretold, but also of all that in clearer vision, and to the perturbation and astonishment of his disciples, Christ had explicitly revealed concerning its then approaching fate. Heathen writers also record many of the facts.

The prophecies from the Old Testament and from the New relative to the siege and destruction of Jerusalem are so numerous, that the insertion of them at length would occupy a greater space than can here be devoted to the consideration of the

* Josephus's History of the Wars of the Jews, book 5, chap. 13, § 6.

subject. The reader may peruse them as they are to be found in the written word: Levit. xxvi. 14, &c.; Deut. xxviii. 15, &c.; Isa. xxix. 1, &c.; Ezek. vi. 7; Jer. xxvi. 18; Micah, iii. 12; Matt. xxi. 33, &c.; xxii. 1-7; xxiv.; Mark, xiii.; Luke, xx. 9-19; xxi.; xxiii. 27-31. They require no other exposition of their meaning. Exclusive of literal predictions, frequent allusions are interspersed throughout the Gospels respecting the abolition of the Mosaic dispensation, and the utter subversion of the Jewish state.

A nation of fierce countenance, of an unknown tongue, and swift as the eagle flieth, were to come from a distant land against the Jews—to despoil them of all their goods—to besiege them in all their gates—to bring down their high and fenced walls. They were to be left few in number—to be slain before their enemies; the pride of their power was to be broken; their cities to be laid waste, and themselves to be destroyed—to be brought to nought—to be plucked from off their own land—to be sold into slavery, and to be so despised that none would buy them. Their high places were to be rendered desolate—their bones to be scattered about their altars; Jerusalem was to be encompassed round about—to be besieged with a mount—to have forts raised against it—to be ploughed over like a field—to become heaps, and to come to an end. The sword, the famine, and the pestilence, were to destroy them.

The Jews lived fearless of judgments like these, when they dwelt in peace, and would not listen to the voice of Jesus. They would have no king but Cæsar; and they trusted in the power of the Roman empire as the security of their state. But He whom they rejected showed how God had rejected them, how they were filling up the measure of their fathers, and how all these judgments that had been denounced of old, and others of which their fathers had not heard, were to be felt by many, and to be all witnessed by some who were living then. And the Man of sorrows, whose face was set as a flint against his own unequalled sufferings, and who shed not a tear on his own account, was moved to pity, and his heart was melted into tenderness, on contemplating the great crimes and the coming calamities of the wicked, impenitent, and devoted city: "when he beheld Jerusalem, he wept over it."

The expiration of thirty-six years from the death of Christ to the destruction of Jerusalem; the death, previous to that event, of at least two of the evangelists who record the prophecies concerning it; the manner in which the predictions and allusions respecting the fate of Jerusalem are interwoven throughout the gospel; the warning given to the disciples of Christ to escape from the impending calamities, and the annunciation of the signs whereby they would know of their approach; the dread that was cherished by some of the earliest converts to the Christian faith that the day of judgment was then at hand, and which had arisen from the prophecies concerning the destruction of Jerusalem being closely connected with those relative to the second coming of Christ and the end of the world (all of which things his disciples had asked him to reveal); the unanimous assent of antiquity to the prior publication of the gospel; and the continued truth of the prophecy still manifested in Jerusalem being yet trodden down of the Gentiles,—afford as full a proof as could now be thought of that the predictions were delivered previous to the event.

No coincidence can be closer in relation to the facts than that which subsists between the predictions of Jesus and the narrative of the Jewish historian. Yet, as the reader will doubtless perceive, this coincidence is not more clear than that which subsists between the testimony of modern unbelievers and those prophecies which refer to the past and present desolation of Judea: wars, rumors of wars, and commotions; nations rising against nation, and kingdom against kingdom; famines, pestilences, and earthquakes in divers places; though the greatest of human evils that mortals fear were to be but the "beginning of sorrows"—the heralds of heavier woes. Many false Christs were to appear, and to deceive many. The disciples of Jesus were to be persecuted, afflicted, imprisoned, hated of all nations, and brought before rulers and kings for his name's sake, and many of them were to be put to death. Iniquity was to abound, and the love of many was to wax cold; but the gospel of the kingdom was to be preached in all the world. The abomination of desolation was to be seen standing in the place where it ought not. Jerusalem was to be compassed about with armies, a trench was to be cast about it, and they were to be hemmed in on every side. And there were to be fearful sights and great signs from heaven. These were to be the signs that the end of Jerusalem was at hand. And there was to be great distress upon the land, and wrath upon the people; the tribulation was to be such as had never been, and would never be. The Jews were to fall by the edge of the sword; a remnant was to be led captive into all nations; of the temple, and of Jerusalem itself, one stone was not to be left upon another; and it was to be trodden down of the Gentiles till the time of the Gentiles should be fulfilled.

The prodigies which preceded the war, as related by Josephus, are these:

A comet, which bore the resemblance of a sword, hung over the city of Jerusalem for the space of a whole year.

A short time before the revolt of the Jews, a most remarkable and extraordinary light was seen about the altar of the temple. It happened at the ninth hour of the night preceding the celebration of the feast of the passover, and continued about half an hour, giving a light equal to that of day. Ignorant persons considered this unusual and wonderful appearance as a happy omen; but those of superior judgment averred that it was a prediction of approaching war; and their opinion was fully confirmed by the event.

The eastern gate of the interior part of the temple was composed of solid brass, and was of such an immense weight that it was the labor of twenty men to make it fast every night. It was secured with iron bolts and bars, which were let down into a large threshold consisting of an entire stone. About the fifth hour of the night this gate opened without any human assistance; immediate notice of which being given to the officer on duty, he lost no time in endeavoring to restore it to its former situation; but it was with the utmost difficulty that he accomplished it. There were likewise some ignorant people who deemed this to be a second good omen, insinuating that Providence had thereby set open a gate of blessings to the people; but persons of superior discernment were of a contrary opinion, and concluded that the opening of the gate predicted the success of the enemy, and destruction of the city.

A short time after the celebration of the feast of the passover, before the setting of the sun, the appearance of chariots and armed men were seen in the air, in various parts of the country, passing round the city among the clouds.

While the priests were going to perform the duties of their function, according to custom, in the inner temple, on the feast of Pentecost, they at first heard an indistinct murmuring, which was succeeded by a voice, repeating, in the most plain and earnest manner, these words: "Let us be gone, let us depart hence."

But the most extraordinary circumstance of the whole was this. Some time before the commencement of the war, and while the city appeared to be in the most perfect peace, and abounded in plenty, there came to the feast of tabernacles a simple countryman, a son of one Ananias, who, without any previous intimation, exclaimed as follows: "A voice from the east; a voice from the west; a voice from the four quarters of the world; a voice to Jerusalem, and a voice to the temple; a voice to men and women newly married; and a voice to the nation at large." In this manner did he continue his exclamations, in various places through all the streets of the city; at which some persons of eminence in the city were so offended, that they ordered him to be apprehended, and severely whipped. This was accordingly done, but he bore his sufferings not only without complaint, but without saying a word in his own defence; and no sooner was his punishment ended, than he proceeded in his exclamations as before. By this time the magistrates were suspicious (and indeed not without reason) that what he had said proceeded from the divine impulse of a superior power, that influenced his words. In consequence of this, they sent him to the governor of Judea, who directed that he should be whipped with the greatest severity. This order was so strictly obeyed, that his very bones were seen, notwithstanding which, he neither wept nor supplicated, but, in a voice of mourning, between each stroke, exclaimed, "Wo, wo to Jerusalem!" From this very extraordinary behavior, the governor was induced to interrogate him with respect to his character, and the places of his birth and residence, and what could prompt him to act as he had done. He would not, however, make any answer to either of these questions; upon which the governor found himself under the necessity of dismissing him, as a man out of his senses. From this period to the commencement of the war, he was never known either to visit or speak to any of the citizens, nor was he heard to say any other words than the melancholy sentence, "Wo, wo to Jerusalem." Those who daily punished him, received no ill language from him; nor did those who fed him receive his thanks; but what he generally said to every one was, an ominous prediction. It was remarked that on public festivals he was more vociferous than at other times; and in the manner before mentioned he continued for the space of more than three years; nor did his voice or strength appear to fail him till his predictions were verified by the siege of Jerusalem. As soon as this event took place, he went for the last time on the wall of the city, and exclaimed with a more powerful voice than usual, "Wo, wo to this city, this temple, and this people;" and concluded his lamentation by saying, "Wo, wo be to myself." He had no sooner spoken these words than, in the midst of these predictions, he was destroyed by a stone thrown from an engine.

Having thus mentioned the very singular prodigies which preceded the destruction of Jerusalem, as related by Josephus, we shall now proceed to give an account of the circumstances which occasioned the war, together with its progress, which at length brought on the final ruin and destruction of the Jewish state.

The commencement of the war was occasioned, partly by the infamous behavior of Albinus, the Roman governor of Judea, and partly by the refractoriness of many of the principal people of Jerusalem. Albinus was a man totally abandoned to every degree of vice. Avarice, corruption, extortion, oppression, public and private, were equally familiar to him. He accepted bribes in civil and personal causes, and oppressed the nation by the weight of arbitrary taxes. If any offender, however atrocious, convicted of robbery or assault by himself, or any other magistrate, was under sentence of the law, a friend and a bribe would insure his liberty; and this governor never found any man guilty who had money to procure his innocence.

At this time there was a strong faction in Jerusalem, who, wishing for a change of government, the most opulent of them privately compounded with Albinus, in case any disturbance should happen. There was likewise a set of men who would not be easy while the state was at peace; and Albinus engaged these in his interest. The leaders of these mutineers were each attended by daring fellows of their own turn of mind; but the governor was the most abandoned villain of the whole, and had guards always ready to execute his orders. The event proved that the injured did not dare to complain; those who were in any danger of losing part of their property were glad to compound to save the rest, and the receiver proved the worst of thieves. In short, there appeared to be no sense of honor remaining; and a new slavery seemed to be predicted from the number of tyrants then in power, through the land of Judea.

Such was the character, and such were the manners, of Albinus, who, in a short time, was, by order of the emperor Nero, removed from his office, and Gessius Florus placed in his stead. This, however, was far from being an advantageous change for the Jews, Florus being so much more abandoned in his principles than the former, as not to admit even of the least comparison. Albinus was treacherous, but observed a secrecy in his crimes that had the appearance of modesty; but Florus was so consummate in his wickedness, that he boasted of his iniquitous behavior, and declared himself the general enemy of the nation. His conduct in the province he governed was more like that of an executioner than a governor; for he treated all the people like criminals, and extended his rapine and tyranny beyond all bounds. He was equally devoid of compassion, and dead to all sense of honor; cruel to the unfortunate, and utterly abandoned in cases so enormous that impudence itself would blush at the recollection of them. He exceeded all the men of his time in making lies and impositions pass for truth; and was equally artful in discovering new modes of doing mischief. He gave such encouragement to the sons of rapine and plunder, that he might as well have proclaimed that every man was at liberty to seize whatever he could lay his hands on, provided that he himself obtained a share of the plunder. His avarice was carried to such an extravagant pitch, that the inhabitants of the province were reduced to degrees of poverty little short of starving; and many of them left the country in absolute want of the necessaries of life.

The daily oppressions of Florus on the people throughout the province of Judea irritated them to the most violent degree, and being fearful lest they should lay a complaint against him before the emperor, Florus, to avoid the consequences of such a proceeding, resolved to continue his oppressions till they should enter into open rebellion, whereby his villanous proceedings would be greatly lessened in the eyes of his master. This had the desired effect, for the factious party in Jerusalem, who for some time had been inclined to revolt, encouraging the greater part of the people of that city to oppose the measures of Florus, an insurrection took place, and a resolution was formed to oppose the Romans with all their might.

It happened at this time that King Agrippa was at Jerusalem, and being fearful of the dreadful consequences that were likely to ensue, he summoned the people together, and strongly exhorted them to desist from any violent proceedings, telling them that if they did, it must inevitably prove their destruction. He advised them to a patient submission to Florus, till another governor should be appointed by the emperor, who, in all probability, would remove the grievances under which they then labored. But this, instead of subsiding, only inflamed the passions of the multitude, who not only made use of the most opprobrious language, but likewise maltreated the king. In consequence of this, Agrippa left Jerusalem; previous to which he despatched messengers to Florus, who was then at Cesarea, informing him of the manner in which he had been treated, and requesting that he would immediately send a proper force to repel the insurgents.

No sooner had Agrippa left Jerusalem than the factious Jews began to carry their design into execution. To this purpose great numbers of them got privately into the Roman garrison called Massada, where they surprised the soldiers, every one of whom they put to death, and, in their stead, substituted a guard of their own people. About this juncture there happened likewise another commotion in the temple of Jerusalem. A bold and factious young man, named Eleazar (son of the then high-priest), who was at that time a military officer, persuaded a number of his friends among the priests not to accept of any offering or sacrifice but from the Jews. This circumstance laid the foundation of a war with the Romans; for, in consequence of the request of Eleazar, when the sacrifices of Nero were presented, according to custom, to be offered up for the success of the people of Rome, they were rejected. So new and extraordinary a proceeding gave great offence to the high-priest and persons of distinction, who protested against it, and earnestly recommended the continuance of so reasonable a custom as that of offering prayers for princes and governors. But the insurgents, relying on the strength of their numbers, were obstinate for obedience to their orders; every one who wished for innovation was on their side, and they considered Eleazar, who was a man of courage, and in office, as the head of their party.

In consequence of the great obstinacy of the insurgents, the high-priest, and most eminent of the Pharisees, assembled together in order to deliberate on the most proper mode of proceeding at so critical a juncture, being apprehensive that if the tumult was not, by some means or other, suppressed, it must be attended with the most fatal consequences. Having consulted for some time, they at length resolved to try what could be done to appease the passions of the multitude; and for this purpose they assembled the people before the brazen gate, on the inside of the temple toward the east. Here they represented to them the rashness of the enterprise in which they had engaged, and which would certainly involve their country in a ruinous war. They then adverted to the unreasonable ground of the dispute, and the evident injustice on which it was founded; they told them that their ancestors were so far from refusing or forbidding the oblations of strangers (which they would have deemed a kind of impiety) that they considered them, in some degree, as a part of their own worship. They likewise mentioned the presents which had, from time to time, been made by strangers to the temple, which were still preserved as ornaments in that sacred place, and in remembrance of those who gave them. They further told them, that the provoking a war with the Romans would be at least disgraceful, if not ruinous, to Jerusalem; that new modes of religion would certainly be adopted, as nothing less could be expected by the interdiction of every sort of people except Jews, from offering oblations and prayers to God in his holy temple. It was urged that this was such an inhuman injunction as could not be excused in the case of a private person; but that it was utterly unpardonable to extend it to the whole people of Rome, and eventually even excommunicating the emperor himself. It was asked what would be the consequence if such contempt should be returned, and those who had refused others the liberty of offering their prayers and oblations, should themselves be denied the privilege of public worship? They concluded with telling them, that if they persisted in their obstinacy, the city would be left void of discipline; and every ill consequence would certainly happen, unless they repented of all the uncharitable things they had done, and made satisfaction, before the emperor should be informed of their violent proceedings.

But all these circumstances were of none effect; the insurgents, who wished for war rather than peace, were determined, to prosecute their design with the utmost vigor; and in this they were further encouraged from the conduct of the Levites, who quitted the altar, and joined themselves to their party.

The high-priest and people of rank, finding the populace despised all obedience to law, and that themselves would probably be the first that would be censured by the Romans, consulted together what means were the most eligible to take in order to save themselves and country from destruction. After deliberating for some time on this head, they at length resolved to send deputies to Florus and Agrippa, representing the conduct of the people in its true light, and requesting them to send forces to to Jerusalem, in order to put a speedy end to the rebellion.

The news of the insurrection at Jerusalem was highly agreeable to Florus, whose disposition led him to inflame rather than to endeavor to suppress the war. This was evidently evinced by his delay in giving an answer to the deputies, knowing thereby that it would afford the rebels an opportunity of augmenting their forces. On the contrary, Agrippa consulted only the general welfare, being desirous of doing all in his power to save both parties; and by this means to secure Jerusalem in the possession of the Jews, and bind the Jews in subjection to the Romans. To effect this he despatched two thousand auxiliary horse to Jerusalem, under the command of Darius, a very able and experienced general. On their arrival at the city they were joined by the rulers and high-priest, together with the rest of the people who wished for peace. The insurgents had already possessed themselves of the temple and lower city; and therefore the royal troops immediately seized on the upper city, being resolved, if possible, to reduce the rebels to subjection. It was not long before a skirmish took place, and the combatants on both sides made use of their bows and arrows, with which they galled each other incessantly. The insurgents made their attacks in the most desperate manner; but the royal forces appeared to have a superior knowledge of the military art. The principal operation the latter had in view was to compel the sacrilegious faction to abandon the temple; while, on the contrary, Eleazar and his adherents labored with equal zeal to get the upper town into their possession. The contest continued without intermission for some days, in all which time, though there was a great slaughter on both sides, not the least advantage was obtained by either. At length, however, the insurgents, being resolved to engage in the most hazardous enterprise, assaulted the king's troops with such violence as to throw them into the greatest confusion and disorder; and this advantage they improved to such a degree, that, equally overcome by superior numbers and more determined resolution, the royal troops were obliged to abandon the upper town, of which the rebels immediately possessed themselves, and thereby became masters of the whole city.

Elated with this success, the insurgents immediately repaired to the house of the high-priest, which they first plundered, and then reduced to ashes. This being done, they resolved, in the next place, to set fire to the offices of record, and consume both them and all their contents. As soon as this was known, the persons who had the care of those places were so terrified, that they immediately abandoned their trust, each man seeking his own security by flight; on which both offices and records were reduced to ashes.

The next day after the insurgents had committed these outrages, they made an attack on the castle of Antonia, and, after only two days' resistance, made themselves masters of it, having done which, they burnt the castle, and put all the garrison to the sword. After this they proceeded to the palace, in which were the troops sent by Agrippa to suppress the insurrection: they immediately invested the place, and having divided themselves into four bodies, made an attempt to undermine the walls; while those within were under the necessity of remaining inactive, as their strength was insufficient for them to sally forth with any hopes of success. The assailants continued their operations with great resolution for several days, till at length the besieged, finding they must either fall by the sword, or be starved into compliance, deserted the place, and fled for security to the castles of Hippon, Phasael and Mariamne. But no sooner had the soldiers quitted the place, than the rebels immediately broke in, and unmercifully put to death every person they met with; having done which, they plundered the palace of all its valuable furniture, and concluded the outrage by setting fire to the camp.

While these things were transacting at Jerusalem, a most dreadful massacre took place in Cesarea, not less than twenty thousand Jews being, at the instigation of Florus, put to death by the Romans in one day. This horrid slaughter so irritated the Jews, that they became universally outrageous, and, dividing themselves into distinct bodies, dispersed into different parts, with a full resolution of seeking revenge on their enemies. They first laid waste a great number of villages in Syria, and then destroyed several principal cities, among which were Philadelphia, Gibonitis, Garasea, Pella, and Scythopolis. They then proceeded to Sebaste and Askelon, both of which places surrendered without opposition. Having effectually reduced these two fortresses, they next proceeded to Gaza, which they totally destroyed; and, continuing their ravages, laid waste a great number of villages on the frontiers of Syria, putting to death all the inhabitants wherever they went.

On the other hand the Syrians wreaked their vengeance on all the Jews they could find, not only in country places, but in many principal cities throughout Syria, all of whom they put to the sword. In short the whole country was in the most deplorable situation, there being, as it were, two armies in every city; nor was any safety to be expected for the one but in the destruction of the other. In the city of Alexandria no less than fifty thousand Jews were put to death by the Romans; and the only places in which the Jews escaped the general carnage were Sidon, Apamia, and Antioch.

Cestius, the governor of Syria, who at this time resided at Antioch, observing the contempt in which the Jews were held throughout the whole province, resolved to take advantage of this circumstance, and prosecute the war against them with the utmost vigor. For this purpose he raised a considerable army, consisting of the whole twelfth legion which he commanded at Antioch; two thousand select men from the other legions, and four divisions of horse, exclusive of the royal auxiliaries, which consisted of two thousand horse and three thousand foot, all armed with bows and arrows.

With this formidable army Cestius left Antioch, and proceeded toward Ptolemais, in his way to which he was joined by a great number of people from different parts of the country. The first material place he came to was Zabulon, otherwise called Andron, the most defensible city of Galilee, and by which Judea was divided from Ptolemais. On his arrival at this place he found that it was amply stored with all kinds of provisions, but not a single person was to be seen in the town, the inhabitants having, on his approach, fled to the mountains for security. In consequence of this Cestius gave his soldiers permission to plunder the city; which being done, he ordered it to be burnt and levelled with the ground. He then proceeded to several other places in the neighborhood of Zabulon, all of which he served in like manner, and then repaired to Ptolemais. On this occasion the Syrians were so anxious for obtaining of plunder, that they could not be prevailed on to retire in time; but many of them remained behind, and, on the retreat of Cestius with the greater part of his forces, the Jews, taking courage, fell on the plunderers, and nearly two thousand of them were put to the sword.

After staying a short time at Ptolemais, Cestius proceeded to Cesarea, whence he despatched a division of his army to Joppa, with orders that, if they could get an easy possession of the place, they should take it; but if they found that the inhabitants made preparations to defend it, they should, in that case, wait till the arrival of the rest of the army. The Romans, however, no sooner arrived at the place than they immediately laid siege to it, and, with very little difficulty, even made themselves masters of it. The inhabitants were so far from being able to resist the attack, that they had not even an opportunity of making their escape; so that the whole, both men, women, and children, were put to the sword, the number amounting to not less than eight thousand. The Romans then plundered the city, and, having reduced it to ashes, they returned to their general at Cesarea. In the meantime a body of Roman horse made similar destruction in the neighborhood of Cesarea, where they ravaged the country, killed great numbers of the inhabitants, took possession of their effects, and then burnt their towns to the ground.

From Cesarea Cestius departed with his army to Antipatris, on his arrival at which place he was informed that a great number of Jews had got into the tower of Aphec, whither he sent a number of his troops to rout them. The Jews, finding themselves totally unable to sustain the shock, abandoned the place to the Romans, who first

39

stripped it of everything that was valuable, and then set fire to it; having done which they departed, but not without destroying several villages in its neighborhood, and putting such of the inhabitants as could not effect their escape to the sword.

Cestius proceeded with his army from Antipatris to Lydda, in which city he found no more than fifty men, all the rest being gone to Jerusalem, in order to be present at the celebration of the feast of tabernacles. The remaining fifty Cestius ordered to be put to death, which being done, he set fire to the town, and then proceeded by the way of Bethoron, to a place named Gabaoh, about fifty furlongs from Jerusalem, where he encamped his army.

The Jews, convinced of the great danger they were in, from the appearance of so formidable an army, laid aside their former scruples with regard to their sacred days, and applied themselves strictly to their arms. Imagining that their force was now sufficient to cope with the Romans, they made a desperate sally on the sabbath-day, regardless of their ancient prejudices, and, with a furious uproar, attacked the enemy. On the first charge they put the front of the Romans into great disorder, and penetrated so far into the main body of the army, that had it not been for a detachment of foot which remained entirely unbroken, and a party of horse that unexpectedly came to their relief, Cestius and his whole army would have been certainly cut to pieces. In this encounter four hundred of the Roman cavalry were slain, and one hundred and fifteen of the infantry; while of the Jews there fell a very small number. The main body of the Jews, retreating in good order, went back into the city; and, in the meantime, the Romans retired toward Bethoron. A strong party of the Jews, however, under the command of one Gioras, pursued the enemy, several of whom they killed: they likewise seized a number of carriages, and a quantity of baggage, which they found in the pursuit, all of which they conveyed safe to Jerusalem.

Cestius and his army remained in the field three days after this action, during which time a party of the Jews was stationed on the adjacent hills to watch his movements. On the fourth day Cestius advanced with his whole army, in a regular manner, to the borders of Jerusalem, where many of the people were so terrified by the faction, that they were afraid to take any step of consequence: while some of the principal promoters of the sedition were so alarmed at the conduct and discipline of the Romans on their march, that they retired from the extremities of the city, and took refuge in the temple. Cestius in his way to Jerusalem burnt Cenopolis, and a place which was denominated the wood-market. Thence he advanced to the upper town of the city, and pitched his camp at a small distance from the palace.

While Cestius was thus situated with his army, Ananus, and several other men among the Jews, called aloud to the Roman general, offering to open the gates to him; but either through diffidence or fear of their fidelity, he was so long in considering whether or not he should accept the offer, that he was at length restrained from it by the people, who were so irritated at Ananus and his companions, that they compelled them to retreat from the walls of the city, and retire to their own houses for protection.

After this the Jews, with a view of defending the walls of the city, repaired to the different turrets, and for five successive days defended them against all the efforts of the Romans, though they pushed the attack with the utmost impetuosity. On the sixth day Cestius made an assault on the north side of the temple, with a select force chosen from his troops and bowmen; but the Jews discharged such a violent quantity of shot and stones from the porch and galleries, that the Romans were not only repeatedly compelled to retire from the severity of the charge, but, for a time, obliged to abandon the enterprise.

Being thus repulsed, the Romans, after some time, had recourse to the following singular invention. Those in front placing their bucklers against the wall of the city, and covering their heads and shoulders with them, those who stood next closed their bucklers to the former, till the whole body was covered, and made the appearance of a tortoise. The bucklers being thus conjoined were proof against all the darts and arrows of the enemy; so that the Romans had the opportunity of undermining the walls without being exposed to danger. The first thing they did was to attempt setting fire to the gates of the temple, which circumstance so terrified the faction, that they considered themselves as ruined, and many absolutely abandoned the town; nor were the quiet party less elevated with joy than the rebels were depressed by despair.

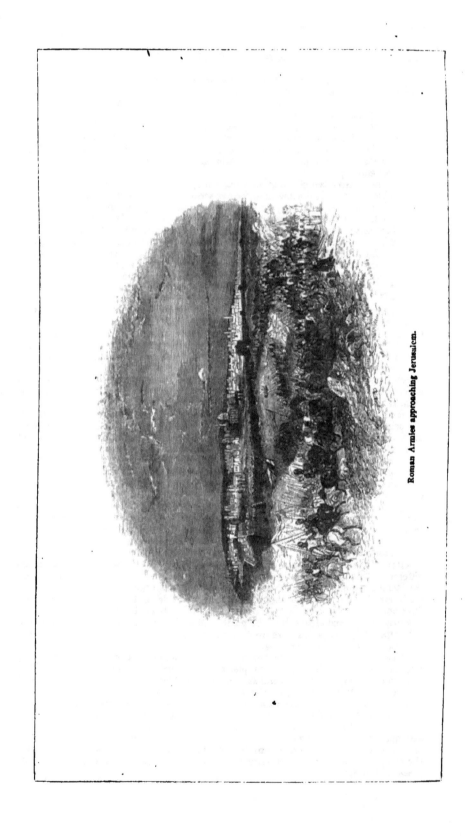

Roman Armies approaching Jerusalem.

While things were in this situation the people demanded that the gates might be opened to Cestius, whom they considered in the light of a friend and preserver. This was a most favorable opportunity for Cestius, and had he maintained the siege only a short time longer, the whole town must have submitted. But, not considering the good disposition of the people in general, or reflecting on the despair into which the rebels were thrown, as if he had been infatuated, he suddenly drew off his men, and, contrary to all sense and reason, abandoned the siege, at a time when his prospects were better than they had been at any former period. The revolters were so much encouraged at this unexpected circumstance, that they attacked the rear of Cestius's army, and destroyed great numbers both of his cavalry and infantry. On the first night after Cestius retreated from the siege, he took up his residence in a camp which he had fortified at a place named Scopus; and on the following day he continued his march, but was closely pursued by the Jews, who annoyed him as he went, and destroyed a considerable number of his troops. On the whole this was a very disastrous attack to the Romans, and attended with very little loss on the part of the Jews.

Cestius having retreated as far as Gabaoh, there encamped with his army, and, during two days, employed his thoughts in what manner he should direct his future conduct. On the third day he found that the Jews were so greatly increased in numbers, that the whole face of the country was covered with them; and that should he continue any longer at Gabaoh, it must be attended with the most fatal consequences. He therefore issued orders that the army should be eased of all their encumbrances, that they might march with the greater expedition; he likewise directed that all the mules, asses, and other beasts of burden, should be killed, except only as many as were necessary to carry such weapons and machines as might afterward be wanted for their own defence.

In this situation the Roman army proceeded toward Bethoron, Cestius marching at their head. While they continued in the open country they did not receive any interruption from the Jews; but as they advanced into hollow ways and defiles, the enemy, who closely pursued, charged them in front and rear, and discharging repeated volleys of arrows and darts, prodigious numbers of them were killed. The Romans, however, with great difficulty, got at length to Bethoron, under cover of the night; upon which all the passes near that place were secured by the Jews, in order to prevent the retreat of their adversaries.

Cestius, finding in what a disagreeable manner he was surrounded, and that it would be impossible to retreat within sight of the enemy, devised a scheme to favor his escape. Having stationed four hundred of his troops on the tops of the houses, he ordered that they should act the part of sentinels, calling as loud as they were able to the watches and guards, as if the army was still in its encampment. While this plan was going forward Cestius collected his troops, with which he left Bethoron, and continued to march with them during the whole course of the night. In the morning, when the Jews found that the place had been deserted by the main body of the army during the night, they were so enraged, that they immediately attacked the four hundred Romans who had acted as sentinels, slew every one of them, and then instantly marched in pursuit of Cestius; but his troops having obtained a whole night's march on them, and proceeded with the utmost rapidity on the following day, it was not possible to overtake them. Such were the hurry and confusion in which the Romans had fled, that they dropped by the way all their slings, machines, and other instruments for battery and attack; which being seized by the pursuers, they afterward turned them to their own advantage. The Jews pursued their enemies as far as Antipatris; but finding it in vain to continue the pursuit, they carefully preserved the engines, stripped the dead, collected all the booty they could, and then returned toward Jerusalem, singing songs of triumph for so important a victory. In this contest there fell, of the Romans and their auxiliaries, three hundred and eighty cavalry, and not less than four thousand of the infantry.

Elated with this distinguished success, the Jews, on their return to Jerusalem, appointed one Joseph, the son of Gorion, a man of great eminence, together with the high-priest, as governors of the city. They likewise sent commanders into the different provinces of Judea and Galilee, in order to secure those places against the power of the Romans. Among others Joseph, or Josephus, the celebrated Jewish historian, was sent to take upon him the government of Galilee, the principal towns in which he immediately ordered to be fortified, and every necessary preparation made for attacking the enemy, should they attempt to invade that province.

In the meantime the emperor Nero, having received intelligence of the defeat of Cestius in Judea, was thrown into the utmost consternation; but he dissembled his fears, by ostentatiously asserting that it was owing to the misconduct of his general, and not to their own valor, that the Jews were indebted for victory; for he imagined that it would be derogatory to the sovereign state of the Roman empire, and to his superiority over other princes, to discover a concern at the common occurrences of life. During this contention between his fear and his pride, he industriously sought for a man qualified to assume the important task of chastizing the revolted Jews, preserving the east in tranquillity, and the allegiance of several other nations who had manifested a disposition to free themselves from the power of the Romans. On mature deliberation, Nero at length judged Vespasian to be the only man possessed of abilities adequate to the important enterprise. Vespasian was then arrived to an advanced age, and from his early years had been engaged in a continued succession of military exploits. From these considerations, together with his approved courage and fidelity, and his having sons for hostages of his loyalty, the emperor determined to appoint him to the command of his army in Syria.

In consequence of this resolution Vespasian, having received his commission from Nero, which he accompanied with the strongest professions of friendship and fidelity, commanded his son Titus to lead the fifth and tenth legions into Alexandria, while himself departed from Achaia, and, crossing the Hellespont, proceeded by land into Syria, where he assembled all the Roman forces, and the auxiliaries which the princes of the adjoining places had gathered together.

In the meantime the Jews, being transported to the most excessive degree of extravagance by the conquest they had gained over the Roman army under the command of Cestius, determined to prosecute the war with the utmost vigor. Accordingly they formed their best troops into a body, and marched against the ancient city of Ascalon, with a resolution of attempting the reduction of that place, against the inhabitants of which they had the most implacable enmity. The Jewish army was under the command of Niger of Perea, Silas, a Babylonian, and John, an Essene, who were men equally celebrated for valor, and skill in the management of war.

Ascalon was surrounded by a wall of surprising strength; but the whole garrison consisted only of a troop of cavalry and a company of foot, under the command of an officer named Anthony. The Jews being impatient to encounter the Romans, marched with the utmost expedition, intending to attack them by surprise; but Anthony, getting intelligence of their design, stationed his cavalry without the town, in order to repulse the enemy. The Roman forces were composed of veteran troops, completely armed, well disciplined, and perfectly obedient to order. The Jews had the superiority in point of numbers; but they were indifferently equipped for, and by no means expert in, the art of war, and the army consisted entirely of infantry. Anthony's troops received the first charge with great resolution: his horse broke the first ranks of the adverse army, which were immediately put to the rout: great numbers were crushed to death by their own people, and wherever they fled they were pursued by the Romans. The Jews exerted their utmost endeavors to rally their forces; but this was prevented by the Romans, who pursued the advantage they had gained till ten thousand of the enemy were slain, among whom were the two generals, John and Silas. Niger, the surviving general, with the rest of the Jews, most of whom were wounded, escaped to a town in Idumea, named Sabis.

The resolution of the Jews, however, was not abated by the terrible defeat they had sustained; but, founding their hopes of success on the recollection of former victories, they were animated to a more violent desire of revenge. They therefore collected together a much more numerous army than before, and determined to make a second attempt against Ascalon, notwithstanding their want of military skill and discipline, the fatal effects of which they had already experienced. But all their hopes were soon vanished; for being surprised by an ambush which Anthony had stationed in the way they were to pass, they were entirely routed, without being able to form themselves into the order of battle. Eight thousand Jews were slain on the spot; and the rest, with Niger, their general, put to flight. Being closely pursued by the Romans, Niger sought refuge in a castle belonging to the village of Bezedel. This castle was supposed to be impregnable; and therefore, as the only effectual means of destroying both Niger and the castle, the Romans set fire to it, after which they departed, triumphing in the idea that the leader of the Jews must inevitably perish in the flames. Niger, being sensible that this must be the case, if he continued in his station, threw himself from the top of the castle into a vault of considerable depth, where, after three days, he was found alive by his friends, who were searching for his remains, in order to give them interment. This unexpected event transported the Jews from a state of despondency into the contrary extreme of joy; and the preservation of their general, whom they considered as an instrument essentially necessary in the prosecution of the war, they attributed to divine interposition.

During these transactions, Vespasian arrived with his army at Antioch, where King Agrippa, attended by his troops, was waiting to receive him. Hence he proceeded to Ptolemais, where the inhabitants of Sepphoris, a city in Galilee, had assembled on occasion of his expected arrival. These were a well-disposed people, and being conscious of the great power of the Romans, as well as desirous of making provision for their own safety, they acknowledged Cestius Gallius as their governor, previous to the arrival of Vespasian, binding themselves to act in perfect obedience to his commands, even against their own countrymen, and at the same time declaring their allegiance to the state of Rome. They received a garrison from Cestius Gallius, and solicited Vespasian to grant them a number of cavalry and infantry sufficient for their defence, in case they should be attacked by the Jews. Vespasian readily complied with this request; for Sepphoris being the most extensive and strongest city in Galilee, he judged it expedient to keep so important a place in a proper state of defence.

The number of troops granted by Vespasian to the people of Sepphoris were, a thousand cavalry and six thousand infantry; the whole of which were placed under the command of Placidus, the tribune. After these troops had been drawn up on the great plain, the foot, for the security of the city, were quartered within the walls, and the horse were ordered into the camp. The Roman troops made daily excursions into the neighborhood, where they committed many acts of violence, and greatly incommoded Joseph (the governor of Galilee) and his friends. Not satisfied with ravaging the country, they made booty of whatever they could obtain from the towns, and treated the inhabitants with so much severity that they were under the necessity of remaining within the walls.

Matters being thus circumstanced, Joseph exerted his utmost efforts to make himself master of Sepphoris; but he found it so strongly fortified, that it appeared to be impregnable, and despairing of success, either by stratagem or force, he abandoned all further thoughts of the enterprise. This so irritated the Romans, that they subjected the people to the most terrible calamities of fire and sword, putting those who attempted resistance to instant death, reducing the rest to slavery, and making booty of all the property they could find.

In the meantime, Titus repaired to his father Vespasian, at Ptolemais, taking with him the fifth, tenth, and fifteenth legions, which were reckoned to be the best disciplined and most courageous of the Roman troops. These were followed by a troop of horse from Cesarea, with a great number of auxiliaries, both horse and foot, from other places. The whole army amounted to sixty thousand, exclusive of the train of baggage, and a great number of domestics, most of whom, having been trained to the practice of war, were but little inferior to the soldiers in courage and dexterity.

During the time Vespasian was with his son Titus at Ptolemais, he ordered every necessary measure to be pursued for the proper regulation and supply of his army. In the meantime, Placidus made an excursion into, and overran, the whole province of Judea, where he took a great number of prisoners, most of whom he put to death. These were people destitute of courage, but such as possessed a greater share of intrepidity made a courageous resistance, and secured themselves in the cities, and other places of strength, which had been fortified by Joseph. Placidus determined to direct his arms against those places where the Galileans had fled for sanctuary; and Jotapata being the strongest hold they possessed, he resolved that his first exploit should be to attempt the reduction of that place. The inhabitants of Jotapata, however, gaining intelligence of the design of Placidus, and that he was marching with all expedition against the place, sallied from the town, in order to give him battle. They attacked the Romans by surprise, and as the fate of their wives, children, and country, depended on the issue of the contest, they fought with the most astonishing bravery, and with such success, that they effectually repulsed the enemy; after which, Placidus drew off his army.

Vespasian, having resolved to make an excursion into Galilee, issued marching orders to his troops, according to the military discipline of the Romans, and departing from Ptolemais, encamped his army on the frontiers of Galilee. He might, indeed, have advanced farther, but his stopping there was designed to strike a terror into the enemy by the formidable appearance of his army. In this conjecture he was not deceived, for the news of his approach threw the Jews into the greatest consternation; and Joseph's followers, who were encamped at some distance from Sepphoris, deserted their leader, even before the enemy came in sight. Being thus abandoned, and finding that the spirits of the Jews were entirely depressed, that the majority of his people had already joined the enemy, and that the rest seemed inclined to follow their example, he retreated to Tiberias, accompanied by a few of his people whom he could trust, and who still maintained their fidelity.

The first place Vespasian laid siege to after his arrival in Galilee, was the city of Gadara, which, not having a sufficient number of inhabitants to defend it, he subdued, with very little difficulty, on the first assault. The natural enmity of the Romans against the Jews, together with a principle of revenge for their having defeated Cestius, induced them to put the inhabitants of the town promiscuously to the sword; and, not satisfied with setting fire to the conquered city, they burnt and utterly laid waste the neighboring small towns and villages, and subjected the inhabitants to slavery.

In the meantime, Joseph (the leader of the Jews in Galilee) left Tiberias, and retired to the strong city of Jotapata, which gave great encouragement to the Jews of that place. Joseph's retreat was soon made known to Vespasian by a deserter, who advised the besieging of Jotapata, observing that, if Joseph could be taken, the war must inevitably terminate to the disadvantage of the Jews. Pleased with this information, and hoping to get into his power the person whom he considered as the most formidable of his enemies, Vespasian despatched Placidus and Æbutius (the latter of whom was one of the most celebrated men of the army for bravery and military skill) with a thousand cavalry, commanding them to environ the city with the greatest expedition, and, if possible, prevent the escape of Joseph.

The next morning Vespasian issued orders for his whole army to march, and, in the afternoon of the same day, encamped about seven furlongs to the north of the city. The Romans being greatly fatigued by their march, did not attempt anything till the next morning, when they began to assault the city, which was defended with great bravery. Vespasian ordered the bowmen and slingers to compel the Jews to desert the walls, while himself, with a body of infantry, began an assault from an eminence convenient for battering the place; but Joseph, at the head of the Jews, made so furious an attack on the enemy, that he compelled them to retreat.

The next day the besiegers renewed the assault, and in this action both parties displayed the most distinguished instances of valor. The Jews were encouraged by the undaunted firmness and resolution with which, contrary to the most sanguine expectations, they had sustained the first assault; and the shame of having been repulsed invigorated the spirits of the Romans. Notwithstanding the great danger and difficulty of the enterprise, the latter continued to pursue their attacks with the utmost vigor, while the Jews, regardless of their great numbers and strength, made frequent sallies against them with considerable advantage.

The city of Jotapata was situated on a rock, and utterly inaccessible, except on the north, where a part of it stood on the brow of a mountain. This quarter Joseph caused to be strongly fortified, thereby precluding the enemy from taking advantage of another mountain by which it was overlooked, and which, with the other mountains adjoining, so entirely enclosed the place, that it could only be seen at a very small distance.

After several days' fruitless attempts, Vespasian, finding the place so admirably situated for defence, and that he had to contend with an intrepid and determined enemy, assembled a council of his principal officers, in order to debate on the most proper means of obtaining a victory. The issue of this deliberation was, that a large terrace should be raised on that side of the city which appeared to be the least capable of resistance. Accordingly, the whole army was employed in the work, which they pursued with surprising rapidity, and the utmost efforts of the Jews to oppose them proved ineffectual.

In the meantime Joseph ordered the wall of the city to be raised in proportion to the advancement of the enemy's works. The Jews at first declined the undertaking, urging the impossibility of pursuing their business, as they should be continually exposed to the enemy. To remove these fears, Joseph suggested the following invention, as a defence against fire, stones, and other weapons. He caused large stakes to be fixed in the ground, and raw hides of beasts to be stretched upon them, the yielding quality of which would prevent any material effect from the lances and stones, and at the same time their moisture would damp the fire of the enemy. The Jews, thinking themselves secure through Joseph's contrivance, continued indefatigably industrious in the work both night and day; and they soon erected a wall several cubits high, on which were formed towers and strong embattlements.

Vespasian now relinquished all hopes of subduing the place by storm; he therefore blocked it up, flattering himself with the expectation, that by cutting off all communication, the consequent necessities of the people would perform the business of the sword, or at least render them incapable of making any advantageous resistance. There was an abundant supply of corn and all other necessaries in the town, excepting water, which latter article they only received from the clouds, there being neither spring nor fountain within the walls of the city. The prospect of a scarcity of water induced Joseph, who was determined not to abandon himself to despair, to limit each man to a daily allowance, in consequence of which a universal discontent prevailed among the people. This circumstance could not be concealed from the Romans, who, from an adjacent hill, observed the people assembled to receive their respective portions, and were otherwise informed of the general discontent which had taken place on that occasion. Vespasian was in continual expectation of making himself master of the town; but Joseph, to convince him that he was not likely to succeed from their distress for want of water, hit upon the following stratagem: he caused great numbers of wet cloths to be hung upon the battlements, which were no sooner observed by the Romans, than they concluded a scarcity of water could not prevail in the town, as in that case they would hardly make use of such an article in so profuse a manner. In consequence of this, Vespasian no longer entertaining hopes that the enemy would surrender through want of the necessaries of life, had again recourse to arms. This proved a circumstance highly agreeable to the Jews, who, being reduced to the greatest distress, entertained the most terrible apprehensions of falling miserable sacrifices to famine, to which they infinitely preferred a glorious death in in the field.

In the midst of this distress, Joseph recollected that on the west side of the city there was a hollow or gutter in a place so little frequented, that it was not likely to have been observed by the enemy. In consequence of this, he sent messengers to the Jews without the city, requesting them to cause water and other necessaries to be conveyed to him through this passage and, as a proper security to the messengers, he ordered them to be covered with hides of beasts, and to go on their hands and feet, that, in case of being observed by the watch, they might be mistaken for dogs and other animals.

This scheme had for some time the desired effect, and an intercourse was maintained between those without the city and those within, to the great satisfaction of the latter. But at length the Romans discovered the project, which they effectually destroyed by closely blocking up the passage, and thereby cutting off all communication whatever.

Joseph now perceived that it would be fruitless to attempt a longer defence of the city, and therefore he joined with several of the principal men in suggesting the means of escape. The people, suspecting on what subject they were met to deliberate, repaired in great multitudes to Joseph, earnestly supplicating, that as he was the only man from whom they could expect relief, he would not desert them in their then extremity; observing, that while he was secure they could not despair of success, and declaring that they could not die more honorably than while acting in obedience to his commands. They told him that if it should prove their misfortune to fall into the power of the Romans, he would acquire the immortal fame of having equally scorned to fly from the enemy, or desert the people under his protection: that by leaving them he would manifest a conduct similar to that of a man taking upon him the command of a ship in temperate weather, and abandoning it in a storm; they likewise added, that after losing the only man in whom they could place a confidence of success, they could no longer cherish the hope of relieving their country.

Joseph, who was unwilling to have it believed that his intention was engrossed on the means of providing for his own safety, told them, that if they were compelled to surrender, his remaining with them could not possibly operate in their favor; whereas, if he obtained his liberty, he might be able to draw an army out of Galilee sufficiently early to raise the siege; and that his continuing in the city would be productive of unfortunate instead of happy consequences, since the expectation of making him a prisoner would induce the Romans to continue a vigorous prosecution of the siege, which they might probably decline if he could effect an escape.

But these arguments, instead of reconciling the multitude, rendered them still more importunate, and with the most bitter lamentations they urgently supplicated that he would still continue his protection to them. Impressed with tenderness and gratitude toward the people, Joseph considered that if he remained in the town, they would attribute his compliance with their request to the influence they had over him, and that if he persisted in a refusal, they might probably detain him by force; and therefore resolved to share the common danger, he addressed them as follows: "My dear friends and faithful countrymen, the period is arrived when we are required to exert our utmost bravery, since in that alone we can place our hopes of safety. If we lose our lives our reward will be a large share of honor, and our names will be endeared to the latest posterity."

This address was received with universal satisfaction by the people, immediately after which Joseph, at the head of the most courageous of the Jews, assaulted the enemy's guards, whom he compelled to desert their trenches and retreat to the camp.

Joseph and his army now defended themselves against the power of the Romans with the most astonishing power and resolution. This they continued to do for the space of forty days, when a deserter represented to Vespasian the state of the town, informing him that through the loss of men, and the hard duty which the survivors were obliged incessantly to perform, the garrison was so reduced that it must necessarily surrender to a vigorous attack, and more especially if advantage was to be taken of a favorable opportunity for making the assault by surprise. He likewise strongly advised the Roman general to attempt the enterprise before daylight, when the Jews would not be apprehensive of danger, and the vigilance of the guard abated by fatigue and an inclination to sleep.

Vespasian, being sensible that the Jews possessed a remarkable fidelity to each other, which the most excruciating torments could not force them to violate, was unwilling at first to put any confidence in what the deserter had related. He had been witness to a recent instance of the amazing constancy and resolution of the Jews, in the case of one of Joseph's people, who being made a prisoner, and interrogated respecting the state of the city, refused to divulge a single circumstance, and persisted in that resolution during the most excessive torments, and while he was undergoing the sentence of crucifixion. Considering, however, that the information of the deserter might possibly be founded in truth, and that no ill consequences were likely to ensue from his appearing to believe that to be the case, Vespasian ordered the man to be secured, and every necessary preparation to be made for the attack.

The Roman army began a silent march at an appointed hour of the night, which had been previously agreed upon according to the plan laid down by the deserter. On their arrival at the walls of the town, finding the sentinels asleep, they immediately despatched them, and without the least molestation entered the city, followed by a large body of troops under the command of the tribune Placidus. Notwithstanding it was open day before the Romans gained possession of the fort and made themselves masters of the town, the Jewish army was so exhausted and fatigued by incessant labor and watching, that they did not entertain the least idea of their danger till the enemy had actually gained their point; and even those who were awake were almost equal strangers to the misfortune, as they could not clearly distinguish objects on account of a thick fog which then prevailed, and continued till the whole Roman army had gained admittance into the city.

The Romans, recollecting the sufferings they had undergone during the course of the siege, laid aside every sentiment of humanity and compassion toward the besieged. They threw many of the Jews from the top of the fort, who were instantly killed by the fall, and others, who had courage enough to make resistance, were either pressed to death by the immense crowds of the enemy, or forced down precipices, and killed by the ruins which fell from above. Such of the guards as first observed the city to be taken fled to a turret on the walls, where they were attacked by the enemy, against whom, for some time, they made a resolute defence. Being oppressed by numbers, they offered to capitulate; but their proposals were rejected and the whole put to the sword. Every Jew who was met by the Romans on that day was put to instant death; and during some following days they carefully searched for such as had concealed themselves in private places, all of whom, except women and children, they destroyed. Having thus obtained a complete victory, Vespasian, after withdrawing his forces from the town, ordered the fortress to be burnt, which was accordingly done, and the whole city laid in ruins.

The Romans, induced partly by personal enmity, and partly by an officious zeal to ingratiate themselves into the favor of their general, assiduously employed themselves in searching every part of the adjoining country, in order to find out the leader of the Jews. It was Joseph's fortune to escape through the midst of his enemies, and to find a deep pit, having a passage leading to a spacious cavern, in which he discovered forty distinguished Jews who had there taken sanctuary, and were supplied with sufficient necessaries to last them several days. The enemy being in possession of the whole adjacent country, Joseph judged it unsafe to venture abroad by day, and therefore he left his retreat only by night, with a view of discovering if there remained any probability of effecting an escape; but finding the enemy exceedingly vigilant, he repeatedly returned to the cavern despairing of success. On the third day he was betrayed by a woman; in consequence of which, Vespasian despatched Paulinus and Gallanicus, two tribunes, to the place where he was secreted, authorizing them to assure Joseph, that, on condition of leaving his retreat, he should meet with a kind and honorable reception. Joseph, conscious that the injuries the Romans had sustained at his hands entitled him to punishment rather than reward, thought it unsafe to rely on Vespasian's word of honor, and therefore he declined the proposal. In consequence of this, Vespasian sent another tribune, named Nicanor, who had long been intimately acquainted with Joseph, and was in fact his most sincere friend. Nicanor forcibly expostulated with him on the impropriety of refusing to comply with Vespasian's request; he represented to him the generosity and benevolence of the Romans toward those they conquered: that, so far from Vespasian's entertaining an enmity against him, he highly esteemed him as being a man of singular intrepidity, and possessed of other eminent virtues; and that the Roman general must indisputably have favorable views, since he condescended to propose terms to a man who was already subject to his power. "Can you imagine," said Nicanor, "that Vespasian would employ a friend in an office of treachery, or that I would accept from him so dishonorable a commission?"

Notwithstanding these remonstrances, Joseph, for some time, declined a compliance; but at length, from the very forcible arguments and advice of Nicanor, he agreed to submit. In consequence of this, his companions instantly drew their swords, and threatened, if he surrendered, to put him to death. Joseph, being apprehensive that they might carry their designs into execution, was desirous of avoiding so horrid an intention; to effect which he addressed them as follows: "Why, my good friends, do you suffer yourselves to be so far transported by the violence of passion as to cherish the idea of separating the soul and body, which are so intimately united by nature? To fall by the hand of a victor in a war maintained according to the laws of arms, is without dispute a glorious fate. I should make no greater difficulty of taking away my own life than of requesting a Roman to perform that office; but if the Romans are inclined to show mercy to an enemy, will reason justify that enemy in having no mercy on himself? No death can be more honorable than that of the man who yields his life to the superior power of an adversary that means to deprive him of the inestimable blessing of liberty. But the Romans wish not our deaths; and all animosity should now cease, for the cause of our contention is at an end. The man who rejects life when his duty requires him to preserve it, is as pusillanimous as he who, in opposition to the dictates of honor, trembles to meet his fate. Is it not from the fear of death alone that we hesitate to yield to the Romans? Shall we precipitate ourselves into certain destruction for the purpose of avoiding a threatened danger, which probably may not arrive? If you conceive that we ought to die to avoid slavery, I must request you to recollect that we enjoy not liberty in the miserable situation to which we are now reduced. If you suppose him to be a brave man who deprives himself of life, I would ask what opinion you would form of the commander of a vessel who during a calm should sink his ship from an apprehension that a tempest might arise? The desire of preserving life is a principle implanted in the whole animal creation; and therefore to deprive ourselves of existence is to violate the order of nature, and offer a sacrilegious insult to God. If we desire to live, may we not indulge that desire, since we have given exemplary proofs of our courage and virtue? But if we are resolved to die, let us fall by the hands of our conquerors. We shall have no cause for regret if the Romans prove treacherous; but, on the contrary, we shall resign our lives with pleasure, since we shall enjoy the satisfaction of knowing that the perfidy of the enemy must necessarily diminish the glory of their victory, and render them infamous to the latest posterity."

Joseph imagined that these arguments would have induced the Jews to relinquish the determination of putting an end to his life; but in this he found himself mistaken, for instead of appeasing, his address provoked them to the utmost extravagance of rage; they approached him with their swords drawn, upbraided him in the most severe terms as being of a contemptibly irresolute disposition, and threatened him with instant death. Thus situated, Joseph addressed his companions in the most soothing manner, which seldom fails to gain respect from those who have been accustomed to obey; he called one by his name, took another by the hand, and endeavored to engage the attention of the rest by arguments and such other means as he conceived to be best adapted for obtaining the end he had in view. Thus, by a singular address in applying to the various humors and dispositions of his companions, Joseph averted the danger that threatened him. The rage of the Jews subsided, their esteem and veneration for their general revived, and they freely gave him his liberty to act as he should think proper. Being thus relieved from the extremity to which he was reduced by the Romans on one hand, and by his own countrymen on the other, Joseph surrendered himself to Nicanor, who immediately conducted him to Vespasian.

The desire of seeing Joseph appear before the Roman general caused prodigious numbers of people to assemble, some of whom rejoiced to see that he was alive, while others vented menaces and the most bitter execrations against him. Those who were sufficiently near to observe his person, recollected the many extraordinary incidents of his life, and reflecting on his then situation, were greatly astonished on the comparison. Notwithstanding the inveteracy which the Roman general had entertained against Joseph, they tenderly compassionated him in his captivity; but Titus was most particularly affected, for on account of his advanced age, and the unconquerable dignity of his mind in the most extreme dangers and distresses, he entertained a great veneration for Joseph, whose former elevated station and great exploits, together with the humiliating condition to which he was now reduced, he most seriously considered, and then proceeded to make some reflections on the chance of war, and the mutability of human affairs. Those who heard Titus adopted his sentiments; and he greatly contributed toward the preservation of Joseph, by influencing Vespasian in his favor.

Vespasian intimated his intentions of sending Joseph to Nero, and ordered him to be kept a close prisoner. In consequence of this Joseph requested to have an audience with Vespasian, which being granted, he was conducted to the general's apartment, whence every person was dismissed, except Titus and two of his friends. In the presence of these Joseph, addressing himself to Vespasian, spoke as follows: "You see me here, sir, your prisoner, and perhaps you consider me in no other character; but believe me, I am no less than a messenger sent by Providence to impart to you a matter of the highest importance.* Had I not been charged with this commission, I should have acted consistent with the character of a Jewish general, and have died rather than have submitted to be made a prisoner. It is unnecessary to send me to Nero, since Vespasian is so near succeeding to the empire, which, upon his decease,

* While Joseph was with his companions in the cavern, he had a most remarkable vision, in which were communicated to him the success and grandeur which the Romans should experience, and the miseries which should attend the Jews. It was likewise revealed to him that Vespasian should become emperor, and that himself should be the messenger of that intelligence; and this it was that made him so strenuous in requesting his companions to spare his life.

will devolve on his son Titus. Let me be kept a prisoner, and guarded with unremitting circumspection; I only request to remain the prisoner of Vespasian, who, by the right of conquest, is become the master of my life and liberty, and will, in a short time, be advanced to the sovereignty of the Roman empire. If it shall hereafter appear that I have made use of any artifice to induce you to repose confidence in an impostor, you will perform an act of justice in subjecting me to the most severe and exemplary punishment."

At first Vespasian considered Joseph's address as a mere fiction, contrived for the purpose of obtaining his favor; but experiencing certain indications, and finding them exactly correspond with what Joseph had related, his doubts gradually subsided, and he gave full confidence to the prediction. One of the persons who was permitted to be present at the interview, observed to Joseph, that since he pretended to a knowledge of future events, he requested to be informed by what means it happened that he remained ignorant of the destruction of Jotapata, and of his own captivity. To which Joseph replied, he had predicted to the inhabitants that the town would be conquered, and himself made a prisoner by the enemy. In consequence of this reply, Vespasian ordered a secret inquiry to be made among the Jewish prisoners relative to the truth of what he had asserted; this was accordingly done, and the Jews confirming every particular related by Joseph, the general was induced to judge more favorably of what he had foretold respecting himself.

Joseph continued to be guarded with the greatest circumspection; but the irksomeness of confinement was in a great degree mitigated, by his being allowed every accommodation and convenience, together with the particular respect and kindness which he received from Titus.

After the conquest of Jotapata, and the total destruction of that city, Vespasian repaired with his army to Cesarea, where he took up his winter quarters; but that he might not overburden the inhabitants of that city, he sent the fifth and tenth legions to Scythopolis.

Early in the ensuing spring Vespasian renewed his operations against the Jews. He sent his son Titus at the head of a considerable army into one part of Judea, while himself went into another; and between them they reduced the most principal places in that country, the inhabitants of some of which quietly submitted; but others, after holding out with the utmost resistance in their power, were conquered, and great numbers put to the sword.

After these conquests Vespasian returned to Cesarea, where he formed the resolution of laying siege to Jerusalem; but while he was making the necessary preparations for this purpose, he received an account of the death of Nero, after a reign of thirteen years and eight days. In consequence of this intelligence, Vespasian suspended his preparations for the expedition toward Jerusalem. Finding that Galba was destined to succeed to the empire, he thought it would not be a prudent measure to take so important a step without express orders for so doing. He therefore despatched his son Titus to wait on Galba, at once to congratulate him on the succession to the empire, and to take his directions how to act in the then emergency of affairs. King Agrippa (who was at this time in Cesarea) being desirous to embark with Titus on this interesting occasion, they set sail in the same vessel; but while they were on their voyage (which was exceedingly tedious owing to the contrariety of the wind) and near to Achaia, they received intelligence that Galba was slain, after having governed only seven months, and that Otho succeeded him, who reigned only three months. This change in affairs did not prevent Agrippa from prosecuting his journey from Achaia to Rome; but Titus sailed thence to Syria, and proceeded with all expedition to his father at Cesarea.

A short time after the return of Titus to Cesarea, Vespasian received intelligence that a civil war had broke out in Rome, occasioned by Vitellius, a daring and enterprising man, who, on the death of Otho, had, with the assistance of a great body of German soldiers, possessed himself of the sovereignty of the empire. Vespasian was a man who had a just opinion of the respect that should be shown to superiors, and was as well calculated to obey as to command; but notwithstanding this, he was greatly chagrined to acknowledge the supreme authority of him who rather seized the empire as a plunder, than became possessed of it as an honor. In a word, this astonishing change in the public affairs affected him to such a degree, that he could no longer entertain any idea of prosecuting foreign wars, when his country at home was distracted by the most disagreeable circumstances. Yet, though his indignation on the one hand urged him to a speedy revenge, yet on the other he was deterred from putting his design into execution, by the consideration of the difficulties and hazards that would attend so long a journey in the midst of winter, beside the probability of many unexpected incidents which might happen before he could arrive in Italy.

While Vespasian was debating this subject in his mind, the officers of his army (all of whom were thoroughly acquainted with the revolutions which had taken place in Rome) associated together, and discoursed with the utmost freedom on the affairs of the state and government. Among other thing they exclaimed most violently against the German soldiers, who were the protectors of Vitellius, ridiculing them as a band of dissolute and effeminate creatures, who would be afraid to face even the usual terrors of war. "What," said they, "shall people like these dispose of armies, or rather sell them to the highest bidder? Is it possible for them to imagine that we who have undergone all the fatigue attending excessive labor, till we are grown old in the use of arms,—that we will ever submit to be governed by an emperor chosen by them, when we have a prince of our own who is much more worthy of the government? Besides, if we omit the present opportunity of testifying our gratitude for the numerous obligations we owe to the generosity of Vespasian, it is not very probable that a similar prospect of paying him the proper compliment will ever again offer. Exclusive of these considerations, the personal merit of Vespasian hath as much better qualified him for the dignity of emperor, than that of Vitellius, as our merits have qualified us for the choice, beyond that of those who have elected him. With regard to Vespasian, there can be no debate or competition; for the senate and people of Rome are entirely in his interest; nor would they even listen to an insinuation of the licentiousness and debauches of Vitellius being put in competition with the modest and temperate behavior of Vespasian; for this, in fact, would be to prefer an abandoned tyrant to an humane prince. After all we have said, let it be considered what a ridiculous figure we should make, and how egregiously we should be duped; we, who of all men living, have the greatest obligations to Vespasian, if the senate themselves should elect him emperor, and thus take out of our hands the merit of so distinguished an action, while we are idly debating on the method of proceeding in such an exigency."

To this purpose was the conversation of the officers under Vespasian. Their first meetings were held in a secret manner; but having publicly declared their sentiments to the soldiers, all of whom agreed with them in opinion, they resolved to make choice of Vespasian as emperor, and entreated him to take under his protection an empire that was shaken to its foundation. Vespasian had for a long time been the support of the empire; but he was so far from being ambitious of the dignity of emperor, that he absolutely declined it, declaring that he chose rather to continue in that line of life to which he had been accustomed, than accept of the pomp and dignity to which he was invited. But the more desirous Vespasian was to avoid this compliment, the more earnestly did the people press his acceptance of it; till at length, on his repeated refusal, they advanced to him with drawn swords, and threatened his destruction if he any longer refused accepting an honor of which he was so deserving. Still, however, for a time, he refused; but at length yielded to an importunity that was not to be resisted.

The government of the empire was no sooner accepted by Vespasian, than Mucianus and the other officers joined with the whole body of the army in requesting that he would immediately march his forces against Vitellius; but Vespasian thought it would be most prudent first to bring over to his interest the people of Alexandria, by means of which he should obtain such advantages as would not only secure himself, but, in all probability, crown his enterprise with success. Egypt, on account of the prodigious quantity of corn which it produced, was deemed one of the most important branches of the empire: wherefore Vespasian was of opinion, that if he could but possess himself of that country, the people of Rome might be induced rather to expel Vitellius, than run the risk of starving if they refused so to do, which would be the natural consequence if they could not obtain proper assistance from Egypt.

These observations being highly approved of by the officers, Vespasian immediately wrote a letter to Tiberius, the then governor of Alexandria, informing him that, at the importunity of his soldiers, he had been prevailed on to take the government into his own hands, and that he thought he could not act more prudently than to request the favor of his advice and assistance in the office of administration. Tiberius had no sooner read this letter than, with the utmost freedom and goodwill, he took an oath of fidelity to Vespasian, and caused the like to be done by all the inhabitants of the city. This oath was taken with every possible demonstration of joy and esteem; for they were previously informed of the good intentions of the new emperor, and confided in his virtue and honor. Tiberius made a generous use of the power intrusted to him for the public welfare, and immediately began to make the necessary preparations for receiving Vespasian.

Intelligence of Vespasian's being advanced to the dignity of ruling the empire was propagated with the utmost speed through every part of the eastern country; and wherever this news arrived, it was so grateful to the people, that the inhabitants of the several cities kept a holyday on the occasion, and offered up their prayers that the reign of Vespasian might be long and happy. Several ambassadors from Syria and other provinces, waited on Vespasian, with congratulatory addresses on his being appointed to the government of the empire. Among the rest was Mucianus, the governor of Syria, who gave him the utmost assurance of the loyalty and affection of the people in general, which they had testified by cheerfully taking the oath of fidelity to his person and authority.

These favorable circumstances struck a deep impression on the mind of Vespasian, who could not help seriously reflecting that they had less the appearance of being the work of chance than the immediate effect of a disposing Providence; and he thought it appeared that he had not been raised to so distinguished an elevation by the power of fortune, but by divine interposition. Reflecting on this subject there occurred to his mind several prophetical hints which had happened in the course of his life, all tending to the same end. Among the rest he could not but recur to the circumstance of Joseph having, while he remained a prisoner, and during the life of Nero, called him by the title of emperor. This singular prediction had great influence on the mind of Vespasian, and the greater, because the party was still a prisoner: wherefore sending for Mucianus and others of his officers, he spoke to them of the singular courage and bravery of Joseph, and how gallantly he had behaved himself at the siege of Jotapata. After this he mentioned several other particulars respecting him, and at length adverted to the subject of his predictions: "Those," said he, "I at first imagined to be nothing more than contrivances for his own preservation; but the event has proved that they were actually the result of divine providence; wherefore, my friends, it would be an indelible disgrace in me longer to detain, in the abject condition of a prisoner, the person who first declared to me the news of my advancement."

Having said this Vespasian instantly sent for Joseph, and, in the presence of the company, restored him to his liberty. From this instance of gratitude in Vespasian, his officers formed the most favorable idea of their own situation, thinking that they, who were his faithful friends and servants, should experience every indulgence under so kind a master. During this scene Titus was present, who, in a most submissive manner, hinted to his father, that the single granting of liberty to Joseph was leaving the generosity of his plan incomplete: that his chains ought not only to be taken off, but broken, for if that was not done the dishonor of his imprisonment would remain with him, though his person was restored to liberty. Vespasian, coinciding in this opinion, gave immediate orders that his chains should be cut to pieces; which circumstance not only gave the most extensive freedom to Joseph, but so raised his reputation as a prophet, that every person was disposed to give credit to any of his future predictions in as full and ample a manner as they had done to what he had already foretold.

A general council was now held to consider the most proper measures to be taken in the then exigency of affairs, in which it was resolved that Titus should prosecute the war against the Jews, and that Vespasian should go to Alexandria, and use such methods as he thought advisable for suppressing the disturbances at Rome, occasioned by the usurper Vitellius.

On Vespasian's arrival at Alexandria he was received by the people of that city with the utmost demonstrations of joy; and measures were instantly concerted for reducing Vitellius, and quieting the disturbances which then took place at Rome. For this purpose he despatched a considerable army of cavalry and foot, under the command of Mucianus, through Cappadocia and Phrygia, into Italy, being afraid to trust his troops by sea during the winter season.

In the meantime Antonius Primus (an excellent soldier who had been banished by Nero, but restored by Galba, a friend to Vespasian) marched at the head of the third legion to give battle to Vitellius, the latter of whom being informed of his intentions, sent a strong army under the command of Cæcinna to oppose him. As soon as Cæcinna met Antonius (which was on the confines of Italy), he was struck with terror at the numbers, order, and discipline of his army. He was totally at a loss how to act: he did not dare to risk a battle, nor could he think of running away from them; and therefore he chose rather to be considered as a deserter than a coward. Having assembled his centurions, tribunes, and all the rest of his officers, he exerted the utmost power of his oratory in a declaration of the different degrees of merit between Vespasian and Vitellius. The one he extolled to the highest degree, and depreciated the character of the other; and all this with a fixed design to prevail on the soldiers of Vitellius to take part with Vespasian. The speech he made on this occasion was to this effect: "Vitellius possesses nothing more than the name of an emperor; whereas the claim of Vespasian is not only founded on the strictest equity, but his person is stamped with the indubitable marks of the imperial character. Besides, the troops of Vespasian are so numerous and well-chosen, that it will be in vain for us to think of entering into a contest with him. This being the case, had we not better now act the same part, as of our own choice and free will, that we shall otherwise be compelled to do through the force of mere necessity? While I say this, I am certain that Vespasian is able to carry his design into execution without our aid or assistance; but Vitellius, so far from being able to protect his adherents, is by no means in a condition to defend himself."

These arguments were urged with so much zeal that Cæcinna obtained the point at which he labored, and prevailed on his troops to go over to Antonius. But on the following night Cæcinna's people, partly repenting of what they had done, and partly in fear of the consequence, in case Vitellius should prove successful in the contest, advanced in a rage, with drawn swords, to despatch Cæcinna, which they would have certainly done, had not the tribunes strongly interposed in his favor. Hereupon they desisted from taking away his life, but insisted that, as a traitor, he should be immediately sent in chains to Vitellius.

As soon as Antonius was informed of this event, he immediately went with a party to attack them as deserters. For some time they made a faint resistance, but receded on the first violent attack, and fled toward Cremona. Antonius interposing with his cavalry between the fugitives and the town, and entirely surrounding them, destroyed great numbers on the spot, and, pursuing the rest, put the whole to the sword, except their general Cæcinna, whom he set at liberty, and despatched to Vespasian with an account of the victory.

After this defeat, Antonius marched with his army toward Rome; information of which being made known to Sabinus, the brother of Vespasian, he that same night assembled the city guards, and possessed himself of the capital. On the following day great numbers of persons of distinguished rank joined his party, among whom was Domitian, brother to Titus, and younger son to Vespasian.

Vitellius paid little regard to the proceedings of Antonius, the principal view of his resentment being directed toward Sabinus, and the other persons who had joined with him in the revolt; and being by nature of a savage and ferocious disposition, but particularly so to those of distinguished rank, he despatched a body of his own troops to attack them. In this enterprise the most singular instances of bravery were displayed on both sides; but in the end, the troops of Vitellius became victorious. Domitian, and other Romans of the first rank, made their escape; but the greater part of the people were destroyed, and the victors, after plundering the temple of Janus, burnt it to the ground. With respect to Sabinus, he was made prisoner, and conducted to Vitellius, who ordered him immediately to be put to death.

The next day Antonius arrived with his army, when a desperate battle ensued between him and the troops of Vitellius. The forces of Antonius being divided, they engaged in three different parts of the city at the same time, and the contest was continued for that day without any material advantage on either side. Early the next morning Mucianus with his army entered Rome, and joining that of Antonius, the attack was renewed with the utmost vigor, and the troops of Vitellius being defeated, were all put to the sword.

Thus was this mighty city taken by her own natural subjects; and as it was fatal to many thousands, so likewise was it to Vitellius himself, whom the soldiers dragged out of his palace, and (without hearkening to any entreaties, binding his hands behind him, and throwing a halter about his neck) drew him into the public Forum, through the main street, called Via Sacra. As he went along, they used the most opprobrious language, and treated him with the greatest indignity they could project; they pelted him with dung and filth, and held the point of a sword under his chin to prevent his concealing his face. At length they conducted him to the common place of execution, where, with many blows and wounds, they despatched him in the 56th year of his age, and after a short reign of only eight months. Having wreaked their vengeance thus, they dragged his body from the spot where they had killed him, and threw it into the river Tiber; after which, they not only made his brother, and only son, but likewise all whom they met with of his party, victims to their resentment.

As soon as the fury of this carnage was over, the Roman senate assembled, and, with unanimous consent, not only declared Vespasian emperor, but conferred the title of Cæsar upon his two sons, Titus and Domitian; nominating the former to be consul with his father for the ensuing year, and the latter to be prætor with consular power. They likewise rewarded Mucianus and Antonius, with several others, for contributing to this happy revolution; and despatched couriers to Vespasian, at Alexandria, to tender him their homage and obedience, and to desire his speedy return to Rome. On this occasion the people made two festivals, one for their deliverance from the tyranny of Vitellius, and the other for the happy advancement of Vespasian to the government of the empire. But it is now time to return to Titus.

Before Vespasian left Judea, he, by the advice of his council, committed the management of the war against the Jews to his son Titus, well knowing his extraordinary valor and skill for such an undertaking. Himself had reduced most of the country, except Jerusalem; but Jerusalem was the capital city, fortified with three walls on every side, except where it was fenced with deep valleys, having the castle of Antonia, the temple, the palace of Acra, the towers on Mount Sion, and several other places almost impregnable; so that great consultation, and a preparation of many materials, were required to carry on such a siege.

The inhabitants of Jerusalem had been for a long time in the most distressed situation, owing to the several parties and factions which had taken possession of different parts of the city, and were not only murdering each other, but, in their rage and madness, destroyed such a quantity of provisions as might have served the city for several months.

Jerusalem was involved in these sad circumstances, when Titus, with a powerful army, and all kinds of warlike engines, approached, and sat down within six or seven furlongs of the city, a little before the feast of the passover. By these means he shut up an infinite number of people who had come from all parts to that solemnity, which, in a short time, occasioned a great consumption of their provisions.

On the first appearance of so formidable an army, the several factions unanimously agreed to oppose it; in consequence of which, they sallied out with great resolution and fury, and putting the Romans to disorder, obliged them to abandon their camp, and fly to the mountains. But the Jews were at last repulsed, and driven into the city by Titus, who particularly distinguished himself as a courageous and expert warrior.

When Titus had properly placed his engines (which was not done without great opposition), he battered the outward walls, and, on the third day of May, making a breach, entered and took possession of the northern quarter of the city, as far as the castle of Antonia, and the valley of Kedron. Having done this, he gave the besieged all possible assurances of pardon and civil treatment if they would but submit: but they, judging his order to be the effect of cowardice, refused to accept of any terms or conditions whatever.

On the fifth day after this Titus broke through the second wall, and though the besieged made several sallies, and drove him out again, yet he recovered the place, and possessed himself of the lower city.

Though Titus was now thoroughly convinced, in his own mind, that he could by

The Forum, Rome.

force of arms easily make a complete conquest of the city, yet he was willing, if possible, to effect it without any further loss of blood. He therefore, in the first place, sent a messenger to the Jews, requesting that they would have so much regard to their own interest as to surrender a place, of which he could, at any time, make himself master. But this not answering his wishes, he despatched Joseph to them, thinking that when they were addressed by their own countryman, and in a language familiar to them, it might probably be attended with success. In conformity to the directions given by Titus, Joseph first walked through several parts of the city, after which, stopping on an elevated spot, within the hearing of the enemy, he addressed them in words to this effect: " Countrymen and friends, it is my earnest request, that if you have any esteem for your lives and liberties, any veneration for your city, your temple, and your country, you will, on the present occasion, give a proper testimony of your sensibility, and learn, even from strangers and enemies, to have a proper regard to your own interest. You may have observed, that the Romans entertain so great a veneration for sacred things, that they make a scruple of seizing anything that is holy; and this they do, though they never presumed to have any share, concern, or interest, in your communion; whereas you, on the contrary, instead of protecting the religion in which you were educated, seem conspiring to complete its destruction. Are you not by this time convinced that, your fortresses being beaten down, and a great part of your walls left in a defenceless condition, your weakness is sufficiently exposed, and that it is an absolute impossibility to support yourselves much longer against so formidable a power as that with which you have to contend? It is true, that engaging in the cause of liberty is a glorious task, provided it be undertaken before that liberty is likely to be lost or forfeited; but when the latter is the case, it is idle to think of attempting to throw it off, and all further endeavors will rather tend to produce a disgraceful death, than give the opportunity of preserving a life of honorable freedom. A state of bondage to a master whom a man of honor would blush to acknowledge his superior, is indeed a scandalous state; but submission to a people whose authority is acknowledged by the whole world, is by no means disgraceful. Conscious of this truth, your ancestors, who were more wise and powerful than you are, were induced to pay allegiance to the Romans, which they certainly would not have done had they not been fully convinced that it was the will of Providence they should submit. But wherefore would you any longer continue a contest that is, in effect, already decided? For if your walls were yet perfect, and the siege actually raised, so long as the Romans resolved not to quit the place, you must soon be starved into submission. Famine has already made great havoc among you, and the calamity will daily increase, as there is no guarding against the consequence of the severities of hunger. It will therefore well become you to recollect yourselves, and take advice while it may be serviceable to you. The Romans are of a liberal disposition, and will be ready to forgive all that is past, if you do not continue to exasperate them till forgiveness would look like weakness. But if you resist till they storm the city, instead of mercy, you will fatally experience their resentment from the point of the sword."

These friendly admonitions made not the least impression on the perverse Jews, who, instead of paying attention to them, treated Joseph with the utmost contempt, and, had he not been properly guarded, would have put him to death. In consequence of this, Titus resolved to proceed with the utmost severity against them. Accordingly, when any fled from the city (which great numbers were constrained to do on account of the want of provisions), they were no sooner taken than Titus ordered them to be scourged and crucified. This, however, he did not do from motives of cruelty, but with a view of striking terror in the multitude, in hopes that they would the sooner give up all opposition, and surrender themselves to the superior force of his arms.

Finding every method ineffectual to bring the Jews to submission, Titus, on the 12th of May, began four mounts for his battering-rams, two near the castle of Antonia, where he was in hopes of taking the temple, and two near the monument of John, the high-priest, where he supposed he might, without much difficulty, break into the upper city. But in two bold sallies, the besieged ruined and destroyed the mounts, and, having burnt several battering-rams, and other engines, pressed forward, and broke into the very camp of the Romans. At length they were repulsed by Titus, who (in a council of war) resolved to surround the whole city with a wall, or intrenchment, to hinder the flight of the besieged, and to prevent all relief from coming into the city, thereby strictly verifying the words of our blessed Redeemer: "The days shall come upon thee, that thine enemies shall cast a trench about thee and compass thee around, and keep thee in on every side." Luke xix. 43.

This work was executed with such astonishing celerity, that the whole was finished within the space of a few days. But it made no impression on the besieged, notwithstanding the famine began to rage with the most horrid violence, and such a mortality ensued, that within the space of three months no less than 115,080 carcasses of the poorer sort were carried to be buried at the public charge, 600,000 were thrown out at the gates; and when the number of dead bodies increased to such a degree that they had no place to bury them, they gathered them together in the largest houses adjoining, and there shut them up.

All this time the famine increased to such a degree, that wives took the meat out of their husbands' mouths, children from their parents, and mothers from their children; old men were driven from their meat as persons of no use, and young men tortured to confess where their provisions lay; sinks and holes were continually raked to find offal for food, and the very soldiers (who were the last that would want) began to eat girdles, shoes, hay, and other articles; and, what was worst of all, and the most shocking to human nature, a woman of quality even boiled her own child with an intent to eat it. This act appeared so detestable in the eyes of Titus, that (after having repeatedly offered peace and pardon to the Jews if they would submit, and as often received a denial) he publicly declared that "he would bury the abominable crime in the ruins of their country, and not suffer the sun to shine upon that city, whose mothers eat their own children, and whose fathers, no less culpable, did, by their obstinacy, reduce them to such an extremity."

With this resolution he ordered all the groves to be cut down within a considerable distance of the city, and, causing more mounts to be raised, on the first of July he began to batter the wall of Antonia, and, on the fifth, entered the castle by force, and pursued the flying Jews even to the temple. Both Titus and Josephus again exhorted them to surrender, but all to no purpose: they absolutely refused every accommodation, and even boasted that rather than submit they would glory in enduring the worst of miseries. Titus, hearing this, in order to make an easy ascent to the temple, ordered the fortress of Antonia to be razed to the ground, and having seized the north and west porticoes, or cloisters of the outward range of the temple, he set them on fire, as the Jews did other porticoes, to hinder the Romans from making their approaches.

On the eighth day of August Titus, perceiving that the walls of the inner temple were too strong for the battering-rams, and that the foundation of the gates could not be undermined, was obliged to set fire to them, yet still with an intent, if possible, to save the temple itself; but it so fell out that, on the tenth, a certain soldier, contrary to the command of the general, cast a flaming firebrand through the golden window into the chambers and buildings on the north side, which immediately set them on fire. The utmost endeavors were used to prevent the fatal effects of this proceeding, but to no purpose. The flames spread throughout the whole fabric, and soon consumed the most beautiful structure that ever was erected; while the Roman soldiers, pursuing their victory with the most imaginable fury and revenge, cut to pieces every person they found about the temple, and then set fire to the rest of the buildings.

During this state of general confusion, those who were the chiefs in the sedition, found means to retire to the upper and strongest part of the city, called Sion, situated upon a steep rock, where they endeavored to defend themselves to the last. But, Titus having raised his batteries and made a breach in the wall, they lost all their courage, abandoned the towers, which were their only strength, and in vain sought to escape by hiding themselves in vaults and privies, whence both John[*] and Simon

* This John was the son of one Levi, and one of the principal men belonging to the city of Grichala. When Titus laid siege to that place, John, under pretence of surrendering it, made his escape, and went, with a party of men to Jerusalem, where, joining with the zealots, and being naturally a crafty man, eloquent in speech, and ambitious beyond measure, he soon began to assume a sovereign power over the rest, and became the commander of one faction, as Simon, the son of Gioras did of another. Simon, having gathered together a great number of robbers and murderers, went into the mountainous parts of the country, reduced all Idumea, and some places in Judea, after which he encamped near Jerusalem, and was at length let in by the citizens to defend them against John, who, at the head of the zealots, did many cruel and tyrannical actions. So that Simon and his army were in the city, while John and his adherents were in the temple, fighting and destroying one another, even while the enemy was at the walls.

(two principal ringleaders of their different factions) were dragged out, and the former condemned to perpetual imprisonment, while the latter was preserved to grace the victor's triumph.

The Romans, having now gained the walls, and with shouts of joy placed their colors upon the towers, broke loose all over the city, and ranged up and down the streets, killing all that fell in their way without distinction, till the passages were filled up with the carcasses, and the channels of the city ran down with blood, as if it had been to quench the fire, which was become, as it were, one general conflagration.

To this fatal end was the famous city of Jerusalem, after a siege of above five months, reduced, in the second year of Vespasian's reign, and thirty-eight years after our Lord's crucifixion. In this siege it was computed that 1,100,000 perished, and 97,000 were taken captives, beside 237,490 (according to Josephus) who fell in the wars which preceded it.

The greater part of the buildings in the city being consumed by fire, and the soldiers having neither rapine nor object left for their rage and indignation to work upon, Titus ordered them to lay the remaining parts of the city and temple level with the ground; which order was so punctually executed that (except three towers, which, for their strength and beauty, were left as monuments to posterity of the once magnificence of the city) the whole was laid so flat that, when the Romans left the place, it looked as if it had never been inhabited.

While these things were transacting at Jerusalem, Vespasian, who entered upon the government in the fifty-ninth year of his age, was received at Rome with all imaginable joy and triumph by the people. They considered him as the only person whose virtues and excellences could recover the languishing state of the empire: nor were they mistaken, for he began immediately to act in conformity to what they had expected, by administering justice, and reforming the laws and customs of Rome, honorably rewarding those who had served him, and pardoning his adversaries with the most singular clemency.

In the meantime the news of the conquest of Jerusalem reached Rome, which occasioned the greatest rejoicings in that city, the people universally proclaiming the praises of Titus, who had shown himself so expert a soldier and commander; and in consequence of this a triumph was decreed both for him and his father, the latter having conducted the beginning of the war with no less eclat than the former had finished it.

When Titus returned to Rome he was received with the universal applause of the people, and within a few days after both the father and son entered upon their triumph, which was more solemn and magnificent than had ever before been seen in Rome. Among other rich and glorious spoils were great quantities of gold taken out of the temple, and the body of the Jewish law, which were exhibited to the view of the people. This was the first time that Rome ever saw the father and son triumph together; and as Vespasian built a new temple to Peace, wherein he deposited most of the Jewish spoils, so Titus had a triumphal arch of great beauty and magnificence erected to his honor, whereon were inscribed all his noble exploits against the Jews, and which, as a lasting monument of the impiety and perverseness of that nation, remains almost entire to this day.

Such was the end of the once famous city of Jerusalem, and such the end of the Jewish polity; from which time those obstinate and perverse people were no longer a nation, but have ever since been dispersed and despised throughout the whole face of the earth.

END OF THE NEW TESTAMENT HISTORY.

Arch of Titus, Rome.

Present Appearance of Jerusalem.

APPENDIX.

LITERARY HISTORY OF THE BIBLE.

THE BIBLE of the Christians is, without exception, the most remarkable work now in existence. In the libraries of the learned, there are frequently seen books of an extraordinary antiquity, and curious and interesting from the nature of their contents; but none approach the Bible, taken in its complete sense, in point of age, while certainly no production whatever has any pretension to rival it in the dignity of composition, or the important nature of the subjects treated of in its pages. The word Bible is of Greek origin, and, in signifying simply The Book, is expressive of its superiority over all other literary productions. The origin and nature of this every way singular work, how it was preserved during the most remote ages, and how it became known to the modern world in its present shape, form a highly interesting chapter of literary history.

The Bible comprehends the entire foundation of the religious belief of the Jews and Christians, and is divided into two distinct portions, entitled the Old and New Testaments, the former being that which is esteemed by the Jewish nation, but both being essential in forming the faith of the Christian. The Old Testament is the largest department of the work, and appears a collection of detached histories, moral essays, and pious poetical effusions, all placed together in the order of time, or, as they may serve, for the purpose of mutual illustration. On taking a glance at the contents, the principal subject of narration seems the history of the Jews, commencing with an account of the creation of the world, and tracing their history genealogically, through a series of striking vicissitudes and changes of situation. But when we examine the narrative minutely, it is found that there is another meaning than that of mere historical elucidation. It is perceived that the whole train of events recorded, the whole of those lofty, impassioned strains of poetry which distinguish the volume, are precursory and prophetic of a great change, which, at a future period, was to be wrought on the moral properties and fate of mankind, by the coming to the earth of a Messiah.

The authorship of the Old Testament has been universally ascribed, by both Jews and Christians, to God himself, though not by direct composition, but by spiritually influencing the minds of certain sages to accomplish the work, or, in ordinary phraseology, by *inspiring* or endowing them with a perfect knowledge of the transactions to be recorded and predicted, in a way suitable to the great end in view. The Bible is hence usually termed the Sacred Scriptures. The periods when the act of writing all or most part of the Scriptures took place, as well as most of the names of those who were instrumental in forming the work, have been ascertained with surprising accuracy, both from written evidence in the narratives themselves, and from the well-preserved traditions of the Jews. At whatever time the different books were written, they were not collected and put into a connected form till long after their immediate authors were deceased; and their present arrangement, as we shall afterward fully explain, is of comparatively modern date.

According to the order in which the books of the Old Testament now stand, those of an historical nature are appropriately placed at the beginning. The first five books, having a chain of connexion throughout, are Genesis, Exodus, Leviticus, Numbers, and Deuteronomy. These are styled the Pentateuch, such being the Greek compound for five books. They are likewise entitled the Books of Moses, from the belief that that enlightened Jewish leader composed them.

The Jews, or Hebrews, take the name of the sacred books from the first word with which each begins; but the Greeks, whom our translators generally follow, take the names from the subject-matter of them. Thus, the first book is called by the Hebrews, Bereshith, which signifies "In the beginning," these being the first words: but the Greeks call it Genesis, which signifies "production," because the creation of the world is the first thing of which it gives an account. It likewise contains an account of the increase of mankind; of their corruption of manners, and its cause; of their punishment by the deluge (an event which, by scientific investigation and historical research, is placed beyond a doubt); of the origin of the Jewish people from Abraham; of the manner in which God was pleased to have them governed; and, particularly, of the nature of the special superintendence vouchsafed to the Jewish nation by the Creator. This comprehensive narrative reaches from the creation of the world till the death of Joseph, or a period of 2,369 years. In another part of the Scriptures, reference is made to the Book of Jasher, and it is believed that Genesis is there meant; for Jasher signifies "the Just," and, according to St. Jerome, a learned Christian writer, the name of the Book of the Just, or the Authentic Book, was applied to it from its containing the history of Abraham, Isaac, and Jacob.

Exodus, the title of the second book of Moses, signifies in the Greek, "The going out," and was applied from the account which it gives of the Israelites going out of Egypt. In it are related the cruel Egyptian slavery under which the Jews groaned; their delivery by flight and passage through the Red sea; the history of the establishment of their very peculiar law, and many remarkable transactions; concluding with the building of the tabernacle, or place appropriated to the service of the Divinity. This book comprises the history of 145 years, from the death of Joseph till the building of the tabernacle. The Hebrews call it Velle Shemoth, that is, in English, "These are the names," which are the words with which it begins.

The third book of Moses is called Leviticus, because it contains the laws which God commanded should be observed by those of the tribe of Levi who ministered at the altar. It treats at large of all the functions of the Levites; of the ceremonial of religion; of the different sorts of sacrifices; of the distinction of clean and unclean beasts; of the different festivals; and of the year of jubilee, or continued holyday. It likewise presents us with an account of what happened to the Jews during the space of one month and a half; that is, from the time the tabernacle was erected, which was the first day of the first month of the second year after the Israelites came out of Egypt, till the second month of the same year, when God commanded the people to be numbered. The Hebrews called this book Vayicre, that is, "And he called," these being the first words; they call it also The Law of the Priests.

In the fourth book, which we call Numbers, Moses numbers the Israelites, and that, too, in the beginning of the book, which shows whence it had its name. The Hebrews call it Vayedavber, that is, "And he spake." This book contains the history of all that passed from the second month of the second year after the Israelites came out of Egypt, till the beginning of the eleventh month of the fortieth year; that is, it contains the history of thirty-nine years, or thereabouts. In it we have also the history of the prophet Balaam, whom the king of the Midianites brought to curse the people of God, and who, on the contrary, heaped blessings upon the Israelites, and foretold the coming of the Messiah. It particularly mentions, also, the two-and-forty encampments of the Israelites in the wilderness.

The fifth book is called Deuteronomy, a Greek term which signifies, "The second law," or, rather, "The repetition of the law," because it does not contain a law different from that which was given on Mount Sinai; but it repeats the same law, for the sake of the children of those who had received it there, and were since dead in the wilderness. The Hebrews call it Elle-haddebarim, that is, "These are the words." Deuteronomy begins with a short account of what had passed in the wilderness, and then Moses repeats what he had before commanded in Exodus, Leviticus, and Numbers, and admonishes the people to be faithful in keeping the commandments of God. After this, he relates what had happened from the beginning of the eleventh month, to the seventh day of the twelfth month of the same year, which was the fortieth after their leaving Egypt. The discourse which is at the beginning of this book was made to the people by Moses, on the first day of the eleventh month. According to Josephus, he died on the first day of the twelfth; and the Israelites, as the Scriptures say, mourned for him in the plains of Moab thirty days, and, consequently, during the whole of the twelfth month.

The Jews called the Pentateuch "The Law," without doubt because the law of God which Moses received on Mount Sinai is the principal part of it; and it is as little to be doubted whether that great man was the writer of the Pentateuch. This is expressly declared both in Exodus and Deuteronomy. But as an account of the death of Moses is given in the last eight verses of this book, it is therefore thought that these verses were added either by Joshua or Ezra. The opinion of Josephus concerning them is very singular; he pretends that Moses, finding his death approaching, and being willing to prevent an error into which the veneration the people had for him might cause the Jews to fall, wrote this account himself, without which the Jews would probably have supposed that God *had taken him away*, like Enoch.

After the death of Moses, Joshua, by the order of the Divine Being, took upon himself the conducting of the Hebrew people, and succeeded Moses, to whom he had been a faithful servant, and by whom he had been instructed in what he ought to do. It is uncertain whether the book which contains the history of this successor of Moses be called Joshua, from the subject of it, or from his having been the writer of it. But it is certain that it contains an account of what passed from the death of Moses to that of Joshua. Nevertheless, there are several things in it which did not come to pass till after the death of this great man, and which, consequently, could not have been written by him. The common opinion as to the length of time it contains is, that Joshua discharged his office only for seventeen years, and that, therefore, this book contains no more than the history of that number of years.

After the death of Joshua, the Israelites were governed by magistrates, who ruled under the general designation of Judges; and the book which contains the history of these rulers is called, The Book of Judges. This history begins with the death of Joshua, and reaches to that of Samson. We here see the people of God often enslaved in punishment of their crimes, and often wonderfully delivered from slavery. Toward the end of it, we have some instances of this people's inclination to idolatry, and of the corruption of their manners, even before they had been brought into slavery. Such are the histories of Micah, and of the Benjamites who abused the Levite's wife. This book contains the history of three hundred and seventy years.

During the time of the government of the Judges, there was a great famine in the land of Israel, which forced Elimelech, a native of Bethlehem, to retire into the land of Moab, with his wife Naomi, and two children. Elimelech died there, as also his two sons, who had married two Moabitish women, one of whom was named Ruth. Naomi, after the death of her husband and her children, returned to Bethlehem, accompanied by Ruth, her daughter-in-law, who was there married to Boaz, Elimelech's near relation, and the heir to his estate. The book which contains this history, is called, The Book of Ruth. The beginning of it shows that it happened in the time of the Judges, but under which of them is not certainly known; some place it in the time of Shamgar, or of Deborah. As to the writer of this book, some think that the books of Judges and Ruth were both written by Samuel; others attribute them to Hezekiah, and others to Ezra. The Jews place the book of Ruth among the five books which they usually read on all the festivals in the year. These five books are, the Song of Songs, Ruth, the Lamentations of Jeremiah, Ecclesiastes, and the book of Esther. In the Hebrew bibles they are printed or written apart by themselves, and are bound up together.

The four books following Ruth are called by the Greeks, and also in some Latin bibles, The History of the Reigns. Others call them all, The Books of Kings, because they give an account of the establishment of the monarchy, and of the succession of the kings, who reigned over the whole kingdom at first, and over the kingdoms of Judah and Israel after its division. At the beginning of these books is given the history of the prophet Samuel, which gives light to that of The Kings. The Jews call the first two of these books, The Books of Samuel: perhaps because they contain the history of the two kings, who were both anointed by Samuel; and because what is said of Saul in *the first*, and of David in *the second*, proves the truth of Samuel's prophecies. They give the name of The Books of Kings only to the other two, which, in the Latin and French bibles, are called the Third and Fourth Books of Kings.

The First Book of Kings, or the First of Samuel, contains the history of the high-priest Eli, of Samuel, and of Saul. As the first year of Eli's high-priesthood falls on the year of the world 2848, and the death of Saul in 2949, the history of this book must comprehend the space of one hundred and one years.

The Second contains the reign of David, which is the history of about forty years. It is commonly believed that Samuel, Nathan, and Gad, were the writers of these two books, and, indeed, they are called, in the end of the first book of Chronicles, David's historians.

The Third, or, according to the Hebrews, the First Book of Kings, begins with a relation of the manner in which Solomon came to the throne, and contains the whole of his reign. After that, an account follows of the division of the kingdom, and the history of four kings of Judah and eight kings of Israel. All these reigns, including that of Solomon, which occupies the first forty years, comprise the space of one hundred and twenty-six years.

The Fourth of these books contains the history of sixteen kings of Judah, and twelve kings of Israel. It likewise gives an account of the prophets who lived during this time. It is quite uncertain who were the writers of the last two mentioned books. They are by some attributed to Jeremiah or Ezra, but no very convincing proofs have been adduced in support of this opinion. It is evident, indeed, that these books form a varied collection of several particular histories.

The name of Paralipomena, which in Greek signifies the "history of things omitted," is given to the two books which follow those of The Kings. These form, in fact, a supplement, containing what had been omitted in the Pentateuch, and the books of Joshua, Judges, and Kings, or rather they contain a fuller description of some things which had been therein only briefly related. Some give them the name of Chronicles, because they are very exact in mentioning the time when every transaction happened. We divide them into two books, as do also the Jews, who call them Dibere Hayanim, that is, an "historical journal," the matters of which they treat having been taken from the journals of the kings. In the original language, however, the word *days* often signifies *the year ;* and, in this sense, we may understand the term to signify properly "annals." The generally-received opinion is, that Ezra was the writer of these. In the first book, he begins with a succinct historical abridgment, from the creation of Adam to the return of the Jews from their captivity ; and then he resumes the history of David, and carries it on to the consecration of Solomon, that is, down to the year before Christ 1015. The history contained in the second book reaches down to the year before Christ 536, when, upon the expiration of the seventy years of captivity, Cyrus gave the Jews leave to return to their own country.

Ezra wrote the history of the return of the Jews from the captivity of Babylon into Judea. It is the history of about eighty-two years, from the year of the world 3468, when Cyrus became master of the eastern empire, by the death of his father, Cambyses, in Persia, and his father-in-law, Cyaxares, in Media, to the year 3550, which was the twentieth year of the reign of Artaxerxes, surnamed Longimanus. This book bears the name of Ezra, who was the writer of it.

The next book is a continuation of that of Ezra, and therefore it is by some called the Second Book of Ezra. It was Nehemiah, however, whose name it also bears, who wrote it, as is said, by the advice of Ezra. It contains the account of the re-establishment of Jerusalem, and the temple, and the worship of God. It is the history of about thirty-one years ; that is to say, from the twentieth year of the reign of Artaxerxes Longimanus, to the reign of Darius Nothus, his son, which began in the year of the world 3581.

After this general history of the Jews, follow two histories of particular persons, viz., Esther and Job. The first contains the account of a miraculous deliverance of the Jews, which was accomplished by means of the heroine named Esther. The Scripture says it happened under the reign of Ahasuerus, king of Persia ; but as there have been several Persian kings of that name, it is not exactly known in which reign it is to be dated. Dr. Lightfoot thinks it was that Artaxerxes who hindered the building of the temple, and who, in the book of Ezra, is called also Ahasuerus, after his great grandfather, the king of the Medes.

The history of Job, which is next in order, is not only a narration of his actions, but contains also the entire discourses which this pious man had with his wife and his friends, and is, indeed, one of the most eloquent books in the Holy Scriptures. It is generally conjectured that Moses was the writer or compiler of this book; but this is very uncertain.

Next to the historical books of Scripture follow those of a moral nature. The first of these is the Book of Psalms, which is likewise in some measure historical; for they recite the miracles which God had wrought, and contain, as it were, an abridgment of all that had been done for the Israelites, and that had happened to them. The Hebrews call them "the Book of Praises," by which they mean, "of the Praises of God." The word psalm is Greek, and properly signifies the sound of a stringed instrument of music. The Hebrews sung the Psalms with different instruments. We make but one book of them all, but the Hebrews divide them into five parts, which all end with the words Amen, Amen. Though the Psalms bear the name of David, yet they were not all composed by him; some of them are more ancient, and others are of a later date than his time; some of them being ascribed to Moses, Samuel, and Ezra. Speaking of the dedication of the second temple, Prideaux says, "In this dedication, the 146th, the 147th, and the 148th psalms seem to have been sung; for in the Septuagint versions they are styled the Psalms of Haggai and Zechariah, as if they had been composed by them for this occasion; and this, no doubt, was from some ancient tradition: but, in the original Hebrew, these Psalms have no such title prefixed to them, neither have they any other to contradict it." It is not probable, however, that all those whose names they bear were the true authors of them; it is more likely that these are only the names of those to whom they were first given to sing.

After the Psalms are the Proverbs, which are a collection of moral sentences, of which Solomon was the writer. This name is given them by the Greeks, but the Hebrews call them Myste, that is, parables, or comparisons; and the word may also signify sentences, or maxims. It is a collection of divine precepts, proper for every age, and every condition of life.

The book which follows is also a moral one, and was likewise composed by Solomon. The Greeks call it Ecclesiastes, which answers to the name of Koheleth, which it bears in the Hebrew. Both these words signify, in our language, a preacher, or one who speaks in an assembly. In this book is given an admirable picture of the vanity of the world.

Among the moral books is also reckoned the Song of Songs; that is to say, according to the Hebrew manner of speaking, a most excellent song. This book has nothing of morality in it, and therefore, it is thought the only reason of its being placed here is because it was a third work of Solomon; for there is not one moral or religious maxim in it, and the name of God is not so much as mentioned in it, except once in the original Hebrew, where it is used adjectively. It is an *Epithalamium*, or nuptial song, wherein, by the expressions of love between a bridegroom and his bride, are set forth and illustrated the mutual affections that pass between God and a distinguished remnant of mankind. It is a sort of dramatic poem or pastoral: the bride and bridegroom, for the more lively representation of humility and innocence, are brought in as a shepherd and shepherdess. We learn from St. Jerome, that the Jews were not permitted to read this song, or the chapters at the beginning of the book of Genesis, till they were thirty years old.

In regard to the prophets, it may be observed, that all the Old Testament is considered to be in substance one continued prophecy of the coming of Jesus Christ; so that all the books of which it consists are understood to be in some sense prophetical. But this name is more especially given to those books which were written by persons who had a clearer knowledge of futurity, who forewarned both kings and people of what would happen to them, and who at the same time pointed out what the Messiah was to do, whom they who are acknowledged to have been prophets had always in view: and this is what ought most especially to be taken notice of in their writings.

The prophecies bear the name of those to whom they belong. Some learned men are of opinion that the prophets made abridgments of the discourses which they had written, and fixed them up at the gates of the temple, that all the people might read them; and that after this the ministers of the temple might take them away, and place them among the archives, which is the reason why we have not the prophecies

in the order in which they were written.   But the interpreters of Scripture have long
since labored to restore that order, according to the course of their history.

The works of the prophets are divided into two parts, the first of which contains
the greater, and the second, the lesser prophets.   This distinction, of course, does not
apply at all to the persons of the prophets, but only to the bulk of their works.   The
greater prophets are Isaiah, Ezekiel, Daniel, and Jeremiah.   The Lamentations of
Jeremiah make a separate book by themselves, containing that prophet's descriptions
of the destruction of the city of Jerusalem, and of the captivity of the people.   The
lesser prophets are Hosea, Joel, Amos, Obadiah, Jonah, Micai, Nahum, Habakkuk,
Zephaniah, Haggai, Zechariah, and Malachi.   They were formerly contained in one
single volume, which the Hebrews call Thereaser, which means twelve, or the book
of the twelve.

The dates of many of the prophecies are uncertain, but the earliest of them was
in the days of Uzziah, king of Judah, and Jeroboam the Second, his contemporary,
king of Israel, about 200 years before the captivity, and not long after Joash had slain
Zechariah, the son of Jehoiada, in the court of the temple.   Hosea was the first of
the writing prophets, and Joel, Amos, and Obadiah, published their prophecies about
the same time.

Isaiah began his remarkable prophecies a short time afterward, but his book is
placed first, because it is the largest of them all, and is more explicit relative to the
advent of Christ than any of the others.   The language of this eminent writer is exceedingly sublime and affecting ; so much so, that it has never been equalled by any
profane poet either in ancient or modern times.   It is impossible to read some of the
chapters without being struck by the force of the prophetic allusions to the character
and sufferings of the Messiah ; and in consequence of these prevailing characteristics,
the author is ordinarily styled the evangelical prophet, and by some of the ancients,
a fifth evangelist.   The Jews say that the spirit of prophecy continued forty years
during the second temple ; and Malachi they call the seal of prophecy, because in him
the succession or series of prophets broke off, and came to a period.   The book of
Malachi, therefore, appropriately closes the sacred record of the Old Testament.

The second and lesser division of the Bible relates entirely to the Christian religion, or the fulfilment of that which was predicted in the preceding and more
ancient department of the work.   This division of the sacred Scriptures is generally
styled the New Testament ; and that portion of it which relates to the history of the
life of Christ is called the Gospel, and by some the Evangel, both these words having
the same meaning, and implying good news, or glad tidings, from the circumstance
that the narratives contain an account of things which are to benefit mankind.

The New Testament, like the Old, is a compilation of books written by different inspired individuals, and all put together in a manner so as to exhibit a regular account of
the birth, actions, and death of Christ—the doctrines he promulgated—and the prophecies regarding the future state of the church which he founded.   The historical books
are the four gospels and the Acts of the Apostles, all these being of the character of
narratives of events ; the doctrinal are the Epistles of St. Paul, and some others ; the
prophetic book is the last, and this is called the Revelation or Apocalypse of St. John,
having been written by that apostle while he was in the island of Patmos.

The writers of the books of the New Testament are generally well known, each
having the name of the author affixed to' it, with the exception of the Acts of the
Apostles, which, it is presumed, was compiled by St. Luke.   It was long disputed
whether St. Paul was the writer of the Epistle to the Hebrews ; Tertullian, an an-
cient Christian writer, and some others, attribute it to St. Barnabas ; others to St.
Luke ; and others to St. Clement ; while some think, with greater probability, that
St. Paul dictated it, and St. Luke acted as the writer ; and that the reason why the
name of the true author was not affixed to it, was because he was disliked by the
Jews.   The four evangelists, or writers of the leading narratives, are St. Matthew,
St. Mark, St. Luke, and St. John ; these having been companions to Christ during
his ministrations, and, therefore, personally acquainted with his life and character.
Each of the four books is principally a repetition of the history of Christ, yet they
all possess a difference of style, and each mentions some circumstances omitted by the
others, so that the whole is essential in making up a complete life of the Messiah.
These distinctions in the tone of the narratives, and other peculiarities, are always
considered as strong circumstantial evidence in proof of their authenticity, and of

there having been no collusion on the part of the writers. But, indeed, the events they record are detailed in so exceedingly simple and unaffected a manner, that it is impossible to suppose that they were written with a view to impose on the credulity of mankind. The veracity and actual belief of the evangelists themselves are placed beyond a doubt.

The first book is written by Matthew, who was by birth a Jew, and exercised the profession of a publican—that is, a collector of the public tax or assessment imposed upon the Jewish people by their conquerors, the Romans. Matthew, who was also called by the name of Levi, was one of the twelve apostles of Christ, and he is said to have written his narrative about eight years after the departure of his Master from the earth. Many of the ancients say that he wrote it in the Hebrew or Syriac language; but Dr. Whitby is clearly of opinion that this tradition is entirely void of foundation, and that it was doubtless written in Greek, as the other parts of the New Testament were. Yet it is probable that there might be an edition of it in Hebrew, published by St. Matthew himself, at the same time that he wrote it in Greek; the former for the Jews, the latter for the Gentiles, when he left Judea to preach among the heathen.

In regard to Mark, the writer of the second Gospel, it may be observed, that although Mark, or Marcus, was a Roman name, and a very common one, yet we have no reason to think but that he was by birth a Jew; but as Saul, when he went among the Gentiles, took the Roman name of Paul, so did this evangelist take that of Mark, his Jewish name, perhaps, being Mardacai, as Grotius observes. Jerome and Tertullian say that he was a disciple of the Apostle Peter, and his interpreter or amanuensis. We have every reason to believe that both he and Luke were of the number of the seventy disciples who companied all along with the apostles, and who had a commission like to theirs: so that it is no diminution at all to the validity or value of this Gospel that Mark was not one of the twelve, as Matthew and John were. Jerome says, that after the writing of this Gospel he went into Egypt, and was the first that preached the gospel at Alexandria, where he founded a church, to which he was a great example of holy living.

The Gospel of St. Mark is much shorter than that of Matthew, not giving so full an account of Christ's sermons as that did, but insisting chiefly on his miracles; and in regard to these, also, it is very much a repetition of what we have in Matthew, many remarkable circumstances being added to the stories there related, but not many new matters. There is a tradition that it was first written in Latin, because it was written at Rome; but this is generally thought to be without foundation, and that it was written in Greek, as was St. Paul's Epistle to the Romans, the Greek being the more universal language.

Luke, the name of the third evangelist, is considered by some to be a contraction of Lucilius, and it is said by St. Jerome to have been borne at Antioch. Some think that he was the only one of all the penmen of the Scriptures that was not of the Israelites; that he was a Jewish proselyte, and was converted to Christianity by the ministry of St. Paul at Antioch, and after his coming into Macedonia he was his constant companion. He had employed himself in the study and practice of physic, and hence Paul calls him "Luke, the beloved physician." It is more than probable, however, as is testified both by Origen and Epiphanius, that he was one of the seventy disciples, and a follower of Christ when he was upon earth; and if so, he was most likely to be a native Israelite. Luke most probably wrote his Gospel at Rome, a little before he wrote his history of the "Acts of the Apostles," which is a continuation of the former, when he was there with Paul, while he was a prisoner, and "preaching in his own hired house," with which the history of the Acts concludes. In this case, it must have been written about twenty-seven years after Christ's departure, and about the fourth year of the reign of Nero. Jerome says that St. Luke died when he was eighty-four years of age, and that he was never married. Dr. Cave observes that "his way and manner of writing are accurate and exact, his style polite and elegant, sublime and lofty, yet perspicuous; and that he expresses himself in a vein of purer Greek than is to be found in the other writers of this holy history." Thus he relates several things more copiously than the other evangelists, and thus he especially treats of those things which relate to the priestly office of Christ.

The fourth evangelist, John, was one of the sons of Zebedee, a fisherman of Galilee, the brother of James, one of the twelve apostles, and distinguished by the honorable appellation, "that disciple whom Jesus loved." The ancients tell us that John lived the longest of all the apostles, and was the only one of them that died a natural death, all the rest suffering martyrdom; and some of them say that he wrote this Gospel at Ephesus, at the request of the ministers of the several churches of Asia, in order to combat certain heresies. It seems most probable that he composed it before his banishment into the isle of Patmos, for there he wrote his Revelation, the close of which seems designed for the closing up of the canon of scripture; in which case this Gospel could not have been written after. It is clear that he wrote the last of the four Evangelists, and, comparing his Gospel with theirs, we may observe that he relates what they had omitted, and thus gleans up what they had passed by.

These four Gospels were early and constantly received by the primitive church, and read in Christian assemblies, as appears by the writings of Justin Martyr and Irenæus, who lived little more than one hundred years after the origin of Christianity; they declared that neither more nor fewer than four were received by the church. A Harmony of these four Evangelists was compiled by Tatian about that time, which he called "The Gospel out of the four." In the third and fourth centuries there were gospels forged by divers sects, and published, one under the name of St. Peter, another of St. Thomas, another of St. Philip, &c. But they were never owned by the church, nor was any credit given to them, as the learned Dr. Whitby shows. And he gives this good reason why we should adhere to these written records: "because," says he, "whatever the pretences of tradition may be, it is not sufficient to preserve things with any certainty, as appears by experience. For whereas Christ said and did many memorable things which were not written, tradition has not preserved any one of them to us, but all is lost except what was written; and that, therefore, is what we must abide by."

After the Gospel, or history of Jesus Christ, follows the history of what passed after his ascension, and was transacted by the apostles. The book, therefore, which contains this history is called "The Acts of the Apostles." It is a history of the rising church for about the space of thirty years. It was written, as has been already observed, by St. Luke the Evangelist, when he was with St. Paul at Rome, during his imprisonment there. In the end of the book he mentions particularly his being with Paul in his dangerous voyage to Rome, when he was carried thither a prisoner; and it is evident that he was with him when, from his prison there, Paul wrote his epistles to the Colossians and Philemon; for in both of these he is named by him.

Next to this come the Epistles of St. Paul, which are fourteen in number: one to the Romans, two to the Corinthians, one to the Galatians, one to the Ephesians, one to the Philippians, one to the Colossians, two to the Thessalonians, two to Timothy, one to Titus, one to Philemon, and one to the Hebrews. They contain that part of ecclesiastical history which immediately follows after what is related in the Acts. The principal matter contained in them is the establishment or confirmation of the doctrine which Jesus Christ taught his disciples. According as the difficulties which raised disputes among the Christians, or the heresies which sprung up in the church from the first age of it, required, St. Paul in these epistles clears up and proves all matters of faith, and gives excellent rules for morality. His epistles may be considered as a commentary on, or an interpretation of, the four books of the Gospel.

The Epistle to the Romans is placed first, not because of the priority of its date, but on account of its superlative excellence, it being one of the longest and fullest of all, and perhaps, also, on account of the dignity of the place to which it is written. It is gathered from some passages in the epistle, that it was written in the year of Christ 56, from Corinth, while Paul made a short stay there in his way to Troas. He was then going up to Jerusalem, with the money that was given to the poor saints there; which is spoken of in the fifteenth chapter of the epistle.

The two epistles to the Corinthians were written about a year after that to the Romans, viz., A. D. 57; that to the Galatians, A. D. 56; to the Ephesians, A. D. 61; to the Philippians, A. D. 62; to the Colossians, A. D. 62; two to the Thessalonians, A. D. 51 and 52; the first to Timothy, A. D. 64; the second to Timothy, A. D. 66; to Titus, A. D. 65; to Philemon, A. D. 62; and that to the Hebrews, A. D. 62. From which chronology it appears that the Epistles of St. Paul are placed in the New

Testament rather according to the dignity of the cities to which they were sent than according to the order of time in which they were written; for the Epistles to the Thessalonians were those he wrote first, though that to the Romans is placed before them. Interpreters are agreed that the last epistle which he wrote was the second to Timothy.

St. Paul wrote to the churches of some particular places, or to some particular persons; but the other epistles which follow his are called catholic, because, with the exception of the second and third of St. John, they were not addressed to any particular church or individual, as his were, but to the whole church in general. These are, one of St. James, two of St. Peter, three of St. John, and one of St. Jude.

The date of most of these epistles is extremely uncertain; but the most generally-received chronology of them is as follows: that of St. James, A. D. 61; of St. Peter, A. D. 66 and 67; of St. John, A. D. 80 and 90; of St. Jude, A. D. 66.

It has sometimes occurred to the minds of many well-disposed persons, that it would have been better for Christianity had there never been any other record of its origin and doctrines than the writings of Matthew, Mark, Luke, and John. But, however plain and satisfactory the histories of these evangelists may be, and however little they admit of controversy, it has to be remembered that it required the strong arguments and illustrations brought forward in the epistles, by Paul and others, to combat the sophistry of the Greeks, and the self-sufficient philosophies of other races of man. Paul, the chief of the epistle writers, who became a Christian by conversion after Christ had departed from the earth, is the great champion of the faith, and exposes, in strong and dauntless language, the hidden depravities of the human heart; so that where the affecting discourses and sufferings of the Messiah fail to convert and convince, the reasoning of this great writer is calculated to silence and subdue those who stubbornly resist the benignant influence of the Christian faith.

The first division of the Scriptures, as already mentioned, is into the Old and New Testaments. The New belongs to the Christians, but the Old was received from the Jews; and it is from them, therefore, that we must learn what the number of the books of it originally was, and everything else relating to this most ancient and interesting production.

The celebrated Jewish writers, Josephus and Philo, reckon two and twenty canonical books in the Old Testament, which is the number of the letters in the Hebrew alphabet: and to make out this, they join the book of Ruth to that of Judges, and the Lamentations of Jeremiah to the book of his Prophecies. But other Jewish doctors divide the book of Ruth from that of Judges, and, making likewise a separate book of the Lamentations of Jeremiah, they reckon four and twenty books in all. In order to accommodate this number to that of the letters of the alphabet, they repeat the letter yod three times, as they say, in honor to the great name of God Jehovah, of which yod is the first letter; and in Chaldee, three yods together were used to express this adorable name: but as the modern Jews thought this savored too much of what Christians call the Trinity, they use only two yods for this purpose. St. Jerome is of opinion that St. John had this division of the Hebrew scriptures in view, when in his Revelation he speaks of the four and twenty elders who paid adoration to the Lamb of God.

The Jews divide the whole of these books into three classes, namely, the Law, the Prophets, and the Hagiographa or Holy Writings, which last division includes more particularly the *poetical* parts; and some are of opinion that Jesus Christ alludes to this division of the Scriptures, when he says that " all things must be fulfilled that were written in the law of Moses, and in the prophets, and in the psalms, concerning" him. For the book of Psalms, they understand all the books of the third class. The Law comprehends the Pentateuch; that is, Genesis, Exodus, Leviticus, Numbers, and Deuteronomy. The Prophetical books are eight, viz: (1) Joshua, (2) Judges, with Ruth, (3) Samuel, (4) Kings, (5) Isaiah, (6) Jeremiah, (7) Ezekiel, and (8) the twelve Lesser Prophets. The first four books of this division are called the Former Prophets, and the last four the Latter Prophets. The Hagiographa, or Holy Writings, are nine, viz: (1) Job, (2) the Psalms, (3) Proverbs, (4) Ecclesiastes, (5) The Song of Songs, (6) Daniel, (7) Chronicles, (8) Ezra, with Nehemiah, and (9) Esther. The Jews do not put Daniel in the rank of a prophet, although they acknowledge him to have been a man inspired by God, and whose writings are full of the clearest prophecies concerning the time of the Messiah's coming, and what should happen to their nation. Jesus Christ, therefore, gives him the name of a Prophet, and the Jewish doctors are much puzzled to find out a proper reason for their not doing the same. " It is," says Maimonides, " because everything that Daniel wrote was not revealed to him when he was awake and had the use of his reason, but in the night, and in obscure dreams." But this is a very unsatisfactory account of the matter; and others are of opinion that the name of a Prophet was commonly given to those only who were of a certain college, and whose business it was to write the annals; and that, therefore, their works were ranked among the prophetical books, though they did not contain a single prediction of anything to come, as the books of Joshua and Judges; while, on the contrary, the works of those who were not of these colleges of the prophets were not ranked among the prophetical books, although they contained true prophecies.

The Latins agree with the Jews as to the number of the Psalms, which is a hundred and fifty; but both they and the Greeks divide them differently from the Hebrews. In the Greek Bible and the Vulgate, or common Latin version, the ninth and tenth, according to the Hebrew, make but one psalm; and therefore, in order to make up the number of a hundred and fifty, they divide the hundred and forty-seventh into two.

This is the general division of the sacred books among the Jews. But they divide the Pentateuch, in particular, into certain paragraphs or sections, which they call *Parashiuth,* and which they subdivide into the Great and Little. A Great section contains as much as is to be read in the synagogue in a week. There are in all fifty-four of these, inasmuch as there may be so many weeks in a year; for the Jews are obliged to read all the Pentateuch over once every year, finishing it on the feast of tabernacles, and beginning it again on the next sabbath day. In the time of the persecution by Antiochus Epiphanes, they also selected fifty-four sections to be read out of the Prophets, which have ever since constituted the second lessons in the Jewish synagogue-service. The Little sections, which are subdivisions of the Greater, are made according to the subjects they treat of; and these Great and Little sections are again of two sorts, one of which is called *Petuchoth,* that is, open sections; and the other *Sethumoth,* that is, close sections. The former commences in the Hebrew Bibles always at the beginning of lines, and are marked with three P's if it be a great section, and with only one if it be a little section; because P is the first letter of the word Petuchoth. Every open section takes its name from its first word; and thus the first section in the whole Bible is called *Bereshith,* which is the first word of the Book of Genesis in Hebrew. The close sections begin the middle of a line, and are marked with the letter *Samech,* which is the first letter of the word Sethumoth; if it be a great section it has three Samechs; if a little section, only one. Every great section is also divided again into seven parts, which are read in the synagogue by so many different persons. If any priest be present, he begins, and a Levite reads after him; and in the choice of the rest, regard is had to their dignity and condition. The divisions of the prophetical books already mentioned are read jointly with those of Moses, in the same manner. These latter divisions they call *Haphteroth,* a term which signifies, in Hebrew, dismissions; because after this reading is over they dismiss the people.

The Jews call the division of the Holy Scriptures into chapters, *Perakim,* which signifies fragments; and the division into verses they call *Pesukim,* a word of nearly the same signification as the former. These last are marked out in the Hebrew Bibles by two great points at the end of them, called hence *Soph-Pasuk,* that is, the end of the verse. But the division of the Scriptures into chapters and verses, as we now have them, is of a much later date. The Psalms, indeed, were always divided as at present; for St. Paul, in his sermon at Antioch in Pisidia, quotes the second Psalm. But as to the rest of the Holy Scriptures, the division of them into such chapters as at present, is what the ancients knew nothing of. Some attribute it to Stephen Langton, who was archbishop of Canterbury in the reigns of King John and his son Henry the Third. But the true author of this invention, as is shown by Dean Prideaux at great length, was Hugo de Sancto Caro, who, being from a Dominican monk advanced to the dignity of a cardinal, and the first of that order that was so, is commonly called Hugo Cardinalis.

This Cardinal Hugo, who flourished about the year 1240, and died in 1262, had labored much in the study of the Holy Scriptures, and made a comment upon the whole of them. The carrying on of this work gave him the occasion of inventing the first concordance that was made of the Scriptures—that is, of the vulgar Latin Bible; for, conceiving that such an index of all the words and phrases in the Bible would be of great use for the attaining of a better understanding of it, he projected a scheme for the making of such an index, and forthwith set a great number of the monks of his order on the collecting of the words under their proper classes in every letter of the alphabet, in order to this design; and, by the help of so many hands, he soon brought it to what he intended. This work was afterward much improved by those who followed him, especially by Arlottus Thuseus, and Conradus Halberstadius, the former a Franciscan and the other a Dominican friar, who both lived about the end of the same century. But the whole intention of the work being for the easier finding of any word or passage in the Scriptures, to make it answer this purpose the cardinal found it necessary, in the first place, to divide the book into sections, and the sections into other divisions, that by these he might the better make the references, and the more exactly point out in the index where any word or passage might be found in the text; and these sections are the chapters into which the Bible has ever since been divided. For, on the publishing of this concordance, the usefulness of it being immediately discerned, all were desirous to have it; and, for the sake of the use of it, they all divided their bibles as Hugo had done; for the references in the concordance being made by these chapters and the subdivisions of them, unless their bibles were so divided too, the concordance would be of no use to them. And thus this division of the several books of the Bible into chapters had its original, which has ever since been made use of in all places and among all people, wherever the Bible itself is used in these western parts of the world; for before this there was no division of the books in the vulgar Latin bibles at all.

But the subdivisions of the chapters were not then by verses as now. Hugo's way of subdividing them was by the letters A, B, C, D, E, F, G, placed in the margin at equal distances from one another, according as the chapters were longer or shorter. In long chapters all these seven letters were used, in others fewer, as the length of the chapters required; for the subdivision of the chapters by verses, which is now in all our bibles, was not introduced into them till some ages after; and then it was from the Jews that the use of it, as we now have it, took its original on the following occasion.

About the year 1430, there lived here among the western Jews a famous rabbi, called by some Rabbi Mordecai Nathan, by others Rabbi Isaac Nathan, and by many by both these names, as if he were first called by one of them, and then, by a change of it, by the other. This rabbi being much conversant with the Christians, and having frequent disputes with their learned men about religion, he thereby came to the knowledge of the great use which they made of the Latin concordance composed by Cardinal Hugo, and the benefit which they had from it, in the ready finding of any place in the Scriptures which they had occasion to consult; which he was so much taken with, that he immediately set about making such a concordance to the Hebrew Bible for the use of the Jews. He began this work in the year 1438, and finished it in 1445, being seven years in composing it; and the first publishing of it happening about the time when printing was invented, it has since undergone several editions from the press. The Buxtorfs, father and son, bestowed much pains on this work; and the edition of it published by them at Basil in 1632 is by far the most complete, and has deservedly the reputation of being the best book of the kind that is extant. Indeed, it is so useful for the understanding of the Hebrew scriptures, that no one who employs his studies in this way can have a better companion; it being the best dictionary, as well as the best concordance to them.

In the composing of this book, Rabbi Nathan finding it necessary to follow the same division of the Scriptures into chapters which Hugo had made in them, it had the like effect as to the Hebrew bibles that Hugo's had as to the Latin, causing the same divisions to be made in all the Hebrew bibles which were afterward either written out or printed for common use; and hence the division into chapters first came into the Hebrew bibles. But Nathan, though he followed Hugo in the division into chapters, yet did not do so in the division of the chapters by the letters A, B, C, &c., in the margin, but introduced a better usage by employing the division that was made by verse. This division, as already mentioned, was very ancient; but it was till now without any numbers put to the verses. The numbering, therefore, of the verses in the chapters, and the quoting of the passages in every chapter by the verses, were Rabbi Nathan's invention; in everything else he followed the pattern which Cardinal Hugo had set him. But it is to be observed, that he did not number the verses any otherwise than by affixing the numerical Hebrew letters in the margin at every fifth verse; and this has been the usage of the Jews in all their Hebrew bibles ever since, except that latterly they have also introduced the common figures for numbering the intermediate verses between every fifth. Vatalibius soon after published a Latin Bible according to this pattern, with the chapters divided into verses, and the verses so numbered; and this example has been followed in all other editions that have been since put forth. So that, as the Jews borrowed the division of the books of the Holy Scriptures into chapters from the Christians, in like manner the Christians borrowed that of the chapters into verses from the Jews. But to this day the book of the law, which is read by the Jews in their synagogues every sabbath day, has none of these distinctions, that is, is not divided into verses as the Bible is.

The division of the books of Scripture into great and little sections, does, without doubt, contribute much to the clearing up of their contents; and for this reason, as well as because they found it practised in the synagogues, the Christians also divided the books of the New Testament into what the Greeks call *pericopes*, that is, sections, that they might be read in their order. Each of these sections contained, under the same title, all the matters that had any relation to one another, and were solemnly read in the churches by the public readers, after the deacons had admonished the faithful to be attentive to it, crying with a loud voice, "Attendance, Let us attend." The name of titles was given to these sections, because each of them had its own title. Robert Stephens, the famous printer, who died at Geneva in 1559, gets the credit of being the first who made the division of the chapters of the New Testament into verses, and for the same reason as Rabbi Nathan had done before him as to the Old Testament; that is, for the sake of a concordance which he was then composing for the Greek Testament, and which was afterward printed by Henry Stephens, his son, who gives this account of the matter in his preface to the concordance. Since that time, this division of the whole Bible by chapters and verses, and the quoting of all passages in them by the numbers of both, has grown into use everywhere among us in these western parts; so that not only all Latin bibles, but all Greek ones also, as well as every other that has been printed in any of the modern languages, have followed this division. They who most approve of this division of the Bible into chapters and verses, as at present used, agree that a much more convenient one might be made; since it often happens that things which ought to be separated are joined together, and many things which ought to be joined together are divided.

The respect which the Jews have for the sacred books, and which even degenerates into superstition, is one of the principal of their religious practices. Nothing can be added to the care they take in writing them. The books of the ancients were of a different form from ours; they did not consist of several leaves, but of one or more skins or parchments sewn together, and fastened at the ends to rollers of wood, upon which they were rolled up; so that a book when thus shut up might easily be sealed in several places. And such was the book mentioned in the Revelations, which St. John says "was sealed with seven seals," and which no one but "the Lion of the tribe of Judah could open and explain."

The Hebrew manuscripts of the Bible are of two kinds—the rolled ones, or those used in the synagogues, and the square ones, or those which are to be found in private collections. The rules laid down by the Jews with respect to their manuscripts have undoubtedly tended much to preserve the integrity of the text. They are directed to be written upon parchment, made from the skin of a clean animal, and to be tied together with strings of similar substance, or sewn with goat's-hair, which has been spun and prepared by a Jewess. It must be likewise a Jew that writes the law, and they are extremely diligent and exact in it, because the least fault in the world profanes the book. Every skin of parchment is to contain a certain number of columns, which are to be of a precise length and breadth, and to contain a certain number of words. They are to be written with the purest ink, and no word is to be written by heart or with the points; it must be first orally pronounced by the copyist. The name of God is directed to be written with the utmost attention and devotion, and the transcriber is to wash his pen before he inscribes it on the parchment. If

41

there should chance to be a word with either a deficient or a redundant letter, or should any of the prosaic part of the Old Testament be written as verse, or *vice versa*, the manuscript is vitiated. No Hebrew manuscript with any illumination is, on any account, admitted into a synagogue, although private individuals are permitted to have them ornamented for their own use; but in the illustrations, the resemblance of any animal denounced by the Jews as unclean can not be admitted. Among the modern Jews, the book of Esther, in particular, is frequently decorated with rude figures of various kinds; but with respect to this book, it must be observed that, owing to its wanting the sacred name of God, it is not held in such repute for holiness as the other books are. The manuscripts for private use may be either upon parchment, vellum, or paper, and of various sizes. "There is," says Prideaux, "in the church of St. Dominic, in Bononia, a copy of the Hebrew Scriptures, kept with a great deal of care, which they pretend to be the original copy written by Ezra himself; and therefore it is there valued at so high a rate, that great sums of money have been borrowed by the Bononians upon the pawn of it, and again repaid for its redemption. It is written in a very fair character upon a sort of leather, and made up in a roll according to the ancient manner; but it having the vowel-points annexed, and the writing being fresh and fair, without any decay, both these particulars prove the novelty of that copy. But such forgeries are no uncommon things among the papistical sect."

To open and shut up the roll or book of the law, to hold it, and to raise and show it to the people, are three offices, which are sold, and bring in a great deal of money. The skins on which the law is written are fastened to two rollers, whose ends jut out at the sides, beyond the skins, and are usually adorned with silver; and it is by them that they hold the book when they lift it up, and exhibit it to the congregation; because they are forbidden to touch the book itself with their hands. All who are in the synagogue kiss it, and they who are not near enough to reach it with their mouths, touch the silken cover of it, and then kiss their hands, and put the two fingers with which they touched it upon their eyes, which they think preserves the sight. They keep it in a cupboard, which supplies the place of the ark of the covenant, and they therefore call this cupboard Aaron, which is the Hebrew name for the ark; and this is always placed in the east end of the synagogue. He who presides chooses any one whom he pleases to read and explain the scripture, which was a mark of distinction; as we see in the thirteenth chapter of the Acts, where we find the rulers of the synagogue desiring the apostles, when they were in the synagogue, to make a discourse to the people. Ordinarily speaking, a priest began, a Levite read on, and at last one of the people, whom the president chose, concluded. He who reads stands upright, and is not suffered so much as to lean against a wall. Before he begins, he says with a loud voice, "Bless ye God;" and the congregation answer, "Blessed be thou, O my God, blessed be thou for ever;" and when the lesson is ended, the book is rolled up, and wrapped in a piece of silk.

The Jews still retain so great a veneration for the Hebrew tongue, that they do not think it lawful to use any other bibles in the synagogues but such as are written in that language. This was what enraged them so much against the Hellenistic or Græcising Jews, who read the Septuagint Greek version in their synagogues; and so much were they grieved that this version was ever made, that they instituted a fast, in which they annually lament this as a misfortune. But because the Hebrew was, after the captivity, no longer the vulgar tongue, there was an interpreter in the synagogues, who explained to the people in the Chaldee, or common tongue, what was read to them in the Hebrew. The use they made of the Scriptures, however, gave the people at least an imperfect knowledge of the Hebrew language. And thus we see the eunuch who is mentioned in the Acts, could read Isaiah, and understand enough of it to form the question which he put to Philip, concerning the passage in the prophecy relating to Jesus Christ.

After having spoken of the books contained in the Bible, and of the divisions of those books which have been used by the Jews and the Christians, both in ancient and modern times, it may now be necessary to examine a little into the language in which they were written. The Old Testament was originally written in the Hebrew tongue; and this language is generally considered as having the best claims to be considered the most ancient at present existing in the world, and, perhaps, as the primeval tongue of the human race. By the Hebrew language, therefore, is meant that which was spoken by Abraham, Isaac, Jacob, and the twelve patriarchs, which was afterward preserved among their posterity, and in which Moses wrote, it being improbable that he would employ any other language than that which was in use among the Jews.

This language is supposed by some to derive its name from Heber, great-grandson to Shem, whose posterity were denominated Hebrews; but it is much more likely that it received its name from its being the mother-tongue of the descendants of Abraham, who were called Hebrews, not because they were descended from Heber, but because Abraham, having received a command from God to leave the country where he lived, which was beyond the Euphrates, passed that river, and came into the land of Canaan, where the inhabitants of the country gave him the name of the Hebrew, that is, one that has passed over; in the same manner as the French call all those that live beyond the mountains, Ultramontanes.

The reasons that demonstrate the antiquity of the Hebrew tongue are many. In the first place, the names which the Scripture explains are therein drawn from Hebrew roots. It was thus that the first man was called Adam, because he had been formed out of the ground, which in Hebrew is called Adamah. The first woman was called Eve, because she was the origin of life to all, *evach* in Hebrew signifying *to live*. The name of Cain, which comes from Canah, signifying *to acquire*, or *get*, alludes to what Eve said when he was born: "I have got a man from the Lord." The explanation of these names is not to be found in any language but the Hebrew; and as this relation between names and things does not occur in any other language, it is in it alone that we can see the reasons why the first human beings were so called.

The names of an immense number of people, also, who are descended from the Hebrews, show the antiquity both of the nation and the language. The Assurians, for instance, derive their name from Ashur, the Elamites from Elam, the Arameans from Aram, the Lydians from Lud, the Medes from Madai, and the Ionians from Javan, who are all traced in the Hebrew bible to Shem, Ham, and Japhet. These names have no signification in any language but the Hebrew, which shows that they are derived thence, as are also the ancient names of the pagan deities; to which we must add the remark which several learned men have made, namely, that there is no language in which some remains of the Hebrew are not to be found.

A very apposite example, in allusion to the meaning of proper names in Hebrew, is to be found in the Book of Ruth, toward the end of the first chapter, where it is said, "And the whole town was in commotion about them; and the women said, Is this Naomi? And she said, Call me not Naomi (which means *Delightful*); call me Marah (which means *Bitter*); for the Almighty (Emer) hath caused bitterness exceedingly to me. I went away full, and Jehovah hath caused me to return empty; wherefore then do ye call me Naomi, since Jehovah hath brought affliction on me, and the Almighty hath caused evil to befall me?"

Thus we see that in Hebrew, as well as in most of the oriental languages, all proper names are significant words; and this is found to be the case also among many of the nations of Africa. This circumstance has a great effect in increasing the energy of the diction in these tongues; for it not unfrequently happens, as in the case of Naomi, that the speaker or writer, in addressing a person by his name, makes use of it at the same time as a word of ordinary signification, to express something in the inward disposition or the outward circumstances of the possessor. Instances of this occur in almost every page of the Hebrew scriptures; and, as may readily be supposed, it is impossible in such cases, for any common translation to do justice to the energy of the original. We have a very remarkable example of this in the twenty-fifth chapter of 1 Samuel, at the twenty-fifth verse, in which Abigail, speaking of her husband Nabal, says to David: "Let not my lord set his mind at all now toward the man of Belial (that is, worthless), this same person, Nabal (which means a scoundrel); for like his name so is he; Nabal is his name, and Nebelah (that is, vileness) is with him."

In speaking of the meaning of proper names, however, the most extraordinary example, perhaps, that can be produced from any book, either ancient or modern, is the following, which is to be found in the fifth chapter of Genesis: the names of the ten antediluvian patriarchs, from Adam to Noah inclusive, are there given; and when these ten names are literally translated, and placed in the order in which they occur, they form altogether the following very remarkable sentence in English: man, appointed, miserable, lamenting, the God of glory, shall descend, to instruct, his death sends to the afflicted, consolation!

We need not be surprised, therefore, at what is mentioned in the Spectator (No. 221), of a certain rabbinical divine having taken the first three of these names as the subject of his discourse, forming thus the text of a regular sermon. "We had a rabbinical divine in England," says Addison, "who was chaplain to the earl of Essex in Queen Elizabeth's time, that had an admirable head for secrets of this nature. Upon his taking the doctor of divinity's degree, he preached before the university of Cambridge upon the first verse of the first chapter of the First Book of Chronicles, 'in which,' says he, 'you have the three following words: 'Adam, Sheth, Enosh.'

"He divided this short text into many parts, and by discovering several mysteries in each word, made a most learned and elaborate discourse. The name of this profound preacher was Dr. Alabaster, of whom the reader may find a more particular account in Dr. Fuller's Book of English Worthies."

It is evident, that although this matter appeared ridiculous enough in Addison's eyes, so as to furnish him with a theme for a very amusing paper, yet, on considering attentively the meaning of the original words here used as proper names, a great deal of very sound doctrine might be elicited by a subtile divine, even from such an apparently insignificant text.

In the same way the names of animals in Hebrew are found to be words expressive of their qualities, which gives support to the idea that this was the language which Adam used when he gave them their names; as we find recorded in the second chapter of Genesis, at the 19th verse: "And Jehovah God formed out of the ground every beast of the field, and he formed also every fowl of the heavens; and he brought them unto Adam to see what he would call them, and whatever Adam called it— the living creature—it is its name."

Some of the names of animals in Hebrew are still found to be clearly descriptive of their qualities, and therefore in regard to what animal is intended there can in such cases be no dispute. But with respect to some others the matter is not so plain, as, from the root not being now found in the language, the ideal meaning of the name can not be so readily ascertained: and hence the eleventh chapter of Leviticus, in which the names of certain clean and unclean animals are enumerated, presents difficulties to a translator of no ordinary description.

There is, perhaps, no language in the world so easily reduced to its original elements as the Hebrew. As Wilson has well expressed it, "We descend from words to their element; and the accurate knowledge of letters is the principal part of Hebrew grammar. Its flexion nearly approaches that of the modern languages, particularly the English. The relations and dependances of nouns are not distinguished by terminations, or cases, but by particles or prepositions prefixed. The persons, moods, or tenses, of verbs are not marked by the changes of their last syllables, but by means of letters of a particular order, which sometimes appear in the middle, sometimes in the beginning, and sometimes in the end of the original word." In fact the structure of the Hebrew language is peculiarly favorable for the expression of energy and sublimity. The words, as is well known, are remarkable for shortness, the greater part consisting of not more than two, three, or four letters; few words have more than ten letters, and those that consist of that number are not many. The sentences are also for the most part short, and are quite free from that complexity which is apt to embarrass the reader when perusing even the best authors of Greece and Rome. The idiom of any language consists in the order of the words; but it is well known that, in this respect, the Greek and Latin tongues are extremely capricious, the words being arranged in them not in the order of the understanding, but of the ear, according to the sound rather than the sense. The Greek and Roman writers place the emphatic words in whatever order the sentence can be made to run most musically, though the sense be suspended till the speaker or reader come to the end; and hence the need of so many flexions and syntax-rules for a learner to arrange them to find out the meaning. Yet even for this purpose more declensions than one were not necessary; nor more tenses than three, a past, a present, and a future.

From this mass of perplexity the Hebrew language is entirely free. Its original words, called roots, consist of a proper number of letters, commonly three, the fewest that make a perfect number; and they express an action finished or expressed by a single agent. It has a proper number of voices, that is, active, passive, and medial—and only the tenses that are in nature. Its primitive words are more sentimental and scientific than sonorous; and they express original ideas, being definitions of things descriptive of their natures.

The Hebrew, Greek, and Latin, and such as are immediately derived from them, or constructed on their model, are the only languages that are formed on a regular artificial plan; and all other tongues of which we know anything, except perhaps the Persian and the Sanscrit, must be considered in comparison as mere gibberish, being quite rude in their original formation; nor is it possible to reduce them to another state, without wholly metamorphosing them. That which was never the language of a cultivated, learned people, and in which there are no literary works of taste, can not be a polished language, although it may have been the language of a civilized nation, or of a court, if they were only an illiterate people. In a word, all languages that have a concourse of consonants, or silent letters, are rude in their writing or pronunciation, whatever their structure may be. The Greek and Latin are free from the latter fault, and the Hebrew from both. "As Solomon possessed the most wisdom and knowledge," says Mr. Ray, "and treated all subjects of natural philosophy, &c., and his court being the most splendid and elegant, as people came to it from all nations, and greatly admired it, the Hebrew must be a copious, elegant language; and its structure is invariable, being the same in Moses and Malachi, at a thousand years' distance." In speaking of the genius of a language, indeed, which is its force, vigor, or energy, the Hebrew, may, without doubt, be said to excel all.

It is evident therefore that if, as Longinus observes, "saying the greatest things in the fewest words" be essential to simplicity and energy in discourse, the Hebrew is the best language in the world for the purpose. In it we have no superfluous parts of a sentence in words, or even in letters. A Hebrew writer conveys his meaning without circumlocution; for, although he were inclined, he would be unable to accomplish it, because the language is quite unsuitable in its nature for being employed in any such way; and therefore if an author's subject be good, even although he should possess but little genius, he will find no great difficulty to clothe his ideas in sublime and energetic language, if he write in Hebrew.

Such is the simple nature of the formation of this primitive language, and which seems, at the same time, to entitle it more to the claim of being a philosophical tongue than, perhaps, any other in the world. It is remarkable that the structure of this very ancient language approaches closely to that of the English, and other modern tongues, as the relations and dependances of nouns, according to what has been already remarked, are not distinguished by terminations, or cases, as in Greek and Latin, but by particles or prepositions (or little words) prefixed, and which are, at the same time, conjoined with the noun, as if they were a part of it.

The advantages which the Hebrew language possesses, above all others, in the simplicity of its formation—its remarkable originality, in that it borrows from no language, while almost all others borrow from it—as also the ideality which is found to pervade its roots or primitive words—have all been considered as entitling it to higher claims in the consideration of philosophers, than any other language in the world, either ancient or modern. These notions have been carried to such a length, indeed, by some learned men, that they gave rise to an entirely new school of philosophy, generally known by the designation of the Hutchinsonian; the disciples of which are remarkable as being opposed in many things to the Newtonian system, and as being possessed with the belief that in the Hebrew language, and in it alone, are to be found the germes of all true philosophy. The system takes its name from John Hutchinson, an English philosopher and critical author, who died in 1737, and was remarkable as an opponent of Dr. Woodward on natural history, and of Sir Isaac Newton in philosophy.

INTEGRITY OF THE TEXT.

The sacred books which were written, as we have seen, in Hebrew, the language of the patriarchs, have been preserved down to our days without any corruption; and the same judgment may also be formed of those other books of Scripture which have been since written in Greek. But before proving the purity and integrity of these original texts, it may be necessary to remove a prejudice which may arise from the variety of different readings that are found in the manuscript and printed copies of the Bible.

The different manner in which some passages are expressed in different manuscripts, together with the omission or insertion of a word, or of a clause, constitute what are called *various readings*. This was occasioned by the oversights or mistakes of transcribers, who deviated from the copy before them, these persons not being, as some have supposed, supernaturally guarded against the possibility of error; and a mistake in one copy would, of course, be propagated through all that were taken from it, each of which copies might likewise have peculiar faults of its own, so that various readings would thus be increased in proportion to the number of transcripts that were made. Besides actual oversights, transcribers might have occasioned various readings by substituting, through ignorance, one word, or even letter, in place of another; they might have mistaken the line on which the copy before them was written, for part of a letter, or they might have mistaken the lower stroke of a letter for the line, and thus have altered the reading; at the same time they were unwilling to correct such mistakes as they detected, lest their pages should appear blotted or defaced; and thus they sacrificed the correctness of their copy to its fair appearance. Copiers seem, not unfrequently, to have added letters to the last word in their lines, in order to preserve them even, and marginal notes have been sometimes introduced into the text. These different circumstances, as well as others with which we may not be acquainted, did no doubt contribute very much to produce and multiply mistakes and variations in the manuscripts of the Hebrew scriptures. This language is more susceptible of corruption, and any alteration would be more detrimental in it than in others. In English, if a letter be omitted, or altered, the mistake can be easily corrected, because the word thus corrupted may have no meaning; but in Hebrew, almost every combination of the letters forms a new word, so that an alteration of even one letter of any description is likely to produce a new word and a new meaning. Thus putting all alterations made knowingly—for the purpose of corrupting the text, out of the question—we must allow that from these circumstances connected with the transcribing, some errata may have found their way into it, and that the sacred Scriptures have in this case suffered the fate of other productions of antiquity.

When we have collected all the differences that are found in manuscripts of the original text, and have selected from them what are really various readings, we are able to determine, from the number and authority of the manuscripts, with tolerable correctness, what is the genuine reading. Beside the authority of the manuscript, we must also be guided in determining the true reading by the scope of the passage, by the interpretations and quotations of ancient writers, by the old versions, and not unfrequently by Scripture itself; for similar or parallel passages will often be found useful for this purpose. When all these things are considered, it will seldom happen that the true reading of a passage will be doubtful; yet should it continue so, either reading may contain a truth, though certainly *both* can not be *authentic*, and in a theological point of view, either of them may be followed without involving a doctrinal error; and in such a case, the common reading should not be relinquished.

To a person who has not considered the subject closely, it may appear sufficient to overthrow the authority of the text, that no less than thirty thousand various readings of the scriptures of the Old and New Testaments have been discovered. But when these are examined closely, and all that are not *properly* various readings are rejected, the number will be considerably diminished; from these again let all be deducted which make no alteration in the several passages to which they refer, and the reduction will be much greater; and out of the remainder there are none found that can invalidate the authority of those doctrines that have been esteemed fundamental, or that can shake a single portion of that internal evidence whereby the divine origin of the Scriptures is supported; so that the friends of revelation had no grounds for the alarm they felt at the time when the subject of various readings began to be discussed. These observations apply strongly to the New Testament, which, as it has been transcribed more frequently, and probably by less skilful transcribers than the Old, has, in proportion, many more various readings. Respecting these, however, it has been said, that "all the omissions of the ancient manuscripts put together, would not countenance the omission of any essential doctrine of the gospel, relative to faith or morals; and all the additions countenanced by the whole mass of manuscripts already collated, do not introduce a single point essential either to faith or morals, beyond what may be found in the Complutensian or Elzevir editions.*

The manner in which the original text of the Scriptures, particularly the Hebrew, has been preserved free from all material corruption, and handed down pure through such a long succession of ages, may now form the subject of our especial consideration.

It has been supposed by many that the Christian fathers accused the Jews of corrupting the text; but from an examination of such passages as seem to imply this, it appears that they spoke not of corrupting the text, but of adopting unfaithful translations. Justin Martyr, one of the most celebrated of the Christian fathers, defends the Jews very well as to this point, and proves that they have not corrupted the Scriptures: and it is past doubt they have not; for, as St. Jerome observes, before the birth of Jesus Christ they had certainly made no malicious alterations in them. If they had done so, our Saviour and his apostles, who cast so many reproaches upon the scribes and Pharisees, would not have passed over in silence so great a crime. To suppose such a thing, indeed, were to know little of the attachment of the Jews for the Scriptures. Josephus and Philo assure us that they would have undergone all sorts of torments rather than have taken a letter from the Scripture, or altered a word in it. A copy which had only one fault in it was by them thought polluted, and was not suffered to be kept above thirty days; and one that had four faults was ordered to be hid in the earth. In the Babylonian Talmud it is laid down as a regulation, that " the books of the law which have been written by a heretic, a traitor, one who is a stranger to the Jewish religion, an idolatrous minister—by which they mean a monk—a slave, a woman, one under age, a Cuthæan, or Christian, or an apostate Israelite, are unlawful."

" This," says St. Augustine, " is a most visible effect of the providence of God over his church. It pleased him that the Jews should be our librarians; that, when the Pagans reject the oracles of the ancient prophets concerning Jesus Christ, which we quote against them as being invented by us, we might refer them to the enemies of our religion, who will show them in their books the same prophecies which we quote against them."

The class of Jewish doctors called Massorites were grammarians, who engaged with peculiar ardor in the revisal of the Hebrew scriptures. The Massoritic notes and criticisms relate to the verses, words, letters, vowel-points, and accents. All the verses of each book and of each section are numbered, and the amount placed at the end of each in numerical letters, or in some symbolical word formed out of them; the middle verse of each book is also marked, and even the very letters are numbered; and all this is done to preserve the text from any alteration, by either fraud or negligence. For instance, Bereshith, or Genesis, is marked as containing 1,534 verses, and the middle one is at—" And by thy sword thou shalt live" (xxvii. 40). The lines are 4,395; its columns are 43, and its chapters 50. The number of its words is 27,713, and its letters are 78,100. The Massoritic notes, or Massorah, as the work is called, contain also observations on the words and letters of the verses; for instance, how many verses end with the letter *samech*; how many there are in which the same word is repeated twice or thrice; and other remarks of a similar nature.

It seems now generally agreed upon that the Massorites of Tiberias, during the fourth century of the Christian era, were the inventors of the system of the *vowel-points and accents* in the Hebrew Bible; and although they multiply them very unnecessarily, it must be allowed that this is the most useful of their works. From the points we learn how the text was read in their time, as we know they were guided in affixing them by the mode of reading which then prevailed, and which they supposed to have been traditionally conveyed down from the sacred writers.

The Massoritic notes were at first written in separate rolls, but they are now usually placed in the margin, or at the top and bottom of the page in printed copies. Many opinions are entertained about the authors of them; some think they were begun by Moses; others regard them as the work of Ezra and the members of the great synagogue, among whom were the later prophets; while others refer them entirely to the rabbins of Tiberias, who are usually styled the Massorites, and suppose that

* Vide Dr. Adam Clarke's Tract on the Editions of the New Testament.

they commenced this system, which was augmented and continued at different times by various authors, so that it was not the work of one man, nor of one age. It is not improbable that these notes were begun about the time of the Maccabees, when the Pharisees, who were called the masters of tradition, first began to make their observations on the *letter* of the law though they were regardless of its *spirit*. They might have commenced by numbering first the verses, next the words and letters; and then, when the vowel-points were added, others continued the system by making observations on them. On the whole, then it appears that what is called the Massorah is entitled to no greater reverence or attention than may be claimed by any other human compilation; but, at the same time, it must be allowed that it has preserved the Hebrew text from the time it was formed, and conveyed it to us as perfect as any ancient work could be given.

The various readings given in the Hebrew Bibles, and which are technically denominated by the Jews the *Keri* and *Cetib*, are not to be ascribed to Moses or the prophets, for it can not be supposed that inspired writers were ignorant of what was the true reading of the scripture text. One principal occasion of the notes of the Keri and Cetib is, that there are several words which the Jews, either from superstitious reverence or from contempt, are never allowed to pronounce. When they meet with them in the text, instead of pronouncing them, they pronounce others that are marked by certain vowels or consonants in the margin. The chief of these is the great name of God JEHOVAH, instead of which they always read *Adonai*, Lord, or *Elohim*, God. This is the word called *Tetragrammaton*, or the ineffable name of God, consisting of the four letters, *Yod, He, Wau, He*. The people were not suffered to pronounce it; the high-priest alone had that privilege, and that only in the temple once a year, when he blessed the people on the great day of atonement; and hence it is, that, as this holy name has not been pronounced since the destruction of the temple, its true pronunciation is now lost. Galatinus, in the sixteenth century, was the first who thought fit to say, that it ought to be pronounced *Jehovah*; "which did not happen," says Pere l'Amy, "without a very particular providence of God, who was pleased, that when the Jews lost the temple in which the true God was worshipped, they should at the same time lose the true pronunciation of his august name. It happened, I say, because, being no longer willing to be their God (for the destruction of the temple was an authentic testimony of the divorce which he gave them), he would not leave them the power of so much as pronouncing his name."[*]

Josephus, himself a priest, says it was unlawful for him to speak of the name whereby God was made known to Moses; and if it be true that the pronunciation of it was connected with the temple service, it is not surprising that all trace of it should be lost when the temple was destroyed, and when the Jews grew every day more superstitiously afraid of pronouncing it. Leusden, the great orientalist, is said to have offered a Jew at Amsterdam a considerable sum of money if he would pronounce it only *once*, but in vain.

Besides the various readings called the Keri and Cetib, which the Jews admit to be the oldest, there are two other kinds of various readings which deserve our notice, because they are given in some printed bibles. The first are those of the eastern and western Jews; the second, those between the manuscripts of Ben Asher and Ben Naphtali. By the eastern Jews we are to understand those of Babylon; by the western, those of Palestine. At Babylon and in Palestine, after the destruction of the city and temple, there were famous schools for many ages, and between the learned men of these places much rivalship existed; so that each party, by following their own copies, gave rise to a collection of various readings, or corrections of the text, whose antiquity is acknowledged, though it does not appear exactly at what time it was made.

The other collection is called after the heads of two celebrated schools—Ben Asher, at Tiberias, and Ben Naphtali, at Babylon, who were two famous Massorites, that lived about the year 1,030, and were the last of them. Both of these rabbies labored to produce a correct copy of the Scriptures, and the followers of each corrected theirs by that of their master. The variations between them relate to the *points*, and in but one instance is there any difference in the writing of a word; so that they do not affect the integrity of the text.

What has been said of the integrity of the text of the Old Testament, may be ap-

* Vide "Apparatus Biblicus, or an Introduction to the Study of the Holy Scriptures."

plied also to the New, in so far as it may be charged with corruptions, in consequence of the negligence of transcribers, as also in consequence of the attempt of heretics to make it conform to their erroneous sentiments. Though it must be admitted that the New Testament text, by being more frequently transcribed than that of the Old, became liable to a greater proportion of various readings, originating from the mistakes of the transcribers, yet this very circumstance was likewise a sure protection against wilful perversion or corruption; for in proportion as copies were multiplied, the difficulty of effecting a general corruption was increased. No such system as that of the Massorites was ever adopted to preserve the purity of the New Testament text; but we have it in our power to use various means for ascertaining what is the true reading of the text, without having recourse to such a plan as that of the Massorah; and concordances, which are now brought to an uncommon degree of perfection, are of great use in preserving it from corruption; in fact, the single one of Buxtorf has done more toward fixing the genuine reading, and pointing out the true meaning of Scripture, than the entire body of the Massoritic notes. We have the consent of the church, in all ages and countries, to prove our copies of the New Testament scriptures authentic, and the authenticity of the Hebrew text is confirmed by Christ and his apostles; and, in concluding this part of the subject, it may be remarked, that the general integrity of the Hebrew text receives additional confirmation from the ancient versions, as will more fully appear hereafter.

ANCIENT VERSIONS.

ORIGINALLY there was but one version of the Scriptures; but a schism of a remarkable nature which broke out between the Jews and the Samaritans, was the cause of producing another version; and of this, and those which followed, we are now about to speak. The Second Book of Kings furnishes us with the history of this schism, which, it will be recollected, was caused by the setting up of certain golden calves to be worshipped at Dan, in Bethel, by Jeroboam. Omri hence built Samaria, and made it the capital of his kingdom, and thus was the separation between Judah and Israel rendered complete. Samaria was, at first, only the name of a city, but afterward it became that of a province. It contained the tribe of Ephraim, and the half-tribe of Manasseh, which was on this side Jordan; so that it was to the north of Judea, and between the Great sea, Galilee, and Jordan; and there was, therefore, no going from Galilee to Jerusalem without passing through this province. The capital of the district, subsequent to the captivity, was Sichem, afterward called Neapolis, or Naplous, which was situated between the mountains Gerizim and Ebal. In the reign of Hezekiah, king of Judah, Samaria was taken by Shalmanezer, and the ten tribes were carried into captivity. Some years after, Esarhaddon sent the Cutheans to supply the place of the Jews, and to inhabit Samaria; and these people, who knew not the true God, but continued their idolatrous practices, and burnt their children in the fire to Moloch, were punished for their idolatry with lions, which made great havoc among them. For this reason, at their request, Esarhaddon sent some of those priests who had been carried into captivity, to instruct them, and teach them the worship of the true God. They did not embrace it with purity, however, but mixed the remains of paganism with their religion; for which reason, in the writings of the Jewish rabbies, they are denominated, in scorn, "The proselytes of the lions;" because it was through fear of them that they mixed the worship of the Creator with that of their idols. Nevertheless, when Manasses, the son of Jaddus, the high-priest of the Jews, had built the temple on Mount Gerizim, the Samaritans then retained their old superstitions no longer, but always contended that their temple was more holy than that of Jerusalem; inferring from the ark's having been a long time at Shiloh, near Ephraim, that the worship of God had rather begun in their country than in Jerusalem. According to Josephus, they claimed kindred with the Jews in their prosperity, but renounced all connexion with them when they were under persecution. From John's gospel we learn, that when the Messiah was on the earth, the Samaritans, who received no part of the Old Testament except the Pentateuch, had lost all tradition of the revolt and subsequent captivity of the ten tribes; they considered themselves descended from the stock of Israel, claimed Jacob for their father, and contended that the "holy mountain" was in the portion assigned to them by Joshua.

There was no particular enmity between the two nations until the time of Ezra. Incensed by the opposition they gave to the building of the temple, from the time their assistance was refused, he is said to have solemnly excommunicated them; and hence arose that enmity, which was carried to such a height that "the Jews had no dealings with the Samaritans;" and, from Ezra's time, Samaria became a refuge for the malcontent Jews. Ptolemy Lagos carried numbers, both of the Samaritans and of the Jews, into Egypt, where a fierce contest took place between them respecting the sanctity of their temples, each party insisting that theirs stood on the holy mount. The point was discussed publicly in presence of the king, and the Samaritan advocates, failing in their proof, were put to death. In the year 109 before Christ, John Hyrcanus destroyed the city and temple of the Samaritans, and, though afterward, viz., in the year 25 before Christ, King Herod built them a city and temple, they still continued to worship on Mount Gerizim. In the twelfth century, Benjamin of Tudela found some remains of these people in that country, where they are still to be found. During the revolt of the Jews, the Samaritans continued in their subjection to the Romans; and since that period they have always remained subject to the different powers who have been in possession of that and the neighboring countries.

It is supposed that the present Hebrew character was first adopted from the Chaldeans by Ezra, at the time when, after the return of the Jews from Babylon, he collected the Scriptures, and formed the entire canon. As the people were familiarized with the Chaldee, he used that character in transcribing the Old Testament. What is now called the *Samaritan*, was the character used by Moses and the prophets; and Ezra relinquished it to the Samaritans, it is said, in order to render the separation between them and the Jews more complete. Since that time, the Jews have used the character we call the Hebrew, and the Samaritans have retained the others.

The value of the Samaritan Pentateuch is very great; for, where its text accords with the Hebrew text, it confirms it most decidedly; because, as the Jews and Samaritans were such inveterate enemies, there never could have been any designed corruption effected by them both. It frequently confirms, and sometimes corrects, the reading of the Hebrew in important places; and it overturns all that system of rabbinical trifling, by which mysterious knowledge is said to be communicated through the shape and positions of certain letters, or certain words, which they pretend Moses learned from God, because such things can not be applied to its characters.

As the Samaritans do not understand the Hebrew text, although in the character of their own language, they have found it necessary to translate it for common use. For, as the Jews, after the Babylonish captivity, degenerated in their language from the Hebrew to the Babylonish dialect, so the Samaritans did the same, most probably, by bringing this dialect out of Assyria with them, when they first came to plant in Samaria. Therefore, as the Jews, for the sake of the vulgar among them who understood only the common language, were forced to make Chaldee versions of the Scriptures, which they called Targums, so the Samaritans, for the same reason, were obliged to do the same thing, and to make a version of their Pentateuch into the vulgar Samaritan, which is, most probably, the most ancient translation of the Bible in existence. This Samaritan version is not made, like the Chaldee versions among the Jews, by way of paraphrase, but by an exact rendering of the text word for word, for the most part without any variation. Being perfectly literal, the same Latin translation answers both to it and the Samaritan Pentateuch; and all the three are published in the Paris and London polyglots.

There were two causes which chiefly conduced to render the Greek language, at one time, of almost universal use in the world. The first cause was the conquests of Alexander the Great, who was, by nation, a Grecian, king of Macedon, and afterward ruler of the greater part of the then known world. His vast empire, although divided, yet subsisted for a great length of time, as his officers divided it among themselves, and reigned in different countries, so that the Greeks still continued to have dominion in the world, particularly the Seleucidæ, in Syria, and the Ptolomies, in Egypt, by which means the Greek language became known and in use, both in Judea and Egypt. The other cause of the extent of this language, was the high reputation the Greeks had acquired for learning and wisdom, which made many people desirous of knowing their language, who were not subject to their dominion.

This, then, was the language which was made use of to give the Gentiles the first knowledge of the Messiah. The Greek version of the Old Testament prepared the way for the gospel. The Gentiles read in these books the prophecies which the apostles showed had been accomplished in Jesus Christ: and they found, also, that the obstinate incredulity of the Jews had been foretold in them. They could not suspect the fidelity of the apostles, because this version of the Scriptures had not been made by them; nor could they accuse the Jews of having altered these books, because, as they were, the Jews were condemned in them. Besides, the time at which it was made, gave this translation of the Bible a prodigious deal of weight; because, from its having appeared before the birth of Jesus Christ, neither Pagans nor Jews could say that the ancient prophecies therein contained had been adapted to the circumstances of his life.

Whoever were the authors of this the first translation of the Scriptures into Greek, commonly known by the name of the SEVENTY, or the SEPTUAGINT, and of which the Jewish historians, Philo and Josephus, have spoken much, no one doubts that it was made long before the time of Jesus Christ; and it is of great authority. Several passages of the Old Testament, which are quoted in the New, are taken thence; and, being thus noticed by the writers of the New Testament, from their mode of using it, we may infer that it was in general circulation among the apostolic churches. All the other ancient versions, likewise, which were publicly read in the different churches of the world, the Arabic, the Ethiopic, the Armenian, the Gothic, the Illyrican, and the ancient Latin, which was in use before St. Jerome's time, were made from it; and, in short, every one of them, except the Syriac, were made from that of the SEVENTY, and to this day the Greek church, and the churches of the east, have no other. It is this version that the fathers and doctors of the church have explained and commented upon. It was from this version that they drew their decisions in matters of faith, and their precepts of morality. It was by this that they confuted heresies, and both general and particular councils explained themselves by it. Thus, whoever the authors of it were, its authority is great; and that upon this account only, if no other, that it was made at a time when the Hebrew was a living language, and, consequently, more easy to be understood than it is now, when it is almost impossible to come at the true understanding of it, otherwise than by the assistance of the ancient versions. For these reasons, we shall turn our attention, somewhat particularly, to the history of this celebrated version.

Alexander the Great, on his building of the city of Alexandria, in Egypt, brought a great many Jews thither to help to plant the new city; and Ptolemy Soter, after his death, having fixed the seat of his government there, and set his heart much upon the enlarging and adorning of it, brought thither many more of this nation for the same purpose; where, having granted to them the same privileges with the Macedonians and other Greeks, they soon grew to be a great part of the inhabitants of that city. Their continual intercourse with the other citizens, among whom they were there mingled, having obliged them to learn and constantly use the Greek language, the same happened to them here, as had happened to them before at Babylon; that is, by accustoming themselves to a foreign language, they forgot their own. Hence, from their no longer understanding the Hebrew language, in which the Scriptures had been hitherto first read, nor the Chaldee, in which they were after that interpreted in every synagogue, they got them translated into Greek for their own use, that this version might serve for the same purpose in Alexandria and Egypt, as the Chaldee paraphrases afterward did in Jerusalem and Judea.

After the time of Ezra, the Scriptures were read to the Jews in Hebrew, and interpreted into the Chaldee language; but at Alexandria, after the writing of this version, it was interpreted to them in Greek, which was afterward done also in all other Grecian cities where the Jews became dispersed.

There are several opinions which modern writers have entertained respecting the origin of the septuagint version, but the commonly-received opinion is that entertained by Bishop Walton, the author of the London polyglot, and is the same which is given in an historical account of the transaction, as related by a Hellenistic Jew, who flourished in the time of Ptolemy Philadelphus, king of Egypt. The account of the affair, as contained in a book written by the person above mentioned, whose name was Aristeas, is as follows:

King Ptolemy Philadelphus, having, by the advice of Demetrius Phalerius, caused a magnificent library to be erected at Alexandria, and given him the direction of it, this philosopher spoke to him of the sacred books of the Jews, as of a work which would do honor to his library. The prince, therefore, resolved to have a copy of the Jewish law translated into Greek, his own language, and that which was then universally understood. For this purpose he sent ambassadors to Jerusalem, to Eleazer, the high-priest, with magnificent presents for the temple. Their instructions were, to desire him to give the king a copy of the sacred books, and to send him some persons of distinction and learning, who might translate them into Greek. Aristeas, who was a chief officer in the king's guards, and a chief man in the kingdom of Egypt, was of this embassy; and Eleazer, who received him with honor, was, according to Josephus, the son of Onias the First, the brother of Simon the Just, who is mentioned in the apocryphal book called Ecclesiasticus, and grandson to Jaddus, who went to meet Alexander the Great, and made him confer favorable terms upon the Jews.

The high-priest consulted with the great council of the nation, called the sanhedrim, in regard to Ptolemy's request, and afterward chose six men out of each tribe—seventy-two in all—gave them a copy of the law, written in letters of gold, upon skins curiously fastened together, and sent them into Egypt. The king received them favorably, and showed a great deal of respect for the divine books; he then assigned them a residence in the isle of Pharos, about seven furlongs distant from Alexandria, where they completed the version in seventy-two days. Demetrius caused it to be read publicly in the presence of the priests, great men, and all the Jews, who were then very numerous at Alexandria, and it was universally applauded; they cried out, with one voice, that the translation was just and faithful; and, in order to render it not only authentic, but also unalterable, they made imprecations against those who should attempt to make any alteration in it. When it was read to the king, he admired the wisdom of the lawgiver, and commanded the books to be deposited in his library, allowing copies to be taken for the use of the Jews; he then sent back the seventy-two elders, after having made them some rich presents. The most magnificent of these presents was the freeing of one hundred and twenty thousand Jewish captives, whose ransom he paid, and gave them liberty to return into Judea. This version soon became common among all the Jews who spoke the Greek language, and was read publicly in their synagogues. It is not accurately ascertained in what year all this took place; Walton thinks the opinion which fixes it in the 7th of Ptolemy, and the 278th before Christ, the most probable.

THE SEPTUAGINT AND VULGATE.

It has generally been admitted that the SEPTUAGINT, which, as has been explained, is so called from the number seventy, or, more properly, seventy-two interpreters, who were said to be employed in the formation of it, was the first Greek version of the Old Testament. No mention has been made of any that preceded it, and it can not be deemed probable that Ptolemy would have taken so much pains to procure a version of the Jewish law, had any other previously existed; and it is equally improbable he should have been unacquainted with it, had it existed at a time when, with the assistance of Demetrius, he was procuring Greek books from every part of the world. It is plainly affirmed by Philo, that before his time the law was not known in any language but the original. The acquaintance with Jewish customs and Jewish history, which many heathen writers, before the reign of Ptolemy, have manifested, has led many persons to conclude that they must have derived their knowledge from a Greek version of at least parts of the Old Testament. Yet we may account for the knowledge of Jewish customs, &c., which these writers display, without supposing that they obtained it from any Greek version; for we have direct evidence that Aristotle, at least, had intercourse with the Jews, for the purpose of gaining information respecting their law; and as the philosophers were certainly acquainted with the doctrine of the Gymnosophists and the Druids, who had not any written law, so we may suppose they obtained their knowledge of the Jewish religion from personal intercourse with individuals of that nation.

At first, it is probable, the law only was translated, for there was no need of the other books in the public worship; no other part of the Scriptures but the law hav-, ing been in early times read in the synagogues. But afterward, when the reading of the prophets also came into use in the synagogues of Judea, in the time of the persecution under Antiochus Epiphanes, and the Jews of Alexandria, who in those times conformed themselves to the usages of Judea and Jerusalem in all matters of religion, were induced hereby to do the same; this caused a translation of the proph- ets also to be there made into the Greek language, in like manner as the law had been before. After this, other persons translated the rest for the private use of the same people; and so that whole version was completed which we now call the sep- tuagint; and after it was thus made, it became of common use among all the churches of the Hellenistical Jews, wherever they were dispersed among the Gre- cian cities.

When the Hebrew language had ceased to be the vulgar tongue, the version of the *seventy* was read in the synagogues, even in Judea itself. It is true, this was not universally done; there was a sort of division among the Jews about it; some were for having the Scripture read only in Hebrew, and were therefore called *He- brews*, or *Hebraizers;* while others read it in Greek, and were called *Hellenists*, that is, *Grecians*, or *Grecizers*, as has been already observed. As the number of the lat- ter was greater than that of the Hebrew-Jews, and the apostles preached most fre- quently to them, it is not to be wondered at, as St. Jerome observes, that the passages of the Old Testament which are quoted in the New, are sometimes borrowed thence. It is thus seen that this version preceded the publication of the gospel; and it has been authorized by the use which the apostles made of it, as well as the whole church. It seems very evident however, from various passages, as Parkhurst has remarked, that the writers of the New Testament, in their citations of the Old, did not intend either literally to translate the Hebrew, or to stamp their authority on the SEVENTY translation, but only to refer us to the original Scriptures.

The septuagint version was continued in public use among the Jews for more than three hundred years; but as it grew into use among the Christians, it went out of credit with the Jews. In the twelfth year of the emperor Adrian, A. D. 128, Aquila, a native of Sinope, a city of Pontus, published a new Greek version of the Old Tes- tament. This man, who had been a Christian, and afterward became a Jew, is supposed to have undertaken this work in opposition to the Christians, not only that the SEVENTY might be superseded, but that a new version might be given of those passages on which they relied most in their controversies with the Jews. The Hel- lenistic Jews received this version, and afterward used it everywhere instead of the septuagint; and, therefore, this Greek translation is often made mention of in the Talmud, or Compendium of Jewish Doctrines, but the septuagint never. The em- peror Justinian published a decree, which is still extant among his institutions, whereby he ordained that the Jews might read the Scriptures in their synagogues, either in the Greek version of the SEVENTY, or in that of Aquila, or in any other lan- guage, according to the country in which they should dwell. But the Jewish doc- tors having determined against this, their decrees prevailed against that of the empe- ror, and, within a little while after, both the septuagint and the version of Aquila was rejected by them; and ever since, the solemn reading of the Scriptures among them, in their public assemblies, has been in the Hebrew and Chaldee languages. "The Chaldee," says Prideaux, "is used in some of their synagogues even to this day, and particularly at Frankfort, in Germany."

Not long after the time of Aquila, there were two other Greek versions of the Old Testament scriptures made; the first by Theodotion, who lived in the time of Com- modus, the Roman emperor, and the other by Symmachus, who flourished a little after him, in the reigns of Severus and Caracalla. The former is supposed to have belonged to Ephesus, and fell into the heretical errors of Ebion and Marcion, to which sect Symmachus also belonged, being by birth a Samaritan, and by profession first a Jew, then a Christian, and, lastly, an Ebionite heretic. They both of them undertook the making their versions with the same design as Aquila did, though not entirely for the same end; for they all three entered on this work for the per- verting of the Old Testament scriptures. Aquila, however, did it for the serving of the interest of the Jewish religion, the other two for promoting the interest of the heretical sect to which they belonged; and all of them wrested the original Scriptures in their versions of them, as much as they could, to make them speak for the different ends which they proposed. From the circumstances, therefore, under which these versions were made, it may be inferred that their authority can not be very great, though from the fragments of them which have been collected, we may derive considerable assistance in understanding particular portions of the Old Testament.

In speaking of the ancient versions of the Bible, it must be observed, that there are two in the Syriac language: the Old, which is a translation of the Old Testament from the Hebrew, and the New, which is a translation of the New Testament from the Greek. This last is, beyond contradiction, the most ancient that ever was formed in the Christian church. It is that which the Christians in the east, called Maronites, make use of in their worship: and they, as well as the other Syrian Christians, boast very much of its antiquity; for they allege that one portion of it was made by the command of Solomon, for the use of Hiram, king of Tyre, and the other part by the command of Abgarus, king of Edessa. It is certain this version was of considerable antiquity, and was in all likelihood made within the first century after Christ, and had for its author some Christian of the Jewish nation that was thoroughly skilled in both the Hebrew and Syriac languages; and as it is among the oldest translations that we have of any part of the Scriptures, so it is the best, without any exception, that has been made of them by the ancients into any language whatsoever. This last character belongs to it in respect of the New Testament, as well as of the Old; and therefore, of all the ancient versions which are now consulted by Christians for the better understanding of the Holy Scriptures, as well of the New Testament as of the Old, none can better serve this end than this old Syriac version, when carefully consulted and well understood. To this purpose the very nature of the language gives much assistance; for, it having been the mother-tongue of those who wrote the New Testament, and a dialect of that in which the Old was first given, many things of both are more happily expressed in it through this whole version than can well be done in any other language.

The languages of princes generally become, in time, the common language of their subjects. The conquests of Alexander made the Greek tongue universal; and by the same means the Latin tongue extended itself, with the Roman empire, all over the world; so that, at length, there was scarce a nation where, by the help of this language, you might not make yourself understood.

It is not known who was the author of the first Latin version of the Scriptures; but St. Augustine, a celebrated bishop of the Latin church, about A. D. 400, tells us that there soon appeared a great number of them. "We know them who translated the Scriptures into Greek," says he, "and the number of them is not great; but the number of the Latin translators is infinite. When the faith came to be established, the first man who found a Greek copy, notwithstanding the little knowledge he had of the two languages, boldly undertook a translation of it." From another passage of his writings, it has been generally concluded that there was one particular version, called "the Italian," in higher estimation than the rest, and which was the authorized version of the Roman churches. However this may be, it is certain the Latin church was in want of a version of the Scriptures formed directly from the Hebrew, as all the Latin translations in existence at that time had been taken from the SEVENTY. St. Jerome, who was contemporary with St. Augustine, was in every respect best suited, of any of the learned men of that time, to the task of making a new translation, which he accordingly undertook. He began by correcting some books of the Old Testament in the Latin bible, particularly the version of the Psalms, and marked those passages wherein any difference existed between the Latin version, the Greek of the SEVENTY, and the Hebrew original. He had early applied himself the study of the Hebrew language, and at different periods had the assistance of five Jewish teachers; he had access also to the works of Origen, who published what is called the Hexapla, that is, the Bible in six different languages. From these he must have derived considerable assistance in the work he undertook: that of translating into Latin all the books of the Old Testament, to which he added a corrected edition of the common version of the new.

This work of St. Jerome is still used in the Roman Catholic church, and is known by the name of the *Vulgate*; for which some have gone so far as to claim the authority and infallibility of an inspired production. At first, however, his version was not generally received; for although many were pleased with it, because it was more consonant to the original, and a more literal translation than that of the SEVENTY, yet others, and among the rest Augustine, considered it a rash attempt, and calculated to diminish the authority of the Greek version. It was approved of by the Jews as conformable to their text, and was received into the church gradually and by tacit consent, rather than by the sanction of public authority.

Nevertheless, the Vulgate which we have at present, and which the celebrated council of Trent declared to be authentic, is not the pure version of St. Jerome; it has in it a great deal of the ancient Italian; but it can not now be discovered by whom, or at what time, this mixture was made. Some think that St. Jerome has no part at all in the present Vulgate; and it is certain that the Psalms in it are not his. Nevertheless, the Latin version comes nearer to the Hebrew, and is more perspicuous, than the Septuagint. Since the time of the council of Trent, namely, in 1589 and 1592, corrected editions of the Vulgate have been published under the authority of the popes Sixtus the Fifth and Clement the Eighth.

MODERN FOREIGN VERSIONS.

We have seen, by the preceding remarks on this subject, that, at some period prior to the promulgation of Christianity, there existed a valuable translation of the Scriptures into Greek, entitled the SEPTUAGINT, or the SEVENTY, from the number of individuals engaged in its arrangement. It has also been shown, that at an early period in the history of the Christian church, a Latin translation of the Scriptures was found called the VULGATE. These Greek and Latin versions of the Bible did not supersede the use of the original Hebrew Scriptures, such being ever preserved by the Jews with the most extraordinary care, and generally made use of by them in their synagogues, while the Septuagint and Vulgate, from being in more modern languages, were in more extensive use among churchmen and the people. The existence of these early versions is therefore an incontestable evidence that the Scriptures as now found in the original tongues, have not been impaired, interpolated, or abused, during the lapse of at least two thousand years.

Almost all the modern nations of Europe, and part of Asia, have had versions of the Scriptures, in whole or in part, taken from other versions, or from the originals. Arabic having become the vulgar language of almost all the east, there are several versions of the Bible in Arabic, which, besides the Syriac version (which is understood by the learned alone), are not only used by the Maronites and other Christians in Asia, but also by the Jews and Samaritans. About the year 900, Rabbi Saadias Gaon, an Arabian Jew, translated the Old Testament, or, at least, the Pentateuch, into Arabic. Another Jew of Mauritania translated the Pentateuch, and Erpenius printed his work. Risius, a monk of Damascus, translated the New Testament. The greater part of these versions were from the Septuagint.

The Persians have some manuscript versions of the Bible. Rabbi Jacob Favos, a Jew, translated the Pentateuch into Persian, and the Jews printed it at Constantinople in 1546. This, with the gospels translated by one Simon, a Christian, are inserted in the London polyglot;* but these gospels are far from being correctly done. There have been several other Persian versions of the Psalms and the New Testament executed in modern times, particularly the New Testament by Henry Martyn, the celebrated English missionary, translated by him in the city of Shiraz in Persia, and printed at Petersburgh in 1815.

The Turks have likewise some translations in manuscript of the Bible in their language. In 1666, a Turkish New Testament was printed at London, for the purpose of being dispersed in the east. It is mentioned, that, in 1721, the Grand Signor ordered an impression of bibles to be produced at Constantinople, that they might be confronted with the Koran, or Bible of the Mohammedans. In the Report of the British and Foreign Bible Society for 1815, it is mentioned, that a Turkish translation in manuscript of the whole Bible had been discovered in the repositories of the University of Leyden, where it had remained for a century and a half. The author of this translation was by birth a Pole, of the name of Albertus Boboosky, and born in the

* Polyglot is a Greek compound word, signifying *many tongues*, and is employed as a title for certain modern Scriptures, printed in divers languages.

beginning of the seventeenth century. While a youth, he was stolen by the Tartars, and, being sold to the Turks in Constantinople, he was by them educated in the Mohammedan faith. His name was changed to Hali Bey, and when he grew up, he was constituted the chief dragoman or translator to Mohammed the Fourth. The learning of Hali Bey was considerable. He understood seventeen languages, and he is said to have spoken in French, German, and English, like a native. He was particularly fond of the English language, and, at the request of the Hon. R. Boyle, translated the Church of England Catechism into Turkish. He also composed different works himself, several of which have been published. His chief work, however, is his translation of the whole Bible into the Turkish language, which was undertaken at the instigation and under the direction of the famous Levin Warner, Dutch ambassador at the court of the sultan at that period; and the translation appears to have been completed about the year 1666, the same year in which Seaman's translation of the New Testament into Turkish was published at Oxford.

The Armenians have a translation of the Old Testament, done from the Septuagint, by Moses Grammaticus, and two others, about 1400 years ago. In 1666, under the direction of an Armenian bishop, it was printed at Amsterdam, corrected or corrupted from the Vulgate. Theodorus Patreus procured an impression of an Armenian New Testament at Antwerp in 1668, and of the whole Bible in 1690. In 1815, the Armenian Bible, in quarto, for the accommodation of the Armenian inhabitants of Russia, who subscribed liberally for the undertaking, was printed at St. Petersburgh. The Armenians are scattered all over Asia.

The Georgians have the Bible in their ancient language; but that being now almost obsolete, and themselves, in general, brutishly ignorant, few of them can either read or understand it. There has never been, till lately, but one edition of the Georgian Bible; it was printed at Moscow in 1743 in a large folio volume.

The modern Greeks have recently received the New Testament in their proper tongue, which is considerably different from that in which the sacred work was originally written. The edition is in the Hellenestic and Romaic dialects, and was printed in England under the direction of a society. It has been approved of by the the patriarch of the Greek church.

The Russians have the Bible in their Sclavonic tongue, done from the Greek by Cyril, their apostle. It was published in 1581, but being too obscure, Ernest Gluk, a Swedish captive, above one hundred years ago, began to form another. He died before he finished it. Peter the Great ordered a number of his most learned clergy to complete the work; and it is supposed that the bibles distributed by imperial authority about 1722 were of this translation. In the course of two hundred and sixty years, from the time when printing was first introduced into Russia, no more than twenty-two editions of the Sclavonian Bible had appeared, prior to the year 1815, consisting of about fifty thousand copies only.

The most ancient German translation is that of Ulphilas, bishop of the Goths, about A. D. 360; but he left out the Books of Kings, lest they should have excited his savage countrymen to war. Toward the end of the 16th century, Junius professed to publish an edition of it, from a manuscript found in the abbey of Verden, written in letters of silver. An anonymous version was printed at Nuremberg in 1477. Between 1521 and 1532, Luther composed his translation, but Michaelis, La Croze, and Bayer, think this was not from the Gothic version of Ulphilas, but one about 200 years later; he published it in seven parts, as it was ready. Some persons of quality, masters of the German language, revised it. Two catholic versions, the one of Eckius on the Old, and Emzer on the New Testament, and another of Ulembergius, were published to depress the credit of Luther's; but the protestants of Germany and Switzerland still use it, a little corrected. About 1604, Piscator turned the Latin translation of Junius and Tremellius into a kind of German, but too much Latinized. About 1680, Athias published a Hebrew-German translation of the Old Testament, for the sake of his Jewish brethren, and Jekuthiel another; but both, especially the latter, distorted several texts relative to the Messiah, &c.

The first Polish version of the Scriptures is ascribed to Hadewich, the wife of Jagellon, Duke of Lithuania, who embraced Christianity A. D. 1390. In 1596, the protestants published another, formed on Luther's translation. There were three other versions, one by James Wick, a Jesuit, and the other two by Socinians, published in the end of the 16th century.

About 1506, the Bohemian Taborites published a Bible in their language, done from the Vulgate. In the end of the 16th century, eight Bohemian divines, after a careful study of the original languages at Wirtemberg and Basil, published a version from the original text.

In 1534, Olaus and Laurence published a Swedish Bible, done from Luther's German translation. About 1617, Gustavus Adolphus ordered some learned men to revise it; and it has been, since, almost universally followed in that kingdom. The translation into the language of Finland is thought to have been done from it. In 1550, Peter Palladius, and three others, published a Danish version, done from the German of Luther; and there are one or two others, as also a version in the Icelandic tongue.

The Flemish or Dutch Bibles, composed by Roman Catholics, are very numerous; but the names of the translators are scarcely known, except that of Nicolas Vink, in 1548. The Calvinists of the Low Countries long used a version done from Luther's; but the synod of Dort appointed some learned men to form a new one from the originals. It was published in 1637, and is considered very exact.

Since the Reformation, a vast number of Latin versions of the Bible have been made by members of the Romish church. Pagnin the Dominican was the first after St. Jerome who translated the Old Testament into Latin from the Hebrew. His version was printed at Lyons in 1528. It is very literal, and generally exact. Arias Montanus retouched it, and made it yet more literal. After Pagnin came a crowd of interpreters, since the Hebrew language has been more studied. Leo of Judah, who, though not a Jew, understood Hebrew extremely well, began one, which has since been printed at Zurich; but death having prevented him from finishing his work, Theodorus Bibliander completed it. This is the version which Robert Stephens printed with the Vulgate and Vatablus's Notes, without naming the authors of it. Of Protestants, Emmanuel Tremillius, who of a Jew became a Christian, and Francis Junius, have also given a Latin translation, as also Castalio and Beza. These are considered tolerably exact, and have been frequently reprinted. Sebastian Munster also published a literal but judicious translation.

In 1471, an Italian Bible, done from the Vulgate by Nicolas Malerme, a Benedictine monk, was published at Venice. Anthony Bruccioli published another in 1530, but the council of Trent prohibited it. The Protestants have two Italian versions—the one, which is rather a paraphrase than a translation, by the celebrated Diodati, published in 1607, and with corrections in 1641—the other by Maximus Theophilus, and dedicated to the Duke of Tuscany, about 1551. By an order of King James of Arragon to burn them, we find there were a number of bibles in Spanish about the year 1270, probably the work of the Waldenses. About 1500, a Spanish version was published, but the translator's name is unknown. In 1543, Driander published his version of the New Testament, and dedicated it to the Emperor Charles the Fifth. In 1553, the Jews published their Spanish version of the Old Testament, after having long used it in private. Cassiodore, a learned Calvinist, published his Bible in 1569, which Cyprian de Valera corrected and republished in 1602.

Peter de Vaux, chief of the Waldenses, published the first translation of the Bible in French about A. D. 1160. Two others were published about the years 1290 and 1380; and in 1550, by order of the Emperor Charles the Fifth, the doctors of Louvain published another. There are various other French versions, particularly of the New Testament; that of Mons, done from the Vulgate, and published in 1665, with the king of Spain and archbishop of Cambray's license, is in a most clear and agreeable style. In 1702, F. Simon published his New Testament, with some literal and critical notes, which the bishops of Paris and Meaux quickly condemned.

There are many French versions of the Bible done by Protestants. Faber's translation of the New Testament was printed for those of Piedmont, in 1534. Next year, Peter Olivetan's Bible was published at Geneva, and, having been reprinted with the corrections of Calvin and others, it is now a work of considerable exactness. After some struggling with the French Protestant clergy, Diodati published his in 1644; but, like his Italian and Latin versions, the translation is too free and paraphrastic. Le Clerc published his New Testament at Amsterdam in 1703, with notes mostly borrowed from Grotius and Hammond. The states-general prohibited it, as inclining to the Sabellian and Socinian heresies. La Cene published another, which shared much the same fate, on account of its fancies and errors.

42

The Bible, or at least portions of it, principally by the labors of the missionaries at Serampore, are now printed in nearly forty Indian languages, and are also to be found in Tartar, in Calmuc, and in Chinese. Upon the whole, out of the 3,064 languages which are said to exist in the world, the Bible is now to be found in one hundred and thirty-nine.

ENGLISH VERSIONS.

It is probable that the inhabitants of Britain, who were first converted to Christianity by St. Augustine, about the beginning of the seventh century, had some of the scripture in their own language. About A. D. 709, Adelm translated the Psalms into English Saxon, and other parts of scripture were translated by Eadfrid, a Saxon, about the same time. Bede, the first ecclesiastical English historian, who was born at Jarrow, on the banks of the Tyne, in 673, commonly denominated the Venerable Bede, made a translation of the Gospels, if not the whole Bible, into his native tongue. The whole Bible was translated into the Anglo-Saxon by order of King Alfred; and he himself, about A. D. 890, undertook a version of the Psalms, but died before it was completed. The next complete translation of the whole Bible, including the apocryphal books, was made by John Wickliffe into English from the Latin, and appeared between 1360 and 1380. This translation was written, but not printed; and great objections were made to it by the clergy; so that, in consequence of a decree of Arundel, archbishop of Canterbury, many persons were committed to the flames for reading Wickliffe's translation of the Old and New Testament. The only portion of Wickliffe's version of the Scriptures which has ever appeared in print, is the New Testament, published in 1731, by the Rev. John Lewis, minister of Margate, in Kent. This was reprinted several years ago, with a life of this earliest of English reformers, by the Rev. H. Baber, A. M., assistant librarian at the British museum. For the gratification of our young readers, we shall transcribe the Lord's prayer in Wickliffe's language, as a curious specimen of the orthography of the times in which this great reformer lived :—

"Our Fadir that art in hevenys; halewid be thi name. Thi kyngdom come to, be thi will done in erthe as in hevene. Give to us this day our breede ouir other substaunce. And forgiue to us our dettis as we forgiven to our dettouris. And lede us not into temptacioun, but delyvere us from yvel. Amen."

In the reign of Henry VIII., William Tyndale made one of the best English translations of the New Testament. It appeared in 1526, being the first that ever was printed in the English language. It was published at Hamburgh or Antwerp, and was dispersed at London and Oxford. Tonstal, bishop of London, and Sir Thomas More, bought up almost the whole impression, and burnt it at St. Paul's Cross. The venders were condemned by the star-chamber to ride with their faces to the horses' tails, with papers on their heads, and with the copies they had dispersed tied about them, to the standard at Cheapside, where they were compelled to throw them in the fire. The price, however, enabled Tyndale to proceed, and, undismayed, he began to translate the Old Testament; for which he was at length seized in Flanders, and, having been strangled by the common hangman, his body was consumed to ashes.

Previous to the Reformation, in the time of Henry VIII., people were so little acquainted with the Scriptures, and so ignorant even in regard to the languages in which they were originally written, that the strangest assertions were made. Upon the appearance of the Scriptures in the Hebrew and Greek originals, some individuals exclaimed that " there was now a new language discovered called GREEK, of which people should beware, since it was that which produced all heresies; that in this language was come forth a book called the New Testament, which was now in everybody's hands, and was full of briars and thorns. And there had also another language now started up, which they called Hebrew, and that they who learnt it were termed Hebrews !"

When the Reformation in England first took place, efforts were made to promote the reading of the Scriptures among the common people. Among other devices for the purpose, the following curious one was adopted. Bonner, bishop of London, caused six bibles to be chained to certain convenient places in St. Paul's church, for all that were so well inclined to resort thither, together with a certain admonition to the readers, fastened upon the pillars to which the bibles were chained, to this tenor: "That whosoever came there to read should prepare himself to be edified, and made the better thereby; that he should bring with him discretion, honest intent, charity, reverence, and quiet behavior; that there should no number meet together there as to make a multitude; that no such exposition be made thereupon but what is declared in the book itself; that it be not read with noise in time of divine service, or that any disputation or contention be used about it; that in case they continued their former misbehavior, and refuse to comply with these directions, the king would be forced, against his will, to remove the occasion, and take the bibles out of the church."

Soon after the death of Tyndale, John Rogers, afterward martyr, finished the correction of Tyndale's translation of the Old Testament, and printed it at Hamburgh, under the name of Thomas Matthews. Archbishop Cranmer and Miles Coverdale further corrected it. Cranmer got it printed by public authority in England, and King Henry ordered a copy of it to be set up in every church, to be read by every one that pleased; but, by advice of the Romish bishops, he soon after revoked this order, and prohibited the Bible. When Coverdale, Knox, Samson, Goodman, Gilby, Cole, and Whittiugham, were exiles during the persecution in the reign of Mary, they framed another translation, with short notes, and got it printed at Geneva. It was much valued by the Puritans, and in about thirty years had as many editions. The bishops being displeased with it, made a new one of their own, which was read in the churches, while the Geneva translation was generally read in families. About 1583 Laurence Thompson published an English version of the New Testament, from the Latin translation, and annotations of the learned Genevan divine Theodore Beza. In the end of the sixteenth and beginning of the seventeenth century, the English catholics at Rheims published a version of the whole Bible, crowded with barbarous terms, and accompanied with notes calculated to support the doctrines of their church.

Of those who translated the Geneva bible, as it is called, in the reign of Mary, besides Coverdale, we have their own and contemporary testimony, that they well understood the grace and propriety both of the Hebrew and Greek tongue. Among the good Hebrew scholars of this period, also, must be reckoned Bishop Alley, afterward one of the translators of the Bishops' Bible, who was the author of a Hebrew grammar, and a person universally learned, especially in divinity and languages; as well as his fellow-laborer, Bishop Benthan, who, about the beginning of the reign of Edward VI., is said to have addicted his mind entirely to the study of theology and the learning of the Hebrew language. To these may be added Bishop Davies, another of the translators of the Bishops' Bible, who, in the time of Mary, fled from this country, and, after his return in the following reign, served Wales, as well as England, with his assistance in translations of the Bible from the original into the languages of both countries.

The knowledge of Hebrew seems sometimes to have formed in those days a part even of female education for ladies of superior rank; and, accordingly, Paschali, in his translation of the Psalms from the Hebrew into Italian verse, dedicated it to Queen Elizabeth, as one who was well acquainted with the eastern tongues.

"Having entered upon the reign of Elizabeth, we soon behold," says Todd, in his Memoirs of Bryan Walton, "with grateful admiration, the goodly company of those who made the present version of our Bible in the reign of her successor. Of these, several, if they have been equalled, have not yet been excelled by any of their countrymen in oriental learning. With men of similar studies the kingdom then abounded. Nor could it well be otherwise, attention having been paid to the cultivation of such learning in public schools (particularly Merchant-Tailors school), founded soon after the accession of Elizabeth, and the pursuit being greatly encouraged at both universities."

At the conference which was held at Hampton Court, soon after the accession of James, for the settling of an ecclesiastical uniformity between the two countries of England and Scotland, the Puritans suggested unanswerable objections to the Bishops' Bible; and the king similarly objected to the Genevan translation. He therefore appointed fifty-four learned persons to translate the Scriptures anew into English, or, at least, compose a better translation, out of many. Seven of the fifty-four either died or declined the assigned task. Forty-seven, who remained, were ranged into six divisions, every individual of each division translating the portion assigned to the division, all of which translations were collected together; and when each company had determined on the construction of their part, it was proposed to the other divisions for general approbation. When they met together, one read the new version, while all the rest held in their hands either copies of the original, or some valuable version: when they observed any objectionable passage, the reader paused till they considered and agreed on it. They met at Oxford, Cambridge, and Westminster, beginning the work in 1607, and after the expiration of three years it was finished, and published in 1611. This Bible, which is now in use, must be pronounced an excellent work, remarkable for the general fidelity of its construction, as well as for the simplicity of its language. Dr. Adam Clarke remarks, that "those who have compared most of the European translations with the original, have not scrupled to say, that the English translation of the Bible, made under the direction of King James the First, is the most accurate and faithful of the whole. Nor is this its only praise: the translators have seized the very spirit and soul of the original, and have expressed this almost everywhere with pathos and energy." It is still of public authority in the British dominions; and, next to the Dutch, is perhaps the best translation of the Bible extant.

It has been asserted by Mr. Bellamy, and some others, that the authors of our authorized translation confined themselves to the Septuagint and the Vulgate, and did not translate from the Hebrew. This assertion, however, can be at once overthrown, by bringing forward the authority of the fifty-four, or rather, as seven of them died before the translation was finished, of the forty-seven learned men, as may be seen by their no less modest than dignified preface, or address to the reader, inserted in the edition of the Bible published in the year 1630, which has this satisfactory passage among many others: "If you ask what they had before them, truly it was the Hebrew text of the Old Testament—the Greek of the New."

Among these translators, two of the most noted for Hebrew erudition were Dr. Adrian Saravia, and Dr. Richard Clarke. Dr. Saravia, well known as a Hebrew critic, "was educated," says Mr. Todd in his life of Bryan Walton, "in all kinds of literature in his younger days, especially in several languages. He was the master of the celebrated oriental scholar, Nicholas Fuller, who gratefully mentions him in the preface to his Miscellanea Theologica; and he was one of those who had successfully answered an objection of the Puritans, which they revived in the conference at Hampton Court, in regard to a verse in the old English version of the Psalms. Next to him in rank is Dr. Richard Clarke, who thoroughly understood three languages, Latin, Greek, and Hebrew. Christ college, in Cambridge, of which he was a fellow, 'had a testimony of his learning in his Hebrew lectures; so had the university, in his disputations and sermons; so had the church, when his majesty (James the First) called many to the work of the last translation of the English bible; in which number he was, like one of the chief of David's worthies, not among the thirty, but among the first three.' To him and to Dr. Saravia, it appears that the portion assigned was from the Pentateuch to the book of Chronicles."

One of the best Hebrew scholars of that time was the celebrated English divine and theological writer, Hugh Broughton, who corresponded with a learned rabbi at Constantinople, and used great exertions for the conversion of the Jews there to Christianity. Mr. Broughton was in continual and most bitter controversy with the bishops, and was not employed, as he thought he should have been, in the translation of the Bible. At the time when our present version was made, he communicated many interpretations to the translators, which, as he afterward complains, they "thrust into the margent;" and whoever compares the text of our version with the marginal readings, will be led to regret that our translators did not associate him with them; though, it must be confessed, he would not have proved a very agreeable fellow-laborer.

It must be observed, that in rendering the original text into English, there are certain words necessarily supplied by the translators, in order to make out the meaning. These supplementary words are printed in our Bible in *italic* letters, to show that they are not in the original. The greatest of these supplements occurs in the 23d verse of the second chapter of the First Epistle of John, where the translators have supplied no fewer than *ten* words, in order to make out what they thought to be the proper meaning.

"From the mutability of language," says Evans, "the variation of customs, and the progress of knowledge, several passages in the Bible require to be newly translated, or materially corrected. Hence, in the present age, when biblical literature has been assiduously cultivated, different parts of the sacred volume have been translated by able hands. The substituting a new translation of the Bible in the room of the one now in common use, has been much debated. Dr. Knox, in his ingenious essays, together with others, argues against it; while Dr. Newcome, the late Lord Primate of Ireland, the late Dr. Geddes, of the Catholic persuasion, and the late Rev. Gilbert Wakefield, contended strenuously for it. Bishop Lowth and Professor Marsh have pointedly shown the necessity of bringing the text of the Scriptures, by the aid of ancient manuscripts and versions, as near as may be to perfection."[a]

Ainsworth, Doddridge, Macknight, Lowth, Blaney, and others, have published new translations of parts of the sacred books in English; and there is no doubt that many improvements might be made upon the present authorized version, particularly in the Old Testament. Dr. Alexander Geddes, above mentioned, at his decease, had proceeded as far as the Psalms in the Translation of the Old Testament; but many of his variations from the common version are extremely injudicious. Archbishop Newcome and Mr. Wakefield published entire translations of the New Testament; and an *improved version* of the New Testament, founded on Newcome, has been published by the Unitarians, accompanied with notes and an excellent introduction.

With the professed object of defeating the attacks on Christianity, a new translation of the Bible was given to the world, some years ago, by Mr. J. Bellamy, of Gray's-Inn lane, London. This version is in many places so very literal in its translation as to be unintelligible, and, therefore, unfit for any good purpose. The writer's forced and erroneous interpretations, as well as his unjustifiable attacks upon other versions and translators, were so far from tending to the accomplishment of his professed object, that they seemed rather calculated to produce the opposite effect; and, consequently, his new translation, which made some noise in its day, was soon judiciously consigned to oblivion. And, upon the whole, it may be observed, that, although it is generally acknowledged that after the lapse of *two hundred and twenty years,* the improvements in critical learning, and the discoveries in the pursuits of knowledge, together with hundreds of manuscripts that have since emerged into light, call for a revision of the present authorized version; yet such an attempt should not be rashly ventured upon, and it should not take place until the necessity of it becomes much more apparent to common apprehension than it is at present.

THE APOCRYPHA.

HAVING given an account of the origin and literary characteristics of the accredited and usually accepted books composing the Old and New Testaments, we now proceed to offer a few details relative to those books styled the Apocrypha, a branch of the subject possessed of considerable interest, and which we shall treat in the same measure of impartiality.

The term *apocrypha* is Greek, signifying *hidden* or *concealed,* and is used to designate a number of books, often placed between the Old and New Testaments, or otherwise bound up with them. Some writers divide the sacred books into three classes, viz., the canonical, the ecclesiastical, and the apocryphal. In the first they place those whose authority has never been questioned in the catholic or universal church; in the second, those which were not received at first, but which were nevertheless read in the public assemblies as books that were useful, though they never placed them upon the same footing of authority as the former; and in the third they placed the books which were of no authority, which could not be made to appear in public, but were kept hidden, and were therefore called apocryphal, that is, concealed, or such as could not be used in public. "Let us lay aside those books which have been called apocryphal," says St. Augustine, "because their authors were not known to the fathers, who have by a constant and certain succession transmitted down to us the authority and truth of the Holy Scriptures. Though some things in these apocryphal books are true, yet, as there are in them multitudes of others which are false, they are of no authority."

[a] Sketches of all Denominations, p. 135.

The Apocrypha consists of fourteen books, viz: First and Second Esdras, Tobit, Judith, the rest of the chapters of the Book of Esther, the Wisdom of Solomon, Ecclesiasticus, Baruch, the Song of the Three Holy Children, the History of Susanna, the Story of Bel and the Dragon, the Prayer of Manasses, and the First and Second Book of the Maccabees. Every attentive reader must perceive that these books want the majesty of inspired scripture; and that there are in them a variety of things wicked, false, and disagreeing with the oracles of God. None of them were ever found in the proper Hebrew tongue; and they were never received into the canon of scripture by the Jews, to whom the oracles of God were originally committed. They were partly read in private by the ancient Christians as useful, but they did not admit them into the canon of scripture. None of them are found in the catalogue of the canonical books by Melita, bishop of Sardis, in the second century; nor does Origen in the third, or Epiphanius in the fourth, in the least acknowledge their authenticity. One or two of the writers of them also ask pardon if they have said anything amiss; which clearly shows that they were not inspired, or at least did not consider themselves to be so; and therefore these books can by no means be considered as having a title to form part of the word of God. A very simple analysis of the books themselves will be sufficient to demonstrate this to every attentive mind.

I. It is not known at what time the First Book of Esdras was written, neither is it known who was the author of it; but Prideaux considers it certain that he wrote before the time of Josephus. It was originally to be found only in Greek; and in the Alexandrian manuscript it is placed before the canonical Book of Ezra, and is there called the First Book of Ezra, because the events related in it occurred prior to the return from the Babylonish captivity. In some editions of the Septuagint it is called the First Book of the Priest (meaning Ezra), the authentic book of Ezra being called the second book. In the editions of the Latin Vulgate previous to the Council of Trent, this and the following book are styled the Third and Fourth Books of Esdras, those of Ezra and Nehemiah being entitled the first and second books. This book is chiefly historical, giving an account of the return of the Jews from the Babylonish captivity, the building of the temple, and the re-establishment of divine worship. It is, in fact, nothing but a bad extract of the last two chapters of Chronicles, and the Book of Ezra; and in a great many instances it even contradicts these. The author falsely makes Zorobabel a young man in the days of Darius Hystaspes, and Joakim to be his son; whereas he was the son of Joshua, the high-priest. He calls Darius king of Assyria, long after that empire was utterly dissolved; and makes some things to be done under Darius which were done under Cyrus.

II. The author of the Second Book of Esdras is likewise unknown. It is supposed to have been originally written in Greek, though the original of it has never been found but in Latin; and there is an Arabic version, differing very materially from it, and having many interpolations. Although the writer personates Ezra, it is manifest from the style and contents of his book, that he lived long after that celebrated Jewish reformer. He pretends to visions and revelations; but they are so fanciful, indigested, ridiculous, and absurd, that it is clear the Holy Spirit could have no concern in the dictating of them. He believed that the day of judgment was at hand, and that the souls of good and wicked men would all be then delivered out of hell. A great many rabbinical fables occur in this book, particularly the account of the six days' creation, and the story of Behemoth (or Euoch, as it is here called) and Leviathan— two monstrous creatures that are designed as a feast for the elect after the day of resurrection, &c. He says that the ten tribes are gone away into a country which he calls Arsareth, and that Ezra restored the whole body of the Scriptures, which had been entirely lost. He also speaks of Jesus Christ and his apostles in so clear a manner, that the gospel itself is scarcely more explicit. On these accounts, and from the numerous traces of the language of the New Testament, and especially of the Revelation of St. John, which are discoverable in this book, several critics have concluded that it was written about the close of the first century, by some converted Jew, who assumed the name of Esdras or Ezra.

III. The Book of Tobit, from the simplicity of the narrative, and the lessons of piety and meekness which it contains, has been always one of the most popular of the apocryphal writings. It was first written in Chaldee by some Babylonian Jew; but there is no authentic information as to his name, or the time when he flourished. It professes to relate the history of Tobit and his family, who were carried into captivity to Nineveh by Shalmanezer, being first begun by Tobit, then continued by his son Tobias, and, lastly, finished by some other of the family, and afterward digested by the Chaldee author into that form in which we now have it. The time of this history ends with the destruction of Nineveh, about six hundred and twelve years before Christ; but most commentators and critics agree in thinking that the book itself was not written till about one hundred and fifty or two hundred years before Christ. It has been generally looked upon, both by Jews and Christians, as a genuine and true history; but it contains so many rabbinical fictions, and allusions to the Babylonian demonology, that it is much more rational to suppose the whole book an entire fable. It is not probable that, in the time of Sennacherib and Esarhaddon, the father should live, as is here said, one hundred and fifty-eight years, and the son one hundred and twenty-seven. It is certain no angel of God could falsely call himself "Azarias the son of Ananias," as this writer affirms. The story of Sarah's seven husbands being successively killed on their marriage-night by an evil spirit, and of that spirit's being driven away by the smell and smoke of the roasted heart and liver of a fish, and bound in the uttermost parts of Egypt, or of the angel Raphael's presenting to God the prayers of the saints, with other matters evidently fabulous, are quite sufficient to justify the rejecting of this book entirely from the sacred canon, upon the score of internal evidence alone.

IV. The Book of Judith professes to relate the defeat of the Assyrians by the Jews, through the instrumentality of their countrywoman of this name, who craftily cut off the head of Holofernes, the Assyrian general. This book was originally written in Chaldee by some Jew of Babylon, and was thence translated by St. Jerome into the Latin tongue. Dr. Prideaux refers this history to the time of Manasseh, king of Judah; Jahn assigns it to the age of the Maccabees, and thinks it was written to animate the Jews against the Syrians; but so many geographical, historical, and chronological difficulties attend this book, that Luther, Grotius, and other eminent critics, have considered it rather as a drama or parable than a real history. It has been received into the canon of scripture by some as being all true; but, on the other hand, it is the opinion of Grotius that it is entirely a parabolical fiction, written in the time of Antiochus Epiphanes, when he came into Judea to raise a persecution against the Jewish church, and that the design of it was to confirm the Jews, under that persecution, in their hope that God would send a deliverer. According to him, by Judith is meant Judea, which, at the time of this persecution, was like a desolate widow: that her sword means the prayers of the saints: that by Bethulia, the name of the town which was attacked, is meant the temple, or the house of the Lord, which is called in Hebrew *Bethel*. Nabuchodonosor denotes the devil, and the kingdom of Assyria the devil's kingdom, pride. Holofernes, whose name signifies a minister of the serpent, means Antiochus Epiphanes, who was the devil's instrument in that persecution, &c., &c. It is plain that in this way, by means of a little ingenuity, anything may be made of anything; and such conjectures as these, as an able commentator remarks, however ingenious, are better calculated to exhibit the powers of fancy and the abuse of learning, than to investigate truth, or throw light on what is uncertain and obscure. The noted deliverance mentioned in this book is there said to have happened after the Jews had returned from their captivity, and had rebuilt the temple, and yet it is said to have been in the eighteenth year of Nebuchadnezzar, which is absurd; and it is said that they had no trouble for *eighty* years or more after this deliverance, which is equally absurd, as the Jews during any period of their history, or indeed any other nation, never enjoyed a peace of such long continuance. It is quite improbable that a small town, as Bethulia is here represented to be, should stand out against so powerful an army, or that the death of the general should have made all the troops betake themselves to a shameful flight. It is certainly wrong, as is done in the case of Judith, to commend a woman as a devout fearer of the Lord, who was guilty of notorious lying, of acting the part of a bawd, of profane swearing, of murder, and of speaking in praise of that committed by the patriarch Simeon, whom she claims as her ancestor.

V. "The rest of the chapters of the Book of Esther, which are found neither in the Hebrew nor in the Chaldee," were originally written in Greek, whence they were translated into Latin, and formed part of the Italic or old Latin version in use before the time of Jerome. Being there annexed to the canonical Book of Esther, they passed without censure, but were rejected by Jerome in his version, because he confined himself to the Hebrew Scriptures, and these chapters never were extant in the Hebrew language. They are evidently the production of a Hellenistic Jew, but are considered both by Jerome and Grotius as a work of pure fiction, which was annexed to the canonical book by way of embellishment. From the coincidence between some of these apocryphal chapters and Josephus, it has been supposed that they are a compilation from the Jewish historian; and this conjecture is further confirmed by the mention of Ptolemy and Cleopatra, who lived but a short time before Josephus. These additions to the Book of Esther are often cited by the father of the church; and the Council of Trent has assigned them a place among the canonical books.[*]

The author of these apocryphal chapters says many things that are in direct contradiction to the inspired historian; as when he affirms that the attempt made by the eunuchs to take away the life of Ahasuerus was in the second year of his reign; that Mordecai was at the very time rewarded for his discovery; that Haman had been advanced before this event, and was provoked with Mordecai for his discovery of the eunuchs; that Haman was a Macedonian, and intended to transfer the government of Persia to the Macedonians. He very stupidly, also, represents Ahasuerus looking upon Esther, "as a fierce lion," and yet "with a countenance full of grace!" and as calling the Jews "the children of the most high and most mighty living God;" and as ordering the heathens to keep the feast of Purim.

VI. The book of "The Wisdom of Solomon" was never written by that monarch, as its author falsely pretends; for it was never extant in Hebrew, nor received into the Jewish canon of scripture, nor is the style like that of Solomon. It consists of two parts: the first, which is written in the name of Solomon, contains a description or encomium of wisdom, by which comprehensive term the ancient Jews understood prudence and foresight, knowledge and understanding, and especially the duties of religion and morality. This division includes the first ten chapters. The second part, comprising the rest of the book, treats on a variety of topics widely differing from the subject of the first, viz., reflections on the history and conduct of the Israelites during their journeyings in the wilderness, and their subsequent proneness to idolatry. Hence the author takes occasion to inveigh against idolatry, the origin of which he investigates, and concludes with reflections on the history of the people of God. His allegorical interpretations of the Pentateuch, and the precept which he gives to worship God before the rising of the sun, have induced some critics to think that the author was of the Jewish sect called Essenes.

Although the fathers of the church, and particularly Jerome, uniformly considered this book as apocryphal, yet they recommended the perusal of it, in consideration of the excellence of its style. The third Council of Carthage, held in the year 397, pronounced it to be a canonical book, under the name of "the Fourth Book of Solomon," and the famous Council of Trent confirmed this decision. Jerome informs us that several writers of the first three centuries ascribed the authorship of it to Philo the Jew, a native of Alexandria who flourished in the first century; and this opinion is generally adopted by the moderns, on account of the Platonic notions that are discoverable in it, as well as from its general style, which evidently shows that it was the production of a Hellenistic Jew of Alexandria. Drusius, indeed, attributes it to another Philo, more ancient than the person just mentioned, and who is cited by Josephus; but this hypothesis is untenable, because the author of the Book of Wisdom was confessedly either a Jew or a heretical Christian, whereas the Philo mentioned by Drusius was a heathen.

It is quite evident that this author had read Plato and the Greek poets; and he employs a great many expressions taken from them, such as Ambrosia, the river of forgetfulness; the kingdom of Pluto, &c.; as also several words borrowed from the Grecian games, which were not in use till long after the time of Solomon, whose name he assumes. A great many of his phrases seem to be taken out of the Prophets, and even from the New Testament. There are numerous passages in the book evidently borrowed from the Prophecies of Isaiah and Jeremiah; particularly in the thirteenth chapter, where there are no less than nine verses plainly copied from the forty-fourth chapter of Isaiah.

This author brings forward many things that are contrary both to the words of inspiration and to common sense. He condemns the marriage-bed as sinful, and also excludes bastards from the hopes of salvation: he talks as if souls were lodged in

* Vide Horne's Introduction to the Scripture, vol. iv. p. 289.

bodies according to their former merits; makes the murder of Abel the cause of the flood; represents the Egyptians as being plagued entirely by their own idols, that is to say, by the beasts which they worshipped, though it is certain they never worshipped *frogs, locusts,* or *lice.* He also calls the divine *Logos,* or second person of the Trinity, a vapor or steam, with many other things that are evidently absurd.

The seventh book of the Apocrypha, is entitled "The Wisdom of Jesus the Son of Sirach, or Ecclesiasticus," which, like the preceding, has sometimes been considered as the production of King Solomon; whence the council of Carthage deemed it canonical, under the title of the Fifth Book of Solomon, and their decision was adopted by the council of Trent. It is, however, manifest, that it was not, and could not be written by Solomon, because in it allusion is made to the captivity; although it is not improbable that the author collected some scattered sentiments ascribed to Solomon, which he arranged with the other materials he had selected for his work. Sonntag is of opinion that this book is a collection of fragments, or miscellaneous hints for a large work, planned out and begun, but not completed. From the book itself it appears that it was written by a person of the name of Jesus the Son of Sirach, who had travelled in pursuit of knowledge. By reading the Scriptures, and other good books, he attained a considerable share of wisdom; and by collecting the grave and short sentences of such as went before him, and adding sundry of his own, he endeavored to produce a work of instruction that might be useful to his countrymen.

This book was originally written in Hebrew, or rather the Syro-Chaldaic dialect then in use in Judea about the year 232 before Christ, when the author was probably about seventy years of age. Jesus, his grandson, who is also called *The Son of Sirach,* translated it into Greek during the reign of Ptolemy Evergetes, king of Egypt, about 140 years before Christ, for the use of the Hellenistical Jews, among whom he had settled in Alexandria. The Hebrew original is now lost; but it was extant in the time of Jerome, for he tells us that he had seen it under the title of *The Parables;* but he says that the common name of it in Greek was The Wisdom of Jesus the Son of Sirach. The Latin version of this book has more in it than the Greek, several particulars being inserted which are not in the other. These seem to have been interpolated by the first author of that version; but now the Hebrew being lost, the Greek, which has been made from it by the grandson of the author, must stand for the original, and from that the English translation has been made. From the supposed resemblance of this book to that of Ecclesiasticus, it has received from the Latin translator the title of Ecclesiasticus, by which name it is most generally known and referred to.

Ecclesiasticus is considered by far the best of all the apocryphal books. The ancients called it *Panareton,* that is, The Treasury of Virtue, as supposing it to contain maxims leading to every virtue. It has met with general esteem, also, in most of the western churches, and was introduced into the public service of the Church of England by the compilers of its Liturgy. It was frequently cited by the fathers of the church under the titles of "The Wisdom of Jesus," "Wisdom," "The Treasures of all the Virtues," or "Logos, the Discourse;" and in those times it was put into the hands of catechumens, or young Christians under examination, on account of the edifying nature of its instruction.

VIII. The Book of "Baruch" is not extant in Hebrew, and only in Greek and Syriac; but in what language it was originally written it is now impossible to ascertain. Grotius is of opinion that it is an entire fiction, and that it was composed by some Hellenistical Jew, under the name of Baruch. The principal subject of the book is an epistle, pretended to be sent by Jehoiakim and the captive Jews in Babylon, to their brethren in Judah and Jerusalem; and the last chapter contains an epistle which falsely bears the name of Jeremiah. This has never been considered as a canonical book, either by the Jews or the Christians; and, indeed, it is little else than an arrant romance. It absurdly pretends to have been written by Baruch at Babylon, when it is probable he never went thither: that it was read to Jechoniah at the river Sud, which is nowhere else mentioned; nor could Jeconiah hear it there, when he was confined in prison. It mentions a collection to buy sacrifices, gathered by the captives in Babylon, and sent to Joakim the priest, along with the sacred vessels which Zedekiah had made; but how could the captives newly enslaved in Babylon be able to make collections? How could they send it to a high-priest that did not then exist? How could the sacred vessels which Zedekiah made be returned from

Babylon, when it does not appear that he made any? Or how could they be returned before they were carried away, along with himself? The author borrows a variety of expressions from Daniel, and must therefore have lived after Baruch was dead. The epistle ascribed to Jeremiah is neither written in his style, nor at all in the style of the Scriptures; and it ridiculously turns the *seventy years* of the captivity into *seven generations.*[*]

IX. "The Song of the Three Children in the Furnace" is placed in the Greek version of Daniel, and also in the Vulgate Latin version, between the twenty-third and twenty-fourth verses of the third chapter. It is partly a poor imitation of the 148th Psalm, and partly deprecatory, not at all suited to such a deliverance. It does not appear to have ever been extant in Hebrew; and although it has met with a good deal of approbation for the piety of its sentiments, it was never admitted to be canonical, until it was recognised by the council of Trent. The account of the flame streaming above the furnace "forty-and-nine cubits," and of the angel's "smiting the flame out of the oven, and making a moist whistling wind in it," seems entirely fabulous and romant.c; nor is it very consistent with the account of the fire's loosening their hands. The fifteenth verse contains a direct falsehood; for it asserts that there was no prophet at that time, when it is well known that Daniel and Ezekiel both exercised the prophetic ministry then in Babylon. This apocryphal fragment is, therefore, most probably the production of some Hellenistic Jew. The hymn resembling the hundred and forty-eighth Psalm, which commences at the 29th verse, was so approved of by the compilers of the Liturgy of the Church of England, that they appointed it to be used instead of the *Te Deum* during Lent.

X. "The History of Susanna," has always been treated with some respect, but has never been considered as canonical, though the council of Trent admitted it into the number of the sacred books. It is evidently, like the rest, the work of some Hellenistic Jew, and in the Vulgate version it forms the thirteenth chapter of the Book of Daniel. In the Septuagint version it is placed at the beginning of that book. Lamy, and some other modern critics after Julius Africanus and Origen, consider it to be both spurious and fabulous. That it was originally written in Greek, is manifest in the punishment pronounced on the elders, from the play which is made upon the Greek names of the mastic and holm trees, under which they said they found Susanna and the young man together. It is evidently absurd to affirm, that in the beginning of the captivity, Joachim, the husband of Susanna, was become exceedingly rich; that there were Jewish judges with the power of life and death in Chaldea; that Daniel, who was bred in the court, had leisure, or being so young, was admitted to be a judge; that Susanna went into her garden to wash at noonday, and did it without searching if anybody was there; or that the elders attempted to force her, when they could not but every moment expect the return of her maids.

XI. "The History of the Destruction of Bel and the Dragon" is a still more romantic story. It is not extant in either the Hebrew or the Chaldee language, and it was always rejected by the Jewish church. Jerome gives it no better title than that of The Fable of Bel and the Dragon; nor has it obtained more credit with posterity, except with the fathers of the council of Trent, who determined it to be a part of the canonical scriptures. It forms the fourteenth chapter of Daniel in the Latin Vulgate; in the Greek it was called the Prophecy of Habakkuk, the son of Jesus, of the tribe of Levi; but this is evidently false, for that prophet lived before the time of Nebuchadnezzar, and the events pretended to have taken place in this fable are assigned to the time of Cyrus. There are two Greek texts of this fragment, that of the Septuagint, and that found in Theodotian's Greek version of Daniel.

The design of this fiction is to render idolatry ridiculous, and to exalt the true God; but the author has destroyed the illusion of his fiction, by transporting to Babylon the worship of animals, which was never practised in that country. It is also quite improbable that Cyrus, a Persian, would worship a Babylonian idol; nay, an idol that was broken to pieces at the taking of the city! It is absurd to imagine that a man of his sense could believe an image of brass and clay did really eat and drink! How pitiful, for Daniel to discover the coming of the priests to devour the provisions, by making the king's servants strew ashes on the floor, when the priest might so easily perceive them, or the servants so readily inform concerning them! It is absurd to suppose that the newly-conquered Babylonians should, by menaces, oblige Cyrus to deliver up his beloved Daniel to them, to be cast into the den of lions; or that

* Brown's Dictionary of the Bible.—Art. Apocrypha.

Habakkuk should be then alive to bring him food; or that Cyrus should be seven days before he went to the den, to see what was become of his favorite minion.

XII. "The Prayer of Manasses," king of Judah, when he was holden captive in Babylon, never appeared in the Hebrew language, and seems to be the product of some Pharisaical spirit. It was never recognised as canonical, and is rejected as spurious even by the Church of Rome. It can not be traced to a higher source than the Vulgate Latin version; and, therefore, it has no claim to be considered as the original prayer which, in the Book of Chronicles, Manasseh is mentioned to have made, and which it pretends to be. The author speaks of just persons, such as Abraham, Isaac, and Jacob, as being *without sin*, and *not called to repent*.

XIII. The Books of the "Maccabees" are thus denominated, because they relate the patriotic and gallant exploits of Judas Maccabeus and his brethren. The Maccabees arose in defence of their brethren the Jews, during the dreadful persecutions to which they were subjected, on account of their religion, under Antiochus Epiphanes, king of Syria, about 100 years before Christ. The most likely derivation of the title Maccabees, is that which takes it from the motto put by Judas in his standard, being this Hebrew sentence, taken out of Exodus xvi. 11, *Mi Camo-ka Baelim Jehovah*, that is, "Who is like unto thee among the gods, O Jehovah?" which being written like the S. P. Q. R., *Senatus Populusque Romanus*, on the Roman standards, by an abbreviation formed by the initial letters of these words put together, made the artificial word *Maccabi;* and hence all who fought under that standard were called Maccabees or Maccabeans.

The First Book of Maccabees is a very valuable historical monument, written with great accuracy and fidelity, on which even more reliance may be placed than on the writings of Josephus, who has borrowed some of his materials from it, and has frequently mistaken its meaning. It is, indeed, an excellent history, and comes the nearest to the style and manner of the sacred historical writings of any extant. It was written originally in the Chaldee language of the Jerusalem dialect, which was the language spoken in Judea, from the return of the Jews thither from the Babylonish captivity; and it was extant in this Syro-Chaldaic language in the time of Jerome, for he tells us that he had seen it. The title which it then bore was, The Sceptre of the Prince of the Sons of God: a title which is certainly suitable to the character of Judas, who was a valiant commander of the persecuted Israelites. It contains the history of the Jews under the government of the priest Matthias and his sons, from the beginning of the reign of Antiochus Epiphanes to the death of Simon Maccabeus, a period of about thirty-four years. The author of this book is not certainly known: some conjecture that it was written by John Hyrcanus, the son of Simon, who was prince and high-priest of the Jews for nearly thirty years, and who commenced his government at the time when this history ends: by others it is ascribed to one of the Maccabees, and many are of opinion that it was compiled by the men of the great synagogue. It is, however, most probable that it was composed in the time of John Hyrcanus, when the wars of the Maccabees are terminated, either by Hyrcanus himself, or by some persons employed by him. There is both a Greek and a Latin translation of it, from the Syro-Chaldaic; and our English version is made from the Greek.

There are many things in this book which show that it was not written by inspiration. The writer often observes, that *there was no prophet* in his times; and, indeed, he has blundered into several mistakes; as, that Alexander the Great parted his kingdom among his honorable servants while he was yet alive; that Antiochus the Great was taken alive by the Romans; that they gave India and Media, parts of his kingdom, to Eumenes, king of Pergamus; that the Roman senate consisted of 320 persons; that Alexander Balas was the son of Antiochus Epiphanes; and several others which are palpably absurd.

XIV. The "Second Book of Maccabees" is a history of fifteen years, from the execution of the commission of Heliodorus, who was sent by Seleucus to bring away the treasures of the temple, to the victory obtained by Judas Maccabeus over Nicanor, that is, from the year of the world 3828 to 3843. It commences with two epistles sent from the Jews of Jerusalem to those of Alexandria and throughout Egypt, exhorting them to observe the feast of the dedication of the new altar, erected by Judas Maccabeus on his purifying the temple. The second of these epistles is not only written in the name of Judas Maccabeus, who was slain thirty-six years before, but also contains such fabulous and absurd stuff, as could never have been written by the great council of the Jews assembled at Jerusalem for the whole nation, as this pretends to be. The epistles, which are confessedly spurious, are followed by the author's preface to his history, which is an abridgment of a larger work, compiled by one Jason, a Hellenistic Jew of Cyrene, who wrote in Greek the history of Judas Maccabeus and his brethren, and an account of the wars against Antiochus Epiphanes, and his son Eupator, in five books. The entire work of Jason has long since perished; and Dr. Prideaux is of opinion that the author of this second book of Maccabees was a Hellenistic Jew of Alexandria, because he makes a distinction between the temple in Egypt and that at Jerusalem, calling the latter "the Great Temple."

The compilation of this unknown author is by no means equal in accuracy to the First Book of the Maccabees, which it contradicts in several instances; it is not arranged in chronological order, and sometimes also it is at variance with the inspired writings. The author concludes it, begging excuse if he had said anything unbecoming the story; and, indeed, he had reason to do so, considering what a number of false and wicked things he retails: as, that Judas Maccabeus was alive in the 188th year of the Seleucidæ, when he died in the 152d; that Antiochus Epiphanes was killed at the temple of Nanea, in Persia, whereas he died on the frontiers of Babylon, of a terrible disease; that Nehemiah built the second temple and altar, whereas they were built sixty years before he came from Persia; that Jeremiah hid the tabernacle, ark, and altar of incense, in a cave; that Persepolis was in being one hundred years after Alexander had burnt it to ashes; that Judas did well in offering prayers and sacrifices to make reconciliation for the dead; and that Rasis did well in murdering himself to escape the fury of the Syrians.

The name of Maccabees was first given to Judas, the son of Matthias, the priest of Modin, and his brethren, for the reason which has been already mentioned; and, therefore, the two books just spoken of, which give us an account of their actions, are called the First and the Second Book of the Maccabees. But because they were sufferers in the cause of their religion, others who were like sufferers in the same cause, and by their sufferings bore witness to the truth, were in after times called also Maccabees by the Jews. For this reason, other two books, giving an account of other persecutions endured by the Jews, are found under the title of the Third and Fourth Books of the Maccabees. The Third Book contains the history of a persecution intended against the Jews in Egypt by Ptolemy Philopator, but which was miraculously prevented. From its style, this book appears to have been written by some Alexandrian Jew; it abounds with absurd fables. With regard to its subject, it ought in strictness to be called the First Book of Maccabees, as the event it professes to relate occurred before the achievements of that heroic family; but as it is of less authority and repute than the other two, it is reckoned after them. It is found in most ancient manuscripts of the Greek Septuagint, particularly in the Alexandrian and Vatican manuscripts; but it was never inserted in the Latin Vulgate, nor in our English bibles.

Of the Fourth Book of the Maccabees very little is known. It is destitute of every internal mark of credibility, and is supposed to be the same as the book "concerning the government or empire of reason," ascribed to Josephus by Philostratus, Eusebius, and Jerome. It is extant in some Greek manuscripts, in which it is placed after the three books of Maccabees. Dr. Lardner thinks it is the work of some unknown Christian writer. The history contained in it extends to about 160 years; beginning at Seleucus's attempt to pillage the temple, and ending just before the birth of Jesus Christ.

Upon the whole, in regard to these apocryphal books, it is to be observed, they appear to have been entirely the work of Hellenistic Jews, and quite destitute of any proper claim to the authority of inspiration. The Jews, after their return from the Babylonish captivity to the time of our Saviour, were much given to religious romances; and of this sort the greater part, if not all, of these books are to be accounted. They were never extant in Hebrew, neither are they quoted in the New Testament, or by the Jewish writers, Philo and Josephus; on the contrary, they contain many things which are fabulous, false, and contradictory to the canonical scriptures. They are nevertheless possessed of some value as ancient writings, which throw considerable light upon the phraseology of Scripture, and upon the history and manners of the east.

FINIS.

NOTICES AND RECOMMENDATIONS

OF

SEARS' BIBLE BIOGRAPHY.

THE Publisher of "BIBLE BIOGRAPHY" respectfully requests of the Christian Public a careful perusal of the following recommendations. In preparing the present volume, his aim has been to make a book *the very best and most useful ever published in modern times*—aiming at universal excellence, that it might justly be entitled to universal patronage and support. On examination, it will be found useful, and eminently adapted to interest, instruct, and improve. It is suited to persons of all ages and of every rank, and is equally worthy of a place in the parlor as in the kitchen, among the limited collection of the young, as well as the various and more extended library of the man of reading. We think it would be difficult to select a more appropriate GIFT at the approaching holydays. The writings of the most eminent divines that have ever lived are laid under contribution, and passages of eminent beauty are taken from them. If, therefore, variety has charms, or religion is lovely, or eloquence is admired, this book will be read with delight: for here is variety without looseness, religion without fanaticism, and eloquence pleading the cause of GOD with man. A few only out of the numerous recommendations the work has already received, will be inserted here :—

From the Rev. Charles G. Sommers, A. M., Corresponding Secretary of the American and Foreign Bible Society.

MR. ROBERT SEARS—*Dear Sir* : Your new and beautiful work on the BIOGRAPHY OF THE BIBLE appears to attract the attention of all classes ; and is undoubtedly destined to become, if it be not already, one of the most popular works ever issued in this country. The HOLY SCRIPTURES, on account of their antiquity, dignity, and other excellences, far exceed all the writings of the ancients. Indeed, if we consider how many centuries have passed away since they were compiled, and how miraculously they have been preserved to the present times, they plainly appear to have been the peculiar care of GOD himself. We ought also to prize the SCRIPTURES, as comprising every species of KNOWLEDGE that is useful and entertaining. Would we know whence natural philosophy, with astronomy, and other appendages on it, derive their origin ? Examine the books of Genesis, Job, and Ecclesiastes. What writings abound more in ethics or moral precepts than the sacred and sententious Proverbs ? What more certain, regular, or pleasing history can we find, than in Genesis, Exodus, Joshua, and Judges ? How free from sophistry are the HOLY SCRIPTURES, and how solid are all the arguments used in them ! Geometry is displayed in the building of the Tabernacle, and the working in metals and wood was known long before the building of Solomon's Temple ; in short, all manner of learning, arts, and sciences, is comprehended within those sacred pages. They are so exactly disposed, that they are a magazine, accommodated to all places, times, and persons : so that St. Basil justly calls them a Pharmacopœia, furnished with medicines for all uses and necessities. From hence, in times of peace and religion, the learned acquired wisdom and eloquence ; in times of heresy, they furnished the orthodox with stability in the faith, and assisted them in the subversion of error. From hence, in prosperity, we learn humility and modesty ; in adversity, magnanimity and patience. In danger, it arms us with an honest zeal ; and finally, if abuses insinuate themselves into discipline, and corrupt our morals, nothing but the rule of GOD's word can restore religion to its pristine state and dignity ; for that alone should be the standard of our thoughts, and guide of our actions.

These reflections have arisen in my mind after a careful and serious perusal of your new and elegant work on SACRED BIOGRAPHY. It leads the mind of the reader, whether he be grave or gay, direct to the SCRIPTURES. All helps to arrive at their true meaning ought to be valued and encouraged. But the humble follower of the SAVIOUR will need no other recommendation to the diligent performance of this duty than that commanded by CHRIST himself—"*Search the Scriptures.*" And in obedience to this precept, the apostles and fathers of the Christian Church made it their great concern to exhort all men to the study of them. The Old Testament is indeed a system of every kind of knowledge useful for the conduct of human life ; and from which the philosophers and legislators of all ages drew the best of their observations, and the authors of both canon and civil law have from thence derived their most useful institutions.

But the excellency of SACRED HISTORY will more evidently appear if we compare it with the accounts of the best and most ancient heathen writers. How obscure and trifling are their stories of Deucalion's flood, of Prometheus, and Hercules, and their general notions of the existence of the world from eternity ! In short, all profane history is filled with obscurity and fables, before the Olympiads, which were their first certain era, and which did not commence till many centuries after the time of Moses. And, indeed, if we pay just deference to it, we shall find it the best guide in the common daily transactions of life. There only we have the true account of the rise and fall of the most early kingdoms of the world ; and by their example, either in prosperity or adversity, learn to be wise and happy. If we compare the Greek and Roman historians with the *Sacred History*, we shall find the latter to abound with the more illustrious examples of heroic virtue. Rome may boast of her Torquatos and Brutas, who, in a more brutal than generous bravery, sacrificed their sons to the public good ; but who would not rather admire the obedience of pious Abraham, who had devoted his beloved Isaac a victim to the will of GOD ? Historians and poets may applaud the courage of the Horatii and others, who, in defence of their country, slew their enemies in single combat ; but how short do they come of the heroic David, who, though but a stripling, encountered and slew the gigantic Goliath, and by his death procured an easy victory over the Philistines ! Alexander's virtue is worthy of praise, who, when he had conquered Darius, would not allow himself the pleasure of surveying his beautiful captives, lest he should be tempted to desire ; but what is this to the continence of Joseph, who fled from the actual solicitations of his lascivious mistress into a loathsome dungeon ? They may talk of the fortitude and success of their warlike heroes—their Cæsar, Pompey, Hannibal, Scipio, and Alexander ; but how much more illustrious the examples of Moses, Joshua, Samson, Gideon, David, and Saul, who, inspired with more than human courage, with a handful of men, trampled on their numerous enemies,—and to facilitate whose conquests, the very elements conspired, and fought on their side !

The time would fail me to go more fully into this subject. In the work before me I find a particular delineation of all the principal personages recorded in the Sacred Records. Who will not delight to read the stories of Moses, Samuel, Ruth, Job—and, above all, the life, death, and sufferings of the REDEEMER himself ? The volume must, from its intrinsic excellence—independent of its pictorial embellishments—prove a rich treat to all lovers of Bible History ; and will be eminently useful in creating and cherishing a taste for the study of the SACRED ORACLES.

Yours, truly,
CHARLES G. SOMMERS.

From the Editors of the New York Observer, July 30, 1842.

THE following editorial notice of Mr. Sears' new and elegant work on the Bible, is from the New York Observer, one of the oldest, most respectable, and best conducted religious newspapers published in the United States. An opinion coming from this high quarter is worth a thousand of the ephemeral puffs that are published in the papers of the day :—

"We have just received this work, published under the editorial auspices of Mr. Sears, the publisher of the 'Pictorial Illustrations.' It is brought out with great neatness, the paper and typography of the first quality, and the engravings, many of them, for wood-cuts, are very fine. The frontispiece, by Lossing, is particularly worthy of commendation, being one of the finest specimens of wood-engraving which we have lately seen.

"The reading matter consists of well-drawn biographies of distinguished Scripture personages, and written for the special instruction of the young, who will be pleased with the general appearance of the book. The Appendix contains a series of selected Biblical articles, carefully condensed and compiled from the most distinguished writers, constituting altogether the most valuable part of the work. —Published and for sale at 122 Nassau st."

From the Rev. Spencer H. Cone, President of the American and Foreign Bible Society.

MR. ROBERT SEARS—*Dear Sir :* I am pleased with your new and elegant volume of 'Bible Biography ;' and, judging from those portions which I have selected for examination, I have great pleasure in stating that I consider it to be a very valuable addition to existing works of a similar description. It contains a vast mass of the results of Biblical criticism, selected with judgment from multifarious sources, most of which are altogether inaccessible to general readers, and many of them even to such as make the Scriptures the subject of professional study. The several hundred engravings are well executed ; and the entire getting up of the work reflects much credit on its editor and publisher.   Yours, &c.

SPENCER H. CONE.

From Charles Van Wyck, Esq., Publisher and Proprietor of the New York Christian Intelligencer.

MR. ROBERT SEARS—*Dear Sir :* From the specimens of the work which you submitted to my examination, while preparing it for the press, I felt fully assured that it would answer well to its title, and meet with general approbation. Since its publication, I am more convinced of its intrinsic beauty and excellency ; and it would answer well to the title of a "Condensed Commentary of the Scriptures." Your new and elegant octavo volume of 500 pages, with its numerous embellishments, does indeed contain a large amount and variety of matter within very narrow bounds ; matter collected from I know not how many of the most esteemed commentators, ancient and modern, interspersed with a due proportion of what is original. But *condensation* is far from being its only merit. There is not only *multum in parvo*, but the *selection* is judicious. There is little that is superfluous. On passages of any difficulty the views of different critics and commentators are given. On the whole, the "Bible Biography" appears to do great credit both to the industry and the judgment of the editor ; and to such students and preachers as may not have access to many books, and to ordinary Christians in the same predicament, to supply an important *desideratum*. It will prove also very useful for reading in the family. Yours, &c.,

CHARLES VAN WYCK.

From the Rev. Duncan Dunbar, Pastor of the MacDougal Street Church, New York.

MR. ROBERT SEARS—*Dear Sir :* I take great pleasure in recommending your elegant volume on "Scripture Biography" to the members of my church and congregation ; and more especially to the YOUNG PEOPLE of my charge. The character and popularity of your previous works are, I presume, known to ALL. I regard the present volume as worthy of the highest commendation. I shall only say, for soundness of doctrine, clear and forcible expression, sterling masculine sense, as well as faithful exhibition of what I believe to be the meaning of the inspired text, your "Bible Biography" cannot be too highly commended. As a whole, it is a work which is eminently calculated to promote correct and Scriptural views of the Word of God. And I should be glad to see it in the libraries not only of our students and ministers, but also of more general readers. Though fitted to be of great service to those who are called to expound the Word of God to others, it is written in a style which any person of intelligence and moderate learning may easily understand and appreciate ; and handling, as it does, *all the leading topics, both in faith and practice*, connected with the Gospel, it is well calculated to correct the loose views which are too often entertained concerning the Word of God, and to diffuse a knowledge of the principles which ought to be followed in interpreting the Word of God. The Dissertations in the last part of the work are on topics of great moment in themselves, and peculiarly important to be correctly understood in the present times. The arguments in these dissertations are conducted with the characteristic force and skill of the author. In short, it is a work of superlative merit, and a "Book of Gems." It presents the evidences of Divine Revelation in a very full, varied, and interesting form. The Christian who carefully reads it, will rise from the perusal, not only more deeply convinced of the truth of Christianity, but more fully acquainted with its important truths. The "Life of Christ" is peculiarly interesting. Persons who have dear relatives to whom they wish to recommend the Gospel, will find Mr. Sears' "Bible Biography" a volume peculiarly suitable to them. Yours, &c.

DUNCAN DUNBAR.

From the Rev. John Dowling, A. M., Pastor of the Pine Street Church, Providence, Rhode Island.

MR. ROBERT SEARS—*Dear Sir :* I am happy to express the conviction that your "Bible Biography" is a valuable accession to the happily abundant and multiplying means of promoting the intelligent study of the divine oracles, while the higher object of practical religion and godly edifying is constantly kept in view, and is well sustained by the reflections at the end of each biography. The explanatory notes of the appendix comprehend a vast amount of historical, antiquarian, and critical illustrations, which are not to be found in many excellent expositions, though far more voluminous. The learned editor has taken a large scope in collecting these illustrations from authors, ancient and modern, heathen, Jewish, and Christian, common and sacred, travellers, naturalists, historians, poets, antiquaries, critics, and divines. By these laborious compilations a welcome light is cast upon obscure passages ; many and serious difficulties are obviated ; facts and minute circumstances which are faintly alluded to, or tacitly implied, in the Scripture text, are brought forward to advantageous application ; the connexion of history, both sacred and profane, and the fulfilment of prophecy, are presented, to the increase of our knowledge and the confirmation of our faith ; and I cannot doubt but that by the use of this work the reading of the word of God will be rendered much more beneficial to all classes, in the present active and inquiring age.   Yours, &c.,

JOHN DOWLING.

From the Rev. James L. Hodge, Pastor of the Baptist Church, Brooklyn, Long Island.

MR. ROBERT SEARS—*Dear Sir :* If my recommendation of your new and elegant volume on "Sacred Biography" can be of any service, I can give it conscientiously and cheerfully. It need not, however, be puffed off ; it is sure to obtain a large sale from the highly respectable names and recommendations by which it is already sanctioned ;

and wherever it goes it will not fail to commend itself, and to extend continually the circles of its possessors. To me as a minister it has already been of great use, by saving me a vast deal of trouble in hunting out the different opinions of critics and commentators ; but of what value must it be to those who have none of these within their reach' You have bestowed a research and a care in your collection of materials, as well as evinced a judgment and accuracy in the disposal of them, which entitle you to great praise ; and it will not be the least of your rewards, that many an humble laborer in the field of Scriptural knowledge, will often, in secret, send an aspiration of gratitude to God for the assistance you have afforded him. I recommend all my people to possess and read this invaluable work.

Yours, &c.,

JAMES L. HODGE.

The following recommendatory notice of the work has been freely furnished by the Rev. B. T. WELCH, D. D., of Albany, N. Y., one of our most distinguished divines and scholars :—

ALBANY, N. Y., AUGUST 4, 1842.

MR. ROBERT SEARS—*Dear Sir :* I thank you for your beautiful and charming volume of " Bible Biography." It has induced in my mind a feeling of gratitude for your continued labours in the cause of God's Holy Oracles, in which I am persuaded the entire taste and intelligence of all evangelical denominations must participate. The examination of the work has afforded me much gratification ; and the more so from the conviction that whatever tends to render the study of the Scriptures interesting to the young mind must necessarily be useful, and, by the blessing of God, may become saving. I am persuaded, however, that its best recommendation is its own attractive appearance and sufficiently obvious excellence. I have rarely, if ever, seen a volume combining so much of important information in a form so attractive. It will be an invaluable aid to the leader of the Bible Class, the Sabbath School teacher, and not less so to the Christian Parent, and must soon be regarded by them as indispensable.

The execution of the work, its typographical neatness, and especially the numerous and beautiful engravings that adorn its pages, are equally honorable to the talent of the artists, and the liberality of the publisher and editor. Should the patronage of the Christian Public be at all commensurate with the merits of the work, your labors will be amply rewarded.

Yours, &c.

B. T. WELCH.

From James A. Sparks, Esq., Publisher of the New York Churchman.

MR. ROBERT SEARS—*Dear Sir :* The design of your work is good ; and if the work is generally executed as well as I have found it to be in those places which I have had occasion to examine, it will be of great service to those students who could neither afford to purchase voluminous works of elaborate criticism, nor find time to read them.

Yours, &c.

JAMES A. SPARKS.

From the Rev. Samuel H. Meeker, Pastor of the Reformed Dutch Church, Bushwick, Long Island.

MR. ROBERT SEARS—*Dear Sir :* I have read with great pleasure a considerable part of the " Bible Biography." The work is indeed *multum in parvo* ; and is all that it professes to be in its excellent and significant title. In your selection of the materials you have evinced uncommon industry, and a profound and accurate judgment. The reflections at the end of the chapters are short, devotional, and suitable for reading either in the family or in the closet. The serious and intelligent Chistian will find here very much to gratify and enlighten his mind ; whilst to the minister who has not access to a large biblical library, there is presented, within the shortest possible compass, the result of the labors of the most eminent interpreters of the word of God. It may safely be asserted that the " Bible Biography" is the cheapest and handsomest work that has ever yet been published. Yours, &c.,

SAMUEL H. MEEKER.

From the Rev. Elisha Tucker, (formerly of Rochester, N. Y.,) Pastor of the Oliver Street Church, New York.

MR. ROBERT SEARS—*Dear Sir :* Accept of my thanks for the copy of " Bible Biography," which you sent me. I cheerfully give my opinion in favor of this excellent and important work. It must have cost my esteemed friend, the editor, research of no ordinary character ; and cannot fail to be appreciated by all who love the Holy Scriptures. I cannot help adverting particularly to the invaluable matter contained in the last hundred pages of the " Biography." This *synopsis of our most valuable English and American critics* must be a great convenience to such ministers, students, and private Christians, who cannot afford to purchase every commentator ; for here are the opinions of many valuable *authors* condensed in a small space. For those who can purchase but *one book*, (next to the Bible,) certainly no 'one can equal it.

In short, I consider this volume a valuable addition to our biblical literature—valuable to the student for its critical selections and references—to the private Christian and the family man for its brief, well-digested, and pious reflections—to all readers of the Sacred Scriptures, for the quantity of important matter which is compressed in very concise limits. I trust it will obtain the extensive circulation which it unquestionably deserves.

Yours, truly,

ELISHA TUCKER.

From the Rev. Sidney A. Corey, Pastor of the Sing Sing Church, N. Y.

MR. ROBERT SEARS—*Dear Sir :* I hesitated to recommend your new and splendid work on Scripture Biography, until I had carefully perused every page. I now feel free to say, that I find it filled with the most valuable information in the most condensed form. The practical reflections at the close of each chapter are pertinent and evangelical. It is no small recommendation to your volume, that while its sentiments are orthodox, and its spirit evangelical and candid, an immense mass of matter is committed to paper and type so good, that the eye is not fatigued by the perusal. Upon the whole, it must be commended as a valuable addition to the means which God now affords to his church for obeying the high command so important for all religious prosperity. " Let the word of Christ dwell in you richly in all wisdom."

Yours, &c.,

SIDNEY A. COREY.

From the Rev. Morgan J. Rhees, Corresponding Secretary of the American Publication Society, and Sunday School Union, dated

PHILADELPHIA, JUNE, 1842.

MR. ROBERT SEARS—*Dear Sir :* I feel much indebted to you for a copy of your beautiful and interesting work, entitled the Lives and Characters of all the prominent persons whose history is furnished in the Sacred Writings. These sketches, or such of them as I have had time to look at, appear to be well drawn, and calculated to produce a good impression on the mind. The embellishments are about five hundred, and they are executed in the best style of wood engraving. They not only ornament but illustrate the book, and make it much more valuable than it would be without them. The title you have selected is beautiful and appropriate—"A Christian Father's Present to his Family," for it is well adapted for this purpose.   Yours, truly,

M. J. RHEES.

☞ The following notice of "Bible Biography" was written by the REV. W. C. BROWNLEE, D. D., after a careful examination of the volume. Dr. B. has been long known throughout the United States, as one of our most useful, learned, and eloquent divines. This candid and impartial review cannot fail, therefore, to have great weight with all who are anxious to know the real merits of the work.

New York, Aug. 6, 1842.

This is, beyond question, one of the most elegant books ever presented to our fellow-citizens, in this Republic. It is a volume of 500 pages, containing about 500 engravings of a most interesting character. The paper, the type, the engravings, are all of them such as might enter into a successful competition with any of the finest London publications. It is a superior specimen of domestic fabrication, both external and internal; and it ought, in this respect, to be patronised by every patriotic citizen. But this is the least valuable thing about it. The volume gives us accurate views of Eastern customs, habits, manners, animals, scenery; and, in addition to statements given in brief, accurate, and elegant details, we have every variety of pictorial exhibitions, which at once amuse, interest, delight, and fascinate. In this volume we have, moreover, admirably well written Biographies of all the principal characters mentioned in the HOLY BIBLE. These are selected with taste, and singular discrimination, from the best authors extant on the subject. And there is a crowning excellence in the last hundred pages, where we possess a rich treasury of Useful and Religious knowledge, carefully condensed and compiled from "Timpson's Key to the HOLY BIBLE," a work accessible to very few.

Mr. SEARS' object in presenting this admirable and beautiful volume, ought to be duly appreciated by every Minister, Parent, and Sabbath School Teacher. His aim is to extend the interest of the HOLY BIBLE—to place in the most attractive light, its divine truths and holy precepts, by instruction, and by captivating examples. It is, in fact, to make it paramount, in our youths' estimation, to all other books, and all other things:—and most captivating in the eyes of the youthful and aged, the beautiful, the gay, the sober, the thoughtless and reflecting. It is designed to set aside as comparatively insignificant, the numerous volumes of light reading, and utter vanity, and to displace them, with all their fascinating and tawdry ornaments of types, and plates, and wit, by what is more beautiful in art, and more valuable in truth, and more fascinating in biography and anecdote.

Hence, Mr. SEARS has an honest and imperative moral claim for patronage and support, on every Minister and every Parent, and on every Sabbath School Teacher, and on every Patriot actuated by Christian principles. I have only to add, to all my friends, and to the people of my numerous charge, that there is, perhaps, no other book, recently from the press, which I would, in preference to this beautiful and judicious volume, put into the hands of my children, to captivate their minds, and woo them over to the study of the antiquities, scenery, biography, and divine truths of the HOLY BIBLE. It ought to be in every Christian Family for its innate value; and in every patriotic family as a splendid specimen of our progress in domestic manufacture, and the advancement of our artists and manufacturers in their rivalship with those of Europe.

W. C. BROWNLEE.

From the Daily Journal.

The "BIBLE BIOGRAPHY," by Mr. Sears, is, in our estimation, the most valuable work of the kind that has ever yet appeared in this country, and so seasonable, that it comes as a desideratum to relieve Christian families from the expense of purchasing a large commentary, which, without being too long, should be sufficiently copious, and without being too critical, should be sufficiently explanatory and practical. A most cordial welcome, therefore, is due to this performance. It must and will receive the entire and hearty commendation of all the friends of religious literature, and the *practical suffrages of many thousands of purchasers!* Few ministers can afford to obtain all those commentaries, the concentrated essence of which is here presented to attention; and to one who possessed the whole of them, this book would be of great utility, as an index. It must have been a work of immense labor and cost to the editor, and it is a matter of congratulation that so much enterprise, judgment, and industry, should have met together, and combined to produce a work which every diligent student of the inspired writings will prize. The paper, typography, and embellishments reflect great credit on all who have been concerned in the production of this Sacred Gem in modern literature.

From the Morning Herald.

This is one of the most beautiful and judicious volumes on the Scriptures we have ever met with. It is impossible for any one to examine this pictorial volume, without wishing to possess a copy for perusal. The work deserves great commendation for the spirit of liberality in which it has been prepared; critics of every creed have been consulted, and the most scrupulous care has been taken to remove every thing sectarian from a volume designed for all denominations of Christians. We are confident every family will purchase the work, after an examination of its merits.

From the Editor of the Protestant Methodist.

It seems, from what we have seen of this beautiful pictorial volume, well to deserve the title, and the strong recommendations it has already received from almost every paper, of all denominations, both political and religious. We trust it may help many to a more diligent and intelligent search of that unfathomable mine of riches—the precious word of the living God.

From the New York Evangelist.

This is a work possessing many novel and uncommonly attractive features. Its appearance is beautiful. Its biographical sketches embrace the most interesting incidents and events in the lives of the principal personages of the Scripture History, woven together in a pleasing and sprightly narrative, and faithfully accompanied with excellent practical lessons. Its chief claim, however, to popularity, consists in its multitudinous pictorial embellishments. Something like five hundred engravings on wood are contained in the volume, many of which are costly and elegant, and in a high style of art, and none discreditable to the theme or the work. These relate to numerous ancient and oriental customs, scenes, manners, history, &c.; and, while they add great spirit and interest to the objects which they illustrate, form of themselves a pleasing and profitable study. The work is a rare combination of the useful and attractive—adapted at once to engage the attention and affect the heart. We should regard its possession by families whose children may obtain from it striking representations of Scriptural truths and events, lasting impressions of their reality, as highly desirable. The Appendix contains thirty brief, but comprehensive and excellent, essays upon the evidences and archæology of the Scriptures, which add greatly to the value of the work as designed for the instruction of youth and families.

From the New York Christian Intelligencer.

This work is an attractive one, not only from the very numerous embellishments which pervade it, but from the interesting matter which it comprises. It furnishes lives of the principal characters of the Old Testament, with accounts of the Creation, Deluge, Dispersion of Mankind, &c., and an extended life of the Saviour, comprising outlines of the Gospel history. The whole is in a spirit and form well adapted for practical usefulness and spiritual improvement. The numerous historical and landscape illustrations of the Sacred Volume introduced into this work, will prove both amusing and instructive to the young especially, and it will be an entertaining and useful volume in the family. The illustrations are neatly executed on wood. The last hundred pages contain *thirty dissertations on the evidences of divine revelation*, from Timpson's Key to the Bible, &c., and are exceedingly valuable. The work is in large octavo, with closely filled pages, and highly decorated by the very numerous illustrations and the binding. It will no doubt meet with a popular demand.

From the Boston American Traveller.

Sears' Bible Biography is even more finely illustrated and beautifully ornamented than his previous works. The typography is clear and plain, the paper and binding handsome, while the gilded figures give it a rich and tasteful appearance. The literary contents are connected biographies of all the principal characters in the Bible. These are well written, and the whole illustrated with several hundred engravings. An appendix is also added, containing some interesting essays upon subjects of importance.

This work, from the information it gives respecting Eastern habits, manners, countries, animals, scenery, and people, all of which are doubly illustrated by language and pictorial representation, will prove a valuable addition to Sabbath-school and family libraries.

There is no series of works, at the present day, of more practical importance, and deserving better encouragement, than that of Mr. Sears. His design is, to add to and extend the interest of the Bible—to place its truths and valuable precepts in an attractive light. It is often remarked, that the young at the present age, though so intelligent, know less of the Bible than children fifty years ago. The reason has been, that their hands have been filled with popular and pleasing books, adapted to their capacity, and rendered attractive by illustrations and beautiful executions; while the Bible has lain neglected by, all its golden tales, and thoughts, and truths, concealed in the sober and formal phraseology of King James' long-winded divines. Mr. Sears, by giving them a popular form, has conferred a great benefit upon the young, and, indeed, upon all classes.

From the New York Public Ledger, July 27.

SEARS' NEW AND ELEGANT WORK ON THE BIBLE.—This superb volume comes to us overflowing with pictorial beauty, and filled with the greatest variety of interesting subjects we have ever seen, compressed in one large octavo volume of five hundred pages. As the editor of the work has had the politeness to send us a copy, and requested of us a very careful and impartial examination of its merits or claims to popular support, we have been induced to review its varied contents with much more care than we should otherwise have done. In giving our opinion of its merits, we shall be as brief as possible, and, at the same time, say enough—to convince ALL who would like to possess the work, of its real character. We, therefore, take great pleasure in introducing this "STRANGER" to our readers—every one of you can *safely* take him home to your dwelling—*he* will be found worthy of a place at the family circle—and your sons and daughters may *converse* with *him* in perfect safety. So rare are good books in these days of "Cheap Literature," and so numerous are the *licentious* publications issuing from the teeming press, that it does one good to meet a work like Mr. SEARS' "Bible Biography." It is indeed worthy of all acceptation—and will carry blessings into every family it enters, as it is well calculated to promote the present and future happiness of its numerous readers.

In preparing the "Scripture Biography," the editor appears to have had special reference to the instruction of the young and rising generation. Every subject is profusely illustrated with hundreds of new and original engravings; and where he has *borrowed* from eminent divines and commentators, he has made such judicious alterations in style and matter as will, we hope and believe, render it worthy of public acceptance. Every sentence is replete with *practical* instruction. He has divested everything of the dryness and tediousness of criticism, and making all his subjects less diffuse, he has sought to give his book a more "popular," though not a less useful character. In delineating the "Scripture Characters" he has brought thousands of topics into a very small compass—and published the whole in the most attractive form. With reference to the "Pictures," it is only necessary to say that those objects have been selected which are the least known in this country; and the very best authorities have been chosen for their representation—all of which are given in the Index of the work.

From the New Brunswicker.

We have received from Mr. Robert Sears, a new work entitled "Bible Biography; or the Lives and Characters of the Principal Personages recorded in the Sacred Writings," illustrated by several hundred beautiful engravings. We pay the editor of this elegant work no gratuitous compliment when we say, that for the interesting matter with which it abounds, the taste and judgment displayed in the engravings, and the neatness of the mechanical department, it has claims on the public which few who feel interested in the events it records will not cheerfully acknowledge; and we recommend it to the attention of our readers, as a volume of undisputed excellence.

From the Morning Star.

ADVICE TO THE YOUNG.—"Search the Scriptures." It is surprising to see how the Bible is neglected by sinful men. The votaries of taste and fashion will spend their days and nights poring over the morbid pages of sensual and fictitious narrative; yet if they were asked if they had read the book which had been sent them from Heaven, where would they look? Make use of all the helps you can procure to understand its beauty and meaning. Go, gentle reader, at once, and examine Mr. SEARS' new and valuable work, entitled "Lives of Scripture Characters." The examination will cost you nothing. Every lover of the Bible *will* possess it.

From the Daily Times.

We are free to say that this, in our opinion, is decidedly the best Family Book we have any knowledge of, on the sublime and interesting subject it embraces. The engravings are about five hundred, designed and executed from new and original designs by the most eminent artists of England and America, and the whole mechanical appearance of the book is extremely prepossessing. The biblical knowledge imparted is in language at once chaste, elegant, and simple, adapted to the comprehension of those for whom it is designed. Every subject is selected with great judgment, and evinces uncommon industry and research. We earnestly hope that parents and teachers will examine and judge for themselves, as we feel confident they will coincide with us in opinion. We only hope the circulation of the work will be commensurate with its merits. No Christian family should be without this beautiful volume. It must become a popular book for all classes; and, in conclusion, we have no hesitation in saying that it meets with our entire approbation, and is highly creditable to the judgment and experience of the editor

From the New York Churchman, August 6.

From a cursory examination of this work, we feel free to commend it to the favorable notice of all our readers. The matter is compiled, generally, from approved authors, is written in an agreeable style, and cannot fail to interest the young, as well as the general reader. The engravings are neatly executed—especially the frontis piece ; and the whole mechanical execution does great credit to its publisher and editor.

From the New York Washingtonian.

It has been beautifully and truly remarked, that of all studies, the study of the Bible tends most to the purity of the heart and the strength and expansion of the intellect. Were we the veriest skeptic that ever mocked the majesty of God, or set at defiance his commands, we would still scatter abroad His holy word, and commend it to those within our influence. Believing, as we do, in its sacred, its elevated character, we cannot but rejoice that means are taking to direct to the Bible the careful and devout attention of all. Whatever is calculated to excite an interest in this volume, or enlighten the understanding in its perusal. we would gladly see encouraged and sustained. The Bible Biography is of this character. It records, as its title indicates, the lives and characters of the persons mentioned in the sacred pages, with a simplicity and fidelity, that cannot fail of enlisting the sympathies of the reader, and urging to further and more elaborate inquiry. To the young the work is invaluable ; and to them we especially commend it.

From the Cleveland (O.) Herald.

This beautiful work contains about five hundred pictures · and we believe it is destined to become one of the most popular and permanent ever issued from the American press. We would respectfully call the attention of all our readers to this invaluable book. It has received the unqualified recommendation of all who have examined it ; and is believed to be admirably adapted to exert a wholesome influence on the minds of the young especially, and lead to the formation of correct moral principles.

From the St. John (N. B.) Courier.

Among the literary pursuits which engage the attention of mankind, there is scarcely any species more instructive than that which traces the march of intellectual energy from obscurity to eminence It records the progress of perseverance in surmounting difficulties ; embodies the virtues by which individuals have been distinguished ; and holds out both invitation and encouragement to those who are climbing the steep ascent to imperishable honors. The statesman, the warrior, and the man of science, claim from their fellow mortals the meed of praise ; and the pen of the biographer is rarely backward to transmit their names and actions to posterity. But while these, and such characters as these, arrest our attention, and command our esteem, we must not forget, that the man who devotes his time to the cultivation of literature, mounts into a still higher region and expatiates at large in the vast empire of the intellectual world. He traces the operations of the mind through the diversified labyrinths of its excursions, connects abstraction with fact, and combines, in new associations, the harmonious agreement of ideas.

We have been irresistibly led into these reflections by a careful perusal of Mr. SEARS' new and beautiful work on the Bible. Of the importance of the above truths, our pious and intelligent author seems to be fully aware. He here brings the results of his speculations to the law and to the testimony, and by this important test learns to distinguish the dross from the pure ore. No reader can rise from the perusal of his " Bible Biography," without feeling wiser and better ; and nothing short of a careful examination can make him acquainted with the intrinsic value of the author's laborious researches. The serious inquirer after divine truth, and the humble Christian, who, laying aside fruitless controversy, is anxious to advance his own spiritual education, will hereby be instructed, confirmed, and comforted, " in the way of righteousness." In short, we are here taught, by faith, to enter an unseen world, to penetrate beyond the grave, to gather indubitable assurances of an hereafter, and to perceive the majesty of a soul possessed of immortality.

The design of the present volume is to point out the proper improvement of the inspired history, many parts of which may appear to common readers dry and uninteresting ; and to offer such reflections upon the various occurrences as a pious mind would wish to indulge. To this end, throughout the whole of the sacred narratives, great plainness of speech is studied, curious researches are avoided, nor is any new information aimed at. Those evangelical doctrines which have been generally received in the Christian church are taken for granted, and a practical application of them is addressed to persons of different descriptions. Neither the limits nor the intent of the work would have permitted a labored defence of each truth therein advanced. And, perhaps, after all the controversial writings with which the world abounds, the important purposes of religion will be more effectually promoted by solemn and earnest exhortations, grounded on acknowledged principles, than by the most ingenious and solid arguments in vindication of even the purest creed. The latter, indeed, may be highly useful, as conveying light to the understanding, and conviction to the judgment ; but the former, in general, have a more powerful influence upon the will and the affections, and are therefore more conducive to practice. One delightful feature of the present work is *its extreme cheapness :* here is a large and handsome octavo, of five hundred pages, bourgeois type, with several hundred fine engravings, handsomely bound in gilt and lettered, afforded at a very low price. It comes within the means of many hundreds of plain people ; and what a mass of precious Biblical instruction does it contain! Surely, every Christian parent will be pleased to purchase it. A more suitable present could not be given to a family

We might enlarge much upon the benefits that would result, to the young especially, from the study of Sacred Biography. It is presumed, however, that these are self-evident to every reflecting mind ; all will admit that it does at once engage the mind, by the variety of remarkable incidents and characters which it brings into view. Nor is it the least considerable recommendation of this study, that it seems particularly calculated to promote SELF-KNOWLEDGE. By looking at the excellences of others, we are convinced of our own duty, and our sad declensions from it, much more forcibly than by the mere reading of dry precepts and directions. After all, however, that is said upon the object and merits of this new work, it must be seen and studied to appreciate its importance and beauty. And, in conclusion, we heartily recommend this book, as a very valuable. cheap, and convenient one for family reading. The price places it within the reach of every clergyman, and of almost every layman. This volume will, we are persuaded, be found a great help to a just and ready understanding of the Sacred Scriptures.

From the New York Union Herald.

We are satisfied that very culpable negligence prevails in many families respecting the character of the books and papers which are read by children, apprentices, &c. That the most mischievous and corrupting sentiments are oftentimes inculcated in books with innocent titles and highly attractive illustrations, we need not say. Such, however, is not the case with the new and beautiful volume on the Bible just issued, and for sale at No. 122 Nassau-street. It is a work of eminent merit, well adapted to the purposes of family instruction ; and we consider it greatly superior to any work now in use for family reading. The five hundred engravings alone are well worth the price of the book. On the whole, it will give complete satisfaction to all classes of readers – the young, the old, the ignorant and the enlightened. We recommend all our young men to procure Mr. Sears' " Bible Biography," and we advise parents to procure it for their sons and daughters.

From the Reading, Pa. Gazette.

This new and splendid work has just been placed in our hands for examination. It is intended as a "Christian Father's Present to his Family;" and indeed we know of no work that would prove a more appropriate and valuable addition to the family library.

From the St. John (N. B.) Morning News.

It is not the province of a journal like the "Morning News," to enter upon a formal or lengthy review of a work like the present. But still, after turning over the pages of this large and beautiful volume, we cannot consent to pass it by without once more bearing our humble testimony to its high value; not only as well written Biographies, but also as a repository of a vast amount of Biblical knowledge, valuable to the parent, teacher, and scholar. The information of the Appendix, is of the most authentic description; and has, evidently, been compiled and condensed with great care. Talk of the heroism of Alexander, Timour, and Napoleon! Let a Christian public, in these pages, contemplate the lives and characters of all the principal "heroes" mentioned in the Sacred Scriptures. Here are to be found, in reality, sublime spectacles of moral heroism in the lives of these "soldiers" engaged in the "holy wars" against the principalities and powers of mental and moral darkness. The plumed soldier, who charges to the cannon's mouth, and falls bravely amid the pomp and pageantry of battle, and dies amid the admiring plaudits of his comrades, with a certainty that his name and deeds are to be heralded through the universe, can do so, and yet possess far less of true moral courage than the Christian missionary, who is called daily to exercise among the burning sands of Africa, or amid the snows of Labrador—among the barbarians of India, or shores of our own country. But how different is the estimate of the world! How will an admiring populace swell their voices in praise of the man who perils his life to take the life of his fellow-man, when, at the same time, the courage of the humble and retiring Bible character, who encounters hunger and cold in the north, and heat and thirst in the south, and lays down his life cheerfully in the cause of his MASTER, at either extremity, is unheeded! But the laurels of the one will fade in the end—the immortal green of the other—never.

But to return from this digression.—We have no hesitation in saying, that Mr. Sears' work is the best of the kind ever published. We consider it an exceedingly valuable one, not only to ministers, and teachers of Sabbath Schools, but to Christians generally. It embodies a vast amount of information, of which every friend who can afford it should be in possession. The work is, in all respects, of superior execution. The five hundred new and original engravings are finely done, and add not a little to its intrinsic value, as well as the ornament of the book. All the leading papers of the day speak of it in the strongest terms of approbation.

From the Philadelphia Daily Ledger.

An interesting volume with the above title has just been published by Mr. Robert Sears, of New York, in which we find the lives and characters of the principal personages recorded in the sacred writings, written out in a clear and comprehensive manner, and illustrated by several hundred engravings, historical and landscape, executed in a very superior style, by American artists of the first character. The work is a large octavo volume of about 500 pages. It is a complete summary of Biblical knowledge, carefully condensed and compiled from the most eminent writers on the Scriptures. It may be justly recommended as a clear medium through which the great events of Scripture may be lastingly impressed upon the minds of youth, and for that reason is admirably suited to their instruction.

From the St. John (N. B.) Herald.

Some few weeks since we announced the arrival of this work in our city, intending to take an early opportunity of again recurring to it, and going more minutely into its merits. After a careful perusal of its contents, we are now prepared to say, that this volume bids fair to be more popular—permanently popular, we mean,—than any of its editor's previous publications; and that is saying much. We go a step farther—it is one of the most interesting and entertaining, and at the same time religious and instructive works, we have for a long time had the pleasure of perusing. There is another considerable recommendation of this work, that there is nothing in it which can offend the most evangelical, the most orthodox, or the most pious persons, whether among churchmen or dissenters. In the whole book we cannot discover the least inclination to favor any one particular denomination; so candid indeed are the expositions, and so catholic is the spirit of the editor, that it would be impossible to tell to what sect he himself belongs. We understand from a source that may be relied on, that the stereotype plates and engravings alone, cost the publisher over $5000; but we believe that the care and pains which he has bestowed in completing his arduous task, and the masterly style in which it is done, must secure it a favorable reception among all classes. The volume is well adapted to promote the interests of spiritual religion.

From the St. John (N. B.) Weekly Chronicle.

MR. ROBERT SEARS, of 122 Nassau street, New York, has issued his promised work, entitled "Bible Biography." On looking over its 500 pages, with some four or five hundred fine Scriptural engravings, we are gratified with the matter of the volume, and the elegant style in which it is printed and bound. With the strictest propriety the work may be called "The History of the Bible." The preparing of such a book has, doubtless, been a great and expensive undertaking, requiring much thought, experience, and judgment. Evidently the editor has had recourse to the best interpreters, critics, and commentators; and the volume closing as it does, with the Life of our blessed Lord and Saviour—every page being replete with evangelical truth and doctrine—appears beautiful and illustrious, of which it is hoped the reader will make a right use and true improvement.

The style, or language, of the whole volume is such as to render it agreeable to modern and intelligent readers. The practical reflections will bear examination, and are purely spiritual, while there is much that throws great light upon some of the obscurer passages in the Old Testament, with which we are furnished in the New. The history of our Saviour's sufferings, death, and resurrection, is full, and beautifully illustrated with numerous engravings of a superior character. And, indeed, throughout the whole work, the author appears to have labored with but one object in view—to render the "Biography" uniformly evangelical. We hope that this new attempt to diffuse Scriptural knowledge in a cheap and popular form, will meet with general approbation, and that this work will be found generally useful to Christians of all denominations.

The composition or language of this volume is not of that common-place and tiresome sort, with a dry detail of facts and events. The writers of biographies ought to be profound, original thinkers, capable of tracing remote causes in the formation of character, and bringing to view the process of its formation and development. The "Lives of Scripture Characters" before us are valuable, as exhibiting, in a good degree, this species of talent in analyzing character, and showing what were its constituent principles, and how it is formed. There is, moreover, in the book itself an unusual measure of excellence. The spirit of piety which it breathes is of the sweetest, purest kind; eminently lovely and winning: while it is also eminently dignified and intellectual. In conclusion, we again cordially recommend this beautiful volume to all our readers, and especially to Christian parents and teachers, as being well adapted to promote their present and future happiness.

From the Poughkeepsie Telegraph.

Among the multitude of books, as various in their character as in their external appearance, which constantly issue from the press, it is pleasant to point to one of real value, and know that we are calling public attention to a work not only unexceptionable in its letter and spirit, but salutary in its tendency and influence. Such is the book to which we would now direct the attention of our readers. This work contains a series of biographical sketches of the most distinguished men mentioned in the Scriptures, from Adam to John the Baptist, with a sketch of the human life of the Redeemer, and dissertations on the fulfilled prophecies, and other matters highly interesting to the Christian; the whole illustrated by about five hundred engravings, many of them beautifully executed. It is handsomely bound in cloth and gilt, and sold at a very low price.

Having examined this work carefully, we do in all sincerity recommend it, believing that it will exert a happy influence in every family circle where it may find its way. It is conceded that biography is one of the most pleasing, and, at the same time, instructive modes of making the young mind acquainted with the character and history of man; for, while it unclasps the volume of grave history, and spreads its varied contents out to view, it "holds the mirror up to nature," and reflects the image of the great and the ignoble, the good and the evil, the wise and the foolish of our species, as exemplars for imitation, or as warning beacons by which we may perceive and avoid the many dangers that lie beneath the surface of society, and on which so many youthful souls have been wrecked. The virtues of the patriarchs, prophets, and sages, which illuminate every page of the Sacred Record, cannot be too closely studied and imitated; and every father, if he is wise for himself and for his children, will not neglect to make the study of such shining examples a part of his child's education. The work before us exhibits a brilliant galaxy of such exemplars, and while the text, recording their virtues, purifies and ennobles the heart, the pictorial illustrations, elucidating every ambiguous passage, enlighten and enlarge the understanding. For this happy combination of influences, effected by the taste and liberality of Mr. Sears, he deserves sincere thanks and pecuniary reward; and we hope that he may receive both, with full measure.

From the Presbyterian.

The title of this book is so full and descriptive, that the reader will want little more to introduce him to a knowledge of its contents. In the Scriptural Biography there is interspersed a great amount of information respecting Eastern customs, and the dissertations are valuable for their argument on the most momentous topics. The wood-cuts are very numerous, and generally very well executed, although sometimes they seem to be stuck in rather for embellishment than illustration of the text. Altogether the book is a beautiful and attractive one, and young persons will be particularly pleased with it, as its instructions are so often relieved by what charms the eye.

From the New York Gazette Extraordinary.

This is indeed a book for every family, illustrated with several hundred new and original engravings, designed and executed by the most eminent artists of Europe and America. This work is worthy of all praise; and must meet the expectations and wants of every serious reader. The conception and arrangement of the work are admirable; and as far as we have had an opportunity of judging, the typographical execution of it equals the plan. We have read various parts of it attentively; and while we have not met with any thing which we could wish to have been omitted, most sincerely can we say that we have found much to edify and amuse, and well calculated to inspire and sustain true religion in the heart. Nor can we refrain from expressing our persuasion that Mr. Sears' "Bible Biography" is well suited, under the divine blessing, to encourage and promote practical Bible religion, not only in the domestic family circle, but throughout the land; and thus to advance the general interests of Scriptural religion. We hope the volume will find a ready welcome in all Christian families at least; and that the number of such families may be increased by the circulation and perusal of this invaluable work on the Bible.

From the United States Literary Advertiser for June, 1842.

This is a work of great attraction and value. This volume must find a welcome at every fireside throughout the country; its contents are as interesting as they are important and instructive, and the judicious and talented author has here contrived to present us with one of the most attractive, and, at the same time, useful books that has ever appeared this side the Atlantic. We trust the public will reward its enterprising publisher.

From the New World.

The engravings, from new and original designs, are well executed. The design of the work is excellent, and we cheerfully recommend it to the notice of our readers.

From the New York Tribune.

This is a very valuable, cheap, and convenient book. The public will soon find it one of the books they must have. May the publisher supply the land with many ten thousands.

From the Baptist Advocate.

We cheerfully commend the book to the readers of the Advocate, as a work of much merit, furnished at a very cheap rate

From the Boston Transcript.

Altogether it is one of the most elegant works of the season, and must prove the most useful ever issued from the American press.

From the Boston Daily Mail.

We cordially recommend this excellent book.

From the Boston Daily Bee.

An elegant work of five hundred pages, and containing about five hundred engravings. The contents of the volume appear to be sound, judicious, and interesting.

☞ Persons in the country would do well to procure a subscription book, and obtain at once the names of their friends and acquaintances, at least, as subscribers to this invaluable literary gem. Will each agent or friend who complies with this request, have the kindness to inform the publisher how many copies will be wanted for his neighborhood, by mail, (*post-paid*,) as soon as possible! It is his intention to spare neither pains nor expense to introduce this entirely new and original volume into every family throughout the Union.

☞ The above will be found one of the most useful and popular works ever published, for enterprising men to undertake the sale of in all our principal cities and towns.

☞ No letter will be taken from the post-office unless the postage is paid. Persons remitting money through the post-office will be careful to pay the whole postage.

Robert Sears,

Editor and Publisher, 122 Nassau Street, New York.

RECOMMENDATIONS.

......◇◇◇◇◇......

GREAT PUBLICATION.—Mr. SEARS has at length given to the public a Book that will never cease to sell, and never can be surpassed for real usefulness and cheapness.—The "WONDERS OF THE WORLD" is its imposing title. It is indeed a curiosity, as well as one of the most useful productions we have ever seen. This *multum in parvo* is the CHEAPEST, the MOST COMPLETE, and the BEST COMPILED PUBLICATION of the sort that has probably ever issued from the press in this country, and one of the most useful practical works of the day. It is brought out in a most commodious form, and at *the cheapest possible price*, and cannot fail to become popular; for it is most unquestionably the best and completest production, for the price, in the English language. We had occasion, some time since, most conscientiously to praise a work called "Sears' Bible Biography," which appeared to us to combine in a small compass the most extensive compendium of religious information we have ever seen. This volume is of a similar size, and equally neat and beautiful; and after a careful examination of Mr. Sears' "Wonders of the World," we can only add to our commendations of the former work, an expression of our feelings that what we now have before us is equally deserving of praise.—*Philadelphia Saturday Post.*

SEARS' WONDERS OF THE WORLD.—An octavo volume of over 500 pages, with this title, has just been published by Sears, of New York. It is a capital work of entertainment and instruction, and almost every department of knowledge has been ransacked and made to contribute to its stores. The work is beautifully embellished with several hundred pictorial illustrations, and contains a vast amount of interesting facts in natural history, natural phenomena, geography, manners and customs of various nations, &c., all of which cannot fail to convey as much instruction to the reader as it will prove interesting and agreeable.—*Philad. Ledger.*

KNOWLEDGE FOR THE PEOPLE!—Mr. Sears' new and elegant volume, entitled the "*Wonders of the World,—*in Nature, Art, and Mind," ought to be considered as one of the greatest! It consists of a little of every thing filled with pictorial embellishments, to the number of about 500; and must long continue to be the "People's Book!" It is published in a neat and handsome style, and only requires to be seen to be admired, and carefully perused to be duly appreciated. The contents comprise a complete storehouse of knowledge on almost every subject that can be thought of. The author has thrown off the shackles of scientific classification, and "roamed through the woods and forests," unfettered by rules, and imparted a vast amount of useful information in a pleasing manner. It is one of the very best books of the day, prepared with a view to the general dissemination of useful information. Rules of classification and the technicalities with which too many works of this kind abound, are very proper and indispensable for teachers and students; but they are not at all calculated for popular reading,—the way in which THE MILLION must become instructed in the great Wonders of Nature and Art. The easier the way to knowledge is made, the more useful it becomes; for thousands are induced to enter it when they no longer see the difficulties of scientific rules to be overcome. To the aspirant after wisdom, in these pages every barrier has been removed, and mountains made to dwindle into molehills. The truth is, that our attainment of objects does not so much depend upon circumstances as upon our inclinations, perseverance, and industry; and interposing obstacles are often only blessings in disguise, for, like the man who toils hard in earning a competence, he more fully appreciates it, and is more frugal in the enjoyment of his gains. We recommend all persons to procure and read these "*Wonders*"—particularly the young, and such as are fainting by the wayside in their ascent up the hill of science and learning. Price only $2.50.—*New York Sun.*

"THE WONDERS OF THE WORLD."—This is the title of a book of 528 pages, just issued by Sears, New York. The book will be warmly greeted by every class of society, and must continue to be the favorite book for *the people—*THE WHOLE PEOPLE—AND NOTHING BUT THE PEOPLE. It abounds with elegant engravings—nay, it overflows with the most vivid embellishments; and sure we are, that nothing to compare with it has ever been produced on this side of the Atlantic. There have been, it is true, many popular books issued—they have had their day, and gone to the tomb; but this work will have no short-lived popularity, no ephemeral existence. It is destined to find its way into every family, and all will buy and read. The character of the literary part of the work is unexceptionable. It treats on thousands of topics, all calculated to lead the tender mind of youth, especially, to the love of knowledge and the practice of virtue. In order to render this volume the best and most attractive one issued of this class, the publisher has incurred an almost incredible expense in preparing the several hundred plates for publication. Many of them are of the first class. We therefore earnestly recommend a careful perusal of Mr. Sears' advertisement in another column, where all particulars are stated; and as it is only by the sale of a large number that the publisher can expect remuneration, all our subscribers would do well to buy the work, and then recommend it to their friends and acquaintances.—*Philad. Daily Chronicle.*

NEW AND BEAUTIFUL VOLUME.—Every reader of this journal is respectfully referred to Mr. Sears' "WONDERS OF THE WORLD," as advertised in another part of this day's paper. Although one or two works of this title, or something similar, have been issued both in England and America, still we believe nothing can be produced that will at all compare with this, either for beauty of embellishment or the amount of correct and useful information contained in its pages. It is, emphatically, "A BOOK FOR ALL!" It may well be called "A Great Enterprise," in these dull times; and we sincerely hope that the enterprising and talented editor will reap a rich reward. We have given the whole volume a careful and impartial examination; and we unhesitatingly pronounce it a Magnificent Book in every sense of the word, and well worthy of all the praises that have been lavished upon it by every respectable press throughout the Union. Nothing, however, from our pen can describe the work. It is a "MUSEUM" in itself—a complete *Picture Gallery.*—*U. S. Gazette.*

SEARS' WONDERS OF THE WORLD—*Illustrated with several hundred new and elegant Engravings.*—This splendid pictorial work, another product of Mr. Sears' skill and talent, comes forth at the appointed time. A single glance at the Frontispiece and Title-page, designed and executed by our most eminent artists, shows that its indefatigable and deserving Editor possesses in an eminent degree all the requisite qualifications for producing entertaining and instructive works of this kind. Labor, industry, and carefulness are their only genuine sources; and when to these, as is very evident in the present case, are superadded an impartial mind, sound judgment, and good abilities, we find the results to be such publications as the "*Wonders of the World,*" and "*Bible Biography.*"—*New World.*

SEARS' WONDERS OF THE WORLD.—This work is in itself a library of useful and entertaining knowledge, presenting well written sketches of Cataracts, Volcanoes, Earthquakes, Caverns, Atmospheric Phenomena, Astronomy, various Animals, Birds, Fishes, Vegetables, Cities, Public Buildings, Manners, Customs, Costumes, &c., all arranged and beautifully embellished with several hundred pictorial illustrations. The department of Natural History is rich, containing a large amount of interesting information, selected from approved writers. To the young, and indeed to readers of every age, it is a highly attractive book, offering them a rich variety of entertaining and useful knowledge in a form happily adapted to win their attention.—*Christian Observer.*

ROBERT SEARS, 122 Nassau Street, } New York.
E. WALKER, 114 Fulton do. }